The Sporting News

PRO FOOTBALL GUIDE

1998 EDITION

Editors/Pro Football Guide
CRAIG CARTER
DAVE SLOAN

The Sporting News

Efrem Zimbalist III, President and Chief Executive Officer, Times Mirror Magazines; **James H. Nuckols,** President, The Sporting News; **Francis X. Farrell,** Senior Vice President, Publisher; **John D. Rawlings,** Senior Vice President, Editorial Director; **John Kastberg,** Vice President, General Manager; **Kathy Kinkeade,** Vice President, Operations; **Steve Meyerhoff,** Executive Editor; **Mike Huguenin,** Assistant Managing Editor; **Joe Hoppel,** Senior Editor; **Mark Bonavita and Brendan Roberts,** Assistant Editors; **Marilyn Kasal,** Production Director; **Michael Bruner,** Prepress Director; **Terry Shea,** Database Analyst; **Michael Behrens,** Art Director, Special Projects; **Christen Webster,** Macintosh Production Artist.

A Times Mirror
Company

CONTENTS

ON THE COVER: Barry Sanders. (Cover design by Michael Behrens/THE SPORTING NEWS. Photos by Albert Dickson/THE SPORTING NEWS.) Spine photo of Troy Aikman by Robert Seale/THE SPORTING NEWS.

NFL week-by-week and postseason highlights written by Mark Bonavita, Dennis Dillon, Joe Hoppel, Leslie Gibson McCarthy, Carl Moritz, Dave Sloan, Ray Slover, Sean Stewart, Larry Wigge and George Winkler of THE SPORTING NEWS.

NFL statistics compiled by STATS, Inc., Lincolnwood, Ill.

Copyright © 1998 by The Sporting News, a division of Times Mirror Magazines, Inc.; 10176 Corporate Square Dr., Suite 200, St. Louis, MO 63132. All rights reserved. Printed in the U.S.A.

No part of the Pro Football Guide may be reproduced or transmitted in any form or by any means, electronic or mechanical, including photocopy, recording or any information storage and retrieval system now known or to be invented, without permission in writing from the publisher, except by a reviewer who wishes to quote brief passages in connection with a review written for inclusion in a magazine, newspaper or broadcast.

The Sporting News is a registered trademark of The Sporting News, a Times Mirror Company.

ISBN: 0-89204-596-5

10 9 8 7 6 5 4 3 2 1

1998 SEASON

NFL directory
Team information
Schedule
College draft
Playoff plan

NFL DIRECTORY

COMMISSIONER'S OFFICE

Address
280 Park Avenue
New York, NY 10017
Phone
212-450-2000
212-681-7573 (FAX)
Commissioner
Paul Tagliabue
President
Neil Austrian
Sr. v.p. of comm. and gov't affairs
Joe Browne
Exec. v.p. of league and football dev.
Roger Goodell
Sr. v.p. of broadcast planning
Dennis Lewin
Sr. v.p. of football operations
George Young
Chief financial officer
Tom Spock
Executive director of special events
Jim Steeg

Vice president-internal audit
Tom Sullivan
V.p.-law/enterprises, broadcast & finance
Frank Hawkins
Exec. v.p. for labor rel./chairman NFLMC
Harold Henderson
Sr. vice president/general counsel
Dennis Curran
Sr. vice president/labor relations
Peter Ruocco
Sr. dir. of player personnel/football op.
Joel Bussert
V.p. of player and employee dev.
Lem Burnham
Vice president of public relations
Greg Aiello
Director of international public relations
Pete Abitante
Director of media services
Leslie Hammond
Director of broadcasting services
Dick Maxwell

Director of broadcasting research
Joe Ferreira
Asst. dir. of broadcasting/productions
Nancy Behar
V.p. club administration and stadium management
Joe Ellis
Director of football development
Gene Washington
Assistant director of game operations
Tim Davey
Senior director of administration
John Buzzeo
Treasurer
Joe Siclare
Senior director of officiating
Jerry Seeman
Supervisors of officials
Al Hynes
Ron DeSouza
Senior director of security
Milt Ahlrich

OTHER ORGANIZATIONS

NFL MANAGEMENT COUNCIL
Address
280 Park Avenue
New York, NY 10017
Phone
212-450-2000
212-681-7590 (FAX)
Exec. v.p. for labor rel./chairman NFLMC
Harold Henderson
Sr. vice president and general counsel
Dennis Curran
Director of labor relations
Lal Heneghan
Assistant general counsel
Buckley Briggs
Labor relations counsel
Belinda Lerner
Rapheal Prevot
Ed Tighe
Sr. v.p. of operations and compliance
Peter Ruocco
Director of compliance
Michael Keenan
V.p. of player & employee development
Lem Burnham
Sr. director of player personnel
Joel Bussert

PRO FOOTBALL HALL OF FAME
Address
2121 George Halas Drive, N.W.
Canton, OH 44708
Phone
330-456-8207
330-456-8175 (FAX)
Executive director
John W. Bankert
V.p./communications & exhibits
Joe Horrigan
V.p./operations and marketing
Dave Motts
V.p./merchandising & licensing
Judy Kuntz

PRO FOOTBALL WRITERS OF AMERICA
President
Steve Schoenfeld, Arizona Republic
First vice president
John Clayton, Tacoma Morning News Tribune
Second vice president
Adam Schefter, Rocky Mountain News
Secretary/treasurer
Howard Balzer

NFL FILMS, INC.
Address
330 Fellowship Road
Mt. Laurel, NJ 08054
Phone
609-778-1600
609-722-6779 (FAX)
President
Steve Sabol

NFL PLAYERS ASSOCIATION
Address
2021 L Street, N.W.
Washington, DC 20036
Phone
202-463-2200
202-835-9775 (FAX)
Executive director
Gene Upshaw
Assistant executive director
Doug Allen
Dir. P.R. and NFLPA retired players org.
Frank Woschitz
General counsel
Richard Berthelsen
Director of communications
Carl Francis
Director of player development
Stacey Robinson

NFL PROPERTIES
Address
280 Park Avenue
New York, NY 10017
Phone
212-450-2000
212-758-4239 (FAX)
Interim chief operating officer
Sara Levinson
V.p., world wide retail licensing
Jim Connelly
V.p., development/special events
David Newman
V.p., corporate sponsorship
Jim Schwebel
V.p., marketing
Howard Handler
V.p., club marketing
Mark Holtzman
V.p., advertising and design
Bruce Burke
V.p., legal and business affairs
Gary Gertzog

NFL ALUMNI ASSOCIATION
Address
6550 N. Federal Highway
Suite 400
Ft. Lauderdale, FL 33308-1400
Phone
954-492-1220
954-492-8297 (FAX)
Executive director/CEO
Frank Krauser
Chairman of the board
Randy Minniear
Vice president/alumni relations
Martin Lerch
Director of communications
Remy Mackowski
Manager of player appearances
Jody Overacre

ARIZONA CARDINALS
NFC EASTERN DIVISION

1997 REVIEW
RESULTS

Aug. 31—at Cincinnati	L	21-24
Sept. 7—DALLAS (OT)	W	25-22
Sept.14—at Washington (OT)	L	13-19
Sept.21—Open date		
Sept.28—at Tampa Bay	L	18-19
Oct. 5—MINNESOTA	L	19-20
Oct. 12—N.Y. GIANTS	L	13-27
Oct. 19—at Philadelphia (OT)	L	10-13
Oct. 26—TENNESSEE	L	14-41
Nov. 2—PHILADELPHIA	W	31-21
Nov. 9—at Dallas	L	6-24
Nov. 16—at N.Y. Giants	L	10-19
Nov. 23—at Baltimore	W	16-13
Nov. 30—PITTSBURGH (OT)	L	20-26
Dec. 7—WASHINGTON	L	28-38
Dec. 14—at New Orleans	L	10-27
Dec. 21—ATLANTA	W	29-26

RECORDS/RANKINGS

1997 regular-season record: 4-12 (5th in NFC East); 2-6 in division; 3-9 in conference; 3-5 at home; 1-7 on road.
Team record last five years: 30-50 (.375, ranks 24th in league in that span).

1997 team rankings:	No.	NFC	NFL
Total offense	*294.6	11	24
Rushing offense	*78.4	15	30
Passing offense	*216.1	3	10
Scoring offense	283	12	25
Total defense	*339.1	14	27
Rushing defense	*136.3	14	27
Passing defense	*202.9	11	15
Scoring defense	379	14	25
Takeaways	20	14	29
Giveaways	42	14	T28
Turnover differential	-22	14	29
Sacks	34	15	26
Sacks allowed	78	15	30

*Yards per game.

TEAM LEADERS

Scoring (kicking): Joe Nedney, 52 pts. (19/19 PATs, 11/17 FGs).
Scoring (touchdowns): Rob Moore, 50 pts. (8 receiving, 1 2-pt. conv.).
Passing: Jake Plummer, 2,203 yds. (296 att., 157 comp., 53.0%, 15 TDs, 15 int.).
Rushing: Leeland McElroy, 424 yds. (135 att., 3.1 avg., 2 TDs).
Receptions: Rob Moore, 97 (1,584 yds., 16.3 avg., 8 TDs).
Interceptions: Aeneas Williams, 6 (95 yds., 2 TDs).
Sacks: Eric Swann, 7.5.
Punting: Jeff Feagles, 44.3 avg. (91 punts, 4,028 yds., 1 blocked).
Punt returns: Kevin Williams, 11.6 avg. (40 att., 462 yds., 0 TDs).
Kickoff returns: Kevin Williams, 24.7 avg. (59 att., 1,458 yds., 0 TDs).

1998 SEASON
CLUB DIRECTORY

President
William V. Bidwill
Vice president
William Bidwill Jr.
Vice president, general counsel
Michael Bidwill
Secretary and general counsel
Thomas J. Guilfoil
Vice president
Larry Wilson
Vice president/player personnel
Bob Ferguson
Treasurer/chief financial officer
Charley Schlegel
Assistant to the president
Rod Graves
Vice president, sales
John Shean
Director/marketing
Joe Castor
Ticket manager
Steve Bomar
Director/community affairs
Adele Harris
Director/public relations
Paul Jensen
Media coordinator
Greg Gladysiewski
Player program/community outreach
Garth Jax
Director/college scouting
Bo Bolinger
Director/pro scouting
Keith Kidd
Scouts
Jim Carmody
Jerry Hardaway
Bob Mazie
Cole Proctor
Jim Stanley

SCHEDULE

Sept. 6—	at Dallas	3:05
Sept. 13—	at Seattle	1:15
Sept. 20—	PHILADELPHIA	5:20
Sept. 27—	at St. Louis	12:01
Oct. 4—	OAKLAND	1:05
Oct. 11—	CHICAGO	1:05
Oct. 18—	at N.Y. Giants	1:01
Oct. 25—	Open date	
Nov. 1—	at Detroit	1:01
Nov. 8—	WASHINGTON	2:05
Nov. 15—	DALLAS	2:15
Nov. 22—	at Washington	1:01
Nov. 29—	at Kansas City	12:01
Dec. 6—	N.Y. GIANTS	2:05
Dec. 13—	at Philadelphia	1:01
Dec. 20—	NEW ORLEANS	2:15
Dec. 27—	SAN DIEGO	2:15

All times are for home team.
All games Sunday unless noted.

Head coach
Vince Tobin

Assistant coaches
George "Geep" Chryst
(quarterbacks)
Alan Everest (special teams)
Joe Greene (defensive line)
David Marmie (defensive backs)
Dave McGinnis (defensive coordinator)
Glenn Pires (linebackers)
Vic Rapp (wide receivers)
Johnny Roland (running backs)
Marc Trestman (offensive coord.)
George Warhop (offensive line)

Head trainer
John Omohundro
Assistant trainers
Jim Shearer
Jeff Herndon
Orthopedist
Russell Chick
Internist
Wayne Kuhl
Equipment manager
Mark Ahlemeier
Assistant equipment manager
Steve Christensen
Video director
Benny Greenberg

DRAFT CHOICES

Andre Wadsworth, DE, Florida State (first round/third pick overall).
Corey Chavous, DB, Vanderbilt (2/33).
Anthony Clement, T, SW Louisiana (2/36).
Michael Pittman, RB, Fresno State (4/95).
Terry Hardy, TE, Southern Mississippi (5/125).
Zack Walz, LB, Dartmouth (6/158).
Phil Savoy, WR, Colorado (7/193).
Jomo Cousins, DE, Florida A&M (7/209).
Pat Tillman, DB, Arizona State (7/226).
Ron Janes, RB, Missouri (7/233).

1998 SEASON
TRAINING CAMP ROSTER

No.	QUARTERBACKS	Ht./Wt.	Born	NFL Exp.	College	How acq.	'97 Games GP/GS
7	Brown, Dave	6-5/230	2-25-70	7	Duke	FA/98	*7/6
15	Case, Stoney	6-3/201	7-7-72	4	New Mexico	D3/95	3/1
16	Plummer, Jake	6-2/197	12-19-74	2	Arizona State	D2/97	10/9
	RUNNING BACKS						
24	Bates, Mario	6-1/217	1-16-73	5	Arizona State	FA/98	*12/7
31	Brown, Rod (FB)	5-11/247	2-28-74	1	North Carolina State	D6a/97	0/0
37	Centers, Larry	6-0/225	6-1-68	9	Stephen F. Austin State	D5/90	15/14
34	Janes, Ron (FB)	6-1/276	2-14-75	R	Missouri	D7c/98	—
30	McElroy, Leeland	5-9/212	6-25-74	3	Texas A&M	D2/96	14/8
20	Moore, Ron	5-10/220	1-26-70	6	Pittsburg (Kan.) State	FA/97	*13/4
29	Murrell, Adrian	5-11/214	10-16-70	6	West Virginia	TR/98	*16/15
32	Pittman, Michael	6-0/214	8-14-75	R	Fresno State	D4/98	—
45	Smith, Cedric (FB)	5-11/250	5-27-68	6	Florida	FA/96	16/3
	RECEIVERS						
89	Brock, Fred	5-11/181	11-15-74	2	Southern Mississippi	FA/96	2/0
12	Carpenter, Chad	5-11/198	7-17-73	1	Washington State	D5/97	0/0
83	Edwards, Anthony	5-10/197	5-26-66	9	New Mexico Highlands	FA/91	16/1
84	Gedney, Chris (TE)	6-5/250	8-9-70	6	Syracuse	FA/97	16/3
80	Hardy, Terry (TE)	6-4/266	5-31-76	R	Southern Mississippi	D5/98	—
86	Junkin, Trey (TE)	6-2/258	1-23-61	16	Louisiana Tech	WV/96	16/0
87	McWilliams, Johnny (TE)	6-4/271	12-14-72	3	Southern California	D3/96	16/7
21	Metcalf, Eric	5-10/188	1-23-68	10	Texas	TR/98	*16/1
85	Moore, Rob	6-3/203	9-27-68	9	Syracuse	TR/95	16/16
81	Sanders, Frank	6-2/197	2-17-73	4	Auburn	D2/95	16/16
82	Savoy, Phil	6-2/195	2-16-75	R	Colorado	D6/98	—
	OFFENSIVE LINEMEN						
75	Brown, Lomas (T)	6-4/290	3-30-63	14	Florida	FA/96	14/14
79	Clark, Jon	6-6/345	4-11-73	3	Temple	FA/98	*1/0
65	Clement, Anthony (T)	6-7/355	4-10-76	R	Southwestern Louisiana	D2b/98	—
72	Daniels, Jerome (T)	6-5/350	9-13-74	1	Northeastern	FA/97	0/0
69	DeGraffenreid, Allen	6-4/293	6-3-74	1	Vanderbilt	FA/97	0/0
62	Devlin, Mike (C)	6-2/318	11-16-69	6	Iowa	FA/96	15/13
64	Dexter, James (T)	6-7/319	3-3-73	3	South Carolina	D5/96	10/9
67	Dishman, Chris (G)	6-3/320	2-27-74	2	Nebraska	D4/97	8/0
54	Graham, Aaron (C)	6-4/293	5-22-73	3	Nebraska	D4/96	16/4
70	Guynes, Thomas (T)	6-5/330	9-9-74	2	Michigan	FA/97	4/0
71	Holmes, Lester (G)	6-4/315	9-27-69	6	Jackson State	FA/98	*15/15
73	Joyce, Matt (G)	6-7/313	3-30-72	4	Richmond	FA/96	9/6
50	McCombs, Tony	6-2/246	8-24-74	2	Eastern Kentucky	D6b/97	12/0
60	Redmon, Anthony (G)	6-5/308	4-9-71	5	Auburn	D5b/94	16/16
74	Selby, Rob (G)	6-3/290	10-11-67	8	Auburn	FA/95	10/9
68	Wolf, Joe	6-6/297	12-28-66	7	Boston College	D1b/89	15/9
	DEFENSIVE LINEMEN						
78	Burnstein, Brent	6-7/268	11-21-73	1	Arizona State	FA/98	0/0
92	Cousins, Jomo (E)	6-5/277	9-2-74	R	Florida A&M	D7a/98	—
76	Drake, Jerry	6-5/310	7-9-69	3	Hastings (Neb.) College	FA/95	0/0
96	Ottis, Brad (T)	6-5/281	8-2-72	5	Wayne State (Neb.)	FA/96	16/4
97	Rice, Simeon (E)	6-5/260	2-24-74	3	Illinois	D1/96	16/15
93	Smith, Mark (E)	6-4/290	8-28-74	2	Auburn	D7/97	16/4
98	Swann, Eric (T)	6-5/313	8-16-70	8	Wake Technical College, N.C.	D1/91	13/13
91	Swinger, Rashod (T)	6-2/286	11-27-74	1	Rutgers	FA/97	1/0
90	Wadsworth, Andre (E)	6-4/278	10-19-74	R	Florida State	D1/98	—
94	Wilson, Bernard (T)	6-3/318	8-17-70	6	Tennessee State	WV/94	16/14
	LINEBACKERS						
51	Cobbins, Lyron	6-0/250	9-17-74	2	Notre Dame	FA/97	6/0
56	Irving, Terry	6-2/236	7-3-71	5	McNeese State	D4c/94	16/6
53	Maddox, Mark	6-1/233	3-23-68	8	Northern Michigan	FA/98	*8/1
57	McKinnon, Ronald	6-0/240	9-20-73	3	North Alabama	FA/96	16/16
95	Miller, Jamir	6-5/266	11-19-73	5	UCLA	D1/94	16/16
55	Sapp, Patrick	6-4/258	5-11-73	3	Clemson	TR/98	*16/9
52	Walz, Zack	6-4/228	2-13-76	R	Dartmouth	D6/98	—
	DEFENSIVE BACKS						
28	Bennett, Tommy (S)	6-2/219	2-19-73	3	UCLA	FA/96	13/7
43	Chavous, Corey	6-0/204	1-15-76	R	Vanderbilt	D2a/98	—
38	Harris, Kenny (S)	6-1/203	4-27-75	2	North Carolina State	FA/96	11/0
27	Howard, Ty (CB)	5-9/185	11-30-73	2	Ohio State	D3/97	15/2

No.	DEFENSIVE BACKS	Ht./Wt.	Born	NFL Exp.	College	How acq.	'97 Games GP/GS
22	Knight, Tom (CB)	5-11/196	12-29-74	2	Iowa	D1/97	15/14
42	Lassiter, Kwamie (S)	6-0/202	12-3-69	4	Kansas	FA/95	16/1
39	Malone, Van (S)	5-11/186	7-1-70	5	Texas	FA/98	*8/4
44	McCleskey, J.J. (CB)	5-8/184	4-10-70	5	Tennessee	WV/96	13/0
23	McGee, Dell (CB)	5-8/185	9-7-73	2	Auburn	D5c/96	0/0
40	Tillman, Pat	5-11/204	11-6-76	R	Arizona State	D7b/98	—
35	Williams, Aeneas (CB)	5-11/202	1-29-68	8	Southern, La	D3/90	16/16
	SPECIALISTS						
6	Nedney, Joe (K)	6-4/215	3-22-73	3	San Jose State	FA/97	10/0
10	Player, Scott (P)	6-0/220	12-17-69	1	Florida State	FA/98	0/0

*Bates played 12 games with Saints in '97; D. Brown played 7 games with Giants; Clark played 1 game with Bears; Holmes played 15 games with Raiders; Maddox played 8 games with Bills; Malone played 8 games with Lions; Metcalf played 16 games with Chargers; Ron Moore played 7 games with Rams and 6 games with Cardinals; Murrell played 16 games with Jets; Sapp played 16 games with Chargers.

Abbreviations: D1—draft pick, first round; SupD2—supplemental draft pick, second round; WV—claimed on waivers; TR— obtained in trade; PlanB—Plan B free-agent acquisition; FA—free-agent acquisition (other than Plan B); ED—expansion draft pick.

MISCELLANEOUS TEAM DATA

Stadium (capacity, surface):
Sun Devil Stadium (73,243, grass)
Business address:
P.O. Box 888
Phoenix, AZ 85001-0888
Business phone:
602-379-0101
Ticket information:
602-379-0102
Team colors:
Cardinal red, black and white
Flagship radio station:
KDUS, 1060 AM
Training site:
Northern Arizona University
Flagstaff, Ariz.
520-523-1818

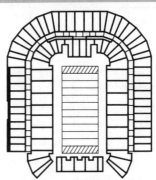

TSN REPORT CARD

Coaching staff	B	This would have been lower had adjustments not been made on the offensive side, where the genius of new coordinator Marc Trestman could cause the grade to go even higher. Defensive coordinator Dave McGinnis and his staff are strong teachers.
Offensive backfield	B +	These guys get the most improved award. Who would you rather go to war with: Adrian Murrell, Mario Bates and Michael Pittman, or Leeland McElroy, LeShon Johnson and Kevin Bouie? At least now the Cardinals can move the ball.
Receivers	B	There are lots of weapons outside in Rob Moore, Frank Sanders and Eric Metcalf. The tight end will be more a part of the offense this year, which is good news to Chris Gedney, a strong receiver. It's time for Johnny McWilliams to step up behind Gedney.
Offensive line	D	Last year it was an F, but there have been massive changes—literally. There are lots of new guys, and they're all big. But are they good? And can they play together effectively to move the ball on the ground and protect scrambling quarterback Jake Plummer?
Defensive line	A	If it's as good as it looks on paper, it will quickly be an A+. The best player in the draft, Andre Wadsworth, lines up next to a Pro Bowl talent in Eric Swann, who is beside an All-Rookie pick in Mark Smith, who is beside a former NFL defensive rookie of the year in Simeon Rice.
Linebackers	C -	Jamir Miller, a stalwart on the left side, lifts this grade. Ron McKinnon was impressive in the middle as a fill-in, but how effective will he be playing every down? And who will take the right-side spot? The list of candidates is not overwhelming.
Secondary	C -	It's fear of the unknown. Both safeties will be new, and of the six contenders only Van Malone has ever started in the NFL (Detroit). At right corner, Tom Knight needs to settle down after an adventurous rookie season. At left corner, perennial Pro Bowl pick Aeneas Williams is in a world of his own.
Special teams	B -	If Joe Nedney loses the hook and gets consistent on his long-range field goal attempts, the grade goes up. A big question is who will succeed Jeff Feagles as punter. The return game is in good hands with Eric Metcalf, and the coverage units are strong.

ATLANTA FALCONS
NFC WESTERN DIVISION

1997 REVIEW
RESULTS

Aug. 31—at Detroit	L	17-28
Sept. 7—CAROLINA	L	6-9
Sept.14—OAKLAND	L	31-36
Sept.21—at San Francisco	L	7-34
Sept.28—DENVER	L	21-29
Oct. 5—Open date		
Oct. 12—at New Orleans	W	23-17
Oct. 19—SAN FRANCISCO	L	28-35
Oct. 26—at Carolina	L	12-21
Nov. 2—ST. LOUIS	W	34-31
Nov. 9—TAMPA BAY	L	10-31
Nov. 16—at St. Louis	W	27-21
Nov. 23—NEW ORLEANS	W	20-3
Nov. 30—at Seattle	W	24-17
Dec. 7—at San Diego	W	14-3
Dec. 14—PHILADELPHIA	W	20-17
Dec. 21—at Arizona	L	26-29

RECORDS/RANKINGS

1997 regular-season record: 7-9 (T2nd in NFC West); 4-4 in division; 5-7 in conference; 3-5 at home; 4-4 on road.
Team record last five years: 32-48 (.400, ranks 21st in league in that span).

1997 team rankings:

	No.	NFC	NFL
Total offense	*294.8	10	23
Rushing offense	*102.7	10	19
Passing offense	*192.1	11	22
Scoring offense	320	6	18
Total defense	*319.1	13	20
Rushing defense	*104.1	4	8
Passing defense	*215	13	20
Scoring defense	361	12	21
Takeaways	28	8	T15
Giveaways	24	6	T13
Turnover differential	4	5	11
Sacks	55	2	2
Sacks allowed	54	13	26

*Yards per game.

TEAM LEADERS

Scoring (kicking): Morten Andersen, 104 pts. (35/35 PATs, 23/27 FGs).
Scoring (touchdowns): Jamal Anderson, 60 pts. (7 rushing, 3 receiving).
Passing: Chris Chandler, 2,692 yds. (342 att., 202 comp., 59.1%, 20 TDs, 7 int.).
Rushing: Jamal Anderson, 1,002 yds. (290 att., 3.5 avg., 7 TDs).
Receptions: Bert Emanuel, 65 (991 yds., 15.2 avg., 9 TDs).
Interceptions: Ray Buchanan, 5 (49 yds., 0 TDs).
Sacks: Chuck Smith, 12.0.
Punting: Dan Stryzinski, 39.3 avg. (89 punts, 3,498 yds., 0 blocked).
Punt returns: Todd Kinchen, 8.6 avg. (52 att., 446 yds., 0 TDs).
Kickoff returns: Byron Hanspard, 24.7 avg. (40 att., 987 yds., 2 TDs).

1998 SEASON
CLUB DIRECTORY

President
Taylor Smith
Special assistant to president
Jerry Rhea
Executive v.p. of administration
Jim Hay
General manager
Harold Richardson
Vice president of football operations
Ron Hill
Vice president and chief financial officer
Kevin Anthony
Administrative assistant
John O. Knox
Vice president of marketing
Rob Jackson
Vice president of corporate development
Tommy Nobis
Marketing/sales assistant
Spencer Treadwell
Marketing/sales assistants
Todd Marble   Spencer Treadwell
Director of public relations
Charlie Taylor
Assistant director of public relations
Frank Kleha
Public relations assistant
Gary Glenn
Director of community relations
Carol Breeding
Coordinator of player programs
Billy "White Shoes" Johnson
Director of ticket operations
Jack Ragsdale
Asst. director of ticket operations
Mike Jennings
Controller
Wallace Norman
Accounting
Carolyn Cathey
Dir. of player personnel/college scouting
Reed Johnson
Admin. assistant/college scouting
LaDonna Jones
Scouts

Ken Blair	Melvin Bratton
Dick Corrick	Boyd Dowler
Elbert Dubenion	Bill Groman
Bob Harrison	

SCHEDULE

Sept. 6— at Carolina	1:01
Sept. 13— PHILADELPHIA	1:01
Sept. 20— Open date	
Sept. 27— at San Francisco	1:15
Oct. 4— CAROLINA	1:01
Oct. 11— at N.Y. Giants	8:20
Oct. 18— NEW ORLEANS	1:01
Oct. 25— at N.Y. Jets	1:01
Nov. 1— ST. LOUIS	1:01
Nov. 8— at New England	1:01
Nov. 15— SAN FRANCISCO	1:01
Nov. 22— CHICAGO	1:01
Nov. 29— at St. Louis	12:01
Dec. 6— INDIANAPOLIS	1:01
Dec. 13— at New Orleans	12:01
Dec. 20— at Detroit	1:01
Dec. 27— MIAMI	1:01

All times are for home team.
All games Sunday unless noted.

Head coach/ executive v.p. for football operations
Dan Reeves

Assistant coaches
Marvin Bass (asst. to head coach/player personnel)
Rich Brooks (assistant head coach/defensive coordinator)
George Sefcik (offensive coordinator/running backs)
Don Blackmon (linebackers)
Jack Burns (quarterbacks)
James Daniel (tight ends)
Joe DeCamillis (special teams)
Tim Jorgensen (assistant strength & conditioning)
Bill Kollar (defensive line)
Ron Meeks (secondary)
Al Miller (strength & conditioning)
Art Shell (offensive line)
Rennie Simmons (wide receivers)
Ed West (off. quality control)
Brian Xanders (def. quality control)

Director of pro personnel
Chuck Connor
Pro personnel assistant
Les Sneed
Admin. assistant/football operations
Kim Mauldin
Head trainer
Ron Medlin
Trainers
Harold King   Matt Smith
Equipment manager
Brian Boigner
Sr. equip. dir./gameday op. coord.
Horace Daniel
Video director
Tom Atcheson

DRAFT CHOICES

Keith Brooking, LB, Georgia Tech (first round/12th pick overall).
Bob Hallen, C, Kent (2/53).
Jammi German, WR, Miami, Fla. (3/74).
Omar Brown, DB, North Carolina (4/103).
Tim Dwight, WR-KR, Iowa (4/114).
Elijah Williams, DB, Florida (6/166).
Ephraim Salaam, T, San Diego State (7/199).
Ken Oxendine, RB, Virginia Tech (7/201).
Henry Slay, DT, West Virginia (7/203).

TRAINING CAMP ROSTER

No.	QUARTERBACKS	Ht./Wt.	Born	NFL Exp.	College	How acq.	'97 Games GP/GS
12	Chandler, Chris	6-4/225	10-12-65	11	Washington	TR/97	14/14
13	Graziani, Tony	6-2/195	12-23-73	2	Oregon	D7/97	3/1
11	Rypien, Mark	6-4/225	10-2-62	13	Washington State	FA/98	*5/0
	RUNNING BACKS						
32	Anderson, Jamal	5-11/234	9-30-72	5	Utah	D7/94	16/15
44	Christian, Bob	5-11/230	11-14-68	7	Northwestern	FA/97	16/12
45	Downs, Gary	6-1/212	6-6-72	5	North Carolina State	FA/97	16/0
28	Green, Harold	6-2/222	1-29-68	9	South Carolina	FA/97	16/1
40	Grenier, Geoff (FB)	6-2/240	1-25-73	1	Oklahoma State	FA/97	0/0
24	Hanspard, Byron	5-10/198	1-23-76	2	Texas Tech	D2b/97	16/0
36	Lester, Fred (FB)	6-1/244	8-1-71	1	Alabama A&M	FA/95	0/0
33	Oxendine, Ken	6-1/228	10-4-75	R	Virginia Tech	D7b/98	—
	RECEIVERS						
82	Crawford, Keith	6-2/195	11-21-70	5	Howard Payne (Tex.)	FA/98	*15/2
83	Dwight, Tim	5-8/184	7-13-75	R	Iowa	D4b/98	—
87	German, Jammi	6-1/187	7-4-74	R	Miami	D3/98	—
84	Hayes, Mercury	5-11/195	1-1-73	3	Michigan	FA/97	*6/0
19	Johnson, Van	6-1/200	8-19-74	1	Temple	FA/98	0/0
89	Kinchen, Todd	5-11/187	1-7-69	7	Louisiana State	FA/97	16/0
85	Kozlowski, Brian (TE)	6-3/255	10-4-70	5	Connecticut	FA/97	16/5
81	Mathis, Terance	5-10/185	6-7-67	9	New Mexico	FA/94	16/16
88	Santiago, O.J. (TE)	6-7/267	4-4-74	2	Kent State	D3/97	11/11
49	Saxton, Brian (TE)	6-6/265	3-13-72	3	Boston College	FA/97	3/0
86	Smith, Ed (TE)	6-4/253	6-5-69	2	None.	FA/97	5/1
80	Thomal, Kevin	6-2/186	11-28-74	1	Southern Methodist	FA/97	0/0
	OFFENSIVE LINEMEN						
71	Adams, Scott (T)	6-5/315	9-28-66	8	Georgia	FA/97	6/0
66	Akers, Jeremy (T)	6-5/304	1-9-74	1	Notre Dame	FA/97	0/0
68	Collins, Calvin (C)	6-2/307	1-5-74	2	Texas A&M	D6/97	15/13
53	Elliott, Matt (C)	6-3/295	10-1-68	6	Michigan	FA/98	*16/6
64	Hallen, Bob (C)	6-4/292	3-9-75	R	Kent	D2/98	—
72	Louchiey, Corey (T)	6-8/305	10-10-71	4	South Carolina	FA/98	*16/6
55	Miller, Nate (T)	6-3/310	10-8-71	2	Lousiana State	FA/95	13/0
74	Salaam, Ephraim (T)	6-7/290	6-19-76	R	San Diego State	D7a/98	—
67	Schreiber, Adam (C)	6-4/298	2-20-62	15	Texas	FA/97	16/0
61	Tobeck, Robbie (C)	6-4/300	3-6-70	5	Washington State	FA/93	16/15
70	Whitfield, Bob (T)	6-5/310	10-18-71	7	Stanford	D1a/92	16/16
79	Widell, Dave (C)	6-7/312	5-14-65	10	Boston College	FA/98	*16/12
65	Williams, Clay (T)	6-6/310	5-6-73	1	Indiana	FA/98	0/0
69	Williams, Gene (T)	6-2/315	10-14-68	8	Iowa State	TR/95	15/15
	DEFENSIVE LINEMEN						
92	Archambeau, Lester (E)	6-5/275	6-27-67	9	Stanford	TR/93	16/16
91	Burrough, John	6-5/275	5-17-72	4	Wyoming	D7/95	16/1
95	Campbell, Mark (E)	6-1/293	9-12-72	3	Florida	FA/98	*5/0
99	Davis, Nathan (E)	6-5/312	2-6-74	2	Indiana	D2a/97	2/0
75	Dronett, Shane (E)	6-6/288	1-12-71	7	Texas	FA/97	16/1
60	Fountaine, Jamal (E)	6-3/240	1-29-71	2	Washington	FA/97	3/0
98	Hall, Travis	6-5/288	8-3-72	4	Brigham Young	D6/95	16/16
73	Michell, Barry (E)	6-3/268	3-18-74	1	Idaho	FA/97	0/0
77	Slay, Henry (T)	6-2/290	4-28-75	R	West Virginia	D7c/98	—
93	Swayda, Shawn (E)	6-5/279	9-4-74	1	Arizona State	D6a/97	0/0
98	Tuaolo, Esera (T)	6-3/276	7-11-68	6	Oregon State	FA/98	*6/1
	LINEBACKERS						
97	Bennett, Cornelius	6-2/238	8-25-65	12	Alabama	FA/96	16/16
51	Brandon, David	6-4/238	2-9-65	12	Memphis State	FA/96	4/4
56	Brooking, Keith	6-2/244	10-30-75	R	Georgia Tech	D1/98	—
94	Crockett, Henri	6-2/251	10-28-74	2	Florida State	D4/97	16/10
54	Hamilton, Ruffin	6-1/238	3-2-71	3	Tulane	FA/97	13/0
52	Sauer, Craig	6-1/240	12-13-72	3	Minnesota	D6/96	16/1
90	Smith, Chuck	6-2/265	12-21-69	7	Tennessee	D2/92	16/15
50	Sutter, Eddie	6-3/239	10-3-69	7	Northwestern	FA/97	16/0
59	Talley, Ben	6-3/248	7-14-72	3	Tennessee	FA/98	0/0
58	Tuggle, Jessie	5-11/230	4-4-65	12	Valdosta (Ga.) State	FA/87	16/15
	DEFENSIVE BACKS						
47	Bayne, Chris	6-1/205	3-22-75	2	Fresno State	D7/97	13/0
43	Bolden, Juran (CB)	6-2/201	6-27-74	3	Mississippi Delta CC	D4b/96	14/1
20	Booker, Michael	6-2/203	4-27-75	2	Nebraska	D1/97	15/2

No.	DEFENSIVE BACKS	Ht./Wt.	Born	NFL Exp.	College	How acq.	'97 Games GP/GS
23	Bradford, Ronnie (CB)	5-10/188	10-1-70	6	Colorado	FA/97	16/15
27	Brown, Omar (S)	5-10/200	3-28-75	R	North Carolina	D4a/98	—
34	Buchanan, Ray	5-9/195	9-29-71	6	Louisville	FA/97	16/16
25	Bush, Devin (S)	5-11/210	7-3-73	4	Florida State	D1/95	16/16
29	Fuller, Randy (CB)	5-10/175	6-2-70	5	Tennessee State	FA/98	*12/3
22	McGill, Lenny (CB)	6-1/202	5-31-71	5	Arizona State	TR/96	15/0
41	Robinson, Eugene (S)	6-1/197	5-28-63	14	Colgate	FA/98	*16/16
35	White, William (S)	5-10/205	2-19-66	11	Ohio State	FA/97	16/16
21	Williams, Elijah (CB)	5-10/181	8-20-75	R	Florida	D6/98	—
48	Wimberly, Marcus (S)	5-11/192	7-8-74	2	Miami (Fla.)	D5/97	6/0
	SPECIALISTS						
66	Akers, David (K)	5-10/180	12-9-74	1	Louisville	FA/97	0/0
5	Andersen, Morten (K)	6-2/225	8-19-60	17	Michigan State	FA/95	16/0
4	Stryzinski, Dan (P)	6-2/200	5-15-65	9	Indiana	FA/95	16/0

*Campbell played 5 games with Cardinals in '97; Crawford played 15 games with Rams; Elliott played 16 games with Panthers; Fuller played 12 games with Steelers; Hayes played 4 games with Saints and 2 games with Falcons; Louchiey played 16 games with Bills; Robinson played 16 games with Packers; Rypien played 5 games with Rams; Tuaolo played 6 games with Jaguars; Widell played 16 games with Jaguars.

Abbreviations: D1—draft pick, first round; SupD2—supplemental draft pick, second round; WV—claimed on waivers; TR—obtained in trade; PlanB—Plan B free-agent acquisition; FA—free-agent acquisition (other than Plan B); ED—expansion draft pick.

MISCELLANEOUS TEAM DATA

Stadium (capacity, surface):
Georgia Dome
(71,228, artificial)
Business address:
Atlanta Falcons
One Falcon Place
Suwanee, Ga. 30024
Business phone:
770-945-1111
Ticket information:
404-223-8444
Team colors:
Black, red, silver and white
Flagship radio station:
WGST, 920 AM
Training site:
Atlanta Falcons
Suwanee, Ga.
770-945-1111

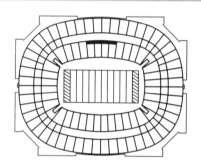

TSN REPORT CARD

Coaching staff	B	Dan Reeves has a knack for keeping games close, and if you do that, you have a chance. His teams aren't exciting, but they're sound and smarter than most. Former NFL head coaches Rich Brooks and Art Shell provide added experience. Defensive line coach Bill Kollar and special teams coach Joe DeCamillis are exceptional.
Offensive backfield	B	Jamal Anderson has rushed for more than 1,000 yards the past two years, and Byron Hanspard ranked third among '97 rookies with 1,375 all-purpose yards. If the line can block for these guys, they'll be productive. Third-down back Harold Green and fullback Bob Christian are more likely to get the ball on pass plays than runs.
Receivers	D	Bert Emanuel signed with the Bucs as a transition free agent, and Michael Haynes, a major disappointment in '97, was waived. That leaves Terance Mathis as the main target and either Todd Kinchen or rookie Jammi German as a likely starter.
Offensive line	C -	The expected offseason overhaul did not occur. Most of the principles are back and they'll be augmented by free agent Corey Louchiey, who started six games for Buffalo last year, and second-round pick Bob Hallen. Ex-Panther Matt Elliott also will get a shot.
Defensive line	B -	Starting right tackle Dan Owens signed with Detroit and wasn't replaced. Chuck Smith, Travis Hall and Lester Archambeau are coming off career years, but critics say they overachieved. Shane Dronett will move from backup to starting right tackle unless '97 second-round pick Nathan Davis comes on.
Linebackers	C	Jessie Tuggle and Cornelius Bennett are nearing the end of their careers, and first-round pick Keith Brooking hasn't played a snap yet. If Brooking pans out, Henri Crockett will move inside and the depth will be better than last year.
Secondary	C +	CBs Ray Buchanan and Ronnie Bradford and Ss Eugene Robinson and William White comprise the best unit the Falcons have had in years. The depth includes former first-round picks Michael Booker and Devin Bush and newcomer Randy Fuller, who started three games for the Steelers last year.
Special teams	A	Morten Andersen is still deadly from long range, and Dan Stryzinski is one of the best hang-time and directional punters in the game. Hanspard returned two kickoffs for touchdowns last year as a rookie. Fourth-round draft choice Tim Dwight takes over on punt returns after leading the nation last year at Iowa.

BALTIMORE RAVENS
AFC CENTRAL DIVISION

1997 REVIEW

RESULTS

Aug. 31—JACKSONVILLE	L	27-28	
Sept. 7—CINCINNATI	W	23-10	
Sept. 14—at N.Y. Giants	W	24-23	
Sept. 21—at Tennessee	W	36-10	
Sept. 28—at San Diego	L	17-21	
Oct. 5—PITTSBURGH	L	34-42	
Oct. 12—Open date			
Oct. 19—MIAMI	L	13-24	
Oct. 26—at Washington	W	20-17	
Nov. 2—at N.Y. Jets (OT)	L	16-19	
Nov. 9—at Pittsburgh	L	0-37	
Nov. 16—PHILADELPHIA (OT)	T	10-10	
Nov. 23—ARIZONA	L	13-16	
Nov. 30—at Jacksonville	L	27-29	
Dec. 7—SEATTLE	W	31-24	
Dec. 14—TENNESSEE	W	21-19	
Dec. 21—at Cincinnati	L	14-16	

RECORDS/RANKINGS

1997 regular-season record: 6-9-1 (5th in AFC Central); 3-5 in division; 4-8 in conference; 3-4-1 at home; 3-5 on road.

1997 team rankings:	No.	AFC	NFL
Total offense	*330.7	5	9
Rushing offense	*99.3	T10	22
Passing offense	*231.4	4	5
Scoring offense	326	11	16
Total defense	*335.2	12	25
Rushing defense	*105.6	5	10
Passing defense	*229.6	14	28
Scoring defense	345	9	18
Takeaways	28	8	T15
Giveaways	32	T11	T20
Turnover differential	-4	13	T22
Sacks	42	T7	T15
Sacks allowed	37	8	13

*Yards per game.

TEAM LEADERS

Scoring (kicking): Matt Stover, 110 pts. (32/32 PATs, 26/34 FGs).
Scoring (touchdowns): Derrick Alexander, 54 pts. (9 receiving).
Passing: Vinny Testaverde, 2,971 yds. (470 att., 271 comp., 57.7%, 18 TDs, 15 int.).
Rushing: Bam Morris, 774 yds. (204 att., 3.8 avg., 4 TDs).
Receptions: Derrick Alexander, 65 (1,009 yds., 15.5 avg., 9 TDs).
Interceptions: Stevon Moore, 4 (56 yds., 0 TDs).
Sacks: Peter Boulware, 11.5.
Punting: Greg Montgomery, 42.7 avg. (83 punts, 3,540 yds., 0 blocked).
Punt returns: Jermaine Lewis, 15.6 avg. (28 att., 437 yds., 2 TDs).
Kickoff returns: Jermaine Lewis, 22.1 avg. (41 att., 905 yds., 0 TDs).

1998 SEASON

CLUB DIRECTORY

Owner/president
Arthur B. Modell
Executive V.P./legal and administration
Jim Bailey
Executive V.P./assistant to the president
David O. Modell
V.P. of player personnel
Ozzie Newsome
Vice president/public relations
Kevin Byrne
Vice president of marketing and sales
David Cope
Chief financial officer
Pat Moriarty
Treasurer
Luis Perez
Director of operations and information
Bob Eller
Director of publications
Francine Lubera
Director of broadcasting
Lisa Bercu
Director of tickets
Roy Sommerhof
Director of pro personnel
James Harris
Director of college scouting
Phil Savage
Scouting/pro personnel
Eric DeCosta
George Kokinis
Ron Marciniak
Terry McDonough
Ernie Plank
Ellis Rainsberger
John Wooten
Art Perkins
Facilities manager
Chuck Cusick
Head trainer
Bill Tessendorf

Head coach
Ted Marchibroda

Assistant coaches
Maxie Baughan (linebackers)
Jacob Burney (defensive line)
Kirk Ferentz (assistant head coach/offense)
Ken Whisenhunt (tight ends)
Al Lavan (running backs)
Marvin Lewis (defensive coordinator)
Lester Erb (quality control-offense)
Scott O'Brien (special teams)
Alvin Reynolds (secondary)
Jim Schwartz (quality control-defense)
Darrin Simmons (strength & conditioning/quality control-special teams)
Richard Mann (receivers)
Jerry Simmons (strength & conditioning)
Don Strock (quarterbacks)

Assistant trainer
Mark Smith
Team physicians
Dr. John Bergfeld
Dr. Claude T. Moorman III
Dr. Andrew Pollak
Dr. Andrew M. Tucker
Equipment manager
Ed Carroll

SCHEDULE

Sept. 6—	PITTSBURGH	1:01
Sept. 13—	at N.Y. Jets	1:01
Sept. 20—	at Jacksonville	4:15
Sept. 27—	CINCINNATI	8:20
Oct. 4—	Open date	
Oct. 11—	TENNESSEE	1:01
Oct. 18—	at Pittsburgh	1:01
Oct. 25—	at Green Bay	12:01
Nov. 1—	JACKSONVILLE	1:01
Nov. 8—	OAKLAND	1:01
Nov. 15—	at San Diego	1:05
Nov. 22—	at Cincinnati	4:15
Nov. 29—	INDIANAPOLIS	1:01
Dec. 6—	at Tennessee	3:15
Dec. 13—	MINNESOTA	4:15
Dec. 20—	at Chicago	12:01
Dec. 27—	DETROIT	1:01

All times are for home team.
All games Sunday unless noted.

DRAFT CHOICES

Duane Starks, DB, Miami, Fla. (first round/10th pick overall).
Pat Johnson, WR, Oregon (2/42).
Martin Chase, DT, Oklahoma (5/124).
Ryan Sutter, DB, Colorado (5/133).
Ron Rogers, LB, Georgia Tech (6/154).
Sammy Williams, T, Oklahoma (6/164).
Cam Quayle, TE, Weber State (7/241).

1998 SEASON
TRAINING CAMP ROSTER

No.	QUARTERBACKS	Ht./Wt.	Born	NFL Exp.	College	How acq.	'97 Games GP/GS
4	Harbaugh, Jim	6-3/215	12-23-63	12	Michigan	TR/98	*12/11
14	Richardson, Wally	6-4/225	2-11-74	2	Penn State	D7b/97	1/0
10	Zeier, Eric	6-1/205	9-6-72	4	Georgia	D3a/95	5/3
	RUNNING BACKS						
23	Cotton, Kenyon (FB)	6-0/255	2-23-74	2	SW Louisiana	FA/97	16/0
34	Graham, Jay	5-11/220	7-14-75	2	Tennessee	D3/97	13/3
33	Holmes, Priest	5-9/205	10-7-73	2	Texas	FA/97	7/0
42	Potts, Roosevelt	6-0/250	1-8-71	5	Northeast Louisiana	FA/98	*8/1
32	Rhett, Errict	5-11/210	12-11-70	5	Florida	TR/98	*11/0
44	Vinson, Tony	6-1/229	3-13-71	2	Towson State	FA/97	0/0
	RECEIVERS						
82	Anderson, Stevie	6-6/216	5-12-70	4	Grambling State	FA/98	0/0
86	Green, Eric (TE)	6-5/285	6-22-67	9	Liberty (Va.)	FA/96	16/15
81	Jackson, Michael	6-4/195	4-12-69	8	Southern Mississippi	D6/91	16/15
85	Johnson, Pat	5-10/180	8-10-76	R	Oregon	D2/98	—
88	Kinchen, Brian (TE)	6-2/240	8-6-65	11	Louisiana State	FA/91	16/6
84	Lewis, Jermaine	5-7/172	10-16-74	3	Maryland	D5/96	14/7
89	Ofodile, A.J. (TE)	6-6/260	10-10-73	2	Missouri	FA/96	12/0
49	Quayle, Cam (TE)	6-7/255	9-24-72	R	Weber State	D7a/98	—
13	Richard, Donald	6-0/180	11-18-72	1	Southwest Louisiana	FA/97	0/0
83	Roe, James	6-1/187	8-23-73	3	Norfolk State	D6b/96	12/4
80	Yarborough, Ryan	6-2/195	4-26-71	4	Wyoming	WV/97	16/3
	OFFENSIVE LINEMEN						
74	Atkins, James (G)	6-6/306	1-28-70	5	Southwestern Louisiana	FA/98	*13/3
76	Bernstein, Alex (G)	6-3/325	8-11-75	1	Massachusetts	FA/97	0/0
69	Blackshear, Jeff (G)	6-6/323	3-29-69	5	Northeast Louisiana	TR/96	16/16
77	Brown, Orlando (T)	6-7/340	12-12-70	6	South Carolina	FA/93	16/16
65	Cavil, Ben (G)	6-2/310	1-31-72	2	Oklahoma	TR/97	15/8
70	Flynn, Mike	6-3/295	6-15-74	1	Maine	FA/97	0/0
71	Folau, Spencer (T)	6-5/300	4-5-73	2	Idaho	FA/96	10/0
64	Isaia, Sale	6-5/315	6-13-72	4	UCLA	FA/95	0/0
60	Mitchell, Jeff (C)	6-4/300	1-29-74	2	Florida	D5/97	0/0
75	Ogden, Jonathan	6-8/318	7-31-74	3	UCLA	D1a/96	16/16
72	Williams, Sammy (T)	6-5/318	12-14-74	R	Oklahoma	D6b/98	—
63	Williams, Wally (G)	6-2/305	2-19-71	6	Florida A&M	FA/93	10/10
	DEFENSIVE LINEMEN						
90	Burnett, Rob (E)	6-4/280	8-27-67	9	Syracuse	D5/90	15/15
92	Chase, Martin (T)	6-2/295	12-19-74	R	Oklahoma	D5a/98	—
94	Frederick, Mike (E)	6-5/280	8-6-72	4	Virginia	D3b/95	16/1
97	Jones, James (T)	6-2/290	2-6-69	8	Northern Iowa	FA/96	16/16
99	McCrary, Michael (E)	6-4/270	7-7-70	6	Wake Forest	FA/97	15/15
98	Siragusa, Tony (T)	6-3/320	5-14-67	9	Pittsburgh	FA/97	14/13
95	Ward, Chris (E)	6-3/275	2-4-74	2	Kentucky	D7a/97	5/0
93	Washington, Keith (E)	6-4/270	12-18-72	3	UNLV	FA/97	10/1
79	Webster, Larry	6-5/288	1-18-69	6	Maryland	FA/95	16/3
	LINEBACKERS						
58	Boulware, Peter	6-4/255	12-18-74	2	Florida State	D1/97	16/16
51	Brown, Cornell	6-0/240	3-15-75	2	Virginia Tech	D6b/97	16/1
52	Lewis, Ray	6-1/240	5-15-75	3	Miami (Fla.)	D1b/96	16/16
54	McCloud, Tyrus	6-1/250	11-23-74	2	Louisville	D4b/97	16/0
53	Peters, Tyrell	6-0/230	8-4-74	2	Oklahoma	FA/97	4/0
50	Rogers, Ron	6-0/245	4-20-75	R	Georgia Tech	D6/98	—
55	Sharper, Jamie	6-3/240	11-23-74	2	Virginia	D2a/97	16/15
	DEFENSIVE BACKS						
24	Brady, Donny	6-2/195	11-24-73	3	Wisconsin	FA/95	16/5
20	Herring, Kim (S)	5-11/210	10-10-75	2	Penn State	D2b/97	15/4
21	Jackson, Alfred	6-0/183	7-10-67	7	San Diego State	FA/98	0/0
25	Jenkins, DeRon (CB)	5-11/190	11-14-73	3	Tennessee	D2/96	16/6
31	Jones, Rondell (S)	6-2/210	5-7-71	6	North Carolina	FA/97	14/12
29	Lyons, Lamar (S)	6-3/210	3-25-73	2	Washington	FA/97	1/0
27	Moore, Stevon (S)	5-11/210	2-9-67	10	Mississippi	PlanB/92	13/12

No.	DEFENSIVE BACKS	Ht./Wt.	Born	NFL Exp.	College	How acq.	'97 Games GP/GS
22	Starks, Duane (CB)	5-10/170	5-23-74	R	Miami	D1/98	—
41	Staten, Ralph (S)	6-3/205	12-3-74	2	Alabama	D7c/97	10/3
35	Sutter, Ryan (S)	6-1/203	9-14-74	R	Colorado	D5/98	—
37	Thompson, Bennie (S)	6-0/214	2-10-63	9	Grambling State	FA/94	16/1
36	Williams, John	5-7/180	7-26-74	1	Southern	FA/97	4/0
26	Woodson, Rod (CB)	6-0/200	3-10-65	12	Purdue	FA/98	*14/14
	SPECIALISTS						
9	Montgomery, Greg (P)	6-4/215	10-29-64	10	Michigan State	FA/96	16/0
5	Richardson, Kyle (P)	6-2/180	2-3-73	2	Arkansas State	FA/98	*5/0
3	Stover, Matt (K)	5-11/178	1-27-68	9	Louisiana Tech	PlanB/91	16/0

*Atkins played 13 games with Seahawks in '97; Harbaugh played 12 games with Colts; Potts played 2 games with Colts and 6 games with Dolphins; Rhett played 11 games with Buccaneers; Richardson played 3 games with Dolphins and 2 games with Eagles; Woodson played 14 games with 49ers.

Abbreviations: D1—draft pick, first round; SupD2—supplemental draft pick, second round; WV—claimed on waivers; TR—obtained in trade; PlanB—Plan B free-agent acquisition; FA—free-agent acquisition (other than Plan B); ED—expansion draft pick.

MISCELLANEOUS TEAM DATA

Stadium (capacity, surface):
Name to be announced
(68,400, grass)
Business address:
11001 Owings Mills Blvd.
Owings Mills, MD 21117
Business phone:
410-654-6200
Ticket information:
410-261-RAVE
Team colors:
Purple, black and metallic gold
Flagship radio stations:
WJFK/WLIF
Training site:
Western Maryland College
Westminster, Md.
401-654-6200

Stadium diagram not available
at press time.

TSN REPORT CARD

Coaching staff	C+	As an overall group, they work well but there is no one accountable for running the offense. Some defensive help is needed. Defensive line coach Jacob Burney, assistant head coach/offense Kirk Ferentz and running backs coach Al Lavan draw high marks.
Offensive backfield	B	This group should function well. Errict Rhett is in excellent condition and Jay Graham has bulked up about 10 pounds. If Roosevelt Potts comes close to his past form with the Indianapolis Colts and Jim Harbaugh stays injury free, watch out.
Receivers	C	It will be interesting to see how Jermaine Lewis plays against top-notch corners on the outside instead of nickel backs and safeties in the slot. Michael Jackson is capable of having a big year, but still is not a model of consistency. Rookie Pat Johnson is a year away from having significant impact. Can anyone block?
Offensive line	B	This could develop into a real fine group. New emphasis on the running game will tell if they are one of the better units in the NFL. Four of the five positions have quality players, but left guard is a big question mark.
Defensive line	C +	They have the potential to be one of the best in the league. The group is solid inside and Michael McCrary is a great, young pass rusher. Quality play is limited at the end positions and the group, as a whole, has a history of knee problems.
Linebackers	B	Strongside linebacker Peter Boulware could join middle linebacker Ray Lewis in the Pro Bowl this season. Boulware, though, has to prove he can handle tight ends on running plays. Weakside linebacker Jamie Sharper had a tendency to disappear once in a while in 1997.
Secondary	C -	There are skeptics around the league questioning the signing of cornerback Rod Woodson. The Ravens will start rookie Duane Starks at left cornerback, and maybe a bigger challenge is strong safety Stevon Moore's comeback from major surgery on both knees.
Special teams	C	The units are promising and should be improved, since many first-year players received playing time last season. Punter Greg Montgomery must become more consistent. Kicker Matt Stover is consistent, but don't bet the farm on him during crunch time. Jermaine Lewis was the NFL's top punt returner last season.

BUFFALO BILLS
AFC EASTERN DIVISION

1997 REVIEW

RESULTS

Aug. 31—MINNESOTA	L	13-34
Sept. 7—at N.Y. Jets	W	28-22
Sept.14—at Kansas City	L	16-22
Sept.21—INDIANAPOLIS	W	37-35
Sept.28—Open date		
Oct. 5—DETROIT	W	22-13
Oct. 12—at New England	L	6-33
Oct. 20—at Indianapolis	W	9-6
Oct. 26—DENVER (OT)	L	20-23
Nov. 2—MIAMI	W	9-6
Nov. 9—NEW ENGLAND	L	10-31
Nov. 17—at Miami	L	13-30
Nov. 23—at Tennessee	L	14-31
Nov. 30—N.Y. JETS	W	20-10
Dec. 7—at Chicago	L	3-20
Dec. 14—JACKSONVILLE	L	14-20
Dec. 20—at Green Bay	L	21-31

RECORDS/RANKINGS

1997 regular-season record: 6-10 (4th in AFC East); 5-3 in division; 5-7 in conference; 4-4 at home; 2-6 on road.
Team record last five years: 45-35 (.563), ranks T7th in league in that span).
1997 team rankings:

	No.	AFC	NFL
Total offense	*291.1	14	25
Rushing offense	*111.4	7	14
Passing offense	*179.7	14	25
Scoring offense	255	15	29
Total defense	*303.3	4	9
Rushing defense	*112	9	15
Passing defense	*191.3	3	12
Scoring defense	367	11	23
Takeaways	22	T14	T26
Giveaways	42	15	T28
Turnover differential	-20	15	28
Sacks	46	T4	T8
Sacks allowed	46	T10	T21

*Yards per game.

TEAM LEADERS

Scoring (kicking): Steve Christie, 93 pts. (21/21 PATs, 24/30 FGs).
Scoring (touchdowns): Antowain Smith, 48 pts. (8 rushing).
Passing: Todd Collins, 2,367 yds. (391 att., 215 comp., 55.0%, 12 TDs, 13 int.).
Rushing: Antowain Smith, 840 yds. (194 att., 4.3 avg., 8 TDs).
Receptions: Andre Reed, 60 (880 yds., 14.7 avg., 5 TDs).
Interceptions: Ken Irvin, 2 (28 yds., 0 TDs); Kurt Schulz, 2 (23 yds., 0 TDs); Marlon Kerner, 2 (20 yds., 0 TDs); Jeff Burris, 2 (19 yds., 0 TDs); Sean Moran, 2 (12 yds., 0 TDs).
Sacks: Bruce Smith, 14.0.
Punting: Chris Mohr, 41.8 avg. (90 punts, 3,764 yds., 1 blocked).
Punt returns: Jeff Burris, 9.4 avg. (21 att., 198 yds., 0 TDs).
Kickoff returns: Eric Moulds, 21.4 avg. (43 att., 921 yds., 0 TDs).

1998 SEASON

CLUB DIRECTORY

President
Ralph C. Wilson Jr.
Exec. vice president/general manager
John Butler
Vice president/administration
Jim Miller
Corporate vice president
Linda Bogdan
Treasurer
Jeffrey C. Littmann
Director of administration/ticket sales
Jerry Foran
Vice president/operations
Bill Munson
Director of business operations
Jim Overdorf
Controller
Frank Wojnicki
Director of merchandising
Christy Wilson Hofmann
Director of player/alumni relations
Jerry Butler
Exec. director of marketing and sales
Russ Brandon
Dir. of public/community relations
Denny Lynch
Director of media relations
Scott Berchtold
Ticket director
June Foran
Video director
Henry Kunttu
Director of stadium operations
George Koch
Director of security
Bill Bambach
Engineering and operations manager
Joe Frandina
Director of pro personnel
A.J. Smith
Director of player personnel
Dwight Adams

SCHEDULE

Sept. 6—	at San Diego	1:15
Sept. 13—	at Miami	1:01
Sept. 20—	ST. LOUIS	1:01
Sept. 27—	Open date	
Oct. 4—	SAN FRANCISCO	1:01
Oct. 11—	at Indianapolis	12:01
Oct. 18—	JACKSONVILLE	1:01
Oct. 25—	at Carolina	8:20
Nov. 1—	MIAMI	1:01
Nov. 8—	at N.Y. Jets	4:15
Nov. 15—	NEW ENGLAND	1:01
Nov. 22—	INDIANAPOLIS	1:01
Nov. 29—	at New England	4:05
Dec. 6—	at Cincinnati	1:01
Dec. 13—	OAKLAND	1:01
Dec. 19—	N.Y. JETS (Mon.)	12:35
Dec. 27—	at New Orleans	12:01

All times are for home team.
All games Sunday unless noted.

Head coach
Wade Phillips

Assistant coaches
Max Bowman (asst. to head coach/tight ends)
Bill Bradley (defensive backs)
Ted Cottrell (def. coordinator)
Bruce DeHaven (special teams)
Chris Dickson (off. quality control)
Bishop Harris (running backs)
Charlie Joiner (receivers)
Rusty Jones (strength & cond.)
Chuck Lester (asst. linebackers)
John Levra (defensive line)
Carl Mauck (offensive line)
Joe Pendry (off. coordinator)
Elijah Pitts (asst. head coach/ running backs—medical leave)
Turk Schonert (quarterbacks)

Scouts

Brad Forsyth	Tom Gibbons
Doug Majeski	Buddy Nix
Bob Ryan	Chink Sengel
Dave G. Smith	Dave W. Smith

Head trainer
Bud Carpenter
Assistant trainer
Melvin Lewis
Greg McMillen
Equipment manager
Dave Hojnowski
Assistant equipment manager
Woody Ribbeck

DRAFT CHOICES

Sam Cowart, LB, Florida State (second round/39th pick overall).
Robert Hicks, T, Mississippi State (3/68).
Jonathan Linton, RB, North Carolina (5/131).
Fred Coleman, WR, Washington (6/160).
Victor Allotey, G, Indiana (7/198).
Kamil Loud, WR, Cal Poly-SLO (7/238).

No.	QUARTERBACKS	Ht./Wt.	Born	NFL Exp.	College	How acq.	'97 Games GP/GS
13	Ballard, Jim	6-3/223	4-16-72	2	Mount Union (Ohio)	FA/97	0/0
15	Collins, Todd	6-4/224	11-5-71	4	Michigan	D2/95	14/13
7	Flutie, Doug	5-10/175	10-23-62	5	Boston College	FA/98	0/0
11	Johnson, Rob	6-4/214	3-18-73	4	Southern California	TR/98	*5/1
10	Van Pelt, Alex	6-0/220	5-1-70	3	Pittsburgh	FA/94	6/3
	RUNNING BACKS						
33	Gash, Sam (FB)	6-0/235	3-7-69	6	Penn State	FA/98	*16/5
44	Holmes, Darick	6-0/226	7-1-71	4	Portland State	D7b/95	13/0
25	Ingoglia, Rene	5-10/202	5-23-72	1	Massachusetts	FA/97	0/0
35	Linton, Jonathan (FB)	6-0/248	10-7-74	R	North Carolina	D5/98	—
23	Smith, Antowain	6-2/224	3-14-72	2	Houston	D1/97	16/0
34	Thomas, Thurman	5-10/198	5-16-66	11	Oklahoma State	D2/88	16/16
	RECEIVERS						
81	Coleman, Fred	6-1/190	1-31-75	R	Washington	D6/98	—
88	Early, Quinn	6-0/190	4-13-65	11	Iowa	FA/96	16/16
48	Fitzgerald, Pat (TE)	6-2/228	12-4-74	1	Texas	D7/97	0/0
17	Galloway, Mitchell	5-8/178	10-8-74	2	East Carolina	FA/97	3/0
84	Johnson, Lonnie (TE)	6-3/240	2-14-71	4	Florida State	D2b/94	16/16
45	Loud, Kamil	6-0/190	6-25-76	R	Cal Poly-SLO	D7b/98	—
80	Moulds, Eric	6-0/204	7-17-73	3	Mississippi State	D1/96	16/8
83	Reed, Andre	6-2/190	1-29-64	14	Kutztown (Pa.) State	D4a/85	15/15
81	Reese, Jerry	5-11/190	3-18-73	2	San Jose State	FA/97	5/0
85	Riemersma, Jay (TE)	6-5/254	5-17-73	2	Michigan	D7b/96	16/8
82	Williams, Kevin	5-9/195	1-25-71	6	Miami (Fla.)	FA/98	*16/0
49	Young, Duane (TE)	6-3/270	5-29-68	6	Michigan State	FA/98	0/0
	OFFENSIVE LINEMEN						
76	Albright, Ethan	6-5/283	5-1-71	4	North Carolina	FA/96	16/0
66	Allotey, Victor (G)	6-3/325	4-8-75	R	Indiana	D7a/98	—
70	Brown, Ruben (G)	6-3/304	2-13-72	4	Pittsburgh	D1/95	16/16
63	Conaty, Billy	6-2/306	3-8-73	2	Virginia Tech	FA/97	1/0
70	Fina, John (T)	6-4/285	3-11-69	7	Arizona	D1/92	16/16
77	Hicks, Robert (T)	6-7/338	11-17-74	R	Mississippi State	D3/98	—
74	Nails, Jamie (T)	6-6/354	6-3-75	1	Florida A&M	D4/97	2/0
60	Ostroski, Jerry (G)	6-4/310	7-12-70	5	Tulsa	FA/93	16/16
72	Panos, Joe (G)	6-2/293	1-24-71	5	Wisconsin	FA/98	*13/13
73	Rockwood, Mike (T)	6-10/345	6-8-73	1	Nevada-Reno	FA/97	1/0
69	Spriggs, Marcus (T)	6-3/295	5-17-74	2	Houston	D6/97	2/0
61	Zeigler, Dusty (C)	6-5/298	9-27-73	2	Notre Dame	D6b/96	13/13
	DEFENSIVE LINEMEN						
90	Hansen, Phil (E)	6-5/278	5-20-68	8	North Dakota State	D2/91	16/16
98	Moran, Sean (E)	6-3/275	6-5-73	3	Colorado State	D4/96	16/7
94	Pike, Mark (E)	6-4/272	12-27-63	12	Georgia Tech	D7b/86	15/0
91	Price, Shawn (E)	6-5/285	3-28-70	6	Pacific	FA/96	10/0
78	Smith, Bruce (E)	6-4/273	6-18-63	14	Virginia Tech	D1a/85	16/16
92	Washington, Ted (NT)	6-4/325	4-13-68	8	Louisville	FA/95	16/16
75	Wiley, Marcellus (E)	6-5/271	11-30-74	2	Columbia	D2/97	16/0
93	Williams, Pat (T)	6-3/270	10-24-72	1	Texas A&M	FA/97	1/0
	LINEBACKERS						
96	Brandenburg, Dan	6-3/240	2-16-73	2	Indiana State	D7a/96	12/0
56	Cowart, Sam	6-2/239	2-26-75	R	Florida State	D2/98	—
51	Cummings, Joe	6-2/242	6-8-74	2	Wyoming	FA/98	0/0
52	Holecek, John	6-2/242	5-7-72	2	Illinois	D5/95	14/8
99	Northern, Gabe	6-2/240	6-8-74	3	Louisiana State	D2/96	16/1
58	Perry, Marlo	6-4/250	8-25-72	4	Jackson State	D3a/94	13/0
59	Rogers, Sam	6-3/245	5-30-70	5	Colorado	D2c/94	15/15
95	Sabb, Dwayne	6-4/248	10-9-69	7	New Hampshire	FA/98	0/0
54	Spielman, Chris	6-0/247	10-11-65	11	Ohio State	FA/96	8/8
	DEFENSIVE BACKS						
27	Irvin, Ken (CB)	5-10/186	7-11-72	4	Memphis	D4a/95	16/0
31	Jackson, Raymond	5-10/189	2-17-73	3	Colorado State	D5/96	9/0
20	Jones, Henry (S)	5-11/197	12-29-67	8	Illinois	D1/91	15/15
46	Kerner, Marlon (CB)	5-10/187	3-18-73	4	Ohio State	D3a/95	13/2

No.	DEFENSIVE BACKS	Ht./Wt.	Born	NFL Exp.	College	How acq.	'97 Games GP/GS
21	Martin, Emanuel (S)	5-11/184	7-31-69	3	Alabama State	FA/96	16/2
24	Schulz, Kurt (S)	6-1/208	12-12-68	7	Eastern Washington	D7/92	15/14
40	Smedley, Eric (S)	5-11/199	7-23-73	3	Indiana	D7c/96	13/1
36	Smith, Adrion (CB)	5-10/175	9-29-71	1	Southwest Missouri	FA/98	0/0
28	Smith, Thomas (CB)	5-11/188	12-5-70	6	North Carolina	D1/93	16/16
37	Woodson, Sean (S)	6-0/214	8-27-74	1	Jackson State	D5/97	1/0
	SPECIALISTS						
2	Christie, Steve (K)	6-0/185	11-13-67	9	William & Mary	PlanB/92	16/0
9	Mohr, Chris (P)	6-5/215	5-11-66	9	Alabama	FA/91	16/0
3	Phair, John (K)	6-8/235	2-23-71	1	Fort Lewis	FA/98	0/0

*Gash played 16 games with Patriots in '97; R. Johnson played 5 games with Jaguars; Panos played 13 games with Eagles; K. Williams played 16 games with Cardinals.

Abbreviations: D1—draft pick, first round; SupD2—supplemental draft pick, second round; WV—claimed on waivers; TR—obtained in trade; PlanB—Plan B free-agent acquisition; FA—free-agent acquisition (other than Plan B); ED—expansion draft pick.

MISCELLANEOUS TEAM DATA

Stadium (capacity, surface):
Rich Stadium (80,091, artificial)
Business address:
One Bills Drive
Orchard Park, N.Y. 14127
Business phone:
716-648-1800
Ticket information:
716-649-0015
Team colors:
Royal blue, scarlet and white
Flagship radio station:
WGRF, 96.9 FM; WEDG 103.3 FM
Training site:
Fredonia State University
Fredonia, N.Y.
716-648-1800

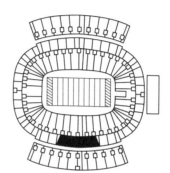

TSN REPORT CARD

Coaching staff	C +	Wade Phillips has only two years of head coaching experience (16-16 record with Denver) and he still has to prove he's more than just a great defensive coordinator. Offensive coordinator Joe Pendry wasn't real popular in Carolina, and Ted Cottrell is in his first year as defensive coordinator. With seven new coaches on board, this staff has some proving to do.
Offensive backfield	B +	Replacing Todd Collins with Rob Johnson at quarterback is akin to trading in a Yugo for a Lexus. Antowain Smith will become the No. 1 back while Thurman Thomas will slide into a specialists role, and both should excel. Sam Gash is the team's first legitimate fullback this decade, and his presence will help make the two-back offense work.
Receivers	B	Andre Reed and Quinn Early are still productive, and Johnson's strong and accurate arm will put their skills to better use. Eric Moulds is a big question mark as the third receiver, and tight end Lonnie Johnson has to start making plays that matter, both as a receiver and a blocker.
Offensive line	C -	Right guard Joe Panos is a big improvement over Corbin Lacina, but the other four positions on a line that allowed 46 sacks remain intact. Jerry Ostroski still has to prove he can play right tackle, and left guard Ruben Brown has to prove his two Pro Bowl appearances were deserved.
Defensive line	A	Right end Bruce Smith will be 35 when the season starts, but he can still rush the passer with a vengeance. Ted Washington is a monster inside, and left end Phil Hansen is vastly underrated. This was the best unit on the team in 1997, and it is again.
Linebackers	B	The switch to the 4-3 defense turns Chris Spielman into a true middle linebacker, but he has to bounce back from serious neck surgery. Bryce Paup is gone, so the heat's on Gabe Northern to replace all those sacks.
Secondary	C	The gang that can't catch needs to do a better job of holding on to interceptions. Right cornerback Thomas Smith is excellent in coverage, but he had no picks in 1997. The team needs big plays, and this unit is due to make a few.
Special teams	C +	It can't get much worse than it was last year, and it won't. Kevin Williams is a superb punt and kickoff returner, the best the Bills have had in years. The coverage teams have vowed to improve dramatically, and kicker Steve Christie and punter Chris Mohr are solid.

CAROLINA PANTHERS
NFC WESTERN DIVISION

1997 REVIEW
RESULTS

Aug. 31—WASHINGTON	L	10-24
Sept. 7—at Atlanta	W	9-6
Sept.14—at San Diego	W	26-7
Sept.21—KANSAS CITY	L	14-35
Sept.29—SAN FRANCISCO	L	21-34
Oct. 5—Open date		
Oct. 12—at Minnesota	L	14-21
Oct. 19—at New Orleans	W	13-0
Oct. 26—ATLANTA	W	21-12
Nov. 2—OAKLAND	W	38-14
Nov. 9—at Denver	L	0-34
Nov. 16—at San Francisco	L	19-27
Nov. 23—at St. Louis	W	16-10
Nov. 30—NEW ORLEANS	L	13-16
Dec. 8—at Dallas	W	23-13
Dec. 14—GREEN BAY	L	10-31
Dec. 20—ST. LOUIS	L	18-30

RECORDS/RANKINGS

1997 regular-season record: 7-9 (T2nd in NFC West); 4-4 in division; 5-7 in conference; 2-6 at home; 5-3 on road.

1997 team rankings:	No.	NFC	NFL
Total offense	*287.8	12	26
Rushing offense	*109.9	8	15
Passing offense	*177.8	12	26
Scoring offense	265	13	27
Total defense	*311.3	9	15
Rushing defense	*123.3	10	22
Passing defense	*187.9	7	9
Scoring defense	314	T7	T13
Takeaways	22	13	T26
Giveaways	39	12	26
Turnover differential	-17	13	27
Sacks	36	14	23
Sacks allowed	44	T9	T18

*Yards per game.

TEAM LEADERS

Scoring (kicking): John Kasay, 91 pts. (25/25 PATs, 22/26 FGs).
Scoring (touchdowns): Fred Lane, 42 pts. (7 rushing).
Passing: Kerry Collins, 2,124 yds. (381 att., 200 comp., 52.5%, 11 TDs, 21 int.).
Rushing: Fred Lane, 809 yds. (182 att., 4.4 avg., 7 TDs).
Receptions: Wesley Walls, 58 (746 yds., 12.9 avg., 6 TDs).
Interceptions: Eric Davis, 5 (25 yds., 0 TDs).
Sacks: Micheal Barrow, 8.5.
Punting: Ken Walter, 42.4 avg. (85 punts, 3,604 yds., 0 blocked).
Punt returns: Tyrone Poole, 7.3 avg. (26 att., 191 yds., 0 TDs).
Kickoff returns: Michael Bates, 27.3 avg. (47 att., 1,281 yds., 0 TDs).

1998 SEASON
CLUB DIRECTORY

Owner & founder
Jerry Richardson
President of Carolina Panthers
Mark Richardson
Director of football administration
Marty Hurney
Director of pro personnel
Jack Bushofsky
President of Carolinas Stadium Corp.
Jon Richardson
Chief financial officer
Dave Olsen
General counsel
Richard Thigpen Jr.
Dir. of marketing & sponsorships
Charles Waddell
Director of sales
Phil Youtsey
Director of communications
Charlie Dayton
Director of player relations
Donnie Shell
Director of facilities
Tom Fellows
Pro scout
Hal Hunter
Sam Mills
Regional scouts
Ralph Hawkins
Area scouts
Hal Athon
Joe Bushofsky
Bob Guarini
Tony Softli
Head groundskeeper
Billy Ball
Equipment manager
Jackie Miles

Head coach
Dom Capers

Assistant coaches
Don Breaux (tight ends)
Billy Davis (outside linebackers)
Vic Fangio (defensive coordinator)
Ted Gill (defensive line)
Chick Harris (running backs)
Gil Haskell (offensive coordinator)
Brett Maxie (assistant def. backs)
Jim McNally (offensive line)
Chip Morton (strength & cond.)
Brad Seely (special teams)
Steve Shafer (def. backs)
John Shoop (quarterbacks)
Kevin Steele (linebackers)
Richard Williamson (wide receivers)

Video director
Dave Sutherby
Head trainer
John Kasik
Assistant trainer
Al Shuford
Orthopedist
Dr. Don D'Alessandro

SCHEDULE

Sept. 6—	ATLANTA	1:01
Sept. 13—	at New Orleans	12:01
Sept. 20—	Open date	
Sept. 27—	GREEN BAY	1:01
Oct. 4—	at Atlanta	1:01
Oct. 11—	at Dallas	12:01
Oct. 18—	at Tampa Bay	1:01
Oct. 25—	BUFFALO	8:20
Nov. 1—	NEW ORLEANS	1:01
Nov. 8—	at San Francisco	1:05
Nov. 15—	MIAMI	1:01
Nov. 22—	at St. Louis	3:05
Nov. 29—	at N.Y. Jets	1:01
Dec. 6—	SAN FRANCISCO	1:01
Dec. 13—	WASHINGTON	1:01
Dec. 20—	ST. LOUIS	1:01
Dec. 27—	at Indianapolis	1:01

All times are for home team.
All games Sunday unless noted.

DRAFT CHOICES

Jason Peter, DT, Nebraska (first round/14th pick overall).
Chuck Wiley, DE, Louisiana State (3/62).
Mitch Marrow, DE, Pennsylvania (3/73).
Donald Hayes, WR, Wisconsin (4/106).
Jerry Jensen, LB, Washington (5/136).
Damien Richardson, DB, Arizona State (6/165).
Viliami Maumau, DT, Colorado (7/196).
Jim Turner, WR, Syracuse (7/228).

1998 SEASON *Carolina Panthers*

No.	QUARTERBACKS	Ht./Wt.	Born	NFL Exp.	College	How acq.	'97 Games GP/GS
7	Beuerlein, Steve	6-3/220	3-7-65	12	Notre Dame	FA/96	7/3
12	Collins, Kerry	6-5/240	12-30-72	4	Penn State	D1a/95	13/13
9	Matthews, Shane	6-3/196	6-1-70	5	Florida	FA/97	0/0
	RUNNING BACKS						
21	Biakabutuka, Tshimanga	6-0/210	1-24-74	2	Michigan	D1/96	8/2
38	Dulaney, Mike (FB)	6-0/245	9-9-70	4	North Carolina	FA/98	*7/0
40	Floyd, William (FB)	6-1/230	2-17-72	5	Florida State	UFA/98	*15/15
43	Greene, Scott (FB)	5-11/225	6-1-72	3	Michigan State	D6/96	16/14
23	Johnson, Anthony	6-0/225	10-25-67	9	Notre Dame	WV/95	16/7
32	Lane, Fred	5-10/205	9-6-75	2	Lane (Tenn.)	FA/97	13/7
20	Oliver, Winslow	5-7/180	3-3-73	3	New Mexico	D3a/96	6/0
22	Smith, Marquette	5-7/190	7-14-72	3	Central Florida	D5/96	0/0
	RECEIVERS						
49	Broughton, Luther (TE)	6-2/248	11-30-74	2	Furman	D5b/97	0/0
83	Carrier, Mark	6-0/185	10-28-65	12	Nicholls State (La.)	ED/95	9/6
86	Carruth, Rae	5-11/194	1-20-74	2	Colorado	D1/97	15/14
	Hayes, Donald	6-5/208	7-13-75	R	Wisconsin	D4/98	—
81	Ismail, Rocket	5-11/176	11-18-69	6	Notre Dame	TR/96	13/2
48	Mangum, Kris (TE)	6-4/249	8-15-73	1	Mississippi	D7/97	2/1
87	Muhammad, Muhsin	6-2/217	5-5-73	3	Michigan State	D2/96	13/5
80	Stone, Dwight	6-0/195	1-28-64	12	Middle Tennessee State	FA/95	16/0
	Turner, Jim	6-4/212	11-13-75	R	Syracuse	D7b/98	—
85	Walls, Wesley (TE)	6-5/250	2-26-66	10	Mississippi	FA/96	15/15
84	Wiggins, Brian	5-11/187	6-14-68	2	Texas Southern	FA/98	0/0
	OFFENSIVE LINEMEN						
78	Brockermeyer, Blake (T)	6-4/300	4-11-73	4	Texas	D1c/95	16/13
66	Campbell, Mathew (T)	6-4/270	7-14-72	4	South Carolina	FA/95	16/14
72	Dafney, Bernard (G)	6-5/329	11-1-68	7	Tennessee	FA/98	*1/0
76	Davidds-Garrido, Norberto (T)	6-6/313	10-4-72	3	Southern California	D4a/96	15/15
65	Garcia, Frank (C)	6-1/295	1-28-72	4	Washington	D4/95	16/16
60	Greeley, Bucky (G)	6-2/285	7-30-72	3	Penn State	FA/96	6/0
61	Hannah, Shane (G)	6-5/320	10-21-71	2	Michigan State	FA/98	0/0
64	Lacina, Corbin (G)	6-4/297	11-2-70	5	Augustana (S.D.)	FA/98	*16/13
63	Rodenhauser, Mark (C)	6-5/280	6-1-61	11	Illinois State	ED/95	16/0
70	Stewart, Todd (T)	6-6/290	9-30-74	1	California	FA/97	0/0
73	Wilson, Jamie (G)	6-7/288	6-6-79	2	Gloucester	FA/97	0/0
	DEFENSIVE LINEMEN						
93	Fox, Mike (E)	6-8/295	8-5-67	9	West Virginia	FA/95	11/9
94	Gilbert, Sean (T)	6-5/318	4-10-70	6	Pittsburgh	FA/98	0/0
96	King, Shawn (E)	6-3/278	6-24-72	4	Northeast Louisiana	D2/95	9/2
	Marrow, Mitch (T)	6-4/280	7-16-75	R	Pennsylvania	D3b/98	—
	Maumau, Viliami (T)	6-2/302	4-3-75	R	Colorado	D7a/98	—
69	Miller, Les (E)	6-7/305	3-1-65	12	Fort Hays State (Kan.)	FA/96	16/11
93	Morabito, Tim (T)	6-3/296	10-12-73	3	Boston College	WV/97	8/0
	Peter, Jason (T)	6-5/288	9-13-74	R	Nebraska	D1/98	—
96	Sasa, Don (T)	6-3/303	9-16-72	3	Washington State	FA/97	1/0
67	Smith, Ryan (E)	6-4/268	10-7-72	1	Idaho	FA/98	0/0
71	Wiley, Chuck (E)	6-4/275	7-16-75	R	Louisiana State	D3a/98	—
	LINEBACKERS						
54	Bailey, Carlton	6-3/242	12-15-64	11	North Carolina	FA/97	8/0
56	Barrow, Micheal	6-2/236	4-19-70	6	Miami (Fla.)	FA/97	16/16
52	Brady, Jeff	6-1/243	11-9-68	8	Kentucky	FA/98	*15/14
56	Dixon, Ernest	6-1/240	10-17-71	5	South Carolina	FA/98	*15/0
54	Gaskins, Percell	6-0/230	4-25-72	3	Kansas State	WV/97	12/0
91	Greene, Kevin	6-3/247	7-31-62	14	Auburn	FA/98	*14/4
	Jensen, Jerry	6-0/237	2-26-75	R	Washington	D5/98	—
57	Lathon, Lamar	6-3/260	12-23-67	9	Houston	FA/95	15/15
58	Mason, Eddie	5-11/245	1-9-72	3	North Carolina	FA/98	0/0
94	Saleh, Tarek	6-1/240	11-7-74	2	Wisconsin	D4/97	3/0
50	Tatum, Kinnon	6-0/222	7-19-75	2	Notre Dame	D3/97	16/0

No.	DEFENSIVE BACKS	Ht./Wt.	Born	NFL Exp.	College	How acq.	'97 Games GP/GS
24	Abraham, Clifton (CB)	5-9/185	12-9-71	3	Florida State	WV/97	1/0
46	Alexander, Brent (S)	5-11/186	7-10-70	5	Tennessee State	FA/98	*16/15
41	Cook, Toi (CB)	5-11/188	12-9-64	12	Stanford	FA/96	16/0
25	Davis, Eric (CB)	5-11/185	1-26-68	9	Jacksonville (Ala.) State	FA/96	14/14
33	Evans, Doug (CB)	6-1/190	5-13-70	6	Louisiana Tech	UFA/98	*15/15
44	Gray, Derwin	5-11/210	4-9-71	6	Brigham Young	FA/98	*11/0
30	Minter, Mike (S)	5-10/188	1-15-74	2	Nebraska	D2/97	16/11
27	Pieri, Damon (S)	6-0/186	9-25-70	4	San Diego State	FA/96	16/0
38	Poole, Tyrone (CB)	5-8/188	2-3-72	4	Fort Valley (Ga.) State	D1b/95	16/16
	Richardson, Damien (S)	6-1/210	4-3-76	R	Arizona State	D6/98	—
31	Smith, Rod (CB)	5-11/187	3-12-70	7	Notre Dame	FA/96	16/2
	Swift, Michael	5-10/165	2-28-74	2	Austin Peay State	FA/98	*12/1
37	Wheeler, Leonard (CB)	5-11/189	1-15-69	7	Troy (Ala.) State	FA/98	*15/0
	SPECIALISTS						
82	Bates, Michael (KR)	5-10/189	12-19-69	6	Arizona	FA/96	16/0
17	Calicchio, Lonnie (P)	6-2/237	10-24-72	1	Mississippi	FA/98	*2/0
4	Kasay, John (K)	5-10/198	10-27-69	8	Georgia	FA/95	16/0
13	Walter, Ken (P)	6-1/195	8-15-72	2	Kent	FA/96	16/0

*Alexander played 16 games with Cardinals in '97; Brady played 15 games with Vikings; Calicchio played 2 games with Eagles; Dafney played 1 game with Ravens; Dixon played 15 games with Saints; Dulaney played 7 games with Bears; Evans played 15 games with Packers; Floyd played 15 games with 49ers; Gray played 11 games with Colts; Greene played 14 games with 49ers; Lacina played 16 games with Bills; Swift played 12 games with Chargers; Wheeler played 15 games with Vikings.

Abbreviations: D1—draft pick, first round; SupD2—supplemental draft pick, second round; WV—claimed on waivers; TR—obtained in trade; PlanB—Plan B free-agent acquisition; FA—free-agent acquisition (other than Plan B); ED—expansion draft pick.

MISCELLANEOUS TEAM DATA

Stadium (capacity, surface):
Ericsson Stadium
(73,248, grass)

Business address:
800 S. Mint St.
Charlotte, NC 28202-1502

Business phone:
704-358-7000

Ticket information:
704-358-7800

Team colors:
Blue, black and silver

Flagship radio station:
WBT-1110 AM

Training site:
Wofford College
Spartanburg, S.C.
704-358-7000

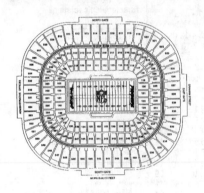

TSN REPORT CARD

Coaching staff	B	Dom Capers and Vic Fangio, the defensive coordinator, have one side of the ball covered and Gil Haskell, the new offensive coordinator, is a vast improvement on the other side over the departed Joe Pendry, now with Buffalo. The rest of the staff is solid.
Offensive backfield	B -	The addition of William Floyd should clear the way to a 1,000-yard season and many touchdowns for Fred Lane. If you don't know who Lane is now, you will by the end of this season. The jury is still out on quarterback Kerry Collins.
Receivers	C -	Outside of tight end Wesley Walls and wideout Mark Carrier, who is getting old and may be phased out, this remains a largely unproven, inexperienced group that did not get the job done last season.
Offensive line	C -	This unit was average at best last season and sometimes much worse. Yet only minor tinkering was done in the offseason, and it remains to be seen how much of a difference Corbin Lacina can make at right guard.
Defensive line	B +	No position group on the team was helped more by offseason attention, with the additions of Sean Gilbert and first-round draft pick Jason Peter expected to help correct last year's most glaring defensive deficiency: inability to stop the run.
Linebackers	B -	Kevin Greene is 36. Lamar Lathon is coming off a two-sack season and knee surgery. Sam Mills has retired. This group still could be great (at least Micheal Barrow will play inside, where he belongs), but there are many questions.
Secondary	B	No team in the league has a combination of three cover cornerbacks like Eric Davis, Doug Evans and Tyrone Poole. The loss of Chad Cota, who signed with the Saints, at strong safety hurts, but the secondary should be solid.
Special teams	B	Michael Bates is one of the game's top kickoff return men, and John Kasay is one of the game's most accurate kickers. The coverage units need to improve on last year's dismal performance.

CHICAGO BEARS
NFC CENTRAL DIVISION

1997 REVIEW
RESULTS

Sept. 1—at Green Bay	L	24-38
Sept. 7—MINNESOTA	L	24-27
Sept.14—DETROIT	L	7-32
Sept.21—at New England	L	3-31
Sept.28—at Dallas	L	3-27
Oct. 5—NEW ORLEANS	L	17-20
Oct. 12—GREEN BAY	L	23-24
Oct. 19—Open date		
Oct. 27—at Miami (OT)	W	36-33
Nov. 2—WASHINGTON	L	8-31
Nov. 9—at Minnesota	L	22-29
Nov. 16—N.Y. JETS	L	15-23
Nov. 23—TAMPA BAY	W	13-7
Nov. 27—at Detroit	L	20-55
Dec. 7—BUFFALO	W	20-3
Dec. 14—at St. Louis	W	13-10
Dec. 21—at Tampa Bay	L	15-31

RECORDS/RANKINGS

1997 regular-season record: 4-12 (5th in NFC Central); 1-7 in division; 2-10 in conference; 2-6 at home; 2-6 on road.
Team record last five years: 36-44 (.450, ranks 17th in league in that span).

1997 team rankings:	No.	NFC	NFL
Total offense	*311.7	7	17
Rushing offense	*109.1	9	16
Passing offense	*202.6	7	T15
Scoring offense	263	14	28
Total defense	*305.5	6	12
Rushing defense	*116.1	8	19
Passing defense	*189.4	9	11
Scoring defense	421	15	29
Takeaways	30	T6	T11
Giveaways	41	13	27
Turnover differential	-11	12	26
Sacks	38	T10	T18
Sacks allowed	43	8	17

*Yards per game.

TEAM LEADERS

Scoring (kicking): Jeff Jaeger, 83 pts. (20/20 PATs, 21/26 FGs).
Scoring (touchdowns): Raymont Harris, 60 pts. (10 rushing).
Passing: Erik Kramer, 3,011 yds. (477 att., 275 comp., 57.7%, 14 TDs, 14 int.).
Rushing: Raymont Harris, 1,033 yds. (275 att., 3.8 avg., 10 TDs).
Receptions: Ricky Proehl, 58 (753 yds., 13.0 avg., 7 TDs).
Interceptions: Walt Harris, 5 (30 yds., 0 TDs).
Sacks: Barry Minter, 6.0; Jim Flanigan, 6.0.
Punting: Todd Sauerbrun, 42.7 avg. (95 punts, 4,059 yds., 0 blocked).
Punt returns: Tyrone Hughes, 7.2 avg. (36 att., 258 yds., 0 TDs).
Kickoff returns: Tyrone Hughes, 23.4 avg. (43 att., 1,008 yds., 0 TDs).

1998 SEASON
CLUB DIRECTORY

Chairman of the board
Edward W. McCaskey
President and chief executive officer
Michael B. McCaskey
Vice president
Timothy E. McCaskey
Secretary
Virginia H. McCaskey
Vice president of operations
Ted Phillips
Director/administration
Bill McGrane
Director/marketing and communications
Ken Valdiserri
Mgr. of promotions and special events
John Bostrom
Manager of sales
Jack Trompeter
Director/public relations
Bryan Harlan
Assistant directors/public relations
Scott Hagel
Phil Handler
Ticket manager
George McCaskey
Vice president, player personnel
Mark Hatley
Director/pro scouting
Rick Spielman
Pro scout
Mike McCartney
Director/college scouting
Bill Rees
Regional scouts
Charles Garcia
Jeff Shiver
Marty Barrett
Gary Smith
Bobby Riggle
Head trainer
Tim Bream

Head coach
Dave Wannstedt

Assistant coaches
Keith Armstrong (special teams)
Joe Brodsky (running backs)
Clarence Brooks (defensive line)
Matt Cavanaugh (offensive coordinator/quarterbacks)
Ivan Fears (wide receivers)
Carlos Mainord (defensive backs)
Tom Rossley (tight ends)
Greg Schiano (defensive backs)
Bob Slowik (defensive coordinator/linebackers)
Tony Wise (assistant head coach/offensive line)

Assistant trainer
Eric Sugerman
Physical development coordinator
Russ Riederer
Asst. physical development coordinator
Steve Little
Equipment manager
Tony Medlin
Assistant equipment managers
Randy Knowles
Carl Piekarski
Director of video services
Dean Pope
Assistant video director
Dave Hendrickson

SCHEDULE

Sept. 6—	JACKSONVILLE	12:01
Sept. 13—	at Pittsburgh	1:01
Sept. 20—	at Tampa Bay	4:05
Sept. 27—	MINNESOTA	3:15
Oct. 4—	DETROIT	12:01
Oct. 11—	at Arizona	1:05
Oct. 18—	DALLAS	3:15
Oct. 25—	at Tennessee	3:05
Nov. 1—	Open date	
Nov. 8—	ST. LOUIS	12:01
Nov. 15—	at Detroit	8:20
Nov. 22—	at Atlanta	1:01
Nov. 29—	TAMPA BAY	12:01
Dec. 6—	at Minnesota	7:20
Dec. 13—	at Green Bay	12:01
Dec. 20—	BALTIMORE	12:01
Dec. 27—	GREEN BAY	12:01

All times are for home team.
All games Sunday unless noted.

DRAFT CHOICES

Curtis Enis, RB, Penn State (first round/fifth pick overall).
Tony Parrish, DB, Washington (2/35).
Olin Kreutz, C, Washington (3/64).
Alonzo Mayes, TE, Oklahoma State (4/94).
Chris Draft, LB, Stanford (6/157).
Patrick Mannelly, T, Duke (6/189).
Chad Overhauser, T, UCLA (7/217).
Moses Moreno, QB, Colorado State (7/232).

TRAINING CAMP ROSTER

No.	QUARTERBACKS	Ht./Wt.	Born	NFL Exp.	College	How acq.	'97 Games GP/GS
12	Kramer, Erik	6-1/204	11-6-64	9	North Carolina State	FA/94	15/13
13	Mirer, Rick	6-2/215	3-19-70	6	Notre Dame	TR/97	7/3
	Moreno, Moses	6-1/195	9-5-75	R	Colorado State	D7b/98	—
18	Stenstrom, Steve	6-2/202	12-23-71	4	Stanford	WV/95	3/0
	RUNNING BACKS						
20	Allen, James	5-10/215	3-28-75	1	Oklahoma	FA/97	0/0
21	Autry, Darnell	5-10/210	6-19-76	2	Northwestern	D4a/97	13/3
32	Bennett, Edgar (FB)	6-0/218	2-15-69	7	Florida State	FA/98	0/0
	Enis, Curtis	6-1/242	6-15-76	R	Penn State	D1/98	—
49	Hallock, Ty (FB)	6-2/256	4-30-71	6	Michigan State	FA/98	*15/8
33	Harmon, Ronnie	5-11/195	5-7-64	13	Iowa	FA/96	*12/0
31	Salaam, Rashaan	6-1/224	10-8-74	4	Colorado	D1/95	3/3
22	Tindale, Tim (FB)	5-10/220	4-15-71	4	Western Ontario	FA/98	*7/0
	RECEIVERS						
85	Allen, Tremayne (TE)	6-2/244	8-9-74	2	Florida	UFA/97	2/0
84	Allred, John (TE)	6-4/249	9-9-74	2	Southern California	D2/97	15/4
82	Bownes, Fabien	5-11/190	2-29-72	2	Western Illinois	FA/95	16/0
80	Conway, Curtis	6-0/194	3-13-71	6	Southern California	D1/93	7/7
81	Engram, Bobby	5-10/192	1-7-73	3	Penn State	D2/96	11/11
87	Lewis, Thomas	6-1/195	1-10-72	5	Indiana	FA/98	*4/2
88	Mayes, Alonzo (TE)	6-4/259	6-4-75	R	Oklahoma State	D4/98	—
15	Miller, Chris	5-10/192	7-10-73	1	Southern California	D7/97	0/0
86	Penn, Chris	6-0/200	4-20-71	5	Tulsa	T-KC/97	14/4
83	Robinson, Marcus	6-3/215	2-27-75	1	South Carolina	D4b/97	0/0
14	Smith, Eric	5-11/183	1-5-71	2	Louisiana State	FA/97	7/0
89	Wetnight, Ryan (TE)	6-2/236	11-5-70	6	Stanford	FA/93	16/3
	OFFENSIVE LINEMEN						
64	Heck, Andy (T)	6-6/298	1-1-67	10	Notre Dame	FA/94	16/16
74	Herndon, Jimmy (T)	6-8/318	8-30-73	3	Houston	D5/96	7/0
67	Huntington, Greg (G)	6-3/308	9-22-70	5	Penn State	FA/96	1/0
57	Kreutz, Olin (C)	6-2/300	6-9-77	R	Washington	D3/98	—
65	Mannelly, Patrick (T)	6-5/285	4-18-75	R	Duke	D6b/98	—
69	Overhauser, Chad (T)	6-4/296	6-17-75	R	UCLA	D7a/98	—
75	Perry, Todd (G)	6-5/308	11-28-70	6	Kentucky	D4a/93	11/11
58	Villarrial, Chris (G)	6-4/310	6-9-73	3	Indiana (Pa.)	D5/96	11/11
60	Wiegmann, Casey (C)	6-3/295	7-20-73	3	Iowa	WV/96	*4/0
71	Williams, James (T)	6-7/340	3-29-68	8	Cheyney (Pa.)	FA/91	16/16
72	Zandofsky, Mike (G)	6-2/308	11-30-65	10	Washington	FA/98	*5/2
73	Zitelli, Emmett (C)	6-3/295	3-13-74	1	Purdue	UFA/97	0/0
	DEFENSIVE LINEMEN						
99	Flanigan, Jim (T)	6-2/286	8-27-71	5	Notre Dame	D3/94	16/16
93	Grasmanis, Paul (T)	6-2/298	8-2-74	3	Notre Dame	D4/96	16/0
76	Lee, Mark (E)	6-4/270	6-4-72	1	Western State Colorado	WV/97	0/0
	Lee, Shawn (T)	6-2/300	10-24-66	11	North Alabama	T/98	*16/5
68	Reeves, Carl (E)	6-4/270	12-17-71	3	North Carolina State	D6b/95	15/11
98	Simpson, Carl (T)	6-2/292	4-18-70	6	Florida State	D2/93	16/16
90	Spellman, Alonzo (E)	6-4/292	9-27-71	7	Ohio State	D1/92	7/5
91	Thierry, John (E)	6-4/265	9-4-71	5	Alcorn State	D1/94	9/9
95	Thomas, Mark (E)	6-5/272	5-6-69	7	North Carolina State	FA/97	16/7
97	Wells, Mike (E)	6-3/310	1-6-71	5	Iowa	FA/98	*16/16
96	Williams, Tyrone (T)	6-4/292	10-22-72	1	Wyoming	WV/97	3/0
	LINEBACKERS						
59	Carter, Daryl	6-2/232	2-24-75	1	Wisconsin.	UFA/97	1/0
	Collins, Andre	6-1/231	5-4-68	9	Penn State	UFA/98	*16/0.
54	Cox, Ron	6-2/235	2-27-68	9	Fresno State	FA/96	15/13
63	Draft, Chris	5-11/222	2-26-76	R	Stanford	D6/98	—
55	Harris, Sean	6-3/248	2-25-72	4	Arizona	D3/95	11/1
94	Hogans, Richard	6-2/249	7-8-75	1	Memphis	D6b/97	0/0
53	Lowery, Michael	6-0/232	2-14-74	3	Mississippi	FA/96	16/0
56	McDonald, Ricardo	6-2/240	11-8-69	7	Pittsburgh	D4/92	13/12
92	Minter, Barry	6-2/242	1-28-70	6	Tulsa	TR/93	16/16
62	Peoples, Shont'e	6-2/249	8-30-72	1	Michigan	FA/98	0/0
	DEFENSIVE BACKS						
30	Bell, Ricky (CB)	5-10/194	10-2-74	3	North Carolina State	WV/96	5/0
25	Carter, Tom (CB)	6-0/189	9-5-72	6	Notre Dame	FA/97	16/16

No.	DEFENSIVE BACKS	Ht./Wt.	Born	NFL Exp.	College	How acq.	'97 Games GP/GS
23	Carter, Marty (S)	6-1/214	12-17-69	8	Middle Tennessee State	FA/95	15/15
24	Cousin, Terry (CB)	5-9/182	3-11-75	2	South Carolina	FA/97	6/0
46	Forbes, Marlon (S)	6-1/215	12-25-71	3	Penn State	FA/95	16/1
27	Harris, Walt (CB)	5-11/195	8-10-74	3	Mississippi State	D1/96	16/16
48	Hiles, Van	6-0/198	11-1-75	2	Kentucky	D5b/97	16/1
35	Johnson, Clyde (S)	5-10/190	5-22-70	1	Kansas State	FA/97	*15/0
44	Mathis, Dedric (CB)	5-10/188	9-26-73	3	Houston	FA/98	*13/4
37	Parrish, Tony (S)	5-11/205	11-23-75	R	Washington	D2/98	—
	SPECIALISTS						
1	Jaeger, Jeff (K)	5-11/190	11-26-64	12	Washington	FA/96	16/0
8	Kanner, Aaron (P)	6-1/220	9-25-70	1	Catawba College (N.C.)	WFA/98	0/0
16	Sauerbrun, Todd (P)	5-10/209	1-4-73	4	West Virginia	D2/95	16/0

*Collins played 16 games with Bengals in '97; Hallock played 15 games with Jaguars; Harmon played 1 game with Bears and 11 games with Oilers; Johnson played 15 games with Chiefs; S. Lee played 16 games with Chargers; Lewis played 4 games with Giants; Mathis played 13 games with Colts; Tindale played 7 games with Bills; Wells played 16 games with Lions; Wiegmann played 3 games with Jets and 1 game with Bears; Zandofsky played 5 games with Eagles.

Abbreviations: D1—draft pick, first round; SupD2—supplemental draft pick, second round; WV—claimed on waivers; TR—obtained in trade; PlanB—Plan B free-agent acquisition; FA—free-agent acquisition (other than Plan B); ED—expansion draft pick.

MISCELLANEOUS TEAM DATA

Stadium (capacity, surface):
Soldier Field (66,944, grass)
Business address:
Halas Hall at Conway Park
1000 Football Drive
Lake Forest, IL 60045
Business phone:
847-295-6600
Ticket information:
847-615-2327
Team colors:
Navy blue, orange and white
Flagship radio station:
WMAQ, 670 AM
Training site:
University of Wisconsin-Platteville
Platteville, Wis.
608-342-1201

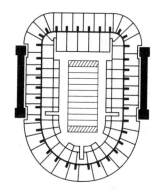

TSN REPORT CARD

Coaching staff	C	Dave Wannstedt was a .500 coach (32-32) in his first four years on the job. He must show that last season's 4-12 record was a blip on the screen in order to save some jobs (his and his assistants'). But the six or seven wins he needs to survive may be hard to get in a tough division.
Offensive backfield	B	After a year of indecision that hurt the entire team, Erik Kramer enters the season as the undisputed starting quarterback. Rookie Curtis Enis and veterans Edgar Bennett and Ty Hallock form the best group of running backs the Bears have assembled under Wannstedt.
Receivers	C -	After Curtis Conway, who missed most of last season with a broken collarbone, the Bears lack long-ball threats. Of the returning wideouts except for Conway, none caught a pass covering more than 33 yards last season. Rookie Alonzo Mayes could make tight end a dangerous position in the Chicago offense for the first time in a long time.
Offensive line	B +	This could be one of the NFL's most consistent offensive lines if a center can be found. The best bet at this point is rookie Olin Kreutz. Left tackle Andy Heck and left guard Todd Perry are entering their fifth season playing alongside each other.
Defensive line	D	These guys are pretty good against the run but pretty woeful, except for Jim Flanigan and Mark Thomas, rushing the passer. The hope is that free-agent signee Mike Wells can alleviate some of the double-teaming Flanigan receives.
Linebackers	C -	Barry Minter is a triple-threat throwback who can cover, rush and plug. Ricardo McDonald is being counted on to upgrade the strong side and pass rush.
Secondary	B	The starting cornerback tandem of Tom Carter and Walt Harris can be very good, and safety has been upgraded with the addition of second-round draft choice Tony Parrish. But the lack of a strong front seven hurts.
Special teams	D -	Jeff Jaeger, who is 40-for-49 on field goals in his two seasons with the team, is the only proven bright spot. The coverage units are poor, the return men are suspect and punter Todd Sauerbrun is inconsistent.

CINCINNATI BENGALS
AFC CENTRAL DIVISION

1997 REVIEW
RESULTS

Aug. 31—ARIZONA	W	24-21
Sept. 7—at Baltimore	L	10-23
Sept.14—Open date		
Sept.21—at Denver	L	20-38
Sept.28—N.Y. JETS	L	14-31
Oct. 5—at Jacksonville	L	13-21
Oct. 12—at Tennessee	L	7-30
Oct. 19—PITTSBURGH	L	10-26
Oct. 26—at N.Y. Giants	L	27-29
Nov. 2—SAN DIEGO	W	38-31
Nov. 9—at Indianapolis	W	28-13
Nov. 16—at Pittsburgh	L	3-20
Nov. 23—JACKSONVILLE	W	31-26
Nov. 30—at Philadelphia	L	42-44
Dec. 4—TENNESSEE	W	41-14
Dec. 14—DALLAS	W	31-24
Dec. 21—BALTIMORE	W	16-14

RECORDS/RANKINGS

1997 regular-season record: 7-9 (4th in AFC Central); 3-5 in division; 5-7 in conference; 6-2 at home; 1-7 on road.
Team record last five years: 28-52 (.350, ranks 25th in league in that span).

1997 team rankings:	No.	AFC	NFL
Total offense	*330.1	6	10
Rushing offense	*122.9	5	9
Passing offense	*207.3	8	13
Scoring offense	355	7	10
Total defense	*355.1	14	28
Rushing defense	*138.9	14	29
Passing defense	*216.2	T8	T21
Scoring defense	405	13	27
Takeaways	23	13	25
Giveaways	22	T5	T7
Turnover differential	1	T8	T14
Sacks	35	T10	T24
Sacks allowed	46	T10	T21

*Yards per game.

TEAM LEADERS

Scoring (kicking): Doug Pelfrey, 77 pts. (41/43 PATs, 12/16 FGs).
Scoring (touchdowns): Corey Dillon, 60 pts. (10 rushing).
Passing: Jeff Blake, 2,125 yds. (317 att., 184 comp., 58.0%, 8 TDs, 7 int.).
Rushing: Corey Dillon, 1,129 yds. (233 att., 4.8 avg., 10 TDs).
Receptions: Darnay Scott, 54 (797 yds., 14.8 avg., 5 TDs).
Interceptions: Corey Sawyer, 4 (44 yds., 0 TDs).
Sacks: Gerald Dixon, 8.5.
Punting: Lee Johnson, 42.9 avg. (81 punts, 3,471 yds., 0 blocked).
Punt returns: Greg Myers, 7.7 avg. (26 att., 201 yds., 0 TDs).
Kickoff returns: Eric Bieniemy, 23.2 avg. (34 att., 789 yds., 1 TD).

1998 SEASON
CLUB DIRECTORY

Chairman of the board
Austin E. Knowlton
President/general manager
Mike Brown
Vice president
John Sawyer
Asst. g.m./director of player personnel
Pete Brown
General counsel/corporate secretary
Katherine Blackburn
Asst. sec./treasurer; scouting/personnel
Paul Brown
Business manager
Bill Connelly
Director of stadium development
Troy Blackburn
Director of community affairs
Jeff Berding
Stadium sales/marketing
Jennifer L. McNally
Stadium construction manager
Eric S. Brown
Scouting/personnel
Jim Lippincott
Scouts
Kale Ane   Earl Biederman
Frank Smouse
Public relations director
Jack Brennan
Assistant public relations director
Patrick J. Combs
Chief financial officer
Bill Scanlon
Comptroller
Johanna Kappner
Director of marketing
Mike Hoffbauer
Director of events
Dave Slyby
Dir. of group sales/corp. entertainment
Michael Alford
Ticket manager
Paul Kelly

Head coach
Bruce Coslet

Assistant coaches
Paul Alexander (offensive line)
Jim Anderson (running backs)
Ken Anderson (offensive coord.)
Louie Cioffi (def. staff assistant)
Mark Duffner (linebackers)
John Garrett (off. staff assistant)
Ray Horton (defensive backs)
Tim Krumrie (defensive line)
Dick LeBeau (defensive coord./
assistant head coach)
Al Roberts (special teams)
Kim Wood (strength & cond.)
Bob Wylie (tight ends)

Ticket office
Tim Kelly   Jo Ann Meyer
Team physicians
Robert Heidt Jr.   Doug Logan
Walter Timperman   Michael Welch
Athletic trainer
Paul Sparling
Assistant athletic trainers
Billy Brooks   Rob Recker
Equipment manager
Tom Gray
Video director
Travis Brammer
Video assistant
Andy Fineberg

SCHEDULE

Sept. 6—	TENNESSEE	1:01
Sept. 13—	at Detroit	1:01
Sept. 20—	GREEN BAY	1:01
Sept. 27—	at Baltimore	8:20
Oct. 4—	Open date	
Oct. 11—	PITTSBURGH	1:01
Oct. 18—	at Tennessee	12:01
Oct. 25—	at Oakland	1:15
Nov. 1—	DENVER	1:01
Nov. 8—	at Jacksonville	1:01
Nov. 15—	at Minnesota	12:01
Nov. 22—	BALTIMORE	4:15
Nov. 29—	JACKSONVILLE	1:01
Dec. 6—	BUFFALO	1:01
Dec. 13—	at Indianapolis	1:01
Dec. 20—	at Pittsburgh	1:01
Dec. 27—	TAMPA BAY	1:01

All times are for home team.
All games Sunday unless noted.

DRAFT CHOICES

Takeo Spikes, LB, Auburn (first round/13th pick overall).
Brian Simmons, LB, North Carolina (1/17).
Artrell Hawkins, DB, Cincinnati (2/43).
Steve Foley, LB, Northeast Louisiana (3/75).
Mike Goff, G, Iowa (3/78).
Glen Steele, DE, Michigan (4/105).
Jason Tucker, WR, Texas Christian (6/167).
Marcus Parker, RB, Virginia Tech (7/202).
Damian Vaughn, TE, Miami of Ohio (7/222).

1998 SEASON

TRAINING CAMP ROSTER

No.	QUARTERBACKS	Ht./Wt.	Born	NFL Exp.	College	How acq.	'97 Games GP/GS
8	Blake, Jeff	6-0/205	12-4-70	7	East Carolina	WV/94	11/11
10	Justin, Paul	6-4/211	5-19-68	4	Arizona State	TR/98	*8/4
15	Kresser, Eric	6-2/223	2-8-73	1	Marshall (W.Va.)	FA/97	0/0
12	May, Chad	6-1/219	9-28-71	3	Kansas State	FA/98	0/0
	RUNNING BACKS						
36	Bennett, Brandon	5-11/223	2-3-73	1	South Carolina	FA/98	0/0
21	Bieniemy, Eric	5-7/205	8-15-69	8	Colorado	FA/95	16/0
32	Carter, Ki-Jana	5-10/222	9-12-73	4	Penn State	D1/95	15/10
28	Dillon, Corey	6-1/220	10-24-75	2	Washington	D2/97	16/6
45	Douthard, Ty (FB)	6-1/214	5-27-73	1	Illinois	FA/97	1/0
44	Milne, Brian (FB)	6-3/254	1-7-73	3	Penn State	WV/98	*16/16
41	Parker, Marcus (FB)	5-9/244	11-12-76	R	Virginia Tech	D7a/98	—
	RECEIVERS						
89	Battaglia, Marco (TE)	6-3/250	1-25-73	3	Rutgers	D2/96	16/0
88	Bush, Steve (TE)	6-3/258	7-4-74	2	Arizona State	FA/97	16/0
87	Doering, Chris	6-4/195	5-19-73	1	Florida	WV/98	*2/0
80	Dunn, David	6-3/220	6-10-72	4	Fresno State	D5/95	14/5
85	Hundon, James	6-1/173	4-9-71	2	Portland State	FA/96	16/0
84	Jenkins, Mike	6-3/191	8-25-74	1	Hampton	FA/97	3/0
82	McGee, Tony (TE)	6-3/246	4-21-71	6	Michigan	D2/93	16/16
81	Pickens, Carl	6-2/206	3-23-70	7	Tennessee	D2/92	12/12
86	Scott, Darnay	6-1/180	7-7-72	5	San Diego State	D2/94	16/15
83	Tucker, Jason	6-1/182	6-24-76	R	Texas Christian	D6/98	—
49	Vaughn, Damian (TE)	6-4/247	6-14-75	R	Miami of Ohio	D7b/98	—
	OFFENSIVE LINEMEN						
71	Anderson, Willie (T)	6-5/335	7-11-75	3	Auburn	D1/96	16/16
66	Blackman, Ken (G)	6-6/315	11-8-72	3	Illinois	D3/96	13/13
74	Braham, Rich (C)	6-4/302	11-6-70	5	West Virginia	WV/94	16/16
65	Brilz, Darrick (C)	6-3/295	2-14-64	12	Oregon State	FA/94	16/16
75	Brown, Anthony (T)	6-5/315	11-6-72	4	Utah	FA/95	6/0
72	Brumfield, Scott (G)	6-8/325	8-19-70	5	Brigham Young	FA/94	15/3
88	Davis, Joel (G)	6-5/310	4-6-73	1	Army	FA/96	0/0
63	Goff, Mike (G)	6-5/311	1-6-76	R	Iowa	D3b/98	—
62	Gutierrez, Brock (C)	6-3/304	8-25-73	3	Central Michigan	FA/98	0/0
60	Jones, Rod (T)	6-4/320	1-11-74	3	Kansas	D7/96	13/8
64	Payne, Rod (C)	6-4/295	6-14-74	2	Michigan	D3/97	0/0
77	Sargent, Kevin (T)	6-6/295	3-31-69	7	Eastern Washington	FA/92	10/8
59	Truitt, Greg (C)	6-0/235	12-8-65	5	Penn State	FA/94	16/0
	DEFENSIVE LINEMEN						
90	Bankston, Michael (E)	6-3/280	3-12-70	7	Sam Houston State	FA/98	*16/16
92	Copeland, John (E)	6-3/280	9-20-70	6	Alabama	D1/93	15/15
94	Langford, Jevon (E)	6-3/276	2-16-74	3	Oklahoma State	D4/96	15/0
97	Purvis, Andre (NT)	6-4/304	7-14-73	2	North Carolina	D5/97	7/1
99	Seals, Ray (E)	6-3/306	6-17-65	11	None	FA/98	*14/7
96	Simmons, Clyde (E)	6-6/281	8-4-64	13	Western Carolina	FA/98	*16/13
79	Stallings, Ramondo (E)	6-7/290	11-21-71	5	San Diego State	D7/94	6/0
96	Steele, Glen	6-4/295	10-4-74	R	Michigan	D4/98	—
93	Thompson, Mike (NT)	6-4/290	12-22-72	2	Wisconsin	FA/97	0/0
67	von Oelhoffen, Kimo (NT)	6-4/305	1-30-71	5	Boise State	D6/94	13/12
	LINEBACKERS						
98	Curtis, Canute	6-2/256	8-4-74	2	West Virginia	FA/97	3/0
95	Foley, Steve	6-4/270	9-9-75	R	Northeast Louisiana	D3a/98	—
50	Francis, James	6-5/257	8-4-68	9	Baylor	D1/90	16/16
91	Granville, Billy	6-3/252	3-11-74	2	Duke	FA/97	12/4
57	Olsavsky, Jerry	6-1/224	3-29-67	10	Pittsburgh	FA/98	*16/0
56	Simmons, Brian	6-3/233	6-21-75	R	North Carolina	D1b/98	—
51	Spikes, Takeo	6-2/221	12-17-76	R	Auburn	D1a/98	—
52	Terry, Tim	6-3/248	7-26-74	2	Temple	FA/97	5/0
58	Tovar, Steve	6-3/244	4-25-70	6	Ohio State	D3/93	14/5
53	Tumulty, Tom	6-3/247	2-11-73	3	Pittsburgh	D6/96	11/11
55	Wilson, Reinard	6-2/251	12-12-73	2	Florida State	D1/97	16/4
	DEFENSIVE BACKS						
33	Ambrose, Ashley (CB)	5-10/185	9-17-70	7	Mississippi Valley State	FA/98	16/16
30	Gilliard, Cory (S)	6-0/210	10-10-74	1	Ball State	FA/97	0/0

No.	DEFENSIVE BACKS	Ht./Wt.	Born	NFL Exp.	College	How acq.	'97 Games GP/GS
27	Hawkins, Artrell (CB)	5-10/190	11-24-75	R	Cincinnati	D2/98	—
34	Mack, Tremain (S)	6-0/193	11-21-74	2	Miami (Fla.)	D4/97	4/4
31	Myers, Greg (S)	6-1/202	9-30-72	3	Colorado State	D5/96	16/14
20	Randolph, Thomas (CB)	5-9/185	10-5-70	5	Kansas State	FA/98	*16/4
23	Sawyer, Corey (CB)	5-11/177	10-4-71	5	Florida State	D4/94	15/2
35	Shade, Sam (S)	6-1/201	6-14-73	4	Alabama	D4/95	16/12
22	Spencer, Jimmy (CB)	5-10/185	3-29-69	7	Florida	FA/96	16/9
42	Wright, Lawrence (S)	6-1/211	9-6-73	2	Florida	FA/97	4/0
	SPECIALISTS						
6	Costello, Brad (P)	6-0/230	12-12-74	R	Boston University	FA/98	—
11	Johnson, Lee (P)	6-2/200	11-27-61	14	Brigham Young	WV/88	16/0
5	Kirchoff, Jay (K)	6-5/205	5-28-70	1	Arizona	FA/98	0/0
4	Kushner, Bill (P)	6-0/203	1-13-70	1	Boston College	FA/97	0/0
9	Pelfrey, Doug (K)	5-11/185	9-25-70	6	Kentucky	D8/93	16/0

*Bankston played 16 games with Cardinals in '97; Doering played 2 games with Colts; Justin played 8 games with Colts; Milne played 16 games with Bengals; Olsavsky played 16 games with Steelers; Randolph played 16 games with Giants; Seals played 14 games with Panthers; C. Simmons played 16 games with Jaguars.

Abbreviations: D1—draft pick, first round; SupD2—supplemental draft pick, second round; WV—claimed on waivers; TR—obtained in trade; PlanB—Plan B free-agent acquisition; FA—free-agent acquisition (other than Plan B); ED—expansion draft pick.

MISCELLANEOUS TEAM DATA

Stadium (capacity, surface):
Cinergy Field
(60,389, artificial)
Business address:
One Bengals Drive
Cincinnati, OH 45204
Business phone:
513-621-3550
Ticket information:
513-621-3550
Team colors:
Black, orange and white
Flagship radio stations:
WBOB 1160 AM; WUBE 105.1 FM
Training site:
Georgetown College
Georgetown, Ky.
502-863-7088

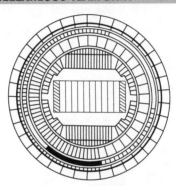

TSN REPORT CARD

Coaching staff	B	Bruce Coslet didn't wait for any players to set the tone for 1998. He did it himself when he sent James Francis and David Dunn home from minicamp for being out of shape. He took good care of defensive coordinator Dick LeBeau, drafting five defensive players among the first six picks.
Offensive backfield	A	It doesn't get much better than Corey Dillon and Ki-Jana Carter sharing time at tailback. Carter brings fresh legs to the lineup when Dillon needs a break. But it'll be Dillon who wears down defenses with his bruising, punishing style behind Brian Milne, one of the league's better blocking fullbacks.
Receivers	A -	Carl Pickens, whose torn groin muscle has healed, continues to be the go-to guy while Darnay Scott will stretch the field. Scott has added strength and bulk but hasn't lost any of his blazing speed. If David Dunn doesn't get his weight under control, James Hundon and Chris Doering are capable third-down replacements.
Offensive line	B +	For the first time in four seasons, the line is set. All five starters return in center Darrick Brilz, guards Rich Braham and Ken Blackman and tackles Kevin Sargent and Willie Anderson. If the often-injured Sargent goes down, the team has faith Rod Jones can get the job done.
Defensive line	C	The loss of ends Dan Wilkinson (trade to Washington) and John Copeland (torn Achilles' tendon) appeared to send the line into a tailspin. But the position gained credibility with the signings of Michael Bankston and Clyde Simmons. Look for some four-man fronts on third down to help get pressure on the quarterback.
Linebackers	B	The Bengals helped themselves in the offseason with the acquisition of Jerry Olsavsky and by drafting Auburn's Takeo Spikes and North Carolina's Brian Simmons in the first round. Speed, which was missing in '97, is finally there to help drive the 3-4 defense. The linebackers won't get gashed as often in '98.
Secondary	C	This deserved an F at midseason last year after a 1-7 start. So a C is a dramatic improvement. Right cornerback, which never got solved last season, was drastically upgraded with free agent Thomas Randolph and second-round pick Artrell Hawkins. There are no complaints with safeties Sam Shade and Greg Myers—yet.
Special teams	C +	Doug Pelfrey, the second most accurate field-goal kicker in NFL history (116 of 144 for 80.56 percent), should get more attempts than the 16 he had in '97. Lee Johnson's status as punter is in jeopardy with the emergence of rookie Brad Costello. Look for big plays from kick returner Eric Bieniemy and punt returners Artrell Hawkins and Greg Myers.

DALLAS COWBOYS
NFC EASTERN DIVISION

1997 REVIEW

RESULTS

Aug. 31—at Pittsburgh	W	37-7	
Sept. 7—at Arizona (OT)	L	22-25	
Sept. 15—PHILADELPHIA	W	21-20	
Sept. 21—Open date			
Sept. 28—CHICAGO	W	27-3	
Oct. 5—at N.Y. Giants	L	17-20	
Oct. 13—at Washington	L	16-21	
Oct. 19—JACKSONVILLE	W	26-22	
Oct. 26—at Philadelphia	L	12-13	
Nov. 2—at San Francisco	L	10-17	
Nov. 9—ARIZONA	W	24-6	
Nov. 16—WASHINGTON	W	17-14	
Nov. 23—at Green Bay	L	17-45	
Nov. 27—TENNESSEE	L	14-27	
Dec. 8—CAROLINA	L	13-23	
Dec. 14—at Cincinnati	L	24-31	
Dec. 21—N.Y. GIANTS	L	7-20	

RECORDS/RANKINGS

1997 regular-season record: 6-10 (4th in NFC East); 3-5 in division; 4-8 in conference; 5-3 at home; 1-7 on road.
Team record last five years: 52-28 (.650), ranks 5th in league in that span.

1997 team rankings:	No.	NFC	NFL
Total offense	*298.6	8	20
Rushing offense	*102.3	11	20
Passing offense	*196.3	10	20
Scoring offense	304	9	22
Total defense	*282.3	2	2
Rushing defense	*124.6	12	24
Passing defense	*157.6	1	1
Scoring defense	314	T7	T13
Takeaways	19	15	30
Giveaways	23	T4	T11
Turnover differential	-4	10	T22
Sacks	38	T10	T18
Sacks allowed	39	6	14

*Yards per game.

TEAM LEADERS

Scoring (kicking): Richie Cunningham, 126 pts. (24/24 PATs, 34/37 FGs).
Scoring (touchdowns): Michael Irvin, 54 pts. (9 receiving).
Passing: Troy Aikman, 3,283 yds. (518 att., 292 comp., 56.4%, 19 TDs, 12 int.).
Rushing: Emmitt Smith, 1,074 yds. (261 att., 4.1 avg., 4 TDs).
Receptions: Michael Irvin, 75 (1,180 yds., 15.7 avg., 9 TDs).
Interceptions: Deion Sanders, 2 (81 yds., 1 TD); Omar Stoutmire, 2 (8 yds., 0 TDs).
Sacks: Shante Carver, 6.0.
Punting: Toby Gowin, 41.8 avg. (86 punts, 3,592 yds., 0 blocked).
Punt returns: Deion Sanders, 12.3 avg. (33 att., 407 yds., 1 TD).
Kickoff returns: Herschel Walker, 23.3 avg. (50 att., 1,167 yds., 0 TDs).

1998 SEASON

CLUB DIRECTORY

President/general manager
Jerry Jones
Vice presidents
Charlotte Anderson
George Hays
Jerry Jones Jr.
Stephen Jones
Treasurer
Robert Nunez
Director of public relations
Rich Dalrymple
Assistant director of public relations
Brett Daniels
Ticket manager
Carol Padgett
Director of college and pro scouting
Larry Lacewell
Scouts
Tom Ciskowski
Jim Garrett
Jim Hess
Walter Juliff
Bobby Marks
Walt Yowarsky
Head trainer
Jim Maurer
Assistant trainers
Britt Brown
Bob Haas
Physicians
Robert Vandermeer
J.R. Zamorano
Equipment/practice fields manager
Mike McCord

Head coach
Chan Gailey

Assistant coaches
Joe Avezzano (special teams)
Jim Bates (asst. head coach/ defensive line)
Dave Campo (def. coordinator)
George Edwards (linebackers)
Buddy Geis (quarterbacks)
Steve Hoffman (kickers/quality control)
Hudson Houck (offensive line)
Jim Jeffcoat (asst. defensive line)
Joe Juraszek (strength & cond.)
Les Miles (tight ends)
Dwain Painter (wide receivers)
Clancy Pendergrast (defensive assistant/quality control)
Tommie Robinson (off. assistant)
Clarence Shelmon (running backs)
Mike Zimmer (defensive backs)

Video director
Robert Blackwell
Director of operations
Bruce Mays

SCHEDULE

Sept. 6— ARIZONA	3:05	
Sept. 13— at Denver	2:15	
Sept. 21— at N.Y. Giants (Mon.)	8:20	
Sept. 27— OAKLAND	12:01	
Oct. 4— at Washington	1:01	
Oct. 11— CAROLINA	12:01	
Oct. 18— at Chicago	3:15	
Oct. 25— Open date		
Nov. 2— at Philadelphia (Mon.)	8:20	
Nov. 8— N.Y. GIANTS	12:01	
Nov. 15— at Arizona	2:15	
Nov. 22— SEATTLE	12:01	
Nov. 26— MINNESOTA (Thanks.)	3:05	
Dec. 6— at New Orleans	12:01	
Dec. 13— at Kansas City	3:15	
Dec. 20— PHILADELPHIA	3:15	
Dec. 27— WASHINGTON	7:20	

All times are for home team.
All games Sunday unless noted.

DRAFT CHOICES

Greg Ellis, DE, North Carolina (first round/eighth pick overall).
Flozell Adams, T, Michigan State (2/38).
Michael Myers, DT, Alabama (4/100).
Darren Hambrick, LB, South Carolina (5/130).
Oliver Ross, T, Iowa State (5/138).
Izell Reese, DB, Alabama-Birmingham (6/188).
Tarik Smith, RB, California (7/223).
Antonio Fleming, G, Georgia (7/227).
Rodrick Monroe, TE, Cincinnati (7/237).

TRAINING CAMP ROSTER

No.	QUARTERBACKS	Ht./Wt.	Born	NFL Exp.	College	How acq.	'97 Games GP/GS
8	Aikman, Troy	6-4/219	11-21-66	10	UCLA	D1/89	16/16
17	Garrett, Jason	6-2/195	3-28-66	6	Princeton	FA/93	1/0
11	Knake, Max	6-2/210	4-11-73	1	Texas Christian	FA/98	0/0

RUNNING BACKS

48	Johnston, Daryl (FB)	6-2/242	2-10-66	10	Syracuse	D2/89	6/6
32	Morgan, Beau	5-10/192	8-4-75	1	Air Force	FA/97	0/0
22	Smith, Emmitt	5-9/209	5-15-69	9	Florida	D1/90	16/16
36	Smith, Tarik	5-10/200	4-16-75	R	California	D7a/98	—
45	Sualua, Nicky (FB)	5-11/257	4-15-75	2	Ohio State	D4c/97	10/1
42	Warren, Chris	6-2/228	1-24-68	9	Ferrum (Va.)	FA/98	*15/13
20	Williams, Sherman	5-8/202	8-13-73	4	Alabama	D2a/95	16/0

RECEIVERS

86	Bjornson, Eric (TE)	6-4/236	12-15-71	4	Washington	D4a/95	14/14
82	Brooks, Macey	6-5/220	2-2-75	2	James Madison	D4b/97	0/0
87	Davis, Billy	6-1/205	7-6-72	4	Pittsburgh	FA/95	16/0
88	Irvin, Michael	6-2/207	3-5-66	11	Miami (Fla.)	D1/88	16/16
89	LaFleur, David (TE)	6-7/280	1-29-74	2	Louisiana State	D1/97	16/5
85	Mills, Ernie	5-11/192	10-28-68	8	Florida	FA/98	*10/5
81	Monroe, Rodrick (TE)	6-4/244	7-30-75	R	Cincinatti	D7c/98	—
83	Oliver, Jimmy	5-10/186	1-30-73	4	Texas Christian	FA/98	0/0
84	Simms, Sean (TE)	6-2/245	7-5-74	1	Nevada	FA/98	0/0
80	Williams, Stepfret	6-0/170	6-14-73	3	Northeast Louisiana	D3b/96	16/0

OFFENSIVE LINEMEN

76	Adams, Flozell (T)	6-7/335	5-10-75	R	Michigan State	D2/98	—
73	Allen, Larry (G)	6-3/326	11-27-71	5	Sonoma State (Calif.)	D2/94	16/16
64	Fleming, Antonio (G)	6-3/309	2-6-74	R	Georgia	D7b/98	—
70	Hellestrae, Dale (G)	6-5/291	7-11-62	14	Southern Methodist	TR/90	16/0
66	Hutson, Tony (G)	6-3/313	3-13-74	2	Northeastern Oklahoma State	FA/97	5/1
69	Jones, John	6-1/325	12-8-72	1	Kansas	FA/98	0/0
63	Kiselak, Mike (C)	6-3/300	3-9-67	1	Maryland	FA/98	0/0
67	McIver, Everett (G)	6-5/318	8-5-70	5	Elizabeth (N.C.) City State	FA/98	*14/14
61	Newton, Nate (G)	6-3/295	12-20-61	13	Florida A&M	FA/86	13/13
62	Perkins, Todd (G)	6-4/295	7-10-73	1	Texas A&M	FA/98	0/0
68	Ross, Oliver	6-4/300	9-27-74	R	Iowa State	D5b/98	—
77	Scifres, Steve (G)	6-4/300	1-22-72	2	Wyoming	D3b/97	5/0
50	Shiver, Clay (C)	6-2/294	12-7-72	3	Florida State	D3a/96	16/16
79	Williams, Erik (T)	6-6/328	9-7-68	8	Central State (Ohio)	D3c/91	15/15

DEFENSIVE LINEMEN

96	Anderson, Antonio (T)	6-6/318	6-4-73	2	Syracuse	D4a/97	16/5
91	Benson, Darren (T)	6-7/308	8-25-74	4	Trinitiy Valley CC (Tex.)	FA/95	6/0
98	Ellis, Greg (E)	6-6/283	8-14-75	R	North Carolina	D1/98	—
95	Hennings, Chad (T)	6-6/291	10-20-65	7	Air Force	D11/88	11/10
78	Lett, Leon	6-6/295	10-12-68	8	Emporia (Kan.) State	D7/91	3/3
99	McCormack, Hurvin	6-5/284	4-6-72	5	Indiana	FA/94	13/0
94	Myers, Michael	6-2/286	1-20-76	R	Alabama	D4/98	—
97	Pittman, Kavika (E)	6-6/267	10-9-74	3	McNeese State	D2a/96	15/0
93	Smith, Herman (E)	6-5/277	1-25-71	3	Portland State	FA/98	0/0
51	Thomas, Broderick (E)	6-4/254	2-20-67	10	Nebraska	FA/96	16/0
92	Tolbert, Tony (E)	6-6/263	12-29-67	10	Texas-El Paso	D4/89	16/16
90	Williams, Brett (E)	6-4/263	10-15-73	1	Clemson	FA/98	0/0

LINEBACKERS

52	Coakley, Dexter	5-10/215	10-20-72	2	Appalachian State	D3a/97	16/16
56	Godfrey, Randall	6-2/237	4-6-73	3	Georgia	D2b/96	16/16
54	Hambrick, Darren	6-2/216	8-30-75	R	South Carolina	D5a/98	—
58	Hemsley, Nate	6-0/219	5-15-74	1	Syracuse	FA/97	2/0
55	Strickland, Fred	6-2/251	8-15-66	11	Purdue	FA/96	15/14

DEFENSIVE BACKS

35	Davis, Wendell (CB)	5-10/183	6-27-73	3	Oklahoma	D6/96	15/0
23	Mathis, Kevin (CB)	5-9/172	4-9-74	2	Texas A&M—Commerce	FA/97	16/3
27	Mobley, Singor (S)	5-11/195	10-12-72	2	Washington State	FA/97	12/0
43	Reese, Izell (S)	6-2/193	5-7-74	R	Alabama-Birmingham	D6/98	—
21	Sanders, Deion (CB)	6-1/195	8-9-67	10	Florida State	FA/95	13/12
26	Smith, Kevin (CB)	5-11/190	4-7-70	7	Texas A&M	D1a/92	16/16

No.	DEFENSIVE BACKS	Ht./Wt.	Born	NFL Exp.	College	How acq.	'97 Games GP/GS
24	Stoutmire, Omar (S)	5-11/198	7-9-74	2	Fresno State	D7/97	16/2
31	Teague, George (S)	6-1/196	2-18-71	6	Alabama	FA/98	*15/6
37	Vaughn, Lee (CB)	5-11/184	11-27-74	2	Wyoming	D6/97	0/0
30	Wheaton, Kenny (CB)	5-10/190	3-8-75	2	Oregon	D3c/97	2/0
25	Williams, Charlie (S)	6-0/189	2-2-72	4	Bowling Green State	D3/95	16/0
28	Woodson, Darren (S)	6-1/219	4-25-69	7	Arizona State	D2b/92	14/14
	SPECIALISTS						
3	Cunningham, Richie (K)	5-10/167	8-18-70	2	Southwestern Louisiana	FA/97	16/0
4	Gowin, Toby (P)	5-10/167	3-30-75	2	North Texas	FA/97	16/0

*McIver played 14 games with Dolphins in '97; Mills played 10 games with Panthers; Teague played 15 games with Dolphins; Warren played 15 games with Seahawks.

Abbreviations: D1—draft pick, first round; SupD2—supplemental draft pick, second round; WV—claimed on waivers; TR—obtained in trade; PlanB—Plan B free-agent acquisition; FA—free-agent acquisition (other than Plan B); ED—expansion draft pick.

MISCELLANEOUS TEAM DATA

Stadium (capacity, surface):
Texas Stadium
(65,812, artificial)
Business address:
One Cowboys Parkway
Irving, TX 75063
Business phone:
972-556-9900
Ticket information:
972-579-5000
Team colors:
Blue, metallic silver blue and white
Flagship radio station:
KVIL, 103.7 FM
Training site:
St. Edward's University
Austin, Tex.
214-556-9900

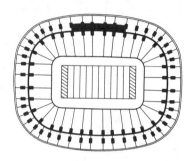

TSN REPORT CARD

Coaching staff — B
Chan Gailey made his mark as an offensive coordinator, and that's why he was hired as the Cowboys new head coach. Early indications of his head coach potential are encouraging. Organized. Disciplined. Even-tempered. Mere presence commands respect. And keeping majority of defensive staff certainly is a plus.

Offensive backfield — B
Those sending Emmitt Smith to pasture are premature. There is nothing wrong with Smith a rebuilt offensive line and an effective passing game won't fix. Not to mention a return of Daryl Johnston, who will attempt to do so after neck surgery, or the addition of Chris Warren. Gailey's arrival has Troy Aikman smiling, a good sign for your team-leading quarterback.

Receivers — C +
Michael Irvin still is the real deal. But after that, who knows. That is why the No. 2 receiver position could be manned by committee, and one loaded with inexperience. Only Ernie Mills has been around the block, but he's trying to make a comeback. Watch for David LaFleur as the complete tight end.

Offensive line — C
How well the Cowboys repair this unit will determine their offensive success. The re-signing of Larry Allen and moving him to left tackle is huge. The turnaround key will be at guard, where Everett McIver was signed to replace Allen on the right side and Nate Newton has been told get in shape or else on the left. Center Clay Shiver must be better.

Defensive line — C +
Having Leon Lett back full-time and Chad Hennings healthy is a good situation to have at defensive tackle. But the mystery remains at end. First-round pick Greg Ellis must be an instant hit, and the club needs production out of Kavika Pittman—an unknown—since veteran Tony Tolbert's health status is a huge question. If this unit does not improve, neither will the Cowboys.

Linebackers — B
Could be a strength of this defense if middle linebacker Fred Strickland can play as well as he did in 1996 when healthy. The outside backers are budding Pro Bowlers, especially strongside linebacker Randall Godfrey. Dexter Coakley should be better with a year's experience. But the backup corps is thin.

Secondary — B +
Was one of the best in the league last year, and should not fall too much with loss of free safety Brock Marion. George Teague gives club some insurance against youthful prospects there, and how good do you really have to be when Deion Sanders and Kevin Smith are on the corners and Pro Bowler Darren Woodson at strong safety?

Special teams — B
With the exception of kickoff return, the specialists are very special, with Deion Sanders returning punts, Richie Cunningham handling place kicks and Toby Gowin punts and kickoffs. Finding a kickoff returner and coverage guys will be the real trick. And if Sanders gets involved in the offense at wide receiver, a punt returner might be needed.

DENVER BRONCOS
AFC WESTERN DIVISION

1997 REVIEW
RESULTS

Aug. 31—KANSAS CITY	W	19-3	
Sept. 7—at Seattle	W	35-14	
Sept. 14—ST. LOUIS	W	35-14	
Sept. 21—CINCINNATI	W	38-20	
Sept. 28—at Atlanta	W	29-21	
Oct. 6—NEW ENGLAND	W	34-13	
Oct. 12—Open date			
Oct. 19—at Oakland	L	25-28	
Oct. 26—at Buffalo (OT)	W	23-20	
Nov. 2—SEATTLE	W	30-27	
Nov. 9—CAROLINA	W	34-0	
Nov. 16—at Kansas City	L	22-24	
Nov. 24—OAKLAND	W	31-3	
Nov. 30—at San Diego	W	38-28	
Dec. 7—at Pittsburgh	L	24-35	
Dec. 15—at San Francisco	L	17-34	
Dec. 21—SAN DIEGO	W	38-3	
Dec. 27—JACKSONVILLE*	W	42-17	
Jan. 4—at Kansas City†	W	14-10	
Jan. 11—at Pittsburgh‡	W	24-21	
Jan. 25—Green Bay§	W	31-24	

*AFC wild-card game.
†AFC divisional playoff game.
‡AFC championship game.
§Super Bowl XXXII.

RECORDS/RANKINGS

1997 regular-season record: 12-4 (2nd in AFC West); 6-2 in division; 9-3 in conference; 8-0 at home; 4-4 on road.
Team record last five years: 49-31 (.613), ranks 6th in league in that span).

1997 team rankings:

	No.	AFC	NFL
Total offense	*367	1	1
Rushing offense	*148.6	3	4
Passing offense	*218.4	7	9
Scoring offense	472	1	1
Total defense	*291.9	1	5
Rushing defense	*112.7	10	16
Passing defense	*179.3	2	5
Scoring defense	287	T2	T6
Takeaways	31	T4	T8
Giveaways	21	4	6
Turnover differential	10	T2	T4
Sacks	44	6	T10
Sacks allowed	35	6	11

*Yards per game.

TEAM LEADERS

Scoring (kicking): Jason Elam, 124 pts. (46/46 PATs, 26/36 FGs).
Scoring (touchdowns): Terrell Davis, 96 pts. (15 rushing, 3 2-pt. conv.).
Passing: John Elway, 3,635 yds. (502 att., 280 comp., 55.8%, 27 TDs, 11 int.).
Rushing: Terrell Davis, 1,750 yds. (369 att., 4.7 avg., 15 TDs).
Receptions: Rod Smith, 70 (1,180 yds., 16.9 avg., 12 TDs).
Interceptions: Tyrone Braxton, 4 (113 yds., 1 TD); Darrien Gordon, 4 (64 yds., 1 TD); Ray Crockett, 4 (18 yds., 0 TDs).
Sacks: Neil Smith, 8.5; Alfred Williams, 8.5; Maa Tanuvasa, 8.5.
Punting: Tom Rouen, 43.3 avg. (60 punts, 2,598 yds., 0 blocked).
Punt returns: Darrien Gordon, 13.6 avg. (40 att., 543 yds., 3 TDs).
Kickoff returns: Vaughn Hebron, 23.5 avg. (43 att., 1,009 yds., 0 TDs).

1998 SEASON
CLUB DIRECTORY

President/chief executive officer
Pat Bowlen
General manager
John Beake
Vice president of business operations
David Wass
Director of player personnel
Neal Dahlen
Chief financial officer
Allen Fears
Dir. of ticket operations/business dev.
Rick Nichols
Stadium operations manager
Gail Stuckey
Director of operations
Bill Harpole
Senior director of media relations
Jim Saccomano
Asst. to the g.m./community relations
Fred Fleming
Director of player relations
Bill Thompson
Community relations coordinator
Steve Sewell
Director of pro personnel
Jack Elway
Director of college scouting
Ted Sundquist
Scouts
Bob Beers
Marv Braden
Scott DiStefano
Dave Gettleman
Cornell Green
Charlie Lee
Head trainer
Steve Antonopulos
Assistant trainers
Ulysses Byas
Jim Keller

Head coach
Mike Shanahan

Assistant coaches
Frank Bush (linebackers)
Alex Gibbs (assistant head coach/ offensive line)
Barney Chavous (defensive assistant)
Rick Dennison (special teams)
Ed Donatell (defensive backs)
George Dyer (defensive line)
Mike Heimerdinger (wide receivers)
Gary Kubiak (offensive coordinator/ quarterbacks)
Brian Pariani (tight ends)
Ricky Porter (offense assistant)
Greg Robinson (defensive coordinator)
Greg Saporta (assistant strength & conditioning)
Rick Smith (defensive assistant)
John Teerlinck (pass rush specialist)
Bobby Turner (running backs)
Rich Tuten (strength & cond.)

Physician
Richard Hawkins
Equipment manager
Doug West
Director/video operations
Kent Erickson

SCHEDULE

Sept. 7—	NEW ENGLAND	6:20
Sept. 13—	DALLAS	2:15
Sept. 20—	at Oakland	1:15
Sept. 27—	at Washington	1:01
Oct. 4—	PHILADELPHIA	2:15
Oct. 11—	at Seattle	1:15
Oct. 18—	Open date	
Oct. 25—	JACKSONVILLE	2:15
Nov. 1—	at Cincinnati	1:01
Nov. 8—	SAN DIEGO	2:15
Nov. 16—	at Kansas City (Mon.)	7:20
Nov. 22—	OAKLAND	2:15
Nov. 29—	at San Diego	5:20
Dec. 6—	KANSAS CITY	2:15
Dec. 13—	at N.Y. Giants	1:01
Dec. 21—	at Miami (Mon.)	8:20
Dec. 27—	SEATTLE	2:15

All times are for home team.
All games Sunday unless noted.

DRAFT CHOICES

Marcus Nash, WR, Tennessee (first round/30th pick overall).
Eric Brown, S, Mississippi State (2/61).
Brian Griese, QB, Michigan (3/91).
Curtis Alexander, RB, Alabama (4/122).
Chris Howard, RB, Michigan (5/153).
Trey Teague, T, Tennessee (7/200).
Nate Wayne, LB, Mississippi (7/219).

1998 SEASON *Denver Broncos*

No.	QUARTERBACKS	Ht./Wt.	Born	NFL Exp.	College	How acq.	'97 Games GP/GS
6	Brister, Bubby	6-3/205	8-15-62	12	Northeast Louisiana	FA/97	1/0
7	Elway, John	6-3/215	6-28-60	16	Stanford	TR/83	16/16
14	Griese, Brian	6-3/215	3-18-75	R	Michigan	D3/98	—
8	Lewis, Jeff	6-2/211	4-17-73	3	Northern Arizona	D4a/96	3/0
13	Nussmeier, Doug	6-3/211	12-11-70	5	Idaho	FA/98	*3/1
	RUNNING BACKS						
40	Alexander, Curtis	6-0/204	6-11-74	R	Alabama	D4/98	—
36	Christopherson, Ryan	5-11/246	7-26-72	3	Wyoming	FA/98	0/0
30	Davis, Terrell	5-11/210	10-28-72	4	Georgia	D6b/95	15/15
29	Griffith, Howard (FB)	6-0/232	11-17-67	6	Illinois	UFA/97	15/13
22	Hebron, Vaughn	5-8/198	10-7-70	6	Virginia Tech	FA/96	16/1
35	Howard, Chris	5-10/223	5-5-75	R	Michigan	D5/98	—
45	Loville, Derek	5-10/205	7-4-68	8	Oregon	FA/97	16/0
42	Smith, Detron (FB)	5-9/230	2-25-74	3	Texas A&M	D3a/96	16/0
	RECEIVERS						
83	Armour, Justin	6-4/209	1-1-73	3	Stanford	FA/98	*1/0
41	Burkett, Jeremy (TE)	6-1/215	4-15-73	1	Colorado State	FA/98	0/0
89	Carswell, Dwayne (TE)	6-3/260	1-18-72	5	Liberty (Va.)	CFA/94	16/3
86	Chamberlain, Byron (TE)	6-1/242	10-17-71	4	Wayne (Neb.) State	D7b/95	10/0
15	Cooper, Andre	6-2/195	6-21-75	1	Florida State	FA/98	0/0
82	Gamble, David	6-1/190	6-14-71	1	New Hampshire	FA/97	2/0
85	Green, Willie	6-4/191	4-2-66	9	Mississippi	UFA-Car/97	16/1
81	Hervey, Edward	6-3/179	5-4-73	2	Southern California	FA/98	0/0
81	Jeffers, Patrick	6-3/218	2-2-73	3	Virginia	D5/96	10/0
11	Jordan, Kevin	6-1/188	12-14-72	2	UCLA	FA/98	0/0
37	Lynn, Anthony (TE)	6-3/230	12-21-68	5	Texas Tech	FA/97	16/0
87	McCaffrey, Ed	6-5/215	8-17-68	8	Stanford	FA/95	15/15
12	Nash, Marcus	6-3/195	2-1-76	R	Tennessee	D1/98	—
84	Sharpe, Shannon (TE)	6-2/228	6-26-68	9	Savannah (Ga.) State	D7/90	16/16
80	Smith, Rod	6-0/196	5-15-70	4	Missouri Southern	FA/95	16/16
88	Wilson, Sir Mawn	6-2/213	6-4-73	1	Syracuse	FA/97	1/0
	OFFENSIVE LINEMEN						
60	Banks, Chris (G)	6-1/286	4-4-73	1	Kansas	FA/97	0/0
63	Diaz-Infante, David	6-3/296	3-31-64	4	San Jose State	FA/96	16/7
67	Goeas, Leo (C)	6-4/300	8-15-66	9	Hawaii	FA/98	*11/7
61	Hall, Courtney (C)	6-1/281	8-26-68	9	Rice	FA/98	0/0
60	Jones, K.C (C)	6-1/275	3-28-74	2	Miami (Florida)	FA/97	0/0
77	Jones, Tony (T)	6-5/291	5-24-66	11	Western Carolina	TR/97	16/16
66	Nalen, Tom (C)	6-2/286	5-13-71	5	Boston College	D7c/94	16/16
62	Neil, Dan (G)	6-2/281	10-21-73	2	Texas	D3/97	3/0
60	Novitsky, Craig (C)	6-5/295	5-12-71	4	UCLA	FA/98	0/0
69	Schlereth, Mark (G)	6-3/287	1-25-66	10	Idaho	FA/95	11/11
74	Swayne, Harry (T)	6-5/293	2-2-65	12	Rutgers	FA/97	7/0
70	Teague, Trey (T)	6-5/307	12-27-74	R	Tennessee	D7a/98	—
65	Zimmerman, Gary (T)	6-6/294	12-13-61	13	Oregon	TR/93	14/14
	DEFENSIVE LINEMEN						
68	Ashman, Duane (E)	6-4/274	12-29-73	1	Virginia	D5b/97	0/0
96	Hasselbach, Harald (E)	6-6/284	9-22-67	5	Washington	FA/94	16/3
75	Ivey, Pat (E)	6-4/247	12-27-72	1	Missouri	FA/98	0/0
76	Jeffries, Dameian (E)	6-4/277	5-7-73	2	Alabama	D4/95	0/0
72	Jones, Ernest (E)	6-2/255	4-1-71	4	Oregon	FA/96	1/0
97	Lodish, Mike (T)	6-3/280	8-11-67	9	UCLA	FA/96	16/0
93	Pryce, Trevor (T)	6-5/284	8-3-75	2	Clemson	D1/97	8/3
99	Richie, David (T)	6-4/280	9-26-73	2	Washington	FA/97	2/0
90	Smith, Neil (E)	6-4/269	4-10-66	11	Nebraska	FA/97	14/13
98	Tanuvasa, Maa (T)	6-2/267	11-6-70	4	Hawaii	FA/95	15/5
94	Traylor, Keith (T)	6-2/304	9-3-69	7	Central Oklahoma	FA/97	16/16
95	Washington, Marvin (E)	6-6/285	10-22-65	10	Idaho	FA/98	*10/1
91	Williams, Alfred (E)	6-6/263	11-6-68	8	Colorado	FA/96	16/16
	LINEBACKERS						
56	Burns, Keith	6-2/236	5-16-72	5	Oklahoma State	D7a/94	16/0
59	Cadrez, Glenn	6-3/249	1-2-70	7	Houston	FA/95	16/0
	Herrin, Errick	6-1/235	4-3-69	2	Southern California	FA/97	0/0
50	Hesse, Jon	6-3/258	6-6-73	1	Nebraska	FA/97	0/0
57	McCoy, Ryan	6-2/237	3-13-72	1	Houston	FA/98	0/0
51	Mobley, John	6-1/236	10-10-73	3	Kutztown (Pa.) University	D1/96	16/16
53	Romanowski, Bill	6-4/245	4-2-66	11	Boston College	FA/96	16/16
58	Russ, Steve	6-4/245	9-16-72	2	Air Force	D7a/95	14/0
	Wayne, Nate	6-0/229	1-12-75	R	Mississippi	D7b/98	—

No.	DEFENSIVE BACKS	Ht./Wt.	Born	NFL Exp.	College	How acq.	'97 Games GP/GS
27	Atwater, Steve (S)	6-3/216	10-28-66	10	Arkansas	D1/89	15/15
28	Barnes, Tomur (CB)	5-10/188	9-8-70	5	North Texas	FA/98	*3/0
34	Braxton, Tyrone (CB)	5-11/185	12-17-64	12	North Dakota State	FA/95	16/16
26	Brown, Eric (S)	6-0/203	3-20-75	R	Mississippi State	D2/98	—
48	Coghill, George (S)	6-0/211	3-30-70	2	Wake Forest	FA/97	0/0
39	Crockett, Ray (CB)	5-10/184	1-5-67	10	Baylor	FA/94	16/16
33	Dodge, Dedrick (S)	6-2/187	6-14-67	7	Florida State	FA/97	16/1
23	Gordon, Darrien (CB)	5-11/178	11-14-70	6	Stanford	UFA/97	16/16
21	Hilliard, Randy (CB)	5-11/168	2-6-67	9	Northwestern (La.) State	FA/94	14/0
20	James, Tory (CB)	6-1/193	5-18-73	3	Louisiana State	D2/96	0/0
25	Johnson, Darrius (CB)	5-9/185	9-17-72	3	Oklahoma	D4b/96	16/0
	Kidd, Carl (CB)	6-1/205	6-14-73	3	Arkansas	FA/98	0/0
27	Paul, Tito	6-0/200	5-24-72	3	Ohio State	D5c/95	*15/5
32	Veland, Tony (S)	6-1/209	3-11-73	2	Nebraska	D6/96	12/0
	SPECIALISTS						
1	Elam, Jason (K)	5-11/200	3-8-70	6	Hawaii	D3b/93	15/0
3	Panasuk, Mike (P)	5-11/198	12-1-68	1	Ferris State	FA/98	0/0
16	Rouen, Tom (P)	6-3/225	6-9-68	6	Colorado	FA/93	16/0

*Armour played 1 game with Eagles in '97; Barnes played 3 games with Oilers; Goeas played 11 games with Ravens; Nussmeier played 3 games with Saints; Paul played 1 game with Cardinals and 14 games with Bengals; Washington played 10 games with 49ers.

Abbreviations: D1—draft pick, first round; SupD2—supplemental draft pick, second round; WV—claimed on waivers; TR—obtained in trade; PlanB—Plan B free-agent acquisition; FA—free-agent acquisition (other than Plan B); ED—expansion draft pick.

MISCELLANEOUS TEAM DATA

Stadium (capacity, surface):
Mile High Stadium
(76,078, grass)
Business address:
13655 Broncos Parkway
Englewood, CO 80112
Business phone:
303-649-9000
Ticket information:
303-433-7466
Team colors:
Orange, navy blue and white
Flagship radio station:
KOA, 850 AM
Training site:
University of Northern Colorado
Greeley, Colo.
303-623-5212

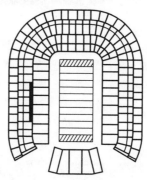

TSN REPORT CARD

Coaching staff — A — Mike Shanahan gives his players more autonomy than most coaches. He has fewer full-pads practices than any other coach in the league, but he gets his message across to the players: Perform on Sunday—or else. Continuity is a major plus. There have been no changes since Shanahan assembled the staff in 1995.

Offensive backfield — A — Even at 38, John Elway can't carry a team on his shoulders any more. But then, with Terrell Davis around, he doesn't have to. The Broncos are a rarity in that, even if they fall behind, they keep running the ball. The idea is for Davis, who gets stronger as the game progresses, to wear down the opposing defense.

Receivers — B — This group needs to make big plays to stretch the defense and keep the pressure off Davis. By midseason, rookie Marcus Nash could be a big part of the offense. As a group, the receivers aren't among the fastest in the league, but the presence of tight end Shannon Sharpe makes it an above-average unit.

Offensive line — A — What do we need to say? You saw the Super Bowl. The Broncos' line, the only one in the league without a 300-pound starter, dominated the Packers. This group doesn't have any prototypical 325-pound tackles, but it's the best-conditioned line in the league. That's another reason the Broncos' running game is so dangerous in the fourth quarter—especially at home in the altitude.

Defensive line — B — If some key players stay healthy, this could be the most improved unit on the team. Neil Smith and Alfred Williams played last season with two healthy arms between them. The No. 1 reason for optimism, though, is the presence of second-year pro Trevor Pryce at right tackle. Shanahan says that if Pryce had stayed for his senior season at Clemson, he would have been a top-five pick in the '98 draft.

Linebackers — C — The most vulnerable position on the roster, bar none. John Mobley is an emerging superstar and Bill Romanowski is as steady as they get, but there isn't much after those two. Glenn Cadrez, a career outside 'backer, will try to replace Allen Aldridge in the middle. If any of the three get hurt, look out.

Secondary — B — If this group plays as well as it did last season, things should be fine. But that's a big if, what with both safeties, Steve Atwater and Tyrone Braxton, well into their 30s. Atwater's shoulder problems could force him to retire a year early. If Tory James, the would-be starting right corner, doesn't bounce back from knee surgery, depth will be a problem.

Special teams — B — Kicker Jason Elam can't be 3-of-8 again from between 40 and 49 yards. If Elam, who has Pro Bowl ability, bounces back, this could be a major strength. For all the inconsistencies the special teams had last season, they won the battle of field position. The Broncos' average starting field position was their 33, compared to the opposition's 25.

DETROIT LIONS
NFC CENTRAL DIVISION

1997 REVIEW
RESULTS

Aug. 31—ATLANTA	W	28-17
Sept. 7—TAMPA BAY	L	17-24
Sept. 14—at Chicago	W	32-7
Sept. 21—at New Orleans	L	17-35
Sept. 28—GREEN BAY	W	26-15
Oct. 5—at Buffalo	L	13-22
Oct. 12—at Tampa Bay	W	27-9
Oct. 19—N.Y. GIANTS (OT)	L	20-26
Sept. 21—Open date		
Nov. 2—at Green Bay	L	10-20
Nov. 9—at Washington	L	7-30
Nov. 16—MINNESOTA	W	38-15
Nov. 23—INDIANAPOLIS	W	32-10
Nov. 27—CHICAGO	W	55-20
Dec. 7—at Miami	L	30-33
Dec. 14—at Minnesota	W	14-13
Dec. 21—N.Y. JETS	W	13-10
Dec. 28—at Tampa Bay*	L	10-20

*NFC wild-card game.

RECORDS/RANKINGS

1997 regular-season record: 9-7 (T3rd in NFC Central); 6-2 in division; 7-5 in conference; 6-2 at home; 3-5 on road.
Team record last five years: 43-37 (.538, ranks 10th in league in that span).

1997 team rankings:	No.	NFC	NFL
Total offense	*362.4	1	2
Rushing offense	*154	1	2
Passing offense	*208.4	5	12
Scoring offense	379	2	4
Total defense	*309.2	8	14
Rushing defense	*114.6	7	18
Passing defense	*194.6	10	13
Scoring defense	306	6	10
Takeaways	25	12	T22
Giveaways	28	7	T16
Turnover differential	-3	9	T19
Sacks	43	T7	T13
Sacks allowed	41	7	16

*Yards per game.

TEAM LEADERS

Scoring (kicking): Jason Hanson, 117 pts. (39/40 PATs, 26/29 FGs).
Scoring (touchdowns): Barry Sanders, 84 pts. (11 rushing, 3 receiving).
Passing: Scott Mitchell, 3,484 yds. (509 att., 293 comp., 57.6%, 19 TDs, 14 int.).
Rushing: Barry Sanders, 2,053 yds. (335 att., 6.1 avg., 11 TDs).
Receptions: Herman Moore, 104 (1,293 yds., 12.4 avg., 8 TDs).
Interceptions: Mark Carrier, 5 (94 yds., 0 TDs).
Sacks: Robert Porcher, 12.5.
Punting: John Jett, 42.6 avg. (84 punts, 3,576 yds., 2 blocked).
Punt returns: Glyn Milburn, 9.2 avg. (47 att., 433 yds., 0 TDs).
Kickoff returns: Glyn Milburn, 23.9 avg. (55 att., 1,315 yds., 0 TDs).

1998 SEASON
CLUB DIRECTORY

Chairman & president
William Clay Ford
Vice-chairman
William Clay Ford Jr.
Exec. V.P./chief operating officer
Chuck Schmidt
Vice president/player personnel
Ron Hughes
V.P. of communications, sales and mktg.
Bill Keenist
V.P. of football administration
Larry Lee
V.P. of finance and chief financial officer
Tom Lesnau
Vice president-general counsel
David Potts
Secretary
David Hempstead
Director/salary cap & stadium dev.
Tom Leward
Executive director/marketing
Steve Harms
Dir./community relations and charities
Tim Pendell
Director of media relations
Mike Murray
Director/ticket sales & customer service
Jennifer Manzo
Box office director
Mark Graham
Director/pro scouting
Kevin Colbert
Scouts

Russ Bolinger	Dirk Dierking
Tom Dimitroff	Scott McEwen
Jim Owens	Charlie Sanders

Head athletic trainer
Kent Falb
Assistant athletic trainers

Bill Ford	Joe Recknagel

Physicians

Keith Burch	David Collon
Terry Lock	

Head coach
Bobby Ross

Assistant coaches
Brian Baker (defensive line)
Sylvester Croom (offensive coord.)
Frank Falks (running backs)
Jack Henry (offensive line)
Bert Hill (strength & conditioning)
John Misciagna (quality control/ offense/admin. asst.)
Gary Moeller (linebackers)
Dennis Murphy (quality control/ defense)
Bob Palcic (tight ends)
Larry Peccatiello (defensive coord.)
Chuck Priefer (special teams)
Dick Selcer (defensive backs)
Jerry Sullivan (wide receivers)
Jim Zorn (quarterbacks)
Don Clemons (defensive asst./ asst. strength coach)
Stan Kwan (offense/special teams assistant)

Groundskeeper
George Karas
Equipment manager
Dan Jaroshewich
Assistant equipment manager
Mark Glenn
Video director
Steve Hermans

SCHEDULE

Sept. 6—	at Green Bay	12:01
Sept. 13—	CINCINNATI	1:01
Sept. 20—	at Minnesota	12:01
Sept. 28—	TAMPA BAY (Mon.)	8:20
Oct. 4—	at Chicago	12:01
Oct. 11—	Open date	
Oct. 15—	GREEN BAY (Thur.)	8:20
Oct. 25—	MINNESOTA	1:01
Nov. 1—	ARIZONA	1:01
Nov. 8—	at Philadelphia	1:01
Nov. 15—	CHICAGO	8:20
Nov. 22—	at Tampa Bay	1:01
Nov. 26—	PITTSBURGH (Thanks.)	12:35
Dec. 6—	at Jacksonville	1:01
Dec. 14—	at San Francisco (Mon.)	5:20
Dec. 20—	ATLANTA	1:01
Dec. 27—	at Baltimore	1:01

All times are for home team.
All games Sunday unless noted.

DRAFT CHOICES

Terry Fair, DB, Tennessee (first round/ 20th pick overall).
Germane Crowell, WR, Virginia (2/50).
Charlie Batch, QB, Eastern Michigan (2/60).
Jamaal Alexander, DB, Southern Mississippi (6/185).
Chris Liwienski, T, Indiana (7/207).

1998 SEASON *Detroit Lions*

No.	QUARTERBACKS	Ht./Wt.	Born	NFL Exp.	College	How acq.	'97 Games GP/GS
10	Batch, Charlie	6-2/216	12-5-74	R	Eastern Michigan	D2b/98	—
16	Miller, Jim	6-2/210	2-9-71	5	Michigan State	FA/98	0/0
19	Mitchell, Scott	6-6/230	1-2-68	9	Utah	FA/94	16/16
14	Reich, Frank	6-4/210	12-4-61	14	Maryland	FA/97	6/0
21	Battle, Terry	5-11/197	2-7-76	2	Arizona State	D7a/97	0/0
	RUNNING BACKS						
34	Rivers, Ron	5-8/205	11-13-71	4	Fresno State	FA/94	16/0
20	Sanders, Barry	5-8/200	7-16-68	10	Oklahoma State	D1/89	16/16
30	Schlesinger, Cory (FB)	6-0/230	6-23-72	4	Nebraska	D6b/95	16/2
44	Vardell, Tommy (FB)	6-2/230	2-20-69	7	Stanford	FA/97	16/10
21	Williams, Allen	5-10/205	9-17-72	2	Georgia	FA/95	0/0
	RECEIVERS						
80	Boyd, Tommie	6-0/195	12-21-71	2	Toledo	FA/96	16/1
81	Chryplewicz, Pete (TE)	6-5/253	4-27-74	2	Notre Dame	D5a/97	10/0
17	Crowell, Germane	6-3/213	9-13-76	R	Virginia	D2a/98	—
9	Maddox, Deon	5-10/175	2-18-74	1	Syracuse	FA/97	0/0
83	McCorvey, Kez	6-0/190	1-23-72	4	Florida State	D5b/95	7/0
84	Moore, Herman	6-4/210	10-20-69	8	Virginia	D1/91	16/16
87	Morton, Johnnie	6-0/190	10-7-71	5	Southern California	D1/94	16/16
89	Rasby, Walter (TE)	6-3/247	9-7-72	5	Wake Forest	FA/98	*14/2
86	Sloan, David (TE)	6-6/254	6-8-72	4	New Mexico	D3/95	14/12
82	Stocz, Eric (TE)	6-4/265	5-25-74	3	Westminster (Pa.)	FA/97	6/0
	OFFENSIVE LINEMEN						
79	Beverly, Eric (G)	6-3/279	3-28-74	1	Miami of Ohio	FA/97	0/0
77	Compton, Mike (G)	6-6/297	9-18-70	6	West Virginia	D3b/93	16/16
74	Harrison, Chris (G)	6-3/290	2-25-72	3	Virginia	FA/96	0/0
64	Hartings, Jeff (G)	6-3/283	9-7-72	3	Penn State	D1b/96	16/16
66	Hempstead, Hessley (G)	6-1/295	1-29-72	4	Kansas	D7/95	16/1
70	Johnson, Andre (T)	6-5/314	8-25-73	3	Penn State	FA/97	0/0
76	Liwienski, Chris (G)	6-5/304	8-2-75	R	Indiana	D7/98	—
61	Pyne, Jim (C)	6-2/297	11-23-71	5	Virginia Tech	FA/98	*15/14
75	Ramirez, Tony (T)	6-6/296	1-26-73	2	Northern Colorado	D6/97	2/0
72	Roberts, Ray (T)	6-6/308	6-3-69	7	Virginia	FA/96	14/14
73	Roque, Juan (T)	6-8/333	1-6-74	2	Arizona State	D2a/97	13/1
62	Semple, Tony (G)	6-4/286	12-20-70	5	Memphis State	D5/94	16/1
71	Tharpe, Larry (T)	6-4/300	11-19-70	8	Tennessee State	FA/97	16/15
	DEFENSIVE LINEMEN						
63	Davis, Jerome (T)	6-4/275	3-4-74	1	Minnesota	FA/97	0/0
94	Elliss, Luther (T)	6-5/291	3-22-73	4	Utah	D1/95	16/16
67	Kirschke, Travis (T)	6-3/286	9-6-74	2	UCLA	FA/97	3/0
90	Owens, Dan (E)	6-3/290	3-16-67	9	Southern California	FA/98	*15/15
91	Porcher, Robert (E)	6-3/270	7-30-69	7	South Carolina State	D1/92	16/15
97	Scroggins, Tracy (E)	6-2/255	9-11-69	7	Tulsa	D2a/92	15/6
68	Sheahan, Kevin (T)	6-1/286	6-19-75	1	Carroll College	FA/97	0/0
92	Spindler, Marc (E)	6-5/290	11-28-69	9	Pittsburgh	FA/97	10/0
98	Thomas, Marvin (E)	6-5/264	10-19-73	1	Memphis	FA/97	0/0
93	Waldroup, Kerwin	6-3/260	8-1-74	3	Central State (Ohio)	D5/96	11/11
69	Whitehead, Willie (E)	6-3/255	1-16-73	1	Auburn	FA/98	0/0
	LINEBACKERS						
55	Aldridge, Allen	6-1/255	5-30-72	5	Houston	FA/98	*16/15
57	Boyd, Stephen	6-0/247	8-22-72	4	Boston College	D5a/95	16/16
53	Fredrickson, Rob	6-4/240	5-13-71	5	Michigan State	TR/98	*16/13
50	Hanks, Ben	6-2/222	7-31-72	3	Florida	FA/97	2/0
58	Jamison, George	6-1/235	9-30-62	13	Cincinnati	FA/97	16/10
99	Jordan, Richard	6-1/245	12-1-74	2	Missouri Southern	FA/97	10/0
52	Kowalkowski, Scott	6-2/228	8-23-68	8	Notre Dame	FA/94	16/0
54	Russell, Matt	6-2/245	7-5-73	2	Colorado	D4/97	14/0
51	Ward, Phillip	6-2/235	11-11-74	1	UCLA	FA/98	0/0
	DEFENSIVE BACKS						
24	Abrams, Kevin (CB)	5-8/175	2-28-74	2	Syracuse	D2b/97	15/4
26	Alexander, Jamaal (S)	5-11/200	9-18-76	R	Southern Mississippi	D6/98	—
35	Bailey, Robert (CB)	5-9/174	9-3-68	8	Miami (Fla.)	FA/97	15/0
27	Carrier, Mark (S)	6-1/192	4-28-68	9	Southern California	FA/97	16/16
23	Fair, Terry (CB)	5-9/185	7-20-76	R	Tennessee	D1/98	—
47	Green, Clifford (CB)	5-8/185	4-15-75	1	Tennessee State	FA/98	0/0

No.	DEFENSIVE BACKS	Ht./Wt.	Born	NFL Exp.	College	How acq.	'97 Games GP/GS
31	Hill, Sean (S)	5-10/195	8-14-71	5	Montana State	FA/98	0/0
25	Jeffries, Greg (CB)	5-9/184	10-16-71	6	Virginia	D6/93	15/2
38	Porter, Daryl (CB).........................	5-9/190	1-16-74	2	Boston College	FA/97	7/0
28	Rice, Ron (S)	6-1/206	11-9-72	4	Eastern Michigan	FA/96	12/8
38	Stewart, Ryan (S).........................	6-1/207	9-30-73	3	Georgia Tech	FA/97	8/0
45	Weems, Cyrill (CB)	6-2/207	8-1-74	1	Wisconsin	FA/98	0/0
32	Westbrook, Bryant (CB)	6-0/199	12-19-74	2	Texas	D1/97	15/14
	SPECIALISTS						
5	Colquitt, Travis (P)	6-1/210	7-16-71	1	Marshall	FA/98	0/0
4	Hanson, Jason (K)	5-11/183	6-17-70	7	Washington State	D2b/92	16/0
18	Jett, John (P)	6-0/199	11-11-68	6	East Carolina	FA/97	16/0

*Aldridge played 16 games with Broncos in '97; Fredrickson played 16 games with Raiders; Owens played 15 games with Falcons; Pyne played 15 games with Buccaneers; Rasby played 14 games with Panthers.

Abbreviations: D1—draft pick, first round; SupD2—supplemental draft pick, second round; WV—claimed on waivers; TR—obtained in trade; PlanB—Plan B free-agent acquisition; FA—free-agent acquisition (other than Plan B); ED—expansion draft pick.

MISCELLANEOUS TEAM DATA

Stadium (capacity, surface):
Pontiac Silverdome
(80,368, artificial)

Business address:
1200 Featherstone Road
Pontiac, MI 48342

Business phone:
248-335-4131

Ticket information:
248-335-4151

Team colors:
Honolulu blue and silver

Flagship radio station:
WXYT, 1270 AM

Training site:
Saginaw Valley State University
Saginaw, Mich.
248-972-3700

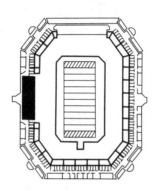

TSN REPORT CARD

Coaching staff	B	Ross hand-picked an entire new group, which has a much better understanding of the players and what makes them tick with a year's experience. Attention to detail is crucial—including officials blowing whistles at each practice. Motivation and teamwork is not overlooked.
Offensive backfield	A	You're going to flunk Barry Sanders? The second-leading rusher of all time disappointed Ross while holding out from training camp, but it's been a good relationship since. Running with a fullback was not the sole reason for Sanders' 2,053-yard season, but it helped. Tommy Vardell and Cory Schlesinger are called on in goal-line situations and provide scoring punch.
Receivers	B +	Herman Moore and Johnnie Morton are at the top of the receiving class, but they want and deserve more downfield opportunities. Get the ball in the same zip code as Moore and the 6-3 receiver can outjump most defenders and pull it down. Morton's breakthrough season was no fluke. Second-round draft pick Germane Crowell will need to contribute immediately as the third receiver.
Offensive line	B	The right side suffered some with Larry Tharpe's injuries and Juan Roque's inexperience. Kevin Glover's loss cannot be underestimated. Jim Pyne will move to center (he played left guard at Tampa Bay), but the Lions are confident he can fill the gap. Guards Mike Compton and Jeff Hartings are solid, although somewhat undersized. When Ray Roberts missed a few games with injuries, the whole line suffered.
Defensive line	B	The line changed philosophy last season and it was a tough switch. Instead of running down the quarterback on every snap, they worked on stopping the run. It worked: Robert Porcher and Luther Elliss had their best seasons. Tracy Scroggins and Kerwin Waldroup were effective at right end. Dan Owens will replace defensive tackle Mike Wells, who signed with the Bears.
Linebackers	C	Two of the three starters are new to the Silverdome—Rob Fredrickson on the strongside and Allen Aldridge on the weakside replacing Reggie Brown. Both are veterans who should step right into coach Bobby Ross' defensive system. Stephen Boyd, a playmaker, is solid in the middle and constantly pushed by Matt Russell.
Secondary	B	They got to know each other last season, which should enhance their coverage this year. Mark Carrier, a veteran, was new to Detroit and working for much of the season with two rookie cornerbacks—Bryant Westbrook and Kevin Abrams. If Ron Rice can stay injury-free, strong safety will no longer be a weak spot.
Special teams	C	Kick and punt returns are the concern. Moves have been made (including the drafting of first-round pick Terry Fair) to improve the numbers. Field position is crucial, and the Lions suffered in that statistical area. Kicker Jason Hanson is the real thing. Punter John Jett needs to return to the form he showed early in the season.

GREEN BAY PACKERS
NFC CENTRAL DIVISION

1997 REVIEW

RESULTS

Sept. 1—CHICAGO	W	38-24
Sept. 7—at Philadelphia	L	9-10
Sept.14—MIAMI	W	23-18
Sept.21—MINNESOTA	W	38-32
Sept.28—at Detroit	L	15-26
Oct. 5—TAMPA BAY	W	21-16
Oct. 12—at Chicago	W	24-23
Oct. 19—Open date		
Oct. 27—at New England	W	28-10
Nov. 2—DETROIT	W	20-10
Nov. 9—ST. LOUIS	W	17-7
Nov. 16—at Indianapolis	L	38-41
Nov. 23—DALLAS	W	45-17
Dec. 1—at Minnesota	W	27-11
Dec. 7—at Tampa Bay	W	17-6
Dec. 14—at Carolina	W	31-10
Dec. 20—BUFFALO	W	31-21
Jan. 4—TAMPA BAY*	W	21-7
Jan. 11—at San Francisco†	W	23-10
Jan. 25—Denver‡	L	24-31

*NFC divisional playoff game.
†NFC championship game.
‡Super Bowl XXXII.

RECORDS/RANKINGS

1997 regular-season record: 13-3 (1st in NFC Central); 7-1 in division; 10-2 in conference; 8-0 at home; 5-3 on road.
Team record last five years: 55-25 (.688, ranks T2nd in league in that span).
1997 team rankings:

	No.	NFC	NFL
Total offense	*350.9	2	4
Rushing offense	*119.3	7	12
Passing offense	*231.6	1	3
Scoring offense	422	1	2
Total defense	*301.7	5	7
Rushing defense	*117.3	9	20
Passing defense	*184.4	6	8
Scoring defense	282	4	5
Takeaways	32	4	T6
Giveaways	32	T10	T20
Turnover differential	0	8	17
Sacks	41	9	17
Sacks allowed	26	1	3

*Yards per game.

TEAM LEADERS

Scoring (kicking): Ryan Longwell, 120 pts. (48/48 PATs, 24/30 FGs).
Scoring (touchdowns): Dorsey Levens, 74 pts. (7 rushing, 5 receiving, 1 2-pt. conv.).
Passing: Brett Favre, 3,867 yds. (513 att., 304 comp., 59.3%, 35 TDs, 16 int.).
Rushing: Dorsey Levens, 1,435 yds. (329 att., 4.4 avg., 7 TDs).
Receptions: Antonio Freeman, 81 (1,243 yds., 15.3 avg., 12 TDs).
Interceptions: LeRoy Butler, 5 (4 yds., 0 TDs).
Sacks: Reggie White, 11.0.
Punting: Craig Hentrich, 45.0 avg. (75 punts, 3,378 yds., 0 blocked).
Punt returns: Bill Schroeder, 10.4 avg. (33 att., 342 yds., 0 TDs).
Kickoff returns: Bill Schroeder, 23.4 avg. (24 att., 562 yds., 0 TDs).

1998 SEASON

CLUB DIRECTORY

President/chief executive officer
Robert E. Harlan
Vice president
John Fabry
Secretary
Peter M. Platten III
Treasurer
John R. Underwood
Executive V.P./general manager
Ron Wolf
Executive assistant to president
Phil Pionek
Chief financial officer
Mike Reinfeldt
General counsel
Lance Lopes
Corporate security officer
Jerry Parins
Accountants
Duke Copp
Vicki Vannieuwenhoven
Executive director/public relations
Lee Remmel
Director/marketing
Jeff Cieply
Asst. directors/public relations
Jeff Blumb
Mark Schiefelbein
Ticket director
Mark Wagner
Director of family programs
Sherry Schuldes
Director of player personnel
Ted Thompson
Director/pro personnel
Reggie McKenzie
Director/college scouting
John Dorsey
College scouts
John "Red" Cochran Will Lewis
Shaun Herock Scot McLoughan
Sam Seale Johnny Meads

SCHEDULE

Sept. 6—	DETROIT	12:01
Sept. 13—	TAMPA BAY	12:01
Sept. 20—	at Cincinnati	1:01
Sept. 27—	at Carolina	1:01
Oct. 5—	MINNESOTA (Mon.)	7:20
Oct. 11—	Open date	
Oct. 15—	at Detroit (Thur.)	8:20
Oct. 25—	BALTIMORE	12:01
Nov. 1—	SAN FRANCISCO	3:15
Nov. 9—	at Pittsburgh (Mon.)	8:20
Nov. 15—	at N.Y. Giants	4:15
Nov. 22—	at Minnesota	12:01
Nov. 29—	PHILADELPHIA	3:15
Dec. 7—	at Tampa Bay (Mon.)	8:20
Dec. 13—	CHICAGO	12:01
Dec. 20—	TENNESSEE	12:01
Dec. 27—	at Chicago	12:01

All times are for home team.
All games Sunday unless noted.

Head coach
Mike Holmgren

Assistant coaches
Larry Brooks (defensive line)
Nolan Cromwell (wide receivers)
Ken Flajole (defensive assistant/ quality control)
Johnny Holland (special teams)
Kent Johnston (strength & cond.)
Sherman Lewis (offensive coord.)
Jim Lind (linebackers)
Tom Lovat (offensive line)
Andy Reid (quarterbacks)
Mike Sherman (tight ends)
Fritz Shurmur (defensive coord.)
Harry Sydney (running backs)
Bob Valesente (secondary)

Head trainer
Pepper Burruss
Assistant trainers
Kurt Fielding Sam Ramsden
Physicians
Patrick McKenzie John Gray
Buildings supervisor
Ted Eisenreich
Fields supervisor
Todd Edlebeck
Equipment manager
Gordon Batty
Assistant equipment managers
Bryan Nehring Tom Bakken
Video director
Al Treml

DRAFT CHOICES

Vonnie Holliday, DT, North Carolina (first round/19th pick overall).
Jonathan Brown, DE, Tennessee (3/90).
Roosevelt Blackmon, DB, Morris Brown (4/121).
Corey Bradford, WR, Jackson State (5/150).
Scott McGarrahan, DB, New Mexico (6/156).
Matt Hasselbeck, QB, Boston College (6/187).
Ed Watson, RB, Purdue (7/218).

1998 SEASON

TRAINING CAMP ROSTER

No.	QUARTERBACKS	Ht./Wt.	Born	NFL Exp.	College	How acq.	'97 Games GP/GS
4	Favre, Brett	6-2/225	10-10-69	8	Southern Mississippi	TR/92	16/16
11	Hasselbeck, Matt	6-4/219	9-25-75	R	Boston College	D6b/98	—
17	McAda, Ronnie	6-3/205	3-6-74	1	Army	D7b/97	0/0
18	Pederson, Doug	6-3/216	1-31-68	6	Northeast Louisiana	FA/95	1/0

No.	RUNNING BACKS	Ht./Wt.	Born	NFL Exp.	College	How acq.	GP/GS
27	Blair, Michael	5-11/240	11-26-74	1	Ball State	FA/98	0/0
44	Darkins, Chris	6-0/210	4-30-74	2	Minnesota	D4/96	14/0
24	Hayden, Aaron	6-0/216	4-13-73	4	Tennessee	W/97	14/0
33	Henderson, William (FB)	6-1/249	2-19-71	4	North Carolina	D3b/95	16/14
32	Jervey, Travis	6-0/222	5-5-72	4	The Citadel	D5b/95	16/0
25	Levens, Dorsey	6-1/230	5-21-70	5	Georgia Tech	D5b/94	16/16
48	McKinney, Anthony (FB)	6-2/250	12-8-74	1	Connecticut	FA/98	0/0
22	Smith, Emory (FB)	6-0/245	5-21-74	1	Clemson	FA/98	0/0
35	Watson, Edwin (FB)	6-0/229	9-29-76	R	Purdue	D7a/98	—

No.	RECEIVERS	Ht./Wt.	Born	NFL Exp.	College	How acq.	GP/GS
82	Anderson, Ronnie	6-1/195	2-27-74	1	Allegheny	FA/97	0/0
85	Bradford, Corey	6-1/200	12-8-75	R	Jackson State	D5/98	—
87	Brooks, Robert	6-0/180	6-23-70	7	South Carolina	D3/92	15/15
89	Chmura, Mark (TE)	6-5/253	2-22-69	7	Boston College	D6/92	15/14
81	Davis, Tyrone (TE)	6-4/245	6-30-72	3	Virginia	FA/97	13/0
46	DeRamus, Lee	6-1/205	8-24-72	3	Wisconsin	FA/98	0/0
86	Freeman, Antonio	6-1/194	5-27-72	4	Virginia Tech	D3d/95	16/16
80	Mayes, Derrick	6-0/205	1-28-74	3	Notre Dame	D2/96	12/3
30	Milburn, Glyn	5-8/177	2-19-71	6	Stanford	TR/98	*16/1
49	Preston, Roell	5-10/185	6-23-72	3	Mississippi	D5/95	*1/0
84	Schroeder, Bill	6-2/200	1-9-71	3	Wisconsin-La Crosse	FA/97	15/1
83	Thomason, Jeff (TE)	6-5/250	12-30-69	6	Oregon	FA/95	13/1
47	Wachholtz, Kyle (TE)	6-4/237	5-17-72	1	Southern California	D7a/96	0/0

No.	OFFENSIVE LINEMEN	Ht./Wt.	Born	NFL Exp.	College	How acq.	GP/GS
70	Andruzzi, Joe (G)	6-3/313	8-23-75	2	Southern Connecticut	FA/97	0/0
60	Davis, Robert (C)	6-3/288	12-10-68	3	Shippensburg (Pa.)	FA/97	7/0
67	Dellenbach, Jeff (C)	6-6/300	2-14-63	13	Wisconsin	FA/96	13/5
72	Dotson, Earl (T)	6-4/315	12-17-70	6	Texas A&I	D3/93	13/13
58	Flanagan, Mike (C)	6-5/290	11-10-73	2	UCLA	D3a/96	0/0
77	Michels, John (T)	6-7/304	3-19-73	3	Southern California	D1/96	9/5
62	Rivera, Marco (G)	6-4/295	4-26-72	2	Penn State	D6/96	14/0
63	Timmerman, Adam (G)	6-4/295	8-14-71	4	South Dakota State	D7/95	16/16
78	Verba, Ross (T)	6-4/299	10-31-73	2	Iowa	D1/97	16/11
74	Widell, Doug (G)	6-4/296	9-23-66	10	Boston College	FA/98	*16/16
64	Wilkerson, Bruce (T)	6-5/310	7-28-64	12	Tennessee	FA/96	16/3
77	Willig, Matt (T)	6-8/317	1-21-69	6	Southern California	TR/96*	*16/13
52	Winters, Frank (C)	6-3/300	1-23-64	12	Western Illinois	PlanB/92	13/13

No.	DEFENSIVE LINEMEN	Ht./Wt.	Born	NFL Exp.	College	How acq.	GP/GS
93	Brown, Gilbert (T)	6-2/345	2-22-71	6	Kansas	WV/93	12/12
91	Brown, Jonathon (E)	6-4/270	11-28-75	R	Tennessee	D3/98	—
68	Bryant, Keif (T)	6-4/285	3-12-73	2	Rutgers	FA/98	0/0
75	Curry, Eric (E)	6-6/275	2-3-70	6	Alabama	FA/98	*6/1
71	Dotson, Santana (T)	6-5/285	12-19-69	7	Baylor	FA/96	16/16
97	Frase, Paul (E)	6-5/267	5-5-65	10	Syracuse	TR/97	9/0
96	Holliday, Vonnie (T)	6-5/300	5-20-76	R	North Carolina	D1/98	—
94	Kuberski, Bob (T)	6-4/295	4-5-71	4	Navy	D7/93	11/3
98	Lyon, Billy (E)	6-5/295	12-10-73	1	Marshall	FA/98	0/0
73	Nottage, Dexter (E)	6-4/280	11-14-70	4	Florida A&M	D6/94	1/0
99	Smith, Jermaine (T)	6-3/289	2-3-72	2	Georgia	D4/97	9/0
92	White, Reggie (E)	6-5/304	12-19-61	14	Tennessee	FA/93	16/16

No.	LINEBACKERS	Ht./Wt.	Born	NFL Exp.	College	How acq.	GP/GS
55	Harris, Bernardo	6-2/247	10-15-71	4	North Carolina	FA/95	16/16
50	Hicks, Anthony	6-1/242	3-31-74	2	Arkansas	D5/97	0/0
56	Hollinquest, Lamont	6-3/250	10-24-70	5	Southern California	FA/96	16/0
59	Joyner, Seth	6-2/245	11-18-64	13	Texas-El Paso	FA/97	11/10
53	Koonce, George	6-1/243	10-15-68	7	East Carolina	FA/92	4/0
57	London, Antonio	6-2/240	4-14-71	6	Alabama	FA/98	*16/6
95	McKenzie, Keith	6-3/255	10-17-73	3	Ball State	D7b/96	16/0
51	Williams, Brian	6-1/240	12-17-72	4	Southern California	D3c/95	16/0

No.	DEFENSIVE BACKS	Ht./Wt.	Born	NFL Exp.	College	How acq.	GP/GS
23	Blackmon, Roosevelt (CB)	6-1/180	9-10-74	R	Morris Brown College (Ga.)	D4/98	—
36	Butler, LeRoy (S)	6-0/200	7-19-68	9	Florida State	D2/90	16/16
29	Fogle, Anthony (CB)	6-0/195	2-23-75	1	Oklahoma	FA/98	0/0

No.	DEFENSIVE BACKS	Ht./Wt.	Born	NFL Exp.	College	How acq.	'97 Games GP/GS
26	Harper, Roger (S)	6-2/223	10-26-70	5	Ohio State	FA/98	0/0
38	McElmurry, Blaine (S)	6-0/188	10-23-73	1	Montana	FA/97	0/0
	McGarrahan, Scott (S)	6-1/200	2-12-74	R	New Mexico	D6a/98	—
28	Mullen, Roderick	6-1/204	12-5-72	4	Grambling State	D5/95	16/1
21	Newsome, Craig (CB)	6-0/190	8-10-71	4	Arizona State	D1/95	1/1
39	Prior, Mike (S)	6-0/208	11-14-63	13	Illinois State	FA/93	16/0
42	Sharper, Darren	6-2/205	11-3-75	2	William & Mary	D2/97	14/0
40	Terrell, Pat (S)	6-1/210	3-18-68	9	Notre Dame	FA/98	*16/5
37	Williams, Tyrone (CB)	5-11/195	5-31-73	3	Nebraska	D3b/96	16/15
	SPECIALISTS						
10	Conway, Brett (K)	6-2/192	3-8-75	2	Penn State	D3/97	0/0
7	Landeta, Sean (P)	6-0/215	1-6-62	13	Towson State	FA/98	*10/0
8	Longwell, Ryan (K)	5-11/185	8-16-74	2	California	WV/97	16/0

*Curry played 6 games with Buccaneers in '97; Landeta played 10 games with Buccaneers; London played 16 games with Lions; Milburn played 16 games with Lions; Preston played 1 game with Packers; Terrell played 16 games with Panthers; Widell played 16 games with Colts; Willig played 16 games with Falcons.

Abbreviations: D1—draft pick, first round; SupD2—supplemental draft pick, second round; WV—claimed on waivers; TR—obtained in trade; PlanB—Plan B free-agent acquisition; FA—free-agent acquisition (other than Plan B); ED—expansion draft pick.

MISCELLANEOUS TEAM DATA

Stadium (capacity, surface):
Lambeau Field
(60,790, grass)
Business address:
P.O. Box 10628
Green Bay, WI 54307-0628
Business phone:
920-496-5700
Ticket information:
920-496-5719
Team colors:
Dark green, gold and white
Flagship radio station:
WTMJ, 620 AM
Training site:
St. Norbert College
West De Pere, Wis.
920-496-5700

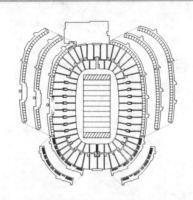

TSN REPORT CARD

Coaching staff	A -	As a possible lame duck coach, Mike Holmgren will be looking to make this season his most memorable. But he'll have to work overtime convincing his players that he's not there just for the ride. They look to him for leadership and if he's thinking about the future they won't follow him.
Offensive backfield	A	Dorsey Levens still has to show he's more than a one-hit wonder, but his rigorous off-season training and strong work ethic make his chances of reaching 1,000 yards again pretty good. Overall, there isn't much depth if he should get injured, although there's a good chance free agent Raymont Harris will be added before training camp.
Receivers	B +	A lack of depth at the wide receiver position is troublesome. The duo of Robert Brooks and Antonio Freeman should be almost impossible to stop, but without two other quality players for nickel situations, the offense will suffer. As usual, the tight end position will be vital.
Offensive line	B	Individually, there are no stars, but as a group the line gets the job done. If last year showed anything it's that the run blocking is a lot better than you would expect from this line. It's up to Holmgren to give them the chance to do it.
Defensive line	C -	The middle is strong with Gilbert Brown and Santana Dotson, but the end position could be a nightmare. The worst case scenario would be for Reggie White's back to hurt, Vonnie Holliday's move to end fail and Brown come into camp overweight and miss most of the season with injuries again. Then the Packers can start planning to be home for the holidays.
Linebackers	C	Only Brian Williams stands as a true playmaker and even he tends to disappear in games. The Packers need a huge performance out of Seth Joyner, who never got in a groove in Fritz Shurmur's scheme, or a return to form from George Koonce.
Secondary	B -	So much depends on the development of Darren Sharper. If he can handle the complexities of the free safety position, it will allow Shurmur to do whatever he likes with his schemes. Craig Newsome's physical play should be an inspiration for an otherwise mild-mannered defense.
Special teams	B -	The coverage and blocking units are outstanding, but new special teams coach Johnny Holland has to find a returner. Neither Glyn Milburn nor Roell Preston are Desmond Howard, but they should be better than what the Packers had a year ago. Sean Landeta's task will be to pin opponents inside the 20, something Craig Hentrich had trouble doing last year.

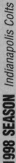

INDIANAPOLIS COLTS
AFC EASTERN DIVISION

1997 REVIEW

RESULTS

Aug. 31—at Miami	L	10-16
Sept. 7—NEW ENGLAND	L	6-31
Sept.14—SEATTLE	L	3-31
Sept.21—at Buffalo	L	35-37
Sept.28—Open date		
Oct. 5—N.Y. JETS	L	12-16
Oct. 12—at Pittsburgh	L	22-24
Oct. 20—BUFFALO	L	6-9
Oct. 26—at San Diego	L	19-35
Nov. 2—TAMPA BAY	L	28-31
Nov. 9—CINCINNATI	L	13-28
Nov. 16—GREEN BAY	W	41-38
Nov. 23—at Detroit	L	10-32
Nov. 30—at New England	L	17-20
Dec. 7—at N.Y. Jets	W	22-14
Dec. 14—MIAMI	W	41-0
Dec. 21—at Minnesota	L	28-39

RECORDS/RANKINGS

1997 regular-season record: 3-13 (5th in AFC East); 2-6 in division; 2-10 in conference; 2-6 at home; 1-7 on road.
Team record last five years: 33-47 (.413, ranks 20th in league in that span).

1997 team rankings:	No.	AFC	NFL
Total offense	*304.3	12	19
Rushing offense	*107.9	8	17
Passing offense	*196.4	10	T18
Scoring offense	313	13	20
Total defense	*303.4	5	10
Rushing defense	*127.1	13	26
Passing defense	*176.3	1	4
Scoring defense	401	12	26
Takeaways	25	T11	T22
Giveaways	28	10	T16
Turnover differential	-3	T11	T19
Sacks	37	9	T21
Sacks allowed	62	15	28

*Yards per game.

TEAM LEADERS

Scoring (kicking): Cary Blanchard, 117 pts. (21/21 PATs, 32/41 FGs).
Scoring (touchdowns): Marshall Faulk, 48 pts. (7 rushing, 1 receiving).
Passing: Jim Harbaugh, 2,060 yds. (309 att., 189 comp., 61.2%, 10 TDs, 4 int.).
Rushing: Marshall Faulk, 1,054 yds. (264 att., 4.0 avg., 7 TDs).
Receptions: Marvin Harrison, 73 (866 yds., 11.9 avg., 6 TDs).
Interceptions: Jason Belser, 2 (121 yds., 1 TD); Quentin Coryatt, 2 (3 yds., 0 TDs); Carlton Gray, 2 (0 yds., 0 TDs).
Sacks: Dan Footman, 10.5.
Punting: Chris Gardocki, 45.3 avg. (67 punts, 3,034 yds., 0 blocked).
Punt returns: Brian Stablein, 7.8 avg. (17 att., 133 yds., 0 TDs).
Kickoff returns: Aaron Bailey, 21.9 avg. (55 att., 1,206 yds., 0 TDs).

1998 SEASON

CLUB DIRECTORY

Owner and CEO
James Irsay
President
Bill Polian
Vice chairman
Michael G. Chernoff
Vice president
Bob Terpening
Vice president/administration
Pete Ward
Controller
Kurt Humphrey
Director/public relations
Craig Kelley
Assistant director/public relations
Todd Stewart
Director of ticket operations
Larry Hall
Exec. director/business develpment
Ray Compton
Director of marketing
Pat Coyle
Director of pro player personnel
Clyde Powers
Director of college player personnel
George Boone
College scouts
Mike Butler
John Goeller
Paul Roell
William Scherer
Duke Tobin
Ron Toman
Head trainer
Hunter Smith
Assistant trainers
Dave Hammer
Dave Walston

Head coach
Jim Mora

Assistant coaches
Bruce Arians (quarterbacks)
Greg Blache (defensive line)
George Catavolos (defensive backs)
Gene Huey (running backs)
Tony Marciano (tight ends)
Tom Moore (offensive coordinator)
Howard Mudd (offensive line)
Mike Murphy (linebackers)
Jay Norvell (receivers)
John Pagano (def. assistant)
Kevin Spencer (special teams)
Rusty Tillman (def. coordinator)
Jon Torine (conditioning)
Tom Zupancic (strength)

Team physician/orthopedic surgeon
K. Donald Shelbourne
Orthopedic surgeon
Arthur C. Rettig
Equipment manager
Jon Scott
Assistant equipment manager
Mike Mays
Video director
Marty Heckscher

SCHEDULE

Sept. 6—	MIAMI	3:15
Sept. 13—	at New England	8:20
Sept. 20—	at N.Y. Jets	1:01
Sept. 27—	NEW ORLEANS	12:01
Oct. 4—	SAN DIEGO	12:01
Oct. 11—	BUFFALO	12:01
Oct. 18—	at San Francisco	1:05
Oct. 25—	Open date	
Nov. 1—	NEW ENGLAND	1:01
Nov. 8—	at Miami	1:01
Nov. 15—	N.Y. JETS	1:01
Nov. 22—	at Buffalo	1:01
Nov. 29—	at Baltimore	1:01
Dec. 6—	at Atlanta	1:01
Dec. 13—	CINCINNATI	1:01
Dec. 20—	at Seattle	1:05
Dec. 27—	CAROLINA	1:01

All times are for home team.
All games Sunday unless noted.

DRAFT CHOICES

Peyton Manning, QB, Tennessee (first round/first pick overall).
Jerome Pathon, WR, Washington (2/32).
E.G. Green, WR, Florida State (3/71).
Steve McKinney, G, Texas A&M (4/93).
Antony Jordon, LB, Vanderbilt (5/135).
Aaron Taylor, G, Nebraska (7/190).
Corey Gaines, DB, Tennessee (7/231).

TRAINING CAMP ROSTER

No.	QUARTERBACKS	Ht./Wt.	Born	NFL Exp.	College	How acq.	'97 Games GP/GS
13	Holcomb, Kelly	6-2/212	7-9-73	2	Middle Tennessee State	FA/96	5/1
7	Kubiak, Jim	6-2/215	5-12-72	1	Navy	FA/98	0/0
18	Manning, Peyton	6-5/230	3-24-76	R	Tennessee	D1/98	—
3	Musgrave, Bill	6-3/220	11-11-67	7	Oregon	FA/98	0/0
	RUNNING BACKS						
32	Crockett, Zack (FB)	6-2/246	12-2-72	4	Florida State	D3/95	16/12
23	Elias, Keith	5-9/203	2-3-72	4	Princeton	FA/98	0/0
28	Faulk, Marshall	5-10/211	2-26-73	5	San Diego State	D1a/94	16/16
33	Groce, Clif	5-11/245	7-30-72	3	Texas A&M	FA/95	7/0
44	Hetherington, Chris	6-3/249	11-27-72	3	Yale	FA/96	16/0
21	Warren, Lamont	5-11/202	1-4-73	5	Colorado	D6/94	13/0
38	Wilson, Abu	6-0/231	1-2-73	1	Utah State	FA/98	0/0
	RECEIVERS						
80	Bailey, Aaron	5-10/185	10-24-71	5	Louisville	FA/94	13/4
83	Banta, Brad (TE)	6-6/260	12-14-70	5	Southern California	D4/94	15/0
85	Dilger, Ken (TE)	6-5/259	2-2-71	4	Illinois	D2/95	14/14
6	Evans, Marlon	5-11/185	2-25-75	1	Stanford	FA/98	0/0
11	Green, E.G.	5-11/187	6-28-75	R	Florida State	D3/98	—
88	Harrison, Marvin	6-0/181	8-25-72	3	Syracuse	D1/96	16/15
86	Jacquet, Nate	6-0/173	9-2-75	2	San Diego State	D5a/97	0/0
48	Jurewicz, Bryan (TE)	6-5/302	2-23-74	1	Wisconsin	FA/98	0/0
10	McGuire, Kaipo	5-10/174	1-16-74	1	Brigham Young	FA/97	3/0
16	Pathon, Jerome	6-0/187	12-16-75	R	Washington	D2/98	—
81	Pollard, Marcus (TE)	6-4/257	2-8-72	4	Bradley (did not play football)	FA/95	16/5
8	Running, Mitch	5-11/185	9-7-72	1	Kansas State	FA/98	0/0
15	Scott, Freddie	5-10/188	8-26-74	3	Penn State	FA/98	*2/0
84	Slutzker, Scott (TE)	6-4/250	12-20-72	3	Iowa	D3/96	12/2
87	Small, Torrance	6-3/209	9-4-70	7	Alcorn State	FA/98	*13/7
	OFFENSIVE LINEMEN						
64	Beaton, Bruce (G)	6-5/291	6-13-68	1	Acadia University	FA/98	0/0
78	Glenn, Tarik (T)	6-5/335	5-25-76	2	California	D1/97	16/16
66	Hardin, Steve (G)	6-6/334	12-30-71	2	Oregon	FA/98	0/0
63	Hayes, Brandon (G)	6-2/305	3-11-73	3	Central State (Ohio)	FA/98	0/0
74	Jackson, Waverly (T)	6-2/310	12-19-72	1	Virginia Tech	FA/98	0/0
60	Johnson, Jason (C)	6-3/281	2-6-74	1	Kansas State	FA/97	0/0
58	Leeuwenburg, Jay (G)	6-3/290	6-18-69	7	Colorado	FA/96	16/16
65	Mahlum, Eric (G)	6-4/302	12-6-70	4	California	D2/94	0/0
79	Mandarich, Tony	6-5/324	9-23-66	7	Michigan State	FA/96	16/16
76	McKinney, Steve (G)	6-4/297	10-15-75	R	Texas A&M	D4/98	—
73	Meadows, Adam (T)	6-5/299	1-25-74	2	Georgia	D2/97	16/16
72	Moore, Larry (G)	6-3/301	6-1-75	1	Brigham Young	FA/98	0/0
67	Myslinski, Tom	6-3/293	12-7-68	7	Tennessee	FA/98	*16/7
69	Taylor, Aaron (G)	6-1/320	1-21-75	R	Nebraska	D7a/98	—
71	Vickers, Kipp (T)	6-2/298	8-27-69	4	Miami (Fla.)	FA/93	9/0
	DEFENSIVE LINEMEN						
96	Carr, William (T)	6-1/314	1-13-75	1	Michigan	FA/98	0/0
93	Ekiyor, Emil (E)	6-4/265	12-25-73	1	Central Florida	FA/98	0/0
68	Embra, Donnie (E)	6-3/286	8-26-74	1	Baylor	FA/98	0/0
99	Fontenot, Al (E)	6-4/287	9-17-70	6	Baylor	FA/97	16/16
78	Footman, Dan (E)	6-5/290	1-13-69	6	Florida State	FA/97	16/10
62	Johnson, Ellis (T)	6-2/292	10-30-73	4	Florida	D1/95	15/15
90	Martin, Steve (T)	6-4/303	5-31-74	3	Missouri	D5/96	12/0
61	McCoy, Tony (NT)	6-0/282	6-10-69	7	Florida	D4b/92	16/11
92	Powell, Carl (E)	6-3/265	1-4-74	2	Louisville	D5b/97	11/0
97	Shello, Kendel (T)	6-3/301	11-24-73	3	Southern	FA/96	6/0
95	Whittington, Bernard (E)	6-6/280	8-20-71	5	Indiana	FA/94	15/6
	LINEBACKERS						
50	Alexander, Elijah	6-2/237	8-8-70	7	Kansas State	FA/96	13/11
94	Baker, Myron	6-1/232	1-6-71	5	Louisiana Tech	FA/98	*2/0
56	Bennett, Tony	6-2/250	7-1-67	9	Mississippi	FA/94	6/6
57	Berry, Bert	6-2/248	8-15-75	2	Notre Dame	D3/97	10/1
53	Burroughs, Sammie	6-0/227	6-21-73	3	Portland State	FA/96	16/1
55	Coryatt, Quentin	6-3/250	8-1-70	7	Texas A&M	D1b/92	15/15
54	Herrod, Jeff	6-0/249	9-29-66	11	Mississippi	FA/98	*10/2
91	Jordan, Antony	6-2/234	12-19-74	R	Vanderbilt	D5b/98	—

No.	LINEBACKERS	Ht./Wt.	Born	NFL Exp.	College	How acq.	'97 Games GP/GS
59	Marshall, Whit	6-2/245	1-6-73	2	Georgia	FA/98	0/0
52	Morrison, Steve	6-3/246	12-28-71	4	Michigan	FA/95	16/9
51	Von Der Ahe, Scott	5-11/242	10-12-75	2	Arizona State	D6/97	9/2
	DEFENSIVE BACKS						
29	Belser, Jason	5-9/196	5-28-70	7	Oklahoma	D8a/92	16/16
25	Blackmon, Robert (S)	6-0/208	5-12-67	9	Baylor	FA/97	14/14
20	Burris, Jeff (CB)	6-0/190	6-7-72	5	Notre Dame	FA/98	*14/14
27	Clark, Rico	5-10/181	6-6-74	1	Louisville	FA/97	4/2
30	Gaines, Cory (S)	5-11/195	5-9-76	R	Tennessee	D7b/98	—
26	Gray, Carlton (CB)	6-0/200	6-26-71	6	UCLA	FA/97	15/13
39	McDaniel, Emmanuel	5-9/180	7-27-72	3	East Carolina	FA/97	3/0
40	McElroy, Ray (CB)	5-11/207	7-31-72	4	Eastern Illinois	D4/95	16/4
34	Montgomery, Monty	5-11/197	12-8-73	2	Houston	D4/97	16/3
41	Reddick, Nakia	5-11/211	9-29-74	1	Central Florida	FA/98	0/0
43	Rosga, Steve (S)	6-1/205	7-10-74	1	Colorado	FA/98	0/0
42	Shamburger, Clifton	5-9/190	7-22-74	1	Troy State	FA/97	0/0
	SPECIALISTS						
14	Blanchard, Cary (K)	6-1/227	11-5-68	6	Oklahoma State	FA/95	16/0
17	Gardocki, Chris (P)	6-1/200	2-7-70	8	Clemson	FA/95	16/0
12	Vanderjagt, Mike (P)	6-5/210	3-24-70	1	West Virginia	FA/98	0/0

*Baker played 2 games with Panthers in '97; Burris played 14 games with Bills; Herrod played 10 games with Eagles; Myslinski played 16 games with Steelers; Scott played 2 games with Falcons; Small played 13 games with Rams.

Abbreviations: D1—draft pick, first round; SupD2—supplemental draft pick, second round; WV—claimed on waivers; TR—obtained in trade; PlanB—Plan B free-agent acquisition; FA—free-agent acquisition (other than Plan B); ED—expansion draft pick.

MISCELLANEOUS TEAM DATA

Stadium (capacity, surface):
RCA Dome (60,599, artificial)
Business address:
P.O. Box 535000
Indianapolis, IN 46253
Business phone:
317-297-2658
Ticket information:
317-297-7000
Team colors:
Royal blue and white
Flagship radio stations:
WNDE, 1260 AM
WFBQ, 94.5 FM
Training site:
Anderson University
Anderson, Ind.
317-649-2200

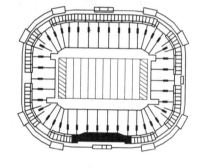

TSN REPORT CARD

Coaching staff	B	Optimism always accompanies a new coaching staff, but the players seem to be embracing Jim Mora. His intent is to better utilize the talent he has inherited. The team underachieved en route to posting an NFL-worst 3-13 record.
Offensive backfield	B	A young, deep corps of running backs, led by Marshall Faulk, will help ease the initiation of rookie quarterback Peyton Manning.
Receivers	C	Wideout Marvin Harrison is the real deal and tight end Ken Dilger could be, if the team would use him. But supporting those two are rookies, free agents and question marks.
Offensive line	C	Developing cohesion and maturity will be vital as the unit will feature new starters at four positions. Tarik Glenn must be up to the task at left tackle.
Defensive line	B	Ends Dan Footman and Tony Bennett are the primary playmakers in a group that is teeming with blue-collar talent. Tackle Ellis Johnson is due for a breakout season.
Linebackers	D	The success of the unit hinges on Quentin Coryatt finally approaching his potential and 32-year-old Jeff Herrod making a triumphant return. Training camp must produce a proven starter on the left side and experienced depth.
Secondary	B	Solid unit that boasts four experienced starters. Another playmaker to complement free safety Jason Belser would be nice. Corners Jeff Burris and Carlton Gray can cover but lack impact potential.
Special teams	C	An area in dire need of a boost. Punter Chris Gardocki is as good as it gets, but kicker Cary Blanchard needs to rebound from an uneven year. The return teams were abysmal.

JACKSONVILLE JAGUARS
AFC CENTRAL DIVISION

1997 REVIEW

RESULTS

Aug. 31—at Baltimore	W	28-27	
Sept. 7—N.Y. GIANTS	W	40-13	
Sept.14—Open date			
Sept.22—PITTSBURGH	W	30-21	
Sept.28—at Washington	L	12-24	
Oct. 5—CINCINNATI	W	21-13	
Oct. 12—PHILADELPHIA	W	38-21	
Oct. 19—at Dallas	L	22-26	
Oct. 26—at Pittsburgh (OT)	L	17-23	
Nov. 2—at Tennessee	W	30-24	
Nov. 9—KANSAS CITY	W	24-10	
Nov. 16—TENNESSEE	W	17-9	
Nov. 23—at Cincinnati	L	26-31	
Nov. 30—BALTIMORE	W	29-27	
Dec. 7—NEW ENGLAND	L	20-26	
Dec. 14—at Buffalo	W	20-14	
Dec. 21—at Oakland	W	20-9	
Dec. 27—at Denver*	L	17-42	

*AFC wild-card game.

RECORDS/RANKINGS

1997 regular-season record: 11-5 (2nd in AFC Central); 6-2 in division; 9-3 in conference; 7-1 at home; 4-4 on road.

1997 team rankings:	No.	AFC	NFL
Total offense	*339	4	7
Rushing offense	*107.5	9	18
Passing offense	*231.5	3	4
Scoring offense	394	2	3
Total defense	*327.4	10	23
Rushing defense	*108.4	8	13
Passing defense	*219	11	24
Scoring defense	318	7	15
Takeaways	29	T6	T13
Giveaways	20	T1	T2
Turnover differential	9	4	T6
Sacks	48	T2	T6
Sacks allowed	40	9	15

*Yards per game.

TEAM LEADERS

Scoring (kicking): Mike Hollis, 134 pts. (41/41 PATs, 31/36 FGs).
Scoring (touchdowns): Natrone Means, 54 pts. (9 rushing); James Stewart, 54 pts. (8 rushing, 1 receiving).
Passing: Mark Brunell, 3,281 yds. (435 att., 264 comp., 60.7%, 18 TDs, 7 int.).
Rushing: Natrone Means, 823 yds. (244 att., 3.4 avg., 9 TDs).
Receptions: Jimmy Smith, 82 (1,324 yds., 16.1 avg., 4 TDs).
Interceptions: Deon Figures, 5 (48 yds., 0 TDs).
Sacks: Clyde Simmons, 8.5.
Punting: Bryan Barker, 44.9 avg. (66 punts, 2,964 yds., 0 blocked).
Punt returns: Reggie Barlow, 11.4 avg. (36 att., 412 yds., 0 TDs).
Kickoff returns: Willie Jackson, 20.4 avg. (32 att., 653 yds., 0 TDs).

1998 SEASON

CLUB DIRECTORY

Chairman, president & CEO
 Wayne Weaver
Senior vice president/football operations
 Michael Huyghue
Senior v.p./marketing
 Dan Connell
Chief financial officer/vice president
 Bill Prescott
General counsel/vice president, admin.
 Paul Vance
Exec. director of communications
 Dan Edwards
Director of pro personnel
 Ron Hill
Director of college scouting
 Rick Reiprish
Director of finance
 Kim Dodson
Director of facilities
 Jeff Cannon
Director of security
 Skip Richardson
Director of information systems
 Bruce Swindell
Director of team operations
 Daren Anderson
Director of broadcasting
 Jennifer Kumik
Head athletic trainer
 Mike Ryan
Video director
 Mike Perkins
Equipment manager
 Bob Monica

Head coach
Tom Coughlin

Assistant coaches
 Joe Baker (asst. special teams)
 Pete Carmichael (wide receivers)
 Perry Fewell (secondary)
 Greg Finnegan (asst. strength & conditioning)
 Fred Hoaglin (tight ends)
 Jerald Ingram (running backs)
 Dick Jauron (defensive coordinator)
 Mike Maser (offensive line)
 Chris Palmer (offensive coordinator)
 Jerry Palmieri (strength & conditioning)
 Larry Pasquale (special teams coordinator)
 John Pease (defensive line)
 Lucious Selmon (outside linebackers)
 Steve Szabo (inside linebackers)

SCHEDULE

Sept. 6— at Chicago	12:01	
Sept. 13— KANSAS CITY	1:01	
Sept. 20— BALTIMORE	4:15	
Sept. 27— at Tennessee	12:01	
Oct. 4— Open date		
Oct. 12— MIAMI (Mon.)	8:20	
Oct. 18— at Buffalo	1:01	
Oct. 25— at Denver	2:15	
Nov. 1— at Baltimore	1:01	
Nov. 8— CINCINNATI	1:01	
Nov. 15— TAMPA BAY	4:15	
Nov. 22— at Pittsburgh	1:01	
Nov. 29— at Cincinnati	1:01	
Dec. 6— DETROIT	1:01	
Dec. 13— TENNESSEE	1:01	
Dec. 20— at Minnesota	7:20	
Dec. 28— PITTSBURGH (Mon.)	8:20	

All times are for home team.
All games Sunday unless noted.

DRAFT CHOICES

Fred Taylor, RB, Florida (first round/ninth pick overall).
Donovin Darius, DB, Syracuse (1/25).
Cordell Taylor, DB, Hampton (2/57).
Jonathan Quinn, QB, Middle Tennessee State (3/86).
Tavian Banks, RB, Iowa (4/101).
Harry Deligianis, DT, Youngstown State (4/118).
John Wade, C, Marshall (5/148).
Lemanzer Williams, DE, Minnesota (6/179).
Kevin McLeod, RB, Auburn (6/182).
Alvis Whitted, WR, North Carolina State (7/192).
Brandon Tolbert, LB, Georgia (7/214).

1998 SEASON *Jacksonville Jaguars*

No.	QUARTERBACKS	Ht./Wt.	Born	NFL Exp.	College	How acq.	'97 Games GP/GS
8	Brunell, Mark	6-1/214	9-17-70	6	Washington	TR/95	14/14
10	Martin, Jamie	6-2/210	2-8-70	4	Weber State	FA/93	0/0
15	Matthews, Steve	6-3/227	10-13-70	3	Memphis State	WV/97	2/1
12	Quinn, Jonathon	6-5/242	2-27-75	R	Middle Tennessee State	D3/98	—
	RUNNING BACKS						
22	Banks, Tavian	5-10/198	2-17-74	R	Iowa	D4a/98	—
43	McLeod, Kevin (FB)	6-0/242	10-17-74	R	Auburn	D6b/98	—
39	Parker, Chris	5-11/213	12-31-72	2	Marshall	FA/97	1/0
31	Shelton, Daimon	6-0/251	9-15-72	2	Cal State Sacramento	D6/97	13/0
33	Stewart, James	6-1/224	12-27-71	4	Tennessee	D1b/95	16/5
28	Taylor, Fred	6-0/228	6-27-76	R	Florida	D1a/98	—
35	Thomas, Malcolm	5-7/202	5-15-74	1	Syracuse	FA/98	0/0
	RECEIVERS						
84	Barlow, Reggie	6-11/191	1-22-73	3	Alabama State	D4/96	16/0
89	Curtis, Isaac (TE)	6-3/245	1-30-74	1	Kentucky	FA/98	0/0
85	Griffith, Rich (TE)	6-5/260	7-31-69	5	Arizona	FA/95	0/0
80	Jackson, Willie	6-1/204	8-16-71	5	Florida	ED/95	16/1
88	Jones, Damon (TE)	6-5/272	9-18-74	2	Southern Illinois	D5/97	11/3
87	McCardell, Keenan	6-1/184	1-6-70	7	UNLV	FA/96	16/16
83	Mitchell, Pete (TE)	6-2/238	10-9-71	4	Boston College	TR/95	16/12
81	Moore, Will	6-1/185	2-21-70	3	Texas Southern	FA/97	11/0
19	Ross, Jermaine	6-0/191	4-27-71	4	Purdue	FA/98	*4/0
82	Smith, Jimmy	6-1/205	2-9-69	6	Jackson State	FA/95	16/16
86	Whitted, Alvis	5-11/187	9-4-74	R	North Carolina State	D7a/98	—
	OFFENSIVE LINEMEN						
71	Boselli, Tony (T)	6-7/322	4-17-72	4	Southern California	D1a/95	12/12
63	Cheever, Michael (C)	6-4/295	6-24-73	3	Georgia Tech	D2b/96	6/4
62	Coleman, Ben (G)	6-5/627	5-18-71	6	Wake Forest	WV/95	16/16
73	DeMarco, Brian (G)	6-7/329	4-9-72	4	Michigan State	D2a/95	14/5
78	Fordham, Todd (G)	6-5/303	10-9-73	2	Florida State	FA/97	1/0
65	Neujahr, Quentin (C)	6-4/305	1-30-71	4	Kansas State	FA/98	*9/7
68	Nori, Mark (G)	6-4/307	1-1-74	1	Boston College	FA/97	0/0
67	Novak, Jeff (G)	6-6/292	7-27-67	5	Southwest Texas State	ED/95	7/2
72	Searcy, Leon (T)	6-3/316	12-21-69	7	Miami (Fla.)	FA/96	16/16
76	Tylski, Rich (G)	6-5/306	2-27-71	3	Utah State	WV/95	13/13
66	Wade, John (C)	6-5/293	1-25-75	R	Marshall (W.Va.)	D5/98	—
	DEFENSIVE LINEMEN						
90	Brackens, Tony (E)	6-4/258	12-26-74	3	Texas	D2a/96	15/3
92	Davey, Don (T)	6-4/270	4-8-68	8	Wisconsin	FA/95	10/10
77	Deligianis, Harry (T)	6-4/302	8-4-75	R	Youngstown State	D4b/98	—
64	Jurkovic, John (T)	6-2/306	8-18-67	8	Eastern Illinois	FA/96	3/3
56	Lageman, Jeff (E)	6-6/265	7-18-67	10	Virginia	FA/95	16/16
91	Payne, Seth (T)	6-4/292	2-12-75	2	Cornell	D4/97	12/5
94	Pritchett, Kelvin (T)	6-3/300	10-24-69	8	Mississippi	FA/95	8/5
75	Robinson, Dwaine (T)	6-4/290	8-26-75	1	Virginia Union	FA/98	0/0
99	Smeenge, Joel (E)	6-6/270	4-1-68	9	Western Michigan	FA/95	16/0
98	Threats, Jabbar (E)	6-5/264	4-26-75	2	Michigan State	FA/97	1/0
93	White, Jose (T)	6-3/274	3-2-73	2	Howard	FA/97	3/0
96	Williams, Lemanzer (E)	6-4/276	11-17-74	R	Minnesota	D6a/98	—
97	Wynn, Renaldo (T)	6-3/290	9-3-74	2	Notre Dame	D1/97	16/8
	LINEBACKERS						
52	Boyer, Brant	6-1/230	6-27-71	5	Arizona	FA/96	16/2
54	Hamilton, James	6-5/238	4-17-74	2	North Carolina	D3/97	9/0
51	Hardy, Kevin	6-4/249	7-24-73	3	Illinois	D1/96	13/11
59	Hines, Tyrone	6-1/244	3-14-73	1	Tennessee	FA/98	0/0
57	Kopp, Jeff	6-3/245	7-8-71	4	Southern California	FA/96	16/3
55	McManus, Tom	6-2/255	7-30-70	4	Boston College	FA/95	0/0
95	Paup, Bryce	6-5/247	2-29-68	9	Northern Iowa	FA/98	*16/16
50	Robinson, Eddie	6-1/233	4-13-70	7	Alabama State	FA/96	16/14
58	Schwartz, Bryan	6-4/251	12-5-71	4	Augustana (S.D.)	D2b/95	16/16
53	Tolbert, Brandon	6-4/225	4-6-75	R	Georgia	D7b/98	—
	DEFENSIVE BACKS						
25	Anderson, Curtis (CB)	6-0/203	9-29-73	2	Pittsburgh	FA/97	9/0
21	Beasley, Aaron	6-0/196	7-7-73	3	West Virginia	D3/96	9/7
20	Darius, Donovin (S)	6-1/213	8-12-75	R	Syracuse	D1b/98	—
45	Davis, Travis (S)	6-0/204	1-10-73	4	Notre Dame	FA/95	16/16

No.	DEFENSIVE BACKS	Ht./Wt.	Born	NFL Exp.	College	How acq.	'97 Games GP/GS
26	Devine, Kevin (CB)	5-9/177	12-11-74	2	California	FA/97	12/0
27	Figures, Deon (CB)	6-0/195	1-10-70	6	Colorado	FA/97	16/12
37	Hudson, Chris (S)	5-10/204	10-6-71	4	Colorado	D3/95	16/16
32	Logan, Mike	6-0/206	9-15-74	2	West Virginia	D2/97	11/0
29	Parker, Ricky	6-1/209	12-4-74	2	San Diego State	FA/97	12/0
23	Taylor, Cordell (CB)	5-11/192	12-22-73	R	Hampton (Va.)	D2/98	—
41	Thomas, Dave (CB)	6-3/214	8-25-68	6	Tennessee	ED/95	16/15
24	Thomas, Tre (S)	6-1/211	9-12-75	1	Texas	FA/98	0/0
	SPECIALISTS						
4	Barker, Bryan (P)	6-2/200	6-28-64	9	Santa Clara	FA/97	16/0
1	Hollis, Mike (K)	5-7/178	5-22-72	4	Idaho	FA/95	16/0

*Neujahr played 9 games with Ravens in '97; Paup played 16 games with Bills; Ross played 4 games with Rams.
Abbreviations: D1—draft pick, first round; SupD2—supplemental draft pick, second round; WV—claimed on waivers; TR—obtained in trade; PlanB—Plan B free-agent acquisition; FA—free-agent acquisition (other than Plan B); ED—expansion draft pick.

MISCELLANEOUS TEAM DATA

Stadium (capacity, surface):
ALLTEL Stadium (73,000, grass)
Business address:
One ALLTEL Stadium Place
Jacksonville, FL 32202
Business phone:
904-633-6000
Ticket information:
904-633-2000
Team colors:
Teal, black and gold
Flagship radio station:
WOKV, 690 AM
Training site:
Alltel Stadium
Jacksonville, Fla.
904-633-6000

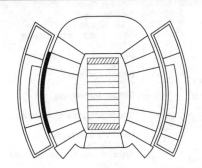

TSN REPORT CARD

Coaching staff   B
Tom Coughlin is a workaholic who continues to earn more and more respect from his players. He runs a tight ship, but players have adjusted to his ways. Offensive coordinator Chris Palmer is a good teacher, who needs to be given more freedom by Coughlin. Defensive coordinator Dick Jauron is a cerebral coach, who has made the best out of a lack of talent in his first three seasons.

Offensive backfield   B -
Quarterback Mark Brunell is coming off an injury-plagued season that slowed his growth. He still went to the Pro Bowl, though, and has a big upside. The team has struggled to find a solid running game, which is why it drafted Fred Taylor with the ninth overall pick. Taylor will push James Stewart for the starting tailback job. The fullback position is a mess, with second-year player Daimon Shelton the only veteran on the roster.

Offensive line   B -
Tony Boselli and Leon Searcy are as good a pair of tackles as there is in the league. Boselli is the best pass-blocking tackle and Searcy improved a bunch in 1997. Left guard Ben Coleman is solid, but the big question is at center, where Michael Cheever is coming off back surgery. When healthy, he is a solid run blocker. The right guard position is a major question area.

Receivers   A
Jimmy Smith and Keenan McCardell are one of the best tandems in the league. Smith is a solid deep threat; McCardell does his damage in the intermediate zones. Both have been to the Pro Bowl. Second-year player Damon Jones has the skills to be the next great tight end in the league. He is big, fast and can block. Pete Mitchell is a solid tight end.

Defensive line   B
The only potential superstar here is third-year end Tony Brackens. Trouble is, he has not played to his potential yet. At the other end, Jeff Lageman and Joel Smeenge are solid but not great. Inside, there are five tackles who have started games, but three—Kelvin Pritchett, Don Davey and John Jurkovic—are coming off major injuries. Second-year player Renaldo Wynn is solid.

Linebackers   B
The addition of Bryce Paup will make this a much better unit. Paup will play the strongside, with Kevin Hardy moving to the weakside. Hardy came into camp last season out of shape, then suffered a knee injury that stunted his play. He takes over for Eddie Robinson, which should help the run defense. The key for this unit will be middle linebacker Bryan Schwartz, who struggled in '97.

Secondary   C
The cornerbacks need to cover better, which is why the team needs a healthy season from Aaron Beasley. He has the skills, but needs to stay on the field. Dave Thomas started on the other side, but he struggles in coverage. Deon Figures is solid. Rookie Donovin Darius may start at free safety, which tells you about the deep secondary. The tackling must improve back there—or else.

Special teams   C
The coverage teams were a major concern last season, but the team feels it has improved there by adding speed. Bryan Barker had an off season in '97, but is still a top-flight punter. Kicker Mike Hollis is solid, but his kickoffs were poor. The return game isn't much, although Bucky Brooks has potential as a kickoff returner. Look for second-year man Mike Logan to take over punt-return duties.

KANSAS CITY CHIEFS
AFC WESTERN DIVISION

1997 REVIEW

RESULTS

Aug. 31—at Denver		L	3-19
Sept. 8—at Oakland		W	28-27
Sept.14—BUFFALO		W	22-16
Sept.21—at Carolina		W	35-14
Sept.28—SEATTLE (OT)		W	20-17
Oct. 5—at Miami		L	14-17
Oct. 12—Open date			
Oct. 16—SAN DIEGO		W	31-3
Oct. 26—at St. Louis		W	28-20
Nov. 3—PITTSBURGH		W	13-10
Nov. 9—at Jacksonville		L	10-24
Nov. 16—DENVER		W	24-22
Nov. 23—at Seattle		W	19-14
Nov. 30—SAN FRANCISCO		W	44-9
Dec. 7—OAKLAND		W	30-0
Dec. 14—at San Diego		W	29-7
Dec. 21—NEW ORLEANS		W	25-13
Jan. 4—DENVER*		L	10-14

*AFC divisional playoff game.

RECORDS/RANKINGS

1997 regular-season record: 13-3 (1st in AFC West); 7-1 in division; 9-3 in conference; 8-0 at home; 5-3 on road.
Team record last five years: 55-25 (.688, ranks T2nd in league in that span).

1997 team rankings:	No.	AFC	NFL
Total offense	*316.5	9	14
Rushing offense	*135.7	4	5
Passing offense	*180.8	13	24
Scoring offense	375	3	T5
Total defense	*305	6	11
Rushing defense	*101.3	4	7
Passing defense	*203.7	5	16
Scoring defense	232	1	1
Takeaways	34	T1	T4
Giveaways	20	T1	T2
Turnover differential	14	1	3
Sacks	54	1	T3
Sacks allowed	32	T4	T5

*Yards per game.

TEAM LEADERS

Scoring (kicking): Pete Stoyanovich, 113 pts. (35/36 PATs, 26/27 FGs).
Scoring (touchdowns): Marcus Allen, 66 pts. (11 rushing).
Passing: Elvis Grbac, 1,943 yds. (314 att., 179 comp., 57.0%, 11 TDs, 6 int.).
Rushing: Greg Hill, 550 yds. (157 att., 3.5 avg., 0 TDs).
Receptions: Andre Rison, 72 (1,092 yds., 15.2 avg., 7 TDs).
Interceptions: Mark McMillian, 8 (274 yds., 3 TDs).
Sacks: Dan Williams, 10.5.
Punting: Louie Aguiar, 42.3 avg. (82 punts, 3,465 yds., 0 blocked).
Punt returns: Tamarick Vanover, 10.9 avg. (35 att., 383 yds., 1 TD).
Kickoff returns: Tamarick Vanover, 25.6 avg. (51 att., 1,308 yds., 1 TD).

1998 SEASON

CLUB DIRECTORY

Founder
Lamar Hunt
Chairman of the board
Jack Steadman
President/g.m./chief executive officer
Carl Peterson
Vice president/administration
Dennis Watley
Executive vice president/assistant g.m.
Dennis Thum
Secretary/legal
Jim Seigfreid
Treasurer and director/finance
Dale Young
Director/sales and marketing
Wallace Bennett
Director/operations
Steve Schneider
Director/development
Ken Blume
Director/corporate sponsorships
Anita Bailey
Director/public relations
Bob Moore
Assistant director/public relations
Jim Carr
Director of player personnel
Terry Bradway
Director of pro personnel
John Schneider
Director of college scouting
Chuck Cook
Scouts
Frank Acevedo
Bill Baker Jr.
Scott Campbell
Jeff Ireland
Quintin Smith
Trainer
Dave Kendall
Assistant trainer
Bud Epps

Head coach
Marty Schottenheimer

Assistant coaches
Russ Ball (administrative assistant to the head coach)
Gunther Cunningham (def. coord.)
Jim Erkenbeck (tight ends)
Jeff Hurd (strength & cond.)
Lionel James (running backs)
Bob Karmelowicz (defensive line)
Woodrow Lowe (defensive & special teams assistant)
Mike McCarthy (quarterbacks)
Jimmy Raye (off. coordinator)
Al Saunders (assistant head coach/receivers)
Brian Schottenheimer (off. asst./quality control)
Kurt Schottenheimer (def. backs)
Mike Solari (offensive line)
Mike Stock (special teams)
Darvin Wallis (quality control/defense)
Roberto Parker (assistant strength & conditioning)

Physicians
Cris Barnthouse
Joseph Brewer
Jon Browne
Mike Monaco
Equipment manager
Mike Davidson

SCHEDULE

Sept. 6—	OAKLAND	7:20
Sept. 13—	at Jacksonville	1:01
Sept. 20—	SAN DIEGO	12:01
Sept. 27—	at Philadelphia	1:01
Oct. 4—	SEATTLE	7:20
Oct. 11—	at New England	1:01
Oct. 18—	Open date	
Oct. 26—	PITTSBURGH (Mon.)	7:20
Nov. 1—	N.Y. JETS	3:05
Nov. 8—	at Seattle	1:15
Nov. 16—	DENVER (Mon.)	7:20
Nov. 22—	at San Diego	1:15
Nov. 29—	ARIZONA	12:01
Dec. 6—	at Denver	2:15
Dec. 13—	DALLAS	3:15
Dec. 20—	at N.Y. Giants	1:01
Dec. 26—	at Oakland (Sat.)	1:05

All times are for home team.
All games Sunday unless noted.

DRAFT CHOICES

Victor Riley, T, Auburn (first round/27th pick overall).
Rashaan Shehee, RB, Washington (3/88).
Greg Favors, LB, Mississippi State (4/120).
Robert Williams, DB, North Carolina (5/128).
Derrick Ransom, DT, Cincinnati (6/181).
Eric Warfield, DB, Nebraska (7/216).
Ernest Blackwell, RB, Missouri (7/224).

TRAINING CAMP ROSTER

No.	QUARTERBACKS	Ht./Wt.	Born	NFL Exp.	College	How acq.	'97 Games GP/GS
17	Barnes, Pat	6-3/215	2-23-75	2	California	D4/97	0/0
12	Gannon, Rich	6-3/210	12-20-65	11	Delaware	FA/95	9/6
11	Grbac, Elvis	6-5/232	8-13-70	6	Michigan	FA/97	10/10
8	Tolliver, Billy Joe	6-1/217	2-7-66	8	Texas Tech	FA/97	6/1
	RUNNING BACKS						
38	Anders, Kimble (FB)	5-11/230	9-10-66	8	Houston	FA/91	15/14
30	Bennett, Donnell (FB)	6-0/232	9-14-72	5	Miami (Fla.)	D2/94	14/1
39	Blackwell, Ernest (FB)	6-2/242	8-7-75	R	Missouri	D7b/98	—
27	Bostic, James	5-11/225	3-13-72	3	Auburn	FA/98	0/0
42	Haynes, Jesse	5-9/210	8-8-72	1	N.W. Missouri	FA/97	0/0
49	Richardson, Tony	6-1/237	12-17-71	4	Auburn	FA/95	14/0
43	Robinson, Greg	5-10/205	8-7-69	4	Northeast Louisiana	FA/97	0/0
22	Shehee, Rashaan	5-10/207	6-20-75	R	Washington	D3/98	—
	RECEIVERS						
82	Alexander, Derrick	6-2/195	11-6-71	5	Michigan	FA/98	*15/13
4	Cotton, Kotto	6-0/182	4-17-73	1	Arkansas	FA/97	0/0
85	Dowdell, Marcus	5-10/179	5-22-70	5	Tennessee State	FA/98	0/0
47	Gaine, Brian (TE)	6-5/255	4-20-73	1	Maine	FA/98	0/0
88	Gonzalez, Tony (TE)	6-4/244	2-27-76	2	California	D1/97	16/0
84	Horn, Joe	6-1/199	1-16-72	3	Itawamba (Miss.) JC	D5/96	8/0
83	Hughes, Danan	6-2/211	12-11-70	6	Iowa	D7/93	16/1
9	Jones, Reggie	6-0/191	5-5-71	3	La. State (did not play football)	FA/97	0/0
81	Lockett, Kevin	6-0/177	9-8-74	2	Kansas State	D2/97	9/0
95	Manuel, Sean (TE)	6-2/245	12-1-73	2	New Mexico State	FA/98	0/0
93	Moore, Jim (TE)	6-3/262	4-29-73	1	Kansas	FA/98	0/0
48	Popson, Ted (TE)	6-4/250	9-10-66	5	Portland State	FA/97	13/12
89	Rison, Andre	6-1/188	3-18-67	10	Michigan State	FA/97	16/16
87	Vanover, Tamarick	5-11/218	2-25-74	4	Florida State	D3a/95	16/0
	OFFENSIVE LINEMEN						
69	Criswell, Jeff (T)	6-7/294	3-7-64	12	Graceland College (Iowa)	FA/95	16/16
60	El-Mashtoub, Hicham (C)	6-2/300	5-11-72	3	Arizona	FA/98	0/0
61	Grunhard, Tim (C)	6-2/307	5-17-68	9	Notre Dame	D2/90	16/16
72	Moore, Brandon (T)	6-7/295	6-21-70	3	Duke	FA/93	0/0
62	Parker, Glenn (G)	6-5/305	4-22-66	9	Arizona	FA/97	15/15
72	Parks, Nathan (T)	6-5/303	10-25-74	2	Stanford	D7/97	1/0
66	Riley, Victor (T)	6-5/321	11-4-74	R	Auburn	D1/98	—
68	Shields, Will (G)	6-3/305	9-15-71	6	Nebraska	D3/93	16/16
65	Smith, Jeffery (C)	6-3/322	5-25-73	3	Tennessee	D7b/96	3/0
70	Spears, Marcus (G)	6-4/305	9-28-71	5	Northwestern (La.) State	FA/97	3/0
73	Swanson, Pete (T)	6-5/307	3-26-74	1	Stanford	FA/97	0/0
79	Szott, David (G)	6-4/293	12-12-67	9	Penn State	D7/90	16/16
64	Tamm, Ralph (G)	6-4/280	3-11-66	11	West Chester (Pa.)	FA/97	16/0
	DEFENSIVE LINEMEN						
71	Barndt, Tom (T)	6-3/301	3-14-72	3	Pittsburgh	D6b/95	16/1
99	Booker, Vaughn (E)	6-5/295	2-24-68	5	Cincinnati	FA/94	13/13
93	Browning, John (T)	6-4/290	9-30-73	3	West Virginia	D3/96	14/13
96	Coleman, Herb (E)	6-4/285	9-4-71	1	Trinity College (Ill.)	FA/97	0/0
90	Holland, Darius (T)	6-5/320	11-10-73	3	Colorado	TR/98	*12/1
77	McDaniels, Pellom (E)	6-3/285	2-21-68	6	Oregon State	FA/93	16/6
75	McGlockton, Chester (T)	6-4/315	9-16-69	7	Clemson	FA/98	*16/16
91	O'Neal, Leslie (E)	6-4/270	5-7-64	13	Oklahoma State	FA/98	*15/14
97	Parten, Ty (E)	6-5/295	10-13-69	4	Arizona	FA/97	2/0
95	Ransom, Derrick (T)	6-3/286	9-13-76	R	Cincinnati	D6/98	—
90	Williams, Dan (E)	6-4/290	12-15-69	6	Toledo	D1/93	15/6
	LINEBACKERS						
57	Clark, Reggie	6-2/240	10-17-67	3	North Carolina	FA/98	0/0
50	Davis, Anthony	6-0/235	3-7-69	6	Utah	FA/94	15/15
59	Edwards, Donnie	6-2/236	4-6-73	3	UCLA	D4/96	16/16
54	Favors, Gregory	6-1/236	9-30-74	R	Mississippi State	D4/98	—
55	George, Ron	6-2/236	3-20-70	6	Stanford	FA/98	*16/0
51	Manusky, Greg	6-1/234	8-12-66	11	Colgate	FA/94	16/1
56	Simmons, Wayne	6-2/250	12-15-69	6	Clemson	TR/97	*16/14
53	Smith, Mark	6-3/242	1-27-74	1	Arkansas	FA/97	0/0
58	Thomas, Derrick	6-3/247	1-1-67	10	Alabama	D1/89	12/10
90	Wooden, Terry	6-3/239	1-14-67	9	Syracuse	FA/97	15/8
	DEFENSIVE BACKS						
26	Adams, Vashone (S)	5-10/196	9-12-73	3	Eastern Michigan	FA/98	*5/4
45	Brooks, Bucky (CB)	6-0/201	1-22-71	4	North Carolina	FA/97	3/0
34	Carter, Dale (CB)	6-1/188	11-28-69	7	Tennessee	D1/92	16/15

No.	DEFENSIVE BACKS	Ht./Wt.	Born	NFL Exp.	College	How acq.	'97 Games GP/GS
23	Dorsett, Matthew (CB)	5-11/190	8-23-73	3	Southern	FA/98	0/0
38	Ellis, Kwame (CB)	5-10/188	2-27-74	2	Stanford	FA/96	0/0
40	Hasty, James (CB)	6-0/208	5-23-65	11	Washington State	FA/95	16/15
25	Johnson, Melvin (S)	6-0/198	4-15-72	4	Kentucky	TR/98	*16/7
29	McMillian, Mark (CB)	5-7/148	4-29-70	7	Alabama	FA/97	16/2
41	Prior, Anthony (CB)	5-11/186	3-27-70	5	Washington State	FA/98	*12/0
31	Ross, Kevin (S)	5-9/185	1-16-62	15	Temple	FA/97	5/0
25	Tongue, Reggie (S)	6-0/201	4-11-73	3	Oregon State	D2/96	16/16
43	Warfield, Eric (S)	6-0/192	3-3-76	R	Nebraska	D7a/98	—
24	Washington, Vann (S)	6-0/212	5-18-74	1	West Virginia	FA/98	0/0
46	Williams, Robert (CB)	5-10/172	5-29-77	R	North Carolina	D5/98	—
21	Woods, Jerome (CB)	6-2/200	3-17-73	3	Memphis	D1/96	16/16
	SPECIALISTS						
5	Aguiar, Louie (P)	6-2/218	6-30-66	8	Utah State	FA/94	16/0
10	Stoyanovich, Pete (K)	5-11/195	4-28-67	10	Indiana	TR/96	16/0

*Adams played 5 games with Saints in '97; Alexander played 15 games with Ravens; Brooks played 3 games with Jaguars, 3 games with Packers and 3 games with Chiefs; George played 16 games with Vikings; Holland played 12 games with Packers; Johnson played 16 games with Buccaneers; McGlockton played 16 games with Raiders; O'Neal played 15 games with Rams; Prior played 12 games with Vikings; Simmons played 6 games with Packers and 10 games with Chiefs.

Abbreviations: D1—draft pick, first round; SupD2—supplemental draft pick, second round; WV—claimed on waivers; TR—obtained in trade; PlanB—Plan B free-agent acquisition; FA—free-agent acquisition (other than Plan B); ED—expansion draft pick.

MISCELLANEOUS TEAM DATA

Stadium (capacity, surface):
Arrowhead Stadium
(79,451, grass)
Business address:
One Arrowhead Drive
Kansas City, MO 64129
Business phone:
816-924-9300
Ticket information:
816-924-9400
Team colors:
Red, gold and white
Flagship radio station:
KCFX, 101.1 FM
Training site:
U. of Wisconsin-River Falls
River Falls, Wis.
715-425-4580

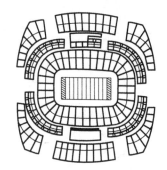

TSN REPORT CARD

Coaching staff	B	Marty Schottenheimer is a great regular-season coach. Gunther Cunningham is a master defensive coordinator. Jimmy Raye replaces Paul Hackett as offensive coordinator and he has the playmakers to fulfill his promise of a better scoring team. But they have to get to a championship game. Anything less isn't enough.
Offensive backfield	B	This team is quarterback Elvis Grbac's to lead. He will have more decision-making power on the field to prove he can. The spotlight is on halfback Donnell Bennett, who can run but has to prove he can be a scorer. The team is strong at fullback, with Pro Bowl selection Kimble Anders and blocking back Tony Richardson.
Receivers	A	The blockbuster move of the offseason was the acquisition of Derrick Alexander. With Andre Rison and Alexander, defenses will have to play the Chiefs honestly. It's obvious that having both improves the offense's ability to score, but second-year tight end Tony Gonzalez is the X factor. He's primed to have a breakout season.
Offensive line	B	The interior is one of the toughest in the NFL, with guards Will Shields and Dave Szott, and center Tim Grunhard. The team is not as strong at tackle. The Chiefs will use the serviceable duo of Jeff Criswell on the left and Glenn Parker on the right and hope rookie Victor Riley can contribute immediately.
Defensive line	A	The Chiefs grabbed two veterans in the offseason—Chester McGlockton to fill in the middle and end Leslie O'Neal to make the pass rush even stronger. This is the club's deepest unit and the reason why expectations are riding so high.
Linebackers	A	The Chiefs want to use their three starters as much as possible, instead of sending in a short-yardage or goal-line group. Wayne Simmons' force on the tight end blends very well with the speed of Donnie Edwards and Anthony Davis.
Secondary	B	This group, led by Pro Bowl corners Dale Carter and James Hasty and third-year safeties Reggie Tongue and Jerome Woods, makes the pass rush that much more powerful. Aside from nickel back Mark McMillian, a new crop of defensive backs has to provide depth or help on special teams.
Special teams	B	Tamarick Vanover is a valuable commodity as a kick returner. Pete Stoyanovich proved 1996 was an aberration with a great performance in '97 that included a couple of game-winning field goals. But the concern about his short kickoffs isn't going away. Punter Louie Aguiar has taken over those duties in the past two seasons.

MIAMI DOLPHINS
AFC EASTERN DIVISION

1997 REVIEW

RESULTS

Aug. 31—INDIANAPOLIS	W	16-10
Sept. 7—TENNESSEE (OT)	W	16-13
Sept.14—at Green Bay	L	18-23
Sept.21—at Tampa Bay	L	21-31
Sept.28—Open date		
Oct. 5—KANSAS CITY	W	17-14
Oct. 12—at N.Y. Jets	W	31-20
Oct. 19—at Baltimore	W	24-13
Oct. 27—CHICAGO (OT)	L	33-36
Nov. 2—at Buffalo	L	6-9
Nov. 9—N.Y. JETS	W	24-17
Nov. 17—BUFFALO	W	30-13
Nov. 23—at New England	L	24-27
Nov. 30—at Oakland	W	34-16
Dec. 7—DETROIT	W	33-30
Dec. 14—at Indianapolis	L	0-41
Dec. 22—NEW ENGLAND	L	12-14
Dec. 28—at New England*	L	3-17

*AFC wild-card game.

RECORDS/RANKINGS

1997 regular-season record: 9-7 (T2nd in AFC East); 4-4 in division; 8-4 in conference; 6-2 at home; 3-5 on road.
Team record last five years: 45-35 (.563), ranks T7th in league in that span).

1997 team rankings:	No.	AFC	NFL
Total offense	*320.3	7	11
Rushing offense	*83.9	15	29
Passing offense	*236.4	2	2
Scoring offense	339	9	13
Total defense	*335.3	13	26
Rushing defense	*113.3	11	17
Passing defense	*221.9	12	25
Scoring defense	327	8	T16
Takeaways	27	9	T17
Giveaways	20	T1	T2
Turnover differential	7	5	8
Sacks	31	T12	T27
Sacks allowed	23	2	2

*Yards per game.

TEAM LEADERS

Scoring (kicking): Olindo Mare, 117 pts. (33/33 PATs, 28/36 FGs).
Scoring (touchdowns): Karim Abdul-Jabbar, 96 pts. (15 rushing, 1 receiving).
Passing: Dan Marino, 3,780 yds. (548 att., 319 comp., 58.2%, 16 TDs, 11 int.).
Rushing: Karim Abdul-Jabbar, 892 yds. (283 att., 3.2 avg., 15 TDs).
Receptions: O.J. McDuffie, 76 (943 yds., 12.4 avg., 1 TD).
Interceptions: Terrell Buckley, 4 (26 yds., 0 TDs).
Sacks: Trace Armstrong, 5.5.
Punting: John Kidd, 43.2 avg. (52 punts, 2,247 yds., 0 blocked).
Punt returns: Charles Jordan, 10.5 avg. (26 att., 273 yds., 0 TDs).
Kickoff returns: Irving Spikes, 23.5 avg. (24 att., 565 yds., 0 TDs).

1998 SEASON

CLUB DIRECTORY

Owner/chairman of the board
H. Wayne Huizenga
President/chief operating officer
Eddie J. Jones
Vice president/administration
Bryan Wiedmeier
Vice president/finance
Jill R. Strafaci
Director of football operations
Bob Ackles
Director/pro personnel
Tom Heckert
Director of college scouting
Tom Braatz
Vice president/media relations
Harvey Greene
Media relations coordinator
Neal Gulkis
Senior director/marketing
David Evans
Director of publications
Scott Stone
Community relations director
Fudge Browne
Vice president/ticket sales
Bill Galante
Scouts
Mike Cartwright
Tom Heckert, Jr.
Ron Labadie
Jeff Smith
Jere Stripling
Head trainer
Kevin O'Neill
Trainers
Troy Mauer
Ryan Vermillion
Physician
Daniel Kanell
John Uribe

**General manager/
head coach**
Jimmy Johnson

Assistant coaches
Larry Beightol (offensive line)
Doug Blevins (kicking)
Kippy Brown (off. coordinator)
Joel Collier (running backs)
Robert Ford (wide receivers)
John Gamble (strength & conditioning)
Cary Godette (defensive line)
George Hill (defensive coordinator/ linebackers)
Pat Jones (tight ends)
Bill Lewis (defensive nickel package)
Rich McGeorge (assistant offensive line)
Mel Phillips (secondary)
Brad Roll (assistant strength and conditioning)
Larry Seiple (quarterbacks)
Randy Shannon (def. assistant)
Mike Westhoff (special teams)

Equipment manager
Tony Egues
Video manager
Dave Hack

SCHEDULE

Sept. 6—	at Indianapolis	3:15
Sept. 13—	BUFFALO	1:01
Sept. 20—	PITTSBURGH	1:01
Sept. 27—	Open date	
Oct. 4—	at N.Y. Jets	1:01
Oct. 12—	at Jacksonville (Mon.)	8:20
Oct. 18—	ST. LOUIS	4:15
Oct. 25—	NEW ENGLAND	1:01
Nov. 1—	at Buffalo	1:01
Nov. 8—	INDIANAPOLIS	1:01
Nov. 15—	at Carolina	1:01
Nov. 23—	at New England (Mon.)	8:20
Nov. 29—	NEW ORLEANS	1:01
Dec. 6—	at Oakland	1:15
Dec. 13—	N.Y. JETS	8:20
Dec. 21—	DENVER (Mon.)	8:20
Dec. 27—	at Atlanta	1:01

All times are for home team.
All games Sunday unless noted.

DRAFT CHOICES

John Avery, RB, Mississippi (first round/29th pick overall).
Patrick Surtain, DB, Southern Mississippi (2/44).
Kenny Mixon, DE, Louisiana State (2/49).
Brad Jackson, LB, Cincinnati (3/79).
Larry Shannon, WR, East Carolina (3/82).
Lorenzo Bromell, DE, Clemson (4/102).
Scott Shaw, G, Michigan State (5/143).
Nathan Strikwerda, C, Northwestern (6/171).
John Dutton, QB, Nevada (6/172).
Jim Bundren, G, Clemson (7/210).

1998 SEASON
TRAINING CAMP ROSTER

No.	QUARTERBACKS	Ht./Wt.	Born	NFL Exp.	College	How acq.	'97 Games GP/GS
16	Dutton, John	6-4/219	9-20-75	R	Nevada	D6b/98	—
7	Erickson, Craig	6-2/210	5-17-69	7	Miami (Fla.)	FA/96	2/0
11	Huard, Damon	6-3/215	7-9-73	2	Washington	FA/97	0/0
13	Marino, Dan	6-4/228	9-15-61	16	Pittsburgh	D1/83	16/16
14	White, Stan	6-2/220	8-14-71	4	Auburn	FA/98	0/0
	RUNNING BACKS						
33	Abdul-Jabbar, Karim	5-10/200	6-28-74	3	UCLA	D3b/96	16/14
20	Avery, John	5-9/184	1-11-76	R	Mississippi	D1/98	—
48	Kitts, Jim (FB)	6-2/243	12-28-72	2	Ferrum (Va.)	FA/97	10/0
32	Nealy, Ray	5-11/235	4-30-75	1	Arkansas-Pine Bluff.	FA/97	1/0
30	Parmalee, Bernie	5-11/210	9-16-67	7	Ball State	FA/92	16/4
21	Phillips, Lawrence	6-0/223	5-12-75	3	Nebraska	FA/97	*12/9
36	Pritchett, Stanley (FB)	6-1/245	12-12-73	3	South Carolina	D4b/96	6/5
	RECEIVERS						
86	Alexander, Kevin	5-9/185	1-23-75	3	Utah State	FA/98	*14/8
15	Dar Dar, Kirby	5-9/188	3-27-72	3	Syracuse	FA/95	0/0
84	Drayton, Troy (TE)	6-3/265	6-29-70	6	Penn State	TR/96	16/15
87	Green, Yatil	6-2/200	11-25-73	2	Miami (Fla.)	D1/97	0/0
88	Jordan, Charles	5-11/185	10-9-69	6	Long Beach (Calif.) City College	FA/96	14/1
83	Manning, Brian	5-11/188	4-22-75	2	Stanford	D6b/97	7/0
81	McDuffie, O.J.	5-10/194	12-2-69	6	Penn State	D1/93	16/16
18	McPhail, Jerris	5-11/210	6-26-72	3	East Carolina	D5a/96	14/1
89	Perry, Ed (TE)	6-4/250	9-1-74	2	James Madison	D6d/97	16/4
19	Shannon, Larry	6-4/210	2-2-75	R	East Carolina	D3b/98	—
85	Thomas, Lamar	6-1/175	2-12-70	6	Miami (Fla.)	FA/96	12/6
46	Tucker, Syii (TE)	6-4/236	7-31-73	2	Miami (Fla.)	FA/98	0/0
82	Wainright, Frank (TE)	6-3/250	10-10-67	8	Northern Colorado	FA/95	9/0
	OFFENSIVE LINEMEN						
60	Bock, John (C)	6-3/295	2-11-71	4	Indiana State	FA/96	14/3
76	Brown, James (T)	6-6/330	1-3-70	6	Virginia State	TR/96	16/16
77	Buckey, Jeff (T)	6-5/305	8-7-74	3	Stanford	D7a/96	16/12
69	Bundren, Jim (G)	6-3/303	10-6-74	R	Clemson	D7/98	—
63	Dixon, Mark (T)	6-4/280	11-6-70	1	Virginia	FA/98	0/0
65	Donnalley, Kevin (G)	6-5/305	6-10-68	8	North Carolina	FA/98	*16/16
61	Ruddy, Tim (C)	6-3/300	4-27-72	5	Notre Dame	D2b/94	15/15
73	Shaw, Scott (G)	6-3/303	6-2-74	R	Michigan State	D5/98	—
68	Sheldon, Mike (T)	6-4/305	6-8-73	2	Grand Valley State	FA/97	11/0
74	Smith, Brent (G)	6-5/305	11-21-73	2	Mississippi State	D3d/97	0/0
67	Stokes, Barry (T)	6-4/312	12-20-73	1	Eastern Michigan	FA/98	0/0
66	Strikwerda, Nathan (C)	6-4/295	8-20-75	R	Northwestern	D6a/98	—
78	Webb, Richmond (T)	6-6/320	1-11-67	9	Texas A&M	D1/90	16/16
64	Wheeler, Randy (G)	6-2/315	5-4-74	1	South Carolina	FA/98	0/0
	DEFENSIVE LINEMEN						
90	Anderson, Dunstan (E)	6-4/270	12-31-70	2	Tulsa	FA/98	9/1
93	Armstrong, Trace (E)	6-4/267	10-5-65	10	Florida	TR/95	16/16
95	Bowens, Tim (T)	6-4/315	2-7-73	5	Mississippi	D1/94	16/16
91	Bromell, Lorenzo (E)	6-6/266	9-23-75	R	Clemson	D4/98	—
75	Burton, Shane (T)	6-6/310	1-18-74	3	Tennessee	D5b/96	16/4
70	Chalenski, Mike (E)	6-5/280	1-28-70	5	UCLA	FA/97	8/0
92	Gardener, Daryl (T)	6-6/315	2-25-73	3	Baylor	D1/96	16/16
79	Mixon, Kenny (E)	6-4/270	5-31-75	R	Louisiana State	D2b/98	—
96	Stubbs, Daniel (E)	6-4/270	1-3-65	10	Miami (Fla.)	FA/96	1/0
72	Tanner, Barron (T)	6-3/310	9-14-73	2	Oklahoma	D5a/97	16/0
99	Taylor, Jason (E)	6-6/255	9-1-74	2	Akron	D3a/97	13/11
	LINEBACKERS						
57	Brigance, O.J.	6-0/236	9-29-69	3	Rice	FA/96	16/0
56	Crawford, Mike	6-1/238	10-29-74	2	Nevada	D6c/97	7/0
51	Harris, Anthony	6-1/235	1-25-73	3	Auburn	FA/96	16/16
50	Hollier, Dwight	6-2/242	4-21-69	7	North Carolina	D4/92	16/3
53	Izzo, Larry	5-10/228	9-26-74	3	Rice	FA/96	0/0
58	Jackson, Brad	6-0/228	1-11-75	R	Cincinnati	D3a/98	—
59	Rodgers, Derrick	6-1/225	10-14-71	2	Arizona State	D3b/97	15/14
54	Thomas, Zach	5-11/235	9-1-73	3	Texas Tech	D5c/96	15/15
55	Ward, Ronnie	6-0/232	2-11-74	2	Kansas	D3c/97	4/0

No.	DEFENSIVE BACKS	Ht./Wt.	Born	NFL Exp.	College	How acq.	'97 Games GP/GS
27	Buckley, Terrell (CB)	5-9/180	6-7-71	7	Florida State	TR/95	16/16
25	Harris, Corey (CB)	5-11/205	10-25-69	7	Vanderbilt	FA/97	16/7
38	Jackson, Calvin (S)	5-9/185	10-28-72	4	Auburn	FA/95	16/16
29	Madison, Sam (CB)	5-11/185	4-23-74	2	Louisville	D2/97	14/3
31	Marion, Brock (S)	5-11/200	6-11-70	6	Nevada	FA/98	*16/16
23	Surtain, Patrick (CB)	5-11/197	5-19-76	R	Southern Mississippi	D2a/98	—
26	Walker, Bracey (S)	6-0/200	10-28-70	5	North Carolina	FA/97	12/0
45	Walker, Brian (S)	6-1/190	5-31-72	3	Washington State	FA/97	5/0
24	Wilson, Jerry (CB)	5-10/187	7-17-73	4	Southern	FA/96	16/0
22	Wooden, Shawn (S)	5-11/205	10-23-73	3	Notre Dame	D6/96	16/15
	SPECIALISTS						
6	Baker, Jonathon (K)	6-1/170	8-13-72	1	Arizona State	FA/98	0/0
5	Cochman, Nate (P)	6-5/215	4-26-75	1	Pittsburgh	FA/98	0/0
	Kidd, John (P)	6-3/214	8-22-61	15	Northwestern	FA/94	13/0
10	Mare, Olindo (K)	5-10/190	6-6-73	2	Syracuse	FA/97	16/0
8	Wilmsmeyer, Klaus (P)	6-1/210	12-4-67	6	Louisville	FA/98	0/0

*Alexander played 14 games with Giants in '97; Donnalley played 16 games with Oilers; Marion played 16 games with Cowboys; Phillips played 10 games with Rams and 2 games with Dolphins.

Abbreviations: D1—draft pick, first round; SupD2—supplemental draft pick, second round; WV—claimed on waivers; TR—obtained in trade; PlanB—Plan B free-agent acquisition; FA—free-agent acquisition (other than Plan B); ED—expansion draft pick.

MISCELLANEOUS TEAM DATA

Stadium (capacity, surface):
Pro Player Stadium
(75,192, grass)
Business address:
7500 S.W. 30th St.
Davie, FL 33314
Business phone:
954-452-7000
Ticket information:
305-620-2578
Team colors:
Aqua, coral, blue and white
Flagship radio station:
WQAM, 560 AM
Training site:
Nova Southeastern University
Davie, Fla.
954-452-7000

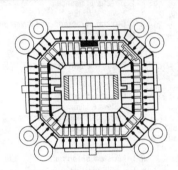

TSN REPORT CARD

Coaching — A - — How can you argue with a guy who has won two Super Bowls in seven seasons as an NFL coach? Jimmy Johnson continued to show restraint in free agency despite the temptation to win right away. One criticism of Johnson, however, may be that he doesn't anticipate the free-agent market very well. The Dolphins should have been more aggressive in their pursuit of Vikings DT John Randle.

Offensive backfield — C + — With QB Dan Marino aging and the offensive emphasis shifting to the running game, the running backs merit a larger part of this grade. As of now, the Dolphins are a little better than average, but a committee running game has its downsides.

Receivers — C - — Until they prove otherwise, there is a lot of mystery to this group and not enough certainty. WR O.J. McDuffie is solid, but not explosive. TE Troy Drayton could be interesting because he'll be on the field more in the new offense. Otherwise, the Dolphins are rolling a lot of dice with the rest of the corps.

Offensive line — B — The addition of G Kevin Donnalley was huge because he's got the nastiness this team hasn't had in years. If the left guard spot can be worked out and a change in attitude brings the rest of the group along, this could develop into a terrific unit.

Defensive line — B — If tackles Daryl Gardener and Tim Bowens play up to their potential, this grade should go way up. The Dolphins were extremely unlucky last year with injuries, but with the addition of rookies Kenny Mixon and Lorenzo Bromell that shouldn't be an issue. If nothing else, the pass rush should be much improved.

Linebackers — B — Zach Thomas is a marvel and fun guy for fans to cheer for. He also has great instincts and makes people around him better. But he isn't a game-changing player. The Dolphins desperately need Derrick Rodgers, Anthony Harris and/or rookie Brad Jackson to take the next step to stardom.

Defensive backs — B — The Dolphins started three players at free safety in each of the past two seasons. With that in mind, free-agent signee Brock Marion must add stability, particularly if the Dolphins are to run the kind of aggressive coverage schemes they want.

Special teams — A - — If Larry Izzo and Kirby Dar Dar return and rookie John Avery is above average as a kickoff and punt returner, the Dolphins might end up with the best special teams in the NFL. This is a great group with a terrific coach in Mike Westhoff. Johnson and Westhoff certainly emphasize it enough.

MINNESOTA VIKINGS
NFC CENTRAL DIVISION

1997 REVIEW
RESULTS

Aug. 31—at Buffalo	W	34-13
Sept. 7—at Chicago	W	27-24
Sept.14—TAMPA BAY	L	14-28
Sept.21—at Green Bay	L	32-38
Sept.28—PHILADELPHIA	W	28-19
Oct. 5—at Arizona	W	20-19
Oct. 12—CAROLINA	W	21-14
Oct. 19—Open date		
Oct. 26—at Tampa Bay	W	10-6
Nov. 2—NEW ENGLAND	W	23-18
Nov. 9—CHICAGO	W	29-22
Nov. 16—at Detroit	L	15-38
Nov. 23—at N.Y. Jets	L	21-23
Dec. 1—GREEN BAY	L	11-27
Dec. 7—at San Francisco	L	17-28
Dec. 14—DETROIT	L	13-14
Dec. 21—INDIANAPOLIS	W	39-28
Dec. 27—at N.Y. Giants*	W	23-22
Jan. 3—at San Francisco†	L	22-38

*NFC wild-card game.
†NFC divisional playoff game.

RECORDS/RANKINGS

1997 regular-season record: 9-7 (T3rd in NFC Central); 3-5 in division; 6-6 in conference; 5-3 at home; 4-4 on road.
Team record last five years: 45-35 (.563, ranks T7th in league in that span).

1997 team rankings:	No.	NFC	NFL
Total offense	*334.6	4	8
Rushing offense	*127.6	2	6
Passing offense	*207.1	6	14
Scoring offense	354	4	11
Total defense	*355.4	15	29
Rushing defense	*123.9	11	23
Passing defense	*231.5	15	29
Scoring defense	359	T10	T19
Takeaways	27	9	T17
Giveaways	22	3	T7
Turnover differential	5	4	T9
Sacks	44	T5	T10
Sacks allowed	33	T4	T9

*Yards per game.

TEAM LEADERS

Scoring (kicking): Eddie Murray, 59 pts. (23/24 PATs, 12/17 FGs).
Scoring (touchdowns): Cris Carter, 84 pts. (13 receiving, 3 2-pt. conv.).
Passing: Brad Johnson, 3,036 yds. (452 att., 275 comp., 60.8%, 20 TDs, 12 int.).
Rushing: Robert Smith, 1,266 yds. (232 att., 5.5 avg., 6 TDs).
Receptions: Jake Reed, 68 (1,138 yds., 16.7 avg., 6 TDs).
Interceptions: Dewayne Washington, 4 (71 yds., 0 TDs).
Sacks: John Randle, 15.5.
Punting: Mitch Berger, 42.9 avg. (73 punts, 3,133 yds., 0 blocked).
Punt returns: David Palmer, 13.1 avg. (34 att., 444 yds., 0 TDs).
Kickoff returns: David Palmer, 22.2 avg. (32 att., 711 yds., 0 TDs).

1998 SEASON
CLUB DIRECTORY

Chairman of the board
John C. Skoglund
President/chief executive officer
Roger Headrick
V.P., administration/team operations
Jeff Diamond
V.P., player personnel
Frank Gilliam
V.P., marketing/business development
Stew Widdess
Assistant general manager, college scouting
Jerry Reichow
Assistant general manager, pro personnel
Paul Wiggin
Director of finance
Nick Valentine
Director of research and development
Mike Eayrs
Director of sales
Kernal Buhler
Public relations assistants
Debra Jones
Bob Hagan
Director of security
Steve Rollins
Player personnel coordinator
Scott Studwell
Head scout
Don Deisch
Assistant head scout
Conrad Cardano
Regional scout
Roger Jackson
Area scout
John Fitzpatrick
Director of team operations
Breck Spinner

Head coach
Dennis Green

Assistant coaches
Hubbard Alexander (receivers)
Dave Atkins (tight ends)
Brian Billick (offensive coord.)
Foge Fazio (defensive coordinator)
Jeff Friday (assistant strength & conditioning)
Carl Hargrave (running backs)
Andre Patterson (defensive line)
Chip Myers (quarterbacks)
Tom Olivadotti (inside linebackers)
Richard Solomon (secondary)
Mike Tice (offensive line)
Trent Walters (outside linebackers)
Steve Wetzel (strength & conditioning)
Gary Zauner (special teams)

Equipment manager
Dennis Ryan
Medical director
Dr. David Fischer
Trainer
Fred Zamberletti
Assistant trainer
Chuck Barta

SCHEDULE

Sept. 6— TAMPA BAY	12:01
Sept. 13— at St. Louis	12:01
Sept. 20— DETROIT	12:01
Sept. 27— at Chicago	3:15
Oct. 5— at Green Bay (Mon.)	7:20
Oct. 11— Open date	
Oct. 18— WASHINGTON	12:01
Oct. 25— at Detroit	1:01
Nov. 1— at Tampa Bay	1:01
Nov. 8— NEW ORLEANS	12:01
Nov. 15— CINCINNATI	12:01
Nov. 22— GREEN BAY	12:01
Nov. 26— at Dallas (Thanks.)	3:05
Dec. 6— CHICAGO	7:20
Dec. 13— at Baltimore	4:15
Dec. 20— JACKSONVILLE	7:20
Dec. 26— at Tennessee (Sat.)	11:35

All times are for home team.
All games Sunday unless noted.

DRAFT CHOICES

Randy Moss, WR, Marshall (first round/21st pick overall).
Kailee Wong, LB, Stanford (2/51).
Ramos McDonald, DB, New Mexico (3/80).
Kivuusama Mays, LB, North Carolina (4/110).
Kerry Cooks, DB, Iowa (5/144).
Matt Birk, T, Harvard (6/173).
Chester Burnett, LB, Arizona (7/208).
Tony Darden, DB, Texas Tech (7/225).

Minnesota Vikings — **1998 SEASON**

No.	QUARTERBACKS	Ht./Wt.	Born	NFL Exp.	College	How acq.	'97 Games GP/GS
8	Bouman, Todd	6-2/195	8-1-72	1	St. Cloud State	FA/97	0/0
7	Cunningham, Randall	6-4/214	3-27-63	13	UNLV	FA/97	6/3
11	Fiedler, Jay	6-1/214	12-29-71	3	Dartmouth	FA/95	0/0
14	Johnson, Brad	6-5/224	9-13-68	7	Florida State	D9/92	13/13
6	Walker, Jay	6-3/229	1-24-72	1	Howard	FA/96	0/0

No.	RUNNING BACKS	Ht./Wt.	Born	NFL Exp.	College	How acq.	'97 Games GP/GS
49	Ayanbadejo, Obafemi (FB)	6-2/230	3-5-75	1	San Diego State	FA/98	0/0
29	Evans, Chuck (FB)	6-1/243	4-16-67	6	Clark Atlanta (Ga.)	D11/92	16/13
44	Hoard, Leroy	5-11/223	5-15-68	9	Michigan	FA/96	12/1
33	Morrow, Harold	5-11/215	2-24-73	3	Auburn	WV/96	16/0
22	Palmer, David	5-8/176	11-19-72	5	Alabama	D2/94	16/0
26	Smith, Robert	6-2/209	3-4-72	6	Ohio State	D1/93	14/14
21	Williams, Moe	6-1/200	7-26-74	3	Kentucky	D3/96	14/0

No.	RECEIVERS	Ht./Wt.	Born	NFL Exp.	College	How acq.	'97 Games GP/GS
45	Baynham, Grant (TE)	6-5/250	10-11-73	1	Georgia Tech	FA/97	0/0
84	Bland, Tony	6-3/213	12-12-72	2	Florida A&M	FA/96	2/0
80	Carter, Cris	6-3/216	11-25-65	12	Ohio State	WV/90	16/16
85	DeLong, Greg (TE)	6-4/247	4-3-73	4	North Carolina	FA/95	16/3
87	Glover, Andrew (TE)	6-6/253	8-12-67	8	Grambling State	FA/97	13/11
87	Goodwin, Hunter (TE)	6-5/273	10-10-72	3	Texas A&M	D4/96	16/5
89	Hatchette, Matthew	6-2/195	5-1-74	2	Langston	D7b/97	16/0
18	Moss, Randy	6-4/194	2-13-77	R	Marshall (W.Va.)	D1/98	—
19	Murphy, Yo	5-10/178	5-11-71	1	Idaho	FA/97	0/0
86	Reed, Jake	6-3/219	9-28-67	8	Grambling State	D3/91	16/16
83	Tate, Robert	5-10/187	10-19-73	2	Cincinnati	D6/97	4/0
81	Walsh, Chris	6-1/198	12-12-68	6	Stanford	FA/94	14/0

No.	OFFENSIVE LINEMEN	Ht./Wt.	Born	NFL Exp.	College	How acq.	'97 Games GP/GS
75	Birk, Matt (T)	6-4/308	7-23-76	R	Harvard	D6/98	—
74	Bobo, Orlando (G)	6-3/296	2-9-74	2	Northeast Louisiana	FA/96	5/0
62	Christy, Jeff (C)	6-3/281	2-3-69	6	Pittsburgh	FA/93	12/12
69	Daniels, LeShun (G)	6-1/304	5-30-74	2	Ohio State	FA/97	1/0
61	Lindsay, Everett (G)	6-4/290	9-18-70	5	Mississippi	D5/93	16/3
64	McDaniel, Randall (G)	6-3/279	12-19-64	11	Arizona State	D1/88	16/16
68	Morris, Mike (C)	6-5/283	2-22-61	12	Northeast Missouri State	FA/91	16/0
79	Moss, Eric	6-4/325	9-25-74	1	Ohio State	FA/97	0/0
78	Sapp, Bob (G)	6-4/303	9-22-73	2	Washington	D3/97	1/0
73	Steussie, Todd (T)	6-6/321	12-1-70	5	California	D1b/94	16/16
77	Stringer, Korey (T)	6-4/353	5-8-74	4	Ohio State	D1/95	15/15

No.	DEFENSIVE LINEMEN	Ht./Wt.	Born	NFL Exp.	College	How acq.	'97 Games GP/GS
90	Alexander, Derrick (E)	6-4/286	11-3-73	4	Florida State	D1a/95	14/14
96	Ball, Jerry (T)	6-1/320	12-15-64	12	Southern Methodist	FA/97	12/6
92	Clemons, Duane (E)	6-5/277	5-23-74	3	California	D1/96	13/3
99	Colinet, Stalin (E)	6-6/274	7-19-74	2	Boston College	D3/97	10/2
72	Fisk, Jason (T)	6-3/295	9-4-72	4	Stanford	D7b/95	16/10
93	Randle, John (T)	6-1/285	12-12-67	9	Texas A&I	FA/90	16/16
95	Smith, Fernando (E)	6-6/283	8-2-71	5	Jackson State	D2b/94	12/11
94	Williams, Tony (T)	6-1/291	7-9-75	2	Memphis	D5/97	6/2
52	Wong, Kailee (E)	6-2/267	5-23-76	R	Stanford	D2/98	—

No.	LINEBACKERS	Ht./Wt.	Born	NFL Exp.	College	How acq.	'97 Games GP/GS
56	Bercich, Pete	6-1/239	12-23-71	4	Notre Dame	D7/94	16/0
50	Burnett, Chester	5-10/226	4-15-75	R	Arizona	D7a/98	—
59	Edwards, Dixon	6-1/237	3-25-68	8	Michigan State	FA/96	16/16
55	Houston, Bobby	6-2/245	10-26-67	8	North Carolina State	FA/98	*7/0
53	Mays, Kivuusama	6-3/244	1-7-75	R	North Carolina	D4/98	—
58	McDaniel, Ed	5-11/230	2-23-69	7	Clemson	D5/92	16/16
57	Rudd, Dwayne	6-2/245	2-3-76	2	Alabama	D1/97	16/2
54	Ulmer, Artie	6-2/243	7-30-73	2	Valdosta State	D7a/97	0/0

No.	DEFENSIVE BACKS	Ht./Wt.	Born	NFL Exp.	College	How acq.	'97 Games GP/GS
30	Banks, Antonio	5-10/199	3-12-73	2	Virginia Tech	D4/97	0/0
43	Briggs, Greg (S)	6-3/215	10-1-68	5	Texas Southern	FA/97	14/0
31	Butler, Duane (S)	6-1/203	11-29-73	2	Illinois State	FA/97	3/0
20	Cooks, Kerry (S)	5-11/198	3-28-74	R	Iowa	D5/98	—
32	Darden, Tony (CB)	5-11/187	8-11-75	R	Texas Tech	D7b/98	—
27	Fuller, Corey (CB)	5-10/206	5-1-71	4	Florida State	D2/95	16/16
23	Gray, Torrian	6-0/198	3-18-74	2	Virginia Tech	D2/97	16/3
24	Griffith, Robert (S)	5-11/198	11-30-70	5	San Diego State	FA/94	16/16

No.	DEFENSIVE BACKS	Ht./Wt.	Born	NFL Exp.	College	How acq.	'97 Games GP/GS
31	Hitchcock, Jimmy (CB)	5-10/188	11-9-71	4	North Carolina	TR/98	*15/15
34	McDonald, Ramos (CB)	5-11/195	4-30-76	R	New Mexico	D3/98	—
28	Phillips, Anthony (CB)	6-2/209	10-5-70	4	Texas A&M	FA/98	0/0
42	Thomas, Orlando (S)	6-1/216	10-21-72	4	Southwestern Louisiana	D2/95	15/13
81	Walker, Anthony	6-0/200	12-6-73	1	Syracuse	FA/97	0/0
	SPECIALISTS						
1	Anderson, Gary (K)	5-11/178	7-16-59	17	Syracuse	FA/98	*16/0
17	Berger, Mitch (P)	6-2/218	6-24-72	3	Colorado	FA/96	14/0
5	Caflisch, Andy (P)	6-3/200	8-7-70	1	Wisconsin-Stout	FA/98	0/0
4	Kurz, Todd (K)	6-3/218	4-20-74	1	Illinois State	FA/98	0/0

*Anderson played 16 games with 49ers in '97; Hitchcock played 15 games with Patriots; Houston played 5 games with Chiefs and 2 games with Chargers.

Abbreviations: D1—draft pick, first round; SupD2—supplemental draft pick, second round; WV—claimed on waivers; TR—obtained in trade; PlanB—Plan B free-agent acquisition; FA—free-agent acquisition (other than Plan B); ED—expansion draft pick.

MISCELLANEOUS TEAM DATA

Stadium (capacity, surface):
Metrodome (64,035, artificial)
Business address:
9520 Viking Drive
Eden Prairie, MN 55344
Business phone:
612-828-6500
Ticket information:
612-333-8828
Team colors:
Purple, gold and white
Flagship radio station:
WCCO, 830 AM
Training site:
Mankato State University
Mankato, Minn.
612-828-6500

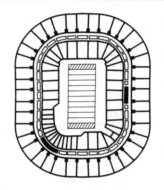

TSN REPORT CARD

Coaching staff	B	Many of Dennis Green's problems are self-inflicted, but he still manages to rate highly within his own locker room and win enough to be among the NFL's top third of coaches. Ending his playoff-victory drought helped, but the pressure is back again as he coaches in the final year of his contract.
Offensive backfield	B +	If quarterback Brad Johnson returns healthy from neck surgery, and running back Robert Smith repeats his impact season of 1997, the team will have among the best weapons in the NFC. Backup quarterback Randall Cunningham proved he can still win games and fullback Charles Evans is a useful, versatile veteran.
Receivers	A +	With gifted first-round draft choice Randy Moss added to the mix, this unit could become the best in the NFL. Cris Carter and Jake Reed have an NFL-record four straight 1,000-yard seasons in tandem, and Moss should help shake some double coverage. Tight end Andrew Glover is an athletic target whose hands are iffy.
Offensive line	A	Two starters went to the Pro Bowl in perennial pick Randall McDaniel (left guard) and first-timer Todd Steussie (left tackle). Right guard David Dixon exceeded expectations last year and right tackle Korey Stringer is one of the best in the NFC. Center Jeff Christy, while undersized, is the unit's leader and his return from a broken ankle is key.
Defensive line	B -	Any unit with NFL sack leader John Randle can't be too bad, but there is more promise than production surrounding Randle. Ends Derrick Alexander and Fernando Smith must re-prove themselves, and nose tackle Jerry Ball might be pushed by Tony Williams. Ends Stalin Colinet and Duane Clemons are in the hunt for starting jobs.
Linebackers	C	This unit had few playmakers last season, with the exception of rookie Dwayne Rudd, who claimed the weakside spot by year's end. Ed McDaniel is undersized but quick, but he shifts to the middle this year, a run-stopping position. Strong-side starter Dixon Edwards slumped last year. Depth remains a concern.
Secondary	C -	Taken individually, the secondary has some talent. But as a unit it struggled, and the pass defense ranked 29th. Corey Fuller is an average corner and newcomer Jimmy Hitchcock was the team's fourth choice. Strong safety Robert Griffith had a great second half, but free safety Orlando Thomas lost his job late last year to rookie Torrian Gray.
Special teams	B	Veteran kicker Gary Anderson should improve the consistency and punter-kickoff specialist Mitch Berger performed fairly well despite a hip injury last year. Return specialist David Palmer made a host of big plays, especially in the season's second half. Kick and punt coverage remains spotty.

NEW ENGLAND PATRIOTS
AFC EASTERN DIVISION

1997 REVIEW

RESULTS

Aug. 31—SAN DIEGO	W	41-7
Sept. 7—at Indianapolis	W	31-6
Sept.14—N.Y. JETS (OT)	W	27-24
Sept.21—CHICAGO	W	31-3
Sept.28—Open date		
Oct. 6—at Denver	L	13-34
Oct. 12—BUFFALO	W	33-6
Oct. 19—at N.Y. Jets	L	19-24
Oct. 27—GREEN BAY	L	10-28
Nov. 2—at Minnesota	L	18-23
Nov. 9—at Buffalo	W	31-10
Nov. 16—at Tampa Bay	L	7-27
Nov. 23—MIAMI	W	27-24
Nov. 30—INDIANAPOLIS	W	20-17
Dec. 7—JACKSONVILLE	W	26-20
Dec. 13—PITTSBURGH (OT)	L	21-24
Dec. 22—at Miami	W	14-12
Dec. 28—MIAMI*	W	17-3
Jan. 3—at Pittsburgh†	L	6-7

*AFC wild-card game.
†AFC divisional playoff game.

RECORDS/RANKINGS

1997 regular-season record: 10-6 (1st in AFC East); 7-1 in division; 9-3 in conference; 6-2 at home; 4-4 on road.
Team record last five years: 42-38 (.525, ranks 11th in league in that span).

1997 team rankings:	No.	AFC	NFL
Total offense	*313.4	10	15
Rushing offense	*91.5	13	26
Passing offense	*221.9	5	7
Scoring offense	369	5	8
Total defense	*317.2	7	19
Rushing defense	*101	3	5
Passing defense	*216.2	T8	T21
Scoring defense	289	4	T8
Takeaways	32	2	T6
Giveaways	22	T5	T7
Turnover differential	10	T2	T4
Sacks	46	T4	T8
Sacks allowed	30	3	4

*Yards per game.

TEAM LEADERS

Scoring (kicking): Adam Vinatieri, 115 pts. (40/40 PATs, 25/29 FGs).
Scoring (touchdowns): Ben Coates, 48 pts. (8 receiving).
Passing: Drew Bledsoe, 3,706 yds. (522 att., 314 comp., 60.2%, 28 TDs, 15 int.).
Rushing: Curtis Martin, 1,160 yds. (274 att., 4.2 avg., 4 TDs).
Receptions: Shawn Jefferson, 54 (841 yds., 15.6 avg., 2 TDs).
Interceptions: Willie Clay, 6 (109 yds., 1 TD).
Sacks: Chris Slade, 9.0.
Punting: Tom Tupa, 45.8 avg. (78 punts, 3,569 yds., 1 blocked).
Punt returns: David Meggett, 10.4 avg. (45 att., 467 yds., 0 TDs).
Kickoff returns: David Meggett, 24.7 avg. (33 att., 816 yds., 0 TDs).

1998 SEASON

CLUB DIRECTORY

President and chief executive officer
Robert K. Kraft
Vice president/owner's representative
Jonathan A. Kraft
Vice president, business operations
Andrew Wasynczuk
Vice president, player personnel
Bobby Grier
Vice president, finance
James Hausmann
Vice president, marketing
Daniel A. Kraft
V.p., player development and community relations
Donald Lowery
Director of pro scouting
Dave Uyrus
Director of media relations
Stacey James
Dir. of marketing and special events
Lou Imbriano
Director of football operations
Ken Deininger
Controller
Jim Nolan
Director of ticketing
Mike Nichols
Corporate sales executive
Jon Levy
General manager of Foxboro Stadium
Dan Murphy
Building services superintendent
Bernie Reinhart

Head coach
Pete Carroll

Assistant coaches
Paul Boudreau (offensive line)
Jeff Davidson (offensive assistant/offensive line)
Ray Hamilton (defensive line)
Ron Lynn (defensive backs)
Johnny Parker (strength & conditioning)
Bo Pelini (linebackers)
Jack Reilly (quarterbacks)
Dante Scarnecchia (special teams)
Steve Sidwell (defensive coord.)
Carl Smith (tight ends)
DeWayne Walker (defensive assistant/defensive backs)
Steve Walters (wide receivers)
Kirby Wilson (running backs)
Ernie Zampese (offensive coord.)

Head trainer
Ron O'Neil
Equipment manager
Don Brocher

SCHEDULE

Sept. 7— at Denver (Mon.)	6:20
Sept. 13— INDIANAPOLIS	8:20
Sept. 20— TENNESSEE	1:01
Sept. 27— Open date	
Oct. 4— at New Orleans	12:01
Oct. 11— KANSAS CITY	1:01
Oct. 19— N.Y. JETS (Mon.)	8:20
Oct. 25— at Miami	1:01
Nov. 1— at Indianapolis	1:01
Nov. 8— ATLANTA	1:01
Nov. 15— at Buffalo	1:01
Nov. 23— MIAMI (Mon.)	8:20
Nov. 29— BUFFALO	4:05
Dec. 6— at Pittsburgh	1:01
Dec. 13— at St. Louis	12:01
Dec. 20— SAN FRANCISCO	1:01
Dec. 27— at N.Y. Jets	1:01

All times are for home team.
All games Sunday unless noted.

DRAFT CHOICES

Robert Edwards, RB, Georgia (first round/18th pick overall).
Tebucky Jones, DB, Syracuse (1/22).
Tony Simmons, WR, Wisconsin (2/52).
Rod Rutledge, TE, Alabama (2/54).
Chris Floyd, RB, Michigan (3/81).
Greg Spires, DE, Florida State (3/83).
Leonta Rheams, DT, Houston (4/115).
Ron Merkerson, LB, Colorado (5/145).
Harold Shaw, RB, Southern Mississippi (6/176).
Jason Andersen, C, Brigham Young (7/211).

1998 SEASON
TRAINING CAMP ROSTER

No.	QUARTERBACKS	Ht./Wt.	Born	NFL Exp.	College	How acq.	'97 Games GP/GS
11	Bledsoe, Drew	6-5/233	2-14-72	6	Washington State	D1/93	16/16
16	Zolak, Scott	6-5/235	12-13-67	8	Maryland	D4/91	4/0
	RUNNING BACKS						
46	Byrd, Rodney	6-2/245	4-28-74	1	Illinois	FA/98	0/0
30	Carter, Tony (FB)	5-11/236	8-23-72	4	Minnesota	FA/98	*16/10
29	Cullors, Derrick	5-11/205	12-26-72	2	Murray State	FA/96	15/1
47	Edwards, Robert	5-11/218	10-2-74	R	Georgia	D1a/98	—
37	Floyd, Chris (FB)	6-0/231	6-23-75	R	Michigan	D3a/98	—
35	Grier, Marrio	5-10/229	12-5-71	3	Tennessee-Chattanooga	D6b/96	16/0
23	Shaw, Sedrick	6-0/214	11-16-73	2	Iowa	D3a/97	1/0
44	Shaw, Harold	6-0/228	9-3-74	R	Southern Mississippi	D6/98	—
	RECEIVERS						
86	Bartrum, Mike (TE)	6-5/245	6-23-70	5	Marshall	TR/96	9/0
82	Brisby, Vincent	6-3/193	1-25-71	6	Northeast Louisiana	D2c/93	16/4
80	Brown, Troy	5-10/190	7-2-71	6	Marshall	D8/93	16/6
87	Coates, Ben (TE)	6-5/245	8-16-69	8	Livingstone College (N.C.)	D5/91	16/16
17	Gaiter, Tony	5-8/170	7-15-74	1	Miami (Fla.)	D6/97	1/0
88	Glenn, Terry	5-11/185	7-23-74	3	Ohio State	D1/96	9/9
84	Jefferson, Shawn	5-11/180	2-22-69	8	Central Florida	FA/96	16/14
83	Jells, Dietrich	5-10/186	4-11-72	3	Pittsburgh	W-KC/96	11/0
18	Ladd, Anthony	6-1/193	12-23-73	1	Cincinnati	FA/97	0/0
12	Montana, Denis	6-1/200	1-5-72	1	Concordia	FA/98	0/0
85	Purnell, Lovett (TE)	6-3/245	4-7-72	3	West Virginia	D7a/96	16/2
49	Rutledge, Rod (TE)	6-5/262	8-12-75	R	Alabama	D2b/98	—
15	Simmons, Tony	6-0/206	12-8-74	R	Wisconsin	D2a/98	—
81	Stablein, Brian	6-1/193	4-14-70	5	Ohio State	FA/98	*16/0
	OFFENSIVE LINEMEN						
67	Andersen, Jason (T)	6-6/312	9-3-75	R	Brigham Young	D7/98	—
78	Armstrong, Bruce (T)	6-4/295	9-7-65	12	Louisville	D1/87	16/16
61	Denson, Damon (G)	6-3/305	2-8-75	2	Michigan	D4/97	2/0
66	Ellis, Ed (T)	6-7/340	10-13-75	2	Buffalo	D4/97	1/0
63	Irwin, Heath (G)	6-4/300	6-27-73	3	Colorado	D4a/96	15/1
68	Lane, Max (T)	6-6/305	2-22-71	5	Navy	D6/94	16/16
75	McGee, Curtis (T)	6-4/285	3-28-74	1	Georgia Tech	FA/98	0/0
77	Moss, Zefross (T)	6-6/325	8-17-66	10	Alabama State	FA/97	15/15
65	Porter, Juan (C)	6-3/295	11-26-73	1	Ohio State	FA/97	0/0
60	Rehberg, Scott (T)	6-8/336	11-17-73	2	Central Michigan	D7/97	6/0
71	Rucci, Todd (G)	6-5/296	7-14-70	6	Penn State	D2b/93	16/16
62	Warren, Brent (T)	6-5/338	2-10-75	R	Syracuse	FA/98	—
64	Wohlabaugh, Dave (C)	6-3/292	4-13-72	4	Syracuse	D4/95	14/14
	DEFENSIVE LINEMEN						
92	Collons, Ferric (E)	6-6/285	12-4-69	5	California	TR/95	6/5
90	Eaton, Chad (T)	6-5/300	4-4-72	2	Washington State	D7/95	16/1
96	Jones, Mike (E)	6-4/280	8-25-69	8	North Carolina State	FA/94	16/7
55	McGinest, Willie (E)	6-5/255	12-11-71	4	Southern California	D1/94	11/11
98	Mitchell, Brandon (T)	6-3/289	6-19-75	2	Texas A&M	D2/97	11/0
94	Rheams, Leonta (T)	6-2/280	8-1-76	R	Houston	D4/98	—
70	Smith, Artie (T)	6-5/305	5-15-70	5	Louisiana Tech	WV/94	0/0
91	Spires, Greg (E)	6-1/260	8-12-74	R	Florida State	D3b/98	—
74	Sullivan, Chris (E)	6-4/279	3-14-73	3	Boston College	D4b/96	16/10
95	Thomas, Henry	6-2/277	1-12-65	12	Louisiana State	FA/95	16/16
97	Wheeler, Mark (T)	6-3/285	4-1-70	7	Texas A&M	FA/96	14/14
72	Wyman, Devin (T)	6-7/290	8-29-73	3	Kentucky State	D6c/96	6/0
	LINEBACKERS						
54	Bruschi, Tedy	6-1/245	6-9-73	3	Arizona	D3/96	16/1
59	Collins, Todd	6-2/248	5-27-70	6	Carson-Newman (Tenn.)	D3a/92	15/15
45	Cottrell, Dana	6-3/244	1-11-74	1	Syracuse	FA/98	0/0
99	Crawford, Vernon	6-3/245	6-25-74	2	Florida State	D5/97	16/0
52	Johnson, Ted	6-3/240	12-4-72	4	Colorado	D2/95	16/16
50	Merkerson, Ron	6-2/247	8-30-75	R	Colorado	D5/98	—
58	Moore, Marty	6-1/244	3-19-71	5	Kentucky	D7/94	16/0
51	Russ, Bernard	6-0/225	11-4-73	1	West Virginia	FA/97	2/0
53	Slade, Chris	6-5/245	1-30-71	6	Virginia	D2/93	16/16
	DEFENSIVE BACKS						
26	Canty, Chris (CB)	5-9/185	3-30-76	2	Kansas State	D1/97	16/1
42	Carter, Chris (S)	6-1/201	9-27-74	2	Texas	D3b/97	16/0
32	Clay, Willie (S)	5-10/200	9-5-70	7	Georgia Tech	FA/96	16/16

No.	DEFENSIVE BACKS	Ht./Wt.	NFL Born	Exp.	College	'97 Games How acq.	GP/GS
21	Israel, Steve (CB)	5-11/194	3-16-69	7	Pittsburgh	FA/97	5/0
34	Jones, Tebucky (S)	6-2/216	10-6-74	R	Syracuse	D1b/98	—
24	Law, Ty (CB)	5-11/200	2-10-74	4	Michigan	D1/95	16/16
38	Lofton, Steve (CB)	5-9/177	11-26-68	7	Texas A&M	FA/95	4/0
36	Milloy, Lawyer (S)	6-0/208	11-14-73	3	Washington	D2/96	16/16
39	Tate, Mark (CB)	6-0/185	3-20-74	1	Penn State	FA/97	0/0
25	Whigham, Larry (S)	6-2/205	6-23-72	5	Northeast Louisiana	FA/94	16/0
	SPECIALISTS						
19	Tupa, Tom (P)	6-4/220	2-6-66	10	Ohio State	FA/96	16/0
4	Vinatieri, Adam (K)	6-0/200	12-28-72	3	South Dakota State	FA/96	16/0

*Carter played 16 games with Bears in '97; Stablein played 16 games with Colts.

Abbreviations: D1—draft pick, first round; SupD2—supplemental draft pick, second round; WV—claimed on waivers; TR—obtained in trade; PlanB—Plan B free-agent acquisition; FA—free-agent acquisition (other than Plan B); ED—expansion draft pick.

MISCELLANEOUS TEAM DATA

Stadium (capacity, surface):
Foxboro Stadium
(60,292, grass)
Business address:
60 Washington St.
Foxboro, MA 02035
Business phone:
508-543-8200
Ticket information:
508-543-1776
Team colors:
Silver, red, white and blue
Flagship radio station:
WBCN, 104.1 FM
Training site:
Bryant College
Smithfield, R.I.
508-543-8200

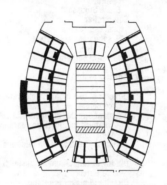

TSN REPORT CARD

Coaching staff — B — Pete Carroll overcame some difficult conditions to establish himself in the minds of the players a year ago. The addition of Ernie Zampese as offensive coordinator should provide the leadership for the offense to find its level. Defensively, coordinator Steve Sidwell's aggressive style and Carroll's philosophy depend on quickness and this team has the physical skills to make it work.

Offensive backfield — B - — Drew Bledsoe has his detractors but he's been to the Pro Bowl three times in the last four seasons and he's led the league in pass attempts over the last four seasons. The running back situation is considerably less stable. With veterans Curtis Martin, Sam Gash, Keith Byars and David Meggett departed, the Patriots running game is in the hands of a number of untested players. Sedrick Shaw was inactive for 17 of the 18 games last year, his rookie season. Derrick Cullors has started one regular season in his three-year career. Robert Edwards is a rookie.

Receivers — B + — Terry Glenn has spent the offseason working out to guard against the injuries that resulted in his slumping from 90 catches as a rookie to 27 last year. If he stays healthy, he's a game breaking outside threat. If Ben Coates stays healthy, he's a game-breaker on the inside and near the goal line. Shawn Jefferson and rookie Tony Simmons provide the outside speed with Troy Brown, Brian Stablein and Vincent Brisby providing veteran relief.

Offensive line — C — Excellent pass protectors starting their second year together as a unit, keeping Bledsoe healthy despite the fact that he throws the ball so often. Their problem has been generating any push on running plays the last three seasons, even with Curtis Martin in place. The same players will start for the second straight year which may lead to improvement in the running game.

Defensive line — C — Basically an undersized group that has to rely on speed. If Willie McGinest stays healthy, he should make a difference on the outside and the return of Ferric Collons on the outside should help. The problem is finding somebody in the middle to supply pressure without requiring the constant aid of blitzing secondary people.

Linebackers — B + — The starters are quality with Ted Johnson and Chris Slade capable of Pro Bowl seasons. Todd Collins, the third starter, is the best athlete but he's slowing. This is an excellent group against the run but has troubles in pass protection. Second-year man Vernon Crawford could help in that area.

Secondary — A - — Ty Law and Lawyer Milloy are coming off excellent seasons and should only get better. If rookie Tebucky Jones can handle the press corner position, he'll fill in the hole in the lineup from a year ago. Free safety Willie Clay has excellent hands and anticipation while Milloy is a terrific pass rusher from the safety position as well as a tough, physical tackler.

Special teams — B — Even without David Meggett, this should be a plus areas. Kicker Adam Vinatieri and punter Tom Tupa were among the best in the conference last year and the coverage teams have always been good. Somebody has to step up as a punt returner but Derrick Cullors showed a year ago he can handle the duties of being a kickoff man.

NEW ORLEANS SAINTS
NFC WESTERN DIVISION

1997 REVIEW

RESULTS

Aug. 31—at St. Louis	L	24-38
Sept. 7—SAN DIEGO	L	6-20
Sept.14—at San Francisco	L	7-33
Sept.21—DETROIT	W	35-17
Sept.28—at N.Y. Giants	L	9-14
Oct. 5—at Chicago	W	20-17
Oct. 12—ATLANTA	L	17-23
Oct. 19—CAROLINA	L	0-13
Oct. 26—SAN FRANCISCO	L	0-23
Nov. 2—Open date		
Nov. 9—at Oakland	W	13-10
Nov. 16—SEATTLE (OT)	W	20-17
Nov. 23—at Atlanta	L	3-20
Nov. 30—at Carolina	W	16-13
Dec. 7—ST. LOUIS	L	27-34
Dec. 14—ARIZONA	W	27-10
Dec. 21—at Kansas City	L	13-25

RECORDS/RANKINGS

1997 regular-season record: 6-10 (4th in NFC West); 1-7 in division; 4-8 in conference; 3-5 at home; 3-5 on road.
Team record last five years: 31-49 (.388), ranks 22nd in league in that span).

1997 team rankings:	No.	NFC	NFL
Total offense	*252.8	15	30
Rushing offense	*91.3	14	27
Passing offense	*161.5	13	27
Scoring offense	237	15	30
Total defense	*290.3	4	4
Rushing defense	*110.3	6	14
Passing defense	*180.1	4	6
Scoring defense	327	9	T16
Takeaways	31	5	T8
Giveaways	55	15	30
Turnover differential	-24	15	30
Sacks	59	1	1
Sacks allowed	50	12	24
*Yards per game.			

TEAM LEADERS

Scoring (kicking): Doug Brien, 91 pts. (22/22 PATs, 23/27 FGs).
Scoring (touchdowns): Andre Hastings, 32 pts. (5 receiving, 1 2-pt. conv.).
Passing: Heath Shuler, 1,288 yds. (203 att., 106 comp., 52.2%, 2 TDs, 14 int.).
Rushing: Ray Zellars, 552 yds. (156 att., 3.5 avg., 4 TDs).
Receptions: Randal Hill, 55 (761 yds., 13.8 avg., 2 TDs).
Interceptions: Sammy Knight, 5 (75 yds., 0 TDs).
Sacks: Wayne Martin, 10.5.
Punting: Mark Royals, 45.9 avg. (88 punts, 4,038 yds., 0 blocked).
Punt returns: Eric Guliford, 10.6 avg. (47 att., 498 yds., 0 TDs).
Kickoff returns: Eric Guliford, 26.2 avg. (43 att., 1,128 yds., 1 TD).

1998 SEASON

CLUB DIRECTORY

Owner
Tom Benson
President/g.m./COO
Bill Kuharich
Sr. v.p. of marketing and administration
Greg Suit
Asst. g.m./v.p. of football operations
Chet Franklin
Treasurer
Bruce Broussard
Comptroller
Charleen Sharpe
NFL salary cap consultant
Terry O'Neil
Director of corporate sales
Greg Seeling
Director of ticket sales
Jasen Feyerherm
Director of media and public relations
Greg Bensel
Assistant director of media and public relations/publications coordinator
Robert Gunn
Assistant director/media relations
Neal Gulkis
Dir. travel/entertainment/special projects
Barra Birrcher
Director of player programs
Austin Dejan
Director of college scouting
Bruce Lemmerman
Scouts

Hamp Cook	Hokie Gajan
Cornell Gowdy	Tom Marino
Phil Neri	Steve Sabo

Trainer
Dean Kleinschmidt
Asst. trainer/director of rehabilitation
Kevin Mangum
Assistant trainer
Buck Oubre
Physicians
Dr. Charles L. Brown Jr.
Dr. Terry Habig
Dr. Timothy Finney

SCHEDULE

Sept. 6—	at St. Louis	12:01
Sept. 13—	CAROLINA	12:01
Sept. 20—	Open date	
Sept. 27—	at Indianapolis	12:01
Oct. 4—	NEW ENGLAND	12:01
Oct. 11—	SAN FRANCISCO	12:01
Oct. 18—	at Atlanta	1:01
Oct. 25—	TAMPA BAY	12:01
Nov. 1—	at Carolina	1:01
Nov. 8—	at Minnesota	12:01
Nov. 15—	ST. LOUIS	12:01
Nov. 22—	at San Francisco	5:20
Nov. 29—	at Miami	1:01
Dec. 6—	DALLAS	12:01
Dec. 13—	ATLANTA	12:01
Dec. 20—	at Arizona	2:15
Dec. 27—	BUFFALO	12:01

All times are for home team.
All games Sunday unless noted.

Head coach
Mike Ditka

Assistant coaches
Danny Abramowicz (offensive coordinator)
Bobby April (special teams)
Tom Clements (quarterbacks)
Walt Corey (defensive line)
Jack Del Rio (linebackers)
Judd Garrett (offensive assistant)
Harold Jackson (wide receivers)
Ned James (defensive assistant)
Larry Kuharich (running backs)
Dan Neal (tight ends/offensive line assistant)
Markus Paul (assistant strength & conditioning)
Dick Stanfel (offensive line)
Rick Venturi (asst. head coach/secondary)
Mike Woicik (strength & cond.)
Zaven Yaralian (def. coordinator)

Facilities manager
Luke Jenkins
Grounds superintendent
Lester Vallet
Equipment manager
Dan Simmons
Assistant equipment manager
Glennon "Silky" Powell
Video director
Joe Malota
Assistant video director
Chad Bogard

DRAFT CHOICES

Kyle Turley, T, San Diego State (first round/seventh pick overall).
Cameron Cleeland, TE, Washington (2/40).
Fred Weary, DB, Florida (4/97).
Julian Pittman, DE, Florida State (4/99).
Wilmont Perry, RB, Livingstone (5/132).
Chris Bordano, LB, Southern Methodist (6/161).
Andy McCullough, WR, Tennessee (7/204).
Ron Warner, LB, Kansas (7/239).

1998 SEASON New Orleans Saints

No.	QUARTERBACKS	Ht./Wt.	Born	NFL Exp.	College	How acq.	'97 Games GP/GS
9	Delhomme, Jake	6-2/205	1-10-75	1	Southwestern Louisiana	FA/97	0/0
12	Hobert, Billy Joe	6-3/230	1-8-71	6	Washington	TR/97	5/4
5	Shuler, Heath	6-2/216	12-31-71	5	Tennessee	TR/97	10/9
7	Wuerffel, Danny	6-1/212	5-27-74	2	Florida	D4a/97	7/2
	RUNNING BACKS						
40	Bender, Wes (FB)	5-10/249	8-2-70	3	Southern California	FA/97	11/0
21	Brown, Derek	5-9/205	4-15-71	6	Nebraska	D4b/93	0/0
32	Craver, Aaron	6-0/220	12-18-68	8	Fresno State	FA/98	*15/5
28	Davis, Troy	5-7/191	9-14-75	2	Iowa State	D3/97	16/7
44	McCrary, Fred (FB)	6-0/232	9-19-72	3	Mississippi State	FA/97	7/0
33	Perry, Wilmont (FB)	6-1/230	2-24-75	R	Livingstone (N.C.)	D5/98	—
25	Smith, Lamar	5-11/218	11-29-70	5	Houston	FA/98	*12/2
34	Zellars, Ray	5-11/233	3-25-73	4	Notre Dame	D2/95	16/16
	RECEIVERS						
89	Bech, Brett	6-1/184	8-20-71	2	Louisiana State	FA/96	10/0
48	Cleeland, Cam (TE)	6-4/272	4-15-75	R	Washington	D2/98	—
86	Dawkins, Sean	6-4/215	2-3-71	5	California	UFA/98	*14/12
87	Farquhar, John (TE)	6-6/278	3-22-72	3	Duke	FA/96	12/8
84	Guliford, Eric	5-8/165	10-25-69	5	Arizona State	FA/97	16/2
80	Harper, Alvin	6-4/218	7-6-68	8	Tennessee	FA/95	12/0
88	Hastings, Andre	6-1/190	11-7-70	6	Georgia	D3/93	16/16
49	Hinton, Marcus (TE)	6-4/265	12-27-71	2	Alcorn State	FA/96	0/0
82	Ismail, Qadry	6-0/196	11-8-70	6	Syracuse	FA/98	*3/0
45	Leshinski, Ron (TE)	6-2/248	3-6-74	1	Army	FA/97	0/0
59	McCullough, Andy	6-3/210	11-11-75	R	Tennessee	D7a/98	—
83	Poole, Keith	6-0/188	6-18-74	2	Arizona State	D4b/97	3/0
85	Savoie, Nicky (TE)	6-5/253	9-21-73	2	Louisiana State	D6/97	1/0
16	Stegall, Milt	6-1/185	1-25-70	4	Miami of Ohio	FA/98	0/0
81	Twyner, Gunnard	5-10/165	7-14-73	2	Western Illinois	FA/97	2/0
	OFFENSIVE LINEMEN						
69	Ackerman, Tom (C)	6-3/290	9-6-72	3	Eastern Washington	D5b/96	14/0
76	Davis, Isaac (G)	6-3/320	4-8-72	5	Arkansas	D2a/94	12/12
62	Fontenot, Jerry (C)	6-3/300	11-21-66	10	Texas A&M	UFA/97	16/16
46	Gammon, Kendall (C)	6-4/288	10-23-68	7	Pittsburg (Kan.) State	FA/96	16/0
76	Hills, Keno (T)	6-6/305	6-13-73	3	Southwestern Louisiana	D6a/96	9/6
72	Jenkins, Trezelle (T)	6-7/317	3-13-73	4	Michigan	FA/97	2/1
74	Jones, Clarence (T)	6-6/280	5-6-68	8	Maryland	FA/96	15/15
67	McCollum, Andy (C)	6-4/295	6-2-70	5	Toledo	FA/94	16/16
65	Naeole, Chris (G)	6-3/313	12-25-74	2	Colorado	D1/97	4/0
77	Roaf, Willie (T)	6-5/300	4-18-70	6	Louisiana Tech	D1/93	16/16
71	Siglar, Ricky (T)	6-7/308	6-14-66	7	San Jose State	FA/93	16/1
68	Turley, Kyle (T)	6-5/307	9-24-75	R	San Diego State	D1/98	—
66	Verstegen, Mike (G)	6-6/311	10-24-71	4	Wisconsin	D3/95	14/8
	DEFENSIVE LINEMEN						
97	Glover, La'Roi (T)	6-1/285	7-4-74	3	San Diego State	D5/96	15/2
94	Johnson, Joe (E)	6-4/270	7-11-72	5	Louisville	D1/94	16/16
86	Johnson, Tony (E)	6-5/255	2-5-72	3	Alabama	FA/96	7/1
93	Martin, Wayne (T)	6-5/275	10-26-65	10	Arkansas	D1/89	16/16
75	Pittman, Julian (T)	6-4/286	4-22-75	R	Florida State	D4b/98	—
95	Robbins, Austin (T)	6-6/290	3-1-71	5	North Carolina	TR/96	12/0
99	Sagapolutele, Pio	6-6/297	11-28-69	8	San Diego State	FA/97	15/13
91	Smith, Brady (E)	6-5/260	6-5-73	3	Colorado State	D3/96	16/2
90	Tomich, Jared (E)	6-2/258	4-24-74	2	Nebraska	D2b/97	16/1
76	Young, Robert (E)	6-6/273	1-29-69	7	Mississippi State	FA/98	0/0
	LINEBACKERS						
54	Aleaga, Ink	6-1/225	4-27-73	2	Washington	FA/97	3/1
92	Bordano, Chris	6-1/241	12-30-74	R	Southern Methodist	D6/98	—
53	Davis, Don	6-1/240	12-17-72	3	Kansas	FA/96	11/0
55	Fields, Mark	6-2/244	11-9-72	4	Washington State	D1/95	16/15
52	Harvey, Richard	6-1/242	9-11-66	9	Tulane	FA/95	14/13
58	Jones, Brian	6-1/250	1-22-68	5	Texas	FA/95	0/0
59	Mitchell, Keith	6-2/240	7-24-74	2	Texas A&M	FA/97	16/2
55	Mitchell, Kevin	6-1/250	1-1-71	5	Syracuse	UFA/98	*16/0
51	Royal, Andre	6-2/238	12-1-72	4	Alabama	RFA/98	*16/13
60	Warner, Ron	6-2/247	9-26-75	R	Kansas	D7b/98	—
	DEFENSIVE BACKS						
30	Cherry, Je'Rod (S)	6-1/210	5-30-73	3	California	D2/96	16/0
27	Cobbs, Anthony	6-1/191	1-9-74	1	UCLA	FA/97	0/0
37	Cota, Chad (S)	6-1/198	8-13-71	4	Oregon	RFA/98	*16/16

No.	DEFENSIVE BACKS	Ht./Wt.	Born	NFL Exp.	College	How acq.	'97 Games GP/GS
22	Drakeford, Tyronne (CB)	5-9/185	6-21-71	5	Virginia Tech	UFA/98	*16/2
38	Greer, Donovan (CB)	5-9/178	9-11-74	2	Texas A&M	FA/97	6/1
23	Hewitt, Chris (S)	6-0/210	7-22-74	2	Cincinnati	FA/97	11/2
24	Kelly, Rob (S)	6-0/199	6-21-74	2	Ohio State	D2a/97	16/2
29	Knight, Sammy (S)	6-0/205	9-10-75	2	Southern California	FA/97	16/12
20	Little, Earl	6-0/191	3-10-73	1	Miami (Fla.)	FA/97	0/0
25	Molden, Alex (CB)	5-10/190	8-4-73	3	Oregon	D1/96	16/15
41	Strong, William (CB)	5-10/191	11-3-71	3	North Carolina State	D5/95	0/0
26	Washington, Mickey (CB)	5-9/195	7-8-68	9	Texas A&M	FA/97	16/2
42	Weary, Fred (CB)	5-10/177	4-12-74	R	Florida	D4a/98	—
	SPECIALISTS						
10	Brien, Doug (K)	6-0/180	11-24-70	5	California	FA/95	16/0
3	Royals, Mark (P)	6-5/215	6-22-64	9	Appalachian State	FA/97	16/0

*Cota played 16 games with Panthers in '97; Craver played 15 games with Chargers; Dawkins played 14 games with Colts; Drakeford played 16 games for 49ers; Ismail played 3 games with Dolphins; Kevin Mitchell played 16 games with 49ers; Royal played 16 games with Panthers; L. Smith played 12 games with Seahawks.

Abbreviations: D1—draft pick, first round; SupD2—supplemental draft pick, second round; WV—claimed on waivers; TR—obtained in trade; PlanB—Plan B free-agent acquisition; FA—free-agent acquisition (other than Plan B); ED—expansion draft pick.

MISCELLANEOUS TEAM DATA

Stadium (capacity, surface):
Louisiana Superdome
(69,028, artificial)

Business address:
5800 Airline Drive
Metairie, LA 70003

Business phone:
504-733-0255

Ticket information:
504-731-1700

Team colors:
Old gold, black and white

Flagship radio station:
WWL, 870 AM

Training site:
University of Wisconsin-La Crosse
La Crosse, Wis.
608-789-4550

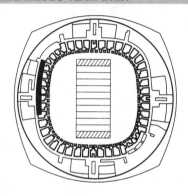

TSN REPORT CARD

Coaching staff	B +	Mike Ditka still has plenty of mountain left to climb following a 6-10 debut. But doubling the team's 1996 victory total was no small feat for him and his staff. Ditka has decided to become more involved in helping coordinator Danny Abramowicz straighten out the NFL's worst offense.
Offensive backfield	C	Signing RB Lamar Smith away from the Seahawks was a major coup. To do so, team officials bested competition from the Chiefs, Rams and Chargers. Making a clean break from RB Mario Bates was another smart move. Standing pat at quarterback, however, was a major mistake.
Receivers	C	Credit general manager Bill Kuharich for the addition of WR Sean Dawkins. Dawkins represents a definite upgrade to a wide receiver corps that didn't exactly strike fear into opposing defenses last year. Opting not to re-sign WR Randal Hill was no major loss. Drafting Cameron Cleeland in the second round brings potential star quality to the tight end position and makes the loss of Irv Smith to the 49ers a wash.
Offensive line	C	This is a group loaded with potential. Three top 10 picks are expected to start in left tackle Willie Roaf, right guard Chris Naeole and rookie Kyle Turley at right tackle. There is plenty of room for improvement after allowing 50 sacks and ranking 27th in rushing in '97.
Defensive line	B +	This group should again be the strongest area of the team despite the retirement of left end Darren Mickell at age 27. Three-year veteran Brady Smith appears ready to take over for Mickell. Left tackle Wayne Martin and right end Joe Johnson continue to be standouts and never take a down off. Right tackle La'Roi Glover is an emerging prospect.
Linebackers	C +	Losing middle linebacker Winfred Tubbs via free agency to the 49ers was a major blow. Tubbs was considered Pro Bowl caliber by the coaching staff after posting a club record 160 tackles in '97. Mark Fields' continued emergence and a healthy and productive season by Brian Jones, Tubbs' replacement, could mean an extra letter grade for this group.
Secondary	C	The question mark here is up the middle at the safety positions. Strong safety Chad Cota is a proven run defender, but can the former Panther hold up against the pass? The same holds true for free safety Sammy Knight. Cornerback appears to be in the capable hands of Alex Molden and ex-49er Tyronne Drakeford. Depth should be no problem.
Special teams	C -	K Doug Brien and P Mark Royals are this group's only salvation. They rank among the best at their position in the league. The same can be said for return specialist Eric Guliford, but he is likely lost for the '98 season with a torn Achilles' tendon. The punt and kickoff coverage units rank among the league's worst.

NEW YORK GIANTS
NFC EASTERN DIVISION

1997 REVIEW

RESULTS

Aug. 31—PHILADELPHIA	W	31-17
Sept. 7—at Jacksonville	L	13-40
Sept.14—BALTIMORE	L	23-24
Sept.21—at St. Louis	L	3-13
Sept.28—NEW ORLEANS	W	14-9
Oct. 5—DALLAS	W	20-17
Oct. 12—at Arizona	W	27-13
Oct. 19—at Detroit (OT)	W	26-20
Oct. 26—CINCINNATI	W	29-27
Nov. 2—Open date		
Nov. 9—at Tennessee	L	6-10
Nov. 16—ARIZONA	W	19-10
Nov. 23—at Washington (OT)	T	7-7
Nov. 30—TAMPA BAY	L	8-20
Dec. 7—at Philadelphia	W	31-21
Dec. 13—WASHINGTON	W	30-10
Dec. 21—at Dallas	W	20-7
Dec. 27—MINNESOTA*	L	22-23

*NFC wild-card game.

RECORDS/RANKINGS

1997 regular-season record: 10-5-1 (1st in NFC East); 7-0-1 in division; 9-2-1 in conference; 6-2 at home; 4-3-1 on road.
Team record last five years: 41-38-1 (.519, ranks T12th in league in that span).

1997 team rankings:	No.	NFC	NFL
Total offense	*282.1	13	27
Rushing offense	*124.3	3	7
Passing offense	*157.8	14	28
Scoring offense	307	8	21
Total defense	*316.7	12	18
Rushing defense	*90.7	2	3
Passing defense	*226	14	26
Scoring defense	265	T2	T3
Takeaways	44	1	1
Giveaways	19	1	1
Turnover differential	25	1	1
Sacks	54	T3	T3
Sacks allowed	32	T2	T5

*Yards per game.

TEAM LEADERS

Scoring (kicking): Brad Daluiso, 93 pts. (27/29 PATs, 22/32 FGs).
Scoring (touchdowns): Chris Calloway, 48 pts. (8 receiving).
Passing: Danny Kanell, 1,740 yds. (294 att., 156 comp., 53.1%, 11 TDs, 9 int.).
Rushing: Charles Way, 698 yds. (151 att., 4.6 avg., 4 TDs).
Receptions: Chris Calloway, 58 (849 yds., 14.6 avg., 8 TDs).
Interceptions: Jason Sehorn, 6 (74 yds., 1 TD).
Sacks: Michael Strahan, 14.0.
Punting: Brad Maynard, 40.8 avg. (111 punts, 4,531 yds., 1 blocked).
Punt returns: Amani Toomer, 9.7 avg. (47 att., 455 yds., 1 TD).
Kickoff returns: Erric Pegram, 17.4 avg. (22 att., 382 yds., 0 TDs).

1998 SEASON

CLUB DIRECTORY

President/co-CEO
  Wellington T. Mara
Chairman/co-CEO
  Preston Robert Tisch
Exec. v.p./general counsel
  John K. Mara
Vice president/general manager
  Ernie Accorsi
Treasurer
  Jonathan Tisch
Assistant general manager
  Rick Donohue
Assistant to the general manager
  Harry Hulmes
V.P. and chief financial officer
  John Pasquali
Controller
  Christine Procops
Director/player personnel
  Tom Boisture
Director of administration
  Jim Phelan
Vice president, marketing
  Rusty Hawley
Director/promotion
  Francis X. Mara
Ticket manager
  John Gorman
Director/pro personnel
  Tim Rooney
Director/research and development
  Raymond J. Walsh Jr.
Director/college scouting
  Jerry Shay
Vice president of communications
  Pat Hanlon
Director of media relations
  Aaron Salkin
Assistant director/marketing
  Bill Smith
Director of player development
  Greg Gabriel
Scouts

Rosey Brown	John Crea
Jeremiah Davis	Ken Kavanaugh
Jerry Reese	Steve Verderosa

Head coach
Jim Fassel

Assistant coaches
  Dave Brazil (def. quality control)
  Rod Dowhower (quarterbacks)
  John Dunn (strength & conditioning)
  John Fox (defensive coordinator)
  Mike Gillhamer (offensive assistant)
  Mike Haluchak (linebackers)
  Johnnie Lynn (defensive backs)
  Larry Mac Duff (special teams)
  Denny Marcin (defensive line)
  John Matsko (offensive line)
  Dick Rehbein (tight ends/asst. offensive line)
  Jimmy Robinson (wide receivers)
  Jim Skipper (offensive coord./ running backs)
  Craig Stoddard (assistant strength & conditioning)

Head trainer
  Ronnie Barnes
Assistant trainers
  Michael Colello
  Steve Kennelly
Team physician
  Russell Warren
Locker room manager
  Ed Wagner
Equipment manager
  Ed Wagner Jr.
Video director
  John Mancuso

SCHEDULE

Sept. 6—	WASHINGTON	1:01
Sept. 13—	at Oakland	1:15
Sept. 21—	DALLAS (Mon.)	8:20
Sept. 27—	at San Diego	1:15
Oct. 4—	at Tampa Bay	4:15
Oct. 11—	ATLANTA	8:20
Oct. 18—	ARIZONA	1:01
Oct. 25—	Open date	
Nov. 1—	at Washington	1:01
Nov. 8—	at Dallas	12:01
Nov. 15—	GREEN BAY	4:15
Nov. 22—	PHILADELPHIA	1:01
Nov. 30—	at San Francisco (Mon.)	5:20
Dec. 6—	at Arizona	2:05
Dec. 13—	DENVER	1:01
Dec. 20—	KANSAS CITY	1:01
Dec. 27—	at Philadelphia	4:05

All times are for home team.
All games Sunday unless noted.

DRAFT CHOICES

Shaun Williams, DB, UCLA (first round/ 24th pick overall).
Joe Jurevicius, WR, Penn State (2/55).
Brian Alford, WR, Purdue (3/70).
Toby Myles, T, Jackson State (5/147).
Todd Pollack, TE, Boston College (6/177).
Ben Fricke, C, Houston (7/213).

1998 SEASON
TRAINING CAMP ROSTER

No.	QUARTERBACKS	Ht./Wt.	Born	NFL Exp.	College	How acq.	'97 Games GP/GS
18	Cherry, Mike	6-3/225	12-15-73	1	Murray State	D6/97	1/0
10	Graham, Kent	6-5/246	11-1-68	7	Ohio State	FA/98	*8/6
13	Kanell, Danny	6-3/215	11-21-73	3	Florida State	D4/96	16/10
	RUNNING BACKS						
21	Barber, Tiki	5-10/205	4-7-75	2	Virginia	D2/97	12/6
33	Brown, Gary	5-11/230	7-1-69	7	Penn State	FA/98	*15/14
23	Johnson, LeShon	6-0/207	1-15-71	5	Northern Illinois	FA/98	*14/0
37	Lane, Eric (FB)	6-2/240	3-17-74	2	Tennessee	FA/97	15/0
24	Walker, Robert	5-10/208	6-26-72	1	West Virginia	FA/96	0/0
30	Way, Charles (FB)	6-0/247	12-27-72	4	Virginia	D6b/95	16/16
28	Wheatley, Tyrone	6-0/230	1-19-72	4	Michigan	D1/95	14/7
	RECEIVERS						
84	Alford, Brian	6-1/187	6-7-75	R	Purdue	D3/98	—
80	Calloway, Chris	5-10/191	3-29-68	9	Michigan	PlanB/92	16/16
87	Cross, Howard (TE)	6-5/270	8-8-67	10	Alabama	D6/89	16/16
82	Douglas, Omar	5-10/180	6-3-72	5	Minnesota	FA/94	0/0
19	Goines, Eddie	6-0/186	8-16-72	3	North Carolina State	D6b/95	0/0
88	Hilliard, Ike	5-11/190	4-5-76	2	Florida	D1/97	2/2
	Jessie, Brandon (TE)	6-6/260	5-20-74	2	Utah	FA/97	0/0
86	Jurevicius, Joe	6-5/231	12-23-74	R	Penn State	D2/98	—
83	Patten, David	5-9/180	8-19-74	2	Western Carolina	FA/97	16/3
89	Pollack, Todd (TE)	6-4/241	12-10-74	R	Boston College	D6/98	—
85	Pupunu, Alfred (TE)	6-2/260	10-17-69	7	Weber State	WV/92	*9/1
81	Toomer, Amani	6-3/202	9-8-74	3	Michigan	D2/96	16/0
15	Washington, John	5-9/170	7-8-74	1	Texas Christian	FA/97	0/0
	OFFENSIVE LINEMEN						
78	Bishop, Greg (G)	6-5/315	5-2-71	6	Pacific	D4/93	16/16
69	Engler, Derek (C)	6-5/300	7-11-74	2	Wisconsin	FA/97	5/5
54	Fricke, Ben (C)	6-0/282	11-13-75	R	Houston	D7/98	—
74	Gragg, Scott (T)	6-8/325	2-28-72	4	Montana	D2/95	16/16
71	Lamb, Marc (C)	6-5/292	5-4-72	1	Montana	FA/97	0/0
70	Myles, Toby (T)	6-4/313	7-23-75	R	Jackson State	D5/98	—
72	Oben, Roman (T)	6-4/310	10-9-72	3	Louisville	D3/96	16/16
66	Reynolds, Jerry (T)	6-6/325	4-2-70	5	UNLV	FA/95	5/0
70	Scott, Lance (C)	6-3/285	2-15-72	4	Utah	D5/95	16/11
60	Stoltenberg, Bryan (C)	6-1/293	8-25-72	3	Colorado	D6b/96	3/0
65	Stone, Ron (G)	6-5/325	7-20-71	6	Boston College	FA/96	16/16
73	Zatechka, Rob (G)	6-4/320	12-1-71	4	Nebraska	D4/95	16/0
	DEFENSIVE LINEMEN						
77	Bratzke, Chad (E)	6-4/285	9-15-71	5	Eastern Kentucky	D5/94	10/10
	Estes, Charles (E)	6-3/265	9-30-75	1	Army	FA/97	0/0
75	Hamilton, Keith (T)	6-6/295	5-25-71	7	Pittsburgh	D4/92	16/16
97	Harris, Robert (T)	6-4/295	6-13-69	7	Southern (La.)	FA/95	16/16
79	Holsey, Bernard (E)	6-2/295	12-10-73	3	Duke	FA/96	16/4
94	Jones, Cedric (E)	6-4/285	4-30-74	3	Oklahoma	D1/96	9/2
99	Peter, Christian (T)	6-3/300	10-5-72	2	Nebraska	FA/96	7/0
92	Strahan, Michael (E)	6-4/285	11-21-71	6	Texas Southern	D2/93	16/16
	LINEBACKERS						
98	Armstead, Jessie	6-1/232	10-26-70	6	Miami (Fla.)	D8/93	16/16
55	Buckley, Marcus	6-3/240	2-3-71	6	Texas A&M	D3/93	12/3
58	Colman, Doug	6-2/250	6-4-73	3	Nebraska	D6a/96	14/0
52	Galyon, Scott	6-2/245	3-23-74	3	Tennessee	D6b/96	16/0
57	Miller, Corey	6-2/248	10-25-68	8	South Carolina	D6/91	14/13
51	Monty, Pete	6-2/250	7-13-74	2	Wisconsin	D4/97	3/0
91	Phillips, Ryan	6-4/252	2-7-74	2	Idaho	D3a/97	10/0
90	Widmer, Corey	6-3/255	12-25-68	7	Montana State	D7/92	16/15
	DEFENSIVE BACKS						
39	Blackwell, Kory (CB)	5-11/185	8-3-72	1	Massachusetts	FA/97	0/0
43	Ellsworth, Percy (S)	6-2/220	10-19-74	2	Virginia	FA/96	16/1
20	Garnes, Sam (S)	6-3/220	7-12-74	2	Cincinnati	D5/97	16/15
41	Hamilton, Conrad (CB)	5-10/195	11-5-74	3	Eastern New Mexico	D7/96	14/0
44	Massey, Robert (CB)	5-11/208	2-17-67	10	North Carolina Central	FA/96	16/0
44	McMullen, Typail	6-2/190	9-3-73	2	Middle Tennessee	FA/97	0/0

No.	DEFENSIVE BACKS	Ht./Wt.	Born	NFL Exp.	College	How acq.	'97 Games GP/GS
34	Sanders, Brandon (S)	5-9/185	6-10-73	2	Arizona	FA/97	12/0
31	Sehorn, Jason (CB)	6-2/210	4-15-71	5	Southern California	D2b/94	16/16
22	Sparks, Phillippi (CB)	5-11/195	4-15-69	7	Arizona State	D2/92	13/13
36	Williams, Shaun (S)	6-2/204	10-10-76	R	UCLA	D1/98	—
29	Wooten, Tito (S)	6-0/195	12-12-71	5	Northeastern Louisiana	SupD4/94	16/16
47	Young, Rodney (S)	6-1/210	1-25-73	4	Louisiana State	D3/95	9/0
	SPECIALISTS						
12	Brice, Will (P)	6-4/225	10-24-74	2	Virginia		6/0
3	Daluiso, Brad (K)	6-2/215	12-31-67	8	UCLA	FA/93	16/0
9	Maynard, Brad (P)	6-1/185	2-9-74	2	Ball State	D3b/97	16/0

*Brown played 15 games with Chargers in '97; Graham played 8 games with Cardinals; Johnson played 14 games with Cardinals; Pupunu played 8 games with Chargers and 1 game with Chiefs.

Abbreviations: D1—draft pick, first round; SupD2—supplemental draft pick, second round; WV—claimed on waivers; TR—obtained in trade; PlanB—Plan B free-agent acquisition; FA—free-agent acquisition (other than Plan B); ED—expansion draft pick.

MISCELLANEOUS TEAM DATA

Stadium (capacity, surface):
Giants Stadium
(79,593, artificial)
Business address:
East Rutherford, NJ 07073
Business phone:
201-935-8111
Ticket information:
201-935-8222
Team colors:
Blue, white and red
Flagship radio station:
WNEW, 102.7 FM
Training site:
University at Albany
Albany, N.Y.
201-935-8111

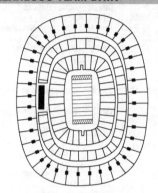

TSN REPORT CARD

Coaching staff	A	Jim Fassel could not have had a more successful debut season, winning over the players, management, fans and media. He must build on that by improving the league's 27th-ranked offense and turning QB Danny Kanell into a weapon instead of a caretaker. Defensive coordinator John Fox is a rising star and offensive coordinator Jim Skipper is Fassel's right-hand man.
Offensive backfield	B	It's hard to argue with Kanell's 7-2-1 mark as a starter, but he must step it up against a tougher schedule. He should get help from a deep running back committee headed by fullback Charles Way. Fassel has to figure out what to do with three tailbacks of differing styles: Tiki Barber, Tyrone Wheatley and Gary Brown.
Receivers	C	This position was a solid F in 1997, but there is hope. Ike Hilliard is due back from the spinal surgery that wrecked his rookie season, and the arrival of high draft picks Joe Jurevicius and Brian Alford could be key. Old reliable Chris Calloway figures to start opposite Hilliard. After that, it should be a scramble. This is Amani Toomer's last chance to show something as a Giant.
Offensive line	C +	This unit improved dramatically during the course of last season, but it still doesn't strike fear in opponents' hearts. If the upward curve continues, keyed by impressive second-year starting left tackle Roman Oben and Pro Bowl-caliber right guard Ron Stone, it could be a very solid group, especially in run blocking.
Defensive line	A -	Michael Strahan, Robert Harris and Keith Hamilton are among the best defensive line trios in the NFL. The concerns are at right end, where Chad Bratzke and Cedric Jones both are coming back from serious leg surgeries, and the overall depth, which was hurt by veteran backup Ray Agnew's free-agent defection to the Rams.
Linebackers	B +	On the weak side, Jessie Armstead is an All-Pro, the team's MVP and its strongest leader. But on the strong side, there are question marks. Corey Miller will battle unproven Marcus Buckley and Ryan Phillips for the starting job. Corey Widmer is a solid run-stopper in the middle.
Secondary	A -	The cornerback tandem of Jason Sehorn and Phillippi Sparks is one of the league's best, but depth was hurt by the departure of Thomas Randolph. There is depth at safety, with first-round pick Shaun Williams joining Tito Wooten, Sam Garnes and Percy Ellsworth. Even if Williams doesn't start, he will play.
Special teams	B -	Brad Daluiso is a solid kicker despite his bad start to last season, but second-year punter Brad Maynard, a third-round choice in '97, must pick it up after a disappointing rookie season. The Giants need a major upgrade in the return games, especially on kickoffs. Fassel is thinking about using Sehorn on occasion.

NEW YORK JETS
AFC EASTERN DIVISION

1997 REVIEW

RESULTS

Aug. 31—at Seattle	W	41-3
Sept. 7—BUFFALO	L	22-28
Sept.14—at New England (OT)	L	24-27
Sept.21—OAKLAND	W	23-22
Sept.28—at Cincinnati	W	31-14
Oct. 5—at Indianapolis	W	16-12
Oct. 12—MIAMI	L	20-31
Oct. 19—NEW ENGLAND	W	24-19
Oct. 26—Open date		
Nov. 2—BALTIMORE (OT)	W	19-16
Nov. 9—at Miami	L	17-24
Nov. 16—at Chicago	W	23-15
Nov. 23—MINNESOTA	W	23-21
Nov. 30—at Buffalo	L	10-20
Dec. 7—INDIANAPOLIS	L	14-22
Dec. 14—TAMPA BAY	W	31-0
Dec. 21—at Detroit	L	10-13

RECORDS/RANKINGS

1997 regular-season record: 9-7 (T2nd in AFC East); 2-6 in division; 6-6 in conference; 5-3 at home; 4-4 on road.
Team record last five years: 27-53 (.338, ranks T26th in league in that span).

1997 team rankings:	No.	AFC	NFL
Total offense	*295.4	13	22
Rushing offense	*92.8	12	25
Passing offense	*202.6	9	T15
Scoring offense	348	8	12
Total defense	*332.5	11	24
Rushing defense	*118.7	12	21
Passing defense	*213.8	7	19
Scoring defense	287	T2	T6
Takeaways	25	T11	T22
Giveaways	22	T5	T7
Turnover differential	3	7	T12
Sacks	29	14	29
Sacks allowed	48	12	23

*Yards per game.

TEAM LEADERS

Scoring (kicking): John Hall, 120 pts. (36/36 PATs, 28/41 FGs).
Scoring (touchdowns): Adrian Murrell, 42 pts. (7 rushing).
Passing: Neil O'Donnell, 2,796 yds. (460 att., 259 comp., 56.3%, 17 TDs, 7 int.).
Rushing: Adrian Murrell, 1,086 yds. (300 att., 3.6 avg., 7 TDs).
Receptions: Keyshawn Johnson, 70 (963 yds., 13.8 avg., 5 TDs).
Interceptions: Otis Smith, 6 (158 yds., 3 TDs).
Sacks: Mo Lewis, 8.0.
Punting: Brian Hansen, 43.2 avg. (71 punts, 3,068 yds., 1 blocked).
Punt returns: Leon Johnson, 12.1 avg. (51 att., 619 yds., 1 TD).
Kickoff returns: Aaron Glenn, 26.5 avg. (28 att., 741 yds., 1 TD).

1998 SEASON

CLUB DIRECTORY

Chairman of the board
Leon Hess
President
Steve Gutman
Treasurer & chief financial officer
Mike Gerstle
Controller
Mike Minarczyk
Director/public relations
Frank Ramos
Assistant director/public relations
Doug Miller
Public relations assistants
Berj Najarian
Sharon Czark
Danny Ferraviola
Coordinator of special projects
Ken Ilchuk
Exec. director of business operations
Bob Parente
Director of marketing
Marc Riccio
Senior marketing manager
Beth Conroy
Director of ticket operations
John Buschhorn
Director/operations
Mike Kensil
Travel coordinator
Kevin Coyle
Director/player personnel
Dick Haley
Director/pro personnel
Scott Pioli
Director/player contract negotiations
Mike Tannenbaum
Scouts
Joey Clinkscales   Michael Davis
Sid Hall   Jesse Kay
Bob Schmitz   Lionel Vitale
Marv Sunderland
Head trainer
David Price

Head coach/ chief football operations officer
Bill Parcells

Assistant coaches
Bill Belichick (assistant head coach/defensive backs)
Maurice Carthon (running backs)
Romeo Crennel (defensive line)
Al Groh (linebackers)
Todd Haley (offensive assistant/ quality control)
Dan Henning (quarterbacks)
Pat Hodgson (tight ends)
John Lott (strength & conditioning)
Eric Mangini (defensive assistant/ quality control)
Bill Muir (offensive line)
Mike Sweatman (special teams)
Charlie Weis (off. coordinator/ wide receivers)
Josh Zitomer (strength & conditioning assistant)

Assistant trainer
John Mellody
Equipment manager
Bill Hampton
Equipment director
Clay Hampton
Groundskeeper
Bob Hansen
Video director
John Seiter

SCHEDULE

Sept. 6—	at San Francisco	1:15
Sept. 13—	BALTIMORE	1:01
Sept. 20—	INDIANAPOLIS	1:01
Sept. 27—	Open date	
Oct. 4—	MIAMI	1:01
Oct. 11—	at St. Louis	3:15
Oct. 19—	at New England (Mon.)	8:20
Oct. 25—	ATLANTA	1:01
Nov. 1—	at Kansas City	3:05
Nov. 8—	BUFFALO	4:15
Nov. 15—	at Indianapolis	1:01
Nov. 22—	at Tennessee	3:15
Nov. 29—	CAROLINA	1:01
Dec. 6—	SEATTLE	1:01
Dec. 13—	at Miami	8:20
Dec. 19—	at Buffalo (Sat.)	12:35
Dec. 27—	NEW ENGLAND	1:01

All times are for home team.
All games Sunday unless noted.

DRAFT CHOICES

Dorian Boose, DE, Washington State (second round/56th pick overall).
Scott Frost, DB, Nebraska (3/67).
Kevin Williams, DB, Oklahoma State (3/87).
Jason Fabini, T, Cincinnati (4/111).
Casey Dailey, LB, Northwestern (5/134).
Doug Karczewski, G, Virginia (5/141).
Blake Spence, TE, Oregon (5/146).
Eric Bateman, G, Brigham Young (5/149).
Eric Ogbogu, DE, Maryland (6/163).
Chris Brazzell, WR, Angelo State (6/174).
Dustin Johnson, RB, Brigham Young (6/183).
Lawrence Hart, TE, Southern University (7/195).

New York Jets

1998 SEASON

No.	QUARTERBACKS	Ht./Wt.	Born	NFL Exp.	College	How acq.	'97 Games GP/GS
7	Clements, Chuck	6-3/214	9-29-73	2	Houston	D6b/97	1/0
4	Foley, Glenn	6-2/210	10-10-70	5	Boston College	D7/94	6/2
6	Lucas, Ray	6-3/201	8-6-72	2	Rutgers	FA/97	5/0
14	O'Donnell, Neil	6-3/228	7-3-66	9	Maryland	FA/96	15/14
	RUNNING BACKS						
20	Anderson, Richie	6-2/225	9-13-71	6	Penn State	D6/93	16/3
41	Byars, Keith (FB)	6-1/255	10-14-63	13	Ohio State	FA/98	*16/8
35	Johnson, Dustin (FB)	6-2/236	8-5-73	R	Brigham Young	D6c/98	—
32	Johnson, Leon	6-0/215	7-13-74	2	North Carolina	D4b/97	16/1
28	Martin, Curtis	5-11/203	5-1-73	4	Pittsburgh	FA/98	*13/13
33	Sowell, Jerald	6-0/248	1-21-74	2	Tulane	D7a/97	9/0
	RECEIVERS						
84	Baxter, Fred (TE)	6-3/265	6-14-71	6	Auburn	D5a/93	16/9
88	Brady, Kyle (TE)	6-6/268	1-14-72	4	Penn State	D1a/95	16/14
87	Brazzell, Chris	6-2/182	5-22-76	R	Angelo State (Texas)	D6b/98	—
80	Chrebet, Wayne	5-10/185	8-14-73	4	Hofstra	FA/95	16/1
83	Hart, Lawrence (TE)	6-4/261	9-19-76	R	Southern	D7/98	—
85	Johnson, Alonzo	5-11/186	4-18-73	1	Central State (Ohio)	FA/97	0/0
19	Johnson, Keyshawn	6-3/210	7-22-72	3	Southern California	D1/96	16/16
82	Spence, Blake (TE)	6-4/249	6-20-75	R	Oregon	D5c/98	—
86	Van Dyke, Alex	6-0/200	7-24-74	3	Nevada	D2/96	5/0
89	Ward, Dedric	5-9/180	9-29-74	2	Northern Iowa	D3/97	11/1
	OFFENSIVE LINEMEN						
74	Bateman, Eric (G)	6-7/319	12-28-73	R	Brigham Young	D5d/98	—
62	Burger, Todd (G)	6-3/303	3-20-70	5	Penn State	FA/98	*15/15
63	Burns, Lamont (G)	6-4/300	3-16-74	2	East Carolina	D5a/97	4/3
64	Conrad, J.R. (T)	6-4/300	2-2-74	2	Oklahoma	FA/97	12/1
76	Elliott, Jumbo (T)	6-7/308	4-1-65	11	Michigan	FA/96	13/13
69	Fabini, Jason (T)	6-7/318	8-25-74	R	Cincinnati	D4/98	—
67	Gisler, Mike (G)	6-4/295	8-26-69	6	Houston	FA/98	*16/2
77	Hagood, Jay (T)	6-4/306	8-9-73	2	Virginia Tech	FA/97	2/0
65	Hudson, John (C)	6-2/270	1-29-68	9	Auburn	FA/96	16/0
71	Jenkins, Kerry (T)	6-5/310	9-6-73	2	Troy State	FA/97	2/2
60	Karczewski, Doug (G)	6-5/298	2-6-75	R	Virginia	D5b/98	—
75	Malamala, Siupeli (G)	6-5/305	1-15-69	7	Washington	D3/92	10/5
68	Mawae, Kevin (C)	6-4/305	1-23-71	5	Louisiana State	FA/98	*16/16
70	O'Dwyer, Matt (G)	6-5/300	9-1-72	4	Northwestern	D2/95	16/16
66	Palelei, Lonnie (G)	6-3/315	10-15-70	3	UNLV	FA/97	15/14
79	Thorpe, Deron (T)	6-8/330	8-31-73	1	Nevada	FA/97	0/0
73	Williams, David (T)	6-5/300	6-21-66	9	Florida	FA/96	12/11
	DEFENSIVE LINEMEN						
97	Boose, Dorian (E)	6-5/283	1-29-74	R	Washington State	D2/98	—
75	Brown, Shannon (T)	6-5/290	5-23-72	1	Alabama	D3/96	0/0
78	Day, Terry (E)	6-4/280	9-18-74	2	Mississippi State	D4a/97	1/0
91	Dixon, Ronnie (T)	6-3/310	5-10-71	5	Cincinnati	FA/97	6/3
72	Ferguson, Jason (T)	6-3/300	11-28-74	2	Georgia	D7b/97	13/1
51	Finkes, Matt (E)	6-3/260	2-12-75	2	Ohio State	D6/97	8/0
92	Hamilton, Bobby (E)	6-5/280	1-7-71	3	Southern Mississippi	FA/96	16/0
76	Keneley, Matt (T)	6-4/286	12-1-73	1	Southern California	D7/97	0/0
93	Logan, Ernie (E)	6-3/290	5-18-68	7	East Carolina	FA/97	15/14
95	Lyle, Rick	6-5/285	2-26-71	4	Missouri	FA/97	16/16
99	Ogbogu, Eric (E)	6-4/266	7-18-75	R	Maryland	D6a/98	—
98	Pleasant, Anthony (E)	6-5/280	1-27-68	9	Tennessee State	FA/98	*11/0
94	Terry, Rick (T)	6-4/302	4-5-74	2	North Carolina	D2/97	14/0
	LINEBACKERS						
53	Cascadden, Chad	6-1/240	5-14-72	4	Wisconsin	FA/95	15/0
49	Dailey, Casey	6-3/249	6-11-75	R	Northwestern	D5a/98	—
58	Farrior, James	6-2/240	1-6-75	2	Virginia	D1/97	16/15
54	Gordon, Dwayne	6-1/240	11-2-69	5	New Hampshire	FA/97	16/8
50	Guest, Craig	6-1/242	12-10-75	1	Buffalo	FA/97	0/0
52	Johnson, Pepper	6-3/259	7-29-64	13	Ohio State	FA/97	8/8
55	Jones, Marvin	6-2/244	6-28-72	6	Florida State	D1/93	16/16
57	Lewis, Mo.	6-3/258	10-21-69	8	Georgia	D3/91	16/16
56	Wing, Chris	6-2/240	5-28-71	1	Boise State	FA/97	2/0

No.	DEFENSIVE BACKS	Ht./Wt.	Born	NFL Exp.	College	How acq.	'97 Games GP/GS
25	Austin, Raymond	5-11/190	12-21-74	2	Tennessee	D5b/97	16/0
44	Brown, Corwin (S)	6-1/200	4-25-70	6	Michigan	FA/97	16/0
42	Coleman, Marcus (S)	6-2/210	5-24-74	3	Texas Tech	D5/96	16/2
47	Frost, Scott (S)	6-3/219	1-4-75	R	Nebraska	D3a/98	—
31	Glenn, Aaron (CB)	5-9/185	7-16-72	5	Texas A&M	D1/94	16/16
21	Green, Victor (S)	5-11/205	12-8-69	6	Akron	FA/93	16/16
30	Hayes, Chris (S)	6-0/200	5-7-72	2	Washington State	D7/96	16/0
26	Henderson, Jerome (CB)	5-10/200	8-8-69	8	Clemson	FA/97	16/14
36	Marshall, Anthony (S)	6-1/212	9-16-70	4	Louisiana State	D/97	14/1
24	Mickens, Ray (CB)	5-8/180	1-4-73	3	Texas A&M	D3/96	16/0
45	Smith, Otis (CB)	5-11/190	10-22-65	8	Missouri	FA/97	16/16
23	Williams, Kevin (CB)	6-0/190	8-4-75	R	Oklahoma State	D3b/98	—
	SPECIALISTS						
8	Deignan, Robert (P)	6-5/230	1-8-74	1	Purdue	FA/98	0/0
3	Gallery, Nick (P)	6-4/239	2-15-75	1	Iowa	FA/97	0/0
9	Hall, John (K)	6-3/223	3-17-74	2	Wisconsin	FA/97	16/0
11	Hansen, Brian (P)	6-4/215	10-26-60	14	Sioux Falls (S.D.) College	FA/97	15/0

*Burger played 15 games with Bears in '97; Byars played 16 games with Patriots; Gisler played 16 games with Patriots; Martin played 13 games with Patriots; Mawae played 16 games with Seahawks; Pleasant played 11 games with Falcons.

Abbreviations: D1—draft pick, first round; SupD2—supplemental draft pick, second round; WV—claimed on waivers; TR—obtained in trade; PlanB—Plan B free-agent acquisition; FA—free-agent acquisition (other than Plan B); ED—expansion draft pick.

MISCELLANEOUS TEAM DATA

Stadium (capacity, surface):
Giants Stadium
(77,716, artificial)
Business address:
1000 Fulton Avenue
Hempstead, NY 11550
Business phone:
516-560-8100
Ticket information:
516-560-8200
Team colors:
Green and white
Flagship radio station:
WFAN, 660 AM
Training site:
Hofstra University
Hempstead, N.Y.
516-560-8100

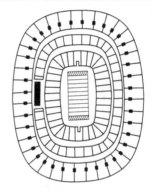

TSN REPORT CARD

Coaching staff	A	Bill Parcells proved again last season why he's one of the best. His assistants don't get much publicity—largely because Parcells forbids them to talk to the media—but they comprise a top-notch staff. Bill Belichick (defense) and Mike Sweatman (special teams) are terrific.
Offensive backfield	B	Curtis Martin is one of the NFL's top six backs, assuming he has recovered from offseason abdominal surgery. The Jets will go as far as he takes them. Quarterback problems, which may include a full-blown controversy between Glenn Foley and Neil O'Donnell, could haunt the team.
Receivers	B -	Keyshawn Johnson and Wayne Chrebet should haul in 140 balls between them. It's time for unproven Alex Van Dyke to step up. No home-run threats here. Tight ends Kyle Brady and Fred Baxter are blue-collar types.
Offensive line	C	The addition of center Kevin Mawae should stabilize the interior. The guards are so-so. Left tackle Jumbo Elliott, completely recovered from Achilles' surgery, still is a long way from being finished. Who starts at right tackle? Good question.
Defensive line	D +	A weakness, but there is some upside here, thanks to improving tackles Jason Ferguson and Rick Terry. At best, this will be a solid, run-stuffing group. Pass rush? Put it this way: Hugh Douglas, traded to the Eagles, is capable of recording more sacks than the entire Jets line.
Linebackers	B	A fast, tenacious group that will get even better if James Farrior, a '97 first rounder, comes into his own. Now that Marvin Jones proved he can stay healthy for an entire season, let's see if he can become a star. Is this the year Mo Lewis makes the Pro Bowl?
Secondary	C -	Big question marks at free safety and right cornerback. The coaching staff will be tickled if former Nebraska quarterback Scott Frost can win the free-safety job. Thank goodness for Pro Bowl cornerback Aaron Glenn, who holds everything together.
Special teams	B	Sweatman has developed a strong nucleus on the return and coverage units. Kicker John Hall has a chance to be special. He can kick 'em long, but he must learn to kick 'em straight. The punting job is up for grabs.

OAKLAND RAIDERS
AFC WESTERN DIVISION

1997 REVIEW

RESULTS

Aug. 31—at Tennessee (OT)	L	21-24	
Sept. 8—KANSAS CITY	L	27-28	
Sept.14—at Atlanta	W	36-31	
Sept.21—at N.Y. Jets	L	22-23	
Sept.28—ST. LOUIS	W	35-17	
Oct. 5—SAN DIEGO	L	10-25	
Oct. 12—Open date			
Oct. 19—DENVER	W	28-25	
Oct. 26—at Seattle	L	34-45	
Nov. 2—at Carolina	L	14-38	
Nov. 9—NEW ORLEANS	L	10-13	
Nov. 16—at San Diego	W	38-13	
Nov. 24—at Denver	L	3-31	
Nov. 30—MIAMI	L	16-34	
Dec. 7—at Kansas City	L	0-30	
Dec. 14—SEATTLE	L	21-22	
Dec. 21—JACKSONVILLE	L	9-20	

RECORDS/RANKINGS

1997 regular-season record: 4-12 (T4th in AFC West); 2-6 in division; 2-10 in conference; 2-6 at home; 2-6 on road.
Team record last five years: 38-42 (.475, ranks 15th in league in that span).

1997 team rankings:	No.	AFC	NFL
Total offense	*318.9	8	13
Rushing offense	*99.3	T10	23
Passing offense	*219.6	6	8
Scoring offense	324	12	17
Total defense	*382.3	15	30
Rushing defense	*140.4	15	30
Passing defense	*241.9	15	30
Scoring defense	419	14	28
Takeaways	22	T14	T26
Giveaways	24	8	T13
Turnover differential	-2	10	18
Sacks	31	T12	T27
Sacks allowed	58	14	27

*Yards per game.

TEAM LEADERS

Scoring (kicking): Cole Ford, 72 pts. (33/35 PATs, 13/22 FGs).
Scoring (touchdowns): James Jett, 72 pts. (12 receiving).
Passing: Jeff George, 3,917 yds. (521 att., 290 comp., 55.7%, 29 TDs, 9 int.).
Rushing: Napoleon Kaufman, 1,294 yds. (272 att., 4.8 avg., 6 TDs).
Receptions: Tim Brown, 104 (1,408 yds., 13.5 avg., 5 TDs).
Interceptions: Eric Turner, 2 (45 yds., 0 TDs); Lionel Washington, 2 (44 yds., 1 TD); James Trapp, 2 (24 yds., 0 TDs); Lorenzo Lynch, 2 (6 yds., 0 TDs).
Sacks: Anthony Smith, 6.5.
Punting: Leo Araguz, 45.0 avg. (93 punts, 4,189 yds., 0 blocked).
Punt returns: Desmond Howard, 7.8 avg. (27 att., 210 yds., 0 TDs).
Kickoff returns: Desmond Howard, 21.6 avg. (61 att., 1,318 yds., 0 TDs).

1998 SEASON

CLUB DIRECTORY

Owner
Al Davis
Executive assistant
Al LoCasale
Chief executive
Amy Trask
Senior assistant
Bruce Allen
Pro football scouting director
George Karras
Senior administrator
Morris Bradshaw
Public relations director
Mike Taylor
Administrative assistants
Mario Perez
Marc McKinney
Finance
Tom Blanda
Marc Badain
Jennifer Levy
General counsel
Jeff Birren
Ticket manager
Peter Eiges
Admin. asst. to the head coach
Mark Arteaga
Head trainer
Rod Martin
Trainers
Jonathan Jones
Scott Touchet
Strength and conditioning
Garrett Giemont
Player personnel
Angelo Coia
Ken Herock
Bruce Kebric

Head coach
Jon Gruden

Assistant coaches
Dave Adolph (linebackers)
Fred Biletnikoff (wide receivers)
Chuck Bresnahan (def. backs)
Bill Callahan (off. coordinator)
Frank Gansz Jr. (special teams)
Skip Peete (running backs)
Keith Rowen (assistant head
coach-offense/offensive line)
David Shaw (quality control-off.)
Willie Shaw (def. coordinator)
Gary Stevens (quarterbacks)
Mike Waufle (defensive line)

Jon Kingdon
Mickey Marvin
David McCloughan
Kent McCloughan
Building and grounds
Ken Irons
Equipment manager
Bob Romanski
Equipment assistant
Richard Romanski
Video coordinators
Dave Nash
John Otten
Jim Otten

SCHEDULE

Sept. 6— at Kansas City	7:20
Sept. 13— N.Y. GIANTS	1:15
Sept. 20— DENVER	1:15
Sept. 27— at Dallas	12:01
Oct. 4— at Arizona	1:05
Oct. 11— SAN DIEGO	1:15
Oct. 18— Open date	
Oct. 25— CINCINNATI	1:15
Nov. 1— at Seattle	5:20
Nov. 8— at Baltimore	1:01
Nov. 15— SEATTLE	1:05
Nov. 22— at Denver	2:15
Nov. 29— WASHINGTON	1:15
Dec. 6— MIAMI	1:15
Dec. 13— at Buffalo	1:01
Dec. 20— at San Diego	1:05
Dec. 26— KANSAS CITY (Sat.)	1:05

All times are for home team.
All games Sunday unless noted.

DRAFT CHOICES

Charles Woodson, DB, Michigan (first round/fourth pick overall).
Mo Collins, T, Florida (1/23).
Leon Bender, DT, Washington State (2/31).
Jon Ritchie, RB, Stanford (3/63).
Gennaro DiNapoli, G, Virginia Tech (4/109).
Jeremy Brigham, TE, Washington (5/127).
Travian Smith, LB, Oklahoma (5/152).
Vince Amey, DE, Arizona State (7/230).
David Sanders, DE, Arkansas (7/235).

1998 SEASON Oakland Raiders

No.	QUARTERBACKS	Ht./Wt.	Born	NFL Exp.	College	How acq.	'97 Games GP/GS
3	George, Jeff	6-4/215	12-8-67	9	Illinois	FA/97	16/16
12	Hollas, Don	6-3/215	11-22-67	5	Rice	FA/97	0/0

No.	RUNNING BACKS	Ht./Wt.	Born	NFL Exp.	College	How acq.	'97 Games GP/GS
35	Aska, Joe	5-11/240	7-14-72	4	Central Oklahoma	D3/95	7/0
	Branch, Calvin	5-11/202	5-8-74	2	Colorado State	D6/97	6/0
48	Davison, Jerone	6-1/235	9-16-70	2	Arizona State	FA/96	8/1
45	Hall, Tim	5-11/218	2-15-74	3	Robert Morris	D6/96	16/0
	Jordan, Randy (FB)	5-10/213	6-6-70	5	North Carolina	FA/98	*7/0
26	Kaufman, Napoleon	5-9/185	6-7-73	4	Washington	D1/95	16/16
31	Levitt, Chad	6-1/231	11-21-75	2	Cornell	D4/97	10/2
	Ritchie, Jon (FB)	6-1/248	9-4-74	R	Stanford	D3/98	—
22	Williams, Harvey	6-2/225	4-22-67	8	Louisiana State	FA/94	14/6

No.	RECEIVERS	Ht./Wt.	Born	NFL Exp.	College	How acq.	'97 Games GP/GS
	Bobo, Phillip	5-11/186	12-6-71	1	Washington State	FA/98	0/0
	Brigham, Jeremy (TE)	6-4/250	3-22-75	R	Washington	D5a/98	—
86	Brown, Derek (TE)	6-6/264	3-31-70	6	Notre Dame	FA/98	*13/8
81	Brown, Tim	6-0/195	7-22-66	10	Notre Dame	D1/88	16/16
86	Cline, Tony (TE)	6-4/247	11-24-71	4	Stanford	D4c/95	10/1
83	Dudley, Rickey (TE)	6-6/250	7-15-72	3	Ohio State	D1/96	16/16
80	Howard, Desmond	5-10/180	5-15-70	7	Michigan	FA/97	15/0
82	Jett, James	5-10/165	12-28-70	6	West Virginia	FA/93	16/16
85	Mickens, Terry	6-0/201	2-21-71	5	Florida A&M	FA/98	*11/0
87	Mills, John Henry (TE)	6-0/235	10-31-69	6	Wake Forest	D5/93	16/0
89	Rosenstiel, Robert (TE)	6-3/240	2-7-74	1	Eastern Illinois	FA/97	4/0
84	Shedd, Kenny	5-10/171	2-14-71	4	Northern Iowa	FA/94	16/0
	Truitt, Olanda	6-0/195	1-4-71	6	Mississippi State	FA/96	14/0

No.	OFFENSIVE LINEMEN	Ht./Wt.	Born	NFL Exp.	College	How acq.	'97 Games GP/GS
77	Ashmore, Darryl (T)	6-7/310	11-1-69	5	Northwestern	D7/92	11/2
	Collins, Mo (T)	6-4/337	9-22-76	R	Florida	D1b/98	—
68	Cunningham, Rick (T)	6-7/315	1-4-67	7	Texas A&M	FA/96	7/0
	DiNapoli, Gennaro (G)	6-2/301	5-25-75	R	Virginia Tech	D4/98	—
77	Harlow, Pat (T)	6-6/290	3-16-69	8	Southern California	TR/96	16/16
72	Kennedy, Lincoln (G)	6-6/325	2-12-71	6	Washington	TR/96	16/16
70	Kohn, Tim (T)	6-5/310	12-6-73	2	Iowa State	D3/97	0/0
63	Robbins, Barret (C)	6-3/315	8-26-73	4	Texas Christian	D2/95	16/16
62	Treu, Adam (T)	6-5/304	6-24-74	2	Nebraska	D3/97	16/0
66	Whitley, Curtis (C)	6-1/295	5-10-69	7	Clemson	ED/95	15/1
78	Whittaker, Scott (T)	6-7/300	5-7-74	2	Kansas	FA/97	0/0
76	Wisniewski, Steve (G)	6-4/295	4-7-67	10	Penn State	D2/89	16/16

No.	DEFENSIVE LINEMEN	Ht./Wt.	Born	NFL Exp.	College	How acq.	'97 Games GP/GS
	Amey, Vince (E)	6-3/289	2-9-75	R	Arizona State	D7b/98	—
99	Bruce, Aundray (E)	6-5/265	4-30-66	10	Auburn	PlanB/92	10/3
95	Faumui, Ta'ase (E)	6-3/278	3-19-71	3	Hawaii	FA/97	0/0
	Folston, James (E)	6-3/235	8-14-71	5	Northeast Louisiana	D2/94	16/7
99	Harris, James (E)	6-6/278	5-13-68	5	Temple	FA/98	0/0
90	Jackson, Grady (E)	6-2/320	1-21-73	2	Knoxville	D6b/97	5/0
51	Johnstone, Lance (E)	6-4/252	6-11-73	3	Temple	D2/96	14/6
67	Maryland, Russell (T)	6-1/279	3-22-69	8	Miami (Fla.)	FA/96	16/16
94	Mims, Chris (E)	6-5/290	9-29-70	7	Tennessee	FA/98	*11/7
96	Russell, Darrell (T)	6-5/310	5-27-76	2	Southern California	D1/97	16/10
	Sanders, David (E)	6-4/308	7-25-75	R	Arkansas	D7b/98	—
56	Swilling, Pat (E)	6-3/245	10-25-64	12	Georgia Tech	FA/98	0/0

No.	LINEBACKERS	Ht./Wt.	Born	NFL Exp.	College	How acq.	'97 Games GP/GS
54	Biekert, Greg	6-2/240	3-14-69	6	Colorado	D7/93	16/16
57	Holmberg, Rob	6-3/230	5-6-71	5	Penn State	D7/94	16/0
50	Morton, Mike	6-4/235	3-28-72	4	North Carolina	D4/95	11/11
	Smith, Travian	6-3/238	8-26-75	R	Oklahoma	D5b/98	—
59	Wallace, Aaron	6-3/240	4-17-67	8	Texas A&M	D2/90	5/0

No.	DEFENSIVE BACKS	Ht./Wt.	Born	NFL Exp.	College	How acq.	'97 Games GP/GS
	Allen, Eric (CB)	5-10/180	11-22-65	11	Arizona State	TR/98	*16/16
	Bates, Patrick (S)	6-3/220	11-27-70	4	Texas A&M	FA/98	0/0
24	Brown, Larry (CB)	5-11/186	11-30-69	8	Texas Christian	FA/96	4/0
33	By'not'e, Butler (CB)	5-9/190	9-29-72	3	Ohio State	WV/95	0/0
20	Carter, Perry (CB)	6-0/190	8-15-71	2	Southern Mississippi	FA/96	16/7
25	Land, Dan (CB)	6-0/195	7-3-65	10	Albany (Ga.) State	FA/89	16/0
29	Lewis, Albert (CB)	6-2/205	10-6-60	16	Grambling State	FA/94	14/11

No.	DEFENSIVE BACKS	Ht./Wt.	Born	NFL Exp.	College	How acq.	'97 Games GP/GS
36	McDaniel, Terry (CB)	5-10/180	2-8-65	10	Tennessee	D1/88	13/12
30	Newman, Anthony (S)	6-0/200	11-21-65	11	Oregon	FA/98	*12/12
37	Trapp, James (CB)	6-0/185	12-28-69	6	Clemson	D3/93	16/16
29	Turner, Eric (S)	6-1/207	9-20-68	8	UCLA	FA/97	16/15
38	Walker, Marquis (CB)	5-10/180	7-6-72	3	Southeast Missouri State	FA/98	11/0
	Woodson, Charles (CB)	6-0/198	10-7-76	R	Michigan	D1a/98	—
	SPECIALISTS						
2	Araguz, Leo (P)	5-11/190	1-18-70	2	Stephen F. Austin	FA/96	16/0
	Dawson, Phil (K)	5-11/195	1-23-75	R	Texas	FA/98	—
5	Ford, Cole (K)	6-2/210	12-31-72	4	Southern California	FA/95	16/0

*Allen played 16 games with Saints in '97; D. Brown played 13 games with Jaguars; Jordan played 7 games with Jaguars; Mickens played 11 games with Packers; Mims played 11 games with Redskins; Newman played 12 games with Saints; Walker played 11 games with Rams.

Abbreviations: D1—draft pick, first round; SupD2—supplemental draft pick, second round; WV—claimed on waivers; TR—obtained in trade; PlanB—Plan B free-agent acquisition; FA—free-agent acquisition (other than Plan B); ED—expansion draft pick.

MISCELLANEOUS TEAM DATA

Stadium (capacity, surface):
Oakland-Alameda County Coliseum
(63,026, grass)

Business address:
1220 Harbor Bay Parkway
Alameda, CA 94502

Business phone:
510-864-5000

Ticket information:
800-949-2626

Team colors:
Silver and black

Flagship radio station:
The Ticket, 1050 AM

Training site:
Napa, Calif.
707-256-1000

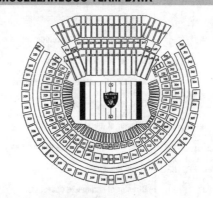

TSN REPORT CARD

Coaching staff	C	Jon Gruden seems well equipped to lead a team—bright mind, strong personality—but the jury remains out on him as a head coach. Gruden surrounded himself with a nice mix of youth and experience. This staff is a decided improvement on the '97 version.
Offensive backfield	B	Jeff George has a mighty arm and abundant weapons. Napoleon Kaufman is one of the most explosive halfbacks around. The team still must figure out how to keep Harvey Williams involved. The rest of the backfield—Jon Ritchie, Tim Hall, Chad Levitt—is young and untested.
Receivers	B +	Tim Brown remains one of the NFL's premier wide receivers. He needs continued production from James Jett and tight end Rickey Dudley, so defenses do not double-team Brown. Another proven wide receiver is needed for third-down situations.
Offensive line	C +	The linemen excel as run blockers and wobble occasionally in pass protection. The Raiders often struggle against the blitz, which means opposing defenses will keep blitzing. This grade would be higher if there was more depth along the line.
Defensive line	D	Chester McGlockton's exit means Darrell Russell will get his chance to become a star. Russell Maryland must raise his production to match his work ethic. Lance Johnstone and the other defensive ends need to put some long-lost pressure on the quarterback.
Linebackers	D	Not much speed, not much play-making ability. The team is reaching into unfamiliar terrain to learn if Mike Morton and James Folston can become effective starters. Middle linebacker Greg Biekert is solid against the run and vulnerable in pass coverage.
Secondary	C	The team made an obvious attempt to upgrade here, drafting cornerback Charles Woodson and trading for cornerback Eric Allen and strong safety Anthony Newman. All three players could start, joining free safety Eric Turner. The team desperately needs to intercept more passes.
Special teams	C -	The ingredients are there, from dangerous return man Desmond Howard to speed among his teammates. But results never came in 1997. Leo Araguz prevents opponents from causing much damage on punt returns; Cole Ford must outkick Phil Dawson in training camp to keep his job.

PHILADELPHIA EAGLES
NFC EASTERN DIVISION

1997 REVIEW
RESULTS

Aug. 31—at N.Y. Giants	L	17-31	
Sept. 7—GREEN BAY	W	10-9	
Sept.15—at Dallas	L	20-21	
Sept.21—Open date			
Sept.28—at Minnesota	L	19-28	
Oct. 5—WASHINGTON	W	24-10	
Oct. 12—at Jacksonville	L	21-38	
Oct. 19—ARIZONA (OT)	W	13-10	
Oct. 26—DALLAS	W	13-12	
Nov. 2—at Arizona	L	21-31	
Nov. 10—SAN FRANCISCO	L	12-24	
Nov. 16—at Baltimore (OT)	T	10-10	
Nov. 23—PITTSBURGH	W	23-20	
Nov. 30—CINCINNATI	W	44-42	
Dec. 7—N.Y. GIANTS	L	21-31	
Dec. 14—at Atlanta	L	17-20	
Dec. 21—at Washington	L	32-35	

RECORDS/RANKINGS

1997 regular-season record: 6-9-1 (3rd in NFC East); 3-5 in division; 4-8 in conference; 6-2 at home; 0-7-1 on road.
Team record last five years: 41-38-1 (.519, ranks T12th in league in that span).

1997 team rankings:

	No.	NFC	NFL
Total offense	*349.4	3	5
Rushing offense	*121.4	5	10
Passing offense	*227.9	2	6
Scoring offense	317	7	19
Total defense	*308.3	7	13
Rushing defense	*125.6	13	25
Passing defense	*182.7	5	7
Scoring defense	372	13	24
Takeaways	26	T10	T19
Giveaways	32	T10	T20
Turnover differential	-6	11	24
Sacks	43	T7	T13
Sacks allowed	64	14	29

*Yards per game.

TEAM LEADERS

Scoring (kicking): Chris Boniol, 99 pts. (33/33 PATs, 22/31 FGs).
Scoring (touchdowns): Ricky Watters, 42 pts. (7 rushing).
Passing: Bobby Hoying, 1,573 yds. (225 att., 128 comp., 56.9%, 11 TDs, 6 int.).
Rushing: Ricky Watters, 1,110 yds. (285 att., 3.9 avg., 7 TDs).
Receptions: Irving Fryar, 86 (1,316 yds., 15.3 avg., 6 TDs).
Interceptions: Brian Dawkins, 3 (76 yds., 1 TD); Troy Vincent, 3 (14 yds., 0 TDs).
Sacks: Rhett Hall, 8.0.
Punting: Tom Hutton, 42.1 avg. (87 punts, 3,660 yds., 1 blocked).
Punt returns: Mark Seay, 10.8 avg. (16 att., 172 yds., 0 TDs).
Kickoff returns: Duce Staley, 24.2 avg. (47 att., 1,139 yds., 0 TDs).

1998 SEASON
CLUB DIRECTORY

Owner/chief executive officer
Jeffrey Lurie
Senior executive vice president
Joe Banner
Sr. vice president/chief financial officer
Mimi Box
Vice president/sales & marketing
Len Komoroski
Exec. dir. of Eagles Youth Partnership
Sarah Helfman
Vice president of corporate sales
Dave Rowan
Director of business development
David Perry
Director of public relations
Ron Howard
Assistant director of public relations
Derek Boyko
Director of administration
Vicki Chatley
Director of merchandising
Steve Strawbridge
Director of advertising & promotions
Kim Babiak
Ticket manager
Leo Carlin
Director of penthouse operations
Christiana Noyalas
Trainer
James Collins
Assistant trainers
Scottie Patton
Scott Trulock

SCHEDULE

Sept. 6—	SEATTLE	1:01
Sept. 13—	at Atlanta	1:01
Sept. 20—	at Arizona	5:20
Sept. 27—	KANSAS CITY	1:01
Oct. 4—	at Denver	2:15
Oct. 11—	WASHINGTON	1:01
Oct. 18—	at San Diego	1:15
Oct. 25—	Open date	
Nov. 2—	DALLAS (Mon.)	8:20
Nov. 8—	DETROIT	1:01
Nov. 15—	at Washington	1:01
Nov. 22—	at N.Y. Giants	1:01
Nov. 29—	at Green Bay	3:15
Dec. 3—	ST. LOUIS (Thur.)	8:20
Dec. 13—	ARIZONA	1:01
Dec. 20—	at Dallas	3:15
Dec. 27—	N.Y. GIANTS	4:05

All times are for home team.
All games Sunday unless noted.

Head coach
Ray Rhodes

Assistant coaches
Dana Bible (offensive coordinator)
Jim Bollman (tight ends)
Gerald Carr (wide receivers)
Juan Castillo (offensive line)
Tom Harbaugh (special teams)
Tom Kanavy (assistant strength & conditioning)
Chuck Knox Jr. (def. assistant)
Sean Payton (quarterbacks)
Danny Smith (defensive backs)
Emmitt Thomas (def. coordinator)
Mike Trgovac (defensive line)
Joe Vitt (linebackers)
Ted Williams (running backs)
Mike Wolf (strength & cond.)
Ken Zampesi (offensive assistant)

Equipment manager
Rusty Sweeney
Video director
Mike Dougherty

DRAFT CHOICES

Tra Thomas, T, Florida State (first round/11th pick overall).
Jeremiah Trotter, LB, Stephen F. Austin State (3/72).
Allen Rossum, DB, Notre Dame (3/85).
Brandon Whiting, DT, California (4/112).
Clarence Love, DB, Toledo (4/116).
Ike Reese, LB, Michigan State (5/142).
Chris Akins, DT, Texas (7/220).
Melvin Thomas, G, Colorado (7/240).

Philadelphia Eagles

1998 SEASON

No.	QUARTERBACKS	Ht./Wt.	Born	NFL Exp.	College	How acq.	'97 Games GP/GS
10	Detmer, Koy	6-0/180	7-5-73	2	Colorado	D7a/97	0/0
7	Hoying, Bobby	6-3/221	9-20-72	2	Ohio State	D3/96	7/6
6	McCoy, Mike	6-2/204	4-1-72	1	Utah	FA/98	0/0
9	Peete, Rodney	6-0/225	3-16-66	10	Southern California	FA/95	5/3

No.	RUNNING BACKS	Ht./Wt.	Born	NFL Exp.	College	How acq.	'97 Games GP/GS
33	Cothran, Jeff (FB)	6-1/249	6-28-71	4	Ohio State	FA/98	0/0
30	Garner, Charlie	5-9/187	2-13-72	5	Tennessee	D2b/94	16/2
22	Staley, Duce	5-11/220	2-27-75	2	South Carolina	D3/97	16/0
34	Turner, Kevin (FB)	6-1/231	6-12-69	7	Alabama	FA/95	16/10
29	Walker, Corey	5-10/188	6-4-73	2	Arkansas State	FA/97	0/0

No.	RECEIVERS	Ht./Wt.	Born	NFL Exp.	College	How acq.	'97 Games GP/GS
86	Copeland, Russell	6-0/200	11-4-71	6	Memphis State	FA/97	0/0
14	Dulick, Jason	6-4/200	5-26-74	1	Illinois	FA/98	0/0
87	Dunn, Jason (TE)	6-4/257	11-15-73	3	Eastern Kentucky	D2a/96	15/4
80	Fryar, Irving	6-0/200	9-28-62	15	Nebraska	FA/96	16/16
81	Graham, Jeff	6-2/206	2-14-69	8	Ohio State	TR/98	*16/16
17	Hankton, Karl	6-2/202	7-24-70	1	Trinity	FA/98	0/0
41	Hickman, Kevin (TE)	6-4/258	8-20-71	3	Navy	FA/98	*4/0
88	Johnson, Jimmie (TE)	6-2/257	10-6-66	10	Howard	FA/95	16/11
82	Jones, Chris T.	6-3/209	8-7-71	4	Miami (Fla.)	D3b/95	4/1
89	Lewis, Chad (TE)	6-6/252	10-5-71	2	Brigham Young	FA/97	16/3
84	Solomon, Freddie	5-10/180	8-15-72	3	South Carolina State	FA/97	15/5
16	Wilson, Sheddrick	6-3/210	11-23-73	2	Louisiana State	FA/98	0/0
85	Wyatt, Antwuan	5-10/199	7-18-75	2	Bethune-Cookman	D6a/97	1/0

No.	OFFENSIVE LINEMEN	Ht./Wt.	Born	NFL Exp.	College	How acq.	'97 Games GP/GS
62	Beckles, Ian (G)	6-1/304	7-20-67	9	Indiana	FA/97	9/8
76	Brooks, Barrett (T)	6-4/309	5-5-72	4	Kansas State	D2b/95	16/14
77	Cooper, Richard (T)	6-5/290	11-1-64	9	Tennessee	FA/96	0/0
66	Crafts, Jerry (T)	6-5/334	1-6-68	5	Louisville	FA/97	15/6
61	Everitt, Steve (C)	6-5/290	8-21-70	6	Michigan	FA/97	16/16
69	Hegamin, George (T)	6-7/331	2-14-73	5	North Carolina State	FA/98	*13/9
73	Kesi, Pat (G)	6-3/319	9-10-73	1	Washington	FA/98	0/0
64	Love, Sean (G)	6-3/305	9-6-68	5	Penn State	FA/97	0/0
71	Mayberry, Jermane (T)	6-4/325	8-29-73	3	Texas A&M-Kingsville	D1/96	16/16
65	Miller, Bubba (T)	6-1/300	1-24-73	3	Tennessee	FA/96	13/3
67	Sims, Keith (G)	6-3/318	6-17-67	9	Iowa State	FA/98	*8/4
63	Storm, Matt (G)	6-3/312	9-2-72	1	Georgia	FA/98	0/0
75	Thomas, Melvin (G)	6-3/322	6-11-75	R	Colorado	D7b/98	—
72	Thomas, Tra (T)	6-7/349	11-20-74	R	Florida State	D1/98	—
68	Unutoa, Morris (C)	6-1/284	3-10-71	3	Brigham Young	FA/96	16/0

No.	DEFENSIVE LINEMEN	Ht./Wt.	Born	NFL Exp.	College	How acq.	'97 Games GP/GS
93	Akins, Chris (T)	6-1/323	1-7-76	R	Texas	D7a/98	—
53	Douglas, Hugh (E)	6-2/280	8-23-71	4	Central State (Ohio)	TR/98	*15/15
97	Hall, Rhett (T)	6-2/276	12-5-68	8	California	FA/95	15/15
90	Harris, Jon (E)	6-7/280	6-9-74	2	Virginia	D1/97	8/4
74	Jasper, Edward (T)	6-2/295	1-18-73	2	Texas A&M	D6b/97	9/1
79	Jefferson, Greg (E)	6-3/257	8-31-71	4	Central Florida	D3a/95	12/11
94	Johnson, Bill	6-4/305	12-9-68	7	Michigan State	FA/98	*16/16
58	Kalu, Ndukwe (E)	6-3/246	8-3-75	2	Rice	D5a/97	3/0
78	Thomas, Hollis (T)	6-0/306	1-10-74	3	Northern Illinois	FA/96	16/16
98	Whiting, Brandon (T)	6-3/278	7-30-76	R	California	D4a/98	—

No.	LINEBACKERS	Ht./Wt.	Born	NFL Exp.	College	How acq.	'97 Games GP/GS
56	Caldwell, Mike	6-2/237	8-31-71	6	Middle Tennessee State	FA/98	*16/0
57	Darling, James	6-0/250	12-29-74	2	Washington State	D2/97	16/6
55	Farmer, Ray	6-3/225	7-1-74	3	Duke	D4/96	14/5
52	Fogle, DeShawn	6-1/220	4-1-75	2	Kansas State	FA/97	5/0
59	Mamula, Mike	6-4/252	8-14-73	4	Boston College	D1/95	16/16
49	Reese, Ike	6-2/222	10-16-73	R	Michigan State	D5/98	—
51	Thomas, William	6-2/223	8-13-68	8	Texas A&M	D4/91	14/14
54	Trotter, Jeremiah	6-0/261	1-20-77	R	Stephen F. Austin	D3a/98	—
96	Wallace, Al	6-5/258	3-25-74	1	Maryland	FA/97	1/0
50	Willis, James	6-2/237	9-2-72	6	Auburn	FA/95	15/15

No.	DEFENSIVE BACKS	Ht./Wt.	Born	NFL Exp.	College	How acq.	'97 Games GP/GS
27	Brice, Alundis (CB)	5-10/178	5-1-70	3	Mississippi	FA/98	0/0
20	Dawkins, Brian (S)	5-11/190	10-13-73	3	Clemson	D2b/96	15/15
47	Emanuel, Charles (S)	6-0/196	6-3-73	2	West Virginia	FA/97	5/1
31	Fisher, John (S)	5-11/200	7-28-73	2	Missouri Western	FA/98	0/0
43	Kinder, Randy (S)	6-1/210	4-4-75	2	Notre Dame	WV/97	6/0

No.	DEFENSIVE BACKS	Ht./Wt.	Born	NFL Exp.	College	How acq.	'97 Games GP/GS
28	Love, Clarence (CB)	5-10/181	6-16-76	R	Toledo	D4b/98	—
24	McTyer, Tim (CB)	5-11/181	12-14-75	2	Brigham Young	FA/97	10/0
26	Rice, Anthony	5-9/185	11-29-73	1	La Verne	FA/97	0/0
25	Rossum, Allen (CB)	5-8/178	10-22-75	R	Notre Dame	D3/98	—
45	Stevens, Matt (S)	6-0/206	6-15-73	3	Appalachian State	WV/97	11/0
21	Taylor, Bobby (CB)	6-3/216	12-28-73	4	Notre Dame	D2a/95	6/5
23	Vincent, Troy (CB)	6-0/194	6-8-70	7	Wisconsin	FA/96	16/16
36	Zordich, Michael (S)	6-1/212	10-12-63	12	Penn State	FA/94	16/16
	SPECIALISTS						
18	Boniol, Chris (K)	5-11/167	12-9-71	4	Louisiana Tech	FA/97	16/0
4	Hutton, Tom (P)	6-1/193	7-8-72	4	Tennessee	FA/95	16/0

*Caldwell played 16 games with Cardinals in '97; Douglas played 15 games with Jets; Graham played 16 games with Jets; Hegamin played 13 games with Cowboys; Hickman played 4 games with Lions; B. Johnson played 16 games with Rams; Sims played 8 games with Dolphins.

Abbreviations: D1—draft pick, first round; SupD2—supplemental draft pick, second round; WV—claimed on waivers; TR—obtained in trade; PlanB—Plan B free-agent acquisition; FA—free-agent acquisition (other than Plan B); ED—expansion draft pick.

MISCELLANEOUS TEAM DATA

Stadium (capacity, surface):
Veterans Stadium
(65,352, artificial)
Business address:
3501 South Broad Street
Philadelphia, PA 19148
Business phone:
215-463-2500
Ticket information:
215-463-5500
Team colors:
Midnight green, silver and white
Flagship radio station:
WYSP, 94.1 FM
Training site:
Lehigh University
Bethlehem, Pa.
610-758-6868

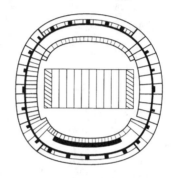

TSN REPORT CARD

Coaching staff	C -	The team has regressed in all three of Ray Rhodes' seasons as coach and most of it stems from his poor drafts and personnel decisions. The staff is inexperienced and overmatched. Other than Bobby Taylor, no young players have developed under their watch, and the offense is going to miss coordinator Jon Gruden.
Offensive backfield	C +	Quarterback Bobby Hoying is going to make his share of youthful mistakes, but it's time for the team to make him the guy. Charlie Garner and Duce Staley will try to make up for the loss of Ricky Watters, now with the Seahawks.
Receivers	C	This area needed to be addressed in the draft. Can the team count on 36-year-old Irving Fryar to have another All-Pro season? They better. Jeff Graham is decent, but nothing sensational, and Chris T. Jones has had serious knee problems. Tight end is a major question with underachieving Jason Dunn getting one more chance to live up to his immense potential.
Offensive line	C	There should be improvement over the group that allowed 64 sacks last year, the third most in franchise history, but how much is the question. Tra Thomas, a first-round pick from Florida State, has a starting spot, but all rookie left tackles take time. Former All-Pro guard Keith Sims might help if he can return to his 1995 form. Center Steve Everitt looked as out of shape in minicamp as he did all of last season.
Defensive line	C -	Hugh Douglas and Mike Mamula are the two lightest pair of ends in the league. Backup Jon Harris might be the tallest, but he still isn't ready for the NFL. Inside, a rotation of underrated Bill Johnson, Hollis Thomas and Rhett Hall is good enough to get by. But the pass rush is average at best, there isn't much depth and teams may run outside all day.
Linebackers	C +	William Thomas needs to return to All-Pro form. He was bothered by nagging injuries and lack of support last year. James Willis is better than people think in the middle. If the tackles in front of him do anything, he'll make plays. James Darling gets his first full season playing on the outside. He has the intensity to make up for a lack of size.
Secondary	C	Troy Vincent and Bobby Taylor are good cornerbacks. The problem comes at safety and in the nickel and dime defenses. Strong safety Mike Zordich, at 34, should not have to start any longer, but he will. Free safety Brian Dawkins took a step backward in his second season after a promising rookie year. There is no experienced depth behind the starters.
Special teams	C	Kicker Chris Boniol needs a big bounce back season and rookie return man Allen Rossum, the third-round draft pick out of Notre Dame, better be as good as advertised, or this group could really falter. John Harbaugh is the team's third special-teams coach in three years and has to do a better job than his two predecessors.

PITTSBURGH STEELERS
AFC CENTRAL DIVISION

1997 REVIEW

RESULTS

Aug. 31—DALLAS	L	7-37
Sept. 7—WASHINGTON	W	14-13
Sept.14—Open date		
Sept.22—at Jacksonville	L	21-30
Sept.28—TENNESSEE	W	37-24
Oct. 5—at Baltimore	W	42-34
Oct. 12—INDIANAPOLIS	W	24-22
Oct. 19—at Cincinnati	W	26-10
Oct. 26—JACKSONVILLE (OT)	W	23-17
Nov. 3—at Kansas City	L	10-13
Nov. 9—BALTIMORE	W	37-0
Nov. 16—CINCINNATI	W	20-3
Nov. 23—at Philadelphia	L	20-23
Nov. 30—at Arizona (OT)	W	26-20
Dec. 7—DENVER	W	35-24
Dec. 13—at New England (OT)	W	24-21
Dec. 21—at Tennessee	L	6-16
Jan. 3—NEW ENGLAND*	W	7-6
Jan.11—DENVER†	L	21-24

*AFC divisional playoff game.
†AFC championship game.

RECORDS/RANKINGS

1997 regular-season record: 11-5 (1st in AFC Central); 6-2 in division; 9-3 in conference; 7-1 at home; 4-0 on road.
Team record last five years: 53-27 (.663, ranks 4th in league in that span).

1997 team rankings:	No.	AFC	NFL
Total offense	*346.4	3	6
Rushing offense	*154.9	1	1
Passing offense	*191.4	12	23
Scoring offense	372	4	7
Total defense	*294.1	2	6
Rushing defense	*82.4	1	1
Passing defense	*211.7	6	18
Scoring defense	307	5	11
Takeaways	34	T1	T4
Giveaways	33	13	24
Turnover differential	1	T8	T14
Sacks	48	T2	T6
Sacks allowed	20	1	1

*Yards per game.

TEAM LEADERS

Scoring (kicking): Norm Johnson, 106 pts. (40/40 PATs, 22/25 FGs).
Scoring (touchdowns): Kordell Stewart, 66 pts. (11 rushing).
Passing: Kordell Stewart, 3,020 yds. (440 att., 236 comp., 53.6%, 21 TDs, 17 int.).
Rushing: Jerome Bettis, 1,665 yds. (375 att., 4.4 avg., 7 TDs).
Receptions: Yancey Thigpen, 79 (1,398 yds., 17.7 avg., 7 TDs).
Interceptions: Donnell Woolford, 4 (91 yds., 0 TDs); Darren Perry, 4 (77 yds., 0 TDs).
Sacks: Carnell Lake, 6.0.
Punting: Josh Miller, 42.6 avg. (64 punts, 2,729 yds., 0 blocked).
Punt returns: Will Blackwell, 6.5 avg. (23 att., 149 yds., 0 TDs).
Kickoff returns: Will Blackwell, 24.7 avg. (32 att., 791 yds., 1 TD).

1998 SEASON

CLUB DIRECTORY

President
Daniel M. Rooney
Vice presidents
John R. McGinley
Arthur J. Rooney Jr.
Vice president/general counsel
Arthur J. Rooney II
Administration advisor
Charles H. Noll
Director of marketing
Mark Fuhrman
Director of business
Mark Hart
Business coordinator
Dan Ferens
Accounts coordinator
Jim Ellenberger
Ticket sales manager
Geraldine Glenn
Director of football operations
Tom Donahoe
Player relations
Anthony Griggs
Communications coordinator
Ron Wahl
Public relations/media manager
Dave Lockett
Director of pro personnel
Tom Modrak
College scouting coordinator
Charles Bailey
College scouts
Mark Gorscak
Phil Kriedler
Bob Lane
Max McCartney
Trainers
John Norwig
Rick Burkholder

Head coach
Bill Cowher

Assistant coaches
Mike Archer (linebackers)
David Culley (wide receivers)
Jim Haslett (defensive coordinator)
Dick Hoak (running backs)
Tim Lewis (defensive backs)
John Mitchell (defensive line)
Mike Mularkey (tight ends)
Ray Sherman (off. coordinator)
Kent Stephenson (offensive line)
Ron Zook (special teams)

Physicians
James P. Bradley
Richard Rydze
Abraham J. Twerski
Anthony P. Yates
Equipment manager
Rodgers Freyvogel
Field manager
Rich Baker
Video director
Bob McCartney
Video assistant
Pat Dolan
Photographer
Mike Fabus

SCHEDULE

Sept. 6— at Baltimore	1:01	
Sept. 13— CHICAGO	1:01	
Sept. 20— at Miami	1:01	
Sept. 27— SEATTLE	4:05	
Oct. 4— Open date		
Oct. 11— at Cincinnati	1:01	
Oct. 18— BALTIMORE	1:01	
Oct. 26— at Kansas City (Mon.)	7:20	
Nov. 1— TENNESSEE	1:01	
Nov. 9— GREEN BAY (Mon.)	8:20	
Nov. 15— at Tennessee	12:01	
Nov. 22— JACKSONVILLE	1:01	
Nov. 26— at Detroit (Thanks.)	12:35	
Dec. 6— NEW ENGLAND	1:01	
Dec. 13— at Tampa Bay	1:01	
Dec. 20— CINCINNATI	1:01	
Dec. 28— at Jacksonville (Mon.)	8:20	

All times are for home team.
All games Sunday unless noted.

DRAFT CHOICES

Alan Faneca, G, Louisiana State (first round/26th pick overall).
Jeremy Staat, DT, Arizona State (2/41).
Chris Conrad, T, Fresno State (3/66).
Hines Ward, WR, Georgia (3/92).
Deshea Townsend, DB, Alabama (4/117).
Carlos King, FB, North Carolina State (4/123).
Jason Simmons, DB, Arizona State (5/137).
Chris Fuamatu-Ma'afala, RB, Utah (6/178).
Ryan Olson, LB, Colorado (6/186).
Angel Rubio, DE, Southeast Missouri State (7/221).

1998 SEASON
TRAINING CAMP ROSTER

No.	QUARTERBACKS	Ht./Wt.	Born	NFL Exp.	College	How acq.	'97 Games GP/GS
7	Gonzalez, Pete	6-1/216	7-4-74	1	Pittsburgh	FA/98	0/0
11	Quinn, Mike	6-3/220	4-15-74	2	Stephen F. Austin	FA/97	1/0
10	Stewart, Kordell	6-1/212	10-16-72	4	Colorado	D2/95	16/16
18	Tomczak, Mike	6-1/207	10-23-62	14	Ohio State	FA/93	16/0

No.	RUNNING BACKS	Ht./Wt.	Born	NFL Exp.	College	How acq.	'97 Games GP/GS
36	Bettis, Jerome	5-11/243	2-16-72	6	Notre Dame	TR/96	15/15
45	Fuamatu-Ma'afala, Chris (FB)	5-11/252	3-4-77	R	Utah	D6a/98	—
33	Huntley, Richard	5-11/224	9-18-72	2	Winston-Salem (N.C.) State	FA/98	0/0
43	Jones, George	5-9/204	12-31-73	2	San Diego State	D5b/97	16/1
35	King, Carlos (FB)	6-0/235	11-27-73	R	North Carolina State	D4b/98	—
34	Lester, Tim (FB)	5-10/238	6-15-68	7	Eastern Kentucky	FA/95	16/13
25	McAfee, Fred	5-10/198	6-20-68	8	Mississippi College	FA/94	14/0
42	McCann, David (FB)	5-11/220	7-27-75	1	Murray State	FA/98	0/0
38	Witman, Jon (FB)	6-1/240	6-1-72	3	Penn State	D3b/96	16/2

No.	RECEIVERS	Ht./Wt.	Born	NFL Exp.	College	How acq.	'97 Games GP/GS
86	Adams, Mike	5-11/184	3-25-74	2	Texas	D7/97	6/0
80	Arnold, Jahine	6-0/187	6-19-73	3	Fresno State	D4b/96	0/0
82	Bailey, Henry	5-8/176	2-28-73	3	UNLV	FA/97	0/0
89	Blackwell, Will	6-0/184	7-9-75	2	San Diego State	D2/97	14/0
84	Botkin, Kirk (TE)	6-3/245	3-19-71	4	Arkansas	WV/96	13/1
87	Bruener, Mark (TE)	6-4/258	9-16-72	4	Washington	D1/95	16/16
19	Coleman, Andre	5-9/165	9-19-72	5	Kansas State	FA/97	*10/0
48	Cushing, Matt (TE)	6-3/260	7-25-75	1	Illinois	FA/98	0/0
88	Hawkins, Courtney	5-9/183	12-12-69	7	Michigan State	FA/97	15/3
83	Holliday, Corey	6-2/208	1-31-71	4	North Carolina	FA/95	2/0
81	Johnson, Charles	6-0/195	1-3-72	5	Colorado	D1/94	13/11
85	Lyons, Mitch (TE)	6-5/265	5-13-70	6	Michigan State	FA/97	10/3
17	Marsh, Curtis	6-2/206	11-24-70	4	Utah	FA/97	5/0
46	Sadowski, Troy (TE)	6-5/252	12-8-65	9	Georgia	FA/97	5/0
15	Ward, Hines	6-0/194	3-8-76	R	Georgia	D3b/98	—

No.	OFFENSIVE LINEMEN	Ht./Wt.	Born	NFL Exp.	College	How acq.	'97 Games GP/GS
78	Conrad, Chris (T)	6-6/301	5-27-75	R	Fresno State	D3a/98	—
63	Dawson, Dermontti (C)	6-2/288	6-17-65	11	Kentucky	D2/88	16/16
62	Duffy, Roger (G)	6-3/305	7-16-67	9	Penn State	FA/98	*15/15
72	Evans, Mike (T)	6-4/315	7-28-73	1	Mercyhurst (Pa.)	FA/98	0/0
65	Faneca, Alan (G)	6-5/322	12-7-76	R	Louisiana State	D1/98	—
64	Henne, Aaron (G)	6-5/299	3-2-74	1	Maryland	FA/98	0/0
68	Stai, Brenden (G)	6-4/305	3-30-72	4	Nebraska	D3/95	10/9
67	Stephens, Jamain (T)	6-6/336	1-9-74	3	North Carolina A&T	D1/96	7/1
73	Strzelczyk, Justin (G)	6-6/305	8-18-68	9	Maine	D11/90	14/14
66	Sweeney, Jim (C)	6-4/298	8-8-62	15	Pittsburgh	FA/96	16/1
79	Wiggins, Paul (T)	6-3/307	8-17-73	2	Oregon	D3a/97	1/0
77	Wolford, Will (T)	6-5/300	5-18-64	14	Vanderbilt	FA/96	16/16

No.	DEFENSIVE LINEMEN	Ht./Wt.	Born	NFL Exp.	College	How acq.	'97 Games GP/GS
90	DeLaTorre, Aaron (NT)	6-1/296	5-6-75	1	Stephen F. Austin	FA/98	0/0
98	Gibson, Oliver (T)	6-3/298	3-15-72	4	Notre Dame	D4a/95	16/0
91	Harper, Matt (E)	6-4/275	4-28-74	1	Texas Christian	FA/98	0/0
74	Harrison, Nolan (E)	6-5/280	1-25-69	8	Indiana	FA/97	16/16
76	Henry, Kevin (E)	6-4/282	10-23-68	6	Mississippi State	D4/93	16/16
97	Manuel, Rod (E)	6-5/290	10-8-74	2	Oklahoma	D6b/97	1/0
55	Olson, Ryan (T)	6-2/275	6-27-75	R	Colorado	D6b/98	—
71	Roye, Orpheus (E)	6-4/290	1-21-74	3	Florida State	D6a/96	16/0
69	Rubio, Angel (E)	6-2/300	4-12-75	R	Southeast Missouri State	D7/98	—
94	Staat, Jeremy (T)	6-5/300	10-10-76	R	Arizona State	D2/98	—
93	Steed, Joel (NT)	6-2/310	2-17-69	7	Colorado	D3/92	16/16
96	Vrabel, Mike (E)	6-4/275	8-14-75	2	Ohio State	D3b/97	15/0

No.	LINEBACKERS	Ht./Wt.	Born	NFL Exp.	College	How acq.	'97 Games GP/GS
56	Brown, Morocco	6-0/230	2-9-76	1	North Carolina State	FA/98	0/0
53	Conley, Steven	6-5/235	1-18-72	3	Arkansas	D3a/96	16/0
51	Emmons, Carlos	6-5/246	9-3-73	3	Arkansas State	D7/96	5/0
57	Fiala, John	6-2/235	11-25-73	2	Washington	FA/98	0/0
92	Gildon, Jason	6-3/245	7-31-72	5	Oklahoma State	D3a/94	16/16
50	Holmes, Earl	6-2/246	4-28-73	3	Florida A&M	D4a/96	16/16
54	Jones, Donta	6-2/234	8-27-72	4	Nebraska	D4b/95	16/4
99	Kirkland, Levon	6-1/274	2-17-69	7	Clemson	D2/92	16/16
95	Lloyd, Greg	6-2/235	5-26-65	12	Fort Valley (Ga.) State College	D6b/87	12/12
44	Ravotti, Eric	6-2/250	3-16-71	4	Penn State	FA/98	0/0

No.	DEFENSIVE BACKS	Ht./Wt.	Born	NFL Exp.	College	How acq.	'97 Games GP/GS
22	Brown, DeAuntae (CB)	5-10/195	4-28-74	1	Central State (Ohio)	FA/98	*1/0
27	Brown, J.B. (CB)	6-0/191	1-5-67	10	Maryland	FA/97	13/0
29	Brown, Lance (CB)	6-2/200	2-2-72	2	Indiana	FA/98	0/0

No.	DEFENSIVE BACKS	Ht./Wt.	Born	NFL Exp.	College	How acq.	'97 Games GP/GS
41	Flowers, Lethon (CB)	6-0/213	1-14-73	4	Georgia Tech	D5a/95	10/0
28	Jenkins, John	6-0/188	5-11-75	1	Pittsburgh	FA/98	0/0
37	Lake, Carnell (S)	6-1/210	7-15-67	10	UCLA	D2/89	16/16
24	Oldham, Chris (CB)	5-9/200	10-26-68	8	Oregon	FA/95	16/0
39	Perry, Darren (S)	5-11/196	12-29-68	7	Penn State	D8a/92	16/16
30	Scott, Chad	6-1/203	9-6-74	2	Maryland	D1/97	13/9
23	Simmons, Jason (CB)	5-8/188	3-30-76	R	Arizona State	D5/98	—
26	Townsend, Deshea (CB)	5-10/180	9-8-75	R	Alabama	D4a/98	—
20	Washington, Dewayne (CB)	6-0/190	12-27-72	5	North Carolina State	FA/98	*16/16
21	Woolford, Donnell (CB)	5-9/200	1-6-66	10	Clemson	FA/97	15/12
	SPECIALISTS						
2	George, Matt (P)	5-11/190	1-13-75	1	Chapman	FA/98	0/0
9	Johnson, Norm (K)	6-2/202	5-31-60	16	UCLA	FA/97	16/0
4	Miller, Josh (P)	6-3/215	7-14-70	3	Arizona	FA/96	16/0

*D. Brown played 1 game with Eagles in '97; Coleman played 2 games with Seahawks and 8 games with Steelers; Duffy played 15 games with Jets; Washington played 16 games with Vikings.

Abbreviations: D1—draft pick, first round; SupD2—supplemental draft pick, second round; WV—claimed on waivers; TR—obtained in trade; PlanB—Plan B free-agent acquisition; FA—free-agent acquisition (other than Plan B); ED—expansion draft pick.

MISCELLANEOUS TEAM DATA

Stadium (capacity, surface):
Three Rivers Stadium
(59,600, artificial)
Business address:
300 Stadium Circle
Pittsburgh, PA 15212
Business phone:
412-323-0300
Ticket information:
412-323-1200
Team colors:
Black and gold
Flagship radio station:
WTAE, 1250 AM
Training site:
St. Vincent College
Latrobe, Pa.
412-539-8515

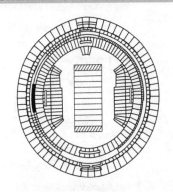

TSN REPORT CARD

Coaching staff — A
Bill Cowher might be the best coach in the game. He has been in the playoffs every year since replacing Chuck Noll six years ago, and only Paul Brown had similar success in his first six seasons. Cowher is daring, well-prepared and his players respond to his bombastic, fiery style.

Offensive backfield — B +
Jerome Bettis is one of the NFL's best backs, certainly the one with the best combination of power and agility. His blocking back, Tim Lester, is a step away from the Pro Bowl. Kordell Stewart made so much progress in his first year as a starting quarterback it's scary.

Receivers — B -
The loss of Yancey Thigpen will hurt, but it might allow Charles Johnson to reach his awesome potential. There are a lot of young receivers to help ease the loss of Thigpen, but it might take them a couple of years to develop.

Offensive line — B
One of the best units in the NFL took a hit with the loss of left tackle John Jackson. But Dermontti Dawson is the best center in the league and guard Will Wolford has played like he belongs in the Pro Bowl the past two seasons. Justin Strzelczyk, who moves from right to left tackle, might be the most underrated offensive lineman in the league.

Defensive line — B -
Joel Steed finally made it to the Pro Bowl last season, but all his play did was overshadow the performance of end Kevin Henry, who got better and better each week. By the end of the season, Henry and Nolan Harrison joined Steed to form a formidable three-man front that stopped the run and got pressure on the quarterback.

Linebackers — A -
Greg Lloyd, a former five-time Pro Bowl player, remains a question mark because of his health. Still, this remains the strongest unit on the team. The inside tandem of Levon Kirkland and Earl Holmes is the biggest and most physical in the league. If Lloyd is gone, his replacement will be Mike Vrabel, who is big, fast and athletic.

Secondary — C
This area remains the biggest question mark on the team because of uncertainty at cornerback. Chad Scott, a first-round pick a year ago, tore the anterior cruciate ligament in his left knee during an offseason workout and could miss the season. Carnell Lake is the best strong safety in the NFL, but he might have to play cornerback again with Scott injured. Donnell Woolford, a free-agent disappointment last year, has been replaced by '98 free agent Dewayne Washington.

Special teams — D
The Steelers did not block a punt, field goal or extra point last year and forced only two fumbles. What's more, they never did settle on a good punt-return man. And punter Josh Miller became a weekly liability despite having a strong leg. The biggest plus turned out to be re-signing kicker Norm Johnson, who refuses to act his age (38).

ST. LOUIS RAMS
NFC WESTERN DIVISION

1997 REVIEW

RESULTS

Aug. 31—NEW ORLEANS	W	38-24
Sept. 7—SAN FRANCISCO	L	12-15
Sept.14—at Denver	L	14-35
Sept.21—N.Y. GIANTS	W	13-3
Sept.28—at Oakland	L	17-35
Oct. 5—Open date		
Oct. 12—at San Francisco	L	10-30
Oct. 19—SEATTLE	L	9-17
Oct. 26—KANSAS CITY	L	20-28
Nov. 2—at Atlanta	L	31-34
Nov. 9—at Green Bay	L	7-17
Nov. 16—ATLANTA	L	21-27
Nov. 23—CAROLINA	L	10-16
Nov. 30—at Washington	W	23-20
Dec. 7—at New Orleans	W	34-27
Dec. 14—CHICAGO	L	10-13
Dec. 20—at Carolina	W	30-18

RECORDS/RANKINGS

1997 regular-season record: 5-11 (5th in NFC West); 3-5 in division; 5-7 in conference; 2-6 at home; 3-5 on road.
Team record last five years: 27-53 (.338, ranks T26th in league in that span).

1997 team rankings:	No.	NFC	NFL
Total offense	*297.6	9	21
Rushing offense	*97.7	13	24
Passing offense	*199.9	8	17
Scoring offense	299	T10	T23
Total defense	*315.9	11	17
Rushing defense	*104.8	5	9
Passing defense	*211.2	12	17
Scoring defense	359	T10	T19
Takeaways	39	3	3
Giveaways	30	9	19
Turnover differential	9	3	T6
Sacks	38	T10	T18
Sacks allowed	44	T9	T18

*Yards per game.

TEAM LEADERS

Scoring (kicking): Jeff Wilkins, 107 pts. (32/32 PATs, 25/37 FGs).
Scoring (touchdowns): Lawrence Phillips, 48 pts. (8 rushing).
Passing: Tony Banks, 3,254 yds. (487 att., 252 comp., 51.7%, 14 TDs, 13 int.).
Rushing: Lawrence Phillips, 633 yds. (183 att., 3.5 avg., 8 TDs).
Receptions: Amp Lee, 61 (825 yds., 13.5 avg., 3 TDs).
Interceptions: Ryan McNeil, 9 (127 yds., 1 TD).
Sacks: Leslie O'Neal, 10.0.
Punting: Mike Horan, 42.9 avg. (53 punts, 2,272 yds., 0 blocked).
Punt returns: Eddie Kennison, 7.3 avg. (34 att., 247 yds., 0 TDs).
Kickoff returns: David Thompson, 22.7 avg. (49 att., 1,110 yds., 0 TDs).

1998 SEASON

CLUB DIRECTORY

Owner/chairman
  Georgia Frontiere
Vice chairman
  Stan Kroenke
President
  John Shaw
Senior vice president
  Jay Zygmunt
Sr. vice president/administration
  Bob Wallace
Vice president/player personnel
  Charley Armey
Vice president/football operations
  Lynn Stiles
Vice president/media and community relations
  Marshall Klein
Vice president/marketing
  Phil Thomas
Director of college scouting
  John Becker
Ticket manager
  Mike Naughton
Director of operations
  John Oswald
Director/public relations
  Rick Smith
Asst. director/public relations
  Duane Lewis
Entertainment coordinator
  Tom Guthrie
Scouts

Billy Campfield	Kevin McCabe
Lawrence McCutcheon	David Razzano
Pete Russell	Harley Sewell
Howard Tippett	

Trainer
  Jim Anderson
Assistant trainers
  Ron DuBuque
  Dake Walden

Head coach
Dick Vermeil

Assistant coaches
  Steve Brown (secondary)
  John Bunting (linebackers/co-def. coordinator)
  Chris Clausen (strength & cond.)
  Dick Coury (wide receivers)
  Frank Gansz (special teams)
  Peter Giunta (asst. head coach/ co-defensive coordinator)
  Kerry Goode (strength & cond.)
  Carl Hairston (defensive line)
  Jim Hanifan (offensive line)
  Todd Howard (defensive assistant)
  Wilbert Montgomery (running backs)
  John Ramsdell (offensive assistant)
  Jerry Rhome (offensive coordinator)
  Lynn Stiles (tight ends)
  Ed White (offensive line)
  Mike White (assistant head coach/quarterbacks)

Physicians
  Dr. Bernard Garfinkel
  Dr. Robert Shively
Equipment manager
  Todd Hewitt
Equipment assistant
  Jim Lake
Video director
  Larry Clerico
Assistant video director
  Rob Zagame

SCHEDULE

Sept. 6—	NEW ORLEANS	12:01
Sept. 13—	MINNESOTA	12:01
Sept. 20—	at Buffalo	1:01
Sept. 27—	ARIZONA	12:01
Oct. 4—	Open date	
Oct. 11—	N.Y. JETS	3:15
Oct. 18—	at Miami	4:15
Oct. 25—	SAN FRANCISCO	12:01
Nov. 1—	at Atlanta	1:01
Nov. 8—	at Chicago	12:01
Nov. 15—	at New Orleans	12:01
Nov. 22—	CAROLINA	3:05
Nov. 29—	ATLANTA	12:01
Dec. 3—	at Philadelphia (Thur.)	8:20
Dec. 13—	NEW ENGLAND	12:01
Dec. 20—	at Carolina	1:01
Dec. 27—	at San Francisco	1:05

All times are for home team.
All games Sunday unless noted.

DRAFT CHOICES

Grant Wistrom, DE, Nebraska (first round/sixth pick overall).
Robert Holcombe, RB, Illinois (2/37).
Leonard Little, LB, Tennessee (3/65).
Az-Zahir Hakim, WR, San Diego State (4/96).
Roland Williams, TE, Syracuse (4/98).
Raymond Priester, RB, Clemson (5/129).
Glenn Roundtree, G, Clemson (6/159).
Jason Chorak, DE, Washington (7/236).

1998 SEASON · *St. Louis Rams*

No.	QUARTERBACKS	Ht./Wt.	Born	NFL Exp.	College	How acq.	'97 Games GP/GS
12	Banks, Tony	6-4/215	4-5-73	3	Michigan State	D2a/96	16/16
13	Bono, Steve	6-4/212	5-11-62	14	UCLA	TR/98	*2/0
9	Furrer, Will	6-3/215	2-5-68	6	Virginia Tech	WV/93	0/0

No.	RUNNING BACKS	Ht./Wt.	Born	NFL Exp.	College	How acq.	'97 Games GP/GS
33	Harris, Derrick	6-0/252	9-18-72	3	Miami (Fla.)	D6a/96	0/0
26	Henley, June	5-10/226	9-4-75	1	Kansas	D5/97	0/0
34	Heyward, Craig (FB)	5-11/265	9-26-66	11	Pittsburgh	FA/97	16/12
25	Holcombe, Robert	5-11/220	12-11-75	R	Illinois	D2/98	—
31	Lee, Amp	5-11/200	10-1-71	7	Florida State	FA/97	16/1
44	Moore, Jerald (FB)	5-9/225	11-20-74	3	Oklahoma	D3/96	9/5
27	Priester, Raymond	6-2/242	2-3-75	R	Clemson	D5/98	—
28	Thompson, David	5-8/200	1-13-75	2	Oklahoma State	FA/97	11/0

No.	RECEIVERS	Ht./Wt.	Born	NFL Exp.	College	How acq.	'97 Games GP/GS
49	Armstrong, Tyji (TE)	6-4/250	10-3-70	6	Mississippi	D3b/92	0/0
19	Baker, Donnell	6-0/200	12-21-73	1	Southern	D7a/96	0/0
80	Bruce, Isaac	6-0/188	11-10-72	5	Memphis State	D2/94	12/12
84	Conwell, Ernie (TE)	6-1/265	8-17-72	3	Washington	D2b/96	16/16
81	Hakim, Az-zahir	5-10/178	6-3-77	R	San Diego State	D4b/98	—
89	Jacoby, Mitch (TE)	6-4/260	12-8-73	2	Northern Illinois	FA/97	14/2
88	Kennison, Eddie	6-0/195	1-20-73	3	Louisiana State	D1b/96	14/9
86	Laing, Aaron (TE)	6-3/260	7-19-71	4	New Mexico State	WV/95	15/3
87	Proehl, Ricky	6-0/190	3-7-68	9	Wake Forest	UFA/98	*15/10
16	Sellers, Donald	6-0/195	12-30-74	1	New Mexico	FA/97	0/0
83	Thomas, J.T.	5-10/180	7-11-71	4	Arizona State	D7/95	5/0
	Williams, Roland (TE)	6-5/269	4-27-75	R	Syracuse	D4b/98	—

No.	OFFENSIVE LINEMEN	Ht./Wt.	Born	NFL Exp.	College	How acq.	'97 Games GP/GS
77	Brooks, Ethan (T)	6-6/299	4-27-72	2	Williams (Conn.)	D7/96	0/0
63	Flannery, John (G)	6-3/304	1-13-69	8	Syracuse	FA/98	*16/4
70	Gandy, Wayne (T)	6-4/310	2-10-71	5	Auburn	D1/94	16/16
66	Gerak, John (G)	6-3/300	1-6-70	6	Penn State	FA/97	16/16
60	Gruttadauria, Mike (C)	6-4/297	12-6-72	3	Central Florida	FA/96	14/14
62	Kempfert, David (G)	6-4/290	5-11-74	1	Montana	FA/98	0/0
73	Miller, Fred (T)	6-7/315	2-6-73	3	Baylor	D5/96	15/7
61	Nutten, Tom (C)	6-4/285	6-8-71	1	Western Michigan	D7a/95	0/0
76	Pace, Orlando (T)	6-7/320	11-4-75	2	Ohio State	D1/97	13/9
71	Reem, Matt (T)	6-6/270	12-23-72	1	Minnesota	FA/98	0/0
65	Roundtree, Glenn (G)	6-3/304	11-24-73	R	Clemson	D6/98	—
	Simmons, Ed (T)	6-5/334	12-31-63	12	Eastern Washington	FA/98	*14/13
50	Tucker, Ryan (C)	6-5/305	6-12-75	2	Texas Christian	D4/97	7/0
72	Wiegert, Zach (T)	6-4/310	8-16-72	4	Nebraska	D2a/95	15/15

No.	DEFENSIVE LINEMEN	Ht./Wt.	Born	NFL Exp.	College	How acq.	'97 Games GP/GS
99	Agnew, Ray (T)	6-3/285	12-9-67	9	North Carolina State	UFA/98	*15/0
93	Carter, Kevin (E)	6-5/280	9-21-73	4	Florida	D1/95	16/16
95	Chorak, Jason (E)	6-4/253	9-23-74	R	Washington	D7a/98	—
75	Farr, D'Marco (T)	6-1/280	6-9-71	5	Washington	FA/94	16/16
97	Manley, James (T)	6-3/320	7-11-74	2	Vanderbilt	FA/98	0/0
91	Maumalanga, Chris (T)	6-3/300	12-15-71	3	Kansas	FA/98	0/0
79	Phillips, Joe (T)	6-5/305	7-15-63	13	Southern Methodist	FA/98	*15/15
92	Robinson, Bryan	6-4/295	6-22-74	2	Fresno State	FA/97	11/0
94	Robinson, Jeff (E)	6-4/275	2-20-70	6	Idaho	FA/97	16/0
96	Williams, Jay (T)	6-3/280	10-13-71	4	Wake Forest	FA/94	16/2
98	Wistrom, Grant (E)	6-5/273	7-3-76	R	Nebraska	D1/98	—
90	Zgonina, Jeff (T)	6-2/300	5-24-70	6	Purdue	FA/97	15/0

No.	LINEBACKERS	Ht./Wt.	Born	NFL Exp.	College	How acq.	'97 Games GP/GS
56	Clemons, Charlie	6-2/255	7-4-72	2	Georgia	FA/97	5/0
55	Dumas, Troy	6-3/242	9-30-72	4	Nebraska	FA/97	8/0
54	Hill, Eric	6-2/258	11-14-66	10	Louisiana State	UFA/98	*11/10
52	Jones, Mike	6-1/240	4-15-69	7	Missouri	FA/97	16/16
59	Kazadi, Muadianvita	6-2/240	12-20-73	2	Tulsa	D6/97	12/0
57	Little, Leonard	6-3/237	10-19-74	R	Tennessee	D3/98	—
58	Phifer, Roman	6-2/240	3-5-68	8	UCLA	D2/91	16/15
51	Styles, Lorenzo	6-1/245	1-31-74	4	Ohio State	FA/97	3/0

No.	DEFENSIVE BACKS	Ht./Wt.	Born	NFL Exp.	College	How acq.	'97 Games GP/GS
20	Allen, Taje	5-10/185	11-6-73	2	Texas	D5/97	14/1
24	Clark, Willie (CB)	5-10/186	1-6-72	5	Notre Dame	FA/98	*16/2
22	Jenkins, Billy (S)	5-10/194	7-8-74	2	Howard	FA/97	16/2
41	Lyght, Todd (CB)	6-0/190	2-9-69	8	Notre Dame	D1/91	16/16
35	Lyle, Keith (S)	6-2/210	4-17-72	5	Virginia	D3/94	16/16
23	McBurrows, Gerald (S)	5-11/205	10-7-73	4	Kansas	D7/95	8/3
21	McCleon, Dexter (CB)	5-10/200	10-9-73	2	Clemson	D2/97	16/1
47	McNeil, Ryan (CB)	6-2/192	10-4-70	6	Miami (Fla.)	FA/97	16/16
42	Rowe, Joe (CB)	6-0/195	12-8-73	1	Virginia	FA/97	2/0
37	Scurlock, Mike (S)	5-10/200	2-26-72	4	Arizona	FA/97	5/0
32	Wright, Toby (S)	5-11/212	11-19-70	5	Nebraska	D2/94	11/11
	SPECIALISTS						
11	Tuten, Rick (P)	6-2/221	1-5-65	10	Florida State	UFA/98	*11/0
14	Wilkins, Jeff (K)	6-2/205	4-19-72	5	Youngstown State	FA/97	16/0

*Agnew played 15 games with Giants in '97; Bono played 2 games with Packers; Clark played 16 games with Eagles; Flannery played 16 games with Cowboys; Hill played 11 games with Cardinals; Phillips played 15 games with Chiefs; Proehl played 15 games with Bears; Simmons played 14 games with Redskins; Tuten played 11 games with Seahawks.

Abbreviations: D1—draft pick, first round; SupD2—supplemental draft pick, second round; WV—claimed on waivers; TR—obtained in trade; PlanB—Plan B free-agent acquisition; FA—free-agent acquisition (other than Plan B); ED—expansion draft pick.

MISCELLANEOUS TEAM DATA

Stadium (capacity, surface):
Trans World Dome (66,000, artificial)
Business address:
1 Rams Way
St. Louis, MO 63045
Business phone:
314-982-7267
Ticket information:
314-425-8830
Team colors:
Royal blue, gold and white
Flagship radio station:
KFNS, 590 AM
Training site:
Western Illinois University
Macomb, Ill.
314-982-7267

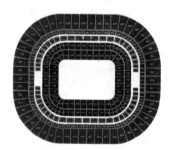

TSN REPORT CARD

Coaching staff	B	There are too many veteran coaches who have had long runs of success in the NFL for this team not to do better. With help from co-coordinator John Bunting, young but talented Peter Giunta should continue the improvement made last season by now-retired Bud Carson on defense.
Offensive backfield	C -	The Rams have two years invested in Tony Banks as a starting quarterback; they're hoping to see some dividends this season. Save for Amp Lee, there's nothing but unproven talent at running back. Robert Holcombe and Jerald Moore should get the tough yards, and more. But there's no home run threat.
Receivers	B -	The signing of Ricky Proehl helps, as does the drafting of Az-zahir Hakim. But this group will be little more than slightly above average—even with Isaac Bruce healthy—unless Eddie Kennison approximates his 1996 play. A more sure-handed Ernie Conwell at tight end would be a big plus.
Offensive line	C	Take away Wayne Gandy, and the rest of the projected starting five has only 59 pro starts. And the NFL isn't exactly the best forum for on-the-job training. Orlando Pace should be fine. But if center Mike Gruttadauria and guards Zach Wiegert and Ryan Tucker aren't up to the task, it will be a long season for the offense.
Defensive line	C	Replacing Leslie O'Neal with Grant Wistrom at end, and Bill Johnson with Ray Agnew and Joe Phillips at tackle looks like a push. The Rams need a breakthrough year from end Kevin Carter and a return to 1995 form by tackle D'Marco Farr. Keep an eye on rookie Leonard Little in passing situations.
Linebackers	C +	This unit needs to make more plays than it did last year, whether it's sacking the quarterback on blitzes, stopping the running back behind the line, forcing a fumble or knocking away a pass. The addition of Eric Hill helps the run defense, but Roman Phifer needs to approach his play of '95 and '96.
Secondary	B -	A healthy Toby Wright at strong safety would work wonders for this unit. When on his game, Wright is the heart and soul of the defense and an intimidating presence on run support. Todd Lyght and Ryan McNeil are above-average corners. Ball-hawking Keith Lyle is a Pro Bowl-caliber free safety.
Special teams	C	There should be improvement across the board here, especially with the addition of Rick Tuten at punter and the potential pairing of David Thompson and rookie Az-zahir Hakim on kickoff returns.

SAN DIEGO CHARGERS
AFC WESTERN DIVISION

1997 REVIEW

RESULTS

Aug. 31—at New England	L	7-41
Sept. 7—at New Orleans	W	20-6
Sept.14—CAROLINA	L	7-26
Sept.21—at Seattle	L	22-26
Sept.28—BALTIMORE	W	21-17
Oct. 5—at Oakland	W	25-10
Oct. 12—Open date		
Oct. 16—at Kansas City	L	3-31
Oct. 26—INDIANAPOLIS	W	35-19
Nov. 2—at Cincinnati	L	31-38
Nov. 9—SEATTLE	L	31-37
Nov. 16—OAKLAND	L	13-38
Nov. 23—at San Francisco	L	10-17
Nov. 30—DENVER	L	28-38
Dec. 7—ATLANTA	L	3-14
Dec. 14—KANSAS CITY	L	7-29
Dec. 21—at Denver	L	3-38

RECORDS/RANKINGS

1997 regular-season record: 4-12 (T4th in AFC West); 1-7 in division; 3-9 in conference; 2-6 at home; 2-6 on road.
Team record last five years: 40-40 (.500, ranks 14th in league in that span).

1997 team rankings:	No.	AFC	NFL
Total offense	*281.6	15	28
Rushing offense	*88.5	14	28
Passing offense	*193.1	11	21
Scoring offense	266	14	26
Total defense	*322.9	8	21
Rushing defense	*106.1	6	11
Passing defense	*216.8	10	23
Scoring defense	425	15	30
Takeaways	26	10	T19
Giveaways	35	14	25
Turnover differential	-9	14	25
Sacks	27	15	30
Sacks allowed	51	13	25

*Yards per game.

TEAM LEADERS

Scoring (kicking): Greg Davis, 78 pts. (21/22 PATs, 19/24 FGs).
Scoring (touchdowns): Tony Martin, 36 pts. (6 receiving).
Passing: Stan Humphries, 1,488 yds. (225 att., 121 comp., 53.8%, 5 TDs, 6 int.).
Rushing: Gary Brown, 945 yds. (253 att., 3.7 avg., 4 TDs).
Receptions: Tony Martin, 63 (904 yds., 14.3 avg., 6 TDs).
Interceptions: Rodney Harrison, 2 (75 yds., 1 TD); Paul Bradford, 2 (56 yds., 1 TD); Dwayne Harper, 2 (43 yds., 0 TDs); Greg Jackson, 2 (37 yds., 1 TD); Junior Seau, 2 (33 yds., 0 TDs).
Sacks: Junior Seau, 7.0.
Punting: Darren Bennett, 44.6 avg. (89 punts, 3,972 yds., 1 blocked).
Punt returns: Eric Metcalf, 10.9 avg. (45 att., 489 yds., 3 TDs).
Kickoff returns: Kenny Bynum, 21.4 avg. (38 att., 814 yds., 0 TDs).

1998 SEASON

CLUB DIRECTORY

Chairman of the board
Alex G. Spanos
President/vice chairman
Dean A. Spanos
Executive vice president
Michael A. Spanos
General manager
Bobby Beathard
Vice president/finance
Jeremiah T. Murphy
Chief financial & administrative officer
Jeanne Bonk
Director/player personnel
Billy Devaney
Director/pro personnel
Rudy Feldman
Coordinator/football operations
Ed McGuire
Business manager
John Hinek
Director/ticket operations
Ron Tuck
Director/public relations
Bill Johnston
Director/premium seating/marketing
Lynn Abramson
Director/security
Dick Lewis
Trainer
Keoki Kamau
Equipment manager
Sid Brooks
Director/video operations
Brian Duddy

Head coach
Kevin Gilbride

Assistant coaches
Mike Cavanaugh (quality control/ offense)
Joe Bugel (offensive line)
John Hastings (strength & conditioning)
June Jones (quarterbacks)
Kevin Lempa (administrative assistant/defense)
Bill MacDermott (tight ends)
Nick Nicolau (asst. head coach)
Frank Novak (special teams)
Wayne Nunnely (defensive line)
Joe Pascale (defensive coordinator)
Derrell Pasquale (quality control/ special teams)
Rod Perry (defensive backs)
Mike Sheppard (offensive coordinator/wide receivers)
Jim Vechiarella (linebackers)
Ollie Wilson (running backs)

SCHEDULE

Sept. 6—	BUFFALO	1:15
Sept. 13—	at Tennessee	12:01
Sept. 20—	at Kansas City	12:01
Sept. 27—	N.Y. GIANTS	1:15
Oct. 4—	at Indianapolis	12:01
Oct. 11—	at Oakland	1:15
Oct. 18—	PHILADELPHIA	1:15
Oct. 25—	SEATTLE	1:15
Nov. 1—	Open date	
Nov. 8—	at Denver	2:15
Nov. 15—	BALTIMORE	1:05
Nov. 22—	KANSAS CITY	1:15
Nov. 29—	DENVER	5:20
Dec. 6—	at Washington	1:01
Dec. 13—	at Seattle	1:05
Dec. 20—	OAKLAND	1:05
Dec. 27—	at Arizona	2:15

All times are for home team.
All games Sunday unless noted.

DRAFT CHOICES

Ryan Leaf, QB, Washington State (first round/second pick overall).
Mikhael Ricks, WR, Stephen F. Austin State (2/59).
Cedric Harden, DE, Florida A&M (5/126).
Clifford Ivory, DB, Troy State (6/155).
Jon Haskins, LB, Stanford (7/194).
Kio Sanford, WR, Kentucky (7/234).

1998 SEASON
TRAINING CAMP ROSTER

No.	QUARTERBACKS	Ht./Wt.	Born	NFL Exp.	College	How acq.	'97 Games GP/GS
16	Leaf, Ryan	6-5/240	5-15-76	R	Washington State	D1/98	—
11	Weldon, Casey	6-1/206	2-3-69	4	Florida State	FA/97	0/0
5	Whelihan, Craig	6-5/220	4-15-71	4	Pacific	D6c/95	9/7

No.	RUNNING BACKS	Ht./Wt.	Born	NFL Exp.	College	How acq.	'97 Games GP/GS
43	Bynum, Kenny	5-11/191	5-29-74	2	South Carolina State	D5a/97	13/0
32	Chancey, Robert (FB)	6-0/260	9-7-72	2	None	FA/97	6/0
26	Filer, Rodney (FB)	6-1/235	6-14-74	1	Iowa	FA/97	0/0
41	Fletcher, Terrell	5-8/196	9-14-73	4	Wisconsin	D2b/95	13/1
4	Means, Natrone	5-10/245	4-26-72	6	North Carolina	FA/98	*14/11

No.	RECEIVERS	Ht./Wt.	Born	NFL Exp.	College	How acq.	'97 Games GP/GS
86	Brown, Tyrone	5-11/168	1-3-73	3	Toledo	FA/98	0/0
83	Burke, John (TE)	6-3/248	9-7-71	4	Virginia Tech	FA/98	*7/1
89	Hartley, Frank (TE)	6-2/268	12-15-67	5	Illinois	FA/97	16/16
82	Jones, Charlie	5-8/175	12-1-72	3	Fresno State	D4/96	16/11
88	Jones, Freddie (TE)	6-4/260	9-16-74	2	North Carolina	D2/97	13/8
81	Martin, Tony	6-0/181	9-5-65	9	Mesa State (Colo.)	TR/94	16/16
85	Rachal, Latario	5-11/183	1-31-73	2	Fresno State	FA/97	14/0
10	Ricks, Mikhael	6-5/237	11-14-74	R	Stephen F. Austin	D2/98	—
87	Roche, Brian (TE)	6-4/255	5-5-73	3	San Jose State	D3/96	5/0
	Rodgers, Anthony	6-3/190	12-11-73	1	Cal State Northridge	FA/97	0/0
19	Sanford, Kio	5-10/180	1-8-75	R	Kentucky	D7b/98	—
84	Slaughter, Webster	6-1/175	10-19-64	11	San Diego State	FA/98	0/0
80	Still, Bryan	5-11/174	6-3-74	3	Virginia Tech	D2a/96	15/4

No.	OFFENSIVE LINEMEN	Ht./Wt.	Born	NFL Exp.	College	How acq.	'97 Games GP/GS
75	Berti, Tony (T)	6-6/300	6-21-72	4	Colorado	D6d/95	16/16
50	Binn, Dave (C)	6-3/240	2-6-72	5	California	FA/94	16/0
69	Bordelon, Ben (T)	6-4/291	4-9-74	2	Louisiana State.	FA/97	16/2
60	Engel, Greg (C)	6-3/285	1-18-71	5	Illinois	FA/94	9/0
67	Fortin, Roman (C)	6-5/297	2-26-67	9	San Diego State	FA/98	*3/3
65	Jackson, John (T)	6-6/297	1-4-65	11	Eastern Kentucky	FA/98	*16/16
63	McKenzie, Raleigh (C)	6-2/283	2-8-63	14	Tennessee	FA/97	16/16
66	Mills, Jim (T)	6-4/290	3-30-73	3	Idaho	D6a/96	1/0
70	Parker, Vaughn (T)	6-3/296	6-5-71	5	UCLA	D2b/94	16/16
79	Price, Marcus (T)	6-6/321	3-3-72	2	Louisiana State	FA/97	2/0
74	Roundtree, Raleigh (T)	6-4/295	8-31-75	2	South Carolina State	D4/97	0/0
72	Sienkiewicz, Troy (G)	6-5/310	5-27-72	4	New Mexico State	D6a/95	14/6
73	Taylor, Aaron (G)	6-4/305	11-14-72	5	Notre Dame	FA/98	*14/14

No.	DEFENSIVE LINEMEN	Ht./Wt.	Born	NFL Exp.	College	How acq.	'97 Games GP/GS
90	Coleman, Marco (E)	6-3/267	12-18-69	7	Georgia Tech	FA/96	16/16
93	Davis, Reuben (T)	6-5/320	5-7-65	11	North Carolina	FA/94	0/0
95	Fuller, William (E)	6-3/280	3-8-62	13	North Carolina	FA/97	16/16
96	Hand, Norman (T)	6-3/313	9-4-72	4	Mississippi	WV/97	15/1
92	Harden, Cedric (E)	6-6/260	10-19-74	R	Florida A&M	D5/98	—
99	Johnson, Raylee (E)	6-3/265	6-1-70	6	Arkansas	D4a/93	16/0
94	Mohring, Mike (T)	6-5/295	3-22-74	1	Pittsburgh	FA/97	2/0
97	Parrella, John (T)	6-3/290	11-22-69	6	Nebraska	FA/94	16/16
91	Tuinei, Van (E)	6-3/266	2-16-71	2	Arizona	FA/97	3/0

No.	LINEBACKERS	Ht./Wt.	Born	NFL Exp.	College	How acq.	'97 Games GP/GS
52	Burgess, James	5-11/230	3-31-74	2	Miami (Fla.)	FA/97	15/4
58	Bush, Lew	6-2/245	12-2-69	6	Washington State	D4b/93	14/13
51	Dixon, Gerald	6-3/250	6-20-69	6	South Carolina	FA/98	*15/13
54	Gouveia, Kurt	6-1/240	9-14-64	13	Brigham Young	FA/96	7/6
53	Hamilton, Michael	6-2/244	12-3-73	2	North Carolina A&T	D3/97	6/0
57	Haskins, Jon	6-2/245	10-6-75	R	Stanford	D7a/98	—
59	James, Toran	6-3/247	3-8-74	2	North Carolina A&T	D7a/97	14/0
55	Seau, Junior	6-3/250	1-19-69	9	Southern California	D1/90	15/15

No.	DEFENSIVE BACKS	Ht./Wt.	Born	NFL Exp.	College	How acq.	'97 Games GP/GS
25	Bradford, Paul	5-9/185	4-20-74	2	Portland State	D5b/97	15/4
22	Brew, Dorian (CB)	5-10/182	7-19-74	3	Kansas	FA/97	*9/0
20	Dumas, Mike (S)	6-0/202	3-18-69	6	Indiana	FA/95	16/15
28	Harper, Dwayne (CB)	5-11/175	3-29-66	11	South Carolina State	FA/94	12/12
37	Harrison, Rodney (S)	6-0/201	12-15-72	5	Western Illinois	D5b/94	16/16

No.	DEFENSIVE BACKS	Ht./Wt.	Born	NFL Exp.	College	How acq.	'97 Games GP/GS
31	Ivory, Clifford (CB)	5-11/183	8-1-75	R	Troy (Ala.) State	D6/98	—
42	Jackson, Greg (S)	6-1/217	8-20-66	10	Louisiana State	FA/94	13/0
40	Montreuil, Mark (CB)	6-2/200	12-29-71	4	Concordia (Canada)	D7/95	6/1
29	Shaw, Terrance (CB)	5-11/190	11-11-73	4	Stephen F. Austin State	D2a/95	16/16
47	Thomas, Johnny (CB)	5-9/191	8-3-64	10	Baylor	FA/97	0/0
23	Williams, Gerome (S)	6-2/210	7-9-73	2	Houston	FA/97	6/0
	SPECIALISTS						
2	Bennett, Darren (P)	6-5/235	1-9-65	4	None	FA/94	16/0
3	Carney, John (K)	5-11/170	4-20-64	10	Notre Dame	FA/90	4/0

*Brew played 3 games with Ravens and 6 games with Chargers in '97; Burke played 7 games with Jets; Dixon played 15 games with Bengals; Fortin played 3 games with Falcons; J. Jackson played 16 games with Steelers; Means played 14 games with Jaguars; Taylor played 14 games with Packers.

Abbreviations: D1—draft pick, first round; SupD2—supplemental draft pick, second round; WV—claimed on waivers; TR—obtained in trade; PlanB—Plan B free-agent acquisition; FA—free-agent acquisition (other than Plan B); ED—expansion draft pick.

MISCELLANEOUS TEAM DATA

Stadium (capacity, surface):
Qualcomm Stadium
(71,000, grass)
Business address:
P.O. Box 609609
San Diego, CA 92160-9609
Business phone:
619-874-4500
Ticket information:
619-280-2121
Team colors:
Navy blue, white and gold
Flagship radio station:
KFMB, 760 AM/STAR 100.7 FM
Training site:
UC San Diego
La Jolla, Calif.
619-874-4500

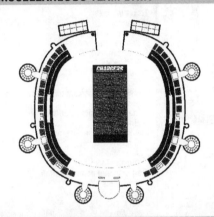

TSN REPORT CARD

Coaching staff	D	Kevin Gilbride's rookie year was torpedoed by numerous injuries. Still, it's unclear whether Gilbride, who had been a successful offensive coordinator with the Oilers and Jaguars, can cut it as a head coach. He needs to distribute responsibility better; he has two able lieutenants in Joe Bugel and June Jones.
Offensive backfield	C	If Natrone Means runs like he did during his first San Diego stint, the team will be pleased. He is still young enough to have an impact, but he also has been slowed by nagging injuries the past two years in Jacksonville. Behind Means, there isn't much: an undersized Terrell Fletcher and a speedy but unproven Kenny Bynum.
Receivers	C -	Tony Martin should be a Pro Bowl player in Gilbride's pass-happy system, but he can't do it alone. Again, he enters the season without a proven receiver on the other side. Bryan Still has been a bust and Eric Metcalf is in Arizona. The team hopes 6-5 rookie Mikhael Ricks can contribute.
Offensive line	B -	The additions of John Jackson, Aaron Taylor and Roman Fortin are huge. Same goes for line guru Joe Bugel, who joined Gilbride's staff after being fired by the Raiders. Still, this unit has to prove it can mesh quickly and be productive.
Defensive line	C -	The middle is decent with the return of Reuben Davis; John Parrella is solid, if not flashy. But the overpriced ends—Marco Coleman and William Fuller—have to step up. The line collected a measly 15 sacks in '97.
Linebackers	C	Any unit with Junior Seau has to be respected. But the energetic Seau isn't a kid anymore and that's also true for Kurt Gouveia (13th year) in the middle. A banged-up Gouveia won't last the year. Lewis Bush is adequate on the outside and Gerald Dixon (8.5 sacks), a free-agent pickup from Cincinnati, will help.
Secondary	C	Keep an eye on strong safety Rodney Harrison. His stellar year got overlooked in the 4-12 pileup. The rest of the defensive backs are average. Veteran corner Dwayne Harper is steady, but he has trouble staying on the field because of injuries. Terrance Shaw, the other corner, is in the last year of his contract and will be motivated.
Special teams	C +	Eric Metcalf's punt returns will be missed; the team hopes Charlie Jones and Bryan Still can compensate. The kickoff-return game should be OK with Latario Rachal. Kicker John Carney is back after missing most of last year with a knee injury; Darren Bennett is among the NFL's top punters.

SAN FRANCISCO 49ERS
NFC WESTERN DIVISION

1997 REVIEW
RESULTS

Aug. 31—at Tampa Bay	L	6-13
Sept. 7—at St. Louis	W	15-12
Sept.14—NEW ORLEANS	W	33-7
Sept.21—ATLANTA	W	34-7
Sept.29—at Carolina	W	34-21
Oct. 5—Open date		
Oct. 12—ST. LOUIS	W	30-10
Oct. 19—at Atlanta	W	35-28
Oct. 26—at New Orleans	W	23-0
Nov. 2—DALLAS	W	17-10
Nov. 10—at Philadelphia	W	24-12
Nov. 16—CAROLINA	W	27-19
Nov. 23—SAN DIEGO	W	17-10
Nov. 30—at Kansas City	L	9-44
Dec. 7—MINNESOTA	W	28-17
Dec. 15—DENVER	W	34-17
Dec. 21—at Seattle	L	9-38
Jan. 3—MINNESOTA*	W	38-22
Jan. 11—GREEN BAY†	L	10-23

*NFC divisional playoff game.
†NFC championship game.

RECORDS/RANKINGS

1997 regular-season record: 13-3 (1st in NFC West); 8-0 in division; 11-1 in conference; 8-0 at home; 5-3 on road.
Team record last five years: 59-21 (.738, ranks 1st in league in that span).

1997 team rankings:	No.	NFC	NFL
Total offense	*319.5	5	12
Rushing offense	*123.1	4	8
Passing offense	*196.4	9	T18
Scoring offense	375	3	T5
Total defense	*250.8	1	1
Rushing defense	*85.4	1	2
Passing defense	*165.4	2	2
Scoring defense	265	T2	T3
Takeaways	41	2	2
Giveaways	20	2	T2
Turnover differential	21	2	2
Sacks	54	T3	T3
Sacks allowed	44	T9	T18

*Yards per game.

TEAM LEADERS

Scoring (kicking): Gary Anderson, 125 pts. (38/38 PATs, 29/36 FGs).
Scoring (touchdowns): Terry Kirby, 52 pts. (6 rushing, 1 receiving, 1 kickoff return, 2 2-pt. conv.).
Passing: Steve Young, 3,029 yds. (356 att., 241 comp., 67.7%, 19 TDs, 6 int.).
Rushing: Garrison Hearst, 1,019 yds. (234 att., 4.4 avg., 4 TDs).
Receptions: Terrell Owens, 60 (936 yds., 15.6 avg., 8 TDs).
Interceptions: Merton Hanks, 6 (103 yds., 1 TD).
Sacks: Dana Stubblefield, 15.0.
Punting: Tommy Thompson, 40.8 avg. (78 punts, 3,182 yds., 1 blocked).
Punt returns: Iheanyi Uwaezuoke, 11.0 avg. (34 att., 373 yds., 0 TDs).
Kickoff returns: Chuck Levy, 22.0 avg. (36 att., 793 yds., 0 TDs).

1998 SEASON
CLUB DIRECTORY

Owners
Edward J. DeBartolo Jr.
Denise DeBartolo York
President
Carmen Policy
V.P./director of football operations
Dwight Clark
V.P./business operations and CFO
Bill Duffy
Director of player personnel
Vinny Cerrato
Ticket manager
Lynn Carrozzi
Pro personnel/AFC
George Streeter
Pro personnel/NFC
Joe Collins
Controller
Melrene Frear
Director of public/community relations
Rodney Knox
Manager of media relations
Kirk Reynolds
Public relations assistants
Kimberly McIntyre
Darla Maeda
Demetra Marcus
Pro personnel administration
Joe Collins
George Streeter
Scouts
Jim Abrams   John Brunner
Mike Faulkiner   Brian Gardner
Jim Gruden   Oscar Lofton
Head trainer
Lindsy McLean
Assistant trainers
Jasen Powell
Todd Lazenby
Physicians
Michael Dillingham, M.D.
James B. Klint, M.D.
Stadium operations director
Murlan "Mo" Fowell

Head coach
Steve Mariucci

Assistant coaches
Jerry Attaway (physical development coordinator)
Mike Barnes (strength development coordinator)
Dwaine Board (defensive line)
Jaime Hill (def. quality control)
Larry Kirksey (wide receivers)
Greg Knapp (offensive assistant/quarterbacks)
John Marshall (def. coordinator)
Bobb McKittrick (offensive line)
Bill McPherson (def. assistant)
Jim Mora Jr. (defensive backs)
Marty Mornhinweg (offensive coordinator/quarterbacks)
Patrick Morris (tight ends/assistant lines)
Tom Rathman (running backs)
Richard Smith (linebackers)
George Stewart (special teams coordinator)
Andy Sugarman (off. quality control)

Equipment manager
Kevin Lartigue
Equipment assistant
Jason Fery
Director/video operations
Robert Yanagi

SCHEDULE

Sept. 6— N.Y. JETS		1:15
Sept. 14— at Washington (Mon.)		8:20
Sept. 20— Open date		
Sept. 27— ATLANTA		1:15
Oct. 4— at Buffalo		1:01
Oct. 11— at New Orleans		12:01
Oct. 18— INDIANAPOLIS		1:05
Oct. 25— at St. Louis		12:01
Nov. 1— at Green Bay		3:15
Nov. 8— CAROLINA		1:05
Nov. 15— at Atlanta		1:01
Nov. 22— NEW ORLEANS		5:20
Nov. 30— N.Y. GIANTS (Mon.)		5:20
Dec. 6— at Carolina		1:01
Dec. 14— DETROIT (Mon.)		5:20
Dec. 20— at New England		1:01
Dec. 27— ST. LOUIS		1:05

All times are for home team.
All games Sunday unless noted.

DRAFT CHOICES

R.W. McQuarters, DB, Oklahoma State (first round/28th pick overall).
Jeremy Newberry, C, California (2/58).
Chris Ruhman, T, Texas A&M (3/89).
Lance Schulters, DB, Hofstra (4/119).
Phil Ostrowski, G, Penn State (5/151).
Fred Beasley, RB, Auburn (6/180).
Ryan Thelwell, WR, Minnesota (7/215).

1998 SEASON *San Francisco 49ers*

No.	QUARTERBACKS	Ht./Wt.	Born	NFL Exp.	College	How acq.	'97 Games GP/GS
11	Detmer, Ty	6-0/194	10-30-67	7	Brigham Young	FA/98	*8/7
14	Druckenmiller, Jim	6-4/241	9-19-72	2	Virginia Tech	D1/97	4/1
8	Young, Steve	6-2/215	10-11-61	14	Brigham Young	TR/87	15/15
	RUNNING BACKS						
40	Beasley, Fred	6-0/220	9-18-74	R	Auburn	D6/98	—
44	Edwards, Marc (FB)	6-0/229	11-17-74	2	Notre Dame	D2/97	15/1
20	Hearst, Garrison	5-11/219	1-4-71	6	Georgia	FA/97	13/13
22	Mitchell, Shon	6-1/218	10-8-73	1	Texas	FA/98	0/0
33	Rutherford, Reynard	6-0/210	5-15-73	1	California	FA/97	0/0
	RECEIVERS						
85	Clark, Greg (TE)	6-4/251	4-7-72	2	Stanford	D3/97	15/4
86	Fann, Chad (TE)	6-3/256	6-7-70	5	Florida A&M	FA/97	11/0
88	Harris, Mark	6-4/201	4-28-70	2	Stanford	FA/97	10/0
32	Levy, Chuck	6-0/206	1-7-72	3	Arizona	FA/96	14/0
81	Owens, Terrell	6-3/217	12-7-73	3	Tennessee-Chattanooga	D3/96	16/15
80	Rice, Jerry	6-2/196	10-13-62	14	Mississippi Valley State	D1/85	2/1
19	Shearer, Curtis	5-10/170	6-8-71	1	San Diego State	FA/98	0/0
82	Smith, Irv (TE)	6-3/262	10-13-71	6	Notre Dame	FA/98	*11/8
83	Stokes, J.J.	6-4/223	10-6-72	4	UCLA	D1/95	16/16
18	Thelwell, Ryan	6-2/188	4-6-73	R	Minnesota	D7/98	—
89	Uwaezuoke, Iheanyi	6-2/198	7-24-73	3	California	D5/96	14/0
	OFFENSIVE LINEMEN						
79	Barton, Harris (T)	6-4/292	4-19-64	12	North Carolina	D1/87	0/0
72	Brown, Jamie (T)	6-8/318	4-24-72	4	Florida A&M	TR/98	*11/2
65	Brown, Ray (G)	6-5/318	12-12-62	13	Arkansas State	FA/96	15/15
67	Dalman, Chris (G)	6-3/297	3-15-70	6	Stanford	D6/93	13/13
63	Deese, Derrick (G)	6-3/289	5-17-70	7	Southern California	FA/92	16/13
74	Fiore, Dave (T)	6-4/288	8-10-74	2	Hofstra	FA/98	0/0
66	Gogan, Kevin (G)	6-7/325	11-2-64	11	Washington	FA/97	16/16
77	Hanshaw, Tim (G)	6-5/302	4-27-70	3	Brigham Young	D4/95	13/3
62	Newberry, Jeremy (C)	6-5/315	3-23-76	R	California	D2/98	—
69	Ostrowski, Phil (G)	6-4/291	9-23-75	R	Penn State	D5/98	—
75	Pollack, Frank (G)	6-5/295	11-5-67	7	Northern Arizona	FA/94	16/0
60	Rudolph, Joe (G)	6-2/284	7-21-72	3	Wisconsin	FA/97	6/1
78	Ruhman, Chris (T)	6-5/321	12-19-74	R	Texas A&M	D3/98	—
	DEFENSIVE LINEMEN						
92	Barker, Roy (E)	6-5/290	2-14-69	7	North Carolina	FA/96	13/12
94	Bonham, Shane	6-2/286	10-18-70	5	Tennessee	FA/98	*16/0
90	Bryant, Junior (E)	6-4/278	1-16-71	4	Notre Dame	FA/93	16/3
	Buckner, Brentson (T)	6-2/315	9-30-71	5	Clemson	UFA/98	*14/4
56	Doleman, Chris (E)	6-5/289	10-16-61	14	Pittsburgh	FA/96	16/16
99	Noble, Brandon (T)	6-2/280	4-10-74	1	Penn State	FA/98	0/0
96	Posey, Jeff (E)	6-5/240	8-14-75	1	Southern Mississippi	FA/98	0/0
91	Price, Daryl (E)	6-3/287	10-23-72	3	Colorado	D4/96	4/0
71	Reese, Albert (T)	6-6/294	4-29-73	2	Grambling State	FA/97	5/0
93	Thornton, Carlos (T)	6-4/308	4-23-74	1	Alcorn State	FA/97	0/0
98	Wilkins, Gabe (E)	6-5/315	9-1-71	5	Gardner-Webb (N.C.)	D4/94	16/16
95	Wilson, Troy (E)	6-4/257	11-22-70	4	Pittsburg (Kan.) State	FA/98	0/0
97	Young, Bryant (T)	6-3/291	1-27-72	5	Notre Dame	D1/94	12/12
	LINEBACKERS						
58	Bradford, Vincent	6-2/231	1-22-73	2	Arkansas	FA/97	0/0
59	Givens, Reggie	6-0/234	10-3-71	1	Penn State	FA/98	0/0
57	Kirk, Randy	6-2/242	12-27-64	11	San Diego State	FA/96	16/0
51	Norton, Ken	6-2/254	9-29-66	11	UCLA	FA/94	16/16
52	Schwantz, Jim	6-2/240	1-23-70	5	Purdue	FA/97	16/0
55	Tubbs, Winfred	6-4/260	9-24-70	5	Texas	FA/98	*16/16
53	Williams, James	6-0/246	10-10-68	8	Mississippi State	FA/98	*16/0
54	Woodall, Lee	6-1/224	10-31-69	5	West Chester (Pa.)	D6/94	16/16
	DEFENSIVE BACKS						
25	Bradley, Mario	6-2/196	4-16-72	1	Southern California	FA/98	0/0
31	Bronson, Zack (S)	6-1/191	1-28-74	2	McNeese State.	FA/97	16/0
28	Buckley, Curtis (S)	6-0/182	9-25-70	6	East Texas State	FA/96	15/0
36	Hanks, Merton (S)	6-2/181	3-12-68	8	Iowa	D5/91	16/16
43	Langham, Antonio (CB)	6-0/184	7-31-72	5	Alabama	FA/98	*16/15

No.	DEFENSIVE BACKS	Ht./Wt.	Born	NFL Exp.	College	How acq.	'97 Games GP/GS
46	McDonald, Tim (S)	6-2/219	1-6-65	12	Southern California	FA/93	15/15
21	McQuarters, R.W. (CB)	5-9/198	12-21-76	R	Oklahoma State	D1/98	—
23	Pope, Marquez (CB)	5-11/193	10-29-70	6	Fresno State	FA/95	5/5
	Schulters, Lance (S)	6-2/188	5-27-75	R	Hofstra	D4/98	—
24	Smith, Tyrone	5-11/193	9-29-72	1	Baylor	FA/98	0/0
38	Walker, Darnell (CB)	5-8/167	1-17-70	6	Oklahoma	FA/97	16/11
	SPECIALISTS						
1	Becksvoort, John (K)	6-1/197	2-26-73	1	Tennessee	FA/98	0/0
4	Phillips, Tucker (P)	6-2/202	2-4-74	1	Rice	FA/98	0/0
3	Thompson, Tommy (P)	5-10/179	4-27-72	4	Oregon	FA/95	16/0

*Bonham played 16 games with Lions in '97; Brown played 11 games with Broncos; Buckner played 14 games with Bengals; Detmer played 8 games with Eagles; Langham played 16 games with Ravens; I. Smith played 11 games with Saints; Tubbs played 16 games with Saints; Williams played 16 games with 49ers.

Abbreviations: D1—draft pick, first round; SupD2—supplemental draft pick, second round; WV—claimed on waivers; TR—obtained in trade; PlanB—Plan B free-agent acquisition; FA—free-agent acquisition (other than Plan B); ED—expansion draft pick.

MISCELLANEOUS TEAM DATA

Stadium (capacity, surface):
3Com Park at Candlestick Point
(70,270, grass)
Business address:
4949 Centennial Blvd.
Santa Clara, CA 95054-1229
Business phone:
408-562-4949
Ticket information:
415-468-2249
Team colors:
Forty Niners gold and cardinal
Flagship radio station:
KGO, 810 AM
Training site:
University of Pacific
Stockton, Calif.
408-562-4949

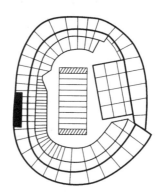

TSN REPORT CARD

Coaching staff	A -	Steve Mariucci did extremely well not letting his spirit or his team sink after a disastrous start last year. Mariucci has all the qualities needed in a head coach: enthusiasm, organization, and intelligence. If there's a knock on him its that he's too organized and too concerned with statistics. Nevertheless, he's well thought of by his fellow coaches, players, and his management.
Offensive backfield	B	The running game was emphasized for the first time in five seasons. Garrison Hearst is quick, has great vision, and is capable of breaking the long run. Marc Edwards takes over at fullback, and most feel he's ready. Chuck Levy has unique skills as a backup and speciality down player. Depth is the only concern.
Offensive line	B	Coaches are concerned about Derrick Deese at right tackle. He's really a guard, and is viewed as undersized. Still, Deese is the best athlete on the line and will improve over last year when he was pressed into duty at left tackle. This year's left tackle, Jamie Brown, is a question mark. He looked good last year backing up Gary Zimmerman in Denver, but it's interesting Denver didn't hang on to him. Otherwise, the line is solid.
Receivers	A -	Jerry Rice hasn't gotten the chance to star in a Steve Mariucci offense, and that could be a winning combination. J.J. Stokes and Terrell Owens came on last year, and will only get better. Iheanyi Uwaezuoke, Mark Harris and seventh-round pick Ryan Thelwell provide excellent depth.
Defensive line	B	With Kevin Greene, Dana Stubblefield and possibly Chris Doleman gone, the line won't be as strong. If free-agent signee Gabe Wilkins isn't ready for the start of the season after knee surgery, the grade drops to a C+. Bryant Young and Roy Barker have to stay healthy for this unit to be effective.
Linebackers	B -	Winfred Tubbs could help ease the loss of Stubblefield, who was an expert run player. Tubbs could be the team's best free-agent signing. Ken Norton routinely leads the team in tackles but may be slowing down. Lee Woodall was inconsistent last year, and there is a lack of depth, particularly at inside linebacker.
Secondary	B +	This backfield could take over as the strength of the defense if Marquez Pope and safety Merton Hanks rebound from injuries. There have been questions about free agent Antonio Langham's cover skills, but he has been impressive in the offseason. Darnell Walker and rookie R.W. McQuarters provide excellent depth at corner. That can't be said for safety.
Special teams	B	McQuarters and Chuck Levy are talented return men. Anthony Peterson will bolster coverage units as will rookies Fred Beasley and Lance Schulters. The kicking game could suffer without a veteran place kicker, but field position is expected to improve with deeper kickoffs.

SEATTLE SEAHAWKS
AFC WESTERN DIVISION

1997 REVIEW
RESULTS

Aug. 31—N.Y. JETS		L	3-41
Sept. 7—DENVER		L	14-35
Sept.14—at Indianapolis		W	31-3
Sept.21—SAN DIEGO		W	26-22
Sept.28—at Kansas City (OT)		L	17-20
Oct. 5—TENNESSEE		W	16-13
Oct. 12—Open date			
Oct. 19—at St. Louis		W	17-9
Oct. 26—OAKLAND		W	45-34
Nov. 2—at Denver		L	27-30
Nov. 9—at San Diego		W	37-31
Nov. 16—at New Orleans (OT)		L	17-20
Nov. 23—KANSAS CITY		L	14-19
Nov. 30—ATLANTA		L	17-24
Dec. 7—at Baltimore		L	24-31
Dec. 14—at Oakland		W	22-21
Dec. 21—SAN FRANCISCO		W	38-9

RECORDS/RANKINGS

1997 regular-season record: 8-8 (3rd in AFC West); 4-4 in division; 6-6 in conference; 4-4 at home; 4-4 on road.

Team record last five years: 35-45 (.438, ranks 18th in league in that span).

1997 team rankings:	No.	AFC	NFL
Total offense	*359.9	2	3
Rushing offense	*112.5	6	13
Passing offense	*247.4	1	1
Scoring offense	365	6	9
Total defense	*303.1	3	8
Rushing defense	*108.2	7	12
Passing defense	*194.9	4	14
Scoring defense	362	10	22
Takeaways	29	T6	T13
Giveaways	32	T11	T20
Turnover differential	-3	T11	T19
Sacks	42	T7	T15
Sacks allowed	36	7	12

*Yards per game.

TEAM LEADERS

Scoring (kicking): Todd Peterson, 103 pts. (37/37 PATs, 22/28 FGs).

Scoring (touchdowns): Joey Galloway, 72 pts. (12 receiving).

Passing: Warren Moon, 3,678 yds. (528 att., 313 comp., 59.3%, 25 TDs, 16 int.).

Rushing: Chris Warren, 847 yds. (200 att., 4.2 avg., 4 TDs).

Receptions: Joey Galloway, 72 (1,049 yds., 14.6 avg., 12 TDs).

Interceptions: Darryl Williams, 8 (172 yds., 1 TD).

Sacks: Michael Sinclair, 12.0.

Punting: Rick Tuten, 41.8 avg. (48 punts, 2,007 yds., 0 blocked).

Punt returns: Ronnie Harris, 6.9 avg. (21 att., 144 yds., 0 TDs).

Kickoff returns: Steve Broussard, 21.5 avg. (50 att., 1,076 yds., 0 TDs).

1998 SEASON
CLUB DIRECTORY

Owner
Paul Allen
Vice chairman
Bert Kolde
President
Bob Whitsitt
Vice president/football operations
Randy Mueller
V.p./chief financial officer
Nathaniel T. "Buster" Brown
V.p./ticket sales & services
Duane McLean
V.P./communications
Gary Wright
Public relations director
Dave Pearson
Community outreach director
Sandy Gregory
Player relations director
Nesby Glasgow
College scouting director
Pat Mondock
Pro scouting director
Bill Quinter
Assistant player personnel director
Rick Thompson
Eastern supervisor
Bill Baker
Scouts
Derrick Jensen
Doug Kretz
Dave Nusz0
John Peterson
Doug Whaley
Head trainer
Jim Whitsel
Assistant trainer
Todd Sperber

Head coach
Dennis Erickson

Assistant coaches
Dave Arnold (special teams)
Tommy Brasher (defensive line)
Bob Bratkowski (offensive coordinator/wide receivers)
Dave Brown (defensive assistant)
Keith Gilbertson (tight ends)
Milt Jackson (wide receivers)
Darren Krein (assistant strength & conditioning)
Dana LeDuc (strength & cond.)
Greg McMackin (def. coordinator)
Howard Mudd (offensive line)
Mike Murphy (linebackers)
Rich Olson (quarterbacks)
Willy Robinson (defensive backs)
Pete Rodriguez (special teams)
Gregg Smith (assistant head coach/offensive line)

Equipment manager
Erik Kennedy
Assistant equipment managers
Howard Baus
Brad Melland
Video director
Thom Fermstad
Assistant video director
Craig Givens

SCHEDULE

Sept. 6—	at Philadelphia	1:01
Sept. 13—	ARIZONA	1:15
Sept. 20—	WASHINGTON	1:05
Sept. 27—	at Pittsburgh	4:05
Oct. 4—	at Kansas City	7:20
Oct. 11—	DENVER	1:15
Oct. 18—	Open date	
Oct. 25—	at San Diego	1:15
Nov. 1—	OAKLAND	5:20
Nov. 8—	KANSAS CITY	1:15
Nov. 15—	at Oakland	1:05
Nov. 22—	at Dallas	12:01
Nov. 29—	TENNESSEE	1:05
Dec. 6—	at N.Y. Jets	1:01
Dec. 13—	SAN DIEGO	1:05
Dec. 20—	INDIANAPOLIS	1:05
Dec. 27—	at Denver	2:15

All times are for home team.
All games Sunday unless noted.

DRAFT CHOICES

Anthony Simmons, LB, Clemson (first round/15th pick overall).
Todd Weiner, T, Kansas State (2/47).
Ahman Green, RB, Nebraska (3/76).
DeShone Myles, LB, Nevada (4/108).
Carl Hansen, DE, Stanford (6/162).
Bobby Shaw, WR, California (6/169).
Jason McEndoo, C, Washington State (7/197).

1998 SEASON

TRAINING CAMP ROSTER

No.	QUARTERBACKS	Ht./Wt.	Born	NFL Exp.	College	How acq.	'97 Games GP/GS
16	Arellanes, Jim	6-3/217	1-30-74	1	Fresno State	FA/97	0/0
17	Friesz, John	6-4/223	5-19-67	9	Idaho	FA/95	2/1
7	Kitna, Jon	6-2/217	9-21-72	2	Central Washington	FA/96	3/1
1	Moon, Warren	6-3/213	11-18-56	15	Washington	FA/97	15/14
	RUNNING BACKS						
31	Broussard, Steve	5-7/201	2-22-67	9	Washington State	FA/95	16/1
34	Brown, Reggie (FB)	6-0/244	6-26-73	3	Fresno State	D3b/96	11/0
35	Gray, Oscar (FB)	6-1/255	8-7-72	2	Arkansas	FA/96	0/0
30	Green, Ahman	6-0/213	2-16-77	R	Nebraska	D3/98	—
38	Strong, Mack (FB)	6-0/235	9-11-71	5	Georgia	FA/93	16/10
32	Watters, Ricky	6-1/217	4-7-69	8	Notre Dame	FA/98	*16/16
	RECEIVERS						
89	Blades, Brian	5-11/190	7-24-65	11	Miami (Fla.)	D2/88	11/3
87	Crumpler, Carlester (TE)	6-6/260	9-5-71	5	East Carolina	D7/94	15/12
83	Davis, Tyree	5-9/175	9-23-70	3	Central Arkansas	FA/97	13/1
86	Fauria, Christian (TE)	6-4/245	9-22-71	4	Colorado	D2/95	16/3
84	Galloway, Joey	5-11/188	11-20-71	4	Ohio State	D1/95	15/15
81	Harris, Ronnie	5-11/179	6-4-70	5	Oregon	FA/94	13/0
88	May, Deems (TE)	6-4/263	3-6-69	7	North Carolina	FA/97	16/0
82	McKnight, James	6-1/198	6-17-72	4	Liberty (Va.)	FA/94	12/5
49	Mili, Itula (TE)	6-4/265	4-20-73	2	Brigham Young	D6/97	0/0
85	Pritchard, Mike	5-10/193	10-26-69	8	Colorado	FA/96	16/15
18	Shaw, Bobby	6-0/186	4-23-75	R	California	D6b/98	—
19	Wilson, Robert	5-11/176	6-23-74	1	Florida A&M	FA/97	0/0
	OFFENSIVE LINEMEN						
75	Ballard, Howard (T)	6-6/325	11-3-63	11	Alabama A&M	FA/94	10/10
63	Beede, Frank (G)	6-4/296	5-1-73	3	Panhandle State (Okla.)	FA/96	16/6
60	Bloedorn, Greg (G)	6-6/278	11-15-72	2	Cornell	FA/96	3/0
53	Glover, Kevin (C)	6-2/282	6-17-63	14	Maryland	FA/98	*16/16
62	Gray, Chris (G)	6-4/305	6-19-70	6	Auburn	FA/98	*8/2
68	Greene, Andrew (G)	6-3/304	9-24-69	2	Indiana	FA/97	0/0
68	Habib, Brian (G)	6-7/299	12-2-64	10	Washington	FA/98	*14/14
71	Jones, Walter (T)	6-5/300	1-19-74	2	Florida State	D1b/97	12/12
66	Kendall, Pete (G)	6-5/292	7-9-73	3	Boston College	D1/96	16/16
52	McEndoo, Jason (G)	6-5/315	2-25-75	R	Washington State	D7/98	—
74	Weiner, Todd (T)	6-4/300	9-16-75	R	Kansas State	D2/98	—
69	Williams, Grant (T)	6-7/323	5-10-74	3	Louisiana Tech	FA/96	16/8
65	Williams, Tashe (T)	6-4/300	9-23-72	1	Northern Colorado	FA/97	0/0
	DEFENSIVE LINEMEN						
98	Adams, Sam (T)	6-3/300	6-13-73	5	Texas A&M	D1/94	16/16
93	Daniels, Phillip (E)	6-5/263	3-4-73	3	Georgia	D4a/96	13/10
91	Hansen, Carl (E)	6-5/282	1-25-76	R	Stanford	D6a/98	—
96	Kennedy, Cortez (T)	6-3/306	8-23-68	9	Miami (Fla.)	D1/90	8/8
99	LaBounty, Matt (E)	6-4/275	1-3-69	6	Oregon	TR/96	15/6
76	Parker, Riddick (T)	6-3/274	11-20-72	2	North Carolina	FA/96	11/0
97	Saleaumua, Dan (T)	6-0/315	11-25-64	12	Arizona State	FA/97	16/8
70	Sinclair, Michael (E)	6-4/267	1-31-68	8	Eastern New Mexico	D6/91	16/16
	LINEBACKERS						
54	Barber, Michael	6-1/246	11-9-71	4	Auburn	FA/95	8/2
94	Brown, Chad	6-2/240	7-12-70	6	Colorado	FA/97	15/15
59	Cain, Joe	6-1/242	6-11-65	10	Oregon Tech	FA/97	12/0
54	Hardy, Darryl	6-2/230	11-22-68	3	Tennessee	WV/97	12/0
57	Kyle, Jason	6-3/242	5-12-72	4	Arizona State	D4b/95	0/0
56	Logan, James	6-2/225	12-6-72	4	Memphis	WV/95	14/1
50	Myles, DeShone	6-2/235	10-31-74	R	Nevada	D4/98	—
51	Simmons, Anthony	6-0/230	6-20-76	R	Clemson	D1/98	—
55	Smith, Darrin	6-1/230	4-15-70	6	Miami, Fla	FA/98	*7/7
95	Wells, Dean	6-3/248	7-20-70	6	Kentucky	D4/93	16/16
	DEFENSIVE BACKS						
20	Bellamy, Jay (S)	5-11/199	7-8-72	5	Rutgers	FA/94	16/7
36	Blades, Bennie (S)	6-1/221	9-3-66	11	Miami (Fla.)	FA/97	10/9
28	Burton, James (CB)	5-9/184	4-27-71	5	Fresno State	FA/98	*5/1
25	Collins, Mark (S)	5-10/196	1-16-64	13	Cal State Fullerton	FA/98	*1/0
21	Cunningham, T.J. (S)	6-0/197	10-24-72	2	Colorado	D6b/96	0/0

No.	DEFENSIVE BACKS	Ht./Wt.	Born	NFL Exp.	College	How acq.	'97 Games GP/GS
39	Jones, Carlos (CB)	5-10/180	8-31-73	1	Miami (Fla.)	FA/98	0/0
21	Rusk, Reggie (CB)	5-10/190	10-19-72	2	Kentucky	FA/97	2/0
24	Springs, Shawn (CB)	6-0/195	3-11-75	2	Ohio State	D1a/97	10/10
37	Stokes, Eric (S)	5-11/201	12-18-73	2	Nebraska	D5/97	7/0
22	Thomas, Fred (CB)	5-9/172	9-11-73	3	Tennessee-Martin	D2/96	16/3
33	Williams, Darryl (S)	6-0/202	1-8-70	7	Miami (Fla.)	FA/96	16/16
27	Williams, Willie (CB)	5-9/180	12-26-70	6	Western Carolina	FA/97	16/16
	SPECIALISTS						
10	Feagles, Jeff (P)	6-1/207	3-7-66	11	Miami (Fla.)	FA/98	*16/0
2	Peterson, Todd (K)	5-10/171	2-4-70	4	Georgia	FA/95	16/0

*Burton played 5 games with Bears in '97; Collins played 1 game with Packers; Feagles played 16 games with Cardinals; Glover played 16 games with Lions; C. Gray played 8 games with Bears; Habib played 14 games with Broncos; Smith played 7 games with Eagles; Watters played 16 games with Eagles.

Abbreviations: D1—draft pick, first round; SupD2—supplemental draft pick, second round; WV—claimed on waivers; TR—obtained in trade; PlanB—Plan B free-agent acquisition; FA—free-agent acquisition (other than Plan B); ED—expansion draft pick.

MISCELLANEOUS TEAM DATA

Stadium (capacity, surface):
Kingdome (66,400, artificial)
Business address:
11220 N.E. 53rd Street
Kirkland, WA 98033
Business phone:
425-827-9777
Ticket information:
206-682-2800
Team colors:
Blue, green and silver
Flagship radio station:
KIRO, 710 AM
Training site:
Eastern Washington University
Cheney, Wash.
206-827-9777

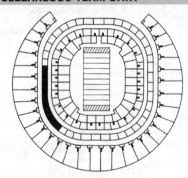

TSN REPORT CARD

Coaching staff	C	Dennis Erickson is not an average coach, but his record in three seasons with the Seahawks is an unimpressive 23-25. Erickson lost five assistants to other teams in the offseason, including three who had the bulk of NFL experience on his staff — Howard Mudd, Mike Murphy and Clarence Shelmon.
Offensive backfield	B +	The Seahawks are hooking their hopes of reaching the playoffs for the first time since 1988 to a 41-year-old quarterback (Warren Moon) and a 29-year-old running back (Ricky Watters). In addition to age, these two have one other thing in common: Production.
Offensive line	C +	The Seahawks are shuffling their starting unit for the 10th straight season. But this time, the moves are upgrades as C Kevin Glover and RG Brian Habib slide in between LT Walter Jones, LG Pete Kendall and RT Howard Ballard. Two questions: How long will it take them to mesh? And, how long will Ballard's right knee hold up?
Receivers	B	Joey Galloway is developing the overall game to complement his speed, but the best thing that has happened to him is the emergence of James McKnight and the rebirth of Mike Pritchard. Now if Brian Blades' battered body can just make it through an entire season.
Defensive line	B	RT Cortez Kennedy and LE Michael Sinclair have been to the Pro Bowl, and LT Sam Adams is close to joining them. But the real keys will be how well RE Phillip Daniels continues to develop, how effectively Dan Saleaumua performs in the three-tackle rotation and, of course, avoiding injuries.
Linebackers	B	Last year, this unit lacked speed and depth. Enter Darrin Smith in free agency and Anthony Simmons and DeShone Myles in the draft. Team them with Chad Brown and Dean Wells and the Seahawks suddenly have the kind of speed Erickson needs to unleash his defensive philosophy.
Secondary	B -	The whole wasn't as good as the parts last season. FS Darryl Williams was voted to his first Pro Bowl, and CBs Willie Williams and Shawn Springs are athletic, fast and can cover. But the Seahawks need either Jay Bellamy or Mark Collins to step in, and step up, at strong safety, and much better play from their third and fourth CBs.
Special teams	C	Only average for now, but a drastic upgrade from last year's F-minus fiasco. There have been changes: rookie Ahman Green joining Steve Broussard on kickoff returns; P Jeff Feagles stepping in for Rick Tuten; and going back to Joey Galloway or perhaps Shawn Springs on punt returns after the Seahawks averaged a league-low 6.7 yards last season. But the most important move was the hiring of Pete Rodriguez to coach these units and the emphasis he is putting on improvement.

TAMPA BAY BUCCANEERS
NFC CENTRAL DIVISION

1997 REVIEW

RESULTS

Aug. 31—SAN FRANCISCO	W	13-6
Sept. 7—at Detroit	W	24-17
Sept.14—at Minnesota	W	28-14
Sept.21—MIAMI	W	31-21
Sept.28—ARIZONA	W	19-18
Oct. 5—at Green Bay	L	16-21
Oct. 12—DETROIT	L	9-27
Oct. 19—Open date		
Oct. 26—MINNESOTA	L	6-10
Nov. 2—at Indianapolis	W	31-28
Nov. 9—at Atlanta	W	31-10
Nov. 16—NEW ENGLAND	W	27-7
Nov. 23—at Chicago	L	7-13
Nov. 30—at N.Y. Giants	W	20-8
Dec. 7—GREEN BAY	L	6-17
Dec. 14—at N.Y. Jets	L	0-31
Dec. 21—CHICAGO	W	31-15
Dec. 28—DETROIT*	W	20-10
Jan. 4—at Green Bay†	L	7-21

*NFC wild-card game.
†NFC divisional playoff game.

RECORDS/RANKINGS

1997 regular-season record: 10-6 (2nd in NFC Central); 3-5 in division; 7-5 in conference; 5-3 at home; 5-3 on road.
Team record last five years: 34-46 (.425, ranks 19th in league in that span).
1997 team rankings:

	No.	NFC	NFL
Total offense	*273.5	14	29
Rushing offense	*120.9	6	11
Passing offense	*152.6	15	30
Scoring offense	299	T10	T23
Total defense	*289.1	3	3
Rushing defense	*101.1	3	6
Passing defense	*188	8	10
Scoring defense	263	1	2
Takeaways	26	T10	T19
Giveaways	23	T4	T11
Turnover differential	3	6	T12
Sacks	44	T5	T10
Sacks allowed	32	T2	T5

*Yards per game.

TEAM LEADERS

Scoring (kicking): Michael Husted, 71 pts. (32/35 PATs, 13/17 FGs).
Scoring (touchdowns): Mike Alstott, 60 pts. (7 rushing, 3 receiving).
Passing: Trent Dilfer, 2,555 yds. (386 att., 217 comp., 56.2%, 21 TDs, 11 int.).
Rushing: Warrick Dunn, 978 yds. (224 att., 4.4 avg., 4 TDs).
Receptions: Karl Williams, 33 (486 yds., 14.7 avg., 4 TDs).
Interceptions: Donnie Abraham, 5 (16 yds., 0 TDs).
Sacks: Warren Sapp, 10.5.
Punting: Sean Landeta, 42.1 avg. (54 punts, 2,274 yds., 1 blocked).
Punt returns: Karl Williams, 13.0 avg. (46 att., 597 yds., 1 TD).
Kickoff returns: Reidel Anthony, 23.7 avg. (25 att., 592 yds., 0 TDs).

1998 SEASON

CLUB DIRECTORY

Owner
Malcolm Glazer
Executive vice president
Bryan Glazer
Executive vice president
Joel Glazer
Executive vice president
Ed Glazer
General manager
Richard McKay
V.p., marketing and communications
Rick McNerney
Vice president, sales administration
Roni Costello
Director of communications
Reggie Roberts
Communications managers
Scott Smith
Nelson Luis
Communications assistant
Jenny Egger
Director of marketing
George Woods
Director of special events
Meredith Chimerine
Director/player personnel
Jerry Angelo
Director/college scouting
Tim Ruskell
College personnel scouts
Mike Ackerley
Dave Boller
Dennis Hickey
Ruston Webster
Mike Yowarsky
Pro personnel assistants
Mark Dominik
Lloyd Richards
Coordinator of football administration
John Idzik

Head coach
Tony Dungy

Assistant coaches
Mark Asanovich (strength & conditioning)
Clyde Christensen (tight ends)
Herman Edwards (assistant head coach/defensive backs)
Chris Foerster (offensive line)
Monte Kiffin (def. coordinator)
Aaron Komarek (asst. strength & conditioning)
Joe Marciano (special teams)
Rod Marinelli (defensive line)
Tony Nathan (running backs)
Kevin O'Dea (defensive assistant)
Mike Shula (off. coordinator)
Lovie Smith (linebackers)
Ricky Thomas (offensive asst.)
Charlie Williams (wide receivers)

Trainer
Todd Toriscelli
Assistant trainer
Mark Shermansky
Team physician
Joseph Diaco
Equipment manager
Darin Kerns
Video director
Dave Levy
Assistant video director
Pat Brazil

SCHEDULE

Sept. 6—	at Minnesota	12:01
Sept. 13—	at Green Bay	12:01
Sept. 20—	CHICAGO	4:05
Sept. 28—	at Detroit (Mon.)	8:20
Oct. 4—	N.Y. GIANTS	4:15
Oct. 11—	Open date	
Oct. 18—	CAROLINA	1:01
Oct. 25—	at New Orleans	12:01
Nov. 1—	MINNESOTA	1:01
Nov. 8—	TENNESSEE	8:20
Nov. 15—	at Jacksonville	4:15
Nov. 22—	DETROIT	1:01
Nov. 29—	at Chicago	12:01
Dec. 7—	GREEN BAY (Mon.)	8:20
Dec. 13—	PITTSBURGH	1:01
Dec. 19—	at Washington (Sat.)	4:05
Dec. 27—	at Cincinnati	1:01

All times are for home team.
All games Sunday unless noted.

DRAFT CHOICES

Jacquez Green, WR, Florida (second round/34th pick overall).
Brian Kelly, DB, Southern California (2/45).
Jamie Duncan, LB, Vanderbilt (3/84).
Todd Washington, G, Virginia Tech (4/104).
James Cannida, DT, Nevada (6/175).
Shevin Smith, DB, Florida State (6/184).
Chance McCarty, DE, Texas Christian (7/212).

1998 SEASON *Tampa Bay Buccaneers*

No.	QUARTERBACKS	Ht./Wt.	Born	NFL Exp.	College	How acq.	'97 Games GP/GS
11	Brohm, Jeff	6-1/205	4-24-71	3	Louisville	FA/98	*5/0
12	Dilfer, Trent	6-4/234	3-13-72	5	Fresno State	D1/94	16/16
13	Milanovich, Scott	6-3/220	1-25-73	3	Maryland	FA/96	0/0
4	Walsh, Steve	6-3/215	12-1-66	10	Miami (Fla.)	FA/97	13/0

	RUNNING BACKS						
40	Alstott, Mike (FB)	6-1/248	12-21-73	3	Purdue	D2/96	15/15
46	Barber, Kantroy (FB)	6-1/243	10-4-73	2	West Virginia	FA/98	0/0
28	Dunn, Warrick	5-8/176	1-5-75	2	Florida State	D1/97	16/10
37	Ellison, Jerry	5-10/204	12-20-71	3	UT-Chattanooga	FA/94	16/0
44	Lee, Steve (FB)	6-0/265	4-16-74	1	Indiana	FA/97	0/0
41	Neal, Lorenzo (FB)	5-11/240	12-27-70	6	Fresno State	TR/98	*16/3

	RECEIVERS						
85	Anthony, Reidel	5-11/178	10-20-76	2	Florida	D1/97	16/12
49	Brady, Rickey (TE)	6-4/264	11-19-70	1	Oklahoma	FA/97	0/0
81	Carter, Nigea	6-1/196	9-1-74	1	Michigan State	D6b/97	0/0
88	Copeland, Horace	6-3/208	1-2-71	6	Miami (Fla.)	D4b/93	13/11
87	Davis, John (TE)	6-4/257	5-14-73	2	Emporia State	FA/97	8/2
80	Emanuel, Bert	5-10/180	10-28-70	5	Rice	FA/98	*16/16
	Green, Jacquez	5-9/172	1-15-76	R	Florida	D2a/98	—
82	Hape, Patrick (TE)	6-4/256	6-6-74	2	Alabama	D5/97	14/3
19	Hunter, Brice	6-0/219	4-21-74	1	Georgia	FA/96	3/0
48	Jordan, Andrew (TE)	6-4/254	6-21-72	5	Western Carolina	FA/97	2/0
89	Marshall, Marvin	5-10/162	6-21-72	2	South Carolina State	FA/95	0/0
83	Moore, Dave (TE)	6-2/242	11-11-69	6	Pittsburgh	FA/92	16/7
17	Simon, Geroy	6-0/183	9-11-75	1	Maryland	FA/97	0/0
84	Thomas, Robb	5-11/178	3-29-66	10	Oregon State	FA/96	16/1
86	Williams, Karl	5-10/174	4-10-71	3	Texas A&M-Kingsville	FA/96	16/8

	OFFENSIVE LINEMEN						
64	Diaz, Jorge (G)	6-4/308	11-15-73	3	Texas A&M-Kingsville	FA/96	16/16
65	Dogins, Kevin (C)	6-1/295	12-7-72	2	Texas A&M-Kingsville	FA/96	0/0
74	Gruber, Paul (T)	6-5/292	2-24-65	11	Wisconsin	D1/88	16/16
67	Mathews, Jason (T)	6-5/304	2-9-71	5	Texas A&M	FA/98	*16/0
61	Mayberry, Tony (C)	6-4/302	12-8-67	9	Wake Forest	D4/90	16/16
73	Middleton, Frank (G)	6-3/340	10-25-74	2	Arizona	D3a/97	15/2
62	Newnam, Brian (G)	6-3/296	2-11-74	2	Tulsa	FA/97	0/0
70	Odom, Jason (T)	6-5/307	3-31-74	3	Florida	D4a/96	16/16
69	Pierson, Pete (T)	6-5/295	2-4-71	3	Washington	D5/94	15/0
	Washington, Todd (G)	6-3/312	7-19-76	R	Virginia Tech	D4/98	—
58	Willis, Donald (G)	6-3/330	7-15-73	1	North Carolina A&T	FA/96	0/0
71	Wunsch, Jerry (T)	6-6/333	1-21-74	2	Wisconsin	D2/97	16/0

	DEFENSIVE LINEMEN						
72	Ahanotu, Chidi (E)	6-2/283	10-11-70	6	California	D6/93	16/15
	Cannida, James (T)	6-2/275	1-3-75	R	Nevada	D6a/98	—
77	Culpepper, Brad (T)	6-1/275	5-8-69	7	Florida	WV/94	16/16
96	DeGrate, Anthony (T)	6-1/333	5-24-74	1	Stephen F. Austin	D7/97	0/0
92	Ifeanyl, Israel (E)	6-3/266	11-21-70	2	Southern California	FA/98	0/0
97	Jackson, Tyoka (E)	6-2/266	11-22-71	3	Penn State	FA/95	12/0
78	Jones, Marcus (T)	6-6/286	8-15-73	3	North Carolina	D1b/96	7/1
90	Maniecki, Jason (T)	6-4/291	8-15-72	3	Wisconsin	D5/96	10/0
	McCarty, Chance (E)	6-3/248	8-29-75	R	Texas Christian	D7a/98	—
99	Sapp, Warren (T)	6-2/276	12-19-72	4	Miami (Fla.)	D1/95	15/15
91	Upshaw, Regan (E)	6-4/268	8-12-75	3	California	D1a/96	15/15

	LINEBACKERS						
52	Bellisari, Greg	6-0/236	6-21-75	2	Ohio State	FA/97	14/0
55	Brooks, Derrick	6-0/235	4-18-73	4	Florida State	D1b/95	16/16
	Duncan, Jamie	6-0/244	7-20-75	R	Vanderbilt	D3/98	—
50	Gooch, Jeff	5-11/224	10-31-74	3	Austin Peay State	FA/96	14/5
56	Nickerson, Hardy	6-2/230	9-1-65	12	California	FA/93	16/16
53	Quarles, Shelton	6-1/236	9-11-71	2	Vanderbilt	FA/97	16/0
51	Singleton, Alshermond	6-2/227	8-7-75	2	Temple	D4/97	12/0
94	White, Steve	6-2/265	10-25-73	3	Tennessee	FA/96	15/1

	DEFENSIVE BACKS						
21	Abraham, Donnie (CB)	5-10/190	10-8-73	3	East Tennessee State	D3/96	16/16
20	Barber, Ronde (CB)	5-10/186	4-7-75	2	Virginia	D3b/97	1/0

No.	DEFENSIVE BACKS	Ht./Wt.	Born	NFL Exp.	College	How acq.	'97 Games GP/GS
23	Bouie, Tony (S)	5-10/193	8-7-72	3	Arizona	FA/95	16/1
30	Harris, Al (CB)	6-0/185	12-7-74	1	Texas A&M-Kingsville	D6/97	0/0
	Kelly, Brian (CB)	5-11/195	1-14-76	R	Southern California	D2/98	—
45	Legette, Tyrone (CB)	5-9/179	2-15-70	7	Nebraska	FA/96	16/1
47	Lynch, John (S)	6-2/214	9-25-71	6	Stanford	D3b/93	16/16
22	Mincy, Charles (S)	5-11/195	12-16-69	8	Washington	FA/96	16/9
27	Parker, Anthony (CB)	5-10/181	2-11-66	9	Arizona State	FA/97	15/14
24	Robinson, Damien (S)	6-2/210	12-22-73	2	Iowa	FA/97	0/0
	Smith, Shevin (S)	5-11/196	6-17-75	R	Florida State	D6b/98	—
33	Vance, Eric (S)	6-2/215	7-14-75	1	Vanderbilt	FA/98	0/0
31	Young, Floyd (CB)	6-0/170	11-23-75	2	Texas A&M-Kingsville	FA/97	12/1
	SPECIALISTS						
6	Barnhardt, Tommy (P)	6-2/228	6-11-63	12	North Carolina	FA/96	6/0
5	Husted, Michael (K)	6-0/190	6-16-70	6	Virginia	FA/93	16/0

*Brohm played 5 games with 49ers in '97; Emanuel played 16 games with Falcons; Mathews played 16 games with Colts; Neal played 16 games with Jets.

Abbreviations: D1—draft pick, first round; SupD2—supplemental draft pick, second round; WV—claimed on waivers; TR—obtained in trade; PlanB—Plan B free-agent acquisition; FA—free-agent acquisition (other than Plan B); ED—expansion draft pick.

MISCELLANEOUS TEAM DATA

Stadium (capacity, surface):
Stadium to be named (65,394, grass)
Business address:
One Buccaneer Place
Tampa, FL 33607
Business phone:
813-870-2700
Ticket information:
813-879-2827
Team colors:
Buccaneer red, pewter, black and orange
Flagship radio station:
WQYK, 99.5 FM
Training site:
University of Tampa
Tampa, Fla.
813-253-6215

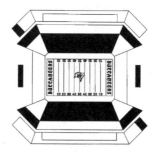

TSN REPORT CARD

Coaching staff — **A -** — Tony Dungy's steady influence has been the key to the team's rise and will be a big factor in determining the next step. The defense, under coordinator Monte Kiffin, already has arrived. The wildcard is the offense. With all the new weapons, coordinator Mike Shula might finally open things up.

Offensive backfield — **B** — TB Warrick Dunn and FB Mike Alstott are the league's best 1-2 punch, and they're young and healthy. Dunn is the one player on this team who can change the outcome of a game by himself, but the Bucs can't afford to ask him to carry too much of the load. QB Trent Dilfer is close to being very good, and now he's got the weapons.

Receivers — **B -** — This group still has a lot to prove. But the arrival of WRs Bert Emanuel and Jacquez Green and the probable improvement of WR Reidel Anthony leaves a surplus of talent. It's doubtful Emanuel will approach the 70+-catch seasons he had in Atlanta because the offense is more conservative, but 45-50 catches would be more than acceptable.

Offensive line — **C +** — C Tony Mayberry and T Paul Gruber are solid, but they're aging. G Jorge Diaz and T Jason Odom are decent, but they'll never be spectacular. That puts the burden on G Frank Middleton as he moves into a starting role. He has the most potential of all the team's young linemen, but he's going to have to develop it quickly.

Defensive line — **A** — DT Warren Sapp has the rare ability to control a game from the defensive line. He is at his best in big games and brings out the most in those around him. If DE Regan Upshaw continues to develop this could become the most ferocious pass rushing unit in the league.

Linebackers — **A** — Derrick Brooks may be the best all-around athlete on the roster; he makes plays all over the field. Hardy Nickerson has been consistently excellent in the middle for years. Alshermond Singleton, Shelton Quarles and Jeff Gooch are competing for the other starting job, but a surplus of talented bodies is something this franchise hasn't seen in years.

Secondary — **C +** — CB Donnie Abraham is one of the league's best-kept secrets. He can take a receiver completely out of a game. If Anthony Parker, Ronde Barber or Brian Kelly plays half as well as Abraham, pass coverage could become a strength. S John Lynch is strong against the run and the pass and Charles Mincy is a solid veteran.

Special teams — **B -** — On paper, this group could be outstanding. P Tommy Barnhardt and K Michael Husted have the potential to be among the league's best. If Green can juice up the return game, the offense will have a lot of easy starting points. The coverage units were inconsistent last season, but improvement in that area will be a training camp focus.

TENNESSEE OILERS
AFC CENTRAL DIVISION

1997 REVIEW

RESULTS

Aug. 31—OAKLAND (OT)	W	24-21
Sept. 7—at Miami (OT)	L	13-16
Sept. 14—Open date		
Sept. 21—BALTIMORE	L	10-36
Sept. 28—at Pittsburgh	L	24-37
Oct. 5—at Seattle	L	13-16
Oct. 12—CINCINNATI	W	30-7
Oct. 19—WASHINGTON	W	28-14
Oct. 26—at Arizona	W	41-14
Nov. 2—JACKSONVILLE	L	24-30
Nov. 9—N.Y. GIANTS	W	10-6
Nov. 16—at Jacksonville	L	9-17
Nov. 23—BUFFALO	W	31-14
Nov. 27—at Dallas	W	27-14
Dec. 4—at Cincinnati	L	14-41
Dec. 14—at Baltimore	L	19-21
Dec. 21—PITTSBURGH	W	16-6

RECORDS/RANKINGS

1997 regular-season record: 8-8 (3rd in AFC Central); 2-6 in division; 4-8 in conference; 6-2 at home; 2-6 on road.
Team record last five years: 37-43 (.463), ranks 16th in league in that span.

1997 team rankings:	No.	AFC	NFL
Total offense	*307.4	11	18
Rushing offense	*150.9	2	3
Passing offense	*156.6	15	29
Scoring offense	333	10	14
Total defense	*326.9	9	22
Rushing defense	*98.3	2	4
Passing defense	*228.6	13	27
Scoring defense	310	6	12
Takeaways	31	T4	T8
Giveaways	26	9	15
Turnover differential	5	6	T9
Sacks	35	T10	T24
Sacks allowed	32	T4	T5

*Yards per game.

TEAM LEADERS

Scoring (kicking): Al Del Greco, 113 pts. (32/32 PATs, 27/35 FGs).
Scoring (touchdowns): Steve McNair, 48 pts. (8 rushing).
Passing: Steve McNair, 2,665 yds. (415 att., 216 comp., 52.0%, 14 TDs, 13 int.).
Rushing: Eddie George, 1,399 yds. (357 att., 3.9 avg., 6 TDs).
Receptions: Frank Wycheck, 63 (748 yds., 11.9 avg., 4 TDs).
Interceptions: Marcus Robertson, 5 (127 yds., 0 TDs); Darryll Lewis, 5 (115 yds., 1 TD).
Sacks: Gary Walker, 7.0; Kenny Holmes, 7.0.
Punting: Reggie Roby, 41.8 avg. (73 punts, 3,049 yds., 0 blocked).
Punt returns: Mel Gray, 8.5 avg. (17 att., 144 yds., 0 TDs).
Kickoff returns: Derrick Mason, 21.2 avg. (26 att., 551 yds., 0 TDs).

1998 SEASON

CLUB DIRECTORY

Owner/president
K.S. "Bud" Adams Jr.
Executive vice president/general manager
Floyd Reese
Executive vice president/administration
Mike McClure
Executive assistant to president
Thomas S. Smith
V.P./player personnel and scouting
Mike Holovak
Vice president/legal counsel
Steve Underwood
Vice president/finance
Jackie Curley
Exec. v.p./broadcasting and marketing
Don MacLachlan
Director of player personnel
Rich Snead
Director/sales operations
Stuart Spears
Dir. of media relations and services
Tony Wyllie
Vice president for community affairs
Bob Hyde
Director/ticket operations
Marty Collins
Director/security
Steve Berk
Director/player programs
Al Smith
Asst. dir. of media relations and services
Robbie Bohren
Head trainer
Brad Brown
Scouts
Ray Biggs
C.O. Brocato
Dub Fesperman
Director of college scouting
Glenn Cumbee

Head coach
Jeff Fisher

Assistant coaches
Les Steckel (offensive coordinator/quarterbacks)
Gregg Williams (defensive coordinator)
Bart Andrus (offensive assistant/quality control)
Greg Brown (defensive backs)
O'Neill Gilbert (linebackers)
Jerry Gray (defensive assistant/quality control)
George Henshaw (offensive line/tight ends)
Alan Lowry (wide receivers)
Mike Munchak (offensive line)
Rex Norris (defensive line)
Russ Purnell (special teams)
Sherman Smith (running backs)
Steve Watterson (strength & rehabilitation)

Equipment manager
Paul Noska
Videotape coordinator
Ken Sparacino
Team physicians
Elrod Burton
Craig Rutlend
John Williams

SCHEDULE

Sept. 6—	at Cincinnati	1:01
Sept. 13—	SAN DIEGO	12:01
Sept. 20—	at New England	1:01
Sept. 27—	JACKSONVILLE	12:01
Oct. 4—	Open date	
Oct. 11—	at Baltimore	1:01
Oct. 18—	CINCINNATI	12:01
Oct. 25—	CHICAGO	3:05
Nov. 1—	at Pittsburgh	1:01
Nov. 8—	at Tampa Bay	8:20
Nov. 15—	PITTSBURGH	12:01
Nov. 22—	N.Y. JETS	3:15
Nov. 29—	at Seattle	1:05
Dec. 6—	BALTIMORE	3:15
Dec. 13—	at Jacksonville	1:01
Dec. 20—	at Green Bay	12:01
Dec. 26—	MINNESOTA (Sat.)	11:35

All times are for home team.
All games Sunday unless noted.

DRAFT CHOICES

Kevin Dyson, WR, Utah (first round/16th pick overall).
Samari Rolle, DB, Florida State (2/46).
Dainon Sidney, DB, Alabama-Birmingham (3/77).
Joe Salave'a, DT, Arizona (4/107).
Benji Olson, G, Washington (5/139).
Lee Wiggins, DB, South Carolina (6/168).
Jimmy Sprotte, LB, Arizona (7/205).
Kevin Long, C, Florida State (7/229).

1998 SEASON *Tennessee Oilers*

No.	QUARTERBACKS	Ht./Wt.	Born	NFL Exp.	College	How acq.	'97 Games GP/GS
17	Krieg, Dave	6-1/202	10-20-58	19	Milton College (Wis.)	FA/97	8/0
9	McNair, Steve	6-2/229	2-14-73	4	Alcorn State	D1/95	16/16
16	Ritchey, James	6-2/210	7-10-73	2	Stephen F. Austin	FA/96	1/0
	RUNNING BACKS						
22	Archie, Mike	5-8/211	10-14-72	3	Penn State	D7/96	5/0
27	George, Eddie	6-3/238	9-24-73	3	Ohio State	D1/96	16/16
35	George, Spencer	5-9/202	10-28-73	1	Rice	FA/97	5/0
20	Thomas, Rodney	5-10/213	3-30-73	4	Texas A&M	D3b/95	16/1
23	Whittle, Ricky	5-9/200	12-21-71	2	Oregon	FA/98	0/0
	RECEIVERS						
1	Byrd, Isaac	6-0/173	11-11-74	2	Kansas	FA/97	2/0
84	Davis, Willie	6-0/182	10-10-67	7	Central Arkansas	FA/96	16/15
	Dyson, Kevin	5-11/199	6-23-75	R	Utah	D1/98	—
81	Harris, Jackie (TE)	6-4/254	1-4-68	9	Northeast Louisiana	FA/98	*12/11
86	Kent, Joey	6-1/186	4-23-74	2	Tennessee	D2/97	12/0
85	Mason, Derrick	5-10/190	1-17-74	2	Michigan State	D4a/97	16/2
87	McKeehan, James (TE)	6-3/251	8-9-73	3	Texas A&M	FA/97	10/0
18	Mustafa, Isaiah	6-2/204	2-11-74	1	Arizona State	FA/97	0/0
80	Roan, Michael (TE)	6-3/242	8-29-72	4	Wisconsin	D4/95	14/13
85	Russell, Derek	6-0/195	6-22-69	8	Arkansas	FA/95	11/2
81	Sanders, Chris	6-1/180	5-8-72	4	Ohio State	D3a/95	15/14
82	Thigpen, Yancey	6-1/202	8-15-69	7	Winston-Salem (N.C.) State	FA/98	*16/15
89	Wycheck, Frank (TE)	6-3/248	10-14-71	6	Maryland	WV/95	16/16
	OFFENSIVE LINEMEN						
71	Hayes, Melvin (T)	6-6/325	4-28-73	4	Mississippi State	D4a/95	0/0
72	Hopkins, Brad (T)	6-3/295	9-5-70	6	Illinois	D1/93	16/16
66	Layman, Jason (T)	6-5/306	7-29-73	3	Tennessee	D2b/96	13/0
	Long, Kevin (C)	6-5/296	5-2-75	R	Florida State	D7b/98	—
74	Matthews, Bruce (G)	6-5/309	8-8-61	16	Southern California	D1/83	16/16
64	Norgard, Erik (G)	6-1/289	11-4-65	10	Colorado	FA/90	15/0
	Olson, Benji (G)	6-4/313	6-5-75	R	Washington	D5/98	—
65	Pilgrim, Evan (G)	6-4/304	8-14-72	3	Brigham Young	FA/98	*13/6
69	Runyan, Jon (T)	6-7/316	11-27-73	3	Michigan	D4b/96	16/16
73	Sanderson, Scott (T)	6-6/278	7-25-74	2	Washington State	D3b/97	10/0
53	Stepnoski, Mark (C)	6-2/263	1-20-67	10	Pittsburgh	FA/95	16/16
76	Washington, T.J.	6-4/335	7-1-74	1	Virginia Tech	FA/97	0/0
	DEFENSIVE LINEMEN						
94	Burton, Kendrick (E)	6-5/288	9-7-73	2	Alabama	D4a/96	0/0
78	Cook, Anthony	6-3/290	5-30-72	4	South Carolina State	D2/95	16/16
92	England, Eric (E)	6-3/273	4-25-71	4	Texas A&M	FA/97	0/0
91	Evans, Josh	6-0/275	9-6-72	4	Alabama-Birmingham	FA/95	15/0
92	Ford, Henry (E)	6-3/292	10-30-71	5	Arkansas	D1/94	16/16
93	Halapin, Mike (T)	6-4/283	7-1-73	3	Pittsburgh	FA/96	3/1
99	Holmes, Kenny (E)	6-4/270	10-24-73	2	Miami (Fla.)	D1/97	16/5
98	Lyons, Pratt (E)	6-5/281	9-17-74	2	Troy (Ala.) State	D4b/97	16/0
97	Mix, Bryant (E)	6-3/293	7-28-72	3	Alcorn State	D2a/96	1/0
90	Roberson, James (E)	6-3/275	5-3-71	3	Florida State	FA/96	15/11
	Salave'a, Joe (T)	6-4/285	3-23-75	R	Arizona	D4/98	—
96	Walker, Gary (E)	6-2/288	2-28-73	4	Auburn	D5/95	15/15
	LINEBACKERS						
54	Adams, Louis	6-1/231	7-8-74	1	Oklahoma State	FA/97	0/0
58	Bowden, Joe	5-11/224	2-25-70	7	Oklahoma	D5a/92	16/16
51	Hall, Lemanski	6-0/230	11-24-70	4	Alabama	D7/94	16/2
57	Jones, Lenoy	6-1/232	9-25-74	3	Texas Christian	FA/96	16/0
50	Killens, Terry	6-1/227	3-24-74	3	Penn State	D3/96	16/0
56	Marts, Lonnie	6-2/241	11-10-68	9	Tulane	FA/97	14/14
	Sprotte, Jimmy	6-3/245	10-2-74	R	Arizona	D7a/98	—
59	Stallings, Dennis	6-0/234	5-25-74	2	Illinois	D6/97	13/0
52	Wortham, Barron	5-11/240	11-1-69	5	Texas-El Paso	D6b/94	16/16
	DEFENSIVE BACKS						
23	Bishop, Blaine (S)	5-9/197	7-24-70	6	Ball State	D8/93	14/14
33	Dorsett, Anthony (CB)	5-11/203	9-14-73	3	Pittsburgh	D6/96	16/0
24	Jackson, Steve (CB)	5-8/188	4-8-69	8	Purdue	D3a/91	12/6
29	Lewis, Darryll (CB)	5-9/186	12-16-68	8	Arizona	D2b/91	16/14
28	McCullough, George	5-10/187	2-18-75	1	Baylor	D5/97	2/0

No.	DEFENSIVE BACKS	Ht./Wt.	Born	NFL Exp.	College	How acq.	'97 Games GP/GS
31	Robertson, Marcus (S)	5-11/202	10-2-69	8	Iowa State	D4b/91	14/14
	Rolle, Samari (CB)	5-11/173	8-10-76	R	Florida State	D2/98	—
	Sidney, Dainon (CB)	6-0/186	5-30-75	R	Alabama-Birmingham	D3/98	—
26	Stewart, Rayna (CB)	5-10/198	6-18-73	3	Northern Arizona	D5/96	16/5
25	Walker, Denard	6-1/192	8-9-73	2	Louisiana State	D3a/97	15/11
36	Wiggins, Lee (CB)	5-11/187	4-27-75	R	South Carolina	D6/98	—
42	Williams, Armon	6-0/215	8-13-73	2	Arizona	D7/97	6/0
	SPECIALISTS						
3	Del Greco, Al (K)	5-10/202	3-2-62	15	Auburn	FA/91	16/0
17	Hentrich, Craig (P)	6-3/200	5-18-71	5	Notre Dame	FA/98	*16/0

*Harris played 12 games with Buccaneers in '97; Hentrich played 16 games with Packers; Pilgrim played 13 games with Bears; Thigpen played 16 games with Steelers.

Abbreviations: D1—draft pick, first round; SupD2—supplemental draft pick, second round; WV—claimed on waivers; TR—obtained in trade; PlanB—Plan B free-agent acquisition; FA—free-agent acquisition (other than Plan B); ED—expansion draft pick.

MISCELLANEOUS TEAM DATA

Stadium (capacity, surface):
Vanderbilt Stadium
(41,600, artificial)

Business address:
Baptist Sports Park
7640 Highway 70 S.
Nashville, TN 37221

Business phone:
615-673-1500

Ticket information:
615-341-7600

Team colors:
Columbia blue, scarlet and white

Flagship radio station:
WGFX, 104.5 FM

Training site:
Tennessee State University
Nashville, Tenn.
615-673-1500

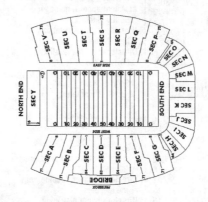

TSN REPORT CARD

Coaching staff	B	Any staff that can achieve an 8-8 mark under the circumstances this club had to play under last year deserves an above-average grade. But coaches were slow to adjust to a poor pass defense and still don't often seem to know what they want to do with Eddie George. Poor play in the division has to cease.
Offensive backfield	A -	The majority of this good grade is attributable to George, but Rodney Thomas is an underrated tailback commodity. Quarterback Steve McNair needs to improve if this team hopes to do anything. Everyone needs to be more productive in the red zone.
Receivers	C -	Frank Wycheck's 63 catches were a highlight. However, the corps had too many dropped passes and ran too many soft routes. The troops didn't beat man coverage when they had to. Some grumbled they didn't have enough chances, but performance wasn't there when they did. Lack of competition in training camp last year may have bred this situation, but that's certainly not a problem this time around with Yancey Thigpen and rookie Kevin Dyson in the mix.
Offensive line	B +	This group did a good job in the power game but allowed 32 sacks. Also, the unit was just 16-of-24 in converting third-and-1 situations, 10-of-17 in third-and-2. But this is a high quality group overall. The line didn't take stupid penalties and is still improving. Veterans Mark Stepnoski, Brad Hopkins and Bruce Matthews are the anchors.
Defensive line	C	There's room for improvement. These guys are stout against the run, but they need to improve their pass rush. Kenny Holmes needs to be more than a role player, while Gary Walker and Henry Ford must be forces in the middle every down instead of occasionally.
Linebackers	B	There are several agile and fast playmakers. However, turnovers were rare and more impact is needed from Lonnie Marts. Barron Wortham isn't a great athlete, but he makes plays. Joe Bowden continues to be a force, but all three looked lost at times last year after being forced to play more conservatively than they wanted.
Secondary	C -	The team finished 27th in pass defense and while injuries were a big part of that, poor play also was a factor. The team showed its desire to improve by using two of its top three picks (Samari Rolle and Dainon Sidney) in the draft for help. The safety tandem of Blaine Bishop and Marcus Robertson augments this unit.
Special teams	C -	The coverage units performed fairly well, but they seemed to surrender the big return at the worst times. Some problems could be averted if Craig Hentrich, who also punts, can boom kickoffs deeper. The return teams need lots of work.

WASHINGTON REDSKINS
NFC EASTERN DIVISION

1997 REVIEW
RESULTS

Aug. 31—at Carolina	W	24-10
Sept. 7—at Pittsburgh	L	13-14
Sept.14—ARIZONA (OT)	W	19-13
Sept.21—Open date		
Sept.28—JACKSONVILLE	W	24-12
Oct. 5—at Philadelphia	L	10-24
Oct. 13—DALLAS	W	21-16
Oct. 19—at Tennessee	L	14-28
Oct. 26—BALTIMORE	L	17-20
Nov. 2—at Chicago	W	31-8
Nov. 9—DETROIT	W	30-7
Nov. 16—at Dallas	L	14-17
Nov. 23—N.Y. GIANTS (OT)	T	7-7
Nov. 30—ST. LOUIS	L	20-23
Dec. 7—at Arizona	W	38-28
Dec. 13—at N.Y. Giants	L	10-30
Dec. 21—PHILADELPHIA	W	35-32

RECORDS/RANKINGS

1997 regular-season record: 8-7-1 (2nd in NFC East); 4-3-1 in division; 7-4-1 in conference; 5-2-1 at home; 3-5 on road.
Team record last five years: 30-49-1 (.381, ranks 23rd in league in that span).

1997 team rankings:	No.	NFC	NFL
Total offense	*312.4	6	16
Rushing offense	*100.9	12	21
Passing offense	*211.4	4	11
Scoring offense	327	5	15
Total defense	*314.4	10	16
Rushing defense	*138.3	15	28
Passing defense	*176.1	3	3
Scoring defense	289	5	T8
Takeaways	30	T6	T11
Giveaways	29	8	18
Turnover differential	1	7	T14
Sacks	37	13	T21
Sacks allowed	33	T4	T9

*Yards per game.

TEAM LEADERS

Scoring (kicking): Scott Blanton, 82 pts. (34/34 PATs, 16/24 FGs).
Scoring (touchdowns): Terry Allen, 30 pts. (4 rushing, 1 receiving); Leslie Shepherd, 30 pts. (5 receiving).
Passing: Gus Frerotte, 2,682 yds. (402 att., 204 comp., 50.7%, 17 TDs, 12 int.).
Rushing: Terry Allen, 724 yds. (210 att., 3.4 avg., 4 TDs).
Receptions: Leslie Shepherd, 29 (562 yds., 19.4 avg., 5 TDs).
Interceptions: Cris Dishman, 4 (47 yds., 1 TD); Stanley Richard, 4 (28 yds., 0 TDs).
Sacks: Ken Harvey, 9.5.
Punting: Matt Turk, 45.1 avg. (84 punts, 3,788 yds., 1 blocked).
Punt returns: Brian Mitchell, 11.6 avg. (38 att., 442 yds., 1 TD).
Kickoff returns: Brian Mitchell, 23.3 avg. (47 att., 1,094 yds., 1 TD).

1998 SEASON
CLUB DIRECTORY

Chairman of the board/CEO
John Kent Cooke Sr.
House counsel
Stuart Haney
Vice president of finance
Greg Dillon
Vice president of marketing
John Kent Cooke Jr.
General manager
Charley Casserly
Assistant general manager
Bobby Mitchell
Director of public relations
Mike McCall
Director of media relations
Chris Helein
Publications/Internet director
Scott McKeen
Director of marketing
John Wagner
Marketing assistant
Ryan Ford
Ticket manager
Jeff Ritter
Director of stadium operations
Jeff Klein
Director of player development
Joe Mendes
Director of administration
Barry Asimos
Director of college scouting
George Saimes
Scouting coordinator
Chuck Banker
Scouting administrator
Dave Sears
Scouts

Gene Bates	Larry Bryan
Scott Cohen	Mike Hagen
Mike MacCagnan	Miller McCalmon
Ron Nay	

Head coach
Norv Turner

Assistant coaches
Jason Arapoff (conditioning director)
Jeff Fitzgerald (def. assistant)
Russ Grimm (offensive line)
Tom Hayes (def. backs)
Bobby Jackson (running backs)
Earl Leggett (defensive line)
Dale Lindsey (linebackers)
Mike Martz (quarterbacks)
LeCharls McDaniel (special teams)
Mike Nolan (defensive coord.)
Michael Pope (tight ends)
Dan Riley (strength)
Terry Robiskie (wide receivers)
Ed Sidwell (offensive assistant)

Head trainer
Bubba Tyer
Assistant trainers
Al Bellamy
Kevin Bastin
Equipment manager
Jay Brunetti
Assistant equipment manager
Jeff Parsons
Director of video
Donnie Schoenmann
Asst. director of video
Hugh McPhillps

SCHEDULE

Sept. 6— at N.Y. Giants	1:01	
Sept. 14— SAN FRANCISCO (Mon.)	8:20	
Sept. 20— at Seattle	1:05	
Sept. 27— DENVER	1:01	
Oct. 4— DALLAS	1:01	
Oct. 11— at Philadelphia	1:01	
Oct. 18— at Minnesota	12:01	
Oct. 25— Open date		
Nov. 1— N.Y. GIANTS	1:01	
Nov. 8— at Arizona	2:05	
Nov. 15— PHILADELPHIA	1:01	
Nov. 22— ARIZONA	1:01	
Nov. 29— at Oakland	1:15	
Dec. 6— SAN DIEGO	1:01	
Dec. 13— at Carolina	1:01	
Dec. 19— TAMPA BAY (Sat.)	4:05	
Dec. 27— at Dallas	7:20	

All times are for home team.
All games Sunday unless noted.

DRAFT CHOICES

Stephen Alexander, TE, Oklahoma (second round/48th pick overall).
Skip Hicks, RB, UCLA (3/69).
Shawn Barber, LB, Richmond (4/113).
Mark Fischer, C, Purdue (5/140).
Pat Palmer, WR, Northwestern (La.) State (6/170).
David Terrell, DB, Texas-El Paso (7/191).
Antwaune Ponds, LB, Syracuse (7/206).

1998 SEASON *Washington Redskins*

No.	QUARTERBACKS	Ht./Wt.	Born	NFL Exp.	College	How acq.	'97 Games GP/GS
12	Frerotte, Gus	6-2/240	7-31-71	5	Tulsa	D7/94	13/13
10	Green, Trent	6-3/215	7-9-70	5	Indiana	FA/95	1/0
15	Hostetler, Jeff	6-3/215	4-22-61	15	West Virginia	FA/97	8/3
	RUNNING BACKS						
21	Allen, Terry	5-10/208	2-21-68	9	Clemson	FA/95	10/10
47	Bowie, Larry	6-0/249	3-21-73	3	Georgia	FA/96	15/13
48	Davis, Stephen	6-0/234	3-1-74	3	Auburn	D4/96	14/6
40	Hicks, Skip	6-0/230	10-13-74	R	UCLA	D3/98	
36	Maston, Le'Shai (FB)	6-1/242	10-7-70	6	Baylor	FA/98	0/0
30	Mitchell, Brian (FB)	5-10/221	8-18-68	9	Southwestern Louisiana	D5/90	16/1
	RECEIVERS						
80	Alexander, Stephen (TE)	6-4/246	11-7-75	R	Oklahoma	D2/98	—
84	Asher, Jamie (TE)	6-3/245	10-31-72	4	Louisville	D5a/95	16/13
83	Connell, Albert	6-0/179	5-13-74	2	Texas A&M	D4/97	5/1
85	Frisch, David (TE)	6-7/260	6-22-70	6	Colorado State	FA/97	2/0
88	Jenkins, James (TE)	6-2/249	8-17-67	8	Rutgers	FA/91	16/4
32	Lusk, Henry (TE)	6-2/250	5-8-72	3	Utah	FA/98	0/0
19	Malveaux, Felman	6-0/179	8-20-73	1	Michigan	FA/98	0/0
17	Matthews, Eric	5-11/185	3-22-72	1	Indiana	FA/98	0/0
14	Palmer, Pat	6-2/181	7-13-75	R	Northwestern State (La.)	D6/98	—
46	Sanders, Chris (TE)	6-3/241	4-22-73	1	Texas A&M	FA/98	1/0
86	Shepherd, Leslie	5-11/186	11-3-69	5	Temple	FA/94	11/9
89	Thomas, Chris	6-2/190	7-16-71	3	Cal Poly-SLO	FA/95	13/0
87	Thrash, James	6-0/200	4-28-75	2	Missouri Southern	FA/97	4/0
82	Westbrook, Michael	6-3/220	7-7-72	4	Colorado	D1/95	13/9
	OFFENSIVE LINEMEN						
74	Badger, Brad (G)	6-4/298	1-11-75	2	Stanford	D5d/97	12/2
61	Batiste, Michael (G)	6-3/325	12-24-70	2	Tulane	FA/97	0/0
75	Drake, Troy (T)	6-6/305	5-15-72	4	Indiana	FA/98	*9/2
60	Fischer, Mark (C)	6-3/293	7-29-74	R	Purdue	D5/98	—
77	Johnson, Tre' (T)	6-2/326	8-30-71	5	Temple	D2/94	11/10
79	Miller, Jeff (T)	6-4/303	11-23-72	3	Mississippi	FA/98	0/0
69	Milstead, Rod (G)	6-2/290	11-10-69	7	Delaware State	FA/98	*4/0
68	Patton, Joe (G)	6-5/306	1-5-72	4	Alabama A&M	D3b/94	16/16
67	Pourdanesh, Shar (T)	6-6/312	7-19-70	3	Nevada	FA/96	16/14
64	Powell, Ozell (T)	6-5/316	11-17-73	1	Alabama	FA/98	0/0
52	Raymer, Cory (C)	6-2/289	3-3-73	4	Wisconsin	D2/95	6/3
66	Turk, Dan (C)	6-4/290	6-25-62	13	Wisconsin	FA/97	16/0
55	Uhlenhake, Jeff (C)	6-3/291	1-28-66	9	Ohio State	FA/96	14/13
	DEFENSIVE LINEMEN						
93	Boutte, Marc (T)	6-4/307	7-26-69	7	Louisiana State	FA/94	16/13
78	Brown, Doug (T)	6-7/290	9-29-74	1	Simon Fraser	FA/98	0/0
92	Duff, Jamal (E)	6-7/285	3-11-72	4	San Diego State	FA/97	13/5
97	Kinney, Kelvin (E)	6-6/264	12-31-72	3	Virginia State	D6/96	4/1
99	Kuehl, Ryan (T)	6-4/289	1-18-72	2	Virginia	FA/97	12/5
90	Lang, Kenard (E)	6-4/277	1-31-75	2	Miami (Fla.)	D1/97	12/11
91	Owens, Rich (E)	6-6/281	5-22-72	4	Lehigh	D5b/95	16/15
94	Stubblefield, Dana (T)	6-2/315	11-14-70	6	Kansas	UFA/98	*16/16
95	Wilkinson, Dan (T)	6-5/313	3-13-73	5	Ohio State	TR/98	*15/15
	LINEBACKERS						
58	Alexander, Patrise	6-1/244	10-23-72	3	Southwestern Louisiana	FA/96	16/0
59	Barber, Shawn	6-2/224	1-14-75	R	Richmond	D4/98	—
56	Hamilton, Malcolm	6-1/235	12-31-72	1	Baylor	FA/98	0/0
57	Harvey, Ken	6-2/237	5-6-65	11	California	FA/94	15/14
54	Jones, Greg	6-4/238	5-22-74	2	Colorado	D2/97	16/3
53	Patton, Marvcus	6-2/236	5-1-67	9	UCLA	FA/95	16/16
51	Ponds, Antwuane	6-2/252	6-29-75	R	Syracuse	D7b/98	—
98	Russell, Twan	6-1/219	4-25-74	2	Miami (Fla.)	D5c/97	14/0
50	Smith, Derek	6-2/239	1-18-75	2	Arizona State	D3/97	16/16
	DEFENSIVE BACKS						
37	Campbell, Jesse (S)	6-1/211	4-11-69	8	North Carolina State	FA/97	16/16
26	Dishman, Cris (CB)	6-0/195	8-13-65	11	Purdue	FA/97	16/15
35	Evans, Leomont (S)	6-1/202	7-12-74	3	Clemson	D5/96	16/0
28	Green, Darrell (CB)	5-8/184	2-15-60	16	Texas A&I	D1/83	16/16
31	Pounds, Darryl (CB)	5-10/189	7-21-72	4	Nicholls State	D3/95	16/0

No.	DEFENSIVE BACKS	Ht./Wt.	Born	NFL Exp.	College	How acq.	'97 Games GP/GS
24	Richard, Stanley (S)	6-2/198	10-21-67	8	Texas	FA/95	16/16
23	Terrell, David	6-2/172	7-8-75	R	Texas-El Paso	D7a/98	—
32	Thibodeaux, Keith	5-11/189	5-16-74	2	Northwestern (La.) State	D5b/97	15/0
29	Turner, Scott (CB)	5-10/180	2-26-72	4	Illinois	D7/95	9/0
22	Williams, Jamel	5-11/205	12-22-73	2	Nebraska	D5a/97	16/0
	SPECIALISTS						
16	Blanton, Scott (K)	6-2/221	7-1-73	4	Oklahoma	FA/95	15/0
4	Howard, Eddie (P)	6-1/203	10-6-72	1	Idaho	FA/98	0/0
1	Turk, Matt (P)	6-5/237	6-16-68	4	Wisconsin-Whitewater	FA/95	16/0

*Drake played 9 games with Eagles in '97; Milstead played 4 games with 49ers; Stubblefield played 16 games with 49ers; Wilkinson played 15 games with Bengals.

Abbreviations: D1—draft pick, first round; SupD2—supplemental draft pick, second round; WV—claimed on waivers; TR—obtained in trade; PlanB—Plan B free-agent acquisition; FA—free-agent acquisition (other than Plan B); ED—expansion draft pick.

MISCELLANEOUS TEAM DATA

Stadium (capacity, surface):
Jack Kent Cooke
Stadium (80,116, grass)
Business address:
P.O. Box 17247
Dulles International Airport
Washington, D.C. 20041
Business phone:
703-478-8900
Ticket information:
301-276-6050
Team colors:
Burgundy and gold
Flagship radio station:
WJFK, 106.7 FM
Training site:
Frostburg State University
Frostburg, Md.
301-687-7975

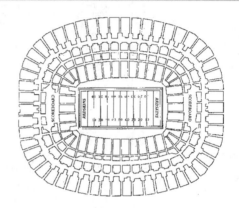

TSN REPORT CARD

| Coaching staff | B - | Norv Turner devises solid game plans and excels at play-calling. His teams, however, have faltered down the stretch the last two seasons. Turner has tried talking his players into performing and now says he will demand that they do. Defensive coordinator Mike Nolan now has a line to go with his back seven. His challenge will be getting consistent performances from his front four. |

| Offensive backfield | C + | Terry Allen excels as a runner, but he was slowed by injuries last season. He has made comebacks before and looks as if he can do it again. Quarterback Gus Frerotte simply has to play better, smarter and with more confidence in 1998. Someone, either Stephen Davis or rookie Skip Hicks, has to become an effective backup for Allen. |

| Receivers | C | Michael Westbrook can be the difference between an average group of receivers and an excellent group of receivers. Westbrook can be a dominant player, but injuries and inconsistency have been his millstones. Leslie Shepherd is steady and sometimes outstanding. Jamie Asher is a dependable tight end and rookie Stephen Alexander might one day be an exceptional one. |

| Offensive line | C | Two new starters, Brad Badger at either tackle or guard, and Cory Raymer at center, highlight a youth movement in a line that was racked by injuries and inconsistency last season. The potential is there to grow and excel, but for now, they're five guys who try hard. |

| Defensive line | B | Dana Stubblefield and Dan Wilkinson might be "A" material, but they have to prove it first. Kenard Lang is solid at left end, but Rich Owens has things to prove at right end. Marc Boutte and Ryan Kuehl are solid, dependable backups, and Kelvin Kinney might push Owens for the starting job. |

| Linebackers | B | It might take an act of Congress to get Marvcus Patton off the field; he has not missed a down on defense in three years. Ken Harvey still strikes fear into left tackles and quarterbacks, and Derek Smith should be even better in his second season than he was in his first. The backups, Greg Jones and Twan Russell, are solid and pushing for playing time, as is rookie Shawn Barber. |

| Secondary | B + | No better pair of cornerbacks exist than Darrell Green and Cris Dishman. Stanley Richard can be an outstanding free safety, but he has yet to be one for an entire season. Jesse Campbell is solid at strong safety. With the exception of cornerback Darryl Pounds, the backups are young and inconsistent. |

| Special teams | C + | The punting of Matt Turk and return skills of Brian Mitchell are exceptional. Scott Blanton is a solid kicker, but he has to improve his kickoffs. The coverage teams need to improve and the return units need to be more consistent in blocking for Mitchell. |

SCHEDULE

PRESEASON

(All times are local, except †American Bowl games, which are Eastern)

WEEK 1

FRIDAY, JULY 31

Seattle at Dallas 8:00

SATURDAY, AUGUST 1

Pittsburgh vs. Tampa Bay at Canton, O.* 7:00
Green Bay vs. Kansas City at Tokyo, Japan .... †10:15
*Hall of Fame Game.

SUNDAY, AUGUST 2

New England at San Francisco 3:00

WEEK 2

THURSDAY, AUGUST 6

N.Y. Jets at Philadelphia 8:00

FRIDAY, AUGUST 7

Arizona at Detroit 7:00
Tennessee at Atlanta 7:30

SATURDAY, AUGUST 8

Buffalo at Pittsburgh 7:30
Chicago at Baltimore 7:30
Cincinnati at N.Y. Giants 8:00
Denver at St. Louis 7:00
Indianapolis at Seattle 7:00
Jacksonville at Carolina 7:30
Kansas City vs. Tampa Bay at Norman, Okla. 7:00
Miami at Washington 7:30
New Orleans at Green Bay 7:00
Oakland at Dallas 8:00
San Francisco at San Diego 7:00

SUNDAY, AUGUST 9

Minnesota at New England 7:30

WEEK 3

THURSDAY, AUGUST 13

Tampa Bay at Miami 8:20

FRIDAY, AUGUST 14

Atlanta at Detroit 7:00
Carolina at Buffalo 7:30
Chicago at Arizona 7:00
New Orleans at Denver 7:00
N.Y. Giants at Jacksonville 8:00
Pittsburgh at Philadelphia 8:00

SATURDAY, AUGUST 15

San Francisco vs. Seattle at Vancouver, B.C. .... †8:00
Baltimore at N.Y. Jets 5:00
Kansas City at Minnesota 7:00
St. Louis at San Diego 8:00
Washington at Tennessee 1:00

SUNDAY, AUGUST 16

Oakland at Green Bay 3:00

MONDAY, AUGUST 17

Dallas vs. New England at Mexico City, Mex. .... †8:00
Indianapolis at Cincinnati 7:30

WEEK 4

THURSDAY, AUGUST 20

N.Y. Giants at N.Y. Jets 8:20

FRIDAY, AUGUST 21

Buffalo at Chicago 7:00

SATURDAY, AUGUST 22

Atlanta vs. Pittsburgh at Morgantown, W.Va. 6:00
Dallas at St. Louis 7:00
Detroit at Cincinnati 7:30
Jacksonville at Kansas City 7:00
Minnesota at Carolina 7:30
New England at Washington 7:30
San Diego at Indianapolis 7:00
Seattle at Arizona 7:00
Tennessee at New Orleans 7:00

SUNDAY, AUGUST 23

Miami at San Francisco 1:00

MONDAY, AUGUST 24

Green Bay at Denver 6:00
Philadelphia at Baltimore 7:30
Tampa Bay at Oakland .... TBA

WEEK 5

THURSDAY, AUGUST 27

Dallas at Jacksonville 8:00
Detroit at Indianapolis 7:30

FRIDAY, AUGUST 28

Baltimore at N.Y. Giants 8:00
Cincinnati at Atlanta 7:30
Green Bay at Miami 7:00
N.Y. Jets at Chicago 7:00
St. Louis at Kansas City 7:00
San Diego at Minnesota 7:00
San Francisco at Seattle 7:00
Tampa Bay at New Orleans 7:30
Washington at Buffalo 7:00

SATURDAY, AUGUST 29

Arizona at Oakland 1:00
Carolina at Pittsburgh 8:20
Denver at Tennessee 1:00
Philadelphia at New England 8:00

REGULAR SEASON

(All times local)

WEEK 1

SUNDAY, SEPTEMBER 6

Arizona at Dallas 3:05
Atlanta at Carolina 1:01
Buffalo at San Diego 1:15
Detroit at Green Bay 12:01
Jacksonville at Chicago 12:01
Miami at Indianapolis 3:15
New Orleans at St. Louis 12:01
N.Y. Jets at San Francisco 1:15
Pittsburgh at Baltimore 1:01
Seattle at Philadelphia 1:01
Tampa Bay at Minnesota 12:01
Tennessee at Cincinnati 1:01
Washington at N.Y. Giants 1:01
Oakland at Kansas City 7:20

MONDAY, SEPTEMBER 7

New England at Denver 6:20

WEEK 2

SUNDAY, SEPTEMBER 13

Arizona at Seattle	1:15
Baltimore at N.Y. Jets	1:01
Buffalo at Miami	1:01
Carolina at New Orleans	12:01
Chicago at Pittsburgh	1:01
Cincinnati at Detroit	1:01
Dallas at Denver	2:15
Kansas City at Jacksonville	1:01
Minnesota at St. Louis	12:01
N.Y. Giants at Oakland	1:15
Philadelphia at Atlanta	1:01
San Diego at Tennessee	12:01
Tampa Bay at Green Bay	12:01
Indianapolis at New England	8:20

MONDAY, SEPTEMBER 14

San Francisco at Washington	8:20

WEEK 3

SUNDAY, SEPTEMBER 20

Baltimore at Jacksonville	4:15
Chicago at Tampa Bay	4:05
Denver at Oakland	1:15
Detroit at Minnesota	12:01
Green Bay at Cincinnati	1:01
Indianapolis at N.Y. Jets	1:01
Pittsburgh at Miami	1:01
St. Louis at Buffalo	1:01
San Diego at Kansas City	12:01
Tennessee at New England	1:01
Washington at Seattle	1:05
Philadelphia at Arizona	5:20

MONDAY, SEPTEMBER 21

Dallas at N.Y. Giants	8:20

Open date: Atlanta, Carolina, New Orleans, San Francisco

WEEK 4

SUNDAY, SEPTEMBER 27

Arizona at St. Louis	12:01
Atlanta at San Francisco	1:15
Denver at Washington	1:01
Green Bay at Carolina	1:01
Jacksonville at Tennessee	12:01
Kansas City at Philadelphia	1:01
Minnesota at Chicago	3:15
New Orleans at Indianapolis	12:01
N.Y. Giants at San Diego	1:15
Oakland at Dallas	12:01
Seattle at Pittsburgh	4:05
Cincinnati at Baltimore	8:20

MONDAY, SEPTEMBER 28

Tampa Bay at Detroit	8:20

Open date: Buffalo, Miami, New England, N.Y. Jets

WEEK 5

SUNDAY, OCTOBER 4

Carolina at Atlanta	1:01
Dallas at Washington	1:01
Detroit at Chicago	12:01
Miami at N.Y. Jets	1:01
New England at New Orleans	12:01
N.Y. Giants at Tampa Bay	4:15
Oakland at Arizona	1:05
Philadelphia at Denver	2:15
San Diego at Indianapolis	12:01
San Francisco at Buffalo	1:01
Seattle at Kansas City	7:20

MONDAY, OCTOBER 5

Minnesota at Green Bay	7:20

Open date: Baltimore, Cincinnati, Jacksonville, Pittsburgh, St. Louis, Tennessee

WEEK 6

SUNDAY, OCTOBER 11

Buffalo at Indianapolis	12:01
Carolina at Dallas	12:01
Chicago at Arizona	1:05
Denver at Seattle	1:15
Kansas City at New England	1:01
N.Y. Jets at St. Louis	3:15
Pittsburgh at Cincinnati	1:01
San Diego at Oakland	1:15
San Francisco at New Orleans	12:01
Tennessee at Baltimore	1:01
Washington at Philadelphia	1:01
Atlanta at N.Y. Giants	8:20

MONDAY, OCTOBER 12

Miami at Jacksonville	8:20

Open date: Detroit, Green Bay, Minnesota, Tampa Bay

WEEK 7

THURSDAY, OCTOBER 15

Green Bay at Detroit	8:20

SUNDAY, OCTOBER 18

Arizona at N.Y. Giants	1:01
Baltimore at Pittsburgh	1:01
Carolina at Tampa Bay	1:01
Cincinnati at Tennessee	12:01
Dallas at Chicago	3:15
Indianapolis at San Francisco	1:05
Jacksonville at Buffalo	1:01
New Orleans at Atlanta	1:01
Philadelphia at San Diego	1:15
St. Louis at Miami	4:15
Washington at Minnesota	12:01

MONDAY, OCTOBER 19

N.Y. Jets at New England	8:20

Open date: Denver, Kansas City, Oakland, Seattle

WEEK 8

SUNDAY, OCTOBER 25

Atlanta at N.Y. Jets	1:01
Baltimore at Green Bay	12:01
Chicago at Tennessee	3:05
Cincinnati at Oakland	1:15
Jacksonville at Denver	2:15
Minnesota at Detroit	1:01
New England at Miami	1:01
San Francisco at St. Louis	12:01
Seattle at San Diego	1:15
Tampa Bay at New Orleans	12:01
Buffalo at Carolina	8:20

MONDAY, OCTOBER 26

Pittsburgh at Kansas City	7:20

Open date: Arizona, Dallas, Indianapolis, N.Y. Giants, Philadelphia, Washington

WEEK 9

SUNDAY, NOVEMBER 1

Arizona at Detroit	1:01
Denver at Cincinnati	1:01
Jacksonville at Baltimore	1:01
Miami at Buffalo	1:01
Minnesota at Tampa Bay	1:01
New England at Indianapolis	1:01

New Orleans at Carolina 1:01
N.Y. Giants at Washington 1:01
N.Y. Jets at Kansas City 3:05
St. Louis at Atlanta 1:01
San Francisco at Green Bay 3:15
Tennessee at Pittsburgh 1:01
Oakland at Seattle 5:20

MONDAY, NOVEMBER 2

Dallas at Philadelphia....................................... 8:20
    Open date: Chicago, San Diego

WEEK 10

SUNDAY, NOVEMBER 8

Atlanta at New England..................................... 1:01
Buffalo at N.Y. Jets 4:15
Carolina at San Francisco 1:05
Cincinnati at Jacksonville.................................. 1:01
Detroit at Philadelphia 1:01
Indianapolis at Miami 1:01
Kansas City at Seattle 1:15
New Orleans at Minnesota 12:01
N.Y. Giants at Dallas 12:01
Oakland at Baltimore 1:01
St. Louis at Chicago 12:01
San Diego at Denver... 2:15
Washington at Arizona....................................... 2:05
Tennessee at Tampa Bay.................................... 8:20

MONDAY, NOVEMBER 9

Green Bay at Pittsburgh..................................... 8:20

WEEK 11

SUNDAY, NOVEMBER 15

Baltimore at San Diego...................................... 1:05
Cincinnati at Minnesota 12:01
Dallas at Arizona 2:15
Green Bay at N.Y. Giants................................... 4:15
Miami at Carolina.. 1:01
New England at Buffalo 1:01
N.Y. Jets at Indianapolis 1:01
Philadelphia at Washington 1:01
Pittsburgh at Tennessee 12:01
St. Louis at New Orleans 12:01
San Francisco at Atlanta 1:01
Seattle at Oakland.. 1:05
Tampa Bay at Jacksonville................................. 4:15
Chicago at Detroit 8:20

MONDAY, NOVEMBER 16

Denver at Kansas City....................................... 7:20

WEEK 12

SUNDAY, NOVEMBER 22

Arizona at Washington....................................... 1:01
Baltimore at Cincinnati....................................... 4:15
Carolina at St. Louis 3:05
Chicago at Atlanta.. 1:01
Detroit at Tampa Bay 1:01
Green Bay at Minnesota..................................... 12:01
Indianapolis at Buffalo 1:01
Jacksonville at Pittsburgh.................................. 1:01
Kansas City at San Diego................................... 1:15
N.Y. Jets at Tennessee 3:15
Oakland at Denver 2:15
Philadelphia at N.Y. Giants 1:01
Seattle at Dallas 12:01
New Orleans at San Francisco 5:20

MONDAY, NOVEMBER 23

Miami at New England.. 8:20

WEEK 13

THURSDAY, NOVEMBER 26

Minnesota at Dallas.. 3:05
Pittsburgh at Detroit... 12:35

SUNDAY, NOVEMBER 29

Arizona at Kansas City....................................... 12:01
Atlanta at St. Louis 12:01
Buffalo at New England 4:05
Carolina at N.Y. Jets... 1:01
Indianapolis at Baltimore................................... 1:01
Jacksonville at Cincinnati.................................. 1:01
New Orleans at Miami 1:01
Philadelphia at Green Bay 3:15
Tampa Bay at Chicago 12:01
Tennessee at Seattle 1:05
Washington at Oakland...................................... 1:15
Denver at San Diego... 5:20

MONDAY, NOVEMBER 30

N.Y. Giants at San Francisco............................. 5:20

WEEK 14

THURSDAY, DECEMBER 3

St. Louis at Philadelphia.................................... 8:20

SUNDAY, DECEMBER 6

Baltimore at Tennessee...................................... 3:15
Buffalo at Cincinnati.. 1:01
Dallas at New Orleans 12:01
Detroit at Jacksonville....................................... 1:01
Indianapolis at Atlanta 1:01
Kansas City at Denver....................................... 2:15
Miami at Oakland.. 1:15
New England at Pittsburgh................................. 1:01
N.Y. Giants at Arizona 2:05
San Diego at Washington 1:01
San Francisco at Carolina 1:01
Seattle at N.Y. Jets.. 1:01
Chicago at Minnesota.. 7:20

MONDAY, DECEMBER 7

Green Bay at Tampa Bay.................................... 8:20

WEEK 15

SUNDAY, DECEMBER 13

Arizona at Philadelphia 1:01
Atlanta at New Orleans 12:01
Chicago at Green Bay 12:01
Cincinnati at Indianapolis.................................. 1:01
Dallas at Kansas City 3:15
Denver at N.Y. Giants 1:01
Minnesota at Baltimore...................................... 4:15
New England at St. Louis 12:01
Oakland at Buffalo 1:01
Pittsburgh at Tampa Bay................................... 1:01
San Diego at Seattle 1:05
Tennessee at Jacksonville................................. 1:01
Washington at Carolina...................................... 1:01
N.Y. Jets at Miami.. 8:20

MONDAY, DECEMBER 14

Detroit at San Francisco 5:20

WEEK 16

SATURDAY, DECEMBER 19

N.Y. Jets at Buffalo 12:35
Tampa Bay at Washington 4:05

SUNDAY, DECEMBER 20

Atlanta at Detroit.. 1:01
Baltimore at Chicago 12:01
Cincinnati at Pittsburgh..................................... 1:01

1998 SEASON *Schedule*

Indianapolis at Seattle 1:05
Kansas City at N.Y. Giants 1:01
New Orleans at Arizona 2:15
Oakland at San Diego 1:05
Philadelphia at Dallas... 3:15
St. Louis at Carolina... 1:01
San Francisco at New England 1:01
Tennessee at Green Bay.. 12:01
Jacksonville at Minnesota.. 7:20

MONDAY, DECEMBER 21

Denver at Miami 8:20

WEEK 17

SATURDAY, DECEMBER 26

Kansas City at Oakland 1:05
Minnesota at Tennessee 11:35

SUNDAY, DECEMBER 27

Buffalo at New Orleans 12:01
Carolina at Indianapolis 1:01
Detroit at Baltimore 1:01
Green Bay at Chicago 12:01
Miami at Atlanta... 1:01
New England at N.Y. Jets 1:01
N.Y. Giants at Philadelphia.. 4:05
St. Louis at San Francisco... 1:05
San Diego at Arizona 2:15
Seattle at Denver 2:15
Tampa Bay at Cincinnati 1:01
Washington at Dallas.. 7:20

MONDAY, DECEMBER 28

Pittsburgh at Jacksonville.. 8:20

NATIONALLY TELEVISED GAMES

(All times local)

REGULAR SEASON

Sun.	Sept. 6—	N.Y. Jets at San Francisco (1:15, CBS)
		Oakland at Kansas City (7:20, ESPN)
Mon.	Sept. 7—	New England at Denver (6:20, ABC)
Sun.	Sept. 13—	Dallas at Denver (2:15, FOX)
		Indianapolis at New England (8:20, ESPN)
Mon.	Sept. 14—	San Francisco at Washington (8:20, ABC)
Sun.	Sept. 20—	Denver at Oakland (1:15, CBS)
		Philadelphia at Arizona (5:20, ESPN)
Mon.	Sept. 21—	Dallas at N.Y. Giants (8:20, ABC)
Sun.	Sept. 27—	Minnesota at Chicago (3:15, FOX)
		Cincinnati at Baltimore (8:20, ESPN)
Mon.	Sept. 28—	Tampa Bay at Detroit (8:20, ABC)
Sun.	Oct. 4—	Philadelphia at Denver (2:15, FOX)
		Seattle at Kansas City (7:20, ESPN)
Mon.	Oct. 5—	Minnesota at Green Bay (7:20, ABC)
Sun.	Oct. 11—	Denver at Seattle (1:15, CBS)
		Atlanta at N.Y. Giants (8:20, ESPN)
Mon.	Oct. 12—	Miami at Jacksonville (8:20, ABC)
Thur.	Oct. 15—	Green Bay at Detroit (8:20, ESPN)
Sun.	Oct. 18—	Dallas at Chicago (3:15, FOX)
Mon.	Oct. 19—	N.Y. Jets at New England (8:20, ABC)
Sun.	Oct. 25—	Jacksonville at Denver (2:15, CBS)
		Buffalo at Carolina (8:20, ESPN)
Mon.	Oct. 26—	Pittsburgh at Kansas City (7:20, ABC)
Sun.	Nov. 1—	San Francisco at Green Bay (3:15, FOX)
		Oakland at Seattle (5:20, ESPN)
Mon.	Nov. 2—	Dallas at Philadelphia (8:20, ABC)
Sun.	Nov. 8—	San Diego at Denver (2:15, CBS)
		Tennessee at Tampa Bay (8:20, ESPN)
Mon.	Nov. 9—	Green Bay at Pittsburgh (8:20, ABC)
Sun.	Nov. 15—	Green Bay at N.Y. Giants (4:15, FOX)
		Chicago at Detroit (8:20, ESPN)
Mon.	Nov. 16—	Denver at Kansas City (7:20, ABC)
Sun.	Nov. 22—	Oakland at Denver (2:15, CBS)
		New Orleans at San Francisco (5:20, ESPN)
Mon.	Nov. 23—	Miami at New England (8:20, ABC)
Thur.	Nov. 26—	Minnesota at Dallas (3:05, FOX)
		Pittsburgh at Detroit (12:35, CBS)
Sun.	Nov. 29—	Philadelphia at Green Bay (3:15, FOX)
		Denver at San Diego (5:20, ESPN)
Mon.	Nov. 30—	N.Y. Giants at San Francisco (5:20, ABC)
Thur.	Dec. 3—	St. Louis at Philadelphia (8:20, ESPN)
Sun.	Dec. 6—	Kansas City at Denver (2:15, CBS)
		Chicago at Minnesota (7:20, ESPN)
Mon.	Dec. 7—	Green Bay at Tampa Bay (8:20, ABC)
Sun.	Dec. 13—	Dallas at Kansas City (3:15, FOX)
		New York Jets at Miami (8:20, ESPN)
Mon.	Dec. 14—	Detroit at San Francisco (5:20, ABC)
Sat.	Dec. 19—	N.Y. Jets at Buffalo (12:35, CBS)
		Tampa Bay at Washington (4:05, FOX)
Sun.	Dec. 20—	Philadelphia at Dallas (3:15, FOX)
		Jacksonville at Minnesota (7:20, ESPN)
Mon.	Dec. 21—	Denver at Miami (8:20, ABC)
Sat.	Dec. 26—	Kansas City at Oakland (1:05, CBS)
		Minnesota at Tennessee (11:35, FOX)
Sun.	Dec. 27—	Seattle at Denver (2:15, CBS)
		Washington at Dallas (7:20, ESPN)
Mon.	Dec. 28—	Pittsburgh at Jacksonville (8:20, ABC)

POSTSEASON

Sat.	Jan. 2—	AFC, NFC wild-card playoffs (ABC)
Sun.	Jan. 3—	AFC, NFC wild-card playoffs (CBS, FOX)
Sat.	Jan. 9—	AFC, NFC divisional playoffs (CBS, FOX)
Sun.	Jan. 10—	AFC, NFC divisional playoffs (CBS, FOX)
Sun.	Jan. 17—	AFC, NFC championship games (CBS, FOX)
Sun.	Jan. 31—	Super Bowl at Pro Player Stadium, Miami (FOX)
Sun.	Feb. 7—	Pro Bowl at Honolulu (ABC)

INTERCONFERENCE GAMES

(All times local)

Sun.	Sept. 6—	Jacksonville at Chicago	12:01
		N.Y. Jets at San Francisco	1:15
		Seattle at Philadelphia	1:01
Sun.	Sept. 13—	Arizona at Seattle...........................	1:15
		Chicago at Pittsburgh	1:01
		Cincinnati at Detroit.......................	1:01
		Dallas at Denver	2:15
		N.Y. Giants at Oakland	1:15
Sun.	Sept. 20—	Green Bay at Cincinnati	1:01
		St. Louis at Buffalo.........................	1:01
		Washington at Seattle.....................	1:05
Sun.	Sept. 27—	Denver at Washington	1:01
		Kansas City at Philadelphia............	1:01
		New Orleans at Indianapolis	12:01
		N.Y. Giants at San Diego................	1:15
		Oakland at Dallas	12:01
Sun.	Oct. 4—	New England at New Orleans.........	12:01
		Oakland at Arizona.........................	1:05
		Philadelphia at Denver...................	2:15
		San Francisco at Buffalo................	1:01
Sun.	Oct. 11—	N.Y. Jets at St. Louis	3:15
Sun.	Oct. 18—	Indianapolis at San Francisco	1:05

		Philadelphia at San Diego	1:15
		St. Louis at Miami	4:15
Sun.	Oct. 25	Atlanta at N.Y. Jets	1:01
		Baltimore at Green Bay	12:01
		Chicago at Tennessee	3:05
		Buffalo at Carolina	8:20
Sun.	Nov. 8	Atlanta at New England	1:01
		Tennessee at Tampa Bay	8:20
Mon.	Nov. 9	Green Bay at Pittsburgh	8:20
Sun.	Nov. 15	Cincinnati at Minnesota	12:01
		Miami at Carolina	1:01
		Tampa Bay at Jacksonville	4:15
Sun.	Nov. 22	Seattle at Dallas	12:01
Thur.	Nov. 26	Pittsburgh at Detroit	12:35
Sun.	Nov. 29	Arizona at Kansas City	12:01
		Carolina at N.Y. Jets	1:01
		New Orleans at Miami	1:01
		Washington at Oakland	1:15
Sun.	Dec. 6	Detroit at Jacksonville	1:01

		Indianapolis at Atlanta	1:01
		San Diego at Washington	1:01
Sun.	Dec. 13	Dallas at Kansas City	3:15
		Denver at N.Y. Giants	1:01
		Minnesota at Baltimore	4:15
		New England at St. Louis	12:01
		Pittsburgh at Tampa Bay	1:01
Sun.	Dec. 20	Baltimore at Chicago	12:01
		Kansas City at N.Y. Giants	1:01
		San Francisco at New England	1:01
		Tennessee at Green Bay	12:01
		Jacksonville at Minnesota	7:20
Sat.	Dec. 26	Minnesota at Tennessee	11:35
Sun.	Dec. 27	Buffalo at New Orleans	12:01
		Carolina at Indianapolis	1:01
		Detroit at Baltimore	1:01
		Miami at Atlanta	1:01
		San Diego at Arizona	2:15
		Tampa Bay at Cincinnati	1:01

1998 STRENGTH OF SCHEDULE

(Teams are ranked from most difficult to easiest schedules, based on 1998 opponents' combined 1997 records)

	Team	Opp. Wins	Opp. Losses	Opp. Ties	Opp. Pct.		Team	Opp. Wins	Opp. Losses	Opp. Ties	Opp. Pct.
1.	Pittsburgh (3)	140	114	2	.551		Denver (T4)	125	128	3	.494
2.	Chicago (T22)	140	115	1	.549		Indianapolis (T16)	126	129	1	.494
3.	Cincinnati (T16)	138	116	2	.543	18.	N.Y. Giants (T25)	124	128	4	.492
	Tampa Bay (21)	138	116	2	.543	19.	Kansas City (2)	123	131	2	.484
5.	Detroit (30)	137	117	2	.539	20.	N.Y. Jets (T13)	123	132	1	.482
	Tennessee (T16)	137	117	2	.539		St. Louis (T9)	123	132	1	.482
7.	Jacksonville (T7)	136	118	2	.535	22.	Atlanta (T13)	122	132	2	.480
8.	Green Bay (12)	132	121	3	.521	23.	Dallas (1)	119	131	6	.477
9.	Oakland (T22)	130	123	3	.514		Seattle (T28)	121	133	2	.477
10.	Minnesota (T4)	129	125	2	.508	25.	New Orleans (24)	121	135	0	.473
11.	Baltimore (T16)	129	127	0	.504		Washington (15)	119	133	4	.473
	New England (T9)	129	127	0	.504	27.	Buffalo (T9)	119	137	0	.465
	Philadelphia (T7)	127	125	4	.504		Miami (T25)	119	137	0	.465
14.	San Diego (T4)	125	127	4	.496		San Francisco (T28)	118	136	2	.465
15.	Carolina (T16)	126	129	1	.494	30.	Arizona (T25)	113	137	6	.453

NOTE: Number in parentheses is 1997 rank.

COLLEGE DRAFT

ROUND-BY-ROUND SELECTIONS

FIRST ROUND

	Team	Player selected	Pos.	College	Draft pick origination
1.	Indianapolis	Peyton Manning	QB	Tennessee	
2.	San Diego	Ryan Leaf	QB	Washington State	From Arizona
3.	Arizona	Andre Wadsworth	DE	Florida State	From San Diego
4.	Oakland	Charles Woodson	DB	Michigan	
5.	Chicago	Curtis Enis	RB	Penn State	
6.	St. Louis	Grant Wistrom	DE	Nebraska	
7.	New Orleans	Kyle Turley	T	San Diego State	
8.	Dallas	Greg Ellis	DE	North Carolina	
9.	Jacksonville	Fred Taylor	RB	Florida	From Buffalo
10.	Baltimore	Duane Starks	DB	Miami, Fla.	
11.	Philadelphia	Tra Thomas	T	Florida State	
12.	Atlanta	Keith Brooking	LB	Georgia Tech	
13.	Cincinnati	Takeo Spikes	LB	Auburn	
14.	Carolina	Jason Peter	DT	Nebraska	
15.	Seattle	Anthony Simmons	LB	Clemson	
16.	Tennessee	Kevin Dyson	WR	Utah	
17.	Cincinnati	Brian Simmons	LB	North Carolina	From Washington
18.	New England	Robert Edwards	RB	Georgia	From N.Y. Jets
19.	Green Bay	Vonnie Holliday	DT	North Carolina	From Miami
20.	Detroit	Terry Fair	DB	Tennessee	
21.	Minnesota	Randy Moss	WR	Marshall	
22.	New England	Tebucky Jones	DB	Syracuse	
23.	Oakland	Mo Collins	T	Florida	From Tampa Bay
24.	New York Giants	Shaun Williams	DB	UCLA	
25.	Jacksonville	Donovin Darius	DB	Syracuse	
26.	Pittsburgh	Alan Faneca	G	Louisiana State	
27.	Kansas City	Victor Riley	T	Auburn	
28.	San Francisco	R.W. McQuarters	DB	Oklahoma State	
29.	Miami	John Avery	RB	Mississippi	From Green Bay
30.	Denver	Marcus Nash	WR	Tennessee	

SECOND ROUND

	Team	Player selected	Pos.	College	Draft pick origination
31.	Oakland*	Leon Bender	DT	Washington State	
32.	Indianapolis	Jerome Pathon	WR	Washington	
33.	Arizona	Corey Chavous	DB	Vanderbilt	From San Diego
34.	Tampa Bay	Jacquez Green	WR	Florida	From Oakland
35.	Chicago	Tony Parrish	DB	Washington	
36.	Arizona	Anthony Clement	T	SW Louisiana	
37.	St. Louis	Robert Holcombe	RB	Illinois	
38.	Dallas	Flozell Adams	T	Michigan State	
39.	Buffalo	Sam Cowart	LB	Florida State	
40.	New Orleans	Cameron Cleeland	TE	Washington	
41.	Pittsburgh	Jeremy Staat	DT	Arizona State	From Philadelphia through N.Y. Jets
42.	Baltimore	Pat Johnson	WR	Oregon	
43.	Cincinnati	Artrell Hawkins	DB	Cincinnati	
44.	Miami	Patrick Surtain	DB	Southern Mississippi	From Carolina
45.	Tampa Bay	Brian Kelly	DB	Southern California	From Atlanta
46.	Tennessee	Samari Rolle	DB	Florida State	
47.	Seattle	Todd Weiner	T	Kansas State	
48.	Washington	Stephen Alexander	TE	Oklahoma	
49.	Miami	Kenny Mixon	DE	Louisiana State	
50.	Detroit	Germane Crowell	WR	Virginia	
51.	Minnesota	Kailee Wong	LB	Stanford	
52.	New England	Tony Simmons	WR	Wisconsin	From N.Y. Jets
53.	Atlanta	Bob Hallen	C	Kent	From Tampa Bay
54.	New England	Rod Rutledge	TE	Alabama	
55.	New York Giants	Joe Jurevicius	WR	Penn State	
56.	New York Jets	Dorian Boose	DE	Washington State	From Pittsburgh
57.	Jacksonville	Cordell Taylor	DB	Hampton	
58.	San Francisco	Jeremy Newberry	C	California	
59.	San Diego	Mikhael Ricks	WR	Stephen F. Austin State	From K.C. through Oakland and T.B.
60.	Detroit	Charlie Batch	QB	Eastern Michigan	From Green Bay through Miami
61.	Denver	Eric Brown	S	Mississippi State	

THIRD ROUND

Team	Player selected	Pos.	College	Draft pick origination
62. Carolina	Chuck Wiley	DE	Louisiana State	From Indianapolis
63. Oakland	Jon Ritchie	RB	Stanford	
64. Chicago	Olin Kreutz	C	Washington	
65. St. Louis	Leonard Little	LB	Tennessee	From Arizona through N.Y. Jets
66. Pittsburgh	Chris Conrad	T	Fresno State	From San Diego
67. New York Jets	Scott Frost	DB	Nebraska	From St. Louis
68. Buffalo	Robert Hicks	T	Mississippi State	
69. Washington	Skip Hicks	RB	UCLA	From New Orleans
70. New York Giants	Brian Alford	WR	Purdue	From Dallas through Philadelphia
71. Indianapolis	E.G. Green	WR	Florida State	From Baltimore
72. Philadelphia	Jeremiah Trotter	LB	Stephen F. Austin State	
73. Carolina	Mitch Marrow	DE	Pennsylvania	
74. Atlanta	Jammi German	WR	Miami, Fla.	
75. Cincinnati	Steve Foley	LB	Northeast Louisiana	
76. Seattle	Ahman Green	RB	Nebraska	
77. Tennessee	Dainon Sydney	DB	Alabama-Birmingham	
78. Cincinnati	Mike Goff	G	Iowa	From Washington
79. Miami	Brad Jackson	LB	Cincinnati	From Detroit
80. Minnesota	Ramos McDonald	DB	New Mexico	
81. New England	Chris Floyd	RB	Michigan	From N.Y. Jets
82. Miami	Larry Shannon	WR	East Carolina	
83. New England	Greg Spires	DE	Florida State	
84. Tampa Bay	Jamie Duncan	LB	Vanderbilt	
85. Philadelphia	Allen Rossum	DB	Notre Dame	From N.Y. Giants
86. Jacksonville	Jonathan Quinn	QB	Middle Tennessee State	
87. New York Jets	Kevin Williams	DB	Oklahoma State	From Pittsburgh
88. Kansas City	Rashaan Shehee	RB	Washington	
89. San Francisco	Chris Ruhman	T	Texas A&M	
90. Green Bay	Jonathan Brown	DE	Tennessee	
91. Denver	Brian Griese	QB	Michigan	
92. Pittsburgh*	Hines Ward	WR	Georgia	

FOURTH ROUND

Team	Player selected	Pos.	College	Draft pick origination
93. Indianapolis	Steve McKinney	G	Texas A&M	From Indianapolis through Baltimore
94. Chicago	Alonzo Mayes	TE	Oklahoma State	
95. Arizona	Michael Pittman	RB	Fresno State	
96. St. Louis	Az-Zahir Hakim	WR	San Diego State	From San Diego
97. New Orleans	Fred Weary	DB	Florida	From Oakland
98. St. Louis	Roland Williams	TE	Syracuse	
99. New Orleans	Julian Pittman	DE	Florida State	
100. Dallas	Michael Myers	DT	Alabama	
101. Jacksonville	Tavian Banks	RB	Iowa	From Buffalo
102. Miami	Lorenzo Bromell	DE	Clemson	From Philadelphia
103. Atlanta	Omar Brown	DB	North Carolina	
104. Tampa Bay	Todd Washington	G	Virginia Tech	From Bal. through Ind. and Bal.
105. Cincinnati	Glen Steele	DE	Michigan	
106. Carolina	Donald Hayes	WR	Wisconsin	
107. Tennessee	Joe Salave'a	DT	Arizona	
108. Seattle	DeShone Myles	LB	Nevada	
109. Oakland	Gennaro DiNapoli	G	Virginia Tech	From Washington
110. Minnesota	Kivuusama Mays	LB	North Carolina	
111. New York Jets	Jason Fabini	T	Cincinnati	
112. Philadelphia	Brandon Whiting	DT	California	From Miami
113. Washington	Shawn Barber	LB	Richmond	From Detroit through Oakland
114. Atlanta	Tim Dwight	WR-KR	Iowa	From Tampa Bay
115. New England	Leonta Rheams	DT	Houston	
116. Philadelphia	Clarence Love	DB	Toledo	From N.Y. Giants
117. Pittsburgh	Deshea Townsend	DB	Alabama	
118. Jacksonville	Harry Deligianis	DT	Youngstown State	
119. San Francisco	Lance Schulters	DB	Hofstra	
120. Kansas City	Greg Favors	LB	Mississippi State	
121. Green Bay	Roosevelt Blackmon	DB	Morris Brown	
122. Denver	Curtis Alexander	RB	Alabama	
123. Pittsburgh*	Carlos King	FB	North Carolina State	

FIFTH ROUND

Team	Player selected	Pos.	College	Draft pick origination
124. Baltimore	Martin Chase	DT	Oklahoma	From Indianapolis
125. Arizona	Terry Hardy	TE	Southern Mississippi	
126. San Diego	Cedric Harden	DE	Florida A&M	
127. Oakland	Jeremy Brigham	TE	Washington	
128. Kansas City	Robert Williams	DB	North Carolina	From Chicago
129. St. Louis	Raymond Priester	RB	Clemson	
130. Dallas	Darren Hambrick	LB	South Carolina	
131. Buffalo	Jonathan Linton	RB	North Carolina	
132. New Orleans	Wilmont Perry	RB	Livingstone	
133. Baltimore	Ryan Sutter	DB	Colorado	
134. New York Jets	Casey Dailey	LB	Northwestern	From Philadelphia
135. Indianapolis	Antony Jordon	LB	Vanderbilt	From Cincinnati
136. Carolina	Jerry Jensen	LB	Washington	
137. Pittsburgh	Jason Simmons	DB	Arizona State	From Atlanta
138. Dallas	Oliver Ross	T	Iowa State	From Seattle
139. Tennessee	Benji Olson	G	Washington	
140. Washington	Mark Fischer	C	Purdue	
141. New York Jets	Doug Karczewski	G	Virginia	
142. Philadelphia	Ike Reese	LB	Michigan State	From Miami
143. Miami	Scott Shaw	G	Michigan State	From Detroit
144. Minnesota	Kerry Cooks	DB	Iowa	
145. New England	Ron Merkerson	LB	Colorado	
146. New York Jets	Blake Spence	TE	Oregon	From Tampa Bay
147. New York Giants	Toby Myles	T	Jackson State	
148. Jacksonville	John Wade	C	Marshall	
149. New York Jets	Eric Bateman	G	Brigham Young	From Pittsburgh
150. Green Bay	Corey Bradford	WR	Jackson State	From Kansas City
151. San Francisco	Phil Ostrowski	G	Penn State	
152. Oakland	Travian Smith	LB	Oklahoma	From Green Bay
153. Denver	Chris Howard	RB	Michigan	

SIXTH ROUND

Team	Player selected	Pos.	College	Draft pick origination
154. Baltimore	Ron Rogers	LB	Georgia Tech	From Indianapolis
155. San Diego	Clifford Ivory	DB	Troy State	
156. Green Bay	Scott McGarrahan	DB	New Mexico	From Oakland
157. Chicago	Chris Draft	LB	Stanford	
158. Arizona	Zack Walz	LB	Dartmouth	
159. St. Louis	Glenn Roundtree	G	Clemson	
160. Buffalo	Fred Coleman	WR	Washington	
161. New Orleans	Chris Bordano	LB	Southern Methodist	
162. Seattle	Carl Hansen	DE	Stanford	From Dallas
163. New York Jets	Eric Ogbogu	DE	Maryland	From Philadelphia
164. Baltimore	Sammy Williams	T	Oklahoma	
165. Carolina	Damien Richardson	DB	Arizona State	
166. Atlanta	Elijah Williams	DB	Florida	
167. Cincinnati	Jason Tucker	WR	Texas Christian	
168. Tennessee	Lee Wiggins	DB	South Carolina	
169. Seattle	Bobby Shaw	WR	California	
170. Washington	Pat Palmer	WR	Northwestern (La.) State	
171. Miami	Nathan Strikwerda	C	Northwestern	
172. Miami	John Dutton	QB	Nevada	From Detroit
173. Minnesota	Matt Birk	T	Harvard	
174. New York Jets	Chris Brazzell	WR	Angelo State	
175. Tampa Bay	James Cannida	DT	Nevada	
176. New England	Harold Shaw	RB	Southern Mississippi	
177. New York Giants	Todd Pollack	TE	Boston College	
178. Pittsburgh	Chris Fuamatu-Ma'afala	RB	Utah	
179. Jacksonville	Lemanzer Williams	DE	Minnesota	
180. San Francisco	Fred Beasley	RB	Auburn	
181. Kansas City	Derrick Ransom	DT	Cincinnati	
182. Jacksonville	Kevin McLeod	RB	Auburn	From Green Bay
183. New York Jets	Dustin Johnson	RB	Brigham Young	From Denver
184. Tampa Bay*	Shevin Smith	DB	Florida State	
185. Detroit*	Jamaal Alexander	DB	Southern Mississippi	
186. Pittsburgh*	Ryan Olson	LB	Colorado	
187. Green Bay*	Matt Hasselbeck	QB	Boston College	
188. Dallas*	Izell Reese	DB	Alabama-Birmingham	
189. Chicago*	Patrick Mannelly	T	Duke	

Team	Player selected	Pos.	College	Draft pick origination
190. Indianapolis	Aaron Taylor	G	Nebraska	
191. Washington	David Terrell	DB	Texas-El Paso	From Oakland
192. Jacksonville	Alvis Whitted	WR	North Carolina State	From Chicago
193. Arizona	Phil Savoy	WR	Colorado	
194. San Diego	Jon Haskins	LB	Stanford	
195. New York Jets	Lawrence Hart	TE	Southern University	From St. Louis
196. Carolina	Viliami Maumau	DT	Colorado	From New Orleans
197. Seattle	Jason McEndoo	C	Washington State	From Dallas
198. Buffalo	Victor Allotey	G	Indiana	
199. Atlanta	Ephraim Salaam	T	San Diego State	From Baltimore through Pittsburgh
200. Denver	Trey Teague	T	Tennessee	From Philadelphia
201. Atlanta	Ken Oxendine	RB	Virginia Tech	
202. Cincinnati	Marcus Parker	RB	Virginia Tech	
203. Atlanta	Henry Slay	DT	West Virginia	From Carolina through Pittsburgh
204. New Orleans	Andy McCullough	WR	Tennessee	From Seattle
205. Tennessee	Jimmy Sprotte	LB	Arizona	
206. Washington	Antwaune Ponds	LB	Syracuse	
207. Detroit	Chris Liwienski	T	Indiana	
208. Minnesota	Chester Burnett	LB	Arizona	
209. Arizona	Jomo Cousins	DE	Florida A&M	From N.Y. Jets
210. Miami	Jim Bundren	G	Clemson	
211. New England	Jason Andersen	C	Brigham Young	
212. Tampa Bay	Chance McCarty	DE	Texas Christian	
213. New York Giants	Ben Fricke	C	Houston	
214. Jacksonville	Brandon Tolbert	LB	Georgia	
215. San Francisco	Ryan Thelwell	WR	Minnesota	From Pittsburgh through Atlanta
216. Kansas City	Eric Warfield	DB	Nebraska	
217. Chicago	Chad Overhauser	T	UCLA	From San Francisco
218. Green Bay	Ed Watson	RB	Purdue	
219. Denver	Nate Wayne	LB	Mississippi	
220. Philadelphia*	Chris Akins	DT	Texas	
221. Pittsburgh*	Angel Rubio	DE	Southeast Missouri State	
222. Cincinnati*	Damian Vaughn	TE	Miami of Ohio	
223. Dallas*	Tarik Smith	RB	California	
224. Kansas City*	Ernest Blackwell	RB	Missouri	
225. Minnesota*	Tony Darden	DB	Texas Tech	
226. Arizona*	Pat Tillman	DB	Arizona State	
227. Dallas*	Antonio Fleming	G	Georgia	
228. Carolina*	Jim Turner	WR	Syracuse	
229. Tennessee*	Kevin Long	C	Florida State	
230. Oakland*	Vince Amey	DE	Arizona State	
231. Indianapolis*	Corey Gaines	DB	Tennessee	
232. Chicago*	Moses Moreno	QB	Colorado State	
233. Arizona*	Ron Janes	RB	Missouri	
234. San Diego*	Kio Sanford	WR	Kentucky	
235. Oakland*	David Sanders	DE	Arkansas	
236. St. Louis*	Jason Chorak	DE	Washington	
237. Dallas*	Rodrick Monroe	TE	Cincinnati	
238. Buffalo*	Kamil Loud	WR	Cal Poly-SLO	
239. New Orleans*	Ron Warner	LB	Kansas	
240. Philadelphia*	Melvin Thomas	G	Colorado	
241. Baltimore*	Cam Quayle	TE	Weber State	

*Pick awarded to team as compensation for loss of a free agent.

1998 SEASON *College draft*

PLAYOFF PLAN

TIEBREAKING PROCEDURES

DIVISION TIES

TWO CLUBS

1. Head-to-head (best won-lost-tied percentage in games between the clubs).
2. Best won-lost-tied percentage in games played within the division.
3. Best won-lost-tied percentage in games played within the conference.
4. Best won-lost-tied percentage in common games, if applicable.
5. Best net points in division games.
6. Best net points in all games.
7. Strength of schedule.
8. Best net touchdowns in all games.
9. Coin toss.

THREE OR MORE CLUBS

(Note: If two clubs remain tied after other clubs are eliminated during any step, tie-breaker reverts to step 1 of two-club format.)
1. Head-to-head (best won-lost-tied percentage in games among the clubs).
2. Best won-lost-tied percentage in games played within the division.
3. Best won-lost-tied percentage in games played within the conference.
4. Best won-lost-tied percentage in common games.
5. Best net points in division games.
6. Best net points in all games.
7. Strength of schedule.
8. Best net touchdowns in all games.
9. Coin toss.

WILD-CARD TIES

If necessary to break ties to determine the three wild-card clubs from each conference, the following steps will be taken:
1. If all the tied clubs are from the same division, apply division tie-breaker.
2. If the tied clubs are from different divisions, apply the steps listed below.
3. When the first wild-card team has been identified, the procedure is repeated to name the second wild card (i.e., eliminate all but the highest-ranked club in each division prior to proceeding to step 2), and repeated a third time, if necessary, to identify the third wild card. In situations where three or more teams - - from the same division are involved in the procedure, the original seeding of the teams remains the same for subsequent applications of the tie-breaker if the top-ranked team in that division qualifies for a wild-card berth.

TWO CLUBS

1. Head-to-head, if applicable.
2. Best won-lost-tied percentage in games played within the conference.
3. Best won-lost-tied percentage in common games, minimum of four.
4. Best average net points in conference games.
5. Best net points in all games.
6. Strength of schedule.
7. Best net touchdowns in all games.
8. Coin toss.

THREE OR MORE CLUBS

(Note: If two clubs remain tied after other clubs are eliminated, tie-breaker reverts to step 1 of two-club format.)
1. Apply division tie-breaker to eliminate all but highest-ranked club in each division prior to proceeding to step 1. The original seeding within a division upon application of the division tie-breaker remains the same for all subsequent applications of the procedure that are necessary to identify the three wild-card participants.
2. Head-to-head sweep (applicable only if one club has defeated each of the others or one club has lost to each of the others).
3. Best won-lost-tied percentage in games played within the conference.
4. Best won-lost-tied percentage in common games, minimum of four.
5. Best average net points in conference games.
6. Best net points in all games.
7. Strength of schedule.
8. Best net touchdowns in all games.
9. Coin toss.

1997 REVIEW

Year in review
Final standings
Weeks 1 through 17
Wild-card games
Divisional playoffs
Conference championships
Super Bowl XXXII
Pro Bowl
Player participation
Attendance
Trades

YEAR IN REVIEW

By KEN SINS

NFL bean counters were the bearers of glad tidings in 1997 as their wealthy bosses got a whole lot richer. The owners' bottom line swelled, and so did the players'. Franchise worth enjoyed another lurch toward the moon. And every fan survey continued to point to pro football as being the king of the Big Four spectator sports.

Television dollars continue to accumulate at a rate that reminds historians of post-World War I inflation. Each of the league's 30 teams will get an equal share of at least $550 million per season under a new record TV contract. Meanwhile, attendance in 1997 was the second-highest in league history at more than 19 million, and labor peace has been assured with an extension of the collective bargaining agreement between owners and players through the 2005 season.

In a move that some might consider to be bad for business, the owners failed to approve a watered-down instant replay proposal. Many observers declared that after a series of aborted attempts at reinstituting the concept, replay was dead.

On the field, tradition took a beating when the heavily favored defending champion Green Bay Packers were upset by the Denver Broncos, 31-24, in the Super Bowl, ending 13 years of NFC domination.

Meanwhile, the balance of power in the once-mighty NFC East shifted from the Dallas Cowboys to the New York Giants. NFL deep thinkers know it's better for business if both teams are strong. They also know that, eventually, new teams must be installed in major markets Los Angeles and Houston.

RECORD TV DEAL

The new contract with the league's TV partners will provide the NFL with an astonishing sum of money—at least $17.6 billion over the next eight seasons, doubling the annual amount of the previous deal. And after the fifth year, the league has the option to throw the contracts back open for bidding, which will garner even more money.

Still, some industry analysts feel the price tag of nearly $18 million might turn out to be a bargain; even with TV ratings down a little, the prestige of pro football means a lot in the television business.

CBS spent its way back into pro football by doling out $4 billion to carry AFC games. Fox retained the NFC package for $4.5 billion. And the Disney Corp., representing ABC and ESPN, forked over $9.2 billion for the rights to show Sunday night and Monday night games for the next eight years.

NBC, which had been the AFC's flagship network, was left out of the picture after finding the bidding too rich for its blood. Super Bowl XXXII marked the final broadcast for a network that had been televising pro football since the days of the AFL.

Was the mind-boggling outlay of funds worth it? CBS thought so, while Turner Network Television owner Ted Turner didn't; he dropped out of the running. CBS, which lost the NFC four years earlier, was determined to regain a piece of the pie even if it had to overpay to do so.

"We will not lose money on this deal," said Sean McManus, president of CBS Sports. "This has tremendous value for our television stations and tremendous value to our affiliates and the network. We have the No. 1 sport in America, which makes us a year-round leader in television."

The escalation of TV money began in earnest four years ago when Fox, at the behest of Cowboys owner Jerry Jones, entered the bidding and shocked the industry with its then-outrageous offer of $2.5 billion for four years' worth of NFC games. At the time, the sanity of Fox execs was seriously questioned, but the purchase gave the then-fledgling network credibility with sponsors and viewers.

Not only is the new deal good for the owners and the league, but the players, who long have contended that they're underpaid compared with their brethren in pro basketball and baseball, also got themselves a nice raise.

Two-thirds of TV revenue goes to the players, which means a total of about $12 billion over eight years. With each of the 30 teams employing about 60 players on their active rosters, injured reserve and practice squad, that means approximately 1,800 players will divide $1.5 billion per year. And that means an average annual salary of $833,000, although superstars obviously will get a lot more than special teams players and backups.

REPLAY REBUFFED AGAIN

With all that TV money pouring in, it was somewhat surprising that league owners again turned down another proposal for instant replay.

The concept continues to be favored by a majority of fans, players, coaches and, yes, owners. But a confirmed group of no voters dug in their heels, and the latest turndown could mean the end of replay forever.

"I think this is it," said Green Bay Packers general manager Ron Wolf, a leading proponent. "I think it's reared its head for the last time. This was as simplistic a form as you could present, and it didn't make it."

For passage of the latest proposal, 23 yes votes were needed. But those in favor could muster only 21 at the winter meetings in Orlando.

The plan under consideration was a "challenge timeout" scheme in which a timeout would have been taken away from a team that challenged a call and was wrong. If a team had three unsuccessful challenges in a half, it would be out of timeouts and unable to question an obviously incorrect call.

In Orlando, the league also extended the current contract with the Players Association through 2005. After assuring labor peace, the owners put a behavior clause into the contract stipulating that any employee of the league can be suspended for "any crime involving the use or threat of physical violence to a person or persons, the use of a deadly weapon in the commission of a crime, involvement in so-called hate crimes or crimes of domestic violence or the destruction of property."

Considering the number of incidents involving players in recent years, that clause figures to come into play very soon.

AFC LIVES

The AFC had grown tired of playing little brother to the big boys of the NFC, and the Broncos finally did something about it. Denver's victory over Green Bay in Super Bowl XXXII ended the NFC's 13-year dominance of the event.

For the 11½-point underdog Broncos, there was redemption on a number of levels. Not only did they allow the AFC to regain bragging rights, the Broncos won their first Super Bowl in five tries.

The victory also was satisfying for John Elway, who had been the losing quarterback in Denver's three previous Super Bowls. Elway did not have a spectacular game, but he was good enough and got help from running back Terrell Davis, who finished with 157 yards on the ground and a Super Bowl record three rushing touchdowns en route to capturing MVP honors.

Denver quarterback John Elway was on top of the world after the Broncos' 31-24 victory over the Packers in Super Bowl XXXII. (Photo by Albert Dickson/THE SPORTING NEWS.)

Another franchise might have given up on the 37-year-old Elway, but the Broncos, losers of four Super Bowls since 1978, stuck with their veteran leader.

"I have wiped the slate clean," he said afterwards.

The Broncos used a stout offensive line and a revitalized ground attack to become only the second wild card team to win the Super Bowl. (The 1980 Oakland Raiders were the first.) Denver's offensive line—Gary Zimmerman, Mark Schlereth, Tom Nalen, Brian Habib and Tony Jones—certainly deserved a share of Davis' MVP award. The veteran group dominated Green Bay's front seven as nobody thought it could. Gilbert Brown, the Packers' 345-pound defensive tackle, was neutralized throughout the game as the Broncos' NFC-style ground game produced 179 net yards.

Denver managed only 123 yards through the air, with Elway going 12-for-22 with one interception and zero touchdowns. But Elway scored one touchdown, made few mistakes and the Broncos controlled the clock with the run.

Davis was an especially poignant story for a Super Bowl played in San Diego. He had starred at San Diego's Lincoln High School and had his jersey

Although he rushed for more than 1,000 yards, Emmitt Smith scored a career-low 4 TDs, a big factor in the Cowboys' offensive decline. (Photo by Albert Dickson/THE SPORTING NEWS.)

retired by the school earlier in the week. He became the first player to win Super Bowl MVP accolades in the city in which he was born.

"I'm numb," Davis said. "It's going to take a while for this to set in."

For a while in the first half, Davis winning MVP honors seemed like a long shot. He suffered symptoms of a migraine in the first half, which clouded his vision. But Davis was not going to miss the ultimate second half of his career, and his one-yard touchdown run with 1:45 to play broke a tie and gave the Broncos their long-awaited victory.

In the end, however, it was Elway's day.

"To finally come out and show the NFC and everyone, it's unbelievable," Elway said.

COWBOYS' DYNASTY CRUMBLES

The Dallas Cowboys, long the NFL's marquee franchise, started the '97 season with a bunker mentality. A series of drug, sex and alcohol escapades had turned the franchise into fodder for talk show hosts and comics.

Step one to restore the team's image came in the offseason, when owner Jerry Jones hired former Dallas running back Calvin Hill and his wife, Janet, to help modify player behavior. Former Cowboys

fullback Robert Newhouse also was hired to handle the day-to-day operation of a program for player assistance and development.

Under tighter scrutiny, the players managed to avoid any scandals in 1997, although coach Barry Switzer was caught at Dallas-Fort Worth International Airport with a gun in his luggage. Switzer said he had forgotten that the firearm was with him, but Jones socked Switzer with a $50,000 fine.

It was the start of what turned out to be a nightmarish season for Switzer. The Cowboys stumbled to a 6-10 record, their worst finish since they were a league-worst 1-15 in 1989. Amid charges that the players had lost all respect for Switzer, Jones allowed his longtime friend to resign at the end of the season.

Following an exhaustive 34-day search for a replacement, Jones hired Pittsburgh Steelers offensive coordinator Chan Gailey as the fourth head coach in the franchise's 37-year history.

Jones reportedly offered the job to former UCLA coach Terry Donahue, but Donahue wanted too much control. Jones also interviewed former 49ers coach George Seifert and Packers offensive coordinator Sherman Lewis. But Gailey emerged late and landed the job with the help of glowing recommendations from highly regarded NFL types such as Atlanta coach Dan Reeves, a former Dallas player and assistant.

Gailey didn't have to be reminded that he was stepping into a pressure situation. The other three coaches in franchise history—Tom Landry, Jimmy Johnson and Switzer—have won Super Bowls. Gailey, 46, accepted the challenge despite the fact Jones serves as his own general manager and may be the most hands-on owner in the league.

Jones settled on Gailey in large part because the Cowboys offense was badly in need of repair. Dallas finished 20th in the league in total offense in 1997, and the once-explosive trio of quarterback Troy Aikman, running back Emmitt Smith and wide receiver Michael Irvin showed signs of slippage. The Dallas offensive line, once considered the best in the league, had deteriorated due to age and injuries.

"I wanted someone who was highly regarded as an innovative and creative mind on the offensive side of the ball," Jones said. "I wanted a proven playcaller who had done it in big games."

RISE OF THE GIANTS

Talk to a couple of NFL executives at happy hour and they'll usually admit, at least off the record, that having at least one strong franchise in New York is good for business. Having a competitive team in the nation's largest market drives interest in the entire league and boosts TV ratings.

The Giants were back in the limelight in 1997, ending the Cowboys' run of five consecutive division titles behind coach Jim Fassel, who as a rookie drove the Giants from worst to first in the NFC East and was voted NFL Coach of the Year.

The 48-year-old Fassel replaced Dan Reeves, who had feuded with Giants management over control of personnel decisions. Fassel let then–GM George Young handle the front office decisions; he stuck to coaching, guiding his young team to a 10-5-1 record and its first NFC East crown since 1990.

BROWNS RETURN

NFL owners voted unanimously at their winter meetings to grant an expansion franchise to Cleveland. It will be known, quite properly, as the Browns.

The league had announced in February 1996 that Cleveland would have a team in 1999 to replace the departing Browns, who moved to Baltimore and became the Ravens. But at that time the league said the new Cleveland team could be either an expansion team or a franchise moving from another city.

When owner Art Modell moved the Browns to Baltimore, Cleveland was up in arms. The NFL headed off what could have been a series of legal skirmishes with Cleveland by promising the city it would have a new team in place by the end of the century.

Possible relocating franchises like Indianapolis and Minnesota firmed up their situations, however, leaving Cleveland with only the expansion option. That was fine with NFL owners, who'll collect a hefty expansion fee from the new team.

The new Browns will be the league's 31st team and will play in the AFC Central, meaning two games each season against the Ravens.

League officials appointed Joe Mack as the team's personnel director, and ownership groups were being screened. A new stadium is under construction.

"I'm like most Clevelanders ... gratified," said Cleveland mayor Michael R. White. "Our goal was to bring a football team back to Cleveland and build them the best home in the world to play in. We're going to do that."

NFL commissioner Paul Tagliabue said the league also was interested in franchises for Los

Marcus Allen is headed for a job in broadcasting after scoring more rushing touchdowns and playing in more games than any back in NFL history. (Photo by Robert Seale/THE SPORTING NEWS.)

Angeles and Houston, other cities that have lost teams in the last five years.

SAVING A LION

Detroit Lions linebacker Reggie Brown suffered the most serious injury of the season. A second-year player from Texas A&M, Brown sustained a severe neck injury during what appeared to be a routine pileup at the Pontiac Silverdome in a December 21 game against the New York Jets.

Quick work by longtime Lions trainer Kent Falb and team doctor Terry Lock not only saved Brown's life, but led to what medical experts said was a miraculous recovery. Brown, 23, will never play football or any other contact sport again, but after some initial paralysis he was walking about a week later.

ALLEN RETIRES

Future Hall of Fame running back Marcus Allen retired from the Kansas City Chiefs to take a job as an analyst for CBS Sports. Allen ended his 16-year career as the NFL's all-time leader in rushing touchdowns with 123 and is sixth on the career rushing list with 12,243 yards. He played in more games (222) than any other running back in NFL history.

Allen, who will be eligible for the Hall of Fame in 2003, said he will enter the Canton shrine as a mem-

Marv Levy, who took the Bills to four straight Super Bowls in the early '90s, decided to hang it up after 34 years as a pro and college head coach. (Photo by Robert Seale/THE SPORTING NEWS.)

ber of the Chiefs and not the Oakland/Los Angeles Raiders, even though his best seasons came in the employment of the Raiders from 1982-92.

JAIL TIME FOR MORRIS

Baltimore Ravens running back Byron "Bam" Morris was sentenced to 90 days in a Texas jail for probation violations, ending a two-year tailspin that started with a marijuana bust in March 1996.

Morris, who spent his 26th birthday in prison, still has visions of resuming his career after being released by the Pittsburgh Steelers and the Ravens.

NITSCHKE DIES

Hall of Fame linebacker Ray Nitschke, whose physical defense was the backbone of the Green Bay Packers' championship teams of the '60s, died of a heart attack March 8 at his winter home in Florida. He was 61.

Nitschke played for the Packers from 1958-72, and his fierce presence was a key factor in the five titles won by Green Bay during his tenure, including the first two Super Bowls. He was a member of the NFL's 75th anniversary all-time team.

Nitschke's death was the second in less than a month involving a former member of the Packers'

championship teams of the '60s. Former defensive end Lionel Aldridge was found dead of natural causes in his suburban Milwaukee apartment February 12. He was 56.

HALL OF FAME HAILS FIVE

The day before the Super Bowl was special for five former NFL stars. That's when the Pro Football Hall of Fame announced the election of its newest members, who will be inducted July 26 in Canton, Ohio.

Heading the group were middle linebacker Mike Singletary, a 10-time Pro Bowl selection in his 12 seasons with the Chicago Bears, and offensive tackle Anthony Munoz, a 13-year star with the Cincinnati Bengals. Both were chosen in their first year of eligibility.

Singletary, who at 6-1 was considered by some scouts to be too short to excel at his position, was the leader of the 1985 Bears defense that swept the team to its only Super Bowl title.

Also selected were former Miami Dolphins center Dwight Stephenson, and defensive back Paul Krause, whose 16-year career with the Minnesota Vikings and Washington Redskins ended with 81 interceptions, most in league history. Stephenson was considered one of the league's top centers before his eight-year career was ended by a knee injury in 1987.

Wide receiver Tommy McDonald, who played for five teams in the 1950s and '60s, was selected by the Seniors Committee. McDonald, who was first eligible for the Hall 24 years ago, had all but abandoned hope of ever joining the shrine despite his 495 career receptions.

COACHING CAROUSEL

The removal of Barry Switzer and installation of Chan Gailey in Dallas was the final move in a relatively light year of coaching changes.

The Buffalo Bills said farewell to venerable Marv Levy, the only man to take a team to four straight Super Bowls. Levy, who coached for five years in the CFL before becoming coach of the Kansas City Chiefs in 1978, retired after 17 NFL seasons and 154 victories, including 11 in the playoffs. He was replaced by Bills defensive coordinator Wade Phillips.

Ousted from the helm of the Indianapolis Colts was Lindy Infante, who was replaced by former Saints coach Jim Mora. And in Oakland, owner Al Davis brought in Jon Gruden to take the place of the fired Joe Bugel. Gruden, 34, had been offensive coordinator of the Philadelphia Eagles the previous three years.

HOT AND COLD

Two striking themes ran concurrently through the 1997 regular season: It was a great year for running backs, and a not-so-hot year for quarterbacks.

Nowhere was it better than in Detroit, where Barry Sanders became the third player to break the 2,000-yard rushing barrier, and first since Eric Dickerson in 1984. All told 16 running backs, eight in each conference, rushed for at least 1,000 yards.

As for the quarterbacks ... San Diego's Stan Humphries suffered a third concussion in 11 months ... San Francisco's Steve Young had to reconsider his career after suffering a third concussion in a year ... Atlanta's Chris Chandler endured two concussions but continued to play ... There were 20 starting quarterback changes during the 1997 season as a result of injury, ranging from a broken jaw (Carolina's Kerry Collins) to a broken collarbone (Kansas City's Elvis Grbac) to a broken hip (Washington's Gus Frerotte).

TRIED RICE

Finally, there was 49ers receiver Jerry Rice's decision to return to action for a Monday night game against Denver in Week 16, just $3\,1/2$ months after undergoing major knee surgery after being injured in the season opener. Rice fractured his kneecap (same knee) making a catch in the end zone for San Francisco's first touchdown. The score ignited his teammates and propelled the 49ers to a 34-17 victory, clinching them home-field advantage for the NFC playoffs.

Pity, but the 49ers could have used Rice for the one game that really counted—the NFC championship game against Green Bay, which they lost 23-10. They didn't need him to get home-field advantage.

FINAL STANDINGS

AMERICAN FOOTBALL CONFERENCE

EASTERN DIVISION

	W	L	T	Pct.	Pts.	Opp.	Home	Away	Vs. AFC	Vs. NFC	Vs.AFC East
New England*	10	6	0	.625	369	289	6-2-0	4-4-0	9-3-0	1-3-0	7-1-0
Miami†	9	7	0	.563	339	327	6-2-0	3-5-0	8-4-0	1-3-0	4-4-0
N.Y. Jets	9	7	0	.563	348	287	5-3-0	4-4-0	6-6-0	3-1-0	2-6-0
Buffalo	6	10	0	.375	255	367	4-4-0	2-6-0	5-7-0	1-3-0	5-3-0
Indianapolis	3	13	0	.188	313	401	2-6-0	1-7-0	2-10-0	1-3-0	2-6-0

CENTRAL DIVISION

	W	L	T	Pct.	Pts.	Opp.	Home	Away	Vs. AFC	Vs. NFC	Vs.AFC Central
Pittsburgh*	11	5	0	.688	372	307	7-1-0	4-4-0	9-3-0	2-2-0	6-2-0
Jacksonville†	11	5	0	.688	394	318	7-1-0	4-4-0	9-3-0	2-2-0	6-2-0
Tennessee	8	8	0	.500	333	310	6-2-0	2-6-0	4-8-0	0-4-0	2-6-0
Cincinnati	7	9	0	.438	355	405	6-2-0	1-7-0	5-7-0	2-2-0	3-5-0
Baltimore	6	9	1	.406	326	345	3-4-1	3-5-0	4-8-0	2-1-1	3-5-0

WESTERN DIVISION

	W	L	T	Pct.	Pts.	Opp.	Home	Away	Vs. AFC	Vs. NFC	Vs.AFC West
Kansas City*	13	3	0	.813	375	232	8-0-0	5-3-0	9-3-0	4-0-0	7-1-0
Denver†	12	4	0	.750	472	287	8-0-0	4-4-0	9-3-0	3-1-0	6-2-0
Seattle	8	8	0	.500	365	362	4-4-0	4-4-0	6-6-0	2-2-0	4-4-0
Oakland	4	12	0	.250	324	419	2-6-0	2-6-0	2-10-0	2-2-0	2-6-0
San Diego	4	12	0	.250	266	425	2-6-0	2-6-0	3-9-0	1-3-0	1-7-0

*Division champion. †Wild-card team.

NATIONAL FOOTBALL CONFERENCE

EASTERN DIVISION

	W	L	T	Pct.	Pts.	Opp.	Home	Away	Vs. AFC	Vs. NFC	Vs.NFC East
N.Y. Giants*	10	5	1	.656	307	265	6-2-0	4-3-1	1-3-0	9-2-1	7-0-1
Washington	8	7	1	.531	327	289	5-2-1	3-5-0	1-3-0	7-4-1	4-3-1
Philadelphia	6	9	1	.406	317	372	6-2-0	0-7-1	2-1-1	4-8-0	3-5-0
Dallas	6	10	0	.375	304	314	5-3-0	1-7-0	2-2-0	4-8-0	3-5-0
Arizona	4	12	0	.250	283	379	3-5-0	1-7-0	1-3-0	3-9-0	2-6-0

CENTRAL DIVISION

	W	L	T	Pct.	Pts.	Opp.	Home	Away	Vs. AFC	Vs. NFC	Vs.NFC Central
Green Bay*	13	3	0	.813	422	282	8-0-0	5-3-0	3-1-0	10-2-0	7-1-0
Tampa Bay†	10	6	0	.625	299	263	5-3-0	5-3-0	3-1-0	7-5-0	3-5-0
Detroit†	9	7	0	.563	379	306	6-2-0	3-5-0	2-2-0	7-5-0	6-2-0
Minnesota†	9	7	0	.563	354	359	5-3-0	4-4-0	3-1-0	6-6-0	3-5-0
Chicago	4	12	0	.250	263	421	2-6-0	2-6-0	2-2-0	2-10-0	1-7-0

WESTERN DIVISION

	W	L	T	Pct.	Pts.	Opp.	Home	Away	Vs. AFC	Vs. NFC	Vs.NFC West
San Francisco*	13	3	0	.813	375	265	8-0-0	5-3-0	2-2-0	11-1-0	8-0-0
Carolina	7	9	0	.438	265	314	2-6-0	5-3-0	2-2-0	5-7-0	4-4-0
Atlanta	7	9	0	.438	320	361	3-5-0	4-4-0	2-2-0	5-7-0	4-4-0
New Orleans	6	10	0	.375	237	327	3-5-0	3-5-0	2-2-0	4-8-0	1-7-0
St. Louis	5	11	0	.313	299	359	2-6-0	3-5-0	0-4-0	5-7-0	3-5-0

*Division champion. †Wild-card team.

AFC PLAYOFFS

AFC wild card: Denver 42, Jacksonville 17
New England 17, Miami 3
AFC semifinals: Pittsburgh 7, New England 6
Denver 14, Kansas City 10
AFC championship: Denver 24, Pittsburgh 21

NFC PLAYOFFS

NFC wild card: Minnesota 23, N.Y. Giants 22
Tampa Bay 20, Detroit 10
NFC semifinals: San Francisco 38, Minnesota 22
Green Bay 21, Tampa Bay 7
NFC championship: Green Bay 23, San Francisco 10

SUPER BOWL

Denver 31, Green Bay 24

WEEK 1

RESULTS

CINCINNATI 24, Arizona 21
Dallas 37, PITTSBURGH 7
DENVER 19, Kansas City 3
DETROIT 28, Atlanta 17
Jacksonville 28, BALTIMORE 27
MIAMI 16, Indianapolis 10
Minnesota 34, BUFFALO 13
NEW ENGLAND 41, San Diego 7
N.Y. GIANTS 31, Philadelphia 17
N.Y. Jets 41, SEATTLE 3
ST. LOUIS 38, New Orleans 24
TAMPA BAY 13, San Francisco 6
TENNESSEE 24, Oakland 21 (OT)
Washington 24, CAROLINA 10
GREEN BAY 38, Chicago 24

Note: All caps denotes home team.

STANDINGS

AFC EAST	W	L	T	Pct.
Miami	1	0	0	1.000
New England	1	0	0	1.000
N.Y. Jets	1	0	0	1.000
Buffalo	0	1	0	.000
Indianapolis	0	1	0	.000

AFC CENTRAL	W	L	T	Pct.
Cincinnati	1	0	0	1.000
Jacksonville	1	0	0	1.000
Tennessee	1	0	0	1.000
Baltimore	0	1	0	.000
Pittsburgh	0	1	0	.000

AFC WEST	W	L	T	Pct.
Denver	1	0	0	1.000
Kansas City	0	1	0	.000
Oakland	0	1	0	.000
San Diego	0	1	0	.000
Seattle	0	1	0	.000

NFC EAST	W	L	T	Pct.
Dallas	1	0	0	1.000
N.Y. Giants	1	0	0	1.000
Washington	1	0	0	1.000
Arizona	0	1	0	.000
Philadelphia	0	1	0	.000

NFC CENTRAL	W	L	T	Pct.
Detroit	1	0	0	1.000
Green Bay	1	0	0	1.000
Minnesota	1	0	0	1.000
Tampa Bay	1	0	0	1.000
Chicago	0	1	0	.000

NFC WEST	W	L	T	Pct.
St. Louis	1	0	0	1.000
Atlanta	0	1	0	.000
Carolina	0	1	0	.000
New Orleans	0	1	0	.000
San Francisco	0	1	0	.000

HIGHLIGHTS

Hero of the week: Neil O'Donnell, a bust with the Jets the year before, threw a career-high five touchdown passes as New York rolled over Seattle, 41-3. He was 18-of-25 for 270 yards and no interceptions. O'Donnell's five touchdown passes were a career high and the most ever yielded by the Seahawks.

Goat of the week: Cardinals fullback Larry Centers, who was stripped of the ball at the Bengals' 37 with 1:10 left in the game as he stretched to get a couple of yards on third down with the Cardinals leading. After Centers fumbled away a chance to run down the clock, Jeff Blake led Cincinnati down the field with sideline completions, ending the drive with a 6-yard touchdown pass to Carl Pickens with 38 seconds left for a 24-21 victory.

Sub of the week: Green Bay tight end Jeff Thomason, who entered after starter Mark Chmura tore his posterior cruciate ligament in the second quarter, caught five passes for 58 yards and one touchdown in the Packers' 38-24 win over Chicago.

Comeback of the week: Through three quarters, Arizona quarterback Kent Graham was picking apart the Bengals' zone-blitz defense, setting up three touchdown runs. It looked as if the Cardinals were on their way to an easy victory when Larry Centers' 1-yard dive put them ahead 21-3 five minutes into the third quarter. Although Cincinnati answered with two Ki-Jana Carter TD runs in the fourth quarter, the Bengals still trailed, 21-16, with 2:14 left. About a minute later, linebacker Gerald Dixon punched the ball loose from Centers' grasp, giving Cincinnati one more chance to score. Quarterback Jeff Blake did not waste the opportunity, driving his team down the field and firing a dramatic game-winning touchdown pass to Carl Pickens in the final minute.

Blowout of the week: The Jets, 1-15 in 1996, served notice they no longer would be a doormat under new coach Bill Parcells. Led by Neil O'Donnell's five TD passes, they trounced Seattle, 41-3, in the Kingdome. The Jets led 27-3 at halftime and did not punt until the fourth quarter.

Nail-biter of the week: Led by tailback Eddie George's 216 yards rushing, the Oilers were leading Oakland late in the fourth quarter. But the Raiders mounted a scoring drive with less than a minute in regulation, and receiver Tim Brown capped the drive with a touchdown catch to send the game into overtime tied at 21. The Oilers regrouped in OT, however, winning on Al Del Greco's 33-yard field goal 3:08 into the extra period.

Hit of the week: When 49ers receiver Jerry Rice took the handoff on an end-around, Tampa Bay defensive tackle Warren Sapp was waiting for him to turn the corner. Rice attempted to avert the pursuing defender, but Sapp grabbed him by the facemask and pulled him to the ground. Rice suffered torn anterior cruciate and medial collateral ligaments, as well as damage to the posterior capsule in his left knee. The injury caused Rice to miss most of the rest of the season.

Oddity of the week: Randall Cunningham returned to the NFL after a one-year absence but was kicking, not throwing, the football with his new team, the Vikings. He handled the team's punting duties after Mitch Berger was sidelined with a hip injury. Cunningham was a two-time All-American punter at UNLV and had punted a dozen times in his 12-year NFL career before 1997. He averaged 42.5 yards on four kicks against Buffalo.

Top rusher: Eddie George's 216-yard effort against the Raiders was the second-highest total on opening day in NFL history. O.J. Simpson had 250 yards for Buffalo at New England in 1973.

Top passer: Drew Bledsoe was 26-of-39 for 340 yards and four touchdowns in directing New England to a 41-7 rout of the Chargers.

Top receiver: Tim Brown caught eight passes for 158 yards and three touchdowns in the Raiders' loss at Tennessee.

Notes: Drew Bledsoe tied Babe Parilli's 30-year-old Patriots team record with four TD passes in a half. . . .

Dallas quarterback Troy Aikman threw four TD passes in a game for the third time in his career in the Cowboys' 37-7 win at Pittsburgh. The loss was the Steelers' worst since a club-record 51-0 setback to Cleveland in the 1989 season opener.... The Panthers' 24-10 loss to Washington was Carolina's first defeat in the 10-game history of Ericsson Stadium.... New England's Dave Meggett returned six punts to set an NFL record with 305 returns in his career. Only he and the Raiders' Tim Brown (301) have returned 300 punts in NFL history.... The Chargers haven't beaten the Patriots since 1970. They are 0-9 since.... Only 30,171 fans turned out to see the Oilers play their inaugural game in Tennessee. One reason for the apathy was that fans in Memphis had lobbied for an NFL team for years, only to be rejected. Another was that Memphis and Nashville are rival cities, unwilling to support the others' teams. The Oilers are calling Memphis home for two years until a new stadium opens in Nashville. As evidenced by a less-than-half-filled Liberty Bowl, the temporary nature of the arrangement did not sit too well with Memphis fans.

Quote of the week: Lions coach Bobby Ross, after Detroit's come-from-behind, 28-17 victory over the Falcons: "They hung in there, and that is what we want to do all year long. Like a chicken on a June bug, we are just going to have to stay after them all the time."

GAME SUMMARIES

OILERS 24, RAIDERS 21

Sunday, August 31

Oakland	0	0	7	14	0—21
Tennessee	10	0	3	8	3—24

First Quarter
Tenn.—FG, Del Greco 30, 10:16.
Tenn.—Sanders 48 pass from McNair (Del Greco kick), 14:59.
Third Quarter
Tenn.—FG, Del Greco 37, 10:11.
Oak.—T. Brown 59 pass from George (Ford kick), 11:17.
Fourth Quarter
Oak.—T. Brown 27 pass from George (Ford kick), 3:14.
Tenn.—George 29 run (George run), 12:51.
Oak.—T. Brown 16 pass from George (Ford kick), 14:38.
Overtime
Tenn.—FG, Del Greco 33, 3:08.
Attendance—30,171.

TEAM STATISTICS

	Oakland	Tennessee
First downs	17	20
Rushes-yards	17-45	42-255
Passing	287	164
Punt returns	2-7	2-23
Kickoff returns	5-154	5-117
Interception returns	1-(-1)	0-0
Comp.-att.-int.	21-38-0	13-25-1
Sacked-yards lost	3-11	3-18
Punts	6-42	5-34
Fumbles-lost	3-1	1-1
Penalties-yards	6-35	7-56
Time of possession	25:31	41:22

INDIVIDUAL STATISTICS
RUSHING—Oakland, Kaufman 12-32, Aska 4-6, Fenner 1-7. Tennessee, George 35-216, McNair 3-23, Thomas 3-4, Harmon 1-12.
PASSING—Oakland, George 21-37-0-298, Kaufman 0-1-0-0. Tennessee, McNair 13-25-1-182.

RECEIVING—Oakland, T. Brown 8-158, Kaufman 3-21, Truitt 2-33, Jett 2-20, Fenner 2-16, Williams 2-14, Dudley 1-26, Shedd 1-10. Tennessee, Harmon 5-50, Wycheck 3-43, Sanders 2-51, Davis 2-27, Mason 1-11.
MISSED FIELD GOAL ATTEMPTS—Oakland, Ford 46.
INTERCEPTIONS—Oakland, Trapp 1-(minus 1).
KICKOFF RETURNS—Oakland, Hall 3-75, Howard 2-79. Tennessee, Gray 4-109, Roan 1-8.
PUNT RETURNS—Oakland, Howard 2-7. Tennessee, Gray 2-23.
SACKS—Oakland, Smith 1.5, Maryland 1, Johnstone 0.5. Tennessee, Bowden 1, Lyons 1, Holmes 1.

BENGALS 24, CARDINALS 21

Sunday, August 31

Arizona	7	7	7	0—21
Cincinnati	0	3	0	21—24

First Quarter
Ariz.—McElroy 17 run (Butler kick), 6:21.
Second Quarter
Cin.—FG, Pelfrey 38, 9:08.
Ariz.—C. Smith 1 run (Butler kick), 14:54.
Third Quarter
Ariz.—Centers 1 run (Butler kick), 4:58.
Fourth Quarter
Cin.—Carter 2 run (Pelfrey kick), 0:47.
Cin.—Carter 1 run (pass failed), 12:46.
Cin.—Pickens 6 pass from Blake (McGee pass from Blake), 14:22.
Attendance—50,298.

TEAM STATISTICS

	Arizona	Cincinnati
First downs	18	21
Rushes-yards	30-75	25-87
Passing	248	230
Punt returns	0-0	4-41
Kickoff returns	4-90	4-83
Interception returns	1-0	1-(-2)
Comp.-att.-int.	20-36-1	24-35-1
Sacked-yards lost	0-0	4-22
Punts	6-43	6-40
Fumbles-lost	1-1	0-0
Penalties-yards	8-73	2-20
Time of possession	31:06	28:54

INDIVIDUAL STATISTICS
RUSHING—Arizona, McElroy 17-52, Centers 11-20, K. Graham 1-2, C. Smith 1-1. Cincinnati, Carter 19-76, Blake 4-6, Bieniemy 2-5.
PASSING—Arizona, K. Graham 20-36-1-248. Cincinnati, Blake 24-35-1-252.
RECEIVING—Arizona, R. Moore 7-96, Sanders 6-105, Centers 5-32, Edwards 2-15. Cincinnati, Pickens 8-79, Scott 5-75, Bieniemy 3-2, Carter 2-40, McGee 2-28, Milne 2-22, Twyner 1-4, Battaglia 1-2.
MISSED FIELD GOAL ATTEMPTS—None.
INTERCEPTIONS—Arizona, A. Williams 1-0. Cincinnati, Spencer 1-(minus 2).
KICKOFF RETURNS—Arizona, Bouie 3-69, C. Smith 1-21. Cincinnati, Twyner 2-42, Dillon 2-41.
PUNT RETURNS—Cincinnati, Myers 4-41.
SACKS—Arizona, Swann 2, Miller 1, Rice 1.

REDSKINS 24, PANTHERS 10

Sunday, August 31

Washington	0	10	0	14—24
Carolina	3	0	0	7—10

First Quarter
Car.—FG, Kasay 52, 12:41.
Second Quarter
Was.—FG, Blanton 38, 2:25.
Was.—Allen 1 run (Blanton kick), 14:32.
Fourth Quarter
Car.—Walls 24 pass from Beuerlein (Kasay kick), 1:28.
Was.—Allen 1 run (Blanton kick), 6:08.
Was.—Shepherd 5 pass from Frerotte (Blanton kick), 8:24.
Attendance—72,633.

TEAM STATISTICS

	Washington	Carolina
First downs	23	16
Rushes-yards	40-198	29-158

	Washington	Carolina
Passing	125	104
Punt returns	2-0	4-30
Kickoff returns	1-11	4-127
Interception returns	2-11	0-0
Comp.-att.-int.	11-29-0	12-26-2
Sacked-yards lost	2-19	1-4
Punts	6-42	5-42
Fumbles-lost	1-0	3-2
Penalties-yards	3-19	10-101
Time of possession	31:32	28:28

INDIVIDUAL STATISTICS

RUSHING—Washington, Allen 25-141, Davis 12-55, Frerotte 2-(minus 2), Shepherd 1-4. Carolina, Johnson 20-134, Lane 6-41, Greene 3-10.

PASSING—Washington, Frerotte 10-27-0-147, Hostetler 1-2-0-(minus 3). Carolina, Beuerlein 12-26-2-108.

RECEIVING—Washington, Asher 4-35, Shepherd 2-48, Mitchell 2-37, Bowie 2-27, Logan 1-(minus 3). Carolina, Greene 3-22, Walls 2-40, Ismail 2-17, Oliver 2-12, Johnson 2-11, Carruth 1-6.

MISSED FIELD GOAL ATTEMPTS—None.

INTERCEPTIONS—Washington, Dishman 1-11, Pounds 1-0.

KICKOFF RETURNS—Washington, Mitchell 1-11. Carolina, Bates 3-94, E. Mills 1-33.

PUNT RETURNS—Washington, Mitchell 2-0. Carolina, Poole 3-21, Oliver 1-9.

SACKS—Washington, Mims 1. Carolina, Poole 1, Lathon 1.

JAGUARS 28, RAVENS 27

Sunday, August 31

Jacksonville	14	7	0	7—28
Baltimore	0	17	7	3—27

First Quarter
Jac.—Johnson 25 run (Hollis kick), 4:43.
Jac.—Means 1 run (Hollis kick), 12:46.

Second Quarter
Bal.—J. Lewis 17 pass from Testaverde (Stover kick), 1:44.
Bal.—J. Lewis 42 pass from Testaverde (Stover kick), 7:44.
Jac.—Smith 20 pass from Johnson (Hollis kick), 13:52.
Bal.—FG, Stover 33, 15:00.

Third Quarter
Bal.—Jackson 54 pass from Testaverde (Stover kick), 1:02.

Fourth Quarter
Bal.—FG, Stover 25, 6:14.
Jac.—Smith 28 pass from Johnson (Hollis kick), 9:13.
Attendance—61,018.

TEAM STATISTICS

	Jacksonville	Baltimore
First downs	19	22
Rushes-yards	31-108	17-72
Passing	303	301
Punt returns	2-6	3-19
Kickoff returns	4-64	5-138
Interception returns	3-23	0-0
Comp.-att.-int.	23-29-0	24-41-3
Sacked-yards lost	3-14	3-21
Punts	5-45	3-44
Fumbles-lost	1-1	0-0
Penalties-yards	11-64	3-20
Time of possession	31:59	28:01

INDIVIDUAL STATISTICS

RUSHING—Jacksonville, Means 25-67, Johnson 4-31, Hallock 1-8, Stewart 1-2. Baltimore, Byner 14-63, Testaverde 2-4, J. Lewis 1-5.

PASSING—Jacksonville, Johnson 20-24-0-294, Matthews 3-5-0-23. Baltimore, Testaverde 24-41-3-322.

RECEIVING—Jacksonville, Smith 6-106, McCardell 6-84, Stewart 4-42, Mitchell 3-38, Means 2-5, Hallock 1-23, Brown 1-19. Baltimore, Jackson 8-143, J. Lewis 4-73, Green 4-41, Byner 3-31, Alexander 2-23, Kinchen 1-10, Yarborough 1-5, Testaverde 1-(minus 4).

MISSED FIELD GOAL ATTEMPTS—Jacksonville, Hollis 43.

INTERCEPTIONS—Jacksonville, Figures 2-0, Hudson 1-23.

KICKOFF RETURNS—Jacksonville, Logan 2-39, Jackson 1-16, Parker 1-9. Baltimore, J. Lewis 4-118, Brew 1-20.

PUNT RETURNS—Jacksonville, Barlow 2-6. Baltimore, J. Lewis 3-19.

SACKS—Jacksonville, Simmons 2, Robinson 1. Baltimore, Burnett 2, Boulware 1.

DOLPHINS 16, COLTS 10

Sunday, August 31

Indianapolis	0	7	0	3—10
Miami	3	7	3	3—16

First Quarter
Mia.—FG, Mare 23, 9:56.

Second Quarter
Ind.—Alexander 43 interception return (Blanchard kick), 0:51.
Mia.—Abdul-Jabbar 9 run (Mare kick), 6:43.

Third Quarter
Mia.—FG, Mare 34, 11:13.

Fourth Quarter
Mia.—FG, Mare 19, 4:15.
Ind.—FG, Blanchard 35, 14:00.
Attendance—70,813.

TEAM STATISTICS

	Indianapolis	Miami
First downs	18	11
Rushes-yards	26-130	28-97
Passing	168	105
Punt returns	1-4	2-16
Kickoff returns	4-91	3-39
Interception returns	1-43	2-10
Comp.-att.-int.	22-42-2	10-26-1
Sacked-yards lost	5-41	0-0
Punts	5-43	6-47
Fumbles-lost	3-1	2-1
Penalties-yards	8-69	4-25
Time of possession	34:01	25:59

INDIVIDUAL STATISTICS

RUSHING—Indianapolis, Faulk 19-94, Harbaugh 3-31, Crockett 3-12, Harrison 1-(minus 7). Miami, Spikes 14-43, Abdul-Jabbar 13-50, Pritchett 1-4.

PASSING—Indianapolis, Harbaugh 14-29-2-109, Justin 8-13-0-100. Miami, Marino 10-26-1-105.

RECEIVING—Indianapolis, Faulk 4-30, Dawkins 4-29, Crockett 4-15, Bailey 2-40, Stablein 2-35, Warren 2-31, Harrison 2-14, Dilger 1-9, Pollard 1-6. Miami, McDuffie 4-31, Barnett 3-28, Drayton 1-29, Abdul-Jabbar 1-10, Spikes 1-7.

MISSED FIELD GOAL ATTEMPTS—Indianapolis, Blanchard 42, 45, 58.

INTERCEPTIONS—Indianapolis, Alexander 1-43. Miami, Wooden 2-10.

KICKOFF RETURNS—Indianapolis, Bailey 4-91. Miami, Ismail 2-39, C. Harris 1-0.

PUNT RETURNS—Indianapolis, Stablein 1-4. Miami, Jordan 2-16.

SACKS—Miami, Rodgers 1, Taylor 1, Armstrong 1, Stubbs 1, Bowens 1.

LIONS 28, FALCONS 17

Sunday, August 31

Atlanta	3	7	0	7—17
Detroit	0	14	0	14—28

First Quarter
Atl.—FG, Andersen 30, 5:15.

Second Quarter
Det.—Moore 43 pass from Mitchell (Hanson kick), 1:55.
Atl.—Haynes 24 pass from Chandler (Andersen kick), 7:04.
Det.—S. Boyd 42 fumble return (Hanson kick), 8:58.

Fourth Quarter
Atl.—Anderson 1 run (Andersen kick), 5:03.
Det.—Moore 25 pass from Mitchell (Hanson kick), 9:55.
Det.—Brown 38 interception return (Hanson kick), 11:03.
Attendance—61,244.

TEAM STATISTICS

	Atlanta	Detroit
First downs	13	10
Rushes-yards	29-55	23-46
Passing	268	175
Punt returns	5-34	3-8
Kickoff returns	3-57	4-103
Interception returns	1-0	3-42
Comp.-att.-int.	20-37-3	12-30-1
Sacked-yards lost	4-22	4-30
Punts	8-41	9-39
Fumbles-lost	5-1	6-2
Penalties-yards	13-93	5-55
Time of possession	35:40	24:20

INDIVIDUAL STATISTICS

RUSHING—Atlanta, Anderson 20-33, Chandler 4-20, Hanspard 3-1, Green 2-1. Detroit, Sanders 15-33, Mitchell 7-13, Vardell 1-0.

PASSING—Atlanta, Chandler 20-36-3-290, Anderson 0-1-0-0. Detroit, Mitchell 12-30-1-205.

RECEIVING—Atlanta, Green 5-55, Emanuel 4-88, Christian 3-23, Santiago 2-47, Haynes 2-34, Anderson 2-26, Mathis 2-17. Detroit, Moore 7-115, Sanders 2-26, Milburn 1-43, Vardell 1-14, Morton 1-7.

MISSED FIELD GOAL ATTEMPTS—Atlanta, Andersen 42.

INTERCEPTIONS—Atlanta, Bradford 1-0. Detroit, Brown 1-38, S. Boyd 1-4, Jeffries 1-0.

KICKOFF RETURNS—Atlanta, Hanspard 2-39, Kinchen 1-18. Detroit, Milburn 4-103.

PUNT RETURNS—Atlanta, Kinchen 5-34. Detroit, Milburn 3-8.

SACKS—Atlanta, Archambeau 1, Hall 1, Burrough 1, Smith 1. Detroit, Porcher 1, Bonham 1, London 0.5, Elliss 0.5, Waldroup 0.5, Wells 0.5.

VIKINGS 34, BILLS 13

Sunday, August 31

Minnesota	0	10	3	21—34
Buffalo	0	7	0	6—13

Second Quarter
Min.—FG, Davis 21, 0:03.
Buf.—Riemersma 19 pass from Collins (Christie kick), 4:05.
Min.—Carter 6 pass from Johnson (Davis kick), 8:41.

Third Quarter
Min.—FG, Davis 43, 11:02.

Fourth Quarter
Buf.—FG, Christie 28, 0:14.
Min.—R. Smith 78 run (Davis kick), 1:13.
Min.—Brady 30 fumble return (Davis kick), 3:57.
Buf.—FG, Christie 46, 9:19.
Min.—Carter 35 pass from Johnson (Davis kick), 12:30.
Attendance—79,139.

TEAM STATISTICS

	Minnesota	Buffalo
First downs	17	22
Rushes-yards	28-185	24-147
Passing	200	279
Punt returns	0-0	2-15
Kickoff returns	1-21	7-145
Interception returns	2-5	1-20
Comp.-att.-int.	17-30-1	25-39-2
Sacked-yards lost	3-18	3-20
Punts	4-43	4-35
Fumbles-lost	0-0	2-2
Penalties-yards	2-15	7-59
Time of possession	29:30	30:30

INDIVIDUAL STATISTICS

RUSHING—Minnesota, R. Smith 16-169, Hoard 7-16, Johnson 3-(minus 3), Evans 1-5, Palmer 1-(minus 2). Buffalo, Thomas 14-63, A. Smith 7-55, Moulds 1-27, Collins 1-2, Zeigler 1-0.

PASSING—Minnesota, Johnson 17-30-1-218. Buffalo, Collins 25-39-2-299.

RECEIVING—Minnesota, Carter 8-121, Goodwin 2-17, Palmer 2-13, Hoard 1-9, Reed 1-30, Reed 1-19, DeLong 1-11, R. Smith 1-5, Evans 1-2. Buffalo, Reed 7-142, Thomas 6-40, A. Smith 5-44, Riemersma 4-54, Johnson 1-8, Holmes 1-7, Moulds 1-4.

MISSED FIELD GOAL ATTEMPTS—None.

INTERCEPTIONS—Minnesota, Washington 1-5, Thomas 1-0. Buffalo, Kerner 1-20.

KICKOFF RETURNS—Minnesota, Morrow 1-21. Buffalo, Moulds 7-145.

PUNT RETURNS—Buffalo, Tasker 2-15.

SACKS—Minnesota, Randle 2, Fisk 1. Buffalo, B. Smith 2, Washington 1.

BUCCANEERS 13, 49ERS 6

Sunday, August 31

San Francisco	3	3	0	0— 6
Tampa Bay	0	0	3	10—13

First Quarter
S.F.—FG, Anderson 30, 13:10.

Second Quarter
S.F.—FG, Anderson 40, 12:03.

Third Quarter
T.B.—FG, Husted 40, 14:37.

Fourth Quarter
T.B.—Moore 1 pass from Dilfer (Husted kick), 5:39.
T.B.—FG, Husted 34, 8:12.
Attendance—62,554.

TEAM STATISTICS

	San Fran.	Tampa Bay
First downs	12	15
Rushes-yards	27-100	27-115
Passing	91	175
Punt returns	2-20	1-8
Kickoff returns	3-56	3-75
Interception returns	0-0	1-0
Comp.-att.-int.	14-21-1	15-26-0
Sacked-yards lost	7-41	2-9
Punts	5-35	4-46
Fumbles-lost	1-0	2-2
Penalties-yards	8-50	6-59
Time of possession	32:31	27:29

INDIVIDUAL STATISTICS

RUSHING—San Francisco, Hearst 18-84, Kirby 5-19, Floyd 2-6, S. Young 1-1, Rice 1-(minus 10). Tampa Bay, Alstott 14-69, Dunn 8-37, Dilfer 4-8, Hape 1-1.

PASSING—San Francisco, Brohm 10-13-0-99, S. Young 4-8-1-33. Tampa Bay, Dilfer 15-26-0-184.

RECEIVING—San Francisco, Rice 4-38, Uwaezuoke 2-29, Kirby 2-22, Jones 2-20, Hearst 2-6, Owens 1-12, Floyd 1-5. Tampa Bay, Williams 3-74, Alstott 3-50, Harris 2-34, Thomas 2-9, Moore 2-6, Dunn 2-4, Anthony 1-7.

MISSED FIELD GOAL ATTEMPTS—San Francisco, Anderson 34. Tampa Bay, Husted 32.

INTERCEPTIONS—Tampa Bay, Legette 1-0.

KICKOFF RETURNS—San Francisco, Owens 2-31, Uwaezuoke 1-25. Tampa Bay, Williams 2-49, Dunn 1-26.

PUNT RETURNS—San Francisco, Uwaezuoke 2-20. Tampa Bay, Williams 1-8.

SACKS—San Francisco, Doleman 1, Walker 1. Tampa Bay, Sapp 2.5, Upshaw 2, Nickerson 1, Brooks 0.5, Porter 0.5, Culpepper 0.5.

JETS 41, SEAHAWKS 3

Sunday, August 31

N.Y. Jets	17	10	14	0—41
Seattle	0	3	0	0— 3

First Quarter
NYJ—Chrebet 35 pass from O'Donnell (Hall kick), 5:53.
NYJ—FG, Hall 55, 7:35.
NYJ—Graham 26 pass from O'Donnell (Hall kick), 10:34.

Second Quarter
NYJ—Brady 1 pass from O'Donnell (Hall kick), 1:18.
NYJ—FG, Hall 28, 6:29.
Sea.—FG, Peterson 31, 14:49.

Third Quarter
NYJ—Chrebet 31 pass from O'Donnell (Hall kick), 2:35.
NYJ—Graham 47 pass from O'Donnell (Hall kick), 6:20.
Attendance—53,893.

TEAM STATISTICS

	N.Y. Jets	Seattle
First downs	28	16
Rushes-yards	40-164	19-84
Passing	270	163
Punt returns	5-30	2-7
Kickoff returns	1-(-11)	3-88
Interception returns	1-0	0-0
Comp.-att.-int.	18-26-0	17-42-1
Sacked-yards lost	0-0	1-5
Punts	2-38	5-45
Fumbles-lost	2-0	2-1
Penalties-yards	5-45	10-56
Time of possession	34:39	25:21

INDIVIDUAL STATISTICS

RUSHING—New York, Murrell 24-131, L. Johnson 11-36, Anderson 2-1, Clements 2-(minus 3), O'Donnell 1-(minus 1). Seattle, Warren 15-64, Smith 2-17, Moon 1-3, Friesz 1-0.

PASSING—New York, O'Donnell 18-25-0-270, L. Johnson 0-1-0-0. Seattle, Moon 7-21-1-89, Friesz 10-21-0-79.

RECEIVING—New York, K. Johnson 6-68, Graham 3-100, Chrebet 3-73, Anderson 2-12, Baxter 2-9, Brady 2-8. Seattle, Pritchard 4-42, Galloway 3-34, Br. Blades 3-33, Smith 2-34, Fauria 2-27, Warren 2-(minus 13), May 1-11.

MISSED FIELD GOAL ATTEMPTS—None.
INTERCEPTIONS—New York, Mickens 1-0.
KICKOFF RETURNS—New York, Baxter 1-(minus 11). Seattle, Broussard 3-88.
PUNT RETURNS—New York, Ward 5-30. Seattle, Harris 2-7.
SACKS—New York, Jones 1.

BRONCOS 19, CHIEFS 3

Sunday, August 31

Kansas City	0	0	3	0— 3
Denver	3	6	0	10—19

First Quarter
Den.—FG, Elam 35, 10:30.

Second Quarter
Den.—FG, Elam 36, 8:51.
Den.—FG, Elam 25, 14:47.

Third Quarter
K.C.—FG, Stoyanovich 20, 13:36.

Fourth Quarter
Den.—Davis 10 run (Elam kick), 2:05.
Den.—FG, Elam 53, 11:16.
Attendance—75,600.

TEAM STATISTICS
	Kansas City	Denver
First downs	12	20
Rushes-yards	19-133	35-146
Passing	108	232
Punt returns	0-0	2-43
Kickoff returns	4-112	2-85
Interception returns	0-0	1-43
Comp.-att.-int.	14-25-1	17-28-0
Sacked-yards lost	3-7	2-14
Punts	5-43	2-33
Fumbles-lost	0-0	1-0
Penalties-yards	9-50	8-69
Time of possession	23:44	36:16

INDIVIDUAL STATISTICS
RUSHING—Kansas City, Hill 7-92, Anders 6-27, Grbac 3-16, Allen 3-(minus 2). Denver, Davis 26-101, Elway 4-24, Hebron 3-8, Griffith 2-13.
PASSING—Kansas City, Grbac 14-25-1-115. Denver, Elway 17-28-0-246.
RECEIVING—Kansas City, Anders 7-29, Dawson 2-30, Rison 2-20, Popson 2-14, Gonzalez 1-22. Denver, R. Smith 5-122, Sharpe 4-41, Davis 3-14, McCaffrey 2-37, Green 2-24, Griffith 1-8.
MISSED FIELD GOAL ATTEMPTS—None.
INTERCEPTIONS—Denver, Braxton 1-43.
KICKOFF RETURNS—Kansas City, Vanover 4-112. Denver, Hebron 2-85.
PUNT RETURNS—Denver, Gordon 2-43.
SACKS—Kansas City, McDaniels 1, Anderson 1. Denver, Tanuvasa 1.5, Gordon 1, Perry 0.5.

GIANTS 31, EAGLES 17

Sunday, August 31

Philadelphia	3	0	7	7—17
N.Y. Giants	7	7	10	7—31

First Quarter
NYG—Brown 3 run (Daluiso kick), 7:08.
Phi.—FG, Boniol 48, 13:21.

Second Quarter
NYG—Calloway 9 pass from Brown (Daluiso kick), 14:54.

Third Quarter
NYG—Barber 1 run (Daluiso kick), 0:58.
NYG—FG, Daluiso 39, 8:17.
Phi.—Watters 3 run (Boniol kick), 13:33.

Fourth Quarter
Phi.—Turner 14 pass from Peete (Boniol kick), 6:45.
NYG—Garnes 95 interception return (Daluiso kick), 10:02.
Attendance—70,296.

TEAM STATISTICS
	Philadelphia	N.Y. Giants
First downs	24	12
Rushes-yards	26-120	26-103
Passing	327	187
Punt returns	4-49	5-43
Kickoff returns	4-71	4-134

	Philadelphia	N.Y. Giants
Interception returns	0-0	1-95
Comp.-att.-int.	26-48-1	13-27-0
Sacked-yards lost	9-44	2-6
Punts	8-42	8-45
Fumbles-lost	3-1	0-0
Penalties-yards	11-85	7-60
Time of possession	35:31	24:29

INDIVIDUAL STATISTICS
RUSHING—Philadelphia, Watters 18-81, Garner 4-12, Detmer 3-20, Turner 1-7. New York, Barber 20-88, Brown 3-10, Way 3-5.
PASSING—Philadelphia, Detmer 9-25-0-103, Peete 17-23-1-268. New York, Brown 13-27-0-193.
RECEIVING—Philadelphia, Timpson 9-125, Watters 4-58, Fryar 4-40, Lewis 3-34, Turner 2-50, Garner 2-23, Seay 1-38, Dunn 1-3. New York, Calloway 4-42, Way 3-63, Barber 3-32, Lewis 1-34, Hilliard 1-19, Cross 1-3.
MISSED FIELD GOAL ATTEMPTS—New York, Daluiso 44.
INTERCEPTIONS—New York, Garnes 1-95.
KICKOFF RETURNS—Philadelphia, Wyatt 2-50, Witherspoon 1-23, Johnson 1-(minus 2). New York, Lewis 4-134.
PUNT RETURNS—Philadelphia, Seay 2-51, Wyatt 2-(minus 2). New York, Toomer 5-43.
SACKS—Philadelphia, H. Thomas 1, J. Jones 1. New York, Strahan 2.5, Harris 1.5, Bratzke 1, K. Hamilton 1, Sehorn 1, Miller 1, Phillips 1.

RAMS 38, SAINTS 24

Sunday, August 31

New Orleans	6	11	0	7—24
St. Louis	0	14	21	3—38

First Quarter
N.O.—FG, Brien 31, 3:27.
N.O.—FG, Brien 53, 12:17.

Second Quarter
St.L.—Phillips 1 run (Wilkins kick), 4:48.
St.L.—Small 30 pass from Banks (Wilkins kick), 13:06.
N.O.—Guliford 102 kickoff return (Hastings pass from Shuler), 13:19.
N.O.—FG, Brien 46, 14:52.

Third Quarter
St.L.—Conwell 46 pass from Banks (Wilkins kick), 7:02.
St.L.—Phillips 25 run (Wilkins kick), 7:26.
St.L.—Phillips 5 run (Wilkins kick), 10:55.

Fourth Quarter
N.O.—Hastings 30 pass from Wuerffel (Brien kick), 7:17.
St.L.—FG, Wilkins 36, 14:05.
Attendance—64,575.

TEAM STATISTICS
	New Orleans	St. Louis
First downs	13	20
Rushes-yards	19-82	43-189
Passing	159	214
Punt returns	4-64	3-25
Kickoff returns	5-197	6-102
Interception returns	1-(-1)	3-6
Comp.-att.-int.	12-33-3	13-21-1
Sacked-yards lost	3-25	2-12
Punts	5-47	6-40
Fumbles-lost	2-2	0-0
Penalties-yards	10-79	7-77
Time of possession	25:39	34:21

INDIVIDUAL STATISTICS
RUSHING—New Orleans, Zellars 8-24, Bates 7-28, T. Davis 4-30. St. Louis, Phillips 26-125, Heyward 6-17, R. Moore 5-5, Lee 3-17, Banks 2-2, Crawford 1-23.
PASSING—New Orleans, Shuler 8-21-2-115, Wuerffel 4-12-1-69. St. Louis, Banks 13-21-1-226.
RECEIVING—New Orleans, Hastings 4-95, Zellars 4-13, I. Smith 2-26, Hill 1-32, T. Davis 1-18. St. Louis, Kennison 4-80, Small 3-67, Conwell 3-63, Phillips 2-8, Lee 1-8.
MISSED FIELD GOAL ATTEMPTS—St. Louis, Wilkins 36.
INTERCEPTIONS—New Orleans, Allen 1-(minus 1). St. Louis, Lyle 2-6, Lyght 1-0.
KICKOFF RETURNS—New Orleans, Guliford 4-168, T. Davis 1-29. St. Louis, Thomas 5-97, Zgonina 1-5.
PUNT RETURNS—New Orleans, Guliford 4-64. St. Louis, Kennison 3-25.
SACKS—New Orleans, Fields 1, Molden 1. St. Louis, Phifer 1, O'Neal 1, Carter 0.5, Farr 0.5.

COWBOYS 37, STEELERS 7

Sunday, August 31

Dallas	0	17	17	3—37
Pittsburgh	0	0	0	7— 7

Second Quarter
Dal.—Miller 12 pass from Aikman (Cunningham kick), 1:35.
Dal.—Irvin 42 pass from Aikman (Cunningham kick), 9:48.
Dal.—FG, Cunningham 52, 14:58.

Third Quarter
Dal.—Irvin 15 pass from Aikman (Cunningham kick), 4:18.
Dal.—FG, Cunningham 24, 6:20.
Dal.—Johnston 13 pass from Aikman (Cunningham kick), 10:36.

Fourth Quarter
Dal.—FG, Cunningham 28, 4:30.
Pit.—Bruener 4 pass from Stewart (N. Johnson kick), 11:56.
   Attendance—60,396.

TEAM STATISTICS

	Dallas	Pittsburgh
First downs	21	15
Rushes-yards	34-85	23-85
Passing	295	89
Punt returns	3-54	3-20
Kickoff returns	1-22	5-109
Interception returns	1-6	0-0
Comp.-att.-int.	19-31-0	13-28-1
Sacked-yards lost	0-0	3-15
Punts	4-46	8-47
Fumbles-lost	0-0	3-1
Penalties-yards	8-74	5-44
Time of possession	32:17	27:43

INDIVIDUAL STATISTICS
RUSHING—Dallas, E. Smith 26-69, S. Williams 5-16, Wilson 2-(minus 3), Johnston 1-3. Pittsburgh, Bettis 15-63, G. Jones 7-18, Stewart 1-4.

PASSING—Dallas, Aikman 19-30-0-295, Wilson 0-1-0-0. Pittsburgh, Stewart 13-28-1-104.

RECEIVING—Dallas, Irvin 7-153, Johnston 5-65, E. Smith 3-25, Miller 2-43, Bjornson 2-9. Pittsburgh, Thigpen 4-43, Hawkins 3-32, C. Johnson 2-19, Bruener 2-3, G. Jones 1-4, Witman 1-3.

MISSED FIELD GOAL ATTEMPTS—None.

INTERCEPTIONS—Dallas, Coakley 1-6.

KICKOFF RETURNS—Dallas, Walker 1-22. Pittsburgh, Blackwell 4-92, Adams 1-17.

PUNT RETURNS—Dallas, Sanders 2-45, Mathis 1-9. Pittsburgh, Blackwell 3-20.

SACKS—Dallas, Stoutmire 1, Hennings 1, Anderson 1.

PATRIOTS 41, CHARGERS 7

Sunday, August 31

San Diego	0	0	7	0— 7
New England	14	17	0	10—41

First Quarter
N.E.—Coates 4 pass from Bledsoe (Vinatieri kick), 5:01.
N.E.—Glenn 25 pass from Bledsoe (Vinatieri kick), 12:16.

Second Quarter
N.E.—FG, Vinatieri 21, 5:14.
N.E.—Gash 12 pass from Bledsoe (Vinatieri kick), 11:09.
N.E.—Byars 2 pass from Bledsoe (Vinatieri kick), 14:23.

Third Quarter
S.D.—F. Jones 44 pass from Humphries (Carney kick), 3:18.

Fourth Quarter
N.E.—FG, Vinatieri 26, 3:33.
N.E.—Clay 53 interception return (Vinatieri kick), 9:28.
   Attendance—60,190.

TEAM STATISTICS

	San Diego	New England
First downs	14	22
Rushes-yards	20-85	26-84
Passing	142	340
Punt returns	2-19	6-99
Kickoff returns	8-186	2-55
Interception returns	0-0	1-53
Comp.-att.-int.	18-38-1	26-39-0
Sacked-yards lost	4-52	0-0
Punts	7-52	4-51
Fumbles-lost	3-2	0-0
Penalties-yards	7-50	6-50
Time of possession	27:20	32:40

INDIVIDUAL STATISTICS
RUSHING—San Diego, Brown 12-49, Fletcher 7-31, Humphries 1-5. New England, Martin 22-75, Bledsoe 2-8, Meggett 1-2, Zolak 1-(minus 1).

PASSING—San Diego, Humphries 12-26-0-131, Everett 6-12-1-63. New England, Bledsoe 26-39-0-340.

RECEIVING—San Diego, F. Jones 4-73, C. Jones 4-55, Fletcher 3-32, Martin 2-18, Still 2-10, Brown 2-0, Hartley 1-6. New England, Jefferson 5-82, Coates 4-60, Brown 4-24, Martin 4-16, Glenn 3-74, Brisby 3-51, Gash 2-31, Byars 1-2.

MISSED FIELD GOAL ATTEMPTS—None.

INTERCEPTIONS—New England, Clay 1-53.

KICKOFF RETURNS—San Diego, Rachal 4-98, Metcalf 4-88. New England, Meggett 2-55.

PUNT RETURNS—San Diego, Metcalf 2-19. New England, Meggett 6-99.

SACKS—New England, Jones 2, Thomas 1, Wheeler 1.

PACKERS 38, BEARS 24

Monday, September 1

Chicago	0	11	0	13—24
Green Bay	3	15	6	14—38

First Quarter
G.B.—FG, Longwell 38, 4:23.

Second Quarter
Chi.—R. Harris 1 run (Flanigan pass from Sauerbrun), 4:57.
G.B.—Thomason 1 pass from Favre (Levens pass from Favre), 9:09.
Chi.—FG, Jaeger 42, 13:04.
G.B.—Brooks 18 pass from Favre (Longwell kick), 14:12.

Third Quarter
G.B.—FG, Longwell 36, 6:36.
G.B.—FG, Longwell 29, 10:45.

Fourth Quarter
G.B.—Levens 1 run (Longwell kick), 6:48.
Chi.—Proehl 22 pass from Kramer (pass failed), 11:32.
G.B.—Wilkins 1 fumble return (Longwell kick), 12:24.
Chi.—R. Harris 68 run (Jaeger kick), 12:52.
   Attendance—60,766.

TEAM STATISTICS

	Chicago	Green Bay
First downs	19	18
Rushes-yards	30-164	31-107
Passing	172	208
Punt returns	1-4	5-107
Kickoff returns	7-148	2-53
Interception returns	1-14	2-44
Comp.-att.-int.	17-41-2	15-22-1
Sacked-yards lost	3-20	2-18
Punts	6-48	4-40
Fumbles-lost	1-1	1-1
Penalties-yards	13-91	6-28
Time of possession	32:11	27:49

INDIVIDUAL STATISTICS
RUSHING—Chicago, Salaam 16-41, R. Harris 13-122, Kramer 1-1. Green Bay, Levens 22-80, Favre 7-18, Henderson 2-9.

PASSING—Chicago, Kramer 17-41-2-192. Green Bay, Favre 15-22-1-226.

RECEIVING—Chicago, R. Harris 4-36, Wetnight 3-32, Engram 3-24, Proehl 2-30, Penn 2-28, Salaam 2-20, Jennings 1-22. Green Bay, Thomason 5-58, Mayes 4-54, Brooks 3-71, Henderson 2-13, Chmura 1-30.

MISSED FIELD GOAL ATTEMPTS—None.

INTERCEPTIONS—Chicago, M. Carter 1-14. Green Bay, Evans 1-27, Mullen 1-17.

KICKOFF RETURNS—Chicago, Hughes 7-148. Green Bay, Schroeder 2-53.

PUNT RETURNS—Chicago, Engram 1-4. Green Bay, Schroeder 5-107.

SACKS—Chicago, R. Cox 1, Spellman 0.5, Simpson 0.5. Green Bay, Brown 1, S. Dotson 1, White 0.5, Wilkins 0.5.

WEEK 2

RESULTS

ARIZONA 25, Dallas 22 (OT)
BALTIMORE 23, Cincinnati 10
Buffalo 28, N.Y. JETS 22
Carolina 9, ATLANTA 6
Denver 35, SEATTLE 14
JACKSONVILLE 40, N.Y. Giants 13
MIAMI 16, Tennessee 13 (OT)
Minnesota 27, CHICAGO 24
New England 31, INDIANAPOLIS 6
PHILADELPHIA 10, Green Bay 9
PITTSBURGH 14, Washington 13
San Diego 20, NEW ORLEANS 6
San Francisco 15, ST. LOUIS 12
Tampa Bay 24, DETROIT 17
Kansas City 28, OAKLAND 27

STANDINGS

AFC EAST	W	L	T	Pct.
Miami	2	0	0	1.000
New England	2	0	0	1.000
Buffalo	1	1	0	.500
N.Y. Jets	1	1	0	.500
Indianapolis	0	2	0	.000

AFC CENTRAL	W	L	T	Pct.
Jacksonville	2	0	0	1.000
Baltimore	1	1	0	.500
Cincinnati	1	1	0	.500
Pittsburgh	1	1	0	.500
Tennessee	1	1	0	.500

AFC WEST	W	L	T	Pct.
Denver	2	0	0	1.000
Kansas City	1	1	0	.500
San Diego	1	1	0	.500
Oakland	0	2	0	.000
Seattle	0	2	0	.000

NFC EAST	W	L	T	Pct.
Arizona	1	1	0	.500
Dallas	1	1	0	.500
N.Y. Giants	1	1	0	.500
Philadelphia	1	1	0	.500
Washington	1	1	0	.500

NFC CENTRAL	W	L	T	Pct.
Minnesota	2	0	0	1.000
Tampa Bay	2	0	0	1.000
Detroit	1	1	0	.500
Green Bay	1	1	0	.500
Chicago	0	2	0	.000

NFC WEST	W	L	T	Pct.
Carolina	1	1	0	.500
St. Louis	1	1	0	.500
San Francisco	1	1	0	.500
Atlanta	0	2	0	.000
New Orleans	0	2	0	.000

HIGHLIGHTS

Hero of the week: For the second consecutive week, Patriots quarterback Drew Bledsoe threw four touchdown passes in a blowout victory, this time 31-6 over the Colts. Bledsoe was 15-of-25 for 267 yards and completed five passes that covered at least 21 yards.

Goat of the week: With the Dolphins driving into Oilers territory in a 13-13 overtime game, Miami wide receiver Fred Barnett caught a pass at the Oilers' 24. After making the tackle, Tennessee cornerback Tomur Barnes shoved Barnett in the head and was hit with a 12-yard penalty, moving the ball to the 12. Miami's Olindo Mare kicked a 29-yard field goal on the next play as the Dolphins won, 16-13.

Sub of the week: Third-string quarterback Steve Matthews, making his first NFL start because of injuries to Mark Brunell and Rob Johnson, was 23-of-35 for 252 yards as the Jaguars routed the Giants, 40-13. Matthews, who never got into a game in three seasons with the Chiefs, had joined the Jaguars three weeks earlier and had a working knowledge of about half the Jacksonville playbook.

Comeback of the week: When Arizona trailed Dallas, 22-7, in the third quarter, it must have been a familiar feeling—the Cardinals had not beaten the Cowboys since 1990. But quarterback Kent Graham's 1-yard touchdown pass to Frank Sanders at the end of the third quarter cut the deficit to 22-14. Graham then engineered an eight-play, 70-yard drive at the end of the fourth quarter, hitting Pat Carter for a touchdown with 1:06 left and throwing to Rob Moore for the two-point conversion, sending the game into overtime. Graham fumbled early in the extra period, but the Cowboys fumbled it back and Graham was able to redeem himself. He completed long passes to Sanders and Larry Centers to set up Kevin Butler's game-winning 20-yard field goal.

Blowout of the week: After trailing, 14-13, at halftime, the Broncos scored 22 consecutive points to beat the Seahawks, 35-14. Keyed by a 32-yard Darrien Gordon interception return for a touchdown at the end of the third quarter, Denver went on to force Seattle to give up the ball on downs twice in the fourth quarter.

Nail-biter of the week: Trailing 9-3 on a wet day in Philadelphia, Ty Detmer and the Eagles put together a 10-minute scoring drive in the fourth quarter to stun the Packers, 10-9. The game-winning points came on a 2-yard touchdown pass from Detmer to Freddie Solomon with 1:56 left. The Packers returned the ensuing kickoff to midfield and drove to the Eagles' 11 with 11 seconds left, but rookie kicker Ryan Longwell pushed a 28-yard field-goal attempt wide right.

Hit of the week: By Eagles linebacker James Willis, who stopped Dorsey Levens short of the first-down marker on third-and-1 at the 11, forcing the Packers into an ill-fated field-goal attempt with 11 seconds left.

Oddity of the week: Barry Sanders had terrorized Tampa Bay defenses by averaging 117.5 rushing yards in his first 15 career games against the Bucs. But in the 16th, Sanders was held to 20 yards on 10 carries as the Bucs beat the Lions, 24-17.

Top rusher: Jerome Bettis ran for 134 yards and a touchdown in leading Pittsburgh to a 14-13 victory over Washington.

Top passer: Detroit's Scott Mitchell was 29-of-50 passes for 331 yards in the Lions' loss to the Buccaneers. Touchdown passes of 73 and 66 yards accounted for 139 of the yardage total.

Top receiver: Andre Rison caught eight passes for 162 yards and one touchdown in Kansas City's 28-27 win over Oakland.

Notes: Andre Rison's touchdown against the Raiders was a game-winner with three seconds left. It gave him at least one TD reception with six teams, an NFL record. . . . Eagles kicker Chris Boniol's streak of successful field goals ended at 28 when he missed a 48-yarder against the Packers. The NFL record is 31 in a row, set by Minnesota's Fuad Reveiz in 1994-95. . . . With 14 yards against Seattle, Broncos quarterback John Elway moved into fourth place on the NFL's career quarterback rushing list with 3,133 yards. Randall Cunningham tops that list with 4,482 yards. . . . The Jaguars were 2-0 despite playing quarterbacks—Rob Johnson and Steve Matthews—who were making their first NFL starts. . . . Troy Aikman broke Roger Staubach's record of 115 starts by a Dallas quarterback. . . . The Redskins had only six possessions in their 14-13 loss to the Steelers . . . Drew Bledsoe's eight TD passes in the first two weeks were caught by eight receivers. He also did not throw an interception in his first 64 attempts. . . . The Broncos' Terrell Davis has 12 career 100-yard rushing games, three against the Seahawks. . . . Barry Sanders had only 53 rushing yards in Detroit's first two games of 1997. He entered the season on the heels of three consecutive 1,500-yard seasons.

Quote of the week: Packers coach Mike Holmgren, after his team lost for the first time in nine games: "It has been a long time since we lost a ballgame. Now I think we can eliminate the 19-0 talk. Every week it's going to be a battle. Maybe it will be a blessing for us."

GAME SUMMARIES

CARDINALS 25, COWBOYS 22

Sunday, September 7

Dallas	6	13	3	0	0—22
Arizona	0	7	7	8	3—25

First Quarter
Dal.—FG, Cunningham 24, 5:44.
Dal.—FG, Cunningham 47, 9:49.
Second Quarter
Ariz.—McElroy 10 run (Butler kick), 2:09.
Dal.—FG, Cunningham 37, 10:00.
Dal.—Hennings 4 fumble return (Cunningham kick), 11:23.
Dal.—FG, Cunningham 34, 14:56.
Third Quarter
Dal.—FG, Cunningham 28, 2:00.
Ariz.—Sanders 7 pass from K. Graham (Butler kick), 13:16.
Fourth Quarter
Ariz.—Carter 1 pass from K. Graham (R. Moore pass from K. Graham), 13:54.
Overtime
Ariz.—FG, Butler 20, 8:30.
Attendance—71,578.

TEAM STATISTICS

	Dallas	Arizona
First downs	10	22
Rushes-yards	29-180	25-66
Passing	147	220
Punt returns	2-30	5-37
Kickoff returns	4-93	4-70
Interception returns	0-0	0-0
Comp.-att.-int.	21-40-0	26-47-0
Sacked-yards lost	3-24	3-29
Punts	8-47	8-44
Fumbles-lost	2-1	6-4
Penalties-yards	12-115	3-20
Time of possession	34:58	33:32

INDIVIDUAL STATISTICS
RUSHING—Dallas, E. Smith 19-132, S. Williams 8-43, Aikman 1-5, Johnston 1-0. Arizona, McElroy 16-53, K. Graham 3-7, Centers 3-5, Bouie 3-1.
PASSING—Dallas, Aikman 21-40-0-171. Arizona, K. Graham 26-47-0-249.
RECEIVING—Dallas, St. Williams 5-53, Irvin 4-18, Bjornson 3-59, E. Smith 3-11, S. Williams 3-10, Johnston 2-11, B. Davis 1-9. Arizona, Sanders 7-44, R. Moore 6-108, Gedney 4-24, McElroy 3-25, Carter 2-10, K. Williams 1-10.

MISSED FIELD GOAL ATTEMPTS—Dallas, Cunningham 40.
INTERCEPTIONS—None.
KICKOFF RETURNS—Dallas, Walker 3-59, Marion 1-34. Arizona, K. Williams 2-30, Bouie 1-27, C. Smith 1-13.
PUNT RETURNS—Dallas, Sanders 2-30. Arizona, K. Williams 5-37.
SACKS—Dallas, Woodson 1, Coakley 1, Tolbert 1. Arizona, Rice 2, Caldwell 1.

PANTHERS 9, FALCONS 6

Sunday, September 7

Carolina	0	0	0	9—9	
Atlanta	0	3	3	0—6	

Second Quarter
Atl.—FG, Andersen 25, 4:07.
Third Quarter
Atl.—FG, Andersen 28, 7:51.
Fourth Quarter
Car.—FG, Kasay 31, 2:21.
Car.—FG, Kasay 31, 12:21.
Car.—FG, Kasay 39, 15:00.
Attendance—51,829.

TEAM STATISTICS

	Carolina	Atlanta
First downs	21	8
Rushes-yards	28-93	27-48
Passing	228	162
Punt returns	2-5	4-11
Kickoff returns	0-0	3-59
Interception returns	0-0	0-0
Comp.-att.-int.	21-35-0	11-23-0
Sacked-yards lost	6-40	0-0
Punts	6-42	8-44
Fumbles-lost	2-2	4-2
Penalties-yards	7-55	5-39
Time of possession	33:20	26:40

INDIVIDUAL STATISTICS
RUSHING—Carolina, Johnson 24-86, Greene 2-6, Beuerlein 1-5, Ismail 1-(minus 4). Atlanta, Anderson 17-42, Green 6-5, Tolliver 2-(minus 1), Hanspard 1-2, Christian 1-0.
PASSING—Carolina, Beuerlein 21-35-0-268. Atlanta, Tolliver 7-17-0-79, Chandler 4-6-0-83.
RECEIVING—Carolina, Muhammad 8-71, Walls 7-147, Ismail 2-25, Carruth 2-18, Johnson 2-7. Atlanta, Emanuel 3-50, Mathis 2-47, Anderson 2-12, Christian 2-8, Santiago 1-26, Green 1-19.
MISSED FIELD GOAL ATTEMPTS—Carolina, Kasay 55.
INTERCEPTIONS—None.
KICKOFF RETURNS—Atlanta, Hanspard 3-59.
PUNT RETURNS—Carolina, Poole 2-5. Atlanta, Kinchen 4-11.
SACKS—Atlanta, Archambeau 2, Dronett 1, Brandon 1, Owens 1, Smith 1.

BILLS 28, JETS 22

Sunday, September 7

Buffalo	0	14	7	7—28	
N.Y. Jets	3	10	6	3—22	

First Quarter
NYJ—FG, Hall 26, 11:01.
Second Quarter
NYJ—Ward 19 pass from O'Donnell (Hall kick), 0:45.
Buf.—Thomas 2 run (Christie kick), 6:02.
Buf.—Reed 10 pass from Collins (Christie kick), 9:03.
NYJ—FG, Hall 19, 15:00.
Third Quarter
Buf.—Early 37 pass from Collins (Christie kick), 8:11.
NYJ—Glenn 96 kickoff return (run failed), 8:28.
Fourth Quarter
NYJ—FG, Hall 52, 5:08.
Buf.—Riemersma 10 pass from Collins (Christie kick), 8:02.
Attendance—72,988.

TEAM STATISTICS

	Buffalo	N.Y. Jets
First downs	15	12
Rushes-yards	33-67	21-39
Passing	193	163

	Buffalo	N.Y. Jets
Punt returns	4-69	3-25
Kickoff returns	1-34	4-151
Interception returns	2-17	2-24
Comp.-att.-int.	15-22-2	16-37-2
Sacked-yards lost	2-17	8-55
Punts	5-50	5-48
Fumbles-lost	2-1	1-0
Penalties-yards	8-82	4-41
Time of possession	30:34	29:26

INDIVIDUAL STATISTICS

RUSHING—Buffalo, A. Smith 14-47, Thomas 12-18, Collins 6-11, Mohr 1-(minus 9). New York, Murrell 14-27, L. Johnson 4-11, O'Donnell 2-1, Anderson 1-0.

PASSING—Buffalo, Collins 15-22-2-210. New York, O'Donnell 16-37-2-218.

RECEIVING—Buffalo, Reed 5-39, Tindale 4-105, Riemersma 2-19, Early 1-37, Johnson 1-8, Moulds 1-8, A. Smith 1-(minus 6). New York, K. Johnson 3-86, Ward 3-51, Chrebet 3-39, Anderson 3-18, L. Johnson 2-14, Brady 1-9, Baxter 1-1.

MISSED FIELD GOAL ATTEMPTS—New York, Hall 39.

INTERCEPTIONS—Buffalo, Burris 1-9, Spielman 1-8. New York, Coleman 1-24, Mickens 1-0.

KICKOFF RETURNS—Buffalo, Moulds 1-34. New York, Glenn 3-140, Ward 1-11.

PUNT RETURNS—Buffalo, Tasker 4-69. New York, Ward 3-25.

SACKS—Buffalo, Paup 3, B. Smith 1.5, Rogers 1, Hansen 1, Washington 0.5, Jeffcoat 0.5, Moran 0.5. New York, Douglas 1, Lyle 1.

CHARGERS 20, SAINTS 6

Sunday, September 7

San Diego	7	3	3	7—20
New Orleans	3	3	0	0— 6

First Quarter
N.O.—FG, Brien 37, 5:17.
S.D.—Harrison fumble recovery in end zone (Carney kick), 9:21.

Second Quarter
N.O.—FG, Brien 31, 2:17.
S.D.—FG, Carney 37, 13:45.

Third Quarter
S.D.—FG, Carney 34, 2:20.

Fourth Quarter
S.D.—F. Jones 21 pass from Everett (Carney kick), 12:50.
Attendance—65,760.

TEAM STATISTICS
	San Diego	New Orleans
First downs	11	14
Rushes-yards	30-59	23-65
Passing	171	178
Punt returns	2-7	3-37
Kickoff returns	2-36	3-67
Interception returns	3-2	1-6
Comp.-att.-int.	17-29-1	20-38-3
Sacked-yards lost	2-24	3-16
Punts	7-39	5-47
Fumbles-lost	2-1	3-3
Penalties-yards	6-49	5-25
Time of possession	29:08	30:52

INDIVIDUAL STATISTICS

RUSHING—San Diego, Brown 21-46, Fletcher 4-3, Everett 2-(minus 4), C. Jones 1-9, Craver 1-3, Pegram 1-2. New Orleans, T. Davis 10-34, Zellars 6-14, Shuler 4-13, Bates 3-4.

PASSING—San Diego, Everett 17-29-1-195. New Orleans, Shuler 20-38-3-194.

RECEIVING—San Diego, Metcalf 4-65, Fletcher 4-35, Still 3-50, F. Jones 2-17, C. Jones 2-7, Hartley 1-13, Martin 1-8. New Orleans, Hill 7-63, Hastings 5-37, T. Davis 4-46, Hobbs 1-21, Guliford 1-11, I. Smith 1-11, Zellars 1-5.

MISSED FIELD GOAL ATTEMPTS—None.

INTERCEPTIONS—San Diego, Coleman 1-2, Gouveia 1-0, Fuller 1-0. New Orleans, Tubbs 1-6.

KICKOFF RETURNS—San Diego, Rachal 1-26, Metcalf 1-10. New Orleans, Guliford 3-67.

PUNT RETURNS—San Diego, Metcalf 2-7. New Orleans, Guliford 3-37.

SACKS—San Diego, Parrella 1.5, Seau 1, Coleman 0.5. New Orleans, Fields 1, B. Smith 1.

PATRIOTS 31, COLTS 6

Sunday, September 7

New England	7	7	7	10—31
Indianapolis	3	3	0	0— 6

First Quarter
N.E.—Jefferson 34 pass from Bledsoe (Vinatieri kick), 9:21.
Ind.—FG, Blanchard 45, 14:59.

Second Quarter
Ind.—FG, Blanchard 38, 9:49.
N.E.—Martin 21 pass from Bledsoe (Vinatieri kick), 11:59.

Third Quarter
N.E.—Brisby 6 pass from Bledsoe (Vinatieri kick), 14:25.

Fourth Quarter
N.E.—Brown 21 pass from Bledsoe (Vinatieri kick), 4:14.
N.E.—FG, Vinatieri 21, 12:47.
Attendance—53,632.

TEAM STATISTICS
	New England	Indianapolis
First downs	15	19
Rushes-yards	26-122	21-41
Passing	260	214
Punt returns	3-26	3-48
Kickoff returns	2-46	5-146
Interception returns	0-0	0-0
Comp.-att.-int.	15-25-0	30-38-0
Sacked-yards lost	1-7	5-27
Punts	5-56	6-50
Fumbles-lost	1-0	1-1
Penalties-yards	8-61	5-44
Time of possession	25:41	34:19

INDIVIDUAL STATISTICS

RUSHING—New England, Martin 25-121, Bledsoe 1-1. Indianapolis, Faulk 15-23, Harbaugh 3-14, Warren 3-4.

PASSING—New England, Bledsoe 15-25-0-267. Indianapolis, Harbaugh 30-38-0-241.

RECEIVING—New England, Coates 4-54, Brisby 3-46, Brown 3-35, Martin 3-34, Jefferson 2-98. Indianapolis, Harrison 9-74, Dawkins 7-61, Stablein 3-35, Bailey 3-25, Dilger 3-15, Faulk 2-22, Warren 2-3, Slutzker 1-6.

MISSED FIELD GOAL ATTEMPTS—None.

INTERCEPTIONS—None.

KICKOFF RETURNS—New England, Meggett 1-23, Cullors 1-23. Indianapolis, Bailey 5-146.

PUNT RETURNS—New England, Meggett 3-26. Indianapolis, Stablein 3-48.

SACKS—New England, Slade 2, Collons 1, McGruder 1, Eaton 1. Indianapolis, Belser 1.

BUCCANEERS 24, LIONS 17

Sunday, September 7

Tampa Bay	10	7	0	7—24
Detroit	0	3	7	7—17

First Quarter
T.B.—FG, Husted 41, 5:03.
T.B.—Hape 1 pass from Dilfer (Husted kick), 9:51.

Second Quarter
T.B.—Dunn 6 run (Husted kick), 9:39.
Det.—FG, Hanson 48, 14:52.

Third Quarter
Det.—Morton 73 pass from Mitchell (Hanson kick), 8:30.

Fourth Quarter
T.B.—Alstott 1 run (Husted kick), 8:18.
Det.—Sanders 66 pass from Mitchell (Hanson kick), 14:45.
Attendance—58,234.

TEAM STATISTICS
	Tampa Bay	Detroit
First downs	20	13
Rushes-yards	41-173	12-24
Passing	99	322
Punt returns	6-33	4-14
Kickoff returns	3-36	3-62
Interception returns	1-14	0-0
Comp.-att.-int.	12-24-0	29-50-1
Sacked-yards lost	3-16	2-9
Punts	7-42	7-50

	Tampa Bay	Detroit
Fumbles-lost	0-0	1-0
Penalties-yards	5-40	11-129
Time of possession	35:01	24:59

INDIVIDUAL STATISTICS

RUSHING—Tampa Bay, Dunn 24-130, Alstott 14-34, Dilfer 3-9. Detroit, Sanders 10-20, Rivers 1-3, Mitchell 1-1.

PASSING—Tampa Bay, Dilfer 12-24-0-115. Detroit, Mitchell 29-50-1-331.

RECEIVING—Tampa Bay, Copeland 4-44, Dunn 2-20, Anthony 2-19, Williams 1-18, Moore 1-8, Thomas 1-5, Hape 1-1. Detroit, Sanders 8-102, Sloan 7-49, Moore 6-51, Morton 4-102, Milburn 2-19, Metzelaars 2-8.

MISSED FIELD GOAL ATTEMPTS—Detroit, Hanson 52.

INTERCEPTIONS—Tampa Bay, Mincy 1-14.

KICKOFF RETURNS—Tampa Bay, Williams 2-36, Moore 1-0. Detroit, Milburn 3-62.

PUNT RETURNS—Tampa Bay, Williams 5-30, Dunn 1-3. Detroit, Milburn 4-14.

SACKS—Tampa Bay, Sapp 1, Jackson 1. Detroit, Porcher 1.5, Elliss 1, Brown 0.5.

JAGUARS 40, GIANTS 13

Sunday, September 7

N.Y. Giants	7	0	6	0—13
Jacksonville	0	20	3	17—40

First Quarter
NYG—Barber 4 run (Daluiso kick), 12:31.

Second Quarter
Jac.—FG, Hollis 29, 0:46.
Jac.—Stewart 1 run (Hollis kick), 4:08.
Jac.—Means 9 run (Hollis kick), 11:48.
Jac.—FG, Hollis 52, 15:00.

Third Quarter
Jac.—FG, Hollis 35, 12:15.
NYG—Calloway 8 pass from Brown (pass failed), 14:30.

Fourth Quarter
Jac.—FG, Hollis 42, 5:17.
Jac.—Means 5 run (Hollis kick), 9:04.
Jac.—Stewart 12 run (Hollis kick), 13:05.
Attendance—70,581.

TEAM STATISTICS
	N.Y. Giants	Jacksonville
First downs	13	23
Rushes-yards	16-39	39-123
Passing	167	249
Punt returns	4-42	5-52
Kickoff returns	5-131	0-0
Interception returns	0-0	1-23
Comp.-att.-int.	16-35-1	23-35-0
Sacked-yards lost	2-15	1-3
Punts	9-45	6-52
Fumbles-lost	2-2	1-1
Penalties-yards	9-80	9-71
Time of possession	20:21	39:39

INDIVIDUAL STATISTICS

RUSHING—New York, Barber 11-17, Wheatley 1-6. Jacksonville, Means 24-85, Stewart 9-24, Shelton 4-2, Matthews 1-10, Hallock 1-2.

PASSING—New York, Brown 16-35-1-182. Jacksonville, Matthews 23-35-0-252.

RECEIVING—New York, Wheatley 4-39, Barber 3-43, Calloway 3-39, Cross 3-12, Hilliard 1-23, Toomer 1-19, Lewis 1-7. Jacksonville, Smith 8-117, McCardell 4-71, Stewart 4-13, Jackson 2-19, Mitchell 2-11, Means 1-20, Brown 1-3, Hallock 1-(minus 2).

MISSED FIELD GOAL ATTEMPTS—None.

INTERCEPTIONS—Jacksonville, Davis 1-23.

KICKOFF RETURNS—New York, Lewis 4-101, Way 1-30.

PUNT RETURNS—New York, Toomer 4-42. Jacksonville, Barlow 5-52.

SACKS—New York, K. Hamilton 1. Jacksonville, Smeenge 1, Simmons 1.

BRONCOS 35, SEAHAWKS 14

Sunday, September 7

Denver	10	3	15	7—35
Seattle	0	14	0	0—14

First Quarter
Den.—FG, Elam 38, 4:23.
Den.—McCaffrey 14 pass from Elway (Elam kick), 10:38.

Second Quarter
Sea.—Crumpler 12 pass from Moon (Peterson kick), 13:49.
Sea.—C. Brown 26 fumble return (Peterson kick), 14:05.
Den.—FG, Elam 51, 14:58.

Third Quarter
Den.—McCaffrey 21 pass from Elway (Sharpe pass from Elway), 14:01.
Den.—Gordon 32 interception return (Elam kick), 15:00.

Fourth Quarter
Den.—Davis 1 run (Elam kick), 7:38.
Attendance—55,859.

TEAM STATISTICS
	Denver	Seattle
First downs	22	16
Rushes-yards	30-143	24-69
Passing	187	220
Punt returns	1-5	0-0
Kickoff returns	3-89	7-101
Interception returns	1-32	0-0
Comp.-att.-int.	18-26-0	20-33-1
Sacked-yards lost	2-10	1-2
Punts	3-36	5-46
Fumbles-lost	1-1	1-0
Penalties-yards	4-25	10-134
Time of possession	29:28	30:32

INDIVIDUAL STATISTICS

RUSHING—Denver, Davis 21-107, Loville 5-22, Elway 4-14. Seattle, Smith 12-54, Warren 11-26, Galloway 1-(minus 11).

PASSING—Denver, Elway 18-26-0-197. Seattle, Moon 20-33-1-222.

RECEIVING—Denver, McCaffrey 8-93, Sharpe 4-62, R. Smith 2-9, Griffith 2-4, Carswell 1-21, Green 1-8. Seattle, Crumpler 5-50, Galloway 4-84, Smith 4-20, Pritchard 3-36, Warren 2-15, Fauria 1-10, Br. Blades 1-7.

MISSED FIELD GOAL ATTEMPTS—None.

INTERCEPTIONS—Denver, Gordon 1-32.

KICKOFF RETURNS—Denver, Hebron 2-81, Burns 1-8. Seattle, Broussard 5-90, R. Brown 1-16, Beede 1-(minus 5).

PUNT RETURNS—Denver, Gordon 1-5.

SACKS—Denver, N. Smith 1. Seattle, Sinclair 2.

RAVENS 23, BENGALS 10

Sunday, September 7

Cincinnati	0	10	0	0—10
Baltimore	0	3	10	10—23

Second Quarter
Cin.—Pickens 8 pass from Blake (Pelfrey kick), 4:57.
Bal.—FG, Stover 37, 10:14.
Cin.—FG, Pelfrey 46, 14:53.

Third Quarter
Bal.—FG, Stover 32, 8:51.
Bal.—Graham 5 run (Stover kick), 13:58.

Fourth Quarter
Bal.—Green 18 pass from Testaverde (Stover kick), 5:24.
Bal.—FG, Stover 41, 11:15.
Attendance—52,968.

TEAM STATISTICS
	Cincinnati	Baltimore
First downs	18	24
Rushes-yards	14-56	35-146
Passing	283	266
Punt returns	2-11	4-21
Kickoff returns	5-118	3-55
Interception returns	1-0	2-18
Comp.-att.-int.	25-45-2	25-36-1
Sacked-yards lost	5-34	1-9
Punts	4-53	2-43
Fumbles-lost	1-0	3-2
Penalties-yards	5-30	4-25
Time of possession	26:18	33:42

INDIVIDUAL STATISTICS

RUSHING—Cincinnati, Carter 10-22, Blake 3-34, Bieniemy 1-0. Baltimore, Byner 17-75, Graham 16-73, Testaverde 2-(minus 2).

PASSING—Cincinnati, Blake 25-45-2-317. Baltimore, Testaverde 25-36-1-275.

RECEIVING—Cincinnati, Pickens 8-99, McGee 4-71, Bieniemy 4-41, Scott 3-42, Twyner 3-41, Carter 2-9, Milne 1-14. Baltimore, Alexander 8-104, Jackson 6-85, Green 4-35, Graham 2-23, Yarborough 2-17, Kinchen 2-10, Byner 1-1.

MISSED FIELD GOAL ATTEMPTS—Cincinnati, Pelfrey 51, 43, 46.

INTERCEPTIONS—Cincinnati, Ambrose 1-0. Baltimore, Moore 2-18.

KICKOFF RETURNS—Cincinnati, Dillon 3-88, Twyner 2-30. Baltimore, Brew 2-33, Ethridge 1-22.

PUNT RETURNS—Cincinnati, Myers 2-11. Baltimore, Ethridge 4-21.

SACKS—Cincinnati, Wilkinson 1. Baltimore, McCrary 1.5, Boulware 1.5, R. Lewis 1, J. Jones 1.

EAGLES 10, PACKERS 9

Sunday, September 7

Green Bay	0	6	3	0— 9
Philadelphia	0	0	3	7—10

Second Quarter
G.B.—FG, Longwell 22, 7:06.
G.B.—FG, Longwell 18, 15:00.
Third Quarter
Phi.—FG, Boniol 32, 2:28.
G.B.—FG, Longwell 27, 9:12.
Fourth Quarter
Phi.—Solomon 2 pass from Detmer (Boniol kick), 13:04.
Attendance—66,803.

TEAM STATISTICS

	Green Bay	Philadelphia
First downs	21	16
Rushes-yards	28-107	30-100
Passing	273	158
Punt returns	3-29	2-0
Kickoff returns	3-105	2-41
Interception returns	0-0	1-39
Comp.-att.-int.	19-41-1	19-32-0
Sacked-yards lost	1-6	3-15
Punts	6-49	7-44
Fumbles-lost	2-1	2-1
Penalties-yards	2-15	5-23
Time of possession	28:29	31:31

INDIVIDUAL STATISTICS

RUSHING—Green Bay, Levens 22-91, Henderson 6-16. Philadelphia, Watters 23-81, Garner 3-18, Detmer 3-0, Turner 1-1.

PASSING—Green Bay, Favre 19-41-1-279. Philadelphia, Detmer 19-32-0-173.

RECEIVING—Green Bay, Brooks 6-90, Freeman 4-63, Henderson 4-41, Mayes 2-40, Thomason 2-32, Levens 1-13. Philadelphia, Fryar 8-125, Watters 3-0, Timpson 2-18, Solomon 2-9, Seay 1-8, Garner 1-5, Lewis 1-5, Turner 1-3.

MISSED FIELD GOAL ATTEMPTS—Green Bay, Longwell 28. Philadelphia, Boniol 48.

INTERCEPTIONS—Philadelphia, Hall 1-39.

KICKOFF RETURNS—Green Bay, Schroeder 2-70, Hayden 1-35. Philadelphia, Witherspoon 2-41.

PUNT RETURNS—Green Bay, Schroeder 3-29. Philadelphia, Seay 2-0.

SACKS—Green Bay, White 1.5, Wilkins 1, Brown 0.5. Philadelphia, W. Thomas 1.

VIKINGS 27, BEARS 24

Sunday, September 7

Minnesota	3	0	10	14—27
Chicago	0	10	7	7—24

First Quarter
Min.—FG, Davis 33, 14:13.
Second Quarter
Chi.—FG, Jaeger 39, 4:37.
Chi.—Proehl 25 pass from Kramer (Jaeger kick), 9:12.
Third Quarter
Min.—FG, Davis 28, 4:41.
Min.—Thomas 22 fumble return (Davis kick), 4:58.
Chi.—Engram 10 pass from Kramer (Jaeger kick), 13:59.
Fourth Quarter
Min.—Reed 21 pass from Johnson (Davis kick), 1:34.
Chi.—R. Harris 59 run (Jaeger kick), 3:08.
Min.—Walsh 9 pass from Johnson (Davis kick), 14:23.
Attendance—59,263.

TEAM STATISTICS

	Minnesota	Chicago
First downs	23	16
Rushes-yards	25-117	23-147
Passing	261	158
Punt returns	5-85	1-6
Kickoff returns	4-81	4-70
Interception returns	0-0	1-0
Comp.-att.-int.	33-44-1	21-36-0
Sacked-yards lost	3-24	2-16
Punts	4-26	5-42
Fumbles-lost	1-0	5-2
Penalties-yards	2-20	3-15
Time of possession	32:04	27:56

INDIVIDUAL STATISTICS

RUSHING—Minnesota, R. Smith 13-85, Hoard 5-19, Evans 5-10, Johnson 2-3. Chicago, Salaam 13-64, R. Harris 8-77, Hughes 1-3, Kramer 1-3.

PASSING—Minnesota, Johnson 33-44-1-285. Chicago, Kramer 21-36-0-174.

RECEIVING—Minnesota, Reed 12-118, Carter 9-107, Palmer 4-18, Evans 3-10, Goodwin 2-14, Walsh 1-9, Hoard 1-7, R. Smith 1-2. Chicago, Engram 6-63, R. Harris 6-15, Proehl 4-51, Hughes 2-22, Wetnight 1-9, Penn 1-8, Jennings 1-6.

MISSED FIELD GOAL ATTEMPTS—Minnesota, Davis 40, 42.

INTERCEPTIONS—Chicago, W. Harris 1-0.

KICKOFF RETURNS—Minnesota, Tate 3-62, Morrow 1-19. Chicago, Hughes 3-54, Bownes 1-16.

PUNT RETURNS—Minnesota, Palmer 5-85. Chicago, Hughes 1-6.

SACKS—Minnesota, Alexander 2. Chicago, B. Cox 1, Flanigan 1, Marshall 1.

DOLPHINS 16, OILERS 13

Sunday, September 7

Tennessee	0	10	3	0—13
Miami	0	3	3	7	3—16

Second Quarter
Mia.—FG, Mare 23, 5:47.
Ten.—George 13 run (Del Greco kick), 11:26.
Ten.—FG, Del Greco 24, 14:46.
Third Quarter
Mia.—FG, Mare 22, 9:33.
Ten.—FG, Del Greco 37, 14:16.
Fourth Quarter
Mia.—Spikes 2 run (Mare kick), 3:39.
Overtime
Mia.—FG, Mare 29, 2:15.
Attendance—64,439.

TEAM STATISTICS

	Tennessee	Miami
First downs	13	21
Rushes-yards	40-185	25-54
Passing	109	300
Punt returns	2-25	3-65
Kickoff returns	2-42	4-106
Interception returns	0-0	1-1
Comp.-att.-int.	7-14-1	24-43-0
Sacked-yards lost	0-0	3-24
Punts	6-43	3-46
Fumbles-lost	1-0	1-1
Penalties-yards	11-105	5-50
Time of possession	29:16	32:59

INDIVIDUAL STATISTICS

RUSHING—Tennessee, George 23-106, McNair 11-62, Thomas 3-26, Harmon 2-(minus 1), Sanders 1-(minus 8). Miami, Abdul-Jabbar 19-33, Spikes 4-18, Parmalee 1-5, Marino 1-(minus 2).

PASSING—Tennessee, McNair 7-14-1-109. Miami, Marino 24-43-0-324.

RECEIVING—Tennessee, Sanders 3-58, Harmon 1-27, Davis 1-11, Wycheck 1-7, Thomas 1-6. Miami, McDuffie 8-135, Barnett 5-56, Spikes 3-39, Parmalee 3-38, Abdul-Jabbar 2-23, Pritchett 1-17, Jordan 1-12, Drayton 1-4.

MISSED FIELD GOAL ATTEMPTS—Tennessee, Del Greco 43. Miami, Mare 25.

INTERCEPTIONS—Miami, Buckley 1-1.

KICKOFF RETURNS—Tennessee, Gray 2-42. Miami, Spikes 3-99, Perry 1-7.

PUNT RETURNS—Tennessee, Gray 2-25. Miami, Jordan 3-65.

SACKS—Tennessee, Hall 1, Holmes 1, Lyons.

49ERS 15, RAMS 12

Sunday, September 7

San Francisco	0	7	0	8—15
St. Louis	3	6	3	0—12

First Quarter
St.L.—FG, Wilkins 40, 5:18.

Second Quarter
St.L.—FG, Wilkins 49, 0:05.
S.F.—Stokes 25 pass from Druckenmiller (Anderson kick), 3:42.
St.L.—FG, Wilkins 52, 8:56.

Third Quarter
St.L.—FG, Wilkins 34, 9:26.

Fourth Quarter
S.F.—Hearst 35 run (Kirby pass from Druckenmiller), 7:10.
Attendance—64,630.

TEAM STATISTICS

	San Fran.	St. Louis
First downs	12	11
Rushes-yards	33-139	35-99
Passing	89	104
Punt returns	3-21	6-56
Kickoff returns	4-85	3-78
Interception returns	0-0	3-51
Comp.-att.-int.	10-28-3	9-24-0
Sacked-yards lost	2-13	3-19
Punts	7-47	5-44
Fumbles-lost	1-1	5-4
Penalties-yards	12-93	7-55
Time of possession	31:40	28:20

INDIVIDUAL STATISTICS
RUSHING—San Francisco, Hearst 16-92, Kirby 7-25, Floyd 5-21, Druckenmiller 5-1. St. Louis, Phillips 23-72, Banks 8-17, Lee 2-9, R. Moore 1-1.

PASSING—San Francisco, Druckenmiller 10-28-3-102. St. Louis, Banks 9-24-0-123.

RECEIVING—San Francisco, Jones 3-39, Stokes 3-35, Owens 2-24, Floyd 1-5, Hearst 1-(minus 1). St. Louis, Conwell 3-28, Small 2-54, Lee 2-21, Kennison 1-11, Ross 1-9.

MISSED FIELD GOAL ATTEMPTS—San Francisco, Anderson 50.

INTERCEPTIONS—St. Louis, McNeil 2-21, Lyle 1-30.

KICKOFF RETURNS—San Francisco, Uwaezuoke 3-61, Drakeford 1-24. St. Louis, Ross 2-59, Lee 1-19.

PUNT RETURNS—San Francisco, Uwaezuoke 3-21. St. Louis, Kennison 4-44, Ross 2-12.

SACKS—San Francisco, Norton 1, Doleman 1, Stubblefield 1. St. Louis, O'Neal 1, Farr 1.

STEELERS 14, REDSKINS 13

Sunday, September 7

Washington	0	3	10	0—13
Pittsburgh	7	0	0	7—14

First Quarter
Pit.—Stewart 1 run (N. Johnson kick), 5:41.

Second Quarter
Was.—FG, Blanton 37, 3:00.

Third Quarter
Was.—Mitchell 97 kickoff return (Blanton kick), 0:18.
Was.—FG, Blanton 28, 11:31.

Fourth Quarter
Pit.—Bettis 1 run (N. Johnson kick), 1:37.
Attendance—58,059.

TEAM STATISTICS

	Washington	Pittsburgh
First downs	19	23
Rushes-yards	21-69	39-222
Passing	285	73
Punt returns	0-0	0-0
Kickoff returns	3-119	4-100
Interception returns	1-5	3-36
Comp.-att.-int.	21-37-3	8-17-1
Sacked-yards lost	0-0	1-9
Punts	1-44	2-45
Fumbles-lost	1-0	0-0
Penalties-yards	8-70	5-44
Time of possession	29:26	30:34

INDIVIDUAL STATISTICS
RUSHING—Washington, Davis 17-66, Mitchell 3-5, Westbrook 1-(minus 2). Pittsburgh, Bettis 27-134, Stewart 10-70, Blackwell 1-11, Hawkins 1-7.

PASSING—Washington, Frerotte 19-35-3-270, Hostetler 2-2-0-15. Pittsburgh, Stewart 8-17-1-82.

RECEIVING—Washington, Asher 6-48, Shepherd 5-87, Ellard 4-78, Davis 2-20, Mitchell 2-13, Westbrook 1-29, Bowie 1-10. Pittsburgh, C. Johnson 3-33, G. Jones 1-14, Hawkins 1-11, Botkin 1-11, Bettis 1-9, Blackwell 1-4.

MISSED FIELD GOAL ATTEMPTS—None.

INTERCEPTIONS—Washington, M. Patton 1-5. Pittsburgh, Perry 1-17, Kirkland 1-11, Oldham 1-8.

KICKOFF RETURNS—Washington, Mitchell 3-119. Pittsburgh, Blackwell 4-100.

PUNT RETURNS—None.

SACKS—Washington, Smith 1.

CHIEFS 28, RAIDERS 27

Monday, September 8

Kansas City	3	10	9	6—28
Oakland	7	3	17	0—27

First Quarter
Oak.—Kaufman 10 run (Ford kick), 8:15.
K.C.—FG, Stoyanovich 23, 12:46.

Second Quarter
K.C.—Anders 5 pass from Grbac (Stoyanovich kick), 6:18.
Oak.—FG, Ford 32, 13:57.
K.C.—FG, Stoyanovich 24, 14:58.

Third Quarter
Oak.—Dudley 37 pass from George (Ford kick), 1:57.
Oak.—Dudley 16 pass from George (Ford kick), 4:37.
Oak.—FG, Ford 34, 5:10.
K.C.—FG, Stoyanovich 23, 9:34.
K.C.—Anderson 55 interception return (pass failed), 13:55.

Fourth Quarter
K.C.—Rison 32 pass from Grbac (pass failed), 14:57.
Attendance—61,523.

TEAM STATISTICS

	Kansas City	Oakland
First downs	21	22
Rushes-yards	26-128	30-108
Passing	300	281
Punt returns	3-31	2-23
Kickoff returns	5-146	7-153
Interception returns	2-64	0-0
Comp.-att.-int.	21-35-0	19-39-2
Sacked-yards lost	1-12	1-14
Punts	6-43	7-45
Fumbles-lost	3-3	0-0
Penalties-yards	8-50	8-69
Time of possession	27:18	32:42

INDIVIDUAL STATISTICS
RUSHING—Kansas City, Hill 16-53, Anders 5-55, Allen 3-13, Grbac 1-5, Rison 1-2. Oakland, Kaufman 22-84, Aska 4-(minus 1), T. Brown 2-19, George 2-6.

PASSING—Kansas City, Grbac 21-35-0-312. Oakland, George 19-39-2-295.

RECEIVING—Kansas City, Rison 8-162, Anders 3-21, Perriman 2-37, Gonzalez 2-23, Dawson 2-21, Popson 1-15, Allen 1-14, Hughes 1-12, Hill 1-7. Oakland, T. Brown 11-155, Dudley 4-90, Kaufman 2-34, Davison 1-9, Jett 1-7.

MISSED FIELD GOAL ATTEMPTS—None.

INTERCEPTIONS—Kansas City, Anderson 1-55, Carter 1-9.

KICKOFF RETURNS—Kansas City, Vanover 5-146. Oakland, Howard 5-114, Hall 2-39.

PUNT RETURNS—Kansas City, Vanover 3-31. Oakland, Howard 2-23.

SACKS—Kansas City, Hasty 1. Oakland, Russell 1.

WEEK 3

RESULTS

Baltimore 24, N.Y. GIANTS 23
Carolina 26, SAN DIEGO 7
DENVER 35, St. Louis 14
Detroit 32, CHICAGO 7
GREEN BAY 23, Miami 18
KANSAS CITY 22, Buffalo 16
NEW ENGLAND 27, N.Y. Jets 24 (OT)
Oakland 36, ATLANTA 31
Tampa Bay 28, MINNESOTA 14
SAN FRANCISCO 33, New Orleans 7
Seattle 31, INDIANAPOLIS 3
WASHINGTON 19, Arizona 13 (OT)
DALLAS 21, Philadelphia 20
   Open date: Cincinnati, Jacksonville,
Pittsburgh, Tennessee.

STANDINGS

AFC EAST

	W	L	T	Pct.
New England	3	0	0	1.000
Miami	2	1	0	.667
Buffalo	1	2	0	.333
N.Y. Jets	1	2	0	.333
Indianapolis	0	3	0	.000

AFC CENTRAL

	W	L	T	Pct.
Jacksonville	2	0	0	1.000
Baltimore	2	1	0	.667
Cincinnati	1	1	0	.500
Pittsburgh	1	1	0	.500
Tennessee	1	1	0	.500

AFC WEST

	W	L	T	Pct.
Denver	3	0	0	1.000
Kansas City	2	1	0	.667
Oakland	1	2	0	.333
San Diego	1	2	0	.333
Seattle	1	2	0	.333

NFC EAST

	W	L	T	Pct.
Dallas	2	1	0	.667
Washington	2	1	0	.667
Arizona	1	2	0	.333
N.Y. Giants	1	2	0	.333
Philadelphia	1	2	0	.333

NFC CENTRAL

	W	L	T	Pct.
Tampa Bay	3	0	0	1.000
Detroit	2	1	0	.667
Green Bay	2	1	0	.667
Minnesota	2	1	0	.667
Chicago	0	3	0	.000

NFC WEST

	W	L	T	Pct.
Carolina	2	1	0	.667
San Francisco	2	1	0	.667
St. Louis	1	2	0	.333
Atlanta	0	3	0	.000
New Orleans	0	3	0	.000

HIGHLIGHTS

Hero of the week: San Francisco cornerback Rod Woodson had three interceptions (returning them for a total of 81 yards), one forced fumble and recovered another in the 49ers' 33-7 victory over the Saints. Woodson, in his 11th NFL season, had the first four-takeaway performance of his career before leaving in the third period because of a pulled calf muscle. It also was the first three-interception game of his career.

Goat of the week: Eagles punter/holder Tom Hutton cost his team a probable victory over the Cowboys at Texas Stadium. With Dallas leading, 21-20, the Eagles lined up for a potential game-winning 22-yard field goal on the final play of regulation. Hutton, holding for kicker Chris Boniol, fumbled the snap, then tried to run with it. He was tackled short of the goal line by Deion Sanders as time expired.

Sub of the week: New England tight end Lovett Purnell caught only two passes for 25 yards in the Patriots' 27-24 overtime victory against the Jets, but one of those catches resulted in a late fourth-quarter touchdown. Quarterback Drew Bledsoe's 10-yard touchdown pass to Purnell with 12:53 left gave the Patriots a 24-17 lead. Purnell was subbing for the temporarily injured Ben Coates, who had suffered bruised ribs earlier in the game.

Comeback of the week: The Cowboys rallied from a 17-3 second-quarter deficit to beat the Eagles, 21-20. With 51 seconds left in regulation, Dallas quarterback Troy Aikman threw a 14-yard touchdown pass to receiver Anthony Miller, who leaped high in the end zone to make the grab.

Blowout of the week: Indianapolis scored first, on a 46-yard field goal by Cary Blanchard, but Seattle scored the next 31 points en route to a 31-3 victory. Seahawks quarterback Warren Moon, at the 40 the oldest player in the NFL, passed for 270 yards and one touchdown. He also scored his first rushing TD in four years.

Nail-biter of the week: Patriots kicker Adam Vinatieri ruined Jets coach Bill Parcells' return to New England by kicking a 34-yard field goal in over-time to give the Pats a 27-24 victory. New York had a chance to win the game in the fourth quarter, but rookie John Hall's 29-yard field goal attempt was blocked by Mike Jones with less than a minute left in regulation.

Hit of the week: Late in the fourth quarter of the Cowboys' victory over Philadelphia, Deion Sanders was running upfield on a punt return. When he quickly changed his direction to avoid being tackled, Philadelphia's Jason Dunn saw his chance to make a play. But Dallas' Billy Davis delivered a vicious hit that knocked Dunn off his feet. Dunn never saw Davis coming and landed several feet from the initial contact.

Oddity of the week: Raiders quarterback Jeff George was hoping for revenge when he took the field at the Georgia Dome in Atlanta for a game against his former team. George, who spent the previous three seasons with the Falcons, clearly was bitter toward the team and its fans. So after downing the ball to run out the clock in Oakland's 36-31 victory, George took a victory lap around the field, pumping his arms and waving the ball as fans booed, shouted insults and pelted him with empty cups.

Top rusher: Curtis Martin rushed 40 times for 199 yards and one touchdown in New England's victory against the Jets.

Top passer: Minnesota's Brad Johnson was 29-of-44 for 334 yards and one touchdown in the Vikings' 28-14 loss to Tampa Bay.

Top receiver: Jake Reed caught six of Brad Johnson's passes for 131 yards in the Vikings' loss.

Notes: The inaugural game at Washington's Jack Kent Cooke Stadium was somewhat less successful than anticipated. Although the Redskins won the game (beating Arizona, 19-13, in overtime), the announced attendance of 78,270 was 1,846 short of capacity. The team claimed a sellout because all general tickets were sold, but many of the expensive club seats had not been sold and sat empty. . . . Chicago's 32-7 loss to the Lions dropped the Bears to 0-3 for the first time since 1969. . . . Until Week 3,

Miami had never lost to Green Bay (8-0). The Packers have now beaten every team in the NFL. . . . Darrien Gordon's 94-yard punt-return touchdown against St. Louis was the first by a Bronco in 10 years, the longest in team history and the longest ever against the Rams. . . . Detroit's Barry Sanders, held to a total of 53 yards in the season's first two games, rushed for 161 and averaged 8.5 yards per carry against the Bears . . . . The Ravens squeaked by the Giants, 24-23, for their first road victory since moving to Baltimore in 1996. . . . Dating to the third quarter of their final game of 1996, the Colts had gone 13 periods (194 minutes, 17 seconds of playing time) in the regular season without scoring an offensive touchdown. . . . John Carney supplanted Rolf Benirschke as the Chargers' leading career scorer.

Quote of the week: San Francisco quarterback Steve Young, on returning from a concussion that kept him on the sidelines the previous week: "It's just nice to get back on the horse and ride a little bit."

GAME SUMMARIES

RAIDERS 36, FALCONS 31

Sunday, September 14

Oakland	7	3	21	5—36
Atlanta	7	7	10	7—31

First Quarter
Atl.—Green 1 run (Andersen kick), 4:54.
Oak.—Kaufman 61 run (Ford kick), 8:00.
Second Quarter
Atl.—Santiago 1 pass from Chandler (Andersen kick), 0:47.
Oak.—FG, Ford 49, 15:00.
Third Quarter
Oak.—Jett 51 pass from George (Ford kick), 3:56.
Atl.—Christian 3 pass from Chandler (Andersen kick), 5:19.
Oak.—Shedd 25 fumble return (Ford kick), 7:19.
Atl.—FG, Andersen 51, 10:51.
Oak.—Kaufman 58 run (Ford kick), 11:14.
Fourth Quarter
Atl.—Mathis 6 pass from Tolliver (Andersen kick), 7:43.
Oak.—FG, Ford 31, 10:36.
Oak.—Safety, Tolliver forced out of the end zone by Russell, 11:41.
Attendance—47,922.

TEAM STATISTICS

	Oakland	Atlanta
First downs	11	24
Rushes-yards	20-149	26-116
Passing	265	250
Punt returns	2-0	4-35
Kickoff returns	3-64	1-34
Interception returns	0-0	0-0
Comp.-att.-int.	12-22-0	26-42-0
Sacked-yards lost	3-21	6-49
Punts	7-45	5-37
Fumbles-lost	2-1	5-2
Penalties-yards	13-99	4-35
Time of possession	23:00	37:00

INDIVIDUAL STATISTICS

RUSHING—Oakland, Kaufman 14-140, Fenner 4-8, T. Brown 1-2, George 1-(minus 1). Atlanta, Green 11-2, Anderson 9-26, Hanspard 4-84, Chandler 2-4.
PASSING—Oakland, George 12-22-0-286. Atlanta, Chandler 16-25-0-199, Tolliver 10-17-0-100.
RECEIVING—Oakland, T. Brown 4-69, Dudley 2-90, Kaufman 2-26, Jett 1-51, Davison 1-25, Shedd 1-16, Fenner 1-9. Atlanta, Mathis 6-55, Santiago 5-40, Emanuel 4-92, Haynes 3-41, Christian 3-24, Hanspard 2-30, Green 2-16, Anderson 1-1.
MISSED FIELD GOAL ATTEMPTS—None.
INTERCEPTIONS—None.

KICKOFF RETURNS—Oakland, Howard 2-57, T. Brown 1-7. Atlanta, Bolden 1-34.
PUNT RETURNS—Oakland, Howard 2-0. Atlanta, Kinchen 4-35.
SACKS—Oakland, Smith 2, Russell 1.5, Fredrickson 1, Biekert 0.5, Morton 0.5, McGlockton 0.5. Atlanta, Hall 2, Bennett 1.

PATRIOTS 27, JETS 24

Sunday, September 14

N.Y. Jets	7	3	7	7	0—24
New England	14	0	3	7	3—27

First Quarter
N.E.—Coates 32 pass from Bledsoe (Vinatieri kick), 1:54.
NYJ—O'Donnell 2 run (Hall kick), 8:58.
N.E.—Martin 2 run (Vinatieri kick), 12:47.
Second Quarter
NYJ—FG, Hall 27, 2:43.
Third Quarter
NYJ—Lewis 43 interception return (Hall kick), 2:55.
N.E.—FG, Vinatieri 33, 10:53.
Fourth Quarter
N.E.—Purnell 10 pass from Bledsoe (Vinatieri kick), 2:07.
NYJ—K. Johnson 24 pass from O'Donnell (Hall kick), 14:29.
Overtime
N.E.—FG, Vinatieri 34, 8:03.
Attendance—60,072.

TEAM STATISTICS

	N.Y. Jets	New England
First downs	22	23
Rushes-yards	21-130	46-213
Passing	225	162
Punt returns	3-51	4-52
Kickoff returns	5-113	4-131
Interception returns	2-43	0-0
Comp.-att.-int.	30-50-0	16-34-2
Sacked-yards lost	7-46	0-0
Punts	5-45	6-34
Fumbles-lost	3-3	1-1
Penalties-yards	7-49	11-85
Time of possession	29:41	38:22

INDIVIDUAL STATISTICS

RUSHING—New York, Murrell 18-110, O'Donnell 3-20. New England, Martin 40-199, Bledsoe 4-6, Byars 2-8.
PASSING—New York, O'Donnell 30-50-0-271. New England, Bledsoe 16-34-2-162.
RECEIVING—New York, Chrebet 6-82, K. Johnson 6-62, Graham 5-54, L. Johnson 5-32, Anderson 3-14, Ward 2-17, Murrell 2-4, Baxter 1-6. New England, Jefferson 5-63, Coates 2-40, Purnell 2-25, Martin 2-15, Brisby 2-15, Byars 2-10, Brown 1-(minus 6).
MISSED FIELD GOAL ATTEMPTS—New York, Hall 29.
INTERCEPTIONS—New York, Lewis 1-43, Smith 1-0.
KICKOFF RETURNS—New York, Glenn 4-93, L. Johnson 1-20. New England, Canty 2-84, Cullors 2-47.
PUNT RETURNS—New York, L. Johnson 3-51. New England, Meggett 4-52.
SACKS—New England, Slade 3, Johnson 2, Wheeler 2.

SEAHAWKS 31, COLTS 3

Sunday, September 14

Seattle	7	10	0	14—31
Indianapolis	3	0	0	0— 3

First Quarter
Ind.—FG, Blanchard 46, 5:52.
Sea.—Smith 3 run (Peterson kick), 9:20.
Second Quarter
Sea.—Moon 1 run (Peterson kick), 1:17.
Sea.—FG, Peterson 27, 14:11.
Fourth Quarter
Sea.—Pritchard 20 pass from Moon (Peterson kick), 1:19.
Sea.—Warren 36 run (Peterson kick), 12:01.
Attendance—49,194.

TEAM STATISTICS

	Seattle	Indianapolis
First downs	27	11
Rushes-yards	25-153	25-95
Passing	270	23

	Seattle	Indianapolis
Punt returns	4-35	2-3
Kickoff returns	2-55	6-213
Interception returns	0-0	1-0
Comp.-att.-int.	24-38-1	11-17-0
Sacked-yards lost	1-0	8-54
Punts	3-41	7-43
Fumbles-lost	0-0	1-0
Penalties-yards	6-60	5-28
Time of possession	31:20	28:40

INDIVIDUAL STATISTICS

RUSHING—Seattle, Smith 12-76, Warren 9-61, Moon 2-18, Kitna 2-(minus 2). Indianapolis, Faulk 17-58, Harbaugh 4-30, Crockett 3-9, Warren 1-(minus 2).

PASSING—Seattle, Moon 24-38-1-270. Indianapolis, Harbaugh 11-17-0-77.

RECEIVING—Seattle, Galloway 6-58, Warren 6-45, Pritchard 4-69, Crumpler 3-26, Harris 2-38, Br. Blades 2-30, Smith 1-4. Indianapolis, Harrison 4-38, Bailey 3-23, Faulk 2-9, Crockett 2-7.

MISSED FIELD GOAL ATTEMPTS—None.

INTERCEPTIONS—Indianapolis, C. Gray 1-0.

KICKOFF RETURNS—Seattle, Broussard 2-55. Indianapolis, Bailey 6-213.

PUNT RETURNS—Seattle, Harris 4-35. Indianapolis, Stablein 2-3.

SACKS—Seattle, C. Brown 3, Daniels 2, Sinclair 1, Adams 1, Kennedy 1. Indianapolis, Coryatt 1.

LIONS 32, BEARS 7

Sunday, September 14

Detroit	3	10	10	9—32
Chicago	7	0	0	0— 7

First Quarter
Chi.—R. Harris 7 run (Jaeger kick), 6:35.
Det.—FG, Hanson 23, 12:11.

Second Quarter
Det.—Morton 16 pass from Mitchell (Hanson kick), 3:42.
Det.—FG, Hanson 33, 14:58.

Third Quarter
Det.—FG, Hanson 29, 7:16.
Det.—Vardell 1 run (Hanson kick), 14:46.

Fourth Quarter
Det.—Moore 27 pass from Mitchell (Mitchell sacked on two-point attempt), 2:51.
Det.—FG, Hanson 32, 14:02.
Attendance—59,147.

TEAM STATISTICS

	Detroit	Chicago
First downs	27	19
Rushes-yards	35-202	29-94
Passing	202	190
Punt returns	2-(-2)	2-17
Kickoff returns	2-43	8-189
Interception returns	1-0	0-0
Comp.-att.-int.	16-25-0	21-40-1
Sacked-yards lost	1-13	4-28
Punts	3-45	4-40
Fumbles-lost	1-1	2-1
Penalties-yards	4-25	8-75
Time of possession	30:38	29:22

INDIVIDUAL STATISTICS

RUSHING—Detroit, Sanders 19-161, Rivers 7-15, Vardell 5-15, Mitchell 4-11. Chicago, R. Harris 22-73, Mirer 4-14, Salaam 2-7, Kramer 1-0.

PASSING—Detroit, Mitchell 16-25-0-215. Chicago, Mirer 10-21-1-90, Kramer 11-19-0-128.

RECEIVING—Detroit, Moore 7-98, Morton 4-49, Sloan 2-14, Vardell 1-37, Metzelaars 1-14, Sanders 1-3. Chicago, Engram 5-60, Proehl 4-46, Hughes 4-33, Penn 3-31, Allred 2-26, R. Harris 2-13, Bownes 1-9.

MISSED FIELD GOAL ATTEMPTS—None.

INTERCEPTIONS—Detroit, Carrier 1-0.

KICKOFF RETURNS—Detroit, Milburn 2-43. Chicago, Hughes 7-180, Wetnight 1-9.

PUNT RETURNS—Detroit, Milburn 2-(minus 2). Chicago, Hughes 2-17.

SACKS—Detroit, Brown 2, Abrams 1, Scroggins 1. Chicago, Thierry 1.

PANTHERS 26, CHARGERS 7

Sunday, September 14

Carolina	10	3	3	10—26
San Diego	7	0	0	0— 7

First Quarter
S.D.—Pegram 6 run (Carney kick), 9:44.
Car.—Walls 8 pass from Collins (Kasay kick), 11:54.
Car.—FG, Kasay 25, 14:11.

Second Quarter
Car.—FG, Kasay 36, 7:15.

Third Quarter
Car.—FG, Kasay 34, 13:03.

Fourth Quarter
Car.—FG, Kasay 28, 0:55.
Car.—Walls 1 pass from Collins (Kasay kick), 4:52.
Attendance—63,149.

TEAM STATISTICS

	Carolina	San Diego
First downs	21	17
Rushes-yards	41-141	21-96
Passing	138	155
Punt returns	1-0	2-26
Kickoff returns	2-75	5-162
Interception returns	0-0	1-26
Comp.-att.-int.	17-36-1	17-34-0
Sacked-yards lost	0-0	7-52
Punts	4-53	5-41
Fumbles-lost	1-0	4-4
Penalties-yards	3-27	8-47
Time of possession	36:13	23:47

INDIVIDUAL STATISTICS

RUSHING—Carolina, Lane 18-52, Biakabutuka 12-54, Greene 5-17, Johnson 5-7, Ismail 1-11. San Diego, Brown 10-35, Fletcher 5-33, Pegram 3-6, Humphries 2-18, Gardner 1-4.

PASSING—Carolina, Collins 17-36-1-138. San Diego, Humphries 13-25-0-145, Everett 4-9-0-62.

RECEIVING—Carolina, Muhammad 4-43, Walls 3-34, Greene 3-18, Ismail 2-21, E. Mills 2-13, Lane 2-2, Johnson 1-7. San Diego, Fletcher 4-8, Martin 3-75, F. Jones 3-26, C. Jones 2-19, Brown 2-11, Metcalf 1-33, Hartley 1-24, Still 1-11.

MISSED FIELD GOAL ATTEMPTS—None.

INTERCEPTIONS—San Diego, Seau 1-26.

KICKOFF RETURNS—Carolina, Bates 2-75. San Diego, Rachal 4-99, Metcalf 1-63.

PUNT RETURNS—Carolina, Poole 1-0. San Diego, Metcalf 2-26.

SACKS—Carolina, Royal 3, Barrow 2, Minter 1, Team 1.

49ERS 33, SAINTS 7

Sunday, September 14

New Orleans	0	0	0	7— 7
San Francisco	13	10	10	0—33

First Quarter
S.F.—FG, Anderson 43, 4:34.
S.F.—Jones 18 pass from S. Young (Anderson kick), 8:30.
S.F.—FG, Anderson 22, 11:44.

Second Quarter
S.F.—FG, Anderson 40, 1:58.
S.F.—Jones 1 pass from S. Young (Anderson kick), 13:03.

Third Quarter
S.F.—Hearst 1 pass from S. Young (Anderson kick), 3:29.
S.F.—FG, Anderson 38, 13:14.

Fourth Quarter
N.O.—Hastings 8 pass from Wuerffel (Brien kick), 0:06.
Attendance—61,838.

TEAM STATISTICS

	New Orleans	San Francisco
First downs	12	17
Rushes-yards	25-84	33-91
Passing	176	213
Punt returns	3-25	1-36
Kickoff returns	8-138	2-71
Interception returns	0-0	6-113
Comp.-att.-int.	12-26-6	22-27-0
Sacked-yards lost	1-9	6-48
Punts	3-38	3-45
Fumbles-lost	3-2	2-1
Penalties-yards	1-5	9-74
Time of possession	23:15	36:45

INDIVIDUAL STATISTICS

RUSHING—New Orleans, Bates 8-28, T. Davis 5-11, Zellars 4-25, Bender 3-8, Hastings 2-8, Wuerffel 1-5, Shuler 1-1, Guliford 1-(minus 2). San Francisco, Hearst 14-29, Kirby 10-43, Floyd 4-3, S. Young 2-12, Edwards 2-5, Druckenmiller 1-(minus 1).

PASSING—New Orleans, Wuerffel 7-15-3-119, Shuler 5-11-3-66. San Francisco, S. Young 18-21-0-220, Druckenmiller 4-6-0-41.

RECEIVING—New Orleans, Hastings 4-58, Guliford 3-61, Hill 3-46, T. Johnson 1-13, Bates 1-7. San Francisco, Jones 5-58, Stokes 4-61, Hearst 4-23, Owens 3-74, Floyd 2-9, Harris 1-14, Uwaezuoke 1-13, Kirby 1-6, Edwards 1-3.

MISSED FIELD GOAL ATTEMPTS—None.

INTERCEPTIONS—San Francisco, Woodson 3-81, Drakeford 2-15, McDonald 1-17.

KICKOFF RETURNS—New Orleans, Guliford 4-83, T. Davis 4-55. San Francisco, Levy 2-71.

PUNT RETURNS—New Orleans, Guliford 3-25. San Francisco, Uwaezuoke 1-36.

SACKS—New Orleans, J. Johnson 2, Mickell 2, Martin 1, Mitchell 1. San Francisco, Washington 1.

RAVENS 24, GIANTS 23

Sunday, September 14

Baltimore	7	7	0	10—24
N.Y. Giants	0	12	8	3—23

First Quarter
Bal.—Alexander 22 pass from Testaverde (Stover kick), 4:14.
Second Quarter
NYG—Barber 1 run (kick blocked), 0:30.
Bal.—Graham 1 run (Stover kick), 11:48.
NYG—Way 1 pass from Brown (pass failed), 14:46.
Third Quarter
NYG—Wheatley 1 run (Barber pass from Brown), 5:47.
Fourth Quarter
NYG—FG, Daluiso 27, 2:38.
Bal.—Jackson 11 pass from Testaverde (Stover kick), 7:52.
Bal.—FG, Stover 37, 14:26.
Attendance—69,768.

TEAM STATISTICS

	Baltimore	N.Y. Giants
First downs	19	29
Rushes-yards	21-63	37-121
Passing	210	269
Punt returns	1-0	4-29
Kickoff returns	3-46	4-77
Interception returns	0-0	1-0
Comp.-att.-int.	22-35-1	28-46-0
Sacked-yards lost	1-13	0-0
Punts	6-46	5-43
Fumbles-lost	2-0	1-0
Penalties-yards	9-66	7-69
Time of possession	24:09	35:51

INDIVIDUAL STATISTICS

RUSHING—Baltimore, Byner 13-57, Graham 6-(minus 4), Testaverde 2-10. New York, Barber 16-64, Wheatley 12-33, Brown 4-14, Way 4-11, Calloway 1-(minus 1).

PASSING—Baltimore, Testaverde 22-35-1-223. New York, Brown 28-46-0-269.

RECEIVING—Baltimore, Green 6-71, Jackson 5-72, Alexander 5-57, Byner 5-20, Graham 1-3. New York, Calloway 8-79, Barber 5-27, Way 4-11, Lewis 3-43, Toomer 3-40, Wheatley 2-16, Cross 1-26, Alexander 1-20, Pierce 1-7.

MISSED FIELD GOAL ATTEMPTS—New York, Daluiso 41, 41.

INTERCEPTIONS—New York, Ellsworth 1-0.

KICKOFF RETURNS—Baltimore, Brew 2-31, Ethridge 1-15. New York, Lewis 3-61, Way 1-16.

PUNT RETURNS—Baltimore, Ethridge 1-0. New York, Toomer 4-29.

SACKS—New York, K. Hamilton 1.

PACKERS 23, DOLPHINS 18

Sunday, September 14

Miami	6	3	3	6—18
Green Bay	0	10	3	10—23

First Quarter
Mia.—FG, Mare 24, 7:06.
Mia.—FG, Mare 31, 13:24.

Second Quarter
G.B.—Freeman 2 pass from Favre (Longwell kick), 3:03.
Mia.—FG, Mare 22, 13:05.
G.B.—FG, Longwell 26, 14:26.
Third Quarter
Mia.—FG, Mare 34, 3:30.
G.B.—FG, Longwell 24, 12:34.
Fourth Quarter
G.B.—FG, Longwell 39, 0:08.
G.B.—Henderson 10 pass from Favre (Longwell kick), 9:27.
Mia.—Jordan 29 pass from Marino (pass failed), 13:13.
Attendance—60,075.

TEAM STATISTICS

	Miami	Green Bay
First downs	20	22
Rushes-yards	22-59	29-142
Passing	240	250
Punt returns	2-28	3-18
Kickoff returns	5-99	4-86
Interception returns	0-0	1-24
Comp.-att.-int.	21-47-1	24-37-0
Sacked-yards lost	0-0	1-3
Punts	4-40	3-49
Fumbles-lost	0-0	2-2
Penalties-yards	7-67	7-69
Time of possession	28:37	31:23

INDIVIDUAL STATISTICS

RUSHING—Miami, Abdul-Jabbar 15-45, Spikes 3-4, Kidd 1-4, Jordan 1-2, McPhail 1-2, Parmalee 1-2. Green Bay, Levens 21-121, Favre 5-11, Henderson 3-10.

PASSING—Miami, Marino 21-47-1-240. Green Bay, Favre 24-37-0-253.

RECEIVING—Miami, Jordan 4-100, McDuffie 4-36, McPhail 4-24, Barnett 3-22, Drayton 2-31, Abdul-Jabbar 2-2, Manning 1-14, Parmalee 1-11. Green Bay, Henderson 7-60, Chmura 5-57, Freeman 5-52, Brooks 4-72, Levens 2-4, Schroeder 1-8.

MISSED FIELD GOAL ATTEMPTS—None.

INTERCEPTIONS—Green Bay, Prior 1-24.

KICKOFF RETURNS—Miami, Ismail 4-81, Spikes 1-18. Green Bay, Hayden 2-49, Schroeder 2-37.

PUNT RETURNS—Miami, Jordan 2-28. Green Bay, Schroeder 3-18.

SACKS—Miami, Rodgers 1.

CHIEFS 22, BILLS 16

Sunday, September 14

Buffalo	0	3	7	6—16
Kansas City	6	3	0	13—22

First Quarter
K.C.—FG, Stoyanovich 46, 6:40.
K.C.—FG, Stoyanovich 45, 13:52.
Second Quarter
Buf.—FG, Christie 46, 7:11.
K.C.—FG, Stoyanovich 42, 13:57.
Third Quarter
Buf.—Reed 77 pass from Collins (Christie kick), 2:45.
Fourth Quarter
Buf.—FG, Christie 33, 0:31.
K.C.—Vanover 94 kickoff return (Stoyanovich kick), 0:47.
Buf.—FG, Christie 30, 3:08.
K.C.—Richardson 1 pass from Grbac (kick blocked), 8:05.
Attendance—78,169.

TEAM STATISTICS

	Buffalo	Kansas City
First downs	16	17
Rushes-yards	23-50	25-107
Passing	275	160
Punt returns	3-25	4-25
Kickoff returns	6-127	5-193
Interception returns	0-0	2-27
Comp.-att.-int.	22-43-2	20-37-0
Sacked-yards lost	4-22	2-19
Punts	7-43	7-48
Fumbles-lost	0-0	0-0
Penalties-yards	6-55	6-93
Time of possession	31:32	28:28

INDIVIDUAL STATISTICS

RUSHING—Buffalo, A. Smith 11-30, Thomas 10-17, Collins 1-3, Reed 1-0. Kansas City, Hill 17-59, Anders 5-25, Grbac 2-15, Allen 1-8.

PASSING—Buffalo, Collins 22-43-2-297. Kansas City, Grbac 20-37-0-179.

RECEIVING—Buffalo, Reed 4-113, Johnson 4-30, Thomas 4-23, Early 3-67, Moulds 3-39, Riemersma 2-22, A. Smith 2-3. Kansas City, Rison 5-75, Anders 5-31, Popson 4-20, Gonzalez 3-34, Hill 1-9, Hughes 1-9, Richardson 1-1.

MISSED FIELD GOAL ATTEMPTS—Kansas City, Stoyanovich 48.

INTERCEPTIONS—Kansas City, McMillian 1-27, Tongue 1-0.

KICKOFF RETURNS—Buffalo, Moulds 6-127. Kansas City, Vanover 5-193.

PUNT RETURNS—Buffalo, Tasker 3-25. Kansas City, Vanover 4-25.

SACKS—Buffalo, Rogers 1, Hansen 1. Kansas City, Tongue 1, Davis 1, McDaniels 1, Barndt 1.

BRONCOS 35, RAMS 14

Sunday, September 14

St. Louis	7	0	0	7—14
Denver	7	7	7	14—35

First Quarter
Den.—R. Smith 72 pass from Elway (Elam kick), 5:04.
St.L.—Phillips 23 run (Wilkins kick), 14:27.

Second Quarter
Den.—Carswell 24 pass from Elway (Elam kick), 10:50.

Third Quarter
Den.—Gordon 94 punt return (Elam kick), 1:33.

Fourth Quarter
Den.—R. Smith 38 pass from Elway (Elam kick), 4:00.
Den.—McCaffrey 23 pass from Elway (Elam kick), 4:57.
St.L.—R. Moore 27 run (Wilkins kick), 12:05.
Attendance—74,338.

TEAM STATISTICS

	St. Louis	Denver
First downs	18	19
Rushes-yards	23-130	34-144
Passing	184	233
Punt returns	2-5	5-121
Kickoff returns	3-47	1-26
Interception returns	1-0	2-4
Comp.-att.-int.	18-33-2	16-28-1
Sacked-yards lost	5-33	1-14
Punts	7-44	4-47
Fumbles-lost	0-0	3-1
Penalties-yards	7-45	10-100
Time of possession	30:29	29:31

INDIVIDUAL STATISTICS

RUSHING—St. Louis, Phillips 13-60, R. Moore 5-48, Banks 2-12, Heyward 2-6, Lee 1-4. Denver, Davis 21-103, Hebron 5-19, Griffith 4-13, Elway 3-10, Lewis 1-(minus 1).

PASSING—St. Louis, Banks 18-33-2-217. Denver, Elway 16-28-1-247.

RECEIVING—St. Louis, Lee 6-90, R. Moore 3-29, Small 3-22, Kennison 2-26, Conwell 2-19, Crawford 1-17, Ross 1-14. Denver, R. Smith 4-126, Carswell 4-47, Sharpe 2-20, Chamberlain 2-18, McCaffrey 1-23, Green 1-5, Davis 1-4, Griffith 1-4.

MISSED FIELD GOAL ATTEMPTS—St. Louis, Wilkins 37. Denver, Elam 43.

INTERCEPTIONS—St. Louis, McNeil 1-0. Denver, Crockett 1-4, McKyer 1-0.

KICKOFF RETURNS—St. Louis, Ross 3-47. Denver, Hebron 1-26.

PUNT RETURNS—St. Louis, Kennison 2-5. Denver, Gordon 4-109, R. Smith 1-12.

SACKS—St. Louis, O'Neal 1. Denver, N. Smith 2, Mobley 1, Traylor 1, Hasselbach 1.

BUCCANEERS 28, VIKINGS 14

Sunday, September 14

Tampa Bay	0	14	7	7—28
Minnesota	3	0	3	8—14

First Quarter
Min.—FG, Davis 25, 13:11.

Second Quarter
T.B.—Harris 5 pass from Dilfer (Husted kick), 1:10.
T.B.—Alstott 1 run (Husted kick), 11:03.

Third Quarter
T.B.—Copeland 27 pass from Dilfer (Husted kick), 5:44.
Min.—FG, Davis 24, 10:23.

Fourth Quarter
T.B.—Dunn 52 run (Husted kick), 2:31.
Min.—Carter 30 pass from Johnson (Johnson run), 14:22.
Attendance—63,697.

TEAM STATISTICS

	Tampa Bay	Minnesota
First downs	17	20
Rushes-yards	37-191	15-72
Passing	185	310
Punt returns	3-39	2-14
Kickoff returns	3-63	4-58
Interception returns	0-0	0-0
Comp.-att.-int.	15-20-0	29-44-0
Sacked-yards lost	1-7	3-24
Punts	5-41	5-41
Fumbles-lost	3-0	2-2
Penalties-yards	6-39	6-40
Time of possession	33:13	26:47

INDIVIDUAL STATISTICS

RUSHING—Tampa Bay, Dunn 16-101, Alstott 8-29, Rhett 8-28, Dilfer 4-7, Anthony 1-26. Minnesota, R. Smith 10-54, Johnson 2-16, Hoard 2-(minus 2), Evans 1-4.

PASSING—Tampa Bay, Dilfer 15-20-0-192. Minnesota, Johnson 29-44-0-334.

RECEIVING—Tampa Bay, Anthony 4-58, Copeland 3-85, Harris 3-13, Thomas 2-26, Alstott 2-9, Dunn 1-1. Minnesota, Reed 6-131, Carter 6-69, R. Smith 6-27, Evans 5-53, Walsh 2-29, Hoard 2-8, Palmer 1-10, DeLong 1-7.

MISSED FIELD GOAL ATTEMPTS—None.

INTERCEPTIONS—None.

KICKOFF RETURNS—Tampa Bay, Dunn 3-63. Minnesota, Palmer 4-58.

PUNT RETURNS—Tampa Bay, Dunn 3-39. Minnesota, Palmer 2-14.

SACKS—Tampa Bay, Brooks 1, Ahanotu 1, Upshaw 0.5, Jackson 0.5. Minnesota, Rudd 1.

REDSKINS 19, CARDINALS 13

Sunday, September 14

Arizona	7	0	3	3	0—13
Washington	3	7	0	3	6—19

First Quarter
Was.—FG, Blanton 20, 6:33.
Ariz.—Bennett recovered blocked punt in end zone (Butler kick), 14:03.

Second Quarter
Was.—Westbrook 5 pass from Frerotte (Blanton kick), 1:23.

Third Quarter
Ariz.—FG, Butler 32, 14:08.

Fourth Quarter
Was.—FG, Blanton 19, 13:47.
Ariz.—FG, Butler 47, 14:58.

Overtime
Was.—Westbrook 40 pass from Frerotte, 1:36.
Attendance—78,270.

TEAM STATISTICS

	Arizona	Washington
First downs	14	17
Rushes-yards	34-118	30-76
Passing	116	252
Punt returns	3-20	4-40
Kickoff returns	5-122	3-48
Interception returns	1-17	0-0
Comp.-att.-int.	17-40-0	19-36-1
Sacked-yards lost	2-16	2-13
Punts	9-42	8-44
Fumbles-lost	4-2	1-0
Penalties-yards	4-44	4-37
Time of possession	32:32	29:04

INDIVIDUAL STATISTICS

RUSHING—Arizona, McElroy 18-49, Centers 6-20, Bouie 5-25, K. Graham 2-9, C. Smith 1-2, Feagles 1-0, K. Williams 1-(minus 2), Gedney 0-15. Washington, Allen 25-56, Frerotte 3-9, Mitchell 1-7, Shepherd 1-4.

PASSING—Arizona, K. Graham 17-40-0-132. Washington, Frerotte 19-36-1-265.

RECEIVING—Arizona, Centers 6-42, Sanders 4-32, R. Moore 3-27, K. Williams 1-16, Gedney 1-9, Edwards 1-5, Carter 1-1. Washington, Shepherd 4-67, Asher 4-29, Westbrook 3-66, Bowie 3-43, Ellard 2-35, Allen 2-14, Mitchell 1-11.

MISSED FIELD GOAL ATTEMPTS—Arizona, Butler 34. Washington, Blanton 51, 51.

INTERCEPTIONS—Arizona, McKinnon 1-17.

KICKOFF RETURNS—Arizona, K. Williams 3-82, Bouie 2-40. Washington, Mitchell 2-42, Jones 1-6.

PUNT RETURNS—Arizona, K. Williams 3-20. Washington, Mitchell 4-40.

SACKS—Arizona, Miller 1, Swann 1. Washington, Boutte 1, Mims 1.

COWBOYS 21, EAGLES 20

Monday, September 15

Philadelphia	10	7	0	3—20
Dallas	3	3	3	12—21

First Quarter
Phi.—FG, Boniol 49, 5:21.
Dal.—FG, Cunningham 46, 9:45.
Phi.—W. Thomas 37 fumble return (Boniol kick), 11:52.

Second Quarter
Phi.—Lewis 12 pass from Detmer (Boniol kick), 5:29.
Dal.—FG, Cunningham 48, 14:58.

Third Quarter
Dal.—FG, Cunningham 25, 3:15.

Fourth Quarter
Phi.—FG, Boniol 44, 0:05.
Dal.—FG, Cunningham 23, 2:08.
Dal.—FG, Cunningham 22, 9:35.
Dal.—Miller 14 pass from Aikman (pass failed), 14:09.
Attendance—63,942.

TEAM STATISTICS

	Philadelphia	Dallas
First downs	16	18
Rushes-yards	29-157	28-92
Passing	176	187
Punt returns	2-13	3-16
Kickoff returns	7-116	5-178
Interception returns	0-0	0-0
Comp.-att.-int.	18-30-0	17-36-0
Sacked-yards lost	2-8	2-18
Punts	6-42	4-38
Fumbles-lost	1-0	2-2
Penalties-yards	13-107	3-34
Time of possession	34:43	25:17

INDIVIDUAL STATISTICS

RUSHING—Philadelphia, Watters 20-106, Garner 7-48, Turner 1-3, Hutton 1-0. Dallas, E. Smith 27-91, Aikman 1-1.

PASSING—Philadelphia, Detmer 18-30-0-184. Dallas, Aikman 17-36-0-205.

RECEIVING—Philadelphia, Watters 5-14, Timpson 3-37, Solomon 2-72, Lewis 2-19, Turner 2-15, Fryar 1-13, Seay 1-6, Vincent 1-5, Dunn 1-3. Dallas, Irvin 4-73, Bjornson 4-48, Miller 3-46, Johnston 2-10, E. Smith 2-7, St. Williams 1-18, Sanders 1-3.

MISSED FIELD GOAL ATTEMPTS—Philadelphia, Boniol 45.

INTERCEPTIONS—None.

KICKOFF RETURNS—Philadelphia, Witherspoon 5-79, Seay 1-28, Johnson 1-9. Dallas, Walker 4-129, Marion 1-49.

PUNT RETURNS—Philadelphia, Seay 2-13. Dallas, Sanders 2-17, Mathis 1-(minus 1).

SACKS—Philadelphia, Taylor 2. Dallas, Carver 1, Thomas 1.

WEEK 4

RESULTS

Baltimore 36, TENNESSEE 10
BUFFALO 37, Indianapolis 35
DENVER 38, Cincinnati 20
GREEN BAY 38, Minnesota 32
Kansas City 35, CAROLINA 14
NEW ENGLAND 31, Chicago 3
NEW ORLEANS 35, Detroit 17
N.Y. JETS 23, Oakland 22
ST. LOUIS 13, N.Y. Giants 3
SAN FRANCISCO 34, Atlanta 7
SEATTLE 26, San Diego 22
TAMPA BAY 31, Miami 21
JACKSONVILLE 30, Pittsburgh 21
  Open date: Arizona, Dallas, Philadelphia,
Washington

STANDINGS

AFC EAST	W	L	T	Pct.
New England	4	0	0	1.000
Buffalo	2	2	0	.500
Miami	2	2	0	.500
N.Y. Jets	2	2	0	.500
Indianapolis	0	4	0	.000

AFC CENTRAL	W	L	T	Pct.
Jacksonville	3	0	0	1.000
Baltimore	3	1	0	.750
Cincinnati	1	2	0	.333
Pittsburgh	1	2	0	.333
Tennessee	1	2	0	.333

AFC WEST	W	L	T	Pct.
Denver	4	0	0	1.000
Kansas City	3	1	0	.750
Seattle	2	2	0	.500
Oakland	1	3	0	.250
San Diego	1	3	0	.250

NFC EAST	W	L	T	Pct.
Dallas	2	1	0	.667
Washington	2	1	0	.667
Arizona	1	2	0	.333
Philadelphia	1	2	0	.333
N.Y. Giants	1	3	0	.250

NFC CENTRAL	W	L	T	Pct.
Tampa Bay	4	0	0	1.000
Green Bay	3	1	0	.750
Detroit	2	2	0	.500
Minnesota	2	2	0	.500
Chicago	0	4	0	.000

NFC WEST	W	L	T	Pct.
San Francisco	3	1	0	.750
Carolina	2	2	0	.500
St. Louis	2	2	0	.500
New Orleans	1	3	0	.250
Atlanta	0	4	0	.000

HIGHLIGHTS

Hero of the week: Denver's Terrell Davis ran for a career-high 215 yards on 27 carries and scored one touchdown in the Broncos' 38-20 victory over Cincinnati.

Goat of the week: Oakland's Cole Ford missed four field goals, including one that was returned for the game-winning touchdown, and botched an extra point in the Raiders' 23-22 loss to the Jets. In fairness to Ford, the snaps were poor or mishandled on three of the kicks.

Sub of the week: Seattle had only 2 yards rushing at halftime, so coach Dennis Erickson inserted Steve Broussard, an eight-year veteran whose primary job had been kickoff returns. Broussard ran for 72 yards in the second half as a replacement for Chris Warren and Lamar Smith, and his 1-yard leap into the end zone with 1:22 left gave the Seahawks their winning points in a 26-22 victory over the Chargers.

Comeback of the week: In many cases, a 26-point lead would be reason to send many of the first-stringers to the bench for a well-deserved rest. But the Colts kept their starters in the game—and still lost. Buffalo rallied from a 26-0 deficit to win, 37-35, in the second-biggest regular-season comeback victory in NFL history. Rookie Antowain Smith's 54-yard TD run with 1:14 left sealed the win.

Blowout of the week: The Bears were 0-4 for the first time in 28 years after a 31-3 defeat at New England. The Patriots gained 402 yards and held Chicago to 199. The final blow came in the fourth quarter, when Curtis Martin's 70-yard touchdown run gave New England a 24-3 lead.

Nail-biter of the week: For the second consecutive Monday night, a failed field-goal attempt on the last play of the game provided a fantastic finish. This time, the Steelers' Norm Johnson lined up for a 40-yard attempt with his team trailing, 23-21. The snap from veteran center Jim Sweeney was low, and Jacksonville's Clyde Simmons blocked the kick. Chris Hudson picked up the loose ball and returned it 58 yards for a touchdown, giving the Jaguars a 30-21 victory.

Hit of the week: Green Bay had blown most of a 31-7 halftime lead as Minnesota quarterback Brad Johnson led four successive scoring drives to close the gap, at one point hitting 13 passes in a row. But Johnson misfired three consecutive times from midfield after the two-minute warning, leaving the Vikings with one last chance. On fourth-and-10 from Minnesota's 46, Reggie White blew past right tackle Korey Stringer and hit Johnson's arm just as he released, which redirected the pass and preserved the Packers' 38-32 victory.

Oddity of the week: Fake field goals and fake punts are trick plays that fans can expect to see every once in a while. But fake onside kicks are even more of a rarity. The Vikings, however, decided to fake an onside kick on each of their six kickoffs against Green Bay. The unorthodox strategy managed to disrupt the Packers' return unit, but Green Bay won anyway.

Top rusher: Terrell Davis' 215-yard effort against the Bengals eclipsed his team record of 194, set a season earlier against Baltimore.

Top passer: Jeff George was 26-of-38 for 374 yards and three touchdowns in the Raiders' 23-22 loss to the Jets.

Top receiver: Oakland's Tim Brown caught 10 passes for 153 yards and scored one touchdown in the losing effort.

Notes: The Jets avoided tying the league record for consecutive home losses (13, set by Dallas in 1988-89) thanks to great special teams play. Corwin Brown blocked a field goal, and Ray Mickens returned it 72 yards for the winning touchdown.... Buffalo's Thurman Thomas had 66 total yards against the Colts to increase his career total to 14,865, moving him past Jim Brown into sixth place on the NFL's career list.... The Patriots improved their record to 3-0 against the Bears since being crushed, 46-10, in Super Bowl XX. . . . In the Dolphins-Bucs game, Trent Dilfer completed 13 of his first 15 passes; Dan Marino completed one of his first nine. . . . Green Bay's Brett Favre threw his 153rd touchdown pass, passing Hall of Famer Bart

Starr to become the Packers' career leader. . . . The Saints converted 10 of 14 third downs in their 35-17 upset of Detroit. . . . Ki-Jana Carter gained 104 yards against Denver, becoming the first Bengal to run for 100 yards since Harold Green on December 20, 1992 (68 games earlier). . . . Only 17,737 people showed up at the 62,320-seat Liberty Bowl in Memphis to watch the Oilers lose, 36-10, to the Ravens. . . . Terrell Davis' big day against Cincinnati put him over the 3,000-yard mark for career rushing yardage. The third-year running back reached the milestone in 34 games.

Quote of the week: Green Bay safety Leroy Butler, expressing how he felt about the rival Vikings after the Packers beat them, 38-32: "This is a team we really don't like, and we really wanted to hammer them. Kill a fly with an ax."

GAME SUMMARIES

PACKERS 38, VIKINGS 32

Sunday, September 21

Minnesota	7	0	15	10—32
Green Bay	7	24	7	0—38

First Quarter
Min.—R. Smith 1 run (Davis kick), 7:36.
G.B.—Brooks 19 pass from Favre (Longwell kick), 11:34.

Second Quarter
G.B.—Freeman 28 pass from Favre (Longwell kick), 4:09.
G.B.—Freeman 15 pass from Favre (Longwell kick), 6:30.
G.B.—Mickens 2 pass from Favre (Longwell kick), 13:51.
G.B.—FG, Longwell 34, 14:57.

Third Quarter
Min.—Carter 3 pass from Johnson (Davis kick), 3:07.
Min.—Reed 7 pass from Johnson (Evans run), 4:40.
G.B.—Chmura 2 pass from Favre (Longwell kick), 10:19.

Fourth Quarter
Min.—FG, Davis 31, 0:48.
Min.—Reed 27 pass from Johnson (Davis kick), 8:16.
Attendance—60,115.

TEAM STATISTICS
	Minnesota	Green Bay
First downs	22	24
Rushes-yards	37-185	22-93
Passing	208	257
Punt returns	1-12	3-65
Kickoff returns	5-87	6-104
Interception returns	2-27	2-2
Comp.-att.-int.	19-34-2	18-31-2
Sacked-yards lost	3-9	2-9
Punts	4-50	4-45
Fumbles-lost	0-0	2-1
Penalties-yards	9-115	5-40
Time of possession	33:05	26:55

INDIVIDUAL STATISTICS
RUSHING—Minnesota, R. Smith 28-132, Evans 5-17, Johnson 3-33, Green 1-3. Green Bay, Levens 17-79, Favre 4-10, Henderson 1-4.
PASSING—Minnesota, Johnson 19-34-2-217. Green Bay, Favre 18-31-2-266.
RECEIVING—Minnesota, Reed 9-119, Carter 5-32, R. Smith 4-38, Glover 1-28. Green Bay, Freeman 7-122, Brooks 5-92, Levens 2-22, Henderson 1-21, Mayes 1-5, Chmura 1-2, Mickens 1-2.
MISSED FIELD GOAL ATTEMPTS—Minnesota, Davis 22.
INTERCEPTIONS—Minnesota, Washington 1-26, Fisk 1-1. Green Bay, Butler 2-2.
KICKOFF RETURNS—Minnesota, Tate 4-77, Morrow 1-10. Green Bay, Darkins 4-68, Schroeder 2-36.
PUNT RETURNS—Minnesota, Palmer 1-12. Green Bay, Schroeder 3-65.
SACKS—Minnesota, E. McDaniel 1, Rudd 1. Green Bay, Wilkins 1, S. Dotson 1, White 1.

JETS 23, RAIDERS 22

Sunday, September 21

Oakland	6	16	0	0—22
N.Y. Jets	3	7	6	7—23

First Quarter
Oak.—Jett 56 pass from George (kick failed), 11:38.
NYJ—FG, Hall 34, 13:46.

Second Quarter
Oak.—T. Brown 29 pass from George (pass failed), 3:29.
NYJ—Murrell 4 run (Hall kick), 5:32.
Oak.—Jett 11 pass from George (Ford kick), 9:28.
Oak.—FG, Ford 43, 12:46.

Third Quarter
NYJ—FG, Hall 47, 4:02.
NYJ—FG, Hall 26, 14:05.

Fourth Quarter
NYJ—Mickens 72 blocked FG return (Hall kick), 2:09.
Attendance—72,586.

TEAM STATISTICS
	Oakland	N.Y. Jets
First downs	26	16
Rushes-yards	28-129	21-83
Passing	339	220
Punt returns	2-26	3-20
Kickoff returns	5-100	3-72
Interception returns	0-0	0-0
Comp.-att.-int.	26-38-0	18-33-0
Sacked-yards lost	4-35	1-4
Punts	4-46	4-37
Fumbles-lost	3-0	2-1
Penalties-yards	4-40	5-55
Time of possession	35:16	24:44

INDIVIDUAL STATISTICS
RUSHING—Oakland, Kaufman 27-126, Aska 1-3. New York, Murrell 15-68, O'Donnell 4-10, L. Johnson 1-10, Anderson 1-(minus 5).
PASSING—Oakland, George 26-38-0-374. New York, O'Donnell 17-32-0-198, Hansen 1-1-0-26.
RECEIVING—Oakland, T. Brown 10-153, Jett 5-148, Kaufman 5-32, Shedd 3-26, Williams 2-10, Dudley 1-5. New York, Chrebet 4-48, Anderson 4-37, Murrell 4-21, Graham 2-54, K. Johnson 2-22, Brown 1-26, Brady 1-16.
MISSED FIELD GOAL ATTEMPTS—Oakland, Ford 44, 27, 35, 47.
INTERCEPTIONS—None.
KICKOFF RETURNS—Oakland, Howard 5-100. New York, Glenn 2-50, Neal 1-22.
PUNT RETURNS—Oakland, Howard 2-26. New York, L. Johnson 3-20.
SACKS—Oakland, Smith 1. New York, Jones 1, Lyle 1, Lewis 1, Farrior 1.

CHIEFS 35, PANTHERS 14

Sunday, September 21

Kansas City	7	7	7	14—35
Carolina	0	7	0	7—14

First Quarter
K.C.—Anders 55 pass from Grbac (Stoyanovich kick), 14:22.

Second Quarter
K.C.—Rison 18 pass from Grbac (Stoyanovich kick), 5:28.
Car.—Lane 8 run (Kasay kick), 11:01.

Third Quarter
K.C.—Allen 1 run (Stoyanovich kick), 8:28.

Fourth Quarter
K.C.—Richardson 3 pass from Grbac (Stoyanovich kick), 0:41.
K.C.—McMillian 62 interception return (Stoyanovich kick), 1:18.
Car.—Walls 19 pass from Collins (Kasay kick), 9:14.
Attendance—67,402.

TEAM STATISTICS
	Kansas City	Carolina
First downs	17	24
Rushes-yards	34-117	24-86
Passing	214	278
Punt returns	1-16	6-31
Kickoff returns	1-19	6-150
Interception returns	4-120	1-0
Comp.-att.-int.	16-29-1	24-47-4
Sacked-yards lost	1-10	5-50

	Kansas City	Carolina
Punts	8-47	5-44
Fumbles-lost	0-0	2-1
Penalties-yards	9-100	8-57
Time of possession	29:31	30:29

INDIVIDUAL STATISTICS

RUSHING—Kansas City, Allen 9-31, Bennett 8-32, Hill 8-5, Anders 7-42, Grbac 2-7. Carolina, Johnson 11-39, Lane 6-21, Biakabutuka 5-28, Collins 1-3, Walter 1-(minus 5).

PASSING—Kansas City, Grbac 16-29-1-224. Carolina, Collins 24-47-4-328.

RECEIVING—Kansas City, Popson 6-49, Anders 4-94, Rison 3-50, Walker 1-22, Hill 1-6, Richardson 1-3. Carolina, Carruth 8-110, Greene 5-57, Johnson 4-48, Carrier 3-59, E. Mills 2-23, Walls 1-19, Ismail 1-12.

MISSED FIELD GOAL ATTEMPTS—Carolina, Kasay 54, 53.

INTERCEPTIONS—Kansas City, McMillian 1-62, Woods 1-27, Hasty 1-19, Edwards 1-12. Carolina, Poole 1-0.

KICKOFF RETURNS—Kansas City, Vanover 1-19. Carolina, Bates 6-150.

PUNT RETURNS—Kansas City, Vanover 1-16. Carolina, Poole 6-31.

SACKS—Kansas City, Browning 1, Barndt 1, Williams 1, Anderson 1, Dumas 1. Carolina, Miller 1.

SAINTS 35, LIONS 17

Sunday, September 21

Detroit	0	7	0	10—17
New Orleans	0	21	7	7—35

Second Quarter
N.O.—Hastings 21 pass from Bates (Brien kick), 1:22.
N.O.—Bates 74 run (Brien kick), 3:43.
N.O.—Hobbs 20 pass from Shuler (Brien kick), 10:33.
Det.—Sanders 17 pass from Mitchell (Hanson kick), 14:01.

Third Quarter
N.O.—Shuler 5 run (Brien kick), 6:38.

Fourth Quarter
Det.—FG, Hanson 47, 0:04.
N.O.—Bates 2 run (Brien kick), 9:13.
Det.—Moore 5 pass from Mitchell (Hanson kick), 11:12.
Attendance—50,016.

TEAM STATISTICS

	Detroit	New Orleans
First downs	22	21
Rushes-yards	19-118	36-172
Passing	237	213
Punt returns	2-22	2-12
Kickoff returns	6-157	1-26
Interception returns	0-0	3-29
Comp.-att.-int.	24-43-3	16-22-0
Sacked-yards lost	5-16	2-10
Punts	3-34	2-55
Fumbles-lost	5-1	0-0
Penalties-yards	5-50	8-62
Time of possession	25:25	34:35

INDIVIDUAL STATISTICS

RUSHING—Detroit, Sanders 18-113, Vardell 1-5. New Orleans, Bates 29-162, T. Davis 4-4, Shuler 3-6.

PASSING—Detroit, Mitchell 24-43-3-253. New Orleans, Shuler 15-21-0-202, Bates 1-1-0-21.

RECEIVING—Detroit, Moore 11-111, Morton 5-72, Metzelaars 3-15, Chryplewicz 2-23, Sanders 1-17, T. Boyd 1-15, Vardell 1-0. New Orleans, Hastings 5-74, Hill 4-36, Guliford 3-43, Zellars 2-27, Farquhar 1-23, Hobbs 1-20.

MISSED FIELD GOAL ATTEMPTS—New Orleans, Brien 50, 48.

INTERCEPTIONS—New Orleans, Newman 2-2, Allen 1-27.

KICKOFF RETURNS—Detroit, Milburn 6-157. New Orleans, Guliford 1-26.

PUNT RETURNS—Detroit, Milburn 2-22. New Orleans, Guliford 2-12.

SACKS—Detroit, Elliss 1.5, Porcher 0.5. New Orleans, Martin 3.5, Glover 1, J. Johnson 0.5.

PATRIOTS 31, BEARS 3

Sunday, September 21

Chicago	0	0	3	0— 3
New England	7	7	0	17—31

First Quarter
N.E.—Brisby 7 pass from Bledsoe (Vinatieri kick), 6:21.

Second Quarter
N.E.—Brown 52 pass from Bledsoe (Vinatieri kick), 13:25.

Third Quarter
Chi.—FG, Jaeger 38, 11:30.

Fourth Quarter
N.E.—FG, Vinatieri 27, 0:54.
N.E.—Martin 70 run (Vinatieri kick), 7:44.
N.E.—Purnell 20 pass from Zolak (Vinatieri kick), 13:58.
Attendance—59,873.

TEAM STATISTICS

	Chicago	New England
First downs	9	23
Rushes-yards	24-79	21-87
Passing	120	315
Punt returns	1-12	5-30
Kickoff returns	5-126	2-59
Interception returns	1-0	2-30
Comp.-att.-int.	17-25-2	27-40-1
Sacked-yards lost	5-34	2-19
Punts	10-41	5-48
Fumbles-lost	1-1	2-2
Penalties-yards	9-75	6-44
Time of possession	30:32	29:28

INDIVIDUAL STATISTICS

RUSHING—Chicago, R. Harris 21-63, Mirer 2-13, Autry 1-3. New England, Martin 14-79, Grier 4-10, Byars 1-1, Gash 1-(minus 1), Meggett 1-(minus 2).

PASSING—Chicago, Mirer 17-25-2-154. New England, Bledsoe 24-37-1-301, Zolak 3-3-0-33.

RECEIVING—Chicago, Engram 5-47, Wetnight 3-46, Penn 3-30, R. Harris 3-17, Proehl 1-8, Jennings 1-5, T. Carter 1-1. New England, Brown 6-124, Coates 6-61, Jefferson 5-55, Brisby 3-29, Martin 3-28, Gash 2-13, Purnell 1-20, Byars 1-4.

MISSED FIELD GOAL ATTEMPTS—None.

INTERCEPTIONS—Chicago, Marshall 1-0. New England, Law 1-30, Moore 1-0.

KICKOFF RETURNS—Chicago, Hughes 4-94, Bownes 1-32. New England, Meggett 2-59.

PUNT RETURNS—Chicago, Hughes 1-12. New England, Meggett 5-30.

SACKS—Chicago, Flanigan 1, Spellman 1. New England, Thomas 2, Whigham 2, Bruschi 1.

RAVENS 36, OILERS 10

Sunday, September 21

Baltimore	3	17	3	13—36
Tennessee	7	3	0	0—10

First Quarter
Bal.—FG, Stover 38, 3:51.
Ten.—Wycheck 36 pass from McNair (Del Greco kick), 10:59.

Second Quarter
Bal.—Alexander 25 pass from Testaverde (Stover kick), 3:00.
Bal.—Alexander 5 pass from Testaverde (Stover kick), 10:44.
Ten.—FG, Del Greco 45, 13:28.
Bal.—FG, Stover 42, 15:00.

Third Quarter
Bal.—FG, Stover 49, 14:12.

Fourth Quarter
Bal.—J. Lewis 16 pass from Testaverde (Stover kick), 4:03.
Bal.—FG, Stover 34, 7:11.
Bal.—FG, Stover 36, 12:53.
Attendance—17,737.

TEAM STATISTICS

	Baltimore	Tennessee
First downs	21	18
Rushes-yards	28-89	18-97
Passing	309	195
Punt returns	2-45	2-2
Kickoff returns	3-49	5-158
Interception returns	1-4	0-0
Comp.-att.-int.	23-37-0	22-35-1
Sacked-yards lost	1-9	3-19
Punts	2-36	3-43
Fumbles-lost	1-0	5-4
Penalties-yards	8-64	5-30
Time of possession	31:15	28:45

INDIVIDUAL STATISTICS

RUSHING—Baltimore, Byner 16-30, Graham 9-51, Testaverde 3-8. Tennessee, George 10-40, McNair 4-36, Thomas 2-8, Harmon 1-7, Ritchey 1-6.

PASSING—Baltimore, Testaverde 23-37-0-318. Tennessee, McNair 20-33-1-199, Ritchey 2-2-0-15.

RECEIVING—Baltimore, J. Lewis 8-124, Alexander 5-66, Jackson 4-73, Kinchen 4-38, Byner 2-17. Tennessee, Davis 4-42, Sanders 4-34, Harmon 4-33, Wycheck 3-55, Russell 3-13, Roan 2-26, Mason 1-8, George 1-3.

MISSED FIELD GOAL ATTEMPTS—Baltimore, Stover 46. Tennessee, Del Greco 41.

INTERCEPTIONS—Baltimore, Sharper 1-0.

KICKOFF RETURNS—Baltimore, J. Lewis 2-35, Holmes 1-14. Tennessee, Mason 4-143, Gray 1-15.

PUNT RETURNS—Baltimore, J. Lewis 2-45. Tennessee, Mason 2-2.

SACKS—Baltimore, Boulware 1, Burnett 1, C. Brown 1. Tennessee, Holmes 1.

RAMS 13, GIANTS 3

Sunday, September 21

N.Y. Giants	0	0	0	3— 3
St. Louis	0	6	0	7—13

Second Quarter
St.L.—FG, Wilkins 23, 5:33.
St.L.—FG, Wilkins 21, 14:47.

Fourth Quarter
NYG—FG, Daluiso 47, 1:34.
St.L.—Heyward 4 run (Wilkins kick), 12:18.
Attendance—64,642.

TEAM STATISTICS

	N.Y. Giants	St. Louis
First downs	11	15
Rushes-yards	24-45	32-92
Passing	147	133
Punt returns	6-56	1-9
Kickoff returns	4-94	1-24
Interception returns	0-0	1-39
Comp.-att.-int.	16-33-1	15-35-0
Sacked-yards lost	4-16	5-43
Punts	7-40	8-43
Fumbles-lost	2-1	1-1
Penalties-yards	10-80	12-80
Time of possession	27:09	32:51

INDIVIDUAL STATISTICS

RUSHING—New York, Barber 9-4, Way 7-25, Wheatley 6-10, Brown 2-6. St. Louis, Phillips 23-72, Banks 5-11, Heyward 2-5, Lee 2-4.

PASSING—New York, Brown 16-31-1-163, Kanell 0-2-0-0. St. Louis, Banks 15-35-0-176.

RECEIVING—New York, Way 6-69, Calloway 4-53, Barber 3-15, Alexander 1-15, Wheatley 1-6, Cross 1-5. St. Louis, Conwell 4-26, Lee 3-58, Kennison 3-28, Small 2-47, Ross 1-14, Laing 1-7, Phillips 1-(minus 4).

MISSED FIELD GOAL ATTEMPTS—New York, Daluiso 54, 42.

INTERCEPTIONS—St. Louis, Lyle 1-39.

KICKOFF RETURNS—New York, Lewis 3-68, Patten 1-26. St. Louis, Ross 1-24.

PUNT RETURNS—New York, Toomer 6-56. St. Louis, Kennison 1-9.

SACKS—New York, Armstead 1, Strahan 1, K. Hamilton 1, Harris 1, Bratzke 1. St. Louis, Phifer 1, Carter 1, Farr 1, Johnson 1.

BILLS 37, COLTS 35

Sunday, September 21

Indianapolis	14	12	0	9—35
Buffalo	0	10	6	21—37

First Quarter
Ind.—Bailey 10 pass from Harbaugh (Blanchard kick), 4:07.
Ind.—Faulk 10 run (Blanchard kick), 12:25.

Second Quarter
Ind.—FG, Blanchard 39, 0:16.
Ind.—FG, Blanchard 36, 4:13.
Ind.—FG, Blanchard 49, 6:14.
Ind.—FG, Blanchard 22, 9:01.
Buf.—Johnson 16 pass from Collins (Christie kick), 12:48.
Buf.—FG, Christie 27, 15:00.

Third Quarter
Buf.—A. Smith 15 run (run failed), 11:34.

Fourth Quarter
Ind.—FG, Blanchard 25, 4:41.
Buf.—Early 4 pass from Collins (Christie kick), 8:35.
Buf.—A. Smith 1 run (Christie kick), 10:17.
Buf.—A. Smith 54 run (Christie kick), 13:46.
Ind.—Harrison 2 pass from Justin (pass failed), 14:46.
Attendance—55,340.

TEAM STATISTICS

	Indianapolis	Buffalo
First downs	17	25
Rushes-yards	30-124	23-163
Passing	198	230
Punt returns	2-13	3-15
Kickoff returns	5-72	8-169
Interception returns	1-18	1-0
Comp.-att.-int.	19-39-1	23-38-1
Sacked-yards lost	2-16	6-45
Punts	6-42	4-40
Fumbles-lost	1-0	6-4
Penalties-yards	14-112	4-45
Time of possession	32:27	27:33

INDIVIDUAL STATISTICS

RUSHING—Indianapolis, Faulk 16-77, Crockett 10-33, Harbaugh 3-15, Bailey 1-(minus 1). Buffalo, A. Smith 12-129, Thomas 7-22, Collins 4-12.

PASSING—Indianapolis, Harbaugh 16-31-0-191, Justin 3-8-1-23. Buffalo, Collins 23-38-1-275.

RECEIVING—Indianapolis, Bailey 7-96, Harrison 6-68, Faulk 3-8, Dilger 2-34, Pollard 1-8. Buffalo, Reed 7-91, Thomas 5-44, Early 4-76, A. Smith 3-32, Johnson 3-25, Riemersma 1-7.

MISSED FIELD GOAL ATTEMPTS—None.

INTERCEPTIONS—Indianapolis, E. Johnson 1-18. Buffalo, Irvin 1-0.

KICKOFF RETURNS—Indianapolis, Bailey 3-38, Warren 1-19, Groce 1-15. Buffalo, Galloway 4-100, Moulds 3-58, Pike 1-11.

PUNT RETURNS—Indianapolis, Stablein 2-13. Buffalo, Galloway 2-15, Jones 1-0.

SACKS—Indianapolis, Bennett 3, Alexander 1, Fontenot 1, McCoy 1. Buffalo, Hansen 1, B. Smith 1.

BRONCOS 38, BENGALS 20

Sunday, September 21

Cincinnati	7	0	10	3—20
Denver	0	14	7	17—38

First Quarter
Cin.—McGee 7 pass from Blake (Pelfrey kick), 14:59.

Second Quarter
Den.—McCaffrey 32 pass from Elway (Elam kick), 3:56.
Den.—R. Smith 1 pass from Elway (Elam kick), 14:35.

Third Quarter
Cin.—Carter 79 run (Pelfrey kick), 0:22.
Cin.—FG, Pelfrey 38, 6:36.
Den.—R. Smith 18 pass from Elway (Elam kick), 12:27.

Fourth Quarter
Cin.—FG, Pelfrey 43, 1:30.
Den.—Davis 50 run (Elam kick), 3:47.
Den.—FG, Elam 25, 11:34.
Den.—Williams 51 fumble return (Elam kick), 14:03.
Attendance—73,871.

TEAM STATISTICS

	Cincinnati	Denver
First downs	22	23
Rushes-yards	25-195	29-222
Passing	194	150
Punt returns	0-0	0-0
Kickoff returns	7-159	5-100
Interception returns	1-29	0-0
Comp.-att.-int.	20-30-0	14-26-1
Sacked-yards lost	4-26	2-12
Punts	3-31	2-37
Fumbles-lost	2-1	0-0
Penalties-yards	12-123	8-90
Time of possession	32:00	28:00

INDIVIDUAL STATISTICS

RUSHING—Cincinnati, Carter 13-104, Dillon 5-58, Blake 4-29, Bieniemy 3-4. Denver, Davis 27-215, Elway 1-5, Hebron 1-2.

PASSING—Cincinnati, Blake 20-30-0-220. Denver, Elway 14-26-1-162.

RECEIVING—Cincinnati, Pickens 8-125, Dillon 4-30, Dunn 2-39, Scott 2-24, McGee 1-7, Battaglia 1-(minus 1), Milne 1-(minus 1), Carter 1-(minus 3). Denver, R. Smith 7-82, McCaffrey 4-62, Davis 2-13, Sharpe 1-5.

MISSED FIELD GOAL ATTEMPTS—Cincinnati, Pelfrey 56.

INTERCEPTIONS—Cincinnati, Mack 1-29.

KICKOFF RETURNS—Cincinnati, Dunn 5-105, Dillon 1-53, Hundon 1-1. Denver, Hebron 4-82, Burns 1-18.

PUNT RETURNS—None.

SACKS—Cincinnati, Dixon 1, Collins 1. Denver, Mobley 1, Romanowski 1, Tanuvasa 1, N. Smith 1.

BUCCANEERS 31, DOLPHINS 21

Sunday, September 21

Miami	0	7	0	14—21
Tampa Bay	7	7	10	7—31

First Quarter
T.B.—Alstott 3 pass from Dilfer (Husted kick), 5:30.

Second Quarter
T.B.—Alstott 1 pass from Dilfer (Husted kick), 7:26.
Mia.—McDuffie 10 pass from Marino (Mare kick), 14:38.

Third Quarter
T.B.—FG, Husted 22, 5:14.
T.B.—Anthony 38 pass from Dilfer (Husted kick), 11:25.

Fourth Quarter
Mia.—Abdul-Jabbar 1 run (Mare kick), 0:50.
T.B.—Dunn 58 pass from Dilfer (Husted kick), 5:42.
Mia.—Barnett 1 pass from Marino (Mare kick), 11:35.
Attendance—73,314.

TEAM STATISTICS

	Miami	Tampa Bay
First downs	21	24
Rushes-yards	17-48	32-109
Passing	235	248
Punt returns	0-0	3-30
Kickoff returns	4-102	3-48
Interception returns	1-10	0-0
Comp.-att.-int.	24-37-0	18-24-1
Sacked-yards lost	0-0	0-0
Punts	3-47	0-0
Fumbles-lost	1-0	1-0
Penalties-yards	8-86	2-35
Time of possession	26:27	33:33

INDIVIDUAL STATISTICS

RUSHING—Miami, Abdul-Jabbar 16-45, McPhail 1-3. Tampa Bay, Alstott 18-95, Dunn 11-17, Dilfer 3-(minus 3).

PASSING—Miami, Marino 24-37-0-235. Tampa Bay, Dilfer 18-24-1-248.

RECEIVING—Miami, McDuffie 6-55, Barnett 5-50, Drayton 3-45, McPhail 3-28, Abdul-Jabbar 3-22, Jordan 1-19, Manning 1-11, Dotson 1-4, Parmalee 1-1. Tampa Bay, Dunn 6-106, Alstott 4-20, Copeland 3-39, Anthony 2-50, Harris 2-20, Williams 1-13.

MISSED FIELD GOAL ATTEMPTS—Miami, Mare 47.

INTERCEPTIONS—Miami, Z. Thomas 1-10.

KICKOFF RETURNS—Miami, Spikes 4-102. Tampa Bay, Williams 2-48, White 1-0.

PUNT RETURNS—Tampa Bay, Williams 3-30.

SACKS—None.

49ERS 34, FALCONS 7

Sunday, September 21

Atlanta	0	0	7	0— 7
San Francisco	3	21	7	3—34

First Quarter
S.F.—FG, Anderson 22, 4:44.

Second Quarter
S.F.—Stokes 10 pass from S. Young (Anderson kick), 6:17.
S.F.—Kirby 1 run (Anderson kick), 9:47.
S.F.—Owens 56 pass from S. Young (Anderson kick), 14:21.

Third Quarter
S.F.—Kirby 15 run (Anderson kick), 5:01.
Atl.—Emanuel 16 pass from Tolliver (Andersen kick), 13:08.

Fourth Quarter
S.F.—FG, Anderson 32, 12:26.
Attendance—60,404.

TEAM STATISTICS

	Atlanta	San Francisco
First downs	15	18
Rushes-yards	29-57	20-71
Passing	154	353
Punt returns	3-18	4-33
Kickoff returns	6-100	1-21
Interception returns	0-0	1-28
Comp.-att.-int.	20-36-1	19-31-0
Sacked-yards lost	3-25	3-15
Punts	9-41	6-44
Fumbles-lost	0-0	1-0
Penalties-yards	8-41	4-27
Time of possession	35:36	24:24

INDIVIDUAL STATISTICS

RUSHING—Atlanta, Anderson 16-46, Green 5-3, Hanspard 5-1, Mathis 1-6, Graziani 1-1, Christian 1-0. San Francisco, Hearst 10-33, Kirby 4-21, Floyd 4-20, Druckenmiller 2-(minus 3).

PASSING—Atlanta, Tolliver 17-31-1-162, Graziani 3-5-0-17. San Francisco, S. Young 17-24-0-336, Druckenmiller 2-7-0-32.

RECEIVING—Atlanta, Emanuel 6-62, Mathis 4-35, Green 4-13, Santiago 2-27, Kinchen 1-28, Christian 1-6, Anderson 1-5, West 1-3. San Francisco, Floyd 7-85, Stokes 3-77, Uwaezuoke 3-41, Hearst 2-83, Jones 2-19, Owens 1-56, Edwards 1-7.

MISSED FIELD GOAL ATTEMPTS—None.

INTERCEPTIONS—San Francisco, Walker 1-28.

KICKOFF RETURNS—Atlanta, Hanspard 5-91, Owens 1-9. San Francisco, Levy 1-21.

PUNT RETURNS—Atlanta, Kinchen 3-18. San Francisco, Uwaezuoke 3-25, Levy 1-8.

SACKS—Atlanta, Owens 1, Smith 1, Tuggle 0.5, Bennett 0.5. San Francisco, Stubblefield 1, B. Young 1, Norton 0.5, Barker 0.5.

SEAHAWKS 26, CHARGERS 22

Sunday, September 21

San Diego	0	16	0	6—22
Seattle	3	10	0	13—26

First Quarter
Sea.—FG, Peterson 41, 4:41.

Second Quarter
S.D.—FG, Carney 22, 0:05.
S.D.—Harrison 75 interception return (Carney kick), 1:23.
S.D.—FG, Carney 27, 7:47.
Sea.—Strong 5 pass from Moon (Peterson kick), 11:26.
Sea.—FG, Peterson 37, 13:10.
S.D.—FG, Carney 26, 14:49.

Fourth Quarter
S.D.—FG, Carney 41, 1:18.
Sea.—Galloway 53 pass from Moon (Peterson kick), 1:59.
S.D.—FG, Carney 41, 9:39.
Sea.—Broussard 1 run (pass failed), 13:38.
Attendance—51,110.

TEAM STATISTICS

	San Diego	Seattle
First downs	20	21
Rushes-yards	26-79	27-92
Passing	230	251
Punt returns	3-47	1-(-3)
Kickoff returns	4-79	7-178
Interception returns	2-86	3-48
Comp.-att.-int.	25-46-3	17-34-2
Sacked-yards lost	2-9	1-2
Punts	4-53	5-45
Fumbles-lost	0-0	2-1
Penalties-yards	6-68	9-60
Time of possession	32:47	27:13

INDIVIDUAL STATISTICS

RUSHING—San Diego, Brown 16-46, Pegram 5-15, Gardner 2-5, Humphries 2-2, C. Jones 1-11. Seattle, Broussard 11-72, Warren 9-21, Smith 4-1, Moon 3-(minus 2).

PASSING—San Diego, Humphries 25-46-3-239. Seattle, Moon 17-34-2-253.

RECEIVING—San Diego, Martin 5-62, F. Jones 5-60, Brown 5-34, C. Jones 4-42, Hartley 2-21, Pegram 2-7, Pupunu 1-7, Metcalf 1-6. Seattle, Pritchard 7-83, Galloway 5-106, Davis 2-48, Smith 1-6, Warren 1-5, Strong 1-5.

MISSED FIELD GOAL ATTEMPTS—None.

INTERCEPTIONS—San Diego, Harrison 1-75, Shaw 1-11. Seattle, D. Williams 3-48.

KICKOFF RETURNS—San Diego, Metcalf 4-79. Seattle, Broussard 4-117, Coleman 2-53, May 1-8.

PUNT RETURNS—San Diego, Metcalf 3-47. Seattle, Davis 1-(minus 3).

SACKS—San Diego, Seau 1. Seattle, LaBounty 1, Sinclair 1.

JAGUARS 30, STEELERS 21

Monday, September 22

Pittsburgh	7	0	7	7—21
Jacksonville	7	10	3	10—30

First Quarter
Jac.—Means 1 run (Hollis kick), 5:12.
Pit.—Stewart 6 run (N. Johnson kick), 8:50.

Second Quarter
Jac.—Smith 11 pass from Brunell (Hollis kick), 2:24.
Jac.—FG, Hollis 20, 14:56.

Third Quarter
Pit.—Thigpen 4 pass from Stewart (N. Johnson kick), 7:39.
Jac.—FG, Hollis 45, 11:35.

Fourth Quarter
Pit.—Bruener 1 pass from Stewart (N. Johnson kick), 0:04.
Jac.—FG, Hollis 27, 10:46.
Jac.—Hudson 58 blocked FG return (Hollis kick), 15:00.
Attendance—73,016.

TEAM STATISTICS

	Pittsburgh	Jacksonville
First downs	19	23
Rushes-yards	29-153	26-40
Passing	153	303
Punt returns	0-0	0-0
Kickoff returns	5-167	4-77
Interception returns	0-0	1-5
Comp.-att.-int.	11-16-1	25-43-0
Sacked-yards lost	3-2	3-25
Punts	2-39	1-38
Fumbles-lost	1-1	0-0
Penalties-yards	6-82	4-35
Time of possession	26:05	33:55

INDIVIDUAL STATISTICS

RUSHING—Pittsburgh, Bettis 21-114, Stewart 6-19, G. Jones 1-18, Witman 1-2. Jacksonville, Means 24-40, Stewart 2-0.

PASSING—Pittsburgh, Stewart 11-16-1-155. Jacksonville, Brunell 24-42-0-306, Barker 1-1-0-22.

RECEIVING—Pittsburgh, Thigpen 5-53, C. Johnson 4-88, Hawkins 1-13, Bruener 1-1. Jacksonville, Smith 10-164, McCardell 6-51, Stewart 2-35, Barlow 2-24, Brown 2-14, Hall 1-22, Mitchell 1-15, Hallock 1-3.

MISSED FIELD GOAL ATTEMPTS—Pittsburgh, N. Johnson 40. Jacksonville, Hollis 29, 38.

INTERCEPTIONS—Jacksonville, Beasley 1-5.

KICKOFF RETURNS—Pittsburgh, Blackwell 4-151, Adams 1-16. Jacksonville, Jackson 3-55, Logan 1-22.

PUNT RETURNS—None.

SACKS—Pittsburgh, Kirkland 1, Gibson 1, Bell 0.5, Henry 0.5. Jacksonville, Brackens 2, Boyer 1.

WEEK 5

RESULTS

DALLAS 27, Chicago 3
Denver 29, ATLANTA 21
DETROIT 26, Green Bay 15
KANSAS CITY 20, Seattle 17 (OT)
MINNESOTA 28, Philadelphia 19
N.Y. GIANTS 14, New Orleans 9
N.Y. Jets 31, CINCINNATI 14
OAKLAND 35, St. Louis 17
PITTSBURGH 37, Tennessee 24
SAN DIEGO 21, Baltimore 17
TAMPA BAY 19, Arizona 18
WASHINGTON 24, Jacksonville 12
San Francisco 34, CAROLINA 21
  Open date: Buffalo, Indianapolis, Miami, New England

STANDINGS

AFC EAST
	W	L	T	Pct.
New England	4	0	0	1.000
N.Y. Jets	3	2	0	.600
Buffalo	2	2	0	.500
Miami	2	2	0	.500
Indianapolis	0	4	0	.000

AFC CENTRAL
	W	L	T	Pct.
Jacksonville	3	1	0	.750
Baltimore	3	2	0	.600
Pittsburgh	2	2	0	.500
Cincinnati	1	3	0	.250
Tennessee	1	3	0	.250

AFC WEST
	W	L	T	Pct.
Denver	5	0	0	1.000
Kansas City	4	1	0	.800
Oakland	2	3	0	.400
San Diego	2	3	0	.400
Seattle	2	3	0	.400

NFC EAST
	W	L	T	Pct.
Dallas	3	1	0	.750
Washington	3	1	0	.750
N.Y. Giants	2	3	0	.600
Arizona	1	3	0	.250
Philadelphia	1	3	0	.250

NFC CENTRAL
	W	L	T	Pct.
Tampa Bay	5	0	0	1.000
Green Bay	3	2	0	.600
Detroit	3	2	0	.600
Minnesota	3	2	0	.600
Chicago	0	5	0	.000

NFC WEST
	W	L	T	Pct.
San Francisco	4	1	0	.800
Carolina	2	3	0	.400
St. Louis	2	3	0	.400
New Orleans	1	4	0	.200
Atlanta	0	5	0	.000

HIGHLIGHTS

Hero of the week: Jets running back Adrian Murrell rushed 40 times for 156 yards and a touchdown in New York's 31-14 victory over the Bengals. The win improved the Jets' record to 3-2 for the first time in nine years. Murrell's 40 attempts tied a Jets record set by Johnny Hector in 1986.

Goat of the week: After a punt by the Vikings' Mitch Berger, the Eagles' Bobby Seay tried to catch the ball on the bounce. But it slipped out of his hands, and Minnesota safety Greg Briggs recovered. Two plays later, Robert Smith scored on a 14-yard run to give the Vikings an insurmountable 21-13 lead en route to a 28-19 victory.

Sub of the week: Beleaguered tailback Tyrone Wheatley, a first-round draft bust, replaced the injured Tiki Barber just as his Giants were about to blow another late fourth-quarter lead. New York took over on its 3 with 3:38 left, but on first down Wheatley rushed for 15 yards to get his team out of trouble. On third-and-4 at the 24, he gained 13 yards. On second-and-7 from the 40, Wheatley rushed for 9 yards. He ended the game with 11 carries for 60 yards and the Giants held on for a 14-9 win.

Comeback of the week: With less than five minutes remaining, the Buccaneers trailed the Cardinals, 18-12, and faced a fourth-and-6 at Arizona's 31. A swirling wind swept away any thoughts of a field goal, so quarterback Trent Dilfer hit wide receiver Karl Williams at the 25, and Williams ran it in for the game-winning score on his only catch of the day.

Blowout of the week: The Cowboys were happy with the victory but extremely unhappy with their effort in a 27-3 rout of the hapless Bears. Dallas managed only 180 total yards, including just 56 rushing (none in the first half) against the second-worst defense in the league. Chicago sacked Cowboys quarterback Troy Aikman three times, pressured him on nearly every play and knocked him down five times. But Bears quarterback Rick Mirer was even worse, going 11-of-21 for 62 yards.

Nail-biter of the week: For the third time in four weeks, the Chiefs managed a fantastic finish as Pete Stoyanovich's 41-yard field goal at 13:04 of overtime sent Kansas City past the Seahawks, 20-17, at Arrowhead Stadium.

Hit of the week: By Rams defensive tackle Jeff Zgonina, who knocked Raiders quarterback Jeff George silly with a late hit. The resulting penalty to Zgonina wiped out an interception and woke up George, who scrambled 11 yards for another first down on the next play. The Raiders, who trailed 14-0 at the time, rallied for a 35-17 win.

Oddity of the week: Adrian Murrell had more carries (40) than the Bengals had offensive plays (39).

Top rusher: Napoleon Kaufman carried 26 times for 162 yards in the Raiders' victory over the Rams.

Top passer: Stan Humphries was 17-of-26 for a career-high 358 yards, including three touchdown passes to Tony Martin, in the Chargers' 21-17 win over the Ravens.

Top receiver: Tony Martin caught four passes for 155 yards and three TDs against Baltimore after entering with only 11 receptions for 163 yards in San Diego's first four games.

Notes: The Broncos-Falcons game marked the first time Denver coach Mike Shanahan and Atlanta coach Dan Reeves were together on the same field since Reeves, then the Broncos' coach, fired Shanahan, then the Broncos' offensive coordinator, for alleged "insubordination" in 1991. The coaches exchanged pleasantries at midfield after Denver's 29-21 victory. . . . Jets quarterback Neil O'Donnell had thrown seven touchdown passes in 1997—all to different receivers. . . . Shannon Sharpe's six receptions against Atlanta increased the Denver tight end's career total to 410. Combined with Sterling Sharpe's 595 receptions for the Packers from 1988 to '94, they became the only brother duo in NFL history with a combined 1,000 catches.

Quote of the week: Jets cornerback Ray Mickens, on teammate Adrian Murrell: "Man, there was blood all over him. I don't know whose blood it was. It was everybody's—his, theirs, ours. But he kept taking it and coming back for more."

GAME SUMMARIES

LIONS 26, PACKERS 15

Sunday, September 28

Green Bay	6	3	6	0	—15
Detroit	0	17	3	6	—26

First Quarter
G.B.—FG, Longwell 36, 6:13.
G.B.—FG, Longwell 19, 11:25.

Second Quarter
Det.—Brown 45 interception return (Hanson kick), 5:00.
Det.—Chryplewicz 4 pass from Mitchell (Hanson kick), 8:28.
G.B.—FG, Longwell 50, 12:44.
Det.—FG, Hanson 53, 15:00.

Third Quarter
G.B.—Schroeder 7 pass from Favre (pass failed), 3:41.
Det.—FG, Hanson 44, 7:26.

Fourth Quarter
Det.—FG, Hanson 22, 5:35.
Det.—FG, Hanson 39, 13:30.
　　Attendance—78,110.

TEAM STATISTICS

	Green Bay	Detroit
First downs	23	18
Rushes-yards	18-107	36-173
Passing	289	203
Punt returns	4-23	2-20
Kickoff returns	2-47	5-99
Interception returns	0-0	3-50
Comp.-att.-int.	22-43-3	17-27-0
Sacked-yards lost	2-6	2-12
Punts	3-50	4-51
Fumbles-lost	2-1	1-0
Penalties-yards	9-65	9-107
Time of possession	29:19	30:41

INDIVIDUAL STATISTICS

RUSHING—Green Bay, Levens 16-107, Favre 1-1, Hayden 1-(minus 1). Detroit, Sanders 28-139, Vardell 3-3, Mitchell 3-(minus 2), Morton 1-20, Rivers 1-13.

PASSING—Green Bay, Favre 22-43-3-295. Detroit, Mitchell 17-27-0-215.

RECEIVING—Green Bay, R. Brooks 9-164, Freeman 5-91, Levens 3-(minus 1), Chmura 2-18, Thomason 1-14, Schroeder 1-7, Henderson 1-2. Detroit, Moore 6-105, Morton 6-61, Sanders 1-20, Milburn 1-11, Vardell 1-8, Metzelaars 1-6, Chryplewicz 1-4.

MISSED FIELD GOAL ATTEMPTS—None.

INTERCEPTIONS—Detroit, Brown 1-45, Porcher 1-5, Carrier 1-0.

KICKOFF RETURNS—Green Bay, Schroeder 1-33, Hayden 1-14. Detroit, Milburn 5-99.

PUNT RETURNS—Green Bay, Schroeder 3-1, Mayes 1-22. Detroit, Milburn 2-20.

SACKS—Green Bay, White 1, Wilkins 1. Detroit, Porcher 1, Abrams 1.

COWBOYS 27, BEARS 3

Sunday, September 28

Chicago	3	0	0	0	— 3
Dallas	0	7	17	3	—27

First Quarter
Chi.—FG, Jaeger 21, 7:48.

Second Quarter
Dal.—Miller 6 pass from Aikman (Cunningham kick), 10:58.

Third Quarter
Dal.—FG, Cunningham 33, 5:00.
Dal.—Irvin 26 pass from Aikman (Cunningham kick), 9:19.
Dal.—Sanders 83 punt return (Cunningham kick), 13:11.

Fourth Quarter
Dal.—FG, Cunningham 23, 3:38.
　　Attendance—64,082.

TEAM STATISTICS

	Chicago	Dallas
First downs	17	13
Rushes-yards	33-141	21-56
Passing	102	124
Punt returns	3-23	4-99
Kickoff returns	5-74	2-51
Interception returns	1-0	2-35
Comp.-att.-int.	18-37-2	12-27-1

	Chicago	Dallas
Sacked-yards lost	5-17	3-20
Punts	8-45	6-55
Fumbles-lost	1-0	1-0
Penalties-yards	8-40	5-45
Time of possession	36:28	23:32

INDIVIDUAL STATISTICS

RUSHING—Chicago, R. Harris 29-120, Autry 3-22, Penn 1-(minus 1). Dallas, E. Smith 13-43, S. Williams 6-23, Aikman 1-1, Sanders 1-(minus 11).

PASSING—Chicago, Mirer 11-21-1-62, Kramer 7-16-1-57. Dallas, Aikman 12-27-1-144.

RECEIVING—Chicago, Proehl 4-33, Engram 3-15, Wetnight 3-13, R. Harris 3-2, Penn 2-22, Jennings 1-14, Smith 1-12, Allred 1-8. Dallas, Irvin 6-105, Johnston 2-25, LaFleur 1-6, Miller 1-6, E. Smith 1-1, Bjornson 1-1.

MISSED FIELD GOAL ATTEMPTS—None.

INTERCEPTIONS—Chicago, T. Carter 1-0. Dallas, K. Smith 1-21, Woodson 1-14.

KICKOFF RETURNS—Chicago, Hughes 4-64, Engram 1-7. Dallas, Walker 2-51.

PUNT RETURNS—Chicago, Hughes 3-23. Dallas, Sanders 4-99.

SACKS—Chicago, Minter 1, Simpson 1, Flanigan 1. Dallas, Tolbert 2, Casillas 1, Carver 1, C. Williams 1.

CHARGERS 21, RAVENS 17

Sunday, September 28

Baltimore	3	3	11	0	—17
San Diego	7	7	7	0	—21

First Quarter
S.D.—Martin 36 pass from Humphries (G. Davis kick), 8:33.
Bal.—FG, Stover 47, 12:36.

Second Quarter
S.D.—Martin 72 pass from Humphries (G. Davis kick), 7:04.
Bal.—FG, Stover 35, 14:31.

Third Quarter
Bal.—FG, Stover 28, 3:38.
Bal.—J. Lewis 37 pass from Testaverde (Jackson pass from Testaverde), 9:00.
S.D.—Martin 38 pass from Humphries (G. Davis kick), 14:57.
　　Attendance—54,094.

TEAM STATISTICS

	Baltimore	San Diego
First downs	18	15
Rushes-yards	25-111	28-88
Passing	217	352
Punt returns	3-61	1-6
Kickoff returns	4-100	4-89
Interception returns	2-12	2-0
Comp.-att.-int.	18-42-2	17-26-2
Sacked-yards lost	2-11	1-6
Punts	5-34	4-51
Fumbles-lost	1-1	1-1
Penalties-yards	7-46	6-50
Time of possession	31:10	28:50

INDIVIDUAL STATISTICS

RUSHING—Baltimore, Morris 17-81, Byner 8-30. San Diego, Brown 18-58, Fletcher 4-17, Gardner 2-8, Humphries 2-4, Bynum 2-1.

PASSING—Baltimore, Testaverde 18-42-2-228. San Diego, Humphries 17-26-2-358.

RECEIVING—Baltimore, Yarborough 5-55, Green 4-29, Jackson 3-24, J. Lewis 2-70, Alexander 2-32, Morris 2-18. San Diego, Martin 4-155, Fletcher 4-15, Metcalf 2-67, Gardner 2-10, Hartley 1-35, F. Jones 1-29, Brown 1-27, Still 1-12, C. Jones 1-8.

MISSED FIELD GOAL ATTEMPTS—San Diego, G. Davis 49.

INTERCEPTIONS—Baltimore, Daniel 1-12, Langham 1-0. San Diego, Dumas 1-0, Harper 1-0.

KICKOFF RETURNS—Baltimore, J. Lewis 3-77, Morris 1-23. San Diego, Metcalf 3-68, Bynum 1-21.

PUNT RETURNS—Baltimore, J. Lewis 2-27, Alexander 1-34. San Diego, Metcalf 1-6.

SACKS—Baltimore, McCrary 1. San Diego, Seau 1, Hand 1.

STEELERS 37, OILERS 24

Sunday, September 28

Tennessee	0	6	3	15	—24
Pittsburgh	10	21	3	3	—37

First Quarter
Pit.—Stewart 7 run (N. Johnson kick), 9:55.
Pit.—FG, N. Johnson 48, 14:27.

1997 REVIEW Week 5

Second Quarter
Pit.—Gildon 12 fumble return (N. Johnson kick), 6:17.
Ten.—FG, Del Greco 37, 11:12.
Pit.—Bruener 18 pass from Stewart (N. Johnson kick), 13:22.
Pit.—Stewart 2 run (N. Johnson kick), 14:38.
Ten.—FG, Del Greco 47, 15:00.

Third Quarter
Ten.—FG, Del Greco 26, 4:29.
Pit.—FG, N. Johnson 25, 11:41.

Fourth Quarter
Pit.—FG, N. Johnson 44, 2:52.
Ten.—Wycheck 10 pass from McNair (Wycheck pass from McNair), 6:44.
Ten.—Davis 11 pass from McNair (Del Greco kick), 11:37.
Attendance—57,507.

TEAM STATISTICS

	Tennessee	Pittsburgh
First downs	20	19
Rushes-yards	15-58	40-137
Passing	226	262
Punt returns	1-8	2-23
Kickoff returns	7-129	3-55
Interception returns	0-0	2-27
Comp.-att.-int.	22-43-2	18-26-0
Sacked-yards lost	7-40	1-8
Punts	4-41	2-39
Fumbles-lost	4-1	2-1
Penalties-yards	6-45	10-112
Time of possession	27:53	32:07

INDIVIDUAL STATISTICS
RUSHING—Tennessee, George 12-29, McNair 3-29. Pittsburgh, Bettis 18-74, G. Jones 14-32, Stewart 6-24, McAfee 1-8, Tomczak 1-(minus 1).
PASSING—Tennessee, McNair 22-43-2-266. Pittsburgh, Stewart 16-24-0-244, Tomczak 2-2-0-26.
RECEIVING—Tennessee, Wycheck 9-72, Davis 5-39, Russell 3-62, Sanders 2-46, Thomas 2-24, Mason 1-12, Harmon 0-11. Pittsburgh, Thigpen 5-89, Blackwell 3-68, Lester 3-11, Hawkins 2-22, Bruener 2-21, Adams 1-39, G. Jones 1-16, C. Johnson 1-4.
MISSED FIELD GOAL ATTEMPTS—Tennessee, Del Greco 43. Pittsburgh, N. Johnson 48.
INTERCEPTIONS—Pittsburgh, Woolford 1-24, Kirkland 1-3.
KICKOFF RETURNS—Tennessee, Mason 6-126, Wycheck 1-3. Pittsburgh, Adams 2-40, Blackwell 1-15.
PUNT RETURNS—Tennessee, Gray 1-8. Pittsburgh, Blackwell 2-23.
SACKS—Tennessee, Roberson 1. Pittsburgh, Kirkland 1, Perry 1, Fuller 1, Holmes 1, Oldham 1, Gildon 1, Lloyd 0.5, Bell 0.5.

REDSKINS 24, JAGUARS 12

Sunday, September 28

Jacksonville	6	3	3	0—12
Washington	0	14	0	10—24

First Quarter
Jac.—FG, Hollis 30, 1:44.
Jac.—FG, Hollis 42, 13:26.

Second Quarter
Jac.—FG, Hollis 25, 2:52.
Was.—Shepherd 10 pass from Frerotte (Blanton kick), 9:05.
Was.—Asher 8 pass from Frerotte (Blanton kick), 13:44.

Third Quarter
Jac.—FG, Hollis 47, 11:32.

Fourth Quarter
Was.—FG, Blanton 41, 3:05.
Was.—Shepherd 13 pass from Frerotte (Blanton kick), 9:12.
Attendance—74,421.

TEAM STATISTICS

	Jacksonville	Washington
First downs	11	20
Rushes-yards	22-70	42-113
Passing	134	223
Punt returns	0-0	2-32
Kickoff returns	5-85	5-88
Interception returns	1-23	2-33
Comp.-att.-int.	16-31-2	16-24-1
Sacked-yards lost	3-19	4-21
Punts	3-46	2-43
Fumbles-lost	0-0	2-2
Penalties-yards	7-68	2-15
Time of possession	24:52	35:08

INDIVIDUAL STATISTICS
RUSHING—Jacksonville, Means 18-62, Brunell 2-4, Stewart 2-4. Washington, Allen 36-122, Frerotte 2-2, Bowie 1-2, Shepherd 1-2, Mitchell 1-1, Westbrook 1-(minus 16).
PASSING—Jacksonville, Brunell 16-31-2-153. Washington, Frerotte 16-24-1-244.
RECEIVING—Jacksonville, Smith 4-52, McCardell 4-37, Stewart 3-16, Jackson 2-28, Hallock 2-11, Barlow 1-9. Washington, Shepherd 4-57, Harper 2-65, Allen 2-41, Bowie 2-28, Westbrook 2-24, Asher 2-22, Ellard 1-12, Mitchell 1-(minus 5).
MISSED FIELD GOAL ATTEMPTS—Washington, Blanton 33.
INTERCEPTIONS—Jacksonville, Thomas 1-23. Washington, Richard 1-23, Boutte 1-10.
KICKOFF RETURNS—Jacksonville, Jackson 3-50, Logan 2-35. Washington, Mitchell 5-88.
PUNT RETURNS—Washington, Mitchell 2-32.
SACKS—Jacksonville, Pritchett 1, Smeenge 1, Davey 1, Brackens 1. Washington, Owens 2, Smith 1.

BUCCANEERS 19, CARDINALS 18

Sunday, September 28

Arizona	0	7	11	0—18
Tampa Bay	6	6	0	7—19

First Quarter
T.B.—Singleton 28 blocked punt return (kick failed), 8:07.

Second Quarter
T.B.—Anthony 8 pass from Dilfer (run failed), 9:14.
Ariz.—R. Moore 21 pass from K. Graham (Butler kick), 13:08.

Third Quarter
Ariz.—FG, Butler 37, 5:12.
Ariz.—A. Williams 42 interception return (Sanders pass from K. Graham), 14:34.

Fourth Quarter
T.B.—Williams 31 pass from Dilfer (Husted kick), 10:12.
Attendance—53,804.

TEAM STATISTICS

	Arizona	Tampa Bay
First downs	23	6
Rushes-yards	25-70	20-44
Passing	294	103
Punt returns	2-21	4-57
Kickoff returns	2-46	3-73
Interception returns	1-42	2-0
Comp.-att.-int.	31-52-2	12-24-1
Sacked-yards lost	6-45	3-22
Punts	6-38	8-49
Fumbles-lost	1-1	2-0
Penalties-yards	5-40	5-45
Time of possession	37:19	22:41

INDIVIDUAL STATISTICS
RUSHING—Arizona, McElroy 13-40, Johnson 5-21, Centers 4-4, McKinnon 1-3, K. Graham 1-2, Swann 1-0. Tampa Bay, Dunn 11-17, Alstott 8-27, Dilfer 1-0.
PASSING—Arizona, K. Graham 31-52-2-339. Tampa Bay, Dilfer 11-23-1-100, Barnhardt 1-1-0-25.
RECEIVING—Arizona, R. Moore 8-147, Centers 8-58, Sanders 5-60, Edwards 3-27, K. Williams 2-15, McElroy 2-11, Gedney 1-17, Carter 1-4, Johnson 1-0. Tampa Bay, Anthony 5-49, Harris 3-10, Dunn 2-10, Williams 1-31, Bouie 1-25.
MISSED FIELD GOAL ATTEMPTS—Arizona, Butler 43, 47.
INTERCEPTIONS—Arizona, A. Williams 1-42. Tampa Bay, Abraham 1-0, Lynch 1-0.
KICKOFF RETURNS—Arizona, K. Williams 2-46. Tampa Bay, Williams 2-43, Dunn 1-30.
PUNT RETURNS—Arizona, K. Williams 2-21. Tampa Bay, Williams 4-57.
SACKS—Arizona, Swann 2, M. Smith 1. Tampa Bay, Culpepper 3, Ahanotu 2, Sapp 1.

JETS 31, BENGALS 14

Sunday, September 28

N.Y. Jets	7	17	0	7—31
Cincinnati	0	7	0	7—14

First Quarter
NYJ—Baxter 2 pass from O'Donnell (Hall kick), 9:13.

Second Quarter
Cin.—Pickens 50 pass from Blake (Pelfrey kick), 0:45.
NYJ—Murrell 12 run (Hall kick), 5:55.
NYJ—FG, Hall 44, 12:37.
NYJ—K. Johnson 12 pass from O'Donnell (Hall kick), 14:45.

1997 REVIEW *Week 5*

Fourth Quarter
NYJ—Anderson 7 pass from O'Donnell (Hall kick), 1:58.
Cin.—Scott 26 pass from Blake (Pelfrey kick), 4:54.
  Attendance—57,209.

TEAM STATISTICS

	N.Y. Jets	Cincinnati
First downs	28	10
Rushes-yards	48-190	16-66
Passing	212	149
Punt returns	3-45	1-13
Kickoff returns	2-40	3-52
Interception returns	1-0	0-0
Comp.-att.-int.	20-34-0	10-21-1
Sacked-yards lost	0-0	2-17
Punts	2-47	5-47
Fumbles-lost	1-1	0-0
Penalties-yards	2-15	5-30
Time of possession	42:50	17:10

INDIVIDUAL STATISTICS
RUSHING—New York, Murrell 40-156, O'Donnell 4-2, L. Johnson 3-17, Anderson 1-15. Cincinnati, Dillon 9-48, Blake 4-18, Bieniemy 1-3, Milne 1-3, Pickens 1-(minus 6).
PASSING—New York, O'Donnell 20-34-0-212. Cincinnati, Blake 10-21-1-166.
RECEIVING—New York, Chrebet 6-68, Anderson 4-28, Graham 3-32, K. Johnson 3-38, Baxter 2-39, Brady 1-13, Murrell 1-4. Cincinnati, Pickens 2-64, Dillon 2-30, Bieniemy 2-18, Scott 1-26, Dunn 1-19, McGee 1-15, Milne 1-(minus 6).
MISSED FIELD GOAL ATTEMPTS—New York, Hall 36.
INTERCEPTIONS—New York, Mickens 1-0.
KICKOFF RETURNS—New York, Glenn 1-26, L. Johnson 1-14. Cincinnati, Dunn 2-34, Hundon 1-18.
PUNT RETURNS—New York, L. Johnson 3-45. Cincinnati, Myers 1-13.
SACKS—New York, Lewis 1, Lyle 1.

CHIEFS 20, SEAHAWKS 17

Sunday, September 28

Seattle	7	3	7	0	0—17
Kansas City	0	7	7	3	3—20

First Quarter
Sea.—Galloway 41 pass from Moon (Peterson kick), 6:27.
Second Quarter
Sea.—FG, Peterson 44, 5:26.
K.C.—Allen 8 run (Stoyanovich kick), 9:49.
Third Quarter
K.C.—Allen 1 run (Stoyanovich kick), 7:57.
Sea.—McKnight 54 pass from Moon (Peterson kick), 9:36.
Fourth Quarter
K.C.—FG, Stoyanovich 29, 1:46.
Overtime
K.C.—FG, Stoyanovich 41, 13:04.
  Attendance—77,877.

TEAM STATISTICS

	Seattle	Kansas City
First downs	16	29
Rushes-yards	26-156	47-203
Passing	220	263
Punt returns	1-4	1-8
Kickoff returns	5-75	4-79
Interception returns	3-51	1-13
Comp.-att.-int.	19-26-1	24-38-3
Sacked-yards lost	3-32	1-11
Punts	5-52	4-37
Fumbles-lost	2-0	0-0
Penalties-yards	2-22	5-40
Time of possession	30:17	42:47

INDIVIDUAL STATISTICS
RUSHING—Seattle, Smith 12-78, Warren 8-53, Broussard 4-12, Pritchard 1-14, Moon 1-(minus 1). Kansas City, Allen 19-78, Hill 16-43, Anders 7-36, Grbac 5-46.
PASSING—Seattle, Moon 19-26-1-252. Kansas City, Grbac 24-38-3-274.
RECEIVING—Seattle, Pritchard 4-88, Smith 4-30, Crumpler 3-16, Br. Blades 2-16, Broussard 2-5, Warren 2-2, McKnight 1-54, Galloway 1-41. Kansas City, Rison 7-78, Anders 4-43, Popson 4-40, Perriman 2-26, Allen 2-18, Vanover 2-12, Hill 1-27, Walker 1-20, Gonzalez 1-10.
MISSED FIELD GOAL ATTEMPTS—Seattle, Peterson 37, 58.
INTERCEPTIONS—Seattle, D. Williams 1-27, Bellamy 1-13, Be. Blades 1-11. Kansas City, Woods 1-13.
KICKOFF RETURNS—Seattle, Broussard 4-63, Coleman 1-12. Kansas City, Vanover 4-79.

PUNT RETURNS—Seattle, Davis 1-4. Kansas City, Vanover 1-8.
SACKS—Seattle, Be. Blades 1. Kansas City, Woods 1, Wooden 1, Edwards 0.5, Tongue 0.5.

GIANTS 14, SAINTS 9

Sunday, September 28

New Orleans	3	3	0	3— 9
N.Y. Giants	7	7	0	0—14

First Quarter
NYG—Alexander 32 pass from Brown (Daluiso kick), 9:12.
N.O.—FG, Brien 36, 14:21.
Second Quarter
NYG—Calloway 14 pass from Brown (Daluiso kick), 9:58.
N.O.—FG, Brien 32, 13:04.
Fourth Quarter
N.O.—FG, Brien 39, 5:41.
  Attendance—68,891.

TEAM STATISTICS

	New Orleans	N.Y. Giants
First downs	14	18
Rushes-yards	24-73	33-105
Passing	193	159
Punt returns	3-23	3-76
Kickoff returns	2-57	3-45
Interception returns	1-32	1-1
Comp.-att.-int.	16-31-1	16-25-1
Sacked-yards lost	2-10	4-35
Punts	5-41	5-34
Fumbles-lost	1-1	2-1
Penalties-yards	6-55	3-25
Time of possession	29:52	30:08

INDIVIDUAL STATISTICS
RUSHING—New Orleans, Bates 18-64, Zellars 3-6, Shuler 2-3, T. Davis 1-0. New York, Wheatley 11-60, Barber 11-42, Way 6-2, Brown 5-1.
PASSING—New Orleans, Shuler 16-31-1-203. New York, Brown 16-25-1-194.
RECEIVING—New Orleans, Farquhar 4-82, Hill 3-26, Hastings 2-36, Guliford 2-26, Zellars 2-12, Bates 2-6, Bech 1-15. New York, Calloway 4-63, Way 4-35, Alexander 3-62, Barber 2-29, Pierce 2-2, Cross 1-3.
MISSED FIELD GOAL ATTEMPTS—New York, Daluiso 46.
INTERCEPTIONS—New Orleans, Knight 1-32. New York, Randolph 1-1.
KICKOFF RETURNS—New Orleans, Guliford 2-57. New York, Patten 3-45.
PUNT RETURNS—New Orleans, Guliford 3-23. New York, Toomer 3-76.
SACKS—New Orleans, Martin 1.5, Molden 1, Sagapolutele 1, Tubbs 0.5. New York, Widmer 1, Strahan 1.

BRONCOS 29, FALCONS 21

Sunday, September 28

Denver	15	8	6	0—29
Atlanta	0	7	7	7—21

First Quarter
Den.—Sharpe 65 pass from Elway (Elam kick), 1:42.
Den.—Green 10 pass from Elway (Davis run), 7:11.
Second Quarter
Den.—Davis 13 run (Davis run), 6:14.
Atl.—West 1 pass from Chandler (Andersen kick), 14:45.
Third Quarter
Atl.—Emanuel 3 pass from Chandler (Andersen kick), 10:48.
Den.—D. Smith 17 pass from Elway (pass failed), 14:23.
Fourth Quarter
Atl.—Anderson 47 pass from Tolliver (Andersen kick), 3:42.
  Attendance—48,211.

TEAM STATISTICS

	Denver	Atlanta
First downs	16	17
Rushes-yards	27-101	21-112
Passing	228	196
Punt returns	1-0	4-40
Kickoff returns	3-52	4-61
Interception returns	1-20	1-0
Comp.-att.-int.	18-32-1	18-31-1
Sacked-yards lost	3-15	4-26
Punts	6-46	7-42
Fumbles-lost	0-0	0-0
Penalties-yards	10-76	5-27
Time of possession	32:09	27:51

INDIVIDUAL STATISTICS

RUSHING—Denver, Davis 23-79, Elway 3-21, D. Smith 1-1. Atlanta, Anderson 13-45, Hanspard 8-67.

PASSING—Denver, Elway 18-32-1-243. Atlanta, Chandler 12-22-1-137, Tolliver 6-9-0-85.

RECEIVING—Denver, Sharpe 6-119, McCaffrey 4-48, R. Smith 3-28, Green 3-26, D. Smith 1-17, Jeffers 1-5. Atlanta, Emanuel 8-58, Anderson 3-68, Santiago 2-22, Mathis 1-49, Green 1-15, Hanspard 1-5, Christian 1-4, West 1-1.

MISSED FIELD GOAL ATTEMPTS—Atlanta, Andersen 52.

INTERCEPTIONS—Denver, Gordon 1-20. Atlanta, Bradford 1-0.

KICKOFF RETURNS—Denver, Hebron 2-52, D. Smith 1-0. Atlanta, Hanspard 3-46, Bolden 1-15.

PUNT RETURNS—Denver, Gordon 1-0. Atlanta, Kinchen 4-40.

SACKS—Denver, Williams 2, Gordon 1, Romanowski 1. Atlanta, Hall 1, Smith 1, Owens 1.

RAIDERS 35, RAMS 17

Sunday, September 28

St. Louis	0	14	0	3—17
Oakland	0	13	15	7—35

Second Quarter
St.L.—Lee 13 pass from Banks (Wilkins kick), 3:51.
St.L.—Laing 3 pass from Banks (Wilkins kick), 6:55.
Oak.—Jett 8 pass from George (Ford kick), 9:53.
Oak.—Dudley 34 pass from George (run failed), 13:19.

Third Quarter
Oak.—Jett 14 pass from George (Williams pass from George), 5:08.
Oak.—Kaufman 1 run (Ford kick), 7:59.

Fourth Quarter
St.L.—FG, Wilkins 38, 0:18.
Oak.—Dudley 5 pass from George (Ford kick), 2:20.
Attendance—42,506.

TEAM STATISTICS

	St. Louis	Oakland
First downs	20	20
Rushes-yards	28-119	33-166
Passing	255	213
Punt returns	2-16	3-27
Kickoff returns	2-35	1-14
Interception returns	1-12	3-45
Comp.-att.-int.	24-49-3	17-30-1
Sacked-yards lost	0-0	1-6
Punts	8-40	7-46
Fumbles-lost	1-0	2-1
Penalties-yards	10-103	9-57
Time of possession	30:09	29:51

INDIVIDUAL STATISTICS

RUSHING—St. Louis, Phillips 16-54, R. Moore 5-24, Lee 4-30, Kennison 1-6, Heyward 1-4, Banks 1-1. Oakland, Kaufman 26-162, George 5-8, Aska 2-(minus 4).

PASSING—St. Louis, Banks 24-49-3-255. Oakland, George 17-30-1-219.

RECEIVING—St. Louis, Lee 10-109, Small 4-44, Thomas 2-25, Conwell 2-14, Phillips 2-5, Crawford 1-20, Jacoby 1-10, Laing 1-3. Oakland, Dudley 5-106, T. Brown 4-56, Jett 4-38, Kaufman 2-(minus 1), Shedd 1-19, Fenner 1-1.

MISSED FIELD GOAL ATTEMPTS—None.

INTERCEPTIONS—St. Louis, McNeil 1-12. Oakland, Turner 2-45, Washington 1-0.

KICKOFF RETURNS—St. Louis, Lee 1-18, R. Moore 1-17. Oakland, Morton 1-14.

PUNT RETURNS—St. Louis, Kennison 2-16. Oakland, Howard 3-27.

SACKS—St. Louis, O'Neal 1.

VIKINGS 28, EAGLES 19

Sunday, September 28

Philadelphia	3	10	6	0—19
Minnesota	7	7	7	7—28

First Quarter
Min.—Reed 48 pass from Johnson (Murray kick), 5:49.
Phi.—FG, Boniol 47, 10:50.

Second Quarter
Phi.—Fryar 6 pass from Detmer (Boniol kick), 5:53.
Min.—R. Smith 12 pass from Johnson (Murray kick), 12:33.
Phi.—FG, Boniol 26, 14:31.

Third Quarter
Min.—R. Smith 14 run (Murray kick), 8:30.
Phi.—Turner 20 pass from Detmer (pass failed), 12:55.

Fourth Quarter
Min.—Carter 18 pass from Johnson (Murray kick), 0:32.
Attendance—55,149.

TEAM STATISTICS

	Philadelphia	Minnesota
First downs	25	17
Rushes-yards	21-100	29-144
Passing	272	221
Punt returns	3-43	2-23
Kickoff returns	5-106	5-84
Interception returns	1-0	2-40
Comp.-att.-int.	28-45-2	17-32-1
Sacked-yards lost	5-26	0-0
Punts	4-48	6-46
Fumbles-lost	5-1	0-0
Penalties-yards	5-50	11-95
Time of possession	31:51	28:09

INDIVIDUAL STATISTICS

RUSHING—Philadelphia, Watters 13-61, Garner 7-30, Detmer 1-9. Minnesota, R. Smith 22-125, Johnson 6-13, Palmer 1-6.

PASSING—Philadelphia, Detmer 28-45-2-298. Minnesota, Johnson 17-32-1-221.

RECEIVING—Philadelphia, Fryar 9-120, Timpson 6-59, Watters 5-27, Turner 4-39, Seay 2-29, Garner 1-18, Dunn 1-6. Minnesota, Reed 6-134, Carter 5-58, R. Smith 3-10, Glover 1-9, Evans 1-8, Palmer 1-2.

MISSED FIELD GOAL ATTEMPTS—None.

INTERCEPTIONS—Philadelphia, Vincent 1-0. Minnesota, Washington 2-40.

KICKOFF RETURNS—Philadelphia, Staley 5-106. Minnesota, Tate 3-57, Palmer 1-17, Walsh 1-10.

PUNT RETURNS—Philadelphia, Seay 3-43. Minnesota, Palmer 2-23.

SACKS—Minnesota, Alexander 2, Edwards 2, Randle 1.

49ERS 34, PANTHERS 21

Monday, September 29

San Francisco	7	13	7	7—34
Carolina	0	7	0	14—21

First Quarter
S.F.—Owens 8 pass from S. Young (Anderson kick), 6:10.

Second Quarter
S.F.—S. Young 2 run (Anderson kick), 0:44.
S.F.—FG, Anderson 25, 2:28.
Car.—Carruth 17 pass from Collins (Kasay kick), 10:50.
S.F.—FG, Anderson 48, 14:43.

Third Quarter
S.F.—Hearst 3 run (Anderson kick), 13:25.

Fourth Quarter
Car.—Ismail 8 pass from Beuerlein (Kasay kick), 2:10.
S.F.—Kirby 3 run (Anderson kick), 12:06.
Car.—Carrier 20 pass from Beuerlein (Kasay kick), 13:46.
Attendance—70,972.

TEAM STATISTICS

	San Fran.	Carolina
First downs	27	16
Rushes-yards	49-219	17-44
Passing	149	210
Punt returns	1-15	4-21
Kickoff returns	3-69	7-151
Interception returns	3-45	0-0
Comp.-att.-int.	16-24-0	20-35-3
Sacked-yards lost	2-3	2-10
Punts	5-46	4-43
Fumbles-lost	1-1	1-1
Penalties-yards	5-45	6-45
Time of possession	37:33	22:27

INDIVIDUAL STATISTICS

RUSHING—San Francisco, Hearst 28-141, Kirby 8-41, Floyd 7-21, S. Young 6-16. Carolina, Johnson 8-21, Collins 4-10, Biakabutuka 4-8, Beuerlein 1-5.

PASSING—San Francisco, S. Young 16-24-0-152. Carolina, Collins 11-24-3-126, Beuerlein 9-11-0-94.

RECEIVING—San Francisco, Owens 5-48, Stokes 4-53, Hearst 3-13, Jones 1-15, Uwaezuoke 1-11, Floyd 1-9, Kirby 1-3. Carolina, Carrier 6-77, Carruth 4-74, Ismail 4-19, Oliver 3-25, Walls 2-24, Greene 1-1.

MISSED FIELD GOAL ATTEMPTS—None.

INTERCEPTIONS—San Francisco, Hanks 2-45, Drakeford 1-0.

KICKOFF RETURNS—San Francisco, Levy 2-44, Uwaezuoke 1-25. Carolina, Bates 4-126, E. Mills 1-12, Rasby 1-9, Greene 1-4.

PUNT RETURNS—San Francisco, Uwaezuoke 1-15. Carolina, Oliver 4-21.

SACKS—San Francisco, Stubblefield 1, Doleman 1. Carolina, Barrow 1, Miller 0.5, Poole 0.5.

RESULTS

BUFFALO 22, Detroit 13
GREEN BAY 21, Tampa Bay 16
JACKSONVILLE 21, Cincinnati 13
MIAMI 17, Kansas City 14
Minnesota 20, ARIZONA 19
New Orleans 20, CHICAGO 17
N.Y. GIANTS 20, Dallas 17
N.Y. Jets 16, INDIANAPOLIS 12
PHILADELPHIA 24, Washington 10
Pittsburgh 42, BALTIMORE 34
San Diego 25, OAKLAND 10
SEATTLE 16, Tennessee 13
DENVER 34, New England 13
 Open date: Atlanta, Carolina, St. Louis, San Francisco

STANDINGS

AFC EAST	W	L	T	Pct.
New England	4	1	0	.800
N.Y. Jets	4	2	0	.667
Buffalo	3	2	0	.600
Miami	3	2	0	.600
Indianapolis	0	5	0	.000

AFC CENTRAL	W	L	T	Pct.
Jacksonville	4	1	0	.800
Pittsburgh	3	2	0	.600
Baltimore	3	3	0	.500
Cincinnati	1	4	0	.200
Tennessee	1	4	0	.200

AFC WEST	W	L	T	Pct.
Denver	6	0	0	1.000
Kansas City	4	2	0	.667
San Diego	3	3	0	.500
Seattle	3	3	0	.500
Oakland	2	4	0	.333

NFC EAST	W	L	T	Pct.
Dallas	3	2	0	.600
Washington	3	2	0	.600
N.Y. Giants	3	3	0	.500
Philadelphia	2	3	0	.400
Arizona	1	4	0	.200

NFC CENTRAL	W	L	T	Pct.
Tampa Bay	5	1	0	.833
Green Bay	4	2	0	.667
Detroit	3	3	0	.500
Minnesota	4	2	0	.667
Chicago	0	6	0	.000

NFC WEST	W	L	T	Pct.
San Francisco	4	1	0	.800
Carolina	2	3	0	.400
St. Louis	2	3	0	.400
New Orleans	2	4	0	.333
Atlanta	0	5	0	.000

1997 REVIEW Week 6

HIGHLIGHTS

Hero of the week: Packers defensive end Gabe Wilkins picked off a Trent Dilfer pass, leaped over the low-flying quarterback (who had jumped in front of Wilkins in an attempt to tackle the 6-5, 305-pounder) and rumbled 77 yards for a touchdown in Green Bay's 21-16 win over Tampa Bay.

Goat of the week: Despite kicking four field goals to help Arizona build a 19-10 lead over Minnesota, Kevin Butler missed a 31-yard attempt when it mattered most—with less than a minute remaining and a chance to seal a victory for the Cardinals. Following Butler's miss, the Vikings mounted a scoring drive to win, 20-19.

Sub of the week: When starting quarterback Dave Brown left with a strained pectoral muscle in the second quarter, the Giants trailed the Cowboys, 6-0. But backup Danny Kanell gave New York the spark it needed for a 20-17, come-from-behind victory. Kanell's numbers weren't spectacular—10-of-17 for 101 yards—but he didn't make a mistake and led the team on three scoring drives.

Comeback of the week: It was a tale of two halves for Steelers quarterback Kordell Stewart against the Ravens. After throwing three interceptions in a first half—which ended with Pittsburgh trailing, 21-0—Stewart rallied the Steelers to a 42-34 triumph to match the biggest comeback in team history. Stewart threw for three touchdowns and ran for two more in the second half, including a 74-yard romp.

Blowout of the week: The Broncos manhandled the Patriots, 34-13, in a much-anticipated Monday night matchup of undefeated teams. Terrell Davis rushed for 171 yards on 32 carries and scored two touchdowns for Denver.

Nail-biter of the week: Trailing 19-17, the Vikings took possession after the Cardinals' Kevin Butler was wide left on a 31-yard field goal attempt with 52 seconds left. Minnesota quarterback Brad Johnson took his team 62 yards in 37 seconds to get in field-goal range, and with 10 seconds left, Eddie Murray kicked a 38-yarder to give the Vikings a 20-19 victory.

Hit of the week: Jacksonville's Kelvin Pritchett had three sacks in the Jaguars' 21-13 victory over the Bengals, but one in particular thwarted Cincinnati's comeback attempt. Down 14-13 early in the fourth quarter, the Bengals tried a play-action fake on third-and-1. But Pritchett wasn't fooled. He sacked quarterback Jeff Blake, and Cincinnati never fully recovered from the loss of momentum.

Oddity of the week: Earlier in the season, the Vikings released kicker Greg Davis; they said he wasn't getting the job done. But when San Diego's John Carney was sidelined because of a knee injury, the Chargers decided to take a chance on Davis. Davis kicked six field goals—one off the NFL record—in a 25-10 victory over Oakland.

Top rusher: Gary Brown rushed 36 times for 181 yards and a touchdown in the Chargers' victory over the Raiders.

Top passer: Troy Aikman was 34-of-52 for 317 yards and one touchdown in the Cowboys' losing effort against the Giants.

Top receiver: Steelers wide receiver Yancey Thigpen caught seven passes for 162 yards in Pittsburgh's come-from-behind win over the Ravens.

Notes: Because of torn cartilage in his knee, Bills defensive end Jim Jeffcoat missed the first game of his NFL career. A 1983 first-round pick by Dallas, Jeffcoat had played in 224 consecutive regular-season games in 12 seasons with the Cowboys and two-plus seasons with Buffalo. . . . Minnesota's Eddie Murray made his 234th consecutive extra point, tying a league record set by the 49ers' Tommy Davis from 1959-65. . . . The Seahawks-Oilers game, because it was the first of the 4 p.m. ET contests completed, was officially recognized as the 10,000th in NFL history.

Quote of the week: New Orleans coach Mike Ditka, after his team's 20-17 victory against his former team, the Bears: "I went nuts. I was an absolute basket case out there. I'm sure every camera in the world was on me, but I don't care anymore. I don't care. I'm going to be me. That's it. If I have to holler at somebody, I'm going to holler at them. I told them before the game, I said, 'I'll holler at you for 10 seconds, it only lasts 10 seconds and it automatically goes away. But for 10 seconds I'm going to be mad.' "

DOLPHINS 17, CHIEFS 14

Sunday, October 5

Kansas City	0	14	0	0—14
Miami	7	7	0	3—17

First Quarter
Mia.—Abdul-Jabbar 10 run (Mare kick), 9:25.

Second Quarter
K.C.—Rison 16 pass from Grbac (Stoyanovich kick), 4:06.
K.C.—Gonzalez 21 pass from Grbac (Stoyanovich kick), 9:20.
Mia.—Parmalee 7 pass from Marino (Mare kick), 13:49.

Fourth Quarter
Mia.—FG, Mare 26, 9:20.
Attendance—71,794.

TEAM STATISTICS

	Kansas City	Miami
First downs	14	19
Rushes-yards	26-96	27-83
Passing	163	254
Punt returns	2-21	2-13
Kickoff returns	2-45	3-45
Interception returns	0-0	0-0
Comp.-att.-int.	23-30-0	19-31-0
Sacked-yards lost	2-14	1-5
Punts	6-43	5-40
Fumbles-lost	1-0	0-0
Penalties-yards	7-49	4-25
Time of possession	29:43	30:17

INDIVIDUAL STATISTICS

RUSHING—Kansas City, Hill 8-10, Allen 7-25, Anders 7-25, Vanover 2-23, Bennett 2-13. Miami, Abdul-Jabbar 17-38, Spikes 4-14, Marino 3-(minus 3), Jordan 1-16, McPhail 1-12, Parmalee 1-6.

PASSING—Kansas City, Grbac 23-30-0-177. Miami, Marino 19-31-0-259.

RECEIVING—Kansas City, Rison 8-86, Anders 7-27, Perriman 2-20, Popson 2-17, Allen 2-0, Gonzalez 1-21, Walker 1-6. Miami, McDuffie 5-86, Drayton 4-80, Parmalee 4-32, L. Thomas 3-43, Barnett 1-10, McPhail 1-6, Perry 1-2.

MISSED FIELD GOAL ATTEMPTS—Miami, Mare 41.

INTERCEPTIONS—None.

KICKOFF RETURNS—Kansas City, Vanover 2-45. Miami, McPhail 2-26, Spikes 1-19.

PUNT RETURNS—Kansas City, Vanover 2-21. Miami, Jordan 2-13.

SACKS—Kansas City, Williams 1. Miami, Bowens 1, Burton 1.

JAGUARS 21, BENGALS 13

Sunday, October 5

Cincinnati	0	7	6	0—13
Jacksonville	7	0	7	7—21

First Quarter
Jac.—Hallock 10 pass from Brunell (Hollis kick), 10:16.

Second Quarter
Cin.—Carter 1 run (Pelfrey kick), 11:51.

Third Quarter
Jac.—Stewart 7 pass from Brunell (Hollis kick), 3:52.
Cin.—Blake 8 run (kick blocked), 10:44.

Fourth Quarter
Jac.—Jackson 12 pass from Brunell (Hollis kick), 6:11.
Attendance—67,128.

TEAM STATISTICS

	Cincinnati	Jacksonville
First downs	17	21
Rushes-yards	29-148	33-160
Passing	200	148
Punt returns	0-0	3-10
Kickoff returns	2-39	1-19
Interception returns	0-0	0-0
Comp.-att.-int.	16-27-0	14-27-0
Sacked-yards lost	5-32	3-16
Punts	5-46	5-51
Fumbles-lost	0-0	1-0
Penalties-yards	11-80	5-40
Time of possession	29:23	30:37

INDIVIDUAL STATISTICS

RUSHING—Cincinnati, Blake 11-75, Carter 9-26, Dillon 7-35, Bieniemy 2-12. Jacksonville, Means 15-75, Stewart 13-58, Brunell 5-27.

PASSING—Cincinnati, Blake 16-27-0-232. Jacksonville, Brunell 14-27-0-164.

RECEIVING—Cincinnati, Pickens 3-53, McGee 3-48, Dunn 2-52, Bieniemy 2-15, Carter 2-9, Battaglia 1-24, Scott 1-17, Dillon 1-9, Milne 1-5. Jacksonville, Smith 4-57, Stewart 3-38, McCardell 3-38, Hallock 2-15, Jackson 1-12, Mitchell 1-4.

MISSED FIELD GOAL ATTEMPTS—Jacksonville, Hollis 27.

INTERCEPTIONS—None.

KICKOFF RETURNS—Cincinnati, Dunn 2-39. Jacksonville, Logan 1-19.

PUNT RETURNS—Jacksonville, Barlow 3-10.

SACKS—Cincinnati, Wilkinson 2, Dixon 1. Jacksonville, Pritchett 3, Brackens 1, Wynn 1.

GIANTS 20, COWBOYS 17

Sunday, October 5

Dallas	3	3	3	8—17
N.Y. Giants	0	3	10	7—20

First Quarter
Dal.—FG, Cunningham 38, 6:08.

Second Quarter
Dal.—FG, Cunningham 31, 7:21.
NYG—FG, Daluiso 27, 14:48.

Third Quarter
NYG—FG, Daluiso 22, 2:25.
Dal.—FG, Cunningham 27, 7:24.
NYG—Wooten 61 interception return (Daluiso kick), 14:20.

Fourth Quarter
NYG—Way 3 run (Daluiso kick), 8:42.
Dal.—Miller 2 pass from Aikman (Bjornson pass from Aikman), 13:06.
Attendance—77,137.

TEAM STATISTICS

	Dallas	N.Y. Giants
First downs	27	13
Rushes-yards	28-118	20-65
Passing	310	101
Punt returns	4-12	3-41
Kickoff returns	3-67	5-56
Interception returns	0-0	2-64
Comp.-att.-int.	34-52-2	12-24-0
Sacked-yards lost	1-7	1-8
Punts	4-40	8-44
Fumbles-lost	2-0	1-0
Penalties-yards	11-119	6-37
Time of possession	40:37	19:23

INDIVIDUAL STATISTICS

RUSHING—Dallas, E. Smith 19-91, S. Williams 8-28, Aikman 1-(minus 1). New York, Wheatley 16-51, Way 4-14.

PASSING—Dallas, Aikman 34-52-2-317. New York, Kanell 10-17-0-101, Brown 2-7-0-8.

RECEIVING—Dallas, Bjornson 7-71, Johnston 7-55, Irvin 6-86, E. Smith 6-24, St. Williams 3-40, Miller 3-28, LaFleur 1-14, Walker 1-(minus 1). New York, Wheatley 2-38, Alexander 2-33, Calloway 2-19, Way 2-8, Toomer 1-6, Pegram 1-2, Pierce 1-2, Cross 1-1.

MISSED FIELD GOAL ATTEMPTS—Dallas, Cunningham 40.

INTERCEPTIONS—New York, Wooten 2-64.

KICKOFF RETURNS—Dallas, Walker 1-47, Marion 1-20, Galbraith 1-0. New York, Patten 4-52, Alexander 1-4.

PUNT RETURNS—Dallas, Sanders 4-16. New York, Toomer 3-41.

SACKS—Dallas, Tolbert 1. New York, Harris 1.

EAGLES 24, REDSKINS 10

Sunday, October 5

Washington	0	3	7	0—10
Philadelphia	7	10	0	7—24

First Quarter
Phi.—Detmer 3 run (Boniol kick), 9:32.

Second Quarter
Phi.—Watters 1 run (Boniol kick), 1:18.
Was.—FG, Blanton 37, 6:12.
Phi.—FG, Boniol 34, 11:50.

Third Quarter
Was.—Allen 5 pass from Frerotte (Blanton kick), 7:04.

Fourth Quarter
Phi.—Watters 1 run (Boniol kick), 1:51.
Attendance—67,008.

1997 REVIEW Week 6

TEAM STATISTICS

	Washington	Philadelphia
First downs	12	26
Rushes-yards	12-30	50-203
Passing	198	246
Punt returns	4-37	1-(-8)
Kickoff returns	5-113	3-67
Interception returns	0-0	1-21
Comp.-att.-int.	16-37-1	17-27-0
Sacked-yards lost	2-18	0-0
Punts	7-45	5-44
Fumbles-lost	0-0	4-1
Penalties-yards	8-55	7-65
Time of possession	20:38	39:22

INDIVIDUAL STATISTICS

RUSHING—Washington, Allen 12-30. Philadelphia, Watters 31-104, Garner 12-60, Detmer 4-1, Turner 3-38.

PASSING—Washington, Frerotte 16-37-1-216. Philadelphia, Detmer 17-27-0-246.

RECEIVING—Washington, Westbrook 3-62, Mitchell 3-31, Asher 3-30, Allen 3-17, Bowie 2-9, Shepherd 1-47, Ellard 1-20. Philadelphia, Solomon 4-45, Turner 4-43, Fryar 3-72, Watters 2-36, Timpson 1-22, Johnson 1-14, C. Jones 1-10, Dunn 1-4.

MISSED FIELD GOAL ATTEMPTS—None.

INTERCEPTIONS—Philadelphia, Zordich 1-21.

KICKOFF RETURNS—Washington, Mitchell 4-103, Logan 1-10. Philadelphia, Staley 3-67.

PUNT RETURNS—Washington, Mitchell 4-37. Philadelphia, Vincent 1-(minus 8).

SACKS—Philadelphia, Hall 1, H. Thomas 1.

STEELERS 42, RAVENS 34

Sunday, October 5

Pittsburgh	0	7	14	21—42
Baltimore	14	10	0	10—34

First Quarter
Bal.—Green 22 pass from Testaverde (Stover kick), 6:08.
Bal.—Morris 1 run (Stover kick), 10:05.

Second Quarter
Bal.—Kinchen 24 pass from Testaverde (Stover kick), 2:07.
Pit.—Stewart 1 run (N. Johnson kick), 11:43.
Bal.—FG, Stover 34, 14:55.

Third Quarter
Pit.—Blackwell 97 kickoff return (N. Johnson kick), 0:17.
Pit.—C. Johnson 8 pass from Stewart (N. Johnson kick), 13:08.

Fourth Quarter
Pit.—Bruener 4 pass from Stewart (N. Johnson kick), 5:29.
Pit.—C. Johnson 17 pass from Stewart (N. Johnson kick), 11:56.
Bal.—Alexander 10 pass from Testaverde (Byner pass from Testaverde), 12:33.
Pit.—Stewart 74 run (N. Johnson kick), 13:13.
Bal.—Safety, Punter J. Miller forced out of end zone, 14:49.
Attendance—64,421.

TEAM STATISTICS

	Pittsburgh	Baltimore
First downs	22	20
Rushes-yards	40-214	18-52
Passing	217	280
Punt returns	4-11	1-37
Kickoff returns	4-148	8-189
Interception returns	2-11	3-86
Comp.-att.-int.	18-28-3	28-47-2
Sacked-yards lost	2-29	4-10
Punts	4-51	5-44
Fumbles-lost	0-0	4-3
Penalties-yards	8-79	3-29
Time of possession	34:42	25:18

INDIVIDUAL STATISTICS

RUSHING—Pittsburgh, Bettis 28-137, Stewart 6-78, Tomczak 3-(minus 1), G. Jones 1-4, Thigpen 1-3, Miller 1-(minus 7). Baltimore, Morris 15-47, Testaverde 2-4, Byner 1-1.

PASSING—Pittsburgh, Stewart 18-28-3-246. Baltimore, Testaverde 28-47-2-290.

RECEIVING—Pittsburgh, Thigpen 7-162, C. Johnson 5-51, Hawkins 3-22, Bruener 2-9, Lester 1-2. Baltimore, Green 8-92, Alexander 6-79, J. Lewis 4-28, Jackson 3-30, Morris 3-25, Byner 3-12, Kinchen 1-24.

MISSED FIELD GOAL ATTEMPTS—None.

INTERCEPTIONS—Pittsburgh, Lake 1-11, Woolford 1-0. Baltimore, Daniel 2-48, Moore 1-38.

KICKOFF RETURNS—Pittsburgh, Blackwell 3-129, Adams 1-19. Baltimore, J. Lewis 6-140, Roe 2-49.

PUNT RETURNS—Pittsburgh, Blackwell 4-11. Baltimore, J. Lewis 1-37.

SACKS—Pittsburgh, Gildon 1, Oldham 1, Conley 1, Vrabel 1. Baltimore, McCrary 1, J. Jones 1.

JETS 16, COLTS 12

Sunday, October 5

N.Y. Jets	7	6	0	3—16
Indianapolis	0	0	3	9—12

First Quarter
NYJ—Murrell 24 run (Hall kick), 11:06.

Second Quarter
NYJ—FG, Hall 53, 8:47.
NYJ—FG, Hall 37, 14:36.

Third Quarter
Ind.—FG, Blanchard 48, 12:00.

Fourth Quarter
Ind.—Faulk 1 run (Blanchard kick), 4:23.
NYJ—FG, Hall 23, 10:35.
Ind.—Safety, O'Donnel threw ball out of end zone, 14:50.
Attendance—48,295.

TEAM STATISTICS

	N.Y. Jets	Indianapolis
First downs	13	20
Rushes-yards	34-78	19-45
Passing	128	265
Punt returns	4-45	2-23
Kickoff returns	2-68	2-31
Interception returns	3-57	1-0
Comp.-att.-int.	15-28-1	24-45-3
Sacked-yards lost	1-1	2-6
Punts	4-52	6-47
Fumbles-lost	1-0	1-0
Penalties-yards	3-14	6-40
Time of possession	29:18	30:42

INDIVIDUAL STATISTICS

RUSHING—New York, Murrell 30-99, O'Donnell 2-(minus 31), Anderson 1-9, L. Johnson 1-1. Indianapolis, Faulk 14-32, Crockett 2-5, Harbaugh 1-6, Justin 1-1, Potts 1-1.

PASSING—New York, O'Donnell 15-28-1-129. Indianapolis, Justin 16-33-2-173, Harbaugh 8-12-1-98.

RECEIVING—New York, Chrebet 4-39, Anderson 3-15, Baxter 2-34, Murrell 2-2, L. Johnson 1-11, Brady 1-11, K. Johnson 1-11, Ward 1-6. Indianapolis, Dawkins 4-59, Stablein 4-47, Faulk 4-38, Harrison 3-36, Pollard 3-31, Crockett 2-20, Slutzker 2-16, Bailey 1-12, Warren 1-12.

MISSED FIELD GOAL ATTEMPTS—None.

INTERCEPTIONS—New York, Green 1-39, P. Johnson 1-13, Glenn 1-5. Indianapolis, C. Gray 1-0.

KICKOFF RETURNS—New York, Glenn 2-68. Indianapolis, Bailey 2-31.

PUNT RETURNS—New York, L. Johnson 4-45. Indianapolis, Harrison 1-19, Stablein 1-4.

SACKS—New York, Lewis 1, Hamilton 1. Indianapolis, Blackmon 1.

PACKERS 21, BUCCANEERS 16

Sunday, October 5

Tampa Bay	3	0	7	6—16
Green Bay	0	21	0	0—21

First Quarter
T.B.—FG, Husted 23, 11:10.

Second Quarter
G.B.—Freeman 31 pass from Favre (Longwell kick), 0:47.
G.B.—Wilkins 77 interception return (Longwell kick), 6:41.
G.B.—Freeman 6 pass from Favre (Longwell kick), 14:16.

Third Quarter
T.B.—Alstott 1 run (Husted kick), 12:06.

Fourth Quarter
T.B.—Dunn 2 run (pass failed), 4:49.
Attendance—60,100.

TEAM STATISTICS

	Tampa Bay	Green Bay
First downs	23	13
Rushes-yards	36-217	18-64
Passing	155	170

	Tampa Bay	Green Bay
Punt returns	1-0	4-40
Kickoff returns	3-44	1-28
Interception returns	0-0	1-77
Comp.-att.-int.	16-29-1	21-31-0
Sacked-yards lost	3-24	3-21
Punts	5-46	7-46
Fumbles-lost	2-1	2-1
Penalties-yards	3-30	5-38
Time of possession	34:21	25:39

INDIVIDUAL STATISTICS

RUSHING—Tampa Bay, Alstott 17-56, Dunn 16-125, Anthony 1-18, Dilfer 1-13, Ellison 1-5. Green Bay, Levens 13-44, Favre 4-17, Hayden 1-3.

PASSING—Tampa Bay, Dilfer 16-29-1-179. Green Bay, Favre 21-31-0-191.

RECEIVING—Tampa Bay, Copeland 5-53, Alstott 4-34, Anthony 3-44, Harris 1-19, Hape 1-13, Moore 1-12, Dunn 1-4. Green Bay, Levens 8-61, R. Brooks 4-29, Freeman 3-57, Chmura 3-23, Henderson 3-21.

MISSED FIELD GOAL ATTEMPTS—Green Bay, Longwell 47.

INTERCEPTIONS—Green Bay, Wilkins 1-77.

KICKOFF RETURNS—Tampa Bay, Anthony 1-28, Copeland 1-16, Alstott 1-0. Green Bay, Schroeder 1-28.

PUNT RETURNS—Tampa Bay, Williams 1-0. Green Bay, Schroeder 4-40.

SACKS—Tampa Bay, Ahanotu 2, Upshaw 1. Green Bay, White 2, Wilkins 1.

BILLS 22, LIONS 13

Sunday, October 5

Detroit	0	3	3	7—13
Buffalo	3	10	0	9—22

First Quarter
Buf.—FG, Christie 47, 5:34.

Second Quarter
Det.—FG, Hanson 28, 2:36.
Buf.—Reed 43 pass from Collins (Christie kick), 3:54.
Buf.—FG, Christie 33, 14:58.

Third Quarter
Det.—FG, Hanson 30, 9:47.

Fourth Quarter
Det.—Mitchell 8 run (Hanson kick), 9:06.
Buf.—Safety, B. Sanders tackled by B. Smith & P. Hansen in end zone, 12:48.
Buf.—A. Smith 56 run (Christie kick), 13:13.
Attendance—78,025.

TEAM STATISTICS

	Detroit	Buffalo
First downs	17	10
Rushes-yards	28-120	30-164
Passing	189	102
Punt returns	2-36	2-3
Kickoff returns	4-69	5-118
Interception returns	0-0	1-6
Comp.-att.-int.	20-38-1	11-18-0
Sacked-yards lost	4-32	3-20
Punts	6-38	8-45
Fumbles-lost	1-0	2-0
Penalties-yards	8-60	7-48
Time of possession	33:31	26:29

INDIVIDUAL STATISTICS

RUSHING—Detroit, Sanders 25-107, Mitchell 2-11, Rivers 1-2. Buffalo, A. Smith 13-88, Thomas 13-73, Collins 4-3.

PASSING—Detroit, Mitchell 20-38-1-221. Buffalo, Collins 11-18-0-122.

RECEIVING—Detroit, Moore 8-116, Morton 2-27, Vardell 2-23, Metzelaars 2-13, Sloan 2-12, Sanders 2-(minus 1), T. Boyd 1-23, Schlesinger 1-8. Buffalo, Reed 5-95, Thomas 5-21, A. Smith 1-6.

MISSED FIELD GOAL ATTEMPTS—None.

INTERCEPTIONS—Buffalo, Covington 1-6.

KICKOFF RETURNS—Detroit, Milburn 3-69, Russell 1-0. Buffalo, Moulds 4-108, Burris 1-10.

PUNT RETURNS—Detroit, Milburn 2-36. Buffalo, Tasker 2-3.

SACKS—Detroit, Wells 1, Elliss 1, London 1. Buffalo, Jones 1, Paup 1, B. Smith 1, Rogers 1.

SEAHAWKS 16, OILERS 13

Sunday, October 5

Tennessee	3	7	0	3—13
Seattle	0	0	10	6—16

First Quarter
Ten.—FG, Del Greco 37, 9:27.

Second Quarter
Ten.—George 11 pass from McNair (Del Greco kick), 8:28.

Third Quarter
Sea.—FG, Peterson 38, 4:54.
Sea.—Broussard 77 run (Peterson kick), 8:15.

Fourth Quarter
Sea.—Broussard 43 run (Tuten missed 2-pt. conversion), 0:48.
Ten.—FG, Del Greco 43, 11:19.
Attendance—49,897.

TEAM STATISTICS

	Tennessee	Seattle
First downs	18	20
Rushes-yards	35-156	19-167
Passing	97	238
Punt returns	2-12	3-34
Kickoff returns	3-50	4-80
Interception returns	0-0	2-0
Comp.-att.-int.	12-28-2	27-40-0
Sacked-yards lost	1-4	2-22
Punts	5-41	5-38
Fumbles-lost	1-0	3-2
Penalties-yards	6-49	7-55
Time of possession	32:48	27:12

INDIVIDUAL STATISTICS

RUSHING—Tennessee, George 26-116, Thomas 4-13, McNair 3-11, Harmon 2-16. Seattle, Smith 10-33, Broussard 6-138, Moon 3-(minus 4).

PASSING—Tennessee, McNair 12-28-2-101. Seattle, Moon 27-40-0-260.

RECEIVING—Tennessee, Wycheck 4-41, Sanders 2-21, George 2-15, Davis 1-14, Russell 1-7, Harmon 1-5, Thomas 1-(minus 2). Seattle, Pritchard 7-75, Smith 4-42, McKnight 3-46, Br. Blades 3-32, Strong 3-16, Crumpler 2-35, Fauria 2-13, Broussard 2-4, Hobbs 1-(minus 3).

MISSED FIELD GOAL ATTEMPTS—None.

INTERCEPTIONS—Seattle, Springs 1-0, D. Williams 1-0.

KICKOFF RETURNS—Tennessee, Mason 3-50. Seattle, Broussard 3-57, Davis 1-23.

PUNT RETURNS—Tennessee, Gray 2-12. Seattle, Davis 3-34.

SACKS—Tennessee, Bowden 1, Ford 1. Seattle, Sinclair 1.

CHARGERS 25, RAIDERS 10

Sunday, October 5

San Diego	6	3	10	6—25
Oakland	0	3	7	0—10

First Quarter
S.D.—FG, G. Davis 30, 5:41.
S.D.—FG, G. Davis 22, 11:47.

Second Quarter
S.D.—FG, G. Davis 38, 7:01.
Oak.—FG, Ford 24, 15:00.

Third Quarter
S.D.—FG, G. Davis 43, 3:56.
Oak.—Kaufman 70 pass from George (Ford kick), 4:57.
S.D.—Brown 1 run (G. Davis kick), 9:17.

Fourth Quarter
S.D.—FG, G. Davis 33, 8:53.
S.D.—FG, G. Davis 33, 12:26.
Attendance—43,648.

TEAM STATISTICS

	San Diego	Oakland
First downs	23	11
Rushes-yards	45-180	13-13
Passing	218	228
Punt returns	4-8	0-0
Kickoff returns	1-16	8-175
Interception returns	0-0	0-0
Comp.-att.-int.	18-33-0	19-42-0
Sacked-yards lost	1-8	6-43
Punts	5-38	7-47
Fumbles-lost	2-0	3-1
Penalties-yards	5-66	6-59
Time of possession	38:57	21:03

INDIVIDUAL STATISTICS

RUSHING—San Diego, Brown 36-181, Fletcher 3-(minus 3), Gardner 2-3, Humphries 2-(minus 1), Metcalf 1-1, Bynum 1-(minus 1). Oakland, Kaufman 11-13, Araguz 1-0, Williams 1-0.

PASSING—San Diego, Humphries 18-33-0-226. Oakland, George 19-42-0-271.

RECEIVING—San Diego, Martin 5-75, C. Jones 5-40, F. Jones 4-53, Fletcher 2-35, Metcalf 1-14, Brown 1-9. Oakland, Dudley 6-68, Kaufman 3-100, Jett 3-30, T. Brown 3-18, Williams 2-31, Fenner 2-24.

MISSED FIELD GOAL ATTEMPTS—None.

INTERCEPTIONS—None.

KICKOFF RETURNS—San Diego, Metcalf 1-16. Oakland, Howard 7-157, Hall 1-18.

PUNT RETURNS—San Diego, Metcalf 4-8.

SACKS—San Diego, Johnson 2, Seau 1, Coleman 1, Fuller 1, Parrella 1. Oakland, McGlockton 1.

VIKINGS 20, CARDINALS 19

Sunday, October 5

Minnesota	7	3	0	10	—20
Arizona	3	10	3	3	—19

First Quarter
Min.—Glover 18 pass from Johnson (Murray kick), 3:29.
Ariz.—FG, Butler 23, 14:20.

Second Quarter
Min.—FG, Murray 49, 8:40.
Ariz.—Gedney 33 pass from K. Graham (Butler kick), 13:44.
Ariz.—FG, Butler 23, 15:00.

Third Quarter
Ariz.—FG, Butler 28, 12:17.

Fourth Quarter
Ariz.—FG, Butler 49, 4:38.
Min.—Carter 1 pass from Johnson (Murray kick), 10:55.
Min.—FG, Murray 38, 14:50.
Attendance—45,550.

TEAM STATISTICS

	Minnesota	Arizona
First downs	20	22
Rushes-yards	23-81	26-108
Passing	272	277
Punt returns	1-6	2-22
Kickoff returns	4-84	4-102
Interception returns	0-0	2-34
Comp.-att.-int.	25-39-2	22-38-0
Sacked-yards lost	2-20	3-16
Punts	2-59	2-41
Fumbles-lost	4-1	1-1
Penalties-yards	6-57	5-70
Time of possession	29:04	30:56

INDIVIDUAL STATISTICS

RUSHING—Minnesota, R. Smith 17-60, Johnson 2-11, Hoard 2-9, Evans 1-1, Berger 1-0. Arizona, McElroy 15-87, Johnson 8-21, Bouie 3-0.

PASSING—Minnesota, Johnson 25-39-2-292. Arizona, K. Graham 22-38-0-293.

RECEIVING—Minnesota, Glover 6-86, Carter 6-64, R. Smith 4-35, Reed 3-55, Evans 2-19, DeLong 2-15, Goodwin 1-11, Palmer 1-7. Arizona, R. Moore 8-108, Sanders 7-99, Gedney 2-41, C. Smith 2-20, Edwards 1-9, K. Williams 1-9, Johnson 1-7.

MISSED FIELD GOAL ATTEMPTS—Arizona, Butler 31.

INTERCEPTIONS—Arizona, A. Williams 1-19, McCleskey 1-15.

KICKOFF RETURNS—Minnesota, M. Williams 4-84. Arizona, K. Williams 4-102.

PUNT RETURNS—Minnesota, Palmer 1-6. Arizona, K. Williams 2-22.

SACKS—Minnesota, Randle 2, F. Smith 1. Arizona, Miller 1, Rice 1.

SAINTS 20, BEARS 17

Sunday, October 5

New Orleans	0	3	10	7	—20
Chicago	3	0	0	14	—17

First Quarter
Chi.—FG, Jaeger 23, 6:23.

Second Quarter
N.O.—FG, Brien 38, 13:04.

Third Quarter
N.O.—Bates 49 run (Brien kick), 2:24.
N.O.—FG, Brien 48, 7:42.

Fourth Quarter
Chi.—Kramer 1 run (Jaeger kick), 7:16.
Chi.—R. Harris 1 run (Jaeger kick), 8:58.
N.O.—Hill 89 pass from Shuler (Brien kick), 9:21.
Attendance—58,865.

TEAM STATISTICS

	New Orleans	Chicago
First downs	11	19
Rushes-yards	30-137	33-101
Passing	185	165
Punt returns	6-77	5-30
Kickoff returns	3-65	5-149
Interception returns	0-0	1-0
Comp.-att.-int.	9-23-1	19-36-0
Sacked-yards lost	2-10	5-24
Punts	9-44	12-44
Fumbles-lost	4-2	1-0
Penalties-yards	9-79	9-60
Time of possession	25:59	34:01

INDIVIDUAL STATISTICS

RUSHING—New Orleans, Zellars 14-65, Bates 9-58, T. Davis 6-14, Shuler 1-0. Chicago, R. Harris 28-82, Mirer 4-18, Kramer 1-1.

PASSING—New Orleans, Shuler 9-23-1-195. Chicago, Kramer 12-20-0-131, Mirer 7-16-0-58.

RECEIVING—New Orleans, Hill 5-121, Farquhar 2-51, Bates 1-15, Hastings 1-8. Chicago, Engram 6-59, Proehl 3-39, R. Harris 3-0, Wetnight 2-36, Penn 2-35, Hughes 2-13, Jennings 1-7.

MISSED FIELD GOAL ATTEMPTS—None.

INTERCEPTIONS—Chicago, Mangum 1-0.

KICKOFF RETURNS—New Orleans, Bech 1-30, T. Davis 1-22, Guliford 1-13. Chicago, Hughes 5-149.

PUNT RETURNS—New Orleans, Guliford 6-77. Chicago, Hughes 5-30.

SACKS—New Orleans, Martin 1, Harvey 1, Sagapolutele 1, Glover 1, Mitchell 1. Chicago, Minter 2.

BRONCOS 34, PATRIOTS 13

Monday, October 6

New England	0	13	0	0	—13
Denver	14	0	17	3	—34

First Quarter
Den.—Davis 2 run (Bentley kick), 9:32.
Den.—Mobley 13 interception return (Bentley kick), 11:09.

Second Quarter
N.E.—Byars 44 pass from Bledsoe (Vinatieri kick), 0:22.
N.E.—FG, Vinatieri 26, 11:48.
N.E.—FG, Vinatieri 49, 15:00.

Third Quarter
Den.—Elway 1 run (Bentley kick), 5:23.
Den.—FG, Bentley 21, 11:23.
Den.—Davis 1 run (Bentley kick), 13:01.

Fourth Quarter
Den.—FG, Bentley 33, 9:36.
Attendance—75,821.

TEAM STATISTICS

	New England	Denver
First downs	13	25
Rushes-yards	19-51	38-192
Passing	211	188
Punt returns	1-20	3-20
Kickoff returns	6-119	2-59
Interception returns	2-30	1-13
Comp.-att.-int.	20-41-1	13-27-2
Sacked-yards lost	3-23	1-8
Punts	7-52	3-50
Fumbles-lost	2-1	3-0
Penalties-yards	10-117	4-20
Time of possession	27:02	32:58

INDIVIDUAL STATISTICS

RUSHING—New England, Martin 15-66, Bledsoe 2-3, Byars 1-0, Brown 1-(minus 18). Denver, Davis 32-171, Hebron 3-22, Elway 3-(minus 1).

PASSING—New England, Bledsoe 20-41-1-234. Denver, Elway 13-27-2-196.

RECEIVING—New England, Coates 5-65, Byars 4-66, Jefferson 3-45, Martin 3-10, Glenn 2-27, Brown 1-10, Purnell 1-6, Brisby 1-5. Denver, R. Smith 5-130, McCaffrey 3-26, Green 2-14, Davis 2-7, Sharpe 1-19.

MISSED FIELD GOAL ATTEMPTS—Denver, Bentley 48.

INTERCEPTIONS—New England, Clay 2-30. Denver, Mobley 1-13.

KICKOFF RETURNS—New England, Meggett 6-119. Denver, Hebron 2-59.

PUNT RETURNS—New England, Meggett 1-20. Denver, Gordon 3-20.

SACKS—New England, Thomas 1. Denver, Tanuvasa 3.

WEEK 7

Atlanta 23, NEW ORLEANS 17
Detroit 27, TAMPA BAY 9
Green Bay 24, CHICAGO 23
JACKSONVILLE 38, Philadelphia 21
Miami 31, N.Y. JETS 20
MINNESOTA 21, Carolina 14
NEW ENGLAND 33, Buffalo 6
N.Y. Giants 27, ARIZONA 13
PITTSBURGH 24, Indianapolis 22
TENNESSEE 30, Cincinnati 7
SAN FRANCISCO 30, St. Louis 10
WASHINGTON 21, Dallas 16
  Open date: Baltimore, Denver, Kansas City,
Oakland, San Diego, Seattle

AFC EAST

	W	L	T	Pct.
New England	5	1	0	.833
Miami	4	2	0	.667
N.Y. Jets	4	3	0	.571
Buffalo	3	3	0	.500
Indianapolis	0	6	0	.000

NFC EAST

	W	L	T	Pct.
Washington	4	2	0	.667
N.Y. Giants	4	3	0	.571
Dallas	3	3	0	.500
Philadelphia	2	4	0	.333
Arizona	1	5	0	.167

AFC CENTRAL

	W	L	T	Pct.
Jacksonville	5	1	0	.833
Pittsburgh	4	2	0	.667
Baltimore	3	3	0	.500
Tennessee	2	4	0	.333
Cincinnati	1	5	0	.167

NFC CENTRAL

	W	L	T	Pct.
Green Bay	5	2	0	.714
Minnesota	5	2	0	.714
Tampa Bay	5	2	0	.714
Detroit	4	3	0	.571
Chicago	0	7	0	.000

AFC WEST

	W	L	T	Pct.
Denver	6	0	0	1.000
Kansas City	4	2	0	.667
San Diego	3	3	0	.500
Seattle	3	3	0	.500
Oakland	2	4	0	.333

NFC WEST

	W	L	T	Pct.
San Francisco	5	1	0	.833
Carolina	2	4	0	.333
St. Louis	2	4	0	.333
New Orleans	2	5	0	.285
Atlanta	1	5	0	.167

Hero of the week: Jaguars running back James Stewart became only the fourth player in NFL history to rush for five touchdowns in a game in leading Jacksonville past the Eagles, 38-21. Stewart's 15-carry, 102-yard effort was only the second 100-yard game of his three-year career. Stewart received most of the carries because Natrone Means left in the first quarter with a sprained ankle.

Goat of the week: Bengals quarterback Jeff Blake passed for 130 yards and no touchdowns in Cincinnati's 30-7 loss to Tennessee. Blake completed just one pass in the second half before being replaced by Boomer Esiason, who guided the team to its only score.

Sub of the week: Redskins running back Stephen Davis, subbing for the injured Terry Allen, had the biggest game of his career by running for two touchdowns and 94 yards on 22 carries in Washington's 21-16 victory over Dallas on Monday night.

Comeback of the week: There weren't many big comebacks in Week 7, but Pittsburgh overcame a 10-point first-quarter deficit to defeat Indianapolis, 24-22. After the Steelers built a 24-13 lead, the Colts scored nine consecutive points, including a touchdown with 3:35 remaining. But Pittsburgh's Chris Oldham batted away the potential tying two-point conversion pass to Brian Stablein after a holding penalty gave the Colts the ball at the 1.

Blowout of the week: Buffalo's chances were diminished early when starting quarterback Todd Collins left the game with a bruised shoulder on the team's second possession. The Bills never recovered and were trounced, 33-6, by New England. Patriots quarterback Drew Bledsoe threw two touchdown passes and Curtis Martin ran for 99 yards and one TD.

Nail-biter of the week: The 0-6 Bears were given virtually no chance of keeping it close against the defending champion Packers. With 1:54 left, though, Chicago trailed, 24-23, with a chance to tie if coach Dave Wannstedt elected to kick the extra point. But Wannstedt went for the win at home, choosing to

attempt a two-point conversion. Erik Kramer's pass sailed past Raymont Harris and Green Bay escaped with a victory.

Hit of the week: With the game tied at 14, Carolina regained possession on its 47 with 5:31 left against the Vikings. On the first play, quarterback Steve Beuerlein threw a pass to receiver Rae Carruth, but linebacker Ed McDaniel ripped the ball away from the rookie receiver. Nose guard Jerry Ball tipped the ball, technically a fumble, into the air, and Fernando Smith caught it and returned it to Carolina's 45. McDaniel's clutch play led to Minnesota's game-winning scoring drive.

Oddity of the week: Vikings quarterback Brad Johnson completed a touchdown pass to himself against Carolina. Early in the fourth quarter, Johnson's third-and-goal pass was batted down by Panthers nose tackle Greg Kragen. The ball went right to Johnson, who caught it, ran by linebacker Micheal Barrow in the backfield and scrambled 3 yards to give the Vikings a 14-7 lead. It was the first time in NFL history that a quarterback completed a touchdown pass to himself.

Top rusher: Barry Sanders carried 24 times for 215 yards and two touchdowns in Detroit's 27-9 win over Tampa Bay.

Top passer: Dan Marino was 27-of-38 for 372 yards and two touchdowns in Miami's 31-20 win over the Jets.

Top receiver: Philadelphia's Irving Fryar made 10 receptions for 124 yards and three touchdowns in the Eagles' loss at Jacksonville.

Notes: Minnesota's Eddie Murray set an NFL record by kicking his 235th, 236th and 237th consecutive extra points in the 21-14 victory over the Panthers. Murray broke a 32-year-old league record of 234 in a row held by the 49ers' Tommy Davis. Not far behind Murray was Pittsburgh's Norm Johnson, who tied Davis' previous record by making all three of his PAT tries against Indianapolis, giving him 234 in a row. . . . Falcons defensive lineman Chuck Smith had five sacks and Atlanta set a team record with 10

1997 REVIEW Week 7

in a 23-17 victory over the Saints. . . . Tyrone Wheatley's career-high 103 yards snapped an NFL-high 23-game streak in which no Giants running back gained 100 yards. . . . Barry Sanders' 215 yards rushing, including the two longest touchdown runs of his career (80 and 82 yards), moved him past Jim Brown into fourth place on the NFL's career rushing list. Sanders also became the first player in league history to score two TDs of at least 80 yards in the same game.

Quote of the week: Bengals coach Bruce Coslet, after his team's 30-7 loss at Tennessee: "We can't run. We can't pass. We can't stop the run. We can't stop the pass. We can't kick. Other than that . . . we're just not a very good football team right now."

GAME SUMMARIES

PACKERS 24, BEARS 23

Sunday, October 12

Green Bay	0	14	7	3—24
Chicago	10	0	7	6—23

First Quarter
Chi.—R. Harris 1 run (Jaeger kick), 2:51.
Chi.—FG, Jaeger 41, 11:02.
Second Quarter
G.B.—Chmura 2 pass from Favre (Longwell kick), 8:22.
G.B.—Levens 1 pass from Favre (Longwell kick), 13:24.
Third Quarter
Chi.—Kramer 3 run (Jaeger kick), 6:42.
G.B.—Chmura 12 pass from Favre (Longwell kick), 14:01.
Fourth Quarter
G.B.—FG, Longwell 37, 12:22.
Chi.—Penn 22 pass from Kramer (pass failed), 13:06.
Attendance—62,212.

TEAM STATISTICS

	Green Bay	Chicago
First downs	22	26
Rushes-yards	25-100	34-121
Passing	177	232
Punt returns	2-23	2-7
Kickoff returns	2-53	4-80
Interception returns	2-25	1-8
Comp.-att.-int.	19-35-1	22-35-2
Sacked-yards lost	0-0	0-0
Punts	4-42	3-47
Fumbles-lost	0-0	0-0
Penalties-yards	5-55	6-53
Time of possession	27:40	32:20

INDIVIDUAL STATISTICS
RUSHING—Green Bay, Levens 12-74, Hayden 7-21, Favre 4-5, Henderson 2-0. Chicago, R. Harris 27-101, Kramer 3-5, Autry 2-7, Conway 1-6, Tony Carter 1-2.
PASSING—Green Bay, Favre 19-35-1-177. Chicago, Kramer 22-35-2-232.
RECEIVING—Green Bay, Freeman 7-86, Henderson 3-20, R. Brooks 2-24, Chmura 2-14, Levens 2-11, Hayden 2-11, Thomason 1-11. Chicago, Penn 7-77, Conway 5-77, Engram 3-17, Jennings 2-34, R. Harris 2-8, Tony Carter 2-4, Wetnight 1-15.
MISSED FIELD GOAL ATTEMPTS—None.
INTERCEPTIONS—Green Bay, B. Williams 1-25, Harris 1-0. Chicago, W. Harris 1-8.
KICKOFF RETURNS—Green Bay, Schroeder 2-53. Chicago, Hughes 3-65, Tony Carter 1-15.
PUNT RETURNS—Green Bay, Schroeder 2-23. Chicago, Hughes 2-7.
SACKS—None.

PATRIOTS 33, BILLS 6

Sunday, October 12

Buffalo	0	0	0	6— 6
New England	10	6	17	0—33

First Quarter
N.E.—Coates 20 pass from Bledsoe (Vinatieri kick), 5:39.
N.E.—FG, Vinatieri 20, 9:38.
Second Quarter
N.E.—FG, Vinatieri 23, 1:40.
N.E.—FG, Vinatieri 41, 5:41.
Third Quarter
N.E.—FG, Vinatieri 52, 1:57.
N.E.—Martin 26 run (Vinatieri kick), 4:18.
N.E.—Byars 4 pass from Bledsoe (Vinatieri kick), 12:24.
Fourth Quarter
Buf.—Holmes 1 run (run failed), 1:01.
Attendance—59,802.

TEAM STATISTICS

	Buffalo	New England
First downs	13	19
Rushes-yards	18-94	39-139
Passing	148	171
Punt returns	2-20	5-54
Kickoff returns	8-151	2-61
Interception returns	1-4	4-73
Comp.-att.-int.	21-41-4	14-27-1
Sacked-yards lost	3-16	1-10
Punts	6-42	3-48
Fumbles-lost	2-0	1-0
Penalties-yards	11-88	1-10
Time of possession	26:11	33:49

INDIVIDUAL STATISTICS
RUSHING—Buffalo, Thomas 6-24, A. Smith 6-22, Holmes 4-41, Hobert 2-7. New England, Martin 22-99, Grier 8-24, Meggett 2-10, Byars 2-4, Bledsoe 2-1, Zolak 2-(minus 2), Cullors 1-3.
PASSING—Buffalo, Hobert 17-30-2-133, Van Pelt 3-7-2-22, Collins 1-4-0-9. New England, Bledsoe 14-27-1-181.
RECEIVING—Buffalo, Early 6-59, Reed 4-42, A. Smith 3-21, Johnson 3-12, Holmes 2-14, Riemersma 2-11, Thomas 1-5. New England, Coates 4-92, Glenn 4-50, Gash 2-7, Jefferson 1-13, Brisby 1-11, Martin 1-4, Byars 1-4.
MISSED FIELD GOAL ATTEMPTS—Buffalo, Christie 34.
INTERCEPTIONS—Buffalo, Perry 1-4. New England, Law 1-40, Clay 1-26, Moore 1-7, Milloy 1-0.
KICKOFF RETURNS—Buffalo, Moulds 8-151. New England, Cullors 2-61.
PUNT RETURNS—Buffalo, Moulds 2-20. New England, Meggett 5-54.
SACKS—Buffalo, B. Smith 1. New England, Slade 2, Bruschi 1.

DOLPHINS 31, JETS 20

Sunday, October 12

Miami	0	17	0	14—31
N.Y. Jets	7	7	0	6—20

First Quarter
NYJ—L. Johnson 1 run (Hall kick), 4:30.
Second Quarter
Mia.—Abdul-Jabbar 36 pass from Marino (Mare kick), 3:23.
NYJ—K. Johnson 7 pass from O'Donnell (Hall kick), 7:56.
Mia.—L. Thomas 22 pass from Marino (Mare kick), 12:14.
Mia.—FG, Mare 23, 15:00.
Fourth Quarter
Mia.—McDuffie 4 run (Mare kick), 10:51.
Mia.—Spikes 8 run (Mare kick), 13:04.
NYJ—Chrebet 8 pass from O'Donnell (pass failed), 13:57.
Attendance—77,716.

TEAM STATISTICS

	Miami	N.Y. Jets
First downs	25	20
Rushes-yards	30-93	20-81
Passing	372	288
Punt returns	3-28	2-13
Kickoff returns	4-52	4-80
Interception returns	0-0	0-0
Comp.-att.-int.	27-38-0	24-37-0
Sacked-yards lost	0-0	5-31
Punts	4-44	5-43
Fumbles-lost	2-0	1-1
Penalties-yards	7-61	5-37
Time of possession	33:23	26:37

RUSHING—Miami, Abdul-Jabbar 18-62, Spikes 8-23, Marino 3-(minus 1), McPhail 1-9. New York, Murrell 13-29, Anderson 4-28, L. Johnson 2-21, O'Donnell 1-3.

PASSING—Miami, Marino 27-38-0-372. New York, O'Donnell 24-37-0-319.

RECEIVING—Miami, Parmalee 6-91, L. Thomas 5-75, Drayton 4-66, McDuffie 4-55, Abdul-Jabbar 3-47, McPhail 3-15, Jordan 1-22, Perry 1-1. New York, Graham 7-77, Chrebet 5-104, K. Johnson 4-80, L. Johnson 3-36, Murrell 2-6, Baxter 1-6, Ward 1-6, Anderson 1-4.

MISSED FIELD GOAL ATTEMPTS—Miami, Mare 30. New York, Hall 30.

INTERCEPTIONS—None.

KICKOFF RETURNS—Miami, Spikes 2-32, C. Harris 1-20, Wooden 1-0. New York, Glenn 2-43, L. Johnson 2-37.

PUNT RETURNS—Miami, Jordan 3-28. New York, L. Johnson 2-13.

SACKS—Miami, Rodgers 2, Taylor 1, Burton 1, Bowens 1.

LIONS 27, BUCCANEERS 9

Sunday, October 12

Detroit	7	3	7	10—27
Tampa Bay	9	0	0	0— 9

First Quarter
T.B.—FG, Husted 25, 6:16.
Det.—Sanders 80 run (Hanson kick), 10:21.
T.B.—Dunn 59 pass from Dilfer (kick failed), 12:59.

Second Quarter
Det.—FG, Hanson 34, 14:54.

Third Quarter
Det.—Sanders 82 run (Hanson kick), 9:17.

Fourth Quarter
Det.—FG, Hanson 39, 2:32.
Det.—Sanders 7 pass from Mitchell (Hanson kick), 8:37.
 Attendance—72,095.

TEAM STATISTICS

	Detroit	Tampa Bay
First downs	17	13
Rushes-yards	33-259	25-72
Passing	188	217
Punt returns	1-40	4-23
Kickoff returns	0-0	4-76
Interception returns	2-17	0-0
Comp.-att.-int.	16-20-0	17-31-2
Sacked-yards lost	4-34	3-20
Punts	5-44	7-42
Fumbles-lost	1-1	4-0
Penalties-yards	2-25	6-41
Time of possession	29:43	30:17

INDIVIDUAL STATISTICS
RUSHING—Detroit, Sanders 24-215, Vardell 4-30, Mitchell 3-7, Rivers 1-7, Schlesinger 1-0. Tampa Bay, Alstott 12-40, Dunn 10-9, Dilfer 3-23.

PASSING—Detroit, Mitchell 16-20-0-222. Tampa Bay, Dilfer 17-31-2-237.

RECEIVING—Detroit, Morton 7-66, Moore 5-120, Schlesinger 1-15, Sloan 1-11, Sanders 1-7, Metzelaars 1-3. Tampa Bay, Copeland 6-105, Dunn 3-71, Anthony 3-22, Williams 2-20, Harris 2-13, Thomas 1-6.

MISSED FIELD GOAL ATTEMPTS—None.

INTERCEPTIONS—Detroit, Raymond 1-17, Bailey 1-0.

KICKOFF RETURNS—Tampa Bay, Anthony 2-75, Williams 2-1.

PUNT RETURNS—Detroit, Milburn 1-40. Tampa Bay, Williams 4-23.

SACKS—Detroit, Porcher 1.5, Waldroup 0.5, Scroggins 0.5, Elliss 0.5. Tampa Bay, Sapp 1, Upshaw 1, Culpepper 1, Ahanotu 1.

VIKINGS 21, PANTHERS 14

Sunday, October 12

Carolina	0	7	0	7—14
Minnesota	0	7	0	14—21

Second Quarter
Min.—Carter 6 pass from Johnson (Murray kick), 4:06.
Car.—Walls 16 pass from Beuerlein (Kasay kick), 9:37.

Fourth Quarter
Min.—Johnson 3 pass from Johnson (Murray kick), 0:52.
Car.—Carruth 5 pass from Beuerlein (Kasay kick), 7:22.
Min.—R. Smith 4 run (Murray kick), 11:13.
 Attendance—62,625.

TEAM STATISTICS

	Carolina	Minnesota
First downs	15	17
Rushes-yards	20-80	29-158
Passing	197	203
Punt returns	4-36	3-35
Kickoff returns	4-72	2-57
Interception returns	1-1	0-0
Comp.-att.-int.	19-35-0	17-34-1
Sacked-yards lost	5-30	0-0
Punts	6-39	7-39
Fumbles-lost	2-2	0-0
Penalties-yards	9-70	10-92
Time of possession	28:03	31:57

INDIVIDUAL STATISTICS
RUSHING—Carolina, Biakabutuka 12-50, Johnson 6-27, Carruth 1-3, Oliver 1-0. Minnesota, R. Smith 23-120, Johnson 4-28, M. Williams 1-8, Evans 1-2.

PASSING—Carolina, Beuerlein 19-35-0-227. Minnesota, Johnson 17-34-1-203.

RECEIVING—Carolina, Carruth 6-107, Walls 5-55, Carrier 4-36, Ismail 2-21, Greene 2-8. Minnesota, Glover 3-15, Reed 2-65, Palmer 2-22, Carter 2-18, Evans 2-15, R. Smith 2-7, Hatchette 1-38, Goodwin 1-14, Walsh 1-6, Johnson 1-3.

MISSED FIELD GOAL ATTEMPTS—None.

INTERCEPTIONS—Carolina, Lathon 1-1.

KICKOFF RETURNS—Carolina, E. Mills 2-18, Bates 1-48, Greene 1-6. Minnesota, M. Williams 2-57.

PUNT RETURNS—Carolina, Oliver 3-28, Bates 1-8. Minnesota, Palmer 3-35.

SACKS—Minnesota, Randle 3, Wheeler 1, Rudd 1.

49ERS 30, RAMS 10

Sunday, October 12

St. Louis	0	7	3	0—10
San Francisco	14	6	10	0—30

First Quarter
S.F.—Owens 5 pass from S. Young (Anderson kick), 5:47.
S.F.—Clark 10 pass from S. Young (Anderson kick), 10:53.

Second Quarter
St.L.—McNeil 75 interception return (Wilkins kick), 3:52.
S.F.—FG, Anderson 20, 13:06.
S.F.—FG, Anderson 46, 14:00.

Third Quarter
S.F.—FG, Anderson 28, 4:21.
S.F.—Owens 17 pass from S. Young (Anderson kick), 5:18.
St.L.—FG, Wilkins 34, 8:16.
 Attendance—63,825.

TEAM STATISTICS

	St. Louis	San Francisco
First downs	7	21
Rushes-yards	13-30	40-156
Passing	83	189
Punt returns	2-(-3)	6-63
Kickoff returns	7-128	0-0
Interception returns	1-75	0-0
Comp.-att.-int.	9-23-0	19-30-1
Sacked-yards lost	4-36	4-34
Punts	8-35	4-45
Fumbles-lost	3-3	1-0
Penalties-yards	5-35	8-72
Time of possession	20:29	39:31

INDIVIDUAL STATISTICS
RUSHING—St. Louis, R. Moore 7-25, Lee 3-(minus 2), Heyward 2-5, Banks 1-2. San Francisco, Hearst 18-81, Floyd 7-13, Levy 6-26, Kirby 4-3, S. Young 3-25, Brohm 2-8.

PASSING—St. Louis, Banks 9-23-0-119. San Francisco, S. Young 19-30-1-223.

RECEIVING—St. Louis, Crawford 3-86, Lee 2-14, Bruce 2-14, R. Moore 1-5, Heyward 1-0. San Francisco, Owens 5-86, Stokes 5-38, Hearst 2-27, Harris 2-25, Clark 2-21, Uwaezuoke 1-13, Floyd 1-11, Kirby 1-2.

MISSED FIELD GOAL ATTEMPTS—None.

INTERCEPTIONS—St. Louis, McNeil 1-75.

KICKOFF RETURNS—St. Louis, Thompson 5-99, Lee 1-15, Kennison 1-14.

PUNT RETURNS—St. Louis, Kennison 2-(minus 3). San Francisco, Uwaezuoke 6-63.

SACKS—St. Louis, Lyle 1, M. Jones 1, Carter 1, Johnson 0.5, O'Neal 0.5. San Francisco, Doleman 2, Stubblefield 1, B. Young 1.

GIANTS 27, CARDINALS 13

Sunday, October 12

N.Y. Giants	3	3	7	14—27
Arizona	0	6	0	7—13

First Quarter
NYG—FG, Daluiso 31, 4:44.

Second Quarter
NYG—FG, Daluiso 48, 0:52.
Ariz.—A. Williams 30 interception return (kick failed), 6:22.

Third Quarter
NYG—Patten 9 pass from Kanell (Daluiso kick), 6:54.

Fourth Quarter
NYG—Wheatley 8 run (Daluiso kick), 0:29.
NYG—Pegram 18 run (Daluiso kick), 9:56.
Ariz.—Case 1 run (Butler kick), 14:07.
Attendance—38,959.

TEAM STATISTICS

	N.Y. Giants	Arizona
First downs	23	19
Rushes-yards	46-239	14-27
Passing	187	208
Punt returns	3-(-28)	1-10
Kickoff returns	2-26	5-104
Interception returns	4-40	1-30
Comp.-att.-int.	13-28-1	22-47-4
Sacked-yards lost	1-11	5-54
Punts	7-35	7-44
Fumbles-lost	0-0	2-1
Penalties-yards	9-67	5-55
Time of possession	34:54	25:06

INDIVIDUAL STATISTICS
RUSHING—New York, Wheatley 22-103, Way 13-91, Pegram 10-47, Cherry 1-(minus 2). Arizona, McElroy 6-1, Centers 4-12, Johnson 2-14, Case 2-0.

PASSING—New York, Kanell 13-28-1-198. Arizona, Case 18-33-2-222, K. Graham 4-14-2-40.

RECEIVING—New York, Patten 3-66, Pegram 3-14, Calloway 2-59, Wheatley 2-18, Way 2-17, Toomer 1-24. Arizona, Sanders 6-59, R. Moore 4-87, Centers 4-37, K. Williams 3-47, Edwards 1-14, Gedney 1-11, Carter 1-8, McElroy 1-2, Johnson 1-(minus 3).

MISSED FIELD GOAL ATTEMPTS—None.

INTERCEPTIONS—New York, Ellsworth 2-40, Sehorn 1-0, Wooten 1-0. Arizona, A. Williams 1-30.

KICKOFF RETURNS—New York, Alexander 2-26. Arizona, K. Williams 4-88, C. Smith 1-16.

PUNT RETURNS—New York, Toomer 3-(minus 28). Arizona, K. Williams 1-10.

SACKS—New York, Strahan 1.5, Harris 1, Galyon 1, Agnew 1, K. Hamilton 0.5. Arizona, Lassiter 1.

FALCONS 23, SAINTS 17

Sunday, October 12

Atlanta	10	6	7	0—23
New Orleans	0	3	0	14—17

First Quarter
Atl.—FG, Andersen 25, 12:11.
Atl.—Emanuel 9 pass from Chandler (Andersen kick), 13:15.

Second Quarter
N.O.—FG, Brien 35, 6:15.
Atl.—FG, Andersen 32, 12:45.
Atl.—FG, Andersen 55, 15:00.

Third Quarter
Atl.—Anderson 2 run (Andersen kick), 2:14.

Fourth Quarter
N.O.—Hastings 16 pass from Wuerffel (Brien kick), 0:05.
N.O.—Bates 1 run (Brien kick), 3:30.
Attendance—65,619.

TEAM STATISTICS

	Atlanta	New Orleans
First downs	14	13
Rushes-yards	31-89	28-80
Passing	77	99
Punt returns	2-20	1-0
Kickoff returns	1-22	1-24
Interception returns	2-10	0-0
Comp.-att.-int.	10-22-0	14-22-2
Sacked-yards lost	5-40	10-76
Punts	6-42	6-41
Fumbles-lost	2-2	5-2
Penalties-yards	6-46	6-39
Time of possession	30:10	29:50

INDIVIDUAL STATISTICS
RUSHING—Atlanta, Anderson 21-62, Hanspard 6-24, Chandler 4-3. New Orleans, Bates 15-31, Zellars 4-18, Shuler 3-9, T. Davis 2-15, Wuerffel 2-6, Bender 1-1, Hastings 1-0.

PASSING—Atlanta, Chandler 10-22-0-117. New Orleans, Wuerffel 9-13-1-120, Shuler 5-9-1-55.

RECEIVING—Atlanta, Emanuel 3-40, Mathis 2-30, Anderson 2-10, Green 1-26, West 1-8, Hanspard 1-3. New Orleans, Hastings 4-96, Farquhar 4-40, Zellars 2-15, T. Davis 2-2, Bates 1-14, Hill 1-8.

MISSED FIELD GOAL ATTEMPTS—None.

INTERCEPTIONS—Atlanta, Booker 2-10.

KICKOFF RETURNS—Atlanta, Hanspard 1-22. New Orleans, Guliford 1-24.

PUNT RETURNS—Atlanta, Kinchen 2-20. New Orleans, Guliford 1-0.

SACKS—Atlanta, Smith 5, Hall 2.5, Owens 1.5, Bennett 1. New Orleans, Fields 2, Harvey 1, J. Johnson 1, Mitchell 1.

JAGUARS 38, EAGLES 21

Sunday, October 12

Philadelphia	0	7	0	14—21
Jacksonville	21	0	7	10—38

First Quarter
Jac.—Stewart 7 run (Hollis kick), 4:02.
Jac.—Stewart 8 run (Hollis kick), 10:58.
Jac.—Stewart 2 run (Hollis kick), 13:18.

Second Quarter
Phi.—Fryar 34 pass from Detmer (Boniol kick), 10:19.

Third Quarter
Jac.—Stewart 1 run (Hollis kick), 11:31.

Fourth Quarter
Jac.—Stewart 1 run (Hollis kick), 2:34.
Phi.—Fryar 9 pass from Peete (Boniol kick), 9:21.
Phi.—Fryar 15 pass from Peete (Boniol kick), 12:24.
Jac.—FG, Hollis 38, 14:05.
Attendance—69,150.

TEAM STATISTICS

	Philadelphia	Jacksonville
First downs	23	21
Rushes-yards	27-90	24-149
Passing	303	157
Punt returns	2-22	3-25
Kickoff returns	6-132	2-31
Interception returns	0-0	1-32
Comp.-att.-int.	27-43-1	15-20-0
Sacked-yards lost	4-22	4-6
Punts	5-32	4-49
Fumbles-lost	2-1	2-1
Penalties-yards	9-65	7-35
Time of possession	36:30	23:30

INDIVIDUAL STATISTICS
RUSHING—Philadelphia, Watters 15-44, Garner 9-37, Detmer 1-7, Peete 1-3, Staley 1-(minus 1). Jacksonville, Stewart 15-102, Means 2-13, Hallock 2-11, Brunell 2-8, Shelton 2-2, Jackson 1-13.

PASSING—Philadelphia, Detmer 15-27-1-202, Peete 12-15-0-123, Johnson 0-1-0-0. Jacksonville, Brunell 14-19-0-153, Johnson 1-1-0-10.

RECEIVING—Philadelphia, Fryar 10-124, Turner 6-59, Watters 4-69, Garner 3-21, Johnson 2-31, C. Jones 1-12, Timpson 1-9. Jacksonville, Smith 5-51, McCardell 4-64, Stewart 2-7, Hallock 1-15, Mitchell 1-13, Moore 1-10, Jackson 1-3.

MISSED FIELD GOAL ATTEMPTS—Philadelphia, Boniol 43.

INTERCEPTIONS—Jacksonville, Figures 1-32.

KICKOFF RETURNS—Philadelphia, Staley 6-132. Jacksonville, Barlow 1-22, Davis 1-9.

PUNT RETURNS—Philadelphia, Solomon 2-22. Jacksonville, Barlow 3-25.

SACKS—Philadelphia, Harris 1, Dent 1, Hall 1, Team 1. Jacksonville, Brackens 1, Simmons 1, Lageman 1, Smeenge 1.

STEELERS 24, COLTS 22

Sunday, October 12

Indianapolis	10	0	3	9—22
Pittsburgh	0	17	7	0—24

First Quarter
Ind.—Harrison 18 pass from Harbaugh (Blanchard kick), 5:14.
Ind.—FG, Blanchard 37, 9:16.

Second Quarter
Pit.—FG, N. Johnson 23, 0:50.
Pit.—Bettis 7 run (N. Johnson kick), 8:27.
Pit.—Lake 38 fumble return (N. Johnson kick), 11:07.

Third Quarter
Ind.—FG, Blanchard 27, 5:35.
Pit.—Hawkins 28 pass from Tomczak (N. Johnson kick), 11:17.

Fourth Quarter
Ind.—FG, Blanchard 35, 7:29.
Ind.—Stablein 5 pass from Harbaugh (pass failed), 11:25.
Attendance—57,925.

TEAM STATISTICS

	Indianapolis	Pittsburgh
First downs	18	17
Rushes-yards	29-79	35-185
Passing	191	142
Punt returns	1-12	3-59
Kickoff returns	4-80	6-143
Interception returns	2-68	1-34
Comp.-att.-int.	19-36-1	11-22-2
Sacked-yards lost	4-28	0-0
Punts	3-48	3-39
Fumbles-lost	1-1	4-4
Penalties-yards	6-69	8-94
Time of possession	33:01	26:59

INDIVIDUAL STATISTICS
RUSHING—Indianapolis, Faulk 20-55, Crockett 7-21, Harbaugh 2-3. Pittsburgh, Bettis 30-164, Stewart 3-11, G. Jones 2-10.
PASSING—Indianapolis, Harbaugh 19-36-1-219. Pittsburgh, Stewart 5-11-0-72, Tomczak 6-11-2-70.
RECEIVING—Indianapolis, Dawkins 6-60, Pollard 3-55, Harrison 3-52, Bailey 2-21, Warren 2-18, Faulk 2-8, Stablein 1-5. Pittsburgh, C. Johnson 3-58, Hawkins 2-39, Thigpen 2-24, Lester 2-8, Bettis 1-14, G. Jones 1-(minus 1).
MISSED FIELD GOAL ATTEMPTS—Indianapolis, Blanchard 42.
INTERCEPTIONS—Indianapolis, Belser 1-37, Mathis 1-31. Pittsburgh, Woolford 1-34.
KICKOFF RETURNS—Indianapolis, Bailey 4-80. Pittsburgh, Adams 5-123, Blackwell 1-20.
PUNT RETURNS—Indianapolis, Stablein 1-12. Pittsburgh, Hawkins 3-59.
SACKS—Pittsburgh, Holmes 1, Lake 1, Steed 1, Conley 1.

OILERS 30, BENGALS 7

Sunday, October 12

Cincinnati	0	0	0	7— 7
Tennessee	7	7	6	10—30

First Quarter
Ten.—Davis 9 pass from McNair (Del Greco kick), 10:22.

Second Quarter
Ten.—Wycheck 39 pass from McNair (Del Greco kick), 12:36.

Third Quarter
Ten.—FG, Del Greco 47, 5:21.
Ten.—FG, Del Greco 45, 12:55.

Fourth Quarter
Ten.—Davis 10 pass from McNair (Del Greco kick), 4:07.
Ten.—FG, Del Greco 19, 9:58.
Cin.—Dillon 21 run (Pelfrey kick), 12:52.
Attendance—17,071.

TEAM STATISTICS

	Cincinnati	Tennessee
First downs	14	26
Rushes-yards	17-55	41-198
Passing	136	193
Punt returns	3-34	3-20
Kickoff returns	6-132	2-31
Interception returns	0-0	0-0
Comp.-att.-int.	18-34-0	16-30-0
Sacked-yards lost	6-33	1-6
Punts	7-49	3-54
Fumbles-lost	2-1	1-0
Penalties-yards	5-71	6-45
Time of possession	22:48	37:12

INDIVIDUAL STATISTICS
RUSHING—Cincinnati, Dillon 8-39, Carter 5-14, Blake 2-10, Milne 1-3, Johnson 1-(minus 11). Tennessee, George 30-106, McNair 6-65, Thomas 4-28, Krieg 1-(minus 1).
PASSING—Cincinnati, Blake 14-28-0-130, Esiason 4-6-0-39. Tennessee, McNair 16-30-0-199.
RECEIVING—Cincinnati, Bieniemy 5-42, Milne 3-29, McGee 3-25, Scott 2-21, Pickens 2-15, Battaglia 1-19, Dillon 1-10, Dunn 1-8. Tennessee, Davis 6-79, Wycheck 4-78, Kent 2-12, Sanders 1-12, Thomas 1-9, George 1-5, Harmon 1-4.
MISSED FIELD GOAL ATTEMPTS—Tennessee, Del Greco 40.
INTERCEPTIONS—None.
KICKOFF RETURNS—Cincinnati, Bieniemy 4-89, Hundon 2-43. Tennessee, Gray 1-19, Roan 1-12.
PUNT RETURNS—Cincinnati, Myers 3-34. Tennessee, Gray 3-20.
SACKS—Cincinnati, Shade 1. Tennessee, Marts 2, Ford 1.5, G. Walker 1, Evans 1, Roberson 0.5.

REDSKINS 21, COWBOYS 16

Monday, October 13

Dallas	3	0	6	7—16
Washington	7	7	7	0—21

First Quarter
Dal.—FG, Cunningham 19, 9:15.
Was.—Davis 2 run (Blanton kick), 12:48.

Second Quarter
Was.—Jenkins 13 pass from Frerotte (Blanton kick), 7:44.

Third Quarter
Was.—Davis 4 run (Blanton kick), 4:11.
Dal.—Coakley 16 fumble return (pass failed), 10:34.

Fourth Quarter
Dal.—Irvin 14 pass from Aikman (Cunningham kick), 5:20.
Attendance—76,159.

TEAM STATISTICS

	Dallas	Washington
First downs	16	16
Rushes-yards	28-115	32-116
Passing	175	139
Punt returns	5-53	0-0
Kickoff returns	3-66	3-67
Interception returns	0-0	0-0
Comp.-att.-int.	17-31-0	12-23-0
Sacked-yards lost	3-18	3-16
Punts	6-41	7-49
Fumbles-lost	1-1	1-1
Penalties-yards	3-20	3-25
Time of possession	30:33	29:27

INDIVIDUAL STATISTICS
RUSHING—Dallas, E. Smith 17-61, S. Williams 8-35, Aikman 3-19. Washington, Davis 22-94, Allen 4-12, Mitchell 3-11, Frerotte 3-(minus 1).
PASSING—Dallas, Aikman 17-31-0-193. Washington, Frerotte 12-23-0-155.
RECEIVING—Dallas, Irvin 5-81, St. Williams 3-34, Miller 3-25, Bjornson 3-17, E. Smith 2-23, LaFleur 1-13. Washington, Bowie 3-6, Shepherd 2-60, Westbrook 2-32, Mitchell 1-20, Allen 1-15, Jenkins 1-13, Asher 1-5, Davis 1-4.
MISSED FIELD GOAL ATTEMPTS—None.
INTERCEPTIONS—None.
KICKOFF RETURNS—Dallas, Walker 2-52, Marion 1-14. Washington, Mitchell 3-67.
PUNT RETURNS—Dallas, Sanders 5-53.
SACKS—Dallas, Godfrey 2, Stoutmire 1. Washington, M. Patton 1, Harvey 1, Jones 1.

WEEK 8

RESULTS

KANSAS CITY 31, San Diego 3
Carolina 13, NEW ORLEANS 0
DALLAS 26, Jacksonville 22
Miami 24, BALTIMORE 13
N.Y. Giants 26, DETROIT 20 (OT)
N.Y. JETS 24, New England 19
OAKLAND 28, Denver 25
PHILADELPHIA 13, Arizona 10 (OT)
Pittsburgh 26, CINCINNATI 10
San Francisco 35, ATLANTA 28
Seattle 17, ST. LOUIS 9
TENNESSEE 28, Washington 14
Buffalo 9, INDIANAPOLIS 6
  Open date: Chicago, Green Bay, Minnesota,
Tampa Bay

STANDINGS

AFC EAST
	W	L	T	Pct.
Miami	5	2	0	.714
New England	5	2	0	.714
N.Y. Jets	5	3	0	.625
Buffalo	4	3	0	.571
Indianapolis	0	7	0	.000

AFC CENTRAL
	W	L	T	Pct.
Jacksonville	5	2	0	.714
Pittsburgh	5	2	0	.714
Baltimore	3	4	0	.429
Tennessee	3	4	0	.429
Cincinnati	1	6	0	.143

AFC WEST
	W	L	T	Pct.
Denver	6	1	0	.857
Kansas City	5	2	0	.714
Seattle	4	3	0	.571
Oakland	3	4	0	.429
San Diego	3	4	0	.429

NFC EAST
	W	L	T	Pct.
N.Y. Giants	5	3	0	.625
Dallas	4	3	0	.571
Washington	4	3	0	.571
Philadelphia	3	4	0	.429
Arizona	1	6	0	.143

NFC CENTRAL
	W	L	T	Pct.
Green Bay	5	2	0	.714
Minnesota	5	2	0	.714
Tampa Bay	5	2	0	.714
Detroit	4	4	0	.500
Chicago	0	7	0	.000

NFC WEST
	W	L	T	Pct.
San Francisco	6	1	0	.857
Carolina	3	4	0	.429
St. Louis	2	5	0	.286
New Orleans	2	6	0	.250
Atlanta	1	6	0	.143

HIGHLIGHTS

Hero of the week: Raiders running back Napoleon Kaufman rushed for 227 yards and one touchdown in carrying Oakland to a 28-25 win over the previously undefeated Broncos. Kaufman ran 57 yards on the first play from scrimmage to set up the game's first touchdown and clinched the victory with an 83-yard TD run in the fourth quarter.

Goat of the week: Jaguars running back James Stewart, who scored five touchdowns the previous week, didn't have any in Jacksonville's 26-22 loss at Dallas. Stewart had only 40 yards on 17 carries as the Cowboys' defense allowed 42 rushing yards.

Sub of the week: Jets coach Bill Parcells benched starting quarterback Neil O'Donnell at halftime and turned to backup Glenn Foley, who came off the bench to pass for 200 yards and one touchdown in rallying the team to a 24-19 win over New England. Foley's 17-of-23 performance included 14 consecutive completions at one point.

Comeback of the week: When Glenn Foley entered the game in the third quarter, the Jets trailed, 12-3. But he rallied New York with consistent passing, including strikes of 20, 18, 23, 21 and 27 yards. With 4:28 left in the game, Foley threw a 5-yard TD pass to complete a 76-yard drive.

Blowout of the week: Everything that could go wrong did go wrong for the Chargers in a 31-3 loss at Kansas City on Thursday night. They committed 19 penalties—three short of the NFL record—for 146 yards. Meanwhile, Elvis Grbac threw two first-half touchdown passes to Andre Rison and also scored on a 1-yard run. Grbac finished with 235 yards.

Nail-biter of the week: Detroit's Scott Mitchell threw a 4-yard touchdown pass with 1:55 remaining, giving the Lions a 20-20 tie with the Giants and sending the game into overtime. But the extra session didn't last long, as Giants quarterback Danny Kanell connected with Chris Calloway on a 68-yard touchdown pass on the third play. Calloway hauled in Kanell's pass at the Lions' 45 just as cornerback Corey Raymond fell down. Calloway went the rest of the way untouched.

Hit of the week: Atlanta quarterback Chris Chandler failed to finish his fourth consecutive home game when he suffered his second concussion of the season in a 35-28 loss to San Francisco. The hit by defensive lineman Junior Bryant knocked out Chandler in the fourth quarter.

Oddity of the week: Jets kicker John Hall continued his strange season when he missed a 68-yard field-goal attempt to conclude the first half. The kick, the longest field-goal attempt in the NFL since the Broncos' Fred Steinfort attempted a 73-yarder at New England in 1980, was short. Hall made a 35-yarder but missed from 35 and 36 yards. For the season, he had made 5-of-6 tries from beyond 40 yards but just 9-of-15 from inside the 40.

Top rusher: Napoleon Kaufman's 227-yard rushing performance broke Bo Jackson's Raiders record of 221 yards set against Seattle on November 30, 1987.

Top passer: Vinny Testaverde was 32-of-47 for 331 yards and one touchdown in Baltimore's 24-13 loss to Miami.

Top receiver: The Giants' Chris Calloway caught five passes for 145 yards and one touchdown against Detroit.

Notes: Since Norv Turner became Redskins coach, they are 0-6 in games played the week after they have played the Cowboys. . . . Saints quarterback Danny Wuerffel had a rough day against the Panthers. He was sacked seven times, hurried 12 times and had three of his passes batted down. Wuerffel had been sacked 14 times in the past six quarters. . . . The Oilers won their second consecutive game before their biggest home crowd of the season as 31,042 fans half-filled the Liberty Bowl in Memphis. The previous high of 30,171 was on opening day. . . . Herschel Walker provided the offensive spark in Dallas' 26-22 victory over Jacksonville. Starting at fullback in place of the injured Daryl Johnston, Walker turned a short reception over the middle into a 64-yard TD to erase a 22-19 Jaguars lead.

Quote of the week: Ravens coach Ted Marchibroda was beside himself about his team's inept defense: "Teams that can't throw, they can't throw until they get to us. Teams that can't run, when they hit us, we make them well."

GAME SUMMARIES

CHIEFS 31, CHARGERS 3

Thursday, October 16

San Diego	0	0	3	0— 3
Kansas City	7	17	0	7—31

First Quarter
K.C.—Grbac 1 run (Stoyanovich kick), 11:43.
Second Quarter
K.C.—Rison 10 pass from Grbac (Stoyanovich kick), 8:10.
K.C.—Rison 5 pass from Grbac (Stoyanovich kick), 12:39.
K.C.—FG, Stoyanovich 45, 14:58.
Third Quarter
S.D.—FG, G. Davis 26, 14:23.
Fourth Quarter
K.C.—Allen 6 run (Stoyanovich kick), 4:26.
Attendance—77,196.

TEAM STATISTICS

	San Diego	Kansas City
First downs	12	25
Rushes-yards	18-69	33-89
Passing	189	224
Punt returns	4-25	4-34
Kickoff returns	3-36	2-43
Interception returns	0-0	2-5
Comp.-att.-int.	14-43-2	20-40-0
Sacked-yards lost	2-6	2-11
Punts	7-40	5-42
Fumbles-lost	3-0	2-1
Penalties-yards	19-146	7-41
Time of possession	25:57	34:03

INDIVIDUAL STATISTICS
RUSHING—San Diego, Brown 12-59, Everett 3-10, Fletcher 3-0. Kansas City, Hill 11-26, Allen 7-29, Bennett 6-14, Grbac 4-21, Anders 3-1, Gannon 2-(minus 2).
PASSING—San Diego, Everett 9-25-2-137, Humphries 3-10-0-45, Whelihan 2-8-0-13. Kansas City, Grbac 20-40-0-235.
RECEIVING—San Diego, Fletcher 5-45, F. Jones 4-81, C. Jones 2-37, Metcalf 2-24, Brown 1-8. Kansas City, Rison 8-86, Popson 4-54, Anders 2-42, Dawson 2-22, Hill 2-8, Allen 1-13, Vanover 1-10.
MISSED FIELD GOAL ATTEMPTS—None.
INTERCEPTIONS—Kansas City, Edwards 1-3, McMillian 1-2.
KICKOFF RETURNS—San Diego, Rachal 2-36, Bordelon 1-0. Kansas City, Vanover 2-43.
PUNT RETURNS—San Diego, Metcalf 4-25. Kansas City, Vanover 4-34.
SACKS—San Diego, Lee 1, Team 1. Kansas City, Edwards 1, Booker 1.

OILERS 28, REDSKINS 14

Sunday, October 19

Washington	0	0	14	0—14
Tennessee	0	14	7	7—28

Second Quarter
Ten.—McNair 2 run (Del Greco kick), 0:41.
Ten.—George 3 run (Del Greco kick), 8:47.
Third Quarter
Ten.—Thomas 5 run (Del Greco kick), 5:03.
Was.—Ellard 13 pass from Frerotte (Blanton kick), 7:15.
Was.—Ellard 10 pass from Frerotte (Blanton kick), 12:14.
Fourth Quarter
Ten.—George 6 run (Del Greco kick), 12:22.
Attendance—31,042.

TEAM STATISTICS

	Washington	Tennessee
First downs	18	23
Rushes-yards	18-92	46-204
Passing	220	185
Punt returns	1-9	1-10
Kickoff returns	4-79	3-45
Interception returns	0-0	3-43
Comp.-att.-int.	16-31-3	13-21-0
Sacked-yards lost	1-8	2-7
Punts	3-51	5-35
Fumbles-lost	1-0	1-0
Penalties-yards	2-15	2-25
Time of possession	24:38	35:22

INDIVIDUAL STATISTICS
RUSHING—Washington, Davis 13-45, Mitchell 3-15, Frerotte 2-32. Tennessee, George 31-125, McNair 10-53, Thomas 4-24, Harmon 1-2.
PASSING—Washington, Frerotte 16-31-3-228. Tennessee, McNair 13-21-0-192.
RECEIVING—Washington, Ellard 6-84, Shepherd 4-81, Davis 2-29, Asher 2-14, Connell 1-14, Bowie 1-6. Tennessee, Davis 5-72, Wycheck 4-54, Roan 2-34, Mason 2-32.
MISSED FIELD GOAL ATTEMPTS—Washington, Blanton 43.
INTERCEPTIONS—Tennessee, Robertson 1-25, D. Walker 1-14, D. Lewis 1-4.
KICKOFF RETURNS—Washington, Mitchell 4-79. Tennessee, Mason 3-45.
PUNT RETURNS—Washington, Mitchell 1-9. Tennessee, Gray 1-10.
SACKS—Washington, Mims 1, M. Patton 0.5, Dishman 0.5. Tennessee, G. Walker 1.

COWBOYS 26, JAGUARS 22

Sunday, October 19

Jacksonville	7	0	7	8—22
Dallas	3	10	6	7—26

First Quarter
Dal.—FG, Cunningham 37, 8:21.
Jac.—Smith 7 pass from Brunell (Hollis kick), 14:09.
Second Quarter
Dal.—E. Smith 1 run (Cunningham kick), 8:24.
Dal.—FG, Cunningham 21, 13:49.
Third Quarter
Dal.—St. Williams 2 pass from Aikman (pass failed), 7:19.
Jac.—McCardell 5 pass from Brunell (Hollis kick), 11:38.
Fourth Quarter
Jac.—Brown 2 pass from Brunell (Jackson pass from Brunell), 5:54.
Dal.—Walker 64 pass from Aikman (Gowin kick), 8:33.
Attendance—64,464.

TEAM STATISTICS

	Jacksonville	Dallas
First downs	15	24
Rushes-yards	18-42	33-99
Passing	229	238
Punt returns	1-12	5-81
Kickoff returns	6-135	4-83
Interception returns	0-0	1-8
Comp.-att.-int.	21-31-1	21-32-0
Sacked-yards lost	2-13	2-24
Punts	5-54	3-44
Fumbles-lost	0-0	1-0
Penalties-yards	10-98	4-40
Time of possession	26:36	33:24

INDIVIDUAL STATISTICS
RUSHING—Jacksonville, Stewart 17-40, Jordan 1-2. Dallas, E. Smith 24-75, S. Williams 4-16, Aikman 4-7, Walker 1-1.
PASSING—Jacksonville, Brunell 21-31-1-242. Dallas, Aikman 21-32-0-262.
RECEIVING—Jacksonville, McCardell 7-120, Mitchell 5-64, Hallock 3-11, Stewart 2-24, Brown 2-13. Dallas, Bjornson 5-36, Walker 4-88, Irvin 3-57, Miller 3-38, St. Williams 3-25, E. Smith 3-18.
MISSED FIELD GOAL ATTEMPTS—Dallas, Gowin 63.
INTERCEPTIONS—Dallas, Stoutmire 1-8.
KICKOFF RETURNS—Jacksonville, Jackson 6-135. Dallas, Walker 3-64, Marion 1-19.
PUNT RETURNS—Jacksonville, Barlow 1-12. Dallas, Sanders 5-81.
SACKS—Jacksonville, Kopp 1, Davey 1. Dallas, Carver 1, Anderson 1.

SEAHAWKS 17, RAMS 9

Sunday, October 19

Seattle	0	3	7	7—17
St. Louis	0	3	3	3— 9

Second Quarter
Sea.—FG, Peterson 24, 4:53.
St.L.—FG, Wilkins 51, 13:48.

Third Quarter
Sea.—Warren 1 run (Peterson kick), 4:00.
St.L.—FG, Wilkins 29, 9:14.

Fourth Quarter
Sea.—Broussard 9 run (Peterson kick), 2:32.
St.L.—FG, Wilkins 46, 10:40.
Attendance—64,819.

TEAM STATISTICS

	Seattle	St. Louis
First downs	27	10
Rushes-yards	30-106	17-37
Passing	251	155
Punt returns	4-35	1-5
Kickoff returns	4-100	4-67
Interception returns	1-0	2-22
Comp.-att.-int.	24-36-2	17-31-1
Sacked-yards lost	1-10	2-9
Punts	5-38	5-45
Fumbles-lost	0-0	2-0
Penalties-yards	7-84	9-51
Time of possession	38:11	21:49

INDIVIDUAL STATISTICS
RUSHING—Seattle, Warren 13-37, Broussard 8-41, Smith 8-21, Moon 1-7. St. Louis, Phillips 9-18, Heyward 3-8, Banks 3-4, Lee 1-7, R. Moore 1-0.
PASSING—Seattle, Moon 24-36-2-261. St. Louis, Banks 17-31-1-164.
RECEIVING—Seattle, Galloway 8-75, Br. Blades 5-39, Smith 3-33, Warren 2-25, McKnight 2-25, Harris 1-34, Broussard 1-16, Crumpler 1-8, Pritchard 1-6. St. Louis, Bruce 6-68, Lee 3-27, Conwell 2-25, Crawford 2-24, Heyward 2-14, Floyd 1-4, Phillips 1-2.
MISSED FIELD GOAL ATTEMPTS—None.
INTERCEPTIONS—Seattle, Be. Blades 1-0. St. Louis, Farr 1-22, McNeil 1-0.
KICKOFF RETURNS—Seattle, Broussard 3-83, Harris 1-17. St. Louis, Thompson 4-67.
PUNT RETURNS—Seattle, Harris 4-35. St. Louis, Floyd 1-5.
SACKS—Seattle, C. Brown 1, Adams 1. St. Louis, McCleon 1.

PANTHERS 13, SAINTS 0
Sunday, October 19

Carolina	10	3	0	0—13
New Orleans	0	0	0	0—0

First Quarter
Car.—FG, Kasay 25, 9:24.
Car.—Johnson 14 pass from Collins (Kasay kick), 14:17.

Second Quarter
Car.—FG, Kasay 23, 14:53.
Attendance—50,963.

TEAM STATISTICS

	Carolina	New Orleans
First downs	15	15
Rushes-yards	29-73	26-111
Passing	196	89
Punt returns	4-53	1-5
Kickoff returns	1-12	4-47
Interception returns	2-10	1-0
Comp.-att.-int.	23-31-1	13-32-2
Sacked-yards lost	1-8	7-43
Punts	6-39	6-49
Fumbles-lost	0-0	2-0
Penalties-yards	3-17	5-32
Time of possession	30:41	29:19

INDIVIDUAL STATISTICS
RUSHING—Carolina, Johnson 14-25, Biakabutuka 9-36, Greene 4-15, Collins 2-(minus 3). New Orleans, T. Davis 12-45, Zellars 11-40, Wuerffel 2-15, Hill 1-11.
PASSING—Carolina, Collins 23-31-1-204. New Orleans, Wuerffel 13-32-2-132.
RECEIVING—Carolina, Carrier 5-51, Johnson 5-31, Walls 4-47, Carruth 4-40, Greene 3-18, Oliver 1-10, Ismail 1-7. New Orleans, Hill 5-79, Farquhar 2-14, Zellars 2-13, T. Davis 2-3, Hastings 1-13, Guliford 1-10.
MISSED FIELD GOAL ATTEMPTS—None.
INTERCEPTIONS—Carolina, Davis 2-10. New Orleans, Knight 1-0.
KICKOFF RETURNS—Carolina, S. Mills 1-12. New Orleans, Guliford 2-46, Bech 1-1, Tomich 1-0.
PUNT RETURNS—Carolina, Oliver 4-53. New Orleans, Guliford 1-5.
SACKS—Carolina, Barrow 2, Royal 1, Minter 1, Seals 1, King 1, Kragen 1. New Orleans, J. Johnson 1.

RAIDERS 28, BRONCOS 25
Sunday, October 19

Denver	7	3	7	8—25
Oakland	7	7	7	7—28

First Quarter
Oak.—Jett 14 pass from George (Ford kick), 2:34.
Den.—Davis 2 run (Elam kick), 14:59.

Second Quarter
Oak.—Dudley 5 pass from George (Ford kick), 4:49.
Den.—FG, Elam 44, 15:00.

Third Quarter
Den.—Davis 3 run (Elam kick), 6:23.
Oak.—Turner 65 fumble return (Ford kick), 12:45.

Fourth Quarter
Oak.—Kaufman 83 run (Ford kick), 7:06.
Den.—McCaffrey 28 pass from Elway (Davis run), 12:45.
Attendance—57,006.

TEAM STATISTICS

	Denver	Oakland
First downs	25	12
Rushes-yards	29-147	32-243
Passing	294	81
Punt returns	4-31	3-10
Kickoff returns	4-73	4-67
Interception returns	1-7	0-0
Comp.-att.-int.	26-46-0	9-12-1
Sacked-yards lost	3-15	2-15
Punts	5-43	5-46
Fumbles-lost	4-1	1-1
Penalties-yards	10-70	7-41
Time of possession	35:10	24:50

INDIVIDUAL STATISTICS
RUSHING—Denver, Davis 23-85, Elway 5-48, R. Smith 1-14. Oakland, Kaufman 28-227, George 1-12, Fenner 1-4, Hall 1-3, T. Brown 1-(minus 3).
PASSING—Denver, Elway 26-46-0-309. Oakland, George 9-12-1-96.
RECEIVING—Denver, Sharpe 8-94, Davis 7-70, R. Smith 5-58, McCaffrey 3-61, Griffith 1-20, D. Smith 1-7, Nalen 1-(minus 1). Oakland, Jett 3-43, T. Brown 2-33, Fenner 2-14, Dudley 2-6.
MISSED FIELD GOAL ATTEMPTS—Denver, Elam 40, 43.
INTERCEPTIONS—Denver, Romanowski 1-7.
KICKOFF RETURNS—Denver, Hebron 3-66, Loville 1-7. Oakland, Howard 4-67.
PUNT RETURNS—Denver, Gordon 4-31. Oakland, Howard 3-10.
SACKS—Denver, Williams 1, N. Smith 1. Oakland, Maryland 1, McGlockton 1, Johnstone 1.

DOLPHINS 24, RAVENS 13
Sunday, October 19

Miami	14	7	0	3—24
Baltimore	3	0	3	7—13

First Quarter
Bal.—FG, Stover 38, 5:25.
Mia.—Abdul-Jabbar 5 run (Mare kick), 10:21.
Mia.—Abdul-Jabbar 5 run (Mare kick), 12:21.

Second Quarter
Mia.—Abdul-Jabbar 6 run (Mare kick), 10:13.

Third Quarter
Bal.—FG, Stover 23, 8:47.

Fourth Quarter
Mia.—FG, Mare 23, 1:08.
Bal.—Alexander 34 pass from Testaverde (Stover kick), 4:09.
Attendance—64,354.

TEAM STATISTICS

	Miami	Baltimore
First downs	24	20
Rushes-yards	41-148	16-54
Passing	189	331
Punt returns	2-23	1-16
Kickoff returns	2-43	5-86
Interception returns	0-0	0-0
Comp.-att.-int.	19-27-0	32-47-0
Sacked-yards lost	0-0	0-0
Punts	2-37	2-38
Fumbles-lost	2-1	3-2
Penalties-yards	5-31	5-55
Time of possession	35:12	24:48

INDIVIDUAL STATISTICS

RUSHING—Miami, Abdul-Jabbar 22-108, Spikes 16-46, Marino 2-0, Jordan 1-(minus 6). Baltimore, Morris 13-44, Testaverde 2-10, Graham 1-0.

PASSING—Miami, Marino 19-27-0-189. Baltimore, Testaverde 32-47-0-331.

RECEIVING—Miami, McDuffie 7-77, Drayton 3-33, Parmalee 3-27, L. Thomas 2-15, Abdul-Jabbar 1-14, Jordan 1-10, Spikes 1-7, McPhail 1-6. Baltimore, Jackson 7-85, J. Lewis 6-105, Alexander 6-79, Green 5-38, Morris 3-12, Graham 3-5, Kinchen 1-4, Yarborough 1-3.

MISSED FIELD GOAL ATTEMPTS—None.

INTERCEPTIONS—None.

KICKOFF RETURNS—Miami, Spikes 1-25, C. Harris 1-18. Baltimore, J. Lewis 3-51, Graham 2-35.

PUNT RETURNS—Miami, Jordan 2-23. Baltimore, J. Lewis 1-16.

SACKS—None.

EAGLES 13, CARDINALS 10

Sunday, October 19

Arizona	0	0	3	7	0—10
Philadelphia	0	7	0	3	3—13

Second Quarter
Phi.—Watters 2 run (Boniol kick), 3:10.

Third Quarter
Ariz.—FG, Nedney 23, 5:24.

Fourth Quarter
Ariz.—K. Williams 31 pass from Plummer (Nedney kick), 11:53.
Phi.—FG, Boniol 38, 14:34.

Overtime
Phi.—FG, Boniol 24, 4:02.
Attendance—66,860.

TEAM STATISTICS

	Arizona	Philadelphia
First downs	15	25
Rushes-yards	28-92	32-130
Passing	143	277
Punt returns	3-39	2-15
Kickoff returns	4-118	2-66
Interception returns	2-10	0-0
Comp.-att.-int.	16-31-0	23-36-2
Sacked-yards lost	7-49	4-21
Punts	7-43	4-51
Fumbles-lost	1-1	2-2
Penalties-yards	4-32	3-25
Time of possession	32:49	31:13

INDIVIDUAL STATISTICS

RUSHING—Arizona, Centers 11-37, Johnson 7-23, Case 5-8, Plummer 3-22, McElroy 2-2. Philadelphia, Watters 24-83, Peete 3-21, Turner 3-1, Garner 2-25.

PASSING—Arizona, Case 11-22-0-94, Plummer 5-9-0-98. Philadelphia, Peete 23-36-2-298.

RECEIVING—Arizona, R. Moore 6-101, Edwards 3-17, K. Williams 2-40, Gedney 2-16, Centers 1-16, Sanders 1-8, McElroy 1-(minus 6). Philadelphia, Fryar 5-85, Turner 5-43, Solomon 4-57, Watters 3-39, Garner 3-38, Johnson 1-18, Seay 1-12, Lewis 1-6.

MISSED FIELD GOAL ATTEMPTS—Arizona, Nedney 40. Philadelphia, Boniol 40.

INTERCEPTIONS—Arizona, Lassiter 1-10, Rice 1-0.

KICKOFF RETURNS—Arizona, K. Williams 4-92. Philadelphia, Staley 2-66.

PUNT RETURNS—Arizona, K. Williams 3-39. Philadelphia, Seay 2-15.

SACKS—Arizona, Lassiter 1, Howard 1, Caldwell 1, M. Smith 1. Philadelphia, W. Thomas 1, Zordich 1, Willis 1, Hall 1, Dent 1, Smith 1, J. Jones 1.

GIANTS 26, LIONS 20

Sunday, October 19

N.Y. Giants	7	3	7	3	6—26
Detroit	0	10	3	7	0—20

First Quarter
NYG—Cross 2 pass from Kanell (Daluiso kick), 7:56.

Second Quarter
Det.—FG, Hanson 22, 3:57.
Det.—Sanders 8 run (Hanson kick), 9:53.
NYG—FG, Daluiso 52, 14:58.

Third Quarter
NYG—Toomer 53 punt return (Daluiso kick), 5:36.
Det.—FG, Hanson 28, 10:48.

Fourth Quarter
NYG—FG, Daluiso 47, 0:57.
Det.—Morton 4 pass from Mitchell (Hanson kick), 13:05.

Overtime
NYG—Calloway 68 pass from Kanell, 1:40.
Attendance—70,069.

TEAM STATISTICS

	N.Y. Giants	Detroit
First downs	15	20
Rushes-yards	29-121	30-111
Passing	210	226
Punt returns	5-78	2-11
Kickoff returns	4-68	4-93
Interception returns	0-0	1-(-5)
Comp.-att.-int.	17-31-1	19-32-0
Sacked-yards lost	1-10	3-17
Punts	8-46	6-44
Fumbles-lost	0-0	2-2
Penalties-yards	11-76	6-53
Time of possession	30:19	31:21

INDIVIDUAL STATISTICS

RUSHING—New York, Way 13-90, Wheatley 13-16, Pegram 3-15. Detroit, Sanders 24-105, Vardell 3-5, Mitchell 2-(minus 1), Schlesinger 1-2.

PASSING—New York, Kanell 17-31-1-220. Detroit, Mitchell 19-32-0-243.

RECEIVING—New York, Calloway 5-145, Pegram 5-28, Cross 3-15, Toomer 1-16, Way 1-8, Patten 1-5, Wheatley 1-3. Detroit, Moore 7-88, Morton 5-72, Vardell 3-39, Sanders 2-21, Schlesinger 1-12, Metzelaars 1-11.

MISSED FIELD GOAL ATTEMPTS—None.

INTERCEPTIONS—Detroit, Malone 1-(minus 5).

KICKOFF RETURNS—New York, Pegram 4-68. Detroit, Milburn 3-82, Rivers 1-11.

PUNT RETURNS—New York, Toomer 5-78. Detroit, Milburn 2-11.

SACKS—New York, Harris 1.5, Strahan 1, Galyon 0.5. Detroit, Porcher 0.5, Bonham 0.5.

JETS 24, PATRIOTS 19

Sunday, October 19

New England	0	5	14	0—19	
N.Y. Jets	3	0	14	7—24	

First Quarter
NYJ—FG, Hall 35, 13:33.

Second Quarter
N.E.—Safety, O'Donnell intentional grounding in the end zone, 7:30.
N.E.—FG, Vinatieri 24, 14:16.

Third Quarter
N.E.—Coates 8 pass from Bledsoe (Vinatieri kick), 1:24.
NYJ—L. Johnson 1 run (Hall kick), 5:36.
N.E.—Brown 23 pass from Bledsoe (Vinatieri kick), 9:24.
NYJ—Murrell 5 run (Hall kick), 13:09.

Fourth Quarter
NYJ—Neal 5 pass from Foley (Hall kick), 4:28.
Attendance—71,061.

TEAM STATISTICS

	New England	N.Y. Jets
First downs	19	22
Rushes-yards	25-105	22-76
Passing	267	254
Punt returns	1-8	1-8
Kickoff returns	4-68	4-64
Interception returns	0-0	1-45
Comp.-att.-int.	24-38-1	23-38-0
Sacked-yards lost	3-27	1-5
Punts	4-41	2-44
Fumbles-lost	0-0	1-0
Penalties-yards	6-74	7-43
Time of possession	33:49	26:11

INDIVIDUAL STATISTICS

RUSHING—New England, Martin 21-87, Bledsoe 3-17, Byars 1-1. New York, Murrell 14-49, L. Johnson 4-8, Foley 2-(minus 4), Ward 1-21, Anderson 1-2.

PASSING—New England, Bledsoe 24-38-1-294. New York, Foley 17-23-0-200, O'Donnell 6-15-0-59.

RECEIVING—New England, Brown 5-125, Martin 5-29, Coates 4-48, Meggett 3-38, Glenn 3-13, Gash 2-22, Jefferson 1-11, Brisby 1-8. New York, Graham 6-79, K. Johnson 4-66, Chrebet 2-39, Brady 2-23, Baxter 2-13, Anderson 2-11, Murrell 2-7, L. Johnson 1-11, Ward 1-5, Neal 1-5.

1997 REVIEW Week 8

MISSED FIELD GOAL ATTEMPTS—New York, Hall 35, 68, 36.
INTERCEPTIONS—New York, Henderson 1-45.
KICKOFF RETURNS—New England, Meggett 2-37, Canty 2-31. New York, Glenn 3-42, L. Johnson 1-22.
PUNT RETURNS—New England, Meggett 1-8. New York, L. Johnson 1-8.
SACKS—New England, Wheeler 1. New York, Lewis 1.5, Green 1, Ferguson 0.5.

49ERS 35, FALCONS 28

Sunday, October 19

San Francisco	7	14	7	7—35
Atlanta	7	7	7	7—28

First Quarter
Atl.—Emanuel 27 pass from Anderson (Andersen kick), 9:36.
S.F.—Owens 5 pass from S. Young (Anderson kick), 12:33.

Second Quarter
S.F.—Kirby 1 run (2-pt conversion failed), 7:19.
S.F.—Kirby 7 run (Kirby run), 11:25.
Atl.—Santiago 7 pass from Chandler (Andersen kick), 14:12.

Third Quarter
S.F.—Owens 31 pass from S. Young (Anderson kick), 11:15.
Atl.—Kinchen 53 pass from Chandler (Andersen kick), 13:02.

Fourth Quarter
S.F.—Floyd 1 run (Anderson kick), 0:03.
Atl.—Mathis 4 pass from Tolliver (Andersen kick), 13:46.
Attendance—53,378.

TEAM STATISTICS

	San Fran.	Atlanta
First downs	24	19
Rushes-yards	35-197	16-39
Passing	241	253
Punt returns	0-0	2-46
Kickoff returns	2-56	6-152
Interception returns	0-0	1-0
Comp.-att.-int.	16-25-1	22-44-0
Sacked-yards lost	3-18	6-46
Punts	3-48	5-46
Fumbles-lost	0-0	2-0
Penalties-yards	11-90	9-80
Time of possession	32:02	27:58

INDIVIDUAL STATISTICS
RUSHING—San Francisco, Hearst 18-105, Floyd 7-39, Kirby 6-24, S. Young 4-29. Atlanta, Anderson 13-19, Tolliver 1-12, Hanspard 1-6, Christian 1-2.
PASSING—San Francisco, S. Young 16-25-1-259. Atlanta, Chandler 15-30-0-230, Tolliver 6-13-0-42, Anderson 1-1-0-27.
RECEIVING—San Francisco, Owens 6-93, Stokes 4-52, Kirby 3-93, Floyd 2-15, Clark 1-6. Atlanta, Mathis 7-75, Emanuel 4-60, Kinchen 3-85, Anderson 2-28, Haynes 2-23, Santiago 2-11, West 1-13, Green 1-4.
MISSED FIELD GOAL ATTEMPTS—None.
INTERCEPTIONS—Atlanta, Bradford 1-0.
KICKOFF RETURNS—San Francisco, Levy 2-56. Atlanta, Hanspard 4-107, Kozlowski 1-26, Bolden 1-19.
PUNT RETURNS—Atlanta, Kinchen 2-9.
SACKS—San Francisco, Stubblefield 2, Barker 2, B. Young 1, Greene 1. Atlanta, Owens 1.5, Bennett 1, Dronett 0.5.

STEELERS 26, BENGALS 10

Sunday, October 19

Pittsburgh	0	13	7	6—26
Cincinnati	7	0	3	0—10

First Quarter
Cin.—Carter 6 run (Pelfrey kick), 11:33.

Second Quarter
Pit.—G. Jones 11 pass from Stewart (pass failed), 0:57.
Pit.—Bettis 1 run (N. Johnson kick), 11:51.

Third Quarter
Pit.—Thigpen 11 pass from Stewart (N. Johnson kick), 6:08.
Cin.—FG, Pelfrey 33, 10:35.

Fourth Quarter
Pit.—FG, N. Johnson 43, 0:15.
Pit.—FG, N. Johnson 32, 13:33.
Attendance—60,020.

TEAM STATISTICS

	Pittsburgh	Cincinnati
First downs	24	14
Rushes-yards	45-166	21-71
Passing	246	165
Punt returns	2-(-1)	1-18
Kickoff returns	3-68	6-119
Interception returns	2-4	2-25
Comp.-att.-int.	16-33-2	15-29-2
Sacked-yards lost	0-0	2-13
Punts	3-42	5-46
Fumbles-lost	0-0	2-2
Penalties-yards	2-15	2-10
Time of possession	36:58	23:02

INDIVIDUAL STATISTICS
RUSHING—Pittsburgh, Bettis 34-135, Stewart 4-16, G. Jones 3-7, Tomczak 2-(minus 2), Lester 1-6, Witman 1-4. Cincinnati, Carter 16-63, Dillon 5-8.
PASSING—Pittsburgh, Stewart 16-33-2-246. Cincinnati, Blake 15-29-2-178.
RECEIVING—Pittsburgh, Thigpen 6-120, Hawkins 3-58, Lyons 3-29, G. Jones 3-25, Lester 1-14. Cincinnati, Pickens 4-81, Bieniemy 3-35, Carter 3-26, Milne 2-3, McGee 1-14, Dillon 1-12, Scott 1-7.
MISSED FIELD GOAL ATTEMPTS—None.
INTERCEPTIONS—Pittsburgh, Lake 1-4, Perry 1-0. Cincinnati, Myers 1-25, Sawyer 1-0.
KICKOFF RETURNS—Pittsburgh, Coleman 3-68. Cincinnati, Bieniemy 3-70, Hundon 3-49.
PUNT RETURNS—Pittsburgh, Coleman 2-(minus 1). Cincinnati, Myers 1-18.
SACKS—Pittsburgh, Henry 1, Conley 1.

BILLS 9, COLTS 6

Monday, October 20

Buffalo	3	3	0	3—9
Indianapolis	0	0	3	3—6

First Quarter
Buf.—FG, Christie 22, 6:18.

Second Quarter
Buf.—FG, Christie 47, 10:44.

Third Quarter
Ind.—FG, Blanchard 39, 14:26.

Fourth Quarter
Ind.—FG, Blanchard 32, 8:48.
Buf.—FG, Christie 27, 14:57.
Attendance—61,139.

TEAM STATISTICS

	Buffalo	Indianapolis
First downs	16	15
Rushes-yards	27-90	25-94
Passing	156	145
Punt returns	2-11	1-2
Kickoff returns	2-34	3-63
Interception returns	0-0	0-0
Comp.-att.-int.	17-22-0	14-18-0
Sacked-yards lost	3-28	5-26
Punts	3-51	4-43
Fumbles-lost	1-0	1-0
Penalties-yards	5-35	6-76
Time of possession	28:14	31:46

INDIVIDUAL STATISTICS
RUSHING—Buffalo, A. Smith 15-42, Thomas 10-42, Collins 2-6. Indianapolis, Faulk 16-54, Crockett 5-20, Warren 3-13, Harbaugh 1-7.
PASSING—Buffalo, Collins 17-22-0-184. Indianapolis, Harbaugh 9-12-0-109, Justin 5-6-0-62.
RECEIVING—Buffalo, Moulds 5-75, Early 4-70, Reed 4-35, Thomas 2-(minus 4), Riemersma 1-4, Johnson 1-2. Indianapolis, Faulk 5-50, Harrison 3-57, Stablein 3-28, Dawkins 2-24, Bailey 1-12.
MISSED FIELD GOAL ATTEMPTS—Buffalo, Christie 32. Indianapolis, Blanchard 51.
INTERCEPTIONS—None.
KICKOFF RETURNS—Buffalo, Moulds 2-34. Indianapolis, Bailey 3-63.
PUNT RETURNS—Buffalo, Burris 2-11. Indianapolis, Stablein 1-2.
SACKS—Buffalo, B. Smith 2, Paup 1, Washington 1, Moran 1. Indianapolis, Footman 2, Blackmon 1.

WEEK 9

RESULTS

Baltimore 20, WASHINGTON 17
CAROLINA 21, Atlanta 12
Denver 23, BUFFALO 20 (OT)
Kansas City 28, ST. LOUIS 20
Minnesota 10, TAMPA BAY 6
N.Y. GIANTS 29, Cincinnati 27
PHILADELPHIA 13, Dallas 12
PITTSBURGH 23, Jacksonville 17 (OT)
SAN DIEGO 35, Indianapolis 19
San Francisco 23, NEW ORLEANS 0
SEATTLE 45, Oakland 34
Tennessee 41, ARIZONA 14
Chicago 36, MIAMI 33 (OT)
Green Bay 28, NEW ENGLAND 10
   Open date: Detroit, N.Y. Jets

STANDINGS

AFC EAST	W	L	T	Pct.
Miami	5	3	0	.625
New England	5	3	0	.625
N.Y. Jets	5	3	0	.625
Buffalo	4	4	0	.500
Indianapolis	0	8	0	.000

AFC CENTRAL	W	L	T	Pct.
Pittsburgh	6	2	0	.750
Jacksonville	5	3	0	.625
Baltimore	4	4	0	.500
Tennessee	4	4	0	.500
Cincinnati	1	7	0	.125

AFC WEST	W	L	T	Pct.
Denver	7	1	0	.875
Kansas City	6	2	0	.750
Seattle	5	3	0	.625
San Diego	4	4	0	.500
Oakland	3	5	0	.375

NFC EAST	W	L	T	Pct.
N.Y. Giants	6	3	0	.667
Dallas	4	4	0	.500
Philadelphia	4	4	0	.500
Washington	4	4	0	.500
Arizona	1	7	0	.125

NFC CENTRAL	W	L	T	Pct.
Green Bay	6	2	0	.750
Minnesota	6	2	0	.750
Tampa Bay	5	3	0	.625
Detroit	4	4	0	.500
Chicago	1	7	0	.125

NFC WEST	W	L	T	Pct.
San Francisco	7	1	0	.875
Carolina	4	4	0	.500
St. Louis	2	6	0	.250
New Orleans	2	7	0	.222
Atlanta	1	7	0	.125

HIGHLIGHTS

Hero of the week: Seattle's Warren Moon was 28-of-44 for 409 yards and five touchdowns, three of them to Joey Galloway, in the Seahawks' 45-34 victory over Oakland. Moon's five TD passes equaled his personal best and tied a club record.

Goat of the week: Falcons rookie Tony Graziani, making his first NFL start, was just 4-of-18 passing for 24 yards and two interceptions in a 21-12 loss to Carolina. Atlanta needed nearly 25 minutes to get a first down, and at halftime coach Dan Reeves decided he had seen enough of the rookie quarterback.

Sub of the week: Running back Leroy Hoard had missed three of Minnesota's last four games with a pulled hamstring and a shoulder injury, but when starter Robert Smith sprained his ankle in the second quarter against Tampa Bay, Hoard came in to gain 40 yards on 18 carries in a 10-6 victory over the Bucs.

Comeback of the week: The Bears rallied from a 15-point deficit in the final 7½ minutes to force overtime and then upset Miami, 36-33, in OT. The win was Chicago's first of the season. Miami's offense went three-and-out on four consecutive possessions late in the game, and Dan Marino's fumble in overtime led to Jeff Jaeger's game-winning 35-yard field goal.

Blowout of the week: Steve McNair accounted for four touchdowns—running for two and throwing for two—in leading Tennessee to a 41-14 victory over Arizona. All five Oilers touchdowns came after turnovers by the Cardinals, who had seven in the game. Arizona's Jake Plummer threw four interceptions in his first NFL start.

Nail-biter of the week: In the fourth quarter at Pittsburgh, the Jaguars recovered a fumble by Steelers running back Jerome Bettis and took advantage of the turnover by taking a 17-14 lead on a 3-yard touchdown pass from Mark Brunell to Pete Mitchell. But Norm Johnson's 19-yard field goal with 2:21 left in regulation forced overtime, and Bettis atoned for his fourth-quarter mistake by fielding Kordell Stewart's quick shovel pass and barreling 17 yards for the winning touchdown 5:47 into overtime to give Pittsburgh a 23-17 victory.

Hit of the week: In overtime of the Denver-Buffalo game, the Bills ran receiver Andre Reed on an end-around pass. Broncos defensive end Alfred Williams dropped Reed for a 17-yard loss, a loss that became 20 yards after Reed fumbled, giving Denver possession at its 42. Eight plays later, the Broncos were on the Bills' 15, setting up Jason Elam's game-winning field goal from 33 yards.

Oddity of the week: For only the second time in NFL history, there were two Monday night games. Because the World Series between the Marlins and Indians went seven games, Game 7 was played at Miami's ProPlayer Stadium on Sunday night, pushing the Bears-Dolphins game back one day. In the regularly scheduled Monday night game, the Packers beat the Patriots, 28-10, in a rematch of Super Bowl XXXI.

Top rusher: Terrell Davis ran for 207 yards and one touchdown on 42 carries in Denver's overtime win at Buffalo.

Top passer: Warren Moon's 409 passing yards accounted for the bulk of Seattle's 554 total yards in the victory over Oakland.

Top receiver: Yancey Thigpen caught 11 passes for 196 yards in the Steelers' overtime win against Jacksonville.

Notes: Brett Favre's 20-yard TD pass to Derrick Mayes was the 1,809th completion of his career, moving him ahead of Bart Starr for the top spot on the Packers' career list. . . . The Steelers are 6-0 in overtime at Three Rivers Stadium. . . . The Jaguars lost consecutive games for the first time in a year (October 20 and 27, 1996). . . . The Falcons extended their string of consecutive games with at least one sack to 20. . . . Jake Plummer became the sixth rookie quarterback to start for the Cardinals since 1960. . . . The Oilers' 41 points were the most by a visiting team since the Cardinals moved to Arizona in 1988. . . . The Chargers were 4-4 for the fifth time in six seasons. The exception was 1994, when they were 7-1 and went to the Super Bowl. . . . Philadelphia was 4-0 at home, 0-4 on the road. . . .

Baltimore quarterback Vinny Testaverde passed for 142 yards in a 20-17 victory against the Redskins to move past Y.A. Tittle into 23rd place on the NFL's career list. Testaverde ended the day with 28,381 passing yards. . . . The 49ers extended their string of quarters without yielding a rushing touchdown to 35. . . . Cincinnati's Eric Bieniemy set a team record with a 102-yard kickoff return. . . . Terrell Davis surpassed 1,000 yards rushing in his eighth game of the season, the fastest in Broncos history. It also was the 16th 100-yard game of Davis' career, a team record. His 207 yards and 42 carries were the most ever given up by the Bills.

Quote of the week: New Orleans coach Mike Ditka, after the Saints lost, 23-0, to the 49ers: "We are just not very good. We are below the floor now. I think I've seen worse teams perform better by accident on offense. You can draw them up in the dirt and make it work better than we make it work."

GAME SUMMARIES

EAGLES 13, COWBOYS 12

Sunday, October 26

Dallas	3	6	0	3—12
Philadelphia	0	0	3	10—13

First Quarter
Dal.—FG, Cunningham 26, 5:33.
Second Quarter
Dal.—FG, Cunningham 24, 2:48.
Dal.—FG, Cunningham 35, 14:19.
Third Quarter
Phi.—FG, Boniol 29, 11:03.
Fourth Quarter
Phi.—FG, Boniol 37, 1:46.
Dal.—FG, Cunningham 43, 6:05.
Phi.—Lewis 8 pass from Peete (Boniol kick), 14:15.
Attendance—67,106.

TEAM STATISTICS

	Dallas	Philadelphia
First downs	14	17
Rushes-yards	31-151	33-154
Passing	93	120
Punt returns	1-0	2-33
Kickoff returns	4-137	4-74
Interception returns	0-0	0-0
Comp.-att.-int.	13-22-0	13-31-0
Sacked-yards lost	6-36	2-6
Punts	5-30	4-31
Fumbles-lost	0-0	2-0
Penalties-yards	10-95	4-25
Time of possession	30:53	29:07

INDIVIDUAL STATISTICS

RUSHING—Dallas, E. Smith 25-126, Aikman 2-15, S. Williams 2-6, Wilson 1-3, Walker 1-1. Philadelphia, Watters 20-88, Garner 9-55, Peete 3-5, Turner 1-6.

PASSING—Dallas, Wilson 11-16-0-108, Aikman 2-6-0-21. Philadelphia, Peete 13-31-0-126.

RECEIVING—Dallas, E. Smith 5-36, Irvin 3-57, Miller 2-16, Walker 1-8, Bjornson 1-7, St. Williams 1-5. Philadelphia, Fryar 6-59, Turner 2-34, Seay 1-11, Lewis 1-8, Garner 1-5, Timpson 1-5, Watters 1-4.

MISSED FIELD GOAL ATTEMPTS—Philadelphia, Boniol 52, 47.

INTERCEPTIONS—None.

KICKOFF RETURNS—Dallas, Walker 3-90, Marion 1-47. Philadelphia, Staley 3-59, Johnson 1-15.

PUNT RETURNS—Dallas, Pittman 1-0. Philadelphia, Seay 2-33.

SACKS—Dallas, Casillas 1, Thomas 1. Philadelphia, Hall 3.5, W. Thomas 2, Jefferson 0.5.

CHIEFS 28, RAMS 20

Sunday, October 26

Kansas City	6	11	11	0—28
St. Louis	7	7	0	6—20

First Quarter
K.C.—FG, Stoyanovich 25, 2:25.
St.L.—Bruce 12 pass from Banks (Wilkins kick), 10:01.
K.C.—FG, Stoyanovich 52, 14:06.
Second Quarter
K.C.—Dawson 21 pass from Grbac (Vanover pass from Grbac), 4:20.
K.C.—FG, Stoyanovich 41, 9:03.
St.L.—Phillips 1 run (Wilkins kick), 13:12.
Third Quarter
K.C.—FG, Stoyanovich 39, 4:51.
K.C.—Allen 2 run (Gonzalez pass from Grbac), 7:59.
Fourth Quarter
St.L.—FG, Wilkins 25, 3:48.
St.L.—FG, Wilkins 49, 9:53.
Attendance—64,864.

TEAM STATISTICS

	Kansas City	St. Louis
First downs	19	20
Rushes-yards	26-87	28-99
Passing	168	261
Punt returns	0-0	3-10
Kickoff returns	4-81	7-160
Interception returns	1-3	0-0
Comp.-att.-int.	20-37-0	18-31-1
Sacked-yards lost	4-36	1-7
Punts	4-49	2-37
Fumbles-lost	1-0	3-3
Penalties-yards	10-90	8-53
Time of possession	30:34	29:26

INDIVIDUAL STATISTICS

RUSHING—Kansas City, Bennett 8-32, Hill 8-30, Grbac 5-5, Allen 3-7, Anders 2-13. St. Louis, Phillips 23-67, Banks 2-17, Lee 2-9, Heyward 1-6.

PASSING—Kansas City, Grbac 20-37-0-204. St. Louis, Banks 18-30-0-268, Rypien 0-1-1-0.

RECEIVING—Kansas City, Popson 5-50, Gonzalez 4-53, Dawson 2-33, Rison 2-33, Anders 2-12, Bennett 2-4, Allen 1-10, Walker 1-6, Hill 1-3. St. Louis, Bruce 5-94, Crawford 4-85, Floyd 3-35, Lee 2-16, Conwell 2-14, Small 1-30, Phillips 1-(minus 6).

MISSED FIELD GOAL ATTEMPTS—St. Louis, Wilkins 45.

INTERCEPTIONS—Kansas City, Hasty 1-3.

KICKOFF RETURNS—Kansas City, Vanover 4-81. St. Louis, Thompson 7-160.

PUNT RETURNS—St. Louis, Floyd 3-10.

SACKS—Kansas City, Thomas 1. St. Louis, O'Neal 4.

49ERS 23, SAINTS 0

Sunday, October 26

San Francisco	7	6	3	7—23
New Orleans	0	0	0	0— 0

First Quarter
S.F.—Hearst 19 pass from S. Young (Anderson kick), 8:19.
Second Quarter
S.F.—FG, Anderson 36, 7:07.
S.F.—FG, Anderson 51, 15:00.
Third Quarter
S.F.—FG, Anderson 29, 7:59.
Fourth Quarter
S.F.—Stokes 5 pass from S. Young (Anderson kick), 9:51.
Attendance—60,443.

	San Fran.	New Orleans
First downs	21	6
Rushes-yards	37-137	18-55
Passing	210	87
Punt returns	5-53	3-29
Kickoff returns	0-0	5-129
Interception returns	1-22	0-0
Comp.-att.-int.	20-32-0	12-25-1
Sacked-yards lost	3-20	4-22
Punts	6-39	8-47

	San Fran.	New Orleans
Fumbles-lost	0-0	1-1
Penalties-yards	5-48	5-36
Time of possession	37:41	22:19

INDIVIDUAL STATISTICS

RUSHING—San Francisco, Hearst 17-53, Kirby 15-73, Floyd 3-4, S. Young 1-8, Brohm 1-(minus 1). New Orleans, Zellars 8-27, Bates 5-18, T. Davis 2-3, Shuler 1-5, Nussmeier 1-2, Bender 1-0.

PASSING—San Francisco, S. Young 20-32-0-230. New Orleans, Wuerffel 7-15-1-60, Nussmeier 4-9-0-36, Shuler 1-1-0-13.

RECEIVING—San Francisco, Owens 7-94, Stokes 5-57, Clark 2-31, Hearst 2-24, Uwaezuoke 1-10, Harris 1-9, Floyd 1-4, Kirby 1-1. New Orleans, Hill 4-34, Zellars 3-21, Hastings 2-33, Guliford 2-16, I. Smith 1-5.

MISSED FIELD GOAL ATTEMPTS—None.

INTERCEPTIONS—San Francisco, Bronson 1-22.

KICKOFF RETURNS—New Orleans, Guliford 5-129.

PUNT RETURNS—San Francisco, Uwaezuoke 5-53. New Orleans, Guliford 3-29.

SACKS—San Francisco, Stubblefield 2, Barker 1, Bryant 1. New Orleans, Fields 1, Glover 1, B. Smith 1.

OILERS 41, CARDINALS 14

Sunday, October 26

Tennessee	3	17	14	7—41
Arizona	0	0	7	7—14

First Quarter
Ten.—FG, Del Greco 52, 3:50.

Second Quarter
Ten.—D. Walker 39 interception return (Del Greco kick), 2:11.
Ten.—FG, Del Greco 42, 13:14.
Ten.—McNair 35 run (Del Greco kick), 14:51.

Third Quarter
Ten.—McNair 2 run (Del Greco kick), 1:12.
Ariz.—R. Moore 12 pass from Plummer (Nedney kick), 9:06.
Ten.—Sanders 55 pass from McNair (Del Greco kick), 13:19.

Fourth Quarter
Ten.—Sanders 20 pass from McNair (Del Greco kick), 3:09.
Ariz.—R. Moore 2 pass from Plummer (Nedney kick), 8:56.
Attendance—44,030.

TEAM STATISTICS

	Tennessee	Arizona
First downs	15	22
Rushes-yards	35-148	24-106
Passing	135	157
Punt returns	3-48	2-16
Kickoff returns	1-1	7-177
Interception returns	4-82	0-0
Comp.-att.-int.	10-19-0	21-40-4
Sacked-yards lost	2-13	6-38
Punts	6-37	4-50
Fumbles-lost	1-0	3-3
Penalties-yards	8-61	8-55
Time of possession	28:55	31:05

INDIVIDUAL STATISTICS

RUSHING—Tennessee, George 17-71, Thomas 10-13, McNair 6-70, Krieg 1-0, Harmon 1-(minus 6). Arizona, Centers 14-57, Plummer 6-34, McElroy 4-15.

PASSING—Tennessee, McNair 9-17-0-146, Krieg 1-2-0-2. Arizona, Plummer 21-40-4-195.

RECEIVING—Tennessee, Wycheck 5-59, Sanders 2-75, George 1-7, Davis 1-5, Harmon 1-2. Arizona, Sanders 10-98, R. Moore 6-58, Centers 3-22, K. Williams 1-12, Gedney 1-5.

MISSED FIELD GOAL ATTEMPTS—None.

INTERCEPTIONS—Tennessee, Robertson 2-39, D. Walker 1-39, D. Lewis 1-4.

KICKOFF RETURNS—Tennessee, Robertson 1-1. Arizona, K. Williams 6-167, Gedney 1-10.

PUNT RETURNS—Tennessee, Gray 3-48. Arizona, K. Williams 2-16.

SACKS—Tennessee, Holmes 3, G. Walker 1, Bishop 0.5, Bowden 0.5, Lyons 0.5, Stewart 0.5. Arizona, Miller 1.5, Swann 0.5.

RAVENS 20, REDSKINS 17

Sunday, October 26

Baltimore	7	7	3	3—20
Washington	7	0	7	3—17

First Quarter
Bal.—Alexander 13 pass from Testaverde (Stover kick), 5:06.
Was.—Shepherd 15 pass from Frerotte (Blanton kick), 8:15.

Second Quarter
Bal.—Morris 4 run (Stover kick), 4:37.

Third Quarter
Bal.—FG, Stover 34, 5:38.
Was.—Mitchell 6 pass from Frerotte (Blanton kick), 12:43.

Fourth Quarter
Bal.—FG, Stover 28, 2:44.
Was.—FG, Blanton 26, 8:18.
Attendance—75,067.

TEAM STATISTICS

	Baltimore	Washington
First downs	20	16
Rushes-yards	44-199	21-67
Passing	133	182
Punt returns	0-0	1-9
Kickoff returns	3-32	4-140
Interception returns	1-18	0-0
Comp.-att.-int.	10-21-0	17-34-1
Sacked-yards lost	2-9	3-17
Punts	4-39	5-45
Fumbles-lost	5-1	2-0
Penalties-yards	4-25	5-60
Time of possession	35:01	24:59

INDIVIDUAL STATISTICS

RUSHING—Baltimore, Morris 36-176, Testaverde 6-11, Byner 1-6, J. Lewis 1-6. Washington, Davis 17-59, Mitchell 2-5, Bowie 1-3, Frerotte 1-0.

PASSING—Baltimore, Testaverde 10-21-0-142. Washington, Frerotte 17-34-1-199.

RECEIVING—Baltimore, Alexander 3-58, Jackson 3-28, J. Lewis 2-48, Morris 2-8. Washington, Asher 5-52, Mitchell 4-36, Ellard 3-44, Bowie 3-36, Shepherd 2-31.

MISSED FIELD GOAL ATTEMPTS—Baltimore, Stover 48.

INTERCEPTIONS—Baltimore, R. Lewis 1-18.

KICKOFF RETURNS—Baltimore, J. Lewis 2-32, McCloud 1-0. Washington, Mitchell 4-140.

PUNT RETURNS—Washington, Mitchell 1-9.

SACKS—Baltimore, R. Lewis 1, Boulware 1, Sharper 1. Washington, Jones 1, Team 1.

VIKINGS 10, BUCCANEERS 6

Sunday, October 26

Minnesota	0	0	10	0—10
Tampa Bay	0	0	0	6— 6

Third Quarter
Min.—FG, Murray 28, 10:54.
Min.—Evans 1 run (Murray kick), 14:32.

Fourth Quarter
T.B.—Anthony 2 pass from Dilfer (kick failed), 4:49.
Attendance—66,815.

TEAM STATISTICS

	Minnesota	Tampa Bay
First downs	16	11
Rushes-yards	35-94	18-52
Passing	214	177
Punt returns	5-84	5-23
Kickoff returns	0-0	3-54
Interception returns	0-0	0-0
Comp.-att.-int.	20-29-0	15-29-0
Sacked-yards lost	2-16	3-11
Punts	6-40	7-43
Fumbles-lost	0-0	1-0
Penalties-yards	6-46	2-15
Time of possession	36:59	23:01

INDIVIDUAL STATISTICS

RUSHING—Minnesota, Hoard 18-40, R. Smith 11-30, Evans 4-17, M. Williams 1-4, Johnson 1-3. Tampa Bay, Dunn 10-39, Alstott 6-8, Dilfer 2-5.

PASSING—Minnesota, Johnson 20-29-0-230. Tampa Bay, Dilfer 15-29-0-188.

RECEIVING—Minnesota, Carter 7-80, Reed 3-46, Walsh 2-30, DeLong 2-29, Glover 2-26, R. Smith 2-10, Goodwin 1-5, Hoard 1-4. Tampa Bay, Anthony 5-92, Moore 2-35, Williams 2-22, Dunn 2-19, Copeland 2-14, Alstott 2-6.

MISSED FIELD GOAL ATTEMPTS—Minnesota, Murray 30.
INTERCEPTIONS—None.
KICKOFF RETURNS—Tampa Bay, Anthony 2-42, Ellison 1-12.
PUNT RETURNS—Minnesota, Palmer 5-84. Tampa Bay, Williams 5-23.
SACKS—Minnesota, F. Smith 2, Rudd 1. Tampa Bay, Ahanotu 1, Sapp 1.

BRONCOS 23, BILLS 20

Sunday, October 26

Denver	0	10	10	0	3	23
Buffalo	0	0	0	20	0	20

Second Quarter
Den.—FG, Elam 23, 5:25.
Den.—Davis 9 run (Elam kick), 13:04.

Third Quarter
Den.—FG, Elam 22, 3:19.
Den.—Traylor 62 interception return (Elam kick), 10:47.

Fourth Quarter
Buf.—Reed 27 pass from Van Pelt (Christie kick), 2:50.
Buf.—FG, Christie 30, 5:20.
Buf.—Early 31 pass from Van Pelt (Christie kick), 12:37.
Buf.—FG, Christie 55, 14:58.

Overtime
Den.—FG, Elam 33, 13:04.
Attendance—78,458.

TEAM STATISTICS

	Denver	Buffalo
First downs	17	19
Rushes-yards	46-225	29-155
Passing	116	160
Punt returns	5-31	2-19
Kickoff returns	4-64	6-125
Interception returns	3-95	2-14
Comp.-att.-int.	16-30-2	19-42-3
Sacked-yards lost	5-17	5-52
Punts	8-40	8-41
Fumbles-lost	1-1	4-3
Penalties-yards	10-113	4-25
Time of possession	42:04	31:00

INDIVIDUAL STATISTICS

RUSHING—Denver, Davis 42-207, Elway 2-14, Hebron 1-6, D. Smith 1-(minus 2). Buffalo, A. Smith 16-92, Thomas 9-47, Moulds 1-9, Van Pelt 1-4, Reed 1-2, Collins 1-1.
PASSING—Denver, Elway 16-30-2-133. Buffalo, Van Pelt 12-24-1-177, Collins 7-18-2-35.
RECEIVING—Denver, Davis 5-29, Sharpe 4-35, R. Smith 3-35, Carswell 2-9, McCaffrey 1-17, D. Smith 1-8. Buffalo, Early 6-91, Reed 4-70, Johnson 4-17, Moulds 3-30, Riemersma 1-4, A. Smith 1-0.
MISSED FIELD GOAL ATTEMPTS—Denver, Elam 38.
INTERCEPTIONS—Denver, Traylor 1-62, Braxton 1-23, Crockett 1-10. Buffalo, Martin 1-12, Schulz 1-2.
KICKOFF RETURNS—Denver, Hebron 3-53, Burns 1-11. Buffalo, Holmes 3-71, Moulds 3-54.
PUNT RETURNS—Denver, Gordon 5-31. Buffalo, Burris 2-19.
SACKS—Denver, N. Smith 2, Traylor 1, Williams 1, Team 1. Buffalo, Hansen 2, B. Smith 1, Moran 1, Covington 0.5, Washington 0.5.

GIANTS 29, BENGALS 27

Sunday, October 26

Cincinnati	7	14	0	6	27
N.Y. Giants	3	7	6	13	29

First Quarter
NYG—FG, Daluiso 35, 4:23.
Cin.—Dillon 1 run (Pelfrey kick), 8:37.

Second Quarter
NYG—Way 1 run (Daluiso kick), 0:10.
Cin.—Bieniemy 102 kickoff return (Pelfrey kick), 0:28.
Cin.—Dunn 39 pass from Blake (Pelfrey kick), 14:54.

Third Quarter
NYG—Way 1 run (run failed), 6:03.

Fourth Quarter
NYG—Wheatley 1 run (pass failed), 0:52.
NYG—Wheatley 3 run (Daluiso kick), 11:36.
Cin.—Blake 4 run (pass failed), 13:29.
Attendance—72,584.

TEAM STATISTICS

	Cincinnati	N.Y. Giants
First downs	22	28
Rushes-yards	27-98	43-109
Passing	225	214
Punt returns	2-17	1-4
Kickoff returns	6-232	4-79
Interception returns	0-0	1-4
Comp.-att.-int.	17-34-1	18-31-0
Sacked-yards lost	2-12	0-0
Punts	4-42	6-41
Fumbles-lost	3-1	2-0
Penalties-yards	10-88	12-127
Time of possession	23:36	36:24

INDIVIDUAL STATISTICS

RUSHING—Cincinnati, Carter 17-70, Dillon 5-8, Bieniemy 3-12, Blake 2-8. New York, Way 20-75, Wheatley 16-39, Kanell 6-0, Pegram 1-(minus 5).
PASSING—Cincinnati, Blake 17-34-1-237. New York, Kanell 18-31-0-214.
RECEIVING—Cincinnati, Hundon 4-42, Dunn 3-61, Milne 3-33, Scott 2-23, Dillon 1-21, Carter 1-16, McGee 1-16, Pickens 1-13, Battaglia 1-12. New York, Alexander 5-100, Calloway 5-56, Way 3-23, Cross 2-23, Pegram 2-8, Wheatley 1-4.
MISSED FIELD GOAL ATTEMPTS—None.
INTERCEPTIONS—New York, Sparks 1-4.
KICKOFF RETURNS—Cincinnati, Bieniemy 5-201, Dunn 1-31. New York, Pegram 3-69, Pierce 1-10.
PUNT RETURNS—Cincinnati, Myers 2-17. New York, Toomer 1-4.
SACKS—New York, Strahan 1, K. Hamilton 0.5, Bratzke 0.5.

STEELERS 23, JAGUARS 17

Sunday, October 26

Jacksonville	0	10	0	7	0	17
Pittsburgh	0	0	7	10	6	23

Second Quarter
Jac.—Jackson 8 pass from Brunell (Hollis kick), 0:52.
Jac.—FG, Hollis 20, 8:36.

Third Quarter
Pit.—Hawkins 28 pass from Stewart (N. Johnson kick), 6:51.

Fourth Quarter
Pit.—Stewart 1 run (N. Johnson kick), 2:39.
Jac.—Mitchell 3 pass from Brunell (Hollis kick), 6:47.
Pit.—FG, N. Johnson 19, 12:39.

Overtime
Pit.—Bettis 17 pass from Stewart, 5:47.
Attendance—57,011.

TEAM STATISTICS

	Jacksonville	Pittsburgh
First downs	16	26
Rushes-yards	23-73	37-141
Passing	194	298
Punt returns	2-2	2-3
Kickoff returns	4-124	5-101
Interception returns	1-9	1-3
Comp.-att.-int.	15-31-1	25-42-1
Sacked-yards lost	4-20	3-19
Punts	7-36	5-43
Fumbles-lost	3-0	3-2
Penalties-yards	11-69	5-54
Time of possession	24:20	41:27

INDIVIDUAL STATISTICS

RUSHING—Jacksonville, Stewart 16-39, Brunell 5-25, Johnson 2-9. Pittsburgh, Bettis 28-99, Stewart 8-37, McAfee 1-5.
PASSING—Jacksonville, Brunell 15-30-0-214, Johnson 0-1-1-0. Pittsburgh, Stewart 25-42-1-317.
RECEIVING—Jacksonville, Smith 4-50, Jackson 3-64, Mitchell 3-36, McCardell 2-22, Stewart 2-13, Barlow 1-29. Pittsburgh, Thigpen 11-196, Hawkins 7-71, Bettis 3-35, Bruener 2-13, Marsh 1-8, G. Jones 1-(minus 6).
MISSED FIELD GOAL ATTEMPTS—None.
INTERCEPTIONS—Jacksonville, Kopp 1-9. Pittsburgh, Scott 1-(minus 4).
KICKOFF RETURNS—Jacksonville, Jackson 4-88. Pittsburgh, Coleman 5-101.
PUNT RETURNS—Jacksonville, Barlow 2-2. Pittsburgh, Coleman 2-3.
SACKS—Jacksonville, Brackens 2, Lageman 1. Pittsburgh, Kirkland 1, Oldham 1, Harrison 1, Gildon 1.

CHARGERS 35, COLTS 19

Sunday, October 26

Indianapolis	0	0	6	13—19
San Diego	3	9	14	9—35

First Quarter
S.D.—FG, G. Davis 45, 8:15.

Second Quarter
S.D.—FG, G. Davis 35, 0:11.
S.D.—FG, G. Davis 34, 9:08.
S.D.—FG, G. Davis 31, 14:49.

Third Quarter
S.D.—Brown 1 run (G. Davis kick), 7:31.
Ind.—Dawkins 36 pass from Justin (pass failed), 8:51.
S.D.—Hartley 2 pass from Humphries (G. Davis kick), 13:02.

Fourth Quarter
S.D.—FG, G. Davis 45, 4:29.
Ind.—Bailey 10 pass from Justin (Blanchard kick), 9:26.
Ind.—McElroy 42 blocked FG return (2-pt conversion failed), 12:43.
S.D.—Harrison 40 kickoff return (kick blocked), 12:51.
Attendance—63,177.

TEAM STATISTICS

	Indianapolis	San Diego
First downs	14	25
Rushes-yards	16-31	38-202
Passing	219	222
Punt returns	0-0	4-30
Kickoff returns	9-165	3-83
Interception returns	0-0	2-44
Comp.-att.-int.	20-39-2	21-34-0
Sacked-yards lost	3-24	1-7
Punts	6-49	2-49
Fumbles-lost	0-0	0-0
Penalties-yards	5-25	6-73
Time of possession	27:01	32:59

INDIVIDUAL STATISTICS

RUSHING—Indianapolis, Faulk 8-11, Crockett 5-9, Warren 3-11. San Diego, Brown 28-169, Craver 5-22, Humphries 3-(minus 4), Fletcher 1-10, C. Jones 1-5.

PASSING—Indianapolis, Justin 20-39-2-243. San Diego, Humphries 21-34-0-229.

RECEIVING—Indianapolis, Dawkins 5-84, Harrison 4-47, Bailey 3-39, Faulk 3-13, Warren 2-34, Dilger 2-12, Stablein 1-14. San Diego, Martin 6-61, F. Jones 4-28, Hartley 3-34, Fletcher 3-6, Metcalf 2-29, Still 1-33, C. Jones 1-23, Brown 1-15.

MISSED FIELD GOAL ATTEMPTS—San Diego, G. Davis 40.

INTERCEPTIONS—San Diego, Harper 1-43, Jackson 1-1.

KICKOFF RETURNS—Indianapolis, Bailey 8-165, Hetherington 1-0. San Diego, Rachal 2-43, Harrison 1-40.

PUNT RETURNS—San Diego, Metcalf 4-30.

SACKS—Indianapolis, Footman 1. San Diego, Harrison 1, Fuller 1, Coleman 0.5, Johnson 0.5.

PANTHERS 21, FALCONS 12

Sunday, October 26

Atlanta	0	3	3	6—12
Carolina	14	0	0	7—21

First Quarter
Car.—Biakabutuka 12 run (Kasay kick), 5:17.
Car.—Carrier 16 pass from Collins (Kasay kick), 14:59.

Second Quarter
Atl.—FG, Andersen 34, 2:56.

Third Quarter
Atl.—FG, Andersen 44, 4:47.

Fourth Quarter
Car.—Biakabutuka 26 run (Kasay kick), 2:40.
Atl.—Anderson 14 pass from Tolliver (run failed), 8:19.
Attendance—54,675.

TEAM STATISTICS

	Atlanta	Carolina
First downs	17	14
Rushes-yards	23-68	36-137
Passing	233	91
Punt returns	5-61	1-0

	Atlanta	Carolina
Kickoff returns	4-99	3-89
Interception returns	1-0	2-30
Comp.-att.-int.	21-46-2	12-25-1
Sacked-yards lost	2-8	3-16
Punts	7-35	8-44
Fumbles-lost	4-1	6-2
Penalties-yards	3-30	3-13
Time of possession	27:58	32:02

INDIVIDUAL STATISTICS

RUSHING—Atlanta, Anderson 15-50, Tolliver 4-(minus 3), Graziani 2-18, Hanspard 2-3. Carolina, Biakabutuka 23-104, Greene 6-27, Collins 5-7, Lane 1-3, Johnson 1-(minus 4).

PASSING—Atlanta, Tolliver 17-28-0-217, Graziani 4-18-2-24. Carolina, Collins 12-25-1-107.

RECEIVING—Atlanta, Mathis 8-107, Emanuel 5-48, Green 3-34, Haynes 2-20, Anderson 1-14, Santiago 1-13, Christian 1-5. Carolina, Carrier 3-34, Ismail 2-24, Walls 2-21, Johnson 2-14, Greene 2-8, Carruth 1-6.

MISSED FIELD GOAL ATTEMPTS—None.

INTERCEPTIONS—Atlanta, Buchanan 1-0. Carolina, Davis 1-17, Cota 1-13.

KICKOFF RETURNS—Atlanta, Hanspard 3-84, Bolden 1-15. Carolina, Bates 3-89.

PUNT RETURNS—Atlanta, Kinchen 5-61. Carolina, Oliver 1-0.

SACKS—Atlanta, Bennett 1.5, Crockett 1, Archambeau 0.5. Carolina, Miller 1, Cook 1.

SEAHAWKS 45, RAIDERS 34

Sunday, October 26

Oakland	14	11	9	0—34
Seattle	3	15	14	13—45

First Quarter
Sea.—FG, Peterson 21, 7:38.
Oak.—Kaufman 55 run (Ford kick), 8:21.
Oak.—Jett 13 pass from George (Ford kick), 11:47.

Second Quarter
Sea.—FG, Peterson 40, 0:52.
Sea.—Br. Blades 7 pass from Moon (pass failed), 8:26.
Sea.—McKnight 42 pass from Moon (pass failed), 10:44.
Oak.—FG, Ford 53, 13:51.
Oak.—Washington 44 interception return (T. Brown pass from George), 14:21.

Third Quarter
Oak.—Jett 49 pass from George (run failed), 1:49.
Sea.—Galloway 17 pass from Moon (Peterson kick), 4:43.
Oak.—FG, Ford 22, 10:41.
Sea.—Galloway 28 pass from Moon (Peterson kick), 13:48.

Fourth Quarter
Sea.—FG, Peterson 38, 2:05.
Sea.—FG, Peterson 25, 7:36.
Sea.—Galloway 2 pass from Moon (Peterson kick), 12:34.
Attendance—66,264.

TEAM STATISTICS

	Oakland	Seattle
First downs	19	26
Rushes-yards	21-119	27-145
Passing	235	409
Punt returns	1-0	3-36
Kickoff returns	10-223	7-165
Interception returns	2-44	0-0
Comp.-att.-int.	18-29-0	28-44-2
Sacked-yards lost	5-25	0-0
Punts	6-41	3-41
Fumbles-lost	2-1	0-0
Penalties-yards	7-73	11-98
Time of possession	26:18	33:42

INDIVIDUAL STATISTICS

RUSHING—Oakland, Kaufman 17-112, Hall 3-2, Fenner 1-5. Seattle, Warren 13-76, Broussard 12-24, Galloway 1-44, Strong 1-1.

PASSING—Oakland, George 18-29-0-260. Seattle, Moon 28-44-2-409.

RECEIVING—Oakland, T. Brown 7-107, Fenner 4-17, Jett 3-78, Dudley 2-49, Williams 1-9. Seattle, Galloway 7-117, McKnight 4-100, Br. Blades 4-58, Broussard 4-30, Warren 3-29, Crumpler 2-48, Strong 2-10, Hobbs 1-10, Pritchard 1-7.

MISSED FIELD GOAL ATTEMPTS—None.

INTERCEPTIONS—Oakland, Washington 1-44, Lynch 1-0.

KICKOFF RETURNS—Oakland, Howard 10-223. Seattle, Harris 7-165.
PUNT RETURNS—Oakland, Howard 1-0. Seattle, Harris 3-36.
SACKS—Seattle, Adams 2, C. Brown 1, Kennedy 1, Sinclair 1.

BEARS 36, DOLPHINS 33

Monday, October 27

Chicago	7	8	3	15	3—36
Miami	7	6	6	14	0—33

First Quarter
Chi.—R. Harris 1 run (Jaeger kick), 5:06.
Mia.—McPhail 71 run (Mare kick), 10:52.
Second Quarter
Chi.—FG, Jaeger 39, 1:00.
Chi.—Safety, Marino sacked by Thierry in end zone, 2:04.
Chi.—FG, Jaeger 23, 11:42.
Mia.—McPhail 10 pass from Marino (pass failed), 14:10.
Third Quarter
Chi.—FG, Jaeger 47, 5:49.
Mia.—Buckley 22 fumble return (pass failed), 11:55.
Fourth Quarter
Mia.—Drayton 22 pass from Marino (Mare kick), 1:54.
Mia.—Abdul-Jabbar 2 run (Mare kick), 7:34.
Chi.—Engram 8 pass from Kramer (Jaeger kick), 9:12.
Chi.—Penn 25 pass from Kramer (Engram pass from Kramer), 13:35.
Overtime
Chi.—FG, Jaeger 35, 9:25.
Attendance—73,156.

TEAM STATISTICS
	Chicago	Miami
First downs	26	18
Rushes-yards	37-128	16-119
Passing	336	246
Punt returns	4-48	0-0
Kickoff returns	4-85	5-90
Interception returns	1-0	0-0
Comp.-att.-int.	32-50-0	18-39-1
Sacked-yards lost	1-7	4-28
Punts	5-40	6-50
Fumbles-lost	3-2	3-2
Penalties-yards	8-82	13-83
Time of possession	44:53	24:32

INDIVIDUAL STATISTICS
RUSHING—Chicago, R. Harris 25-106, Autry 7-21, Kramer 4-1, Tony Carter 1-0. Miami, Abdul-Jabbar 11-38, McPhail 2-77, Spikes 2-4, Parmalee 1-0.
PASSING—Chicago, Kramer 32-50-0-343. Miami, Marino 18-39-1-274.
RECEIVING—Chicago, Engram 8-63, Conway 6-100, Wetnight 6-61, Proehl 4-40, Jennings 3-23, Penn 2-33, Allred 1-12, Autry 1-8, R. Harris 1-3. Miami, McDuffie 7-137, Perriman 3-52, Drayton 2-29, McPhail 2-19, Parmalee 2-16, Jordan 1-13, Abdul-Jabbar 1-8.
MISSED FIELD GOAL ATTEMPTS—None.

INTERCEPTIONS—Chicago, Marshall 1-0.
KICKOFF RETURNS—Chicago, Bownes 2-46, Engram 1-20, Tony Carter 1-19. Miami, Spikes 2-47, McPhail 2-43, A. Harris 1-0.
PUNT RETURNS—Chicago, Hughes 4-48.
SACKS—Chicago, Thierry 2, Minter 1, Thomas 1. Miami, Bowens 0.5, Gardener 0.5.

PACKERS 28, PATRIOTS 10

Monday, October 27

Green Bay	7	7	7	7—28
New England	0	10	0	0—10

First Quarter
G.B.—Levens 6 pass from Favre (Longwell kick), 11:41.
Second Quarter
N.E.—Coates 11 pass from Bledsoe (Vinatieri kick), 4:05.
N.E.—FG, Vinatieri 38, 12:48.
G.B.—Chmura 32 pass from Favre (Longwell kick), 14:38.
Third Quarter
G.B.—R. Brooks 20 pass from Favre (Longwell kick), 14:45.
Fourth Quarter
G.B.—Levens 3 run (Longwell kick), 12:14.
Attendance—59,972.

TEAM STATISTICS
	Green Bay	New England
First downs	27	18
Rushes-yards	39-144	20-69
Passing	227	255
Punt returns	1-13	3-24
Kickoff returns	3-63	4-83
Interception returns	3-33	0-0
Comp.-att.-int.	23-34-0	20-36-3
Sacked-yards lost	1-12	2-13
Punts	4-45	3-37
Fumbles-lost	2-1	2-1
Penalties-yards	4-25	3-15
Time of possession	34:20	25:40

INDIVIDUAL STATISTICS
RUSHING—Green Bay, Levens 26-100, Favre 9-32, Hayden 2-6, Henderson 2-6. New England, Martin 18-65, Meggett 1-4, Bledsoe 1-0.
PASSING—Green Bay, Favre 23-34-0-239. New England, Bledsoe 20-36-3-268.
RECEIVING—Green Bay, Levens 7-40, R. Brooks 6-67, Chmura 4-60, Freeman 3-32, Henderson 2-20, Mayes 1-20. New England, Glenn 7-163, Martin 4-52, Jefferson 3-18, Coates 3-14, Meggett 1-15, Byars 1-3, Gash 1-3.
MISSED FIELD GOAL ATTEMPTS—None.
INTERCEPTIONS—Green Bay, Robinson 1-26, B. Williams 1-5, Butler 1-2.
KICKOFF RETURNS—Green Bay, Schroeder 3-63. New England, Meggett 4-83.
PUNT RETURNS—Green Bay, Schroeder 1-13. New England, Meggett 3-24.
SACKS—Green Bay, Butler 1, Wilkins 0.5, Brown 0.5.

WEEK 10

RESULTS

ARIZONA 31, Philadelphia 21
ATLANTA 34, St. Louis 31
BUFFALO 9, Miami 6
CAROLINA 38, Oakland 14
CINCINNATI 38, San Diego 31
DENVER 30, Seattle 27
GREEN BAY 20, Detroit 10
Jacksonville 30, TENNESSEE 24
MINNESOTA 23, New England 18
N.Y. JETS 19, Baltimore 16 (OT)
SAN FRANCISCO 17, Dallas 10
Tampa Bay 31, INDIANAPOLIS 28
Washington 31, CHICAGO 8
KANSAS CITY 13, Pittsburgh 10
Open date: New Orleans, N.Y. Giants

STANDINGS

AFC EAST	W	L	T	Pct.
N.Y. Jets	6	3	0	.667
Buffalo	5	4	0	.556
Miami	5	4	0	.556
New England	5	4	0	.556
Indianapolis	0	9	0	.000

AFC CENTRAL	W	L	T	Pct.
Jacksonville	6	3	0	.667
Pittsburgh	6	3	0	.667
Baltimore	4	5	0	.444
Tennessee	4	5	0	.444
Cincinnati	2	7	0	.222

AFC WEST	W	L	T	Pct.
Denver	8	1	0	.889
Kansas City	7	2	0	.778
Seattle	5	4	0	.556
San Diego	4	5	0	.444
Oakland	3	6	0	.333

NFC EAST	W	L	T	Pct.
N.Y. Giants	6	3	0	.667
Washington	5	4	0	.556
Dallas	4	5	0	.444
Philadelphia	4	5	0	.444
Arizona	2	7	0	.222

NFC CENTRAL	W	L	T	Pct.
Green Bay	7	2	0	.778
Minnesota	7	2	0	.778
Tampa Bay	6	3	0	.667
Detroit	4	5	0	.444
Chicago	1	8	0	.111

NFC WEST	W	L	T	Pct.
San Francisco	8	1	0	.889
Carolina	5	4	0	.556
Atlanta	2	7	0	.222
New Orleans	2	7	0	.222
St. Louis	2	7	0	.222

HIGHLIGHTS

Hero of the week: Two weeks after replacing Neil O'Donnell and leading the Jets to a comeback win over the Patriots, Glenn Foley did it again, this time against the Ravens. The fourth-year quarterback led the Jets on a 60-yard drive in overtime, resulting in John Hall's 37-yard game-winning field goal with 10:02 left.

Goat of the week: With the score tied at 28 and three minutes left, winless Indianapolis had the ball at Tampa Bay's 5. But on a fake handoff to Lamont Warren, Colts quarterback Kelly Holcomb lost the ball before embarking on a bootleg. His fumble was recovered by defensive end Chidi Ahanotu and the Bucs went on to win, 31-28.

Sub of the week: Filling in for Tim Biakabutuka, who suffered bruised ribs on the fifth play of the game, Panthers running back Fred Lane rushed for a franchise-record 147 yards and three touchdowns in Carolina's 38-14 victory. Lane, an undrafted rookie from Division II Lane College (Tenn.), had some incredible runs, including a 15-yard TD on Carolina's opening drive when he appeared stopped at the line of scrimmage but broke three tackles and ran past five others on his way to the end zone.

Comeback of the week: Cardinals quarterback Kent Graham scored two touchdowns in the final 3:10 to lead Arizona over Philadelphia, 31-21. Graham, sidelined by a leg injury since October 12, replaced struggling rookie Jake Plummer. Arizona's defense and special teams set up Graham's touchdowns. The Eagles' Mark Seay fumbled a punt, leading to the Cardinals' first fourth-quarter score, and Mike Caldwell intercepted a pass that led to Arizona's second fourth-quarter touchdown.

Blowout of the week: The Raiders came into their game against the Panthers with 15 plays of 40 or more yards, but they made just one against Carolina—a 41-yard pass from Jeff George to Tim Brown. The Raiders also struggled on defense as the Panthers tied a team record with 28 points in the first half.

Nail-biter of the week: After William Floyd's 1-yard touchdown run with 5:57 left put the 49ers ahead 14-10, the Cowboys had one more chance to take the lead. But on second and long from the 49ers' 40, a Troy Aikman pass to Michael Irvin fell incomplete when Irvin and 49ers cornerback Rod Woodson got tangled up at the goal line. One official threw a flag, but after a discussion, the officiating crew ruled the contact was incidental. On the next play, safety Tim McDonald intercepted an Aikman pass, sealing the 49ers' victory.

Hit of the week: Cincinnati linebacker Reinard Wilson delivered a late hit on San Diego quarterback Stan Humphries in the third quarter that will be remembered more for Humphries' reaction to the hit than the hit itself. After Wilson slammed the veteran quarterback to the turf, Humphries' eyes rolled around in their sockets as he tried to refocus them, a site that was unnerving to even the most blood-thirsty of fans. Humphries suffered a concussion on the play and his career was put in jeopardy. The Bengals won, 38-31.

Oddity of the week: Two weeks after defeating the Colts 9-6, the Bills defeated the Dolphins by the same score.

Top rusher: Jamal Anderson gained 159 yards and scored a touchdown in the Falcons' 34-31 overtime victory against the Rams.

Top passer: Tony Banks was 23-of-34 for 401 yards and two touchdowns in the Rams' loss.

Top receiver: Isaac Bruce was on the receiving end of 10 Banks passes, burning Falcons cornerback Ray Buchanan early and often. Bruce caught TD passes of 9 and 29 yards in the first half before the Falcons started rolling coverage toward him.

Notes: The Chargers' Eric Metcalf returned two punts for touchdowns against the Bengals, giving him an NFL-record 10 TDs on punt and kickoff returns in his career. Of his eight punt returns for touchdowns, four have come against the Bengals. . . . On their first 15 plays against Buffalo, the Dolphins gained 23 yards. . . . Corey Dillon became the first Bengals rookie to rush for 100 yards in a game since Ickey Woods in 1988. . . . Dan Marino's 33 percent completion rate (5-of-15) against the Bills was the worst of his career. . . . Running back Marcus Allen threw the fifth touchdown pass of his career (this one to Danan Hughes) to help the Chiefs defeat the Steelers, 13-10. . . . The Cowboys are 1-4 against the 49ers in the Barry Switzer era. . . . In a battle of old guys, John Elway, 37, led the Broncos to a 30-27 win over Warren Moon, 40, and the Seahawks. Elway passed two career milestones in the process. He became the third player in NFL history to reach the 50,000-yard mark in total offense, and he moved past Fran Tarkenton in passing yards by upping his total to 47,019. . . . The Jaguars' Clyde Simmons recorded his 106th career sack in a game against the Oilers. . . . Chicago receiver Curtis Conway was ejected from a 31-8 loss to the Redskins when he made contact with an official and threw his helmet after a play in the end zone.

Quote of the week: Patriots running back Keith Byars after his team's third straight loss, to the Vikings: "There will always be some peaks and valleys. We can't seem to find the bottom of this valley."

GAME SUMMARIES

REDSKINS 31, BEARS 8

Sunday, November 2

Washington	14	10	7	0—	31
Chicago	0	0	0	8—	8

First Quarter
Was.—Jenkins 9 pass from Frerotte (Blanton kick), 3:41.
Was.—Bowie 5 run (Blanton kick), 9:05.

Second Quarter
Was.—Frerotte 1 run (Blanton kick), 1:26.
Was.—FG, Blanton 38, 9:12.

Third Quarter
Was.—Shepherd 39 pass from Frerotte (Blanton kick), 2:19.

Fourth Quarter
Chi.—Proehl 2 pass from Kramer (Proehl pass from Kramer), 9:57.
Attendance—53,032.

TEAM STATISTICS

	Washington	Chicago
First downs	24	23
Rushes-yards	42-203	16-62
Passing	185	274
Punt returns	3-46	1-0
Kickoff returns	2-29	6-96
Interception returns	2-7	0-0
Comp.-att.-int.	14-20-0	25-42-2
Sacked-yards lost	1-7	2-13
Punts	3-40	6-42
Fumbles-lost	1-1	3-2
Penalties-yards	6-56	7-68
Time of possession	32:47	27:13

INDIVIDUAL STATISTICS
RUSHING—Washington, Allen 20-125, Davis 12-41, Bowie 5-17, Logan 2-2, Frerotte 2-1, Shepherd 1-17. Chicago, R. Harris 13-43, Kramer 3-19.
PASSING—Washington, Frerotte 14-20-0-192. Chicago, Kramer 21-37-1-237, Stenstrom 4-5-1-50.
RECEIVING—Washington, Bowie 4-53, Shepherd 3-68, Asher 3-35, Allen 2-25, Jenkins 1-9, Mitchell 1-2. Chicago, Tony Carter 5-48, Bownes 4-54, Conway 3-57, Wetnight 3-32, Proehl 3-24, Penn 2-27, Engram 2-16, Jennings 1-15, Autry 1-12, R. Harris 1-2.
MISSED FIELD GOAL ATTEMPTS—None.
INTERCEPTIONS—Washington, Dishman 1-7, Richard 1-0.
KICKOFF RETURNS—Washington, Mitchell 1-19, M. Patton 1-10. Chicago, Bownes 4-69, Hughes 1-16, Allred 1-11.
PUNT RETURNS—Washington, Mitchell 3-46. Chicago, Hughes 1-0.
SACKS—Washington, Boutte 1, Pounds 1. Chicago, Thomas 1.

JETS 19, RAVENS 16

Sunday, November 2

Baltimore	6	3	0	7	0—	16
N.Y. Jets	7	3	3	3	3—	19

First Quarter
NYJ—Baxter 13 pass from O'Donnell (Hall kick), 2:04.
Bal.—FG, Stover 41, 8:19.
Bal.—FG, Stover 22, 12:30.

Second Quarter
NYJ—FG, Hall 28, 5:46.
Bal.—FG, Stover 24, 14:41.

Third Quarter
NYJ—FG, Hall 33, 11:05.

Fourth Quarter
NYJ—FG, Hall 31, 3:21.
Bal.—Alexander 16 pass from Testaverde (Stover kick), 14:57.

Overtime
NYJ—FG, Hall 37, 4:58.
Attendance—77,716.

TEAM STATISTICS

	Baltimore	N.Y. Jets
First downs	23	15
Rushes-yards	35-159	30-65
Passing	288	160
Punt returns	2-18	6-117
Kickoff returns	4-60	4-43
Interception returns	0-0	1-25
Comp.-att.-int.	25-46-1	18-33-0
Sacked-yards lost	0-0	2-8
Punts	6-43	6-48
Fumbles-lost	4-1	4-0
Penalties-yards	8-58	7-56
Time of possession	33:50	31:08

INDIVIDUAL STATISTICS
RUSHING—Baltimore, Morris 31-130, Testaverde 4-29. New York, Murrell 19-42, L. Johnson 8-19, O'Donnell 3-4.
PASSING—Baltimore, Testaverde 25-46-1-288. New York, O'Donnell 12-20-0-96, Foley 6-13-0-72.
RECEIVING—Baltimore, Green 9-80, Alexander 5-69, J. Lewis 4-72, Jackson 2-25, Byner 2-13, Morris 2-7, Yarborough 1-22. New York, Chrebet 5-46, K. Johnson 4-63, Brady 2-17, Graham 2-13, Ward 2-9, Baxter 1-13, Murrell 1-5, Anderson 1-2.
MISSED FIELD GOAL ATTEMPTS—New York, Hall 47.
INTERCEPTIONS—New York, Smith 1-25.
KICKOFF RETURNS—Baltimore, J. Lewis 3-39, Graham 1-21. New York, L. Johnson 1-21, Glenn 1-21, Ferguson 1-1, Neal 1-0.
PUNT RETURNS—Baltimore, J. Lewis 2-18. New York, L. Johnson 6-117.
SACKS—Baltimore, J. Jones 1, Boulware 1.

VIKINGS 23, PATRIOTS 18

Sunday, November 2

New England	0	3	0	15—	18
Minnesota	10	3	3	7—	23

First Quarter
Min.—FG, Murray 24, 2:58.
Min.—M. Williams 1 run (Murray kick), 5:56.

Second Quarter
N.E.—FG, Vinatieri 22, 8:15.
Min.—FG, Murray 23, 12:35.

Third Quarter
Min.—FG, Murray 41, 8:22.

Fourth Quarter
N.E.—Jefferson 5 pass from Bledsoe (conversion failed), 4:59.
N.E.—FG, Vinatieri 25, 9:14.
Min.—Carter 28 pass from Johnson (Murray kick), 12:21.
N.E.—Glenn 3 pass from Bledsoe (pass failed), 14:18.
Attendance—62,917.

TEAM STATISTICS

	New England	Minnesota
First downs	21	18
Rushes-yards	24-117	29-66
Passing	293	222

	New England	Minnesota
Punt returns	2-23	4-58
Kickoff returns	6-160	4-137
Interception returns	0-0	1-1
Comp.-att.-int.	27-42-1	18-31-0
Sacked-yards lost	3-20	1-5
Punts	5-46	5-40
Fumbles-lost	0-0	1-0
Penalties-yards	8-88	5-28
Time of possession	30:18	29:42

INDIVIDUAL STATISTICS

RUSHING—New England, Martin 21-104, Bledsoe 2-10, Meggett 1-3. Minnesota, M. Williams 19-43, Green 5-19, Evans 3-6, Johnson 2-(minus 2).

PASSING—New England, Bledsoe 27-42-1-313. Minnesota, Johnson 18-31-0-227.

RECEIVING—New England, Martin 6-36, Coates 5-58, Glenn 5-45, Jefferson 4-108, Brown 2-37, Byars 2-8, Brisby 1-10, Meggett 1-6, Gash 1-5. Minnesota, Carter 8-116, Reed 3-65, M. Williams 3-14, Evans 1-10, Hatchette 1-10, Walsh 1-7, Green 1-5.

MISSED FIELD GOAL ATTEMPTS—None.

INTERCEPTIONS—Minnesota, Thomas 1-1.

KICKOFF RETURNS—New England, Meggett 5-148, Cullors 1-12. Minnesota, M. Williams 4-137.

PUNT RETURNS—New England, Meggett 2-23. Minnesota, Palmer 4-58.

SACKS—New England, Collins 0.5, Law 0.5. Minnesota, Clemons 2, Randle 1.

BILLS 9, DOLPHINS 6

Sunday, November 2

Miami	0	3	0	3—6
Buffalo	3	3	0	3—9

First Quarter
Buf.—FG, Christie 41, 10:20.

Second Quarter
Buf.—FG, Christie 40, 3:18.
Mia.—FG, Mare 27, 14:37.

Fourth Quarter
Mia.—FG, Mare 35, 0:39.
Buf.—FG, Christie 39, 4:18.
Attendance—78,011.

TEAM STATISTICS

	Miami	Buffalo
First downs	13	17
Rushes-yards	23-54	41-179
Passing	176	86
Punt returns	2-14	4-26
Kickoff returns	4-123	2-22
Interception returns	0-0	2-10
Comp.-att.-int.	13-33-2	13-22-0
Sacked-yards lost	2-21	1-3
Punts	7-43	6-40
Fumbles-lost	3-0	6-1
Penalties-yards	5-69	6-50
Time of possession	26:04	33:56

INDIVIDUAL STATISTICS

RUSHING—Miami, Abdul-Jabbar 16-39, Erickson 4-8, Spikes 2-(minus 1), McPhail 1-8. Buffalo, A. Smith 22-59, Thomas 11-68, Van Pelt 6-17, Moulds 1-29, Holmes 1-6.

PASSING—Miami, Erickson 8-18-1-121, Marino 5-15-1-76. Buffalo, Van Pelt 13-22-0-89.

RECEIVING—Miami, McDuffie 3-42, McPhail 3-34, Drayton 2-50, Parmalee 2-21, Jordan 1-25, Perriman 1-16, Abdul-Jabbar 1-9. Buffalo, Reed 3-32, Early 3-25, Moulds 3-18, Johnson 3-14, A. Smith 1-0.

MISSED FIELD GOAL ATTEMPTS—Miami, Mare 32. Buffalo, Christie 41, 65.

INTERCEPTIONS—Buffalo, Burris 1-10, Moran 1-0.

KICKOFF RETURNS—Miami, McPhail 2-76, Spikes 2-47. Buffalo, Holmes 1-22, Cline 1-0.

PUNT RETURNS—Miami, Jordan 2-14. Buffalo, Burris 4-26.

SACKS—Miami, Burton 1. Buffalo, Moran 1, B. Smith 1.

CARDINALS 31, EAGLES 21

Sunday, November 2

Philadelphia	7	0	14	0—21
Arizona	7	3	7	14—31

First Quarter
Ariz.—Wilson 66 interception return (Nedney kick), 5:09.
Phi.—Clark 39 kickoff return (Boniol kick), 5:19.

Second Quarter
Ariz.—FG, Nedney 45, 12:30.

Third Quarter
Ariz.—R. Moore 31 pass from Plummer (Nedney kick), 6:24.
Phi.—Seay 19 pass from Detmer (Boniol kick), 9:44.
Phi.—Solomon 18 pass from Detmer (Boniol kick), 11:28.

Fourth Quarter
Ariz.—K. Graham 1 run (Nedney kick), 11:50.
Ariz.—K. Graham 1 run (Nedney kick), 14:36.
Attendance—39,549.

TEAM STATISTICS

	Philadelphia	Arizona
First downs	18	17
Rushes-yards	28-95	33-90
Passing	265	141
Punt returns	3-17	4-65
Kickoff returns	4-134	2-86
Interception returns	1-0	3-77
Comp.-att.-int.	18-40-3	12-27-1
Sacked-yards lost	2-13	5-24
Punts	7-46	7-42
Fumbles-lost	2-1	1-1
Penalties-yards	15-140	5-38
Time of possession	30:00	30:00

INDIVIDUAL STATISTICS

RUSHING—Philadelphia, Watters 21-73, Garner 6-14, Peete 1-8. Arizona, McElroy 13-67, Centers 9-1, K. Graham 6-3, Plummer 3-17, Johnson 1-2, C. Smith 1-0.

PASSING—Philadelphia, Detmer 15-27-2-224, Peete 3-13-1-54. Arizona, Plummer 7-18-1-132, K. Graham 5-9-0-33.

RECEIVING—Philadelphia, Solomon 4-77, Timpson 4-48, Watters 4-31, Fryar 2-53, Garner 2-22, Johnson 1-28, Seay 1-19. Arizona, R. Moore 3-82, Gedney 3-42, McWilliams 3-28, Centers 2-4, Sanders 1-9.

MISSED FIELD GOAL ATTEMPTS—Philadelphia, Boniol 37. Arizona, Nedney 51, 48.

INTERCEPTIONS—Philadelphia, Dawkins 1-0. Arizona, Wilson 1-66, McKinnon 1-6, Caldwell 1-5.

KICKOFF RETURNS—Philadelphia, Staley 3-95, Clark 1-39. Arizona, K. Williams 2-86.

PUNT RETURNS—Philadelphia, Seay 3-17. Arizona, K. Williams 3-66, Edwards 1-(minus 1).

SACKS—Philadelphia, H. Thomas 1.5, Willis 1, Hall 1, Jefferson 0.5, Mamula 0.5, Dent 0.5. Arizona, Rice 1, Swann 1.

FALCONS 34, RAMS 31

Sunday, November 2

St. Louis	3	21	0	7—31
Atlanta	0	17	14	3—34

First Quarter
St.L.—FG, Wilkins 38, 6:14.

Second Quarter
Atl.—Emanuel 28 pass from Chandler (Andersen kick), 3:36.
St.L.—Phillips 16 run (Wilkins kick), 6:06.
Atl.—Emanuel 33 pass from Chandler (Andersen kick), 9:47.
St.L.—Bruce 29 pass from Banks (Wilkins kick), 13:02.
St.L.—Bruce 9 pass from Banks (Wilkins kick), 14:20.
Atl.—FG, Andersen 37, 14:58.

Third Quarter
Atl.—Anderson 2 run (Andersen kick), 3:59.
Atl.—Mathis 11 pass from Chandler (Andersen kick), 8:48.

Fourth Quarter
St.L.—Banks 1 run (Wilkins kick), 13:50.
Atl.—FG, Andersen 27, 14:58.
Attendance—36,583.

TEAM STATISTICS

	St. Louis	Atlanta
First downs	24	28
Rushes-yards	29-108	26-197
Passing	399	265
Punt returns	2-(-5)	2-18
Kickoff returns	4-50	4-102
Interception returns	1-0	1-14

	St. Louis	Atlanta
Comp.-att.-int.	23-34-1	19-32-1
Sacked-yards lost	1-2	2-11
Punts	4-42	4-42
Fumbles-lost	1-0	0-0
Penalties-yards	12-57	9-64
Time of possession	30:59	29:01

INDIVIDUAL STATISTICS

RUSHING—St. Louis, Phillips 22-74, Banks 3-18, J. Moore 2-14, Kennison 1-2, Heyward 1-0. Atlanta, Anderson 20-162, Green 3-24, Chandler 1-6, Hanspard 1-4, Christian 1-1.

PASSING—St. Louis, Banks 23-34-1-401. Atlanta, Chandler 19-32-1-276.

RECEIVING—St. Louis, Bruce 10-233, Lee 5-91, Small 4-49, Conwell 2-18, Kennison 1-10, Gruttadauria 1-0. Atlanta, Mathis 7-73, Emanuel 6-108, Kinchen 2-42, Santiago 1-20, Green 1-19, Christian 1-8, Haynes 1-6.

MISSED FIELD GOAL ATTEMPTS—None.

INTERCEPTIONS—St. Louis, Lyght 1-0. Atlanta, Buchanan 1-14.

KICKOFF RETURNS—St. Louis, Thompson 3-45, Williams 1-5. Atlanta, Hanspard 1-33, Bolden 1-23, Green 1-23, Kozlowski 1-23.

PUNT RETURNS—St. Louis, Kennison 2-(minus 5). Atlanta, Kinchen 2-18.

SACKS—St. Louis, Lyle 1, O'Neal 1. Atlanta, Crockett 1.

49ERS 17, COWBOYS 10

Sunday, November 2

Dallas	7	0	3	0	10
San Francisco	0	0	7	10	17

First Quarter
Dal.—Irvin 5 pass from Aikman (Cunningham kick), 14:29.

Third Quarter
S.F.—Hearst 8 run (Anderson kick), 5:50.
Dal.—FG, Cunningham 21, 10:34.

Fourth Quarter
S.F.—Floyd 1 run (Anderson kick), 9:03.
S.F.—FG, Anderson 28, 12:45.
Attendance—68,657.

TEAM STATISTICS

	Dallas	San Francisco
First downs	16	18
Rushes-yards	25-87	33-128
Passing	184	173
Punt returns	3-42	3-52
Kickoff returns	4-61	3-57
Interception returns	1-31	2-15
Comp.-att.-int.	22-36-2	15-23-1
Sacked-yards lost	4-34	1-7
Punts	6-39	5-45
Fumbles-lost	0-0	2-1
Penalties-yards	5-30	7-49
Time of possession	31:12	28:48

INDIVIDUAL STATISTICS

RUSHING—Dallas, S. Williams 17-54, E. Smith 7-31, Aikman 1-2. San Francisco, Hearst 22-104, Kirby 4-13, Floyd 4-8, S. Young 3-3.

PASSING—Dallas, Aikman 22-36-2-218. San Francisco, S. Young 15-23-1-180.

RECEIVING—Dallas, Irvin 6-51, St. Williams 5-36, Miller 4-85, Bjornson 4-22, S. Williams 1-11, Walker 1-7, E. Smith 1-6. San Francisco, Owens 3-57, Uwaezuoke 3-29, Floyd 3-14, Stokes 2-31, Levy 1-30, Clark 1-12, Hearst 1-5, Jones 1-2.

MISSED FIELD GOAL ATTEMPTS—None.

INTERCEPTIONS—Dallas, Sanders 1-31. San Francisco, McDonald 1-15, Drakeford 1-0.

KICKOFF RETURNS—Dallas, Walker 3-43, Sanders 1-18. San Francisco, Levy 2-37, Uwaezuoke 1-20.

PUNT RETURNS—Dallas, Sanders 3-42. San Francisco, Uwaezuoke 3-52.

SACKS—Dallas, Casillas 1. San Francisco, Stubblefield 2, Greene 1, Doleman 1.

BRONCOS 30, SEAHAWKS 27

Sunday, November 2

Seattle	3	7	10	7	27
Denver	3	10	14	3	30

First Quarter
Sea.—FG, Peterson 52, 5:47.
Den.—FG, Elam 23, 13:08.

Second Quarter
Den.—Green 10 pass from Elway (Elam kick), 3:50.
Den.—FG, Elam 48, 9:51.
Sea.—McKnight 20 pass from Moon (Peterson kick), 11:48.

Third Quarter
Den.—Johnson 6 fumble return (Elam kick), 0:11.
Sea.—FG, Peterson 41, 9:42.
Sea.—Strong 4 pass from Moon (Peterson kick), 11:09.
Den.—R. Smith 59 pass from Elway (Elam kick), 13:14.

Fourth Quarter
Sea.—Br. Blades 8 pass from Moon (Peterson kick), 2:58.
Den.—FG, Elam 22, 7:32.
Attendance—74,212.

TEAM STATISTICS

	Seattle	Denver
First downs	22	19
Rushes-yards	18-104	31-140
Passing	245	245
Punt returns	3-5	2-18
Kickoff returns	6-91	6-114
Interception returns	0-0	0-0
Comp.-att.-int.	28-46-0	19-30-0
Sacked-yards lost	2-11	1-7
Punts	5-41	4-47
Fumbles-lost	5-2	4-2
Penalties-yards	7-50	7-55
Time of possession	28:20	31:40

INDIVIDUAL STATISTICS

RUSHING—Seattle, Warren 12-55, Broussard 4-33, Galloway 2-16. Denver, Davis 21-101, Elway 7-24, Hebron 2-12, R. Smith 1-3.

PASSING—Seattle, Moon 28-46-0-256. Denver, Elway 19-30-0-252.

RECEIVING—Seattle, Galloway 8-98, Warren 5-28, Pritchard 4-33, Br. Blades 3-27, Crumpler 3-19, McKnight 2-41, Broussard 2-6, Strong 1-4. Denver, Davis 6-17, R. Smith 5-114, Sharpe 3-85, Green 2-22, McCaffrey 1-8, Carswell 1-6, Griffith 1-0.

MISSED FIELD GOAL ATTEMPTS—None.

INTERCEPTIONS—None.

KICKOFF RETURNS—Seattle, Broussard 3-60, Harris 2-33, Daniels 1-(minus 2). Denver, Hebron 6-114.

PUNT RETURNS—Seattle, Harris 3-5. Denver, Gordon 2-18.

SACKS—Seattle, Bellamy 1. Denver, Braxton 1, Hasselbach 1.

PANTHERS 38, RAIDERS 14

Sunday, November 2

Oakland	0	7	7	0	14
Carolina	14	14	3	7	38

First Quarter
Car.—Lane 15 run (Kasay kick), 5:25.
Car.—Lane 18 run (Kasay kick), 14:58.

Second Quarter
Car.—Collins 6 run (Kasay kick), 9:06.
Oak.—Kaufman 23 pass from George (Ford kick), 11:36.
Car.—Greene 10 run (Kasay kick), 13:55.

Third Quarter
Oak.—Jett 16 pass from George (Ford kick), 3:28.
Car.—FG, Kasay 54, 11:59.

Fourth Quarter
Car.—Lane 32 run (Kasay kick), 8:41.
Attendance—71,064.

TEAM STATISTICS

	Oakland	Carolina
First downs	20	27
Rushes-yards	16-38	41-216
Passing	319	192
Punt returns	1-31	2-25
Kickoff returns	6-136	3-95
Interception returns	0-0	2-18
Comp.-att.-int.	28-45-2	18-32-0
Sacked-yards lost	2-12	1-6
Punts	5-43	4-32
Fumbles-lost	1-0	1-0
Penalties-yards	7-60	5-40
Time of possession	24:58	35:02

INDIVIDUAL STATISTICS

RUSHING—Oakland, Kaufman 10-16, Hall 2-16, Williams 2-5, George 1-1, Klingler 1-0. Carolina, Lane 28-147, Greene 4-17, Collins 3-29, Biakabutuka 3-6, Johnson 1-8, Ismail 1-7, Carruth 1-2.

PASSING—Oakland, George 24-38-1-304, Klingler 4-7-1-27. Carolina, Collins 18-32-0-198.

RECEIVING—Oakland, T. Brown 10-163, Kaufman 7-70, Dudley 5-51, Jett 2-22, Howard 2-14, Fenner 2-11. Carolina, Walls 5-73, Ismail 5-43, Greene 2-35, Johnson 2-12, Lane 2-11, Carruth 1-14, Carrier 1-10.

MISSED FIELD GOAL ATTEMPTS—Oakland, Ford 45.

INTERCEPTIONS—Carolina, S. Mills 1-18, Poole 1-0.

KICKOFF RETURNS—Oakland, Howard 4-101, Hall 2-35. Carolina, Bates 2-58, Stone 1-37.

PUNT RETURNS—Oakland, Howard 1-31. Carolina, Poole 2-25.

SACKS—Oakland, Lewis 1. Carolina, Royal 1, Lathon 1.

JAGUARS 30, OILERS 24

Sunday, November 2

Jacksonville	17	7	3	3—30
Tennessee	7	3	7	7—24

First Quarter
Ten.—D. Lewis 47 interception return (Del Greco kick), 4:46.
Jac.—FG, Hollis 30, 12:11.
Jac.—Hudson 32 fumble return (Hollis kick), 12:31.
Jac.—Mitchell 6 pass from Brunell (Hollis kick), 14:49.
Second Quarter
Ten.—FG, Del Greco 36, 3:27.
Jac.—Brunell 6 run (Hollis kick), 13:02.
Third Quarter
Jac.—FG, Hollis 30, 5:49.
Ten.—Thomas 3 run (Del Greco kick), 9:55.
Fourth Quarter
Jac.—FG, Hollis 37, 1:31.
Ten.—George 5 run (Del Greco kick), 2:22.
Attendance—27,208.

TEAM STATISTICS

	Jacksonville	Tennessee
First downs	17	15
Rushes-yards	31-135	27-107
Passing	155	195
Punt returns	3-76	2-0
Kickoff returns	5-105	7-131
Interception returns	1-6	1-47
Comp.-att.-int.	17-31-1	13-22-1
Sacked-yards lost	3-14	2-16
Punts	4-52	3-50
Fumbles-lost	1-1	3-1
Penalties-yards	6-65	9-59
Time of possession	33:24	26:36

INDIVIDUAL STATISTICS

RUSHING—Jacksonville, Stewart 17-99, Means 9-20, Brunell 4-16, Barker 1-0. Tennessee, George 17-51, McNair 6-34, Thomas 4-22.

PASSING—Jacksonville, Brunell 17-31-1-169. Tennessee, McNair 13-22-1-211.

RECEIVING—Jacksonville, Smith 5-50, Mitchell 4-34, McCardell 3-22, Stewart 2-44, Hallock 1-10, Jackson 1-9, Means 1-0. Tennessee, Wycheck 5-77, Davis 4-83, Roan 3-51, Sanders 1-0.

MISSED FIELD GOAL ATTEMPTS—Tennessee, Del Greco 33, 41.

INTERCEPTIONS—Jacksonville, Hudson 1-6. Tennessee, D. Lewis 1-47.

KICKOFF RETURNS—Jacksonville, Jackson 5-105. Tennessee, Mason 6-126, Layman 1-5.

PUNT RETURNS—Jacksonville, Barlow 3-76. Tennessee, Gray 2-0.

SACKS—Jacksonville, Simmons 1, Team 1. Tennessee, Evans 1, Ford 1, Hall 1.

PACKERS 20, LIONS 10

Sunday, November 2

Detroit	7	3	0	0—10
Green Bay	0	14	3	3—20

First Quarter
Det.—Vardell 1 run (Hanson kick), 9:32.
Second Quarter
G.B.—R. Brooks 26 pass from Favre (Longwell kick), 0:50.
G.B.—Sharper 50 interception return (Longwell kick), 10:17.
Det.—FG, Hanson 34, 14:48.

Third Quarter
G.B.—FG, Longwell 23, 4:36.
Fourth Quarter
G.B.—FG, Longwell 44, 8:16.
Attendance—60,126.

TEAM STATISTICS

	Detroit	Green Bay
First downs	18	11
Rushes-yards	28-125	25-81
Passing	131	163
Punt returns	4-16	4-22
Kickoff returns	5-120	3-44
Interception returns	1-17	4-56
Comp.-att.-int.	21-47-4	15-28-1
Sacked-yards lost	4-27	2-18
Punts	8-38	8-42
Fumbles-lost	2-0	2-1
Penalties-yards	4-20	7-54
Time of possession	32:41	27:19

INDIVIDUAL STATISTICS

RUSHING—Detroit, Sanders 23-105, Mitchell 3-18, Vardell 2-2. Green Bay, Levens 20-59, Favre 4-13, Henderson 1-9.

PASSING—Detroit, Mitchell 21-47-4-158. Green Bay, Favre 15-28-1-181.

RECEIVING—Detroit, Moore 9-50, Sloan 5-29, Morton 4-35, Schlesinger 1-33, Metzelaars 1-7, Vardell 1-4. Green Bay, R. Brooks 5-77, Freeman 5-44, Levens 3-6, Chmura 1-28, Davis 1-26.

MISSED FIELD GOAL ATTEMPTS—None.

INTERCEPTIONS—Detroit, Carrier 1-17. Green Bay, Butler 2-0, Sharper 1-50, Evans 1-6.

KICKOFF RETURNS—Detroit, Milburn 5-120. Green Bay, Schroeder 2-24, Hayden 1-20.

PUNT RETURNS—Detroit, Milburn 4-16. Green Bay, Schroeder 3-22, Prior 1-0.

SACKS—Detroit, Elliss 1, Team 1. Green Bay, White 1, McKenzie 1, Smith 1, Robinson 0.5, Brown 0.5.

BUCCANEERS 31, COLTS 28

Sunday, November 2

Tampa Bay	7	14	0	10—31
Indianapolis	3	7	11	7—28

First Quarter
T.B.—Alstott 1 run (Husted kick), 7:31.
Ind.—FG, Blanchard 43, 11:23.
Second Quarter
Ind.—Faulk 4 run (Blanchard kick), 1:38.
T.B.—Moore 2 pass from Dilfer (Husted kick), 8:29.
T.B.—Williams 6 pass from Dilfer (Husted kick), 14:25.
Third Quarter
Ind.—FG, Blanchard 36, 4:56.
Ind.—Warren 1 run (Pollard pass from Holcomb), 14:05.
Fourth Quarter
Ind.—Blackmon 18 fumble return (Blanchard kick), 4:14.
T.B.—Williams 24 pass from Dilfer (Husted kick), 8:08.
T.B.—FG, Husted 36, 14:52.
Attendance—58,512.

TEAM STATISTICS

	Tampa Bay	Indianapolis
First downs	18	23
Rushes-yards	25-84	34-147
Passing	150	212
Punt returns	3-99	3-17
Kickoff returns	5-117	4-60
Interception returns	1-0	0-0
Comp.-att.-int.	16-25-0	20-33-1
Sacked-yards lost	3-14	2-13
Punts	6-43	3-48
Fumbles-lost	1-1	4-2
Penalties-yards	10-87	5-25
Time of possession	26:09	33:51

INDIVIDUAL STATISTICS

RUSHING—Tampa Bay, Alstott 16-45, Dunn 7-17, Anthony 1-17, Dilfer 1-5. Indianapolis, Crockett 14-81, Faulk 14-40, Warren 4-8, Bailey 1-18, Justin 1-0.

PASSING—Tampa Bay, Dilfer 16-25-0-164. Indianapolis, Holcomb 19-30-1-181, Justin 1-3-0-44.

RECEIVING—Tampa Bay, Moore 6-53, Dunn 3-39, Williams 2-30, Copeland 2-25, Anthony 2-16, Hape 1-1. Indianapolis, Dawkins 4-55, Warren 4-37, Harrison 3-57, Dilger 3-37, Crockett 3-29, Stablein 2-11, Faulk 1-(minus 1).

MISSED FIELD GOAL ATTEMPTS—Indianapolis, Blanchard 30.

INTERCEPTIONS—Tampa Bay, Abraham 1-0.

KICKOFF RETURNS—Tampa Bay, Anthony 4-97, Williams 1-20. Indianapolis, Bailey 4-60.

PUNT RETURNS—Tampa Bay, Williams 3-99. Indianapolis, Stablein 3-17.

SACKS—Tampa Bay, Sapp 1, Team 1. Indianapolis, Morrison 1, Fontenot 1, Footman 1.

BENGALS 38, CHARGERS 31

Sunday, November 2

San Diego	7	10	0	14—31
Cincinnati	0	24	7	7—38

First Quarter
S.D.—Brown 1 run (G. Davis kick), 12:48.

Second Quarter
Cin.—FG, Pelfrey 27, 2:12.
Cin.—Pickens 15 pass from Blake (Pelfrey kick), 3:41.
S.D.—Metcalf 85 punt return (G. Davis kick), 6:14.
Cin.—Milne 2 run (Pelfrey kick), 13:00.
Cin.—Copeland 25 fumble return (Pelfrey kick), 13:40.
S.D.—FG, G. Davis 45, 15:00.

Third Quarter
Cin.—Dillon 71 run (Pelfrey kick), 14:41.

Fourth Quarter
S.D.—Metcalf 67 punt return (G. Davis kick), 2:36.
Cin.—Blake 13 run (Pelfrey kick), 7:58.
S.D.—C. Jones 44 pass from Whelihan (G. Davis kick), 9:00.
Attendance—53,754.

TEAM STATISTICS

	San Diego	Cincinnati
First downs	14	18
Rushes-yards	21-67	37-174
Passing	168	162
Punt returns	4-168	5-26
Kickoff returns	5-102	5-110
Interception returns	0-0	1-37
Comp.-att.-int.	20-41-1	19-33-0
Sacked-yards lost	6-37	3-10
Punts	10-49	11-43
Fumbles-lost	2-2	3-1
Penalties-yards	7-58	6-54
Time of possession	27:12	32:48

INDIVIDUAL STATISTICS
RUSHING—San Diego, Brown 14-34, Craver 3-23, Fletcher 2-7, Whelihan 1-3, Humphries 1-0. Cincinnati, Dillon 19-123, Carter 9-25, Blake 7-21, Bieniemy 1-3, Milne 1-2.

PASSING—San Diego, Humphries 12-25-1-115, Whelihan 8-16-0-90. Cincinnati, Blake 19-32-0-172, Carter 0-1-0-0.

•

RECEIVING—San Diego, Martin 7-69, F. Jones 5-37, Fletcher 4-36, Still 2-15, C. Jones 1-44, Metcalf 1-4. Cincinnati, Scott 6-52, Pickens 4-45, McGee 4-44, Bieniemy 1-12, Milne 1-9, Carter 1-5, Dillon 1-4, Graham 1-1.

MISSED FIELD GOAL ATTEMPTS—None.

INTERCEPTIONS—Cincinnati, Sawyer 1-37.

KICKOFF RETURNS—San Diego, Rachal 2-44, Bynum 2-36, Metcalf 1-22. Cincinnati, Dunn 3-72, Bieniemy 2-38.

PUNT RETURNS—San Diego, Metcalf 4-168. Cincinnati, Myers 5-26.

SACKS—San Diego, Seau 1, Parrella 1, Lee 1. Cincinnati, Wilson 2, Dixon 2, Collins 1.5, Copeland 0.5.

CHIEFS 13, STEELERS 10

Monday, November 3

Pittsburgh	10	0	0	0—10
Kansas City	0	13	0	0—13

First Quarter
Pit.—Hawkins 44 pass from Stewart (N. Johnson kick), 6:55.
Pit.—FG, N. Johnson 27, 14:28.

Second Quarter
K.C.—FG, Stoyanovich 35, 5:47.
K.C.—FG, Stoyanovich 44, 12:06.
K.C.—Hughes 14 pass from Allen (Stoyanovich kick), 13:20.
Attendance—78,301.

TEAM STATISTICS

	Pittsburgh	Kansas City
First downs	12	24
Rushes-yards	23-142	42-183
Passing	93	209
Punt returns	1-3	3-23
Kickoff returns	4-83	3-53
Interception returns	1-33	1-17
Comp.-att.-int.	11-21-1	22-35-1
Sacked-yards lost	1-8	0-0
Punts	7-44	3-38
Fumbles-lost	1-0	2-1
Penalties-yards	4-40	4-36
Time of possession	23:28	36:32

INDIVIDUAL STATISTICS
RUSHING—Pittsburgh, Bettis 17-103, Stewart 3-24, G. Jones 2-14, McAfee 1-1. Kansas City, Allen 10-49, Hill 9-18, Bennett 8-38, Anders 5-17, Grbac 4-35, Gannon 4-10, Vanover 2-16.

PASSING—Pittsburgh, Stewart 11-21-1-101. Kansas City, Grbac 16-29-1-172, Gannon 5-5-0-23, Allen 1-1-0-14.

RECEIVING—Pittsburgh, Hawkins 5-76, Lester 2-9, Bettis 2-7, Thigpen 1-11, G. Jones 1-(minus 2). Kansas City, Anders 7-40, Gonzalez 4-56, Rison 4-52, Hughes 2-24, Dawson 2-19, Popson 2-12, Walker 1-6.

MISSED FIELD GOAL ATTEMPTS—None.

INTERCEPTIONS—Pittsburgh, Woolford 1-33. Kansas City, Woods 1-17.

KICKOFF RETURNS—Pittsburgh, Coleman 4-83. Kansas City, Vanover 3-53.

PUNT RETURNS—Pittsburgh, Coleman 1-3. Kansas City, Vanover 3-23.

SACKS—Kansas City, Williams 1.

RESULTS

Cincinnati 28, INDIANAPOLIS 13
DALLAS 24, Arizona 6
DENVER 34, Carolina 0
GREEN BAY 17, St. Louis 7
JACKSONVILLE 24, Kansas City 10
MIAMI 24, N.Y. Jets 17
MINNESOTA 29, Chicago 22
New England 31, BUFFALO 10
New Orleans 13, OAKLAND 10
PITTSBURGH 37, Baltimore 0
Seattle 37, SAN DIEGO 31
Tampa Bay 31, ATLANTA 10
TENNESSEE 10, N.Y. Giants 6
WASHINGTON 30, Detroit 7
San Francisco 24, PHILADELPHIA 12

STANDINGS

AFC EAST

	W	L	T	Pct.
Miami	6	4	0	.600
New England	6	4	0	.600
N.Y. Jets	6	4	0	.600
Buffalo	5	5	0	.500
Indianapolis	0	10	0	.000

AFC CENTRAL

	W	L	T	Pct.
Jacksonville	7	3	0	.700
Pittsburgh	7	3	0	.700
Tennessee	5	5	0	.500
Baltimore	4	6	0	.400
Cincinnati	3	7	0	.300

AFC WEST

	W	L	T	Pct.
Denver	9	1	0	.900
Kansas City	7	3	0	.700
Seattle	6	4	0	.600
San Diego	4	6	0	.400
Oakland	3	7	0	.300

NFC EAST

	W	L	T	Pct.
N.Y. Giants	6	4	0	.600
Washington	6	4	0	.600
Dallas	5	5	0	.500
Philadelphia	4	6	0	.400
Arizona	2	8	0	.200

NFC CENTRAL

	W	L	T	Pct.
Green Bay	8	2	0	.800
Minnesota	8	2	0	.800
Tampa Bay	7	3	0	.700
Detroit	4	6	0	.400
Chicago	1	9	0	.100

NFC WEST

	W	L	T	Pct.
San Francisco	9	1	0	.900
Carolina	5	5	0	.500
New Orleans	3	7	0	.300
Atlanta	2	8	0	.200
St. Louis	2	8	0	.200

HIGHLIGHTS

Hero of the week: Denver's Darrien Gordon set the tone for the Broncos' 34-0 rout of Carolina by returning two punts for touchdowns in the first quarter. Gordon, the top-ranked punt returner in NFL history, went virtually untouched on 82- and 75-yard returns at a snowy Mile High Stadium.

Goat of the week: The Ravens' quarterback tandem of Vinny Testaverde and Eric Zeier combined to give up six turnovers in an embarrassing 37-0 loss at Pittsburgh. Testaverde, weakened by the flu and frustrated by the Steelers' ever-changing defense, threw interceptions on Baltimore's first three possessions, and backup Zeier threw one interception and fumbled twice. During one stretch in the first half, Testaverde and Zeier threw three interceptions in three passes.

Sub of the week: Bengals quarterback Boomer Esiason replaced starter Jeff Blake, who left the game because of a slight concussion in the third quarter, and sparked Cincinnati to a 28-13 victory over Indianapolis. Esiason led the Bengals on three second-half touchdown drives to break open a game that was tied at 7 at halftime.

Comeback of the week: In the first quarter of the Seattle-San Diego game, the Chargers scored two touchdowns to take a 14-0 lead. After an exchange of field goals made the score 17-3, Seattle began its comeback. Thanks to quarterback Warren Moon going 24-of-45 for 295 yards and two touchdowns, the Seahawks rallied to beat San Diego, 37-31.

Blowout of the week: The Steelers dominated nearly every statistical category and the Ravens committed seven turnovers in Pittsburgh's 37-0 win. Steelers running back Jerome Bettis' rushing yardage (114) was more than the combined passing yardage (112) of Baltimore quarterbacks Vinny Testaverde and Eric Zeier.

Nail-biter of the week: After leading, 21-10, at halftime, the Vikings allowed the Bears to take a 22-21 lead late in the fourth quarter. With less than four minutes left, Vikings quarterback Brad Johnson led his team on a 75-yard drive in nine plays. Running back Leroy Hoard capped it off by scoring a touchdown with 54 seconds remaining, and Minnesota added a two-point conversion for a 29-22 victory.

Hit of the week: The Seahawks sacked Chargers quarterback Craig Whelihan—making his first NFL start—on fourth-and-6 at midfield with 43 seconds left, causing a fumble to secure Seattle's 37-31 victory.

Oddity of the week: After losing a bet that his defense would be unable to stop a crossing pattern by Oakland wide receiver Tim Brown, Saints coach Mike Ditka handed $50 to defensive coordinator Zaven Yaralian on the sidelines late in the game. Ditka laughed as Yaralian counted out $25 in change. The NFL did not laugh; it fined Ditka a few days later.

Top rusher: Glenn Foley was 25-of-48 for 322 yards and one touchdown in the Jets' 24-17 loss to Miami.

Top passer: Eddie George had 32 carries for 122 yards and one touchdown in the Oilers' 10-6 victory over the Giants.

Top receiver: Denver's Shannon Sharpe caught eight passes for 174 yards against Carolina.

Notes: Darrien Gordon became the first Bronco to return two punts for touchdowns in the same game since Rick Upchurch did it against Cleveland on September 26, 1976. . . . Arizona tackle Lomas Brown aggravated a foot injury before the game, ending a 189-game streak. . . . Dallas' Emmitt Smith scored his 110th career rushing touchdown, tying him with Walter Payton for second on the career list. . . . Mike Holmgren coached his 100th game with the Packers. . . . New England's Adam Vinatieri had a streak of consecutive field goals stopped at 25. . . . Kansas City's Marcus Allen gained 37 yards to join six others in NFL history with 12,000 yards rushing. . . . Detroit's Barry Sanders became the first NFL player to rush for 1,000 yards in nine consecutive seasons. He also surpassed the 100-yard mark for the eighth consecutive road game, breaking a league record he had shared with Allen.

Quote of the week: Oakland receiver Tim Brown, on the grim state of affairs for the 3-7 Raiders:

"I looked up in the stands and saw a sign that said, 'PSL: Please Stop Losing.' That's about as low as it gets at your home stadium."

GAME SUMMARIES

VIKINGS 29, BEARS 22

Sunday, November 9

Chicago	7	3	9	3—22
Minnesota	7	14	0	8—29

First Quarter
Min.—Palmer 8 run (Murray kick), 8:16.
Chi.—R. Harris 1 run (Jaeger kick), 14:22.
Second Quarter
Min.—Palmer 7 pass from Johnson (Murray kick), 5:14.
Chi.—FG, Jaeger 29, 11:36.
Min.—Evans 3 run (Murray kick), 13:04.
Third Quarter
Chi.—FG, Jaeger 22, 4:46.
Chi.—Proehl 59 pass from Kramer (pass failed), 9:07.
Fourth Quarter
Chi.—FG, Jaeger 36, 11:27.
Min.—Hoard 1 run (Carter pass from Johnson), 14:06.
    Attendance—63,443.

TEAM STATISTICS

	Chicago	Minnesota
First downs	20	19
Rushes-yards	29-90	27-109
Passing	251	193
Punt returns	5-31	2-12
Kickoff returns	5-116	6-158
Interception returns	2-4	1-2
Comp.-att.-int.	23-35-1	22-33-2
Sacked-yards lost	2-5	2-10
Punts	4-45	5-45
Fumbles-lost	2-1	0-0
Penalties-yards	4-29	4-49
Time of possession	33:19	26:41

INDIVIDUAL STATISTICS
RUSHING—Chicago, Autry 13-59, R. Harris 13-22, Kramer 2-(minus 3), Smith 1-12. Minnesota, Hoard 13-31, Evans 8-50, Johnson 3-9, Palmer 2-15, M. Williams 1-4.
PASSING—Chicago, Kramer 23-35-1-256. Minnesota, Johnson 22-33-2-203.
RECEIVING—Chicago, Proehl 9-132, Tony Carter 3-29, Wetnight 3-26, Engram 2-23, Bownes 2-20, R. Harris 2-16, Smith 1-10, Autry 1-0. Minnesota, Carter 8-69, Hoard 4-25, Palmer 3-41, Glover 2-20, Reed 1-21, Evans 1-12, Walsh 1-11, DeLong 1-4, M. Williams 1-0.
MISSED FIELD GOAL ATTEMPTS—Minnesota, Murray 53.
INTERCEPTIONS—Chicago, Mangum 1-4, W. Harris 1-0. Minnesota, Fuller 1-2.
KICKOFF RETURNS—Chicago, Hughes 5-114. Minnesota, M. Williams 5-96, Palmer 1-62.
PUNT RETURNS—Chicago, Hughes 5-31. Minnesota, Palmer 2-12.
SACKS—Chicago, B. Cox 1, Simpson 1. Minnesota, Randle 1, Clemons 1.

BRONCOS 34, PANTHERS 0

Sunday, November 9

Carolina	0	0	0	0— 0
Denver	14	3	10	7—34

First Quarter
Den.—Gordon 82 punt return (Elam kick), 7:05.
Den.—Gordon 75 punt return (Elam kick), 14:14.
Second Quarter
Den.—FG, Elam 25, 14:15.
Third Quarter
Den.—FG, Elam 50, 4:04.
Den.—R. Smith 20 pass from Elway (Elam kick), 11:07.
Fourth Quarter
Den.—Braxton 27 interception return (Elam kick), 1:47.
    Attendance—71,408.

TEAM STATISTICS

	Carolina	Denver
First downs	7	20
Rushes-yards	14-34	42-160
Passing	113	233
Punt returns	1-0	5-168
Kickoff returns	7-177	1-24
Interception returns	0-0	3-31
Comp.-att.-int.	13-29-3	15-24-0
Sacked-yards lost	4-28	3-15
Punts	9-47	3-37
Fumbles-lost	3-1	2-1
Penalties-yards	4-62	3-15
Time of possession	22:41	37:19

INDIVIDUAL STATISTICS
RUSHING—Carolina, Lane 8-18, Carruth 2-9, Johnson 2-6, Greene 1-1, Collins 1-0. Denver, Davis 21-104, Hebron 9-42, Elway 8-11, Lewis 4-3.
PASSING—Carolina, Collins 13-29-3-141. Denver, Elway 14-23-0-227, Lewis 1-1-0-21.
RECEIVING—Carolina, Carrier 4-62, Walls 4-57, Ismail 2-12, Greene 2-6, Lane 1-4. Denver, Sharpe 8-174, R. Smith 4-40, Lynn 1-21, Davis 1-12, Griffith 1-1.
MISSED FIELD GOAL ATTEMPTS—Denver, Elam 42.
INTERCEPTIONS—Denver, Crockett 2-4, Braxton 1-27.
KICKOFF RETURNS—Carolina, Bates 6-166, Rasby 1-11. Denver, Hebron 1-24.
PUNT RETURNS—Carolina, Oliver 1-0. Denver, Gordon 5-168.
SACKS—Carolina, Miller 1, Barrow 1, Kragen 1. Denver, Mobley 1, Tanuvasa 1, Lodish 1, Williams 0.5, Pryce 0.5.

BENGALS 28, COLTS 13

Sunday, November 9

Cincinnati	0	7	14	7—28
Indianapolis	0	7	3	3—13

Second Quarter
Cin.—McGee 15 pass from Blake (Pelfrey kick), 10:37.
Ind.—Harrison 6 pass from Holcomb (Blanchard kick), 13:52.
Third Quarter
Ind.—FG, Blanchard 42, 5:31.
Cin.—Dillon 46 run (Pelfrey kick), 8:27.
Cin.—Pickens 5 pass from Esiason (Pelfrey kick), 13:27.
Fourth Quarter
Cin.—McGee 5 pass from Esiason (Pelfrey kick), 7:57.
Ind.—FG, Blanchard 45, 9:20.
    Attendance—58,473.

TEAM STATISTICS

	Cincinnati	Indianapolis
First downs	17	22
Rushes-yards	33-144	30-150
Passing	129	191
Punt returns	0-0	2-25
Kickoff returns	3-78	5-117
Interception returns	3-63	0-0
Comp.-att.-int.	16-25-0	19-32-3
Sacked-yards lost	3-16	7-45
Punts	5-41	2-45
Fumbles-lost	3-1	2-1
Penalties-yards	3-60	11-101
Time of possession	25:26	34:34

INDIVIDUAL STATISTICS
RUSHING—Cincinnati, Dillon 22-97, Carter 4-7, Milne 3-9, Blake 2-22, Bieniemy 1-10, Esiason 1-(minus 1). Indianapolis, Faulk 18-110, Warren 6-27, Crockett 3-8, Holcomb 3-5.
PASSING—Cincinnati, Blake 9-15-0-63, Esiason 7-10-0-82. Indianapolis, Holcomb 19-32-3-236.
RECEIVING—Cincinnati, Dunn 3-43, Battaglia 3-35, McGee 2-20, Pickens 2-15, Milne 2-3, Bieniemy 1-15, Scott 1-8, Dillon 1-5, Carter 1-1. Indianapolis, Harrison 8-83, Dawkins 4-32, Dilger 3-44, Faulk 1-41, Warren 1-15, Crockett 1-14, Stablein 1-7.
MISSED FIELD GOAL ATTEMPTS—Indianapolis, Blanchard 31.
INTERCEPTIONS—Cincinnati, Ambrose 2-56, Francis 1-7.
KICKOFF RETURNS—Cincinnati, Dunn 2-58, Bieniemy 1-20. Indianapolis, Bailey 4-94, Hetherington 1-23.
PUNT RETURNS—Indianapolis, Stablein 2-25.
SACKS—Cincinnati, Ambrose 1, Francis 1, Shade 1, Copeland 1, Langford 1, Wilkinson 1, McDonald 1. Indianapolis, Footman 1, Burroughs 1, Team 1.

COWBOYS 24, CARDINALS 6

Sunday, November 9

Arizona	3	0	3	0— 6
Dallas	0	10	14	0—24

First Quarter
Ariz.—FG, Nedney 42, 10:38.
Second Quarter
Dal.—FG, Cunningham 23, 4:41.
Dal.—Walker 11 pass from Aikman (Cunningham kick), 13:56.
Third Quarter
Ariz.—FG, Nedney 39, 2:18.
Dal.—S. Williams 1 run (Cunningham kick), 6:10.
Dal.—E. Smith 5 run (Cunningham kick), 11:27.
Attendance—64,302.

TEAM STATISTICS

	Arizona	Dallas
First downs	18	19
Rushes-yards	26-101	35-125
Passing	173	204
Punt returns	3-7	0-0
Kickoff returns	5-93	2-36
Interception returns	1-17	0-0
Comp.-att.-int.	18-36-0	15-22-1
Sacked-yards lost	9-49	2-12
Punts	4-36	6-37
Fumbles-lost	2-1	0-0
Penalties-yards	8-60	7-70
Time of possession	30:45	29:15

INDIVIDUAL STATISTICS

RUSHING—Arizona, Plummer 7-51, Centers 7-18, McElroy 7-5, R. Moore 5-27. Dallas, S. Williams 16-53, E. Smith 15-64, Aikman 2-10, Wilson 2-(minus 2).

PASSING—Arizona, Plummer 13-22-0-148, K. Graham 5-14-0-74. Dallas, Aikman 15-22-1-216.

RECEIVING—Arizona, R. Moore 6-95, Centers 3-20, Edwards 2-33, McWilliams 2-21, Gedney 2-17, Sanders 2-7, Brock 1-29. Dallas, Miller 3-77, E. Smith 3-12, Irvin 2-36, Bjornson 2-26, Walker 2-23, St. Williams 1-20, B. Davis 1-12, LaFleur 1-10.

MISSED FIELD GOAL ATTEMPTS—Arizona, Nedney 46, 51.

INTERCEPTIONS—Arizona, McKinnon 1-17.

KICKOFF RETURNS—Arizona, K. Williams 5-93. Dallas, Walker 2-36.

PUNT RETURNS—Arizona, K. Williams 3-7.

SACKS—Arizona, Bankston 1, Miller 1. Dallas, Carver 2, Tolbert 2, Woodson 1, Bates 1, Thomas 1, C. Williams 1, Coakley 0.5, McCormack 0.5.

REDSKINS 30, LIONS 7

Sunday, November 9

Detroit	0	0	7	0— 7
Washington	3	10	7	10—30

First Quarter
Was.—FG, Blanton 22, 7:34.
Second Quarter
Was.—Jenkins 1 pass from Frerotte (Blanton kick), 10:35.
Was.—FG, Blanton 50, 15:00.
Third Quarter
Was.—Allen 1 run (Blanton kick), 9:41.
Det.—Sanders 51 run (Hanson kick), 10:03.
Fourth Quarter
Was.—FG, Blanton 45, 5:36.
Was.—Pounds 22 interception return (Blanton kick), 6:04.
Attendance—75,261.

TEAM STATISTICS

	Detroit	Washington
First downs	11	25
Rushes-yards	15-105	44-141
Passing	163	247
Punt returns	4-69	5-82
Kickoff returns	5-131	2-38
Interception returns	0-0	3-38
Comp.-att.-int.	15-43-3	20-41-0
Sacked-yards lost	0-0	0-0
Punts	8-45	7-48
Fumbles-lost	1-1	0-0
Penalties-yards	7-83	7-62
Time of possession	19:57	40:03

INDIVIDUAL STATISTICS

RUSHING—Detroit, Sanders 15-105. Washington, Allen 31-94, Bowie 4-17, Frerotte 4-2, Davis 3-2, Mitchell 2-26.

PASSING—Detroit, Reich 10-28-2-110, Mitchell 5-14-0-53, Blundin 0-1-1-0. Washington, Frerotte 20-41-0-247.

RECEIVING—Detroit, Morton 5-69, Moore 5-36, Vardell 2-42, Sanders 1-9, Milburn 1-4, Sloan 1-3. Washington, Westbrook 4-93, Mitchell 4-37, Bowie 3-33, Allen 3-21, Shepherd 2-16, Davis 1-19, Ellard 1-16, Asher 1-11, Jenkins 1-1.

MISSED FIELD GOAL ATTEMPTS—Washington, Blanton 40, 46.

INTERCEPTIONS—Washington, Pounds 2-31, Campbell 1-7.

KICKOFF RETURNS—Detroit, Milburn 5-131. Washington, Mitchell 2-38.

PUNT RETURNS—Detroit, Milburn 4-69. Washington, Mitchell 5-82.

SACKS—None.

DOLPHINS 24, JETS 17

Sunday, November 9

N.Y. Jets	0	10	0	7—17
Miami	7	7	7	3—24

First Quarter
Mia.—Abdul-Jabbar 4 run (Mare kick), 6:31.
Second Quarter
NYJ—FG, Hall 29, 9:05.
NYJ—Brady 18 pass from Foley (Hall kick), 13:24.
Mia.—Perriman 23 pass from Marino (Mare kick), 14:55.
Third Quarter
Mia.—Abdul-Jabbar 5 run (Mare kick), 7:07.
Fourth Quarter
Mia.—FG, Mare 21, 6:10.
NYJ—Murrell 43 run (Hall kick), 7:23.
Attendance—73,809.

TEAM STATISTICS

	N.Y. Jets	Miami
First downs	20	22
Rushes-yards	18-79	36-120
Passing	305	176
Punt returns	6-37	2-15
Kickoff returns	5-117	3-41
Interception returns	0-0	1-23
Comp.-att.-int.	25-48-1	18-29-0
Sacked-yards lost	2-17	1-10
Punts	4-41	7-46
Fumbles-lost	2-1	0-0
Penalties-yards	7-78	3-22
Time of possession	26:40	33:20

INDIVIDUAL STATISTICS

RUSHING—New York, Murrell 12-69, L. Johnson 4-7, Ward 1-4, Foley 1-(minus 1). Miami, Abdul-Jabbar 25-103, Spikes 8-18, Marino 2-(minus 2), McPhail 1-1.

PASSING—New York, Foley 25-48-1-322. Miami, Marino 18-29-0-186.

RECEIVING—New York, Ward 6-108, K. Johnson 6-79, Chrebet 4-30, Baxter 3-35, Graham 3-31, Brady 2-29, Neal 1-10. Miami, McDuffie 3-23, Perry 3-19, Perriman 2-39, L. Thomas 2-30, McPhail 2-21, Abdul-Jabbar 2-19, Drayton 2-18, Jordan 1-10, Spikes 1-7.

MISSED FIELD GOAL ATTEMPTS—New York, Hall 39.

INTERCEPTIONS—Miami, Teague 1-23.

KICKOFF RETURNS—New York, Glenn 3-93, L. Johnson 1-24, Hamilton 1-0. Miami, McPhail 1-20, Spikes 1-15, Jordan 1-6.

PUNT RETURNS—New York, L. Johnson 6-37. Miami, Jordan 2-15.

SACKS—New York, Ferguson 1. Miami, Rodgers 1, Taylor 1.

OILERS 10, GIANTS 6

Sunday, November 9

N.Y. Giants	0	3	3	0— 6
Tennessee	3	7	0	0—10

First Quarter
Ten.—FG, Del Greco 31, 11:26.
Second Quarter
Ten.—George 1 run (Del Greco kick), 14:10.
NYG—FG, Daluiso 42, 15:00.
Third Quarter
NYG—FG, Daluiso 40, 10:06.
Attendance—26,744.

TEAM STATISTICS

	N.Y. Giants	Tennessee
First downs	10	19
Rushes-yards	20-107	40-153
Passing	111	173
Punt returns	3-13	0-0
Kickoff returns	3-29	1-17
Interception returns	1-0	1-15
Comp.-att.-int.	15-28-1	13-23-1
Sacked-yards lost	3-22	1-10
Punts	8-36	5-41
Fumbles-lost	1-0	2-1
Penalties-yards	6-35	3-25
Time of possession	24:16	35:44

INDIVIDUAL STATISTICS

RUSHING—New York, Wheatley 13-94, Way 4-1, Barber 2-(minus 1), Pegram 1-13. Tennessee, George 32-122, McNair 8-31.

PASSING—New York, Kanell 15-28-1-133. Tennessee, McNair 13-23-1-183.

RECEIVING—New York, Calloway 4-65, Pegram 3-11, Alexander 2-22, Pierce 2-15, Toomer 1-9, Wheatley 1-6, Way 1-5, Cross 1-0. Tennessee, Sanders 3-64, Russell 3-45, Harmon 2-23, Roan 2-11, Davis 1-23, Wycheck 1-9, Kent 1-8.

MISSED FIELD GOAL ATTEMPTS—Tennessee, Del Greco 44.

INTERCEPTIONS—New York, Widmer 1-0. Tennessee, Robertson 1-15.

KICKOFF RETURNS—New York, Pegram 3-29. Tennessee, Mason 1-17.

PUNT RETURNS—New York, Toomer 3-13.

SACKS—New York, Harris 0.5, Bratzke 0.5. Tennessee, Ford 2, Holmes 1.

SEAHAWKS 37, CHARGERS 31

Sunday, November 9

Seattle	0	10	14	13—37
San Diego	14	3	7	7—31

First Quarter

S.D.—Jackson 41 fumble return (G. Davis kick), 1:30.

S.D.—Martin 10 pass from Whelihan (G. Davis kick), 12:43.

Second Quarter

Sea.—FG, Peterson 27, 8:02.

S.D.—FG, G. Davis 33, 13:44.

Sea.—Galloway 30 pass from Moon (Peterson kick), 14:38.

Third Quarter

Sea.—Warren 1 run (Peterson kick), 6:00.

Sea.—Sinclair recovered fumble in end zone (Peterson kick), 6:16.

S.D.—Bradford 56 interception return (G. Davis kick), 14:30.

Fourth Quarter

S.D.—Martin 61 pass from Whelihan (G. Davis kick), 3:40.

Sea.—FG, Peterson 28, 8:58.

Sea.—Galloway 40 pass from Moon (Peterson kick), 12:40.

Sea.—FG, Peterson 27, 13:42.

Attendance—64,616.

TEAM STATISTICS

	Seattle	San Diego
First downs	24	13
Rushes-yards	27-92	25-81
Passing	281	179
Punt returns	1-9	5-33
Kickoff returns	5-109	8-109
Interception returns	1-29	1-56
Comp.-att.-int.	24-45-1	17-29-1
Sacked-yards lost	2-14	4-27
Punts	6-41	6-43
Fumbles-lost	1-1	4-1
Penalties-yards	3-20	6-52
Time of possession	31:38	28:22

INDIVIDUAL STATISTICS

RUSHING—Seattle, Warren 16-59, Broussard 7-14, Moon 2-11, Galloway 1-9, Strong 1-(minus 1). San Diego, Brown 18-53, Whelihan 3-2, Fletcher 2-5, C. Jones 1-17, Craver 1-4.

PASSING—Seattle, Moon 24-45-1-295. San Diego, Whelihan 17-29-1-206.

RECEIVING—Seattle, Br. Blades 4-47, Warren 4-21, Galloway 3-84, Crumpler 3-41, Broussard 3-6, Strong 2-34, Pritchard 2-28, McKnight 2-27, Hobbs 1-7. San Diego, Martin 5-100, F. Jones 4-38, Metcalf 2-19, Craver 1-20, Still 1-15, Hartley 1-7, Fletcher 1-5, C. Jones 1-3, Brown 1-(minus 1).

MISSED FIELD GOAL ATTEMPTS—None.

INTERCEPTIONS—Seattle, D. Williams 1-29. San Diego, Bradford 1-56.

KICKOFF RETURNS—Seattle, Harris 3-81, Broussard 2-28. San Diego, Bynum 4-67, Craver 2-42, Metcalf 1-0, Bordelon 1-0.

PUNT RETURNS—Seattle, Harris 1-9. San Diego, Metcalf 4-33, Jackson 1-0.

SACKS—Seattle, C. Brown 1.5, Daniels 1, Adams 0.5, Team 1. San Diego, Seau 1, Lee 1.

JAGUARS 24, CHIEFS 10

Sunday, November 9

Kansas City	0	3	0	7—10
Jacksonville	7	17	0	0—24

First Quarter

Jac.—Mitchell 5 pass from Brunell (Hollis kick), 3:30.

Second Quarter

Jac.—Stewart 1 run (Hollis kick), 1:57.

K.C.—FG, Stoyanovich 45, 4:00.

Jac.—Means 14 run (Hollis kick), 8:03.

Jac.—FG, Hollis 52, 13:45.

Fourth Quarter

K.C.—Hughes 7 fumble return (Stoyanovich kick), 5:11.

Attendance—70,444.

TEAM STATISTICS

	Kansas City	Jacksonville
First downs	22	16
Rushes-yards	29-159	27-150
Passing	265	182
Punt returns	5-28	2-16
Kickoff returns	4-81	3-66
Interception returns	1-22	2-(-2)
Comp.-att.-int.	29-50-2	9-21-1
Sacked-yards lost	6-49	3-17
Punts	4-46	7-42
Fumbles-lost	5-3	1-1
Penalties-yards	6-48	5-39
Time of possession	36:14	23:46

INDIVIDUAL STATISTICS

RUSHING—Kansas City, Anders 7-32, Gannon 7-32, Hill 6-36, Bennett 5-16, Allen 3-37, Aguiar 1-6. Jacksonville, Means 14-62, Stewart 10-54, Brunell 2-26, Jackson 1-8.

PASSING—Kansas City, Gannon 29-50-2-314. Jacksonville, Brunell 9-20-0-199, Johnson 0-1-1-0.

RECEIVING—Kansas City, Anders 8-62, Gonzalez 7-69, Dawson 6-49, Rison 3-54, Hill 2-16, Horn 1-47, Hughes 1-10, Allen 1-7. Jacksonville, Smith 4-112, Mitchell 2-30, McCardell 1-23, Brown 1-17, Hallock 1-17.

MISSED FIELD GOAL ATTEMPTS—None.

INTERCEPTIONS—Kansas City, McMillian 1-22. Jacksonville, Figures 1-1, Hudson 1-(minus 3).

KICKOFF RETURNS—Kansas City, Vanover 3-65, Manusky 1-16. Jacksonville, Jackson 2-61, Mitchell 1-5.

PUNT RETURNS—Kansas City, Vanover 5-28. Jacksonville, Barlow 2-16.

SACKS—Kansas City, Davis 1, Simmons 1, Browning 0.5, Thomas 0.5. Jacksonville, Simmons 2, Lageman 2, Davey 1, Brackens 1.

BUCCANEERS 31, FALCONS 10

Sunday, November 9

Tampa Bay	7	10	7	7—31
Atlanta	0	7	3	0—10

First Quarter

T.B.—Alstott 47 run (Husted kick), 4:17.

Second Quarter

Atl.—Emanuel 30 pass from Chandler (Andersen kick), 11:30.

T.B.—Dunn 24 pass from Dilfer (Husted kick), 14:15.

T.B.—FG, Husted 54, 14:56.

Third Quarter

Atl.—FG, Andersen 34, 6:36.

T.B.—Moore 14 pass from Dilfer (Husted kick), 14:55.

Fourth Quarter

T.B.—Dunn 30 run (Husted kick), 8:16.

Attendance—46,018.

TEAM STATISTICS

	Tampa Bay	Atlanta
First downs	20	18
Rushes-yards	38-199	24-102

	Tampa Bay	Atlanta
Passing	150	173
Punt returns	0-0	4-25
Kickoff returns	3-55	3-53
Interception returns	0-0	0-0
Comp.-att.-int.	12-20-0	19-27-0
Sacked-yards lost	0-0	5-39
Punts	5-36	5-32
Fumbles-lost	1-0	2-2
Penalties-yards	5-45	5-35
Time of possession	29:21	30:39

INDIVIDUAL STATISTICS

RUSHING—Tampa Bay, Alstott 14-77, Dunn 14-76, Rhett 6-30, Dilfer 3-16, Walsh 1-0. Atlanta, Anderson 14-49, Chandler 4-11, Hanspard 3-34, Green 2-5, Christian 1-3.

PASSING—Tampa Bay, Dilfer 12-20-0-150. Atlanta, Chandler 19-27-0-212.

RECEIVING—Tampa Bay, Williams 4-38, Dunn 3-57, Moore 2-25, Copeland 2-23, Hape 1-7. Atlanta, Anderson 7-47, Green 4-54, Mathis 3-32, Emanuel 2-43, Kinchen 2-25, Christian 1-11.

MISSED FIELD GOAL ATTEMPTS—None.

INTERCEPTIONS—None.

KICKOFF RETURNS—Tampa Bay, Anthony 3-55. Atlanta, Hanspard 3-53.

PUNT RETURNS—Atlanta, Kinchen 4-25.

SACKS—Tampa Bay, Culpepper 3, Ahanotu 1, Maniecki 1.

PACKERS 17, RAMS 7

Sunday, November 9

St. Louis	0	0	7	0— 7
Green Bay	0	3	7	7—17

Second Quarter
G.B.—FG, Longwell 44, 10:58.

Third Quarter
G.B.—Freeman 25 pass from Favre (Longwell kick), 3:34.
St.L.—Phillips 8 run (Wilkins kick), 11:29.

Fourth Quarter
G.B.—Favre 7 run (Longwell kick), 0:07.
Attendance—60,093.

TEAM STATISTICS

	St. Louis	Green Bay
First downs	16	18
Rushes-yards	25-66	25-96
Passing	203	291
Punt returns	2-16	6-23
Kickoff returns	4-99	1-24
Interception returns	2-5	1-(-1)
Comp.-att.-int.	18-41-1	18-37-2
Sacked-yards lost	4-32	2-15
Punts	9-40	6-44
Fumbles-lost	1-0	1-1
Penalties-yards	15-110	9-66
Time of possession	32:20	27:40

INDIVIDUAL STATISTICS

RUSHING—St. Louis, Phillips 15-41, Lee 4-8, J. Moore 2-9, Banks 2-6, Heyward 1-1, Rypien 1-1. Green Bay, Levens 21-81, Favre 4-15.

PASSING—St. Louis, Banks 9-23-0-103, Rypien 9-18-1-132. Green Bay, Favre 18-37-2-306.

RECEIVING—St. Louis, Lee 5-104, J. Moore 4-38, Small 4-38, Bruce 3-34, Kennison 1-17, Heyward 1-4. Green Bay, Freeman 7-160, R. Brooks 4-48, Chmura 3-45, Henderson 2-39, Levens 2-14.

MISSED FIELD GOAL ATTEMPTS—St. Louis, Wilkins 37, 36.

INTERCEPTIONS—St. Louis, O'Neal 1-5, McNeil 1-0. Green Bay, Prior 1-(minus 1).

KICKOFF RETURNS—St. Louis, Thompson 4-99. Green Bay, Schroeder 1-24.

PUNT RETURNS—St. Louis, Kennison 2-16. Green Bay, Schroeder 6-23.

SACKS—St. Louis, Johnson 1, O'Neal 1. Green Bay, Butler 1, S. Dotson 1, Robinson 1, Joyner 0.5, McKenzie 0.5.

SAINTS 13, RAIDERS 10

Sunday, November 9

New Orleans	0	3	0	10—13
Oakland	0	10	0	0—10

Second Quarter
Oak.—Williams 1 run (Ford kick), 3:11.
Oak.—FG, Ford 43, 10:45.
N.O.—FG, Brien 48, 15:00.

Fourth Quarter
N.O.—Zellars 1 run (Brien kick), 0:03.
N.O.—FG, Brien 44, 12:03.
Attendance—40,091.

TEAM STATISTICS

	New Orleans	Oakland
First downs	17	12
Rushes-yards	35-59	20-32
Passing	154	189
Punt returns	7-90	5-61
Kickoff returns	2-44	3-49
Interception returns	1-39	1-13
Comp.-att.-int.	21-34-1	17-39-1
Sacked-yards lost	3-27	3-22
Punts	8-45	8-45
Fumbles-lost	0-0	1-1
Penalties-yards	12-94	9-91
Time of possession	34:03	25:57

INDIVIDUAL STATISTICS

RUSHING—New Orleans, Bates 14-31, Zellars 11-32, T. Davis 5-1, Shuler 5-(minus 5). Oakland, Kaufman 15-14, George 2-11, Williams 2-6, T. Brown 1-1.

PASSING—New Orleans, Shuler 21-34-1-181. Oakland, George 17-39-1-211.

RECEIVING—New Orleans, Hill 5-52, Guliford 3-37, Zellars 3-26, I. Smith 3-25, Hastings 3-23, T. Davis 2-9, Bech 1-13, McCrary 1-(minus 4). Oakland, Dudley 5-116, T. Brown 5-43, Kaufman 4-23, Shedd 2-22, Williams 1-7.

MISSED FIELD GOAL ATTEMPTS—None.

INTERCEPTIONS—New Orleans, Knight 1-39. Oakland, Land 1-13.

KICKOFF RETURNS—New Orleans, Guliford 2-44. Oakland, Howard 2-37, Levitt 1-12.

PUNT RETURNS—New Orleans, Guliford 7-90. Oakland, Howard 5-61.

SACKS—New Orleans, Fields 1, Molden 1, Mickell 1. Oakland, Smith 1, Russell 1, Johnstone 1.

PATRIOTS 31, BILLS 10

Sunday, November 9

New England	7	10	7	7—31
Buffalo	3	0	7	0—10

First Quarter
Buf.—FG, Christie 23, 14:08.
N.E.—Cullors 86 kickoff return (Vinatieri kick), 14:26.

Second Quarter
N.E.—FG, Vinatieri 42, 0:59.
N.E.—Coates 6 pass from Bledsoe (Vinatieri kick), 12:21.

Third Quarter
N.E.—Slade 1 interception return (Vinatieri kick), 8:55.
Buf.—A. Smith 1 run (Christie kick), 14:12.

Fourth Quarter
N.E.—Martin 1 run (Vinatieri kick), 2:30.
Attendance—65,783.

TEAM STATISTICS

	New England	Buffalo
First downs	11	14
Rushes-yards	32-103	27-122
Passing	164	119
Punt returns	3-16	1-20
Kickoff returns	3-157	6-107
Interception returns	4-5	0-0
Comp.-att.-int.	15-22-0	15-33-4
Sacked-yards lost	3-36	2-8
Punts	6-39	5-45
Fumbles-lost	3-0	0-0
Penalties-yards	4-48	9-46
Time of possession	31:35	28:25

INDIVIDUAL STATISTICS

RUSHING—New England, Martin 26-93, Grier 4-5, Byars 2-5. Buffalo, A. Smith 12-43, Thomas 8-41, Holmes 4-25, Van Pelt 2-8, Collins 1-5.

PASSING—New England, Bledsoe 15-22-0-200. Buffalo, Collins 12-21-1-89, Van Pelt 3-12-3-38.

RECEIVING—New England, Glenn 3-59, Coates 3-17, Brown 2-61, Jefferson 2-33, Meggett 2-10, Gash 2-6, Martin 1-14. Buffalo, Johnson 4-34, Early 3-25, Reed 3-21, Cline 1-29, Moulds 1-9, Holmes 1-6, Riemersma 1-2, A. Smith 1-1.

MISSED FIELD GOAL ATTEMPTS—New England, Vinatieri 42, 45.

INTERCEPTIONS—New England, Hitchcock 1-4, Slade 1-1, Clay 1-0, Law 1-0.

KICKOFF RETURNS—New England, Cullors 2-134, Meggett 1-23. Buffalo, Holmes 6-107.

PUNT RETURNS—New England, Meggett 3-16. Buffalo, Burris 1-20.

SACKS—New England, McGinest 1, Thomas 1. Buffalo, Paup 1.5, Hansen 0.5, Holecek 0.5, Washington 0.5.

STEELERS 37, RAVENS 0

Sunday, November 9

Baltimore	0	0	0	0— 0
Pittsburgh	10	10	10	7—37

First Quarter
Pit.—Bettis 1 run (N. Johnson kick), 3:54.
Pit.—FG, N. Johnson 52, 12:36.
Second Quarter
Pit.—Stewart 1 run (N. Johnson kick), 1:38.
Pit.—FG, N. Johnson 22, 9:19.
Third Quarter
Pit.—FG, N. Johnson 39, 4:08.
Pit.—Thigpen 52 pass from Stewart (N. Johnson kick), 8:24.
Fourth Quarter
Pit.—G. Jones 1 run (N. Johnson kick), 6:11.
Attendance—56,669.

TEAM STATISTICS

	Baltimore	Pittsburgh
First downs	11	19
Rushes-yards	21-58	39-143
Passing	112	198
Punt returns	2-21	4-22
Kickoff returns	8-157	1-28
Interception returns	0-0	4-48
Comp.-att.-int.	15-39-4	15-29-0
Sacked-yards lost	3-24	1-8
Punts	6-44	6-31
Fumbles-lost	5-3	0-0
Penalties-yards	11-73	9-60
Time of possession	25:07	34:53

INDIVIDUAL STATISTICS
RUSHING—Baltimore, Morris 14-39, Graham 4-11, Montgomery 1-11, Byner 1-(minus 1), Zeier 1-(minus 2). Pittsburgh, Bettis 24-114, G. Jones 12-24, Stewart 2-2, Hawkins 1-3.

PASSING—Baltimore, Testaverde 13-32-3-120, Zeier 2-7-1-16. Pittsburgh, Stewart 14-27-0-196, Quinn 1-2-0-10.

RECEIVING—Baltimore, Green 4-24, Alexander 3-47, Jackson 2-20, Roe 2-15, Yarborough 1-13, Morris 1-9, Kinchen 1-5, J. Lewis 1-3. Pittsburgh, Thigpen 6-130, Hawkins 5-48, Blackwell 1-20, C. Johnson 1-10, Lyons 1-0, G. Jones 1-(minus 2).

MISSED FIELD GOAL ATTEMPTS—None.

INTERCEPTIONS—Pittsburgh, Perry 1-42, Oldham 1-8, Lake 1-1, Conley 1-(minus 3).

KICKOFF RETURNS—Baltimore, Graham 3-59, J. Lewis 3-55, Roe 2-43. Pittsburgh, Blackwell 1-28.

PUNT RETURNS—Baltimore, J. Lewis 1-13, Roe 1-8. Pittsburgh, Blackwell 4-22.

SACKS—Baltimore, R. Lewis 1. Pittsburgh, Holmes 1, Harrison 1, Lloyd 1.

49ERS 24, EAGLES 12

Monday, November 10

San Francisco	7	17	0	0—24
Philadelphia	3	3	0	6—12

First Quarter
S.F.—Hanks 38 fumble return (Anderson kick), 1:07.
Phi.—FG, Boniol 28, 12:21.
Second Quarter
Phi.—FG, Boniol 34, 1:44.
S.F.—Hearst 1 run (Anderson kick), 5:34.
S.F.—Levy 73 punt return (Anderson kick), 10:56.
S.F.—FG, Anderson 31, 14:56.
Fourth Quarter
Phi.—Lewis 6 pass from Hoying (pass failed), 13:46.
Attendance—67,133.

TEAM STATISTICS

	San Fran.	Philadelphia
First downs	13	18
Rushes-yards	38-117	20-69
Passing	96	188
Punt returns	3-82	2-7
Kickoff returns	3-50	5-102
Interception returns	1-10	1-0
Comp.-att.-int.	13-23-1	21-45-1
Sacked-yards lost	1-7	8-43
Punts	8-37	7-40
Fumbles-lost	2-0	2-2
Penalties-yards	4-50	4-40
Time of possession	32:18	27:42

INDIVIDUAL STATISTICS
RUSHING—San Francisco, Hearst 26-77, S. Young 5-26, Floyd 4-2, Kirby 2-10, Levy 1-2. Philadelphia, Watters 14-42, Garner 4-18, Detmer 2-9.

PASSING—San Francisco, S. Young 13-23-1-103. Philadelphia, Detmer 13-31-1-137, Hoying 8-14-0-94.

RECEIVING—San Francisco, Owens 3-50, Kirby 3-32, Stokes 3-18, Floyd 2-2, Harris 1-5, Hearst 1-(minus 4). Philadelphia, Fryar 9-138, Solomon 3-29, Turner 3-3, Watters 2-22, Lewis 2-12, Garner 1-14, Timpson 1-13.

MISSED FIELD GOAL ATTEMPTS—San Francisco, Anderson 43.

INTERCEPTIONS—San Francisco, Walker 1-10. Philadelphia, Dimry 1-0.

KICKOFF RETURNS—San Francisco, Levy 2-36, Kirby 1-14. Philadelphia, Staley 4-91, Lewis 1-11.

PUNT RETURNS—San Francisco, Levy 3-82. Philadelphia, Solomon 2-7.

SACKS—San Francisco, Stubblefield 3.5, Doleman 2, Greene 1.5, Bryant 1. Philadelphia, Conner 1.

WEEK 12

RESULTS

Atlanta 27, ST. LOUIS 21
BALTIMORE 10, Philadelphia 10 (OT)
DALLAS 17, Washington 14
DETROIT 38, Minnesota 15
INDIANAPOLIS 41, Green Bay 38
JACKSONVILLE 17, Tennessee 9
KANSAS CITY 24, Denver 22
NEW ORLEANS 20, Seattle 17 (OT)
N.Y. GIANTS 19, Arizona 10
N.Y. Jets 23, CHICAGO 15
Oakland 38, SAN DIEGO 13
PITTSBURGH 20, Cincinnati 3
SAN FRANCISCO 27, Carolina 19
TAMPA BAY 27, New England 7
MIAMI 30, Buffalo 13

STANDINGS

AFC EAST

	W	L	T	Pct.
Miami	7	4	0	.636
N.Y. Jets	7	4	0	.636
New England	6	5	0	.545
Buffalo	5	6	0	.454
Indianapolis	1	10	0	.090

AFC CENTRAL

	W	L	T	Pct.
Jacksonville	8	3	0	.727
Pittsburgh	8	3	0	.727
Tennessee	5	6	0	.454
Baltimore	4	6	1	.409
Cincinnati	3	8	0	.273

AFC WEST

	W	L	T	Pct.
Denver	9	2	0	.818
Kansas City	8	3	0	.727
Seattle	6	5	0	.545
Oakland	4	7	0	.364
San Diego	4	7	0	.364

NFC EAST

	W	L	T	Pct.
N.Y. Giants	7	4	0	.636
Dallas	6	5	0	.545
Washington	6	5	0	.545
Philadelphia	4	6	1	.409
Arizona	2	9	0	.181

NFC CENTRAL

	W	L	T	Pct.
Green Bay	8	3	0	.727
Minnesota	8	3	0	.727
Tampa Bay	8	3	0	.727
Detroit	5	6	0	.454
Chicago	1	10	0	.090

NFC WEST

	W	L	T	Pct.
San Francisco	10	1	0	.909
Carolina	5	6	0	.454
New Orleans	4	7	0	.364
Atlanta	3	8	0	.273
St. Louis	2	9	0	.181

HIGHLIGHTS

Hero of the week: With no time left, Pete Stoyanovich booted a 54-yard field goal just over the crossbar to give the Chiefs a dramatic 24-22 victory over the Broncos at Arrowhead Stadium. The win put Kansas City one game behind Denver in the AFC West and preserved the Chiefs' perfect record (5-0) at home.

Goat of the week: With the score tied at 17 and 22 seconds left in regulation, Seattle kicker Todd Peterson was wide right on a 45-yard field-goal attempt. Warren Moon then threw an interception on the first play in overtime. With an offense that had been inept most of the day, Saints coach Mike Ditka didn't waste any time, sending the field-goal unit onto the field on the next play. Doug Brien made Ditka's decision pay off by kicking a 38-yarder to win it, 20-17, for New Orleans.

Sub of the week: Harvey Williams, playing for the injured Derrick Fenner (sprained ankle), scored a career-high four touchdowns as the Raiders defeated the Chargers, 38-13. Coming into the game, Williams had five carries and eight catches on the season.

Comeback of the week: In an ending reminiscent of the days of Clint Longley, the Cowboys scored 11 points in the final 1:55 to defeat the Redskins, 17-14. Troy Aikman capped an 11-play, 97-yard drive with a 6-yard scoring pass to Michael Irvin to cut the Redskins' lead to two points and threw to Emmitt Smith for the tying two-point conversion. After Dallas' defense forced the Redskins to go three-and-out, the Cowboys drove 28 yards on eight plays to Washington's 25, setting up Richie Cunningham's game-winning 42-yard field goal with four seconds left.

Blowout of the week: Jeff George came out gunning as the Raiders opened with six consecutive passes, and the Oakland offense never let up. George finished with 226 yards and three touchdowns as the Raiders rolled over San Diego, 38-13.

Nail-biter of the week: In perhaps the biggest surprise of the 1997 season, the previously winless Colts defeated the defending Super Bowl champion Packers, 41-38. The Colts were led by backup quarterback Paul Justin, who was 24-of-30 for 340 yards and one touchdown. The Colts' defense scored two touchdowns as Indianapolis battled back from 14-3, 28-24 and 31-30 deficits.

Hit of the week: Jaguars defensive tackle Seth Payne, a rookie from Cornell making his first NFL start in place of the injured Don Davey, sent a strong message to the Oilers' Eddie George on the first two plays of the game. Payne stuffed George twice, including a tackle for no gain, as the Jaguars held George, who was averaging 98.2 rushing yards per game, to 54. Jacksonville won, 17-9.

Oddity of the week: A 10-10 tie between the Eagles and Ravens was the NFL's first since the Chiefs and Browns played to a 10-10 tie on November 19, 1989.

Top rusher: Baltimore rookie Jay Graham rushed for 154 yards on 35 carries in the Ravens' 10-10 tie with the Eagles.

Top passer: Arizona's Jake Plummer was 22-of-33 for 388 yards with one touchdown and two interceptions in the Cardinals' 19-10 loss to the Giants.

Top receiver: The Cardinals' Frank Sanders was the recipient of nine of Jake Plummer's passes for 188 yards and a score.

Notes: Steve Mariucci became the first NFL coach to have a 10-game winning streak in his first season as the 49ers defeated the Panthers, 27-19, to clinch the NFC West crown. . . . The Chiefs' Derrick Thomas became the 15th player in league history to amass 100 sacks. . . . With their 27-7 win over the Patriots, the Buccaneers were assured of ending their NFL-record streak of 14 consecutive seasons of double-digit losses. . . . With their 20-3 loss to the Steelers, the Bengals were assured their seventh consecutive non-winning season. . . . The Rams' Jeff Wilkins, who had never missed two consecutive field-goal attempts in his three-plus seasons in the league, missed two in St. Louis' 27-21 loss to Atlanta, making it four consecutive misses. . . . The Jets' Otis Smith intercepted two passes and caused another interception with a tipped pass. He scored on one of the interceptions as New York defeated Chicago, 23-

15. . . . Falcons kicker Morten Andersen became the sixth player in NFL history to score 1,600 points, joining George Blanda, Nick Lowery, Jan Stenerud, Gary Anderson and Lou Groza. . . . The Cardinals lost for the 13th time in their past 14 games against the Giants in New York. . . . It took Denver's Terrell Davis 41 games to rush for 4,000 career yards. Only Eric Dickerson (33 games), Jim Brown (38) and Earl Campbell (39) reached the plateau in fewer games. **Quote of the week:** Steelers running back Jerome Bettis, on a wind-chill near zero for Pittsburgh's game against Cincinnati: "I like it cold, but not that cold. Woo-o-o, it was cold."

GAME SUMMARIES

GIANTS 19, CARDINALS 10

Sunday, November 16

Arizona	0	0	10	0—10
N.Y. Giants	0	10	0	9—19

Second Quarter
NYG—FG, Daluiso 33, 10:15.
NYG—Toomer 56 pass from Kanell (Daluiso kick), 13:16.
Third Quarter
Ariz.—Sanders 70 pass from Plummer (Nedney kick), 1:08.
Ariz.—FG, Nedney 34, 12:55.
Fourth Quarter
NYG—Cross 1 pass from Kanell (kick failed), 6:50.
NYG—FG, Daluiso 34, 10:11.
Attendance—68,316.

TEAM STATISTICS

	Arizona	N.Y. Giants
First downs	21	21
Rushes-yards	23-49	40-201
Passing	350	172
Punt returns	1-4	1-15
Kickoff returns	2-41	0-0
Interception returns	0-0	2-65
Comp.-att.-int.	22-33-2	14-21-0
Sacked-yards lost	8-38	1-10
Punts	3-39	3-35
Fumbles-lost	2-1	0-0
Penalties-yards	6-44	5-55
Time of possession	28:00	32:00

INDIVIDUAL STATISTICS

RUSHING—Arizona, Centers 10-34, R. Moore 7-(minus 5), Plummer 3-16, McElroy 3-4. New York, Wheatley 17-48, Way 14-114, Barber 7-42, Kanell 2-(minus 3).

PASSING—Arizona, Plummer 22-33-2-388. New York, Kanell 14-21-0-182.

RECEIVING—Arizona, Sanders 9-188, R. Moore 8-139, K. Williams 2-28, Edwards 1-15, Gedney 1-14, Centers 1-4. New York, Barber 4-44, Toomer 2-64, Patten 2-35, Calloway 2-22, Pegram 2-12, Pierce 1-4, Cross 1-1.

MISSED FIELD GOAL ATTEMPTS—None.

INTERCEPTIONS—New York, Sehorn 1-41, Wooten 1-24.

KICKOFF RETURNS—Arizona, K. Williams 2-41.

PUNT RETURNS—Arizona, K. Williams 1-4. New York, Toomer 1-15.

SACKS—Arizona, Bankston 1. New York, Strahan 3, Armstead 2, Harris 1, Galyon 1, Sehorn 0.5, Widmer 0.5.

FALCONS 27, RAMS 21

Sunday, November 16

Atlanta	7	3	7	10—27
St. Louis	0	7	14	0—21

First Quarter
Atl.—Anderson 4 run (Andersen kick), 13:25.
Second Quarter
Atl.—FG, Andersen 27, 10:34.
St.L.—Conwell 1 pass from Banks (Wilkins kick), 14:38.

Third Quarter
Atl.—Anderson 1 run (Andersen kick), 6:13.
St.L.—Lee 19 pass from Banks (Wilkins kick), 10:31.
St.L.—Phillips 1 run (Wilkins kick), 14:20.
Fourth Quarter
Atl.—Kozlowski 2 pass from Chandler (Andersen kick), 8:57.
Atl.—FG, Andersen 44, 12:17.
Attendance—64,299.

TEAM STATISTICS

	Atlanta	St. Louis
First downs	22	22
Rushes-yards	29-100	23-89
Passing	214	237
Punt returns	3-21	1-(-2)
Kickoff returns	3-62	5-117
Interception returns	0-0	1-4
Comp.-att.-int.	20-30-1	21-38-0
Sacked-yards lost	2-18	4-29
Punts	3-40	5-42
Fumbles-lost	1-1	0-0
Penalties-yards	8-45	8-79
Time of possession	30:30	29:30

INDIVIDUAL STATISTICS

RUSHING—Atlanta, Anderson 19-72, Hanspard 4-9, Green 3-19, Chandler 3-0. St. Louis, Phillips 13-50, J. Moore 6-18, Banks 3-17, Heyward 1-4.

PASSING—Atlanta, Chandler 20-30-1-232. St. Louis, Banks 21-38-0-266.

RECEIVING—Atlanta, Mathis 6-85, Emanuel 3-52, Christian 3-32, Green 2-9, Kozlowski 2-7, West 1-23, Santiago 1-11, Anderson 1-8, Kinchen 1-5. St. Louis, Lee 5-61, Conwell 5-20, Kennison 3-97, Bruce 3-50, Phillips 3-28, J. Moore 1-6, Laing 1-4.

MISSED FIELD GOAL ATTEMPTS—St. Louis, Wilkins 28, 48.

INTERCEPTIONS—St. Louis, McNeil 1-4.

KICKOFF RETURNS—Atlanta, Hanspard 3-62. St. Louis, Thompson 5-117.

PUNT RETURNS—Atlanta, Kinchen 3-21. St. Louis, Kennison 1-(minus 2).

SACKS—Atlanta, Bennett 1, Hall 1, Smith 1, Dronett 1. St. Louis, Carter 1, J. Robinson 0.5, Farr 0.5.

STEELERS 20, BENGALS 3

Sunday, November 16

Cincinnati	0	0	3	0— 3
Pittsburgh	3	3	7	7—20

First Quarter
Pit.—FG, N. Johnson 34, 6:19.
Second Quarter
Pit.—FG, N. Johnson 25, 14:55.
Third Quarter
Pit.—Thigpen 20 pass from Stewart (N. Johnson kick), 9:53.
Cin.—FG, Pelfrey 25, 13:50.
Fourth Quarter
Pit.—Bruener 5 pass from Stewart (N. Johnson kick), 2:58.
Attendance—55,226.

TEAM STATISTICS

	Cincinnati	Pittsburgh
First downs	16	20
Rushes-yards	30-116	39-190
Passing	126	119
Punt returns	1-12	1-4
Kickoff returns	4-59	2-42
Interception returns	0-0	0-0
Comp.-att.-int.	15-21-0	11-22-0
Sacked-yards lost	4-32	2-9
Punts	3-42	3-44
Fumbles-lost	3-3	0-0
Penalties-yards	5-40	4-31
Time of possession	28:19	31:41

INDIVIDUAL STATISTICS

RUSHING—Cincinnati, Dillon 19-78, Blake 5-12, Bieniemy 2-15, Carter 2-8, Milne 1-4, Graham 1-(minus 1). Pittsburgh, Bettis 25-101, G. Jones 8-64, Stewart 3-9, Hawkins 3-9, Lester 1-3, Witman 1-2.

PASSING—Cincinnati, Blake 15-21-0-158. Pittsburgh, Stewart 11-22-0-128.

RECEIVING—Cincinnati, Pickens 6-71, Scott 3-34, Dunn 2-13, Dillon 1-21, McGee 1-12, Milne 1-8, Bieniemy 1-(minus 1). Pittsburgh, Thigpen 5-101, Hawkins 2-8, C. Johnson 1-12, Lester 1-7, Bruener 1-5, Bettis 1-(minus 5).

MISSED FIELD GOAL ATTEMPTS—None.
INTERCEPTIONS—None.
KICKOFF RETURNS—Cincinnati, Dunn 2-36, Bieniemy 2-23. Pittsburgh, Blackwell 2-42.
PUNT RETURNS—Cincinnati, Myers 1-12. Pittsburgh, Blackwell 1-4.
SACKS—Cincinnati, Tumulty 1, Dixon 1. Pittsburgh, Henry 1, Lloyd 1, Harrison 1, Roye 1.

CHIEFS 24, BRONCOS 22

Sunday, November 16

Denver	3	10	3	6—22
Kansas City	0	14	7	3—24

First Quarter
Den.—FG, Elam 21, 10:17.
Second Quarter
Den.—Sharpe 5 pass from Elway (Elam kick), 0:04.
Den.—FG, Elam 38, 8:33.
K.C.—Allen 6 run (Stoyanovich kick), 10:32.
K.C.—Hughes 5 pass from Gannon (Stoyanovich kick), 13:52.
Third Quarter
K.C.—Allen 1 run (Stoyanovich kick), 6:56.
Den.—FG, Elam 38, 10:24.
Fourth Quarter
Den.—FG, Elam 28, 0:46.
Den.—FG, Elam 34, 14:00.
K.C.—FG, Stoyanovich 54, 15:00.
Attendance—77,963.

TEAM STATISTICS

	Denver	Kansas City
First downs	26	15
Rushes-yards	40-135	30-106
Passing	194	96
Punt returns	1-(-1)	2-16
Kickoff returns	4-96	7-199
Interception returns	1-12	0-0
Comp.-att.-int.	18-31-0	11-21-1
Sacked-yards lost	6-38	1-2
Punts	4-42	7-40
Fumbles-lost	2-1	1-0
Penalties-yards	8-84	11-120
Time of possession	37:25	22:35

INDIVIDUAL STATISTICS

RUSHING—Denver, Davis 34-127, Elway 4-21, Hebron 1-0, R. Smith 1-(minus 13). Kansas City, Allen 16-43, Gannon 6-20, Hill 3-38, Bennett 3-(minus 1), Anders 2-6.
PASSING—Denver, Elway 18-31-0-232. Kansas City, Gannon 11-21-1-98.
RECEIVING—Denver, R. Smith 7-114, Green 3-58, Sharpe 3-27, McCaffrey 2-16, Davis 2-13, Carswell 1-4. Kansas City, Anders 2-19, Hughes 2-10, Horn 1-18, Anders 1-6, Bennett 1-1.
MISSED FIELD GOAL ATTEMPTS—Denver, Elam 59.
INTERCEPTIONS—Denver, Gordon 1-12.
KICKOFF RETURNS—Denver, Hebron 2-75, Chamberlain 1-13, Burns 1-8. Kansas City, Vanover 6-199, Hughes 1-0.
PUNT RETURNS—Denver, Gordon 1-(minus 1). Kansas City, Vanover 2-16.
SACKS—Denver, Tanuvasa 1. Kansas City, Thomas 2, Davis 1, Edwards 1, Browning 1, Barndt 1.

LIONS 38, VIKINGS 15

Sunday, November 16

Minnesota	0	7	0	8—15
Detroit	3	21	14	0—38

First Quarter
Det.—FG, Hanson 27, 11:10.
Second Quarter
Det.—Vardell 1 run (Hanson kick), 1:25.
Det.—Vardell 1 run (Hanson kick), 6:51.
Min.—R. Smith 27 run (Murray kick), 12:53.
Det.—Morton 14 pass from Mitchell (Hanson kick), 13:47.
Third Quarter
Det.—Vardell 1 run (Hanson kick), 4:42.
Det.—Moore 10 pass from Mitchell (Hanson kick), 12:37.
Fourth Quarter
Min.—Hoard 3 run (Carter pass from Johnson), 4:23.
Attendance—68,910.

TEAM STATISTICS

	Minnesota	Detroit
First downs	18	27
Rushes-yards	28-126	32-211
Passing	174	266
Punt returns	0-0	2-12
Kickoff returns	5-130	3-41
Interception returns	0-0	1-66
Comp.-att.-int.	19-37-1	21-30-0
Sacked-yards lost	1-3	2-5
Punts	6-44	4-40
Fumbles-lost	0-0	0-0
Penalties-yards	7-36	5-28
Time of possession	30:18	29:42

INDIVIDUAL STATISTICS

RUSHING—Minnesota, R. Smith 10-61, Hoard 10-36, Palmer 4-8, Johnson 3-21, Evans 1-0. Detroit, Sanders 19-108, Vardell 5-45, Rivers 4-51, Reich 2-(minus 2), Morton 1-9, Schlesinger 1-0.
PASSING—Minnesota, Johnson 19-37-1-177. Detroit, Mitchell 21-29-0-271, Reich 0-1-0-0.
RECEIVING—Minnesota, Glover 5-50, Reed 4-61, Carter 4-38, R. Smith 3-9, Hoard 1-9, Palmer 1-6, Evans 1-4. Detroit, Moore 10-130, Morton 6-59, Sloan 2-12, Sanders 1-34, T. Boyd 1-32, Vardell 1-4.
MISSED FIELD GOAL ATTEMPTS—None.
INTERCEPTIONS—Detroit, Carrier 1-66.
KICKOFF RETURNS—Minnesota, Palmer 2-67, Morrow 2-49, M. Williams 1-14. Detroit, Milburn 2-26, Vardell 1-15.
PUNT RETURNS—Detroit, Milburn 2-12.
SACKS—Minnesota, Wheeler 1, F. Smith 1. Detroit, Elliss 1.

BUCCANEERS 27, PATRIOTS 7

Sunday, November 16

New England	0	0	0	7— 7
Tampa Bay	7	3	7	10—27

First Quarter
T.B.—Rhett 1 run (Husted kick), 12:30.
Second Quarter
T.B.—FG, Husted 44, 14:55.
Third Quarter
T.B.—Moore 7 pass from Dilfer (Husted kick), 4:00.
Fourth Quarter
T.B.—Alstott 1 run (Husted kick), 4:00.
T.B.—FG, Husted 44, 9:44.
N.E.—Purnell 6 pass from Zolak (Vinatieri kick), 14:52.
Attendance—70,479.

TEAM STATISTICS

	New England	Tampa Bay
First downs	10	21
Rushes-yards	16-75	41-141
Passing	93	202
Punt returns	1-5	3-37
Kickoff returns	4-86	1-10
Interception returns	0-0	2-13
Comp.-att.-int.	16-31-2	21-29-0
Sacked-yards lost	5-58	1-7
Punts	7-42	2-48
Fumbles-lost	2-1	5-2
Penalties-yards	6-38	3-15
Time of possession	20:32	39:28

INDIVIDUAL STATISTICS

RUSHING—New England, Martin 8-26, Cullors 4-41, Byars 2-5, Gash 1-4, Bledsoe 1-(minus 1). Tampa Bay, Alstott 16-91, Dunn 14-36, Rhett 8-15, Walsh 2-(minus 6), Williams 1-5.
PASSING—New England, Bledsoe 13-25-2-117, Zolak 3-6-0-34. Tampa Bay, Dilfer 21-29-0-209.
RECEIVING—New England, Brown 5-58, Martin 4-23, Coates 3-27, Jefferson 2-28, Jells 1-9, Purnell 1-6. Tampa Bay, Dunn 4-20, Harris 3-51, Williams 3-36, Alstott 3-35, Anthony 3-24, Copeland 3-20, Moore 2-23.
MISSED FIELD GOAL ATTEMPTS—None.
INTERCEPTIONS—Tampa Bay, Brooks 1-13, Abraham 1-0.
KICKOFF RETURNS—New England, Meggett 3-77, Cullors 1-9. Tampa Bay, Dunn 1-10.
PUNT RETURNS—New England, Meggett 1-5. Tampa Bay, Williams 3-37.
SACKS—New England, Canty 1. Tampa Bay, Culpepper 1, Parker 1, Sapp 1, Jackson 1, Upshaw 1.

SAINTS 20, SEAHAWKS 17

Sunday, November 16

Seattle	0	10	0	7	0—17
New Orleans	0	7	0	10	3—20

Second Quarter
Sea.—FG, Peterson 36, 2:16.
Sea.—D. Williams 44 interception return (Peterson kick), 3:29.
N.O.—Zellars 1 run (Brien kick), 14:23.
Fourth Quarter
N.O.—Zellars 2 run (Brien kick), 1:24.
N.O.—FG, Brien 19, 5:33.
Sea.—McKnight 34 pass from Moon (Peterson kick), 13:20.
Overtime
N.O.—FG, Brien 38, 0:17.
Attendance—50,493.

TEAM STATISTICS

	Seattle	New Orleans
First downs	19	14
Rushes-yards	29-111	30-72
Passing	229	101
Punt returns	2-6	2-39
Kickoff returns	3-64	4-120
Interception returns	2-68	2-22
Comp.-att.-int.	23-46-2	10-18-2
Sacked-yards lost	3-22	3-8
Punts	4-30	5-45
Fumbles-lost	3-2	3-3
Penalties-yards	6-41	7-65
Time of possession	33:41	26:36

INDIVIDUAL STATISTICS
RUSHING—Seattle, Warren 22-87, Broussard 3-16, Moon 1-7, Strong 1-2, K. Richardson 1-0, Galloway 1-(minus 1). New Orleans, Zellars 14-49, Bates 10-15, Shuler 2-6, McCrary 2-2, Nussmeier 2-0.
PASSING—Seattle, Moon 23-46-2-251. New Orleans, Shuler 6-14-2-64, Nussmeier 4-4-0-45.
RECEIVING—Seattle, Warren 7-38, Galloway 5-68, Pritchard 4-30, McKnight 3-67, Br. Blades 3-30, Crumpler 1-18. New Orleans, Hastings 3-35, Guliford 2-27, Hill 2-25, Zellars 2-21, McCrary 1-1.
MISSED FIELD GOAL ATTEMPTS—Seattle, Peterson 33, 45.
INTERCEPTIONS—Seattle, D. Williams 2-68. New Orleans, Tubbs 1-15, Harvey 1-7.
KICKOFF RETURNS—Seattle, Broussard 2-42, Harris 1-22. New Orleans, Guliford 4-120.
PUNT RETURNS—Seattle, Harris 2-6. New Orleans, Guliford 2-39.
SACKS—Seattle, Adams 2, Saleaumua 1. New Orleans, Martin 1, J. Johnson 1, Glover 1.

JAGUARS 17, OILERS 9

Sunday, November 16

Tennessee	0	3	0	6— 9	
Jacksonville	0	7	7	3—17	

Second Quarter
Jac.—McCardell 17 pass from Brunell (Hollis kick), 10:40.
Ten.—FG, Del Greco 35, 14:30.
Third Quarter
Jac.—Means 1 run (Hollis kick), 7:45.
Fourth Quarter
Ten.—Wycheck 22 pass from Davis (run failed), 2:19.
Jac.—FG, Hollis 23, 7:43.
Attendance—70,070.

TEAM STATISTICS

	Tennessee	Jacksonville
First downs	17	21
Rushes-yards	33-136	36-103
Passing	184	249
Punt returns	1-(-2)	3-44
Kickoff returns	4-60	3-51
Interception returns	0-0	2-11
Comp.-att.-int.	9-23-2	22-30-0
Sacked-yards lost	0-0	2-18
Punts	6-42	5-45
Fumbles-lost	0-0	2-2
Penalties-yards	6-37	4-58
Time of possession	27:07	32:53

INDIVIDUAL STATISTICS
RUSHING—Tennessee, George 18-49, Thomas 9-54, McNair 6-33. Jacksonville, Means 23-64, Stewart 7-12, Brunell 6-27.
PASSING—Tennessee, McNair 8-22-2-162, Davis 1-1-0-22. Jacksonville, Brunell 22-30-0-267.
RECEIVING—Tennessee, Wycheck 3-70, Davis 3-57, Harmon 1-34, Russell 1-12, Roan 1-11. Jacksonville, Smith 8-158, McCardell 6-64, Means 3-13, Stewart 2-11, Hallock 2-11, Jackson 1-10.
MISSED FIELD GOAL ATTEMPTS—Tennessee, Del Greco 41.
INTERCEPTIONS—Jacksonville, Thomas 1-11, Robinson 1-0.
KICKOFF RETURNS—Tennessee, Mason 3-44, Harmon 1-16. Jacksonville, Jackson 3-51.
PUNT RETURNS—Tennessee, Gray 1-(minus 2). Jacksonville, Barlow 3-44.
SACKS—Tennessee, G. Walker 1, Holmes 1.

COLTS 41, PACKERS 38

Sunday, November 16

Green Bay	14	14	0	10—38	
Indianapolis	9	18	3	11—41	

First Quarter
G.B.—Levens 3 pass from Favre (Longwell kick), 1:57.
Ind.—FG, Blanchard 42, 7:12.
G.B.—Levens 52 run (Longwell kick), 8:08.
Ind.—Harrison 7 pass from Justin (pass failed), 12:37.
Second Quarter
Ind.—Fontenot 33 fumble return (Stablein pass from Justin), 0:10.
Ind.—Belser 50 interception return (Blanchard kick), 6:24.
G.B.—Levens 1 run (Longwell kick), 10:28.
G.B.—Freeman 16 pass from Favre (Longwell kick), 13:58.
Ind.—FG, Blanchard 41, 15:00.
Third Quarter
Ind.—FG, Blanchard 35, 11:52.
Fourth Quarter
G.B.—FG, Longwell 18, 2:56.
Ind.—Warren 3 run (Harrison pass from Justin), 8:32.
G.B.—Freeman 26 pass from Favre (Longwell kick), 9:41.
Ind.—FG, Blanchard 20, 15:00.
Attendance—60,928.

TEAM STATISTICS

	Green Bay	Indianapolis
First downs	20	26
Rushes-yards	16-107	34-147
Passing	334	320
Punt returns	1-0	1-5
Kickoff returns	7-211	6-124
Interception returns	0-0	2-52
Comp.-att.-int.	18-25-2	24-30-0
Sacked-yards lost	3-29	2-20
Punts	1-65	1-52
Fumbles-lost	1-1	3-1
Penalties-yards	8-53	6-45
Time of possession	23:06	36:54

INDIVIDUAL STATISTICS
RUSHING—Green Bay, Levens 14-103, Henderson 1-4, Favre 1-0. Indianapolis, Faulk 17-116, Crockett 10-27, Justin 4-1, Warren 3-3.
PASSING—Green Bay, Favre 18-25-2-363. Indianapolis, Justin 24-30-0-340.
RECEIVING—Green Bay, Freeman 5-93, Levens 4-92, Henderson 4-45, Mayes 3-119, Chmura 2-14. Indianapolis, Harrison 8-98, Dilger 6-96, Dawkins 5-83, Bailey 2-33, Crockett 1-19, Warren 1-6, Faulk 1-5.
MISSED FIELD GOAL ATTEMPTS—Indianapolis, Blanchard 42.
INTERCEPTIONS—Indianapolis, Blackmon 1-2, Coryatt 1-0.
KICKOFF RETURNS—Green Bay, Preston 7-211. Indianapolis, Bailey 6-124.
PUNT RETURNS—Green Bay, Preston 1-0. Indianapolis, Stablein 1-5.
SACKS—Green Bay, S. Dotson 2. Indianapolis, Footman 1, Shello 1, Montgomery 1.

JETS 23, BEARS 15

Sunday, November 16

N.Y. Jets	10	13	0	0—23	
Chicago	0	0	7	8—15	

First Quarter
NYJ—FG, Hall 34, 6:55.
NYJ—K. Johnson 35 pass from Foley (Hall kick), 10:01.

Second Quarter
NYJ—FG, Hall 36, 6:13.
NYJ—FG, Hall 34, 8:26.
NYJ—Smith 38 interception return (Hall kick), 9:33.

Third Quarter
Chi.—Penn 4 pass from Kramer (Jaeger kick), 6:09.

Fourth Quarter
Chi.—Proehl 5 pass from Kramer (Autry run), 14:30.
Attendance—45,642.

TEAM STATISTICS

	N.Y. Jets	Chicago
First downs	11	27
Rushes-yards	32-77	20-49
Passing	116	307
Punt returns	2-26	6-34
Kickoff returns	2-25	6-123
Interception returns	4-87	0-0
Comp.-att.-int.	12-25-0	33-65-4
Sacked-yards lost	3-20	5-48
Punts	7-40	4-33
Fumbles-lost	1-1	4-1
Penalties-yards	9-70	8-55
Time of possession	28:06	31:54

INDIVIDUAL STATISTICS
RUSHING—New York, Murrell 21-61, Neal 6-10, Anderson 2-6, O'Donnell 2-(minus 2), L. Johnson 1-2. Chicago, Autry 19-39, Kramer 1-10.

PASSING—New York, Foley 8-13-0-111, O'Donnell 4-12-0-25. Chicago, Kramer 32-60-3-354, Stenstrom 1-5-1-1.

RECEIVING—New York, Graham 3-19, Murrell 2-26, Chrebet 2-12, Ward 2-10, K. Johnson 1-35, Brady 1-21, Anderson 1-13. Chicago, Proehl 11-118, Penn 7-85, Wetnight 4-32, Tony Carter 4-27, Bownes 3-40, Jennings 2-30, Autry 2-23.

MISSED FIELD GOAL ATTEMPTS—New York, Hall 48. Chicago, Jaeger 34, 32.

INTERCEPTIONS—New York, Green 2-50, Smith 2-37.

KICKOFF RETURNS—New York, Glenn 1-20, Chrebet 1-5. Chicago, Bownes 5-113, Allred 1-10.

PUNT RETURNS—New York, L. Johnson 2-26. Chicago, Hughes 5-34, Dulaney 1-0.

SACKS—New York, Douglas 2, Jones 1, Mickens 1, Lewis 1. Chicago, Minter 1, Flanigan 1, B. Cox 0.5, Thomas 0.5.

49ERS 27, PANTHERS 19
Sunday, November 16

Carolina	0	6	13	0—19
San Francisco	3	14	7	3—27

First Quarter
S.F.—FG, Anderson 28, 7:02.

Second Quarter
S.F.—S. Young 1 run (Anderson kick), 0:04.
S.F.—Floyd 44 pass from S. Young (Anderson kick), 7:00.
Car.—FG, Kasay 46, 10:29.
Car.—FG, Kasay 27, 14:56.

Third Quarter
S.F.—Kirby 101 kickoff return (Anderson kick), 0:18.
Car.—Lane 4 run (Kasay kick), 4:02.
Car.—Walls 5 pass from Collins (run failed), 10:46.

Fourth Quarter
S.F.—FG, Anderson 43, 5:16.
Attendance—61,500.

TEAM STATISTICS

	Carolina	San Francisco
First downs	18	20
Rushes-yards	23-85	35-99
Passing	169	221
Punt returns	2-18	0-0
Kickoff returns	5-109	5-165
Interception returns	0-0	3-2
Comp.-att.-int.	18-33-3	17-22-0
Sacked-yards lost	3-21	0-0
Punts	3-40	3-40
Fumbles-lost	0-0	0-0
Penalties-yards	5-59	7-48
Time of possession	27:09	32:51

INDIVIDUAL STATISTICS
RUSHING—Carolina, Lane 16-66, Greene 5-15, Collins 1-6, Johnson 1-(minus 2). San Francisco, Hearst 18-48, S. Young 6-22, Kirby 6-8, Floyd 5-21.

PASSING—Carolina, Collins 18-33-3-190. San Francisco, S. Young 17-22-0-221.

RECEIVING—Carolina, Carrier 6-87, Walls 4-47, Carruth 4-35, Ismail 2-23, Greene 1-2, Lane 1-(minus 4). San Francisco, Stokes 5-56, Floyd 3-59, Owens 4-48, Clark 2-26, Kirby 2-16, Hearst 1-13, Jones 1-11.

MISSED FIELD GOAL ATTEMPTS—San Francisco, Anderson 47.

INTERCEPTIONS—San Francisco, McDonald 1-2, Hanks 1-0, Woodall 1-0.

KICKOFF RETURNS—Carolina, Bates 3-86, Rasby 1-12, Garcia 1-11. San Francisco, Levy 3-55, Kirby 2-110.

PUNT RETURNS—Carolina, Poole 2-18.

SACKS—San Francisco, B. Young 1, Doleman 1, Greene 1.

COWBOYS 17, REDSKINS 14
Sunday, November 16

Washington	0	0	7	7—14
Dallas	0	6	0	11—17

Second Quarter
Dal.—FG, Cunningham 34, 2:39.
Dal.—FG, Cunningham 40, 13:56.

Third Quarter
Was.—Allen 4 run (Blanton kick), 12:29.

Fourth Quarter
Was.—Ellard 24 pass from Frerotte (Blanton kick), 1:23.
Dal.—Irvin 6 pass from Aikman (E. Smith pass from Aikman), 13:05.
Dal.—FG, Cunningham 42, 14:56.
Attendance—64,559.

TEAM STATISTICS

	Washington	Dallas
First downs	16	20
Rushes-yards	28-104	25-105
Passing	155	207
Punt returns	2-27	3-15
Kickoff returns	4-67	3-95
Interception returns	0-0	0-0
Comp.-att.-int.	16-31-0	25-45-0
Sacked-yards lost	1-2	1-10
Punts	8-41	6-42
Fumbles-lost	0-0	2-0
Penalties-yards	7-41	6-41
Time of possession	27:11	32:49

INDIVIDUAL STATISTICS
RUSHING—Washington, Allen 18-57, Mitchell 4-29, Bowie 4-15, Logan 2-3. Dallas, E. Smith 21-99, Aikman 3-6, S. Williams 1-0.

PASSING—Washington, Frerotte 16-31-0-157. Dallas, Aikman 25-45-0-217.

RECEIVING—Washington, Allen 6-42, Ellard 4-64, Thomas 2-23, Asher 2-21, Mitchell 1-9, Bowie 1-(minus 2). Dallas, Irvin 7-91, Bjornson 6-42, E. Smith 4-31, LaFleur 3-8, St. Williams 2-22, B. Davis 1-12, Miller 1-8, Walker 1-3.

MISSED FIELD GOAL ATTEMPTS—None.

INTERCEPTIONS—None.

KICKOFF RETURNS—Washington, Mitchell 3-50, Asher 1-17. Dallas, Walker 2-49, Marion 1-46.

PUNT RETURNS—Washington, Mitchell 2-27. Dallas, Sanders 3-15.

SACKS—Washington, M. Patton 1. Dallas, Hennings 1.

RAVENS 10, EAGLES 10
Sunday, November 16

Philadelphia	0	0	3	7	0—10
Baltimore	7	0	0	3	0—10

First Quarter
Bal.—Jackson 29 pass from Testaverde (Stover kick), 10:59.

Third Quarter
Phi.—FG, Boniol 33, 4:48.

Fourth Quarter
Bal.—FG, Stover 23, 11:20.
Phi.—Garner 2 run (Boniol kick), 13:35.
Attendance—63,546.

TEAM STATISTICS

	Philadelphia	Baltimore
First downs	18	19
Rushes-yards	23-63	44-204

	Philadelphia	Baltimore
Passing	210	125
Punt returns	3-19	7-64
Kickoff returns	3-58	3-39
Interception returns	2-11	0-0
Comp.-att.-int.	26-38-0	19-32-2
Sacked-yards lost	9-66	2-15
Punts	9-45	7-46
Fumbles-lost	1-1	2-0
Penalties-yards	4-20	2-15
Time of possession	35:48	39:07

INDIVIDUAL STATISTICS

RUSHING—Philadelphia, Watters 12-36, Garner 10-21, Hoying 1-6. Baltimore, Graham 35-154, Testaverde 7-48, Byner 2-2.

PASSING—Philadelphia, Hoying 26-38-0-276. Baltimore, Testaverde 19-32-2-140.

RECEIVING—Philadelphia, Fryar 6-71, Turner 5-57, Watters 4-33, Garner 4-28, Johnson 3-29, Solomon 2-42, Timpson 1-13, Seay 1-3. Baltimore, Graham 5-15, Alexander 4-39, Green 4-23, Jackson 2-37, Byner 2-13, Yarborough 1-9, Kinchen 1-4.

MISSED FIELD GOAL ATTEMPTS—Philadelphia, Boniol 40. Baltimore, Stover 53.

INTERCEPTIONS—Philadelphia, W. Thomas 1-11, Willis 1-0.

KICKOFF RETURNS—Philadelphia, Staley 3-58. Baltimore, Roe 2-37, Byner 1-2.

PUNT RETURNS—Philadelphia, Solomon 3-19. Baltimore, Roe 7-64.

SACKS—Philadelphia, W. Thomas 1, Conner 1. Baltimore, McCrary 3, Boulware 2, J. Jones 2, Burnett 1, Sharper 1.

RAIDERS 38, CHARGERS 13

Sunday, November 16

Oakland	7	14	14	3—38
San Diego	7	6	0	0—13

First Quarter
S.D.—Jackson 36 interception return (G. Davis kick), 7:55.
Oak.—Williams 8 pass from George (Ford kick), 9:54.

Second Quarter
Oak.—Williams 1 run (Ford kick), 2:12.
S.D.—FG, G. Davis 45, 5:50.
Oak.—Jett 9 pass from George (Ford kick), 9:43.
S.D.—FG, G. Davis 22, 14:34.

Third Quarter
Oak.—Williams 1 run (Ford kick), 7:56.
Oak.—Williams 32 pass from George (Ford kick), 13:14.

Fourth Quarter
Oak.—FG, Ford 23, 4:22.
Attendance—65,714.

TEAM STATISTICS

	Oakland	San Diego
First downs	22	11
Rushes-yards	34-140	25-91
Passing	225	157
Punt returns	4-23	3-18
Kickoff returns	4-92	5-98
Interception returns	0-0	2-36
Comp.-att.-int.	16-34-2	14-26-0
Sacked-yards lost	1-1	3-45
Punts	4-46	7-40
Fumbles-lost	0-0	3-2
Penalties-yards	5-46	11-99
Time of possession	32:07	27:53

INDIVIDUAL STATISTICS

RUSHING—Oakland, Kaufman 20-109, Hall 7-24, Williams 4-7, Aska 2-1, George 1-(minus 1). San Diego, Brown 21-86, Fletcher 4-5.

PASSING—Oakland, George 16-34-2-226. San Diego, Whelihan 14-26-0-202.

RECEIVING—Oakland, Jett 4-58, T. Brown 4-30, Williams 3-59, Kaufman 3-35, Dudley 2-44. San Diego, Metcalf 4-43, C. Jones 3-86, Martin 3-58, Brown 2-4, F. Jones 1-11, Fletcher 1-0.

MISSED FIELD GOAL ATTEMPTS—San Diego, G. Davis 27.

INTERCEPTIONS—San Diego, Jackson 1-36, Bradford 1-0.

KICKOFF RETURNS—Oakland, Howard 3-77, Holmberg 1-15. San Diego, Bynum 5-98.

PUNT RETURNS—Oakland, Howard 4-23. San Diego, Metcalf 2-18, Harrison 1-0.

SACKS—Oakland, Maryland 2, Lynch 1. San Diego, Harrison 1.

DOLPHINS 30, BILLS 13

Monday, November 17

Buffalo	0	0	10	3—13
Miami	3	10	3	14—30

First Quarter
Mia.—FG, Mare 37, 4:51.

Second Quarter
Mia.—Perry 3 pass from Marino (Mare kick), 5:30.
Mia.—FG, Mare 30, 10:22.

Third Quarter
Buf.—Holmes 1 run (Christie kick), 4:15.
Mia.—FG, Mare 35, 7:41.
Buf.—FG, Christie 36, 13:02.

Fourth Quarter
Buf.—FG, Christie 24, 1:04.
Mia.—Drayton 30 pass from Marino (Mare kick), 9:49.
Mia.—Abdul-Jabbar 1 run (Mare kick), 11:15.
Attendance—74,155.

TEAM STATISTICS

	Buffalo	Miami
First downs	15	16
Rushes-yards	29-92	31-96
Passing	131	218
Punt returns	2-20	1-7
Kickoff returns	3-74	4-101
Interception returns	1-0	1-2
Comp.-att.-int.	19-37-1	18-24-1
Sacked-yards lost	3-21	2-16
Punts	4-36	3-41
Fumbles-lost	1-1	2-1
Penalties-yards	1-9	6-60
Time of possession	30:10	29:50

INDIVIDUAL STATISTICS

RUSHING—Buffalo, A. Smith 13-41, Thomas 11-43, Holmes 2-3, Reed 1-9, Collins 1-2, Moulds 1-(minus 6). Miami, Abdul-Jabbar 26-83, Spikes 2-11, Marino 2-(minus 2), McPhail 1-4.

PASSING—Buffalo, Collins 19-37-1-152. Miami, Marino 18-24-1-234.

RECEIVING—Buffalo, Early 7-57, Reed 4-37, Thomas 2-39, Holmes 2-14, Johnson 2-11, Moulds 2-(minus 6). Miami, Drayton 4-62, Perriman 3-48, L. Thomas 2-49, Abdul-Jabbar 2-29, McDuffie 2-10, Perry 2-4, Jordan 1-25, Spikes 1-10, McPhail 1-(minus 3).

MISSED FIELD GOAL ATTEMPTS—None.

INTERCEPTIONS—Buffalo, Kerner 1-0. Miami, Teague 1-2.

KICKOFF RETURNS—Buffalo, Holmes 1-36, Moulds 1-26, Wiley 1-12. Miami, Spikes 4-101.

PUNT RETURNS—Buffalo, Burris 2-20. Miami, Jordan 1-7.

SACKS—Buffalo, B. Smith 2. Miami, A. Harris 1, Armstrong 1, Wilson 1.

RESULTS

Arizona 16, BALTIMORE 13
ATLANTA 20, New Orleans 3
Carolina 16, ST. LOUIS 10
CHICAGO 13, Tampa Bay 7
CINCINNATI 31, Jacksonville 26
DETROIT 32, Indianapolis 10
GREEN BAY 45, Dallas 17
Kansas City 19, SEATTLE 14
NEW ENGLAND 27, Miami 24
N.Y. Giants 7, WASHINGTON 7 (OT)
N.Y. JETS 23, Minnesota 21
PHILADELPHIA 23, Pittsburgh 20
SAN FRANCISCO 17, San Diego 10
TENNESSEE 31, Buffalo 14
DENVER 31, Oakland 3

STANDINGS

AFC EAST

	W	L	T	Pct.
N.Y. Jets	8	4	0	.667
Miami	7	5	0	.583
New England	7	5	0	.583
Buffalo	5	7	0	.417
Indianapolis	1	11	0	.083

AFC CENTRAL

	W	L	T	Pct.
Jacksonville	8	4	0	.667
Pittsburgh	8	4	0	.667
Tennessee	6	6	0	.500
Baltimore	4	7	1	.375
Cincinnati	4	8	0	.333

AFC WEST

	W	L	T	Pct.
Denver	10	2	0	.833
Kansas City	9	3	0	.750
Seattle	6	6	0	.500
Oakland	4	8	0	.333
San Diego	4	8	0	.333

NFC EAST

	W	L	T	Pct.
N.Y. Giants	7	4	1	.625
Washington	6	5	1	.542
Dallas	6	6	0	.500
Philadelphia	5	6	1	.458
Arizona	3	9	0	.250

NFC CENTRAL

	W	L	T	Pct.
Green Bay	9	3	0	.750
Minnesota	8	4	0	.667
Tampa Bay	8	4	0	.667
Detroit	6	6	0	.500
Chicago	2	10	0	.167

NFC WEST

	W	L	T	Pct.
San Francisco	11	1	0	.917
Carolina	6	6	0	.500
Atlanta	4	8	0	.333
New Orleans	4	8	0	.333
St. Louis	2	10	0	.167

HIGHLIGHTS

Hero of the week: Lions running back Barry Sanders carried 24 times for 216 yards, including touchdown runs of 80 and 4 yards, in Detroit's 32-10 win over Indianapolis. It was the fourth 200-yard game of Sanders' career, two shy of O.J. Simpson's NFL record.

Goat of the week: Redskins receiver Michael Westbrook didn't have a good day. In the final minute of overtime, after his team had reached the Giants' 38, Westbrook was penalized 15 yards for slamming his helmet to the ground after an official had ruled that he didn't catch a pass along the sideline. The Redskins subsequently recovered some of the yardage, but Scott Blanton's 54-yard field goal attempt was short and wide right and the game ended in a 7-7 tie.

Sub of the week: Defensive back Roger Jones, a six-year NFL veteran signed by Baltimore 18 days earlier, intercepted a pass and got in on 18 snaps in his first game of the year, helping the Ravens to a 31-14 win over Buffalo.

Comeback of the week: In one of the few games of Week 13 in which a team rallied to win, Carolina rebounded from a 7-0 second-quarter deficit to defeat the Rams, 16-10. The Rams scored the game's first touchdown on Leslie O'Neal's 66-yard fumble return, but the Panthers answered with a touchdown catch by Rocket Ismail and three field goals by John Kasay. A goal-line stand by Carolina with 1:13 left preserved the victory.

Blowout of the week: Green Bay routed Dallas, 45-17, at Lambeau Field to avenge eight consecutive losses to the Cowboys, the last seven in Dallas. Dorsey Levens rushed for a club-record 190 yards, including two touchdowns, and Brett Favre passed for four TDs. The Packers scored every time they had the ball in the second half.

Nail-biter of the week: A 7-7 tie between the Redskins and the Giants included Michael Westbrook's unsportsmanlike penalty in overtime and Washington quarterback Gus Frerotte head-butting a concrete wall during a first-half touchdown celebration. (He suffered a sprained neck and left the game.) Each team missed a field-goal attempt in overtime.

Hit of the week: Left end Rick Lyle preserved the Jets' 23-21 win over the Vikings by grabbing hold of running back Robert Smith's foot and pulling him down before he could reach the goal line on a two-point conversion attempt on the final play of the game. A TD catch by tight end Andrew Glover had cut the Jets' lead to two points.

Oddity of the week: With Kansas City punter Louis Aguiar in punt formation, he took the snap and unleashed a towering spiral—with his hands, not his foot. The Seahawks appeared confused and Chiefs rookie Kevin Lockett grabbed the ball over punt returner Ronnie Harris deep in Seattle territory, setting up a 1-yard touchdown run by Marcus Allen that helped lead the Chiefs to a 19-14 win. Harris said he knew it was a pass, but some of his teammates didn't. They stood around, reacting as if the ball was a punt that was either going to bounce into the end zone or be fair caught.

Top rusher: Barry Sanders had 24 carries for 216 yards and two touchdowns in the Lions' victory over the Colts.

Top passer: Dan Marino was 38-of-60 for 389 yards in the Dolphins' 27-24 loss to New England.

Top receiver: Minnesota's Jake Reed caught eight passes for 150 yards and two touchdowns against the Jets.

Notes: Barry Sanders became the first running back to run for 100 yards in 10 consecutive games in the same season. He also became the first player to score three touchdowns on runs of at least 80 yards in a season. . . . Chicago linebacker Bryan Cox lost his composure after he was called for a roughing penalty on Tampa Bay quarterback Trent Dilfer in the Bears' 13-7 upset win. Cox's outburst caused referees to throw another flag, this time for unsportsmanlike conduct. After lectures from teammates and coaches, Cox quit as team captain after the game. . . . Detroit's Jason Hanson broke Eddie Murray's team record by making his 21st consecutive field goal. After tying Murray's record of 19 with a 38-yarder, Hanson broke it with a 52-yarder, then extended his streak with a 55-yarder. . . . Attendance for the Carolina-St. Louis game was 64,609, the 23rd consecutive sellout for the Rams, who have played to capacity crowds in every game since moving to St. Louis in 1995. . . . The Steelers are winless against the Eagles (0-7) at Philadelphia's Veterans Stadium, which opened in 1971. . . . Buffalo's Andre Reed had five catches in a 31-14 defeat to the Oilers, giving him 821 in his career, surpassing Steve Largent (819) for third place on the NFL's career list. . . . New England's four interception returns for touchdowns this season is a franchise record. . . . Miami's Karim Abdul-Jabbar set a club record for rushing touchdowns in a season (13). . . . After going eight years without a tie game, the NFL had its second in as many weeks.

Quote of the week: Saints coach Mike Ditka, after his team lost to Atlanta, 20-3, to fall to 4-8 on the season: "I'm probably the wrong guy for this job, I'll say that. They are probably better off getting somebody else. I don't have it any more. They say God puts people in places for reasons. He probably put me here to be humbled. And I deserve it."

GAME SUMMARIES

FALCONS 20, SAINTS 3

Sunday, November 23

New Orleans	0	3	0	0— 3
Atlanta	3	3	7	7—20

First Quarter
Atl.—FG, Andersen 43, 13:16.
Second Quarter
Atl.—FG, Andersen 22, 11:03.
N.O.—FG, Brien 22, 14:52.
Third Quarter
Atl.—Emanuel 36 pass from Chandler (Andersen kick), 9:50.
Fourth Quarter
Atl.—Mathis 4 pass from Chandler (Andersen kick), 0:07.
Attendance—48,620.

TEAM STATISTICS
	New Orleans	Atlanta
First downs	11	16
Rushes-yards	19-58	33-92
Passing	115	177
Punt returns	1-10	4-39
Kickoff returns	4-88	2-30
Interception returns	0-0	4-23
Comp.-att.-int.	14-29-4	17-27-0
Sacked-yards lost	7-35	4-34
Punts	6-48	6-33
Fumbles-lost	2-1	4-1
Penalties-yards	3-20	4-40
Time of possession	24:13	35:47

INDIVIDUAL STATISTICS
RUSHING—New Orleans, Zellars 11-19, Nussmeier 4-28, McCrary 4-11. Atlanta, Anderson 21-65, Hanspard 6-14, Chandler 5-13, Christian 1-0.
PASSING—New Orleans, Nussmeier 10-19-3-101, Hobert 4-10-1-49. Atlanta, Chandler 17-26-0-211, Anderson 0-1-0-0.
RECEIVING—New Orleans, Guliford 4-40, I. Smith 2-30, McCrary 2-20, Zellars 2-13, Bech 1-22, Hastings 1-15, Hill 1-7, T. Davis 1-3. Atlanta, Emanuel 4-96, Mathis 3-30, Christian 3-17, Anderson 2-16, West 2-15, Green 1-21, Haynes 1-12, Kinchen 1-4.
MISSED FIELD GOAL ATTEMPTS—New Orleans, Brien 42. Atlanta, Andersen 43.
INTERCEPTIONS—Atlanta, Bradford 1-9, Booker 1-6, Bush 1-4, Buchanan 1-4.

KICKOFF RETURNS—New Orleans, Guliford 4-88. Atlanta, Hanspard 1-24, Burrough 1-6.
PUNT RETURNS—New Orleans, Guliford 1-10. Atlanta, Kinchen 4-39.
SACKS—New Orleans, B. Smith 2, Tomich 1, J. Johnson 1. Atlanta, Dronett 2.5, Hall 2.5, Archambeau 1, Pleasant 1.

EAGLES 23, STEELERS 20

Sunday, November 23

Pittsburgh	3	3	7	7—20
Philadelphia	14	3	3	3—23

First Quarter
Phi.—Dunn 31 pass from Hoying (Boniol kick), 4:33.
Phi.—Fryar 8 pass from Hoying (Boniol kick), 9:22.
Pit.—FG, N. Johnson 46, 13:41.
Second Quarter
Pit.—FG, N. Johnson 40, 9:36.
Phi.—FG, Boniol 23, 13:18.
Third Quarter
Phi.—FG, Boniol 35, 9:15.
Pit.—Bettis 19 pass from Stewart (N. Johnson kick), 12:56.
Fourth Quarter
Phi.—FG, Boniol 25, 1:22.
Pit.—Blackwell 30 pass from Stewart (N. Johnson kick), 14:50.
Attendance—67,166.

TEAM STATISTICS
	Pittsburgh	Philadelphia
First downs	22	19
Rushes-yards	25-111	35-97
Passing	272	229
Punt returns	1-2	0-0
Kickoff returns	6-101	4-62
Interception returns	0-0	3-25
Comp.-att.-int.	20-43-3	15-31-0
Sacked-yards lost	2-22	3-17
Punts	2-37	4-42
Fumbles-lost	3-2	1-0
Penalties-yards	6-54	3-15
Time of possession	27:53	32:07

INDIVIDUAL STATISTICS
RUSHING—Pittsburgh, Bettis 20-80, Stewart 3-33, G. Jones 1-8, Hawkins 1-(minus 10). Philadelphia, Watters 20-48, Garner 8-42, Hoying 5-(minus 4), Turner 2-11.
PASSING—Pittsburgh, Stewart 20-43-3-294. Philadelphia, Hoying 15-31-0-246.
RECEIVING—Pittsburgh, C. Johnson 7-106, Thigpen 5-87, Blackwell 4-58, Hawkins 2-21, Bettis 1-19, G. Jones 1-3. Philadelphia, Fryar 7-116, Johnson 4-37, Watters 2-50, Dunn 1-31, Solomon 1-12.
MISSED FIELD GOAL ATTEMPTS—None.
INTERCEPTIONS—Philadelphia, Dimry 1-25, Stevens 1-0, Vincent 1-0.
KICKOFF RETURNS—Pittsburgh, Blackwell 5-84, Coleman 1-17. Philadelphia, Staley 4-62.
PUNT RETURNS—Pittsburgh, Blackwell 1-2.
SACKS—Pittsburgh, Kirkland 1, Henry 1, Lloyd 1. Philadelphia, Zordich 1, Mamula 0.5, J. Jones 0.5.

LIONS 32, COLTS 10

Sunday, November 23

Indianapolis	7	3	0	0—10
Detroit	9	9	7	7—32

First Quarter
Det.—Vardell 1 run (Hanson kick), 8:50.
Det.—Safety, Justin sacked by Scroggins in end zone, 9:50.
Ind.—Harrison 20 pass from Justin (Blanchard kick), 12:35.
Second Quarter
Det.—FG, Hanson 38, 0:05.
Ind.—FG, Blanchard 35, 5:45.
Det.—FG, Hanson 52, 13:06.
Det.—FG, Hanson 55, 15:00.
Third Quarter
Det.—Sanders 80 run (Hanson kick), 0:18.
Fourth Quarter
Det.—Sanders 4 run (Hanson kick), 6:43.
Attendance—62,803.

TEAM STATISTICS

	Indianapolis	Detroit
First downs	12	21
Rushes-yards	19-53	36-249
Passing	120	142
Punt returns	3-18	5-25
Kickoff returns	2-33	2-29
Interception returns	0-0	1-29
Comp.-att.-int.	18-28-1	16-28-0
Sacked-yards lost	8-61	1-8
Punts	6-48	5-40
Fumbles-lost	0-0	0-0
Penalties-yards	7-54	6-61
Time of possession	28:22	31:38

INDIVIDUAL STATISTICS

RUSHING—Indianapolis, Faulk 12-38, Harbaugh 3-21, Crockett 2-(minus 7), Bailey 1-3, Warren 1-(minus 2). Detroit, Sanders 24-216, Rivers 6-29, Mitchell 2-4, Vardell 2-2, Reich 2-(minus 2).

PASSING—Indianapolis, Harbaugh 10-16-0-112, Justin 6-8-0-61, Holcomb 2-3-1-8, Warren 0-1-0-0. Detroit, Mitchell 16-28-0-150.

RECEIVING—Indianapolis, Dawkins 4-55, Warren 4-16, Faulk 3-45, Harrison 3-30, Crockett 2-8, Pollard 1-14, Dilger 1-13. Detroit, Morton 5-39, Sloan 3-43, Metzelaars 2-26, T. Boyd 2-16, Moore 2-16, Sanders 2-10.

MISSED FIELD GOAL ATTEMPTS—None.

INTERCEPTIONS—Detroit, Abrams 1-29.

KICKOFF RETURNS—Indianapolis, Bailey 2-33. Detroit, Milburn 2-29.

PUNT RETURNS—Indianapolis, Jacquet 3-18. Detroit, Milburn 5-25.

SACKS—Indianapolis, Footman 1. Detroit, Porcher 3.5, Scroggins 3, Elliss 1.5.

CARDINALS 16, RAVENS 13

Sunday, November 23

Arizona	3	0	3	10—16
Baltimore	0	3	7	3—13

First Quarter
Ariz.—FG, Nedney 22, 7:04.

Second Quarter
Bal.—FG, Stover 46, 15:00.

Third Quarter
Ariz.—FG, Nedney 27, 5:08.
Bal.—Morris 1 run (Stover kick), 11:32.

Fourth Quarter
Ariz.—Sanders 4 pass from Plummer (Nedney kick), 6:26.
Bal.—FG, Stover 34, 14:26.
Ariz.—FG, Nedney 43, 15:00.
Attendance—53,976.

TEAM STATISTICS

	Arizona	Baltimore
First downs	15	17
Rushes-yards	24-71	28-129
Passing	202	185
Punt returns	6-110	3-19
Kickoff returns	2-60	3-61
Interception returns	0-0	2-15
Comp.-att.-int.	19-34-2	21-37-0
Sacked-yards lost	2-16	2-8
Punts	6-44	9-42
Fumbles-lost	0-0	1-0
Penalties-yards	2-20	8-63
Time of possession	27:46	32:14

INDIVIDUAL STATISTICS

RUSHING—Arizona, McElroy 11-16, Centers 8-36, Plummer 5-19. Baltimore, Morris 20-88, Testaverde 4-16, Byner 3-22, Graham 1-3.

PASSING—Arizona, Plummer 19-34-2-218. Baltimore, Testaverde 21-37-0-193.

RECEIVING—Arizona, R. Moore 8-112, Centers 6-49, Edwards 3-44, Sanders 2-13. Baltimore, Morris 6-35, Jackson 4-56, Alexander 3-48, Yarborough 3-35, J. Lewis 2-13, Green 1-6, Graham 1-5, Byner 1-(minus 5).

MISSED FIELD GOAL ATTEMPTS—None.

INTERCEPTIONS—Baltimore, R. Jones 1-15, Moore 1-0.

KICKOFF RETURNS—Arizona, K. Williams 2-60. Baltimore, J. Lewis 1-21, Roe 1-21, Singleton 1-19.

PUNT RETURNS—Arizona, K. Williams 6-110. Baltimore, J. Lewis 3-19.

SACKS—Arizona, Swann 1, M. Smith 1. Baltimore, Boulware 1, McCrary 1.

BEARS 13, BUCCANEERS 7

Sunday, November 23

Tampa Bay	0	0	7	0— 7
Chicago	10	3	0	0—13

First Quarter
Chi.—R. Harris 2 run (Jaeger kick), 2:47.
Chi.—FG, Jaeger 32, 5:12.

Second Quarter
Chi.—FG, Jaeger 25, 9:38.

Third Quarter
T.B.—Anthony 12 pass from Dilfer (Husted kick), 14:12.
Attendance—43,955.

TEAM STATISTICS

	Tampa Bay	Chicago
First downs	14	17
Rushes-yards	18-35	42-169
Passing	237	110
Punt returns	3-40	2-15
Kickoff returns	3-62	2-54
Interception returns	0-0	0-0
Comp.-att.-int.	19-33-0	15-28-0
Sacked-yards lost	2-10	0-0
Punts	4-42	7-41
Fumbles-lost	3-3	0-0
Penalties-yards	3-20	6-58
Time of possession	23:13	36:47

INDIVIDUAL STATISTICS

RUSHING—Tampa Bay, Dunn 9-4, Alstott 7-18, Dilfer 1-13, Anthony 1-0. Chicago, R. Harris 33-116, Autry 5-11, Kramer 4-42.

PASSING—Tampa Bay, Dilfer 19-33-0-247. Chicago, Kramer 15-28-0-110.

RECEIVING—Tampa Bay, Anthony 4-59, Thomas 4-53, Harris 3-54, Williams 3-53, Dunn 2-13, Alstott 2-10, Copeland 1-5. Chicago, Penn 6-53, Bownes 2-23, Proehl 2-4, Allred 1-9, Jennings 1-8, Wetnight 1-6, Tony Carter 1-4, R. Harris 1-3.

MISSED FIELD GOAL ATTEMPTS—Tampa Bay, Husted 50, 40. Chicago, Jaeger 41.

INTERCEPTIONS—None.

KICKOFF RETURNS—Tampa Bay, Williams 3-62. Chicago, Bownes 2-54.

PUNT RETURNS—Tampa Bay, Williams 3-40. Chicago, Hughes 2-15.

SACKS—Chicago, Thomas 1, Simpson 1.

JETS 23, VIKINGS 21

Sunday, November 23

Minnesota	0	7	0	14—21
N.Y. Jets	7	13	3	0—23

First Quarter
NYJ—L. Johnson 66 punt return (Hall kick), 2:21.

Second Quarter
Min.—Reed 7 pass from Johnson (Murray kick), 1:29.
NYJ—FG, Hall 28, 5:16.
NYJ—Baxter 3 pass from O'Donnell (Hall kick), 10:22.
NYJ—FG, Hall 27, 14:49.

Third Quarter
NYJ—FG, Hall 51, 6:43.

Fourth Quarter
Min.—Reed 6 pass from Johnson (Johnson run), 3:41.
Min.—Glover 1 pass from Johnson (run failed), 15:00.
Attendance—77,716.

TEAM STATISTICS

	Minnesota	N.Y. Jets
First downs	19	22
Rushes-yards	27-74	32-130
Passing	312	227
Punt returns	0-0	3-81
Kickoff returns	5-122	3-71
Interception returns	0-0	0-0
Comp.-att.-int.	24-35-0	23-34-0
Sacked-yards lost	0-0	3-15
Punts	5-40	3-34
Fumbles-lost	2-1	4-3
Penalties-yards	3-36	1-0
Time of possession	27:05	32:55

INDIVIDUAL STATISTICS

RUSHING—Minnesota, R. Smith 18-46, Johnson 4-7, Hoard 3-15, Evans 1-4, Palmer 1-2. New York, Murrell 28-95, Lucas 1-15, O'Donnell 1-11, Neal 1-8, L. Johnson 1-1.

PASSING—Minnesota, Johnson 24-35-0-312. New York, O'Donnell 23-34-0-242.

RECEIVING—Minnesota, Reed 8-150, Carter 6-105, Glover 3-28, R. Smith 3-5, Palmer 1-9, Walsh 1-9, Evans 1-3, DeLong 1-3. New York, K. Johnson 9-104, Chrebet 4-66, Baxter 4-33, Neal 3-19, Murrell 2-10, Brady 1-10.

MISSED FIELD GOAL ATTEMPTS—Minnesota, Murray 49. New York, Hall 42.

INTERCEPTIONS—None.

KICKOFF RETURNS—Minnesota, Palmer 5-122. New York, Glenn 3-71.

PUNT RETURNS—New York, L. Johnson 3-81.

SACKS—Minnesota, Clemons 2, Fisk 1.

PANTHERS 16, RAMS 10

Sunday, November 23

Carolina	0	10	3	3—16
St. Louis	0	7	3	0—10

Second Quarter
St.L.—O'Neal 66 fumble return (Wilkins kick), 3:49.
Car.—Ismail 59 pass from Collins (Kasay kick), 5:03.
Car.—FG, Kasay 36, 12:21.

Third Quarter
St.L.—FG, Wilkins 26, 4:19.
Car.—FG, Kasay 53, 8:19.

Fourth Quarter
Car.—FG, Kasay 27, 6:56.
Attendance—64,609.

TEAM STATISTICS

	Carolina	St. Louis
First downs	17	12
Rushes-yards	27-48	22-81
Passing	254	187
Punt returns	4-56	2-28
Kickoff returns	2-43	5-89
Interception returns	1-(-2)	0-0
Comp.-att.-int.	23-30-0	16-32-1
Sacked-yards lost	4-32	2-12
Punts	5-42	6-50
Fumbles-lost	1-1	0-0
Penalties-yards	6-41	9-61
Time of possession	33:57	26:03

INDIVIDUAL STATISTICS

RUSHING—Carolina, Lane 19-41, Collins 4-(minus 1), Greene 3-10, Johnson 1-(minus 2). St. Louis, J. Moore 19-60, Banks 2-20, Lee 1-1.

PASSING—Carolina, Collins 23-30-0-286. St. Louis, Rypien 10-19-0-138, Banks 6-13-1-61.

RECEIVING—Carolina, Walls 8-106, Ismail 5-93, Greene 5-23, Muhammad 3-39, Carrier 1-20, Carruth 1-5. St. Louis, Bruce 5-48, Conwell 4-75, Kennison 4-62, Heyward 1-9, Lee 1-5, Jacoby 1-0.

MISSED FIELD GOAL ATTEMPTS—St. Louis, Wilkins 40.

INTERCEPTIONS—Carolina, Davis 1-(minus 2).

KICKOFF RETURNS—Carolina, Bates 1-23, Stone 1-20. St. Louis, Thompson 4-70, Lee 1-19.

PUNT RETURNS—Carolina, Poole 4-56. St. Louis, Kennison 2-28.

SACKS—Carolina, Turnbull 1, Barrow 0.5, Miller 0.5. St. Louis, Carter 2, M. Jones 1, B. Robinson 1.

49ERS 17, CHARGERS 10

Sunday, November 23

San Diego	0	0	10	0—10
San Francisco	3	7	7	0—17

First Quarter
S.F.—FG, Anderson 29, 7:15.

Second Quarter
S.F.—Owens 37 pass from S. Young (Anderson kick), 14:32.

Third Quarter
S.D.—FG, G. Davis 31, 3:47.
S.F.—Stokes 3 pass from S. Young (Anderson kick), 8:07.
S.D.—Bradford 78 fumble return (G. Davis kick), 12:07.
Attendance—61,195.

TEAM STATISTICS

	San Diego	San Francisco
First downs	8	19
Rushes-yards	23-92	34-110
Passing	111	228
Punt returns	4-1	5-60
Kickoff returns	4-117	3-59
Interception returns	0-0	3-3
Comp.-att.-int.	10-28-3	20-30-0
Sacked-yards lost	4-27	2-17
Punts	6-47	8-39
Fumbles-lost	0-0	3-2
Penalties-yards	7-40	5-41
Time of possession	24:35	35:25

INDIVIDUAL STATISTICS

RUSHING—San Diego, Bynum 11-64, Fletcher 5-20, Craver 4-4, Philcox 1-3, Metcalf 1-2, Whelihan 1-(minus 1). San Francisco, Hearst 22-87, Floyd 6-19, S. Young 4-7, Kirby 2-(minus 3).

PASSING—San Diego, Whelihan 4-18-3-81, Philcox 6-10-0-57. San Francisco, S. Young 20-30-0-245.

RECEIVING—San Diego, F. Jones 3-48, Metcalf 2-25, Fletcher 2-16, Still 1-39, Hartley 1-5, Martin 1-5. San Francisco, Jones 5-83, Owens 4-84, Stokes 3-21, Floyd 3-15, Hearst 2-5, Levy 1-27, Kirby 1-7, Uwaezuoke 1-3.

MISSED FIELD GOAL ATTEMPTS—San Diego, G. Davis 43.

INTERCEPTIONS—San Francisco, Hanks 2-3, Maxie 1-0.

KICKOFF RETURNS—San Diego, Bynum 4-117. San Francisco, Levy 3-59.

PUNT RETURNS—San Diego, Metcalf 4-1. San Francisco, Uwaezuoke 5-60.

SACKS—San Diego, Seau 1, Harrison 1. San Francisco, Greene 2, Stubblefield 2.

CHIEFS 19, SEAHAWKS 14

Sunday, November 23

Kansas City	7	3	7	2—19
Seattle	7	7	0	0—14

First Quarter
K.C.—Allen 1 run (Stoyanovich kick), 5:08.
Sea.—Galloway 20 pass from Moon (Peterson kick), 12:14.

Second Quarter
K.C.—FG, Stoyanovich 22, 2:45.
Sea.—Broussard 22 run (Peterson kick), 13:54.

Third Quarter
K.C.—Gannon 1 run (Stoyanovich kick), 5:34.

Fourth Quarter
K.C.—Safety, punt blocked out of end zone, 3:35.
Attendance—66,264.

TEAM STATISTICS

	Kansas City	Seattle
First downs	22	18
Rushes-yards	34-120	23-68
Passing	204	223
Punt returns	3-27	2-11
Kickoff returns	4-77	4-80
Interception returns	1-0	0-0
Comp.-att.-int.	16-29-0	20-37-1
Sacked-yards lost	2-6	5-25
Punts	5-45	7-28
Fumbles-lost	3-2	3-2
Penalties-yards	7-57	7-59
Time of possession	30:56	29:04

INDIVIDUAL STATISTICS

RUSHING—Kansas City, Bennett 7-35, Hill 7-27, Gannon 7-21, Allen 7-19, Anders 5-7, Vanover 1-11. Seattle, Warren 10-32, Broussard 7-33, Smith 3-(minus 2), Moon 2-(minus 1), Strong 1-6.

PASSING—Kansas City, Gannon 15-28-0-175, Aguiar 1-1-0-35. Seattle, Moon 20-37-1-248.

RECEIVING—Kansas City, Rison 6-90, Gonzalez 4-37, Vanover 2-22, Lockett 1-35, Dawson 1-13, Anders 1-9, Bennett 1-4. Seattle, Warren 5-38, McKnight 4-66, Pritchard 4-56, Galloway 3-36, Crumpler 2-29, Hobbs 1-21, Broussard 1-2.

MISSED FIELD GOAL ATTEMPTS—None.

INTERCEPTIONS—Kansas City, Hasty 1-0.

KICKOFF RETURNS—Kansas City, Vanover 4-77. Seattle, Broussard 4-80.

PUNT RETURNS—Kansas City, Vanover 3-27. Seattle, Harris 2-11.

SACKS—Kansas City, Booker 2, Tongue 1, Davis 1, Edwards 0.5, Phillips 0.5. Seattle, Wells 1, Sinclair 1.

PATRIOTS 27, DOLPHINS 24

Sunday, November 23

Miami	0	3	7	14—24
New England	3	21	3	0—27

First Quarter
N.E.—FG, Vinatieri 36, 13:18.

Second Quarter
Mia.—FG, Mare 25, 4:12.
N.E.—Brown 35 pass from Meggett (Vinatieri kick), 12:23.
N.E.—Whigham 60 interception return (Vinatieri kick), 13:16.
N.E.—Hitchcock 100 interception return (Vinatieri kick), 14:49.

Third Quarter
N.E.—FG, Vinatieri 27, 5:00.
Mia.—Abdul-Jabbar 1 run (Mare kick), 7:40.

Fourth Quarter
Mia.—Abdul-Jabbar 1 run (Mare kick), 3:04.
Mia.—Abdul-Jabbar 1 run (Mare kick), 14:50.
Attendance—59,002.

TEAM STATISTICS

	Miami	New England
First downs	33	15
Rushes-yards	22-36	24-84
Passing	370	234
Punt returns	2-14	2-12
Kickoff returns	6-101	3-65
Interception returns	0-0	3-160
Comp.-att.-int.	38-60-3	16-27-0
Sacked-yards lost	3-19	1-8
Punts	3-37	2-44
Fumbles-lost	0-0	0-0
Penalties-yards	3-35	8-76
Time of possession	34:15	25:45

INDIVIDUAL STATISTICS

RUSHING—Miami, Abdul-Jabbar 18-33, Nealy 1-2, McPhail 1-1, Parmalee 1-1, Marino 1-(minus 1). New England, Martin 22-80, Bledsoe 1-3, Gash 1-1.

PASSING—Miami, Marino 38-60-3-389. New England, Bledsoe 15-26-0-207, Meggett 1-1-0-35.

RECEIVING—Miami, McDuffie 9-110, Jordan 5-78, Manning 5-60, McPhail 5-47, L. Thomas 4-53, Abdul-Jabbar 4-14, Drayton 3-18, Perry 5-9. New England, Jefferson 4-71, Byars 3-58, Brown 3-46, Coates 3-39, Martin 2-18, Gash 1-10.

MISSED FIELD GOAL ATTEMPTS—New England, Vinatieri 30.

INTERCEPTIONS—New England, Whigham 2-60, Hitchcock 1-100.

KICKOFF RETURNS—Miami, C. Harris 5-101, Hollier 1-0. New England, Meggett 2-49, Cullors 1-26.

PUNT RETURNS—Miami, Jordan 2-14. New England, Meggett 2-12.

SACKS—Miami, Taylor 1. New England, Slade 2, Jones 1.

OILERS 31, BILLS 14

Sunday, November 23

Buffalo	0	7	0	7—14
Tennessee	14	7	3	7—31

First Quarter
Ten.—Robertson 25 fumble return (Del Greco kick), 0:19.
Ten.—McNair 1 run (Del Greco kick), 8:40.

Second Quarter
Ten.—McNair 3 run (Del Greco kick), 11:07.
Buf.—Early 9 pass from Collins (Christie kick), 13:34.

Third Quarter
Ten.—FG, Del Greco 51, 5:50.

Fourth Quarter
Buf.—Early 5 pass from Collins (Christie kick), 2:35.
Ten.—Russell 2 pass from McNair (Del Greco kick), 10:58.
Attendance—23,571.

TEAM STATISTICS

	Buffalo	Tennessee
First downs	12	21
Rushes-yards	14-4	42-163
Passing	286	159
Punt returns	2-16	4-42
Kickoff returns	6-104	2-46
Interception returns	0-0	1-24
Comp.-att.-int.	25-40-1	15-24-0
Sacked-yards lost	0-0	2-8
Punts	5-42	5-40
Fumbles-lost	2-1	1-1
Penalties-yards	5-31	5-40
Time of possession	21:25	38:35

INDIVIDUAL STATISTICS

RUSHING—Buffalo, A. Smith 9-7, Thomas 3-1, Collins 1-(minus 1), Holmes 1-(minus 3). Tennessee, E. George 25-93, Thomas 8-33, McNair 6-45, Krieg 2-(minus 1), Mason 1-(minus 7).

PASSING—Buffalo, Collins 25-40-1-286. Tennessee, McNair 15-24-0-167.

RECEIVING—Buffalo, Early 8-103, Reed 5-93, Riemersma 5-29, Johnson 3-18, A. Smith 2-27, Holmes 2-16. Tennessee, Wycheck 6-51, Davis 3-37, Mason 2-40, Thomas 2-22, E. George 1-15, Russell 1-2.

MISSED FIELD GOAL ATTEMPTS—Buffalo, Christie 36.

INTERCEPTIONS—Tennessee, Roger Jones 1-24.

KICKOFF RETURNS—Buffalo, Moulds 3-59, Holmes 3-45. Tennessee, Thomas 2-46.

PUNT RETURNS—Buffalo, Burris 2-16. Tennessee, Mason 3-42, Robertson 1-0.

SACKS—Buffalo, Washington 1, Paup 1.

PACKERS 45, COWBOYS 17

Sunday, November 23

Dallas	3	7	0	7—17
Green Bay	7	3	14	21—45

First Quarter
G.B.—Levens 7 pass from Favre (Longwell kick), 9:12.
Dal.—FG, Cunningham 29, 14:27.

Second Quarter
Dal.—Sanders 50 interception return (Cunningham kick), 13:41.
G.B.—FG, Longwell 32, 14:59.

Third Quarter
G.B.—Chmura 4 pass from Favre (Longwell kick), 4:34.
G.B.—Chmura 2 pass from Favre (Longwell kick), 14:50.

Fourth Quarter
Dal.—E. Smith 21 run (Cunningham kick), 1:38.
G.B.—Freeman 23 pass from Favre (Longwell kick), 6:42.
G.B.—Levens 5 run (Longwell kick), 13:05.
G.B.—Sharper 34 fumble return (Longwell kick), 13:27.
Attendance—60,111.

TEAM STATISTICS

	Dallas	Green Bay
First downs	11	29
Rushes-yards	20-93	41-220
Passing	120	189
Punt returns	1-0	4-25
Kickoff returns	7-148	4-84
Interception returns	1-50	0-0
Comp.-att.-int.	12-25-0	22-35-1
Sacked-yards lost	1-10	2-14
Punts	6-43	3-41
Fumbles-lost	3-2	0-0
Penalties-yards	11-103	3-23
Time of possession	22:41	37:19

INDIVIDUAL STATISTICS

RUSHING—Dallas, E. Smith 11-59, Walker 3-16, S. Williams 3-15, Aikman 3-3. Green Bay, Levens 33-190, Henderson 5-9, Favre 3-21.

PASSING—Dallas, Aikman 12-24-0-130, Wilson 0-1-0-0. Green Bay, Favre 22-35-1-203.

RECEIVING—Dallas, Irvin 4-57, Bjornson 4-38, E. Smith 2-2, Miller 1-26, St. Williams 1-7. Green Bay, Chmura 5-52, Henderson 5-12, Mayes 4-30, Levens 4-17, Freeman 3-56, R. Brooks 1-36.

MISSED FIELD GOAL ATTEMPTS—Green Bay, Longwell 34.

INTERCEPTIONS—Dallas, Sanders 1-50.

KICKOFF RETURNS—Dallas, Walker 6-137, Galbraith 1-11. Green Bay, Schroeder 4-84.

PUNT RETURNS—Dallas, Sanders 1-0. Green Bay, Mayes 4-25.

SACKS—Dallas, Coakley 1, Hennings 1. Green Bay, Harris 1.

REDSKINS 7, GIANTS 7

Sunday, November 23

N.Y. Giants	0	0	7	0	0—7
Washington	0	7	0	0	0—7

Second Quarter

Was.—Frerotte 1 run (Blanton kick), 12:44.

Third Quarter

NYG—Calloway 4 pass from Kanell (Daluiso kick), 8:02.
Attendance—75,703.

TEAM STATISTICS

	N.Y. Giants	Washington
First downs	18	23
Rushes-yards	37-157	32-82
Passing	105	292
Punt returns	2-1	4-24
Kickoff returns	2-39	3-68
Interception returns	3-3	1-11
Comp.-att.-int.	20-37-1	28-60-3
Sacked-yards lost	6-63	4-25
Punts	13-41	9-41
Fumbles-lost	5-1	2-1
Penalties-yards	7-47	7-64
Time of possession	33:54	41:04

INDIVIDUAL STATISTICS

RUSHING—New York, Way 17-84, Wheatley 11-39, Barber 6-23, Pegram 2-3, Kanell 1-8. Washington, Allen 27-64, Hostetler 2-9, Frerotte 2-2, Mitchell 1-7.

PASSING—New York, Kanell 20-37-1-168. Washington, Hostetler 19-41-3-213, Frerotte 9-19-0-104.

RECEIVING—New York, Barber 7-65, Way 4-14, Calloway 3-22, Toomer 2-42, Pegram 2-9, Alexander 1-9, Pierce 1-7. Washington, Westbrook 9-125, Ellard 7-77, Asher 4-45, Mitchell 2-22, Thomas 2-22, Logan 2-9, Jenkins 1-20, Allen 1-(minus 3).

MISSED FIELD GOAL ATTEMPTS—New York, Daluiso 54. Washington, Blanton 45, 54.

INTERCEPTIONS—New York, Sparks 2-0, Sehorn 1-(minus 2). Washington, M. Patton 1-0.

KICKOFF RETURNS—New York, Pegram 2-39. Washington, Davis 2-46, Mitchell 1-22.

PUNT RETURNS—New York, Toomer 2-1. Washington, Mitchell 4-24.

SACKS—New York, K. Hamilton 1.5, Sparks 1, Strahan 1, Harris 0.5. Washington, Harvey 4, Duff 1, Zorich 1.

BENGALS 31, JAGUARS 26

Sunday, November 23

Jacksonville	7	3	13	3—26
Cincinnati	21	7	3	0—31

First Quarter

Cin.—Carter 1 run (Pelfrey kick), 5:57.
Cin.—McGee 9 pass from Esiason (Pelfrey kick), 7:47.
Jac.—Mitchell 24 pass from Brunell (Hollis kick), 13:47.
Cin.—Dillon 3 run (Pelfrey kick), 14:11.

Second Quarter

Cin.—Scott 11 pass from Esiason (Pelfrey kick), 12:46.
Jac.—FG, Hollis 21, 15:00.

Third Quarter

Jac.—FG, Hollis 35, 3:31.
Jac.—Means 5 run (Hollis kick), 5:04.
Cin.—FG, Pelfrey 20, 10:06.
Jac.—FG, Hollis 29, 12:58.

Fourth Quarter

Jac.—FG, Hollis 25, 5:48.
Attendance—55,158.

TEAM STATISTICS

	Jacksonville	Cincinnati
First downs	20	24
Rushes-yards	24-135	36-124
Passing	280	203
Punt returns	3-79	0-0
Kickoff returns	6-92	6-197
Interception returns	0-0	1-3
Comp.-att.-int.	20-33-1	26-36-0
Sacked-yards lost	1-6	1-8
Punts	1-56	6-35
Fumbles-lost	2-2	1-0
Penalties-yards	5-41	5-79
Time of possession	24:19	35:41

INDIVIDUAL STATISTICS

RUSHING—Jacksonville, Means 19-96, Brunell 3-29, Stewart 2-10. Cincinnati, Dillon 26-88, Carter 5-11, Esiason 2-15, Milne 2-8, Bieniemy 1-2.

PASSING—Jacksonville, Brunell 20-33-1-286. Cincinnati, Esiason 26-36-0-211.

RECEIVING—Jacksonville, McCardell 8-109, Smith 5-106, Mitchell 4-46, Stewart 2-4, Brown 1-21. Cincinnati, Dillon 5-48, Scott 5-45, Pickens 4-35, Milne 4-12, Hundon 3-25, McGee 3-25, Carter 2-21.

MISSED FIELD GOAL ATTEMPTS—None.

INTERCEPTIONS—Cincinnati, Orlando 1-3.

KICKOFF RETURNS—Jacksonville, Jackson 6-92. Cincinnati, Hundon 3-58, Dunn 2-112, Bieniemy 1-27.

PUNT RETURNS—Jacksonville, Barlow 3-79.

SACKS—Jacksonville, Payne 1. Cincinnati, Francis 1.

BRONCOS 31, RAIDERS 3

Monday, November 24

Oakland	0	3	0	0— 3
Denver	0	14	17	0—31

Second Quarter

Den.—Davis 3 run (Elam kick), 6:35.
Den.—Davis 19 run (Elam kick), 13:12.
Oak.—FG, Ford 41, 14:44.

Third Quarter

Den.—Davis 2 run (Elam kick), 3:59.
Den.—FG, Elam 36, 6:58.
Den.—R. Smith 15 pass from Elway (Elam kick), 12:59.
Attendance—75,307.

TEAM STATISTICS

	Oakland	Denver
First downs	14	23
Rushes-yards	21-110	30-110
Passing	150	260
Punt returns	1-0	4-31
Kickoff returns	5-86	1-33
Interception returns	0-0	0-0
Comp.-att.-int.	22-41-0	21-33-0
Sacked-yards lost	4-35	3-20
Punts	8-44	5-43
Fumbles-lost	2-2	1-1
Penalties-yards	12-82	8-75
Time of possession	29:06	30:54

INDIVIDUAL STATISTICS

RUSHING—Oakland, Kaufman 13-53, Hall 4-31, Williams 3-21, George 1-5. Denver, Davis 21-69, Loville 6-36, Elway 3-5.

PASSING—Oakland, George 22-41-0-185. Denver, Elway 21-32-0-280, Lewis 0-1-0-0.

RECEIVING—Oakland, T. Brown 8-55, Jett 5-68, Williams 4-10, Dudley 2-26, Shedd 1-14, Howard 1-7, Kaufman 1-5. Denver, Sharpe 10-142, McCaffrey 4-51, Davis 4-46, R. Smith 3-41.

MISSED FIELD GOAL ATTEMPTS—None.

INTERCEPTIONS—None.

KICKOFF RETURNS—Oakland, Howard 5-86. Denver, Hebron 1-33.

PUNT RETURNS—Oakland, Howard 1-0. Denver, Gordon 4-31.

SACKS—Oakland, McGlockton 1, Johnstone 1, Russell 1. Denver, Mobley 1, Williams 1, Atwater 1, N. Smith 1.

WEEK 14

RESULTS

DETROIT 55, Chicago 20
Tennessee 27, DALLAS 14
Atlanta 24, SEATTLE 17
BUFFALO 20, N.Y. Jets 10
Denver 38, SAN DIEGO 28
JACKSONVILLE 29, Baltimore 27
KANSAS CITY 44, San Francisco 9
Miami 34, OAKLAND 16
NEW ENGLAND 20, Indianapolis 17
New Orleans 16, CAROLINA 13
PHILADELPHIA 44, Cincinnati 42
Pittsburgh 26, ARIZONA 20 (OT)
St. Louis 23, WASHINGTON 20
Tampa Bay 20, N.Y. GIANTS 8
Green Bay 27, MINNESOTA 11

STANDINGS

AFC EAST	W	L	T	Pct.
Miami	8	5	0	.615
New England	8	5	0	.615
N.Y. Jets	8	5	0	.615
Buffalo	6	7	0	.462
Indianapolis	1	12	0	.077

AFC CENTRAL	W	L	T	Pct.
Jacksonville	9	4	0	.692
Pittsburgh	9	4	0	.692
Tennessee	7	6	0	.538
Baltimore	4	8	1	.346
Cincinnati	4	9	0	.308

AFC WEST	W	L	T	Pct.
Denver	11	2	0	.846
Kansas City	10	3	0	.769
Seattle	6	7	0	.462
Oakland	4	9	0	.308
San Diego	4	9	0	.308

NFC EAST	W	L	T	Pct.
N.Y. Giants	7	5	1	.577
Philadelphia	6	6	1	.500
Washington	6	6	1	.500
Dallas	6	7	0	.462
Arizona	3	10	0	.231

NFC CENTRAL	W	L	T	Pct.
Green Bay	10	3	0	.769
Tampa Bay	9	4	0	.692
Minnesota	8	5	0	.615
Detroit	7	6	0	.538
Chicago	2	11	0	.154

NFC WEST	W	L	T	Pct.
San Francisco	11	2	0	.846
Carolina	6	7	0	.462
Atlanta	5	8	0	.385
New Orleans	5	8	0	.385
St. Louis	3	10	0	.231

HIGHLIGHTS

Hero of the week: Barry Sanders ran for 167 yards and scored three touchdowns as Detroit defeated Chicago, 55-20, on Thanksgiving Day. It was the 11th consecutive game Sanders rushed for at least 100 yards, tying a league record held by Marcus Allen.

Goat of the week: In another Thanksgiving Day game, Cowboys quarterback Troy Aikman threw three interceptions in a 27-14 loss to the Oilers. Aikman was unusually wild early on as Tennessee intercepted two of his passes in the first quarter, turning both into touchdowns.

Sub of the week: Baltimore quarterback Eric Zeier, subbing for the injured Vinny Testaverde, rallied the Ravens to two fourth-quarter touchdowns and a near upset over Jacksonville. His second TD pass, a 7-yarder to Eric Green, cut the Jaguars' lead to 29-27 with 1:10 left. But on the 2-point conversion attempt that would have tied the game, Zeier tripped over the leg of left tackle Jonathan Ogden on a quarterback draw and was stopped short of the goal line.

Comeback of the week: The Lions rallied from a 17-3 second-quarter deficit by scoring 45 consecutive points to run away with a 55-20 victory over Chicago. Detroit's onslaught began after the Bears took a 20-10 lead on Jeff Jaeger's 32-yard field goal with 1:32 left in the first half.

Blowout of the week: In one of the more stunning scores of the season, the Chiefs whipped the 49ers, 44-9, handing San Francisco only its second loss of the season and ending its 11-game winning streak. Led by quarterback Rich Gannon, the Chiefs scored their most points in a game in 12 seasons and handed the 49ers their worst regular-season defeat in 17 years.

Nail-biter of the week: The Eagles built a 41-28 lead over Cincinnati, then had to rally in the final minute for a 44-42 victory. Boomer Esiason nearly pulled off a comeback for the Bengals, throwing two of his four touchdown passes in the fourth quarter. Cincinnati went ahead 42-41 with a minute to play on Brian Milne's 1-yard touchdown run, but Philadelphia's Chris Boniol kicked a game-winning 31-yard field goal as time expired.

Hit of the week: A sack by Steelers defensive end Nolan Harrison on Arizona's last drive in the fourth quarter set the Cardinals back to the 28, enough to force Joe Nedney to attempt a field goal from a longer distance than his career best of 45 yards. Nedney missed and the Steelers went on to win 26-20 in overtime, the winning score coming on a 10-yard TD run by Jerome Bettis.

Oddity of the week: Green Bay finally put to rest a Metrodome hex by beating the Vikings, 27-11, in Minneapolis. Packers coach Mike Holmgren had been 0-5 at Minnesota's home stadium since taking over for Lindy Infante after the 1991 season. Most of the losses were close, including three game-winning field goals by Minnesota's Fuad Reveiz. But this time the Packers sacked Vikings quarterback Brad Johnson six times and never trailed en route to a convincing victory.

Top rusher: Terrell Davis rushed 26 times for 178 yards and one touchdown in Denver's 38-28 victory over San Diego.

Top passer: Boomer Esiason was 27-of-47 for 378 yards and four touchdowns in the Bengals' loss at Philadelphia.

Top receiver: Rob Moore caught eight passes for 188 yards in Arizona's overtime loss to Pittsburgh.

Notes: Barry Sanders became the No. 2 rusher in NFL history with his 167-yard performance against Chicago. Sanders (13,319) moved past Eric Dickerson (13,259) and trailed only Walter Payton (16,726). . . . Bills running back Thurman Thomas gained 104 yards in 18 carries to move into ninth place on the career rushing list with 11,325 yards. Thomas passed O.J. Simpson (11,236). . . . Andre Reed's first-quarter touchdown was Buffalo's first in the opening quarter in 17 games. . . . Miami quarterback Dan Marino recorded his 12th 3,000-yard passing season, the first NFL quarterback to have that many. . . . Giants cornerback Phillippi Sparks had two interceptions for the second game in a row. . . . Seattle's Warren Moon (274) passed Joe Montana (273) to move into fourth place on the career touchdown pass list. . . . The Dolphins, who never had won in eight previous tries in Oakland, broke the streak with a 34-16 victory over the Raiders. . . . Atlanta beat Seattle despite being outgained (351 yards to 273), having fewer first downs (19-14), running fewer plays (66-49) and having less time of possession (33:33-26:27). The Falcons had no first downs in the second half.

Quote of the week: Bears linebacker Barry Minter, on his inability to chase down Barry Sanders: "Somebody made the comparison that he was in a Lamborghini and I was in a Chevy S-10. You can't ask just one guy to tackle Barry Sanders when you're 10 yards off the ball and have to catch up."

GAME SUMMARIES

LIONS 55, BEARS 20

Thursday, November 27

Chicago	14	6	0	0—20
Detroit	3	14	17	21—55

First Quarter
Chi.—R. Harris 2 run (Jaeger kick), 7:16.
Chi.—Proehl 78 pass from Kramer (Jaeger kick), 10:15.
Det.—FG, Hanson 40, 11:24.

Second Quarter
Chi.—FG, Jaeger 52, 3:32.
Det.—Moore 8 pass from Mitchell (Hanson kick), 8:55.
Chi.—FG, Jaeger 32, 13:28.
Det.—Sanders 40 run (Hanson kick), 14:13.

Third Quarter
Det.—FG, Hanson 29, 4:35.
Det.—Morton 50 pass from Mitchell (Hanson kick), 8:03.
Det.—Sanders 25 run (Hanson kick), 9:41.

Fourth Quarter
Det.—Sanders 15 run (Hanson kick), 1:32.
Det.—Rivers 13 run (Hanson kick), 4:26.
Det.—Scroggins 17 fumble return (Hanson kick), 6:02.
Attendance—77,904.

INDIVIDUAL STATISTICS

	Chicago	Detroit
First downs	16	25
Rushes-yards	32-71	29-222
Passing	262	274
Punt returns	1-11	4-57
Kickoff returns	8-190	5-189
Interception returns	1-12	0-0
Comp.-att.-int.	16-30-0	20-31-1
Sacked-yards lost	3-16	2-8
Punts	5-54	3-41
Fumbles-lost	4-4	0-0
Penalties-yards	4-45	6-43
Time of possession	30:48	29:12

INDIVIDUAL STATISTICS
RUSHING—Chicago, R. Harris 19-49, Autry 6-10, Kramer 4-3, Stenstrom 1-6, Tony Carter 1-1, Conway 1-1. Detroit, Sanders 19-167, Rivers 5-44, Schlesinger 4-9, Vardell 1-2.
PASSING—Chicago, Kramer 13-26-0-259, Stenstrom 3-4-0-19. Detroit, Mitchell 20-31-1-282.
RECEIVING—Chicago, Wetnight 5-34, Proehl 4-164, Penn 4-66, Tony Carter 1-6, Autry 1-4, Allred 1-4. Detroit, Morton 7-120, Moore 6-89, Sloan 3-40, Sanders 2-8, Metzelaars 1-22, McCorvey 1-3.
MISSED FIELD GOAL ATTEMPTS—Chicago, Jaeger 45.
INTERCEPTIONS—Chicago, Tom Carter 1-12.
KICKOFF RETURNS—Chicago, Hughes 4-124, Bownes 4-66. Detroit, Milburn 5-189.
PUNT RETURNS—Chicago, Hughes 1-11. Detroit, Milburn 4-57.
SACKS—Chicago, Minter 1, Simpson 1. Detroit, Scroggins 1.5, Bailey 1, Porcher 0.5.

OILERS 27, COWBOYS 14

Thursday, November 27

Tennessee	14	10	0	3—27
Dallas	0	7	7	0—14

First Quarter
Ten.—Norgard 2 pass from McNair (Del Greco kick), 7:32.
Ten.—McNair 1 run (Del Greco kick), 13:06.

Second Quarter
Dal.—Irvin 19 pass from Aikman (Cunningham kick), 4:21.
Ten.—FG, Del Greco 29, 9:08.
Ten.—Robertson 42 fumble return (Del Greco kick), 13:27.

Third Quarter
Dal.—Irvin 37 pass from Aikman (Cunningham kick), 6:49.

Fourth Quarter
Ten.—FG, Del Greco 19, 5:16.
Attendance—63,421.

TEAM STATISTICS

	Tennessee	Dallas
First downs	14	16
Rushes-yards	49-164	13-46
Passing	81	340
Punt returns	2-19	4-21
Kickoff returns	3-40	6-149
Interception returns	3-108	0-0
Comp.-att.-int.	9-17-0	27-42-3
Sacked-yards lost	0-0	2-16
Punts	5-45	4-47
Fumbles-lost	3-1	5-2
Penalties-yards	6-64	6-59
Time of possession	36:02	23:58

INDIVIDUAL STATISTICS
RUSHING—Tennessee, E. George 34-110, McNair 9-26, Thomas 6-28. Dallas, E. Smith 10-22, S. Williams 2-12, Aikman 1-12.
PASSING—Tennessee, McNair 9-17-0-81. Dallas, Aikman 27-42-3-356.
RECEIVING—Tennessee, Wycheck 3-39, Thomas 2-20, Sanders 1-14, R. Lewis 1-7, Norgard 1-2, E. George 1-(minus 1). Dallas, S. Williams 7-56, Irvin 5-118, Miller 5-86, Bjornson 5-66, E. Smith 3-20, Galbraith 1-5, LaFleur 1-5.
MISSED FIELD GOAL ATTEMPTS—None.
INTERCEPTIONS—Tennessee, D. Lewis 2-60, Robertson 1-48.
KICKOFF RETURNS—Tennessee, Thomas 3-40. Dallas, Walker 6-149.
PUNT RETURNS—Tennessee, Mason 2-19. Dallas, Mathis 3-11, Sanders 1-10.
SACKS—Tennessee, Bishop 1, G. Walker 1.

SAINTS 16, PANTHERS 13

Sunday, November 30

New Orleans	0	13	0	3—16
Carolina	0	3	0	10—13

Second Quarter
N.O.—FG, Brien 50, 1:02.
N.O.—Zellars 10 run (Brien kick), 3:32.
Car.—FG, Kasay 44, 5:15.
N.O.—FG, Brien 51, 13:54.

Fourth Quarter
Car.—Lane 2 run (Kasay kick), 0:04.
Car.—FG, Kasay 31, 8:42.
N.O.—FG, Brien 45, 14:55.
Attendance—57,957.

TEAM STATISTICS

	New Orleans	Carolina
First downs	18	21
Rushes-yards	32-136	23-186
Passing	190	241
Punt returns	2-9	1-0
Kickoff returns	4-83	4-73
Interception returns	3-21	1-0
Comp.-att.-int.	14-30-1	24-42-3
Sacked-yards lost	0-0	2-9
Punts	4-42	3-37
Fumbles-lost	1-1	3-1
Penalties-yards	5-36	9-60
Time of possession	29:50	30:10

INDIVIDUAL STATISTICS

RUSHING—New Orleans, Zellars 18-95, T. Davis 9-37, Hobert 4-4, McCrary 1-0. Carolina, Lane 13-112, Greene 7-30, Beuerlein 1-20, Ismail 1-18, Johnson 1-6.

PASSING—New Orleans, Hobert 14-30-1-190. Carolina, Beuerlein 17-27-1-168, Collins 7-15-2-82.

RECEIVING—New Orleans, Hill 4-40, I. Smith 4-39, Zellars 3-58, Hastings 2-39, Savoie 1-14. Carolina, Walls 8-63, Ismail 6-102, Greene 5-35, Muhammad 3-40, Lane 1-7, E. Mills 1-3.

MISSED FIELD GOAL ATTEMPTS—Carolina, Kasay 26.

INTERCEPTIONS—New Orleans, Knight 2-4, Newman 1-17. Carolina, Davis 1-0.

KICKOFF RETURNS—New Orleans, T. Davis 3-67, Bech 1-16. Carolina, Bates 3-73, S. Mills 1-0.

PUNT RETURNS—New Orleans, Guliford 1-11, Hastings 1-(minus 2). Carolina, Poole 1-0.

SACKS—New Orleans, Molden 1, Glover 1.

PATRIOTS 20, COLTS 17

Sunday, November 30

Indianapolis	3	0	7	7—17
New England	7	6	0	7—20

First Quarter
N.E.—Gash 3 pass from Bledsoe (Vinatieri kick), 6:13.
Ind.—FG, Blanchard 24, 12:28.

Second Quarter
N.E.—FG, Vinatieri 32, 2:16.
N.E.—FG, Vinatieri 48, 15:00.

Third Quarter
Ind.—Bailey 18 pass from Harbaugh (Blanchard kick), 10:06.

Fourth Quarter
N.E.—Brown 18 pass from Bledsoe (Vinatieri kick), 0:04.
Ind.—Dawkins 11 pass from Harbaugh (Blanchard kick), 13:52.
Attendance—58,507.

TEAM STATISTICS

	Indianapolis	New England
First downs	23	17
Rushes-yards	26-118	25-71
Passing	285	187
Punt returns	1-9	2-57
Kickoff returns	4-68	3-83
Interception returns	0-0	0-0
Comp.-att.-int.	22-41-0	20-33-0
Sacked-yards lost	4-25	2-17
Punts	3-45	5-51
Fumbles-lost	1-1	0-0
Penalties-yards	5-34	10-65
Time of possession	33:23	26:37

INDIVIDUAL STATISTICS

RUSHING—Indianapolis, Faulk 12-44, Crockett 7-23, Warren 4-18, Harbaugh 3-33. New England, Martin 20-66, Bledsoe 3-1, Meggett 2-4.

PASSING—Indianapolis, Harbaugh 22-41-0-310. New England, Bledsoe 20-33-0-204.

RECEIVING—Indianapolis, Dawkins 7-120, Stablein 4-36, Faulk 3-43, Harrison 3-40, Bailey 2-28, Warren 1-20, Dilger 1-20, Glenn 1-3. New England, Coates 5-41, Jefferson 4-74, Brown 3-35, Martin 3-17, Brisby 2-25, Gash 2-10, Byars 1-2.

MISSED FIELD GOAL ATTEMPTS—Indianapolis, Blanchard 42.

INTERCEPTIONS—None.

KICKOFF RETURNS—Indianapolis, Bailey 4-68. New England, Meggett 3-83.

PUNT RETURNS—Indianapolis, Jacquet 1-9. New England, Meggett 2-57.

SACKS—Indianapolis, Fontenot 1, E. Johnson 0.5, McCoy 0.5. New England, Thomas 2, McGinest 1, Jones 1.

RAMS 23, REDSKINS 20

Sunday, November 30

St. Louis	0	10	7	6—23
Washington	7	3	0	10—20

First Quarter
Was.—Bowie 39 pass from Frerotte (Blanton kick), 4:51.

Second Quarter
St.L.—FG, Wilkins 30, 1:15.
Was.—FG, Blanton 43, 12:51.
St.L.—Lee 36 pass from Banks (Wilkins kick), 13:41.

Third Quarter
St.L.—J. Moore 5 run (Wilkins kick), 9:13.

Fourth Quarter
Was.—FG, Blanton 19, 1:29.
St.L.—FG, Wilkins 23, 10:18.
Was.—Mitchell 2 run (Blanton kick), 13:10.
St.L.—FG, Wilkins 25, 14:56.
Attendance—74,772.

TEAM STATISTICS

	St. Louis	Washington
First downs	19	19
Rushes-yards	30-114	22-49
Passing	284	240
Punt returns	3-14	4-37
Kickoff returns	5-125	6-116
Interception returns	2-18	0-0
Comp.-att.-int.	19-38-0	20-45-2
Sacked-yards lost	1-14	3-18
Punts	7-45	6-49
Fumbles-lost	4-0	3-0
Penalties-yards	7-40	4-14
Time of possession	31:56	28:04

INDIVIDUAL STATISTICS

RUSHING—St. Louis, J. Moore 22-92, Banks 4-21, Heyward 2-5, Thompson 2-(minus 4). Washington, Allen 12-23, Bowie 3-9, Frerotte 3-8, Davis 3-7, Mitchell 1-2.

PASSING—St. Louis, Banks 19-38-0-298. Washington, Frerotte 20-45-2-258.

RECEIVING—St. Louis, Lee 6-128, Bruce 5-41, Small 4-62, Kennison 1-35, Conwell 1-25, J. Moore 1-6, Wiegert 1-1. Washington, Mitchell 6-58, Bowie 4-84, Westbrook 3-40, Asher 3-31, Thomas 2-11, Ellard 1-19, Davis 1-15.

MISSED FIELD GOAL ATTEMPTS—St. Louis, Wilkins 43.

INTERCEPTIONS—St. Louis, Lyle 1-18, McCleon 1-0.

KICKOFF RETURNS—St. Louis, Thompson 5-125. Washington, Mitchell 4-91, Davis 1-16, D. Green 1-9.

PUNT RETURNS—St. Louis, Kennison 3-14. Washington, Mitchell 4-37.

SACKS—St. Louis, Zgonina 2, O'Neal 1. Washington, M. Patton 1.

JAGUARS 29, RAVENS 27

Sunday, November 30

Baltimore	7	7	0	13—27
Jacksonville	3	13	10	3—29

First Quarter
Bal.—Langham 40 interception return (Stover kick), 7:52.
Jac.—FG, Hollis 41, 12:02.

Second Quarter
Bal.—J. Lewis 15 pass from Testaverde (Stover kick), 1:23.
Jac.—Means 3 run (Hollis kick), 6:34.
Jac.—FG, Hollis 42, 9:18.
Jac.—FG, Hollis 31, 14:58.

Third Quarter
Jac.—Jones 26 pass from Brunell (Hollis kick), 4:06.
Jac.—FG, Hollis 29, 11:20.

Fourth Quarter
Jac.—FG, Hollis 22, 5:56.
Bal.—Cotton 1 run (Stover kick), 7:47.
Bal.—Green 7 pass from Zeier (run failed), 13:50.
Attendance—63,712.

TEAM STATISTICS

	Baltimore	Jacksonville
First downs	17	23
Rushes-yards	22-58	31-91
Passing	163	313
Punt returns	1-13	4-43
Kickoff returns	7-127	4-104
Interception returns	1-40	0-0
Comp.-att.-int.	18-29-0	25-40-1
Sacked-yards lost	4-25	1-4
Punts	6-43	2-42
Fumbles-lost	1-0	0-0
Penalties-yards	6-71	11-122
Time of possession	24:49	35:11

INDIVIDUAL STATISTICS

RUSHING—Baltimore, Graham 9-11, Byner 6-26, Morris 3-10, Zeier 3-10, Cotton 1-1. Jacksonville, Means 16-34, Stewart 9-40, Brunell 6-17.

PASSING—Baltimore, Testaverde 11-17-0-101, Zeier 7-12-0-87. Jacksonville, Brunell 25-40-1-317.

RECEIVING—Baltimore, Jackson 5-50, Green 5-35, Roe 4-80, J. Lewis 2-16, Morris 2-7. Jacksonville, McCardell 7-97, Stewart 5-44, Smith 4-93, Jones 2-34, Jackson 2-30, Mitchell 2-14, Means 2-4, Hallock 1-1.

MISSED FIELD GOAL ATTEMPTS—None.

INTERCEPTIONS—Baltimore, Langham 1-40.

KICKOFF RETURNS—Baltimore, J. Lewis 5-94, Singleton 2-33. Jacksonville, Logan 2-59, Barlow 2-45.

PUNT RETURNS—Baltimore, J. Lewis 1-13. Jacksonville, Barlow 4-43.

SACKS—Baltimore, Herring 1. Jacksonville, Hardy 1, Smeenge 1, Wynn 1, Davis 1.

CHIEFS 44, 49ERS 9

Sunday, November 30

San Francisco	3	3	3	0—9
Kansas City	7	21	0	16—44

First Quarter
K.C.—Rison 6 pass from Gannon (Stoyanovich kick), 7:57.
S.F.—FG, Anderson 33, 14:05.

Second Quarter
K.C.—Gonzalez 2 pass from Gannon (Stoyanovich kick), 5:54.
K.C.—Allen 3 run (Stoyanovich kick), 7:56.
K.C.—Popson 1 pass from Allen (Stoyanovich kick), 14:34.
S.F.—FG, Anderson 33, 15:00.

Third Quarter
S.F.—FG, Anderson 40, 2:43.

Fourth Quarter
K.C.—Rison 29 pass from Gannon (Stoyanovich kick), 2:20.
K.C.—Safety, Kirby tackled by Phillips and Edwards in end zone, 6:34.
K.C.—McMillian 12 interception return (Stoyanovich kick), 10:47.
Attendance—77,535.

TEAM STATISTICS

	San Fran.	Kansas City
First downs	13	22
Rushes-yards	21-127	42-153
Passing	152	187
Punt returns	1-3	2-28
Kickoff returns	7-119	3-82
Interception returns	1-11	2-12
Comp.-att.-int.	17-24-2	13-22-1
Sacked-yards lost	5-32	0-0
Punts	4-28	4-35
Fumbles-lost	3-1	1-0
Penalties-yards	7-50	6-55
Time of possession	24:56	35:04

INDIVIDUAL STATISTICS

RUSHING—San Francisco, Kirby 9-28, Hearst 7-85, Floyd 3-7, S. Young 2-7. Kansas City, Hill 19-54, Allen 13-48, Bennett 7-36, Gannon 3-15.

PASSING—San Francisco, S. Young 17-23-1-184, Brohm 0-1-1-0. Kansas City, Gannon 12-21-1-186, Allen 1-1-0-1.

RECEIVING—San Francisco, Owens 6-68, Stokes 4-65, Floyd 4-18, Jones 3-33. Kansas City, Rison 5-117, Dawson 2-38, Gonzalez 2-19, Vanover 1-6, Hill 1-5, Bennett 1-1, Popson 1-1.

MISSED FIELD GOAL ATTEMPTS—None.

INTERCEPTIONS—San Francisco, Walker 1-11. Kansas City, McMillian 1-12, Carter 1-0.

KICKOFF RETURNS—San Francisco, Levy 6-119, Fann 1-0. Kansas City, Vanover 3-82.

PUNT RETURNS—San Francisco, Uwaezuoke 1-3. Kansas City, Vanover 2-28.

SACKS—Kansas City, Williams 2, McDaniels 2, Thomas 1.

BILLS 20, JETS 10

Sunday, November 30

N.Y. Jets	0	3	7	0—10
Buffalo	7	3	0	10—20

First Quarter
Buf.—Reed 22 pass from Collins (Christie kick), 3:49.

Second Quarter
NYJ—FG, Hall 22, 5:59.
Buf.—FG, Christie 49, 14:24.

Third Quarter
NYJ—K. Johnson 29 pass from O'Donnell (Hall kick), 7:41.

Fourth Quarter
Buf.—Johnson 62 pass from Collins (Christie kick), 2:13.
Buf.—FG, Christie 34, 9:39.
Attendance—47,776.

INDIVIDUAL STATISTICS

	N.Y. Jets	Buffalo
First downs	16	19
Rushes-yards	15-30	34-197
Passing	264	139
Punt returns	5-39	6-49
Kickoff returns	5-79	3-63
Interception returns	1-2	1-12
Comp.-att.-int.	25-47-1	12-31-1
Sacked-yards lost	3-28	3-25
Punts	7-45	8-42
Fumbles-lost	3-1	3-0
Penalties-yards	5-45	5-50
Time of possession	27:59	32:01

INDIVIDUAL STATISTICS

RUSHING—New York, Murrell 9-27, O'Donnell 3-(minus 2), Neal 1-4, L. Johnson 1-2, Anderson 1-(minus 1). Buffalo, Thomas 18-104, A. Smith 13-78, Collins 3-15.

PASSING—New York, O'Donnell 25-47-1-292. Buffalo, Collins 12-31-1-164.

RECEIVING—New York, Chrebet 6-86, K. Johnson 5-99, Murrell 4-3, Brady 3-37, Baxter 2-29, Graham 2-23, L. Johnson 2-15, Neal 1-0. Buffalo, Johnson 4-81, Reed 2-33, Early 2-21, Riemersma 2-8, Thomas 1-15, A. Smith 1-6.

MISSED FIELD GOAL ATTEMPTS—New York, Hall 53.

INTERCEPTIONS—New York, Mickens 1-2. Buffalo, Moran 1-12.

KICKOFF RETURNS—New York, L. Johnson 4-80, Ward 1-(minus 1). Buffalo, Holmes 3-63.

PUNT RETURNS—New York, L. Johnson 5-39. Buffalo, Burris 6-49.

SACKS—New York, Lewis 2, Douglas 1. Buffalo, B. Smith 1, Paup 1, Hansen 1.

EAGLES 44, BENGALS 42

Sunday, November 30

Cincinnati	14	0	7	21—42
Philadelphia	7	17	10	10—44

First Quarter
Phi.—Timpson 23 pass from Hoying (Boniol kick), 5:03.
Cin.—Scott 10 pass from Esiason (Pelfrey kick), 12:14.
Cin.—Hundon 36 pass from Esiason (Pelfrey kick), 14:38.

Second Quarter
Phi.—Lewis 2 pass from Hoying (Boniol kick), 9:36.
Phi.—Johnson 14 pass from Hoying (Boniol kick), 11:27.
Phi.—FG, Boniol 33, 14:58.

Third Quarter
Phi.—FG, Boniol 25, 4:57.
Cin.—Carter 1 run (Pelfrey kick), 8:31.
Phi.—Turner 23 pass from Hoying (Boniol kick), 13:16.

Fourth Quarter
Cin.—McGee 9 pass from Esiason (Pelfrey kick), 5:47.
Phi.—Watters 16 run (Boniol kick), 9:31.
Cin.—Hundon 13 pass from Esiason (Pelfrey kick), 11:40.
Cin.—Milne 1 run (Pelfrey kick), 14:00.
Phi.—FG, Boniol 31, 15:00.
Attendance—66,623.

TEAM STATISTICS

	Cincinnati	Philadelphia
First downs	29	27
Rushes-yards	27-124	35-196
Passing	373	311
Punt returns	2-16	3-7
Kickoff returns	8-137	7-195
Interception returns	1-21	1-0
Comp.-att.-int.	27-47-1	26-42-1
Sacked-yards lost	1-5	2-2
Punts	3-36	4-39
Fumbles-lost	3-2	2-1
Penalties-yards	5-30	5-54
Time of possession	27:01	32:59

INDIVIDUAL STATISTICS

RUSHING—Cincinnati, Dillon 19-114, Carter 4-0, Scott 1-6, Bieniemy 1-3, Milne 1-1, Esiason 1-0. Philadelphia, Watters 20-98, Garner 9-29, Hoying 5-62, Turner 1-7.

PASSING—Cincinnati, Esiason 27-47-1-378. Philadelphia, Hoying 26-42-1-313.

RECEIVING—Cincinnati, Scott 6-99, Hundon 5-118, Dunn 4-54, Bieniemy 4-25, McGee 3-41, Dillon 2-17, Carter 2-17, Battaglia 1-7. Philadelphia, Fryar 7-122, Timpson 6-73, Turner 4-41, Johnson 2-20, Solomon 2-18, Watters 2-7, Seay 1-22, Garner 1-8, Lewis 1-2.

MISSED FIELD GOAL ATTEMPTS—None.

INTERCEPTIONS—Cincinnati, Shade 1-21. Philadelphia, W. Thomas 1-0.

KICKOFF RETURNS—Cincinnati, Bieniemy 8-137. Philadelphia, Staley 7-195.

PUNT RETURNS—Cincinnati, Myers 2-16. Philadelphia, Solomon 3-7.

SACKS—Cincinnati, Francis 1, Wilkinson 1. Philadelphia, Mamula 1.

STEELERS 26, CARDINALS 20

Sunday, November 30

Pittsburgh	7	3	7	3	6—26
Arizona	0	3	14	3	0—20

First Quarter
Pit.—Bettis 2 run (N. Johnson kick), 8:13.

Second Quarter
Ariz.—FG, Nedney 32, 8:34.
Pit.—FG, N. Johnson 40, 13:47.

Third Quarter
Ariz.—Sanders 3 pass from Plummer (Nedney kick), 4:14.
Pit.—Bettis 7 run (N. Johnson kick), 10:40.
Ariz.—Gedney 11 pass from Plummer (Nedney kick), 14:00.

Fourth Quarter
Pit.—FG, N. Johnson 39, 5:48.
Ariz.—FG, Nedney 19, 10:40.

Overtime
Pit.—Bettis 10 run, 5:34.
Attendance—66,341.

TEAM STATISTICS

	Pittsburgh	Arizona
First downs	25	18
Rushes-yards	44-177	17-48
Passing	165	243
Punt returns	4-34	2-20
Kickoff returns	4-97	5-82
Interception returns	0-0	0-0
Comp.-att.-int.	18-35-0	16-27-0
Sacked-yards lost	2-14	10-53
Punts	5-47	6-45
Fumbles-lost	0-0	0-0
Penalties-yards	4-20	4-30
Time of possession	39:22	26:12

INDIVIDUAL STATISTICS

RUSHING—Pittsburgh, Bettis 36-142, Stewart 6-27, Hawkins 1-6, G. Jones 1-2. Arizona, McElroy 9-33, Centers 5-(minus 4), Plummer 3-19.

PASSING—Pittsburgh, Stewart 18-35-0-179. Arizona, Plummer 15-26-0-270, Sanders 1-1-0-26.

RECEIVING—Pittsburgh, Thigpen 5-78, C. Johnson 5-41, Bettis 2-19, Bruener 2-15, Blackwell 2-5, Hawkins 1-15, G. Jones 1-6. Arizona, R. Moore 8-188, Sanders 4-71, Centers 2-15, Gedney 1-11, McWilliams 1-11.

MISSED FIELD GOAL ATTEMPTS—Arizona, Nedney 46.

INTERCEPTIONS—None.

KICKOFF RETURNS—Pittsburgh, Coleman 2-51, Blackwell 2-46. Arizona, K. Williams 4-66, Gedney 1-16.

PUNT RETURNS—Pittsburgh, Blackwell 3-25, Hawkins 1-9. Arizona, K. Williams 2-20.

SACKS—Pittsburgh, Lake 3, Henry 1.5, Kirkland 1, Gildon 1, Holmes 1, Harrison 1, Oldham 1, Vrabel 0.5. Arizona, McCleskey 1, M. Smith 1.

BUCCANEERS 20, GIANTS 8

Sunday, November 30

Tampa Bay	0	7	7	6—20
N.Y. Giants	0	3	3	2— 8

Second Quarter
T.B.—Alstott 1 pass from Dilfer (Husted kick), 7:06.
NYG—FG, Daluiso 45, 14:56.

Third Quarter
T.B.—Alstott 9 run (Husted kick), 3:34.
NYG—FG, Daluiso 30, 14:25.

Fourth Quarter
NYG—Safety, Dilfer penalized for intentional grounding in end zone, 0:52.
T.B.—Rhett 1 run (pass failed), 7:38.
Attendance—68,678.

TEAM STATISTICS

	Tampa Bay	N.Y. Giants
First downs	21	13
Rushes-yards	41-147	21-99
Passing	152	103
Punt returns	4-87	1-0
Kickoff returns	3-92	5-72
Interception returns	2-16	3-121
Comp.-att.-int.	12-22-3	14-31-2
Sacked-yards lost	0-0	2-14
Punts	3-36	5-46
Fumbles-lost	1-0	1-0
Penalties-yards	10-93	9-107
Time of possession	35:40	24:20

INDIVIDUAL STATISTICS

RUSHING—Tampa Bay, Dunn 24-120, Alstott 11-30, Dilfer 4-(minus 4), Rhett 2-1. New York, Wheatley 9-64, Way 7-28, Barber 3-4, Kanell 2-3.

PASSING—Tampa Bay, Dilfer 12-22-3-152. New York, Kanell 14-31-2-117.

RECEIVING—Tampa Bay, Moore 3-55, Dunn 2-49, Williams 2-17, Alstott 2-9, Thomas 1-13, Ellison 1-8, Davis 1-3. New York, Way 4-29, Calloway 3-56, Wheatley 2-10, Alexander 2-6, Patten 1-10, Barber 1-7, Pegram 1-(minus 1).

MISSED FIELD GOAL ATTEMPTS—New York, Daluiso 47.

INTERCEPTIONS—Tampa Bay, Abraham 1-16, Brooks 1-0. New York, Sparks 2-68, Wooten 1-53.

KICKOFF RETURNS—Tampa Bay, Anthony 2-43, Ellison 1-49. New York, Pegram 4-64, Sparks 1-8.

PUNT RETURNS—Tampa Bay, Williams 4-87. New York, Toomer 1-0.

SACKS—Tampa Bay, Ahanotu 2.

DOLPHINS 34, RAIDERS 16

Sunday, November 30

Miami	3	14	14	3—34
Oakland	7	0	3	6—16

First Quarter
Oak.—T. Brown 24 pass from George (Ford kick), 5:55.
Mia.—FG, Mare 28, 13:37.

Second Quarter
Mia.—Jordan 8 pass from Marino (Mare kick), 7:56.
Mia.—Jordan 44 pass from Marino (Mare kick), 13:01.

Third Quarter
Oak.—FG, Ford 44, 7:15.
Mia.—Abdul-Jabbar 2 run (Mare kick), 10:48.
Mia.—Bowens recovered fumble in end zone (Mare kick), 11:53.

Fourth Quarter
Oak.—Jett 27 pass from George (kick failed), 3:04.
Mia.—FG, Mare 42, 8:35.
Attendance—50,569.

TEAM STATISTICS

	Miami	Oakland
First downs	23	18
Rushes-yards	38-137	19-114
Passing	241	212
Punt returns	4-41	1-2
Kickoff returns	4-87	3-48
Interception returns	1-21	1-6
Comp.-att.-int.	19-34-1	17-34-1
Sacked-yards lost	0-0	6-60
Punts	3-38	5-47
Fumbles-lost	2-1	1-1
Penalties-yards	4-30	5-66
Time of possession	40:11	19:49

INDIVIDUAL STATISTICS

RUSHING—Miami, Abdul-Jabbar 23-85, Parmalee 11-46, Marino 2-(minus 1), McPhail 1-8, Pritchett 1-(minus 1). Oakland, Kaufman 12-69, Hall 4-30, Williams 3-15.

PASSING—Miami, Marino 19-34-1-241. Oakland, George 17-34-1-272.

RECEIVING—Miami, Jordan 5-106, McDuffie 4-34, Drayton 3-22, L. Thomas 2-31, Perriman 2-24, McPhail 2-12, Parmalee 1-12. Oakland, T. Brown 8-125, Jett 3-86, Kaufman 2-32, Hall 1-9, Howard 1-9, Williams 1-7, Dudley 1-4.

MISSED FIELD GOAL ATTEMPTS—Miami, Mare 44. Oakland, Ford 47.

INTERCEPTIONS—Miami, Madison 1-21. Oakland, Lynch 1-6.

KICKOFF RETURNS—Miami, McPhail 4-87. Oakland, Howard 3-48.

PUNT RETURNS—Miami, Jordan 4-41. Oakland, Howard 1-2.

SACKS—Miami, Armstrong 1.5, Z. Thomas 1, Bowens 1, Burton 1, Wilson 1, Jackson 0.5.

FALCONS 24, SEAHAWKS 17

Sunday, November 30

Atlanta	7	10	7	0—24
Seattle	0	7	7	3—17

First Quarter
Atl.—Anderson 1 run (Andersen kick), 7:48.

Second Quarter
Atl.—Anderson 13 pass from Chandler (Andersen kick), 4:32.
Atl.—FG, Andersen 18, 9:30.
Sea.—Galloway 16 pass from Moon (Peterson kick), 13:58.

Third Quarter
Sea.—Broussard 20 pass from Moon (Peterson kick), 6:53.
Atl.—Hanspard 93 kickoff return (Andersen kick), 7:10.

Fourth Quarter
Sea.—FG, Peterson 35, 6:03.
Attendance—52,584.

TEAM STATISTICS

	Atlanta	Seattle
First downs	14	19
Rushes-yards	25-72	25-123
Passing	201	228
Punt returns	4-53	1-11
Kickoff returns	3-145	5-89
Interception returns	1-7	0-0
Comp.-att.-int.	15-23-0	24-38-1
Sacked-yards lost	1-3	3-12
Punts	5-37	5-39
Fumbles-lost	1-0	1-0
Penalties-yards	3-20	5-35
Time of possession	26:27	33:33

INDIVIDUAL STATISTICS

RUSHING—Atlanta, Anderson 16-41, Chandler 6-8, Hanspard 2-7, Mathis 1-16. Seattle, Warren 15-87, Smith 6-27, Broussard 2-8, Moon 1-2, Galloway 1-(minus 1).

PASSING—Atlanta, Chandler 15-23-0-204. Seattle, Moon 24-38-1-240.

RECEIVING—Atlanta, Emanuel 4-71, Mathis 3-42, Green 2-28, Christian 2-14, Kozlowski 1-28, Anderson 1-13, Kinchen 1-6, E. Smith 1-2. Seattle, Pritchard 6-66, McKnight 5-61, Broussard 4-30, Galloway 3-34, Warren 3-13, Fauria 1-25, Smith 1-6, Crumpler 1-5.

MISSED FIELD GOAL ATTEMPTS—Seattle, Peterson 48.

INTERCEPTIONS—Atlanta, McGill 1-7.

KICKOFF RETURNS—Atlanta, Hanspard 3-145. Seattle, Broussard 3-59, Strong 1-16, Smith 1-14.

PUNT RETURNS—Atlanta, Kinchen 4-53. Seattle, Davis 1-11.

SACKS—Atlanta, C. Smith 1, Burrough 1, Hall 0.5, Archambeau 0.5. Seattle, Sinclair 1.

BRONCOS 38, CHARGERS 28

Sunday, November 30

Denver	7	21	7	3—38
San Diego	0	7	7	14—28

First Quarter
Den.—McCaffrey 4 pass from Elway (Elam kick), 10:04.

Second Quarter
Den.—R. Smith 5 pass from Elway (Elam kick), 3:18.
S.D.—Martin 4 pass from Whelihan (G. Davis kick), 9:09.
Den.—Davis 5 run (Elam kick), 13:45.
Den.—Atwater 22 interception return (Elam kick), 13:59.

Third Quarter
S.D.—Metcalf 83 punt return (G. Davis kick), 2:19.
Den.—McCaffrey 21 pass from Elway (Elam kick), 5:51.

Fourth Quarter
S.D.—Brown 1 run (G. Davis kick), 8:41.
Den.—FG, Elam 32, 10:44.
S.D.—Metcalf 10 pass from Whelihan (G. Davis kick), 14:32.
Attendance—54,245.

TEAM STATISTICS

	Denver	San Diego
First downs	28	22
Rushes-yards	29-198	21-47
Passing	240	222
Punt returns	2-24	1-83
Kickoff returns	3-64	7-158
Interception returns	2-42	0-0
Comp.-att.-int.	20-33-0	23-51-2
Sacked-yards lost	0-0	1-0
Punts	1-50	4-44
Fumbles-lost	0-0	2-0
Penalties-yards	12-92	10-71
Time of possession	29:59	30:01

INDIVIDUAL STATISTICS

RUSHING—Denver, Davis 26-178, R. Smith 1-21, Griffith 1-0, Elway 1-(minus 1). San Diego, Brown 12-21, Fletcher 6-17, Whelihan 2-9, Craver 1-0.

PASSING—Denver, Elway 20-33-0-240. San Diego, Whelihan 23-51-2-222.

RECEIVING—Denver, McCaffrey 7-111, Sharpe 4-46, R. Smith 4-40, Davis 4-36, Carswell 1-7. San Diego, Martin 8-78, Still 4-44, Metcalf 4-38, Fletcher 3-32, Hartley 2-17, C. Jones 1-4.

MISSED FIELD GOAL ATTEMPTS—Denver, Elam 35.

INTERCEPTIONS—Denver, Atwater 1-22, Braxton 1-20.

KICKOFF RETURNS—Denver, Hebron 3-64. San Diego, Bynum 7-158.

PUNT RETURNS—Denver, Gordon 2-24. San Diego, Metcalf 1-83.

SACKS—Denver, N. Smith 1.

PACKERS 27, VIKINGS 11

Monday, December 1

Green Bay	3	7	7	10—27
Minnesota	0	3	0	8—11

First Quarter
G.B.—FG, Longwell 30, 9:44.

Second Quarter
Min.—FG, Murray 42, 0:09.
G.B.—R. Brooks 18 pass from Favre (Longwell kick), 12:50.

Third Quarter
G.B.—Levens 3 run (Longwell kick), 3:36.

Fourth Quarter
G.B.—FG, Longwell 19, 6:58.
Min.—Hoard 4 run (Carter pass from Cunningham), 11:30.
G.B.—Levens 5 run (Longwell kick), 13:17.
Attendance—64,001.

TEAM STATISTICS

	Green Bay	Minnesota
First downs	17	17
Rushes-yards	36-139	24-99
Passing	187	154
Punt returns	6-78	5-68
Kickoff returns	1-11	6-146
Interception returns	1-0	0-0
Comp.-att.-int.	15-29-0	21-42-1
Sacked-yards lost	1-9	6-35
Punts	7-48	8-47
Fumbles-lost	0-0	2-1
Penalties-yards	6-41	7-40
Time of possession	30:30	29:30

INDIVIDUAL STATISTICS

RUSHING—Green Bay, Levens 31-108, Favre 4-17, Freeman 1-14. Minnesota, R. Smith 16-54, Cunningham 3-39, Hoard 3-2, Evans 2-4.

PASSING—Green Bay, Favre 15-29-0-196. Minnesota, Johnson 15-30-1-117, Cunningham 6-12-0-72.

RECEIVING—Green Bay, Freeman 6-85, Levens 4-25, R. Brooks 2-43, Henderson 2-34, Chmura 1-9. Minnesota, Carter 6-52, Palmer 5-35, Reed 3-50, Glover 2-32, Walsh 2-13, R. Smith 2-6, Hoard 1-1.

MISSED FIELD GOAL ATTEMPTS—Green Bay, Longwell 35. Minnesota, Murray 44.

INTERCEPTIONS—Green Bay, Evans 1-0.

KICKOFF RETURNS—Green Bay, Beebe 1-11. Minnesota, Palmer 6-146.

PUNT RETURNS—Green Bay, Mayes 6-78. Minnesota, Palmer 5-68.

SACKS—Green Bay, White 2.5, Joyner 1, S. Dotson 0.5, Team 2. Minnesota, E. McDaniel 0.5, Alexander 0.5.

WEEK 15

RESULTS

CINCINNATI 41, Tennessee 14
Atlanta 14, SAN DIEGO 3
BALTIMORE 31, Seattle 24
CHICAGO 20, Buffalo 3
Green Bay 17, TAMPA BAY 6
Indianapolis 22, N.Y. JETS 14
KANSAS CITY 30, Oakland 0
MIAMI 33, Detroit 30
New England 26, JACKSONVILLE 20
N.Y. Giants 31, PHILADELPHIA 21
PITTSBURGH 35, Denver 24
St. Louis 34, NEW ORLEANS 27
SAN FRANCISCO 28, Minnesota 17
Washington 38, ARIZONA 28
Carolina 23, DALLAS 13

STANDINGS

AFC EAST	W	L	T	Pct.
Miami	9	5	0	.643
New England	9	5	0	.643
N.Y. Jets	8	6	0	.571
Buffalo	6	8	0	.429
Indianapolis	2	12	0	.143

AFC CENTRAL	W	L	T	Pct.
Pittsburgh	10	4	0	.714
Jacksonville	9	5	0	.643
Tennessee	7	7	0	.500
Baltimore	5	8	1	.393
Cincinnati	5	9	0	.357

AFC WEST	W	L	T	Pct.
Denver	11	3	0	.786
Kansas City	11	3	0	.786
Seattle	6	8	0	.429
Oakland	4	10	0	.286
San Diego	4	10	0	.286

NFC EAST	W	L	T	Pct.
N.Y. Giants	8	5	1	.607
Washington	7	6	1	.536
Philadelphia	6	7	1	.464
Dallas	6	8	0	.429
Arizona	3	11	0	.214

NFC CENTRAL	W	L	T	Pct.
Green Bay	11	3	0	.786
Tampa Bay	9	5	0	.643
Minnesota	8	6	0	.571
Detroit	7	7	0	.500
Chicago	3	11	0	.214

NFC WEST	W	L	T	Pct.
San Francisco	12	2	0	.857
Carolina	7	7	0	.500
Atlanta	6	8	0	.429
New Orleans	5	9	0	.357
St. Louis	4	10	0	.286

HIGHLIGHTS

Hero of the week: Pittsburgh quarterback Kordell Stewart passed for three touchdowns and ran for two more as the Steelers rallied from a 21-7 first-half deficit to defeat Denver, 35-24, at Three Rivers Stadium. Stewart was 18-of-29 for 303 yards and ran for another 49 yards on 10 carries.

Goat of the week: Philadelphia quarterback Bobby Hoying committed three first-half turnovers—all of which led to Giants touchdowns—as the Eagles lost to New York, 31-21, at Veterans Stadium. It was Hoying's first loss in four NFL starts.

Sub of the week: Jeff Hostetler, making his first start of the season for injured Washington starter Gus Frerotte (who was put on injured reserve with a hip injury suffered the week before), threw for 226 yards and three touchdowns as the Redskins kept their playoff hopes alive by defeating the Cardinals, 38-28.

Comeback of the week: Thanks to a 56-yard kickoff return by David Thompson and heroic efforts by quarterback Tony Banks and receiver Isaac Bruce, the Rams scored 21 consecutive points in the final 11:10 to defeat the Saints, 34-27, at the Superdome. Banks was 22-of-41 for 267 yards and three touchdowns. Bruce caught nine passes for 144 yards and two touchdowns.

Blowout of the week: The Chiefs rushed for a season-high 214 yards, controlled the ball for 41:30 and held the Raiders to 93 yards of total offense and five first downs in whipping Oakland, 30-0.

Nail-biter of the week: Despite 137 yards rushing from Barry Sanders, the Lions botched two extra points and Scott Mitchell threw two interceptions as Detroit lost at Miami, 33-30. Olindo Mare's fourth field goal of the game, a 42-yarder with no time left, won it for the Dolphins.

Hits of the week: New England cornerback Steve Israel delivered a blindside hit to Jaguars quarterback Mark Brunell, forcing a fumble the Patriots recovered on Jacksonville's 48. Four plays later, New England scored a touchdown. On the ensuing kickoff, the Pats' Vernon Crawford jarred the ball loose from the Jaguars' Reggie Barlow, leading to another Patriots touchdown in their 26-20 victory.

Oddity of the week: The Bucs completed a 35-yard pass on their first passing play against the Packers but had only 32 passing yards at halftime, thanks to three sacks of quarterback Trent Dilfer.

Top rusher: Cincinnati's Corey Dillon broke Jim Brown's 40-year-old NFL single-game record for rushing yards by a rookie with 246 yards on 39 carries in the Bengals' 41-14 victory over the Oilers. Dillon also scored a club-record four rushing touchdowns against what had been the NFL's third-ranked run defense.

Top passer: Arizona's Jake Plummer was 19-of-38 for 337 yards and four touchdowns in the Cardinals' 38-28 loss to Washington.

Top receiver: Pittsburgh's Yancey Thigpen caught six passes for 175 yards and three touchdowns in the Steelers' 35-24 victory over the Broncos.

Notes: Jermaine Lewis returned two punts for touchdowns in the Ravens' 31-24 victory over the Seahawks. Until Lewis' feat, no Raven had returned a kick for a touchdown in the team's two-year history. . . . The Colts are 17-5 in their past 22 games against the Jets and 9-2 in their past 11 games against them in the Meadowlands. . . . The Packers' Brett Favre became the first quarterback to throw at least 30 TD passes in four consecutive seasons. . . . Warren Moon completed 12 passes against Baltimore to break Dave Krieg's Seattle record for completions in a season (297). . . . The Chiefs set an NFL record by not allowing a second-half touchdown for the ninth consecutive game, breaking a mark set by the 1934 Lions. . . . Darrell Green played in his 216th game, tying him with Monte Coleman for the most in Redskins history. . . . The Cowboys lost a third consecutive game for the first time since 1990. . . . Dillon became the ninth rookie to rush for 200 yards in a game. . . . Raymont Harris became only the seventh Bear to rush for 1,000 yards in a season. Of the previous six, only three—Walter Payton (10 times total), Neal Anderson (three) and Gale Sayers (two)—did it again. . . . The 49ers' 28-17 victory over the Vikings at 3Com Park was overshadowed by the resignation of owner Eddie Debartolo Jr. in the wake of a gambling investigation.

Quote of the week: Dillon, after his record-setting performance: "When I was growing up playing Pop Warner (football), I watched a lot of film of Brown, Payton, Dorsett, Sayers, Dickerson and a lot of runners. As I watched, I tried to steal a little bit of their running style and add it to mine. It's paid off."

GAME SUMMARIES

BENGALS 41, OILERS 14

Thursday, December 4

Tennessee	0	0	0	14	14
Cincinnati	14	14	10	3	41

First Quarter
Cin.—Dillon 2 run (Pelfrey kick), 4:16.
Cin.—McGee 1 pass from Esiason (Pelfrey kick), 8:57.
Second Quarter
Cin.—Dillon 31 run (Pelfrey kick), 5:11.
Cin.—Dillon 1 run (Pelfrey kick), 9:03.
Third Quarter
Cin.—Dillon 2 run (Pelfrey kick), 7:55.
Cin.—FG, Pelfrey 26, 14:16.
Fourth Quarter
Ten.—Davis 5 pass from McNair (Del Greco kick), 2:40.
Cin.—FG, Pelfrey 40, 9:30.
Ten.—Kent 11 pass from McNair (Del Greco kick), 11:29.
Attendance—49,086.

TEAM STATISTICS

	Tennessee	Cincinnati
First downs	12	34
Rushes-yards	12-44	54-276
Passing	131	239
Punt returns	0-0	1-6
Kickoff returns	8-173	3-76
Interception returns	0-0	0-0
Comp.-att.-int.	14-25-0	20-28-0
Sacked-yards lost	3-15	1-6
Punts	6-43	1-23
Fumbles-lost	4-0	0-0
Penalties-yards	10-81	8-73
Time of possession	19:21	40:39

INDIVIDUAL STATISTICS
RUSHING—Tennessee, McNair 5-16, E. George 5-11, Roby 1-12, Thomas 1-5. Cincinnati, Dillon 39-246, Carter 11-29, Milne 2-2, Bieniemy 1-0, Esiason 1-(minus 1).
PASSING—Tennessee, McNair 14-25-0-146. Cincinnati, Esiason 20-28-0-245.
RECEIVING—Tennessee, Davis 4-45, Thomas 3-24, Roan 2-26, Wycheck 2-21, Sanders 2-19, Kent 1-11. Cincinnati, Scott 6-83, McGee 4-43, Bieniemy 3-18, Dunn 2-44, Dillon 2-30, Hundon 1-13, Battaglia 1-9, Carter 1-5.
MISSED FIELD GOAL ATTEMPTS—None.
INTERCEPTIONS—None.
KICKOFF RETURNS—Tennessee, Thomas 6-149, Archie 2-24. Cincinnati, Bieniemy 3-76.
PUNT RETURNS—Cincinnati, Myers 1-6.
SACKS—Tennessee, Jackson 1. Cincinnati, Shade 1, Collins 1, Dixon 1.

PACKERS 17, BUCCANEERS 6

Sunday, December 7

Green Bay	7	0	7	3	17
Tampa Bay	3	3	0	0	6

First Quarter
T.B.—FG, Husted 24, 6:18.
G.B.—R. Brooks 43 pass from Favre (Longwell kick), 10:14.
Second Quarter
T.B.—FG, Husted 48, 13:15.
Third Quarter
G.B.—Levens 8 pass from Favre (Longwell kick), 8:57.

Fourth Quarter
G.B.—FG, Longwell 27, 8:36.
Attendance—73,523.

TEAM STATISTICS

	Green Bay	Tampa Bay
First downs	20	8
Rushes-yards	31-82	22-67
Passing	280	94
Punt returns	3-16	1-13
Kickoff returns	2-60	4-83
Interception returns	1-0	1-28
Comp.-att.-int.	25-33-1	10-26-1
Sacked-yards lost	0-0	4-23
Punts	4-40	6-43
Fumbles-lost	2-2	1-1
Penalties-yards	3-21	6-33
Time of possession	34:41	25:19

INDIVIDUAL STATISTICS
RUSHING—Green Bay, Levens 22-54, Favre 6-13, Henderson 2-11, R. Brooks 1-4. Tampa Bay, Dunn 12-33, Alstott 10-34.
PASSING—Green Bay, Favre 25-33-1-280. Tampa Bay, Dilfer 6-17-0-67, Walsh 4-9-1-50.
RECEIVING—Green Bay, Levens 8-64, Freeman 5-73, Chmura 5-37, R. Brooks 3-71, Mayes 3-22, Henderson 1-13. Tampa Bay, Williams 5-87, Thomas 2-19, Dunn 2-9, Harris 1-2.
MISSED FIELD GOAL ATTEMPTS—Green Bay, Longwell 31.
INTERCEPTIONS—Green Bay, Prior 1-0. Tampa Bay, Lynch 1-28.
KICKOFF RETURNS—Green Bay, Beebe 2-60. Tampa Bay, Anthony 2-45, Williams 1-22, Rhett 1-16.
PUNT RETURNS—Green Bay, Mayes 3-16. Tampa Bay, Williams 1-13.
SACKS—Green Bay, Robinson 1, Joyner 1, Wilkins 1, White 1.

BEARS 20, BILLS 3

Sunday, December 7

Buffalo	0	3	0	0	3
Chicago	0	17	0	3	20

Second Quarter
Chi.—FG, Jaeger 41, 0:44.
Chi.—Wetnight 30 pass from Kramer (Jaeger kick), 8:25.
Chi.—Proehl 3 pass from Kramer (Jaeger kick), 14:28.
Buf.—FG, Christie 43, 15:00.
Fourth Quarter
Chi.—FG, Jaeger 38, 2:57.
Attendance—39,784.

TEAM STATISTICS

	Buffalo	Chicago
First downs	10	23
Rushes-yards	16-55	43-120
Passing	105	272
Punt returns	0-0	4-24
Kickoff returns	5-68	1-20
Interception returns	2-46	0-0
Comp.-att.-int.	13-32-0	24-36-2
Sacked-yards lost	5-33	1-7
Punts	7-43	5-30
Fumbles-lost	2-1	2-0
Penalties-yards	4-26	6-61
Time of possession	19:32	40:28

INDIVIDUAL STATISTICS
RUSHING—Buffalo, Thomas 7-22, A. Smith 6-17, Collins 2-10, Johnson 1-6. Chicago, R. Harris 24-59, Autry 14-40, Conway 1-10, Sauerbrun 1-8, Tony Carter 1-3, Kramer 1-1, Mirer 1-(minus 1).
PASSING—Buffalo, Collins 13-32-0-138. Chicago, Kramer 23-33-2-270, Mirer 1-3-0-9.
RECEIVING—Buffalo, Holmes 3-41, Early 2-37, Reed 2-29, Thomas 2-10, A. Smith 2-9, Johnson 1-6, Moulds 1-6. Chicago, Conway 7-115, Wetnight 5-70, Tony Carter 5-24, Penn 3-41, Proehl 3-23, Allred 1-6.
MISSED FIELD GOAL ATTEMPTS—Buffalo, Christie 41.
INTERCEPTIONS—Buffalo, Maddox 1-25, Schulz 1-21.
KICKOFF RETURNS—Buffalo, Holmes 4-56, Tasker 1-12. Chicago, Smith 1-20.
PUNT RETURNS—Chicago, Hughes 4-24.
SACKS—Buffalo, Moran 1. Chicago, Marshall 2, B. Cox 1, Thomas 1, Flanigan 1.

STEELERS 35, BRONCOS 24

Sunday, December 7

Denver 14   7   3   0—24
Pittsburgh. . . . . 7 14 7 7—35

First Quarter
Den.—R. Smith 37 pass from Elway (Elam kick), 5:22.
Pit.—Thigpen 33 pass from Stewart (N. Johnson kick), 9:34.
Den.—Davis 3 run (Elam kick), 13:42.

Second Quarter
Den.—R. Smith 25 pass from Elway (Elam kick), 4:14.
Pit.—Thigpen 69 pass from Stewart (N. Johnson kick), 8:25.
Pit.—Thigpen 21 pass from Stewart (N. Johnson kick), 13:55.

Third Quarter
Den.—FG, Elam 35, 6:06.
Pit.—Stewart 4 run (N. Johnson kick), 12:44.

Fourth Quarter
Pit.—Stewart 9 run (N. Johnson kick), 13:03.
    Attendance—59,739.

TEAM STATISTICS

	Denver	Pittsburgh
First downs	18	22
Rushes-yards	24-89	36-186
Passing	231	290
Punt returns	3-24	1-15
Kickoff returns	6-114	5-75
Interception returns	1-0	1-3
Comp.-att.-int.	17-42-1	18-29-1
Sacked-yards lost	2-17	1-13
Punts	4-44	3-45
Fumbles-lost	1-0	3-1
Penalties-yards	4-33	5-35
Time of possession	27:31	32:29

INDIVIDUAL STATISTICS

RUSHING—Denver, Davis 21-75, Elway 2-23, R. Smith 1-(minus 9). Pittsburgh, Bettis 24-125, Stewart 10-49, G. Jones 2-12.

PASSING—Denver, Elway 17-42-1-248. Pittsburgh, Stewart 18-29-1-303.

RECEIVING—Denver, R. Smith 4-115, Griffith 4-18, Green 3-54, Davis 3-26, Jeffers 2-19, Sharpe 1-16. Pittsburgh, Thigpen 6-175, C. Johnson 4-29, Hawkins 3-42, G. Jones 3-37, Blackwell 1-13, Bruener 1-7.

MISSED FIELD GOAL ATTEMPTS—Denver, Elam 53. Pittsburgh, N. Johnson 51.

INTERCEPTIONS—Denver, Gordon 1-0. Pittsburgh, Bell 1-3.

KICKOFF RETURNS—Denver, Hebron 6-114. Pittsburgh, Blackwell 3-41, Coleman 2-34.

PUNT RETURNS—Denver, Gordon 3-24. Pittsburgh, Blackwell 1-15.

SACKS—Denver, McKyer 1. Pittsburgh, Lake 2.

RAVENS 31, SEAHAWKS 24

Sunday, December 7

Seattle . . . . 7 10 7 0—24
Baltimore . . . . 3 14 7 7—31

First Quarter
Sea.—Smith 4 run (Peterson kick), 6:58.
Bal.—FG, Stover 24, 9:56.

Second Quarter
Sea.—Safety, Zeier sacked in end zone, 3:29.
Bal.—J. Lewis 89 punt return (Stover kick), 5:22.
Sea.—C. Brown 42 fumble return (Smith run), 12:25.
Bal.—J. Lewis 66 punt return (Stover kick), 14:25.

Third Quarter
Sea.—McKnight 60 pass from Moon (Peterson kick), 3:06.
Bal.—J. Lewis 29 pass from Zeier (Stover kick), 10:18.

Fourth Quarter
Bal.—Morris 1 run (Stover kick), 4:18.
    Attendance—54,395.

TEAM STATISTICS

	Seattle	Baltimore
First downs	14	15
Rushes-yards	27-103	28-88
Passing	170	286
Punt returns	3-30	5-184
Kickoff returns	7-98	4-103
Interception returns	0-0	4-48
Comp.-att.-int.	17-34-4	17-28-0
Sacked-yards lost	4-29	3-16
Punts	9-41	5-33
Fumbles-lost	0-0	3-3
Penalties-yards	8-45	7-40
Time of possession	33:20	26:40

INDIVIDUAL STATISTICS

RUSHING—Seattle, Smith 12-47, Warren 11-20, Broussard 3-21, Galloway 1-15. Baltimore, Morris 24-86, Zeier 3-2, Alexander 1-0.

PASSING—Seattle, Moon 12-19-1-140, Friesz 5-15-3-59. Baltimore, Zeier 17-28-0-302.

RECEIVING—Seattle, Galloway 3-31, Broussard 3-24, McKnight 2-65, Pritchard 2-36, Fauria 2-19, Strong 2-9, Crumpler 1-14, Smith 1-2, Warren 1-(minus 1). Baltimore, Alexander 6-150, Jackson 4-40, J. Lewis 2-33, Morris 2-20, Roe 1-29, Yarborough 1-24, Green 1-6.

MISSED FIELD GOAL ATTEMPTS—Baltimore, Stover 45, 42.

INTERCEPTIONS—Baltimore, Staten 2-12, C. Brown 1-21, Jenkins 1-15.

KICKOFF RETURNS—Seattle, Broussard 5-82, McKnight 1-14, Davis 1-2. Baltimore, J. Lewis 3-91, Singleton 1-12.

PUNT RETURNS—Seattle, Davis 3-30. Baltimore, J. Lewis 5-184.

SACKS—Seattle, Saleaumua 2, LaBounty 1. Baltimore, Boulware 2, McCrary 1, Sharper 1.

CHIEFS 30, RAIDERS 0

Sunday, December 7

Oakland 0   0   0   0— 0
Kansas City. . . . . 10 10   0 10—30

First Quarter
K.C.—FG, Stoyanovich 44, 3:39.
K.C.—Bennett 9 run (Stoyanovich kick), 11:55.

Second Quarter
K.C.—FG, Stoyanovich 27, 1:34.
K.C.—Gannon 5 run (Stoyanovich kick), 12:47.

Fourth Quarter
K.C.—FG, Stoyanovich 40, 0:39.
K.C.—Richardson 2 pass from Gannon (Stoyanovich kick), 8:18.
    Attendance—76,379.

TEAM STATISTICS

	Oakland	Kansas City
First downs	5	27
Rushes-yards	15-36	48-214
Passing	57	204
Punt returns	0-0	2-(-3)
Kickoff returns	7-129	1-24
Interception returns	0-0	0-0
Comp.-att.-int.	8-18-0	15-21-0
Sacked-yards lost	6-45	3-21
Punts	5-48	2-35
Fumbles-lost	1-1	0-0
Penalties-yards	6-58	7-54
Time of possession	18:30	41:30

INDIVIDUAL STATISTICS

RUSHING—Oakland, Kaufman 8-7, Williams 3-16, Davison 2-4, George 1-6, Hall 1-3. Kansas City, Bennett 24-85, Anders 10-64, Allen 6-26, Hill 5-14, Gannon 3-25.

PASSING—Oakland, George 8-18-0-102. Kansas City, Gannon 15-21-0-225.

RECEIVING—Oakland, Jett 3-42, Dudley 3-38, T. Brown 2-22. Kansas City, Rison 5-93, Anders 3-10, Hill 2-45, Popson 2-33, Vanover 1-42, Richardson 1-2, Bennett 1-0.

MISSED FIELD GOAL ATTEMPTS—Oakland, Ford 38.

INTERCEPTIONS—None.

KICKOFF RETURNS—Oakland, Howard 5-98, Biekert 1-16, Hall 1-15. Kansas City, Vanover 1-24.

PUNT RETURNS—Kansas City, Vanover 2-(minus 3).

SACKS—Oakland, Fredrickson 1, Biekert 1, McGlockton 1. Kansas City, Simmons 2, Williams 1, Browning 1, Thomas 1, Booker 1.

GIANTS 31, EAGLES 21

Sunday, December 7

N.Y. Giants . . . . 7 14   0 10—31
Philadelphia 7   0   7   7—21

First Quarter
NYG—Armstead 57 interception return (Daluiso kick), 2:41.
Phi.—Watters 1 run (Boniol kick), 8:09.

Second Quarter
NYG—Barber 11 pass from Kanell (Daluiso kick), 9:45.
NYG—Patten 40 pass from Kanell (Daluiso kick), 10:43.
Third Quarter
Phi.—Dawkins 64 interception return (Boniol kick), 7:15.
Fourth Quarter
NYG—Calloway 5 pass from Kanell (Daluiso kick), 4:21.
NYG—FG, Daluiso 19, 11:20.
Phi.—Fryar 72 pass from Hoying (Boniol kick), 12:01.
Attendance—67,084.

TEAM STATISTICS

	N.Y. Giants	Philadelphia
First downs	18	15
Rushes-yards	46-208	20-70
Passing	137	186
Punt returns	3-19	0-0
Kickoff returns	3-56	3-54
Interception returns	3-57	1-64
Comp.-att.-int.	14-27-1	16-35-3
Sacked-yards lost	2-16	4-23
Punts	6-28	5-34
Fumbles-lost	3-1	3-2
Penalties-yards	6-45	4-30
Time of possession	35:49	24:11

INDIVIDUAL STATISTICS
RUSHING—New York, Barber 21-114, Way 18-76, Wheatley 5-20, Kanell 2-(minus 2). Philadelphia, Watters 12-39, Garner 5-18, Turner 2-7, Hoying 1-6.

PASSING—New York, Kanell 14-27-1-153. Philadelphia, Hoying 16-35-3-209.

RECEIVING—New York, Calloway 4-38, Barber 4-28, Patten 3-54, Toomer 1-15, Alexander 1-9, Cross 1-9. Philadelphia, Timpson 5-54, Seay 3-39, Watters 3-15, Fryar 2-78, Turner 2-10, Garner 1-13.

MISSED FIELD GOAL ATTEMPTS—New York, Daluiso 50. Philadelphia, Boniol 48.

INTERCEPTIONS—New York, Armstead 2-57, Ellsworth 1-0. Philadelphia, Dawkins 1-64.

KICKOFF RETURNS—New York, Pegram 3-56. Philadelphia, Turner 2-40, Gray 1-8.

PUNT RETURNS—New York, Toomer 3-19.

SACKS—New York, Armstead 1, K. Hamilton 1, Galyon 1, Holsey 1. Philadelphia, Dent 1, Team 1.

PATRIOTS 26, JAGUARS 20

Sunday, December 7

New England	13	7	3	3—26
Jacksonville	0	7	0	13—20

First Quarter
N.E.—FG, Vinatieri 44, 3:07.
N.E.—Brown 9 pass from Bledsoe (Vinatieri kick), 9:41.
N.E.—FG, Vinatieri 41, 11:16.
Second Quarter
Jac.—McCardell 20 pass from Brunell (Hollis kick), 13:44.
N.E.—Coates 5 pass from Bledsoe (Vinatieri kick), 14:57.
Third Quarter
N.E.—FG, Vinatieri 33, 14:08.
Fourth Quarter
Jac.—McCardell 12 pass from Brunell (pass failed), 9:10.
N.E.—FG, Vinatieri 39, 12:30.
Jac.—Barlow 92 kickoff return (Hollis kick), 12:45.
Attendance—73,446.

TEAM STATISTICS

	New England	Jacksonville
First downs	17	23
Rushes-yards	20-55	27-107
Passing	227	234
Punt returns	1-2	2-22
Kickoff returns	2-30	6-176
Interception returns	0-0	0-0
Comp.-att.-int.	26-35-0	25-42-0
Sacked-yards lost	2-7	4-17
Punts	4-42	3-38
Fumbles-lost	1-0	2-2
Penalties-yards	5-31	9-63
Time of possession	27:31	32:29

INDIVIDUAL STATISTICS
RUSHING—New England, Grier 10-20, Meggett 5-22, Cullors 2-9, Gash 2-4, Bledsoe 1-0. Jacksonville, Means 15-51, Brunell 6-41, Stewart 5-22, Jackson 1-(minus 7).

PASSING—New England, Bledsoe 26-35-0-234. Jacksonville, Brunell 25-42-0-251.

RECEIVING—New England, Coates 6-54, Gash 6-46, Meggett 5-39, Brisby 4-58, Brown 3-26, Jefferson 1-9, Byars 1-2. Jacksonville, McCardell 11-152, Smith 5-51, Mitchell 3-23, Stewart 3-5, Hallock 1-8, Jackson 1-7, Means 1-5.

MISSED FIELD GOAL ATTEMPTS—New England, Vinatieri 32. Jacksonville, Hollis 44.

INTERCEPTIONS—None.

KICKOFF RETURNS—New England, Cullors 2-30. Jacksonville, Barlow 5-157, Mitchell 1-12.

PUNT RETURNS—New England, Meggett 1-2. Jacksonville, Barlow 2-22.

SACKS—New England, Johnson 1, Slade 1, Israel 1, Bruschi 1. Jacksonville, Smeenge 2.

COLTS 22, JETS 14

Sunday, December 7

Indianapolis	0	12	3	7—22
N.Y. Jets	0	0	0	14—14

Second Quarter
Ind.—FG, Blanchard 38, 3:10.
Ind.—FG, Blanchard 20, 10:34.
Ind.—Crockett 2 run (pass failed), 13:12.
Third Quarter
Ind.—FG, Blanchard 42, 11:09.
Fourth Quarter
Ind.—Faulk 2 run (Blanchard kick), 0:03.
NYJ—Van Dyke 17 pass from O'Donnell (Hall kick), 8:48.
NYJ—Van Dyke 18 pass from O'Donnell (Hall kick), 13:26.
Attendance—61,168.

TEAM STATISTICS

	Indianapolis	N.Y. Jets
First downs	19	12
Rushes-yards	46-193	11-33
Passing	173	93
Punt returns	5-50	4-51
Kickoff returns	1-23	6-138
Interception returns	1-14	0-0
Comp.-att.-int.	15-24-0	14-32-1
Sacked-yards lost	0-0	8-58
Punts	5-39	7-45
Fumbles-lost	1-0	1-0
Penalties-yards	8-79	6-42
Time of possession	40:07	19:53

INDIVIDUAL STATISTICS
RUSHING—Indianapolis, Faulk 23-133, Crockett 15-36, Harbaugh 7-13, Groce 1-11. New York, Murrell 5-7, L. Johnson 2-13, Anderson 2-6, O'Donnell 1-4, Neal 1-3.

PASSING—Indianapolis, Harbaugh 15-24-0-173. New York, O'Donnell 14-32-1-151.

RECEIVING—Indianapolis, Faulk 5-87, Dawkins 5-38, Harrison 3-48, Pollard 1-2, Stablein 1-(minus 2). New York, K. Johnson 7-79, Van Dyke 2-35, Graham 2-14, L. Johnson 1-11, Brady 1-7, Neal 1-5.

MISSED FIELD GOAL ATTEMPTS—New York, Hall 42.

INTERCEPTIONS—Indianapolis, Clark 1-14.

KICKOFF RETURNS—Indianapolis, Neal 1-23. New York, Van Dyke 6-138.

PUNT RETURNS—Indianapolis, Jacquet 5-50. New York, L. Johnson 4-51.

SACKS—Indianapolis, E. Johnson 3, Footman 2, Coryatt 1, Fontenot 1, McCoy 1.

REDSKINS 38, CARDINALS 28

Sunday, December 7

Washington	7	10	7	14—38
Arizona	0	14	7	7—28

First Quarter
Was.—Mitchell 63 punt return (Blanton kick), 10:02.
Second Quarter
Was.—Bowie 3 pass from Hostetler (Blanton kick), 0:46.
Was.—FG, Blanton 40, 5:34.
Ariz.—R. Moore 4 pass from Plummer (Nedney kick), 11:24.
Ariz.—R. Moore 29 pass from Plummer (Nedney kick), 14:53.

Third Quarter
Was.—Dishman 29 interception return (Blanton kick), 1:41.
Ariz.—Gedney 37 pass from Plummer (Nedney kick), 2:46.
Fourth Quarter
Was.—Ellard 23 pass from Hostetler (Blanton kick), 0:55.
Ariz.—R. Moore 47 pass from Plummer (Nedney kick), 4:57.
Was.—Connell 7 pass from Hostetler (Blanton kick), 10:43.
   Attendance—41,537.

TEAM STATISTICS

	Washington	Arizona
First downs	17	14
Rushes-yards	35-139	20-57
Passing	223	301
Punt returns	3-63	2-11
Kickoff returns	3-62	7-174
Interception returns	2-29	1-4
Comp.-att.-int.	18-34-1	19-38-2
Sacked-yards lost	1-3	5-36
Punts	7-45	7-51
Fumbles-lost	0-0	1-1
Penalties-yards	6-46	8-60
Time of possession	35:17	24:43

INDIVIDUAL STATISTICS
RUSHING—Washington, Davis 20-92, Hostetler 7-17, Bowie 6-14, Mitchell 1-9, Westbrook 1-7. Arizona, R. Moore 13-38, Plummer 3-9, Centers 3-5, Sanders 1-5.

PASSING—Washington, Hostetler 18-34-1-226. Arizona, Plummer 19-38-2-337.

RECEIVING—Washington, Davis 6-27, Bowie 3-34, Mitchell 2-79, Westbrook 2-30, Connell 2-21, Ellard 1-23, Thomas 1-9, Asher 1-3. Arizona, R. Moore 5-114, Centers 5-41, Sanders 3-87, Gedney 2-45, Edwards 2-18, K. Williams 1-17, McWilliams 1-15.

MISSED FIELD GOAL ATTEMPTS—None.

INTERCEPTIONS—Washington, Dishman 2-29. Arizona, A. Williams 1-4.

KICKOFF RETURNS—Washington, Mitchell 1-26, Logan 1-21, Bowie 1-15. Arizona, K. Williams 7-174.

PUNT RETURNS—Washington, Mitchell 3-63. Arizona, K. Williams 2-11.

SACKS—Washington, Harvey 1.5, M. Patton 1, Lang 1, Duff 1, Jones 0.5. Arizona, Lassiter 1.

49ERS 28, VIKINGS 17

Sunday, December 7

Minnesota	7	7	3	0—17
San Francisco	14	7	7	0—28

First Quarter
S.F.—Kirby 16 pass from S. Young (Anderson kick), 3:43.
S.F.—Floyd 1 run (Anderson kick), 11:09.
Min.—Carter 10 pass from Cunningham (Murray kick), 14:48.
Second Quarter
S.F.—Owens 21 pass from S. Young (Anderson kick), 2:39.
Min.—Carter 22 pass from Cunningham (Murray kick), 11:14.
Third Quarter
S.F.—S. Young 4 run (Anderson kick), 9:42.
Min.—FG, Murray 42, 14:39.
   Attendance—55,761.

TEAM STATISTICS

	Minnesota	San Francisco
First downs	20	24
Rushes-yards	25-143	37-98
Passing	155	270
Punt returns	0-0	2-26
Kickoff returns	5-61	3-72
Interception returns	0-0	1-0
Comp.-att.-int.	16-31-1	20-25-0
Sacked-yards lost	5-23	2-10
Punts	4-35	2-32
Fumbles-lost	2-1	1-0
Penalties-yards	7-60	5-55
Time of possession	28:07	31:53

INDIVIDUAL STATISTICS
RUSHING—Minnesota, R. Smith 11-69, Hoard 8-35, Cunningham 3-24, Evans 3-15. San Francisco, Kirby 17-39, S. Young 10-31, Floyd 10-28.

PASSING—Minnesota, Cunningham 16-31-1-178. San Francisco, S. Young 20-25-0-280.

RECEIVING—Minnesota, Reed 3-58, Carter 3-43, Glover 3-29, Palmer 2-19, Evans 2-15, R. Smith 2-8, Hatchette 1-6. San Francisco, Stokes 6-87, Owens 6-74, Floyd 3-49, Fann 2-28, Jones 1-23, Kirby 1-16, Levy 1-3.

MISSED FIELD GOAL ATTEMPTS—San Francisco, Anderson 37, 51.

INTERCEPTIONS—San Francisco, Drakeford 1-0.

KICKOFF RETURNS—Minnesota, Palmer 4-51, George 1-10. San Francisco, Levy 2-42, Edwards 1-30.

PUNT RETURNS—San Francisco, Uwaezuoke 2-26.

SACKS—Minnesota, Clemons 1, Fisk 1. San Francisco, Doleman 3.5, Greene 1.5.

FALCONS 14, CHARGERS 3

Sunday, December 7

Atlanta	0	7	7	0—14
San Diego	0	0	3	0— 3

Second Quarter
Atl.—Mathis 19 pass from Chandler (Andersen kick), 0:50.
Third Quarter
Atl.—Hanspard 99 kickoff return (Andersen kick), 0:19.
S.D.—FG, G. Davis 37, 7:47.
   Attendance—46,317.

TEAM STATISTICS

	Atlanta	San Diego
First downs	13	16
Rushes-yards	28-96	17-47
Passing	108	221
Punt returns	1-6	2-(-5)
Kickoff returns	1-99	3-59
Interception returns	3-45	1-0
Comp.-att.-int.	10-23-1	22-41-3
Sacked-yards lost	1-7	4-38
Punts	5-38	4-39
Fumbles-lost	1-0	0-0
Penalties-yards	9-79	9-53
Time of possession	30:13	29:47

INDIVIDUAL STATISTICS
RUSHING—Atlanta, Anderson 22-60, Hanspard 3-3, Chandler 2-20, Mathis 1-13. San Diego, Brown 11-24, Fletcher 5-16, Whelihan 1-7.

PASSING—Atlanta, Chandler 10-23-1-115. San Diego, Whelihan 22-41-3-259.

RECEIVING—Atlanta, Emanuel 3-32, Kinchen 2-32, Mathis 1-19, Haynes 1-18, Kozlowski 1-7, Hanspard 1-5, Christian 1-2. San Diego, Metcalf 8-109, Still 3-39, Fletcher 3-27, Hartley 2-30, Martin 2-28, Brown 2-3, Mitchell 1-14, C. Jones 1-9.

MISSED FIELD GOAL ATTEMPTS—San Diego, G. Davis 42.

INTERCEPTIONS—Atlanta, Buchanan 2-31, Owens 1-14. San Diego, Harrison 1-0.

KICKOFF RETURNS—Atlanta, Hanspard 1-99. San Diego, Bynum 3-59.

PUNT RETURNS—Atlanta, Kinchen 1-6. San Diego, Metcalf 2-(minus 5).

SACKS—Atlanta, Tuggle 1, Hall 1, Bennett 1, Archambeau 1. San Diego, Harrison 1.

RAMS 34, SAINTS 27

Sunday, December 7

St. Louis	0	13	0	21—34
New Orleans	10	3	7	7—27

First Quarter
N.O.—FG, Brien 49, 5:33.
N.O.—Fields 21 fumble return (Brien kick), 5:56.
Second Quarter
St.L.—Conwell 3 pass from Banks (Wilkins kick), 2:57.
St.L.—FG, Wilkins 37, 8:33.
N.O.—FG, Brien 53, 10:40.
St.L.—FG, Wilkins 34, 14:15.
Third Quarter
N.O.—Hastings 34 pass from Hobert (Brien kick), 13:21.
Fourth Quarter
N.O.—I. Smith 1 pass from Hobert (Brien kick), 3:26.
St.L.—J. Moore 3 run (Wilkins kick), 3:50.
St.L.—Bruce 30 pass from Banks (Wilkins kick), 9:14.
St.L.—Bruce 5 pass from Banks (Wilkins kick), 11:09.
   Attendance—54,803.

TEAM STATISTICS

	St. Louis	New Orleans
First downs	23	16
Rushes-yards	35-114	12-44
Passing	229	240
Punt returns	5-87	5-37
Kickoff returns	6-162	5-117
Interception returns	2-12	1-0
Comp.-att.-int.	22-42-1	18-42-2
Sacked-yards lost	5-38	2-19
Punts	5-39	6-44
Fumbles-lost	3-2	4-2
Penalties-yards	10-78	4-63
Time of possession	38:54	21:06

INDIVIDUAL STATISTICS

RUSHING—St. Louis, J. Moore 13-39, Thompson 9-18, Heyward 8-22, Banks 4-28, Lee 1-7. New Orleans, Zellars 8-21, T. Davis 4-23.

PASSING—St. Louis, Banks 22-41-1-267, Rypien 0-1-0-0. New Orleans, Hobert 18-42-2-259.

RECEIVING—St. Louis, Bruce 9-144, Kennison 3-27, Small 2-32, Heyward 2-25, Lee 2-18, Conwell 2-15, Laing 1-6, J. Moore 1-0. New Orleans, Hastings 6-120, Hill 5-67, Farquhar 3-35, I. Smith 2-26, Zellars 2-11.

MISSED FIELD GOAL ATTEMPTS—St. Louis, Wilkins 45, 48.

INTERCEPTIONS—St. Louis, Lyght 1-12, Lyle 1-0. New Orleans, Washington 1-0.

KICKOFF RETURNS—St. Louis, Thompson 6-162. New Orleans, Guliford 4-102, McCrary 1-15.

PUNT RETURNS—St. Louis, Kennison 5-87. New Orleans, Guliford 5-37.

SACKS—St. Louis, Lyght 1, Farr 1. New Orleans, Tubbs 1, Martin 1, J. Johnson 1, Mitchell 0.5, B. Smith 0.5, Glover 0.5, Dixon 0.5.

DOLPHINS 33, LIONS 30

Sunday, December 7

Detroit	3	7	6	14	—30
Miami	14	6	3	10	—33

First Quarter
Mia.—Drayton 27 pass from Marino (Mare kick), 2:24.
Det.—FG, Hanson 26, 6:53.
Mia.—Abdul-Jabbar 1 run (Mare kick), 13:50.

Second Quarter
Mia.—FG, Mare 19, 9:29.
Det.—Sanders 7 run (Hanson kick), 14:04.
Mia.—FG, Mare 33, 15:00.

Third Quarter
Mia.—FG, Mare 21, 5:10.
Det.—Morton 35 pass from Mitchell (pass failed), 10:08.

Fourth Quarter
Det.—Westbrook 64 interception return (kick failed), 0:57.
Mia.—Drayton 23 pass from Marino (Mare kick), 5:46.
Det.—Moore 16 pass from Mitchell (Moore pass from Mitchell), 13:46.
Mia.—FG, Mare 42, 15:00.
Attendance—72,266.

TEAM STATISTICS

	Detroit	Miami
First downs	24	19
Rushes-yards	33-145	27-81
Passing	279	310
Punt returns	4-26	1-9
Kickoff returns	6-97	6-109
Interception returns	1-64	2-18
Comp.-att.-int.	19-29-2	24-39-1
Sacked-yards lost	1-9	0-0
Punts	2-36	5-42
Fumbles-lost	3-3	0-0

	Detroit	Miami
Penalties-yards	4-47	4-19
Time of possession	29:39	30:21

INDIVIDUAL STATISTICS

RUSHING—Detroit, Sanders 30-137, Mitchell 2-2, Vardell 1-6. Miami, Abdul-Jabbar 23-70, McPhail 2-8, Pritchett 1-4, Parmalee 1-(minus 1).

PASSING—Detroit, Mitchell 19-29-2-288. Miami, Marino 24-39-1-310.

RECEIVING—Detroit, Morton 9-171, Moore 5-64, Sloan 2-32, Metzelaars 2-19, Sanders 1-2. Miami, Jordan 5-51, Perriman 4-75, Drayton 4-62, McDuffie 4-41, McPhail 3-31, Parmalee 2-18, L. Thomas 1-26, Pritchett 1-6.

MISSED FIELD GOAL ATTEMPTS—None.

INTERCEPTIONS—Detroit, Westbrook 1-64. Miami, Buckley 2-18.

KICKOFF RETURNS—Detroit, Milburn 6-97. Miami, Spikes 3-60, McPhail 2-33, Potts 1-16.

PUNT RETURNS—Detroit, Milburn 3-26, Carrier 1-0. Miami, Jordan 1-9.

SACKS—Miami, Armstrong 1.

PANTHERS 23, COWBOYS 13

Monday, December 8

Carolina	3	7	7	6	—23
Dallas	0	6	0	7	—13

First Quarter
Car.—FG, Kasay 34, 10:15.

Second Quarter
Car.—Carruth 15 pass from Collins (Kasay kick), 10:32.
Dal.—FG, Cunningham 43, 12:33.
Dal.—FG, Cunningham 32, 15:00.

Third Quarter
Car.—Greene 1 pass from Collins (Kasay kick), 6:57.

Fourth Quarter
Car.—FG, Kasay 40, 6:59.
Dal.—Irvin 52 pass from Aikman (Cunningham kick), 8:27.
Car.—FG, Kasay 18, 14:07.
Attendance—63,251.

TEAM STATISTICS

	Carolina	Dallas
First downs	22	9
Rushes-yards	45-155	21-78
Passing	169	138
Punt returns	3-19	2-14
Kickoff returns	3-58	6-141
Interception returns	0-0	0-0
Comp.-att.-int.	17-30-0	14-27-0
Sacked-yards lost	1-5	4-42
Punts	4-38	6-38
Fumbles-lost	2-1	3-1
Penalties-yards	4-30	10-70
Time of possession	36:39	23:21

INDIVIDUAL STATISTICS

RUSHING—Carolina, Lane 34-138, Biakabutuka 7-13, Greene 3-6, Collins 1-(minus 2). Dallas, S. Williams 19-75, E. Smith 2-3.

PASSING—Carolina, Collins 16-28-0-136, Beuerlein 1-2-0-38. Dallas, Aikman 14-26-0-180, Wilson 0-1-0-0.

RECEIVING—Carolina, Muhammad 4-73, Carruth 4-36, Greene 4-31, Walls 2-13, Johnson 1-13, Lane 1-7, Rasby 1-1. Dallas, LaFleur 4-26, S. Williams 3-33, St. Williams 3-32, Irvin 2-67, Miller 1-19, Walker 1-3.

MISSED FIELD GOAL ATTEMPTS—None.

INTERCEPTIONS—None.

KICKOFF RETURNS—Carolina, Bates 2-50, Greene 1-8. Dallas, Walker 4-115, Marion 1-20, Galbraith 1-6.

PUNT RETURNS—Carolina, Poole 3-19. Dallas, St. Williams 1-14, Mathis 1-0.

SACKS—Carolina, Barrow 1, Cota 1, Miller 1, King 1. Dallas, Carver 1.

WEEK 16

N.Y. GIANTS 30, Washington 10
Pittsburgh 24, NEW ENGLAND 21 (OT)
ATLANTA 20, Philadelphia 17
BALTIMORE 21, Tennessee 19
Chicago 13, ST. LOUIS 10
CINCINNATI 31, Dallas 24
Detroit 14, MINNESOTA 13
Green Bay 31, CAROLINA 10
INDIANAPOLIS 41, Miami 0
Jacksonville 20, BUFFALO 14
Kansas City 29, SAN DIEGO 7
NEW ORLEANS 27, Arizona 10
N.Y. JETS 31, Tampa Bay 0
Seattle 22, OAKLAND 21
SAN FRANCISCO 34, Denver 17

STANDINGS

AFC EAST	W	L	T	Pct.
Miami	9	6	0	.600
New England	9	6	0	.600
N.Y. Jets	9	6	0	.600
Buffalo	6	9	0	.400
Indianapolis	3	12	0	.200

AFC CENTRAL	W	L	T	Pct.
Pittsburgh	11	4	0	.733
Jacksonville	10	5	0	.667
Tennessee	7	8	0	.467
Baltimore	6	8	1	.433
Cincinnati	6	9	0	.400

AFC WEST	W	L	T	Pct.
Kansas City	12	3	0	.800
Denver	11	4	0	.733
Seattle	7	8	0	.467
Oakland	4	11	0	.267
San Diego	4	11	0	.267

NFC EAST	W	L	T	Pct.
N.Y. Giants	9	5	1	.633
Washington	7	7	1	.500
Philadelphia	6	8	1	.433
Dallas	6	9	0	.400
Arizona	3	12	0	.200

NFC CENTRAL	W	L	T	Pct.
Green Bay	12	3	0	.800
Tampa Bay	9	6	0	.600
Detroit	8	7	0	.533
Minnesota	8	7	0	.533
Chicago	4	11	0	.267

NFC WEST	W	L	T	Pct.
San Francisco	13	2	0	.867
Atlanta	7	8	0	.467
Carolina	7	8	0	.467
New Orleans	6	9	0	.400
St. Louis	4	11	0	.267

HIGHLIGHTS

Hero of the week: Colts quarterback Jim Harbaugh was 20-of-26 for 255 yards and a career-best four touchdowns in Indianapolis' 41-0 victory over Miami. The Colts scored on every first-half possession.

Goat of the week: In an equally stunning result, Tampa Bay's Trent Dilfer was just 2-of-15 for 38 yards and no touchdowns in a 31-0 loss to the Jets. Dilfer also threw two interceptions, both of which were returned for touchdowns by New York cornerback Otis Smith.

Sub of the week: Seahawks quarterback Jon Kitna, who came into the Seattle-Oakland game having never thrown an NFL pass, was 23-of-37 for 283 yards and one touchdown in a 22-21 come-from-behind victory. Kitna played in relief of starter Warren Moon, who was sidelined with bruised ribs.

Comeback of the week: Seattle had to rally from a 21-3 third-quarter deficit to beat the Raiders. Led by Kitna, the Seahawks closed the gap to 21-19 early in the fourth quarter. Todd Peterson then kicked a game-winning 49-yard field goal with 2:20 left.

Blowout of the week: Miami entered Week 16 with a 9-5 record and Indianapolis was 2-12, but the Colts pulled off a stunning 41-0 win. The Colts defense sacked Dan Marino twice and forced him to fumble twice deep in Miami territory. Both turnovers led to Indianapolis scores.

Nail-biter of the week: Scott Mitchell's 1-yard pass to Herman Moore with three seconds left lifted the Lions to a 14-13 victory against the Vikings. Mitchell engineered a nine-play, 72-yard drive in 1:53 that culminated with the game-winning touchdown.

Hit of the week: In the Detroit-Minnesota game, Lions defensive tackle Luther Elliss stopped Vikings fullback Charles Evans for a 3-yard loss on third down with about two minutes remaining. On the next play, Eddie Murray pushed a 37-yard field goal attempt wide. The Lions took advantage of the Vikings' gaffes by driving for a game-winning touchdown.

Oddity of the week: The Ravens had a unique postgame ceremony after their 21-19 victory over the Oilers. It involved former Baltimore Colts players who ran a play to symbolize the end of an era in the last game at Memorial Stadium. Several former Colts, including Johnny Unitas and Art Donovan, ran the final play in the stadium before handing off the ball to Ravens receiver Michael Jackson to take to the new stadium at Camden Yards.

Top rusher: Barry Sanders rushed 19 times for 138 yards in Detroit's 14-13 victory over Minnesota.

Top passer: Mark Brunell was 24-of-32 for 317 yards in the Jaguars' 20-14 victory over Buffalo.

Top receiver: Green Bay's Antonio Freeman caught 10 passes for 166 yards and two touchdowns.

Notes: Rams rookie David Thompson increased his kickoff-return yardage total to 1,065, making him the third player in club history with more than 1,000 yards in kickoff returns in a season. . . . San Diego native Marcus Allen has scored more touchdowns against the Chargers (23) than any other opponent. . . . Dallas' Emmitt Smith became the fourth NFL running back to gain 1,000 yards in seven consecutive seasons. . . . Corey Dillon set a Bengals rookie rushing record with 1,069 yards. Ickey Woods had 1,066 yards in 1988. . . . The Cardinals allowed five sacks against the Saints, increasing their total for the season to 76, the second-most in NFL history to Philadelphia's 106 in 1986. . . . Tim Brown became Oakland's career all-purpose yardage leader (12,858 yards). . . . Jeff George set a Raiders single-season mark with 3,673 passing yards. . . . Miami offensive tackle Richmond Webb started his 109th consecutive game, tying Hall of Fame center Jim Langer for most in franchise history. . . . The Jets equaled the mark for the greatest turnaround in NFL history with their win against the Buccaneers. The Jets, 1-15 in 1996, improved to 9-6. The last team to make an eight-game turnaround was Indianapolis, in 1992. . . . Detroit wide receiver Herman Moore's six catches gave him 100 for the third consecutive season, tying an NFL record held by San Francisco's Jerry Rice. . . . Lions running back Barry Sanders rushed for at least 100 yards for a record-setting 13th time this season.

1997 REVIEW *Week 16*

Quote of the week: Bengals quarterback Boomer Esiason wasn't very happy when his team fell behind Dallas, 10-0: "I just think some of our guys were looking for autographs instead of playing football. I just told them to calm down and relax, make them realize that just because they had a star on their helmet doesn't mean we couldn't play with them."

GAME SUMMARIES

STEELERS 24, PATRIOTS 21

Saturday, December 13

Pittsburgh	0	7	3	11	3—24
New England	0	14	0	7	0—21

Second Quarter
N.E.—Coates 18 pass from Bledsoe (Vinatieri kick), 2:34.
N.E.—Gash 1 pass from Bledsoe (Vinatieri kick), 8:58.
Pit.—Stewart 1 run (N. Johnson kick), 14:29.
Third Quarter
Pit.—FG, N. Johnson 36, 6:03.
Fourth Quarter
Pit.—FG, N. Johnson 34, 2:05.
N.E.—Meggett 49 pass from Bledsoe (Vinatieri kick), 4:29.
Pit.—Bruener 1 pass from Stewart (Thigpen pass from Stewart), 14:22.
Overtime
Pit.—FG, N. Johnson 31, 4:43.
Attendance—60,013.

TEAM STATISTICS

	Pittsburgh	New England
First downs	22	15
Rushes-yards	40-138	18-42
Passing	266	211
Punt returns	4-27	2-18
Kickoff returns	5-102	4-109
Interception returns	2-54	2-15
Comp.-att.-int.	26-48-2	21-36-2
Sacked-yards lost	0-0	0-0
Punts	5-43	6-45
Fumbles-lost	1-0	0-0
Penalties-yards	10-72	5-35
Time of possession	41:04	23:39

INDIVIDUAL STATISTICS
RUSHING—Pittsburgh, Bettis 28-80, Stewart 10-57, G. Jones 2-1. New England, Grier 6-14, Cullors 5-19, Meggett 4-8, Bledsoe 2-(minus 1), Gash 1-2.
PASSING—Pittsburgh, Stewart 26-48-2-266. New England, Bledsoe 21-36-2-211.
RECEIVING—Pittsburgh, C. Johnson 6-87, Hawkins 5-77, Thigpen 5-45, Bruener 5-43, Bettis 4-12, G. Jones 1-2. New England, Jefferson 5-57, Coates 5-39, Meggett 4-66, Brown 3-32, Brisby 1-9, Byars 1-5, Cullors 1-2, Gash 1-1.
MISSED FIELD GOAL ATTEMPTS—None.
INTERCEPTIONS—Pittsburgh, Henry 1-36, Perry 1-18. New England, Milloy 1-15, Clay 1-0.
KICKOFF RETURNS—Pittsburgh, Coleman 5-102. New England, Meggett 2-70, Cullors 2-39.
PUNT RETURNS—Pittsburgh, Blackwell 4-27. New England, Meggett 2-18.
SACKS—None.

GIANTS 30, REDSKINS 10

Saturday, December 13

Washington	0	3	7	0—10	
N.Y. Giants	17	3	0	10—30	

First Quarter
NYG—FG, Daluiso 41, 2:16.
NYG—Way 15 run (Daluiso kick), 4:57.
NYG—Calloway 7 pass from Kanell (Daluiso kick), 13:46.
Second Quarter
Was.—FG, Blanton 33, 4:49.
NYG—FG, Daluiso 28, 14:34.

Third Quarter
Was.—Connell 41 pass from Hostetler (Blanton kick), 2:43.
Fourth Quarter
NYG—FG, Daluiso 28, 0:36.
NYG—Sehorn 35 interception return (Daluiso kick), 0:57.
Attendance—77,571.

TEAM STATISTICS

	Washington	N.Y. Giants
First downs	18	14
Rushes-yards	15-45	37-130
Passing	275	110
Punt returns	2-5	2-5
Kickoff returns	6-127	3-57
Interception returns	2-5	4-53
Comp.-att.-int.	23-42-4	13-25-2
Sacked-yards lost	3-13	2-15
Punts	3-41	6-40
Fumbles-lost	4-2	2-0
Penalties-yards	4-40	5-46
Time of possession	25:15	34:45

INDIVIDUAL STATISTICS
RUSHING—Washington, Davis 10-41, Hostetler 2-1, Connell 1-3, Bowie 1-0, M. Turk 1-0. New York, Barber 13-32, Way 11-49, Hampton 11-43, Kanell 1-4, Patten 1-2.
PASSING—Washington, Hostetler 23-42-4-288. New York, Kanell 13-25-2-125.
RECEIVING—Washington, Connell 5-89, Mitchell 5-70, Asher 4-48, Davis 3-23, Thomas 3-21, Thrash 2-24, Ellard 1-13. New York, Cross 5-52, Way 2-17, Calloway 2-17, Toomer 1-14, Patten 1-9, Pierce 1-9, Barber 1-7.
MISSED FIELD GOAL ATTEMPTS—None.
INTERCEPTIONS—Washington, Richard 2-5. New York, Sehorn 2-35, C. Hamilton 1-18, Widmer 1-0.
KICKOFF RETURNS—Washington, Mitchell 4-88, Logan 2-39. New York, Pegram 3-57.
PUNT RETURNS—Washington, Mitchell 2-5. New York, Toomer 2-5.
SACKS—Washington, Harvey 1, Mims 1. New York, Strahan 1, Holsey 1, Harris 1.

JETS 31, BUCCANEERS 0

Sunday, December 14

Tampa Bay	0	0	0	0— 0	
N.Y. Jets	3	14	14	0—31	

First Quarter
NYJ—FG, Hall 32, 13:55.
Second Quarter
NYJ—Smith 45 interception return (Hall kick), 3:55.
NYJ—Smith 51 interception return (Hall kick), 8:41.
Third Quarter
NYJ—L. Johnson 101 kickoff return (Hall kick), 0:17.
NYJ—Murrell 7 run (Hall kick), 4:04.
Attendance—60,122.

TEAM STATISTICS

	Tampa Bay	N.Y. Jets
First downs	6	14
Rushes-yards	25-90	43-122
Passing	21	112
Punt returns	4-40	4-45
Kickoff returns	5-97	1-101
Interception returns	1-5	2-96
Comp.-att.-int.	3-22-2	14-22-1
Sacked-yards lost	3-25	0-0
Punts	10-37	6-37
Fumbles-lost	2-1	0-0
Penalties-yards	3-28	5-45
Time of possession	22:29	37:31

INDIVIDUAL STATISTICS
RUSHING—Tampa Bay, Dunn 23-88, Rhett 1-2, Dilfer 1-0. New York, Murrell 26-73, Sowell 7-35, O'Donnell 4-(minus 2), Lucas 2-10, Anderson 2-3, Neal 1-3, L. Johnson 1-0.
PASSING—Tampa Bay, Dilfer 2-15-2-38, Walsh 1-7-0-8. New York, O'Donnell 14-22-1-112.
RECEIVING—Tampa Bay, Dunn 1-22, Davis 1-16, Copeland 1-8. New York, K. Johnson 3-22, Baxter 2-26, Graham 2-20, Van Dyke 1-18, L. Johnson 1-12, Sowell 1-8, Murrell 1-3, Brady 1-3, Neal 1-1, Anderson 1-(minus 1).
MISSED FIELD GOAL ATTEMPTS—Tampa Bay, Husted 51.

INTERCEPTIONS—Tampa Bay, Parker 1-5. New York, Smith 2-96.

KICKOFF RETURNS—Tampa Bay, Anthony 5-97. New York, L. Johnson 1-101.

PUNT RETURNS—Tampa Bay, Williams 4-40. New York, L. Johnson 4-45.

SACKS—New York, Ferguson 1, Terry 1, Farrior 0.5, Lewis 0.5.

JAGUARS 20, BILLS 14

Sunday, December 14

Jacksonville	7	7	3	3—20
Buffalo	0	3	0	11—14

First Quarter
Jac.—Brunell 13 run (Hollis kick), 4:50.

Second Quarter
Jac.—Means 2 run (Hollis kick), 2:10.
Buf.—FG, Christie 38, 14:58.

Third Quarter
Jac.—FG, Hollis 19, 5:19.

Fourth Quarter
Buf.—FG, Christie 31, 0:52.
Buf.—A. Smith 1 run (Moulds pass from Van Pelt), 6:57.
Jac.—FG, Hollis 47, 10:42.
Attendance—41,231.

TEAM STATISTICS

	Jacksonville	Buffalo
First downs	20	24
Rushes-yards	31-91	33-143
Passing	297	192
Punt returns	1-13	1-1
Kickoff returns	4-82	5-131
Interception returns	1-15	1-28
Comp.-att.-int.	24-32-1	19-41-1
Sacked-yards lost	2-20	2-18
Punts	4-39	4-38
Fumbles-lost	0-0	3-2
Penalties-yards	3-35	0-0
Time of possession	31:33	28:27

INDIVIDUAL STATISTICS

RUSHING—Jacksonville, Means 22-74, Stewart 5-7, Brunell 4-10. Buffalo, A. Smith 15-70, Holmes 8-35, Thomas 8-30, Collins 2-8.

PASSING—Jacksonville, Brunell 24-32-1-317. Buffalo, Collins 13-26-0-107, Van Pelt 6-15-1-103.

RECEIVING—Jacksonville, McCardell 6-94, Means 4-52, Mitchell 3-44, Jackson 3-24, Stewart 3-17, Smith 2-51, Jones 2-27, Hallock 1-8. Buffalo, Moulds 6-80, Early 4-65, Johnson 3-30, Thomas 2-13, Reed 1-8, Holmes 1-6, Riemersma 1-6, A. Smith 1-2.

MISSED FIELD GOAL ATTEMPTS—None.

INTERCEPTIONS—Jacksonville, Figures 1-15. Buffalo, Irvin 1-28.

KICKOFF RETURNS—Jacksonville, Logan 2-55, Barlow 1-21, Hallock 1-6. Buffalo, Moulds 2-89, Galloway 2-30, Coons 1-12.

PUNT RETURNS—Jacksonville, Barlow 1-13. Buffalo, Tasker 1-1.

SACKS—Jacksonville, Robinson 1, Schwartz 0.5, Boyer 0.5. Buffalo, Jones 1, Paup 1.

LIONS 14, VIKINGS 13

Sunday, December 14

Detroit	0	7	0	7—14
Minnesota	7	6	0	0—13

First Quarter
Min.—R. Smith 22 run (Murray kick), 10:38.

Second Quarter
Det.—Schlesinger 1 pass from Mitchell (Hanson kick), 0:38.
Min.—FG, Murray 21, 4:52.
Min.—FG, Murray 28, 12:34.

Fourth Quarter
Det.—Moore 1 pass from Mitchell (Hanson kick), 14:57.
Attendance—60,982.

TEAM STATISTICS

	Detroit	Minnesota
First downs	21	13
Rushes-yards	27-148	37-214
Passing	242	43
Punt returns	4-52	2-31
Kickoff returns	3-82	3-34
Interception returns	0-0	1-18

	Detroit	Minnesota
Comp.-att.-int.	24-39-1	9-18-0
Sacked-yards lost	3-24	2-34
Punts	5-35	7-43
Fumbles-lost	1-0	2-0
Penalties-yards	7-44	4-31
Time of possession	28:55	31:05

INDIVIDUAL STATISTICS

RUSHING—Detroit, Sanders 19-138, Mitchell 3-7, Vardell 2-0, Rivers 2-(minus 1), Morton 1-4. Minnesota, R. Smith 20-101, Cunningham 6-71, Evans 6-20, Hoard 3-15, Palmer 2-7.

PASSING—Detroit, Mitchell 23-38-1-255, Reich 1-1-0-11. Minnesota, Cunningham 9-18-0-77.

RECEIVING—Detroit, Morton 8-95, Moore 6-65, Sanders 5-37, Vardell 2-36, T. Boyd 2-32, Schlesinger 1-1. Minnesota, Palmer 3-11, R. Smith 2-20, Reed 2-19, Glover 1-19, Carter 1-8.

MISSED FIELD GOAL ATTEMPTS—Detroit, Hanson 50, 38. Minnesota, Murray 37.

INTERCEPTIONS—Minnesota, E. McDaniel 1-18.

KICKOFF RETURNS—Detroit, Milburn 3-82. Minnesota, Palmer 3-34.

PUNT RETURNS—Detroit, Milburn 4-52. Minnesota, Palmer 2-31.

SACKS—Detroit, Jeffries 1, Bailey 1. Minnesota, Randle 3.

BENGALS 31, COWBOYS 24

Sunday, December 14

Dallas	10	0	0	14—24
Cincinnati	0	17	14	0—31

First Quarter
Dal.—FG, Cunningham 23, 5:14.
Dal.—S. Williams 3 run (Cunningham kick), 13:52.

Second Quarter
Cin.—FG, Pelfrey 42, 5:08.
Cin.—Bieniemy 20 run (Pelfrey kick), 11:48.
Cin.—Scott 48 pass from Esiason (Pelfrey kick), 14:35.

Third Quarter
Cin.—Dillon 14 run (Pelfrey kick), 8:32.
Cin.—Dunn 32 pass from Esiason (Pelfrey kick), 12:26.

Fourth Quarter
Dal.—LaFleur 13 pass from Aikman (Cunningham kick), 6:09.
Dal.—LaFleur 12 pass from Aikman (Cunningham kick), 8:33.
Attendance—60,043.

TEAM STATISTICS

	Dallas	Cincinnati
First downs	29	17
Rushes-yards	31-128	31-157
Passing	274	262
Punt returns	1-0	1-0
Kickoff returns	6-116	4-72
Interception returns	1-0	2-7
Comp.-att.-int.	28-53-2	13-25-1
Sacked-yards lost	1-11	1-7
Punts	5-37	4-48
Fumbles-lost	0-0	1-1
Penalties-yards	6-55	8-44
Time of possession	37:57	22:03

INDIVIDUAL STATISTICS

RUSHING—Dallas, S. Williams 16-53, E. Smith 12-68, Miller 1-6, Walker 1-2, Aikman 1-(minus 1). Cincinnati, Dillon 26-127, Carter 3-2, Bieniemy 2-28.

PASSING—Dallas, Aikman 28-53-2-285. Cincinnati, Esiason 13-25-1-269.

RECEIVING—Dallas, Irvin 9-117, Miller 9-93, S. Williams 6-44, LaFleur 3-29, Walker 1-2. Cincinnati, Scott 4-112, Hundon 2-75, Dunn 2-45, Bieniemy 2-27, Dillon 2-7, Carter 1-3.

MISSED FIELD GOAL ATTEMPTS—None.

INTERCEPTIONS—Dallas, Stoutmire 1-0. Cincinnati, Sawyer 2-7.

KICKOFF RETURNS—Dallas, Walker 5-88, Marion 1-28. Cincinnati, Bieniemy 3-63, Carter 1-9.

PUNT RETURNS—Dallas, St. Williams 1-0. Cincinnati, Myers 1-0.

SACKS—Dallas, V. Smith 1. Cincinnati, Copeland 1.

COLTS 41, DOLPHINS 0

Sunday, December 14

Miami	0	0	0	0— 0
Indianapolis	3	31	0	7—41

First Quarter

Ind.—FG, Blanchard 21, 8:08.

Second Quarter

Ind.—Faulk 10 pass from Harbaugh (Blanchard kick), 0:35.
Ind.—Dilger 7 pass from Harbaugh (Blanchard kick), 6:46.
Ind.—FG, Blanchard 50, 9:21.
Ind.—Dilger 31 pass from Harbaugh (Blanchard kick), 13:05.
Ind.—Dilger 8 pass from Harbaugh (Blanchard kick), 14:07.

Fourth Quarter

Ind.—Faulk 7 run (Blanchard kick), 8:26.
　Attendance—61,282.

TEAM STATISTICS

	Miami	Indianapolis
First downs	10	23
Rushes-yards	27-76	36-148
Passing	107	253
Punt returns	1-3	2-5
Kickoff returns	5-108	1-27
Interception returns	0-0	0-0
Comp.-att.-int.	12-25-0	20-26-0
Sacked-yards lost	2-8	1-2
Punts	2-47	1-35
Fumbles-lost	3-2	1-1
Penalties-yards	7-45	7-55
Time of possession	25:58	34:02

INDIVIDUAL STATISTICS

RUSHING—Miami, Phillips 13-36, Abdul-Jabbar 8-27, McPhail 3-10, Potts 1-3, Marino 1-0, Parmalee 1-0. Indianapolis, Faulk 20-67, Groce 6-52, Crockett 6-10, Harbaugh 3-19, Harrison 1-0.

PASSING—Miami, Marino 7-15-0-71, Erickson 5-10-0-44. Indianapolis, Harbaugh 20-26-0-255.

RECEIVING—Miami, Perriman 2-26, McDuffie 2-23, L. Thomas 1-16, Potts 1-13, Perry 1-10, Parmalee 1-9, McPhail 1-7, Phillips 1-6, Abdul-Jabbar 1-4, Pritchett 1-1. Indianapolis, Dilger 5-100, Harrison 5-63, Faulk 5-50, Dawkins 4-38, Stablein 1-4.

MISSED FIELD GOAL ATTEMPTS—Miami, Mare 50.

INTERCEPTIONS—None.

KICKOFF RETURNS—Miami, C. Harris 3-62, Ismail 2-46. Indianapolis, Jacquet 1-27.

PUNT RETURNS—Miami, McDuffie 1-3. Indianapolis, Jacquet 2-5.

SACKS—Miami, Taylor 1. Indianapolis, Footman 1, Team 1.

FALCONS 20, EAGLES 17

Sunday, December 14

Philadelphia	7	0	0	10	17
Atlanta	0	7	7	6	20

First Quarter

Phi.—Timpson 3 pass from Hoying (Boniol kick), 6:12.

Second Quarter

Atl.—Hanspard 10 pass from Chandler (Andersen kick), 5:22.

Third Quarter

Atl.—Anderson 2 run (Andersen kick), 7:07.

Fourth Quarter

Atl.—FG, Andersen 21, 4:21.
Phi.—Watters 1 run (Boniol kick), 7:12.
Phi.—FG, Boniol 39, 13:05.
Atl.—FG, Andersen 33, 15:00.
　Attendance—42,866.

TEAM STATISTICS

	Philadelphia	Atlanta
First downs	15	21
Rushes-yards	20-106	36-211
Passing	171	175
Punt returns	0-0	3-24
Kickoff returns	4-88	4-70
Interception returns	0-0	1-0
Comp.-att.-int.	16-34-1	12-21-0
Sacked-yards lost	1-9	5-35
Punts	6-42	4-39
Fumbles-lost	0-0	2-1
Penalties-yards	6-50	4-35
Time of possession	24:20	35:40

INDIVIDUAL STATISTICS

RUSHING—Philadelphia, Watters 15-95, Garner 3-5, Hoying 2-6. Atlanta, Anderson 21-78, Chandler 8-38, Hanspard 4-76, Green 3-19.

PASSING—Philadelphia, Hoying 16-34-1-180. Atlanta, Chandler 12-21-0-210.

RECEIVING—Philadelphia, Watters 4-35, Fryar 3-35, Solomon 2-64, Turner 2-2, Dunn 1-15, C. Jones 1-11, Lewis 1-8, Garner 1-7, Timpson 1-3. Atlanta, Mathis 4-57, Kinchen 3-39, Kozlowski 2-41, Green 1-47, Emanuel 1-16, Hanspard 1-10.

MISSED FIELD GOAL ATTEMPTS—Atlanta, Andersen 42.

INTERCEPTIONS—Atlanta, Archambeau 1-0.

KICKOFF RETURNS—Philadelphia, Staley 4-88. Atlanta, Hanspard 4-70.

PUNT RETURNS—Atlanta, Kinchen 3-24.

SACKS—Philadelphia, Jefferson 2, Farmer 1, Dent 1, Hall 0.5, Mamula 0.5. Atlanta, Archambeau 0.5, C. Smith 0.5.

RAVENS 21, OILERS 19

Sunday, December 14

Tennessee	3	3	6	7	19
Baltimore	7	7	0	7	21

First Quarter

Bal.—Jackson 8 pass from Zeier (Stover kick), 3:10.
Ten.—FG, Del Greco 25, 11:46.

Second Quarter

Ten.—FG, Del Greco 40, 3:33.
Bal.—Green 37 pass from Zeier (Stover kick), 9:58.

Third Quarter

Ten.—McNair 15 run (run failed), 14:36.

Fourth Quarter

Bal.—Alexander 15 pass from Zeier (Stover kick), 5:40.
Ten.—McNair 1 run (Del Greco kick), 13:57.
　Attendance—60,558.

TEAM STATISTICS

	Tennessee	Baltimore
First downs	23	11
Rushes-yards	37-190	21-54
Passing	200	192
Punt returns	6-15	2-21
Kickoff returns	3-50	4-108
Interception returns	0-0	1-0
Comp.-att.-int.	22-45-1	13-28-0
Sacked-yards lost	3-19	2-12
Punts	3-51	6-48
Fumbles-lost	4-3	1-1
Penalties-yards	7-45	4-27
Time of possession	37:35	22:25

INDIVIDUAL STATISTICS

RUSHING—Tennessee, E. George 26-129, McNair 8-50, Thomas 3-11. Baltimore, Morris 18-51, Byner 1-3, Cotton 1-1, Zeier 1-(minus 1).

PASSING—Tennessee, McNair 22-45-1-219. Baltimore, Zeier 13-28-0-204.

RECEIVING—Tennessee, Wycheck 8-56, Sanders 7-100, Mason 4-36, Davis 2-19, Thomas 1-8. Baltimore, Jackson 4-56, Green 3-59, Alexander 2-47, J. Lewis 2-15, Byner 1-17, Morris 1-10.

MISSED FIELD GOAL ATTEMPTS—Baltimore, Stover 50, 27.

INTERCEPTIONS—Baltimore, Langham 1-0.

KICKOFF RETURNS—Tennessee, Thomas 3-50. Baltimore, J. Lewis 4-108.

PUNT RETURNS—Tennessee, Mason 5-10, Archie 1-5. Baltimore, J. Lewis 2-21.

SACKS—Tennessee, G. Walker 2. Baltimore, J. Jones 1, Washington 1, Boulware 1.

SEAHAWKS 22, RAIDERS 21

Sunday, December 14

Seattle	0	3	9	10	22
Oakland	14	7	0	0	21

First Quarter

Oak.—Truitt 19 pass from George (Ford kick), 9:22.
Oak.—Jett 37 pass from George (Ford kick), 12:22.

Second Quarter

Sea.—FG, Peterson 27, 5:30.
Oak.—Dudley 5 pass from George (Ford kick), 13:04.

Third Quarter

Sea.—Galloway 8 pass from Kitna (pass failed), 2:15.
Sea.—FG, Peterson 27, 9:39.

Fourth Quarter
Sea.—Warren 9 run (Peterson kick), 1:02.
Sea.—FG, Peterson 49, 12:40.
  Attendance—40,124.

TEAM STATISTICS

	Seattle	Oakland
First downs	22	15
Rushes-yards	34-103	17-34
Passing	278	241
Punt returns	3-17	0-0
Kickoff returns	3-63	6-135
Interception returns	0-0	2-42
Comp.-att.-int.	23-37-2	21-31-0
Sacked-yards lost	1-5	5-33
Punts	3-39	3-55
Fumbles-lost	1-0	3-2
Penalties-yards	7-47	9-60
Time of possession	34:58	25:02

INDIVIDUAL STATISTICS

RUSHING—Seattle, Warren 19-70, Kitna 7-11, Smith 6-22, Galloway 1-1, Broussard 1-(minus 1). Oakland, Kaufman 16-36, George 1-(minus 2).

PASSING—Seattle, Kitna 23-37-2-283. Oakland, George 21-31-0-274.

RECEIVING—Seattle, Galloway 7-82, Pritchard 5-98, McKnight 3-33, Strong 2-13, Crumpler 1-14, Warren 1-11, Broussard 1-11, May 1-10, Fauria 1-7, Smith 1-4. Oakland, Dudley 5-66, Jett 4-75, T. Brown 4-57, Kaufman 3-15, Truitt 2-29, Levitt 2-24, Shedd 1-8.

MISSED FIELD GOAL ATTEMPTS—Seattle, Peterson 35. Oakland, Ford 24.

INTERCEPTIONS—Oakland, Trapp 1-25, McDaniel 1-17.

KICKOFF RETURNS—Seattle, Broussard 3-63. Oakland, Truitt 2-51, Aska 2-46, Shedd 2-38.

PUNT RETURNS—Seattle, Davis 3-17.

SACKS—Seattle, Daniels 2, Bellamy 1, Sinclair 1, Saleaumua 0.5, Adams 0.5. Oakland, Lewis 1.

PACKERS 31, PANTHERS 10

Sunday, December 14

Green Bay	14	3	7	7—31
Carolina	0	3	0	7—10

First Quarter
G.B.—Freeman 58 pass from Favre (Longwell kick), 7:22.
G.B.—R. Brooks 20 pass from Favre (Longwell kick), 14:34.
Second Quarter
Car.—FG, Kasay 43, 6:55.
G.B.—FG, Longwell 31, 13:37.
Third Quarter
G.B.—Freeman 6 pass from Favre (Longwell kick), 7:10.
Fourth Quarter
Car.—Lane 35 run (Kasay kick), 0:44.
G.B.—Hayden 6 run (Longwell kick), 10:54.
  Attendance—70,887.

TEAM STATISTICS

	Green Bay	Carolina
First downs	26	9
Rushes-yards	41-218	24-140
Passing	240	32
Punt returns	5-7	1-5
Kickoff returns	3-63	6-121
Interception returns	0-0	1-15
Comp.-att.-int.	18-34-1	7-26-0
Sacked-yards lost	3-16	3-24
Punts	5-43	9-42
Fumbles-lost	2-0	2-1
Penalties-yards	1-10	0-0
Time of possession	37:44	22:16

INDIVIDUAL STATISTICS

RUSHING—Green Bay, Levens 17-73, Hayden 14-86, Henderson 5-32, Bono 3-(minus 3), R. Brooks 1-15, Favre 1-15. Carolina, Lane 19-119, Collins 2-10, Carruth 1-6, Johnson 1-4, Greene 1-1.

PASSING—Green Bay, Favre 18-34-1-256. Carolina, Collins 7-26-0-56.

RECEIVING—Green Bay, Freeman 10-166, R. Brooks 2-43, Beebe 2-28, Levens 2-0, Chmura 1-11, Henderson 1-8. Carolina, Carruth 4-28, E. Mills 1-22, Muhammad 1-6, Walls 1-0.

MISSED FIELD GOAL ATTEMPTS—None.

INTERCEPTIONS—Carolina, Cota 1-15.

KICKOFF RETURNS—Green Bay, Beebe 3-63. Carolina, Bates 5-93, Stone 1-28.

PUNT RETURNS—Green Bay, Sharper 5-7. Carolina, Poole 1-5.

SACKS—Green Bay, Evans 1, B. Williams 1, Butler 1. Carolina, Minter 1.5, Barrow 1, Raybon 0.5.

CHIEFS 29, CHARGERS 7

Sunday, December 14

Kansas City	7	7	8	7—29
San Diego	0	7	0	0— 7

First Quarter
K.C.—Allen 1 run (Stoyanovich kick), 11:58.
Second Quarter
S.D.—Metcalf 14 pass from Whelihan (G. Davis kick), 0:51.
K.C.—Dawson 21 pass from Gannon (Stoyanovich kick), 6:55.
Third Quarter
K.C.—FG, Stoyanovich 40, 4:17.
K.C.—Safety, Philcox sacked by D.Thomas in end zone, 9:19.
K.C.—FG, Stoyanovich 48, 13:18.
Fourth Quarter
K.C.—McMillian 87 interception return (Stoyanovich kick), 8:14.
  Attendance—54,594.

TEAM STATISTICS

	Kansas City	San Diego
First downs	14	22
Rushes-yards	27-131	28-63
Passing	108	219
Punt returns	1-(-1)	5-24
Kickoff returns	3-68	6-125
Interception returns	1-87	0-0
Comp.-att.-int.	8-25-0	23-38-1
Sacked-yards lost	1-8	7-34
Punts	7-39	6-40
Fumbles-lost	1-0	5-1
Penalties-yards	9-76	10-137
Time of possession	24:58	35:02

INDIVIDUAL STATISTICS

RUSHING—Kansas City, Allen 8-44, Hill 7-13, Bennett 6-32, Anders 5-43, Gannon 1-(minus 1). San Diego, Brown 16-57, Bynum 6-(minus 1), Craver 3-11, Whelihan 2-4, Metcalf 1-(minus 8).

PASSING—Kansas City, Gannon 8-25-0-116. San Diego, Whelihan 13-21-0-137, Philcox 10-17-1-116.

RECEIVING—Kansas City, Gonzalez 3-15, Rison 2-52, Dawson 2-48, Anders 1-1. San Diego, Martin 7-66, Hartley 4-54, Metcalf 3-48, Still 3-41, C. Jones 3-33, Craver 2-0, Brown 1-11.

MISSED FIELD GOAL ATTEMPTS—None.

INTERCEPTIONS—Kansas City, McMillian 1-87.

KICKOFF RETURNS—Kansas City, Vanover 2-47, Hughes 1-21. San Diego, Bynum 6-125.

PUNT RETURNS—Kansas City, Vanover 1-(minus 1). San Diego, Metcalf 4-24, Shaw 1-0.

SACKS—Kansas City, Thomas 3, Williams 2, Wooden 1, Davis 1. San Diego, Fuller 1.

SAINTS 27, CARDINALS 10

Sunday, December 14

Arizona	7	3	0	0—10
New Orleans	0	3	7	17—27

First Quarter
Ariz.—Plummer 10 run (Nedney kick), 9:32.
Second Quarter
N.O.—FG, Brien 20, 2:59.
Ariz.—FG, Nedney 30, 11:55.
Third Quarter
N.O.—Hill 9 pass from Hobert (Brien kick), 10:17.
Fourth Quarter
N.O.—FG, Brien 33, 1:32.
N.O.—Guliford 16 pass from Hobert (Brien kick), 4:50.
N.O.—Farquhar 8 pass from Hobert (Brien kick), 13:05.
  Attendance—45,517.

TEAM STATISTICS

	Arizona	New Orleans
First downs	18	17
Rushes-yards	28-111	34-130

	Arizona	New Orleans
Passing	154	252
Punt returns	4-65	2-14
Kickoff returns	5-124	1-29
Interception returns	1-0	2-45
Comp.-att.-int.	17-37-2	14-24-1
Sacked-yards lost	5-26	0-0
Punts	6-50	6-57
Fumbles-lost	2-2	0-0
Penalties-yards	9-59	13-107
Time of possession	29:40	30:20

INDIVIDUAL STATISTICS

RUSHING—Arizona, R. Moore 22-79, Plummer 3-21, Centers 3-11. New Orleans, Zellars 19-72, Hobert 7-17, T. Davis 6-13, Hastings 1-27, Bates 1-1.

PASSING—Arizona, Plummer 17-37-2-180. New Orleans, Hobert 14-24-1-252.

RECEIVING—Arizona, Sanders 4-55, K. Williams 4-54, R. Moore 4-31, Carter 1-15, Centers 1-9, Gedney 1-8, Edwards 1-6, Plummer 1-2. New Orleans, Hill 5-124, Guliford 2-38, Zellars 2-22, Hastings 2-6, Poole 1-49, Farquhar 1-8, I. Smith 1-5.

MISSED FIELD GOAL ATTEMPTS—None.

INTERCEPTIONS—Arizona, A. Williams 1-0. New Orleans, Washington 1-30, Kelly 1-15.

KICKOFF RETURNS—Arizona, K. Williams 5-124. New Orleans, Guliford 1-29.

PUNT RETURNS—Arizona, K. Williams 4-65. New Orleans, Guliford 2-14.

SACKS—New Orleans, B. Smith 1.5, J. Johnson 1.5, Glover 1, Martin 1.

BEARS 13, RAMS 10

Sunday, December 14

Chicago	0	7	0	6—13
St. Louis	7	0	0	3—10

First Quarter
St.L.—J. Moore 1 run (Wilkins kick), 11:08.
Second Quarter
Chi.—Conway 55 pass from Kramer (Jaeger kick), 5:25.
Fourth Quarter
St.L.—FG, Wilkins 28, 4:17.
Chi.—FG, Jaeger 27, 9:52.
Chi.—FG, Jaeger 20, 12:09.
Attendance—66,030.

TEAM STATISTICS

	Chicago	St. Louis
First downs	13	12
Rushes-yards	37-120	20-49
Passing	189	116
Punt returns	4-29	3-11
Kickoff returns	3-55	4-121
Interception returns	3-22	2-33
Comp.-att.-int.	15-30-2	13-28-3
Sacked-yards lost	1-5	5-31
Punts	5-43	6-41
Fumbles-lost	3-3	3-2
Penalties-yards	5-30	9-85
Time of possession	35:09	24:51

INDIVIDUAL STATISTICS

RUSHING—Chicago, Autry 26-62, Mirer 5-28, Tony Carter 3-24, Hicks 2-5, Kramer 1-1. St. Louis, J. Moore 13-35, Thompson 2-5, Heyward 2-0, Crawford 1-9, Banks 1-0, Lee 1-0.

PASSING—Chicago, Kramer 14-22-1-186, Mirer 1-7-1-8, Conway 0-1-0-0. St. Louis, Banks 13-28-3-147.

RECEIVING—Chicago, Conway 7-109, Wetnight 4-37, Penn 3-40, Autry 1-8. St. Louis, Lee 4-38, Bruce 3-46, Conwell 3-23, J. Moore 1-19, Small 1-13, Kennison 1-8.

MISSED FIELD GOAL ATTEMPTS—Chicago, Jaeger 22. St. Louis, Wilkins 40.

INTERCEPTIONS—Chicago, W. Harris 2-22, Tom Carter 1-0. St. Louis, McNeil 1-20, Lyght 1-13.

KICKOFF RETURNS—Chicago, Smith 3-55. St. Louis, Thompson 4-121.

PUNT RETURNS—Chicago, Proehl 4-29. St. Louis, Kennison 3-11.

SACKS—Chicago, B. Cox 1.5, M. Carter 1, Flanigan 1, Grasmanis 0.5, Reeves 0.5, Spellman 0.5. St. Louis, Carter 1.

49ERS 34, BRONCOS 17

Monday, December 15

Denver	10	0	7	0—17
San Francisco	0	14	10	10—34

First Quarter
Den.—Davis 4 run (Elam kick), 6:46.
Den.—FG, Elam 49, 13:29.
Second Quarter
S.F.—Rice 14 pass from S. Young (Anderson kick), 8:07.
S.F.—Kirby 1 run (Anderson kick), 14:38.
Third Quarter
Den.—Hebron 1 run (Elam kick), 4:30.
S.F.—FG, Anderson 32, 8:01.
S.F.—Hanks 55 interception return (Anderson kick), 9:03.
Fourth Quarter
S.F.—FG, Anderson 20, 5:55.
S.F.—Greene 40 fumble return (Anderson kick), 10:55.
Attendance—68,461.

TEAM STATISTICS

	Denver	San Francisco
First downs	15	18
Rushes-yards	23-96	26-58
Passing	141	265
Punt returns	1-0	4-19
Kickoff returns	7-152	4-86
Interception returns	0-0	2-110
Comp.-att.-int.	16-41-2	22-34-0
Sacked-yards lost	1-9	2-11
Punts	4-49	5-36
Fumbles-lost	2-1	1-1
Penalties-yards	5-46	11-95
Time of possession	27:46	32:14

INDIVIDUAL STATISTICS

RUSHING—Denver, Hebron 12-64, Davis 10-28, Griffith 1-4. San Francisco, Kirby 15-27, Floyd 7-19, S. Young 3-11, Levy 1-1.

PASSING—Denver, Elway 16-41-2-150. San Francisco, S. Young 22-34-0-276.

RECEIVING—Denver, R. Smith 5-73, Sharpe 5-60, Davis 2-0, Green 1-17, McCaffrey 1-5, Carswell 1-0, Hebron 1-(minus 5). San Francisco, Kirby 6-76, Jones 4-68, Rice 3-40, Owens 3-39, Stokes 3-32, Floyd 3-21.

MISSED FIELD GOAL ATTEMPTS—Denver, Elam 44, 29. San Francisco, Anderson 35.

INTERCEPTIONS—San Francisco, Hanks 1-55, Woodall 1-55.

KICKOFF RETURNS—Denver, Hebron 4-50, Loville 3-102. San Francisco, Levy 4-86.

PUNT RETURNS—Denver, Gordon 1-0. San Francisco, Levy 2-19, Uwaezuoke 1-0, Woodson 1-0.

SACKS—Denver, Williams 2. San Francisco, Greene 1.

WEEK 17

RESULTS

GREEN BAY 31, Buffalo 21
St. Louis 30, CAROLINA 18
ARIZONA 29, Atlanta 26
CINCINNATI 16, Baltimore 14
DENVER 38, San Diego 3
DETROIT 13, N.Y. Jets 10
Jacksonville 20, OAKLAND 9
KANSAS CITY 25, New Orleans 13
MINNESOTA 39, Indianapolis 28
N.Y. Giants 20, DALLAS 7
SEATTLE 38, San Francisco 9
TAMPA BAY 31, Chicago 15
TENNESSEE 16, Pittsburgh 6
WASHINGTON 35, Philadelphia 32
New England 14, MIAMI 12

STANDINGS

AFC EAST

	W	L	T	Pct.
New England	10	6	0	.625
Miami	9	7	0	.563
N.Y. Jets	9	7	0	.563
Buffalo	6	10	0	.375
Indianapolis	3	13	0	.188

AFC CENTRAL

	W	L	T	Pct.
Pittsburgh	11	5	0	.688
Jacksonville	11	5	0	.688
Tennessee	8	8	0	.500
Cincinnati	7	9	0	.438
Baltimore	6	9	1	.406

AFC WEST

	W	L	T	Pct.
Kansas City	13	3	0	.813
Denver	12	4	0	.750
Seattle	8	8	0	.500
Oakland	4	12	0	.250
San Diego	4	12	0	.250

NFC EAST

	W	L	T	Pct.
N.Y. Giants	10	5	1	.656
Washington	8	7	1	.531
Philadelphia	6	9	1	.406
Dallas	6	10	0	.375
Arizona	4	12	0	.250

NFC CENTRAL

	W	L	T	Pct.
Green Bay	13	3	0	.813
Tampa Bay	10	6	0	.625
Detroit	9	7	0	.563
Minnesota	9	7	0	.563
Chicago	4	12	0	.250

NFC WEST

	W	L	T	Pct.
San Francisco	13	3	0	.813
Atlanta	7	9	0	.438
Carolina	7	9	0	.438
New Orleans	6	10	0	.375
St. Louis	5	11	0	.313

HIGHLIGHTS

Hero of the week: Needing 131 yards to become only the third player in NFL history to rush for 2,000 in a season, Barry Sanders didn't disappoint, rushing for 184 yards on 23 carries in the Lions' 13-10 victory over the Jets. Sanders started slowly (20 yards in the first half) and finished fast (112 in the fourth quarter), hitting the 2,000-yard plateau on a 2-yard run with 2:15 left.

Goat of the week: In a week when many teams rested their best players in preparation for the playoffs, one player who had plenty at stake—Panthers quarterback Kerry Collins—was dreadful. Needing a strong performance to keep his team from having a losing season and to persuade management he was worthy of a $6 million bonus he was eligible for in the offseason, Collins bombed, going 11-of-25 and throwing three interceptions in a 20-13 loss to the Rams. Before being yanked by coach Dom Capers in the third quarter, Collins had compiled a quarterback rating of 34.5, including 8.3 in the first half.

Sub of the week: Although the Eagles lost, it wasn't running back Charlie Garner's fault. Subbing for the injured Ricky Watters, Garner rushed for 115 yards on 18 carries and scored two touchdowns in Philadelphia's 35-32 loss at Washington.

Comeback of the week: After spotting the Jets a 10-0 first-quarter lead, the Lions—who needed to win to secure a playoff spot—scored 13 consecutive points over the next three periods to beat New York. Detroit's winning points came on a 15-yard run by Sanders early in the fourth quarter.

Blowout of the week: Needing a win to assure home-field advantage for its first playoff game, the Broncos didn't fail, routing San Diego, 38-3. Playing without star running back Terrell Davis, the Broncos raced to a 24-3 halftime lead and cruised behind quarterback John Elway's four touchdown passes, including a 68-yarder to Shannon Sharpe on the first play of the second half.

Nail-biter of the week: Trailing 26-14 with less than five minutes left, the Cardinals scored 15 points in the final 4:45 to beat Atlanta, 29-26. The Cardinals'

game-winning drive covered 80 yards in 12 plays, ending in a 1-yard touchdown pass from rookie quarterback Jake Plummer to fullback Larry Centers with five seconds left.

Hit of the week: By Redskins cornerback Darryl Pounds, who forced, recovered and then returned a fumble by Eagles quarterback Bobby Hoying 18 yards for a touchdown 1:30 into the game.

Oddity of the week: The Panthers had a 98-yard drive against the Rams—and failed to score.

Top rusher: Sanders' 184-yard effort against the Jets was his 14th consecutive 100-yard game, extending his NFL record.

Top passer: Eric Zeier was 28-of-41 for 349 yards and two touchdowns in Baltimore's 16-14 loss at Cincinnati.

Top receiver: Tim Brown caught a Raiders-record 14 passes for 164 yards in Oakland's 20-9 loss to Jacksonville.

Notes: The Jets-Lions game was marred by a life-threatening injury sustained by Detroit linebacker Reggie Brown. Brown, a second-year player from Texas A&M, hurt his neck trying to tackle running back Adrian Murrell early in the fourth quarter. Brown, who was knocked unconscious, lay on the field for about 20 minutes barely moving or breathing before being taken off on a stretcher. It was later revealed that Brown, who was up and walking less than a month later, would have died on the field in not for miraculous work by the Lions' medical staff. . . . The Packers had two 1,000-yard receivers in the same season for the first time: Antonio Freeman (1,243) and Robert Brooks (1,010). . . . Bills special-teams ace Steve Tasker, who earlier had announced his retirement, ended his 13-year career on a sour note. He was ejected from a game against the Packers for arguing after Green Bay's first touchdown—an end-zone fumble recovery by Tyrone Davis. It was Tasker's first ejection. . . . The Giants (7-0-1) became the first team to go undefeated in the NFC East since the division was formed in 1970. . . . Carolina finished 2-6 at home after going 8-0 at

Ericsson Stadium the year before. . . . The Eagles (0-7-1) failed to win a road game for the first time since 1970. . . . Seahawks quarterback Warren Moon threw for 232 yards against San Francisco to end the season with 3,678 yards, breaking a club record set by Dave Krieg in 1984. Moon holds the single season passing records for three NFL teams: Houston/Tennessee (4,690), Minnesota (4,264) and Seattle. . . . The Raiders ended the season at 4-12, their worst record of the Al Davis era. . . . 49ers kicker Gary Anderson booted three field goals against Seattle to increase his career total to 385, breaking Nick Lowery's NFL record of 383. Falcons kicker Morten Andersen, like Anderson a 16-year vet, tied a record held by Lowery for most 100-point seasons (11). . . . The Cardinals allowed 78 sacks in 1997, the second-highest total in NFL history. The Eagles allowed 104 in 1986. . . . The Cowboys finished the season with six rushing touchdowns, their fewest since the 1960 and '61 teams also had six. . . . Did the Seahawks have an average season, or what? They were 8-8 overall, 4-4 at home, 4-4 on the road, 4-4 in division games, 6-6 vs. the AFC and 2-2 vs. the NFC. They also scored 365 points and allowed 362, the closest differential of any team in the league. . . . In the persistence pays off category, Redskins third-string quarterback Trent Green finally played in an NFL game. Green, an eighth-round draft choice of the Chargers in 1993, took one snap against the Eagles and threw an incomplete pass. It came in the 64th game of Green's career.

Quote of the week: Raiders coach Joe Bugel, when informed that a "source" from within the team was making critical comments about him, the players and the team's dismal season: "I'd like to meet 'source.' I'd really like to meet that sucker. I've got a few things I'd like to say to him."

GAME SUMMARIES

RAMS 30, PANTHERS 18

Saturday, December 20

St. Louis	10	6	7	7—30
Carolina	0	0	8	10—18

First Quarter
St.L.—Wiegert recovered fumble in end zone (Wilkins kick), 8:01.
St.L.—FG, Wilkins 49, 14:32.
Second Quarter
St.L.—FG, Wilkins 42, 4:29.
St.L.—FG, Wilkins 47, 15:00.
Third Quarter
St.L.—Thompson 7 run (Wilkins kick), 4:59.
Fourth Quarter
St.L.—Conwell 1 pass from Banks (Wilkins kick), 3:29.
Car.—E. Mills 2 pass from Beuerlein (Johnson run), 9:52.
Car.—Safety, Horan ran out of end zone, forced by Stone, 14:14.
Attendance—58,101.

TEAM STATISTICS
	St. Louis	Carolina
First downs	23	21
Rushes-yards	39-148	20-83
Passing	149	233
Punt returns	2-2	1-10
Kickoff returns	2-45	7-146
Interception returns	3-9	0-0
Comp.-att.-int.	16-25-0	21-42-3

	St. Louis	Carolina
Sacked-yards lost	1-14	3-28
Punts	4-45	4-48
Fumbles-lost	1-0	1-0
Penalties-yards	7-53	12-86
Time of possession	34:09	25:51

INDIVIDUAL STATISTICS
RUSHING—St. Louis, J. Moore 27-113, Thompson 3-11, Lee 3-10, Banks 2-11, Heyward 2-1, Kennison 1-5, Horan 1-(minus 3). Carolina, Lane 14-78, Collins 2-(minus 5), Carruth 1-3, Johnson 1-3, Beuerlein 1-2, Greene 1-2.
PASSING—St. Louis, Banks 16-25-0-163. Carolina, Collins 11-25-3-132, Beuerlein 10-17-0-129.
RECEIVING—St. Louis, Bruce 5-43, Lee 4-37, Conwell 3-39, Small 2-30, Laing 1-11, Kennison 1-3. Carolina, E. Mills 5-66, Carruth 4-66, Mangum 4-56, Muhammad 4-45, Johnson 2-15, Greene 2-13.
MISSED FIELD GOAL ATTEMPTS—None.
INTERCEPTIONS—St. Louis, Lyle 2-9, M. Jones 1-0.
KICKOFF RETURNS—St. Louis, Thompson 2-45. Carolina, Bates 6-141, Poole 1-5.
PUNT RETURNS—St. Louis, Kennison 2-2. Carolina, Poole 1-10.
SACKS—St. Louis, Carter 2, Williams 1. Carolina, Minter 0.5, Saleh 0.5.

PACKERS 31, BILLS 21

Saturday, December 20

Buffalo	0	0	8	13—21
Green Bay	14	7	3	7—31

First Quarter
G.B.—T. Davis recovered fumble in end zone (Longwell kick), 1:37.
G.B.—Freeman 4 pass from Favre (Longwell kick), 11:41.
Second Quarter
G.B.—T. Davis 2 pass from Favre (Longwell kick), 7:34.
Third Quarter
G.B.—FG, Longwell 35, 11:22.
Buf.—A. Smith 5 run (Riemersma pass from Van Pelt), 14:37.
Fourth Quarter
Buf.—A. Smith 1 run (pass failed), 3:36.
G.B.—Sharper 20 interception return (Longwell kick), 10:18.
Buf.—Van Pelt 1 run (Christie kick), 12:55.
Attendance—60,108.

TEAM STATISTICS
	Buffalo	Green Bay
First downs	21	14
Rushes-yards	21-51	34-102
Passing	274	170
Punt returns	3-37	2-25
Kickoff returns	5-77	4-83
Interception returns	0-0	3-69
Comp.-att.-int.	24-45-3	17-28-0
Sacked-yards lost	1-10	1-15
Punts	7-30	6-45
Fumbles-lost	3-1	3-3
Penalties-yards	10-93	13-115
Time of possession	27:52	32:08

INDIVIDUAL STATISTICS
RUSHING—Buffalo, A. Smith 10-20, Thomas 7-28, Van Pelt 2-4, Holmes 2-(minus 1). Green Bay, Levens 22-71, Hayden 7-33, Pederson 3-(minus 4), Henderson 1-3, Favre 1-(minus 1).
PASSING—Buffalo, Van Pelt 23-44-3-255, Mohr 1-1-0-29. Green Bay, Favre 12-18-0-156, Bono 5-10-0-29.
RECEIVING—Buffalo, Early 7-120, Johnson 4-44, Riemersma 4-42, A. Smith 4-32, Moulds 3-31, Reese 1-13, Holmes 1-2. Green Bay, Freeman 6-63, R. Brooks 4-83, Henderson 3-18, Chmura 2-17, Levens 1-2, T. Davis 1-2.
MISSED FIELD GOAL ATTEMPTS—Green Bay, Longwell 45.
INTERCEPTIONS—Green Bay, Prior 1-49, Sharper 1-20, Ty.Williams 1-0.
KICKOFF RETURNS—Buffalo, Moulds 3-47, Holmes 2-30. Green Bay, Schroeder 2-57, Hayden 1-23, Sharper 1-3.
PUNT RETURNS—Buffalo, Burris 2-37, Jackson 1-0. Green Bay, Sharper 2-25.
SACKS—Buffalo, Holecek 1. Green Bay, White 1.

JAGUARS 20, RAIDERS 9

Sunday, December 21

Jacksonville	14	0	0	6—20
Oakland	0	3	6	0— 9

First Quarter
Jac.—McCardell 35 pass from Brunell (Hollis kick), 6:47.
Jac.—Jones 26 pass from Brunell (Hollis kick), 12:17.

Oak.—FG, Ford 33, 9:07.

Third Quarter
Oak.—Dudley 2 pass from George (pass failed), 7:54.

Fourth Quarter
Jac.—FG, Hollis 19, 2:05.
Jac.—FG, Hollis 23, 10:00.
Attendance—40,032.

TEAM STATISTICS

	Jacksonville	Oakland
First downs	20	19
Rushes-yards	31-143	24-108
Passing	274	192
Punt returns	2-12	0-0
Kickoff returns	1-22	4-74
Interception returns	0-0	0-0
Comp.-att.-int.	19-28-0	24-37-0
Sacked-yards lost	1-9	6-52
Punts	4-37	6-42
Fumbles-lost	1-0	1-1
Penalties-yards	3-11	5-40
Time of possession	28:25	31:35

INDIVIDUAL STATISTICS
RUSHING—Jacksonville, Means 18-80, Stewart 6-42, Johnson 4-(minus 6), Brunell 3-27. Oakland, Kaufman 21-94, Levitt 2-3, Hall 1-11.
PASSING—Jacksonville, Brunell 18-27-0-243, Johnson 1-1-0-40. Oakland, George 24-37-0-244.
RECEIVING—Jacksonville, McCardell 7-116, Smith 6-93, Stewart 2-23, Jones 1-26, Barlow 1-12, Mitchell 1-8, Means 1-5. Oakland, T. Brown 14-164, Jett 3-38, Truitt 3-29, Kaufman 3-11, Dudley 1-2.
MISSED FIELD GOAL ATTEMPTS—None.
INTERCEPTIONS—None.
KICKOFF RETURNS—Jacksonville, Barlow 1-22. Oakland, Howard 4-74.
PUNT RETURNS—Jacksonville, Barlow 2-12.
SACKS—Jacksonville, Davis 1, Tuaolo 1, Simmons 1, Hamilton 1, Lageman 1, Wynn 0.5, Smeenge 0.5. Oakland, Maryland 1.

BUCCANEERS 31, BEARS 15

Sunday, December 21

Chicago	0	7	0	8—15
Tampa Bay	14	7	10	0—31

First Quarter
T.B.—Dilfer 7 run (Husted kick), 12:51.
T.B.—Williams 61 punt return (Husted kick), 15:00.

Second Quarter
Chi.—Autry 3 run (Jaeger kick), 5:08.
T.B.—Williams 7 pass from Dilfer (Husted kick), 14:49.

Third Quarter
T.B.—FG, Husted 20, 6:44.
T.B.—Rhett 5 run (Husted kick), 11:59.

Fourth Quarter
Chi.—Mirer 1 run (Mirer run), 2:07.
Attendance—70,930.

TEAM STATISTICS

	Chicago	Tampa Bay
First downs	15	12
Rushes-yards	27-90	33-183
Passing	106	86
Punt returns	4-30	6-116
Kickoff returns	6-119	3-90
Interception returns	0-0	2-19
Comp.-att.-int.	18-29-2	11-19-0
Sacked-yards lost	3-15	1-8
Punts	7-42	5-47
Fumbles-lost	1-1	1-0
Penalties-yards	3-30	2-35
Time of possession	31:29	28:31

INDIVIDUAL STATISTICS
RUSHING—Chicago, Autry 16-45, Mirer 4-6, Tony Carter 2-25, Hicks 2-9, Harmon 2-6, Kramer 1-(minus 1). Tampa Bay, Dunn 16-119, Rhett 6-20, Alstott 5-12, Walsh 3-(minus 3), Anthony 1-23, Dilfer 1-7, Ellison 1-5.
PASSING—Chicago, Kramer 12-19-1-82, Mirer 6-10-1-39. Tampa Bay, Dilfer 10-18-0-94, Walsh 1-1-0-0.
RECEIVING—Chicago, Proehl 4-41, Conway 2-18, Wetnight 2-15, Engram 2-12, Tony Carter 2-9, Harmon 2-8, Autry 2-4, T. Allen 1-9, Allred 1-5. Tampa Bay, Williams 4-47, Dunn 3-18, Davis 1-16, Anthony 1-8, Alstott 1-5, Jordan 1-0.

MISSED FIELD GOAL ATTEMPTS—None.
INTERCEPTIONS—Tampa Bay, Johnson 1-19, Abraham 1-0.
KICKOFF RETURNS—Chicago, Smith 6-119. Tampa Bay, Anthony 3-90.
PUNT RETURNS—Chicago, Proehl 4-30. Tampa Bay, Williams 6-116.
SACKS—Chicago, Mangum 1. Tampa Bay, Sapp 2, Upshaw 1.

VIKINGS 39, COLTS 28

Sunday, December 21

Indianapolis	7	3	8	10—28
Minnesota	7	22	7	3—39

First Quarter
Ind.—Faulk 1 run (Blanchard kick), 7:01.
Min.—Carter 16 pass from Cunningham (Murray kick), 11:11.

Second Quarter
Min.—FG, Murray 29, 0:03.
Ind.—FG, Blanchard 27, 7:57.
Min.—Carter 3 pass from Cunningham (Murray kick), 9:24.
Min.—Hoard 6 run (kick blocked), 11:05.
Min.—Glover 14 pass from Cunningham (pass failed), 13:58.

Third Quarter
Ind.—Faulk 3 run (Harrison pass from Harbaugh), 8:44.
Min.—Carter 13 pass from Cunningham (Murray kick), 12:05.

Fourth Quarter
Ind.—FG, Blanchard 21, 0:46.
Ind.—Harrison 2 pass from Harbaugh (Blanchard kick), 6:35.
Min.—FG, Murray 25, 12:40.
Attendance—54,107.

TEAM STATISTICS

	Indianapolis	Minnesota
First downs	21	17
Rushes-yards	34-132	30-180
Passing	166	165
Punt returns	2-14	2-16
Kickoff returns	7-129	6-154
Interception returns	3-39	3-48
Comp.-att.-int.	20-35-3	13-27-3
Sacked-yards lost	4-30	1-9
Punts	3-45	3-44
Fumbles-lost	2-2	0-0
Penalties-yards	3-25	8-40
Time of possession	33:48	26:12

INDIVIDUAL STATISTICS
RUSHING—Indianapolis, Faulk 23-102, Harbaugh 3-14, Crockett 3-13, Groce 3-3, Holcomb 3-3. Minnesota, R. Smith 17-160, Hoard 6-19, Cunningham 6-(minus 1), Evans 1-2.
PASSING—Indianapolis, Harbaugh 15-27-0-167, Holcomb 5-8-3-29. Minnesota, Cunningham 13-27-3-174.
RECEIVING—Indianapolis, Dawkins 7-66, Harrison 7-65, Faulk 3-23, Doering 2-12, Stablein 1-30. Minnesota, Carter 5-89, Glover 3-36, R. Smith 2-15, Reed 1-21, DeLong 1-12, Evans 1-1.
MISSED FIELD GOAL ATTEMPTS—None.
INTERCEPTIONS—Indianapolis, Belser 1-34, Coryatt 1-3, Morrison 1-2. Minnesota, Griffith 2-26, Fuller 1-22.
KICKOFF RETURNS—Indianapolis, Jacquet 7-129. Minnesota, Palmer 6-154.
PUNT RETURNS—Indianapolis, Jacquet 2-14. Minnesota, Palmer 2-16.
SACKS—Indianapolis, Blackmon 1. Minnesota, Randle 2, Rudd 1, Clemons 1.

CHIEFS 25, SAINTS 13

Sunday, December 21

New Orleans	0	0	7	6—13
Kansas City	3	9	0	13—25

First Quarter
K.C.—FG, Stoyanovich 30, 11:27.

Second Quarter
K.C.—FG, Stoyanovich 25, 6:33.
K.C.—Vanover 82 punt return (pass failed), 9:13.

Third Quarter
N.O.—Poole 32 pass from Hobert (Brien kick), 9:03.

Fourth Quarter
K.C.—Allen 3 run (pass failed), 3:39.
K.C.—Popson 3 pass from Gannon (Stoyanovich kick), 5:29.
N.O.—Poole 14 pass from Wuerffel (run failed), 12:37.
Attendance—66,772.

TEAM STATISTICS

	New Orleans	Kansas City
First downs	17	14
Rushes-yards	25-103	41-156
Passing	149	20
Punt returns	3-25	2-130
Kickoff returns	6-143	2-43
Interception returns	0-0	3-62
Comp.-att.-int.	13-29-3	9-19-0
Sacked-yards lost	2-10	3-30
Punts	4-47	6-36
Fumbles-lost	2-2	1-0
Penalties-yards	3-14	9-80
Time of possession	26:51	33:09

INDIVIDUAL STATISTICS

RUSHING—New Orleans, Zellars 18-47, T. Davis 5-41, Hobert 1-15, Wuerffel 1-0. Kansas City, Bennett 10-37, Hill 10-32, Allen 9-50, Grbac 4-18, Anders 3-4, Richardson 2-11, Tolliver 2-(minus 1), Aguiar 1-5.

PASSING—New Orleans, Hobert 11-25-3-141, Wuerffel 2-4-0-18. Kansas City, Grbac 5-14-0-51, Gannon 3-4-0-7, Tolliver 1-1-0-(minus 8).

RECEIVING—New Orleans, Guliford 4-53, Poole 3-49, Hastings 3-34, I. Smith 1-13, Zellars 1-6, T. Davis 1-4. Kansas City, Anders 4-26, Popson 2-15, Gonzalez 1-9, Allen 1-5, Bennett 1-(minus 1).

MISSED FIELD GOAL ATTEMPTS—New Orleans, Brien 41.

INTERCEPTIONS—Kansas City, McMillian 2-62, Woods 1-0.

KICKOFF RETURNS—New Orleans, Guliford 5-132, McCrary 1-11. Kansas City, Horn 1-25, Vanover 1-18.

PUNT RETURNS—New Orleans, Guliford 3-25. Kansas City, Vanover 2-130.

SACKS—New Orleans, Fields 2, Tubbs 1. Kansas City, Williams 1, Thomas 1.

REDSKINS 35, EAGLES 32

Sunday, December 21

Philadelphia	7	7	3	15	—32
Washington	14	14	0	7	—35

First Quarter

Was.—Pounds 18 fumble return (Jacke kick), 1:30.
Was.—D. Green 83 interception return (Jacke kick), 10:03.
Phi.—Dunn 31 pass from Hoying (Boniol kick), 11:42.

Second Quarter

Was.—Davis 1 run (Jacke kick), 0:54.
Phi.—Garner 9 run (Boniol kick), 4:21.
Was.—Bowie 3 run (Jacke kick), 9:19.

Third Quarter

Phi.—FG, Boniol 33, 9:48.

Fourth Quarter

Phi.—Garner 1 run (Solomon pass from Hoying), 8:19.
Was.—Westbrook 7 pass from Hostetler (Jacke kick), 10:00.
Phi.—Solomon 14 pass from Hoying (Boniol kick), 13:51.
Attendance—75,939.

TEAM STATISTICS

	Philadelphia	Washington
First downs	24	17
Rushes-yards	36-193	20-78
Passing	208	143
Punt returns	2-17	1-31
Kickoff returns	6-154	5-111
Interception returns	2-26	1-83
Comp.-att.-int.	21-31-1	16-24-2
Sacked-yards lost	6-47	2-17
Punts	3-39	3-47
Fumbles-lost	2-2	2-0
Penalties-yards	7-72	2-20
Time of possession	35:16	24:44

INDIVIDUAL STATISTICS

RUSHING—Philadelphia, Garner 18-115, Watters 8-30, Staley 6-30, Turner 2-16, Hoying 2-2. Washington, Davis 12-65, Hostetler 4-0, Bowie 3-23, Mitchell 1-(minus 10).

PASSING—Philadelphia, Hoying 21-31-1-255. Washington, Hostetler 16-23-2-160, T. Green 0-1-0-0.

RECEIVING—Philadelphia, Turner 6-44, Fryar 4-65, Solomon 3-30, Garner 3-23, C. Jones 2-40, Staley 2-22, Dunn 1-31. Washington, Westbrook 5-58, Asher 4-45, Bowie 2-21, Davis 2-(minus 3), Mitchell 1-18, Connell 1-14, Thomas 1-7.

MISSED FIELD GOAL ATTEMPTS—None.

INTERCEPTIONS—Philadelphia, Vincent 1-14, Dawkins 1-12. Washington, D. Green 1-83.

KICKOFF RETURNS—Philadelphia, Staley 3-114, Dunn 2-32, Turner 1-8. Washington, Mitchell 5-111.

PUNT RETURNS—Philadelphia, Gray 2-17. Washington, Mitchell 1-31.

SACKS—Philadelphia, Mamula 1, H. Thomas 1. Washington, Harvey 2, Pounds 1, Dishman 1, Jones 1, Lang 0.5, Owens 0.5.

GIANTS 20, COWBOYS 7

Sunday, December 21

N.Y. Giants	10	10	0	0	—20
Dallas	0	0	7	0	— 7

First Quarter

NYG—FG, Daluiso 28, 5:16.
NYG—Calloway 21 pass from Kanell (Daluiso kick), 14:29.

Second Quarter

NYG—FG, Daluiso 42, 7:01.
NYG—Hampton 1 run (Daluiso kick), 13:41.

Third Quarter

Dal.—E. Smith 4 run (Cunningham kick), 1:03.
Attendance—63,746.

TEAM STATISTICS

	N.Y. Giants	Dallas
First downs	17	11
Rushes-yards	44-147	21-79
Passing	136	105
Punt returns	2-23	6-75
Kickoff returns	0-0	3-70
Interception returns	1-0	0-0
Comp.-att.-int.	10-25-0	17-32-1
Sacked-yards lost	3-7	4-31
Punts	8-40	7-42
Fumbles-lost	2-1	2-2
Penalties-yards	4-50	9-88
Time of possession	35:11	24:49

INDIVIDUAL STATISTICS

RUSHING—New York, Barber 17-82, Hampton 12-38, Way 7-15, Lane 5-13, Pegram 2-(minus 1), Brown 1-0. Dallas, E. Smith 13-40, S. Williams 6-39, Aikman 1-0, Wilson 1-0.

PASSING—New York, Kanell 8-16-0-129, Brown 2-9-0-14. Dallas, Aikman 6-16-1-73, Garrett 10-14-0-56, Wilson 1-2-0-7.

RECEIVING—New York, Calloway 3-74, Patten 2-47, Toomer 2-14, Way 1-5, Barber 1-2, Pierce 1-1. Dallas, Miller 5-49, LaFleur 3-11, Walker 2-16, St. Williams 2-16, Irvin 2-13, E. Smith 1-15, Galbraith 1-11, S. Williams 1-5.

MISSED FIELD GOAL ATTEMPTS—New York, Daluiso 38. Dallas, Cunningham 44.

INTERCEPTIONS—New York, Sehorn 1-0.

KICKOFF RETURNS—Dallas, Walker 2-36, Marion 1-34.

PUNT RETURNS—New York, Toomer 2-23. Dallas, Mathis 6-75.

SACKS—New York, Harris 1, Agnew 1, Holsey 1, Edwards 1. Dallas, Hennings 2, Pittman 1.

OILERS 16, STEELERS 6

Sunday, December 21

Pittsburgh	3	0	0	3	— 6
Tennessee	3	10	3	0	—16

First Quarter

Ten.—FG, Del Greco 34, 5:49.
Pit.—FG, N. Johnson 23, 13:56.

Second Quarter

Ten.—Thomas 25 run (Del Greco kick), 6:03.
Ten.—FG, Del Greco 29, 14:49.

Third Quarter

Ten.—FG, Del Greco 26, 12:03.

Fourth Quarter

Pit.—FG, N. Johnson 36, 3:29.
Attendance—50,677.

TEAM STATISTICS

	Pittsburgh	Tennessee
First downs	19	14
Rushes-yards	36-93	29-156
Passing	176	85
Punt returns	0-0	1-22
Kickoff returns	5-74	3-61
Interception returns	1-0	1-9
Comp.-att.-int.	14-27-1	10-26-1
Sacked-yards lost	0-0	2-17
Punts	4-40	4-38

	Pittsburgh	Tennessee
Fumbles-lost	4-2	0-0
Penalties-yards	4-25	6-45
Time of possession	34:38	25:22

INDIVIDUAL STATISTICS

RUSHING—Pittsburgh, G. Jones 16-21, McAfee 10-27, Stewart 5-20, Witman 2-3, Tomczak 1-17, Blackwell 1-3, Marsh 1-2. Tennessee, E. George 16-25, McNair 7-90, Thomas 6-41.

PASSING—Pittsburgh, Stewart 6-16-1-87, Tomczak 8-11-0-89. Tennessee, McNair 10-26-1-102.

RECEIVING—Pittsburgh, Thigpen 6-84, C. Johnson 4-30, McAfee 2-44, Sadowski 1-12, Marsh 1-6. Tennessee, Mason 3-47, Kent 2-24, Wycheck 2-16, Davis 1-11, Sanders 1-4, Thomas 1-0.

MISSED FIELD GOAL ATTEMPTS—None.

INTERCEPTIONS—Pittsburgh, Scott 1-0. Tennessee, Bowden 1-9.

KICKOFF RETURNS—Pittsburgh, Blackwell 2-43, Coleman 2-31, Vrabel 1-0. Tennessee, Thomas 3-61.

PUNT RETURNS—Tennessee, Mason 1-22.

SACKS—Pittsburgh, Conley 1, Gildon 0.5, Oldham 0.5.

LIONS 13, JETS 10

Sunday, December 21

N.Y. Jets	10	0	0	0—10
Detroit	0	3	3	7—13

First Quarter
NYJ—FG, Hall 32, 7:33.
NYJ—Murrell 14 run (Hall kick), 11:48.

Second Quarter
Det.—FG, Hanson 44, 15:00.

Third Quarter
Det.—FG, Hanson 25, 4:15.

Fourth Quarter
Det.—Sanders 15 run (Hanson kick), 1:49.
Attendance—77,624.

TEAM STATISTICS
	N.Y. Jets	Detroit
First downs	20	13
Rushes-yards	23-108	31-206
Passing	207	95
Punt returns	5-38	3-27
Kickoff returns	3-74	2-49
Interception returns	0-0	3-29
Comp.-att.-int.	24-40-3	15-28-0
Sacked-yards lost	4-23	3-27
Punts	6-39	8-41
Fumbles-lost	0-0	1-0
Penalties-yards	5-40	5-36
Time of possession	33:48	26:12

INDIVIDUAL STATISTICS

RUSHING—New York, Murrell 12-43, L. Johnson 4-10, Lucas 3-30, Anderson 3-6, O'Donnell 1-19. Detroit, Sanders 23-184, Mitchell 5-12, Vardell 2-7, Rivers 1-3.

PASSING—New York, O'Donnell 21-35-1-202, Lucas 3-4-1-28, L. Johnson 0-1-1-0. Detroit, Mitchell 15-28-0-122.

RECEIVING—New York, K. Johnson 6-59, Chrebet 4-67, Baxter 4-32, Murrell 4-15, Brady 3-34, Graham 2-26, Anderson 1-(minus 3). Detroit, Moore 4-39, T. Boyd 3-24, Sanders 3-10, Morton 2-13, Sloan 1-19, Vardell 1-11, McCorvey 1-6.

MISSED FIELD GOAL ATTEMPTS—None.

INTERCEPTIONS—Detroit, Rice 1-18, Carrier 1-11, Westbrook 1-0.

KICKOFF RETURNS—New York, Glenn 3-74. Detroit, Milburn 1-26, Rivers 1-23.

PUNT RETURNS—New York, L. Johnson 5-38. Detroit, Milburn 3-27.

SACKS—New York, Ferguson 2, Green 1. Detroit, Rice 1, Porcher 1, Elliss 1, Scroggins 1.

BRONCOS 38, CHARGERS 3

Sunday, December 21

San Diego	3	0	0	0—3
Denver	0	24	7	7—38

First Quarter
S.D.—FG, G. Davis 26, 11:31.

Second Quarter
Den.—R. Smith 11 pass from Elway (Elam kick), 1:22.
Den.—R. Smith 15 pass from Elway (Elam kick), 5:55.
Den.—McCaffrey 1 pass from Elway (Elam kick), 10:51.
Den.—FG, Elam 25, 14:47.

Third Quarter
Den.—Sharpe 68 pass from Elway (Elam kick), 0:23.

Fourth Quarter
Den.—Loville 6 run (Elam kick), 10:25.
Attendance—69,632.

TEAM STATISTICS
	San Diego	Denver
First downs	9	24
Rushes-yards	23-70	33-130
Passing	133	321
Punt returns	1-3	2-40
Kickoff returns	7-159	2-58
Interception returns	1-7	1-20
Comp.-att.-int.	15-28-1	23-35-1
Sacked-yards lost	2-14	0-0
Punts	6-46	2-53
Fumbles-lost	0-0	0-0
Penalties-yards	6-41	5-43
Time of possession	27:17	32:43

INDIVIDUAL STATISTICS

RUSHING—San Diego, Bynum 10-34, Brown 8-27, Whelihan 3-5, Craver 2-4. Denver, Loville 14-66, Hebron 12-47, Brister 4-2, D. Smith 2-11, Griffith 1-4.

PASSING—San Diego, Whelihan 15-28-1-147. Denver, Elway 17-26-1-273, Brister 6-9-0-48.

RECEIVING—San Diego, Martin 4-46, Metcalf 3-52, Brown 2-16, C. Jones 2-13, Bynum 2-4, Still 1-10, Craver 1-6. Denver, Sharpe 8-162, R. Smith 4-53, McCaffrey 4-32, Hebron 2-41, Loville 2-10, Green 1-12, D. Smith 1-9, Carswell 1-2.

MISSED FIELD GOAL ATTEMPTS—None.

INTERCEPTIONS—San Diego, Seau 1-7. Denver, Atwater 1-20.

KICKOFF RETURNS—San Diego, Bynum 6-133, Craver 1-26. Denver, Hebron 1-31, Loville 1-27.

PUNT RETURNS—San Diego, Metcalf 1-3. Denver, Gordon 2-40.

SACKS—Denver, Pryce 1, Williams 1.

CARDINALS 29, FALCONS 26

Sunday, December 21

Atlanta	14	3	3	6—26
Arizona	7	7	0	15—29

First Quarter
Atl.—Emanuel 38 pass from Chandler (Andersen kick), 1:40.
Ariz.—Gedney 1 pass from Plummer (Nedney kick), 7:13.
Atl.—Mathis 17 pass from Chandler (Andersen kick), 13:55.

Second Quarter
Atl.—FG, Andersen 25, 6:52.
Ariz.—Plummer 1 run (Nedney kick), 12:02.

Third Quarter
Atl.—FG, Andersen 31, 9:02.

Fourth Quarter
Atl.—FG, Andersen 20, 0:04.
Atl.—FG, Andersen 26, 6:19.
Ariz.—R. Moore 21 pass from Plummer (Nedney kick), 10:05.
Ariz.—Centers 1 pass from Plummer (Plummer run), 14:55.
Attendance—32,003.

TEAM STATISTICS
	Atlanta	Arizona
First downs	22	20
Rushes-yards	40-189	18-66
Passing	167	231
Punt returns	2-32	0-0
Kickoff returns	3-53	7-207
Interception returns	2-15	1-0
Comp.-att.-int.	13-20-1	19-39-2
Sacked-yards lost	3-9	2-6
Punts	2-35	4-46
Fumbles-lost	1-0	0-0
Penalties-yards	6-53	9-75
Time of possession	36:29	23:31

INDIVIDUAL STATISTICS

RUSHING—Atlanta, Anderson 33-152, Chandler 5-35, Christian 1-2, Green 1-0. Arizona, R. Moore 10-36, Centers 3-20, Plummer 3-8, C. Smith 1-2, McElroy 1-0.

PASSING—Atlanta, Chandler 13-19-0-176, Anderson 0-1-1-0. Arizona, Plummer 19-39-2-237.

RECEIVING—Atlanta, Emanuel 5-75, Anderson 4-36, Mathis 3-49, Kozlowski 1-16. Arizona, R. Moore 7-91, Sanders 4-82, Centers 4-32, K. Williams 2-25, Carter 1-6, Gedney 1-1.

MISSED FIELD GOAL ATTEMPTS—None.
INTERCEPTIONS—Atlanta, White 1-11, C. Smith 1-4. Arizona, Bennett 1-0.
KICKOFF RETURNS—Atlanta, Hanspard 3-53. Arizona, K. Williams 7-207.
PUNT RETURNS—Atlanta, Kinchen 2-32.
SACKS—Atlanta, Owens 2. Arizona, M. Smith 2, McKinnon 1.

BENGALS 16, RAVENS 14

Sunday, December 21

Baltimore	0	0	7	7—14
Cincinnati	7	0	3	6—16

First Quarter
Cin.—Battaglia 8 pass from Esiason (Pelfrey kick), 4:50.
Third Quarter
Bal.—Alexander 83 pass from Zeier (Stover kick), 4:58.
Cin.—FG, Pelfrey 44, 8:09.
Fourth Quarter
Cin.—Scott 77 pass from Esiason (kick failed), 11:19.
Bal.—Green 12 pass from Zeier (Stover kick), 13:20.
Attendance—50,917.

TEAM STATISTICS

	Baltimore	Cincinnati
First downs	15	18
Rushes-yards	17-51	29-65
Passing	304	237
Punt returns	5-25	3-7
Kickoff returns	4-83	2-45
Interception returns	0-0	0-0
Comp.-att.-int.	28-41-0	21-34-0
Sacked-yards lost	7-45	3-17
Punts	9-47	9-43
Fumbles-lost	1-0	1-0
Penalties-yards	12-100	6-45
Time of possession	27:58	32:02

INDIVIDUAL STATISTICS
RUSHING—Baltimore, Morris 13-22, Zeier 2-6, J. Lewis 1-24, Byner 1-(minus 1). Cincinnati, Dillon 24-60, Esiason 3-(minus 2), Carter 1-7, Milne 1-0.
PASSING—Baltimore, Zeier 28-41-0-349. Cincinnati, Esiason 21-34-0-254.
RECEIVING—Baltimore, Jackson 7-94, Green 7-62, Alexander 5-111, Morris 5-25, J. Lewis 3-48, Byner 1-9. Cincinnati, Scott 6-129, Dunn 5-36, Dillon 3-15, Battaglia 2-42, Carter 2-8, Hundon 1-12, Milne 1-7, McGee 1-5.
MISSED FIELD GOAL ATTEMPTS—Baltimore, Stover 44.
INTERCEPTIONS—None.
KICKOFF RETURNS—Baltimore, J. Lewis 2-44, Roe 2-39. Cincinnati, Bieniemy 2-45.
PUNT RETURNS—Baltimore, J. Lewis 5-25. Cincinnati, Myers 3-7.
SACKS—Baltimore, R. Lewis 1, Washington 1, Team 1. Cincinnati, Dixon 3.5, Shade 1, Wilson 1, Orlando 1, Francis 0.5.

SEAHAWKS 38, 49ERS 9

Sunday, December 21

San Francisco	6	0	3	0— 9
Seattle	7	14	7	10—38

First Quarter
S.F.—FG, Anderson 33, 4:35.
S.F.—FG, Anderson 40, 12:34.
Sea.—Galloway 37 pass from Moon (Peterson kick), 14:54.
Second Quarter
Sea.—McKnight 21 pass from Moon (Peterson kick), 3:55.
Sea.—Pritchard 21 pass from Moon (Peterson kick), 6:58.
Third Quarter
S.F.—FG, Anderson 23, 7:50.
Sea.—Galloway 35 pass from Moon (Peterson kick), 11:35.
Fourth Quarter
Sea.—FG, Peterson 39, 1:47.
Sea.—Kitna 1 run (Peterson kick), 12:06.
Attendance—66,253.

TEAM STATISTICS

	San Fran.	Seattle
First downs	17	24
Rushes-yards	24-125	25-124
Passing	199	283
Punt returns	1-(-1)	3-11
Kickoff returns	7-167	4-109
Interception returns	0-0	1-0
Comp.-att.-int.	18-33-1	24-33-0
Sacked-yards lost	2-17	5-37
Punts	5-36	3-45
Fumbles-lost	3-1	1-0
Penalties-yards	7-92	5-45
Time of possession	28:52	31:08

INDIVIDUAL STATISTICS
RUSHING—San Francisco, Kirby 11-47, Levy 8-61, Edwards 3-12, Brohm 1-4, Druckenmiller 1-1. Seattle, Warren 17-99, Smith 4-18, Broussard 2-7, Kitna 2-0.
PASSING—San Francisco, S. Young 7-12-0-87, Druckenmiller 5-11-1-64, Brohm 6-10-0-65. Seattle, Moon 16-25-0-232, Kitna 8-8-0-88.
RECEIVING—San Francisco, Stokes 4-50, Edwards 4-38, Fann 3-50, Owens 2-37, Levy 2-8, Uwaezuoke 1-16, Jones 1-12, Kirby 1-5. Seattle, Galloway 6-101, Pritchard 6-90, McKnight 3-52, Crumpler 3-38, Broussard 1-9, Fauria 1-9, Harris 1-9, Hobbs 1-9, Smith 1-2, Warren 1-1.
MISSED FIELD GOAL ATTEMPTS—None.
INTERCEPTIONS—Seattle, W. Williams 1-0.
KICKOFF RETURNS—San Francisco, Levy 7-167. Seattle, Broussard 4-109.
PUNT RETURNS—San Francisco, Uwaezuoke 1-(minus 1). Seattle, Davis 3-11.
SACKS—San Francisco, Greene 2, Maxie 1, Doleman 1, Barker 1. Seattle, Sinclair 2.

PATRIOTS 14, DOLPHINS 12

Monday, December 22

New England	0	0	7	7—14
Miami	3	3	0	6—12

First Quarter
Mia.—FG, Mare 50, 6:06.
Second Quarter
Mia.—FG, Mare 41, 13:41.
Third Quarter
N.E.—Grier 2 run (Vinatieri kick), 7:07.
Fourth Quarter
N.E.—Meggett 5 run (Vinatieri kick), 2:53.
Mia.—L. Thomas 8 pass from Marino (pass failed), 11:14.
Attendance—74,379.

TEAM STATISTICS

	New England	Miami
First downs	10	17
Rushes-yards	17-47	20-42
Passing	160	243
Punt returns	4-20	5-59
Kickoff returns	1-0	3-52
Interception returns	1-0	1-7
Comp.-att.-int.	18-26-1	28-44-1
Sacked-yards lost	2-13	4-32
Punts	7-47	5-44
Fumbles-lost	2-1	2-0
Penalties-yards	2-10	8-76
Time of possession	23:53	36:07

INDIVIDUAL STATISTICS
RUSHING—New England, Cullors 10-29, Meggett 3-9, Bledsoe 3-7, Grier 1-2. Miami, Abdul-Jabbar 13-33, Phillips 5-8, McPhail 1-3, Marino 1-(minus 2).
PASSING—New England, Bledsoe 18-26-1-173. Miami, Marino 28-44-1-275.
RECEIVING—New England, Jefferson 7-76, Coates 4-28, Meggett 3-29, Byars 2-25, Brisby 1-9, Cullors 1-6. Miami, L. Thomas 6-64, Abdul-Jabbar 6-60, McDuffie 4-48, McPhail 3-15, Perriman 2-29, Parmalee 2-25, Potts 2-14, Pritchett 2-11, Drayton 1-9.
MISSED FIELD GOAL ATTEMPTS—Miami, Mare 51.
INTERCEPTIONS—New England, Milloy 1-0. Miami, Buckley 1-7.
KICKOFF RETURNS—New England, Cullors 1-0. Miami, McPhail 2-29, C. Harris 1-23.
PUNT RETURNS—New England, Meggett 4-20. Miami, Buckley 4-58, McDuffie 1-1.
SACKS—New England, Johnson 1, Collins 1, Canty 1, Team 1. Miami, Gardener 1, Armstrong 1.

DENVER 42, JACKSONVILLE 17

Why the Broncos won: Their offense dominated, rolling up 511 yards against an overmatched Jacksonville defense. The Broncos rushed for a team playoff-record 310 yards and enjoyed a time of possession advantage of more than 2-1.

Why the Jaguars lost: Beside being unable to stop Denver, the Jaguars did little with the ball when they had it. Mark Brunell, who ran for 44 yards and threw for 245 in a playoff upset on the same field against the Broncos a year earlier, was held to 4 and 203, respectively, in the rematch. Natrone Means, who torched Denver for 140 yards rushing in '96, had 40.

The turning points:

1. The Broncos drove 73 yards on 15 plays on their first possession, scoring on a 2-yard run by Terrell Davis to take a 7-0 lead.

2. With the Broncos up, 14-0, and facing third-and-6 at their 12 in the second quarter, the Jaguars came after quarterback John Elway with an all-out blitz. Elway read it perfectly and unloaded a 40-yard pass to Rod Smith to get the ball near midfield. The Broncos subsequently scored their third touchdown to take a 21-0 lead.

3. After whittling the Broncos' lead to 21-17, Jacksonville had the ball at the Broncos' 16 late in the third quarter. But center Doug Widell, a former Bronco, could not hear Brunell's signal-calling because of the roar of the Mile High Stadium crowd and hiked the ball early. Brunell wasn't ready for the snap and fumbled; linebacker Allen Aldridge recovered for Denver to snuff out Jacksonville's last, best chance. Denver dominated the fourth quarter.

Notable: The Broncos set team playoff records for points and margin of victory as well as rushing yards. . . . Davis (184 yards) and Derek Loville (103) became the third pair of NFL teammates to each rush for 100 yards in the same playoff game. . . . Denver converted its first nine third-down opportunities. . . . The Broncos' offensive line was so dominant it was named NFL "player" of the week.

Quotable: Jaguars coach Tom Coughlin: "It seemed like the line of scrimmage was controlled by Denver from the midpoint of the third quarter on." . . . Broncos defensive end Alfred Williams, after the Jaguars cut a 21-0 deficit to 21-17: "The emotions were so crazy. We go from being up 21-0 to it being a four-point game and all they had was 80 yards of total offense. We got the defense together in a tight huddle on the sidelines. We promised each other that we were not going to let it happen. We just couldn't let it happen again." . . . Elway: "Going into the wind was tough. The first thing I said to myself during warmups was, 'Thank God we have a good running game.'"

BRONCOS 42, JAGUARS 17

Saturday, December 27

Jacksonville	0	7	10	0—17
Denver	14	7	0	21—42

First Quarter
Den.—Davis 2 run (Elam kick), 7:21.
Den.—R. Smith 43 pass from Elway (Elam kick), 12:23.

Second Quarter
Den.—Davis 5 run (Elam kick), 4:14.
Jac.—Means 1 run (Hollis kick), 9:51.

Third Quarter
Jac.—FG, Hollis 38, 1:27.
Jac.—Davis 29 blocked punt return (Hollis kick), 5:44.

Fourth Quarter
Den.—Loville 25 run (Elam kick), 1:39.
Den.—Loville 8 run (Elam kick), 11:17.
Den.—Hebron 6 run (Elam kick), 13:49.
  Attendance—74,481.

TEAM STATISTICS

	Jacksonville	Denver
First downs	14	28
Rushes-yards	14-50	49-310
Passing	187	201
Punt returns	1-5	1-14
Kickoff returns	7-166	3-87
Interception returns	0-0	1-0
Comp.-att.-int.	18-32-1	16-24-0
Sacked-yards lost	3-16	3-22
Punts	4-30	3-33
Fumbles-lost	1-1	3-2
Penalties-yards	9-54	9-94
Time of possession	19:01	40:59

INDIVIDUAL STATISTICS

RUSHING—Jacksonville, Means 10-40, Brunell 3-4, Stewart 1-6. Denver, Davis 31-184, Loville 11-103, Hebron 6-23, Elway 1-0.

PASSING—Jacksonville, Brunell 18-32-1-203. Denver, Elway 16-24-0-223.

RECEIVING—Jacksonville, McCardell 6-55, Smith 6-55, Stewart 3-46, Jones 1-37, Mitchell 1-7, Means 1-3. Denver, Davis 4-11, R. Smith 3-99, McCaffrey 2-33, Green 2-32, Sharpe 2-29, Griffith 2-9, Loville 1-10.

MISSED FIELD GOAL ATTEMPTS—None.

INTERCEPTIONS—Denver, Gordon 1-0.

KICKOFF RETURNS—Jacksonville, Barlow 3-118, Logan 3-44, Hallock 1-6. Denver, Hebron 3-87.

PUNT RETURNS—Jacksonville, Barlow 1-5. Denver, Gordon 1-14.

SACKS—Jacksonville, Simmons 2, Hudson 1. Denver, Gordon 1, Tanuvasa 1, Pryce 1.

1997 REVIEW Wild-card games

NEW ENGLAND 17, MIAMI 3

Why the Patriots won: They didn't play particularly well, especially on offense, but it was good enough to beat a weak Miami team. Whereas the Dolphins committed two critical turnovers, New England didn't have any, and the Patriots' defense hasseled Dolphins quarterback Dan Marino all day. **Why the Dolphins lost:** Marino was awful, something that could be attributed to his offensive teammates and the New England defense. He was just 17-of-41, was sacked four times, hurried on many other occasions and finished with a QB rating of 29.3.

The turning points:

1. After a scoreless first quarter, Pats cornerback Larry Whigham deflected a Marino pass toward teammate Chris Slade, who returned the ball 22 yards to Miami's 29. Three plays later, New England scored the first touchdown on Drew Bledsoe's 24-yard pass to Troy Brown.

2. On Miami's first possession of the second half, Marino threw his second interception. Linebacker Todd Collins returned the ball 40 yards for a touchdown and a 14-0 New England lead.

3. On the ensuing kickoff, the Dolphins surprised the Patriots by pulling off a successful onside kick, with Corey Harris recovering for Miami. But on the first play from scrimmage, Marino had the ball jarred loose by a blitzing Chris Canty, and the Patriots recovered.

Notable: The win was the Patriots' third over the Dolphins in five weeks and second in six days. Miami had just 42 yards rushing in each of the last two games. . . . After the game, many Patriots defenders said they knew the plays the Dolphins were going to run beforehand; Miami's offensive coaches apparently had changed little of the terminology from six days earlier, when the teams met in the NFL's regular-season finale. . . . Marino had his NFL-record streak of 13 consecutive playoff games with at least one touchdown pass come to an end. . . . Miami's 162 yards of total offense was its lowest ever in a playoff game. . . . New England had just one offensive drive longer than 30 yards.

Quotable: Miami coach Jimmy Johnson: "Yeah, they knew exactly what our audibles were. They were laughing at our players during the game about it." . . . Dolphins receiver O.J. McDuffie: "It was frustrating all day. We couldn't get anything going. They were running around, calling out our plays every time we tried to audible. It was like they had a headset on." . . . Dolphins receiver Charles Jordan: "Basically, their defense was better prepared for what we were doing than our offense was." . . . Bledsoe, on Marino: "Dan wasn't able to get rid of it quick because the guys were covered. I sympathize for him. It was a tough experience, but I was happy to see it."

Sunday, December 28

Miami	0	0	0	3—	3
New England	0	7	10	0—	17

Second Quarter
N.E.—Brown 24 pass from Bledsoe (Vinatieri kick), 4:33.
Third Quarter
N.E.—Collins 40 interception return (Vinatieri kick), 0:55.
N.E.—FG, Vinatieri 22, 13:02.
Fourth Quarter
Mia.—FG, Mare 38, 0:09.
Attendance—60,041.

TEAM STATISTICS

	Miami	New England
First downs	10	15
Rushes-yards	17-42	31-108
Passing	120	120
Punt returns	5-45	2-10
Kickoff returns	3-77	1-17
Interception returns	0-0	2-62
Comp.-att.-int.	17-43-2	16-32-0
Sacked-yards lost	4-21	3-19
Punts	7-37	7-37
Fumbles-lost	1-1	2-0
Penalties-yards	5-21	5-31
Time of possession	26:09	33:51

INDIVIDUAL STATISTICS

RUSHING—Miami, Parmalee 9-22, Abdul-Jabbar 5-16, McPhail 1-4, Marino 1-2, Pritchett 1-(minus 2). New England, Cullors 22-86, Grier 6-16, Bledsoe 2-4, Meggett 1-2.

PASSING—Miami, Marino 17-43-2-141. New England, Bledsoe 16-32-0-139.

RECEIVING—Miami, McPhail 5-28, L. Thomas 3-62, Parmalee 3-13, McDuffie 3-6, Perriman 1-13, Jordan 1-11, Drayton 1-8. New England, Glenn 4-57, Coates 4-25, Brown 2-32, Meggett 2-11, Jefferson 1-7, Purnell 1-4, Gash 1-3, Cullors 1-0.

MISSED FIELD GOAL ATTEMPTS—New England, Vinatieri 48, 47.

INTERCEPTIONS—New England, Collins 1-40, Slade 1-22.

KICKOFF RETURNS—Miami, C. Harris 3-77. New England, Cullors 1-17.

PUNT RETURNS—Miami, McDuffie 4-34, Buckley 1-11. New England, Meggett 1-10, Brown 1-0.

SACKS—Miami, Gardener 1, Brigance 1, Armstrong 1. New England, Johnson 1, McGinest 1, Slade 1, Canty 1.

MINNESOTA 23, N.Y. GIANTS 22

Why the Vikings won: After putting his team in a huge hole with a terrible first half, quarterback Randall Cunningham dug the Vikings out of it with a solid second half. His quarterback rating says it all: first half, 16.1; second, 91.5.

Why the Giants lost: The league's youngest team seemed to wilt under playoff pressure. After building a 19-3 halftime lead, the Giants scored just three points the rest of the way. After playing aggressively in the first two periods, they seemed to play not to lose in the final two, and failed to make many routine plays.

The turning points:

1. With his team holding a 16-point lead, Giants running back Tiki Barber fumbled on his 4 on the first possession of the second half. Minnesota recovered, and cut New York's lead to nine points on the next play on a 4-yard touchdown run by Leroy Hoard.

2. With the Giants leading, 22-13, in the final two minutes, Cunningham capped a four-play, 49-yard drive by tossing a 30-yard TD pass to Jake Reed with 1:30 left to cut the deficit to 22-20.

3. On the ensuing kickoff, an onside kick by the Vikings' Eddie Murray bounced off the chest of one of the Giants' "hands" men, wide receiver Chris Calloway. Chris Walsh pounced on the ball for Minnesota at his 39 with 1:25 left. Cunningham then drove the Vikings 56 yards in six plays to set up a 24-yard field goal by Murray with 10 seconds left.

Notable: The 16-point comeback was the fifth biggest in NFL playoff history and the largest by a road team in 25 years. . . . It was the Vikings' first playoff win in nine years and Dennis Green's first as an NFL coach (1-4). . . . It was the Giants' first loss in five wild-card playoff games. . . . Brad Daluiso tied a Giants playoff record with five field goals. . . . Minnesota held New York to 8 yards rushing (82 total yards) in the second half. ... Of Cunningham's 203 yards passing, 97 came in the last two minutes.

Quotable: Reed, who appeared to be out of bounds on his 30-yard TD reception: "If the referee called it in, it was in. A catch is a catch if they count it." . . . Giants coach Jim Fassel: "The Vikings kept fighting on every play. It's a very bitter pill to swallow. They just made the plays." . . . Green: "The victory feels great because I know a lot of guys in this business who have never been in the playoffs. I'm a lucky man."

VIKINGS 23, GIANTS 22

Saturday, December 27

Minnesota	0	3	7	13—23
N.Y. Giants	6	13	0	3—22

First Quarter
NYG—FG, Daluiso 43, 8:25.
NYG—FG, Daluiso 22, 12:40.

Second Quarter
NYG—Pierce 2 pass from Kanell (Daluiso kick), 3:27.
NYG—FG, Daluiso 41, 10:06.
Min.—FG, Murray 26, 13:13.
NYG—FG, Daluiso 51, 14:47.

Third Quarter
Min.—Hoard 4 run (Murray kick), 4:34.

Fourth Quarter
Min.—FG, Murray 26, 0:15.
NYG—FG, Daluiso 22, 7:57.
Min.—Reed 30 pass from Cunningham (Murray kick), 13:30.
Min.—FG, Murray 24, 14:50.
Attendance—77,497.

TEAM STATISTICS

	Minnesota	N.Y. Giants
First downs	16	13
Rushes-yards	28-106	36-76
Passing	187	190
Punt returns	2-23	3-11
Kickoff returns	7-121	4-43
Interception returns	0-0	1-36
Comp.-att.-int.	15-36-1	16-32-0
Sacked-yards lost	2-16	1-9
Punts	6-39	6-38
Fumbles-lost	4-2	2-2
Penalties-yards	3-21	4-28
Time of possession	27:57	32:03

INDIVIDUAL STATISTICS

RUSHING—Minnesota, R. Smith 16-40, Cunningham 7-38, Hoard 3-14, Evans 2-14. New York, Barber 17-29, Way 10-28, Hampton 8-18, Lane 1-1.

PASSING—Minnesota, Cunningham 15-36-1-203. New York, Kanell 16-32-0-199.

RECEIVING—Minnesota, Carter 6-83, Reed 5-89, Glover 2-18, Hoard 1-9, DeLong 1-4. New York, Calloway 6-53, Patten 5-86, Barber 3-31, Way 1-27, Pierce 1-2.

MISSED FIELD GOAL ATTEMPTS—Minnesota, Murray 48.

INTERCEPTIONS—New York, Sehorn 1-36.

KICKOFF RETURNS—Minnesota, Palmer 4-106, M. Williams 1-14, Wheeler 1-1, DeLong 1-0. New York, Barber 2-34, Way 1-7, Colman 1-2.

PUNT RETURNS—Minnesota, Palmer 2-23. New York, Toomer 3-11.

SACKS—Minnesota, Fisk 1. New York, Strahan 1, K. Hamilton 1.

1997 REVIEW *Wild-card games*

TAMPA BAY 20, DETROIT 10

Why the Buccaneers won: They played well on both sides of the ball, scoring the game's first 20 points and holding the Lions' high-powered offense in check. Tampa Bay linebacker Derrick Brooks had 10 tackles and cornerback Anthony Parker had eight.

Why the Lions lost: Their three biggest offensive weapons—running back Barry Sanders, wide receiver Herman Moore and quarterback Scott Mitchell—did little. Sanders was held to 65 yards on 18 carries, Moore caught four passes (none in the first half) for 44 yards and Mitchell was just 10-of-25 for 78 yards before being forced out of the game with a concussion late in the third quarter.

The turning points:

1. Leading 3-0, the Bucs drove 89 yards in 17 plays to increase their lead to 10-0 midway through the second quarter. Trent Dilfer completed a 12-yard pass to Mike Alstott and 10- and 20-yarders to Reidel Anthony before hooking up with Horace Copeland on a 9-yard touchdown pass.

2. On the Lions' next possession, Parker intercepted a Mitchell pass and returned it 19 yards to Detroit's 19, setting up Michael Husted's second field goal of the game and giving the Bucs a 13-0 lead.

Notable: The Bucs won their first playoff game since December 29, 1979, when they advanced to the NFC championship game with a 24-17 win over Philadelphia. . . . Sanders was held to fewer than 100 yards rushing for the first time since the Bucs held him to 20 yards in Week 2 (15 games earlier). Sanders had just 15 yards on six carries at halftime. . . . The Lions lost their fifth consecutive playoff game.

Quotable: Detroit coach Bobby Ross: "Offensively speaking, we never got into any kind of rhythm. Their plan was even simpler than we anticipated." . . . Bucs defensive tackle Brad Culpepper: "There's really not a plan to stop Barry; you've just always got to hustle. All week, we'd been hearing Barry this and Barry that. Maybe that was fodder for us." . . . Tampa Bay coach Tony Dungy, on the differences between Sanders and Packers quarterback Brett Favre, who shared MVP honors this season and players the Bucs face twice a year: "With Barry, sometimes like today, circumstances can take him out of the game. You can get ahead, or your offense can control the ball. With Favre, you know he's going to have the ball in his hands every play. He creates more problems to game plan for."

BUCCANEERS 20, LIONS 10

Sunday, December 28

Detroit	0	0	3	7—10
Tampa Bay	3	10	7	0—20

First Quarter
T.B.—FG, Husted 22, 9:36.

Second Quarter
T.B.—Copeland 9 pass from Dilfer (Husted kick), 4:36.
T.B.—FG, Husted 42, 8:11.

Third Quarter
T.B.—Alstott 31 run (Husted kick), 3:54.
Det.—FG, Hanson 33, 14:32.

Fourth Quarter
Det.—Vardell 1 run (Hanson kick), 7:12.
Attendance—73,361.

TEAM STATISTICS

	Detroit	Tampa Bay
First downs	18	15
Rushes-yards	27-109	32-141
Passing	198	175
Punt returns	2-5	2-8
Kickoff returns	5-140	3-52
Interception returns	1-2	1-19
Comp.-att.-int.	21-40-1	13-26-1
Sacked-yards lost	2-9	2-6
Punts	4-38	5-40
Fumbles-lost	1-0	2-1
Penalties-yards	4-20	4-25
Time of possession	28:23	31:37

INDIVIDUAL STATISTICS

RUSHING—Detroit, Sanders 18-65, Mitchell 4-20, Vardell 2-1, Rivers 1-17, Reich 1-5, Jett 1-1. Tampa Bay, Dunn 18-72, Alstott 11-68, Dilfer 2-0, Anthony 1-1.

PASSING—Detroit, Mitchell 10-25-1-78, Reich 11-15-0-129. Tampa Bay, Dilfer 13-26-1-181.

RECEIVING—Detroit, Morton 7-69, Sanders 5-43, Moore 4-44, T. Boyd 2-11, Scroggins 1-19, Vardell 1-12, Sloan 1-9. Tampa Bay, Anthony 3-62, Dunn 3-0, Thomas 2-66, Copeland 2-14, Williams 1-23, Alstott 1-12, Harris 1-4.

MISSED FIELD GOAL ATTEMPTS—None.

INTERCEPTIONS—Detroit, Rice 1-2. Tampa Bay, Parker 1-19.

KICKOFF RETURNS—Detroit, Milburn 5-140. Tampa Bay, Anthony 3-52.

PUNT RETURNS—Detroit, Milburn 2-5. Tampa Bay, Williams 2-8.

SACKS—Detroit, Elliss 1, London 1. Tampa Bay, Ahanotu 1, Jackson 1.

DIVISIONAL PLAYOFFS

DENVER 14, KANSAS CITY 10

Why the Broncos won: They played well on offense and defense and weren't intimidated by a loud crowd at sold-out Arrowhead Stadium. Terrell Davis scored both Denver touchdowns on 1-yard runs, and John Elway—though his final numbers were modest—threw no interceptions and completed key passes when needed.

Why the Chiefs lost: In the frantic final moments, their offense looked as if it were being choreographed by the Three Stooges. After Andre Rison caught a 23-yard pass from Elvis Grbac to take the ball to Denver's 28 at the two-minute warning, the Chiefs took more than 90 seconds to complete three more passes for a total of 8 yards, primarily because their receivers failed to get out of bounds. Then, needing 2 yards for a first down at Denver's 20 with 19 seconds left, Grbac lofted a fourth-down pass to a double-covered Lake Dawson in the end zone that was batted away.

The turning points:
1. In the first quarter of a scoreless game, Pete Stoyanovich kicked a 34-yard field goal for the Chiefs. But Greg Manusky was called for holding, and Stoyanovich was forced to try again, from 44 yards. He did—and missed.
2. After Kansas City took its only lead of the game on a 12-yard touchdown pass from Grbac to rookie tight end Tony Gonzalez late in the third quarter, the Broncos bounced right back, with Elway hitting wide receiver Ed McCaffrey on a crossing pattern for a 43-yard gain to Kansas City's 1. After being stopped twice, Davis scored the game's final touchdown on his third attempt.

Notable: The teams combined for just 68 rushing yards in the first half. . . . Of Grbac's first nine completions, only one was longer than 10 yards. . . . Elway (3,940) moved into second place behind Joe Montana (5,772) on the NFL's career playoff passing yardage list.

Quotable: Grbac on why the Chiefs went for broke when all they needed was 2 yards on fourth down on the final drive: "I knew it was fourth down, and we had some communication problems with the headset. I couldn't really hear, and I had to call the plays on my own. We didn't play very smart, and we couldn't make the plays when it counted." . . . Broncos linebacker Bill Romanowski on the final drive: "They (the Chiefs) were hurrying, they were scattering, they were trying to make something happen. They were rattled." . . . Elway: "It's tough to come in here and win. (Coach) Marty's (Schottenheimer) teams are always ready to play. When you play him, you know it's going to come right down to the end like it did today. And whoever makes the plays usually wins."

BRONCOS 14, CHIEFS 10

Sunday, January 4

Denver	0	7	0	7—14
Kansas City	0	0	10	0—10

Second Quarter
Den.—Davis 1 run (Elam kick), 13:04.
Third Quarter
K.C.—FG, Stoyanovich 20, 5:18.
K.C.—Gonzalez 12 pass from Grbac (Stoyanovich kick), 14:50.
Fourth Quarter
Den.—Davis 1 run (Elam kick), 2:28.
Attendance—76,965.

TEAM STATISTICS

	Denver	Kansas City
First downs	16	18
Rushes-yards	32-109	24-77
Passing	163	226
Punt returns	1-36	1-10
Kickoff returns	3-71	3-69
Interception returns	0-0	0-0
Comp.-att.-int.	10-19-0	24-37-0
Sacked-yards lost	1-7	4-34
Punts	6-36	5-46
Fumbles-lost	4-2	2-0
Penalties-yards	8-64	7-65
Time of possession	28:54	31:06

INDIVIDUAL STATISTICS

RUSHING—Denver, Davis 25-101, Griffith 4-9, Loville 2-0, Elway 1-(minus 1). Kansas City, Allen 12-37, Grbac 4-22, Anders 3-9, Bennett 3-4, Aguiar 1-3, Hill 1-2.

PASSING—Denver, Elway 10-19-0-170. Kansas City, Grbac 24-37-0-260.

RECEIVING—Denver, McCaffrey 3-56, Sharpe 2-33, R. Smith 2-19, Carswell 1-26, Green 1-19, Davis 1-17. Kansas City, Rison 8-110, Popson 5-26, Gonzalez 3-26, Dawson 2-20, Anders 2-4, Horn 1-50, Hughes 1-13, Allen 1-8, Vanover 1-3.

MISSED FIELD GOAL ATTEMPTS—Kansas City, Stoyanovich 44.

INTERCEPTIONS—None.

KICKOFF RETURNS—Denver, Hebron 2-51, Loville 1-20. Kansas City, Vanover 3-69.

PUNT RETURNS—Denver, Gordon 1-36. Kansas City, Vanover 1-10.

SACKS—Denver, N. Smith 2, Williams 2. Kansas City, Woods 1.

1997 REVIEW *Divisional playoffs*

PITTSBURGH 7, NEW ENGLAND 6

Why the Steelers won: Their defense played a solid game, giving up just two field goals and making big plays when needed. With running back Jerome Bettis shut down, quarterback Kordell Stewart stepped up, rushing for a team-high 68 yards and scoring the game's only touchdown.

Why the Patriots lost: Injuries. Running back Curtis Martin didn't play because of an abdominal tear, and tight end Ben Coates (thumb and knee) and wide receiver Terry Glenn (collarbone) were hurt during the game. New England's leading rusher was rookie Sedrick Shaw, a third-stringer who had no carries from scrimmage during the regular season.

The turning points:

1. On New England's first possession, Steelers rookie cornerback Chad Scott picked off a Drew Bledsoe pass and returned it 27 yards to Pittsburgh's 38. Stewart then completed two third-down passes to Charles Johnson before tip-toeing down the sideline on a 40-yard touchdown run.

2. With Pittsburgh clinging to a one-point lead with 3:29 left, Steelers coach Bill Cowher eschewed an almost-certain field goal on fourth down to go for a touchdown. Stewart was stopped for no gain by linebackers Ted Johnson and Tedy Bruschi, giving the Patriots both possession and momentum.

3. With Bledsoe completing six of seven passes and New England driving into scoring range in the final two minutes, Steelers rookie defensive end Mike Vrabel beat Pro Bowl left tackle Bruce Armstrong and stripped the ball from Bledsoe, forcing a fumble that teammate Jason Gildon recovered at Pittsburgh's 34 to preserve the victory.

Notable: Of Stewart's 68 yards rushing, 55 came in the first half. . . . Bettis' 67 yards was his lowest total since he had 63 against Dallas in the season opener. . . . Glenn caught five passes for 96 yards before breaking his collarbone making a third-down catch on the last play of the third quarter.

Quotable: Bledsoe: "When you score only six points, it's hard to win any game. We didn't put the ball in the end zone and we put our defense in some terrible positions. Without Curtis, we knew we weren't going to be able to go out and run it a bunch." . . . New England linebacker Todd Collins, who admitted to pulling up in his pursuit of Stewart, thinking the quarterback had been forced out of bounds: "I should have just unloaded on him, but I hesitated. Why I did that is beyond me. In a 7-6 game, that's something you'll re-live forever." . . . Steelers backup center Jim Sweeney, after the Patriots began moving the ball on offense late in the game: "I was praying on the sideline—praying for somebody to make a big play."

STEELERS 7, PATRIOTS 6

Saturday, January 3

New England	0	3	0	3—6
Pittsburgh	7	0	0	0—7

First Quarter
Pit.—Stewart 40 run (N. Johnson kick), 5:11.
Second Quarter
N.E.—FG, Vinatieri 31, 7:20.
Fourth Quarter
N.E.—FG, Vinatieri 46, 2:44.
Attendance—61,228.

TEAM STATISTICS

	New England	Pittsburgh
First downs	15	16
Rushes-yards	19-36	37-145
Passing	244	134
Punt returns	3-24	4-78
Kickoff returns	2-36	3-44
Interception returns	1-0	2-48
Comp.-att.-int.	23-44-2	14-31-1
Sacked-yards lost	2-20	2-0
Punts	7-42	9-33
Fumbles-lost	2-2	0-0
Penalties-yards	7-68	5-41
Time of possession	24:23	35:37

INDIVIDUAL STATISTICS

RUSHING—New England, Shaw 10-22, Cullors 7-18, Bledsoe 2-(minus 4). Pittsburgh, Bettis 25-67, Stewart 11-68, McAfee 1-10.

PASSING—New England, Bledsoe 23-44-2-264. Pittsburgh, Stewart 14-31-1-134.

RECEIVING—New England, Jefferson 9-104, Glenn 5-96, Brisby 3-37, Byars 2-1, Shaw 1-13, Brown 1-6, Gash 1-6, Cullors 1-1. Pittsburgh, Hawkins 4-28, Thigpen 3-54, C. Johnson 3-28, Lester 2-3, Blackwell 1-14, Bettis 1-7.

MISSED FIELD GOAL ATTEMPTS—None.

INTERCEPTIONS—New England, Israel 1-0. Pittsburgh, Scott 1-27, Kirkland 1-21.

KICKOFF RETURNS—New England, Canty 2-36. Pittsburgh, Blackwell 3-36.

PUNT RETURNS—New England, Meggett 3-24. Pittsburgh, Blackwell 4-78.

SACKS—New England, McGinest 1.5, Slade 0.5. Pittsburgh, Vrabel 1, Gildon 1.

SAN FRANCISCO 38, MINNESOTA 22

Why the 49ers won: They carved up a suspect Minnesota defense that finished 29th in the league during the regular season. Steve Young was 21-of-30 for 224 yards and a touchdown, and Terry Kirby rushed 25 times for 120 yards, both career highs. The first 10 times the 49ers had the ball, they went three-and-out only once.

Why the Vikings lost: After squeaking past a weak Giants team in the first round, they were simply overmatched in the second round. The outcome was never in doubt.

The turning points:

1. After failing to move the ball on their first possession, the Vikings were forced to punt from deep in their end. But Mitch Berger's kick traveled just 12 yards, giving San Francisco possession on Minnesota's 26. Four plays later, William Floyd scored from a yard out for the game's first points.

2. With the score tied at 7 in the second quarter, Vikings cornerback Torrian Gray was flagged for pass interference and fellow rookie Dwayne Rudd, a linebacker, was slapped with an unsportsmanlike penalty, moving the ball to Minnesota's 2. Kirby scored on a 1-yard run to give the Niners a 14-7 lead.

3. On the Vikings' next possession, linebacker Ken Norton Jr. intercepted a Randall Cunningham pass and returned it 23 yards for another 49ers touchdown.

Notable: The victory was San Francisco's team-record 11th in a row at home. . . . 49ers receiver J.J. Stokes caught a career-high nine passes. . . . San Francisco scored a season-high 38 points. . . . Kirby's 100-yard performance was only the third of his five-year career.

Quotable: 49ers tight end Brent Jones: "We thought our receivers versus their secondary was a good matchup, so we went after them. I really felt like if we protected (Young), we could really gash those guys in the secondary." . . . Young: "We just played our offense. That's us. That was kind of a nice display of who we are." . . . Norton on his interception return: "It was strange. I had the tight end covered so well, you really don't think he's going to throw it in there." . . . 49ers coach Steve Mariucci: "It's what we hoped for, what we expected, what we all set out to do way back when. There's still more out there in front of us." . . . 49ers linebacker Gary Plummer on critics of the team's "soft" schedule: "Before we played Minnesota the first time this year, (Vikings coach) Denny Green said our schedule has been nothing but hiccups and giggles. So what I want to know is what was Minnesota—the hiccup or the giggle?"

49ERS 38, VIKINGS 22

Saturday, January 3

Minnesota	7	0	7	8—22
San Francisco	7	14	10	7—38

First Quarter
S.F.—Floyd 1 run (Anderson kick), 6:57.
Min.—Carter 66 pass from Cunningham (Murray kick), 7:34.

Second Quarter
S.F.—Kirby 1 run (Anderson kick), 8:32.
S.F.—Norton 23 interception return (Anderson kick), 9:19.

Third Quarter
S.F.—FG, Anderson 34, 6:43.
Min.—Carter 3 pass from Cunningham (Murray kick), 9:47.
S.F.—Owens 15 pass from S. Young (Anderson kick), 13:00.

Fourth Quarter
S.F.—Kirby 1 run (Anderson kick), 7:28.
Min.—Hatchette · 13 pass from Cunningham (Walsh pass from Cunningham), 11:13.
Attendance—65,018.

TEAM STATISTICS

	Minnesota	San Francisco
First downs	16	31
Rushes-yards	16-57	41-175
Passing	321	219
Punt returns	4-22	0-0
Kickoff returns	5-109	2-28
Interception returns	0-0	1-23
Comp.-att.-int.	18-40-1	21-30-0
Sacked-yards lost	1-10	1-5
Punts	7-30	6-39
Fumbles-lost	1-0	0-0
Penalties-yards	12-91	7-69
Time of possession	21:56	38:04

INDIVIDUAL STATISTICS

RUSHING—Minnesota, R. Smith 8-33, Hoard 5-11, Cunningham 2-14, Evans 1-(minus 1). San Francisco, Kirby 25-120, Levy 9-5, S. Young 4-37, Floyd 3-13.

PASSING—Minnesota, Cunningham 18-40-1-331. San Francisco, S. Young 21-30-0-224.

RECEIVING—Minnesota, Carter 6-93, Reed 5-114, Glover 3-84, R. Smith 3-27, Hatchette 1-13. San Francisco, Stokes 9-101, Owens 4-49, Jones 3-39, Kirby 3-24, Levy 1-6, Floyd 1-5.

MISSED FIELD GOAL ATTEMPTS—None.

INTERCEPTIONS—San Francisco, Norton 1-23.

KICKOFF RETURNS—Minnesota, Palmer 5-109. San Francisco, Levy 2-28.

PUNT RETURNS—Minnesota, Palmer 4-22.

SACKS—Minnesota, Randle 1. San Francisco, Barker 1.

1997 REVIEW Divisional playoffs

GREEN BAY 21, TAMPA BAY 7

Why the Packers won: On a day their offense was rusty from a one-week layoff, the Green Bay defense was terrific, forcing Tampa Bay quarterback Trent Dilfer to go 11-of-36 with two interceptions.

Why the Buccaneers lost: They went 0-for-3 in field-goal opportunities early in the game, when they were clearly outplaying the Packers and had a chance to take the lead. One field-goal attempt was blocked, a high snap foiled another, and the Bucs failed to pick up a first down on a shovel pass on a fake field-goal attempt.

The turning points:

1. After defensive tackle Warren Sapp forced a fumble by Packers running back Dorsey Levens and recovered the ball himself at Green Bay's 30, the Bucs botched their third field-goal attempt when Dave Moore's snap sailed over the head of holder Steve Walsh.

2. With the Packers leading 10-0 late in the first half, Tyrone Williams picked off a Dilfer pass and returned it 14 yards to the Bucs' 27. Seven plays later, Ryan Longwell kicked a 32-yard field goal to increase the lead to 13-0.

3. After the Bucs cut the Packers' lead to 13-7 late in the third period, Green Bay responded with a nine-play, 54-yard drive to put the game away. Favre completed two third-down passes to keep the drive alive: a 13-yarder to Levens on third-and-6 and a 23-yarder to a diving Derrick Mayes on third-and-18.

Notable: Levens' 112 yards rushing was a Green Bay playoff record. . . . Sapp finished with seven tackles, three sacks, two forced fumbles and a fumble recovery. . . . The Packers haven't allowed a touchdown pass in 27 quarters. . . . Of Dilfer's 200 yards passing, 80 came on two passes in a 94-yard scoring drive. . . . Green Bay's Antonio Freeman had a 90-yard kickoff return for a touchdown called back because of a holding penalty.

Quotable: Favre on the talking he did with Sapp throughout the game: "It was a friendly conversation most of the time. It was out of respect. He said, 'I'm going to chase you down all day, get used to seeing me.' I said, 'OK.' What could I say? He was back there all day." . . . Bucs coach Tony Dungy on the early field-goal problems: "We wanted nine points and got none. That was the story of the day." . . . Sapp on the end of the Buccaneers' season: "There is no crying going on in this locker room. We know we can build on it. This team is strong in every phase. We just weren't up to the challenge."

PACKERS 21, BUCCANEERS 7

Sunday, January 4

Tampa Bay	0	0	7	0— 7
Green Bay	7	6	0	8—21

First Quarter
G.B.—Chmura 3 pass from Favre (Longwell kick), 9:24.
Second Quarter
G.B.—FG, Longwell 21, 13:08.
G.B.—FG, Longwell 32, 14:58.
Third Quarter
T.B.—Alstott 6 run (Husted kick), 8:43.
Fourth Quarter
G.B.—Levens 2 run (Favre run), 1:23.
Attendance—60,327.

TEAM STATISTICS

	Tampa Bay	Green Bay
First downs	15	16
Rushes-yards	27-90	32-118
Passing	173	171
Punt returns	1-21	3-47
Kickoff returns	5-78	2-36
Interception returns	2-0	2-27
Comp.-att.-int.	12-37-2	15-28-2
Sacked-yards lost	2-27	4-19
Punts	4-42	5-43
Fumbles-lost	2-0	3-1
Penalties-yards	3-38	7-90
Time of possession	27:57	32:03

INDIVIDUAL STATISTICS

RUSHING—Tampa Bay, Dunn 18-64, Alstott 7-21, Anthony 1-5, Walsh 1-0. Green Bay, Levens 25-112, Favre 5-2, Henderson 2-4.

PASSING—Tampa Bay, Dilfer 11-36-2-200, Walsh 1-1-0-0. Green Bay, Favre 15-28-2-190.

RECEIVING—Tampa Bay, Copeland 4-44, Moore 3-54, Dunn 2-34, Anthony 1-52, Thomas 1-16, Davis 1-0. Green Bay, Freeman 4-75, Levens 4-29, Mayes 2-37, Chmura 2-20, Henderson 2-8, R. Brooks 1-21.

MISSED FIELD GOAL ATTEMPTS—Tampa Bay, Husted 43.

INTERCEPTIONS—Tampa Bay, Abraham 2-0. Green Bay, Ty. Williams 1-14, Prior 1-13.

KICKOFF RETURNS—Tampa Bay, Anthony 4-68, White 1-6. Green Bay, Freeman 2-36.

PUNT RETURNS—Tampa Bay, Anthony 1-21. Green Bay, R. Brooks 3-47.

SACKS—Tampa Bay, Sapp 3, Culpepper 1. Green Bay, Butler 1, McKenzie 1.

CONFERENCE CHAMPIONSHIPS

DENVER 24, PITTSBURGH 21

Why the Broncos won: Running back Terrell Davis and quarterback John Elway were superb, rallying Denver from an early deficit to its first AFC championship in eight years. Davis ran for 139 yards on 26 carries against the NFL's top-ranked rushing defense and Elway completed one key pass after another, especially late in the first half and late in the game.

Why the Steelers lost: Besides being unable to stop Davis and Elway, quarterback Kordell Stewart was dreadful. He committed four turnovers (three interceptions, one fumble) and looked like the first-year starting quarterback he was. You also have to wonder about the Pittsburgh coaching staff, which removed running back Jerome Bettis on many plays in the red zone.

The turning points:

1. The Steelers were leading, 14-10, in the second quarter and had the ball at Denver's 35 when Stewart inexplicably threw into double coverage in the end zone. The pass was intercepted by Broncos cornerback Ray Crockett.

2. After the Steelers drove to Denver's 5 in the third quarter, Stewart was intercepted again, this time by linebacker Allen Aldridge, killing another scoring opportunity for Pittsburgh.

3. Despite Stewart's struggles, the Steelers still had a chance if they could pin the Broncos deep in their territory and force a punt with Denver clinging to a three-point lead late in the game. But with the Broncos facing third-and-6 at their 15 with 1:46 left, Elway completed an 18-yard pass to tight end Shannon Sharpe, and Pittsburgh never got the ball again.

Notable: Denver became only the fourth of 92 wild-card teams since 1978 to advance to the Super Bowl. . . . Elway was 6-of-6 for 68 yards on back-to-back scoring drives that helped the Broncos turn a 14-10 deficit into a 24-14 lead. . . . Davis gained 43 yards on his first carry of the game and became the first player to rush for 100 yards against the Steelers since New England's Curtis Martin did it in the 1996 playoffs. . . . Elway improved his record in AFC title games to 4-1. He also became the second-oldest quarterback to lead a team to the Super Bowl. Johnny Unitas was 44 days older when he led the Baltimore Colts to Super Bowl V against the Cowboys in 1971. . . . The Steelers allowed only two rushing touchdowns at Three Rivers Stadium all season—and both were scored by Davis. . . . After winning only one road playoff game (the 1986 AFC championship game at Cleveland) in their history before the 1997 season, the Broncos had two in two weeks (Kansas City and Pittsburgh).

Quotable: Elway on the key completion to Sharpe:

"I had to make a quick decision, and fortunately it was the right one." . . . Davis: "We knew we had to run the ball to even have a chance. We were committed to the run." . . . Stewart: "I didn't play my best game. I think if I would have played my best game, we would have won." . . . Broncos defensive end Neil Smith on Stewart: "This was a big game, and he made his mistakes. He'll have his time, but his time isn't now." . . . Elway: "I'm not satisfied. We've won the AFC before. I won't be satisfied until we win the next one."

BRONCOS 24, STEELERS 21

Sunday, January 11

Denver	7	17	0	0—24
Pittsburgh	7	7	0	7—21

First Quarter
Den.—Davis 8 run (Elam kick), 5:42.
Pit.—Stewart 33 run (N. Johnson kick), 8:44.

Second Quarter
Pit.—Bettis 1 run (N. Johnson kick), 2:18.
Den.—FG, Elam 43, 6:40.
Den.—Griffith 15 pass from Elway (Elam kick), 13:13.
Den.—McCaffrey 1 pass from Elway (Elam kick), 14:47.

Fourth Quarter
Pit.—C. Johnson 14 pass from Stewart (N. Johnson kick), 12:14.
Attendance—61,382.

TEAM STATISTICS

	Denver	Pittsburgh
First downs	23	23
Rushes-yards	30-150	27-161
Passing	195	193
Punt returns	2-19	1-19
Kickoff returns	4-69	4-62
Interception returns	3-6	1-0
Comp.-att.-int.	18-31-1	18-36-3
Sacked-yards lost	2-15	3-8
Punts	5-31	4-42
Fumbles-lost	2-1	1-1
Penalties-yards	4-21	4-71
Time of possession	30:01	29:59

INDIVIDUAL STATISTICS

RUSHING—Denver, Davis 26-139, Elway 2-9, Hebron 2-2. Pittsburgh, Bettis 23-105, Stewart 3-44, McAfee 1-12.

PASSING—Denver, Elway 18-31-1-210. Pittsburgh, Stewart 18-36-3-201.

RECEIVING—Denver, R. Smith 6-87, McCaffrey 5-37, Sharpe 3-49, Griffith 2-26, Hebron 1-9, Davis 1-2. Pittsburgh, Thigpen 6-92, Hawkins 4-30, C. Johnson 3-34, Blackwell 2-19, Bruener 1-16, Lester 1-7, Bettis 1-3.

MISSED FIELD GOAL ATTEMPTS—Pittsburgh, N. Johnson 38.

INTERCEPTIONS—Denver, Braxton 1-6, Crockett 1-0, Aldridge 1-0. Pittsburgh, Kirkland 1-0.

KICKOFF RETURNS—Denver, Hebron 4-69. Pittsburgh, Blackwell 3-52, Witman 1-10.

PUNT RETURNS—Denver, Gordon 2-19. Pittsburgh, Blackwell 1-19.

SACKS—Denver, Crockett 1, N. Smith 1, Traylor 1. Pittsburgh, Kirkland 1, Bell 1.

1997 REVIEW *Conference championships*

GREEN BAY 23, SAN FRANCISCO 10

Why the Packers won: Quarterback Brett Favre and the defense were outstanding. Favre was 16-of-27 for 222 yards and a touchdown, and the Green Bay defense smothered quarterback Steve Young and the 49ers' running game.

Why the 49ers lost: The game was played on a muddy field, an apt analogy for the 49ers' performance. They never got untracked. The Niners were held to 33 yards rushing, committed 59 yards in penalties in the first half alone and began eight drives inside their 20.

The turning points:

1. With Green Bay leading, 3-0, Young hit wide receiver J.J. Stokes for a 43-yard gain deep into Packers' territory early in the second quarter. But Terrell Owens fumbled on a reverse for a 7-yard loss, and Eugene Robinson picked off a Young pass on the next play, returning the ball 58 yards to San Francisco's 28. Two plays later, Favre tossed a 27-yard touchdown pass to Antonio Freeman.

2. After the 49ers cut the Packers' lead to 10-3 on Gary Anderson's 28-yard field goal with 58 seconds left in the first half, Green Bay bounced right back, with Favre completing a 40-yard pass to Freeman with three seconds left in the half, setting up a 43-yard Ryan Longwell field goal. The Packers had their 10-point lead back and were never threatened.

Notable: Green Bay beat San Francisco for the fourth consecutive time. . . . The Packers became only the third team to eliminate the same opponent from the playoffs three consecutive years. Dallas eliminated San Francisco from 1970 through '72 and Green Bay in 1993, '94 and '95. . . . Dorsey Levens set a Packers playoff rushing record for the second consecutive game. One week after gaining 112 yards against the Buccaneers, he gained 114 against the 49ers. . . . Levens became the first back to rush for 100 yards against San Francisco this season. . . . Young completed his first 10 passes and had 198 yards passing at halftime. In the second half, he threw for only 52 yards. . . . The 49ers had a team record 11-game home-field winning streak come to an end. . . . The average start for a 49ers possession was their 17; the Packers' average was their 47. . . . Robinson's interception was only the seventh thrown by Young this season. . . . Longwell, a rookie, had been cut by the 49ers before the start of training camp.

Quotable: Young on the 49ers' performance: "I liken it to a train wreck. We were making mistake after mistake." . . . Favre on the playing conditions that deteriorated as the game wore on: "It was terrible. I feel bad for Steve, having to throw the ball in those types of conditions. It was impossible to make anything happen. So we were fortunate to have a chance to run the ball." . . . 49ers linebacker Gary Plummer: "The thing that was so distressing is that the plays (the Packers) were effective on were the things we worked on. They'd go to three wide receivers to one side and just throw that slant." . . . Robinson on his interception: "I just wanted to get to the ball. Then the more I ran, the more my legs got tired from the mud."

PACKERS 23, 49ERS 10

Sunday, January 11

Green Bay	3	10	0	10—23
San Francisco	0	3	0	7—10

First Quarter
G.B.—FG, Longwell 19, 12:12.

Second Quarter
G.B.—Freeman 27 pass from Favre (Longwell kick), 3:30.
S.F.—FG, Anderson 28, 14:02.
G.B.—FG, Longwell 43, 15:00.

Fourth Quarter
G.B.—FG, Longwell 25, 9:48.
G.B.—Levens 5 run (Longwell kick), 11:50.
S.F.—Levy 95 kickoff return (Anderson kick), 12:08.
Attendance—68,987.

TEAM STATISTICS

	Green Bay	San Francisco
First downs	19	15
Rushes-yards	32-106	18-33
Passing	219	224
Punt returns	2-27	3-2
Kickoff returns	2-37	4-134
Interception returns	1-58	0-0
Comp.-att.-int.	16-27-0	23-38-1
Sacked-yards lost	1-3	4-26
Punts	5-37	6-34
Fumbles-lost	1-0	4-1
Penalties-yards	9-62	6-64
Time of possession	31:40	28:20

INDIVIDUAL STATISTICS

RUSHING—Green Bay, Levens 27-114, Henderson 3-2, Favre 2-(minus 10). San Francisco, Hearst 8-12, Kirby 6-21, S. Young 2-1, Floyd 2-(minus 1).

PASSING—Green Bay, Favre 16-27-0-222. San Francisco, S. Young 23-38-1-250.

RECEIVING—Green Bay, Freeman 4-107, Levens 4-27, R. Brooks 3-36, Chmura 2-18, T. Davis 1-17, Mayes 1-10, Henderson 1-7. San Francisco, Owens 6-100, Stokes 6-87, Kirby 4-7, Hearst 3-14, Uwaezuoke 2-14, Clark 1-16, Jones 1-12.

MISSED FIELD GOAL ATTEMPTS—Green Bay, Longwell 47.

INTERCEPTIONS—Green Bay, Robinson 1-58.

KICKOFF RETURNS—Green Bay, Hayden 1-19, Freeman 1-18. San Francisco, Levy 3-127, Pollack 1-7.

PUNT RETURNS—Green Bay, R. Brooks 2-27. San Francisco, Levy 3-2.

SACKS—Green Bay, McKenzie 2, Harris 1, White 1. San Francisco, McDonald 1.

SUPER BOWL XXXII

AT QUALCOMM STADIUM, SAN DIEGO, JANUARY 25, 1998

DENVER 31, GREEN BAY 24

Why the Broncos won: Their offensive line was indomitable and running back Terrell Davis was unstoppable, carrying 30 times for 157 yards and scoring a Super Bowl-record three rushing touchdowns. Denver's offensive line continually pushed around Green Bay's much larger defensive line, and Davis' only mistake was a fumble on the first play of the second half that led to a Packers field goal.

Why the Packers lost: They made too many mistakes. Quarterback Brett Favre committed two first-half turnovers that resulted in 10 Denver points, and the defense—besides being unable to stop Davis—shot itself in the foot with ill-timed errors. No NFC team had committed a Super Bowl turnover in three years, but the Packers, with three, made up for it.

The turning points:

1. After the Packers scored first on a 22-yard TD pass from Favre to Antonio Freeman four minutes into the game, the Broncos bounced right back, driving 58 yards in 10 plays after Vaughn Hebron returned the kickoff 32 yards to his 42. The drive appeared stalled when John Elway threw incomplete on third-and-10 from the Packers' 46, but a holding penalty against cornerback Doug Evans kept the drive alive.

2. After Green Bay scored 10 points to erase a 17-7 Denver lead, the Broncos drove 92 yards in 13 plays to regain the lead on a 1-yard TD run by Davis. Elway and wide receiver Ed McCaffrey hooked up for a 36-yard completion to the Packers' 33, and Elway later scrambled eight yards for a first down at the 4.

3. With the game tied at 24 with 3:27 left, the Broncos took over at the Packers' 49 after a 39-yard punt by Green Bay's Craig Hentrich. Davis gained 2 yards on first down, but defensive tackle Darius Holland was penalized 15 yards for grabbing Davis' facemask, moving the ball to the Packers' 32. After a 1-yard gain by Davis, fullback Howard Griffith picked up a block by McCaffrey to turn a short pass into a 23-yard gain to the Packers' 8. Davis ran 7 yards to the 1 on the following play. The run was nullified by a holding penalty, but Davis responded with a 17-yard gallop to the same spot on the next play, setting up his 1-yard TD run.

Notable: The Super Bowl victory was the first by an AFC team since January 22, 1984, when the Raiders beat the Redskins, 38-9. . . . At 37 years, 6 months, 28 days, Elway became the oldest quarterback to win a Super Bowl. . . . The Broncos joined the 1980 Raiders as the only wild-card teams to win the Super Bowl. . . . For the first time in the game's history, both teams scored a touchdown on their first possession. . . . Elway and defensive backs Tyrone Braxton and Steve Atwater were the only players left from Denver's last Super Bowl team (1989 season). . . . Elway joined Roger Staubach, Terry Bradshaw and Joe Montana as the only quarterbacks to start four Super Bowls. . . . Including Denver's four post-

season games, Davis set an NFL record for most carries in one season with 481.

Quotable: Packers defensive coordinator Fritz Shurmur: "(The Broncos) didn't do anything really that we hadn't seen on tape. But in the last three games, their offensive line was playing as well as I had seen anyone play all year." . . . Elway on his personal Super Bowl travails (0-3 before this one): "You wonder if you're going to win or if you're going to run out of years." . . . Packers coach Mike Holmgren: "In kind of a strange way—John Elway, I've always enjoyed him. I just wished he hadn't done it against me." . . . Braxton on Favre: "We knew from watching films that he can be careless at times. We were looking for that at some point. We just wanted to disguise things the best we could." . . . Sharpe on the underdog Broncos' win: "So many people have told me, 'I can't believe the Broncos won.' Deal with it. It's history."

BRONCOS 31, PACKERS 24

Sunday, January 25

Green Bay	7	7	3	7—24
Denver	7	10	7	7—31

First Quarter
G.B.—Freeman 22 pass from Favre (Longwell kick), 4:02.
Den.—Davis 1 run (Elam kick), 9:21.
Second Quarter
Den.—Elway 1 run (Elam kick), 0:05.
Den.—FG, Elam 51, 2:39.
G.B.—Chmura 6 pass from Favre (Longwell kick), 14:48.
Third Quarter
G.B.—FG, Longwell 27, 3:01.
Den.—Davis 1 run (Elam kick), 14:26.
Fourth Quarter
G.B.—Freeman 13 pass from Favre (Longwell kick), 1:28.
Den.—Davis 1 run (Elam kick), 13:15.
Attendance—68,912.

TEAM STATISTICS

	Green Bay	Denver
First downs	21	21
Rushes-yards	20-95	39-179
Passing	255	123
Punt returns	0-0	0-0
Kickoff returns	6-104	5-95
Interception returns	1-17	1-0
Comp.-att.-int.	25-42-1	12-22-1
Sacked-yards lost	1-1	0-0
Punts	4-36	4-37
Fumbles-lost	2-2	1-1
Penalties-yards	9-59	7-65
Time of possession	27:35	32:25

INDIVIDUAL STATISTICS

RUSHING—Green Bay, Levens 19-90, R. Brooks 1-5. Denver, Davis 30-157, Elway 5-17, Hebron 3-3, Griffith 1-2.

PASSING—Green Bay, Favre 25-42-1-256. Denver, Elway 12-22-1-123.

RECEIVING—Green Bay, Freeman 9-126, Levens 6-56, Chmura 4-43, R. Brooks 3-16, Henderson 2-9, Mickens 1-6. Denver, Sharpe 5-38, McCaffrey 2-45, Davis 2-8, Griffith 1-23, Hebron 1-5, Carswell 1-4.

MISSED FIELD GOAL ATTEMPTS—None.

INTERCEPTIONS—Green Bay, Robinson 1-17. Denver, Braxton 1-0.

KICKOFF RETURNS—Green Bay, Freeman 6-104. Denver, Hebron 4-79, Burns 1-16.

PUNT RETURNS—None.

SACKS—Denver, Atwater 1.

PRO BOWL

AFC 29, NFC 24

Why the AFC won: The third quarterback it used in the game, 41-year-old Seattle starter Warren Moon, had just enough gas left to rally the AFC from a 10-point fourth-quarter deficit. Moon, who was summoned to Hawaii after Denver's John Elway asked out because of impending shoulder surgery, completed four of eight passes for 89 yards on the final drive before scoring the winning touchdown himself on a 1-yard run with 1:49 left.

Why the NFC lost: After leading or being tied for the lead for the first 51 minutes, the NFC fell apart in the last nine minutes, giving up two touchdowns and one field goal to blow the lead. Both touchdowns came after fumbles—by Bucs running back Warrick Dunn and Falcons quarterback Chris Chandler.

The turning points:
1. The NFC saw its 21-7 halftime lead shrink to seven points when Pats quarterback Drew Bledsoe and Jaguars receiver Jimmy Smith hooked up on a 14-yard TD pass early in the third quarter.
2. After the teams exchanged field goals early in the fourth period, the AFC cashed in on fumbles by Dunn, a rookie, and Chandler, a 10-year veteran, to score the game's final two touchdowns. Moon threw a 57-yard pass to Oakland's Tim Brown to set up a 4-yard TD run by Eddie George with 2:31 left, and Moon ran one yard for the game-winning TD four plays after Chandler fumbled at his own 16.

Notable: The AFC won the Super Bowl and Pro Bowl in the same season for the first time in 21 years. . . . Moon, the game's MVP, became the oldest player to score a touchdown in the Pro Bowl. He was three years and three months older than the next-oldest player (Redskins cornerback Darrell Green) and even older than his coach, Pittsburgh's Bill Cowher (40). . . . The 49ers' Steve Young threw TD passes to the Lions' Herman Moore and the Cardinals' Rob Moore to increase his career Pro Bowl total to four, the most of any player. . . . Chandler was an injury replacement for Packers quarterback Brett Favre who, like Elway, did not play because of injury. . . . The game was spiced by a fight between 49ers guard Kevin Gogan and Broncos defensive end Neil Smith early in the fourth quarter. . . . For the second consecutive year, a fan kicked a 35-yard field goal at halftime as part of a promotion to win $1 million. A year ago, it was a 26-year-old New York investment banker named Lance Alstodt. This year, it was a 32-year-old home improvement store manager from Cleveland, Tenn., named Dennis Crawford.

Quotable: Moon, who was playing for the first time since the Seahawks' season ended six weeks earlier: "I've been staying in shape since the season ended, but I haven't been throwing, so I was a little rusty." . . . Moon, who likely snatched the MVP award from Young with his big fourth quarter: "Steve played great in the first half and he was the front-runner if the NFC would have won. But I guess when you make the plays at the important time of the game, that has a lot to do with being the most valuable player." . . . Cowher: "Even though (Moon) is older than I am, I thought he could run the quarterback sneak pretty well.". . . Young, on Chandler: "Poor Chris Chandler showed up on Friday. That's not fair. He hadn't played in a month." . . . Moon, on accepting the invitation to his ninth Pro Bowl: "It's an honor, playing in the Pro Bowl. And when you have an opportunity to come over here, you don't turn it away. If I was voted in, I would be here. I guarantee you. I might not be here on time, but I'll be here."

AFC 29, NFC 24

Sunday, February 1

NFC	7	14	0	3 —24
AFC	7	0	7	15 —29

First Quarter
NFC—H. Moore 22 pass from Young (Hanson kick), 5:25.
AFC—Rison 17 pass from Brunell (Hollis kick), 14:30.

Second Quarter
NFC—R. Moore 36 pass from Young (Hanson kick), 2:50.
NFC—Levens 12 run (Hanson kick), 13:24.

Third Quarter
AFC—J. Smith 14 pass from Bledsoe (Hollis kick), 3:29.

Fourth Quarter
NFC—FG Hanson 35, :41.
AFC—FG Hollis 48, 6:09.
AFC—George 4 run (pass failed), 12:29.
AFC—Moon 1 run (pass failed), 13:11.
Attendance—49,995.

TEAM STATISTICS

	NFC	AFC
First downs	19	20
Rushes-yards	33-107	34-110
Passing	197	254
Punt returns	3-28	2-10
Kickoff returns	6-122	5-109
Interception returns	0-0	0-0
Comp.-att.-int.	14-36-0	15-33-0
Sacked-yards lost	4-15	0-0
Punts	3-36	4-40
Fumbles-lost	3-3	3-3
Penalties-yards	3-20	7-37
Time of possession	32:22	27:38

INDIVIDUAL STATISTICS

RUSHING—NFC, Dunn 11-26, Levens 6-24, B. Sanders 7-22, Alstott 4-14, Young 2-20, Chandler 3-1. AFC, George 12-43, Bettis 11-34, Davis 6-27, Metcalf 1-6, Brunell 1-2, Moon 2-0, T. Brown 1-(minus 2).

PASSING—NFC, Young 5-11-0-103, Dilfer 8-18-0-98, Chandler 1-7-0-11. AFC, Brunell 6-11-0-98, Bledsoe 5-14-0-67, Moon 4-8-0-89.

RECEIVING—NFC, Fryar 3-46, Walls 3-36, R. Moore 2-47, Carter 2-12, Alstott 1-23, H. Moore 1-22, Chmura 1-16, Dunn 1-10. AFC, T. Brown 5-129, J. Smith 2-31, Anders 2-29, Bettis 2-9, George 1-23, Rison 1-17, Coates 1-8, Metcalf 1-8.

MISSED FIELD GOAL ATTEMPTS—NFC, Hanson 44.
INTERCEPTIONS—None.
KICKOFF RETURNS—NFC, Bates 6-122. AFC, Metcalf 5-109.
PUNT RETURNS—NFC, Dunn 3-28. AFC, Metcalf 2-10.
SACKS—AFC, B. Smith 2.5, McGlockton 1.0, Sinclair 0.5.

AFC SQUAD

OFFENSE

WR—Tim Brown, Oakland*
  Yancey Thigpen, Pittsburgh*
  Andre Rison, Kansas City
  Jimmy Smith, Jacksonville
TE— Shannon Sharpe, Denver*
  Ben Coates, New England
T— Tony Boselli, Jacksonville*
  Jonathan Ogden, Baltimore*
  Bruce Armstrong, New England
G— Bruce Matthews, Tennessee*
  Will Shields, Kansas City*
  Ruben Brown, Buffalo
C— Dermontti Dawson, Pittsburgh*
  Tom Nalen, Denver
QB— John Elway, Denver*
  Mark Brunell, Jacksonville
  Drew Bledsoe, New England
  Warren Moon, Seattle
RB— Terrell Davis, Denver*
  Jerome Bettis, Pittsburgh*
  Eddie George, Tennessee
FB— Kimble Anders, Kansas City
NOTE: QB Elway replaced due to injury by Moon.

DEFENSE

DE— Bruce Smith, Buffalo*
  Neil Smith, Denver*
  Michael Sinclair, Seattle
DT— Ted Washington, Buffalo*
  Joel Steed, Pittsburgh*
  Chester McGlockton, Oakland
OLB— Bryce Paup, Buffalo*
  Chris Slade, New England*
  Derrick Thomas, Kansas City
ILB— Levon Kirkland, Pittsburgh*
  Junior Seau, San Diego
  Ray Lewis, Baltimore†
CB— Aaron Glenn, New York Jets*
  Dale Carter, Kansas City*
  James Hasty, Kansas City
SS— Carnell Lake, Pittsburgh*
  Blaine Bishop, Tennessee
FS— Darryl Williams, Seattle*

SPECIALISTS

P— Bryan Barker, Jacksonville
K— Mike Hollis, Jacksonville
KR— Eric Metcalf, San Diego
ST— Larry Whigham, New England

NFC SQUAD

OFFENSE

WR—Herman Moore, Detroit*
  Cris Carter, Minnesota*
  Rob Moore, Arizona
  Irving Fryar, Philadelphia
TE— Wesley Walls, Carolina*
  Mark Chmura, Green Bay
T— William Roaf, New Orleans*
  Todd Steussie, Minnesota*
  Erik Williams, Dallas
G— Larry Allen, Dallas*
  Randall McDaniel, Minnesota*
  Kevin Gogan, San Francisco
C— Kevin Glover, Detroit*
  Tony Mayberry, Tampa Bay
QB— Brett Favre, Green Bay*
  Steve Young, San Francisco
  Trent Dilfer, Tampa Bay
  Chris Chandler, Atlanta
RB— Barry Sanders, Detroit*
  Dorsey Levens, Green Bay*
  Warrick Dunn, Tampa Bay
FB— Mike Alstott, Tampa Bay
NOTE: QB Favre replaced due to injury by Chandler.

DEFENSE

DE— Reggie White, Green Bay*
  Michael Strahan, N.Y. Giants*
  Chris Doleman, San Francisco
DT— Dana Stubblefield, San Francisco*
  John Randle, Minnesota*
  Warren Sapp, Tampa Bay
OLB— Jessie Armstead, New York Giants*
  Ken Harvey, Washington*
  Derrick Brooks, Tampa Bay
  Lee Woodall, San Francisco
ILB— Hardy Nickerson, Tampa Bay*
  Jessie Tuggle, Atlanta
  Ken Norton Jr., San Francisco†
CB— Aeneas Williams, Arizona*
  Deion Sanders, Dallas*
  Darrell Green, Washington
  Cris Dishman, Washington
SS— LeRoy Butler, Green Bay*
  Darren Woodson, Dallas
  John Lynch, Tampa Bay
FS— Merton Hanks, San Francisco*
NOTE: OLB Harvey replaced due to injury by Woodall, CB
  Sanders replaced due to injury by Dishman, SS
  Woodson replaced due to injury by Lynch.

SPECIALISTS

P— Matt Turk, Washington
K— Jason Hanson, Detroit
KR— Michael Bates, Carolina
ST— Travis Jervey, Green Bay
  *Elected starter.
  †Selected as need player.

PLAYER PARTICIPATION

COMPLETE LIST

Player, Team	GP	GS
Abdul-Jabbar, Karim, Miami	16	14
Abraham, Clifton, Carolina	1	0
Abraham, Donnie, Tampa Bay	16	16
Abrams, Kevin, Detroit	15	4
Ackerman, Tom, New Orleans	14	0
Adams, Michael, Pittsburgh	6	0
Adams, Sam, Seattle	16	15
Adams, Scott, Atlanta	6	0
Adams, Vashone, New Orleans	5	4
Agnew, Ray, N.Y. Giants	15	0
Aguiar, Louie, Kansas City	16	0
Ahanotu, Chidi, Tampa Bay	16	15
Aikman, Troy, Dallas	16	16
Albright, Ethan, Buffalo	16	0
Aldridge, Allen, Denver	16	15
Aleaga, Ink, New Orleans	3	1
Alexander, Brent, Arizona	16	15
Alexander, Derrick, Minnesota	14	14
Alexander, Derrick S., Baltimore	15	13
Alexander, Elijah, Indianapolis	13	11
Alexander, Kevin, N.Y. Giants	14	8
Alexander, Patrise, Washington	16	0
Allen, Eric, New Orleans	16	16
Allen, Larry, Dallas	16	16
Allen, Marcus, Kansas City	16	0
Allen, Taje, St. Louis	14	1
Allen, Terry, Washington	10	10
Allen, Tremayne, Chicago	2	0
Allred, John, Chicago	15	4
Alstott, Mike, Tampa Bay	15	15
Ambrose, Ashley, Cincinnati	16	16
Anders, Kimble, Kansas City	15	14
Andersen, Morten, Atlanta	16	0
Anderson, Antonio, Dallas	16	5
Anderson, Curtis, Jacksonville	9	0
Anderson, Darren, Kansas City	11	0
Anderson, Dunstan, Miami	9	1
Anderson, Eddie, Oakland	11	1
Anderson, Flipper, Denver	4	0
Anderson, Gary, San Francisco	16	0
Anderson, Jamal, Atlanta	16	15
Anderson, Richie, N.Y. Jets	16	3
Anderson, Willie, Cincinnati	16	16
Anthony, Reidel, Tampa Bay	16	13
Araguz, Leo, Oakland	16	0
Archambeau, Lester, Atlanta	16	16
Archie, Mike, Tennessee	5	0
Armour, Justin, Philadelphia	1	0
Armstead, Jessie, N.Y. Giants	16	16
Armstrong, Bruce, N.E.	16	16
Armstrong, Trace, Miami	16	16
Asher, Jamie, Washington	16	13
Ashmore, Darryl, Washington	11	2
Aska, Joe, Oakland	7	0
Atkins, James, Seattle	13	3
Atwater, Steve, Denver	15	15
Austin, Raymond, N.Y. Jets	16	0
Autry, Darnell, Chicago	13	3
Badger, Brad, Washington	12	1
Bailey, Aaron, Indianapolis	13	4
Bailey, Carlton, Carolina	8	0
Bailey, Robert, Detroit	15	0
Baker, Myron, Carolina	2	0
Ball, Jerry, Minnesota	12	6
Ballard, Howard, Seattle	10	10
Banks, Tony, St. Louis	16	16
Bankston, Michael, Arizona	16	16
Banta, Brad, Indianapolis	15	0
Barber, Michael, Seattle	8	2
Barber, Ronde, Tampa Bay	1	0
Barber, Tiki, N.Y. Giants	12	6
Barker, Bryan, Jacksonville	16	0
Barker, Roy, San Francisco	13	12
Barlow, Reggie, Jacksonville	16	0
Barndt, Tom, Kansas City	16	1
Barnes, Derrick, New Orleans	1	0
Barnes, Tomur, Tennessee	3	0
Barnett, Fred, Miami	6	5
Barnhardt, Tommy, Tampa Bay	6	0
Barrow, Micheal, Carolina	16	16
Bartrum, Mike, New England	9	0
Bates, Bill, Dallas	16	0
Bates, Mario, New Orleans	12	7
Bates, Michael, Carolina	16	0
Battaglia, Marco, Cincinnati	16	0
Baxter, Fred, N.Y. Jets	16	9
Bayne, Chris, Atlanta	13	0
Beasley, Aaron, Jacksonville	9	7
Bech, Brett, New Orleans	10	0
Beckles, Ian, Philadelphia	9	8
Beebe, Don, Green Bay	10	0
Beede, Frank, Seattle	16	6
Bell, Myron, Pittsburgh	16	8
Bell, Ricky, Chicago	5	0
Bellamy, Jay, Seattle	16	7
Bellisari, Greg, Tampa Bay	14	0
Belser, Jason, Indianapolis	16	16
Bender, Wes, New Orleans	11	0
Bennett, Cornelius, Atlanta	16	16
Bennett, Darren, San Diego	16	0
Bennett, Donnell, Kansas City	14	1
Bennett, Tommy, Arizona	13	7
Bennett, Tony, Indianapolis	6	6
Benson, Darren, Dallas	6	0
Bentley, Scott, Den.-Atl.	3	0
Bercich, Pete, Minnesota	16	0
Berger, Mitch, Minnesota	16	0
Berry, Bert, Indianapolis	10	1
Berti, Tony, San Diego	16	16
Bettis, Jerome, Pittsburgh	15	15
Beuerlein, Steve, Carolina	7	3
Biakabutuka, Tim, Carolina	8	2
Biekert, Greg, Oakland	16	16
Bieniemy, Eric, Cincinnati	16	0
Binn, David, San Diego	16	0
Bishop, Blaine, Tennessee	14	14
Bishop, Greg, N.Y. Giants	16	16
Bjornson, Eric, Dallas	14	14
Blackman, Ken, Cincinnati	13	13
Blackmon, Robert, Indianapolis	14	14
Blackshear, Jeff, Baltimore	16	16
Blackwell, Will, Pittsburgh	14	0
Blades, Bennie, Seattle	10	9
Blades, Brian, Seattle	11	3
Blake, Jeff, Cincinnati	11	11
Blanchard, Cary, Indianapolis	16	0
Bland, Tony, Minnesota	2	0
Blanton, Scott, Washington	15	0
Bledsoe, Drew, New England	16	16
Bloedorn, Greg, Seattle	2	0
Blundin, Matt, Detroit	1	0
Bobo, Orlando, Minnesota	5	0
Bock, John, Miami	14	3
Bolden, Juran, Atlanta	14	1
Bonham, Shane, Detroit	16	0
Boniol, Chris, Philadelphia	16	0
Bono, Steve, Green Bay	2	0
Booker, Michael, Atlanta	15	3
Booker, Vaughn, Kansas City	13	13
Bordelon, Ben, San Diego	16	2
Boselli, Tony, Jacksonville	12	12
Botkin, Kirk, Pittsburgh	13	1
Bouie, Kevin, Arizona	5	0
Bouie, Tony, Tampa Bay	16	1
Boulware, Peter, Baltimore	16	16
Boutte, Marc, Washington	16	14
Bowden, Joe, Tennessee	16	16
Bowens, Tim, Miami	16	16
Bowie, Larry, Washington	15	12
Bownes, Fabien, Chicago	16	0
Boyd, Stephen, Detroit	16	16
Boyd, Tommie, Detroit	16	1
Boyer, Brant, Jacksonville	16	2
Brackens, Tony, Jacksonville	15	3
Bradford, Paul, San Diego	15	4
Bradford, Ronnie, Atlanta	16	14
Brady, Donny, Baltimore	16	5
Brady, Jeff, Minnesota	15	14
Brady, Kyle, N.Y. Jets	16	14
Braham, Rich, Cincinnati	16	16
Branch, Calvin, Oakland	6	0
Brandenburg, Dan, Buffalo	12	0
Brandon, David, Atlanta	4	4
Bratzke, Chad, N.Y. Giants	10	10
Braxton, Tyrone, Denver	16	16
Brew, Dorian, Bal.-S.D.	9	0
Brice, Will, St. Louis	6	0
Brien, Doug, New Orleans	16	0
Brigance, O.J., Miami	16	0
Briggs, Greg, Minnesota	14	0
Brilz, Darrick, Cincinnati	16	16
Brisby, Vincent, New England	16	4
Brister, Bubby, Denver	1	0
Brock, Fred, Arizona	2	0
Brockermeyer, Blake, Carolina	16	13
Brohm, Jeff, San Francisco	5	0
Bronson, Zack, San Francisco	16	0
Brooks, Barrett, Philadelphia	16	14
Brooks, Bucky, Jac.-G.B.-K.C.	9	0
Brooks, Derrick, Tampa Bay	16	16
Brooks, Robert, Green Bay	15	15
Brostek, Bern, St. Louis	1	1
Broussard, Steve, Seattle	16	1
Brown, Anthony, Cincinnati	6	0
Brown, Chad, Seattle	15	15
Brown, Cornell, Baltimore	16	1
Brown, Corwin, N.Y. Jets	16	0
Brown, Dave, N.Y. Giants	7	6
Brown, DeAuntae, Philadelphia	1	0
Brown, Derek, Jacksonville	13	8
Brown, Gary, San Diego	15	14
Brown, Gilbert, Green Bay	12	12
Brown, James, Miami	16	16
Brown, Jamie, Denver	11	2
Brown, J.B., Pittsburgh	13	0
Brown, Larry, Oakland	4	0
Brown, Lomas, Arizona	14	14
Brown, Orlando, Baltimore	16	16

Player, Team	GP	GS	Player, Team	GP	GS	Player, Team	GP	GS
Brown, Ray, San Francisco	15	15	Centers, Larry, Arizona	15	14	Crockett, Ray, Denver	16	16
Brown, Reggie, Seattle	11	0	Chalenski, Mike, Miami	8	0	Crockett, Zack, Indianapolis	16	11
Brown, Reggie D., Detroit	16	16	Chamberlain, Byron, Denver	10	0	Cross, Howard, N.Y. Giants	16	16
Brown, Ruben, Buffalo	16	16	Chancey, Robert, San Diego	6	0	Crumpler, Carlester, Seattle	15	12
Brown, Tim, Oakland	16	16	Chandler, Chris, Atlanta	14	14	Cullors, Derrick, New England	15	1
Brown, Troy, New England	16	6	Cheever, Michael, Jacksonville	6	4	Culpepper, Brad, Tampa Bay	16	16
Browning, John, Kansas City	14	13	Cherry, Je'Rod, New Orleans	16	0	Cunningham, Randall, Min.	6	3
Bruce, Aundray, Oakland	10	3	Cherry, Mike, N.Y. Giants	1	0	Cunningham, Richie, Dallas	16	0
Bruce, Isaac, St. Louis	12	12	Chmura, Mark, Green Bay	15	14	Cunningham, Rick, Oakland	7	0
Bruener, Mark, Pittsburgh	16	16	Chrebet, Wayne, N.Y. Jets	16	1	Curry, Eric, Tampa Bay	6	1
Brumfield, Scott, Cincinnati	15	3	Christian, Bob, Atlanta	16	12	Curtis, Canute, Cincinnati	3	0
Brunell, Mark, Jacksonville	14	14	Christie, Steve, Buffalo	16	0	Dafney, Bernard, Baltimore	1	0
Bruschi, Tedy, New England	16	1	Christy, Jeff, Minnesota	12	12	Dahl, Bob, Washington	11	9
Bryant, Junior, San Francisco	16	3	Chryplewicz, Pete, Detroit	10	0	Dalman, Chris, San Francisco	13	13
Buchanan, Ray, Atlanta	16	16	Chung, Eugene, Indianapolis	10	0	Daluiso, Brad, N.Y. Giants	16	0
Buckey, Jeff, Miami	16	12	Clark, Greg, San Francisco	15	4	Daniel, Eugene, Baltimore	9	6
Buckley, Curtis, San Francisco	15	0	Clark, Jon, Chicago	1	0	Daniels, LeShun, Minnesota	1	0
Buckley, Marcus, N.Y. Giants	12	3	Clark, Rico, Indianapolis	4	2	Daniels, Phillip, Seattle	13	10
Buckley, Terrell, Miami	16	16	Clark, Willie, Philadelphia	16	2	Darby, Matt, Arizona	11	7
Buckner, Brentson, Cincinnati	14	4	Clavelle, Shannon, G.B.-K.C.	7	0	Darkins, Chris, Green Bay	14	0
Burger, Todd, Chicago	15	15	Clay, Willie, New England	16	16	Darling, James, Philadelphia	16	6
Burgess, James, San Diego	15	4	Clements, Chuck, N.Y. Jets	1	0	Davey, Don, Jacksonville	10	10
Burke, John, N.Y. Jets	7	1	Clemons, Charlie, St. Louis	5	0	Davidds-Garrido, Norbert, Car.	15	15
Burnett, Rob, Baltimore	15	15	Clemons, Duane, Minnesota	13	3	Davis, Anthony, Kansas City	15	15
Burns, Keith, Denver	16	0	Cline, Tony, Buffalo	10	1	Davis, Antone, Atlanta	3	3
Burns, Lamont, N.Y. Jets	4	3	Coakley, Dexter, Dallas	16	16	Davis, Billy, Dallas	16	0
Burris, Jeff, Buffalo	14	14	Coates, Ben, New England	16	16	Davis, Don, New Orleans	11	0
Burrough, John, Atlanta	16	1	Cobbins, Lyron, Arizona	6	0	Davis, Eric, Carolina	14	14
Burroughs, Sammie, Ind.	16	1	Cocozzo, Joe, San Diego	16	12	Davis, Greg, Min.-S.D.	14	0
Burton, James, Chicago	5	1	Coleman, Andre, Sea.-Pit.	10	2	Davis, Isaac, S.D.-N.O.	15	14
Burton, Shane, Miami	16	4	Coleman, Ben, Jacksonville	16	16	Davis, John, Tampa Bay	8	2
Bush, Devin, Atlanta	16	16	Coleman, Marco, San Diego	16	16	Davis, Nathan, Atlanta	2	0
Bush, Lewis, San Diego	14	13	Coleman, Marcus, N.Y. Jets	16	2	Davis, Rob, Green Bay	7	0
Bush, Steve, Cincinnati	16	0	Colinet, Stalin, Minnesota	10	2	Davis, Scott, Atlanta	2	2
Butler, Duane, Minnesota	3	0	Collins, Andre, Cincinnati	16	0	Davis, Stephen, Washington	14	6
Butler, Kevin, Arizona	6	0	Collins, Calvin, Atlanta	15	13	Davis, Terrell, Denver	15	15
Butler, LeRoy, Green Bay	16	16	Collins, Kerry, Carolina	13	13	Davis, Travis, Jacksonville	16	16
Byars, Keith, New England	16	8	Collins, Mark, Green Bay	1	0	Davis, Troy, New Orleans	16	7
Byner, Earnest, Baltimore	16	5	Collins, Todd, Buffalo	14	13	Davis, Tyree, Seattle	13	1
Bynum, Kenny, San Diego	13	0	Collins, Todd F., New England	15	15	Davis, Tyrone, Green Bay	13	0
Byrd, Isaac, Tennessee	2	0	Collons, Ferric, New England	5	5	Davis, Wendell, Dallas	15	0
Cadrez, Glenn, Denver	16	0	Colman, Doug, N.Y. Giants	14	0	Davis, Willie, Tennessee	16	15
Cain, Joe, Seattle	11	0	Colon, Harry, Detroit	8	4	Davison, Jerone, Oakland	8	1
Caldwell, Mike, Arizona	16	0	Compton, Mike, Detroit	16	16	Dawkins, Brian, Philadelphia	15	15
Calicchio, Lonny, Philadelphia	2	0	Conaty, Billy, Buffalo	1	0	Dawkins, Sean, Indianapolis	14	12
Calloway, Chris, N.Y. Giants	16	16	Conley, Steve, Pittsburgh	16	0	Dawson, Dermontti, Pittsburgh	16	16
Campbell, Jesse, Washington	16	16	Connell, Albert, Washington	5	1	Dawson, Lake, Kansas City	11	11
Campbell, Mark, Arizona	5	0	Conner, Darion, Philadelphia	14	0	Day, Terry, N.Y. Jets	1	0
Campbell, Matthew, Carolina	16	14	Conrad, J.R., N.Y. Jets	12	1	Deese, Derrick, San Francisco	16	13
Canty, Chris, New England	16	1	Conway, Curtis, Chicago	7	7	Del Greco, Al, Tennessee	16	0
Carney, John, San Diego	4	0	Conwell, Ernie, St. Louis	16	16	Dellenbach, Jeff, Green Bay	14	5
Carrier, Mark A., Detroit	16	16	Cook, Anthony, Tennessee	16	16	DeLong, Greg, Minnesota	16	3
Carrier, J. Mark, Carolina	9	6	Cook, Toi, Carolina	16	0	DeMarco, Brian, Jacksonville	14	5
Carruth, Rae, Carolina	15	14	Coons, Rob, Buffalo	12	0	Denson, Damon, New England	1	0
Carswell, Dwayne, Denver	16	3	Copeland, Horace, Tampa Bay	13	11	Dent, Richard, Philadelphia	15	0
Carter, Chris, New England	16	0	Copeland, John, Cincinnati	15	15	Detmer, Ty, Philadelphia	8	7
Carter, Cris, Minnesota	16	16	Coryatt, Quentin, Indianapolis	15	15	Devine, Kevin, Jacksonville	12	0
Carter, Dale, Kansas City	16	15	Cota, Chad, Carolina	16	16	Devlin, Mike, Arizona	15	13
Carter, Daryl, Chicago	1	0	Cotton, Kenyon, Baltimore	15	0	Dexter, James, Arizona	10	9
Carter, Kevin, St. Louis	16	16	Cousin, Terry, Chicago	6	0	Diaz, Jorge, Tampa Bay	16	16
Carter, Ki-Jana, Cincinnati	15	10	Covington, Damien, Buffalo	8	8	Diaz-Infante, David, Denver	16	7
Carter, Marty, Chicago	15	15	Cox, Bryan, Chicago	16	15	Dilfer, Trent, Tampa Bay	16	16
Carter, Pat, Arizona	16	10	Cox, Ron, Chicago	15	13	Dilger, Ken, Indianapolis	14	14
Carter, Perry, Oakland	16	7	Crafts, Jerry, Philadelphia	15	6	Dill, Scott, Minnesota	13	5
Carter, Tom, Chicago	16	16	Craver, Aaron, San Diego	15	5	Dillon, Corey, Cincinnati	16	6
Carter, Tony, Chicago	16	10	Crawford, Keith, St. Louis	15	2	Dimry, Charles, Philadelphia	15	9
Carver, Shante, Dallas	16	16	Crawford, Mike, Miami	7	0	Dingle, Nate, St. Louis	9	0
Cascadden, Chad, N.Y. Jets	15	0	Crawford, Vernon, New England	16	0	Dishman, Chris, Arizona	8	0
Case, Stoney, Arizona	3	1	Criswell, Jeff, Kansas City	16	16	Dishman, Cris, Washington	16	15
Casillas, Tony, Dallas	15	14	Crittenden, Ray, San Diego	2	0	Dixon, David, Minnesota	13	3
Cavil, Ben, Baltimore	15	8	Crockett, Henri, Atlanta	16	10	Dixon, Ernest, New Orleans	15	0

Player, Team	GP	GS
Dixon, Gerald, Cincinnati	15	13
Dixon, Ronnie, N.Y. Jets	5	3
Dodge, Dedrick, Denver	16	1
Doering, Chris, Indianapolis	2	0
Doleman, Chris, San Francisco	16	16
Donnalley, Kevin, Tennessee	16	16
Dorsett, Anthony, Tennessee	16	0
Dotson, DeWayne, Miami	10	2
Dotson, Earl, Green Bay	13	13
Dotson, Santana, Green Bay	16	16
Douglas, Hugh, N.Y. Jets	15	15
Douthard, Ty, Cincinnati	1	0
Dowden, Corey, Chicago	2	0
Downs, Gary, Atlanta	16	0
Drake, Troy, Philadelphia	9	2
Drakeford, Tyronne, S.F.	16	2
Drayton, Troy, Miami	16	15
Dronett, Shane, Atlanta	16	1
Druckenmiller, Jim, S.F.	4	1
Dudley, Rickey, Oakland	16	16
Duff, Jamal, Washington	13	5
Duffy, Roger, N.Y. Jets	15	15
Dulaney, Mike, Chicago	7	0
Dumas, Mike, San Diego	16	15
Dumas, Troy, K.C.-St.L.	10	0
Dunn, David, Cincinnati	14	5
Dunn, Jason, Philadelphia	15	4
Dunn, Warrick, Tampa Bay	16	10
Dye, Ernest, St. Louis	13	0
Early, Quinn, Buffalo	16	16
Eaton, Chad, New England	16	1
Edwards, Anthony, Arizona	16	1
Edwards, Antonio, Sea.-NYG	4	0
Edwards, Dixon, Minnesota	16	16
Edwards, Donnie, Kansas City	16	16
Edwards, Marc, San Francisco	15	1
Elam, Jason, Denver	15	0
Ellard, Henry, Washington	16	11
Elliott, Jumbo, N.Y. Jets	13	13
Elliott, Matt, Carolina	16	6
Ellis, Ed, New England	1	0
Ellison, Jerry, Tampa Bay	16	0
Elliss, Luther, Detroit	16	16
Ellsworth, Percy, N.Y. Giants	16	1
Elway, John, Denver	16	16
Emanuel, Bert, Atlanta	16	16
Emanuel, Charles, Philadelphia	5	1
Emmons, Carlos, Pittsburgh	5	0
Emtman, Steve, Washington	3	0
Engel, Greg, San Diego	9	0
Engler, Derek, N.Y. Giants	5	5
Engram, Bobby, Chicago	11	11
Erickson, Craig, Miami	2	0
Esiason, Boomer, Cincinnati	7	5
Ethridge, Ray, Baltimore	2	0
Evans, Charles, Minnesota	16	13
Evans, Doug, Green Bay	15	15
Evans, Josh, Tennessee	15	0
Evans, Leomont, Washington	16	0
Everett, Jim, San Diego	4	1
Everitt, Steve, Philadelphia	16	16
Fann, Chad, San Francisco	11	0
Farmer, Ray, Philadelphia	14	5
Farquhar, John, New Orleans	11	8
Farr, D'Marco, St. Louis	16	16
Farrior, James, N.Y. Jets	16	15
Faulk, Marshall, Indianapolis	16	16
Fauria, Christian, Seattle	16	3
Favre, Brett, Green Bay	16	16
Feagles, Jeff, Arizona	16	0
Fenner, Derrick, Oakland	9	7
Ferguson, Jason, N.Y. Jets	13	1
Fields, Mark, New Orleans	16	15
Figures, Deon, Jacksonville	16	12
Fina, John, Buffalo	16	16
Finkes, Matt, N.Y. Jets	8	0
Fisk, Jason, Minnesota	16	10
Flanigan, Jim, Chicago	16	16
Flannery, John, Dallas	16	4
Fletcher, Terrell, San Diego	13	1
Flowers, Lethon, Pittsburgh	10	0
Floyd, Malcolm, Ten.-St.L.	5	0
Floyd, William, San Francisco	15	15
Fogle, DeShawn, Philadelphia	5	0
Folau, Spencer, Baltimore	10	0
Foley, Glenn, N.Y. Jets	6	2
Folston, James, Oakland	16	7
Fontenot, Al, Indianapolis	16	16
Fontenot, Jerry, New Orleans	16	16
Footman, Dan, Indianapolis	16	10
Forbes, Marlon, Chicago	16	1
Ford, Cole, Oakland	16	0
Ford, Henry, Tennessee	16	16
Fordham, Todd, Jacksonville	1	0
Fortin, Roman, Atlanta	3	3
Fountaine, Jamal, Atlanta	3	0
Fox, Mike, Carolina	11	9
Francis, James, Cincinnati	16	16
Frase, Paul, Green Bay	9	0
Frederick, Mike, Baltimore	16	1
Fredrickson, Rob, Oakland	16	13
Freeman, Antonio, Green Bay	16	16
Frerotte, Gus, Washington	13	13
Friesz, John, Seattle	2	1
Frisch, David, Washington	2	0
Fryar, Irving, Philadelphia	16	16
Fuller, Corey, Minnesota	16	16
Fuller, Randy, Pittsburgh	12	3
Fuller, William, San Diego	16	16
Gaines, William, Washington	13	6
Gaiter, Tony, New England	1	0
Galbraith, Scott, Dallas	16	0
Galloway, Joey, Seattle	15	15
Galloway, Mitchell, Buffalo	3	0
Galyon, Scott, N.Y. Giants	16	0
Gamble, David, Denver	2	0
Gammon, Kendall, New Orleans	16	0
Gandy, Wayne, St. Louis	16	16
Gannon, Rich, Kansas City	9	6
Gant, Kenneth, Tampa Bay	9	0
Garcia, Frank, Carolina	16	16
Gardener, Daryl, Miami	16	16
Gardner, Carwell, San Diego	5	2
Gardocki, Chris, Indianapolis	16	0
Garner, Charlie, Philadelphia	16	2
Garnes, Sam, N.Y. Giants	16	15
Garrett, Jason, Dallas	1	0
Gash, Sam, New England	16	5
Gaskins, Percell, Carolina	12	0
Gedney, Chris, Arizona	16	3
George, Eddie, Tennessee	16	16
George, Jeff, Oakland	16	16
George, Ron, Minnesota	16	0
George, Spencer, Tennessee	5	0
Gerak, John, St. Louis	16	16
Gibson, Oliver, Pittsburgh	16	0
Gildon, Jason, Pittsburgh	16	16
Gilliard, Cory, Cincinnati	1	0
Gisler, Mike, New England	16	2
Glenn, Aaron, N.Y. Jets	16	16
Glenn, Tarik, Indianapolis	16	16
Glenn, Terry, New England	9	9
Glover, Andrew, Minnesota	13	11
Glover, Kevin, Detroit	16	16
Glover, La'Roi, New Orleans	15	2
Godfrey, Randall, Dallas	16	16
Goeas, Leo, Baltimore	11	7
Gogan, Kevin, San Francisco	16	16
Gonzalez, Tony, Kansas City	16	0
Gooch, Jeff, Tampa Bay	14	5
Goodwin, Hunter, Minnesota	16	5
Gordon, Darrien, Denver	16	16
Gordon, Dwayne, N.Y. Jets	16	8
Gouveia, Kurt, San Diego	7	6
Gowin, Toby, Dallas	16	0
Gragg, Scott, N.Y. Giants	16	16
Graham, Aaron, Arizona	16	4
Graham, Derrick, Seattle	9	9
Graham, Jay, Baltimore	13	3
Graham, Jeff, N.Y. Jets	16	16
Graham, Kent, Arizona	8	6
Graham, Scottie, Cincinnati	5	0
Grant, Stephen, Indianapolis	9	9
Granville, Billy, Cincinnati	12	4
Grasmanis, Paul, Chicago	16	1
Gray, Carlton, Indianapolis	15	13
Gray, Chris, Chicago	8	2
Gray, Derwin, Indianapolis	11	0
Gray, Mel, Ten.-Phi.	14	0
Gray, Torrian, Minnesota	16	3
Graziani, Tony, Atlanta	3	1
Grbac, Elvis, Kansas City	10	10
Greeley, Bucky, Carolina	6	0
Green, Darrell, Washington	16	16
Green, Eric, Baltimore	15	15
Green, Harold, Atlanta	16	1
Green, Robert, Minnesota	3	1
Green, Trent, Washington	1	0
Green, Victor, N.Y. Jets	16	16
Green, Willie, Denver	16	1
Greene, Kevin, San Francisco	14	4
Greene, Scott, Carolina	16	14
Greer, Donovan, Atl.-N.O.	7	1
Grier, Marrio, New England	16	0
Griffith, Howard, Denver	15	13
Griffith, Rich, Jacksonville	16	1
Griffith, Robert, Minnesota	16	16
Groce, Clif, Indianapolis	7	0
Gruber, Paul, Tampa Bay	16	16
Grunhard, Tim, Kansas City	16	16
Gruttadauria, Mike, St. Louis	14	14
Guliford, Eric, New Orleans	16	2
Gutierrez, Brock, Cincinnati	5	0
Guynes, Thomas, Arizona	4	0
Habib, Brian, Denver	14	14
Hager, Britt, St. Louis	13	0
Hagood, Jay, N.Y. Jets	2	0
Halapin, Mike, Tennessee	3	1
Hall, Dana, Jacksonville	16	0
Hall, John, N.Y. Jets	16	0
Hall, Lemanski, Tennessee	16	2
Hall, Rhett, Philadelphia	15	15
Hall, Tim, Oakland	16	0
Hall, Travis, Atlanta	16	16
Hallock, Ty, Jacksonville	15	7
Hamilton, Bobby, N.Y. Jets	16	0
Hamilton, Conrad, N.Y. Giants	14	0
Hamilton, James, Jacksonville	9	0
Hamilton, Keith, N.Y. Giants	16	16
Hamilton, Michael, San Diego	6	0
Hamilton, Ruffin, Atlanta	12	0
Hampton, Rodney, N.Y. Giants	2	0
Hand, Norman, San Diego	15	1

Player, Team	GP	GS
Hanks, Ben, Detroit	2	0
Hanks, Merton, San Francisco	16	16
Hansen, Brian, N.Y. Jets	15	0
Hansen, Phil, Buffalo	16	16
Hanshaw, Tim, San Francisco	13	3
Hanson, Jason, Detroit	16	0
Hanspard, Byron, Atlanta	16	0
Hape, Patrick, Tampa Bay	14	3
Harbaugh, Jim, Indianapolis	12	11
Hardy, Darryl, Dal.-Sea.	14	0
Hardy, Kevin, Jacksonville	13	11
Harlow, Pat, Oakland	16	16
Harmon, Andy, Philadelphia	5	0
Harmon, Ronnie, Ten.-Chi.	12	0
Harper, Alvin, Washington	12	0
Harper, Dwayne, San Diego	12	12
Harris, Anthony, Miami	16	16
Harris, Bernardo, Green Bay	16	16
Harris, Corey, Miami	16	7
Harris, Jackie, Tampa Bay	12	11
Harris, Jon, Philadelphia	8	4
Harris, Kenny, Arizona	11	0
Harris, Mark, San Francisco	10	0
Harris, Raymont, Chicago	13	13
Harris, Robert, N.Y. Giants	16	16
Harris, Ronnie, Seattle	13	0
Harris, Sean, Chicago	11	1
Harris, Walt, Chicago	16	16
Harrison, Martin, Seattle	8	0
Harrison, Marvin, Indianapolis	16	15
Harrison, Nolan, Pittsburgh	16	16
Harrison, Rodney, San Diego	16	16
Hartings, Jeff, Detroit	16	16
Hartley, Frank, San Diego	16	16
Harvey, Ken, Washington	15	14
Harvey, Richard, New Orleans	14	13
Hasselbach, Harald, Denver	16	3
Hastings, Andre, New Orleans	16	16
Hasty, James, Kansas City	16	15
Hatchette, Matthew, Minnesota	16	0
Hauck, Tim, Seattle	16	0
Hawkins, Courtney, Pittsburgh	15	13
Hayden, Aaron, Green Bay	14	0
Hayes, Chris, N.Y. Jets	16	0
Hayes, Mercury, N.O.-Atl.	6	0
Haynes, Michael, Atlanta	12	0
Hearst, Garrison, San Francisco	13	13
Hebron, Vaughn, Denver	16	1
Heck, Andy, Chicago	16	16
Hegamin, George, Dallas	13	9
Hellestrae, Dale, Dallas	16	0
Hempstead, Hessley, Detroit	16	1
Hemsley, Nate, Dallas	2	0
Henderson, Jerome, N.Y. Jets	16	14
Henderson, William, Green Bay	16	14
Hendrix, David, San Diego	4	0
Hennings, Chad, Dallas	11	10
Henry, Kevin, Pittsburgh	16	16
Hentrich, Craig, Green Bay	16	0
Herndon, Jimmy, Chicago	7	0
Herring, Kim, Baltimore	15	4
Herrod, Jeff, Philadelphia	10	2
Hetherington, Chris, Ind.	16	0
Hewitt, Chris, New Orleans	11	2
Heyward, Craig, St. Louis	16	12
Hickman, Kevin, Detroit	4	0
Hicks, Kerry, Kansas City	2	0
Hicks, Michael, Chicago	3	0
Hiles, Van, Chicago	16	1
Hill, Eric, Arizona	11	10
Hill, Greg, Kansas City	16	16
Hill, Keno, New Orleans	9	6
Hill, Randal, New Orleans	15	15
Hilliard, Ike, N.Y. Giants	2	2
Hilliard, Randy, Denver	14	0
Hitchcock, Jimmy, New England	15	15
Hoard, Leroy, Minnesota	12	1
Hobbs, Daryl, N.O.-Sea.	14	0
Hobert, Billy Joe, Buf.-N.O.	7	4
Holcomb, Kelly, Indianapolis	5	1
Holecek, John, Buffalo	14	8
Holland, Darius, Green Bay	12	1
Holliday, Corey, Pittsburgh	2	0
Hollier, Dwight, Miami	16	3
Hollinquest, Lamont, Green Bay	16	0
Hollis, Mike, Jacksonville	16	0
Holmberg, Rob, Oakland	16	0
Holmes, Darick, Buffalo	13	0
Holmes, Earl, Pittsburgh	16	16
Holmes, Kenny, Tennessee	16	5
Holmes, Lester, Oakland	15	15
Holmes, Priest, Baltimore	7	0
Holsey, Bernard, N.Y. Giants	16	4
Hopkins, Brad, Tennessee	16	16
Horan, Mike, St. Louis	10	0
Horn, Joe, Kansas City	8	0
Hostetler, Jeff, Washington	6	3
Houston, Bobby, K.C.-S.D.	7	0
Howard, Desmond, Oakland	15	0
Howard, Ty, Arizona	15	2
Hoying, Bobby, Philadelphia	7	6
Hudson, Chris, Jacksonville	16	16
Hudson, John, N.Y. Jets	16	0
Hughes, Danan, Kansas City	16	1
Hughes, Tyrone, Chicago	14	0
Humphries, Stan, San Diego	8	8
Hundon, James, Cincinnati	16	0
Hunter, Brice, Tampa Bay	3	0
Huntington, Greg, Chicago	1	0
Husted, Michael, Tampa Bay	16	0
Hutson, Tony, Dallas	5	1
Hutton, Tom, Philadelphia	16	0
Irvin, Ken, Buffalo	16	0
Irvin, Michael, Dallas	16	16
Irving, Terry, Arizona	16	6
Irwin, Heath, New England	16	1
Ismail, Qadry, Miami	3	0
Ismail, Raghib, Carolina	13	2
Israel, Steve, New England	5	0
Jacke, Chris, Washington	1	0
Jackson, Calvin, Miami	16	16
Jackson, Grady, Oakland	5	0
Jackson, Greg, San Diego	13	0
Jackson, John, Pittsburgh	16	16
Jackson, Michael, Baltimore	16	15
Jackson, Ray, Buffalo	9	0
Jackson, Steve, Tennessee	12	5
Jackson, Tyoka, Tampa Bay	12	0
Jackson, Willie, Jacksonville	16	1
Jacobs, Tim, Miami	16	1
Jacoby, Mitch, St. Louis	14	2
Jacquet, Nate, Indianapolis	5	0
Jaeger, Jeff, Chicago	16	0
James, Toran, San Diego	14	0
Jamison, George, Detroit	16	10
Jasper, Edward, Philadelphia	10	1
Jeffcoat, Jim, Buffalo	7	0
Jeffers, Patrick, Denver	10	0
Jefferson, Greg, Philadelphia	12	11
Jefferson, Shawn, New England	16	14
Jeffries, Greg, Detroit	15	2
Jells, Dietrich, New England	11	0
Jenkins, Billy, St. Louis	16	2
Jenkins, DeRon, Baltimore	16	16
Jenkins, James, Washington	16	5
Jenkins, Kerry, N.Y. Jets	2	2
Jenkins, Mike, Cincinnati	4	0
Jenkins, Trezelle, Kansas City	2	1
Jennings, Keith, Chicago	12	12
Jervey, Travis, Green Bay	16	0
Jett, James, Oakland	16	16
Jett, John, Detroit	16	0
Johnson, Anthony, Carolina	16	7
Johnson, Bill, St. Louis	16	16
Johnson, Brad, Minnesota	13	13
Johnson, Charles, Pittsburgh	13	11
Johnson, Clyde, Kansas City	15	0
Johnson, Darrius, Denver	16	0
Johnson, Ellis, Indianapolis	15	15
Johnson, Jimmie, Philadelphia	16	11
Johnson, Joe, New Orleans	16	16
Johnson, Kevin, Oakland	15	0
Johnson, Keyshawn, N.Y. Jets	16	16
Johnson, Lee, Cincinnati	16	0
Johnson, Leon, N.Y. Jets	16	1
Johnson, LeShon, Arizona	14	0
Johnson, Lonnie, Buffalo	16	16
Johnson, Melvin, Tampa Bay	16	7
Johnson, Norm, Pittsburgh	16	0
Johnson, Pepper, N.Y. Jets	8	8
Johnson, Raylee, San Diego	16	0
Johnson, Reggie, Green Bay	4	0
Johnson, Rob, Jacksonville	5	1
Johnson, Ted, New England	16	16
Johnson, Tony, New Orleans	7	1
Johnson, Tre, Washington	11	11
Johnston, Daryl, Dallas	6	6
Johnstone, Lance, Oakland	14	6
Jones, Brent, San Francisco	13	12
Jones, Cedric, N.Y. Giants	9	2
Jones, Charlie, San Diego	16	11
Jones, Chris, Philadelphia	4	1
Jones, Clarence, New Orleans	15	15
Jones, Damon, Jacksonville	11	3
Jones, Donta, Pittsburgh	16	4
Jones, Ernest, Denver	1	0
Jones, Freddie, San Diego	13	8
Jones, George, Pittsburgh	16	1
Jones, Greg, Washington	16	3
Jones, Henry, Buffalo	15	15
Jones, James, Baltimore	16	16
Jones, Jimmie, Philadelphia	14	0
Jones, Lenoy, Tennessee	16	0
Jones, Marcus, Tampa Bay	7	1
Jones, Marvin, N.Y. Jets	16	16
Jones, Mike A., St. Louis	16	16
Jones, Mike D., New England	16	7
Jones, Robert, St. Louis	16	15
Jones, Rod, Cincinnati	13	8
Jones, Roger, Tennessee	2	0
Jones, Rondell, Baltimore	14	12
Jones, Tony, Denver	16	16
Jones, Walter, Seattle	12	12
Jordan, Andrew, Min.-T.B.	4	0
Jordan, Charles, Miami	14	1
Jordan, Randy, Jacksonville	7	0
Jordan, Richard, Detroit	10	0
Joyce, Matt, Arizona	9	6
Joyner, Seth, Green Bay	11	10
Junkin, Trey, Arizona	16	0
Jurkovic, John, Jacksonville	3	3
Justin, Paul, Indianapolis	8	4
Kalu, Ndukwe, Philadelphia	3	0

Player, Team	GP	GS	Player, Team	GP	GS	Player, Team	GP	GS
Kanell, Danny, N.Y. Giants	16	10	Lewis, Ray, Baltimore	16	16	McCaffrey, Ed, Denver	15	15
Kasay, John, Carolina	16	0	Lewis, Roderick, Tennessee	10	1	McCardell, Keenan, Jacksonville	16	16
Kaufman, Napoleon, Oakland	16	16	Lewis, Thomas, N.Y. Giants	4	2	McCleon, Dexter, St. Louis	16	1
Kazadi, Muadianvita, St. Louis	12	0	Lincoln, Jeremy, Seattle	12	3	McCleskey, J.J., Arizona	13	0
Kelly, Rob, New Orleans	16	2	Lindsay, Everett, Minnesota	16	3	McCloud, Tyrus, Baltimore	16	0
Kendall, Pete, Seattle	16	16	Lloyd, Greg, Pittsburgh	12	12	McCollum, Andy, New Orleans	16	16
Kennedy, Cortez, Seattle	8	8	Lockett, Kevin, Kansas City	9	0	McCombs, Tony, Arizona	12	0
Kennedy, Lincoln, Oakland	16	16	Lodish, Mike, Denver	16	0	McCormack, Hurvin, Dallas	13	0
Kennison, Eddie, St. Louis	14	9	Lofton, Steve, New England	4	0	McCorvey, Kez, Detroit	7	0
Kent, Joey, Tennessee	12	0	Logan, Ernie, N.Y. Jets	15	14	McCoy, Tony, Indianapolis	16	11
Kerner, Marlon, Buffalo	13	2	Logan, James, Seattle	14	1	McCrary, Fred, New Orleans	7	0
Kidd, John, Miami	13	0	Logan, Marc, Washington	15	1	McCrary, Michael, Baltimore	15	15
Killens, Terry, Tennessee	16	0	Logan, Mike, Jacksonville	11	0	McCullough, George, Tennessee	2	0
Kinchen, Brian, Baltimore	16	7	London, Antonio, Detroit	16	6	McDaniel, Ed, Minnesota	16	16
Kinchen, Todd, Atlanta	16	0	Longwell, Ryan, Green Bay	16	0	McDaniel, Emmanuel, Ind.	3	0
Kinder, Randy, G.B.-Phi.	12	0	Lott, Anthone, Cincinnati	5	0	McDaniel, Randall, Minnesota	16	16
King, Ed, New Orleans	2	0	Louchiey, Corey, Buffalo	16	6	McDaniel, Terry, Oakland	13	12
King, Shawn, Carolina	9	2	Loville, Derek, Denver	16	0	McDaniels, Pellom, Kansas City	16	6
Kinney, Kelvin, Washington	4	1	Lowery, Michael, Chicago	16	0	McDonald, Ricardo, Cincinnati	13	12
Kirby, Terry, San Francisco	16	3	Lucas, Ray, N.Y. Jets	5	0	McDonald, Tim, San Francisco	15	15
Kirk, Randy, San Francisco	16	0	Lyght, Todd, St. Louis	16	16	McDuffie, O.J., Miami	16	16
Kirkland, Levon, Pittsburgh	16	16	Lyle, Keith, St. Louis	16	16	McElmurry, Blaine, Green Bay	1	0
Kirschke, Travis, Detroit	3	0	Lyle, Rick, N.Y. Jets	16	16	McElroy, Leeland, Arizona	14	8
Kitna, Jon, Seattle	3	1	Lynch, John, Tampa Bay	16	16	McElroy, Ray, Indianapolis	16	4
Kitts, Jim, Miami	10	0	Lynch, Lorenzo, Oakland	15	0	McGee, Tony, Cincinnati	16	16
Klingler, David, Oakland	·1	0	Lynn, Anthony, Denver	16	0	McGill, Lenny, Atlanta	15	0
Knight, Sammy, New Orleans	16	12	Lyons, Lamar, Baltimore	1	0	McGinest, Willie, New England	11	11
Knight, Tom, Arizona	15	14	Lyons, Mitch, Pittsburgh	10	3	McGlockton, Chester, Oakland	16	16
Koonce, George, Green Bay	4	0	Lyons, Pratt, Tennessee	16	0	McGruder, Scooter, N.E.	3	0
Kopp, Jeff, Jacksonville	16	3	Mack, Tremain, Cincinnati	4	4	McGuire, Kaipo, Indianapolis	3	0
Kowalkowski, Scott, Detroit	16	0	Maddox, Mark, Buffalo	8	1	McIver, Everett, Miami	14	14
Kozlowski, Brian, Atlanta	16	5	Madison, Sam, Miami	14	3	McKeehan, James, Tennessee	10	0
Kragen, Greg, Carolina	16	0	Malamala, Siupeli, N.Y. Jets	10	5	McKenzie, Keith, Green Bay	16	0
Kramer, Erik, Chicago	15	13	Malone, Van, Detroit	8	4	McKenzie, Raleigh, San Diego	16	16
Krieg, Dave, Tennessee	8	0	Mamula, Mike, Philadelphia	16	16	McKinnon, Ronald, Arizona	16	16
Kuberski, Bob, Green Bay	11	3	Mandarich, Tony, Indianapolis	16	16	McKnight, James, Seattle	12	6
Kuehl, Ryan, Washington	12	5	Mangum, John, Chicago	16	16	McKyer, Tim, Denver	16	1
LaBounty, Matt, Seattle	16	6	Mangum, Kris, Carolina	2	1	McMillian, Mark, Kansas City	16	2
Lacina, Corbin, Buffalo	16	13	Maniecki, Jason, Tampa Bay	10	0	McNair, Steve, Tennessee	16	16
LaFleur, David, Dallas	16	5	Manning, Brian, Miami	7	0	McNeil, Ryan, St. Louis	16	16
Lageman, Jeff, Jacksonville	16	16	Manuel, Rod, Pittsburgh	1	0	McPhail, Jerris, Miami	14	1
Laing, Aaron, St. Louis	15	3	Manusky, Greg, Kansas City	16	1	McTyer, Tim, Philadelphia	10	0
Lake, Carnell, Pittsburgh	16	16	Mare, Olindo, Miami	16	0	McWilliams, Johnny, Arizona	16	7
Land, Dan, Oakland	16	0	Marino, Dan, Miami	16	16	Meadows, Adam, Indianapolis	16	16
Landeta, Sean, Tampa Bay	10	0	Marion, Brock, Dallas	16	16	Means, Natrone, Jacksonville	14	11
Lane, Eric, N.Y. Giants	15	0	Marsh, Curtis, Pittsburgh	5	0	Meggett, Dave, New England	16	2
Lane, Fred, Carolina	13	7	Marshall, Anthony, Chicago	14	1	Metcalf, Eric, San Diego	16	1
Lane, Max, New England	16	16	Martin, Curtis, New England	13	13	Metzelaars, Pete, Detroit	16	6
Lang, Kenard, Washington	11	11	Martin, Emanuel, Buffalo	16	1	Michels, John, Green Bay	9	5
Langford, Jevon, Cincinnati	14	0	Martin, Steve, Indianapolis	12	0	Mickell, Darren, New Orleans	14	13
Langham, Antonio, Baltimore	16	15	Martin, Tony, San Diego	16	16	Mickens, Ray, N.Y. Jets	16	0
Lassiter, Kwamie, Arizona	16	1	Martin, Wayne, New Orleans	16	16	Mickens, Terry, Green Bay	11	0
Lathon, Lamar, Carolina	15	15	Marts, Lonnie, Tennessee	14	14	Middleton, Frank, Tampa Bay	15	2
Law, Ty, New England	16	16	Maryland, Russell, Oakland	16	16	Milburn, Glyn, Detroit	16	1
Layman, Jason, Tennessee	14	0	Mason, Derrick, Tennessee	16	2	Miller, Anthony, Dallas	16	16
Le Bel, Harper, Chicago	16	0	Massey, Robert, N.Y. Giants	16	0	Miller, Bubba, Philadelphia	13	3
Lee, Amp, St. Louis	16	1	Mathews, Jason, Indianapolis	16	0	Miller, Corey, N.Y. Giants	14	13
Lee, Shawn, San Diego	16	15	Mathis, Dedric, Indianapolis	13	5	Miller, Fred, St. Louis	15	7
Leeuwenburg, Jay, Indianapolis	16	16	Mathis, Kevin, Dallas	16	3	Miller, Jamir, Arizona	16	16
Legette, Tyrone, Tampa Bay	16	1	Mathis, Terance, Atlanta	16	16	Miller, Josh, Pittsburgh	16	0
Lester, Tim, Pittsburgh	16	13	Matthews, Bruce, Tennessee	16	16	Miller, Les, Carolina	16	11
Levens, Dorsey, Green Bay	16	16	Matthews, Steve, Jacksonville	2	1	Miller, Nate, Atlanta	13	0
Levitt, Chad, Oakland	10	2	Mawae, Kevin, Seattle	16	16	Milloy, Lawyer, New England	16	16
Levy, Chuck, San Francisco	14	0	Maxie, Brett, San Francisco	2	1	Mills, Ernie, Carolina	10	5
Lewis, Albert, Oakland	14	11	May, Deems, Seattle	16	0	Mills, Jim, San Diego	1	0
Lewis, Chad, Philadelphia	16	3	Mayberry, Jermane, Phi.	16	16	Mills, John Henry, Oakland	16	0
Lewis, Darryll, Tennessee	16	16	Mayberry, Tony, Tampa Bay	16	16	Mills, Sam, Carolina	16	16
Lewis, Jeff, Denver	3	0	Mayes, Derrick, Green Bay	12	3	Milne, Brian, Cincinnati	16	16
Lewis, Jermaine, Baltimore	14	7	Maynard, Brad, N.Y. Giants	16	0	Milstead, Rod, San Francisco	4	0
Lewis, Mo, N.Y. Jets	16	16	McAfee, Fred, Pittsburgh	14	0	Mims, Chris, Washington	11	7
			McBurrows, Gerald, St. Louis	8	3	Mincy, Charles, Tampa Bay	16	9

Player, Team	GP	GS
Miniefield, Kevin, Arizona	3	0
Minter, Barry, Chicago	16	16
Minter, Mike, Carolina	16	11
Mirer, Rick, Chicago	7	3
Mitchell, Brandon, New England	12	0
Mitchell, Brian, Washington	16	1
Mitchell, Keith, New Orleans	16	2
Mitchell, Kevin, San Francisco	16	0
Mitchell, Pete, Jacksonville	16	12
Mitchell, Scott, Detroit	16	16
Mitchell, Shannon, San Diego	4	1
Mix, Bryant, Tennessee	1	0
Mobley, John, Denver	16	16
Mobley, Singor, Dallas	12	0
Mohr, Chris, Buffalo	16	0
Mohring, Mike, San Diego	2	0
Molden, Alex, New Orleans	16	15
Montgomery, Delmonico, Ind.	16	3
Montgomery, Greg, Baltimore	16	0
Montreuil, Mark, San Diego	6	1
Monty, Pete, N.Y. Giants	3	0
Moon, Warren, Seattle	15	14
Moore, Dave, Tampa Bay	16	7
Moore, Herman, Detroit	16	16
Moore, Jerald, St. Louis	9	5
Moore, Marty, New England	16	0
Moore, Rob, Arizona	16	16
Moore, Ronald, St.L.-Ari.	13	4
Moore, Stevon, Baltimore	13	13
Moore, Will, Jacksonville	11	0
Morabito, Tim, Carolina	8	0
Moran, Sean, Buffalo	16	7
Morris, Bam, Baltimore	11	8
Morris, Mike, Minnesota	16	0
Morrison, Steve, Indianapolis	16	9
Morrow, Harold, Minnesota	16	0
Morton, Johnnie, Detroit	16	16
Morton, Mike, Oakland	11	11
Moss, Winston, Seattle	14	14
Moss, Zefross, New England	15	15
Moulds, Eric, Buffalo	16	8
Muhammad, Muhsin, Carolina	13	5
Mullen, Roderick, Green Bay	16	1
Murray, Eddie, Minnesota	12	0
Murrell, Adrian, N.Y. Jets	16	15
Myers, Greg, Cincinnati	16	14
Myslinski, Tom, Pittsburgh	16	7
Naeole, Chris, New Orleans	4	0
Nails, Jamie, Buffalo	2	0
Nalen, Tom, Denver	16	16
Neal, Leon, Indianapolis	1	0
Neal, Lorenzo, N.Y. Jets	16	3
Nealy, Ray, Miami	1	0
Nedney, Joe, Arizona	10	0
Neil, Dan, Denver	3	0
Neujahr, Quentin, Baltimore	9	7
Newman, Anthony, New Orleans	12	12
Newsome, Craig, Green Bay	1	1
Newton, Nate, Dallas	13	13
Nickerson, Hardy, Tampa Bay	16	16
Norgard, Erik, Tennessee	16	0
Northern, Gabe, Buffalo	16	1
Norton, Ken, San Francisco	16	16
Nottage, Dexter, Kansas City	1	0
Novak, Jeff, Jacksonville	7	2
Nussmeier, Doug, New Orleans	3	1
Oben, Roman, N.Y. Giants	16	16
Odom, Jason, Tampa Bay	16	16
O'Donnell, Neil, N.Y. Jets	15	14
O'Dwyer, Matt, N.Y. Jets	16	16
Ofodile, A.J., Baltimore	12	0
Ogden, Jonathan, Baltimore	16	16
Oldham, Chris, Pittsburgh	16	0
Oliver, Winslow, Carolina	6	0
Olsavsky, Jerry, Pittsburgh	16	0
O'Neal, Leslie, St. Louis	15	14
Orlando, Bo, Cincinnati	16	2
Ostroski, Jerry, Buffalo	16	16
Ottis, Brad, Arizona	16	4
Owens, Dan, Atlanta	15	15
Owens, Rich, Washington	16	15
Owens, Terrell, San Francisco	16	15
Pace, Orlando, St. Louis	13	9
Palelei, Lonnie, N.Y. Jets	15	14
Palmer, David, Minnesota	16	0
Panos, Joe, Philadelphia	13	13
Parker, Anthony, Tampa Bay	15	14
Parker, Chris, Jacksonville	1	0
Parker, Glenn, Kansas City	15	15
Parker, Ricky, Jacksonville	12	0
Parker, Riddick, Seattle	12	0
Parker, Vaughn, San Diego	16	16
Parmalee, Bernie, Miami	16	4
Parrella, John, San Diego	16	16
Parten, Ty, Kansas City	2	0
Patten, David, N.Y. Giants	16	3
Patton, Joe, Washington	16	16
Patton, Marvcus, Washington	16	16
Paul, Tito, Ari.-Cin.	15	5
Paup, Bryce, Buffalo	16	16
Payne, Seth, Jacksonville	12	5
Pederson, Doug, Green Bay	1	0
Peete, Rodney, Philadelphia	5	3
Pegram, Erric, S.D.-NYG	15	0
Pelfrey, Doug, Cincinnati	16	0
Penn, Chris, Chicago	14	4
Perriman, Brett, K.C.-Mia.	13	9
Perry, Darren, Pittsburgh	16	16
Perry, Ed, Miami	16	4
Perry, Marlo, Buffalo	13	0
Perry, Michael Dean, Den.-K.C.	10	8
Perry, Todd, Chicago	11	11
Peter, Christian, N.Y. Giants	7	0
Peters, Tyrell, Baltimore	4	0
Peterson, Anthony, Chicago	16	0
Peterson, Todd, Seattle	16	0
Phifer, Roman, St. Louis	16	15
Philcox, Todd, San Diego	2	0
Phillips, Joe, Kansas City	15	15
Phillips, Lawrence, St.L.-Mia.	12	9
Phillips, Ryan, N.Y. Giants	10	0
Pickens, Carl, Cincinnati	12	12
Pierce, Aaron, N.Y. Giants	16	4
Pieri, Damon, Carolina	16	0
Pierson, Pete, Tampa Bay	15	0
Pike, Mark, Buffalo	15	0
Pilgrim, Evan, Chicago	13	6
Pittman, Kavika, Dallas	15	0
Pleasant, Anthony, Atlanta	11	0
Plummer, Gary, San Francisco	16	16
Plummer, Jake, Arizona	10	9
Pollack, Frank, San Francisco	16	0
Pollard, Marcus, Indianapolis	16	6
Poole, Keith, New Orleans	3	0
Poole, Tyrone, Carolina	16	16
Pope, Marquez, San Francisco	5	5
Popson, Ted, Kansas City	13	12
Porcher, Robert, Detroit	16	15
Porter, Daryl, Detroit	7	0
Porter, Rufus, Tampa Bay	11	10
Potts, Roosevelt, Ind.-Mia.	8	1
Pounds, Darryl, Washington	16	0
Pourdanesh, Shar, Washington	16	14
Powell, Carl, Indianapolis	11	0
Preston, Roell, Green Bay	1	0
Price, Daryl, San Francisco	5	0
Price, Marcus, San Diego	2	0
Price, Shawn, Buffalo	10	0
Prior, Anthony, Minnesota	12	0
Prior, Mike, Green Bay	16	0
Pritchard, Mike, Seattle	16	15
Pritchett, Kelvin, Jacksonville	8	5
Pritchett, Stanley, Miami	6	5
Proehl, Ricky, Chicago	15	10
Pryce, Trevor, Denver	8	3
Pupunu, Alfred, S.D.-K.C.	9	1
Purnell, Lovett, New England	16	2
Purvis, Andre, Cincinnati	7	1
Pyne, Jim, Tampa Bay	15	14
Quarles, Shelton, Tampa Bay	16	0
Quinn, Mike, Pittsburgh	1	0
Rachal, Latorio, San Diego	14	0
Ramirez, Tony, Detroit	2	0
Randle, John, Minnesota	16	16
Randolph, Thomas, N.Y. Giants	16	4
Rasby, Walter, Carolina	14	2
Raybon, Israel, Carolina	9	0
Raymer, Cory, Washington	6	3
Raymond, Corey, Detroit	13	12
Redmon, Anthony, Arizona	16	16
Reed, Andre, Buffalo	15	15
Reed, Jake, Minnesota	16	16
Reese, Albert, San Francisco	5	0
Reese, Jerry, Buffalo	5	0
Reeves, Carl, Chicago	15	10
Rehberg, Scott, New England	6	0
Reich, Frank, Detroit	6	0
Reynolds, Jerry, N.Y. Giants	5	0
Rhett, Errict, Tampa Bay	11	0
Rice, Jerry, San Francisco	2	1
Rice, Ron, Detroit	12	8
Rice, Simeon, Arizona	16	15
Richard, Stanley, Washington	16	16
Richardson, C.J., Seattle	14	0
Richardson, Kyle, Mia.-Sea.	5	0
Richardson, Tony, Kansas City	14	0
Richie, David, Denver	2	0
Riemersma, Jay, Buffalo	16	8
Rison, Andre, Kansas City	16	16
Ritchey, James, Tennessee	1	0
Rivera, Marco, Green Bay	14	0
Rivers, Ron, Detroit	16	0
Roaf, Willie, New Orleans	16	16
Roan, Michael, Tennessee	14	13
Robbins, Austin, New Orleans	12	0
Robbins, Barret, Oakland	16	16
Roberson, James, Tennessee	15	11
Roberts, Ray, Detroit	14	14
Roberts, William, N.Y. Jets	12	0
Robertson, Marcus, Tennessee	14	14
Robinson, Bryan, St. Louis	11	0
Robinson, Eddie, Jacksonville	16	13
Robinson, Eugene, Green Bay	16	16
Robinson, Jeff, St. Louis	16	0
Robinson, Rafael, Tennessee	3	0
Roby, Reggie, Tennessee	16	0
Roche, Brian, San Diego	5	0
Rodenhauser, Mark, Carolina	16	0
Rodgers, Derrick, Miami	15	14
Roe, James, Baltimore	12	4
Rogers, Sam, Buffalo	15	15
Romanowski, Bill, Denver	16	16
Roque, Juan, Detroit	13	1

Player, Team	GP	GS	Player, Team	GP	GS	Player, Team	GP	GS
Rosenstiel, Bob, Oakland	4	0	Semple, Tony, Detroit	16	1	Spikes, Irving, Miami	12	1
Ross, Jermaine, St. Louis	4	0	Shade, Sam, Cincinnati	16	12	Spindler, Marc, Detroit	10	0
Ross, Kevin, Kansas City	5	0	Sharpe, Shannon, Denver	16	16	Spriggs, Marcus, Buffalo	2	0
Rouen, Tom, Denver	16	0	Sharper, Darren, Green Bay	14	0	Springs, Shawn, Seattle	10	10
Rowe, Joe, St. Louis	2	0	Sharper, Jamie, Baltimore	16	15	Stablein, Brian, Indianapolis	16	0
Royal, Andre, Carolina	16	13	Shaw, Sedrick, New England	1	0	Stai, Brenden, Pittsburgh	11	9
Royals, Mark, New Orleans	16	0	Shaw, Terrance, San Diego	16	16	Staley, Duce, Philadelphia	16	0
Roye, Orpheus, Pittsburgh	16	0	Shedd, Kenny, Oakland	16	0	Stallings, Dennis, Tennessee	13	0
Rucci, Todd, New England	16	16	Sheldon, Mike, Miami	11	0	Stallings, Ramondo, Cincinnati	6	0
Rucker, Keith, Washington	2	0	Shelling, Chris, Atlanta	2	0	Stargell, Tony, Chicago	1	0
Rudd, Dwayne, Minnesota	16	2	Shello, Kendel, Indianapolis	6	0	Stark, Rohn, Seattle	4	0
Ruddy, Tim, Miami	15	15	Shelton, Daimon, Jacksonville	13	0	Staten, Ralph, Baltimore	10	3
Rudolph, Joe, San Francisco	6	1	Shepherd, Leslie, Washington	11	9	Steed, Joel, Pittsburgh	16	16
Runyan, Jon, Tennessee	16	16	Shields, Will, Kansas City	16	16	Stenstrom, Steve, Chicago	3	0
Rusk, Reggie, T.B.-Sea.	6	0	Shiver, Clay, Dallas	16	16	Stephens, Jamain, Pittsburgh	8	1
Russ, Bernard, New England	2	0	Shuler, Heath, New Orleans	10	9	Stepnoski, Mark, Tennessee	16	16
Russ, Steve, Denver	14	0	Sienkiewicz, Troy, San Diego	14	6	Steussie, Todd, Minnesota	16	16
Russell, Darrell, Oakland	16	10	Siglar, Ricky, New Orleans	16	1	Stevens, Matt, Philadelphia	11	0
Russell, Derek, Tennessee	11	2	Simien, Tracy, Kansas City	16	0	Stewart, James, Jacksonville	16	5
Russell, Matt, Detroit	14	0	Simmons, Clyde, Jacksonville	16	13	Stewart, Kordell, Pittsburgh	16	16
Russell, Twan, Washington	15	0	Simmons, Ed, Washington	14	13	Stewart, Rayna, Tennessee	16	4
Rypien, Mark, St. Louis	5	0	Simmons, Wayne, G.B.-K.C.	16	14	Stewart, Ryan, Detroit	8	0
Sadowski, Troy, Pittsburgh	6	0	Simpson, Carl, Chicago	16	16	Still, Bryan, San Diego	15	4
Sagapolutele, Pio, New Orleans	14	13	Sims, Keith, Miami	8	4	Stocz, Eric, Detroit	6	0
Salaam, Rashaan, Chicago	3	3	Sinclair, Michael, Seattle	16	16	Stokes, Eric, Seattle	7	0
Saleaumua, Dan, Seattle	16	9	Singleton, Alsheemond, T.B.	12	0	Stokes, J.J., San Francisco	16	16
Saleh, Tarek, Carolina	3	0	Singleton, Nate, Baltimore	4	0	Stoltenberg, Bryan, N.Y. Giants	3	0
Salmon, Mike, San Francisco	1	0	Siragusa, Tony, Baltimore	14	13	Stone, Dwight, Carolina	16	0
Sanders, Barry, Detroit	16	16	Skrepenak, Greg, Carolina	16	16	Stone, Ron, N.Y. Giants	16	16
Sanders, Brandon, N.Y. Giants	12	0	Slade, Chris, New England	16	16	Stoutmire, Omar, Dallas	16	2
Sanders, Chris, Tennessee	15	14	Sloan, David, Detroit	14	12	Stover, Matt, Baltimore	16	0
Sanders, Chris, Washington	1	0	Slutzker, Scott, Indianapolis	12	2	Stoyanovich, Pete, Kansas City	16	0
Sanders, Deion, Dallas	13	12	Small, Torrance, St. Louis	13	7	Strahan, Michael, N.Y. Giants	16	16
Sanders, Frank, Arizona	16	16	Smedley, Eric, Buffalo	13	1	Strickland, Fred, Dallas	15	14
Sanderson, Scott, Tennessee	10	0	Smeenge, Joel, Jacksonville	16	0	Stringer, Korey, Minnesota	15	15
Santiago, O.J., Atlanta	11	11	Smith, Anthony, Oakland	13	14	Strong, Mack, Seattle	16	9
Sapolu, Jesse, San Francisco	12	3	Smith, Antowain, Buffalo	16	0	Stryzinski, Dan, Atlanta	16	0
Sapp, Bob, Minnesota	1	0	Smith, Brady, New Orleans	16	2	Strzelczyk, Justin, Pittsburgh	14	14
Sapp, Patrick, San Diego	16	9	Smith, Bruce, Buffalo	16	16	Stubblefield, Dana, S.F.	16	16
Sapp, Warren, Tampa Bay	15	15	Smith, Cedric, Arizona	16	3	Stubbs, Daniel, Miami	1	0
Sargent, Kevin, Cincinnati	10	8	Smith, Chuck, Atlanta	16	15	Styles, Lorenzo, St. Louis	3	0
Sasa, Don, Washington	1	0	Smith, Darrin, Philadelphia	7	7	Sualua, Nicky, Dallas	10	1
Sauer, Craig, Atlanta	16	1	Smith, Derek, Washington	16	16	Sullivan, Chris, New England	16	10
Sauerbrun, Todd, Chicago	16	0	Smith, Detron, Denver	16	0	Sutter, Eddie, Atlanta	16	0
Savoie, Nicky, New Orleans	1	0	Smith, Ed, Atlanta	5	1	Swann, Eric, Arizona	13	13
Sawyer, Corey, Cincinnati	15	2	Smith, Emmitt, Dallas	16	16	Swayne, Harry, Denver	7	0
Saxton, Brian, Atlanta	3	0	Smith, Eric, Chicago	7	0	Sweeney, Jim, Pittsburgh	16	1
Schlereth, Mark, Denver	11	11	Smith, Fernando, Minnesota	12	11	Swift, Michael, San Diego	12	1
Schlesinger, Cory, Detroit	16	2	Smith, Frankie, San Francisco	16	0	Swinger, Rashod, Arizona	1	0
Schreiber, Adam, Atlanta	16	0	Smith, Irv, New Orleans	11	8	Szott, David, Kansas City	16	16
Schroeder, Bill, Green Bay	15	1	Smith, Jeff, Kansas City	3	0	Tamm, Ralph, Kansas City	16	0
Schultz, Bill, Chicago	8	3	Smith, Jermaine, Green Bay	9	0	Tanner, Barron, Miami	16	0
Schulz, Kurt, Buffalo	15	15	Smith, Jimmy, Jacksonville	16	16	Tanuvasa, Maa, Denver	15	5
Schwantz, Jim, San Francisco	16	0	Smith, Kevin, Dallas	16	16	Tasker, Steve, Buffalo	14	0
Schwartz, Bryan, Jacksonville	16	16	Smith, Lamar, Seattle	12	2	Tate, David, Indianapolis	8	2
Scifres, Steve, Dallas	6	0	Smith, Mark, Arizona	16	4	Tate, Robert, Minnesota	4	0
Scott, Chad, Pittsburgh	13	9	Smith, Neil, Denver	14	13	Tatum, Kinnon, Carolina	16	0
Scott, Darnay, Cincinnati	16	15	Smith, Otis, N.Y. Jets	16	16	Taylor, Aaron, Green Bay	14	14
Scott, Freddie, Atlanta	2	0	Smith, Robert, Minnesota	14	14	Taylor, Bobby, Philadelphia	6	5
Scott, Lance, N.Y. Giants	16	11	Smith, Rod, Denver	16	16	Taylor, Jason, Miami	13	11
Scott, Todd, Kansas City	10	0	Smith, Rod M., Carolina	16	2	Taylor, Leland, Baltimore	1	0
Scrafford, Kirk, San Francisco	16	16	Smith, Thomas, Buffalo	16	16	Teague, George, Miami	15	6
Scroggins, Tracy, Detroit	15	6	Smith, Vernice, St. Louis	10	2	Terrell, Pat, Carolina	16	5
Scurlock, Mike, St. Louis	5	0	Smith, Vinson, Dallas	14	13	Terry, Rick, N.Y. Jets	14	0
Seals, Ray, Carolina	14	7	Solomon, Freddie, Philadelphia	15	5	Terry, Tim, Cincinnati	5	0
Searcy, Leon, Jacksonville	16	16	Sowell, Jerald, N.Y. Jets	9	0	Testaverde, Vinny, Baltimore	13	13
Seau, Junior, San Diego	15	15	Sparks, Phillippi, N.Y. Giants	13	13	Tharpe, Larry, Detroit	16	15
Seay, Mark, Philadelphia	12	2	Spears, Marcus, Kansas City	3	0	Thibodeaux, Keith, Washington	15	0
Sehorn, Jason, N.Y. Giants	16	16	Spellman, Alonzo, Chicago	7	5	Thierry, John, Chicago	9	9
Seigler, Dexter, Seattle	2	0	Spencer, Jimmy, Cincinnati	16	9	Thigpen, Yancey, Pittsburgh	16	15
Selby, Rob, Arizona	10	9	Spielman, Chris, Buffalo	8	8	Thomas, Broderick, Dallas	16	0

Player, Team	GP	GS
Thomas, Chris, Washington	13	0
Thomas, Dave, Jacksonville	16	16
Thomas, Derrick, Kansas City	12	10
Thomas, Fred, Seattle	16	3
Thomas, Henry, New England	16	16
Thomas, Hollis, Philadelphia	16	16
Thomas, J.T., St. Louis	4	0
Thomas, Lamar, Miami	12	6
Thomas, Mark, Chicago	16	7
Thomas, Orlando, Minnesota	15	13
Thomas, Robb, Tampa Bay	16	1
Thomas, Rodney, Tennessee	16	1
Thomas, Thurman, Buffalo	16	16
Thomas, William, Philadelphia	14	14
Thomas, Zach, Miami	15	15
Thomason, Jeff, Green Bay	13	1
Thompson, Bennie, Baltimore	16	0
Thompson, David, St. Louis	11	0
Thompson, Tommy, S.F.	16	0
Thornton, Carlos, San Francisco	16	0
Thrash, James, Washington	4	0
Threats, Jabbar, Jacksonville	2	0
Timmerman, Adam, Green Bay	16	16
Timpson, Michael, Philadelphia	15	10
Tindale, Tim, Buffalo	7	0
Tobeck, Robbie, Atlanta	16	15
Tolbert, Tony, Dallas	16	16
Tolliver, Billy Joe, Atl.-K.C.	9	1
Tomczak, Mike, Pittsburgh	16	0
Tomich, Jared, New Orleans	16	1
Tongue, Reggie, Kansas City	16	16
Toomer, Amani, N.Y. Giants	16	0
Tovar, Steve, Cincinnati	14	5
Townsend, Greg, Oakland	4	0
Trapp, James, Oakland	16	16
Traylor, Keith, Denver	16	16
Treu, Adam, Oakland	16	0
Truitt, Greg, Cincinnati	16	0
Truitt, Olanda, Oakland	14	0
Tuaolo, Esera, Jacksonville	6	1
Tubbs, Winfred, New Orleans	16	16
Tucker, Ryan, St. Louis	7	0
Tuggle, Jessie, Atlanta	16	15
Tuinei, Mark, Dallas	6	6
Tuinei, Van, San Diego	3	0
Tumulty, Tom, Cincinnati	11	11
Tupa, Tom, New England	16	0
Turk, Dan, Washington	16	0
Turk, Matt, Washington	16	0
Turnbull, Renaldo, Carolina	16	2
Turner, Eric, Oakland	16	15
Turner, Kevin, Philadelphia	16	10
Turner, Scott, Washington	9	0
Tuten, Rick, Seattle	11	0
Twyner, Gunnard, Cin.-N.O.	4	0
Tylski, Rich, Jacksonville	13	13
Uhlenhake, Jeff, Washington	14	13
Unutoa, Morris, Philadelphia	16	0
Unverzagt, Eric, Seattle	1	0
Upshaw, Regan, Tampa Bay	15	15
Uwaezuoke, Iheanyi, S.F.	14	0
Van Dyke, Alex, N.Y. Jets	5	0
Vanover, Tamarick, Kansas City	16	0
Van Pelt, Alex, Buffalo	6	3
Vardell, Tommy, Detroit	16	10
Veland, Tony, Denver	12	0
Verba, Ross, Green Bay	16	11
Verstegen, Mike, New Orleans	14	8
Vickers, Kipp, Indianapolis	9	0
Villa, Danny, New England	7	0
Villarrial, Chris, Chicago	11	11
Vinatieri, Adam, New England	16	0
Vincent, Troy, Philadelphia	16	16
Vanover, Tamarick, Kansas City	16	0
Vinson, Tony, Baltimore	13	0
Von der Ahe, Scott, Ind.	9	2
von Oelhoffen, Kimo, Cincinnati	13	13
Vrabel, Mike, Pittsburgh	15	0
Wainright, Frank, Miami	9	0
Waldroup, Kerwin, Detroit	11	11
Walker, Bracey, Miami	12	0
Walker, Brian, Washington	5	0
Walker, Darnell, San Francisco	16	11
Walker, Denard, Tennessee	15	11
Walker, Derrick, Kansas City	16	5
Walker, Gary, Tennessee	15	15
Walker, Herschel, Dallas	16	6
Walker, Marquis, St. Louis	11	0
Wallace, Aaron, Oakland	5	0
Wallace, Al, Philadelphia	1	0
Wallace, Steve, Kansas City	10	0
Wallerstedt, Brett, St. Louis	2	0
Walls, Wesley, Carolina	15	15
Walsh, Chris, Minnesota	14	0
Walsh, Steve, Tampa Bay	12	0
Walter, Joe, Cincinnati	5	0
Walter, Ken, Carolina	16	0
Ward, Chris, Baltimore	5	0
Ward, Dedric, N.Y. Jets	11	1
Ward, Ronnie, Miami	4	0
Warren, Chris, Seattle	15	13
Warren, Lamont, Indianapolis	13	0
Washington, Dewayne, Min.	16	16
Washington, Keith, Baltimore	10	1
Washington, Lionel, Oakland	9	3
Washington, Marvin, S.F.	10	1
Washington, Mickey, N.O.	16	2
Washington, Ted, Buffalo	16	16
Watson, Tim, Philadelphia	3	0
Watters, Ricky, Philadelphia	16	16
Watts, Damon, Indianapolis	8	5
Way, Charles, N.Y. Giants	16	16
Webb, Richmond, Miami	16	16
Webster, Larry, Baltimore	16	3
Wells, Dean, Seattle	16	16
Wells, Mike, Detroit	16	16
West, Derek, Indianapolis	1	0
West, Ed, Atlanta	12	3
Westbrook, Bryant, Detroit	15	14
Westbrook, Michael, Was.	13	9
Wetnight, Ryan, Chicago	16	3
Wheatley, Tyrone, N.Y. Giants	14	7
Wheaton, Kenny, Dallas	2	0
Wheeler, Leonard, Minnesota	15	0
Wheeler, Mark, New England	14	14
Whelihan, Craig, San Diego	9	7
Whigham, Larry, New England	16	0
White, Jose, Jacksonville	3	0
White, Reggie, Green Bay	16	16
White, Steve, Tampa Bay	15	1
White, William, Atlanta	16	16
Whitfield, Bob, Atlanta	16	16
Whitley, Curtis, Oakland	15	1
Whittington, Bernard, Ind.	15	6
Widell, Dave, Jacksonville	16	12
Widell, Doug, Indianapolis	16	16
Widmer, Corey, N.Y. Giants	16	15
Wiegert, Zach, St. Louis	15	15
Wiegmann, Casey, NYJ-Chi.	4	0
Wiggins, Paul, Pittsburgh	1	0
Wiley, Marcellus, Buffalo	16	0
Wilkerson, Bruce, Green Bay	16	3
Wilkins, Gabe, Green Bay	16	16
Wilkins, Jeff, St. Louis	16	0
Wilkinson, Dan, Cincinnati	15	15
Williams, Aeneas, Arizona	16	16
Williams, Alfred, Denver	16	16
Williams, Armon, Tennessee	6	0
Williams, Brian, Green Bay	16	16
Williams, Charlie, Dallas	16	0
Williams, Dan, Kansas City	15	6
Williams, Darryl, Seattle	16	16
Williams, David, N.Y. Jets	12	11
Williams, Erik, Dallas	15	15
Williams, Gene, Atlanta	15	15
Williams, Gerald, Car.-G.B.	9	5
Williams, Gerome, San Diego	6	0
Williams, Grant, Seattle	16	8
Williams, Harvey, Oakland	14	6
Williams, Jamel, Washington	16	0
Williams, James E., S.F.	16	0
Williams, James O., Chicago	16	16
Williams, Jay, St. Louis	16	2
Williams, John, Baltimore	4	0
Williams, Karl, Tampa Bay	16	7
Williams, Kevin, Arizona	16	0
Williams, Moe, Minnesota	14	0
Williams, Pat, Buffalo	1	0
Williams, Sherman, Dallas	16	0
Williams, Stepfret, Dallas	16	0
Williams, Tony, Minnesota	6	2
Williams, Tyrone, Chicago	3	0
Williams, Tyrone, Green Bay	16	15
Williams, Wally, Baltimore	10	10
Williams, Willie, Seattle	16	16
Willig, Matt, Atlanta	16	13
Willis, James, Philadelphia	15	15
Wilson, Bernard, Arizona	16	14
Wilson, Jerry, Miami	16	0
Wilson, Reinard, Cincinnati	16	3
Wilson, Wade, Dallas	7	0
Wimberly, Marcus, Atlanta	6	0
Wing, Chris, N.Y. Jets	2	0
Winters, Frank, Green Bay	13	13
Wisniewski, Steve, Oakland	16	16
Witherspoon, Derrick, Phi.	3	0
Witman, Jon, Pittsburgh	16	2
Wohlabaugh, Dave, N.E.	14	14
Wolf, Joe, Arizona	15	9
Wolford, Will, Pittsburgh	16	16
Woodall, Lee, San Francisco	16	16
Wooden, Shawn, Miami	16	15
Wooden, Terry, Kansas City	15	8
Woods, Jerome, Kansas City	16	16
Woodson, Darren, Dallas	14	14
Woodson, Rod, San Francisco	14	14
Woolford, Donnell, Pittsburgh	15	12
Wooten, Tito, N.Y. Giants	16	16
Wortham, Barron, Tennessee	16	16
Wright, Lawrence, Cincinnati	4	0
Wright, Toby, St. Louis	11	11
Wuerffel, Danny, New Orleans	7	2
Wunsch, Jerry, Tampa Bay	16	0
Wyatt, Antwuan, Philadelphia	1	0
Wycheck, Frank, Tennessee	16	16
Wyman, Devin, New England	6	0
Wynn, Renaldo, Jacksonville	16	8
Yarborough, Ryan, Baltimore	16	3
Young, Bryant, San Francisco	12	12
Young, Floyd, Tampa Bay	12	1
Young, Rodney, N.Y. Giants	9	0
Young, Steve, San Francisco	15	15
Zandofsky, Mike, Philadelphia	5	2

Player, Team	GP	GS	Player, Team	GP	GS	Player, Team	GP	GS
Zatechka, Rob, N.Y. Giants	16	0	Zellars, Ray, New Orleans	16	16	Zolak, Scott, New England	4	0
Zeier, Eric, Baltimore	5	3	Zgonina, Jeff, St. Louis	15	0	Zordich, Michael, Philadelphia	16	16
Zeigler, Dusty, Buffalo	13	13	Zimmerman, Gary, Denver	14	14	Zorich, Chris, Chi.-Was.	8	0

PLAYERS WITH TWO OR MORE CLUBS

Player, Team	GP	GS	Player, Team	GP	GS	Player, Team	GP	GS
Bentley, Scott, Denver	1	0	Hardy, Darryl, Dallas	12	0	Perry, Michael Dean, K.C.	1	0
Bentley, Scott, Atlanta	2	0	Hardy, Darryl, Seattle	2	0	Phillips, Lawrence, St. Louis	10	9
Brew, Dorian, Baltimore	3	0	Harmon, Ronnie, Chicago	1	0	Phillips, Lawrence, Miami	2	0
Brew, Dorian, San Diego	6	0	Harmon, Ronnie, Tennessee	11	0	Potts, Roosevelt, Indianapolis	2	0
Brooks, Bucky, Jacksonville	3	0	Hayes, Mercury, New Orleans	4	0	Potts, Roosevelt, Miami	6	1
Brooks, Bucky, Green Bay	3	0	Hayes, Mercury, Atlanta	2	0	Pupunu, Alfred, San Diego	8	1
Brooks, Bucky, Kansas City	3	0	Hobbs, Daryl, New Orleans	4	0	Pupunu, Alfred, Kansas City	1	0
Clavelle, Shannon, Green Bay	6	0	Hobbs, Daryl, Seattle	10	0	Richardson, Kyle, Miami	3	0
Clavelle, Shannon, Kansas City	1	0	Hobert, Billy Joe, Buffalo	2	0	Richardson, Kyle, Seattle	2	0
Coleman, Andre, Seattle	2	0	Hobert, Billy Joe, New Orleans	5	4	Rusk, Reggie, Tampa Bay	4	0
Coleman, Andre, Pittsburgh	8	0	Houston, Bobby, Kansas City	5	0	Rusk, Reggie, Seattle	2	0
Davis, Greg, Minnesota	4	0	Houston, Bobby, San Diego	2	0	Simmons, Wayne, Green Bay	6	6
Davis, Greg, San Diego	12	0	Jordan, Andrew, Minnesota	2	0	Simmons, Wayne, Kansas City	10	8
Davis, Isaac, San Diego	12	12	Jordan, Andrew, Tampa Bay	2	0	Tolliver, Billy Joe, Atlanta	6	1
Davis, Isaac, New Orleans	3	2	Kinder, Randy, Green Bay	6	0	Tolliver, Billy Joe, Kansas City	3	0
Dumas, Troy, Kansas City	8	0	Kinder, Randy, Philadelphia	6	0	Twyner, Gunnard, Cincinnati	2	0
Dumas, Troy, St. Louis	2	0	Moore, Ronald, St. Louis	7	2	Twyner, Gunnard, New Orleans	2	0
Edwards, Antonio, Seattle	1	0	Moore, Ronald, Arizona	6	2	Wiegmann, Casey, N.Y. Jets	3	0
Edwards, Antonio, N.Y. Giants	3	0	Paul, Tito, Arizona	1	0	Wiegmann, Casey, Chicago	1	0
Floyd, Malcolm, Tennessee	1	0	Paul, Tito, Cincinnati	14	5	Williams, Gerald, Carolina	5	5
Floyd, Malcolm, St. Louis	4	0	Pegram, Erric, San Diego	4	0	Williams, Gerald, Green Bay	4	0
Gray, Mel, Tennessee	11	0	Pegram, Erric, N.Y. Giants	11	0	Zorich, Chris, Chicago	3	0
Gray, Mel, Philadelphia	3	0	Perriman, Brett, Kansas City	5	4	Zorich, Chris, Washington	5	0
Greer, Donovan, Atlanta	1	0	Perriman, Brett, Miami	8	5			
Greer, Donovan, New Orleans	6	1	Perry, Michael Dean, Denver	9	8			

ATTENDANCE

REGULAR SEASON

Team	Home Attendance	Average	NFL Rank	Road Attendance	Average	NFL Rank
Arizona	379,547	47,443	27	484,689	60,586	14
Atlanta	375,427	46,928	29	437,145	54,643	29
Baltimore	475,236	59,405	19	447,488	55,936	28
Buffalo	523,763	65,470	11	469,716	58,715	20
Carolina	523,691	65,461	12	489,334	61,167	13
Chicago	421,900	52,738	26	536,184	67,023	4
Cincinnati	439,831	54,979	25	463,944	57,993	25
Dallas	511,767	63,971	14	541,187	67,648	2
Denver	590,189	73,774	3	499,942	62,493	12
Detroit	554,898	69,362	7	527,918	65,990	6
Green Bay	481,494	60,187	17	536,436	67,055	3
Indianapolis	451,455	56,432	23	483,840	60,480	15
Jacksonville	557,547	69,693	6	420,543	52,568	30
Kansas City	610,192	76,274	1	532,485	66,561	5
Miami	574,811	71,851	4	522,208	65,276	8
Minnesota	486,921	60,865	16	505,684	63,211	10
New England	477,431	59,679	18	547,518	68,440	1
New Orleans	443,614	55,452	24	467,609	58,451	21
N.Y. Giants	573,241	71,655	5	477,528	59,691	18
N.Y. Jets	543,181	67,898	9	464,320	58,040	24
Oakland	375,499	46,937	28	505,407	63,176	11
Philadelphia	535,783	66,973	10	480,437	60,055	17
Pittsburgh	462,532	57,817	21	519,955	64,994	9
St. Louis	518,468	64,809	13	465,021	58,128	23
San Diego	465,906	58,238	20	482,485	60,311	16
San Francisco	501,641	62,705	15	522,898	65,362	7
Seattle	462,124	57,766	22	475,730	59,466	19
Tampa Bay	543,514	67,939	8	459,316	57,415	26
Tennessee	224,221	28,028	30	459,008	57,376	27
Washington	605,592	75,699	2	465,441	58,180	22
NFL total	14,691,416	61,214		14,691,416	61,214	

Note: Attendance figures are unofficial and are based on box scores of games.

HISTORICAL

TOP REGULAR-SEASON HOME CROWDS

Team	Attendance	Date	Site	Opponent
Arizona	73,400	October 30, 1994	Sun Devil Stadium	Pittsburgh
Atlanta	71,253	November 21, 1993	Georgia Dome	Dallas
Baltimore	64,421	October 5, 1997	Memorial Stadium	Pittsburgh
Buffalo	80,368	October 4, 1992	Rich Stadium	Miami
Carolina	76,136	December 10, 1995	Clemson Memorial Stadium	San Francisco
Chicago	66,900	September 5, 1993	Soldier Field	N.Y. Giants
Cincinnati	60,284	October 17, 1971	Riverfront Stadium	Cleveland
Dallas	80,259	November 24, 1966	Cotton Bowl	Cleveland
Denver	76,089	October 26, 1986	Mile High Stadium	Seattle
Detroit	80,444	December 20, 1981	Pontiac Silverdome	Tampa Bay
Green Bay	60,766	September 1, 1997	Lambeau Field	Chicago
Indianapolis	61,282	December 14, 1997	RCA Dome	Miami
Jacksonville	73,446	December 7, 1997	ALLTEL Stadium	New England
Kansas City	82,094	November 5, 1972	Arrowhead Stadium	Oakland
Miami	78,914	November 19, 1972	Orange Bowl	N.Y. Jets
Minnesota	64,168	September 22, 1996	Metrodome	Green Bay
New England	61,457	December 5, 1971	Schaefer Stadium*	Miami
New Orleans	83,437	November 12, 1967	Tulane Stadium	Dallas
		November 26, 1967	Tulane Stadium	Atlanta
New York Giants	77,571	December 13, 1997	Giants Stadium	Washington
New York Jets	75,606	November 27, 1994	Giants Stadium	Miami
Oakland	74,121	September 23, 1973	Memorial Stadium; Berkeley, Cal.	Miami
Philadelphia	72,111	November 1, 1981	Veterans Stadium	Dallas
Pittsburgh	60,808	December 18, 1994	Three Rivers Stadium	Cleveland
St. Louis	66,030	December 14, 1997	Trans World Dome	Chicago

Team	Attendance	Date	Site	Opponent
San Diego	65,714	November 16, 1997	Qualcomm Stadium	Oakland
San Francisco	69,014	November 13, 1994	Candlestick Park	Dallas
Seattle	66,264	October 26, 1997	Kingdome	Oakland
Tampa Bay	73,523	December 12, 1997	Houlihan's Stadium	Green Bay
Tennessee	50,677	December 21, 1997	Liberty Bowl Memorial Stadium	Pittsburgh
Washington	78,270	September 14, 1997	Jack Kent Cooke Stadium	Arizona

*Now known as Foxboro Stadium.

YEAR BY YEAR

NATIONAL FOOTBALL LEAGUE

Year	Regular season*		Average	Postseason†	
1934	492,684	(60)	8,211	35,059	(1)
1935	638,178	(53)	12,041	15,000	(1)
1936	816,007	(54)	15,111	29,545	(1)
1937	963,039	(55)	17,510	15,878	(1)
1938	937,197	(55)	17,040	48,120	(1)
1939	1,071,200	(55)	19,476	32,279	(1)
1940	1,063,025	(55)	19,328	36,034	(1)
1941	1,108,615	(55)	20,157	55,870	(2)
1942	887,920	(55)	16,144	36,006	(1)
1943	969,128	(50)	19,383	71,315	(2)
1944	1,019,649	(50)	20,393	46,016	(1)
1945	1,270,401	(50)	25,408	32,178	(1)
1946	1,732,135	(55)	31,493	58,346	(1)
1947	1,837,437	(60)	30,624	66,268	(2)
1948	1,525,243	(60)	25,421	36,309	(1)
1949	1,391,735	(60)	23,196	27,980	(1)
1950	1,977,753	(78)	25,356	136,647	(3)
1951	1,913,019	(72)	26,570	57,522	(1)
1952	2,052,126	(72)	28,502	97,507	(2)
1953	2,164,585	(72)	30,064	54,577	(1)
1954	2,190,571	(72)	30,425	43,827	(1)
1955	2,521,836	(72)	35,026	85,693	(1)
1956	2,551,263	(72)	35,434	56,836	(1)
1957	2,836,318	(72)	39,393	119,579	(2)
1958	3,006,124	(72)	41,752	123,659	(2)
1959	3,140,000	(72)	43,617	57,545	(1)
1960	3,128,296	(78)	40,106	67,325	(1)
1961	3,986,159	(98)	40,675	39,029	(1)
1962	4,003,421	(98)	40,851	64,892	(1)
1963	4,163,643	(98)	42,486	45,801	(1)
1964	4,563,049	(98)	46,562	79,544	(1)
1965	4,634,021	(98)	47,296	100,304	(2)
1966	5,337,044	(105)	50,829	135,098	(2)
1967	5,938,924	(112)	53,026	241,754	(4)
1968	5,882,313	(112)	52,521	291,279	(4)
1969	6,096,127	(112)	54,430	242,841	(4)
1970	9,533,333	(182)	52,381	410,371	(7)
1971	10,076,035	(182)	55,363	430,244	(7)
1972	10,445,827	(182)	57,395	435,466	(7)
1973	10,730,933	(182)	58,961	458,515	(7)
1974	10,236,322	(182)	56,224	412,180	(7)
1975	10,213,193	(182)	56,116	443,811	(7)
1976	11,070,543	(196)	56,482	428,733	(7)
1977	11,018,632	(196)	56,218	483,588	(7)
1978	12,771,800	(224)	57,017	578,107	(9)
1979	13,182,039	(224)	58,848	582,266	(9)
1980	13,392,230	(224)	59,787	577,186	(9)
1981	13,606,990	(224)	60,745	587,361	(9)
1982§	7,367,438	(126)	58,472	985,952	(15)
1983	13,277,222	(224)	59,273	625,068	(9)
1984	13,398,112	(224)	59,813	614,809	(9)
1985	13,345,047	(224)	59,567	660,667	(9)
1986	13,588,551	(224)	60,663	683,901	(9)
1987∞	10,032,493	(168)	59,717	606,864	(9)
1988	13,539,848	(224)	60,446	608,204	(9)
1989	13,625,662	(224)	60,829	635,326	(9)
1990	14,266,240	(224)	63,689	797,198	(11)
1991	13,187,478	(224)	58,873	758,186	(11)
1992	13,159,387	(224)	58,747	756,005	(11)
1993	13,328,760	(224)	59,503	755,625	(11)
1994	13,479,680	(224)	60,177	719,143	(11)
1995	14,196,205	(240)	59,151	733,729	(11)
1996	13,695,748	(240)	57,066	711,601	(11)
1997	14,691,416	(240)	61,214	751,884	(11)

*Number of tickets sold, including no-shows; number of regular-season games in parentheses.

†Includes conference, league championship and Super Bowl games, but not Pro Bowl; number of postseason games in parentheses.

‡A 57-day players strike reduced 224-game schedule to 126 games.

§A 24-day players strike reduced 224-game schedule to 168 non-strike games.

AMERICAN FOOTBALL LEAGUE

Year	Regular season*	Average	AFL Champ. Game
1960	926,156 (56)	16,538	32,183
1961	1,002,657 (56)	17,904	29,556
1962	1,147,302 (56)	20,487	37,981
1963	1,241,741 (56)	22,174	30,127
1964	1,447,875 (56)	25,855	40,242
1965	1,782,384 (56)	31,828	30,361
1966	2,160,369 (63)	34,291	42,080
1967	2,295,697 (63)	36,439	53,330
1968	2,635,004 (70)	37,643	62,627
1969	2,843,373 (70)	40,620	53,564

*Number of regular-season games in parentheses.

TRADES

(Covering June 1997 through May 1998)

JUNE 5

N.Y. Jets traded CB Carl Greenwood to Green Bay for S Chris Hayes.

JUNE 25

N.Y. Jets traded TE Henry Lusk to Green Bay to complete an earlier trade.

JULY 2

Pittsburgh traded RB Erric Pegram to San Diego for a 1999 seventh-round draft choice.

AUGUST 22

N.Y. Jets traded G Sean Love to Philadelphia for past considerations.

Pittsburgh traded T/G Bernard Dafney to Baltimore for a 1998 seventh-round draft choice. Pittsburgh traded the pick to Atlanta.

Pittsburgh traded DE Israel Raybon to Carolina for a 1998 seventh-round draft choice. Pittsburgh traded the pick to Atlanta.

Philadelphia traded G Ben Cavil to Baltimore for a 1999 seventh-round draft choice.

Green Bay traded WR/PR Qadry Ismail to Miami for a conditional draft choice.

Jacksonville traded DE Paul Frase to Green Bay for a 1998 sixth-round draft choice. Jacksonville selected RB Kevin McLeod (Auburn).

Jacksonville traded T Jimmy Herndon to Chicago for a 1998 seventh-round draft choice. Jacksonville selected WR Alvis Whitted (North Carolina State).

Kansas City traded WR Chris Penn to Chicago for a 1998 fifth-round draft choice. Kansas City selected DB Robert Williams (North Carolina).

AUGUST 25

N.Y. Jets traded TE Tyrone Davis to Green Bay for past considerations.

SEPTEMBER 30

New Orleans traded WR Daryl Hobbs to Seattle for a 1998 seventh-round 1998 draft choice. New Orleans selected WR Andy McCullough (Tennessee).

OCTOBER 7

Green Bay traded LB Wayne Simmons to Kansas City for a 1998 fifth-round draft choice. Green Bay selected WR Corey Bradford (Jackson State).

FEBRUARY 13

Jacksonville traded QB Rob Johnson to Buffalo for 1998 first- and fourth-round draft choices. Jacksonville selected RB Fred Taylor (Florida) in the first round and RB Tavian Banks (Iowa) in the fourth round.

FEBRUARY 14

Indianapolis traded QB Jim Harbaugh and a 1998 fourth-round draft pick to Baltimore for 1998 third- and fourth-round draft choices. Indianapolis selected WR E.G. Green (Florida State) in the third round and traded the fourth-round pick.

FEBRUARY 17

Tampa Bay traded RB Errict Rhett to Baltimore for a 1999 third-round draft choice.

FEBRUARY 26

Cincinnati traded DT Dan Wilkinson to Washington for 1998 first- and third-round draft choices. Cincinnati selected LB Brian Simmons (North Carolina) in the first round and G Mike Goff (Iowa) in the third round.

MARCH 5

New Orleans traded CB Eric Allen to Oakland Raiders for a 1998 fourth-round draft choice. New Orleans selected DB Fred Weary (Florida).

MARCH 12

N.Y. Jets traded FB Lorenzo Neal to Tampa Bay for a 1998 fifth-round draft choice. The Jets selected TE Blake Spence (Oregon).

San Diego traded KR Eric Metcalf, LB Patrick Sapp, 1998 first- and second-round draft choices and a 1999 first-round choice to Arizona for a 1998 first-round draft choice. San Diego selected QB Ryan Leaf (Washington State). Arizona selected DE Andre Wadsworth (Florida State) in the first round and DB Corey Chavous (Vanderbilt) in the second round.

MARCH 13

N.Y. Jets traded DE Hugh Douglas to Philadelphia for 1998 second- and fifth-round draft choices. The Jets selected LB Casey Dailey (Northwestern) in the fifth round and traded the second-round pick to Pittsburgh.

MARCH 25

Oakland traded LB Rob Frederickson to Detroit for a 1998 fourth-round draft choice. Oakland traded the fourth-round pick to Washington.

MARCH 26

Indianapolis traded QB Paul Justin to Cincinnati for a 1998 fifth-round draft choice. Indianapolis selected LB Antony Jordan (Vanderbilt).

APRIL 4

Green Bay traded QB Steve Bono to St. Louis for a 1999 draft choice.

APRIL 7

N.Y. Jets traded RB Adrian Murrell and a 1998 seventh-round draft choice to Arizona for a 1998 third-round draft choice. The Jets traded the third-round pick to St. Louis. Arizona selected DE Jomo Cousins (Florida A&M).

APRIL 15

Denver traded OT Jamie Brown to San Francisco for a 1999 second-round draft choice.

Chicago traded LB Anthony Peterson to San Francisco for a 1998 seventh-round draft choice. Chicago selected T Chad Overhauser (UCLA).

APRIL 16

Miami traded a 2000 first-round draft choice to Carolina for a 1998 second-round choice. Miami selected DB Patrick Surtain (Southern Mississippi).

APRIL 18

Miami traded a 1998 first-round draft choice to Green Bay for 1998 first- and second-round draft choices. Green Bay selected DT Vonnie Holliday (North Carolina). Miami selected RB John

– 235 –

Avery (Mississippi) in the first round and traded the second-round pick to Detroit.

N.Y. Jets traded WR Jeff Graham to Philadelphia for a 1998 sixth-round draft choice. The Jets selected DE Eric Ogbogu (Maryland).

Tampa Bay traded S Melvin Johnson to Kansas City for an undisclosed 1999 draft choice.

APRIL 21

Detroit traded KR/WR Glyn Milburn to Green Bay for a 1999 conditional draft choice.

MAY 13

Green Bay traded DT Darius Holland to Kansas City for DE Vaughn Booker.

1997 STATISTICS

Rushing
Passing
Receiving
Scoring
Interceptions
Sacks
Fumbles
Field goals
Punting
Punt returns
Kickoff returns
Miscellaneous

RUSHING

TEAM

AFC

Team	Att.	Yds.	Avg.	Long	TD
Pittsburgh	572	2479	4.3	t74	19
Tennessee	541	2414	4.5	47	17
Denver	520	2378	4.6	t50	18
Kansas City	529	2171	4.1	43	15
Cincinnati	452	1966	4.3	t79	23
Seattle	404	1800	4.5	t77	13
Buffalo	422	1782	4.2	t56	12
Indianapolis	450	1727	3.8	45	10
Jacksonville	454	1720	3.8	33	20
Baltimore	420	1589	3.8	25	7
Oakland	360	1588	4.4	t83	9
N.Y. Jets	431	1485	3.4	t43	10
New England	398	1464	3.7	t70	6
San Diego	409	1416	3.5	32	5
Miami	430	1343	3.1	t71	18
AFC total	6792	27322	4.0	t83	202
AFC average	452.8	1821.5	4.0	...	13.5

t—touchdown.

NFC

Team	Att.	Yds.	Avg.	Long	TD
Detroit	447	2464	5.5	t82	19
Minnesota	449	2041	4.5	t78	14
N.Y. Giants	521	1988	3.8	42	14
San Francisco	523	1969	3.8	51	16
Philadelphia	465	1943	4.2	30	11
Tampa Bay	479	1934	4.0	76	15
Green Bay	459	1909	4.2	t52	9
Carolina	441	1770	4.0	50	11
Chicago	490	1746	3.6	t68	14
Atlanta	442	1643	3.7	77	8
Dallas	423	1637	3.9	44	6
Washington	453	1615	3.6	34	12
St. Louis	443	1563	3.5	28	15
New Orleans	417	1461	3.5	t74	9
Arizona	395	1255	3.2	31	9
NFC total	6847	26938	3.9	t82	182
NFC average	456.5	1795.9	3.9	...	12.1
NFL total	13639	54260	...	t83	384
NFL average	454.6	1808.7	4.0	...	12.8

INDIVIDUAL

BESTS OF THE SEASON

Yards, season
NFC: 2053—Barry Sanders, Detroit.
AFC: 1750—Terrell Davis, Denver.

Yards, game
AFC: 246—Corey Dillon, Cincinnati vs. Tennessee, Dec. 4 (39 attempts, 4 TDs).
NFC: 216—Barry Sanders, Detroit vs. Indianapolis, Nov. 23 (24 attempts, 2 TDs).

Longest gain
AFC: 83—Napoleon Kaufman, Oakland vs. Denver, Oct. 19 (TD).
NFC: 82—Barry Sanders, Detroit at Tampa Bay, Oct. 12 (TD).

Attempts, season
AFC: 375—Jerome Bettis, Pittsburgh.
NFC: 335—Barry Sanders, Detroit.

Attempts, game
AFC: 42—Terrell Davis, Denver at Buffalo, Oct. 26 (207 yards, 1 TD).
NFC: 36—Terry Allen, Washington vs. Jacksonville, Sept. 28 (122 yards, 0 TDs).

Yards per attempt, season
AFC: 6.7—Steve McNair, Tennessee.
NFC: 6.1—Barry Sanders, Detroit.

Touchdowns, season
AFC: 15—Karim Abdul-Jabbar, Miami; Terrell Davis, Denver.
NFC: 11—Barry Sanders, Detroit.

Team leaders, yards
AFC:

Baltimore	774	Bam Morris
Buffalo	840	Antowain Smith
Cincinnati	1129	Corey Dillon
Denver	1750	Terrell Davis
Indianapolis	1054	Marshall Faulk
Jacksonville	823	Natrone Means
Kansas City	550	Greg Hill
Miami	892	Karim Abdul-Jabbar
New England	1160	Curtis Martin
N.Y. Jets	1086	Adrian Murrell
Oakland	1294	Napoleon Kaufman
Pittsburgh	1665	Jerome Bettis
San Diego	945	Gary Brown
Seattle	847	Chris Warren
Tennessee	1399	Eddie George

NFC:

Arizona	424	Leeland McElroy
Atlanta	1002	Jamal Anderson
Carolina	809	Fred Lane
Chicago	1033	Raymont Harris
Dallas	1074	Emmitt Smith
Detroit	2053	Barry Sanders
Green Bay	1435	Dorsey Levens
Minnesota	1266	Robert Smith
New Orleans	552	Ray Zellars
N.Y. Giants	698	Charles Way
Philadelphia	1110	Ricky Watters
St. Louis	633	Lawrence Phillips
San Francisco	1019	Garrison Hearst
Tampa Bay	978	Warrick Dunn
Washington	724	Terry Allen

NFL LEADERS

Player, Team	Att.	Yds.	Avg.	Long	TD
Sanders, Barry, Detroit	335	2053	6.1	t82	11
Davis, Terrell, Denver*	369	1750	4.7	t50	15
Bettis, Jerome, Pittsburgh*	375	1665	4.4	34	7
Levens, Dorsey, Green Bay*	329	1435	4.4	t52	7
George, Eddie, Tennessee*	357	1399	3.9	30	6
Kaufman, Napoleon, Oakland*	272	1294	4.8	t83	6
Smith, Robert, Minnesota	232	1266	5.5	t78	6
Martin, Curtis, New England*	274	1160	4.2	t70	4
Dillon, Corey, Cincinnati*	233	1129	4.8	t71	10
Watters, Ricky, Philadelphia	285	1110	3.9	28	7
Murrell, Adrian, N.Y. Jets*	300	1086	3.6	t43	7
Smith, Emmitt, Dallas	261	1074	4.1	44	4
Faulk, Marshall, Indianapolis*	264	1054	4.0	45	7
Harris, Raymont, Chicago	275	1033	3.8	t68	10
Hearst, Garrison, San Francisco	234	1019	4.4	51	4
Anderson, Jamal, Atlanta	290	1002	3.5	39	7
Dunn, Warrick, Tampa Bay	224	978	4.4	76	4
Brown, Gary, San Diego*	253	945	3.7	32	4
Abdul-Jabbar, Karim, Miami*	283	892	3.2	22	15
Warren, Chris, Seattle*	200	847	4.2	t36	4
Smith, Antowain, Buffalo*	194	840	4.3	t56	8
Means, Natrone, Jacksonville*	244	823	3.4	20	9
Lane, Fred, Carolina	182	809	4.4	50	7

Player, Team	Att.	Yds.	Avg.	Long	TD
Morris, Bam, Baltimore*	204	774	3.8	25	4
Allen, Terry, Washington	210	724	3.4	34	4
Way, Charles, N.Y. Giants	151	698	4.6	42	4
Phillips, Lawrence, Miami*	201	677	3.4	28	8
McNair, Steve, Tennessee*	101	674	6.7	47	8
Alstott, Mike, Tampa Bay	176	665	3.8	t47	7
Thomas, Thurman, Buffalo*	154	643	4.2	24	1

*AFC.
t—touchdown.
Leader based on yards gained.

AFC

Player, Team	Att.	Yds.	Avg.	Long	TD
Abdul-Jabbar, Karim, Miami	283	892	3.2	22	15
Aguiar, Louie, Kansas City	2	11	5.5	6	0
Alexander, Derrick, Baltimore	1	0	0.0	0	0
Allen, Marcus, Kansas City	124	505	4.1	30	11
Anders, Kimble, Kansas City	79	397	5.0	43	0
Anderson, Richie, N.Y. Jets	21	70	3.3	19	0
Araguz, Leo, Oakland	1	0	0.0	0	0
Aska, Joe, Oakland	12	10	0.8	4	0
Bailey, Aaron, Indianapolis	3	20	6.7	18	0
Barker, Bryan, Jacksonville	1	0	0.0	0	0
Bennett, Donnell, Kansas City	94	369	3.9	14	1
Bettis, Jerome, Pittsburgh	375	1665	4.4	34	7
Bieniemy, Eric, Cincinnati	21	97	4.6	t20	1
Blackwell, Will, Pittsburgh	2	14	7.0	11	0
Blake, Jeff, Cincinnati	45	234	5.2	16	3
Bledsoe, Drew, New England	28	55	2.0	8	0
Brister, Bubby, Denver	4	2	0.5	2	0
Broussard, Steve, Seattle	70	418	6.0	t77	5
Brown, Gary, San Diego	253	945	3.7	32	4
Brown, Tim, Oakland	5	19	3.8	12	0
Brown, Troy, New England	1	-18	-18.0	-18	0
Brunell, Mark, Jacksonville	48	257	5.4	15	2
Byars, Keith, New England	11	24	2.2	5	0
Byner, Earnest, Baltimore	84	313	3.7	19	0
Bynum, Kenny, San Diego	30	97	3.2	19	0
Carter, Ki-Jana, Cincinnati	128	464	3.6	t79	7
Clements, Chuck, N.Y. Jets	2	-3	-1.5	-1	0
Collins, Todd, Buffalo	30	77	2.6	11	0
Cotton, Kenyon, Baltimore	2	2	1.0	t1	1
Craver, Aaron, San Diego	20	71	3.6	22	0
Crockett, Zack, Indianapolis	95	300	3.2	20	1
Cullors, Derrick, New England	22	101	4.6	24	0
Davis, Terrell, Denver	369	1750	4.7	t50	15
Davison, Jerone, Oakland	2	4	2.0	5	0
Dillon, Corey, Cincinnati	233	1129	4.8	t71	10
Elway, John, Denver	50	218	4.4	23	1
Erickson, Craig, Miami	4	8	2.0	4	0
Esiason, Boomer, Cincinnati	8	11	1.4	8	0
Everett, Jim, San Diego	5	6	1.2	6	0
Faulk, Marshall, Indianapolis	264	1054	4.0	45	7
Fenner, Derrick, Oakland	7	24	3.4	7	0
Fletcher, Terrell, San Diego	51	161	3.2	13	0
Foley, Glenn, N.Y. Jets	3	-5	-1.7	-1	0
Friesz, John, Seattle	1	0	0.0	0	0
Galloway, Joey, Seattle	9	72	8.0	44	0
Gannon, Rich, Kansas City	33	109	3.3	13	2
Gardner, Carwell, San Diego	7	20	2.9	5	0
Gash, Sam, New England	6	10	1.7	4	0
George, Eddie, Tennessee	357	1399	3.9	30	6
George, Jeff, Oakland	17	44	2.6	12	0
Graham, Jay, Baltimore	81	299	3.7	19	2
Graham, Scottie, Cincinnati	1	-1	-1.0	-1	0
Grbac, Elvis, Kansas City	30	168	5.6	20	1
Grier, Marrio, New England	33	75	2.3	12	1
Griffith, Howard, Denver	9	34	3.8	9	0
Groce, Clif, Indianapolis	10	66	6.6	29	0
Hall, Tim, Oakland	23	120	5.2	15	0
Hallock, Ty, Jacksonville	4	21	5.3	11	0
Harbaugh, Jim, Indianapolis	36	206	5.7	18	0
Harrison, Marvin, Indianapolis	2	-7	-3.5	0	0
Hawkins, Courtney, Pittsburgh	5	17	3.4	11	0
Hebron, Vaughn, Denver	49	222	4.5	46	1
Hill, Greg, Kansas City	157	550	3.5	38	0
Holcomb, Kelly, Indianapolis	5	5	1.0	3	0
Holmes, Darick, Buffalo	22	106	4.8	19	2
Humphries, Stan, San Diego	13	24	1.8	11	0
Jackson, Willie, Jacksonville	3	14	4.7	13	0
Johnson, Lee, Cincinnati	1	0	0.0	0	0
Johnson, Leon, N.Y. Jets	48	158	3.3	20	2
Johnson, Lonnie, Buffalo	1	6	6.0	6	0
Johnson, Rob, Jacksonville	10	34	3.4	t25	1
Jones, Charlie, San Diego	4	42	10.5	17	0
Jones, George, Pittsburgh	72	235	3.3	32	1
Jordan, Charles, Miami	3	12	4.0	16	0
Jordan, Randy, Jacksonville	1	2	2.0	2	0
Justin, Paul, Indianapolis	6	2	0.3	3	0
Kaufman, Napoleon, Oakland	272	1294	4.8	t83	6
Kidd, John, Miami	1	4	4.0	4	0
Kitna, Jon, Seattle	10	9	0.9	8	1
Klingler, David, Oakland	1	0	0.0	0	0
Krieg, Dave, Tennessee	4	-2	-0.5	0	0
Lester, Tim, Pittsburgh	2	9	4.5	6	0
Levitt, Chad, Oakland	2	3	1.5	2	0
Lewis, Jeff, Denver	5	2	0.4	5	0
Lewis, Jermaine, Baltimore	3	35	11.7	24	0
Loville, Derek, Denver	25	124	5.0	17	1
Lucas, Ray, N.Y. Jets	6	55	9.2	17	0
Marino, Dan, Miami	18	-14	-0.8	1	0
Marsh, Curtis, Pittsburgh	1	2	2.0	2	0
Martin, Curtis, New England	274	1160	4.2	t70	4
Mason, Derrick, Tennessee	1	-7	-7.0	-7	0
Matthews, Steve, Jacksonville	1	10	10.0	10	0
McAfee, Fred, Pittsburgh	13	41	3.2	9	0
McNair, Steve, Tennessee	101	674	6.7	47	8
McPhail, Jerris, Miami	17	146	8.6	t71	1
Means, Natrone, Jacksonville	244	823	3.4	20	9
Meggett, Dave, New England	20	60	3.0	10	1
Metcalf, Eric, San Diego	3	-5	-1.7	2	0
Miller, Josh, Pittsburgh	1	-7	-7.0	-7	0
Milne, Brian, Cincinnati	13	32	2.5	5	2
Mohr, Chris, Buffalo	1	0	0.0	0	0
Montgomery, Greg, Baltimore	1	11	11.0	11	0
Moon, Warren, Seattle	17	40	2.4	17	1
Morris, Bam, Baltimore	204	774	3.8	25	4
Moulds, Eric, Buffalo	4	59	14.8	29	0
Murrell, Adrian, N.Y. Jets	300	1086	3.6	t43	7
Neal, Lorenzo, N.Y. Jets	10	28	2.8	8	0
Nealy, Ray, Miami	1	2	2.0	2	0
O'Donnell, Neil, N.Y. Jets	32	36	1.1	19	1
Parmalee, Bernie, Miami	18	59	3.3	12	0
Philcox, Todd, San Diego	1	3	3.0	3	0
Phillips, Lawrence, St.L.-Mia.*	201	677	3.4	28	8
Pickens, Carl, Cincinnati	1	-6	-6.0	-6	0
Potts, Roosevelt, Ind.-Mia.	2	4	2.0	3	0
Pritchard, Mike, Seattle	1	14	14.0	14	0
Pritchett, Stanley, Miami	3	7	2.3	4	0
Reed, Andre, Buffalo	3	11	3.7	9	0
Richardson, Kyle, Seattle	1	0	0.0	0	0
Richardson, Tony, Kansas City	2	11	5.5	6	0
Rison, Andre, Kansas City	1	2	2.0	2	0
Ritchey, James, Tennessee	1	6	6.0	6	0
Roby, Reggie, Tennessee	1	12	12.0	12	0
Sanders, Chris, Tennessee	1	-8	-8.0	-8	0
Scott, Darnay, Cincinnati	1	6	6.0	6	0
Shelton, Daimon, Jacksonville	6	4	0.7	2	0
Smith, Antowain, Buffalo	194	840	4.3	t56	8
Smith, Detron, Denver	4	10	2.5	11	0
Smith, Lamar, Seattle	91	392	4.3	35	2

1997 STATISTICS Rushing

Player, Team	Att.	Yds.	Avg.	Long	TD
Smith, Rod, Denver	5	16	3.2	21	0
Sowell, Jerald, N.Y. Jets	7	35	5.0	10	0
Spikes, Irving, Miami	63	180	2.9	14	2
Stewart, James, Jacksonville	136	555	4.1	33	8
Stewart, Kordell, Pittsburgh	88	476	5.4	t74	11
Strong, Mack, Seattle	4	8	2.0	6	0
Testaverde, Vinny, Baltimore	34	138	4.1	16	0
Thigpen, Yancey, Pittsburgh	1	3	3.0	3	0
Thomas, Rodney, Tennessee	67	310	4.6	t25	3
Thomas, Thurman, Buffalo	154	643	4.2	24	1
Tolliver, Billy Joe, Atl.-K.C.*	9	7	0.8	12	0
Tomczak, Mike, Pittsburgh	7	13	1.9	17	0
Vanover, Tamarick, Kansas City	5	50	10.0	17	0
Van Pelt, Alex, Buffalo	11	33	3.0	9	1
Ward, Dedric, N.Y. Jets	2	25	12.5	21	0
Warren, Chris, Seattle	200	847	4.2	t36	4
Warren, Lamont, Indianapolis	28	80	2.9	11	2
Whelihan, Craig, San Diego	13	29	2.2	7	0
Williams, Harvey, Oakland	18	70	3.9	13	3
Witman, Jon, Pittsburgh	5	11	2.2	4	0
Zeier, Eric, Baltimore	10	17	1.7	12	0
Zolak, Scott, New England	3	-3	-1.0	-1	0

*Includes both NFC and AFC statistics.
t—touchdown.

NFC

Player, Team	Att.	Yds.	Avg.	Long	TD
Aikman, Troy, Dallas	25	79	3.2	13	0
Allen, Terry, Washington	210	724	3.4	34	4
Alstott, Mike, Tampa Bay	176	665	3.8	t47	7
Anderson, Jamal, Atlanta	290	1002	3.5	39	7
Anthony, Reidel, Tampa Bay	5	84	16.8	26	0
Autry, Darnell, Chicago	112	319	2.8	17	1
Banks, Tony, St. Louis	47	186	4.0	23	1
Barber, Tiki, N.Y. Giants	136	511	3.8	42	3
Bates, Mario, New Orleans	119	440	3.7	t74	4
Bender, Wes, New Orleans	5	9	1.8	6	0
Berger, Mitch, Minnesota	1	0	0.0	0	0
Beuerlein, Steve, Carolina	4	32	8.0	20	0
Biakabutuka, Tim, Carolina	75	299	4.0	t26	2
Bono, Steve, Green Bay	3	-3	-1.0	-1	0
Bouie, Kevin, Arizona	11	26	2.4	6	0
Bowie, Larry, Washington	28	100	3.6	18	2
Brohm, Jeff, San Francisco	4	11	2.8	10	0
Brooks, Robert, Green Bay	2	19	9.5	15	0
Brown, Dave, N.Y. Giants	17	29	1.7	7	1
Calloway, Chris, N.Y. Giants	1	-1	-1.0	-1	0
Carruth, Rae, Carolina	6	23	3.8	6	0
Carter, Tony, Chicago	9	56	6.2	16	0
Case, Stoney, Arizona	7	8	1.1	3	1
Centers, Larry, Arizona	101	276	2.7	14	1
Chandler, Chris, Atlanta	43	158	3.7	19	0
Cherry, Mike, N.Y. Giants	1	-2	-2.0	-2	0
Christian, Bob, Atlanta	7	8	1.1	3	0
Collins, Kerry, Carolina	26	65	2.5	21	1
Connell, Albert, Washington	1	3	3.0	3	0
Conway, Curtis, Chicago	3	17	5.7	10	0
Crawford, Keith, St. Louis	2	32	16.0	23	0
Cunningham, Randall, Minnesota	19	127	6.7	28	0
Davis, Stephen, Washington	141	567	4.0	18	3
Davis, Troy, New Orleans	75	271	3.6	20	0
Detmer, Ty, Philadelphia	14	46	3.3	14	1
Dilfer, Trent, Tampa Bay	33	99	3.0	17	1
Druckenmiller, Jim, San Francisco	10	-6	-0.6	2	0
Dunn, Warrick, Tampa Bay	224	978	4.4	76	4
Edwards, Marc, San Francisco	5	17	3.4	6	0
Ellison, Jerry, Tampa Bay	2	10	5.0	5	0
Evans, Charles, Minnesota	43	157	3.7	13	2
Favre, Brett, Green Bay	58	187	3.2	16	1
Floyd, William, San Francisco	78	231	3.0	22	3
Freeman, Antonio, Green Bay	1	14	14.0	14	0
Frerotte, Gus, Washington	25	65	2.6	26	2
Garner, Charlie, Philadelphia	116	547	4.7	26	3
Gedney, Chris, Arizona	1	15	15.0	15	0
Graham, Kent, Arizona	13	23	1.8	10	2
Graziani, Tony, Atlanta	3	19	6.3	10	0
Green, Harold, Atlanta	36	78	2.2	22	1
Green, Robert, Minnesota	6	22	3.7	8	0
Greene, Scott, Carolina	45	157	3.5	t10	1
Guliford, Eric, New Orleans	1	-2	-2.0	-2	0
Hampton, Rodney, N.Y. Giants	23	81	3.5	22	1
Hanspard, Byron, Atlanta	53	335	6.3	77	0
Hape, Patrick, Tampa Bay	1	1	1.0	1	0
Harmon, Ronnie, Ten.-Chi.*	10	36	3.6	14	0
Harris, Raymont, Chicago	275	1033	3.8	t68	10
Hastings, Andre, New Orleans	4	35	8.8	27	0
Hayden, Aaron, Green Bay	32	148	4.6	21	1
Hearst, Garrison, San Francisco	234	1019	4.4	51	4
Henderson, William, Green Bay	31	113	3.6	15	0
Heyward, Craig, St. Louis	34	84	2.5	8	1
Hicks, Michael, Chicago	4	14	3.5	8	0
Hill, Randal, New Orleans	1	11	11.0	11	0
Hoard, Leroy, Minnesota	80	235	2.9	20	4
Hobert, Billy Joe, Buf.-N.O.*	14	43	3.1	15	0
Horan, Mike, St. Louis	1	-3	-3.0	-3	0
Hostetler, Jeff, Washington	14	28	2.0	11	0
Hoying, Bobby, Philadelphia	16	78	4.9	30	0
Hughes, Tyrone, Chicago	1	3	3.0	3	0
Hutton, Tom, Philadelphia	1	0	0.0	0	0
Ismail, Raghib, Carolina	4	32	8.0	18	0
Johnson, Anthony, Carolina	97	358	3.7	20	0
Johnson, Brad, Minnesota	35	139	4.0	28	0
Johnson, LeShon, Arizona	23	81	3.5	11	0
Johnston, Daryl, Dallas	2	3	1.5	3	0
Kanell, Danny, N.Y. Giants	15	2	0.1	8	0
Kennison, Eddie, St. Louis	3	13	4.3	6	0
Kirby, Terry, San Francisco	125	418	3.3	38	6
Kramer, Erik, Chicago	27	83	3.1	31	2
Lane, Eric, N.Y. Giants	5	13	2.6	6	0
Lane, Fred, Carolina	182	809	4.4	50	7
Le Bel, Harper, Chicago	1	0	0.0	0	0
Lee, Amp, St. Louis	28	104	3.7	14	0
Levens, Dorsey, Green Bay	329	1435	4.4	t52	7
Levy, Chuck, San Francisco	16	90	5.6	24	0
Logan, Marc, Washington	4	5	1.3	4	0
Mathis, Terance, Atlanta	3	35	11.7	16	0
McCrary, Fred, New Orleans	8	15	1.9	8	0
McElroy, Leeland, Arizona	135	424	3.1	18	2
McKinnon, Ronald, Arizona	1	3	3.0	3	0
Miller, Anthony, Dallas	1	6	6.0	6	0
Mirer, Rick, Chicago	20	78	3.9	20	1
Mitchell, Brian, Washington	23	107	4.7	26	1
Mitchell, Scott, Detroit	37	83	2.2	13	1
Moore, Jerald, St. Louis	104	380	3.7	26	3
Moore, Ronald, St.L.-Ari.	81	278	3.4	t27	1
Morton, Johnnie, Detroit	3	33	11.0	20	0
Nussmeier, Doug, New Orleans	8	30	3.8	15	0
Oliver, Winslow, Carolina	1	0	0.0	0	0
Palmer, David, Minnesota	11	36	3.3	10	1
Patten, David, N.Y. Giants	1	2	2.0	2	0
Pederson, Doug, Green Bay	3	-4	-1.3	-1	0
Peete, Rodney, Philadelphia	8	37	4.6	16	0
Pegram, Erric, S.D.-NYG*	28	95	3.4	t18	2
Penn, Chris, Chicago	1	-1	-1.0	-1	0
Plummer, Jake, Arizona	39	216	5.5	31	2
Reich, Frank, Detroit	4	-4	-1.0	-1	0
Rhett, Errict, Tampa Bay	31	96	3.1	21	3
Rice, Jerry, San Francisco	1	-10	-10.0	-10	0
Rivers, Ron, Detroit	29	166	5.7	31	1
Rypien, Mark, St. Louis	1	1	1.0	1	0
Salaam, Rashaan, Chicago	31	112	3.6	17	0

Player, Team	Att.	Yds.	Avg.	Long	TD
Sanders, Barry, Detroit	335	2053	6.1	t82	11
Sanders, Deion, Dallas	1	-11	-11.0	-11	0
Sanders, Frank, Arizona	1	5	5.0	5	0
Sauerbrun, Todd, Chicago	2	8	4.0	8	0
Schlesinger, Cory, Detroit	7	11	1.6	4	0
Shepherd, Leslie, Washington	4	27	6.8	17	0
Shuler, Heath, New Orleans	22	38	1.7	8	1
Smith, Cedric, Arizona	4	5	1.3	2	1
Smith, Emmitt, Dallas	261	1074	4.1	44	4
Smith, Eric, Chicago	1	12	12.0	12	0
Smith, Robert, Minnesota	232	1266	5.5	t78	6
Staley, Duce, Philadelphia	7	29	4.1	12	0
Stenstrom, Steve, Chicago	1	6	6.0	6	0
Swann, Eric, Arizona	1	0	0.0	0	0
Thompson, David, St. Louis	16	30	1.9	9	1
Turk, Matt, Washington	1	0	0.0	0	0
Turner, Kevin, Philadelphia	18	96	5.3	29	0
Vardell, Tommy, Detroit	32	122	3.8	41	6
Walker, Herschel, Dallas	6	20	3.3	11	0
Walsh, Steve, Tampa Bay	6	-4	-0.7	0	0
Walter, Ken, Carolina	1	-5	-5.0	-5	0
Watters, Ricky, Philadelphia	285	1110	3.9	28	7
Way, Charles, N.Y. Giants	151	698	4.6	42	4
Westbrook, Michael, Washington	3	-11	-3.7	7	0
Wheatley, Tyrone, N.Y. Giants	152	583	3.8	38	4
Williams, Karl, Tampa Bay	1	5	5.0	5	0
Williams, Kevin, Arizona	1	-2	-2.0	-2	0
Williams, Moe, Minnesota	22	59	2.7	8	1
Williams, Sherman, Dallas	121	468	3.9	18	2
Wilson, Wade, Dallas	6	-2	-0.3	3	0
Wuerffel, Danny, New Orleans	6	26	4.3	10	0
Young, Steve, San Francisco	50	199	4.0	13	3
Zellars, Ray, New Orleans	156	552	3.5	27	4

*Includes both NFC and AFC statistics.
t—touchdown.

PLAYERS WITH TWO CLUBS

Player, Team	Att.	Yds.	Avg.	Long	TD
Harmon, Ronnie, Tennessee	8	30	3.8	14	0
Harmon, Ronnie, Chicago	2	6	3.0	4	0
Hobert, Billy Joe, Buffalo	2	7	3.5	7	0
Hobert, Billy Joe, New Orleans	12	36	3.0	15	0
Moore, Ronald, St. Louis	24	103	4.3	t27	1
Moore, Ronald, Arizona	57	175	3.1	16	0
Pegram, Erric, San Diego	9	23	2.6	t6	1
Pegram, Erric, N.Y. Giants	19	72	3.8	t18	1
Phillips, Lawrence, St. Louis	183	633	3.5	28	8
Phillips, Lawrence, Miami	18	44	2.4	8	0
Potts, Roosevelt, Indianapolis	1	1	1.0	1	0
Potts, Roosevelt, Miami	1	3	3.0	3	0
Tolliver, Billy Joe, Atlanta	7	8	1.1	12	0
Tolliver, Billy Joe, Kansas City	2	-1	-0.5	0	0

PASSING

TEAM

AFC

Team	Att.	Comp.	Pct. Comp.	Gross Yds.	Sack	Yds. Lost	Net Yds.	Yds./ Att.	Yds./ Comp.	TD	Pct. TD	Long	Had Int.	Pct. Int.
Seattle	609	359	58.9	4187	36	228	3959	6.88	11.66	26	4.27	61	21	3.4
Miami	576	332	57.6	3945	22	153	3792	6.85	11.88	16	2.78	55	12	2.1
Oakland	529	294	55.6	3944	58	430	3514	7.46	13.41	29	5.48	76	10	1.9
Baltimore	586	338	57.7	3929	37	227	3702	6.70	11.62	25	4.27	92	16	2.7
Jacksonville	504	313	62.1	3922	40	218	3704	7.78	12.53	20	3.97	75	9	1.8
New England	532	321	60.3	3808	30	258	3550	7.16	11.86	31	5.83	76	15	2.8
Denver	513	287	55.9	3704	35	210	3494	7.22	12.91	27	5.26	78	11	2.1
Cincinnati	504	302	59.9	3603	46	287	3316	7.15	11.93	21	4.17	t77	9	1.8
Indianapolis	523	317	60.6	3560	62	418	3142	6.81	11.23	16	3.06	58	17	3.3
N.Y. Jets	564	319	56.6	3555	48	313	3242	6.30	11.14	20	3.55	70	10	1.8
San Diego	565	291	51.5	3475	51	386	3089	6.15	11.94	12	2.12	t72	21	3.7
Pittsburgh	466	253	54.3	3215	20	152	3063	6.90	12.71	22	4.72	t69	19	4.1
Buffalo	546	293	53.7	3213	46	338	2875	5.88	10.97	14	2.56	t77	25	4.6
Kansas City	493	281	57.0	3129	32	236	2893	6.35	11.14	20	4.06	t55	10	2.0
Tennessee	420	220	52.4	2704	32	199	2505	6.44	12.29	15	3.57	t55	13	3.1
AFC total	7930	4520	...	53893	595	4053	49840	...	...	314	...	92	218	...
AFC average	528.7	301.3	57.0	3592.9	39.7	270.9	3322.7	6.80	11.92	20.9	4.00	...	14.5	2.7

t—touchdown.

NFC

Team	Att.	Comp.	Pct. Comp.	Gross Yds.	Sack	Yds. Lost	Net Yds.	Yds./ Att.	Yds./ Comp.	TD	Pct. TD	Long	Had Int.	Pct. Int.
Philadelphia	587	330	56.2	4009	64	362	3647	6.83	12.15	22	3.75	t72	16	2.7
Arizona	602	317	52.7	3953	78	495	3458	6.57	12.47	19	3.16	t70	22	3.7
Green Bay	523	309	59.1	3896	26	191	3705	7.45	12.61	35	6.69	74	16	3.1
Detroit	540	304	56.3	3605	41	271	3334	6.68	11.86	19	3.52	79	17	3.1
Washington	547	283	51.7	3581	33	198	3383	6.55	12.65	22	4.02	69	22	4.0
Minnesota	540	319	59.1	3537	33	224	3313	6.55	11.09	26	4.81	56	16	3.0
St. Louis	526	271	51.5	3524	44	326	3198	6.70	13.00	14	2.66	76	15	2.9
Chicago	595	336	56.5	3501	43	257	3244	5.88	10.42	14	2.35	t78	22	3.7
Dallas	553	314	56.8	3454	39	313	3141	6.25	11.00	19	3.44	t64	12	2.2
Atlanta	484	273	56.4	3445	54	372	3073	7.12	12.62	26	5.37	56	11	2.3
San Francisco	432	278	64.4	3432	44	289	3143	7.94	12.35	20	4.63	82	11	2.5
Carolina	534	289	54.1	3156	44	311	2845	5.91	10.92	17	3.18	t59	24	4.5
New Orleans	458	228	49.8	2901	50	317	2584	6.33	12.72	13	2.84	t89	33	7.2
N.Y. Giants	474	249	52.5	2763	32	238	2525	5.83	11.10	16	3.38	t68	12	2.5
Tampa Bay	404	224	55.4	2638	32	196	2442	6.53	11.78	21	5.20	t59	12	3.0
NFC total	7799	4324	...	51395	657	4360	47035	...	...	303	...	t89	261	...
NFC average	519.9	288.3	55.4	3426.3	43.8	290.7	3135.7	6.59	11.89	20.2	3.90	...	17.4	3.3
NFL total	15729	8844	...	105288	1252	8413	96875	...	...	617	...	92	479	...
NFL average	524.3	294.8	56.2	3509.6	41.7	280.4	3229.2	6.69	11.91	20.6	3.90	...	16	3.0

INDIVIDUAL

BESTS OF THE SEASON

Highest rating, season
NFC: 104.7—Steve Young, San Francisco.
AFC: 91.2—Mark Brunell, Jacksonville.

Completion percentage, season
NFC: 67.7—Steve Young, San Francisco.
AFC: 61.2—Jim Harbaugh, Indianapolis.

Attempts, season
AFC: 548—Dan Marino, Miami.
NFC: 518—Troy Aikman, Dallas.

Completions, season
AFC: 319—Dan Marino, Miami.
NFC: 304—Brett Favre, Green Bay.

Yards, season
AFC: 3917—Jeff George, Oakland.
NFC: 3867—Brett Favre, Green Bay.

Yards, game
AFC: 409—Warren Moon, Seattle vs. Oakland, Oct. 26 (28-44, 5 TDs).
NFC: 401—Tony Banks, St. Louis at Atlanta, Nov. 2 (23-34, 2 TDs).

Longest gain
AFC: 92—Eric Zeier (to Derrick Alexander), Baltimore vs. Seattle, Dec. 7.
NFC: 89—Heath Shuler (to Randal Hill), New Orleans at Chicago, Oct. 5 (TD).

Yards per attempt, season
NFC: 8.51—Steve Young, San Francisco.
AFC: 7.54—Mark Brunell, Jacksonville.

Touchdown passes, season
NFC: 35—Brett Favre, Green Bay.
AFC: 29—Jeff George, Oakland.

Touchdown passes, game
AFC: 5—Neil O'Donnell, N.Y. Jets at Seattle, Aug. 31 (18-25, 270
yards); Warren Moon, Seattle vs. Oakland, Oct. 26 (28-44,
409 yards).
NFC: 5—Brett Favre, Green Bay vs. Minnesota, Sept. 21 (18-31,
266 yards).

Lowest interception percentage, season
AFC: 1.3—Jim Harbaugh, Indianapolis.
NFC: 1.7—Steve Young, San Francisco.

NFL LEADERS

Player, Team	Att.	Comp.	Pct. Comp.	Yds.	Avg. Gain	TD	Pct. TD	Long	Int.	Pct. Int.	Sack	Yds. Lost	Rat. Pts.
Young, Steve, San Francisco	356	241	67.7	3029	8.51	19	5.3	82	6	1.7	35	220	104.7
Chandler, Chris, Atlanta	342	202	59.1	2692	7.87	20	5.8	56	7	2.0	39	261	95.1
Favre, Brett, Green Bay	513	304	59.3	3867	7.54	35	6.8	74	16	3.1	25	176	92.6
Brunell, Mark, Jacksonville*	435	264	60.7	3281	7.54	18	4.1	75	7	1.6	33	189	91.2
George, Jeff, Oakland*	521	290	55.7	3917	7.52	29	5.6	76	9	1.7	58	430	91.2
Bledsoe, Drew, New England*	522	314	60.2	3706	7.10	28	5.4	76	15	2.9	30	258	87.7
Elway, John, Denver*	502	280	55.8	3635	7.24	27	5.4	78	11	2.2	34	203	87.5
Harbaugh, Jim, Indianapolis*	309	189	61.2	2060	6.67	10	3.2	58	4	1.3	41	256	86.2
Johnson, Brad, Minnesota	452	275	60.8	3036	6.72	20	4.4	56	12	2.7	26	164	84.5
Hoying, Bobby, Philadelphia	225	128	56.9	1573	6.99	11	4.9	t72	6	2.7	28	183	83.8
Moon, Warren, Seattle*	528	313	59.3	3678	6.97	25	4.7	t60	16	3.0	30	192	83.7
Dilfer, Trent, Tampa Bay	386	217	56.2	2555	6.62	21	5.4	t59	11	2.8	32	196	82.8
Marino, Dan, Miami*	548	319	58.2	3780	6.90	16	2.9	55	11	2.0	20	132	80.7
O'Donnell, Neil, N.Y. Jets*	460	259	56.3	2796	6.08	17	3.7	70	7	1.5	45	289	80.3
Mitchell, Scott, Detroit	509	293	57.6	3484	6.84	19	3.7	79	14	2.8	41	271	79.6
Grbac, Elvis, Kansas City*	314	179	57.0	1943	6.19	11	3.5	t55	6	1.9	19	150	79.1
Aikman, Troy, Dallas	518	292	56.4	3283	6.34	19	3.7	t64	12	2.3	33	269	78.0
Blake, Jeff, Cincinnati*	317	184	58.0	2125	6.70	8	2.5	t50	7	2.2	39	244	77.6
Testaverde, Vinny, Baltimore*	470	271	57.7	2971	6.32	18	3.8	t54	15	3.2	20	129	75.9
Stewart, Kordell, Pittsburgh*	440	236	53.6	3020	6.86	21	4.8	t69	17	3.9	20	152	75.2
Kramer, Erik, Chicago	477	275	57.7	3011	6.31	14	2.9	t78	14	2.9	25	149	74.0
Detmer, Ty, Philadelphia	244	134	54.9	1567	6.42	7	2.9	57	6	2.5	19	94	73.9
Frerotte, Gus, Washington	402	204	50.7	2682	6.67	17	4.2	52	12	3.0	23	146	73.8
Plummer, Jake, Arizona	296	157	53.0	2203	7.44	15	5.1	t70	15	5.1	52	291	73.1
Banks, Tony, St. Louis	487	252	51.7	3254	6.68	14	2.9	76	13	2.7	43	317	71.5
Humphries, Stan, San Diego*	225	121	53.8	1488	6.61	5	2.2	t72	6	2.7	18	144	70.8
Kanell, Danny, N.Y. Giants	294	156	53.1	1740	5.92	11	3.7	t68	9	3.1	19	171	70.7
McNair, Steve, Tennessee*	415	216	52.0	2665	6.42	14	3.4	t55	13	3.1	31	190	70.4
Collins, Todd, Buffalo*	391	215	55.0	2367	6.05	12	3.1	t77	13	3.3	39	278	69.5
Graham, Kent, Arizona	250	130	52.0	1408	5.63	4	1.6	47	5	2.0	16	115	65.9

*AFC.
t—touchdown.
Leader based on rating points, minimum 224 attempts.

AFC

Player, Team	Att.	Comp.	Pct. Comp.	Yds.	Avg. Gain	TD	Pct. TD	Long	Int.	Pct. Int.	Sack	Yds. Lost	Rat. Pts.
Aguiar, Louie, Kansas City	1	1	100.0	35	35.00	0	0.0	35	0	0.0	0	0	118.8
Allen, Marcus, Kansas City	2	2	100.0	15	7.50	2	100.0	t14	0	0.0	0	0	137.5
Barker, Bryan, Jacksonville	1	1	100.0	22	22.00	0	0.0	22	0	0.0	0	0	118.8
Blake, Jeff, Cincinnati	317	184	58.0	2125	6.70	8	2.5	t50	7	2.2	39	244	77.6
Bledsoe, Drew, New England	522	314	60.2	3706	7.10	28	5.4	76	15	2.9	30	258	87.7
Brister, Bubby, Denver	9	6	66.7	48	5.33	0	0.0	15	0	0.0	0	0	79.9
Brunell, Mark, Jacksonville	435	264	60.7	3281	7.54	18	4.1	75	7	1.6	33	189	91.2
Carter, Ki-Jana, Cincinnati	1	0	0.0	0	0.00	0	0.0	0	0	0.0	0	0	39.6
Collins, Todd, Buffalo	391	215	55.0	2367	6.05	12	3.1	t77	13	3.3	39	278	69.5
Davis, Willie, Tennessee	1	1	100.0	22	22.00	1	100.0	t22	0	0.0	0	0	158.3
Elway, John, Denver	502	280	55.8	3635	7.24	27	5.4	78	11	2.2	34	203	87.5
Erickson, Craig, Miami	28	13	46.4	165	5.89	0	0.0	27	1	3.6	2	21	50.4
Esiason, Boomer, Cincinnati	186	118	63.4	1478	7.95	13	7.0	t77	2	1.1	7	43	106.9
Everett, Jim, San Diego	75	36	48.0	457	6.09	1	1.3	62	4	5.3	4	30	49.7
Foley, Glenn, N.Y. Jets	97	56	57.7	705	7.27	3	3.1	t35	1	1.0	3	24	86.5
Friesz, John, Seattle	36	15	41.7	138	3.83	0	0.0	22	3	8.3	2	11	18.1
Galloway, Joey, Seattle	0	0	...	0	...	0	...	0	0	...	1	15	...
Gannon, Rich, Kansas City	175	98	56.0	1144	6.54	7	4.0	47	4	2.3	13	86	79.8
George, Jeff, Oakland	521	290	55.7	3917	7.52	29	5.6	76	9	1.7	58	430	91.2
Grbac, Elvis, Kansas City	314	179	57.0	1943	6.19	11	3.5	t55	6	1.9	19	150	79.1
Hansen, Brian, N.Y. Jets	1	1	100.0	26	26.00	0	0.0	26	0	0.0	0	0	118.8
Harbaugh, Jim, Indianapolis	309	189	61.2	2060	6.67	10	3.2	58	4	1.3	41	256	86.2
Holcomb, Kelly, Indianapolis	73	45	61.6	454	6.22	1	1.4	41	8	11.0	11	76	44.3
Humphries, Stan, San Diego	225	121	53.8	1488	6.61	5	2.2	t72	6	2.7	18	144	70.8

Player, Team	Att.	Comp.	Pct. Comp.	Yds.	Avg. Gain	TD	Pct. TD	Long	Int.	Pct. Int.	Sack	Yds. Lost	Rat. Pts.
Johnson, Leon, N.Y. Jets	2	0	0.0	0	0.00	0	0.0	0	1	50.0	0	0	0.0
Johnson, Rob, Jacksonville	28	22	78.6	344	12.29	2	7.1	40	2	7.1	6	29	111.9
Justin, Paul, Indianapolis	140	83	59.3	1046	7.47	5	3.6	44	5	3.6	10	86	79.6
Kaufman, Napoleon, Oakland	1	0	0.0	0	0.00	0	0.0	0	0	0.0	0	0	39.6
Kitna, Jon, Seattle	45	31	68.9	371	8.24	1	2.2	61	2	4.4	3	10	82.7
Klingler, David, Oakland	7	4	57.1	27	3.86	0	0.0	8	1	14.3	0	0	26.2
Krieg, Dave, Tennessee	2	1	50.0	2	1.00	0	0.0	2	0	0.0	0	0	56.3
Lewis, Jeff, Denver	2	1	50.0	21	10.50	0	0.0	21	0	0.0	1	7	87.5
Lucas, Ray, N.Y. Jets	4	3	75.0	28	7.00	0	0.0	19	1	25.0	0	0	54.2
Marino, Dan, Miami	548	319	58.2	3780	6.90	16	2.9	55	11	2.0	20	132	80.7
Matthews, Steve, Jacksonville	40	26	65.0	275	6.88	0	0.0	43	0	0.0	1	0	84.9
McNair, Steve, Tennessee	415	216	52.0	2665	6.42	14	3.4	t55	13	3.1	31	190	70.4
Meggett, David, New England	1	1	100.0	35	35.00	1	100.0	t35	0	0.0	0	0	158.3
Mohr, Chris, Buffalo	1	1	100.0	29	29.00	0	0.0	29	0	0.0	0	0	118.8
Moon, Warren, Seattle	528	313	59.3	3678	6.97	25	4.7	t60	16	3.0	30	192	83.7
O'Donnell, Neil, N.Y. Jets	460	259	56.3	2796	6.08	17	3.7	70	7	1.5	45	289	80.3
Philcox, Todd, San Diego	28	16	57.1	173	6.18	0	0.0	29	1	3.6	8	44	60.6
Quinn, Mike, Pittsburgh	2	1	50.0	10	5.00	0	0.0	10	0	0.0	0	0	64.6
Reed, Andre, Buffalo	0	0	...	0	...	0		...	0	...	1	20	
Ritchey, James, Tennessee	2	2	100.0	15	7.50	0	0.0	11	0	0.0	1	9	97.9
Stewart, Kordell, Pittsburgh	440	236	53.6	3020	6.86	21	4.8	t69	17	3.9	20	152	75.2
Testaverde, Vinny, Baltimore	470	271	57.7	2971	6.32	18	3.8	t54	15	3.2	20	129	75.9
Tolliver, Billy Joe, Atl.-K.C.*	116	64	55.2	677	5.84	5	4.3	t47	1	0.9	14	104	83.2
Tomczak, Mike, Pittsburgh	24	16	66.7	185	7.71	1	4.2	t28	2	8.3	0	0	68.9
Van Pelt, Alex, Buffalo	124	60	48.4	684	5.52	2	1.6	39	10	8.1	4	33	37.2
Warren, Lamont, Indianapolis	1	0	0.0	0	0.00	0	0.0	0	0	0.0	0	0	39.6
Whelihan, Craig, San Diego	237	118	49.8	1357	5.73	6	2.5	t61	10	4.2	21	168	58.3
Zeier, Eric, Baltimore	116	67	57.8	958	8.26	7	6.0	92	1	0.9	17	98	101.1
Zolak, Scott, New England	9	6	66.7	67	7.44	2	22.2	t20	0	0.0	0	0	128.2

*Includes both AFC and NFC statistics.
t—touchdown.

NFC

Player, Team	Att.	Comp.	Pct. Comp.	Yds.	Avg. Gain	TD	Pct. TD	Long	Int.	Pct. Int.	Sack	Yds. Lost	Rat. Pts.
Aikman, Troy, Dallas	518	292	56.4	3283	6.34	19	3.7	t64	12	2.3	33	269	78.0
Anderson, Jamal, Atlanta	4	1	25.0	27	6.75	1	25.0	t27	1	25.0	0	0	55.2
Banks, Tony, St. Louis	487	252	51.7	3254	6.68	14	2.9	76	13	2.7	43	317	71.5
Barnhardt, Tommy, Tampa Bay	1	1	100.0	25	25.00	0	0.0	25	0	0.0	0	0	118.8
Bates, Mario, New Orleans	1	1	100.0	21	21.00	1	100.0	t21	0	0.0	0	0	158.3
Beuerlein, Steve, Carolina	153	89	58.2	1032	6.75	6	3.9	52	3	2.0	17	111	83.6
Blundin, Matt, Detroit	1	0	0.0	0	0.0	0	0.0	0	1	100.0	0	0	0.0
Bono, Steve, Green Bay	10	5	50.0	29	2.90	0	0.0	14	0	0.0	1	15	56.3
Brohm, Jeff, San Francisco	24	16	66.7	164	6.83	0	0.0	21	1	4.2	5	37	68.8
Brown, Dave, N.Y. Giants	180	93	51.7	1023	5.68	5	2.8	62	3	1.7	13	67	71.1
Case, Stoney, Arizona	55	29	52.7	316	5.75	0	0.0	30	2	3.6	10	89	54.8
Chandler, Chris, Atlanta	342	202	59.1	2692	7.87	20	5.8	56	7	2.0	39	261	95.1
Collins, Kerry, Carolina	381	200	52.5	2124	5.57	11	2.9	t59	21	5.5	27	200	55.7
Conway, Curtis, Chicago	1	0	0.0	0	0.00	0	0.0	0	0	0.0	0	0	39.6
Cunningham, Randall, Minnesota	88	44	50.0	501	5.69	6	6.8	34	4	4.5	7	60	71.3
Detmer, Ty, Philadelphia	244	134	54.9	1567	6.42	7	2.9	57	6	2.5	19	94	73.9
Dilfer, Trent, Tampa Bay	386	217	56.2	2555	6.62	21	5.4	t59	11	2.8	32	196	82.8
Druckenmiller, Jim, San Francisco	52	21	40.4	239	4.60	1	1.9	33	4	7.7	4	32	29.2
Favre, Brett, Green Bay	513	304	59.3	3867	7.54	35	6.8	74	16	3.1	25	176	92.6
Frerotte, Gus, Washington	402	204	50.7	2682	6.67	17	4.2	52	12	3.0	23	146	73.8
Garrett, Jason, Dallas	14	10	71.4	56	4.00	0	0.0	12	0	0.0	2	18	78.3
Graham, Kent, Arizona	250	130	52.0	1408	5.63	4	1.6	47	5	2.0	16	115	65.9
Graziani, Tony, Atlanta	23	7	30.4	41	1.78	0	0.0	13	2	8.7	1	7	3.7
Green, Trent, Washington	1	0	0.0	0	0.00	0	0.0	0	0	0.0	0	0	39.6
Hill, Randal, New Orleans	0	0	...	0	...	0		...	0	...	1	8	
Hobert, Billy Joe, Buf.-N.O.*	161	78	48.4	1024	6.36	6	3.7	49	10	6.2	6	36	55.5
Hostetler, Jeff, Washington	144	79	54.9	899	6.24	5	3.5	69	10	6.9	10	52	56.5
Hoying, Bobby, Philadelphia	225	128	56.9	1573	6.99	11	4.9	t72	6	2.7	28	183	83.8
Johnson, Brad, Minnesota	452	275	60.8	3036	6.72	20	4.4	56	12	2.7	26	164	84.5
Kanell, Danny, N.Y. Giants	294	156	53.1	1740	5.92	11	3.7	t68	9	3.1	19	171	70.7
Kramer, Erik, Chicago	477	275	57.7	3011	6.31	14	2.9	t78	14	2.9	25	149	74.0
Mirer, Rick, Chicago	103	53	51.5	420	4.08	0	0.0	34	6	5.8	16	89	37.7
Mitchell, Scott, Detroit	509	293	57.6	3484	6.84	19	3.7	79	14	2.8	41	271	79.6
Nussmeier, Doug, New Orleans	32	18	56.3	183	5.72	0	0.0	24	3	9.4	6	32	33.7
Peete, Rodney, Philadelphia	118	68	57.6	869	7.36	4	3.4	38	4	3.4	17	85	78.0

Player, Team	Att.	Comp.	Pct. Comp.	Yds.	Avg. Gain	TD	Pct. TD	Long	Int.	Pct. Int.	Sack	Yds. Lost	Rat. Pts.
Plummer, Jake, Arizona	296	157	53.0	2203	7.44	15	5.1	t70	15	5.1	52	291	73.1
Reich, Frank, Detroit	30	11	36.7	121	4.03	0	0.0	27	2	6.7	0	0	21.7
Rypien, Mark, St. Louis	39	19	48.7	270	6.92	0	0.0	62	2	5.1	1	9	50.2
Sanders, Frank, Arizona	1	1	100.0	26	26.00	0	0.0	26	0	0.0	0	0	118.8
Shuler, Heath, New Orleans	203	106	52.2	1288	6.34	2	1.0	t89	14	6.9	21	132	46.6
Stenstrom, Steve, Chicago	14	8	57.1	70	5.00	0	0.0	18	2	14.3	2	19	31.0
Walsh, Steve, Tampa Bay	17	6	35.3	58	3.41	0	0.0	38	1	5.9	0	0	21.2
Wilson, Wade, Dallas	21	12	57.1	115	5.48	0	0.0	32	0	0.0	4	26	72.5
Wuerffel, Danny, New Orleans	91	42	46.2	518	5.69	4	4.4	47	8	8.8	18	116	42.3
Young, Steve, San Francisco	356	241	67.7	3029	8.51	19	5.3	82	6	1.7	35	220	104.7

*Includes both NFC and AFC statistics.
t—touchdown.

PLAYERS WITH TWO CLUBS

Player, Team	Att.	Comp.	Pct. Comp.	Yds.	Avg. Gain	TD	Pct. TD	Long	Int.	Pct. Int.	Sack	Yds. Lost	Rat. Pts.
Hobert, Billy Joe, Buffalo	30	17	56.7	133	4.43	0	0.0	20	2	6.7	2	7	40.0
Hobert, Billy Joe, New Orleans	131	61	46.6	891	6.80	6	4.6	49	8	6.1	4	29	59.0
Tolliver, Billy Joe, Atlanta	115	63	54.8	685	5.96	5	4.3	t47	1	0.9	14	104	83.4
Tolliver, Billy Joe, Kansas City	1	1	100.0	-8	-8.00	0	0.0	0	0	0.0	0	0	79.2

1997 STATISTICS Passing

RECEIVING

BESTS OF THE SEASON

Receptions, season
AFC: 104—Tim Brown, Oakland.
NFC: 104—Herman Moore, Detroit.

Receptions, game
AFC: 14—Tim Brown, Oakland vs. Jacksonville, Dec. 21 (164 yards) (0 TDs).
NFC: 12—Jake Reed, Minnesota at Chicago, Sept. 7 (118 yards) (1 TD).

Yards, season
NFC: 1584—Rob Moore, Arizona.
AFC: 1408—Tim Brown, Oakland.

Yards, game
NFC: 233—Isaac Bruce, St. Louis at Atlanta, Nov. 2 (10 receptions, 2 TDs).
AFC: 196—Yancey Thigpen, Pittsburgh vs. Jacksonville, Oct. 26 (11 receptions, 0 TDs).

Longest gain
AFC: 92—Derrick Alexander (from Eric Zeier), Baltimore vs. Seattle, Dec. 7.
NFC: 89—Randal Hill (from Heath Shuler), New Orleans at Chicago, Oct. 5 (TD).

Yards per reception, season
AFC: 18.7—James McKnight, Seattle.
NFC: 16.8—Robert Brooks, Green Bay.

Touchdowns, season
NFC: 13—Cris Carter, Minnesota.
AFC: 12—James Jett, Oakland; Joey Galloway, Seattle; Rod Smith, Denver.

Team leaders, receptions
AFC:

Baltimore	69	Michael Jackson
Buffalo	60	Andre Reed
		Quinn Early
Cincinnati	54	Darnay Scott
Denver	72	Shannon Sharpe
Indianapolis	73	Marvin Harrison
Jacksonville	85	Keenan McCardell
Kansas City	72	Andre Rison
Miami	76	O.J. McDuffie
New England	66	Ben Coates
N.Y. Jets	70	Keyshawn Johnson
Oakland	104	Tim Brown
Pittsburgh	79	Yancey Thigpen
San Diego	63	Tony Martin
Seattle	72	Joey Galloway
Tennessee	63	Frank Wycheck

NFC:

Arizona	97	Rob Moore
Atlanta	65	Bert Emanuel
Carolina	58	Wesley Walls
Chicago	58	Ricky Proehl
Dallas	75	Michael Irvin
Detroit	104	Herman Moore
Green Bay	81	Antonio Freeman
Minnesota	89	Cris Carter
New Orleans	55	Randal Hill
N.Y. Giants	58	Chris Calloway
Philadelphia	86	Irving Fryar
St. Louis	61	Amp Lee
San Francisco	60	Terrell Owens
Tampa Bay	39	Warrick Dunn
Washington	49	Jamie Asher

NFL LEADERS

Player, Team	No.	Yds.	Avg.	Long	TD
Brown, Tim, Oakland*	104	1408	13.5	t59	5
Moore, Herman, Detroit	104	1293	12.4	79	8
Moore, Rob, Arizona	97	1584	16.3	t47	8
Carter, Cris, Minnesota	89	1069	12.0	43	13
Fryar, Irving, Philadelphia	86	1316	15.3	t72	6
McCardell, Keenan, Jacksonville*	85	1164	13.7	60	5
Smith, Jimmy, Jacksonville*	82	1324	16.1	75	4
Freeman, Antonio, Green Bay	81	1243	15.3	t58	12
Morton, Johnnie, Detroit	80	1057	13.2	t73	6
Thigpen, Yancey, Pittsburgh*	79	1398	17.7	t69	7
McDuffie, O.J., Miami*	76	943	12.4	55	1
Irvin, Michael, Dallas	75	1180	15.7	55	9
Sanders, Frank, Arizona	75	1017	13.6	t70	4
Harrison, Marvin, Indianapolis*	73	866	11.9	44	6
Sharpe, Shannon, Denver*	72	1107	15.4	t68	3
Rison, Andre, Kansas City*	72	1092	15.2	45	7
Galloway, Joey, Seattle*	72	1049	14.6	t53	12
Smith, Rod, Denver*	70	1180	16.9	78	12
Johnson, Keyshawn, N.Y. Jets*	70	963	13.8	39	5
Jackson, Michael, Baltimore*	69	918	13.3	t54	4
Reed, Jake, Minnesota	68	1138	16.7	56	6
Dawkins, Sean, Indianapolis*	68	804	11.8	51	2
Coates, Ben, New England*	66	737	11.2	35	8
Alexander, Derrick, Baltimore*	65	1009	15.5	92	9
Emanuel, Bert, Atlanta	65	991	15.2	56	9
Green, Eric, Baltimore*	65	601	9.2	t37	5
Pritchard, Mike, Seattle*	64	843	13.2	61	2
Martin, Tony, San Diego*	63	904	14.3	t72	6
Wycheck, Frank, Tennessee*	63	748	11.9	42	4
Mathis, Terance, Atlanta	62	802	12.9	49	6

*AFC.
t—touchdown.
Leader based on most passes caught.

AFC

Player, Team	No.	Yds.	Avg.	Long	TD
Abdul-Jabbar, Karim, Miami	29	261	9.0	t36	1
Adams, Michael, Pittsburgh	1	39	39.0	39	0
Alexander, Derrick, Baltimore	65	1009	15.5	92	9
Allen, Marcus, Kansas City	11	86	7.8	18	0
Anders, Kimble, Kansas City	59	453	7.7	t55	2
Anderson, Richie, N.Y. Jets	26	150	5.8	19	1
Bailey, Aaron, Indianapolis	26	329	12.7	22	3
Barlow, Reggie, Jacksonville	5	74	14.8	29	0
Barnett, Fred, Miami	17	166	9.8	20	1
Battaglia, Marco, Cincinnati	12	149	12.4	34	1
Baxter, Fred, N.Y. Jets	27	276	10.2	37	3
Bennett, Donnell, Kansas City	7	5	0.7	4	0
Bettis, Jerome, Pittsburgh	15	110	7.3	t19	2
Bieniemy, Eric, Cincinnati	31	249	8.0	21	0
Blackwell, Will, Pittsburgh	12	168	14.0	46	1
Blades, Brian, Seattle	30	319	10.6	27	2
Botkin, Kirk, Pittsburgh	1	11	11.0	11	0
Brady, Kyle, N.Y. Jets	22	238	10.8	24	2
Brisby, Vincent, New England	23	276	12.0	31	2
Broussard, Steve, Seattle	24	143	6.0	t20	1
Brown, Corwin, N.Y. Jets	1	26	26.0	26	0
Brown, Derek, Jacksonville	8	84	10.5	21	1
Brown, Gary, San Diego	21	137	6.5	27	0
Brown, Tim, Oakland	104	1408	13.5	t59	5
Brown, Troy, New England	41	607	14.8	67	6

Player, Team	No.	Yds.	Avg.	Long	TD
Bruener, Mark, Pittsburgh	18	117	6.5	t18	6
Byars, Keith, New England	20	189	9.5	51	3
Byner, Earnest, Baltimore	21	128	6.1	17	0
Bynum, Kenny, San Diego	2	4	2.0	3	0
Carswell, Dwayne, Denver	12	96	8.0	t24	1
Carter, Ki-Jana, Cincinnati	21	157	7.5	35	0
Chamberlain, Byron, Denver	2	18	9.0	9	0
Chrebet, Wayne, N.Y. Jets	58	799	13.8	70	3
Cline, Tony, Buffalo	1	29	29.0	29	0
Coates, Ben, New England	66	737	11.2	35	8
Craver, Aaron, San Diego	4	26	6.5	20	0
Crockett, Zack, Indianapolis	15	112	7.5	19	0
Crumpler, Carlester, Seattle	31	361	11.6	30	1
Cullors, Derrick, New England	2	8	4.0	6	0
Davis, Terrell, Denver	42	287	6.8	25	0
Davis, Tyree, Seattle	2	48	24.0	37	0
Davis, Willie, Tennessee	43	564	13.1	46	4
Davison, Jerone, Oakland	2	34	17.0	29	0
Dawkins, Sean, Indianapolis	68	804	11.8	51	2
Dawson, Lake, Kansas City	21	273	13.0	27	2
Dilger, Ken, Indianapolis	27	380	14.1	43	3
Dillon, Corey, Cincinnati	27	259	9.6	28	0
Doering, Chris, Indianapolis	2	12	6.0	8	0
Dotson, Dewayne, Miami	1	4	4.0	4	0
Drayton, Troy, Miami	39	558	14.3	t30	4
Dudley, Rickey, Oakland	48	787	16.4	76	7
Dunn, David, Cincinnati	27	414	15.3	t39	2
Early, Quinn, Buffalo	60	853	14.2	45	5
Faulk, Marshall, Indianapolis	47	471	10.0	58	1
Fauria, Christian, Seattle	10	110	11.0	25	0
Fenner, Derrick, Oakland	14	92	6.6	13	0
Fletcher, Terrell, San Diego	39	292	7.5	25	0
Galloway, Joey, Seattle	72	1049	14.6	t53	12
Gardner, Carwell, San Diego	2	10	5.0	8	0
Gash, Sam, New England	22	154	7.0	19	3
George, Eddie, Tennessee	7	44	6.3	15	1
Glenn, Tarik, Indianapolis	1	3	3.0	3	0
Glenn, Terry, New England	27	431	16.0	50	2
Gonzalez, Tony, Kansas City	33	368	11.2	30	2
Graham, Jay, Baltimore	12	51	4.3	19	0
Graham, Jeff, N.Y. Jets	42	542	12.9	t47	2
Graham, Scottie, Cincinnati	1	1	1.0	1	0
Green, Eric, Baltimore	65	601	9.2	t37	5
Green, Willie, Denver	19	240	12.6	31	2
Griffith, Howard, Denver	11	55	5.0	20	0
Hall, Dana, Jacksonville	1	22	22.0	22	0
Hall, Tim, Oakland	1	9	9.0	9	0
Hallock, Ty, Jacksonville	18	131	7.3	23	1
Harris, Ronnie, Seattle	4	81	20.3	34	0
Harrison, Marvin, Indianapolis	73	866	11.9	44	6
Hartley, Frank, San Diego	19	246	12.9	35	1
Hawkins, Courtney, Pittsburgh	45	555	12.3	t44	3
Hebron, Vaughn, Denver	3	36	12.0	21	0
Hill, Greg, Kansas City	12	126	10.5	39	0
Hobbs, Daryl, N.O.-Sea.*	7	85	12.1	21	1
Holmes, Darick, Buffalo	13	106	8.2	22	0
Horn, Joe, Kansas City	2	65	32.5	47	0
Howard, Desmond, Oakland	4	30	7.5	9	0
Hughes, Danan, Kansas City	7	65	9.3	t14	2
Hundon, James, Cincinnati	16	285	17.8	61	2
Jackson, Michael, Baltimore	69	918	13.3	t54	4
Jackson, Willie, Jacksonville	17	206	12.1	45	2
Jeffers, Patrick, Denver	3	24	8.0	10	0
Jefferson, Shawn, New England	54	841	15.6	76	2
Jells, Dietrich, New England	1	9	9.0	9	0
Jett, James, Oakland	46	804	17.5	t56	12
Johnson, Charles, Pittsburgh	46	568	12.3	49	2
Johnson, Keyshawn, N.Y. Jets	70	963	13.8	39	5
Johnson, Leon, N.Y. Jets	16	142	8.9	20	0
Johnson, Lonnie, Buffalo	41	340	8.3	t62	2
Jones, Charlie, San Diego	32	423	13.2	t44	1
Jones, Damon, Jacksonville	5	87	17.4	t26	2
Jones, Freddie, San Diego	41	505	12.3	62	2
Jones, George, Pittsburgh	16	96	6.0	25	1
Jordan, Charles, Miami	27	471	17.4	t44	3
Kaufman, Napoleon, Oakland	40	403	10.1	t70	2
Kent, Joey, Tennessee	6	55	9.2	19	1
Kinchen, Brian, Baltimore	11	95	8.6	t24	1
Lester, Tim, Pittsburgh	10	51	5.1	14	0
Levitt, Chad, Oakland	2	24	12.0	22	0
Lewis, Jermaine, Baltimore	42	648	15.4	t42	6
Lewis, Roderick, Tennessee	1	7	7.0	7	0
Lockett, Kevin, Kansas City	1	35	35.0	35	0
Loville, Derek, Denver	2	10	5.0	7	0
Lynn, Anthony, Denver	1	21	21.0	21	0
Lyons, Mitch, Pittsburgh	4	29	7.3	13	0
Manning, Brian, Miami	7	85	12.1	21	0
Marsh, Curtis, Pittsburgh	2	14	7.0	8	0
Martin, Curtis, New England	41	296	7.2	22	1
Martin, Tony, San Diego	63	904	14.3	t72	6
Mason, Derrick, Tennessee	14	186	13.3	38	0
May, Deems, Seattle	2	21	10.5	11	0
McAfee, Fred, Pittsburgh	2	44	22.0	30	0
McCaffrey, Ed, Denver	45	590	13.1	35	8
McCardell, Keenan, Jacksonville	85	1164	13.7	60	5
McDuffie, O.J., Miami	76	943	12.4	55	1
McGee, Tony, Cincinnati	34	414	12.2	37	6
McKnight, James, Seattle	34	637	18.7	t60	6
McPhail, Jerris, Miami	34	262	7.7	19	1
Means, Natrone, Jacksonville	15	104	6.9	21	0
Meggett, Dave, New England	19	203	10.7	t49	1
Metcalf, Eric, San Diego	40	576	14.4	62	2
Milne, Brian, Cincinnati	23	138	6.0	20	0
Mitchell, Pete, Jacksonville	35	380	10.9	33	4
Mitchell, Shannon, San Diego	1	14	14.0	14	0
Moore, Will, Jacksonville	1	10	10.0	10	0
Morris, Bam, Baltimore	29	176	6.1	15	0
Moulds, Eric, Buffalo	29	294	10.1	32	0
Murrell, Adrian, N.Y. Jets	27	106	3.9	23	0
Nalen, Tom, Denver	1	-1	-1.0	-1	0
Neal, Lorenzo, N.Y. Jets	8	40	5.0	14	1
Norgard, Erik, Tennessee	1	2	2.0	t2	1
Parmalee, Bernie, Miami	28	301	10.8	29	1
Perriman, Brett, K.C.-Mia.	25	392	15.7	27	1
Perry, Ed, Miami	11	45	4.1	10	1
Phillips, Lawrence, St.L.-Mia.*	11	39	3.5	17	0
Pickens, Carl, Cincinnati	52	695	13.4	t50	5
Pollard, Marcus, Indianapolis	10	116	11.6	28	0
Popson, Ted, Kansas City	35	320	9.1	21	2
Potts, Roosevelt, Miami	3	27	9.0	13	0
Pritchard, Mike, Seattle	64	843	13.2	61	2
Pritchett, Stanley, Miami	5	35	7.0	17	0
Pupunu, Alfred, San Diego	1	7	7.0	7	0
Purnell, Lovett, New England	5	57	11.4	t20	3
Reed, Andre, Buffalo	60	880	14.7	t77	5
Reese, Jerry, Buffalo	1	13	13.0	13	0
Richardson, Tony, Kansas City	3	6	2.0	t3	3
Riemersma, Jay, Buffalo	26	208	8.0	22	2
Rison, Andre, Kansas City	72	1092	15.2	45	7
Roan, Michael, Tennessee	12	159	13.3	26	0
Roe, James, Baltimore	7	124	17.7	29	0
Russell, Derek, Tennessee	12	141	11.8	23	1
Sadowski, Troy, Pittsburgh	1	12	12.0	12	0
Sanders, Chris, Tennessee	31	498	16.1	t55	3
Scott, Darnay, Cincinnati	54	797	14.8	t77	5
Sharpe, Shannon, Denver	72	1107	15.4	t68	3
Shedd, Kenny, Oakland	10	115	11.5	19	0
Slutzker, Scott, Indianapolis	3	22	7.3	11	0
Smith, Antowain, Buffalo	28	177	6.3	19	0
Smith, Detron, Denver	4	41	10.3	t17	1

Player, Team	No.	Yds.	Avg.	Long	TD
Smith, Jimmy, Jacksonville	82	1324	16.1	75	4
Smith, Lamar, Seattle	23	183	8.0	22	0
Smith, Rod, Denver	70	1180	16.9	78	12
Sowell, Jerald, N.Y. Jets	1	8	8.0	8	0
Spikes, Irving, Miami	7	70	10.0	24	0
Stablein, Brian, Indianapolis	25	253	10.1	30	1
Stewart, James, Jacksonville	41	336	8.2	40	1
Still, Bryan, San Diego	24	324	13.5	39	0
Strong, Mack, Seattle	13	91	7.0	20	2
Testaverde, Vinny, Baltimore	1	-4	-4.0	-4	0
Thigpen, Yancey, Pittsburgh	79	1398	17.7	t69	7
Thomas, Lamar, Miami	28	402	14.4	26	2
Thomas, Rodney, Tennessee	14	111	7.9	22	0
Thomas, Thurman, Buffalo	30	208	6.9	30	0
Tindale, Tim, Buffalo	4	105	26.3	45	0
Truitt, Olanda, Oakland	7	91	13.0	t19	1
Twyner, Gunnard, Cincinnati	4	45	11.3	16	0
Van Dyke, Alex, N.Y. Jets	3	53	17.7	t18	2
Vanover, Tamarick, Kansas City	7	92	13.1	42	0
Walker, Derrick, Kansas City	5	60	12.0	22	0
Ward, Dedric, N.Y. Jets	18	212	11.8	33	1
Warren, Chris, Seattle	45	257	5.7	20	0
Warren, Lamont, Indianapolis	20	192	9.6	31	0
Williams, Harvey, Oakland	16	147	9.2	t32	2
Witman, Jon, Pittsburgh	1	3	3.0	3	0
Wycheck, Frank, Tennessee	63	748	11.9	42	4
Yarborough, Ryan, Baltimore	16	183	11.4	26	0

*Includes both NFC and AFC statistics.
t—touchdown.

NFC

Player, Team	No.	Yds.	Avg.	Long	TD
Alexander, Kevin, N.Y. Giants	18	276	15.3	40	1
Allen, Terry, Washington	20	172	8.6	38	1
Allen, Tremayne, Chicago	1	9	9.0	9	0
Allred, John, Chicago	8	70	8.8	18	0
Alstott, Mike, Tampa Bay	23	178	7.7	26	3
Anderson, Jamal, Atlanta	29	284	9.8	t47	3
Anthony, Reidel, Tampa Bay	35	448	12.8	t38	4
Asher, Jamie, Washington	49	474	9.7	24	1
Autry, Darnell, Chicago	9	59	6.6	14	0
Barber, Tiki, N.Y. Giants	34	299	8.8	29	1
Bates, Mario, New Orleans	5	42	8.4	15	0
Bech, Brett, New Orleans	3	50	16.7	22	0
Beebe, Don, Green Bay	2	28	14.0	23	0
Bjornson, Eric, Dallas	47	442	9.4	32	0
Bouie, Tony, Tampa Bay	1	25	25.0	25	0
Bowie, Larry, Washington	34	388	11.4	t39	2
Bownes, Fabien, Chicago	12	146	12.2	21	0
Boyd, Tommie, Detroit	10	142	14.2	32	0
Brock, Fred, Arizona	1	29	29.0	29	0
Brooks, Robert, Green Bay	60	1010	16.8	48	7
Bruce, Isaac, St. Louis	56	815	14.6	59	5
Calloway, Chris, N.Y. Giants	58	849	14.6	t68	8
Carrier, Mark, Carolina	33	436	13.2	36	2
Carruth, Rae, Carolina	44	545	12.4	52	4
Carter, Cris, Minnesota	89	1069	12.0	43	13
Carter, Pat, Arizona	7	44	6.3	15	1
Carter, Tony, Chicago	24	152	6.3	19	0
Centers, Larry, Arizona	54	409	7.6	29	1
Chmura, Mark, Green Bay	38	417	11.0	t32	6
Christian, Bob, Atlanta	22	154	7.0	19	1
Chrylewicz, Pete, Detroit	3	27	9.0	12	1
Clark, Greg J., San Francisco	8	96	12.0	23	1
Connell, Albert, Washington	9	138	15.3	t41	2
Conway, Curtis, Chicago	30	476	15.9	t55	1
Conwell, Ernie, St. Louis	38	404	10.6	t46	4
Copeland, Horace, Tampa Bay	33	431	13.1	49	1
Crawford, Keith, St. Louis	11	232	21.1	69	0
Cross, Howard, N.Y. Giants	21	150	7.1	26	2
Davis, Billy, Dallas	3	33	11.0	12	0

Player, Team	No.	Yds.	Avg.	Long	TD
Davis, John, Tampa Bay	3	35	11.7	16	0
Davis, Stephen, Washington	18	134	7.4	19	0
Davis, Troy, New Orleans	13	85	6.5	18	0
Davis, Tyrone, Green Bay	2	28	14.0	26	1
DeLong, Greg, Minnesota	8	75	9.4	23	0
Dunn, Jason, Philadelphia	7	93	13.3	t31	2
Dunn, Warrick, Tampa Bay	39	462	11.8	t59	3
Edwards, Anthony, Arizona	20	203	10.2	33	0
Edwards, Marc, San Francisco	6	48	8.0	19	0
Ellard, Henry, Washington	32	485	15.2	27	4
Ellison, Jerry, Tampa Bay	1	8	8.0	8	0
Emanuel, Bert, Atlanta	65	991	15.2	56	9
Engram, Bobby, Chicago	45	399	8.9	23	2
Evans, Charles, Minnesota	21	152	7.2	17	0
Fann, Chad, San Francisco	5	78	15.6	21	0
Farquhar, John, New Orleans	17	253	14.9	42	1
Floyd, Malcolm, St. Louis	4	39	9.8	14	0
Floyd, William, San Francisco	37	321	8.7	t44	1
Freeman, Antonio, Green Bay	81	1243	15.3	t58	12
Fryar, Irving, Philadelphia	86	1316	15.3	t72	6
Galbraith, Scott, Dallas	2	16	8.0	11	0
Garner, Charlie, Philadelphia	24	225	9.4	27	0
Gedney, Chris, Arizona	23	261	11.3	t37	4
Glover, Andrew, Minnesota	32	378	11.8	43	3
Goodwin, Hunter, Minnesota	7	61	8.7	14	0
Green, Harold, Atlanta	29	360	12.4	47	0
Green, Robert, Minnesota	1	5	5.0	5	0
Greene, Scott, Carolina	40	277	6.9	25	1
Gruttadauria, Mike, St. Louis	1	0	0.0	0	0
Guliford, Eric, New Orleans	27	362	13.4	47	1
Hanspard, Byron, Atlanta	6	53	8.8	21	1
Hape, Patrick, Tampa Bay	4	22	5.5	13	1
Harmon, Ronnie, Ten.-Chi.	18	197	10.9	27	0
Harper, Alvin, Washington	2	65	32.5	52	0
Harris, Jackie, Tampa Bay	19	197	10.4	39	1
Harris, Mark, San Francisco	5	53	10.6	16	0
Harris, Raymont, Chicago	28	115	4.1	16	0
Hastings, Andre, New Orleans	48	722	15.0	39	5
Hatchette, Matthew, Minnesota	3	54	18.0	38	0
Hayden, Aaron, Green Bay	2	11	5.5	7	0
Haynes, Michael, Atlanta	12	154	12.8	t24	1
Hearst, Garrison, San Francisco	21	194	9.2	69	2
Henderson, William, Green Bay	41	367	9.0	25	1
Heyward, Craig, St. Louis	8	77	9.6	25	0
Hill, Randal, New Orleans	55	761	13.8	t89	2
Hilliard, Ike, N.Y. Giants	2	42	21.0	23	0
Hoard, Leroy, Minnesota	11	84	7.6	30	0
Hughes, Tyrone, Chicago	8	68	8.5	16	0
Irvin, Michael, Dallas	75	1180	15.7	55	9
Ismail, Raghib, Carolina	36	419	11.6	t59	2
Jacoby, Mitch, St. Louis	2	10	5.0	10	0
Jenkins, James, Washington	4	43	10.8	20	3
Jennings, Keith, Chicago	14	164	11.7	23	0
Johnson, Anthony, Carolina	21	158	7.5	25	1
Johnson, Brad, Minnesota	1	3	3.0	t3	1
Johnson, Jimmie, Philadelphia	14	177	12.6	28	1
Johnson, LeShon, Arizona	3	4	1.3	7	0
Johnson, Tony, New Orleans	1	13	13.0	13	0
Johnston, Daryl, Dallas	18	166	9.2	21	1
Jones, Brent, San Francisco	29	383	13.2	33	2
Jones, Chris T., Philadelphia	5	73	14.6	32	0
Jordan, Andrew, Tampa Bay	1	0	0.0	0	0
Kennison, Eddie, St. Louis	25	404	16.2	76	0
Kinchen, Todd, Atlanta	16	266	16.6	t53	1
Kirby, Terry, San Francisco	23	279	12.1	82	1
Kozlowski, Brian, Atlanta	7	99	14.1	29	1
LaFleur, David, Dallas	18	122	6.8	17	2
Laing, Aaron, St. Louis	5	31	6.2	11	1
Lane, Fred, Carolina	8	27	3.4	7	0
Lee, Amp, St. Louis	61	825	13.5	62	3
Levens, Dorsey, Green Bay	53	370	7.0	56	5

Player, Team	No.	Yds.	Avg.	Long	TD
Levy, Chuck, San Francisco	5	68	13.6	30	0
Lewis, Chad, Philadelphia	12	94	7.8	17	4
Lewis, Thomas, N.Y. Giants	5	84	16.8	34	0
Logan, Marc, Washington	3	6	2.0	5	0
Mangum, Kris, Carolina	4	56	14.0	22	0
Mathis, Terance, Atlanta	62	802	12.9	49	6
Mayes, Derrick, Green Bay	18	290	16.1	74	0
McCorvey, Kez, Detroit	2	9	4.5	6	0
McCrary, Fred, New Orleans	4	17	4.3	11	0
McElroy, Leeland, Arizona	7	32	4.6	17	0
McWilliams, Johnny, Arizona	7	75	10.7	15	0
Metzelaars, Pete, Detroit	17	144	8.5	22	0
Mickens, Terry, Green Bay	1	2	2.0	t2	1
Milburn, Glyn, Detroit	5	77	15.4	43	0
Miller, Anthony, Dallas	46	645	14.0	54	4
Mills, Ernie, Carolina	11	127	11.5	37	1
Mitchell, Brian, Washington	36	438	12.2	69	1
Moore, Dave, Tampa Bay	19	217	11.4	28	4
Moore, Herman, Detroit	104	1293	12.4	79	8
Moore, Jerald, St. Louis	8	69	8.6	19	0
Moore, Rob, Arizona	97	1584	16.3	t47	8
Moore, Ronald, St. Louis	4	34	8.5	13	0
Morton, Johnnie, Detroit	80	1057	13.2	t73	6
Muhammad, Muhsin, Carolina	27	317	11.7	38	0
Oliver, Winslow, Carolina	6	47	7.8	11	0
Owens, Terrell, San Francisco	60	936	15.6	t56	8
Palmer, David, Minnesota	26	193	7.4	23	1
Patten, David, N.Y. Giants	13	226	17.4	t40	2
Pegram, Erric, S.D.-NYG*	21	90	4.3	14	0
Penn, Chris, Chicago	47	576	12.3	33	3
Pierce, Aaron, N.Y. Giants	10	47	4.7	14	0
Plummer, Jake, Arizona	1	2	2.0	2	0
Poole, Keith, New Orleans	4	98	24.5	49	2
Proehl, Ricky, Chicago	58	753	13.0	t78	7
Rasby, Walter, Carolina	1	1	1.0	1	0
Reed, Jake, Minnesota	68	1138	16.7	56	6
Rice, Jerry, San Francisco	7	78	11.1	16	1
Ross, Jermaine, St. Louis	3	37	12.3	14	0
Salaam, Rashaan, Chicago	2	20	10.0	18	0
Sanders, Barry, Detroit	33	305	9.2	t66	3
Sanders, Frank, Arizona	75	1017	13.6	t70	4
Santiago, O.J., Atlanta	17	217	12.8	30	2
Savoie, Nicky, New Orleans	1	14	14.0	14	0
Schlesinger, Cory, Detroit	5	69	13.8	33	1
Schroeder, Bill, Green Bay	2	15	7.5	8	1
Seay, Mark, Philadelphia	13	187	14.4	38	1
Shepherd, Leslie, Washington	29	562	19.4	48	5
Sloan, David, Detroit	29	264	9.1	25	0
Small, Torrance, St. Louis	32	488	15.3	46	1
Smith, Cedric, Arizona	2	20	10.0	18	0
Smith, Ed, Atlanta	1	2	2.0	2	0
Smith, Emmitt, Dallas	40	234	5.9	24	0
Smith, Eric, Chicago	2	22	11.0	12	0
Smith, Irv, New Orleans	17	180	10.6	25	1
Smith, Robert, Minnesota	37	197	5.3	20	1
Solomon, Freddie, Philadelphia	29	455	15.7	56	3
Staley, Duce, Philadelphia	2	22	11.0	22	0
Stokes, J.J., San Francisco	58	733	12.6	36	4
Thomas, Chris, Washington	11	93	8.5	17	0
Thomas, J.T., St. Louis	2	25	12.5	16	0
Thomas, Robb, Tampa Bay	13	129	9.9	21	0
Thomason, Jeff, Green Bay	9	115	12.8	27	1
Thrash, James, Washington	2	24	12.0	17	0
Timpson, Michael, Philadelphia	42	484	11.5	26	2
Toomer, Amani, N.Y. Giants	16	263	16.4	t56	1
Turner, Kevin, Philadelphia	48	443	9.2	36	3
Uwaezuoke, Iheanyi, San Francisco	14	165	11.8	25	0
Vardell, Tommy, Detroit	16	218	13.6	37	0
Walker, Herschel, Dallas	14	149	10.6	t64	2
Walls, Wesley, Carolina	58	746	12.9	52	6
Walsh, Chris, Minnesota	11	114	10.4	19	1
Watters, Ricky, Philadelphia	48	440	9.2	37	0
Way, Charles, N.Y. Giants	37	304	8.2	62	1
West, Ed, Atlanta	7	63	9.0	23	1
Westbrook, Michael, Washington	34	559	16.4	t40	3
Wetnight, Ryan, Chicago	46	464	10.1	34	1
Wheatley, Tyrone, N.Y. Giants	16	140	8.8	27	0
Wiegert, Zach, St. Louis	1	1	1.0	1	0
Williams, Karl, Tampa Bay	33	486	14.7	55	4
Williams, Kevin, Arizona	20	273	13.7	t31	1
Williams, Moe, Minnesota	4	14	3.5	7	0
Williams, Sherman, Dallas	21	159	7.6	18	0
Williams, Stepfret, Dallas	30	308	10.3	20	1
Zellars, Ray, New Orleans	31	263	8.5	38	0

*Includes both NFC and AFC statistics.
t—touchdown.

PLAYERS WITH TWO CLUBS

Player, Team	No.	Yds.	Avg.	Long	TD
Harmon, Ronnie, Tennessee	16	189	11.8	27	0
Harmon, Ronnie, Chicago	2	8	4.0	6	0
Hobbs, Daryl, New Orleans	2	41	20.5	21	1
Hobbs, Daryl, Seattle	5	44	8.8	21	0
Pegram, Erric, San Diego	2	7	3.5	4	0
Pegram, Erric, N.Y. Giants	19	83	4.4	14	0
Perriman, Brett, Kansas City	6	83	13.8	27	0
Perriman, Brett, Miami	19	309	16.3	26	1
Phillips, Lawrence, St. Louis	10	33	3.3	17	0
Phillips, Lawrence, Miami	1	6	6.0	6	0

SCORING

TEAM

AFC

Team	Total TD	TD Rush	TD Pass	TD Misc.	XP	2Pt.	XPA	FG	FGA	Safeties	Total Pts.
Denver	55	18	27	10	50	4	50	28	39	0	472
Jacksonville	43	20	20	3	41	1	41	31	36	0	394
Kansas City	42	15	20	7	35	2	36	26	27	3	375
Pittsburgh	44	19	22	3	40	1	40	22	25	0	372
New England	42	6	31	5	40	0	40	25	29	1	369
Seattle	43	13	26	4	37	1	37	22	28	1	365
Cincinnati	46	23	21	2	41	1	43	12	16	0	355
N.Y. Jets	38	10	20	8	36	0	36	28	41	0	348
Miami	37	18	16	3	33	0	33	28	36	0	339
Tennessee	36	17	15	4	32	2	32	27	35	0	333
Baltimore	35	7	25	3	32	2	32	26	34	1	326
Oakland	41	9	29	3	33	2	35	13	22	1	324
Indianapolis	31	10	16	5	21	4	21	32	41	1	313
San Diego	27	5	12	10	26	0	27	26	31	0	266
Buffalo	26	12	14	0	21	2	21	24	30	1	255
AFC total	586	202	314	70	518	22	524	370	470	9	5206
AFC average	39.1	13.5	20.9	4.7	34.5	1.5	34.9	24.7	31.3	0.6	347.1

NFC

Team	Total TD	TD Rush	TD Pass	TD Misc.	XP	2Pt.	XPA	FG	FGA	Safeties	Total Pts.
Green Bay	50	9	35	6	48	1	48	24	30	0	422
Detroit	43	19	19	5	39	1	40	26	29	1	379
San Francisco	41	16	20	5	38	2	38	29	36	0	375
Minnesota	42	14	26	2	33	6	34	19	27	0	354
Washington	40	12	22	6	39	0	39	16	24	0	327
Atlanta	36	8	26	2	35	0	35	23	27	0	320
Philadelphia	36	11	22	3	33	1	33	22	31	0	317
N.Y. Giants	35	14	16	5	27	1	29	22	32	1	307
Dallas	29	6	19	4	24	2	24	34	38	0	304
St. Louis	32	15	14	3	32	0	32	25	37	0	299
Tampa Bay	38	15	21	2	32	0	35	13	17	0	299
Arizona	32	9	19	4	28	3	29	19	29	0	283
Carolina	28	11	17	0	25	2	25	22	26	1	265
Chicago	28	14	14	0	20	5	20	21	26	1	263
New Orleans	24	9	13	2	22	1	22	23	27	0	237
NFC total	534	182	303	49	475	25	483	338	436	4	4751
NFC average	35.6	12.1	20.2	3.3	31.7	1.7	32.2	22.5	29.1	0.3	316.7
NFL total	1120	384	617	119	993	47	1007	708	906	13	9957
NFL average	37.3	12.8	20.6	4.0	33.1	1.6	33.6	23.6	30.2	0.4	331.9

INDIVIDUAL

BESTS OF THE SEASON

Points, season
AFC: 134—Mike Hollis, Jacksonville.
NFC: 126—Richie Cunningham, Dallas.

Touchdowns, season
AFC: 16—Karim Abdul-Jabbar, Miami.
NFC: 14—Barry Sanders, Detroit.

Extra points, season
NFC: 48—Ryan Longwell, Green Bay.
AFC: 46—Jason Elam, Denver.

Field goals, season
NFC: 34—Richie Cunningham, Dallas.
AFC: 32—Cary Blanchard, Indianapolis.

Field goal attempts, season
AFC: 41—Cary Blanchard, Indianapolis; John Hall, N.Y. Jets.
NFC: 37—Jeff Wilkins, St. Louis; Richie Cunningham, Dallas.

Longest field goal
AFC: 55—John Hall, N.Y. Jets at Seattle, Aug. 31; Steve Christie, Denver vs. Buffalo, Oct. 26 (OT).
NFC: 55—Morten Andersen, Atlanta at New Orleans, Oct. 12; Jason Hanson, Indianapolis vs. Detroit, Nov. 23.

Most points, game
AFC: 6—Held by many players.
NFC: 6—Held by many players.

Team leaders, points
AFC:

Baltimore	110	Matt Stover
Buffalo	93	Steve Christie
Cincinnati	77	Doug Pelfrey
Denver	124	Jason Elam
Indianapolis	117	Cary Blanchard
Jacksonville	134	Mike Hollis
Kansas City	113	Pete Stoyanovich
Miami	117	Olindo Mare

Team	Pts	Kicker
New England	115	Adam Vinatieri
N.Y. Jets	120	John Hall
Oakland	72	James Jett
		Cole Ford
Pittsburgh	106	Norm Johnson
San Diego	78	Greg Davis
Seattle	103	Todd Peterson
Tennessee	113	Al Del Greco

NFC:

Team	Pts	Kicker
Arizona	52	Joe Nedney
Atlanta	104	Morten Andersen
Carolina	91	John Kasay
Chicago	83	Jeff Jaeger
Dallas	126	Richie Cunningham
Detroit	117	Jason Hanson
Green Bay	120	Ryan Longwell
Minnesota	84	Cris Carter
New Orleans	91	Doug Brien
N.Y. Giants	93	Brad Daluiso
Philadelphia	99	Chris Boniol
St. Louis	107	Jeff Wilkins
San Francisco	125	Gary Anderson
Tampa Bay	71	Michael Husted
Washington	82	Scott Blanton

NFL LEADERS

KICKERS

Player, Team	XPM	XPA	FGM	FGA	Tot. Pts.
Hollis, Mike, Jacksonville*	41	41	31	36	134
Cunningham, Richie, Dallas	24	24	34	37	126
Anderson, Gary, San Francisco	38	38	29	36	125
Elam, Jason, Denver*	46	46	26	36	124
Longwell, Ryan, Green Bay	48	48	24	30	120
Hall, John, N.Y. Jets*	36	36	28	41	120
Hanson, Jason, Detroit	39	40	26	29	117
Blanchard, Cary, Indianapolis*	21	21	32	41	117
Mare, Olindo, Miami*	33	33	28	36	117
Vinatieri, Adam, New England*	40	40	25	29	115
Del Greco, Al, Tennessee*	32	32	27	35	113
Stoyanovich, Pete, Kansas City*	35	36	26	27	113
Stover, Matt, Baltimore*	32	32	26	34	110
Davis, Greg, San Diego*	31	32	26	34	109
Wilkins, Jeff, St. Louis	32	32	25	37	107
Johnson, Norm, Pittsburgh*	40	40	22	25	106
Andersen, Morten, Atlanta	35	35	23	27	104
Peterson, Todd, Seattle*	37	37	22	28	103
Boniol, Chris, Philadelphia	33	33	22	31	99
Christie, Steve, Buffalo*	21	21	24	30	93

*AFC.

NON-KICKERS

Player, Team	TD	RTD	PTD	MTD	2Pt.	Tot. Pts.
Davis, Terrell, Denver*	15	15	0	0	3	96
Abdul-Jabbar, Karim, Miami*	16	15	1	0	0	96
Carter, Cris, Minnesota	13	0	13	0	3	84
Sanders, Barry, Detroit	14	11	3	0	0	84
Levens, Dorsey, Green Bay	12	7	5	0	1	74
Jett, James, Oakland*	12	0	12	0	0	72
Galloway, Joey, Seattle*	12	0	12	0	0	72
Smith, Rod, Denver*	12	0	12	0	0	72
Freeman, Antonio, Green Bay	12	0	12	0	0	72
Allen, Marcus, Kansas City*	11	11	0	0	0	66
Stewart, Kordell, Pittsburgh*	11	11	0	0	0	66
Harris, Raymont, Chicago	10	10	0	0	0	60
Anderson, Jamal, Atlanta	10	7	3	0	0	60
Alstott, Mike, Tampa Bay	10	7	3	0	0	60
Dillon, Corey, Cincinnati*	10	10	0	0	0	60
Irvin, Michael, Dallas	9	0	9	0	0	54
Bettis, Jerome, Pittsburgh*	9	7	2	0	0	54
Means, Natrone, Jacksonville*	9	9	0	0	0	54

Player, Team	TD	RTD	PTD	MTD	2Pt.	Tot. Pts.
Alexander, Derrick, Baltimore*	9	0	9	0	0	54
Emanuel, Bert, Atlanta	9	0	9	0	0	54
Stewart, James, Jacksonville*	9	8	1	0	0	54
Kirby, Terry, San Francisco	8	6	1	1	2	52
Moore, Rob, Arizona	8	0	8	0	1	50
Moore, Herman, Detroit	8	0	8	0	1	50
Calloway, Chris, N.Y. Giants	8	0	8	0	0	48
McCaffrey, Ed, Denver*	8	0	8	0	0	48
Coates, Ben, New England*	8	0	8	0	0	48
Faulk, Marshall, Indianapolis*	8	7	1	0	0	48
McNair, Steve, Tennessee*	8	8	0	0	0	48
Kaufman, Napoleon, Oakland*	8	6	2	0	0	48

*AFC.

AFC

KICKERS

Player, Team	XPM	XPA	FGM	FGA	Tot. Pts.
Bentley, Scott, Denver	4	4	2	3	10
Blanchard, Cary, Indianapolis	21	21	32	41	117
Carney, John, San Diego	5	5	7	7	26
Christie, Steve, Buffalo	21	21	24	30	93
Davis, Greg, Min.-S.D.*	31	32	26	34	109
Del Greco, Al, Tennessee	32	32	27	35	113
Elam, Jason, Denver	46	46	26	36	124
Ford, Cole, Oakland	33	35	13	22	72
Hall, John, N.Y. Jets	36	36	28	41	120
Hollis, Mike, Jacksonville	41	41	31	36	134
Johnson, Norm, Pittsburgh	40	40	22	25	106
Mare, Olindo, Miami	33	33	28	36	117
Pelfrey, Doug, Cincinnati	41	43	12	16	77
Peterson, Todd, Seattle	37	37	22	28	103
Stover, Matt, Baltimore	32	32	26	34	110
Stoyanovich, Pete, Kansas City	35	36	26	27	113
Vinatieri, Adam, New England	40	40	25	29	115

*Includes both NFC and AFC statistics.

NON-KICKERS

Player, Team	TD	RTD	PTD	MTD	2Pt.	Tot. Pts.
Abdul-Jabbar, Karim, Miami	16	15	1	0	0	96
Alexander, Derrick, Baltimore	9	0	9	0	0	54
Alexander, Elijah, Indianapolis	1	0	0	1	0	6
Allen, Marcus, Kansas City	11	11	0	0	0	66
Anders, Kimble, Kansas City	2	0	2	0	0	12
Anderson, Darren, Kansas City	1	0	0	1	0	6
Anderson, Richie, N.Y. Jets	1	0	1	0	0	6
Atwater, Steve, Denver	1	0	0	1	0	6
Bailey, Aaron, Indianapolis	3	0	3	0	0	18
Barlow, Reggie, Jacksonville	1	0	0	1	0	6
Barnett, Fred, Miami	1	0	1	0	0	6
Battaglia, Marco, Cincinnati	1	0	1	0	0	6
Baxter, Fred, N.Y. Jets	3	0	3	0	0	18
Belser, Jason, Indianapolis	1	0	0	1	0	6
Bennett, Donnell, Kansas City	1	1	0	0	0	6
Bettis, Jerome, Pittsburgh	9	7	2	0	0	54
Bieniemy, Eric, Cincinnati	2	1	0	1	0	12
Blackmon, Robert, Indianapolis	1	0	0	1	0	6
Blackwell, Will, Pittsburgh	2	0	1	1	0	12
Blades, Brian, Seattle	2	0	2	0	0	12
Blake, Jeff, Cincinnati	3	3	0	0	0	18
Bowens, Tim, Miami	1	0	0	1	0	6
Bradford, Paul, San Diego	2	0	0	2	0	12
Brady, Kyle, N.Y. Jets	2	0	2	0	0	12
Braxton, Tyrone, Denver	1	0	0	1	0	6
Brisby, Vincent, New England	2	0	2	0	0	12
Broussard, Steve, Seattle	6	5	1	0	0	36
Brown, Chad, Seattle	2	0	0	2	0	12
Brown, Derek, Jacksonville	1	0	1	0	0	6
Brown, Gary, San Diego	4	4	0	0	0	24

Player, Team	Tot. TD	RTD	PTD	MTD	2Pt.	Tot. Pts.
Brown, Tim, Oakland	5	0	5	0	1	32
Brown, Troy, New England	6	0	6	0	0	36
Bruener, Mark, Pittsburgh	6	0	6	0	0	36
Brunell, Mark, Jacksonville	2	2	0	0	0	12
Buckley, Terrell, Miami	1	0	0	1	0	6
Byars, Keith, New England	3	0	3	0	0	18
Byner, Earnest, Baltimore	0	0	0	0	1	2
Carswell, Dwayne, Denver	1	0	1	0	0	6
Carter, Ki-Jana, Cincinnati	7	7	0	0	0	42
Chrebet, Wayne, N.Y. Jets	3	0	3	0	0	18
Clay, Willie, New England	1	0	0	1	0	6
Coates, Ben, New England	8	0	8	0	0	48
Copeland, John, Cincinnati	1	0	0	1	0	6
Cotton, Kenyon, Cincinnati	1	1	0	0	0	6
Crockett, Zack, Indianapolis	1	1	0	0	0	6
Crumpler, Carlester, Seattle	1	0	1	0	0	6
Cullors, Derrick, New England	1	0	0	1	0	6
Davis, Terrell, Denver	15	15	0	0	3	96
Davis, Willie, Tennessee	4	0	4	0	0	24
Dawkins, Sean, Indianapolis	2	0	2	0	0	12
Dawson, Lake, Kansas City	2	0	2	0	0	12
Dilger, Ken, Indianapolis	3	0	3	0	0	18
Dillon, Corey, Cincinnati	10	10	0	0	0	60
Drayton, Troy, Miami	4	0	4	0	0	24
Dudley, Rickey, Oakland	7	0	7	0	0	42
Dunn, David, Cincinnati	2	0	2	0	0	12
Early, Quinn, Buffalo	5	0	5	0	0	30
Elway, John, Denver	1	1	0	0	0	6
Faulk, Marshall, Indianapolis	8	7	1	0	0	48
Fontenot, Al, Indianapolis	1	0	0	1	0	6
Galloway, Joey, Seattle	12	0	12	0	0	72
Gannon, Rich, Kansas City	2	2	0	0	0	12
Gash, Sam, New England	3	0	3	0	0	18
George, Eddie, Tennessee	7	6	1	0	1	44
Gildon, Jason, Pittsburgh	1	0	0	1	0	6
Glenn, Aaron, N.Y. Jets	1	0	0	1	0	6
Glenn, Terry, New England	2	0	2	0	0	12
Gonzalez, Tony, Kansas City	2	0	2	0	1	14
Gordon, Darrien, Denver	4	0	0	4	0	24
Graham, Jay, Baltimore	2	2	0	0	0	12
Graham, Jeff, N.Y. Jets	2	0	2	0	0	12
Grbac, Elvis, Kansas City	1	1	0	0	0	6
Green, Eric, Baltimore	5	0	5	0	0	30
Green, Willie, Denver	2	0	2	0	0	12
Grier, Marrio, New England	1	1	0	0	0	6
Hallock, Ty, Jacksonville	1	0	1	0	0	6
Hansen, Phil, Buffalo	0	0	0	0	0	*2
Harrison, Marvin, Indianapolis	6	0	6	0	2	40
Harrison, Rodney, San Diego	3	0	0	3	0	18
Hartley, Frank, San Diego	1	0	1	0	0	6
Hawkins, Courtney, Pittsburgh	3	0	3	0	0	18
Hebron, Vaughn, Denver	1	1	0	0	0	6
Hitchcock, Jimmy, N.E.	1	0	0	1	0	6
Holmes, Darick, Buffalo	2	2	0	0	0	12
Hudson, Chris, Jacksonville	2	0	0	2	0	12
Hughes, Danan, Kansas City	3	0	2	1	0	18
Hundon, James, Cincinnati	2	0	2	0	0	12
Jackson, Greg, San Diego	2	0	0	2	0	12
Jackson, Michael, Baltimore	4	0	4	0	1	26
Jackson, Willie, Jacksonville	2	0	2	0	1	14
Jefferson, Shawn, N.E.	2	0	2	0	0	12
Jett, James, Oakland	12	0	12	0	0	72
Johnson, Charles, Pittsburgh	2	0	2	0	0	12
Johnson, Darrius, Denver	1	0	0	1	0	6
Johnson, Keyshawn, N.Y. Jets	5	0	5	0	0	30
Johnson, Leon, N.Y. Jets	4	2	0	2	0	24
Johnson, Lonnie, Buffalo	2	0	2	0	0	12
Johnson, Rob, Jacksonville	1	1	0	0	0	6
Jones, Charlie, San Diego	1	0	1	0	0	6
Jones, Damon, Jacksonville	2	0	2	0	0	12
Jones, Freddie, San Diego	2	0	2	0	0	12

Player, Team	Tot. TD	RTD	PTD	MTD	2Pt.	Tot. Pts.
Jones, George, Pittsburgh	2	1	1	0	0	12
Jordan, Charles, Miami	3	0	3	0	0	18
Kaufman, Napoleon, Oakland	8	6	2	0	0	48
Kent, Joey, Tennessee	1	0	1	0	0	6
Kinchen, Brian, Baltimore	1	0	1	0	0	6
Kitna, Jon, Seattle	1	1	0	0	0	6
Lake, Carnell, Pittsburgh	1	0	0	1	0	6
Langham, Antonio, Baltimore	1	0	0	1	0	6
Lewis, Darryll, Tennessee	1	0	0	1	0	6
Lewis, Jermaine, Baltimore	8	0	6	2	0	48
Lewis, Mo, N.Y. Jets	1	0	0	1	0	6
Loville, Derek, Denver	1	1	0	0	0	6
Martin, Curtis, New England	5	4	1	0	0	30
Martin, Tony, San Diego	6	0	6	0	0	36
McCaffrey, Ed, Denver	8	0	8	0	0	48
McCardell, Keenan, Jac.	5	0	5	0	0	30
McDuffie, O.J., Miami	2	0	1	1	0	12
McElroy, Ray, Indianapolis	1	0	0	1	0	6
McGee, Tony, Cincinnati	6	0	6	0	1	38
McKnight, James, Seattle	6	0	6	0	0	36
McMillian, Mark, Kansas City	3	0	0	3	0	18
McNair, Steve, Tennessee	8	8	0	0	0	48
McPhail, Jerris, Miami	2	1	1	0	0	12
Means, Natrone, Jacksonville	9	9	0	0	0	54
Meggett, David, New England	2	1	1	0	0	12
Metcalf, Eric, San Diego	5	0	2	3	0	30
Mickens, Ray, N.Y. Jets	1	0	0	1	0	6
Milne, Brian, Cincinnati	2	2	0	0	0	12
Mitchell, Pete, Jacksonville	4	0	4	0	0	24
Mobley, John, Denver	1	0	0	1	0	6
Moon, Warren, Seattle	1	1	0	0	0	6
Morris, Bam, Baltimore	4	4	0	0	0	24
Moulds, Eric, Buffalo	0	0	0	0	1	2
Murrell, Adrian, N.Y. Jets	7	7	0	0	0	42
Neal, Lorenzo, N.Y. Jets	1	0	1	0	0	6
Norgard, Erik, Tennessee	1	0	1	0	0	6
O'Donnell, Neil, N.Y. Jets	1	1	0	0	0	6
Parmalee, Bernie, Miami	1	0	1	0	0	6
Perriman, Brett, Miami	1	0	1	0	0	6
Perry, Ed, Miami	1	0	1	0	0	6
Phillips, Joe, Kansas City	0	0	0	0	0	*2
Pickens, Carl, Cincinnati	5	0	5	0	0	30
Pollard, Marcus, Indianapolis	0	0	0	0	1	2
Popson, Ted, Kansas City	2	0	2	0	0	12
Pritchard, Mike, Seattle	2	0	2	0	0	12
Purnell, Lovett, New England	3	0	3	0	0	18
Reed, Andre, Buffalo	5	0	5	0	0	30
Richardson, Tony, Kansas City	3	0	3	0	0	18
Riemersma, Jay, Buffalo	2	0	2	0	1	14
Rison, Andre, Kansas City	7	0	7	0	0	42
Robertson, Marcus, Tennessee	2	0	0	2	0	12
Russell, Derek, Tennessee	1	0	1	0	0	6
Saleaumua, Dan, Seattle	0	0	0	0	0	*2
Sanders, Chris, Tennessee	3	0	3	0	0	18
Scott, Darnay, Cincinnati	5	0	5	0	0	30
Sharpe, Shannon, Denver	3	0	3	0	1	20
Shedd, Kenny, Oakland	1	0	0	1	0	6
Sinclair, Michael, Seattle	1	0	0	1	0	6
Slade, Chris, New England	1	0	0	1	0	6
Smith, Anthony, Oakland	0	0	0	0	0	*2
Smith, Antowain, Buffalo	8	8	0	0	0	48
Smith, Detron, Denver	1	0	1	0	0	6
Smith, Jimmy, Jacksonville	4	0	4	0	0	24
Smith, Lamar, Seattle	2	2	0	0	1	14
Smith, Otis, N.Y. Jets	3	0	0	3	0	18
Smith, Rod, Denver	12	0	12	0	0	72
Spikes, Irving, Miami	2	2	0	0	0	12
Stablein, Brian, Indianapolis	1	0	1	0	1	8
Stewart, James, Jacksonville	9	8	1	0	0	54
Stewart, Kordell, Pittsburgh	11	11	0	0	0	66
Strong, Mack, Seattle	2	0	2	0	0	12

Player, Team	Tot. TD	RTD	PTD	MTD	2Pt.	Tot. Pts.
Thigpen, Yancey, Pittsburgh ...	7	0	7	0	1	44
Thomas, Derrick, Kansas City.	0	0	0	0	0	*2
Thomas, Lamar, Miami	2	0	2	0	0	12
Thomas, Rodney, Tennessee ..	3	3	0	0	0	18
Thomas, Thurman, Buffalo	1	1	0	0	0	6
Traylor, Keith, Denver	1	0	0	1	0	6
Truitt, Olanda, Oakland	1	0	1	0	0	6
Turner, Eric, Oakland	1	0	0	1	0	6
Van Dyke, Alex, N.Y. Jets	2	0	2	0	0	12
Vanover, Tamarick, Kansas City.	2	0	0	2	1	14
Van Pelt, Alex, Buffalo	1	1	0	0	0	6
Walker, Denard, Tennessee	1	0	0	1	0	6
Ward, Dedric, N.Y. Jets	1	0	1	0	0	6
Warren, Chris, Seattle	4	4	0	0	0	24
Warren, Lamont, Indianapolis.	2	2	0	0	0	12
Washington, Lionel, Oakland ..	1	0	0	1	0	6
Whigham, Larry, New England .	1	0	0	1	0	6
Williams, Alfred, Denver	1	0	0	1	0	6
Williams, Darryl, Seattle	1	0	0	1	0	6
Williams, Harvey, Oakland	5	3	2	0	1	32
Wycheck, Frank, Tennessee	4	0	4	0	1	26

*Includes safety.

NOTE: One team safety apiece credited to Indianapolis; Kansas City; New England and Baltimore.

NFC

KICKERS

Player, Team	XPM	XPA	FGM	FGA	Tot. Pts.
Andersen, Morten, Atlanta	35	35	23	27	104
Anderson, Gary, San Francisco	38	38	29	36	125
Blanton, Scott, Washington	34	34	16	24	82
Boniol, Chris, Philadelphia	33	33	22	31	99
Brien, Doug, New Orleans	22	22	23	27	91
Butler, Kevin, Arizona	9	10	8	12	33
Cunningham, Richie, Dallas	24	24	34	37	126
Daluiso, Brad, N.Y. Giants	27	29	22	32	93
Hanson, Jason, Detroit	39	40	26	29	117
Husted, Michael, Tampa Bay	32	35	13	17	71
Jacke, Chris, Washington	5	5	0	0	5
Jaeger, Jeff, Chicago	20	20	21	26	83
Kasay, John, Carolina	25	25	22	26	91
Longwell, Ryan, Green Bay	48	48	24	30	120
Murray, Eddie, Minnesota	23	24	12	17	59
Nedney, Joe, Arizona	19	19	11	17	52
Wilkins, Jeff, St. Louis	32	32	25	37	107
Gowin, Toby, Dallas	0	0	0	1	0

NON-KICKERS

Player, Team	Tot. TD	RTD	PTD	MTD	2Pt.	Tot. Pts.
Alexander, Kevin, N.Y. Giants..	1	0	1	0	0	6
Allen, Terry, Washington	5	4	1	0	0	30
Alstott, Mike, Tampa Bay	10	7	3	0	0	60
Anderson, Jamal, Atlanta	10	7	3	0	0	60
Anthony, Reidel, Tampa Bay ...	4	0	4	0	0	24
Armstead, Jessie, N.Y. Giants..	1	0	0	1	0	6
Asher, Jamie, Washington	1	0	1	0	0	6
Autry, Darnell, Chicago	1	1	0	0	1	8
Banks, Tony, St. Louis	1	1	0	0	0	6
Barber, Tiki, N.Y. Giants	4	3	1	0	1	26
Bates, Mario, New Orleans	4	4	0	0	0	24
Bennett, Tommy, Arizona	1	0	0	1	0	6
Biakabutuka, Tim, Carolina	2	2	0	0	0	12
Bjornson, Eric, Dallas	0	0	0	0	1	2
Bowie, Larry, Washington	4	2	2	0	0	24
Boyd, Stephen, Detroit	1	0	0	1	0	6
Brady, Jeff, Minnesota	1	0	0	1	0	6
Brooks, Robert, Green Bay	7	0	7	0	0	42
Brown, Dave, N.Y. Giants	1	1	0	0	0	6
Brown, Reggie, Detroit	2	0	0	2	0	12

Player, Team	Tot. TD	RTD	PTD	MTD	2Pt.	Tot. Pts.
Bruce, Isaac, St. Louis	5	0	5	0	0	30
Calloway, Chris, N.Y. Giants....	8	0	8	0	0	48
Carrier, Mark, Carolina	2	0	2	0	0	12
Carruth, Rae, Carolina	4	0	4	0	0	24
Carter, Cris, Minnesota	13	0	13	0	3	84
Carter, Pat, Arizona	1	0	1	0	0	6
Case, Stoney, Arizona	1	1	0	0	0	6
Centers, Larry, Arizona	2	1	1	0	0	12
Chmura, Mark, Green Bay	6	0	6	0	0	36
Christian, Bob, Atlanta	1	0	1	0	0	6
Chryplewicz, Pete, Detroit	1	0	1	0	0	6
Clark, Greg J., San Francisco..	1	0	1	0	0	6
Clark, Willie, Philadelphia	1	0	0	1	0	6
Coakley, Dexter, Dallas	1	0	0	1	0	6
Collins, Kerry, Carolina	1	1	0	0	0	6
Connell, Albert, Washington ...	2	0	2	0	0	12
Conway, Curtis, Chicago	1	0	1	0	0	6
Conwell, Ernie, St. Louis	4	0	4	0	0	24
Copeland, Horace, Tampa Bay	1	0	1	0	0	6
Cross, Howard, N.Y. Giants	2	0	2	0	0	12
Davis, Stephen, Washington...	3	3	0	0	0	18
Davis, Tyrone, Green Bay	2	0	1	1	0	12
Dawkins, Brian, Philadelphia...	1	0	0	1	0	6
Detmer, Ty, Philadelphia	1	1	0	0	0	6
Dilfer, Trent, Tampa Bay	1	1	0	0	0	6
Dishman, Cris, Washington	1	0	0	1	0	6
Dunn, Jason, Philadelphia	2	0	2	0	0	12
Dunn, Warrick, Tampa Bay	7	4	3	0	0	42
Ellard, Henry, Washington	4	0	4	0	0	24
Emanuel, Bert, Atlanta	9	0	9	0	0	54
Engram, Bobby, Chicago	2	0	2	0	1	14
Evans, Charles, Minnesota	2	2	0	0	1	14
Farquhar, John, New Orleans..	1	0	1	0	0	6
Favre, Brett, Green Bay	1	1	0	0	0	6
Fields, Mark, New Orleans	1	0	0	1	0	6
Flanigan, Jim, Chicago	0	0	0	0	1	2
Floyd, William, San Francisco.	4	3	1	0	0	24
Freeman, Antonio, Green Bay .	12	0	12	0	0	72
Frerotte, Gus, Washington	2	2	0	0	0	12
Fryar, Irving, Philadelphia	6	0	6	0	0	36
Garner, Charlie, Philadelphia..	3	3	0	0	0	18
Garnes, Sam, N.Y. Giants	1	0	0	1	0	6
Gedney, Chris, Arizona	4	0	4	0	0	24
Glover, Andrew, Minnesota	3	0	3	0	0	18
Graham, Kent, Arizona	2	2	0	0	0	12
Green, Darrell, Washington.....	1	0	0	1	0	6
Green, Harold, Atlanta	1	1	0	0	0	6
Greene, Kevin, San Francisco .	1	0	0	1	0	6
Greene, Scott, Carolina	2	1	1	0	0	12
Guliford, Eric, New Orleans.....	2	0	1	1	0	12
Hampton, Rodney, N.Y. Giants .	1	1	0	0	0	6
Hanks, Merton, San Francisco .	2	0	0	2	0	12
Hanspard, Byron, Atlanta	3	0	1	2	0	18
Hape, Patrick, Tampa Bay	1	0	1	0	0	6
Harris, Jackie, Tampa Bay	1	0	1	0	0	6
Harris, Raymont, Chicago	10	10	0	0	0	60
Hastings, Andre, New Orleans	5	0	5	0	1	32
Hayden, Aaron, Green Bay	1	1	0	0	0	6
Haynes, Michael, Atlanta	1	0	1	0	0	6
Hearst, Garrison, San Fran.	6	4	2	0	0	36
Henderson, William, G.B.	1	0	1	0	0	6
Hennings, Chad, Dallas	1	0	0	1	0	6
Heyward, Craig, St. Louis	1	1	0	0	0	6
Hill, Randal, New Orleans	2	0	2	0	0	12
Hoard, Leroy, Minnesota	4	4	0	0	0	24
Hobbs, Daryl, New Orleans.....	1	0	1	0	0	6
Irvin, Michael, Dallas	9	0	9	0	0	54
Ismail, Raghib, Carolina	2	0	2	0	0	12
Jenkins, James, Washington ..	3	0	3	0	0	18
Johnson, Anthony, Carolina.....	1	0	0	1	1	8
Johnson, Brad, Minnesota	1	0	1	0	2	10

Player, Team	Tot. TD	RTD	PTD	MTD	2Pt.	Tot. Pts.
Johnson, Jimmie, Philadelphia.	1	0	1	0	0	6
Johnston, Daryl, Dallas	1	0	1	0	0	6
Jones, Brent, San Francisco	2	0	2	0	0	12
Kinchen, Todd, Atlanta	1	0	1	0	0	6
Kirby, Terry, San Francisco	8	6	1	1	2	52
Kozlowski, Brian, Atlanta	1	0	1	0	0	6
Kramer, Erik, Chicago	2	2	0	0	0	12
LaFleur, David, Dallas	2	0	2	0	0	12
Laing, Aaron, St. Louis	1	0	1	0	0	6
Lane, Fred, Carolina	7	7	0	0	0	42
Lee, Amp, St. Louis	3	0	3	0	0	18
Levens, Dorsey, Green Bay	12	7	5	0	1	74
Levy, Chuck, San Francisco	1	0	0	1	0	6
Lewis, Chad, Philadelphia	4	0	4	0	0	24
Mathis, Terance, Atlanta	6	0	6	0	0	36
McElroy, Leeland, Arizona	2	2	0	0	0	12
McNeil, Ryan, St. Louis	1	0	0	1	0	6
Mickens, Terry, Green Bay	1	0	1	0	0	6
Miller, Anthony, Dallas	4	0	4	0	0	24
Mills, Ernie, Carolina	1	0	1	0	0	6
Mirer, Rick, Chicago	1	1	0	0	1	8
Mitchell, Brian, Washington	4	1	1	2	0	24
Mitchell, Scott, Detroit	1	1	0	0	0	6
Moore, Dave, Tampa Bay	4	0	4	0	0	24
Moore, Herman, Detroit	8	0	8	0	1	50
Moore, Jerald, St. Louis	3	3	0	0	0	18
Moore, Rob, Arizona	8	0	8	0	1	50
Moore, Ronald, St. Louis	1	1	0	0	0	6
Morton, Johnnie, Detroit	6	0	6	0	0	36
Muhammad, Muhsin, Carolina.	0	0	0	0	1	2
O'Neal, Leslie, St. Louis	1	0	0	1	0	6
Owens, Terrell, San Francisco.	8	0	8	0	0	48
Palmer, David, Minnesota	2	1	1	0	0	12
Patten, David, N.Y. Giants	2	0	2	0	0	12
Pegram, Erric, S.D.-NYG†	2	2	0	0	0	12
Penn, Chris, Chicago	3	0	3	0	0	18
Phillips, Lawrence, St. Louis	8	8	0	0	0	48
Plummer, Jake, Arizona	2	2	0	0	1	14
Poole, Keith, New Orleans	2	0	2	0	0	12
Pounds, Darryl, Washington	2	0	0	2	0	12
Proehl, Ricky, Chicago	7	0	7	0	1	44
Reed, Jake, Minnesota	6	0	6	0	0	36
Rhett, Errict, Tampa Bay	3	3	0	0	0	18
Rice, Jerry, San Francisco	1	0	1	0	0	6
Rivers, Ron, Detroit	1	1	0	0	0	6
Sanders, Barry, Detroit	14	11	3	0	0	84
Sanders, Deion, Dallas	2	0	0	2	0	12
Sanders, Frank, Arizona	4	0	4	0	1	26
Santiago, O.J., Atlanta	2	0	2	0	0	12
Schlesinger, Cory, Detroit	1	0	1	0	0	6
Schroeder, Bill, Green Bay	1	0	1	0	0	6
Scroggins, Tracy, Detroit	1	0	0	1	0	*8
Seay, Mark, Philadelphia	1	0	1	0	0	6
Sehorn, Jason, N.Y. Giants	1	0	0	1	0	6
Sharper, Darren, Green Bay	3	0	0	3	0	18
Shepherd, Leslie, Washington	5	0	5	0	0	30
Shuler, Heath, New Orleans	1	1	0	0	0	6
Singleton, Alsheemond, T.B.	1	0	0	1	0	6
Small, Torrance, St. Louis	1	0	1	0	0	6
Smith, Cedric, Arizona	1	1	0	0	0	6
Smith, Emmitt, Dallas	4	4	0	0	1	26
Smith, Irv, New Orleans	1	0	1	0	0	6
Smith, Robert, Minnesota	7	6	1	0	0	42
Solomon, Freddie, Philadelphia.	3	0	3	0	1	20
Stokes, J.J., San Francisco	4	0	4	0	0	24
Stone, Dwight, Carolina	0	0	0	0	0	*2
Thomas, Orlando, Minnesota	1	0	0	1	0	6
Thomas, William, Philadelphia	1	0	0	1	0	6
Thomason, Jeff, Green Bay	1	0	1	0	0	6
Thompson, David, St. Louis	1	1	0	0	0	6
Timpson, Michael, Philadelphia	2	0	2	0	0	12
Toomer, Amani, N.Y. Giants	2	0	1	1	0	12
Turner, Kevin, Philadelphia	3	0	3	0	0	18
Vardell, Tommy, Detroit	6	6	0	0	0	36
Walker, Herschel, Dallas	2	0	2	0	0	12
Walls, Wesley, Carolina	6	0	6	0	0	36
Walsh, Chris, Minnesota	1	0	1	0	0	6
Watters, Ricky, Philadelphia	7	7	0	0	0	42
Way, Charles, N.Y. Giants	5	4	1	0	0	30
West, Ed, Atlanta	1	0	1	0	0	6
Westbrook, Bryant, Detroit	1	0	0	1	0	6
Westbrook, Michael, Was.	3	0	3	0	0	18
Wetnight, Ryan, Chicago	1	0	1	0	0	6
Wheatley, Tyrone, N.Y. Giants	4	4	0	0	0	24
Wiegert, Zach, St. Louis	1	0	0	1	0	6
Wilkins, Gabe, Green Bay	2	0	0	2	0	12
Williams, Aeneas, Arizona	2	0	0	2	0	12
Williams, Karl, Tampa Bay	5	0	4	1	0	30
Williams, Kevin, Arizona	1	0	1	0	0	6
Williams, Moe, Minnesota	1	1	0	0	0	6
Williams, Sherman, Dallas	2	2	0	0	0	12
Williams, Stepfret, Dallas	1	0	1	0	0	6
Wilson, Bernard, Arizona	1	0	0	1	0	6
Wooten, Tito, N.Y. Giants	1	0	0	1	0	6
Young, Steve, San Francisco	3	3	0	0	0	18
Zellars, Ray, New Orleans	4	4	0	0	0	24

*Includes safety.

†Includes both NFC and AFC statistics.

NOTE: One team safety apiece credited to Chicago and N.Y. Giants.

PLAYERS WITH TWO CLUBS

KICKERS

Player, Team	XPM	XPA	FGM	FGA	Tot. Pts.
Davis, Greg, Minnesota	10	10	7	10	31
Davis, Greg, San Diego	21	22	19	24	78

NON-KICKERS

Player, Team	Tot. TD	RTD	PTD	MTD	2Pt.	Tot. Pts.
Pegram, Erric, San Diego	1	1	0	0	0	6
Pegram, Erric, N.Y. Giants	1	1	0	0	0	6

INTERCEPTIONS

TEAM

AFC

Team	No.	Yds.	Avg.	Long	TD
Kansas City	21	432	20.6	t87	4
Pittsburgh	20	253	12.7	42	0
New England	19	366	19.3	t100	4
N.Y. Jets	18	379	21.1	t51	4
Denver	18	319	17.7	t62	5
Baltimore	17	241	14.2	43	1
San Diego	15	257	17.1	t75	3
Buffalo	15	157	10.5	28	0
Tennessee	14	328	23.4	48	2
Jacksonville	14	145	10.4	32	0
Seattle	13	196	15.1	t44	1
Cincinnati	13	183	14.1	37	0
Indianapolis	12	234	19.5	t52	2
Oakland	10	149	14.9	t44	1
Miami	10	92	9.2	23	0
AFC total	229	3731	16.3	t100	27
AFC average	15.3	248.7	16.3	...	1.8

t—touchdown.

NFC

Team	No.	Yds.	Avg.	Long	TD
N.Y. Giants	27	503	18.6	t95	4
San Francisco	25	366	14.6	t55	1
St. Louis	25	281	11.2	t75	1
Green Bay	21	329	15.7	t77	3
Atlanta	18	114	6.3	31	0
Detroit	17	309	18.2	66	3
Washington	16	222	13.9	t83	3
New Orleans	16	194	12.1	39	0
Arizona	15	231	15.4	t66	3
Philadelphia	14	186	13.3	t64	1
Tampa Bay	13	95	7.3	28	0
Chicago	13	60	4.6	14	0
Minnesota	12	141	11.8	27	0
Carolina	11	72	6.5	18	0
Dallas	7	130	18.6	t50	1
NFC total	250	3233	12.9	t95	20
NFC average	16.7	215.5	12.9	...	1.3
NFL total	479	6964	...	t100	47
NFL average	16.0	232.1	14.5	...	1.6

INDIVIDUAL

BESTS OF THE SEASON

Interceptions, season
NFC: 9—Ryan McNeil, St. Louis.
AFC: 8—Mark McMillian, Kansas City.

Interceptions, game
AFC: 3—Darryl Williams, Seattle vs. San Diego, Sept. 21.
NFC: 3—Rod Woodson, San Francisco vs. New Orleans, Sept. 14.

Yards, season
AFC: 274—Mark McMillian, Kansas City.
NFC: 146—Tito Wooten, N.Y. Giants.

Longest
AFC: 100—Jimmy Hitchcock, New England vs. Miami, Nov. 23 (TD).
NFC: 95—Sam Garnes, N.Y. Giants vs. Philadelphia, Aug. 31 (TD).

Touchdowns, season
AFC: 3—Otis Smith, N.Y. Jets; Mark McMillian, Kansas City.
NFC: 2—Aeneas Williams, Arizona; Reggie Brown, Detroit; Darren Sharper, Green Bay.

Team leaders, interceptions

AFC:

Baltimore	4	Stevon Moore
Buffalo	2	Ken Irvin
		Kurt Schulz
		Marlon Kerner
		Jeff Burris
		Sean Moran
Cincinnati	4	Corey Sawyer
Denver	4	Tyrone Braxton
		Darrien Gordon
		Ray Crockett
Indianapolis	2	Jason Belser
		Quentin Coryatt
		Carlton Gray
Jacksonville	5	Deon Figures
Kansas City	8	Mark McMillian
Miami	4	Terrell Buckley
New England	6	Willie Clay
N.Y. Jets	6	Otis Smith
Oakland	2	Eric Turner
		Lionel Washington
		James Trapp
		Lorenzo Lynch
Pittsburgh	4	Donnell Woolford
		Darren Perry
San Diego	2	Rodney Harrison
		Paul Bradford
		Dwayne Harper
		Greg Jackson
		Junior Seau
Seattle	8	Darryl Williams
Tennessee	5	Marcus Robertson
		Darryll Lewis

NFC:

Arizona	6	Aeneas Williams
Atlanta	5	Ray Buchanan
Carolina	5	Eric Davis
Chicago	5	Walt Harris
Dallas	2	Deion Sanders
		Omar Stoutmire
Detroit	5	Mark Carrier
Green Bay	5	LeRoy Butler
Minnesota	4	Dewayne Washington
New Orleans	5	Sammy Knight
N.Y. Giants	6	Jason Sehorn
Philadelphia	3	Brian Dawkins
		Troy Vincent
St. Louis	9	Ryan McNeil
San Francisco	6	Merton Hanks
Tampa Bay	5	Donnie Abraham
Washington	4	Cris Dishman
		Stanley Richard

NFL LEADERS

Player, Team	No.	Yds.	Avg.	Long	TD
McNeil, Ryan, St. Louis	9	127	14.1	t75	1
McMillian, Mark, Kansas City*	8	274	34.3	t87	3
Williams, Darryl, Seattle*	8	172	21.5	t44	1
Lyle, Keith, St. Louis	8	102	12.8	39	0
Smith, Otis, N.Y. Jets*	6	158	26.3	t51	3
Clay, Willie, New England*	6	109	18.2	t53	1
Hanks, Merton, San Francisco	6	103	17.2	t55	1

Player, Team	No.	Yds.	Avg.	Long	TD
Williams, Aeneas, Arizona	6	95	15.8	t42	2
Sehorn, Jason, N.Y. Giants	6	74	12.3	41	1

*AFC.
t—touchdown.
Leader based on most interceptions.

AFC

Player, Team	No.	Yds.	Avg.	Long	TD
Alexander, Elijah, Indianapolis	1	43	43.0	t43	1
Ambrose, Ashley, Cincinnati	3	56	18.7	29	0
Anderson, Darren, Kansas City	1	55	55.0	t55	1
Atwater, Steve, Denver	2	42	21.0	t22	1
Beasley, Aaron, Jacksonville	1	5	5.0	5	0
Bell, Myron, Pittsburgh	1	10	10.0	7	0
Bellamy, Jay, Seattle	1	13	13.0	13	0
Belser, Jason, Indianapolis	2	121	60.5	t50	1
Blackmon, Robert, Indianapolis	1	2	2.0	2	0
Blades, Bennie, Seattle	2	11	5.5	11	0
Bowden, Joe, Tennessee	1	9	9.0	9	0
Bradford, Paul, San Diego	2	56	28.0	t56	1
Braxton, Tyrone, Denver	4	113	28.3	43	1
Brown, Cornell, Baltimore	1	21	21.0	21	0
Buckley, Terrell, Miami	4	26	6.5	12	0
Burris, Jeff, Buffalo	2	19	9.5	10	0
Carter, Dale, Kansas City	2	9	4.5	9	0
Clark, Rico, Indianapolis	1	14	14.0	14	0
Clay, Willie, New England	6	109	18.2	t53	1
Coleman, Marco, San Diego	1	2	2.0	2	0
Coleman, Marcus, N.Y. Jets	1	24	24.0	24	0
Conley, Steve, Pittsburgh	1	-3	-3.0	0	0
Coryatt, Quentin, Indianapolis	2	3	1.5	3	0
Covington, Damien, Buffalo	1	6	6.0	6	0
Crockett, Ray, Denver	4	18	4.5	10	0
Daniel, Eugene, Baltimore	3	60	20.0	43	0
Davis, Travis, Jacksonville	1	23	23.0	23	0
Dumas, Mike, San Diego	1	0	0.0	0	0
Edwards, Donnie, Kansas City	2	15	7.5	12	0
Figures, Deon, Jacksonville	5	48	9.6	32	0
Francis, James, Cincinnati	1	7	7.0	7	0
Fuller, William, San Diego	1	0	0.0	0	0
Glenn, Aaron, N.Y. Jets	1	5	5.0	5	0
Gordon, Darrien, Denver	4	64	16.0	t32	1
Gouveia, Kurt, San Diego	1	0	0.0	0	0
Gray, Carlton, Indianapolis	2	0	0.0	0	0
Green, Victor, N.Y. Jets	3	89	29.7	39	0
Harper, Dwayne, San Diego	2	43	21.5	43	0
Harrison, Rodney, San Diego	2	75	37.5	t75	1
Hasty, James, Kansas City	3	22	7.3	19	0
Henderson, Jerome, N.Y. Jets	1	45	45.0	45	0
Henry, Kevin, Pittsburgh	1	36	36.0	36	0
Hitchcock, Jimmy, New England	2	104	52.0	t100	1
Hudson, Chris, Jacksonville	3	26	8.7	23	0
Irvin, Ken, Buffalo	2	28	14.0	28	0
Jackson, Greg, San Diego	2	37	18.5	t36	1
Jenkins, DeRon, Baltimore	1	15	15.0	15	0
Johnson, Ellis, Indianapolis	1	18	18.0	18	0
Johnson, Pepper, N.Y. Jets	1	13	13.0	13	0
Jones, Roger, Tennessee	1	24	24.0	24	0
Jones, Rondell, Baltimore	1	15	15.0	15	0
Kerner, Marlon, Buffalo	2	20	10.0	20	0
Kirkland, Levon, Pittsburgh	2	14	7.0	11	0
Kopp, Jeff, Jacksonville	1	9	9.0	9	0
Lake, Carnell, Pittsburgh	3	16	5.3	11	0
Land, Dan, Oakland	1	13	13.0	13	0
Langham, Antonio, Baltimore	3	40	13.3	t40	1
Law, Ty, New England	3	70	23.3	40	0
Lewis, Darryll, Tennessee	5	115	23.0	t47	1
Lewis, Mo, N.Y. Jets	1	43	43.0	t43	1
Lewis, Ray, Baltimore	1	18	18.0	18	0
Lynch, Lorenzo, Oakland	2	6	3.0	6	0

Player, Team	No.	Yds.	Avg.	Long	TD
Mack, Tremain, Cincinnati	1	29	29.0	29	0
Maddox, Mark, Buffalo	1	25	25.0	25	0
Madison, Sam, Miami	1	21	21.0	21	0
Martin, Emanuel, Buffalo	1	12	12.0	12	0
Mathis, Dedric, Indianapolis	1	31	31.0	31	0
McDaniel, Terry, Oakland	1	17	17.0	17	0
McKyer, Tim, Denver	1	0	0.0	0	0
McMillian, Mark, Kansas City	8	274	34.3	t87	3
Mickens, Ray, N.Y. Jets	4	2	0.5	2	0
Milloy, Lawyer, New England	3	15	5.0	15	0
Mobley, John, Denver	1	13	13.0	t13	1
Moore, Marty, New England	2	7	3.5	7	0
Moore, Stevon, Baltimore	4	56	14.0	38	0
Moran, Sean, Buffalo	2	12	6.0	12	0
Morrison, Steve, Indianapolis	1	2	2.0	2	0
Myers, Greg, Cincinnati	1	25	25.0	25	0
Oldham, Chris, Pittsburgh	2	16	8.0	8	0
Orlando, Bo, Cincinnati	1	3	3.0	3	0
Perry, Darren, Pittsburgh	4	77	19.3	42	0
Perry, Marlo, Buffalo	1	4	4.0	4	0
Robertson, Marcus, Tennessee	5	127	25.4	48	0
Robinson, Eddie, Jacksonville	1	0	0.0	0	0
Romanowski, Bill, Denver	1	7	7.0	7	0
Sawyer, Corey, Cincinnati	4	44	11.0	37	0
Schulz, Kurt, Buffalo	2	23	11.5	21	0
Scott, Chad, Pittsburgh	2	-4	-2.0	0	0
Seau, Junior, San Diego	2	33	16.5	26	0
Shade, Sam, Cincinnati	1	21	21.0	21	0
Sharper, Jamie, Baltimore	1	4	4.0	4	0
Shaw, Terrance, San Diego	1	11	11.0	11	0
Slade, Chris, New England	1	1	1.0	t1	1
Smith, Otis, N.Y. Jets	6	158	26.3	t51	3
Spencer, Jimmy, Cincinnati	1	-2	-2.0	0	0
Spielman, Chris, Buffalo	1	8	8.0	8	0
Springs, Shawn, Seattle	1	0	0.0	0	0
Staten, Ralph, Baltimore	2	12	6.0	9	0
Teague, George, Miami	2	25	12.5	23	0
Thomas, Dave, Jacksonville	2	34	17.0	23	0
Thomas, Zach, Miami	1	10	10.0	10	0
Tongue, Reggie, Kansas City	1	0	0.0	0	0
Trapp, James, Oakland	2	24	12.0	25	0
Traylor, Keith, Denver	1	62	62.0	t62	1
Turner, Eric, Oakland	2	45	22.5	29	0
Walker, Denard, Tennessee	2	53	26.5	t39	1
Washington, Lionel, Oakland	2	44	22.0	t44	1
Whigham, Larry, New England	2	60	30.0	t60	1
Williams, Darryl, Seattle	8	172	21.5	t44	1
Williams, Willie, Seattle	1	0	0.0	0	0
Wooden, Shawn, Miami	2	10	5.0	10	0
Woods, Jerome, Kansas City	4	57	14.3	27	0
Woolford, Donnell, Pittsburgh	4	91	22.8	34	0

t—touchdown.

NFC

Player, Team	No.	Yds.	Avg.	Long	TD
Abraham, Donnie, Tampa Bay	5	16	3.2	16	0
Abrams, Kevin, Detroit	1	29	29.0	29	0
Allen, Eric, New Orleans	2	27	13.5	27	0
Archambeau, Lester, Atlanta	1	0	0.0	0	0
Armstead, Jesse, N.Y. Giants	2	57	28.5	t57	1
Bailey, Robert, Detroit	1	0	0.0	0	0
Bennett, Tommy, Arizona	1	0	0.0	0	0
Booker, Michael, Atlanta	3	16	5.3	10	0
Boutte, Marc, Washington	1	10	10.0	10	0
Boyd, Stephen, Detroit	1	4	4.0	4	0
Bradford, Ronnie, Atlanta	4	9	2.3	9	0
Bronson, Zack, San Francisco	1	22	22.0	22	0
Brooks, Derrick, Tampa Bay	2	13	6.5	13	0
Brown, Reggie, Detroit	2	83	41.5	t45	2
Buchanan, Ray, Atlanta	5	49	9.8	31	0

Player, Team	No.	Yds.	Avg.	Long	TD
Bush, Devin, Atlanta	1	4	4.0	4	0
Butler, LeRoy, Green Bay	5	4	0.8	2	0
Caldwell, Mike, Arizona	1	5	5.0	5	0
Campbell, Jesse, Washington	1	7	7.0	7	0
Carrier, Mark, Detroit	5	94	18.8	66	0
Carter, Marty, Chicago	1	14	14.0	14	0
Carter, Tom, Chicago	3	12	4.0	12	0
Coakley, Dexter, Dallas	1	6	6.0	6	0
Cota, Chad, Carolina	2	28	14.0	15	0
Davis, Eric, Carolina	5	25	5.0	17	0
Dawkins, Brian, Philadelphia	3	76	25.3	t64	1
Dimry, Charles, Philadelphia	2	25	12.5	25	0
Dishman, Cris, Washington	4	47	11.8	t29	1
Drakeford, Tyronne, S.F.	5	15	3.0	15	0
Ellsworth, Percy, N.Y. Giants	4	40	10.0	25	0
Evans, Doug, Green Bay	3	33	11.0	27	0
Farr, D'Marco, St. Louis	1	22	22.0	22	0
Fisk, Jason, Minnesota	1	1	1.0	1	0
Fuller, Corey, Minnesota	2	24	12.0	22	0
Garnes, Sam, N.Y. Giants	1	95	95.0	t95	1
Green, Darrell, Washington	1	83	83.0	t83	1
Griffith, Robert, Minnesota	2	26	13.0	21	0
Hall, Rhett, Philadelphia	1	39	39.0	39	0
Hamilton, Conrad, N.Y. Giants	1	18	18.0	18	0
Hanks, Merton, San Francisco	6	103	17.2	t55	1
Harris, Bernardo, Green Bay	1	0	0.0	0	0
Harris, Walt, Chicago	5	30	6.0	12	0
Harvey, Richard, New Orleans	1	7	7.0	7	0
Jeffries, Greg, Detroit	1	0	0.0	0	0
Johnson, Melvin, Tampa Bay	1	19	19.0	19	0
Jones, Mike, St. Louis	1	0	0.0	0	0
Kelly, Rob, New Orleans	1	15	15.0	15	0
Knight, Sammy, New Orleans	5	75	15.0	39	0
Lassiter, Kwamie, Arizona	1	10	10.0	10	0
Lathon, Lamar, Carolina	1	1	1.0	1	0
Legette, Tyrone, Tampa Bay	1	0	0.0	0	0
Lyght, Todd, St. Louis	4	25	6.3	13	0
Lyle, Keith, St. Louis	8	102	12.8	39	0
Lynch, John, Tampa Bay	2	28	14.0	28	0
Malone, Van, Detroit	1	-5	-5.0	0	0
Mangum, John, Chicago	2	4	2.0	4	0
Marshall, Anthony, Chicago	2	0	0.0	0	0
Maxie, Brett, San Francisco	1	0	0.0	0	0
McCleon, Dexter, St. Louis	1	0	0.0	0	0
McCleskey, J.J., Arizona	1	15	15.0	15	0
McDaniel, Ed, Minnesota	1	18	18.0	18	0
McDonald, Tim, San Francisco	3	34	11.3	17	0
McGill, Lenny, Atlanta	1	7	7.0	7	0
McKinnon, Ronald, Arizona	3	40	13.3	17	0
McNeil, Ryan, St. Louis	9	127	14.1	t75	1
Mills, Sam, Carolina	1	18	18.0	18	0
Mincy, Charles, Tampa Bay	1	14	14.0	14	0
Mullen, Roderick, Green Bay	1	17	17.0	17	0
Newman, Anthony, New Orleans	3	19	6.3	17	0
O'Neal, Leslie, St. Louis	1	5	5.0	5	0
Owens, Dan, Atlanta	1	14	14.0	14	0
Parker, Anthony, Tampa Bay	1	5	5.0	5	0
Patton, Marvcus, Washington	2	5	2.5	5	0
Poole, Tyrone, Carolina	2	0	0.0	0	0
Pope, Marquez, San Francisco	1	7	7.0	7	0
Porcher, Robert, Detroit	1	5	5.0	5	0
Pounds, Darryl, Washington	3	42	14.0	t22	1
Prior, Mike, Green Bay	4	72	18.0	49	0
Randolph, Thomas, N.Y. Giants	1	1	1.0	1	0
Raymond, Corey, Detroit	1	17	17.0	17	0
Rice, Ron, Detroit	1	18	18.0	18	0
Rice, Simeon, Arizona	1	0	0.0	0	0
Richard, Stanley, Washington	4	28	7.0	23	0
Robinson, Eugene, Green Bay	1	26	26.0	26	0
Sanders, Deion, Dallas	2	81	40.5	t50	1
Sehorn, Jason, N.Y. Giants	6	74	12.3	41	1
Sharper, Darren, Green Bay	2	70	35.0	t50	2
Smith, Chuck, Atlanta	1	4	4.0	4	0
Smith, Kevin, Dallas	1	21	21.0	21	0
Sparks, Phillippi, N.Y. Giants	5	72	14.4	68	0
Stevens, Matt, Philadelphia	1	0	0.0	0	0
Stoutmire, Omar, Dallas	2	8	4.0	8	0
Thomas, Orlando, Minnesota	2	1	0.5	1	0
Thomas, William, Philadelphia	2	11	5.5	11	0
Tubbs, Winfred, New Orleans	2	21	10.5	15	0
Vincent, Troy, Philadelphia	3	14	4.7	14	0
Walker, Darnell, San Francisco	3	49	16.3	28	0
Washington, Dewayne, Minnesota	4	71	17.8	27	0
Washington, Mickey, New Orleans	2	30	15.0	30	0
Westbrook, Bryant, Detroit	2	64	32.0	t64	1
White, William, Atlanta	1	11	11.0	11	0
Widmer, Corey, N.Y. Giants	2	0	0.0	0	0
Wilkins, Gabe, Green Bay	1	77	77.0	t77	1
Williams, Aeneas, Arizona	6	95	15.8	t42	2
Williams, Brian, Green Bay	2	30	15.0	25	0
Williams, Tyrone, Green Bay	1	0	0.0	0	0
Willis, James, Philadelphia	1	0	0.0	0	0
Wilson, Bernard, Arizona	1	66	66.0	t66	1
Woodall, Lee, San Francisco	2	55	27.5	55	0
Woodson, Darren, Dallas	1	14	14.0	14	0
Woodson, Rod, San Francisco	3	81	27.0	41	0
Wooten, Tito, N.Y. Giants	5	146	29.2	t61	1
Zordich, Michael, Philadelphia	1	21	21.0	21	0

t—touchdown.

SACKS

TEAM

AFC

Team	Sacks	Yards
Kansas City	54	359
Jacksonville	48	331
Pittsburgh	48	294
Buffalo	46	344
New England	45	303
Denver	44	298
Baltimore	42	293
Seattle	42	238
Indianapolis	37	247
Tennessee	35	240
Cincinnati	35	209
Oakland	31	239
Miami	31	231
N.Y. Jets	29	242
San Diego	27	164
AFC total	594	4032
AFC average	39.6	268.8

NFC

Team	Sacks	Yards
New Orleans	59	408
Atlanta	55	354
San Francisco	54	364
N.Y. Giants	54	341
Tampa Bay	44	331
Minnesota	44	253
Detroit	43	287
Philadelphia	43	278
Green Bay	41	274
St. Louis	38	296
Chicago	38	259
Dallas	38	195
Washington	37	280
Carolina	36	246
Arizona	34	215
NFC total	658	4381
NFC average	43.9	292.1
NFL total	1252	8413
NFL average	41.7	280.4

INDIVIDUAL

BESTS OF THE SEASON

Sacks, season
NFC: 15.5—John Randle, Minnesota.
AFC: 14.0—Bruce Smith, Buffalo.
Sacks, game
NFC: 5.0—Chuck Smith, Atlanta at New Orleans, Oct. 12.
AFC: 3.5—Gerald Dixon, Cincinnati vs. Baltimore, Dec. 21.

NFL LEADERS

Player, Team	No.
Randle, John, Minnesota	15.5
Stubblefield, Dana, San Francisco	15.0
Smith, Bruce, Buffalo*	14.0
Strahan, Michael, N.Y. Giants	14.0
Porcher, Robert, Detroit	12.5
Smith, Chuck, Atlanta	12.0
Doleman, Chris, San Francisco	12.0
Sinclair, Michael, Seattle*	12.0
Boulware, Peter, Baltimore*	11.5
White, Reggie, Green Bay	11.0
Sapp, Warren, Tampa Bay	10.5
Greene, Kevin, San Francisco	10.5
Footman, Dan, Indianapolis*	10.5
Hall, Travis, Atlanta	10.5
Martin, Wayne, New Orleans	10.5
Williams, Dan, Kansas City*	10.5
O'Neal, Leslie, St. Louis	10.0
Ahanotu, Chidi, Tampa Bay	10.0
Harris, Robert, N.Y. Giants	10.0
Harvey, Ken, Washington	9.5
Paup, Bryce, Buffalo*	9.5
Thomas, Derrick, Kansas City*	9.5
*AFC.	

AFC

Player, Team	No.
Adams, Sam, Seattle	7.0
Alexander, Elijah, Indianapolis	1.0
Ambrose, Ashley, Cincinnati	1.0
Anderson, Darren, Kansas City	2.0
Armstrong, Trace, Miami	5.5

Player, Team	No.
Atwater, Steve, Denver	1.0
Barndt, Tom, Kansas City	2.0
Bell, Myron, Pittsburgh	1.5
Bellamy, Jay, Seattle	2.0
Belser, Jason, Indianapolis	1.0
Bennett, Tony, Indianapolis	3.0
Biekert, Greg, Oakland	2.5
Bishop, Blaine, Tennessee	1.5
Blackmon, Robert, Indianapolis	3.0
Blades, Bennie, Seattle	1.0
Booker, Vaughn, Kansas City	4.0
Boulware, Peter, Baltimore	11.5
Bowden, Joe, Tennessee	2.5
Bowens, Tim, Miami	5.0
Boyer, Brant, Jacksonville	1.5
Brackens, Tony, Jacksonville	7.0
Braxton, Tyrone, Denver	0.5
Brown, Chad, Seattle	6.5
Brown, Cornell, Baltimore	0.5
Browning, John, Kansas City	4.0
Bruce, Aundray, Oakland	1.0
Bruschi, Tedy, New England	4.0
Burnett, Rob, Baltimore	4.0
Burroughs, Sammie, Indianapolis	1.0
Burton, Shane, Miami	4.0
Canty, Chris, New England	2.0
Coleman, Marco, San Diego	2.0
Collins, Andre, Cincinnati	3.0
Collins, Todd, New England	1.5
Collons, Ferric, New England	1.0
Conley, Steve, Pittsburgh	4.0
Copeland, John, Cincinnati	3.0
Coryatt, Quentin, Indianapolis	2.0
Covington, Damien, Buffalo	0.5
Daniels, Phillip, Seattle	4.0
Davey, Don, Jacksonville	3.0
Davis, Anthony, Kansas City	3.5
Davis, Travis, Jacksonville	2.0
Dixon, Gerald, Cincinnati	8.5
Douglas, Hugh, N.Y. Jets	4.0
Dumas, Mike, San Diego	1.0
Dumas, Troy, Kansas City	1.0
Eaton, Chad, New England	1.0

Player, Team	No.
Edwards, Donnie, Kansas City	2.5
Evans, Josh, Tennessee	2.0
Farrior, James, N.Y. Jets	1.5
Ferguson, Jason, N.Y. Jets	3.5
Fontenot, Al, Indianapolis	4.5
Footman, Dan, Indianapolis	10.5
Ford, Henry, Tennessee	5.0
Francis, James, Cincinnati	3.5
Fredrickson, Rob, Oakland	2.0
Fuller, Randy, Pittsburgh	1.0
Fuller, William, San Diego	3.0
Gardener, Daryl, Miami	1.5
Gibson, Oliver, Pittsburgh	1.0
Gildon, Jason, Pittsburgh	5.0
Gordon, Darrien, Denver	2.0
Gordon, Dwayne, N.Y. Jets	1.0
Green, Victor, N.Y. Jets	1.0
Hall, Lemanski, Tennessee	2.0
Hamilton, Bobby, N.Y. Jets	1.0
Hamilton, James, Jacksonville	1.0
Hand, Norman, San Diego	1.0
Hansen, Phil, Buffalo	6.0
Hardy, Kevin, Jacksonville	2.5
Harris, Anthony, Miami	1.0
Harrison, Nolan, Pittsburgh	4.0
Harrison, Rodney, San Diego	4.0
Hasselbach, Harald, Denver	1.5
Hasty, James, Kansas City	2.0
Henry, Kevin, Pittsburgh	4.5
Herring, Kim, Baltimore	1.0
Holecek, John, Buffalo	1.5
Holmes, Earl, Pittsburgh	4.0
Holmes, Kenny, Tennessee	7.0
Israel, Steve, New England	1.0
Jackson, Calvin, Miami	0.5
Jackson, Steve, Tennessee	1.0
Jeffcoat, Jim, Buffalo	0.5
Johnson, Ellis, Indianapolis	4.5
Johnson, Raylee, San Diego	2.5
Johnson, Ted, New England	4.0
Johnstone, Lance, Oakland	3.5
Jones, Henry, Buffalo	2.0
Jones, James, Baltimore	6.0
Jones, Lenoy, Tennessee	1.0
Jones, Marvin, N.Y. Jets	3.0
Jones, Mike, New England	4.0
Kennedy, Cortez, Seattle	2.0
Kirkland, Levon, Pittsburgh	5.0
Kopp, Jeff, Jacksonville	1.0
LaBounty, Matt, Seattle	3.0
Lageman, Jeff, Jacksonville	5.0
Lake, Carnell, Pittsburgh	6.0
Langford, Jevon, Cincinnati	1.0
Langham, Antonio, Baltimore	1.0
Law, Ty, New England	0.5
Lee, Shawn, San Diego	3.0
Lewis, Albert, Oakland	2.0
Lewis, Mo, N.Y. Jets	8.0
Lewis, Ray, Baltimore	4.0
Lloyd, Greg, Pittsburgh	3.5
Lodish, Mike, Denver	1.0
Lyle, Rick, N.Y. Jets	3.0
Lynch, Lorenzo, Oakland	1.0
Lyons, Pratt, Tennessee	2.5
Marts, Lonnie, Tennessee	1.0
Maryland, Russell, Oakland	4.5
McCoy, Tony, Indianapolis	2.5
McCrary, Michael, Baltimore	9.0
McDaniels, Pellom, Kansas City	3.5
McDonald, Ricardo, Cincinnati	1.0
McGinest, Willie, New England	2.0
McGlockton, Chester, Oakland	4.5
McGruder, Scooter, New England	1.0
McKyer, Tim, Denver	1.0

Player, Team	No.
Mickens, Ray, N.Y. Jets	1.0
Mobley, John, Denver	4.0
Montgomery, Delmonico, Indianapolis	1.0
Moran, Sean, Buffalo	4.5
Morrison, Steve, Indianapolis	1.0
Oldham, Chris, Pittsburgh	4.0
Orlando, Bo, Cincinnati	1.0
Parrella, John, San Diego	3.5
Paup, Bryce, Buffalo	9.5
Perry, Darren, Pittsburgh	1.0
Phillips, Joe, Kansas City	0.5
Pritchett, Kelvin, Jacksonville	3.0
Pryce, Trevor, Denver	2.0
Richie, David, Denver	0.5
Roberson, James, Tennessee	2.0
Robinson, Eddie, Jacksonville	2.0
Rodgers, Derrick, Miami	5.0
Rogers, Sam, Buffalo	3.5
Romanowski, Bill, Denver	2.0
Roye, Orpheus, Pittsburgh	1.0
Russell, Darrell, Oakland	3.5
Saleaumua, Dan, Seattle	3.5
Schwartz, Bryan, Jacksonville	0.5
Seau, Junior, San Diego	7.0
Shade, Sam, Cincinnati	4.0
Sharper, Jamie, Baltimore	3.0
Shello, Kendel, Indianapolis	1.0
Simmons, Clyde, Jacksonville	8.5
Simmons, Wayne, Kansas City	3.5
Sinclair, Michael, Seattle	12.0
Slade, Chris, New England	9.0
Smeenge, Joel, Jacksonville	6.5
Smith, Anthony, Oakland	6.5
Smith, Bruce, Buffalo	14.0
Smith, Neil, Denver	8.5
Steed, Joel, Pittsburgh	1.0
Stewart, Rayna, Tennessee	0.5
Stubbs, Daniel, Miami	1.0
Tanuvasa, Maa, Denver	8.5
Taylor, Jason, Miami	5.0
Terry, Rick, N.Y. Jets	2.0
Thomas, Derrick, Kansas City	9.5
Thomas, Henry, New England	7.0
Thomas, Zach, Miami	0.5
Tongue, Reggie, Kansas City	2.5
Traylor, Keith, Denver	2.0
Tuaolo, Esera, Jacksonville	1.0
Tumulty, Tom, Cincinnati	1.0
Vrabel, Mike, Pittsburgh	1.5
Walker, Gary, Tennessee	7.0
Washington, Keith, Baltimore	2.0
Washington, Ted, Buffalo	4.0
Wells, Dean, Seattle	1.0
Wheeler, Mark, New England	4.0
Whigham, Larry, New England	2.0
Wilkinson, Dan, Cincinnati	5.0
Williams, Alfred, Denver	8.5
Williams, Dan, Kansas City	10.5
Wilson, Jerry, Miami	2.0
Wilson, Reinard, Cincinnati	3.0
Wooden, Terry, Kansas City	2.0
Woods, Jerome, Kansas City	1.0
Wynn, Renaldo, Jacksonville	2.5

NFC

Player, Team	No.
Abrams, Kevin, Detroit	2.0
Agnew, Ray, N.Y. Giants	2.0
Ahanotu, Chidi, Tampa Bay	10.0
Alexander, Derrick, Minnesota	4.5
Anderson, Antonio, Dallas	2.0
Archambeau, Lester, Atlanta	8.5
Armstead, Jesse, N.Y. Giants	3.5

Player, Team	No.	Player, Team	No.
Bailey, Robert, Detroit	2.0	Lang, Kenard, Washington	1.5
Bankston, Michael, Arizona	2.0	Lassiter, Kwamie, Arizona	3.0
Barker, Roy, San Francisco	5.5	Lathon, Lamar, Carolina	2.0
Barrow, Micheal, Carolina	8.5	Lett, Leon, Dallas	0.5
Bates, Bill, Dallas	1.0	London, Antonio, Detroit	2.0
Bennett, Cornelius, Atlanta	7.0	Lyght, Todd, St. Louis	1.0
Bonham, Shane, Detroit	1.0	Lyle, Keith, St. Louis	2.0
Boutte, Marc, Washington	2.0	Mamula, Mike, Philadelphia	4.0
Brandon, David, Atlanta	1.0	Mangum, John, Chicago	1.0
Bratzke, Chad, N.Y. Giants	3.5	Maniecki, Jason, Tampa Bay	1.0
Brooks, Derrick, Tampa Bay	1.5	Marshall, Anthony, Chicago	3.0
Brown, Gilbert, Green Bay	3.0	Martin, Wayne, New Orleans	10.5
Brown, Reggie, Detroit	2.5	Maxie, Brett, San Francisco	1.0
Bryant, Junior, San Francisco	2.5	McCleon, Dexter, St. Louis	1.0
Burrough, John, Atlanta	1.0	McCleskey, J.J., Arizona	1.0
Butler, LeRoy, Green Bay	3.0	McCormack, Hurvin, Dallas	0.5
Caldwell, Mike, Arizona	2.0	McDaniel, Ed, Minnesota	1.5
Carter, Kevin, St. Louis	7.5	McKenzie, Keith, Green Bay	1.5
Carter, Marty, Chicago	1.0	McKinnon, Ronald, Arizona	1.0
Carver, Shante, Dallas	6.0	Mickell, Darren, New Orleans	3.5
Casillas, Tony, Dallas	3.0	Miller, Corey, N.Y. Giants	1.0
Clemons, Duane, Minnesota	7.0	Miller, Jamir, Arizona	5.5
Coakley, Dexter, Dallas	2.5	Miller, Les, Carolina	5.5
Conner, Darion, Philadelphia	1.5	Mims, Chris, Washington	4.0
Cook, Toi, Carolina	1.0	Minter, Barry, Chicago	6.0
Cota, Chad, Carolina	1.0	Minter, Mike, Carolina	3.5
Cox, Bryan, Chicago	5.0	Mitchell, Keith, New Orleans	4.0
Cox, Ron, Chicago	1.0	Molden, Alex, New Orleans	4.0
Crockett, Henri, Atlanta	2.0	Nickerson, Hardy, Tampa Bay	1.0
Culpepper, Brad, Tampa Bay	8.5	Norton, Ken, San Francisco	1.5
Dent, Richard, Philadelphia	4.5	O'Neal, Leslie, St. Louis	10.0
Dishman, Cris, Washington	1.5	Owens, Dan, Atlanta	8.0
Dixon, Ernest, New Orleans	0.5	Owens, Rich, Washington	2.5
Doleman, Chris, San Francisco	12.0	Parker, Anthony, Tampa Bay	1.0
Dotson, Santana, Green Bay	5.5	Patton, Marvcus, Washington	4.5
Dronett, Shane, Atlanta	3.0	Peter, Christian, N.Y. Giants	0.5
Duff, Jamal, Washington	2.0	Phifer, Roman, St. Louis	2.0
Edwards, Dixon, Minnesota	1.5	Phillips, Ryan, N.Y. Giants	1.0
Elliss, Luther, Detroit	8.5	Pittman, Kavika, Dallas	1.0
Evans, Doug, Green Bay	1.0	Pleasant, Anthony, Atlanta	0.5
Farmer, Ray, Philadelphia	1.0	Poole, Tyrone, Carolina	1.0
Farr, D'Marco, St. Louis	3.0	Porcher, Robert, Detroit	12.5
Fields, Mark, New Orleans	8.0	Porter, Rufus, Tampa Bay	0.5
Fisk, Jason, Minnesota	3.0	Pounds, Darryl, Washington	2.0
Flanigan, Jim, Chicago	6.0	Randle, John, Minnesota	15.5
Galyon, Scott, N.Y. Giants	3.0	Raybon, Israel, Carolina	0.5
Glover, La'Roi, New Orleans	6.5	Reeves, Carl, Chicago	0.5
Godfrey, Randall, Dallas	1.0	Rice, Ron, Detroit	1.0
Grasmanis, Paul, Chicago	0.5	Rice, Simeon, Arizona	5.0
Greene, Kevin, San Francisco	10.5	Robinson, Bryan, St. Louis	1.0
Hall, Rhett, Philadelphia	8.0	Robinson, Eugene, Green Bay	2.5
Hall, Travis, Atlanta	10.5	Robinson, Jeff, St. Louis	0.5
Hamilton, Keith, N.Y. Giants	8.0	Royal, Andre, Carolina	5.0
Harris, Bernardo, Green Bay	1.0	Rudd, Dwayne, Minnesota	5.0
Harris, Jon, Philadelphia	1.0	Sagapolutele, Pio, New Orleans	2.0
Harris, Robert, N.Y. Giants	10.0	Saleh, Tarek, Carolina	1.0
Harvey, Ken, Washington	9.5	Sapp, Warren, Tampa Bay	10.5
Harvey, Richard, New Orleans	3.0	Scroggins, Tracy, Detroit	7.5
Hennings, Chad, Dallas	4.5	Seals, Ray, Carolina	1.0
Holsey, Bernard, N.Y. Giants	3.5	Sehorn, Jason, N.Y. Giants	1.5
Howard, Ty, Arizona	1.0	Simpson, Carl, Chicago	4.5
Jackson, Tyoka, Tampa Bay	2.5	Smith, Brady, New Orleans	5.0
Jamison, George, Detroit	1.0	Smith, Chuck, Atlanta	12.0
Jasper, Edward, Philadelphia	1.0	Smith, Darrin, Philadelphia	1.0
Jefferson, Greg, Philadelphia	3.0	Smith, Derek, Washington	2.0
Jeffries, Greg, Detroit	1.0	Smith, Fernando, Minnesota	4.0
Johnson, Bill, St. Louis	4.0	Smith, Jermaine, Green Bay	1.0
Johnson, Joe, New Orleans	8.5	Smith, Mark, Arizona	6.0
Jones, Greg, Washington	3.5	Smith, Vinson, Dallas	1.0
Jones, Jimmie, Philadelphia	2.5	Sparks, Phillippi, N.Y. Giants	1.0
Jones, Mike, St. Louis	2.0	Spellman, Alonzo, Chicago	2.0
Jones, Robert, St. Louis	1.0	Stoutmire, Omar, Dallas	2.0
Joyner, Seth, Green Bay	3.0	Strahan, Michael, N.Y. Giants	14.0
King, Shawn, Carolina	2.0	Strickland, Fred, Dallas	0.5
Kragen, Greg, Carolina	2.0	Stubblefield, Dana, San Francisco	15.0

Player, Team	No.	Player, Team	No.
Swann, Eric, Arizona	7.5	Washington, Marvin, San Francisco	1.0
Taylor, Bobby, Philadelphia	2.0	Wells, Mike, Detroit	1.0
Thierry, John, Chicago	3.0	Wheeler, Leonard, Minnesota	2.0
Thomas, Broderick, Dallas	3.5	White, Reggie, Green Bay	11.0
Thomas, Hollis, Philadelphia	2.5	Widmer, Corey, N.Y. Giants	1.5
Thomas, Mark, Chicago	4.5	Wilkins, Gabe, Green Bay	5.5
Thomas, William, Philadelphia	5.0	Williams, Brian, Green Bay	1.0
Tolbert, Tony, Dallas	5.0	Williams, Charlie, Dallas	2.0
Tomich, Jared, New Orleans	1.0	Williams, Jay, St. Louis	1.0
Tubbs, Winfred, New Orleans	2.5	Willis, James, Philadelphia	2.0
Tuggle, Jessie, Atlanta	1.5	Woodson, Darren, Dallas	2.0
Turnbull, Renaldo, Carolina	1.0	Young, Bryant, San Francisco	4.0
Upshaw, Regan, Tampa Bay	7.5	Zgonina, Jeff, St. Louis	2.0
Waldroup, Kerwin, Detroit	1.0	Zordich, Michael, Philadelphia	2.0
Walker, Darnell, San Francisco	1.0	Zorich, Chris, Washington	1.0

1997 STATISTICS Sacks

FUMBLES

AFC

Team	Fum.	Own Fum. Rec.	Own Fum. *O.B.	Own Fum. Lost	TD	Opp Fum. Rec.	TD	†Yards	Total Rec.
Jacksonville	17	4	2	11	0	15	1	19	19
New England	17	9	1	7	0	13	0	10	22
Kansas City	21	9	2	10	0	13	1	23	22
Indianapolis	23	9	3	11	0	13	2	71	22
Miami	23	13	2	8	1	17	2	-3	30
Cincinnati	25	11	2	12	0	10	1	18	21
Denver	25	12	3	10	0	13	2	74	25
Oakland	25	10	1	14	0	12	2	52	22
Pittsburgh	25	9	2	14	1	13	1	136	22
Seattle	26	12	3	11	0	16	3	57	28
N.Y. Jets	27	13	2	12	0	7	0	45	20
San Diego	30	16	0	14	1	11	2	108	27
Tennessee	31	15	3	13	0	17	2	139	32
Baltimore	37	18	3	16	0	11	0	-16	29
Buffalo	39	21	1	17	0	7	0	-23	28
AFC total	391	181	30	180	3	188	19	710	369
AFC average	26.0	12.1	2.0	12.0	0.2	12.5	1.3	47.3	24.6

*Fumbled out of bounds.

†Includes all fumble yardage (aborted plays and recoveries of own and opponents' fumbles).

NFC

Team	Fum.	Own Fum. Rec.	Own Fum. *O.B.	Own Fum. Lost	TD	Opp Fum. Rec.	TD	†Yards	Total Rec.
Minnesota	16	9	1	6	0	15	2	58	24
Washington	21	12	2	7	0	14	1	-10	26
San Francisco	22	13	0	9	0	16	2	70	29
Dallas	23	10	2	11	0	12	2	28	22
N.Y. Giants	23	12	4	7	0	17	0	14	29
Green Bay	24	7	1	16	0	11	3	19	18
Detroit	26	12	3	11	0	8	2	48	20
Arizona	27	7	0	20	0	5	0	-1	12
St. Louis	29	11	3	15	1	14	1	78	25
Carolina	30	11	4	15	0	11	0	2	22
Tampa Bay	31	17	3	11	0	13	0	-2	30
Chicago	33	12	2	19	0	17	0	-14	29
Atlanta	34	16	5	13	0	10	0	-16	26
New Orleans	34	12	0	22	0	15	1	15	27
Philadelphia	35	17	2	16	0	12	1	70	29
NFC total	408	178	32	198	1	190	15	359	368
NFC average	27.2	11.9	2.1	13.2	0.1	12.7	1.0	23.9	24.5
NFL total	799	359	62	378	4	378	34	1069	737
NFL average	26.6	12.0	2.1	12.6	0.1	12.6	1.1	35.6	24.6

INDIVIDUAL

BESTS OF THE SEASON

Fumbles, season

AFC: 16—Steve McNair, Tennessee.

NFC: 15—Scott Mitchell, Detroit; Tony Banks, St. Louis.

Fumbles, game

AFC: 4—Rich Gannon, Kansas City at Jacksonville, Nov. 9; Steve McNair, Tennessee at Cincinnati, Dec. 4.

NFC: 4—Scott Mitchell, Detroit vs. Atlanta, Aug. 31.

Own fumbles recovered, season

AFC: 7—Steve McNair, Tennessee.

NFC: 4—Scott Mitchell, Detroit; Zach Wiegert, St. Louis; Charles Way, N.Y. Giants; Warrick Dunn, Tampa Bay.

Own fumbles recovered, game

NFC: 3—Scott Mitchell, Detroit vs. Atlanta, Aug. 31.

AFC: 2—Held by nine players.

Opponents' fumbles recovered, season

AFC: 4—Chad Brown, Seattle.

NFC: 3—Held by nine players.

Opponents' fumbles recovered, game

AFC: 2—Blaine Bishop, Tennessee at Seattle, Oct. 5; Chad Brown, Seattle at New Orleans, Nov. 16.

NFC: 2—Held by five players.

Yards returning fumbles, season

AFC: 78—Paul Bradford, San Diego.

NFC: 66—Leslie O'Neal, St. Louis.

Longest fumble return

AFC: 78—Paul Bradford, San Diego at San Francisco, Nov. 23 (TD).

NFC: 66—Leslie O'Neal, St. Louis vs. Carolina, Nov. 23 (TD).

1997 STATISTICS *Fumbles*

Player, Team	Fum.	Own Rec.	Opp. Rec.	Yds.	Tot. Rec.	TD
Abdul-Jabbar, Karim, Miami ...	3	0	0	0	0	0
Adams, Michael, Pittsburgh....	1	0	0	0	0	0
Alexander, Derrick, Baltimore .	1	0	0	0	0	0
Allen, Marcus, Kansas City	4	2	0	0	2	0
Ambrose, Ashley, Cincinnati ...	0	0	2	0	2	0
Anders, Kimble, Kansas City...	3	1	0	0	1	0
Anderson, Dunstan, Miami	0	0	1	0	1	0
Anderson, Richie, N.Y. Jets.....	2	1	0	0	1	0
Araguz, Leo, Oakland.............	1	1	0	-21	1	0
Archie, Mike, Tennessee	0	1	0	0	1	0
Armstrong, Trace, Miami	0	0	3	0	3	0
Atkins, James, Seattle............	0	1	0	0	1	0
Atwater, Steve, Denver...........	0	0	2	0	2	0
Bailey, Aaron, Indianapolis......	2	1	0	0	1	0
Barber, Michael, Seattle	0	0	1	0	1	0
Barker, Bryan, Jacksonville.....	1	0	0	-19	0	0
Barlow, Reggie, Jacksonville ..	2	1	0	0	1	0
Barnett, Fred, Miami	1	0	0	0	0	0
Battaglia, Marco, Cincinnati	2	1	1	0	2	0
Baxter, Fred, N.Y. Jets............	1	0	0	0	0	0
Beede, Frank, Seattle	1	0	0	0	0	0
Bell, Myron, Pittsburgh...........	0	0	1	0	1	0
Berti, Tony, San Diego	0	1	0	0	1	0
Bettis, Jerome, Pittsburgh	6	1	0	0	1	0
Bieniemy, Eric, Cincinnati	2	0	0	0	0	0
Bishop, Blaine, Tennessee	0	0	2	0	2	0
Blackmon, Robert, Ind.	0	0	1	18	1	1
Blackwell, Will, Pittsburgh	3	2	0	0	2	0
Blades, Brian, Seattle.............	1	0	0	0	0	0
Blake, Jeff, Cincinnati	7	0	0	0	0	0
Bledsoe, Drew, New England..	4	3	0	-4	3	0
Booker, Vaughn, Kansas City..	0	0	1	0	1	0
Bowden, Joe, Tennessee.........	0	0	1	0	1	0
Bowens, Tim, Miami	0	0	1	0	1	1
Brackens, Tony, Jacksonville ..	0	0	1	0	1	0
Bradford, Paul, San Diego	0	0	1	78	1	1
Brady, Donny, Baltimore	0	0	1	0	1	0
Brady, Kyle, N.Y. Jets.............	1	0	0	0	0	0
Brandenburg, Dan, Buffalo	0	1	0	0	1	0
Braxton, Tyrone, Denver	0	0	3	45	3	0
Brigance, O.J., Miami	0	0	1	0	1	0
Brilz, Darrick, Cincinnati	0	1	0	0	1	0
Brown, Chad, Seattle	0	0	4	68	4	2
Brown, Gary, San Diego	2	0	0	0	0	0
Brown, Ruben, Buffalo............	0	1	0	0	1	0
Brown, Tim, Oakland	1	0	0	0	0	0
Browning, John, Kansas City..	0	0	1	0	1	0
Bruener, Mark, Pittsburgh.......	1	0	0	0	0	0
Brunell, Mark, Jacksonville	4	0	0	-5	0	0
Bruschi, Tedy, New England ...	0	0	2	0	2	0
Buckley, Terrell, Miami...........	0	0	2	23	2	1
Burnett, Rob, Baltimore	0	0	1	0	1	0
Burris, Jeff, Buffalo.................	3	1	0	0	1	0
Burton, Shane, Miami	0	0	1	0	1	0
Byars, Keith, New England......	1	0	0	0	0	0
Byner, Earnest, Baltimore	2	2	1	0	3	0
Cain, Joe, Seattle	0	0	1	0	1	0
Canty, Chris, New England......	0	2	0	9	2	0
Carswell, Dwayne, Denver	0	0	1	0	1	0
Carter, Ki-Jana, Cincinnati......	3	2	0	0	2	0
Cascadden, Chad, N.Y. Jets ...	0	0	1	0	1	0
Chamberlain, Byron, Denver....	1	0	0	0	0	0
Clay, Willie, New England	0	0	2	0	2	0
Coleman, Andre, Sea.-Pit.	2	0	0	0	0	0
Coleman, Marcus, N.Y. Jets....	0	0	1	0	1	0
Collins, Andre, Cincinnati.......	0	0	1	0	1	0
Collins, Todd, Buffalo.............	10	0	0	-30	0	0
Collons, Ferric, New England..	0	0	1	5	1	0
Cook, Anthony, Tennessee	0	0	2	0	2	0
Copeland, John, Cincinnati	0	0	2	25	2	1
Craver, Aaron, San Diego.......	0	1	0	0	1	0
Crawford, Vernon, N.E.	0	1	0	0	1	0
Crockett, Zack, Indianapolis....	3	0	0	0	0	0
Cullors, Derrick, New England..	3	0	0	0	0	0
Daniels, Phillip, Seattle	1	0	0	0	0	0
Davis, Anthony, Kansas City ...	0	0	1	2	1	0
Davis, Terrell, Denver.............	4	2	0	-7	2	0
Davis, Travis, Jacksonville	0	0	3	10	3	0
Davis, Tyree, Seattle	1	1	0	0	1	0
Dillon, Corey, Cincinnati..........	1	1	0	4	1	0
Dodge, Dedrick, Denver	0	0	1	0	1	0
Duffy, Roger, N.Y. Jets...........	2	1	0	-22	1	0
Dumas, Mike, San Diego	0	0	1	0	1	0
Dunn, David, Cincinnati	1	1	0	0	1	0
Edwards, Donnie, K.C.	0	0	1	0	1	0
Elway, John, Denver	11	1	0	-21	1	0
Erickson, Craig, Miami	2	2	0	-13	2	0
Esiason, Boomer, Cincinnati ...	1	0	0	0	0	0
Ethridge, Ray, Baltimore	2	0	0	0	0	0
Evans, Josh, Tennessee	0	0	1	0	1	0
Everett, Jim, San Diego	2	1	0	-8	1	0
Faulk, Marshall, Indianapolis ..	5	1	0	0	1	0
Fenner, Derrick, Oakland.........	1	0	0	0	0	0
Fina, John, Buffalo..................	0	1	0	0	1	0
Fletcher, Terrell, San Diego	4	0	0	0	0	0
Flowers, Lethon, Pittsburgh.....	0	1	0	0	1	0
Foley, Glenn, N.Y. Jets...........	1	0	0	0	0	0
Folston, James, Oakland.........	0	0	3	35	3	1
Fontenot, Al, Indianapolis	0	0	2	14	2	0
Footman, Dan, Indianapolis	0	0	2	13	2	0
Ford, Henry, Tennessee..........	0	1	0	0	1	0
Francis, James, Cincinnati	0	0	1	0	1	0
Frederick, Mike, Baltimore	0	0	1	0	1	0
Friesz, John, Seattle...............	1	1	0	-2	1	0
Galloway, Joey, Seattle	1	1	0	0	1	0
Galloway, Mitchell, Buffalo......	1	0	0	0	0	0
Gannon, Rich, Kansas City	5	0	0	0	0	0
Gardener, Daryl, Miami	0	0	1	0	1	0
George, Eddie, Tennessee.......	4	0	0	0	0	0
George, Jeff, Oakland	7	3	0	-14	3	0
Gibson, Oliver, Pittsburgh.......	0	0	1	0	1	0
Gildon, Jason, Pittsburgh	0	1	1	32	2	1
Glenn, Aaron, N.Y. Jets..........	1	0	0	0	0	0
Glenn, Tarik, Indianapolis.......	1	0	0	0	0	0
Glenn, Terry, New England......	1	0	0	0	0	0
Gordon, Darrien, Denver.........	3	3	1	0	4	0
Graham, Jay, Baltimore...........	2	1	0	0	1	0
Graham, Jeff, N.Y. Jets	0	1	0	0	1	0
Grant, Stephen, Indianapolis ..	0	0	1	0	1	0
Gray, Mel, Tennessee.............	1	0	0	0	0	0
Grbac, Elvis, Kansas City	1	0	0	0	0	0
Green, Eric, Baltimore.............	1	0	0	0	0	0
Griffith, Howard, Denver	0	1	0	0	1	0
Grunhard, Tim, Kansas City....	0	1	0	0	1	0
Harbaugh, Jim, Indianapolis...	4	1	0	0	1	0
Harper, Dwayne, San Diego	0	0	1	0	1	0
Harris, Ronnie, Seattle............	4	2	0	0	2	0
Harrison, Martin, Seattle..........	0	0	1	0	1	0
Harrison, Marvin, Indianapolis..	2	1	0	5	1	0
Harrison, Rodney, San Diego..	0	1	2	0	3	1
Hasty, James, Kansas City......	0	0	1	0	1	0
Hauck, Tim, Seattle.................	0	0	1	8	1	0
Hawkins, Courtney, Pittsburgh .	1	0	0	0	0	0
Hebron, Vaughn, Denver.........	1	1	0	0	1	0
Henry, Kevin, Pittsburgh.........	0	0	2	0	2	0
Herring, Kim, Baltimore	0	0	1	0	1	0
Hill, Greg, Kansas City	1	0	0	0	0	0

1997 STATISTICS Fumbles

Player, Team	Fum.	Own Rec.	Opp. Rec.	Yds.	Tot. Rec.	TD
Hobbs, Daryl, Seattle	1	0	0	0	0	0
Holcomb, Kelly, Indianapolis	4	1	0	-8	1	0
Holmberg, Rob, Oakland	0	0	1	0	1	0
Holmes, Darick, Buffalo	1	1	0	0	1	0
Holmes, Earl, Pittsburgh	0	0	1	0	1	0
Holmes, Kenny, Tennessee	0	0	1	0	1	0
Hopkins, Brad, Tennessee	0	1	0	0	1	0
Howard, Desmond, Oakland	2	2	0	0	2	0
Hudson, Chris, Jacksonville	1	0	2	32	2	1
Hughes, Danan, Kansas City	0	1	1	7	2	0
Humphries, Stan, San Diego	7	1	0	-10	1	0
Hundon, James, Cincinnati	1	0	0	0	0	0
Jackson, Calvin, Miami	0	1	0	0	1	0
Jackson, Greg, San Diego	0	0	1	41	1	1
Jackson, Michael, Baltimore	2	0	0	0	0	0
Jackson, Ray, Buffalo	1	0	0	0	0	0
Jackson, Willie, Jacksonville	1	0	0	0	0	0
Jacquet, Nate, Indianapolis	1	1	0	0	1	0
Jefferson, Shawn, N.E.	2	0	0	0	0	0
Jenkins, DeRon, Baltimore	0	0	1	0	1	0
Jett, James, Oakland	2	1	0	0	1	0
Johnson, Darrius, Denver	0	0	1	6	1	1
Johnson, Ellis, Indianapolis	0	0	2	0	2	0
Johnson, Lee, Cincinnati	0	2	0	0	2	0
Johnson, Leon, N.Y. Jets	5	5	0	0	5	0
Johnson, Lonnie, Buffalo	2	1	0	0	1	0
Johnstone, Lance, Oakland	0	0	1	2	1	0
Jones, Donta, Pittsburgh	0	1	0	6	1	0
Jones, George, Pittsburgh	3	1	0	0	1	0
Jones, Henry, Buffalo	1	0	1	0	1	0
Jones, James, Baltimore	0	1	0	0	1	0
Jones, Marvin, N.Y. Jets	0	0	1	0	1	0
Jones, Mike, New England	0	1	0	0	1	0
Jordan, Charles, Miami	2	1	0	0	1	0
Justin, Paul, Indianapolis	1	0	0	0	0	0
Kaufman, Napoleon, Oakland	7	1	0	0	1	0
Kerner, Marlon, Buffalo	0	1	0	0	1	0
Kirkland, Levon, Pittsburgh	0	0	1	0	1	0
Kitna, Jon, Seattle	1	1	0	-2	1	0
Klingler, David, Oakland	1	1	0	-5	1	0
Lacina, Corbin, Buffalo	0	1	0	0	1	0
Lageman, Jeff, Jacksonville	0	0	1	0	1	0
Lake, Carnell, Pittsburgh	0	0	1	38	1	1
Lane, Max, New England	0	1	0	0	1	0
Law, Ty, New England	1	0	1	0	1	0
Leeuwenburg, Jay, Ind.	1	0	0	-20	0	0
Lewis, Darryll, Tennessee	1	1	2	68	3	0
Lewis, Jermaine, Baltimore	3	2	0	0	2	0
Lewis, Mo, N.Y. Jets	0	0	1	26	1	0
Lewis, Ray, Baltimore	0	1	0	0	1	0
Lincoln, Jeremy, Seattle	0	0	1	0	1	0
Lloyd, Greg, Pittsburgh	1	0	3	61	3	0
Lodish, Mike, Denver	0	0	1	0	1	0
Logan, James, Seattle	0	0	1	0	1	0
Lott, Anthone, Cincinnati	0	1	0	0	1	0
Loville, Derek, Denver	1	0	0	0	0	0
Lyle, Rick, N.Y. Jets	0	0	1	2	1	0
Mandarich, Tony, Indianapolis	0	1	0	0	1	0
Manning, Brian, Miami	0	1	0	-1	1	0
Manusky, Greg, Kansas City	0	1	0	0	1	0
Marino, Dan, Miami	8	3	0	-17	3	0
Martin, Curtis, New England	3	0	0	0	0	0
Marts, Lonnie, Tennessee	0	0	1	0	1	0
Mason, Derrick, Tennessee	5	0	0	0	0	0
Matthews, Bruce, Tennessee	0	2	0	0	2	0
Matthews, Steve, Jacksonville	1	0	0	0	0	0
Mawae, Kevin, Seattle	0	1	1	0	2	0
McAfee, Fred, Pittsburgh	1	0	0	0	0	0
McCaffrey, Ed, Denver	0	1	1	0	2	0
McCloud, Tyrus, Baltimore	1	0	1	0	1	0
McCrary, Michael, Baltimore	0	0	2	0	2	0
McDaniel, Terry, Oakland	1	0	0	0	0	0
McDaniels, Pellom, K.C.	0	0	1	0	1	0
McDuffie, O.J., Miami	0	2	0	3	2	1
McGinest, Willie, New England	0	0	3	0	3	0
McGlockton, Chester, Oakland	0	0	1	0	1	0
McKenzie, Raleigh, San Diego	0	1	0	0	1	0
McKnight, James, Seattle	1	0	0	0	0	0
McNair, Steve, Tennessee	16	7	0	-2	7	0
McPhail, Jerris, Miami	1	0	0	4	0	0
Means, Natrone, Jacksonville	5	0	0	0	0	0
Meggett, David, New England	2	1	0	0	1	0
Metcalf, Eric, San Diego	4	2	0	0	2	0
Milloy, Lawyer, New England	0	0	2	0	2	0
Mitchell, Pete, Jacksonville	0	1	0	0	1	0
Mobley, John, Denver	0	0	1	0	1	0
Mohr, Chris, Buffalo	1	1	0	-10	1	0
Moon, Warren, Seattle	7	1	0	-2	1	0
Moran, Sean, Buffalo	0	0	1	0	1	0
Morris, Bam, Baltimore	4	4	0	0	4	0
Morrison, Steve, Indianapolis	0	0	2	27	2	0
Morton, Mike, Oakland	0	0	1	0	1	0
Moss, Winston, Seattle	0	0	1	0	1	0
Moulds, Eric, Buffalo	3	1	0	0	1	0
Murrell, Adrian, N.Y. Jets	4	2	0	0	2	0
Myers, Greg, Cincinnati	3	2	0	0	2	0
Norgard, Erik, Tennessee	0	1	0	0	1	0
O'Donnell, Neil, N.Y. Jets	9	2	0	-1	2	0
Orlando, Bo, Cincinnati	0	0	1	0	1	0
Ostroski, Jerry, Buffalo	0	3	0	0	3	0
Palelei, Lonnie, N.Y. Jets	0	1	0	0	1	0
Parker, Vaughn, San Diego	0	2	0	0	2	0
Parmalee, Bernie, Miami	1	0	0	-2	0	0
Parrella, John, San Diego	0	0	1	0	1	0
Paul, Tito, Cincinnati	0	0	1	0	1	0
Paup, Bryce, Buffalo	0	0	1	0	1	0
Perry, Ed, Miami	0	1	0	0	1	0
Perry, Marlo, Buffalo	0	1	0	0	1	0
Philcox, Todd, San Diego	2	0	0	0	0	0
Phillips, Joe, Kansas City	0	0	1	0	1	0
Pickens, Carl, Cincinnati	1	0	0	0	0	0
Pritchard, Mike, Seattle	2	0	0	0	0	0
Pritchett, Kelvin, Jacksonville	0	0	1	0	1	0
Pupunu, Alfred, San Diego	0	1	0	0	1	0
Purnell, Lovett, New England	0	1	0	0	1	0
Rachal, Latorio, San Diego	1	0	1	0	1	0
Reed, Andre, Buffalo	1	0	0	0	0	0
Richardson, Kyle, Seattle	1	0	0	-13	0	0
Riemersma, Jay, Buffalo	1	0	0	0	0	0
Roberson, James, Tennessee	0	0	1	0	1	0
Robertson, Marcus, Tennessee	0	0	3	67	3	2
Robinson, Eddie, Jacksonville	0	0	2	0	2	0
Rodgers, Derrick, Miami	0	0	1	0	1	0
Roe, James, Baltimore	1	1	0	0	1	0
Saleaumua, Dan, Seattle	0	0	1	0	1	0
Sanders, Chris, Tennessee	1	0	0	0	0	0
Schlereth, Mark, Denver	0	1	0	0	1	0
Schwartz, Bryan, Jacksonville	0	0	1	0	1	0
Seau, Junior, San Diego	1	0	2	5	2	0
Shade, Sam, Cincinnati	1	0	1	0	1	0
Sharpe, Shannon, Denver	1	0	0	0	0	0
Sharper, Jamie, Baltimore	1	0	0	0	0	0
Shaw, Terrance, San Diego	0	1	0	0	1	0
Shedd, Kenny, Oakland	0	0	2	25	2	1
Shelton, Daimon, Jacksonville	1	0	0	0	0	0
Sienkiewicz, Troy, San Diego	0	2	0	7	2	0
Sinclair, Michael, Seattle	0	0	1	0	1	1
Siragusa, Tony, Baltimore	0	0	1	7	1	0
Slutzker, Scott, Indianapolis	0	1	1	0	2	0
Smeenge, Joel, Jacksonville	0	0	2	1	2	0

Player, Team	Fum.	Own Rec.	Opp. Rec.	Yds.	Tot. Rec.	TD
Smith, Anthony, Oakland	0	0	1	0	1	0
Smith, Antowain, Buffalo	4	0	0	0	0	0
Smith, Jimmy, Jacksonville	1	1	0	0	1	0
Smith, Otis, N.Y. Jets	0	0	2	40	2	0
Smith, Rod, Denver	3	1	0	0	1	0
Smith, Thomas, Buffalo	1	0	1	1	1	0
Spikes, Irving, Miami	3	2	0	0	2	0
Steed, Joel, Pittsburgh	0	0	1	0	1	0
Stepnoski, Mark, Tennessee	2	1	0	-7	1	0
Stewart, Kordell, Pittsburgh	6	1	0	-1	1	0
Stewart, Rayna, Tennessee	0	0	1	0	1	0
Strong, Mack, Seattle	0	1	0	0	1	0
Swift, Michael, San Diego	0	0	1	6	1	0
Szott, David, Kansas City	0	1	0	0	1	0
Tasker, Steve, Buffalo	1	1	1	0	2	0
Taylor, Jason, Miami	0	0	2	0	2	0
Testaverde, Vinny, Baltimore	11	5	0	-9	5	0
Thigpen, Yancey, Pittsburgh	1	1	0	0	1	0
Thomas, Dave, Jacksonville	0	0	1	0	1	0
Thomas, Henry, New England	0	0	1	0	1	0
Thomas, Lamar, Miami	1	0	0	0	0	0
Thomas, Rodney, Tennessee	1	0	0	0	0	0
Thomas, Thurman, Buffalo	2	0	0	0	0	0
Thompson, Bennie, Baltimore	0	2	0	0	2	0
Tolliver, Billy Joe, Atl.-K.C.*	7	2	0	-1	2	0
Trapp, James, Oakland	0	1	1	0	2	0
Truitt, Greg, Cincinnati	2	0	0	-11	0	0
Truitt, Olanda, Oakland	1	0	0	0	0	0
Turner, Eric, Oakland	1	0	3	65	3	1
Vanover, Tamarick, K.C.	6	1	0	0	1	0
Van Pelt, Alex, Buffalo	3	3	0	-7	3	0
Veland, Tony, Denver	0	1	0	0	1	0
Vrabel, Mike, Pittsburgh	0	0	1	0	1	0
Walker, Bracey, Miami	0	0	1	0	1	0
Ward, Dedric, N.Y. Jets	1	0	0	0	0	0
Warren, Chris, Seattle	2	0	0	0	0	0
Warren, Lamont, Indianapolis	0	0	1	0	1	0
Washington, Ted, Buffalo	0	0	1	0	1	0
Wells, Dean, Seattle	0	0	1	0	1	0
Whelihan, Craig, San Diego	7	2	0	-11	2	0
Widell, Dave, Jacksonville	0	1	0	0	1	0
Wiley, Marcellus, Buffalo	1	1	1	40	2	0
Williams, Alfred, Denver	0	0	1	51	1	1
Williams, Dan, Kansas City	0	0	2	2	2	0
Williams, Darryl, Seattle	0	0	1	0	1	0
Williams, Grant, Seattle	0	2	0	0	2	0
Wilson, Jerry, Miami	0	0	1	0	1	0
Wooden, Shawn, Miami	1	0	2	0	2	0
Wooden, Terry, Kansas City	0	0	1	0	1	0
Woods, Jerome, Kansas City	0	0	2	13	2	0
Wycheck, Frank, Tennessee	0	1	0	0	1	0
Wynn, Renaldo, Jacksonville	0	0	1	0	1	0
Yarborough, Ryan, Baltimore	3	0	0	0	0	0
Zeier, Eric, Baltimore	3	0	0	-14	0	0
Zeigler, Dusty, Buffalo	1	1	0	-12	1	0

*Includes both NFC and AFC statistics.

NFC

Player, Team	Fum.	Own Rec.	Opp. Rec.	Yds.	Tot. Rec.	TD
Abraham, Donnie, Tampa Bay	0	0	1	2	1	0
Agnew, Ray, N.Y. Giants	0	0	1	0	1	0
Ahanotu, Chidi, Tampa Bay	0	0	2	0	2	0
Aikman, Troy, Dallas	6	0	0	-5	0	0
Alexander, Derrick, Minnesota	0	1	0	0	1	0
Allen, Terry, Washington	2	1	0	0	1	0
Alstott, Mike, Tampa Bay	5	0	0	0	0	0
Anderson, Jamal, Atlanta	4	1	0	0	1	0
Archambeau, Lester, Atlanta	0	0	3	0	3	0

Player, Team	Fum.	Own Rec.	Opp. Rec.	Yds.	Tot. Rec.	TD
Armstead, Jesse, N.Y. Giants	0	0	1	0	1	0
Asher, Jamie, Washington	0	2	0	0	2	0
Autry, Darnell, Chicago	2	0	0	0	0	0
Ball, Jerry, Minnesota	0	0	2	0	2	0
Banks, Tony, St. Louis	15	3	0	-27	3	0
Barber, Tiki, N.Y. Giants	3	0	0	0	0	0
Barrow, Micheal, Carolina	0	0	2	0	2	0
Bates, Mario, New Orleans	2	0	0	0	0	0
Bates, Michael, Carolina	4	2	0	0	2	0
Bech, Brett, New Orleans	0	0	1	0	1	0
Beckles, Ian, Philadelphia	0	2	0	0	2	0
Bender, Wes, New Orleans	1	0	0	0	0	0
Bennett, Cornelius, Atlanta	0	0	1	0	1	0
Berger, Mitch, Minnesota	1	0	0	-9	0	0
Beuerlein, Steve, Carolina	1	0	0	0	0	0
Biakabutuka, Tim, Carolina	1	0	0	0	0	0
Bishop, Greg, N.Y. Giants	0	1	0	0	1	0
Bjornson, Eric, Dallas	2	0	0	0	0	0
Blanton, Scott, Washington	0	0	1	0	1	0
Bono, Steve, Green Bay	1	0	0	0	0	0
Bouie, Tony, Tampa Bay	0	1	0	0	1	0
Bowie, Larry, Washington	2	1	0	0	1	0
Bownes, Fabien, Chicago	0	0	1	0	1	0
Boyd, Stephen, Detroit	0	0	1	42	1	1
Brady, Jeff, Minnesota	0	0	3	30	3	1
Bratzke, Chad, N.Y. Giants	0	0	2	0	2	0
Briggs, Greg, Minnesota	0	0	1	0	1	0
Brohm, Jeff, San Francisco	3	0	0	0	0	0
Bronson, Zack, San Francisco	0	0	1	3	1	0
Brooks, Barrett, Philadelphia	0	2	0	0	2	0
Brooks, Derrick, Tampa Bay	1	0	1	0	1	0
Brown, Dave, N.Y. Giants	1	0	0	0	0	0
Bruce, Isaac, St. Louis	1	0	0	0	0	0
Buckley, Curtis, San Francisco	0	0	1	0	1	0
Buckley, Marcus, N.Y. Giants	0	0	1	0	1	0
Burger, Todd, Chicago	0	1	0	0	1	0
Bush, Devin, Atlanta	0	0	1	0	1	0
Butler, LeRoy, Green Bay	0	1	0	0	1	0
Campbell, Jesse, Washington	0	1	1	-1	2	0
Carrier, Mark, Carolina	1	0	0	0	0	0
Carrier, Mark, Detroit	1	0	0	0	0	0
Carruth, Rae, Carolina	2	0	0	0	0	0
Carter, Cris, Minnesota	3	0	0	0	0	0
Carter, Kevin, St. Louis	0	0	2	5	2	0
Carter, Tony, Chicago	0	1	0	0	1	0
Case, Stoney, Arizona	3	0	0	0	0	0
Centers, Larry, Arizona	1	0	0	0	0	0
Chandler, Chris, Atlanta	9	3	0	-18	3	0
Chmura, Mark, Green Bay	1	0	0	0	0	0
Christian, Bob, Atlanta	3	1	0	0	1	0
Clemons, Duane, Minnesota	0	0	1	0	1	0
Coakley, Dexter, Dallas	0	0	1	16	1	1
Collins, Kerry, Carolina	8	2	0	-14	2	0
Conwell, Ernie, St. Louis	0	0	1	0	1	0
Copeland, Horace, Tampa Bay	3	0	0	0	0	0
Cota, Chad, Carolina	0	0	1	0	1	0
Cox, Bryan, Chicago	0	0	1	0	1	0
Crawford, Keith, St. Louis	0	1	0	0	1	0
Crockett, Henri, Atlanta	0	0	1	0	1	0
Cross, Howard, N.Y. Giants	1	1	0	0	1	0
Cunningham, Randall, Min.	4	2	0	0	2	0
Dahl, Bob, Washington	0	1	0	0	1	0
Dalman, Chris, San Francisco	0	1	0	0	1	0
Darby, Matt, Arizona	0	0	2	0	2	0
Davis, Antone, Atlanta	0	1	0	0	1	0
Davis, Eric, Carolina	0	0	1	2	1	0
Davis, Stephen, Washington	1	1	0	0	1	0
Davis, Troy, New Orleans	3	0	0	0	0	0
Davis, Tyrone, Green Bay	0	0	1	0	1	1
Davis, Wendell, Dallas	0	1	1	0	2	0

Player, Team	Fum.	Own Rec.	Opp. Rec.	Yds.	Tot. Rec.	TD
Deese, Derrick, San Francisco	0	1	0	0	1	0
DeLong, Greg, Minnesota	1	0	0	0	0	0
Detmer, Ty, Philadelphia	6	1	0	0	1	0
Devlin, Mike, Arizona	0	1	0	0	1	0
Diaz, Jorge, Tampa Bay	0	1	0	0	1	0
Dilfer, Trent, Tampa Bay	9	3	0	-12	3	0
Dimry, Charles, Philadelphia	1	1	1	34	2	0
Dishman, Cris, Washington	0	0	1	0	1	0
Doleman, Chris, S.F.	0	0	1	0	1	0
Dotson, Earl, Green Bay	0	1	0	0	1	0
Dulaney, Mike, Chicago	1	0	0	0	0	0
Dunn, Warrick, Tampa Bay	4	4	0	0	4	0
Edwards, Anthony, Arizona	0	1	0	0	1	0
Edwards, Dixon, Minnesota	0	0	1	0	1	0
Ellison, Jerry, Tampa Bay	0	1	0	0	1	0
Elliss, Luther, Detroit	0	0	2	0	2	0
Ellsworth, Percy, N.Y. Giants	0	0	2	24	2	0
Emanuel, Bert, Atlanta	2	1	1	0	2	0
Engler, Derek, N.Y. Giants	1	0	0	-2	0	0
Engram, Bobby, Chicago	1	1	0	0	1	0
Evans, Charles, Minnesota	0	1	0	0	1	0
Evans, Leomont, Washington	0	0	1	0	1	0
Everitt, Steve, Philadelphia	0	1	0	0	1	0
Farmer, Ray, Philadelphia	0	0	1	0	1	0
Farr, D'Marco, St. Louis	0	0	2	0	2	0
Favre, Brett, Green Bay	7	1	0	-10	1	0
Feagles, Jeff, Arizona	1	1	0	0	1	0
Fields, Mark, New Orleans	0	0	2	28	2	1
Fisk, Jason, Minnesota	0	0	1	0	1	0
Flanigan, Jim, Chicago	0	0	3	3	3	0
Floyd, William, San Francisco	2	0	0	0	0	0
Fontenot, Jerry, New Orleans	3	0	0	0	0	0
Freeman, Antonio, Green Bay	1	0	0	0	0	0
Frerotte, Gus, Washington	8	2	0	-16	2	0
Fryar, Irving, Philadelphia	1	0	0	0	0	0
Garner, Charlie, Philadelphia	1	0	0	0	0	0
Gedney, Chris, Arizona	1	0	0	0	0	0
Glover, Kevin, Detroit	0	1	0	0	1	0
Glover, La'Roi, New Orleans	0	0	1	0	1	0
Godfrey, Randall, Dallas	0	0	1	0	1	0
Gragg, Scott, N.Y. Giants	0	1	0	0	1	0
Graham, Aaron, Arizona	0	1	0	0	1	0
Graham, Kent, Arizona	5	0	0	0	0	0
Grasmanis, Paul, Chicago	0	0	1	0	1	0
Green, Harold, Atlanta	0	1	0	0	1	0
Green, Robert, Minnesota	0	1	0	0	1	0
Greene, Kevin, San Francisco	0	0	2	40	2	1
Greene, Scott, Carolina	1	0	0	0	0	0
Gruber, Paul, Tampa Bay	0	1	0	0	1	0
Guliford, Eric, New Orleans	2	1	0	0	1	0
Hall, Travis, Atlanta	0	0	1	0	1	0
Hamilton, Keith, N.Y. Giants	0	0	3	0	3	0
Hanks, Merton, San Francisco	0	0	2	38	2	1
Hanspard, Byron, Atlanta	3	2	0	0	2	0
Hape, Patrick, Tampa Bay	1	0	0	0	0	0
Harris, Raymont, Chicago	1	0	0	0	0	0
Harris, Robert, N.Y. Giants	0	0	2	0	2	0
Harris, Walt, Chicago	1	0	1	0	1	0
Harvey, Richard, New Orleans	0	0	1	0	1	0
Hastings, Andre, New Orleans	1	0	0	0	0	0
Hearst, Garrison, S.F.	2	2	0	0	2	0
Hegamin, George, Dallas	0	1	0	0	1	0
Henderson, William, G.B.	1	2	0	0	2	0
Hennings, Chad, Dallas	0	0	1	4	1	1
Hewitt, Chris, New Orleans	0	0	1	0	1	0
Heyward, Craig, St. Louis	1	0	0	0	0	0
Hill, Randal, New Orleans	0	1	0	0	1	0
Hobert, Billy Joe, Buf.-N.O.*	3	1	0	-5	1	0
Hostetler, Jeff, Washington	3	1	0	0	1	0
Hoying, Bobby, Philadelphia	7	1	0	0	1	0
Hughes, Tyrone, Chicago	2	2	0	0	2	0
Hutton, Tom, Philadelphia	1	1	0	-1	1	0
Irving, Terry, Arizona	0	0	1	0	1	0
Jamison, George, Detroit	0	0	1	0	1	0
Jefferson, Greg, Philadelphia	0	0	1	0	1	0
Johnson, Anthony, Carolina	2	2	0	0	2	0
Johnson, Bill, St. Louis	0	0	1	0	1	0
Johnson, Brad, Minnesota	4	3	0	0	3	0
Johnson, Jimmie, Phi.	1	0	0	0	0	0
Johnson, Joe, New Orleans	0	0	1	0	1	0
Johnson, Tony, New Orleans	1	0	0	0	0	0
Johnston, Daryl, Dallas	1	0	0	0	0	0
Jones, Brent, San Francisco	1	0	0	0	0	0
Jones, Clarence, New Orleans	0	2	0	0	2	0
Jones, Marcus, Tampa Bay	0	0	1	0	1	0
Kanell, Danny, N.Y. Giants	6	0	0	-10	0	0
Kennison, Eddie, St. Louis	2	0	0	0	0	0
Kinchen, Todd, Atlanta	5	2	0	0	2	0
Kirby, Terry, San Francisco	3	2	0	0	2	0
Knight, Sammy, New Orleans	0	0	1	0	1	0
Kramer, Erik, Chicago	11	3	0	-14	3	0
LaFleur, David, Dallas	1	0	0	0	0	0
Lane, Fred, Carolina	4	2	0	0	2	0
Lang, Kenard, Washington	0	0	2	0	2	0
Le Bel, Harper, Chicago	1	0	1	0	1	0
Levens, Dorsey, Green Bay	5	1	0	-7	1	0
Levy, Chuck, San Francisco	1	0	0	0	0	0
Logan, Marc, Washington	1	1	0	0	1	0
Lyght, Todd, St. Louis	0	0	2	0	2	0
Lynch, John, Tampa Bay	0	0	2	0	2	0
Malone, Van, Detroit	1	0	0	0	0	0
Mangum, John, Chicago	0	0	3	0	3	0
Maniecki, Jason, Tampa Bay	0	0	1	0	1	0
Marion, Brock, Dallas	0	0	1	13	1	0
Marshall, Anthony, Chicago	1	1	1	10	2	0
Martin, Wayne, New Orleans	0	0	1	0	1	0
Mathis, Kevin, Dallas	2	1	1	0	2	0
Mayberry, Jermane, Phi.	0	0	1	0	1	0
McDonald, Tim, S.F.	0	0	3	0	3	0
McElroy, Leeland, Arizona	3	0	0	0	0	0
McNeil, Ryan, St. Louis	1	0	1	0	1	0
Mickell, Darren, New Orleans	0	0	1	11	1	0
Milburn, Glyn, Detroit	3	2	0	0	2	0
Miller, Anthony, Dallas	1	1	0	0	1	0
Miller, Les, Carolina	0	0	1	3	1	0
Mills, Sam, Carolina	1	0	0	0	0	0
Mincy, Charles, Tampa Bay	0	1	0	0	1	0
Minter, Barry, Chicago	0	0	3	0	3	0
Minter, Mike, Carolina	0	0	2	0	2	0
Mirer, Rick, Chicago	4	1	0	-4	1	0
Mitchell, Brian, Washington	3	0	0	0	0	0
Mitchell, Scott, Detroit	15	4	0	-15	4	0
Molden, Alex, New Orleans	0	0	2	0	2	0
Moore, Jerald, St. Louis	4	2	0	0	2	0
Morabito, Tim, Carolina	0	0	1	0	1	0
Morton, Johnnie, Detroit	2	0	0	0	0	0
Mullen, Roderick, Green Bay	0	0	1	1	1	0
Newman, Anthony, N.O.	0	0	1	0	1	0
Newton, Nate, Dallas	0	1	0	0	1	0
Nickerson, Hardy, Tampa Bay	0	1	1	0	2	0
Norton, Ken, San Francisco	0	0	2	0	2	0
Nussmeier, Doug, N.O.	1	0	0	-4	0	0
Oliver, Winslow, Carolina	2	0	0	0	0	0
O'Neal, Leslie, St. Louis	0	0	2	66	2	1
Owens, Dan, Atlanta	1	0	1	2	1	0
Owens, Rich, Washington	0	0	1	0	1	0
Owens, Terrell, San Francisco	1	1	0	0	1	0
Pace, Orlando, St. Louis	0	1	0	0	1	0
Palmer, David, Minnesota	2	0	0	0	0	0
Panos, Joe, Philadelphia	0	1	0	0	1	0

Player, Team	Fum.	Own Rec.	Opp. Rec.	Yds.	Tot. Rec.	TD
Parker, Anthony, Tampa Bay ...	1	0	0	0	0	0
Patten, David, N.Y. Giants	2	0	1	0	1	0
Patton, Joe, Washington.........	0	1	0	0	1	0
Patton, Marvcus, Washington.	0	0	1	0	1	0
Peete, Rodney, Philadelphia....	5	2	0	-2	2	0
Pegram, Erric, N.Y. Giants	1	1	0	0	1	0
Penn, Chris, Chicago.............	1	0	0	0	0	0
Peterson, Anthony, Chicago....	0	1	0	0	1	0
Phillips, Lawrence, St. Louis ..	3	0	0	0	0	0
Pilgrim, Evan, Chicago............	0	1	0	0	1	0
Plummer, Jake, Arizona	6	1	0	-1	1	0
Poole, Tyrone, Carolina..........	3	2	1	11	3	0
Pounds, Darryl, Washington...	0	0	3	18	3	1
Prior, Mike, Green Bay............	1	0	0	0	0	0
Proehl, Ricky, Chicago............	2	0	0	0	0	0
Pyne, Jim, Tampa Bay	1	0	0	-5	0	0
Quarles, Shelton, Tampa Bay..	0	0	2	0	2	0
Randle, John, Minnesota	0	0	2	5	2	0
Reeves, Carl, Chicago	0	0	1	0	1	0
Richard, Stanley, Washington.	0	0	1	0	1	0
Rivers, Ron, Detroit	0	1	0	0	1	0
Roberts, Ray, Detroit	0	2	0	4	2	0
Robinson, Eugene, Green Bay	1	0	2	0	2	0
Royal, Andre, Carolina	0	0	1	0	1	0
Russell, Matt, Detroit	0	0	1	0	1	0
Salaam, Rashaan, Chicago	2	0	0	0	0	0
Sanders, Barry, Detroit	3	1	0	0	1	0
Sanders, Deion, Dallas............	1	0	0	0	0	0
Sanders, Frank, Arizona	3	0	0	0	0	0
Santiago, O.J., Atlanta	1	0	0	0	0	0
Sapp, Warren, Tampa Bay	0	0	1	23	1	0
Sauer, Craig, Atlanta	0	0	1	0	1	0
Sauerbrun, Todd, Chicago	1	0	0	-9	0	0
Schroeder, Bill, Green Bay	4	1	0	0	1	0
Scroggins, Tracy, Detroit	0	0	1	17	1	1
Seay, Mark, Philadelphia.........	3	1	0	0	1	0
Sehorn, Jason, N.Y. Giants	0	0	1	2	1	0
Sharper, Darren, Green Bay	1	0	1	34	1	1
Shiver, Clay, Dallas	2	1	0	0	1	0
Shuler, Heath, New Orleans	8	3	0	-20	3	0
Smith, Cedric, Arizona	0	0	1	0	1	0
Smith, Darrin, Philadelphia.....	0	0	1	0	1	0
Smith, Derek, Washington.......	0	0	2	5	2	0
Smith, Emmitt, Dallas.............	1	1	0	0	1	0
Smith, Fernando, Minnesota...	0	0	1	6	1	0
Smith, Frankie, San Francisco..	0	1	0	0	1	0
Smith, Irv, New Orleans	1	0	0	0	0	0
Smith, Robert, Minnesota.......	0	1	0	0	1	0
Solomon, Freddie, Phi.	3	1	0	0	1	0
Staley, Duce, Philadelphia.......	0	1	0	0	1	0
Stenstrom, Steve, Chicago......	1	0	0	0	0	0
Stevens, Matt, Philadelphia.....	0	0	1	0	1	0
Stokes, J.J., San Francisco.....	1	2	0	0	2	0
Stoltenberg, Bryan, NYG........	1	0	0	0	0	0
Stone, Dwight, Carolina	0	0	1	0	1	0
Stone, Ron, N.Y. Giants	0	1	0	0	1	0
Stoutmire, Omar, Dallas.........	0	1	0	0	1	0
Strahan, Michael, N.Y. Giants .	0	0	1	0	1	0
Strickland, Fred, Dallas..........	0	0	2	0	2	0
Swann, Eric, Arizona...............	1	0	1	0	1	0
Terrell, Pat, Carolina	0	1	0	0	1	0
Thomas, Broderick, Dallas......	0	0	1	0	1	0
Thomas, Hollis, Philadelphia..	0	0	1	0	1	0
Thomas, Mark, Chicago..........	0	0	1	0	1	0
Thomas, Orlando, Minnesota..	1	0	2	26	2	1
Thomas, William, Phi.	0	0	1	37	1	1
Thomason, Jeff, Green Bay.....	1	0	0	0	0	0
Thompson, David, St. Louis ...	2	0	1	0	1	0
Timpson, Michael, Phi.	1	0	0	0	0	0
Tobeck, Robbie, Atlanta	0	1	0	0	1	0
Tomich, Jared, New Orleans ...	1	1	0	0	1	0
Tubbs, Winfred, New Orleans .	0	0	2	0	2	0
Turk, Matt, Washington	1	0	0	-16	0	0
Turner, Kevin, Philadelphia......	1	0	0	0	0	0
Upshaw, Regan, Tampa Bay ...	0	0	1	0	1	0
Uwaezuoke, Iheanyi, S.F.	4	1	1	0	2	0
Vardell, Tommy, Detroit	1	1	0	0	1	0
Vincent, Troy, Philadelphia......	1	1	1	5	2	0
Waldroup, Kerwin, Detroit	0	0	1	0	1	0
Walker, Herschel, Dallas	0	1	1	0	2	0
Walker, Marquis, St. Louis......	0	0	1	0	1	0
Walsh, Steve, Tampa Bay........	1	2	0	0	2	0
Washington, Marvin, S.F.	0	0	1	0	1	0
Watters, Ricky, Philadelphia ...	3	1	0	0	1	0
Way, Charles, N.Y. Giants	3	4	1	0	5	0
Wells, Mike, Detroit	0	0	1	0	1	0
Wetnight, Ryan, Chicago	1	0	0	0	0	0
Wheatley, Tyrone, N.Y. Giants .	3	3	0	0	3	0
Wheeler, Leonard, Minnesota .	0	0	1	0	1	0
White, Reggie, Green Bay	0	0	2	0	2	0
Wiegert, Zach, St. Louis	0	4	0	0	4	1
Wilkins, Gabe, Green Bay	0	0	3	1	3	1
Williams, Brian, Green Bay	0	0	1	0	1	0
Williams, Gene, Atlanta...........	0	2	0	0	2	0
Williams, James, S.F.	0	0	1	0	1	0
Williams, Karl, Tampa Bay	5	1	0	0	1	0
Williams, Kevin, Arizona	3	1	0	0	1	0
Williams, Sherman, Dallas......	5	1	0	0	1	0
Willis, James, Philadelphia	0	0	2	0	2	0
Wolf, Joe, Arizona..................	0	1	0	0	1	0
Woodson, Darren, Dallas........	1	0	2	0	2	0
Woodson, Rod, San Francisco.	0	0	1	0	1	0
Wooten, Tito, N.Y. Giants........	1	0	1	0	1	0
Wright, Toby, St. Louis	0	0	1	34	1	0
Wuerffel, Danny, New Orleans .	2	2	0	0	2	0
Wunsch, Jerry, Tampa Bay	0	1	0	0	1	0
Young, Steve, San Francisco ..	4	2	0	-11	2	0
Zellars, Ray, New Orleans	6	2	0	0	2	0
Zordich, Michael, Philadelphia .	0	0	1	-1	1	0

*Includes both NFC and AFC statistics.

PLAYERS WITH TWO CLUBS

Player, Team	Fum.	Own Rec.	Opp. Rec.	Yds.	Tot. Rec.	TD
Coleman, Andre, Seattle	1	0	0	0	0	0
Coleman, Andre, Pittsburgh....	1	0	0	0	0	0
Hobert, Billy Joe, Buffalo	1	1	0	-5	1	0
Hobert, Billy Joe, New Orleans.	2	0	0	0	0	0
Tolliver, Billy Joe, Atlanta........	6	1	0	0	1	0
Tolliver, Billy Joe, Kansas City..	1	1	0	-1	1	0

FIELD GOALS

TEAM

AFC

Team	Made	Att.	Pct.	Long
Kansas City	26	27	.963	54
Pittsburgh	22	25	.880	52
New England	25	29	.862	52
Jacksonville	31	36	.861	52
San Diego	26	31	.839	45
Buffalo	24	30	.800	55
Seattle	22	28	.786	52
Indianapolis	32	41	.780	50
Miami	28	36	.778	50
Tennessee	27	35	.771	52
Baltimore	26	34	.765	49
Cincinnati	12	16	.750	46
Denver	28	39	.718	53
N.Y. Jets	28	41	.683	55
Oakland	13	22	.591	53
AFC total	370	470	...	55
AFC average	24.7	31.3	.787	...

NFC

Team	Made	Att.	Pct.	Long
Detroit	26	29	.897	55
Dallas	34	38	.895	53
Atlanta	23	27	.852	55
New Orleans	23	27	.852	53
Carolina	22	26	.846	54
Chicago	21	26	.808	52
San Francisco	29	36	.806	51
Green Bay	24	30	.800	50
Tampa Bay	13	17	.765	54
Philadelphia	22	31	.710	49
Minnesota	19	27	.704	49
N.Y. Giants	22	32	.688	52
St. Louis	25	37	.676	52
Washington	16	24	.667	50
Arizona	19	29	.655	49
NFC total	338	436	...	55
NFC average	22.5	29.1	.775	...
NFL total	708	906	...	55
NFL average	23.6	30.2	.781	...

INDIVIDUAL

BESTS OF THE SEASON

Field goal percentage, season
AFC: .963—Pete Stoyanovich, Kansas City.
NFC: .919—Richie Cunningham, Dallas.

Field goals, season
NFC: 34—Richie Cunningham, Dallas.
AFC: 32—Cary Blanchard, Indianapolis.

Field goal attempts, season
AFC: 41—Cary Blanchard, Indianapolis; John Hall, N.Y.Jets.
NFC: 37—Richie Cunningham, Dallas; Jeff Wilkins, St. Louis.

Longest field goal
AFC: 55—John Hall, N.Y.Jets at Seattle, Aug. 31; Steve Christie, Buffalo vs. Denver, Oct. 26 (OT).
NFC: 55—Morten Andersen, Atlanta at New Orleans, Oct. 12; Jason Hanson, Detroit vs. Indianapolis, Nov. 23.

Average yards made, season
NFC: 39.0—Doug Brien, New Orleans.
AFC: 36.5—Pete Stoyanovich, Kansas City.

NFL LEADERS

Team	Made	Att.	Pct.	Long
Stoyanovich, Pete, Kansas City*..	26	27	.963	54
Cunningham, Richie, Dallas	34	37	.919	53
Hanson, Jason, Detroit	26	29	.897	55
Johnson, Norm, Pittsburgh*	22	25	.880	52
Vinatieri, Adam, New England*	25	29	.862	52
Hollis, Mike, Jacksonville*	31	36	.861	52
Andersen, Morten, Atlanta	23	27	.852	55
Brien, Doug, New Orleans	23	27	.852	53
Kasay, John, Carolina	22	26	.846	54
Jaeger, Jeff, Chicago	21	26	.808	52

*AFC.
Leader based on percentage, minimum 16 attempts.

AFC

Player, Team	1-19	20-29	30-39	40-49	Over	Totals	Avg. Yds. Att.	Avg. Yds. Made	Avg. Yds. Miss	Long
Bentley, Scott	0-0	1-1	1-1	0-1	0-0	2-3	34.0	27.0	48.0	33
Denver	...	1.000	1.000	.000	...	.667				
Blanchard, Cary	0-0	9-9	12-14	10-15	1-3	32-41	37.0	35.5	42.6	50
Indianapolis	...	1.000	.857	.667	.333	.780				
Carney, John	0-0	3-3	2-2	2-2	0-0	7-7	32.6	32.6	...	41
San Diego	...	1.000	1.000	1.000	...	1.000				
Christie, Steve	0-0	6-6	9-12	8-10	1-2	24-30	37.3	36.2	41.5	55
Buffalo	...	1.000	.750	.800	.500	.800				
Davis, Greg	0-0	8-10	12-12	6-12	0-0	26-34	34.2	33.0	38.1	45
Min.-S.D.*	...	.800	1.000	.500	...	.765				
Del Greco, Al	2-2	6-6	10-11	7-14	2-2	27-35	36.6	35.4	40.8	52
Tennessee	1.000	1.000	.909	.500	1.000	.771				
Elam, Jason	0-0	10-11	10-12	3-8	3-5	26-36	36.5	34.2	42.6	53
Denver	...	.909	.833	.375	.600	.722				
Ford, Cole	0-0	3-5	4-6	5-10	1-1	13-22	37.5	36.3	39.2	53
Oakland	...	.600	.667	.500	1.000	.591				
Hall, John	1-1	10-11	11-17	2-6	4-6	28-41	36.7	34.3	41.8	55
N.Y. Jets	1.000	.909	.647	.333	.667	.683				

Player, Team	1-19	20-29	30-39	40-49	Over	Totals	Avg. Yds. Att.	Avg. Yds. Made	Avg. Yds. Miss	Long
Hollis, Mike	2-2	12-14	8-9	7-9	2-2	31-36	33.0	32.5	36.2	52
Jacksonville	1.000	.857	.889	.778	1.000	.861				
Johnson, Norm	1-1	6-6	8-8	6-8	1-2	22-25	35.9	34.5	46.3	52
Pittsburgh	1.000	1.000	1.000	.750	.500	.880				
Mare, Olindo	2-2	14-15	8-10	3-6	1-3	28-36	31.6	29.3	40.0	50
Miami	1.000	.933	.800	.500	.333	.778				
Pelfrey, Doug	0-0	4-4	3-3	5-7	0-2	12-16	38.6	35.2	49.0	46
Cincinnati	...	1.000	1.000	.714	.000	.750				
Peterson, Todd	0-0	9-9	7-10	5-7	1-2	22-28	36.1	34.3	42.7	52
Seattle	...	1.000	.700	.714	.500	.786				
Stover, Matt	0-0	8-9	12-12	6-11	0-2	26-34	36.5	34.0	44.4	49
Baltimore	...	.889	1.000	.545	.000	.765				
Stoyanovich, Pete	0-0	9-9	3-3	12-13	2-2	26-27	36.9	36.5	48.0	54
Kansas City	...	1.000	1.000	.923	1.000	.963				
Vinatieri, Adam	0-0	11-11	7-9	6-8	1-1	25-29	33.6	33.0	37.3	52
New England	...	1.000	.778	.750	1.000	.862				

*Includes both NFC and AFC statistics.

NFC

Player, Team	1-19	20-29	30-39	40-49	Over	Totals	Avg. Yds. Att.	Avg. Yds. Made	Avg. Yds. Miss	Long
Andersen, Morten	1-1	10-10	7-7	3-6	2-3	23-27	33.7	31.8	44.8	55
Atlanta	1.000	1.000	1.000	.500	.667	.852				
Anderson, Gary	0-0	11-11	9-12	8-10	1-3	29-36	35.0	33.2	42.4	51
San Francisco	...	1.000	.750	.800	.333	.806				
Blanton, Scott	2-2	4-4	5-6	4-8	1-4	16-24	37.5	33.5	45.4	50
Washington	1.000	1.000	.833	.500	.250	.667				
Boniol, Chris	0-0	7-7	11-12	4-11	0-1	22-31	37.0	34.0	44.4	49
Philadelphia	...	1.000	.917	.364	.000	.710				
Brien, Doug	1-1	2-2	10-10	6-9	4-5	23-27	40.0	39.0	45.3	53
New Orleans	1.000	1.000	1.000	.667	.800	.852				
Butler, Kevin	0-0	4-4	2-4	2-4	0-0	8-12	34.5	32.4	38.8	49
Arizona	...	1.000	.500	.500	...	.667				
Cunningham, Richie	1-1	16-16	9-9	7-10	1-1	34-37	32.6	31.9	41.3	53
Dallas	1.000	1.000	1.000	.700	1.000	.919				
Daluiso, Brad	1-1	6-6	6-7	8-14	1-4	22-32	38.8	35.7	45.7	52
N.Y. Giants	1.000	1.000	.857	.571	.250	.688				
Gowin, Toby	0-0	0-0	0-0	0-0	0-1	0-1	63.0	...	63.0	0
Dallas	...	...	...	...	.000	.000				
Hanson, Jason	0-0	10-10	8-9	5-5	3-5	26-29	36.6	35.4	46.7	55
Detroit	...	1.000	.889	1.000	.600	.897				
Husted, Michael	0-0	5-5	2-3	5-6	1-3	13-17	36.9	35.0	43.3	54
Tampa Bay	...	1.000	.667	.833	.333	.765				
Jaeger, Jeff	0-0	8-9	8-10	4-6	1-1	21-26	33.7	33.4	34.8	52
Chicago	...	.889	.800	.667	1.000	.808				
Kasay, John	1-1	6-7	8-8	4-4	3-6	22-26	37.1	35.3	47.0	54
Carolina	1.000	.857	1.000	1.000	.500	.846				
Longwell, Ryan	4-4	7-8	10-13	2-4	1-1	24-30	31.9	30.8	36.7	50
Green Bay	1.000	.875	.769	.500	1.000	.800				
Murray, Eddie	0-0	7-7	1-3	4-6	0-1	12-17	35.5	32.5	42.6	49
Minnesota	...	1.000	.333	.667	.000	.706				
Nedney, Joe	1-1	3-3	4-4	3-7	0-2	11-17	37.5	32.4	47.0	45
Arizona	1.000	1.000	1.000	.429	.000	.647				
Wilkins, Jeff	0-0	8-9	8-12	7-14	2-2	25-37	37.5	36.2	40.3	52
St. Louis	...	.889	.667	.500	1.000	.676				

PLAYERS WITH TWO CLUBS

Player, Team	1-19	20-29	30-39	40-49	Over	Totals	Avg. Yds. Att.	Avg. Yds. Made	Avg. Yds. Miss	Long
Davis, Greg	0-0	4-5	2-2	1-3	0-0	7-10	30.9	29.3	34.7	43
Minnesota	...	.800	1.000	.333	...	.700				
Davis, Greg	0-0	4-5	10-10	5-9	0-0	19-24	31.1	34.4	18.4	45
San Diego	...	.800	1.000	.556	...	.792				

1997 STATISTICS Field goals

PUNTING

AFC

Team	Total Punts	Yards	Long	Avg.	TB	Blocked	Opp. Ret.	Ret. Yards	Inside 20	Net Avg.
Indianapolis	67	3034	72	45.3	6	0	43	491	18	36.2
New England	79	3569	73	45.2	14	1	38	437	24	36.1
Oakland	93	4189	63	45.0	6	0	52	431	28	39.1
Jacksonville	66	2964	64	44.9	8	0	29	241	27	38.8
San Diego	90	3972	66	44.1	8	1	39	416	26	37.7
Miami	68	2962	58	43.6	6	0	43	323	15	37.0
Denver	60	2598	57	43.3	4	0	26	235	22	38.1
Cincinnati	81	3471	66	42.9	8	0	35	407	27	35.9
N.Y. Jets	75	3212	58	42.8	5	1	47	459	20	35.4
Baltimore	83	3540	60	42.7	2	0	53	460	24	36.6
Pittsburgh	64	2729	72	42.6	11	0	23	271	17	35.0
Kansas City	83	3489	65	42.0	4	0	39	255	29	38.0
Tennessee	74	3081	59	41.6	2	0	36	430	25	35.3
Buffalo	91	3764	59	41.4	6	1	44	366	24	36.0
Seattle	78	3144	65	40.3	8	2	38	463	24	32.3
AFC total	1152	49718	73	...	98	6	585	5685	350	...
AFC average	76.8	3314.5	...	43.2	6.5	0.4	39.0	379.0	23.3	36.5

Leader based on average.

NFC

Team	Total Punts	Yards	Long	Avg.	TB	Blocked	Opp. Ret.	Ret. Yards	Inside 20	Net Avg.
New Orleans	88	4038	66	45.9	13	0	50	706	21	34.9
Green Bay	75	3378	65	45.0	21	0	32	255	26	36.0
Washington	85	3788	62	44.6	11	1	33	237	32	39.2
Arizona	92	4028	62	43.8	10	1	40	441	24	36.8
Tampa Bay	84	3578	74	42.6	9	1	42	388	27	35.8
Chicago	96	4077	67	42.5	11	0	52	727	26	32.6
Carolina	85	3604	62	42.4	4	0	38	428	29	36.4
Minnesota	81	3407	65	42.1	5	0	49	566	25	33.8
St. Louis	95	3985	61	41.9	8	1	60	618	16	33.8
Dallas	86	3592	72	41.8	9	0	40	365	26	35.4
Philadelphia	88	3660	61	41.6	5	1	48	515	19	34.6
Detroit	86	3576	60	41.6	4	2	51	434	24	35.6
N.Y. Giants	112	4531	57	40.5	14	1	40	378	33	34.6
San Francisco	79	3182	55	40.3	7	1	41	307	22	34.6
Atlanta	89	3498	57	39.3	9	0	21	55	20	36.7
NFC total	1321	55922	74	...	140	9	637	6420	370	...
NFC average	88.1	3728.1	...	42.3	9.3	0.6	42.5	428.0	24.7	35.4
NFL total	2473	105640	74	...	238	15	1222	12105	720	...
NFL average	82.4	3521.3	...	42.7	7.9	0.5	40.7	403.5	24.0	35.9

INDIVIDUAL

BESTS OF THE SEASON

Average yards per punt, season
NFC: 45.9—Mark Royals, New Orleans.
AFC: 45.8—Tom Tupa, New England.

Net average yards per punt, season
NFC: 39.2—Matt Turk, Washington.
AFC: 39.1—Leo Araguz, Oakland.

Longest
NFC: 74—Sean Landeta, Tampa Bay at N.Y. Jets, Dec. 14.
AFC: 73—Tom Tupa, New England at Denver, Oct. 6.

Punts, season
NFC: 111—Brad Maynard, N.Y. Giants.
AFC: 93—Leo Araguz, Oakland.

Punts, game
NFC: 13—Brad Maynard, N.Y. Giants at Washington, Nov. 23 (OT).
AFC: 11—Lee Johnson, Cincinnati vs. San Diego, Nov. 2.

NFL LEADERS

Player, Team	Net Punts	Yards	Long	Avg.	Total Punts	TB	Blk.	Opp. Ret.	Ret. Yds.	In 20	Net Avg.
Tupa, Tom, New England	78	3569	73	45.8	79	14	1	38	437	24	36.1
Gardocki, Chris, Indianapolis	67	3034	72	45.3	67	6	0	43	491	18	36.2
Araguz, Leo, Oakland	93	4189	63	45.0	93	6	0	52	431	28	39.1

Player, Team	Net Punts	Yards	Long	Avg.	Total Punts	TB	Blk.	Opp. Ret.	Ret. Yds.	In 20	Net Avg.
Barker, Bryan, Jacksonville..............	66	2964	64	44.9	66	8	0	29	241	27	38.8
Bennett, Darren, San Diego	89	3972	66	44.6	90	8	1	39	416	26	37.7
Rouen, Tom, Denver.........................	60	2598	57	43.3	60	4	0	26	235	22	38.1
Hansen, Brian, N.Y. Jets	71	3068	58	43.2	72	5	1	45	429	20	35.3
Kidd, John, Miami	52	2247	58	43.2	52	4	0	35	243	13	37.0
Johnson, Lee, Cincinnati	81	3471	66	42.9	81	8	0	35	407	27	35.9
Montgomery, Greg, Baltimore	83	3540	60	42.7	83	2	0	53	460	24	36.6
Miller, Josh, Pittsburgh	64	2729	72	42.6	64	11	0	23	271	17	35.0
Aguiar, Louie, Kansas City	82	3465	65	42.3	82	4	0	39	255	28	38.2
Mohr, Chris, Buffalo.........................	90	3764	59	41.8	91	6	1	44	366	24	36.0
Roby, Reggie, Tennessee..................	73	3049	59	41.8	73	1	0	36	430	25	35.6
Tuten, Rick, Seattle.........................	48	2007	65	41.8	48	5	0	23	161	15	36.4

*AFC.

Leader based on average, minimum 40 punts.

AFC

Player, Team	Net Punts	Yards	Long	Avg.	Total Punts	TB	Blk.	Opp. Ret.	Ret. Yds.	In 20	Net Avg.
Aguiar, Louie, Kansas City	82	3465	65	42.3	82	4	0	39	255	28	38.2
Araguz, Leo, Oakland.........................	93	4189	63	45.0	93	6	0	52	431	28	39.1
Barker, Bryan, Jacksonville.................	66	2964	64	44.9	66	8	0	29	241	27	38.8
Bennett, Darren, San Diego	89	3972	66	44.6	90	8	1	39	416	26	37.7
Del Greco, Al, Tennessee...................	1	32	32	32.0	1	1	0	0	0	0	12.0
Gardocki, Chris, Indianapolis..............	67	3034	72	45.3	67	6	0	43	491	18	36.2
Hall, John, N.Y. Jets........................	3	144	57	48.0	3	0	0	2	30	0	38.0
Hansen, Brian, N.Y. Jets	71	3068	58	43.2	72	5	1	45	429	20	35.3
Johnson, Lee, Cincinnati	81	3471	66	42.9	81	8	0	35	407	27	35.9
Kidd, John, Miami	52	2247	58	43.2	52	4	0	35	243	13	37.0
Mare, Olindo, Miami	5	235	53	47.0	5	0	0	1	4	2	46.2
Miller, Josh, Pittsburgh	64	2729	72	42.6	64	11	0	23	271	17	35.0
Mohr, Chris, Buffalo.........................	90	3764	59	41.8	91	6	1	44	366	24	36.0
Montgomery, Greg, Baltimore	83	3540	60	42.7	83	2	0	53	460	24	36.6
Richardson, Kyle, Mia.-Sea...............	19	804	54	42.3	21	3	2	12	142	2	28.7
Roby, Reggie, Tennessee..................	73	3049	59	41.8	73	1	0	36	430	25	35.6
Rouen, Tom, Denver.........................	60	2598	57	43.3	60	4	0	26	235	22	38.1
Stark, Rohn, Seattle........................	20	813	52	40.7	20	2	0	10	236	7	26.9
Stoyanovich, Pete, Kansas City	1	24	24	24.0	1	0	0	0	0	1	24.0
Tupa, Tom, New England	78	3569	73	45.8	79	14	1	38	437	24	36.1
Tuten, Rick, Seattle..........................	48	2007	65	41.8	48	5	0	23	161	15	36.4

NFC

Player, Team	Net Punts	Yards	Long	Avg.	Total Punts	TB	Blk.	Opp. Ret.	Ret. Yds.	In 20	Net Avg.
Barnhardt, Tommy, Tampa Bay..........	29	1304	61	45.0	29	3	0	14	110	12	39.1
Berger, Mitch, Minnesota...................	73	3133	65	42.9	73	5	0	46	545	22	34.1
Brice, Will, St. Louis	41	1713	61	41.8	42	4	1	27	352	6	30.5
Cunningham, Randall, Minnesota.......	8	274	65	34.3	8	0	0	3	21	3	31.6
Feagles, Jeff, Arizona......................	91	4028	62	44.3	92	10	1	40	441	24	36.8
Gowin, Toby, Dallas.........................	86	3592	72	41.8	86	9	0	40	365	26	35.4
Hentrich, Craig, Green Bay	75	3378	65	45.0	75	21	0	32	255	26	36.0
Horan, Mike, St. Louis	53	2272	60	42.9	53	4	0	33	266	10	36.3
Hutton, Tom, Philadelphia	87	3660	61	42.1	88	5	1	48	515	19	34.6
Jaeger, Jeff, Chicago	1	18	18	18.0	1	0	0	0	0	0	18.0
Jett, John, Detroit...........................	84	3576	60	42.6	86	4	2	51	434	24	35.6
Landeta, Sean, Tampa Bay...............	54	2274	74	42.1	55	6	1	28	278	15	34.1
Maynard, Brad, N.Y. Giants	111	4531	57	40.8	112	14	1	40	378	33	34.6
Royals, Mark, New Orleans	88	4038	66	45.9	88	13	0	50	706	21	34.9
Sauerbrun, Todd, Chicago	95	4059	67	42.7	95	11	0	52	727	26	32.8
Stryzinski, Dan, Atlanta....................	89	3498	57	39.3	89	9	0	21	55	20	36.7
Thompson, Tommy, San Francisco.....	78	3182	55	40.8	79	7	1	41	307	22	34.6
Turk, Matt, Washington	84	3788	62	45.1	85	11	0	33	237	32	39.2
Walter, Ken, Carolina	85	3604	62	42.4	85	4	0	38	428	29	36.4

PLAYERS WITH TWO CLUBS

Player, Team	Net Punts	Yards	Long	Avg.	Total Punts	TB	Blk.	Opp. Ret.	Ret. Yds.	In 20	Net Avg.
Richardson, Kyle, Miami...................	11	480	54	43.6	11	2	0	7	76	0	33.1
Richardson, Kyle, Seattle..................	8	324	52	40.5	10	1	2	5	66	2	23.8

1997 STATISTICS Punting

PUNT RETURNS

TEAM

AFC

Team	No.	FC	Yds.	Avg.	Long	TD
Denver............	41	22	555	13.5	t94	3
Baltimore.........	42	14	564	13.4	t89	2
Jacksonville......	36	16	412	11.4	52	0
N.Y. Jets..........	59	8	674	11.4	t66	1
Kansas City......	35	14	383	10.9	t82	1
Miami..............	32	16	335	10.5	38	0
San Diego........	47	8	489	10.4	t85	3
New England.....	45	8	467	10.4	47	0
Buffalo.............	39	19	346	8.9	47	0
Indianapolis......	31	10	248	8.0	20	0
Oakland............	27	20	210	7.8	31	0
Cincinnati.........	26	19	201	7.7	18	0
Tennessee........	32	13	244	7.6	30	0
Pittsburgh.........	32	10	222	6.9	30	0
Seattle.............	37	18	248	6.7	28	0
AFC total......	561	215	5598	10.0	t94	10
AFC average .	37.4	14.3	373.2	10.0	...	0.7

t—touchdown.

NFC

Team	No.	FC	Yds.	Avg.	Long	TD
Minnesota........	34	19	444	13.1	57	0
Tampa Bay........	51	12	645	12.6	63	1
San Francisco ...	41	16	482	11.8	t73	1
Washington	38	23	442	11.6	t63	1
Arizona	41	16	461	11.2	50	0
Dallas..............	47	14	512	10.9	t83	1
New Orleans	48	26	496	10.3	32	0
N.Y. Giants.......	47	19	455	9.7	t53	1
Atlanta	52	14	483	9.3	38	0
Green Bay	56	17	515	9.2	46	0
Detroit..............	48	26	433	9.0	40	0
Carolina	41	23	310	7.6	40	0
Philadelphia	31	21	234	7.5	42	0
Chicago............	46	8	321	7.0	19	0
St. Louis	40	23	274	6.9	43	0
NFC total.......	661	277	6507	9.8	t83	5
NFC average .	44.1	18.5	433.8	9.8	...	0.3
NFL total.......	1222	492	12105	...	t94	15
NFL average .	40.7	16.4	403.5	9.9	...	0.5

INDIVIDUAL

BESTS OF THE SEASON

Yards per attempt, season
AFC: 15.6—Jermaine Lewis, Baltimore.
NFC: 13.1—David Palmer, Minnesota.

Yards, season
AFC: 619—Leon Johnson, N.Y. Jets.
NFC: 597—Karl Williams, Tampa Bay.

Yards, game
AFC: 184—Jermaine Lewis, Baltimore vs. Seattle, Dec. 7 (5 returns, 2 TDs).
NFC: 116—Karl Williams, Tampa Bay vs. Chicago, Dec. 21 (6 returns, 1 TD).

Longest
AFC: 94—Darrien Gordon, Denver vs. St. Louis, Sept. 14 (TD).
NFC: 83—Deion Sanders, Dallas vs. Chicago, Sept. 28 (TD).

Returns, season
NFC: 52—Todd Kinchen, Atlanta.
AFC: 51—Leon Johnson, N.Y. Jets.

Returns, game
AFC: 7—James Roe, Baltimore vs. Philadelphia, Nov. 16 (64 yards).
NFC: 7—Eric Guliford, New Orleans at Oakland, Nov. 9 (90 yards).

Fair catches, season
NFC: 26—Glyn Milburn, Detroit; Eric Guliford, New Orleans.
AFC: 22—Darrien Gordon, Denver.

Touchdowns, season
AFC: 3—Darrien Gordon, Denver; Eric Metcalf, San Diego.
NFC: 1—Held by five players.

NFL LEADERS

Player, Team	No.	FC	Yds.	Avg.	Long	TD
Lewis, Jermaine, Baltimore*....	28	13	437	15.6	t89	2
Gordon, Darrien, Denver*........	40	22	543	13.6	t94	3
Palmer, David, Minnesota	34	19	444	13.1	57	0
Williams, Karl, Tampa Bay	46	12	597	13.0	63	1
Sanders, Deion, Dallas............	33	12	407	12.3	t83	1
Johnson, Leon, N.Y. Jets*	51	6	619	12.1	t66	1
Mitchell, Brian, Washington	38	23	442	11.6	t63	1
Williams, Kevin, Arizona	40	15	462	11.6	50	0
Barlow, Reggie, Jacksonville*...	36	16	412	11.4	52	0

NFC

Player, Team	No.	FC	Yds.	Avg.	Long	TD
Uwaezuoke, Iheanyi, S.F.	34	14	373	11.0	36	0
Vanover, Tamarick, K.C.*	35	14	383	10.9	t82	1
Metcalf, Eric, San Diego*.........	45	8	489	10.9	t85	3
Guliford, Eric, New Orleans......	47	26	498	10.6	32	0
Jordan, Charles, Miami*	26	15	273	10.5	38	0
Meggett, David, New England* .	45	8	467	10.4	47	0

*AFC.
t—touchdown.
Leader based on average return, minimum 20.

AFC

Player, Team	No.	FC	Yds.	Avg.	Long	TD
Alexander, Derrick, Baltimore...	1	0	34	34.0	34	0
Archie, Mike, Tennessee..........	1	0	5	5.0	5	0
Bailey, Aaron, Indianapolis.......	1	0	19	19.0	19	0
Barlow, Reggie, Jacksonville....	36	16	412	11.4	52	0
Blackwell, Will, Pittsburgh	23	6	149	6.5	15	0
Buckley, Terrell, Miami	4	0	58	14.5	26	0
Burris, Jeff, Buffalo	21	8	198	9.4	32	0
Coleman, Andre, Pittsburgh.....	5	2	5	1.0	5	0
Davis, Tyree, Seattle...............	16	6	104	6.5	28	0
Ethridge, Ray, Baltimore	5	1	21	4.2	16	0
Galloway, Mitchell, Buffalo.......	2	2	15	7.5	15	0
Gordon, Darrien, Denver	40	22	543	13.6	t94	3
Harris, Ronnie, Seattle............	21	12	144	6.9	19	0
Harrison, Marvin, Indianapolis...	0	1	0	...	0	0
Harrison, Rodney, San Diego ...	1	0	0	0.0	0	0
Hawkins, Courtney, Pittsburgh ..	4	2	68	17.0	30	0
Howard, Desmond, Oakland	27	20	210	7.8	31	0
Jackson, Greg, San Diego	1	0	0	0.0	0	0
Jackson, Ray, Buffalo	1	0	0	0.0	0	0
Jacquet, Nate, Indianapolis	13	0	96	7.4	17	0
Johnson, Leon, N.Y. Jets	51	6	619	12.1	t66	1
Jones, Henry, Buffalo	1	0	0	0.0	0	0
Jordan, Charles, Miami	26	15	273	10.5	38	0
Lewis, Jermaine, Baltimore......	28	13	437	15.6	t89	2
Mason, Derrick, Tennessee......	13	3	95	7.3	29	0
McDuffie, O.J., Miami	2	1	4	2.0	3	0
Meggett, David, New England ..	45	8	467	10.4	47	0
Metcalf, Eric, San Diego..........	45	8	489	10.9	t85	3

Player, Team	No.	FC	Yds.	Avg.	Long	TD
Moulds, Eric, Buffalo	2	0	20	10.0	10	0
Myers, Greg, Cincinnati	26	19	201	7.7	18	0
Robertson, Marcus, Tennessee	1	0	0	0.0	0	0
Roe, James, Baltimore	8	0	72	9.0	14	0
Smith, Rod, Denver	1	0	12	12.0	12	0
Stablein, Brian, Indianapolis	17	9	133	7.8	20	0
Tasker, Steve, Buffalo	12	9	113	9.4	47	0
Vanover, Tamarick, Kansas City	35	14	383	10.9	t82	1
Ward, Dedric, N.Y. Jets	8	2	55	6.9	12	0

t—touchdown.

NFC

Player, Team	No.	FC	Yds.	Avg.	Long	TD
Bates, Michael, Carolina	1	0	8	8.0	8	0
Buchanan, Ray, Atlanta	0	1	37	...	37	0
Carrier, Mark, Detroit	1	0	0	0.0	0	0
Dulaney, Mike, Chicago	1	0	0	0.0	0	0
Dunn, Warrick, Tampa Bay	5	0	48	9.6	25	0
Edwards, Anthony, Arizona	1	1	-1	-1.0	-1	0
Engram, Bobby, Chicago	1	0	4	4.0	4	0
Floyd, Malcolm, St. Louis	4	2	15	3.8	8	0
Gray, Mel, Ten.-Phi.*	19	15	161	8.5	30	0
Guliford, Eric, New Orleans	47	26	498	10.6	32	0
Hastings, Andre, New Orleans	1	0	-2	-2.0	-2	0
Hughes, Tyrone, Chicago	36	7	258	7.2	19	0
Kennison, Eddie, St. Louis	34	20	247	7.3	43	0
Kinchen, Todd, Atlanta	52	13	446	8.6	38	0
Lee, Amp, St. Louis	0	1	0	...	...	0
Levy, Chuck, San Francisco	6	2	109	18.2	t73	1
Mathis, Kevin, Dallas	11	2	91	8.3	45	0
Mayes, Derrick, Green Bay	14	3	141	10.1	26	0
Milburn, Glyn, Detroit	47	26	433	9.2	40	0
Mitchell, Brian, Washington	38	23	442	11.6	t63	1
Oliver, Winslow, Carolina	14	5	111	7.9	26	0
Palmer, David, Minnesota	34	19	444	13.1	57	0
Pittman, Kavika, Dallas	1	0	0	0.0	0	0
Poole, Tyrone, Carolina	26	18	191	7.3	40	0
Preston, Roell, Green Bay	1	0	0	0.0	0	0
Prior, Mike, Green Bay	1	3	0	0.0	0	0
Proehl, Ricky, Chicago	8	1	59	7.4	14	0
Ross, Jermaine, St. Louis	2	0	12	6.0	6	0
Sanders, Deion, Dallas	33	12	407	12.3	t83	1
Schroeder, Bill, Green Bay	33	8	342	10.4	46	0
Seay, Mark, Philadelphia	16	8	172	10.8	42	0
Sharper, Darren, Green Bay	7	3	32	4.6	23	0
Solomon, Freddie, Philadelphia	10	7	55	5.5	14	0
Toomer, Amani, N.Y. Giants	47	19	455	9.7	t53	1
Uwaezuoke, Iheanyi, S.F.	34	14	373	11.0	36	0
Vincent, Troy, Philadelphia	1	0	-8	-8.0	-8	0
Williams, Karl, Tampa Bay	46	12	597	13.0	63	1
Williams, Kevin, Arizona	40	15	462	11.6	50	0
Williams, Stepfret, Dallas	2	0	14	7.0	14	0
Woodson, Rod, San Francisco	1	0	0	0.0	0	0
Wyatt, Antwuan, Philadelphia	2	1	-2	-1.0	0	0

t—touchdown.
*Includes both AFC and NFC statistics.

PLAYERS WITH TWO CLUBS

Player, Team	No.	FC	Yds.	Avg.	Long	TD
Gray, Mel, Tennessee	17	10	144	8.5	30	0
Gray, Mel, Philadelphia	2	5	17	8.5	11	0

KICKOFF RETURNS

AFC

Team	No.	Yds.	Avg.	Long	TD
New England................	53	1337	25.2	t86	1
Kansas City................	54	1345	24.9	t94	1
Cincinnati....................	74	1708	23.1	t102	1
N.Y. Jets	54	1236	22.9	t101	2
Pittsburgh...................	67	1493	22.3	t97	1
Denver........................	54	1203	22.3	61	0
San Diego	75	1613	21.5	63	1
Jacksonville	58	1233	21.3	t92	1
Indianapolis	68	1442	21.2	61	0
Oakland......................	81	1699	21.0	45	0
Miami	63	1298	20.6	48	0
Seattle	76	1550	20.4	43	0
Baltimore	71	1435	20.2	51	0
Tennessee..................	58	1150	19.8	54	0
Buffalo	78	1538	19.7	53	0
AFC total	984	21280	21.6	t102	8
AFC average	65.6	1418.7	21.6	...	0.5

t—touchdown.

NFC

Team	No.	Yds.	Avg.	Long	TD
Arizona	70	1696	24.2	63	0
Dallas.........................	63	1520	24.1	49	0
New Orleans	58	1374	23.7	t102	1
Atlanta	51	1198	23.5	t99	2
Carolina	64	1500	23.4	56	0
Detroit	59	1364	23.1	69	0
Green Bay	49	1119	22.8	43	0
San Francisco	50	1133	22.7	t101	1
Philadelphia	69	1520	22.0	57	1
Minnesota	65	1414	21.8	74	0
Washington	59	1283	21.7	t97	1
Chicago......................	79	1694	21.4	58	0
St. Louis	68	1454	21.4	56	0
Tampa Bay	51	1075	21.1	51	0
N.Y. Giants.................	51	963	18.9	84	0
NFC total................	906	20307	22.4	t102	6
NFC average	60.4	1353.8	22.4	...	0.4
NFL total	1890	41587	...	t102	14
NFL average	63.0	1386.2	22.0	...	0.5

BESTS OF THE SEASON

Yards per attempt, season
NFC: 27.3—Michael Bates, Carolina.
AFC: 26.5—Aaron Glenn, N.Y. Jets.

Yards, season
NFC: 1458—Kevin Williams, Arizona.
AFC: 1318—Desmond Howard, Oakland.

Yards, game
AFC: 223—Desmond Howard, Oakland at Seattle, Oct. 26 (10 returns).
NFC: 211—Roell Preston, Green Bay at Indianapolis, Nov. 16 (7 returns).

Longest
AFC: 102—Eric Bieniemy, Cincinnati at N.Y. Giants, Oct. 26 (TD).
NFC: 102—Eric Guliford, New Orleans at St. Louis, Aug. 31 (TD).

Returns, season
AFC: 61—Desmond Howard, Oakland.
NFC: 59—Kevin Williams, Arizona.

Returns, game
AFC: 10—Desmond Howard, Oakland at Seattle, Oct. 26 (223 yards).
NFC: 7—Held by eight players.

Touchdowns, season
NFC: 2—Byron Hanspard, Atlanta.
AFC: 1—Held by eight players.

NFL LEADERS

Player, Team	No.	Yds.	Avg.	Long	TD
Bates, Michael, Carolina	47	1281	27.3	56	0
Glenn, Aaron, N.Y. Jets*................	28	741	26.5	t96	1
Guliford, Eric, New Orleans	43	1128	26.2	t102	1
Vanover, Tamarick, Kansas City*...	51	1308	25.6	t94	1
Meggett, David, New England*	33	816	24.7	61	0
Blackwell, Will, Pittsburgh*..........	32	791	24.7	t97	1
Williams, Kevin, Arizona................	59	1458	24.7	63	0
Hanspard, Byron, Atlanta..............	40	987	24.7	t99	2
Staley, Duce, Philadelphia	47	1139	24.2	57	0
Milburn, Glyn, Detroit...................	55	1315	23.9	69	0

Player, Team	No.	Yds.	Avg.	Long	TD
Anthony, Reidel, Tampa Bay	25	592	23.7	51	0
Spikes, Irving, Miami*	24	565	23.5	48	0
Hebron, Vaughn, Denver*	43	1009	23.5	46	0
Hughes, Tyrone, Chicago..............	43	1008	23.4	58	0
Schroeder, Bill, Green Bay.............	24	562	23.4	40	0

*AFC.
t—touchdown.
Leader based on average return, minimum 20.

AFC

Player, Team	No.	Yds.	Avg.	Long	TD
Adams, Michael, Pittsburgh	10	215	21.5	31	0
Anders, Kimble, Kansas City	1	0	0.0	0	0
Archie, Mike, Tennessee	2	24	12.0	15	0
Aska, Joe, Oakland	2	46	23.0	26	0
Bailey, Aaron, Indianapolis	55	1206	21.9	61	0
Barlow, Reggie, Jacksonville	10	267	26.7	t92	1
Baxter, Fred, N.Y. Jets..................	1	0	0.0	0	0
Beede, Frank, Seattle	1	0	0.0	0	0
Biekert, Greg, Oakland	1	16	16.0	16	0
Bieniemy, Eric, Cincinnati	34	789	23.2	t102	1
Blackwell, Will, Pittsburgh............	32	791	24.7	t97	1
Bordelon, Ben, San Diego	2	0	0.0	0	0
Brew, Dorian, Baltimore	5	88	17.6	24	0
Broussard, Steve, Seattle	50	1076	21.5	43	0
Brown, Reggie, Seattle	1	16	16.0	16	0
Brown, Tim, Oakland	1	7	7.0	7	0
Burns, Keith, Denver	4	45	11.3	18	0
Burris, Jeff, Buffalo	1	10	10.0	10	0
Byner, Earnest, Baltimore	1	0	0.0	0	0
Bynum, Kenny, San Diego	38	814	21.4	57	0
Canty, Chris, New England	4	115	28.8	63	0
Carter, Ki-Jana, Cincinnati	1	9	9.0	9	0
Chamberlain, Byron, Denver..........	1	13	13.0	13	0
Chrebet, Wayne, N.Y. Jets	1	5	5.0	5	0
Cline, Tony, Buffalo......................	1	0	0.0	0	0
Coates, Ben, New England............	1	20	20.0	20	0
Coleman, Andre, Sea.-Pit..............	27	552	20.4	29	0
Coons, Rob, Buffalo	1	12	12.0	12	0
Craver, Aaron, San Diego	3	68	22.7	27	0

Player, Team	No.	Yds.	Avg.	Long	TD
Cullors, Derrick, New England	15	386	25.7	t86	1
Daniels, Phillip, Seattle	1	-2	-2.0	-2	0
Davis, Travis, Jacksonville	1	9	9.0	9	0
Davis, Tyree, Seattle	2	25	12.5	23	0
Dillon, Corey, Cincinnati	6	182	30.3	58	0
Dunn, David, Cincinnati	19	487	25.6	85	0
Ethridge, Ray, Baltimore	2	37	18.5	22	0
Ferguson, Jason, N.Y. Jets	1	1	1.0	1	0
Galloway, Mitchell, Buffalo	6	130	21.7	30	0
Glenn, Aaron, N.Y. Jets	28	741	26.5	t96	1
Graham, Jay, Baltimore	6	115	19.2	24	0
Groce, Clif, Indianapolis	1	15	15.0	15	0
Hall, Tim, Oakland	9	182	20.2	34	0
Hallock, Ty, Jacksonville	1	6	6.0	6	0
Hamilton, Bobby, N.Y. Jets	1	0	0.0	0	0
Harmon, Ronnie, Tennessee	1	16	16.0	16	0
Harris, Anthony, Miami	1	0	0.0	0	0
Harris, Corey, Miami	11	224	20.4	34	0
Harris, Ronnie, Seattle	14	318	22.7	34	0
Harrison, Rodney, San Diego	1	40	40.0	t40	1
Hebron, Vaughn, Denver	43	1009	23.5	46	0
Hetherington, Chris, Indianapolis	2	23	11.5	23	0
Hollier, Dwight, Miami	1	0	0.0	0	0
Holmberg, Rob, Oakland	1	15	15.0	15	0
Holmes, Darick, Buffalo	23	430	18.7	36	0
Holmes, Priest, Baltimore	1	14	14.0	14	0
Horn, Joe, Kansas City	1	25	25.0	25	0
Howard, Desmond, Oakland	61	1318	21.6	45	0
Hughes, Danan, Kansas City	1	21	21.0	21	0
Hundon, James, Cincinnati	10	169	16.9	28	0
Ismail, Qadry, Miami	8	166	20.8	27	0
Jackson, Willie, Jacksonville	32	653	20.4	38	0
Jacquet, Nate, Indianapolis	8	156	19.5	27	0
Johnson, Leon, N.Y. Jets	12	319	26.6	t101	1
Jordan, Charles, Miami	1	6	6.0	6	0
Layman, Jason, Tennessee	1	5	5.0	5	0
Levitt, Chad, Oakland	1	12	12.0	12	0
Lewis, Jermaine, Baltimore	41	905	22.1	51	0
Logan, Mike, Jacksonville	10	236	23.6	39	0
Loville, Derek, Denver	5	136	27.2	61	0
Manusky, Greg, Kansas City	1	16	16.0	16	0
Mason, Derrick, Tennessee	26	551	21.2	54	0
May, Deems, Seattle	1	8	8.0	8	0
McCloud, Tyrus, Baltimore	1	0	0.0	0	0
McKnight, James, Seattle	1	14	14.0	14	0
McPhail, Jerris, Miami	15	314	20.9	39	0
Meggett, David, New England	33	816	24.7	61	0
Metcalf, Eric, San Diego	16	355	22.2	63	0
Mitchell, Pete, Jacksonville	2	17	8.5	12	0
Moore, Will, Jacksonville	1	36	36.0	36	0
Morris, Bam, Baltimore	1	23	23.0	23	0
Morton, Mike, Oakland	1	14	14.0	14	0
Moulds, Eric, Buffalo	43	921	21.4	53	0
Neal, Leon, Indianapolis	1	23	23.0	23	0
Neal, Lorenzo, N.Y. Jets	2	22	11.0	22	0
Parker, Chris, Jacksonville	1	9	9.0	9	0
Perry, Ed, Miami	1	7	7.0	7	0
Pike, Mark, Buffalo	1	11	11.0	11	0
Potts, Roosevelt, Miami	1	16	16.0	16	0
Rachal, Latorio, San Diego	15	336	22.4	30	0
Roan, Michael, Tennessee	2	20	10.0	12	0
Roe, James, Baltimore	9	189	21.0	33	0
Shedd, Kenny, Oakland	2	38	19.0	23	0
Singleton, Nate, Baltimore	4	64	16.0	19	0
Smith, Detron, Denver	1	0	0.0	0	0
Smith, Lamar, Seattle	1	14	14.0	14	0
Spikes, Irving, Miami	24	565	23.5	48	0
Strong, Mack, Seattle	1	16	16.0	16	0
Tasker, Steve, Buffalo	1	12	12.0	12	0
Thomas, Rodney, Tennessee	17	346	20.4	33	0
Truitt, Olanda, Oakland	2	51	25.5	30	0

Player, Team	No.	Yds.	Avg.	Long	TD
Twyner, Gunnard, Cincinnati	4	72	18.0	24	0
Van Dyke, Alex, N.Y. Jets	6	138	23.0	30	0
Vanover, Tamarick, Kansas City	51	1308	25.6	t94	1
Vrabel, Mike, Pittsburgh	1	0	0.0	0	0
Ward, Dedric, N.Y. Jets	2	10	5.0	11	0
Warren, Lamont, Indianapolis	1	19	19.0	19	0
Wiley, Marcellus, Buffalo	1	12	12.0	12	0
Wycheck, Frank, Tennessee	1	3	3.0	3	0

t—touchdown.
f—includes at least one fair catch.

NFC

Player, Team	No.	Yds.	Avg.	Long	TD
Alexander, Kevin, N.Y. Giants	3	30	10.0	15	0
Allred, John, Chicago	2	21	10.5	11	0
Alstott, Mike, Tampa Bay	1	0	0.0	0	0
Anthony, Reidel, Tampa Bay	25	592	23.7	51	0
Asher, Jamie, Washington	1	17	17.0	17	0
Bates, Michael, Carolina	47	1281	27.3	56	0
Bech, Brett, New Orleans	3	47	15.7	30	0
Beebe, Don, Green Bay	6	134	22.3	39	0
Bolden, Juran, Atlanta	5	106	21.2	34	0
Bouie, Kevin, Arizona	6	136	22.7	27	0
Bowie, Larry, Washington	1	15	15.0	15	0
Bownes, Fabien, Chicago	19	396	20.8	36	0
Burrough, John, Atlanta	1	6	6.0	6	0
Carter, Tony, Chicago	2	34	17.0	19	0
Clark, Willie, Philadelphia	1	39	39.0	t39	1
Darkins, Chris, Green Bay	4	68	17.0	20	0
Davis, Stephen, Washington	3	62	20.7	28	0
Davis, Troy, New Orleans	9	173	19.2	29	0
Drakeford, Tyronne, San Francisco	1	24	24.0	24	0
Dunn, Jason, Philadelphia	2	32	16.0	16	0
Dunn, Warrick, Tampa Bay	6	129	21.5	30	0
Edwards, Marc, San Francisco	1	30	30.0	30	0
Ellison, Jerry, Tampa Bay	2	61	30.5	49	0
Engram, Bobby, Chicago	2	27	13.5	20	0
Fann, Chad, San Francisco	1	0	0.0	0	0
Galbraith, Scott, Dallas	2	24	12.0	13	0
Garcia, Frank, Carolina	1	11	11.0	11	0
Gedney, Chris, Arizona	2	26	13.0	16	0
George, Ron, Minnesota	1	10	10.0	10	0
Gray, Mel, Ten.-Phi.*	9	193	21.4	33	0
Green, Darrell, Washington	1	9	9.0	9	0
Green, Harold, Atlanta	1	23	23.0	23	0
Greene, Scott, Carolina	3	18	6.0	8	0
Guliford, Eric, New Orleans	43	1128	26.2	t102	1
Hanspard, Byron, Atlanta	40	987	24.7	t99	2
Hayden, Aaron, Green Bay	6	141	23.5	35	0
Hughes, Tyrone, Chicago	43	1008	23.4	58	0
Johnson, Jimmie, Philadelphia	3	22	7.3	15	0
Johnson, LeShon, Arizona	0	26	...	26	0
Jones, Greg, Washington	1	6	6.0	6	0
Kennison, Eddie, St. Louis	1	14	14.0	7	0
Kinchen, Todd, Atlanta	1	18	18.0	18	0
Kirby, Terry, San Francisco	3	124	41.3	t101	1
Kozlowski, Brian, Atlanta	2	49	24.5	26	0
Lee, Amp, St. Louis	4	71	17.8	19	0
Levy, Chuck, San Francisco	36	793	22.0	59	0
Lewis, Chad, Philadelphia	1	11	11.0	11	0
Lewis, Thomas, N.Y. Giants	14	364	26.0	84	0
Logan, Marc, Washington	4	70	17.5	24	0
Marion, Brock, Dallas	10	311	31.1	49	0
Marshall, Anthony, Chicago	0	3	...	3	0
McCrary, Fred, New Orleans	2	26	13.0	15	0
Mickens, Terry, Green Bay	1	0	0.0	0	0
Milburn, Glyn, Detroit	55	1315	23.9	69	0
Mills, Ernie, Carolina	4	65	16.3	33	0
Mills, Sam, Carolina	2	12	6.0	12	0

Player, Team	No.	Yds.	Avg.	Long	TD
Mitchell, Brian, Washington	47	1094	23.3	t97	1
Moore, Ronald, St. Louis	1	17	17.0	17	0
Morrow, Harold, Minnesota	5	99	19.8	42	0
Owens, Dan, Atlanta	1	9	9.0	9	0
Owens, Terrell, San Francisco	2	31	15.5	23	0
Palmer, David, Minnesota	32	711	22.2	62	0
Patten, David, N.Y. Giants	8	123	15.4	26	0
Patton, Marvcus, Washington	1	10	10.0	10	0
Pegram, Erric, N.Y. Giants	22	382	17.4	50	0
Pierce, Aaron, N.Y. Giants	1	10	10.0	10	0
Poole, Tyrone, Carolina	1	5	5.0	5	0
Preston, Roell, Green Bay	7	211	30.1	43	0
Rasby, Walter, Carolina	3	32	10.7	12	0
Rhett, Errict, Tampa Bay	1	16	16.0	16	0
Rivers, Ron, Detroit	2	34	17.0	23	0
Ross, Jermaine, St. Louis	6	130	21.7	42	0
Russell, Matt, Detroit	1	0	0.0	0	0
Sanders, Deion, Dallas	1	18	18.0	18	0
Schroeder, Bill, Green Bay	24	562	23.4	40	0
Sharper, Darren, Green Bay	1	3	3.0	3	0
Smith, Cedric, Arizona	3	50	16.7	21	0
Smith, Eric, Chicago	10	196	19.6	28	0
Sparks, Phillippi, N.Y. Giants	1	8	8.0	8	0
Staley, Duce, Philadelphia	47	1139	24.2	57	0
Stone, Dwight, Carolina	3	76	25.3	37	0
Tate, Robert, Minnesota	10	196	19.6	36	0
Thomas, J.T., St. Louis	5	97	19.4	24	0
Thompson, David, St. Louis	49	1110	22.7	56	0
Tomich, Jared, New Orleans	1	0	0.0	0	0
Turner, Kevin, Philadelphia	3	48	16.0	22	0
Uwaezuoke, Iheanyi, S.F.	6	131	21.8	25	0
Vardell, Tommy, Detroit	1	15	15.0	15	0
Walker, Herschel, Dallas	50	1167	23.3	49	0
Walsh, Chris, Minnesota	1	10	10.0	10	0
Way, Charles, N.Y. Giants	2	46	23.0	30	0
Wetnight, Ryan, Chicago	1	9	9.0	9	0
White, Steve, Tampa Bay	1	0	0.0	0	0
Williams, Jay, St. Louis	1	10	10.0	10	0
Williams, Karl, Tampa Bay	15	277	18.5	28	0
Williams, Kevin, Arizona	59	1458	24.7	63	0
Williams, Moe, Minnesota	16	388	24.3	74	0
Witherspoon, Derrick, Philadelphia	9	171	19.0	28	0
Wyatt, Antwuan, Philadelphia	2	50	25.0	30	0
Zgonina, Jeff, St. Louis	1	5	5.0	5	0

*Includes both NFC and AFC statistics.
t—touchdown.
f—includes at least one fair catch.

PLAYERS WITH TWO CLUBS

Player, Team	No.	Yds.	Avg.	Long	TD
Coleman, Andre, Seattle	3	65	21.7	29	0
Coleman, Andre, Pittsburgh	24	487	20.3	28	0
Gray, Mel, Tennessee	8	185	23.1	33	0
Gray, Mel, Philadelphia	1	8	8.0	8	0

MISCELLANEOUS

CLUB RANKINGS BY YARDS

Team	OFFENSE Total	Rush	Pass	DEFENSE Total	Rush	Pass
Arizona	24	30	10	27	27	15
Atlanta	23	19	22	20	8	20
Baltimore	9	22	5	25	10	28
Buffalo	25	14	25	9	15	12
Carolina	26	15	26	15	22	9
Chicago	17	16	15	12	19	11
Cincinnati	10	9	13	28	29	21
Dallas	20	20	20	2	24	1
Denver	1	4	9	5	16	5
Detroit	2	2	12	14	18	13
Green Bay	4	12	3	7	20	8
Indianapolis	19	17	19	10	26	4
Jacksonville	7	18	4	23	13	24
Kansas City	14	5	24	11	7	16
Miami	11	29	2	26	17	25
Minnesota	8	6	14	29	23	29
New England	15	26	7	19	5	21
New Orleans	30	27	27	4	14	6
N.Y. Giants	27	7	28	18	3	26
N.Y. Jets	22	25	16	24	21	19
Oakland	13	23	8	30	30	30
Philadelphia	5	10	6	13	25	7
Pittsburgh	6	1	23	6	1	18
St. Louis	21	24	17	17	9	17
San Diego	28	28	21	21	11	22
San Francisco	12	8	18	1	2	2
Seattle	3	13	1	8	12	14
Tampa Bay	29	11	30	3	6	10
Tennessee	18	3	29	22	4	27
Washington	16	21	11	16	28	3

*NFL leader.

TAKEAWAYS/GIVEAWAYS

	TAKEAWAYS Int.	Fum.	Tot.	GIVEAWAYS Int.	Fum.	Tot.	Net Diff.
Washington	16	14	30	22	7	29	1
Green Bay	21	11	32	16	16	32	0
Detroit	17	8	25	17	11	28	-3
Dallas	7	12	19	12	11	23	-4
Philadelphia	14	12	26	16	16	32	-6
Chicago	13	17	30	22	19	41	-11
Carolina	11	11	22	24	15	39	-17
Arizona	15	5	20	22	20	42	-22
New Orleans	16	15	31	33	22	55	-24

AFC

	TAKEAWAYS Int.	Fum.	Tot.	GIVEAWAYS Int.	Fum.	Tot.	Net Diff.
Kansas City	21	13	34	10	10	20	14
Denver	18	13	31	11	10	21	10
New England	19	13	32	15	7	22	10
Jacksonville	14	15	29	9	11	20	9
Miami	10	17	27	12	8	20	7
Tennessee	14	18	32	13	13	26	6
N.Y. Jets	18	7	25	10	12	22	3
Cincinnati	13	10	23	9	13	22	1
Pittsburgh	20	14	34	19	14	33	1
Oakland	10	12	22	10	14	24	-2
Indianapolis	12	13	25	17	11	28	-3
Seattle	13	16	29	21	11	32	-3
Baltimore	17	11	28	16	17	33	-5
San Diego	15	11	26	21	14	35	-9
Buffalo	15	7	22	25	17	42	-20

NFC

	TAKEAWAYS Int.	Fum.	Tot.	GIVEAWAYS Int.	Fum.	Tot.	Net Diff.
N.Y. Giants	27	17	44	12	7	19	25
San Francisco	25	16	41	11	9	20	21
St. Louis	25	14	39	15	15	30	9
Minnesota	12	15	27	16	6	22	5
Atlanta	18	10	28	11	13	24	4
Tampa Bay	13	13	26	12	11	23	3

CLUB LEADERS

	Offense	Defense
First downs	Den. 340	S.F. 242
Rushing	Pit. 154	S.F. 67
Passing	Sea. 207	Dal. 139
Penalty	NYG 36	Was. 14
Rushes	Pit. 572	Den. 381
Net yards gained	Pit. 2479	Pit. 1318
Average gain	Det. 5.5	Pit. 3.3
Passes attempted	Sea. 609	Ind. 453
Completed	Sea. 359	Dal. 253
Percent completed	S.F. 64.4	S.F. 50.7
Total yards gained	Sea. 4187	Dal. 2717
Times sacked	Pit. 20	N.O. 59
Yards lost	Pit. 152	N.O. 408
Net yards gained	Sea. 3959	Dal. 2522
Net yards per pass play	Jac. 6.81	S.F. 4.70
Yards gained per completion	Oak. 13.41	N.E. 10.25
Combined net yards gained	Den. 5872	S.F. 4013
Percent total yards rushing	Ten. 49.1	Pit. 28.0
Percent total yards passing	Mia. 73.8	Dal. 55.8
Ball-control plays	Chi. 1128	Ind. 928
Average yards per play	Det. 5.64	S.F. 4.23
Avg. time of possession	Chi. 33:08	—
Third-down efficiency	Pit. 44.7	Den. 31.4
Interceptions	—	N.O. 33
Yards returned	—	Phi. 425
Returned for TD	—	Four tied 4
Punts	NYG 112	—
Yards punted	NYG 4531	—
Average yards per punt	N.O. 45.9	—
Punt returns	NYJ 59	Atl. 21
Yards returned	NYJ 674	Atl. 55
Average yds. per return	Den. 13.5	Atl. 2.6
Returned for TD	Den., S.D. 3	—
Kickoff returns	Oak. 81	Ari. 42
Yards returned	Cin. 1708	Ari. 945
Average yards per return	N.E. 25.2	Dal. 18.0
Returned for TD	Atl., NYJ 2	—
Total points scored	Den. 472	K.C. 232
Total TDs	Den. 55	K.C. 23
TDs rushing	Cin. 23	Pit., S.F. 5
TDs passing	G.B. 35	G.B., NYG 10
TDs on ret. and recov.	Den., S.D. 10	K.C. 0
Extra points	Den. 50	G.B. 18
2-point conversions	Min. 6	—
Safeties	K.C. 3	—
Field goals made	Dal. 34	Atl., Den. 14
Field goals attempted	Ind., NYJ 41	Den. 19
Percent successful	K.C. 96.3	T.B. 62.1

1997 STATISTICS Miscellaneous

OFFENSE

	Bal.	Buf.	Cin.	Den.	Ind.	Jac.	K.C.	Mia.	N.E.	NYJ	Oak.	Pit.	S.D.	Sea.	Ten.
First downs	292	268	310	340	301	308	315	311	267	291	263	326	251	331	288
Rushing	99	98	104	138	109	103	129	87	71	97	74	154	70	98	130
Passing	176	144	171	172	171	187	163	199	173	173	170	157	157	207	136
Penalty	17	26	35	30	21	18	23	25	23	21	19	15	21	26	22
Rushes	420	422	452	520	450	454	529	430	398	431	360	572	409	404	541
Net yards gained	1589	1782	1966	2378	1727	1720	2171	1343	1464	1485	1588	2479	1416	1800	2414
Average gain	3.8	4.2	4.3	4.6	3.8	3.8	4.1	3.1	3.7	3.4	4.4	4.3	3.5	4.5	4.5
Average yards per game	99.3	111.4	122.9	148.6	107.9	107.5	135.7	83.9	91.5	92.8	99.3	154.9	88.5	112.5	150.9
Passes attempted	586	546	504	513	523	504	493	576	532	564	529	466	565	609	420
Completed	338	293	302	287	317	313	281	332	321	319	294	253	291	359	220
Percent completed	57.7	53.7	59.9	55.9	60.6	62.1	57.0	57.6	60.3	56.6	55.6	54.3	51.5	58.9	52.4
Total yards gained	3929	3213	3603	3704	3560	3922	3129	3945	3808	3555	3944	3215	3475	4187	2704
Times sacked	37	46	46	35	62	40	32	22	30	48	58	20	51	36	32
Yards lost	227	338	287	210	418	218	236	153	258	313	430	152	386	228	199
Net yards gained	3702	2875	3316	3494	3142	3704	2893	3792	3550	3242	3514	3063	3089	3959	2505
Average yards per game	231.4	179.7	207.3	218.4	196.4	231.5	180.8	237.0	221.9	202.6	219.6	191.4	193.1	247.4	156.6
Net yards per pass play	5.94	4.86	6.03	6.38	5.37	6.81	5.51	6.34	6.32	5.30	5.99	6.30	5.01	6.14	5.54
Yards gained per completion	11.62	10.97	11.93	12.91	11.23	12.53	11.14	11.88	11.86	11.14	13.41	12.71	11.94	11.66	12.29
Combined net yards gained	5291	4657	5282	5872	4869	5424	5064	5135	5014	4727	5102	5542	4505	5759	4919
Percent total yards rushing	30.0	38.3	37.2	40.5	35.5	31.7	42.9	26.2	29.2	31.4	31.1	44.7	31.4	31.3	49.1
Percent total yards passing	70.0	61.7	62.8	59.5	64.5	68.3	57.1	73.8	70.8	68.6	68.9	55.3	68.6	68.7	50.9
Average yards per game	330.7	291.1	330.1	367.0	304.3	339.0	316.5	320.9	313.4	295.4	318.9	346.4	281.6	359.9	307.4
Ball-control plays	1043	1014	1002	1068	1035	998	1054	1028	960	1043	947	1058	1025	1049	993
Average yards per play	5.1	4.6	5.3	5.5	4.7	5.4	4.8	5.0	5.2	4.5	5.4	5.2	4.4	5.5	5.0
Average time of possession	28:30	27:59	27:56	32:07	32:56	29:40	31:16	30:29	28:08	29:42	26:24	32:05	29:22	30:47	31:27
Third-down efficiency	36.1	25.0	41.1	42.4	37.9	39.2	41.3	37.8	40.4	38.2	31.9	44.7	32.9	40.6	42.0
Had intercepted	16	25	9	11	17	9	10	12	15	10	10	19	21	21	13
Yards opponents returned	118	359	26	193	285	184	148	307	213	100	192	270	387	372	48
Returned by oppponents for TD	0	3	0	1	0	2	0	4	2	0	2	0	3	4	0
Punts	83	91	81	60	67	66	83	68	79	75	93	64	90	78	74
Yards punted	3540	3764	3471	2598	3034	2964	3489	2962	3569	3212	4189	2729	3972	3144	3081
Average yards per punt	42.7	41.4	42.9	43.3	45.3	44.9	42.0	43.6	45.2	42.8	45.0	42.6	44.1	40.3	41.6
Punt returns	42	39	26	41	31	36	35	32	45	59	27	32	47	37	32
Yards returned	564	346	201	555	248	412	383	335	467	674	210	222	489	248	244
Average yards per return	13.4	8.9	7.7	13.5	8.0	11.4	10.9	10.5	10.4	11.4	7.8	6.9	10.4	6.7	7.6
Returned for TD	2	0	0	3	0	0	1	0	0	1	0	0	3	0	0
Kickoff returns	71	78	74	54	68	58	54	63	53	54	81	67	75	76	58
Yards returned	1435	1538	1708	1203	1442	1233	1345	1298	1337	1236	1699	1493	1613	1550	1150
Average yards per return	20.2	19.7	23.1	22.3	21.2	21.3	24.9	20.6	25.2	22.9	21.0	22.3	21.5	20.4	19.8
Returned for TD	0	0	1	0	0	1	1	0	1	2	0	1	1	0	0
Fumbles	37	39	25	25	23	17	21	22	17	27	25	25	30	26	31
Lost	17	17	13	10	11	11	10	8	7	12	14	14	14	11	13
Out of bounds	3	1	2	3	3	2	2	2	1	2	1	2	0	3	3
Recovered for TD	0	0	0	0	0	0	0	1	0	0	0	1	1	0	0
Penalties	101	92	98	116	106	110	120	93	99	83	117	95	129	109	103
Yards penalized	777	742	877	1006	880	914	1035	783	845	678	976	861	1101	911	814
Total points scored	326	255	355	472	313	394	375	339	369	348	324	372	266	365	333
Total TDs	35	26	46	55	31	43	42	37	42	38	41	44	27	43	36
TDs rushing	7	12	23	18	10	20	15	18	6	10	9	19	5	13	17
TDs passing	25	14	21	27	16	20	20	16	31	20	29	22	12	26	15
TDs on returns and recoveries	3	0	2	10	5	3	7	3	5	8	3	3	10	4	4
Extra points	34	23	42	54	25	42	37	33	40	36	35	41	26	38	34
Safeties	1	1	0	0	1	0	3	0	1	0	1	0	0	1	0
Field goals made	26	24	12	28	32	31	26	28	25	28	13	22	26	22	27
Field goals attempted	34	30	16	39	41	36	27	36	29	41	22	25	31	28	35
Percent successful	76.5	80.0	75.0	71.8	78.0	86.1	96.3	77.8	86.2	68.3	59.1	88.0	83.9	78.6	77.1
2-Pt. conversions	2	2	1	4	4	1	2	0	0	0	2	1	0	1	2
Field goals blocked	2	1	1	2	0	0	0	1	0	1	2	1	3	1	0

DEFENSE

	Bal.	Buf.	Cin.	Den.	Ind.	Jac.	K.C.	Mia.	N.E.	NYJ	Oak.	Pit.	S.D.	Sea.	Ten.
First downs	306	265	351	258	280	318	278	299	322	301	345	285	308	286	292
Rushing	101	85	141	83	95	107	94	106	114	103	121	82	92	96	79
Passing	180	160	188	145	163	190	158	176	183	177	199	177	181	166	193
Penalty	25	20	22	30	22	21	26	17	25	21	25	26	35	24	20
Rushes	470	493	514	381	438	455	413	443	435	470	525	403	453	455	414
Net yards gained	1690	1792	2223	1803	2034	1734	1621	1813	1616	1899	2246	1318	1698	1731	1573
Average gain	3.6	3.6	4.3	4.7	4.6	3.8	3.9	4.1	3.7	4.0	4.3	3.3	3.7	3.8	3.8
Average yards per game	105.6	112.0	138.9	112.7	127.1	108.4	101.3	113.3	101.0	118.7	140.4	82.4	106.1	108.2	98.3
Passes attempted	556	502	542	526	453	532	507	530	619	558	552	554	568	462	543
Completed	332	287	309	290	261	320	271	329	368	304	324	295	297	276	321
Percent completed	59.7	57.2	57.0	55.1	57.6	60.2	53.5	62.1	59.5	54.5	58.7	53.2	52.3	59.7	59.1
Total yards gained	3966	3405	3668	3166	3067	3835	3618	3782	3772	3663	4109	3681	3632	3356	3898
Times sacked	42	46	35	44	37	48	54	31	45	29	31	48	27	42	35
Yards lost	293	344	209	298	247	331	359	231	303	242	239	294	164	238	240
Net yards gained	3673	3061	3459	2868	2820	3504	3259	3551	3469	3421	3870	3387	3468	3118	3658
Average yards per game	229.6	191.3	216.2	179.3	176.3	219.0	203.7	221.9	216.8	213.8	241.9	211.7	216.8	194.9	228.6
Net yards per pass play	6.14	5.59	5.99	5.03	5.76	6.04	5.81	6.33	5.22	5.83	6.64	5.63	5.83	6.19	6.33
Yards gained per completion	11.95	11.86	11.87	10.92	11.75	11.98	13.35	11.50	10.25	12.05	12.68	12.48	12.23	12.16	12.14
Combined net yards gained	5363	4853	5682	4671	4854	5238	4880	5364	5085	5320	6116	4705	5166	4849	5231
Percent total yards rushing	31.5	36.9	39.1	38.6	41.9	33.1	33.2	33.8	31.8	35.7	36.7	28.0	32.9	35.7	30.1
Percent total yards passing	68.5	63.1	60.9	61.4	58.1	66.9	66.8	66.2	68.2	64.3	63.3	72.0	67.1	64.3	69.9
Average yards per game	335.2	303.3	355.1	291.9	303.4	327.4	305.0	335.3	317.8	332.5	382.3	294.1	322.9	303.1	326.9
Ball-control plays	1068	1041	1091	951	928	1035	974	1004	1100	1057	1108	1005	1048	959	992
Average yards per play	5.0	4.7	5.2	4.9	5.2	5.1	5.0	5.3	4.6	5.0	5.5	4.7	4.9	5.1	5.3
Average time of possession	31:30	32:01	32:04	27:53	27:04	30:20	28:44	29:31	31:52	30:18	33:36	27:55	30:38	29:13	28:33
Third-down efficiency	40.3	35.4	44.9	31.4	41.7	45.1	31.6	42.8	38.6	31.6	39.0	44.7	38.5	33.3	39.0
Intercepted by	17	15	13	18	12	14	21	10	19	18	10	20	15	13	14
Yards returned by	241	157	183	319	234	145	432	92	366	379	149	253	257	196	328
Returned for TD	1	0	0	5	2	0	4	0	4	4	1	0	3	1	2
Punts	82	86	69	94	64	73	84	63	74	92	77	66	85	74	69
Yards punted	3611	3608	3082	4091	2948	3060	3468	2679	3288	3862	3035	2804	3702	3111	3007
Average yards per punt	44.0	42.0	44.7	43.5	46.1	41.9	41.3	42.5	44.4	42.0	39.4	42.5	43.6	42.0	43.6
Punt returns	53	44	35	26	43	29	39	43	38	47	52	23	39	38	36
Yards returned	460	366	407	235	491	241	255	323	437	459	431	271	416	463	430
Average yards per return	8.7	8.3	11.6	9.0	11.4	8.3	6.5	7.5	11.5	9.8	8.3	11.8	10.7	12.2	11.9
Returned for TD	0	0	2	1	0	0	0	0	0	0	0	0	0	2	0
Kickoff returns	58	55	67	89	64	77	80	53	75	54	48	74	63	77	71
Yards returned	1323	1385	1406	1827	1544	1730	1672	1018	1651	1134	1124	1556	1517	1779	1528
Average yards per return	22.8	25.2	21.0	20.5	24.1	22.5	20.9	19.2	22.0	21.0	23.4	21.0	24.1	23.1	21.5
Returned for TD	1	3	0	0	1	0	0	0	2	0	0	1	1	1	0
Fumbles	23	23	23	27	23	26	30	31	30	27	26	26	21	33	32
Recovered by	11	7	10	13	13	15	13	17	13	7	12	14	11	16	18
Out of bounds	2	3	2	1	0	3	2	3	2	0	2	5	3	5	4
Recovered for TD	0	0	0	0	0	0	0	0	1	0	0	0	0	0	1
Penalties	106	98	107	130	102	90	113	92	106	99	117	90	101	100	94
Yards penalized	828	992	951	1118	861	800	977	892	763	832	977	708	784	820	830
Total points scored	345	367	405	287	401	318	232	327	289	287	419	307	425	362	310
Total TDs	39	37	48	35	46	39	23	36	33	33	44	31	50	38	35
TDs rushing	17	11	15	10	18	12	8	9	16	9	19	5	12	10	12
TDs passing	20	17	30	20	26	24	15	23	14	23	21	24	31	19	21
TDs on returns and recoveries	2	9	3	5	2	3	0	4	3	1	4	2	7	9	2
Extra points	35	34	45	35	42	32	22	32	30	29	39	30	47	37	34
Safeties	1	0	0	0	1	0	0	1	0	2	0	1	1	1	0
Field goals made	24	37	24	14	27	17	24	25	20	18	38	29	25	31	22
Field goals attempted	34	46	29	19	31	25	33	35	29	27	43	35	26	34	30
Percent successful	70.6	80.4	82.8	73.7	87.1	68.0	72.7	71.4	69.0	66.7	88.4	82.9	96.2	91.2	73.3
2-Pt. conversions	2	0	0	0	0	1	0	2	1	2	2	2	1	2	0
Field goals blocked	1	0	0	0	1	1	0	0	1	1	3	0	1	0	4

OFFENSE

	Ari.	Atl.	Car.	Chi.	Dal.	Det.	G.B.	Min.	N.O.	NYG	Phi.	S.F.	St.L.	T.B.	Was.
First downs	295	281	284	305	279	304	325	293	229	273	326	294	271	249	300
Rushing	79	88	91	94	82	120	103	96	78	113	105	106	85	88	86
Passing	186	168	170	188	170	166	191	177	127	124	203	167	161	134	192
Penalty	30	25	23	23	27	18	31	20	24	36	18	21	25	27	22
Rushes	395	442	441	490	423	447	459	449	417	521	465	523	443	479	453
Net yards gained	1255	1643	1770	1746	1637	2464	1909	2041	1461	1988	1943	1969	1563	1934	1615
Average gain	3.2	3.7	4.0	3.6	3.9	5.5	4.2	4.5	3.5	3.8	4.2	3.8	3.5	4.0	3.6
Average yards per game	78.4	102.7	110.6	109.1	102.3	154.0	119.3	127.6	91.3	124.3	121.4	123.1	97.7	120.9	100.9
Passes attempted	602	484	534	595	553	540	523	540	458	474	587	432	526	404	547
Completed	317	273	289	336	314	304	309	319	228	249	330	278	271	224	283
Percent completed	52.7	56.4	54.1	56.5	56.8	56.3	59.1	59.1	49.8	52.5	56.2	64.4	51.5	55.4	51.7
Total yards gained	3953	3445	3156	3501	3454	3605	3896	3537	2901	2763	4009	3432	3524	2638	3581
Times sacked	78	54	44	43	39	41	26	33	50	32	64	44	44	32	33
Yards lost	495	372	311	260	313	271	191	224	317	238	362	289	326	196	198
Net yards gained	3458	3073	2845	3241	3141	3334	3705	3313	2584	2525	3647	3143	3198	2442	3383
Average yards per game	216.1	192.1	177.8	202.6	196.3	208.4	231.6	207.1	161.5	157.8	227.9	196.4	199.9	152.6	211.4
Net yards per pass play	5.09	5.71	4.92	5.08	5.31	5.74	6.75	5.78	5.09	4.99	5.60	6.60	5.61	5.60	5.83
Yards gained per completion	12.47	12.62	10.92	10.42	11.00	11.86	12.61	11.09	12.72	11.10	12.15	12.35	13.00	11.78	12.65
Combined net yards gained	4713	4716	4615	4990	4778	5798	5614	5354	4045	4513	5590	5112	4761	4376	4998
Percent total yards rushing	26.6	34.8	38.4	35.0	34.3	42.5	34.0	38.1	36.1	44.1	34.8	38.5	32.8	44.2	32.3
Percent total yards passing	73.4	65.2	61.6	65.0	65.7	57.5	66.0	61.9	63.9	55.9	65.2	61.5	67.2	55.8	67.7
Average yards per game	294.6	294.8	288.4	311.9	298.6	362.4	350.9	334.6	252.8	282.1	349.4	319.5	297.6	273.5	312.4
Ball-control plays	1075	980	1019	1128	1015	1028	1008	1022	925	1027	1116	999	1013	915	1034
Average yards per play	4.4	4.8	4.5	4.4	4.7	5.6	5.6	5.2	4.4	4.4	5.0	5.1	4.7	4.8	4.8
Average time of possession	29:02	31:29	29:43	33:08	29:53	28:37	30:05	29:46	27:47	29:27	31:09	32:28	29:47	29:22	29:27
Third-down efficiency	35.1	35.2	44.0	36.0	36.2	35.3	39.6	39.5	26.1	31.2	37.2	36.4	32.7	38.7	42.3
Had intercepted	22	11	24	22	12	17	16	16	33	12	16	11	15	12	22
Yards opponents returned	289	124	265	328	211	191	305	166	342	230	425	169	85	370	262
Returned by opponents for TD	2	1	2	1	1	2	3	0	1	2	4	2	0	4	1
Punts	92	89	85	96	86	86	75	81	88	112	88	79	95	84	85
Yards punted	4028	3498	3604	4077	3592	3576	3378	3407	4038	4531	3660	3182	3985	3578	3788
Average yards per punt	43.8	39.3	42.4	42.5	41.8	41.6	45.0	42.1	45.9	40.5	41.6	40.3	41.9	42.6	44.6
Punt returns	41	52	41	46	47	48	56	34	48	47	31	41	40	51	38
Yards returned	461	483	310	321	512	433	515	444	496	455	234	482	274	645	442
Average yards per return	11.2	9.3	7.6	7.0	10.9	9.0	9.2	13.1	10.3	9.7	7.5	11.8	6.9	12.6	11.6
Returned for TD	0	0	0	0	1	0	0	0	0	1	0	1	0	1	1
Kickoff returns	70	51	64	79	63	59	49	65	58	51	69	50	68	51	59
Yards returned	1696	1198	1500	1694	1520	1364	1119	1414	1374	963	1520	1133	1454	1075	1283
Average yards per return	24.2	23.5	23.4	21.4	24.1	23.1	22.8	21.8	23.7	18.9	22.0	22.7	21.4	21.1	21.7
Returned for TD	0	2	0	0	0	0	0	0	0	1	0	1	0	0	1
Fumbles	27	34	30	33	23	26	24	16	34	23	35	22	29	31	21
Lost	20	13	15	19	11	11	16	6	22	7	16	9	15	11	7
Out of bounds	0	5	4	2	2	3	1	1	0	4	2	0	3	3	2
Recovered for TD	0	0	0	0	0	0	0	0	0	0	0	1	0	0	0
Penalties	93	101	94	107	116	94	93	97	101	116	104	115	142	77	78
Yards penalized	775	773	763	867	1058	866	718	800	811	1005	866	979	1065	660	639
Total points scored	283	320	265	263	304	379	422	354	237	307	317	375	299	299	327
Total TDs	32	36	28	28	29	43	50	42	24	35	36	41	32	38	40
TDs rushing	9	8	11	14	6	19	9	14	9	14	11	16	15	15	12
TDs passing	19	26	17	14	19	19	35	26	13	16	22	20	14	21	22
TDs on returns and recoveries	4	2	0	0	4	5	6	2	2	5	3	5	3	2	6
Extra points	31	35	27	25	26	40	49	39	23	28	34	40	32	32	39
Safeties	0	0	1	1	0	1	0	0	0	1	0	0	0	0	0
Field goals made	19	23	22	21	34	26	24	19	23	22	22	29	25	13	16
Field goals attempted	29	27	26	26	38	29	30	27	27	32	31	36	37	17	24
Percent successful	65.5	85.2	84.6	80.8	89.5	89.7	80.0	70.4	85.2	68.8	71.0	80.6	67.6	76.5	66.7
2-Pt. conversions	3	0	2	5	2	1	1	6	1	1	1	2	0	0	0
Field goals blocked	0	0	1	1	1	0	2	0	1	0	0	2	1	0	0

1997 STATISTICS Miscellaneous

DEFENSE

	Ari.	Atl.	Car.	Chi.	Dal.	Det.	G.B.	Min.	N.O.	NYG	Phi.	S.F.	St.L.	T.B.	Was.
First downs	298	274	290	281	281	268	288	325	280	310	286	242	296	265	291
Rushing	112	76	112	97	104	98	105	104	95	82	115	67	84	96	129
Passing	167	180	163	156	139	152	156	195	168	195	150	145	177	155	149
Penalty	19	18	15	28	38	18	27	26	17	33	21	30	35	14	14
Rushes	524	409	497	421	511	471	443	442	496	432	476	386	440	420	508
Net yards gained	2180	1666	1973	1858	1994	1833	1876	1983	1764	1451	2009	1366	1687	1617	2212
Average gain	4.2	4.1	4.0	4.4	3.9	3.9	4.2	4.5	3.6	3.4	4.2	3.5	3.8	3.9	4.4
Average yards per game	136.3	104.1	123.3	116.1	124.6	114.6	117.3	123.9	110.3	90.7	125.6	85.4	105.4	101.1	138.3
Passes attempted	491	496	490	476	473	507	563	542	518	596	490	509	543	518	513
Completed	279	275	260	273	253	281	288	336	293	325	259	258	288	325	267
Percent completed	56.8	55.4	53.1	57.4	53.5	55.4	51.2	62.0	56.6	54.5	52.9	50.7	53.0	62.7	52.0
Total yards gained	3461	3794	3253	3289	2717	3401	3225	3957	3289	3957	3201	3011	3675	3342	3098
Times sacked	34	55	36	38	38	43	41	44	59	54	43	54	38	44	37
Yards lost	215	354	246	259	195	287	274	253	408	341	278	364	296	331	280
Net yards gained	3246	3440	3007	3030	2522	3114	2951	3704	2881	3616	2923	2647	3379	3011	2818
Average yards per game	202.9	215.0	187.9	189.4	157.6	194.6	184.4	231.5	180.1	226.0	182.7	165.4	211.2	188.2	176.1
Net yards per pass play	6.18	6.24	5.72	5.89	4.94	5.66	4.89	6.32	4.99	5.56	5.48	4.70	5.82	5.36	5.12
Yards gained per completion	12.41	13.80	12.51	12.05	10.74	12.10	11.20	11.78	11.23	12.18	12.36	11.67	12.76	10.28	11.60
Combined net yards gained	5426	5106	4980	4888	4516	4947	4827	5687	4645	5067	4932	4013	5066	4628	5030
Percent total yards rushing	40.2	32.6	39.6	38.0	44.2	37.1	38.9	34.9	38.0	28.6	40.7	34.0	33.3	34.9	44.0
Percent total yards passing	59.8	67.4	60.4	62.0	55.8	62.9	61.1	65.1	62.0	71.4	59.3	66.0	66.7	65.1	56.0
Average yards per game	339.1	319.1	311.3	305.5	282.3	309.2	301.7	355.4	290.3	316.7	308.3	250.8	316.6	289.3	314.4
Ball-control plays	1049	960	1023	935	1022	1021	1047	1028	1073	1082	1009	949	1021	982	1058
Average yards per play	5.2	5.3	4.9	5.2	4.4	4.8	4.6	5.5	4.3	4.7	4.9	4.2	5.0	4.7	4.8
Average time of possession	30:58	28:31	30:17	26:52	30:07	31:23	29:55	30:14	32:13	30:33	28:51	27:32	30:13	30:38	30:33
Third-down efficiency	34.2	36.6	36.9	31.7	38.2	36.0	33.2	41.5	40.5	34.4	36.9	34.7	35.3	34.1	33.3
Intercepted by	15	18	11	13	7	17	21	12	16	27	14	25	25	13	16
Yards returned by	231	114	72	60	130	309	329	141	194	503	186	366	281	95	222
Returned for TD	3	0	0	0	1	3	3	0	0	4	1	1	1	0	3
Punts	94	90	88	81	95	97	90	70	92	89	87	83	82	88	95
Yards punted	4130	3835	3756	3526	4142	4296	3828	2932	3668	3748	3603	3473	3648	3661	4038
Average yards per punt	43.9	42.6	42.7	43.5	43.6	44.3	42.5	41.9	39.9	42.1	41.4	41.8	44.5	41.6	42.5
Punt returns	40	21	38	52	40	51	32	49	50	40	48	41	60	42	33
Yards returned	441	55	428	727	365	434	255	566	706	378	515	307	618	388	237
Average yards per return	11.0	2.6	11.3	14.0	9.1	8.5	8.0	11.6	14.1	9.5	10.7	7.5	10.3	9.2	7.2
Returned for TD	1	0	2	2	0	1	0	1	1	0	1	0	1	0	0
Kickoff returns	42	52	55	52	65	61	78	67	51	49	66	82	54	44	67
Yards returned	945	1167	1276	1237	1172	1269	1599	1398	1139	1163	1548	1746	1262	957	1515
Average yards per return	22.5	22.4	23.2	23.8	18.0	20.8	20.5	20.9	22.3	23.7	23.5	21.3	23.4	21.8	22.6
Returned for TD	1	0	1	0	0	0	0	0	0	1	0	0	1	1	0
Fumbles	16	27	26	25	27	24	25	31	31	33	25	24	27	21	36
Recovered	5	10	11	17	12	8	11	15	15	17	12	16	14	13	14
Out of bounds	1	3	2	1	1	3	2	3	2	2	0	1	2	0	2
Recovered for TD	0	0	1	0	0	0	0	0	1	0	0	0	0	0	0
Penalties	113	115	97	93	99	112	114	81	110	122	86	91	133	93	96
Yards penalized	981	872	757	763	757	841	945	668	895	1056	708	742	1064	814	849
Total points scored	379	361	314	421	314	306	282	359	327	265	372	265	359	263	289
Total TDs	42	45	36	50	36	33	30	42	35	30	43	31	39	29	32
TDs rushing	13	18	12	18	12	15	16	13	11	17	16	5	10	10	15
TDs passing	23	24	17	25	20	15	10	28	21	10	20	23	26	13	14
TDs on returns and recoveries	6	3	7	7	4	3	4	1	3	3	7	3	3	6	3
Extra points	36	43	35	47	36	30	24	37	33	27	42	29	38	29	31
Safeties	0	1	0	0	0	1	0	0	0	0	0	1	1	1	0
Field goals made	30	14	21	24	20	25	24	23	28	19	24	16	26	18	21
Field goals attempted	35	20	25	32	27	32	30	30	36	25	33	20	31	29	25
Percent successful	85.7	70.0	84.0	75.0	74.1	78.1	80.0	76.7	77.8	76.0	72.7	80.0	83.9	62.1	84.0
2-Pt. conversions	1	4	1	2	2	1	6	1	0	1	0	0	0	7	3
Field goals blocked	1	2	1	0	0	0	1	1	1	0	0	0	2	2	0

1997 STATISTICS *Miscellaneous*

	AFC Offense Total	AFC Offense Average	AFC Defense Total	AFC Defense Average	NFC Offense Total	NFC Offense Average	NFC Defense Total	NFC Defense Average	NFL Total	NFL Average
First downs	4462	297.5	4494	299.6	4307	287.2	4276	285.1	8770	292.3
Rushing	1561	104.1	1499	99.9	1414	94.3	1476	98.4	2975	99.2
Passing	2559	170.6	2636	175.7	2524	168.3	2447	163.1	5083	169.4
Penalty	342	22.8	359	23.9	370	24.7	353	23.5	712	23.7
Rushes	6792	452.8	6763	450.9	6847	456.5	6876	458.4	13639	454.6
Net yards gained	27322	1821.5	26791	1786.1	26938	1795.9	27469	1831.3	54260	1808.7
Average gain	...	4.0	...	4.0	...	3.9	...	4.0	...	4.0
Average yards per game	...	113.8	...	111.6	...	112.2	...	114.5	...	113.0
Passes attempted	7930	528.7	8004	533.6	7799	519.9	7725	515.0	15729	524.3
Completed	4520	301.3	4584	305.6	4324	288.3	4260	284.0	8844	294.8
Percent completed	...	57.0	...	57.3	...	55.4	...	55.1	...	56.2
Total yards gained	53893	3592.9	54618	3641.2	51395	3426.3	50670	3378.0	105288	3509.6
Times sacked	595	39.7	594	39.6	657	43.8	658	43.9	1252	41.7
Yards lost	4053	270.2	4032	268.8	4360	290.7	4381	292.1	8413	280.4
Net yards gained	49840	3322.7	50586	3372.4	47035	3135.7	46289	3085.9	96875	3229.2
Average yards per game	...	207.7	...	210.8	...	196.0	...	192.9	...	201.8
Net yards per pass play	...	5.85	...	5.88	...	5.56	...	5.52	...	5.70
Yards gained per completion	...	11.92	...	11.91	...	11.89	...	11.89	...	11.91
Combined net yards gained	77162	5144.1	77377	5158.5	73973	4931.5	73758	4917.2	151135	5037.8
Percent total yards rushing	...	35.4	...	34.6	...	36.4	...	37.2	...	35.9
Percent total yards passing	...	64.6	...	65.4	...	63.6	...	62.8	...	64.1
Average yards per game	...	321.5	...	322.4	...	308.2	...	307.3	...	314.9
Ball-control plays	15317	1021.1	15361	1024.1	15303	1020.2	15259	1017.3	30620	1020.7
Average yards per play	...	5.0	...	5.0	...	4.8	...	4.8	...	4.9
Third-down efficiency	...	38.1	...	38.6	...	36.4	...	35.9	...	37.2
Interceptions	218	14.5	229	15.3	261	17.4	250	16.7	479	16.0
Yards returned	3202	213.5	3731	248.7	3762	250.8	3233	215.5	6964	232.1
Returned for TD	21	1.4	27	1.8	26	1.7	20	1.3	47	1.6
Punts	1152	76.8	1152	76.8	1321	88.1	1321	88.1	2473	82.4
Yards punted	49718	3314.5	49356	3290.4	55922	3728.1	56284	3752.3	105640	3521.3
Average yards per punt	...	43.2	...	42.8	...	42.3	...	42.6	...	42.7
Punt returns	561	37.4	585	39.0	661	44.1	637	42.5	1222	40.7
Yards returned	5598	373.2	5685	379.0	6507	433.8	6420	428.0	12105	403.5
Average yards per return	...	10.0	...	9.7	...	9.8	...	10.1	...	9.9
Returned for TD	10	0.7	5	0.3	5	0.3	10	0.7	15	0.5
Kickoff returns	984	65.6	1005	67.0	906	60.4	885	59.0	1890	63.0
Yards returned	21280	1418.7	22194	1479.6	20307	1353.8	19393	1292.9	41587	1386.2
Average yards per return	...	21.6	...	22.1	...	22.4	...	21.9	...	22.0
Returned for TD	8	0.5	9	0.6	6	0.4	5	0.3	14	0.5
Fumbles	391	26.1	401	26.7	408	27.2	398	26.5	799	26.6
Lost	182	12.1	190	12.7	198	13.2	190	12.7	380	12.7
Out of bounds	30	2.0	37	2.5	32	2.1	25	1.7	62	2.1
Own recovered for TD	3	0.2	2	0.1	1	0.1	2	0.1	4	0.1
Opponents recovered by	188	12.5	180	12.0	190	12.7	198	13.2	378	12.6
Opponents recovered for TD	19	1.3	16	1.1	15	1.0	18	1.2	34	1.1
Penalties	1572	104.8	1545	103.0	1528	101.9	1555	103.7	3100	103.3
Yards penalized	13200	880.0	13133	875.5	12645	843.0	12712	847.5	25845	861.5
Total points scored	5206	347.1	5081	338.7	4751	316.7	4876	325.1	9957	331.9
Total TDs	586	39.1	567	37.8	534	35.6	553	36.9	1120	37.3
TDs rushing	202	13.5	183	12.2	182	12.1	201	13.4	384	12.8
TDs passing	314	20.9	328	21.9	303	20.2	289	19.3	617	20.6
TDs on returns and recoveries	70	4.7	56	3.7	49	3.3	63	4.2	119	4.0
Extra points	540	34.5	523	33.9	500	31.7	517	32.3	1040	33.1
Safeties	9	0.6	8	0.5	4	0.3	5	0.3	13	0.4
Field goals made	370	24.7	375	25.0	338	22.5	333	22.2	708	23.6
Field goals attempted	470	31.3	476	31.7	436	29.1	430	28.7	906	30.2
Percent successful	...	78.7	...	78.8	...	77.5	...	77.4	...	41.2
2-Pt. conversions	22	1.5	15	1.0	25	1.7	32	2.1	47	1.6
Field goals blocked	15	1.0	13	0.9	9	0.6	11	0.7	24	0.8

1997 STATISTICS *Miscellaneous*

Player, Team	Opponent	Date	Att.	Yds.	TD
Corey Dillon, Cincinnati	vs. Tennessee	December 4	39	246	4
Napoleon Kaufman, Oakland	vs. Denver	October 19	28	227	1
Barry Sanders, Detroit	vs. Indianapolis	November 23	24	216	2
Eddie George, Tennessee	vs. Oakland	August 31*	35	216	1
Barry Sanders, Detroit	at Tampa Bay	October 12	24	215	2
Terrell Davis, Denver	vs. Cincinnati	September 21	27	215	1
Terrell Davis, Denver	at Buffalo	October 26*	42	207	1
Curtis Martin, New England	vs. N.Y. Jets	September 14*	40	199	1
Dorsey Levens, Green Bay	vs. Dallas	November 23	33	190	1
Barry Sanders, Detroit	vs. N.Y. Jets	December 21	23	184	1
Gary Brown, San Diego	at Oakland	October 5	36	181	1
Terrell Davis, Denver	at San Diego	November 30	26	178	1
Bam Morris, Baltimore	at Washington	October 26	36	176	1
Terrell Davis, Denver	vs. New England	October 6	32	171	2
Robert Smith, Minnesota	at Buffalo	August 31	16	169	1
Gary Brown, San Diego	vs. Indianapolis	October 26	28	169	1
Barry Sanders, Detroit	vs. Chicago	November 27	19	167	3
Jerome Bettis, Pittsburgh	vs. Indianapolis	October 12	30	164	1
Napoleon Kaufman, Oakland	vs. St. Louis	September 28	26	162	1
Mario Bates, New Orleans	vs. Detroit	September 21	29	162	2
Jamal Anderson, Atlanta	vs. St. Louis	November 2	20	162	1
Barry Sanders, Detroit	at Chicago	September 14	19	161	0
Robert Smith, Minnesota	vs. Indianapolis	December 21	17	160	0
Adrian Murrell, N.Y. Jets	at Cincinnati	September 28	40	156	1
Jay Graham, Baltimore	vs. Philadelphia	November 16*	35	154	0
Jamal Anderson, Atlanta	at Arizona	December 21	33	152	0
Fred Lane, Carolina	vs. Oakland	November 2	28	147	3
Jerome Bettis, Pittsburgh	at Arizona	November 30*	36	142	3
Terry Allen, Washington	at Carolina	August 31	25	141	2
Garrison Hearst, San Francisco	at Carolina	September 29	28	141	1
Napoleon Kaufman, Oakland	at Atlanta	September 14	14	140	2
Barry Sanders, Detroit	vs. Green Bay	September 28	28	139	0
Steve Broussard, Seattle	vs. Tennessee	October 5	6	138	2
Fred Lane, Carolina	at Dallas	December 8	34	138	0
Barry Sanders, Detroit	at Minnesota	December 14	19	138	0
Barry Sanders, Detroit	at Miami	December 7	30	137	1
Jerome Bettis, Pittsburgh	at Baltimore	October 5	28	137	0
Jerome Bettis, Pittsburgh	at Cincinnati	October 19	34	135	1
Anthony Johnson, Carolina	vs. Washington	August 31	20	134	0
Jerome Bettis, Pittsburgh	vs. Washington	September 7	27	134	1
Marshall Faulk, Indianapolis	at N.Y. Jets	December 7	23	133	1
Emmitt Smith, Dallas	at Arizona	September 7*	19	132	0
Robert Smith, Minnesota	at Green Bay	September 21	28	132	1
Adrian Murrell, N.Y. Jets	at Seattle	August 31	24	131	0
Bam Morris, Baltimore	at N.Y. Jets	November 2*	31	130	0
Warrick Dunn, Tampa Bay	at Detroit	September 7	24	130	1
Eddie George, Tennessee	at Baltimore	December 14	26	129	0
Antowain Smith, Buffalo	vs. Indianapolis	September 21	12	129	3
Terrell Davis, Denver	at Kansas City	November 16	34	127	0
Corey Dillon, Cincinnati	vs. Dallas	December 14	26	127	1
Emmitt Smith, Dallas	at Philadelphia	October 26	25	126	0
Napoleon Kaufman, Oakland	at N.Y. Jets	September 21	27	126	0
Warrick Dunn, Tampa Bay	at Green Bay	October 5	16	125	1
Jerome Bettis, Pittsburgh	vs. Denver	December 7	24	125	0
Eddie George, Tennessee	vs. Washington	October 19	31	125	2
Robert Smith, Minnesota	vs. Philadelphia	September 28	22	125	1
Lawrence Phillips, St. Louis	vs. New Orleans	August 31	26	125	3
Terry Allen, Washington	at Chicago	November 2	20	125	0
Corey Dillon, Cincinnati	vs. San Diego	November 2	19	123	1
Raymont Harris, Chicago	at Green Bay	September 1	13	122	2
Terry Allen, Washington	vs. Jacksonville	September 28	36	122	0
Eddie George, Tennessee	vs. N.Y. Giants	November 9	32	122	1
Dorsey Levens, Green Bay	vs. Miami	September 14	21	121	0
Curtis Martin, New England	at Indianapolis	September 7	25	121	1
Raymont Harris, Chicago	at Dallas	September 28	29	120	0
Warrick Dunn, Tampa Bay	at N.Y. Giants	November 30	24	120	0
Robert Smith, Minnesota	vs. Carolina	October 12	23	120	1
Fred Lane, Carolina	vs. Green Bay	December 14	19	119	1

Player, Team	Opponent	Date	Att.	Yds.	TD
Warrick Dunn, Tampa Bay	vs. Chicago	December 21	16	119	0
Marshall Faulk, Indianapolis	vs. Green Bay	November 16	17	116	0
Eddie George, Tennessee	at Seattle	October 5	26	116	0
Raymont Harris, Chicago	vs. Tampa Bay	November 23	33	116	1
Charlie Garner, Philadelphia	at Washington	December 21	18	115	2
Tiki Barber, N.Y. Giants	at Philadelphia	December 7	21	114	0
Charles Way, N.Y. Giants	vs. Arizona	November 16	14	114	0
Jerome Bettis, Pittsburgh	vs. Baltimore	November 9	24	114	1
Jerome Bettis, Pittsburgh	at Jacksonville	September 22	21	114	0
Corey Dillon, Cincinnati	at Philadelphia	November 30	19	114	0
Barry Sanders, Detroit	at New Orleans	September 21	18	113	0
Jerald Moore, St. Louis	at Carolina	December 20	27	113	0
Napoleon Kaufman, Oakland	at Seattle	October 26	17	112	1
Fred Lane, Carolina	vs. New Orleans	November 30	13	112	1
Marshall Faulk, Indianapolis	vs. Cincinnati	November 9	18	110	0
Adrian Murrell, N.Y. Jets	at New England	September 14*	18	110	0
Eddie George, Tennessee	at Dallas	November 27	34	110	0
Napoleon Kaufman, Oakland	at San Diego	November 16	20	109	0
Karim Abdul-Jabbar, Miami	at Baltimore	October 19	22	108	3
Dorsey Levens, Green Bay	at Minnesota	December 1	31	108	2
Barry Sanders, Detroit	vs. Minnesota	November 16	19	108	0
Barry Sanders, Detroit	at Buffalo	October 5	25	107	0
Terrell Davis, Denver	at Seattle	September 7	21	107	1
Dorsey Levens, Green Bay	at Detroit	September 28	16	107	0
Ricky Watters, Philadelphia	at Dallas	September 15	20	106	0
Eddie George, Tennessee	at Miami	September 7*	23	106	1
Eddie George, Tennessee	vs. Cincinnati	October 12	30	106	0
Raymont Harris, Chicago	at Miami	October 27*	25	106	1
Garrison Hearst, San Francisco	at Atlanta	October 19	18	105	0
Barry Sanders, Detroit	at Washington	November 9	15	105	1
Barry Sanders, Detroit	at Green Bay	November 2	23	105	0
Barry Sanders, Detroit	vs. N.Y. Giants	October 19*	24	105	1
Terrell Davis, Denver	vs. Carolina	November 9	21	104	0
Curtis Martin, New England	at Minnesota	November 2	21	104	0
Garrison Hearst, San Francisco	vs. Dallas	November 2	22	104	1
Tshimanga Biakabutuka, Carolina	vs. Atlanta	October 26	23	104	2
Ricky Watters, Philadelphia	vs. Washington	October 5	31	104	2
Thurman Thomas, Buffalo	vs. N.Y. Jets	November 30	18	104	0
Ki-Jana Carter, Cincinnati	at Denver	September 21	13	104	1
Dorsey Levens, Green Bay	at Indianapolis	November 16	14	103	2
Terrell Davis, Denver	vs. St. Louis	September 14	21	103	0
Jerome Bettis, Pittsburgh	at Kansas City	November 3	17	103	0
Karim Abdul-Jabbar, Miami	vs. N.Y. Jets	November 9	25	103	2
Tyrone Wheatley, N.Y. Giants	at Arizona	October 12	22	103	1
James Stewart, Jacksonville	vs. Philadelphia	October 12	15	102	5
Marshall Faulk, Indianapolis	at Minnesota	December 21	23	102	2
Warrick Dunn, Tampa Bay	at Minnesota	September 14	16	101	1
Terrell Davis, Denver	vs. Kansas City	August 31	26	101	1
Robert Smith, Minnesota	vs. Detroit	December 14	20	101	1
Raymont Harris, Chicago	vs. Green Bay	October 12	27	101	1
Terrell Davis, Denver	vs. Seattle	November 2	21	101	0
Jerome Bettis, Pittsburgh	vs. Cincinnati	November 16	25	101	0
Dorsey Levens, Green Bay	at New England	October 27	26	100	1

*Overtime game.

PASSING

Player, Team	Opponent	Date	Att.	Comp.	Yds.	TD	Int.
Warren Moon, Seattle	vs. Oakland	October 26	44	28	409	5	2
Tony Banks, St. Louis	at Atlanta	November 2	34	23	401	2	1
Dan Marino, Miami	at New England	November 23	60	38	389	0	3
Jake Plummer, Arizona	at N.Y. Giants	November 16	33	22	388	1	2
Boomer Esiason, Cincinnati	at Philadelphia	November 30	47	27	378	4	1
Jeff George, Oakland	at N.Y. Jets	September 21	38	26	374	3	0
Dan Marino, Miami	at N.Y. Jets	October 12	38	27	372	2	0
Brett Favre, Green Bay	at Indianapolis	November 16	25	18	363	3	2
Stan Humphries, San Diego	vs. Baltimore	September 28	26	17	358	3	2
Troy Aikman, Dallas	vs. Tennessee	November 27	42	27	356	2	3
Erik Kramer, Chicago	vs. N.Y. Jets	November 16	60	32	354	2	3
Eric Zeier, Baltimore	at Cincinnati	December 21	41	28	349	2	0
Erik Kramer, Chicago	at Miami	October 27*	50	32	343	2	0
Paul Justin, Indianapolis	vs. Green Bay	November 16	30	24	340	1	0

Player, Team	Opponent	Date	Att.	Comp.	Yds.	TD	Int.
Drew Bledsoe, New England	vs. San Diego	August 31	39	26	340	4	0
Kent Graham, Arizona	at Tampa Bay	September 28	52	31	339	1	2
Jake Plummer, Arizona	vs. Washington	December 7	38	19	337	4	2
Steve Young, San Francisco	vs. Atlanta	September 21	24	17	336	2	0
Brad Johnson, Minnesota	vs. Tampa Bay	September 14	44	29	334	1	0
Vinny Testaverde, Baltimore	vs. Miami	October 19	47	32	331	1	0
Scott Mitchell, Detroit	vs. Tampa Bay	September 7	50	29	331	2	1
Kerry Collins, Carolina	vs. Kansas City	September 21	47	24	328	1	4
Dan Marino, Miami	vs. Tennessee	September 7*	43	24	324	0	0
Vinny Testaverde, Baltimore	vs. Jacksonville	August 31	41	24	322	3	3
Glenn Foley, N.Y. Jets	at Miami	November 9	48	25	322	1	1
Neil O'Donnell, N.Y. Jets	vs. Miami	October 12	37	24	319	2	0
Vinny Testaverde, Baltimore	at Tennessee	September 21	37	23	318	3	0
Kordell Stewart, Pittsburgh	vs. Jacksonville	October 26*	42	25	317	2	1
Mark Brunell, Jacksonville	at Buffalo	December 14	32	24	317	0	1
Mark Brunell, Jacksonville	vs. Baltimore	November 30	40	25	317	1	1
Jeff Blake, Cincinnati	at Baltimore	September 7	45	25	317	1	2
Troy Aikman, Dallas	at N.Y. Giants	October 5	52	34	317	1	2
Rich Gannon, Kansas City	at Jacksonville	November 9	50	29	314	0	2
Bobby Hoying, Philadelphia	vs. Cincinnati	November 30	42	26	313	4	1
Drew Bledsoe, New England	at Minnesota	November 2	42	27	313	2	1
Elvis Grbac, Kansas City	at Oakland	September 8	35	21	312	2	0
Brad Johnson, Minnesota	at N.Y. Jets	November 23	35	24	312	3	0
Jim Harbaugh, Indianapolis	at New England	November 30	41	22	310	2	0
Dan Marino, Miami	vs. Detroit	December 7	39	24	310	2	1
John Elway, Denver	at Oakland	October 19	46	26	309	1	0
Brett Favre, Green Bay	vs. St. Louis	November 9	37	18	306	1	2
Mark Brunell, Jacksonville	vs. Pittsburgh	September 22	42	24	306	1	0
Jeff George, Oakland	at Carolina	November 2	38	24	304	2	1
Kordell Stewart, Pittsburgh	vs. Denver	December 7	29	18	303	3	1
Eric Zeier, Baltimore	vs. Seattle	December 7	28	17	302	1	0
Drew Bledsoe, New England	vs. Chicago	September 21	37	24	301	2	0

*Overtime game.

RECEIVING

Player, Team	Opponent	Date	Rec.	Yds.	TD
Isaac Bruce, St. Louis	at Atlanta	November 2	10	233	2
Yancey Thipgen, Pittsburgh	vs. Jacksonville	October 26*	11	196	0
Frank Sanders, Arizona	at N.Y. Giants	November 16	9	188	1
Rob Moore, Arizona	vs. Pittsburgh	November 30*	8	188	0
Yancey Thipgen, Pittsburgh	vs. Denver	December 7	6	175	3
Shannon Sharpe, Denver	vs. Carolina	November 9	8	174	0
Johnnie Morton, Detroit	at Miami	December 7	9	171	1
Antonio Freeman, Green Bay	at Carolina	December 14	10	166	2
Tim Brown, Oakland	vs. Jacksonville	December 21	14	164	0
Ricky Proehl, Chicago	at Detroit	November 27	4	164	1
Jimmy Smith, Jacksonville	vs. Pittsburgh	September 22	10	164	1
Robert Brooks, Green Bay	at Detroit	September 28	9	164	0
Terry Glenn, New England	vs. Green Bay	October 27	7	163	0
Tim Brown, Oakland	at Carolina	November 2	10	163	0
Yancey Thipgen, Pittsburgh	at Baltimore	October 5	7	162	0
Andre Rison, Kansas City	at Oakland	September 8	8	162	1
Shannon Sharpe, Denver	vs. San Diego	December 21	8	162	0
Antonio Freeman, Green Bay	vs. St. Louis	November 9	7	160	1
Tim Brown, Oakland	at Tennessee	August 31*	8	158	3
Jimmy Smith, Jacksonville	vs. Tennessee	November 16	8	158	0
Tim Brown, Oakland	vs. Kansas City	September 8	11	155	0
Tony Martin, San Diego	vs. Baltimore	September 28	4	155	3
Tim Brown, Oakland	at N.Y. Jets	September 21	10	153	1
Michael Irvin, Dallas	at Pittsburgh	August 31	7	153	2
Keenan McCardell, Jacksonville	vs. New England	December 7	11	152	2
Derrick Alexander, Baltimore	vs. Seattle	December 7	6	150	0
Jake Reed, Minnesota	at N.Y. Jets	November 23	8	150	2
James Jett, Oakland	at N.Y. Jets	September 21	5	148	2
Wesley Walls, Carolina	at Atlanta	September 7	7	147	0
Rob Moore, Arizona	at Tampa Bay	September 28	8	147	1
Chris Calloway, N.Y. Giants	at Detroit	October 19*	5	145	1
Isaac Bruce, St. Louis	at New Orleans	December 7	9	144	2
Michael Jackson, Baltimore	vs. Jacksonville	August 31	8	143	1
Andre Reed, Buffalo	vs. Minnesota	August 31	7	142	0
Shannon Sharpe, Denver	vs. Oakland	November 24	10	142	0

Player, Team	Opponent	Date	Rec.	Yds.	TD
Rob Moore, Arizona	at N.Y. Giants	November 16	8	139	0
Irving Fryar, Philadelphia	vs. San Francisco	November 10	9	138	0
O.J. McDuffie, Miami	vs. Chicago	October 27*	7	137	0
O.J. McDuffie, Miami	vs. Tennessee	September 7*	8	135	0
Jake Reed, Minnesota	vs. Philadelphia	September 28	6	134	1
Ricky Proehl, Chicago	at Minnesota	November 9	9	132	1
Jake Reed, Minnesota	vs. Tampa Bay	September 14	6	131	0
Yancey Thigpen, Pittsburgh	vs. Baltimore	November 9	6	130	1
Herman Moore, Detroit	vs. Minnesota	November 16	10	130	1
Rod Smith, Denver	vs. New England	October 6	5	130	0
Darnay Scott, Cincinnati	vs. Baltimore	December 21	6	129	1
Amp Lee, St. Louis	at Washington	November 30	6	128	1
Rod Smith, Denver	vs. St. Louis	September 14	4	126	2
Tim Brown, Oakland	vs. Miami	November 30	8	125	1
Michael Westbrook, Washington	vs. N.Y. Giants	November 23*	9	125	0
Troy Brown, New England	at N.Y. Jets	October 19	5	125	1
Irving Fryar, Philadelphia	vs. Green Bay	September 7	8	125	0
Carl Pickens, Cincinnati	at Denver	September 21	8	125	0
Michael Timpson, Philadelphia	at N.Y. Giants	August 31	9	125	0
Troy Brown, New England	vs. Chicago	September 21	6	124	1
Irving Fryar, Philadelphia	at Jacksonville	October 12	10	124	3
Randal Hill, New Orleans	vs. Arizona	December 14	5	124	1
Jermaine Lewis, Baltimore	at Tennessee	September 21	8	124	1
Rod Smith, Denver	vs. Kansas City	August 31	5	122	0
Antonio Freeman, Green Bay	vs. Minnesota	September 21	7	122	2
Irving Fryar, Philadelphia	vs. Cincinnati	November 30	7	122	0
Randal Hill, New Orleans	at Chicago	October 5	5	121	1
Cris Carter, Minnesota	at Buffalo	August 31	8	121	2
Keenan McCardell, Jacksonville	at Dallas	October 19	7	120	1
Sean Dawkins, Indianapolis	at New England	November 30	7	120	1
Andre Hastings, New Orleans	vs. St. Louis	December 7	6	120	1
Quinn Early, Buffalo	at Green Bay	December 20	7	120	0
Irving Fryar, Philadelphia	at Minnesota	September 28	9	120	1
Johnnie Morton, Detroit	vs. Chicago	November 27	7	120	1
Herman Moore, Detroit	at Tampa Bay	October 12	5	120	0
Yancey Thigpen, Pittsburgh	at Cincinnati	October 19	6	120	1
Jake Reed, Minnesota	at Green Bay	September 21	9	119	2
Shannon Sharpe, Denver	at Atlanta	September 28	6	119	1
Derrick Mayes, Green Bay	at Indianapolis	November 16	3	119	0
Michael Irvin, Dallas	vs. Tennessee	November 27	5	118	2
Jake Reed, Minnesota	at Chicago	September 7	12	118	1
Ricky Proehl, Chicago	vs. N.Y. Jets	November 16	11	118	1
James Hundon, Cincinnati	at Philadelphia	November 30	5	118	2
Andre Rison, Kansas City	vs. San Francisco	November 30	5	117	2
Michael Irvin, Dallas	at Cincinnati	December 14	9	117	0
Joey Galloway, Seattle	vs. Oakland	October 26	7	117	3
Jimmy Smith, Jacksonville	vs. N.Y. Giants	September 7	8	117	0
Cris Carter, Minnesota	vs. New England	November 2	8	116	1
Irving Fryar, Philadelphia	vs. Pittsburgh	November 23	7	116	1
Herman Moore, Detroit	at Buffalo	October 5	8	116	0
Rickey Dudley, Oakland	vs. New Orleans	November 9	5	116	0
Keenan McCardell, Jacksonville	at Oakland	December 21	7	116	1
Rod Smith, Denver	at Pittsburgh	December 7	4	115	2
Herman Moore, Detroit	vs. Atlanta	August 31	7	115	2
Curtis Conway, Chicago	vs. Buffalo	December 7	7	115	0
Rod Smith, Denver	at Kansas City	November 16	7	114	0
Rod Smith, Denver	vs. Seattle	November 2	5	114	1
Rob Moore, Arizona	vs. Washington	December 7	5	114	3
Andre Reed, Buffalo	at Kansas City	September 14	4	113	1
Jimmy Smith, Jacksonville	vs. Kansas City	November 9	4	112	0
Darnay Scott, Cincinnati	vs. Dallas	December 14	4	112	1
Rob Moore, Arizona	at Baltimore	November 23	8	112	0
Herman Moore, Detroit	at New Orleans	September 21	11	111	1
Derrick Alexander, Baltimore	at Cincinnati	December 21	5	111	1
Ed McCaffrey, Denver	at San Diego	November 30	7	111	2
O.J. McDuffie, Miami	at New England	November 23	9	110	0
Rae Carruth, Carolina	vs. Kansas City	September 21	8	110	1
Amp Lee, St. Louis	at Oakland	September 28	10	109	1
Eric Metcalf, San Diego	vs. Atlanta	December 7	8	109	0
Curtis Conway, Chicago	at St. Louis	December 14	7	109	1
Keenan McCardell, Jacksonville	at Cincinnati	November 23	8	109	0
Bert Emanuel, Atlanta	vs. St. Louis	November 2	6	108	2

Player, Team	Opponent	Date	Rec.	Yds.	TD
Shawn Jefferson, New England	at Minnesota	November 2	4	108	1
Dedric Ward, N.Y. Jets	at Miami	November 9	6	108	0
Rob Moore, Arizona	vs. Dallas	September 7*	6	108	0
Rob Moore, Arizona	vs. Minnesota	October 5	8	108	0
Terance Mathis, Atlanta	at Carolina	October 26	8	107	0
Tim Brown, Oakland	at Seattle	October 26	7	107	0
Cris Carter, Minnesota	at Chicago	September 7	9	107	0
Rae Carruth, Carolina	at Minnesota	October 12	6	107	1
Wesley Walls, Carolina	at St. Louis	November 23	8	106	0
Jimmy Smith, Jacksonville	at Cincinnati	November 23	5	106	0
Jimmy Smith, Jacksonville	at Baltimore	August 31	6	106	2
Joey Galloway, Seattle	vs. San Diego	September 21	5	106	1
Rickey Dudley, Oakland	vs. St. Louis	September 28	5	106	2
Charles Johnson, Pittsburgh	at Philadelphia	November 23	7	106	0
Warrick Dunn, Tampa Bay	vs. Miami	September 21	6	106	1
Charles Jordan, Miami	at Oakland	November 30	5	106	2
Michael Irvin, Dallas	vs. Chicago	September 28	6	105	1
Tim Tindale, Buffalo	at N.Y. Jets	September 7	4	105	0
Frank Sanders, Arizona	at Cincinnati	August 31	6	105	0
Cris Carter, Minnesota	at N.Y. Jets	November 23	6	105	0
Horace Copeland, Tampa Bay	vs. Detroit	October 12	6	105	0
Jermaine Lewis, Baltimore	vs. Miami	October 19	6	105	0
Herman Moore, Detroit	vs. Green Bay	September 28	6	105	0
Derrick Alexander, Baltimore	vs. Cincinnati	September 7	8	104	0
Amp Lee, St. Louis	at Green Bay	November 9	5	104	0
Keyshawn Johnson, N.Y. Jets	vs. Minnesota	November 23	9	104	0
Wayne Chrebet, N.Y. Jets	vs. Miami	October 12	5	104	1
Quinn Early, Buffalo	at Tennessee	November 23	8	103	2
Barry Sanders, Detroit	vs. Tampa Bay	September 7	8	102	1
Johnnie Morton, Detroit	vs. Tampa Bay	September 7	4	102	1
Rocket Ismail, Carolina	vs. New Orleans	November 30	6	102	0
Yancey Thigpen, Pittsburgh	vs. Cincinnati	November 16	5	101	1
Joey Galloway, Seattle	vs. San Francisco	December 21	6	101	2
Rob Moore, Arizona	at Philadelphia	October 19*	6	101	0
James McKnight, Seattle	vs. Oakland	October 26	4	100	1
Jeff Graham, N.Y. Jets	at Seattle	August 31	3	100	2
Kevin Alexander, N.Y. Giants	vs. Cincinnati	October 26	5	100	0
Curtis Conway, Chicago	at Miami	October 27*	6	100	0
Napoleon Kaufman, Oakland	vs. San Diego	October 5	3	100	1
Chris Sanders, Tennessee	at Baltimore	December 14	7	100	0
Tony Martin, San Diego	vs. Seattle	November 9	5	100	2
Charles Jordan, Miami	at Green Bay	September 14	4	100	1
Ken Dilger, Indianapolis	vs. Miami	December 14	5	100	3

*Overtime game.

OFFENSE

TOTAL SCORES

Team	Series	TD Rush	TD Pass	Total TDs	TD Efficiency Pct.	FGM	Total Scores	Scoring Efficiency Pct.
Jacksonville	63	19	14	33	52.38	23	56	88.89
San Francisco	58	15	14	29	50.00	24	53	91.38
Green Bay	60	8	24	32	53.33	20	52	86.67
Denver	57	17	13	30	52.63	20	50	87.72
Miami	56	17	7	24	42.86	24	48	85.71
Dallas	54	5	14	19	35.19	27	46	85.19
Pittsburgh	53	18	15	33	62.26	13	46	86.79
Indianapolis	52	10	13	23	44.23	21	44	84.62
Kansas City	49	15	14	29	59.18	15	44	89.80
Minnesota	51	11	19	30	58.82	14	44	86.27
Philadelphia	51	11	15	26	50.98	18	44	86.27
Atlanta	48	8	17	25	52.08	18	43	89.58
Tennessee	46	15	9	24	52.17	18	42	91.30
New England	48	4	21	25	52.08	17	42	87.50
N.Y. Jets	55	8	13	21	38.18	21	42	76.36
Washington	47	12	16	28	59.57	13	41	87.23
Detroit	49	13	12	25	51.02	15	40	81.63
Cincinnati	40	17	14	31	77.50	8	39	97.50
N.Y. Giants	42	14	11	25	59.52	13	38	90.48
Baltimore	42	7	13	20	47.62	18	38	90.48
St. Louis	49	13	9	22	44.90	14	36	73.47
Seattle	44	9	11	20	45.45	16	36	81.82
Carolina	45	8	13	21	46.67	15	36	80.00
Tampa Bay	46	12	14	26	56.52	8	34	73.91
Chicago	46	12	7	19	41.30	14	33	71.74
Arizona	41	9	11	20	48.78	13	33	80.49
Buffalo	38	10	7	17	44.74	14	31	81.58
San Diego	40	5	5	10	25.00	19	29	72.50
Oakland	36	5	15	20	55.56	8	28	77.78
New Orleans	30	7	8	15	50.00	11	26	86.67
Totals	1436	334	388	722	50.28	492	1214	84.54
Average	47.9	11.1	12.9	24.1	50.28	16.4	40.5	84.54

SCORING EFFICIENCY

Team	Series	TD Rush	TD Pass	Total TDs	TD Efficiency Pct.	FGM	Total Scores	Scoring Efficiency Pct.
Cincinnati	40	17	14	31	77.50	8	39	97.50
San Francisco	58	15	14	29	50.00	24	53	91.38
Tennessee	46	15	9	24	52.17	18	42	91.30
N.Y. Giants	42	14	11	25	59.52	13	38	90.48
Baltimore	42	7	13	20	47.62	18	38	90.48
Kansas City	49	15	14	29	59.18	15	44	89.80
Atlanta	48	8	17	25	52.08	18	43	89.58
Jacksonville	63	19	14	33	52.38	23	56	88.89
Denver	57	17	13	30	52.63	20	50	87.72
New England	48	4	21	25	52.08	17	42	87.50
Washington	47	12	16	28	59.57	13	41	87.23
Pittsburgh	53	18	15	33	62.26	13	46	86.79
Green Bay	60	8	24	32	53.33	20	52	86.67
New Orleans	30	7	8	15	50.00	11	26	86.67
Minnesota	51	11	19	30	58.82	14	44	86.27
Philadelphia	51	11	15	26	50.98	18	44	86.27
Miami	56	17	7	24	42.86	24	48	85.71
Dallas	54	5	14	19	35.19	27	46	85.19
Indianapolis	52	10	13	23	44.23	21	44	84.62
Seattle	44	9	11	20	45.45	16	36	81.82
Detroit	49	13	12	25	51.02	15	40	81.63
Buffalo	38	10	7	17	44.74	14	31	81.58
Arizona	41	9	11	20	48.78	13	33	80.49
Carolina	45	8	13	21	46.67	15	36	80.00
Oakland	36	5	15	20	55.56	8	28	77.78
N.Y. Jets	55	8	13	21	38.18	21	42	76.36
Tampa Bay	46	12	14	26	56.52	8	34	73.91
St. Louis	49	13	9	22	44.90	14	36	73.47
San Diego	40	5	5	10	25.00	19	29	72.50
Chicago	46	12	7	19	41.30	14	33	71.74
Totals	1436	334	388	722	50.28	492	1214	84.54
Average	47.9	11.1	12.9	24.1	50.28	16.4	40.5	84.54

1997 STATISTICS *Miscellaneous*

TOTAL SCORES

Team	Series	TD Rush	TD Pass	Total TDs	TD Efficiency Pct.	FGM	Total Scores	Scoring Efficiency Pct.
Tampa Bay	38	8	6	14	36.84	13	27	71.05
Denver	35	6	13	19	54.29	9	28	80.00
San Francisco	35	5	14	19	54.29	9	28	80.00
Detroit	39	11	5	16	41.03	16	32	82.05
St. Louis	41	9	10	19	46.34	13	32	78.05
Green Bay	42	13	7	20	47.62	13	33	78.57
Kansas City	42	7	9	16	38.10	17	33	78.57
N.Y. Jets	45	9	12	21	46.67	12	33	73.33
Carolina	44	13	10	23	52.27	10	33	75.00
N.Y. Giants	42	17	5	22	52.38	14	36	85.71
Atlanta	42	13	15	28	66.67	9	37	88.10
Seattle	42	9	9	18	42.86	19	37	88.10
Washington	43	14	9	23	53.49	14	37	86.05
New England	51	16	9	25	49.02	13	38	74.51
Miami	47	8	13	21	44.68	18	39	82.98
Tennessee	51	8	16	24	47.06	16	40	78.43
Baltimore	48	15	10	25	52.08	15	40	83.33
Dallas	49	11	15	26	53.06	17	43	87.76
Jacksonville	48	12	18	30	62.50	13	43	89.58
Buffalo	50	9	12	21	42.00	25	46	92.00
New Orleans	53	10	14	24	45.28	22	46	86.79
Philadelphia	51	16	13	29	56.86	18	47	92.16
Pittsburgh	54	5	17	22	40.74	25	47	87.04
Arizona	54	12	16	28	51.85	21	49	90.74
Chicago	58	13	16	29	50.00	21	50	86.21
Indianapolis	53	12	19	31	58.49	19	50	94.34
Minnesota	58	11	21	32	55.17	18	50	86.21
San Diego	57	11	19	30	52.63	21	51	89.47
Cincinnati	63	14	23	37	58.73	17	54	85.71
Oakland	61	17	13	30	49.18	25	55	90.16
Totals	1436	334	388	722	50.28	492	1214	84.54
Average	47.9	11.1	12.9	24.1	50.28	16.4	40.5	84.54

SCORING EFFICIENCY

Team	Series	TD Rush	TD Pass	Total TDs	TD Efficiency Pct.	FGM	Total Scores	Scoring Efficiency Pct.
Tampa Bay	38	8	6	14	36.84	13	27	71.05
N.Y. Jets	45	9	12	21	46.67	12	33	73.33
New England	51	16	9	25	49.02	13	38	74.51
Carolina	44	13	10	23	52.27	10	33	75.00
St. Louis	41	9	10	19	46.34	13	32	78.05
Tennessee	51	8	16	24	47.06	16	40	78.43
Green Bay	42	13	7	20	47.62	13	33	78.57
Kansas City	42	7	9	16	38.10	17	33	78.57
Denver	35	6	13	19	54.29	9	28	80.00
San Francisco	35	5	14	19	54.29	9	28	80.00
Detroit	39	11	5	16	41.03	16	32	82.05
Miami	47	8	13	21	44.68	18	39	82.98
Baltimore	48	15	10	25	52.08	15	40	83.33
N.Y. Giants	42	17	5	22	52.38	14	36	85.71
Cincinnati	63	14	23	37	58.73	17	54	85.71
Washington	43	14	9	23	53.49	14	37	86.05
Chicago	58	13	16	29	50.00	21	50	86.21
Minnesota	58	11	21	32	55.17	18	50	86.21
New Orleans	53	10	14	24	45.28	22	46	86.79
Pittsburgh	54	5	17	22	40.74	25	47	87.04
Dallas	49	11	15	26	53.06	17	43	87.76
Atlanta	42	13	15	28	66.67	9	37	88.10
Seattle	42	9	9	18	42.86	19	37	88.10
San Diego	57	11	19	30	52.63	21	51	89.47
Jacksonville	48	12	18	30	62.50	13	43	89.58
Oakland	61	17	13	30	49.18	25	55	90.16
Arizona	54	12	16	28	51.85	21	49	90.74
Buffalo	50	9	12	21	42.00	25	46	92.00
Philadelphia	51	16	13	29	56.86	18	47	92.16
Indianapolis	53	12	19	31	58.49	19	50	94.34
Totals	1436	334	388	722	50.28	492	1214	84.54
Average	47.9	11.1	12.9	24.1	50.28	16.4	40.5	84.54

1997 STATISTICS Miscellaneous

HISTORY

Championship games

Year-by-year standings

Super Bowls

Pro Bowls

Records

Statistical leaders

Coaching records

Hall of Fame

The Sporting News awards

Team by team

CHAMPIONSHIP GAMES

RESULTS

HISTORY Championship games

Sea.	Date	Winner (Share)	Loser (Share)	Score	Site	Attendance
1933	Dec. 17	Chicago Bears ($210.34)	N.Y. Giants ($140.22)	23-21	Chicago	26,000
1934	Dec. 9	N.Y. Giants ($621)	Chicago Bears ($414.02)	30-13	N.Y. Giants	35,059
1935	Dec. 15	Detroit ($313.35)	N.Y. Giants ($200.20)	26-7	Detroit	15,000
1936	Dec. 13	Green Bay ($250)	Boston Redskins ($180)	21-6	N.Y. Giants	29,545
1937	Dec. 12	Washington ($225.90)	Chicago Bears ($127.78)	28-21	Chicago	15,870
1938	Dec. 11	N.Y. Giants ($504.45)	Green Bay ($368.81)	23-17	N.Y. Giants	48,120
1939	Dec. 10	Green Bay ($703.97)	N.Y. Giants ($455.57)	27-0	Milwaukee	32,279
1940	Dec. 8	Chicago Bears ($873)	Washington ($606)	73-0	Washington	36,034
1941	Dec. 21	Chicago Bears ($430)	N.Y. Giants ($288)	37-9	Chicago	13,341
1942	Dec. 13	Washington ($965)	Chicago Bears ($637)	14-6	Washington	36,006
1943	Dec. 26	Chicago Bears ($1,146)	Washington ($765)	41-21	Chicago	34,320
1944	Dec. 17	Green Bay ($1,449)	N.Y. Giants ($814)	14-7	N.Y. Giants	46,016
1945	Dec. 16	Cleveland Rams ($1,469)	Washington ($902)	15-14	Cleveland	32,178
1946	Dec. 15	Chicago Bears ($1,975)	N.Y. Giants ($1,295)	24-14	N.Y. Giants	58,346
1947	Dec. 28	Chi. Cardinals ($1,132)	Philadelphia ($754)	28-21	Chicago	30,759
1948	Dec. 19	Philadelphia ($1,540)	Chi. Cardinals ($874)	7-0	Philadelphia	36,309
1949	Dec. 18	Philadelphia ($1,094)	L.A. Rams ($739)	14-0	L.A. Rams	27,980
1950	Dec. 24	Cleveland Browns ($1,113)	L.A. Rams ($686)	30-28	Cleveland	29,751
1951	Dec. 23	L. A. Rams ($2,108)	Cleve. Browns ($1,483)	24-17	L.A. Rams	57,522
1952	Dec. 28	Detroit ($2,274)	Cleveland Browns ($1,712)	17-7	Cleveland	50,934
1953	Dec. 27	Detroit ($2,424)	Cleveland Browns ($1,654)	17-16	Detroit	54,577
1954	Dec. 26	Cleveland Browns ($2,478)	Detroit ($1,585)	56-10	Cleveland	43,827
1955	Dec. 26	Cleveland Browns ($3,508)	L.A. Rams ($2,316)	38-14	L.A. Rams	85,693
1956	Dec. 30	N.Y. Giants ($3,779)	Chicago Bears ($2,485)	47-7	N.Y. Giants	56,836
1957	Dec. 29	Detroit ($4,295)	Cleveland Browns ($2,750)	59-14	Detroit	55,263
1958	Dec. 28	Baltimore ($4,718)	N.Y. Giants ($3,111)	23-17*	N.Y. Giants	64,185
1959	Dec. 27	Baltimore ($4,674)	N.Y. Giants ($3,083)	31-16	Baltimore	57,545
1960	Dec. 26	Philadelphia ($5,116)	Green Bay ($3,105)	17-13	Philadelphia	67,325
1961	Dec. 31	Green Bay ($5,195)	N.Y. Giants ($3,339)	37-0	Green Bay	39,029
1962	Dec. 30	Green Bay ($5,888)	N.Y. Giants ($4,166)	16-7	N.Y. Giants	64,892
1963	Dec. 29	Chicago Bears ($5,899)	N.Y. Giants ($4,218)	14-10	Chicago	45,801
1964	Dec. 27	Cleveland Browns ($8,052)	Baltimore ($5,571)	27-0	Cleveland	79,544
1965	Jan. 2	Green Bay ($7,819)	Cleveland Browns ($5,288)	23-12	Green Bay	50,777
1966	Jan. 1	Green Bay ($9,813)	Dallas ($6,527)	34-27	Dallas	74,152
1967	Dec. 31	Green Bay ($7,950)	Dallas ($5,299)	21-17	Green Bay	50,861
1968	Dec. 29	Baltimore ($9,306)	Cleveland Browns ($5,963)	34-0	Cleveland	78,410
1969	Jan. 4	Minnesota ($7,930)	Cleveland Browns ($5,118)	27-7	Minnesota	46,503
1970	Jan. 3	Dallas ($8,500)	San Francisco ($5,500)	17-10	San Francisco	59,364
1971	Jan. 2	Dallas ($8,500)	San Francisco ($5,500)	14-3	Dallas	63,409
1972	Dec. 31	Washington ($8,500)	Dallas ($5,500)	26-3	Washington	53,129
1973	Dec. 30	Minnesota ($8,500)	Dallas ($5,500)	27-10	Dallas	64,422
1974	Dec. 29	Minnesota ($8,500)	L.A. Rams ($5,500)	14-10	Minnesota	48,444
1975	Jan. 4	Dallas ($8,500)	L.A. Rams ($5,500)	37-7	L.A. Rams	88,919
1976	Dec. 26	Minnesota ($8,500)	L.A. Rams ($5,500)	24-13	Minnesota	48,379
1977	Jan. 1	Dallas ($9,000)	Minnesota ($9,000)	23-6	Dallas	64,293
1978	Jan. 7	Dallas ($9,000)	L.A. Rams ($9,000)	28-0	L.A. Rams	71,086
1979	Jan. 6	L.A. Rams ($9,000)	Tampa Bay ($9,000)	9-0	Tampa Bay	72,033
1980	Jan. 11	Philadelphia ($9,000)	Dallas ($9,000)	20-7	Philadelphia	70,696
1981	Jan. 10	San Francisco ($9,000)	Dallas ($9,000)	28-27	San Francisco	60,525
1982	Jan. 22	Washington ($18,000)	Dallas ($18,000)	31-17	Washington	55,045
1983	Jan. 8	Washington ($18,000)	San Francisco ($18,000)	24-21	Washington	55,363
1984	Jan. 6	San Francisco ($18,000)	Chicago Bears ($18,000)	23-0	San Francisco	61,040
1985	Jan. 12	Chicago Bears ($18,000)	L.A. Rams ($18,000)	24-0	Chicago	63,522
1986	Jan. 11	N. Y. Giants ($18,000)	Washington ($18,000)	17-0	N.Y. Giants	76,633
1987	Jan. 17	Washington ($18,000)	Minnesota ($18,000)	17-10	Washington	55,212
1988	Jan. 8	San Francisco ($18,000)	Chicago Bears ($18,000)	28-3	Chicago	64,830
1989	Jan. 14	San Francisco ($18,000)	L.A. Rams ($18,000)	30-3	San Francisco	64,769
1990	Jan. 20	N. Y. Giants ($18,000)	San Francisco ($18,000)	15-13	San Francisco	65,750
1991	Jan. 12	Washington ($18,000)	Detroit ($18,000)	41-10	Washington	55,585
1992	Jan. 17	Dallas ($18,000)	San Francisco ($18,000)	30-20	San Francisco	64,920
1993	Jan. 23	Dallas ($23,500)	San Francisco ($23,500)	38-21	Dallas	64,902
1994	Jan. 15	San Francisco ($26,000)	Dallas ($26,000)	38-28	San Francisco	69,125
1995	Jan. 14	Dallas ($27,000)	Green Bay ($27,000)	38-27	Dallas	65,135
1996	Jan. 12	Green Bay ($29,000)	Carolina ($29,000)	30-13	Green Bay	60,216
1997	Jan. 11	Green Bay ($30,000)	San Francisco ($30,000)	23-10	San Francisco	68,987

*Sudden-death overtime.

– 292 –

COMPOSITE STANDINGS

	W	L	Pct.	PF	PA		W	L	Pct.	PF	PA
Philadelphia Eagles	4	1	.800	79	48	Phoenix Cardinals*	1	1	.500	28	28
Green Bay Packers	10	3	.769	303	177	San Francisco 49ers	5	7	.417	245	222
Baltimore Colts	3	1	.750	88	60	Cleveland Browns	4	7	.364	224	253
Detroit Lions	4	2	.667	139	141	New York Giants	5	11	.313	240	322
Minnesota Vikings	4	2	.667	108	80	Los Angeles Rams‡	3	9	.250	123	270
Washington Redskins†	7	5	.583	222	255	Carolina Panthers	0	1	.000	13	30
Chicago Bears	7	6	.538	286	245	Tampa Bay Buccaneers	0	1	.000	0	9
Dallas Cowboys	8	8	.500	361	319						

*Both games played when franchise was in Chicago; won 28-21, lost 7-0.
†One game played when franchise was in Boston; lost 21-6.
‡One game played when franchise was in Cleveland; won 15-14.

AFL (1960-1969); AFC (1970-1997)
RESULTS

Sea.	Date	Winner (Share)	Loser (Share)	Score	Site	Attendance
1960	Jan. 1	Houston ($1,025)	L.A. Chargers ($718)	24-16	Houston	32,183
1961	Dec. 24	Houston ($1,792)	San Diego ($1,111)	10-3	San Diego	29,556
1962	Dec. 23	Dallas Texans ($2,206)	Houston ($1,471)	20-17*	Houston	37,981
1963	Jan. 5	San Diego ($2,498)	Boston Patriots ($1,596)	51-10	San Diego	30,127
1964	Dec. 26	Buffalo ($2,668)	San Diego ($1,738)	20-7	Buffalo	40,242
1965	Dec. 26	Buffalo ($5,189)	San Diego ($3,447)	23-0	San Diego	30,361
1966	Jan. 1	Kansas City ($5,309)	Buffalo ($3,799)	31-7	Buffalo	42,080
1967	Dec. 31	Oakland ($6,321)	Houston ($4,996)	40-7	Oakland	53,330
1968	Dec. 29	N.Y. Jets ($7,007)	Oakland ($5,349)	27-23	New York	62,627
1969	Jan. 4	Kansas City ($7,755)	Oakland ($6,252)	17-7	Oakland	53,564
1970	Jan. 3	Baltimore ($8,500)	Oakland ($5,500)	27-17	Baltimore	54,799
1971	Jan. 2	Miami ($8,500)	Baltimore ($5,500)	21-0	Miami	76,622
1972	Dec. 31	Miami ($8,500)	Pittsburgh ($5,500)	21-17	Pittsburgh	50,845
1973	Dec. 30	Miami ($8,500)	Oakland ($5,500)	27-10	Miami	79,325
1974	Dec. 29	Pittsburgh ($8,500)	Oakland ($5,500)	24-13	Oakland	53,800
1975	Jan. 4	Pittsburgh ($8,500)	Oakland ($5,500)	16-10	Pittsburgh	50,609
1976	Dec. 28	Oakland ($8,500)	Pittsburgh ($5,500)	24-7	Oakland	53,821
1977	Jan. 1	Denver ($9,000)	Oakland ($9,000)	20-17	Denver	75,044
1978	Jan. 7	Pittsburgh ($9,000)	Houston ($9,000)	34-5	Pittsburgh	50,725
1979	Jan. 6	Pittsburgh ($9,000)	Houston ($9,000)	27-13	Pittsburgh	50,475
1980	Jan. 11	Oakland ($9,000)	San Diego ($9,000)	34-27	San Diego	52,428
1981	Jan. 10	Cincinnati ($9,000)	San Diego ($9,000)	27-7	Cincinnati	46,302
1982	Jan. 23	Miami ($18,000)	N.Y. Jets ($18,000)	14-0	Miami	67,396
1983	Jan. 8	L.A. Raiders ($18,000)	Seattle ($18,000)	30-14	Los Angeles	88,734
1984	Jan. 6	Miami ($18,000)	Pittsburgh ($18,000)	45-28	Miami	76,029
1985	Jan. 12	New England ($18,000)	Miami ($18,000)	31-14	Miami	74,978
1986	Jan. 11	Denver ($18,000)	Cleveland ($18,000)	23-20*	Cleveland	79,915
1987	Jan. 17	Denver ($18,000)	Cleveland ($18,000)	38-33	Denver	75,993
1988	Jan. 8	Cincinnati ($18,000)	Buffalo ($18,000)	21-10	Cincinnati	59,747
1989	Jan. 14	Denver ($18,000)	Cleveland ($18,000)	37-21	Denver	76,046
1990	Jan. 20	Buffalo ($18,000)	L.A. Raiders ($18,000)	51-3	Buffalo	80,234
1991	Jan. 12	Buffalo ($18,000)	Denver ($18,000)	10-7	Buffalo	80,272
1992	Jan. 17	Buffalo ($18,000)	Miami ($18,000)	29-10	Miami	72,703
1993	Jan. 23	Buffalo ($23,500)	Kansas City ($23,500)	30-13	Buffalo	76,642
1994	Jan. 15	San Diego ($26,000)	Pittsburgh ($26,000)	17-13	Pittsburgh	61,545
1995	Jan. 14	Pittsburgh ($27,000)	Indianapolis ($27,000)	20-16	Pittsburgh	61,062
1996	Jan. 12	New England ($29,000)	Jacksonville ($29,000)	20-6	New England	60,190
1997	Jan. 11	Denver ($30,000)	Pittsburgh ($30,000)	24-21	Pittsburgh	61,382

*Sudden-death overtime.

COMPOSITE STANDINGS

	W	L	Pct.	PF	PA		W	L	Pct.	PF	PA
Cincinnati Bengals	2	0	1.000	48	17	Houston Oilers	2	4	.333	76	140
Denver Broncos	5	1	.833	149	122	Indianapolis Colts∞	1	2	.333	43	58
Buffalo Bills	6	2	.750	180	92	Oakland Raiders§	4	8	.333	228	264
Kansas City Chiefs†	3	1	.750	81	61	San Diego Chargers*	2	6	.250	128	161
Miami Dolphins	5	2	.714	152	115	Seattle Seahawks	0	1	.000	14	30
New England Patriots‡	2	1	.667	61	71	Jacksonville Jaguars	0	1	.000	6	20
Pittsburgh Steelers	5	5	.500	207	188	Cleveland Browns	0	3	.000	74	98
New York Jets	1	1	.500	27	37						

*One game played when franchise was in Los Angeles; lost 24-16.
†One game played when franchise was in Dallas (Texans); won 20-17.
‡One game played when franchise was in Boston; lost 51-10.
§Two games played when franchise was in Los Angeles; record of 1-1.
∞Two games played when franchise was in Baltimore; record of 1-1.

POSTSEASON GAME COMPOSITE STANDINGS

	W	L	Pct.	PF	PA		W	L	Pct.	PF	PA
Green Bay Packers	22	9	.710	745	528	Detroit Lions	7	9	.438	352	377
San Francisco 49ers	23	14	.622	936	712	New England Patriots§	7	9	.438	310	332
Dallas Cowboys	32	19	.627	1254	932	Seattle Seahawks	3	4	.429	128	139
Washington Redskins‡	21	14	.600	738	625	New York Giants	14	19	.424	551	616
Pittsburgh Steelers	21	15	.583	801	707	Kansas City Chiefs*	8	11	.421	301	384
Oakland Raiders◆	21	15	.583	855	659	Cincinnati Bengals	5	7	.417	246	257
Denver Broncos	13	11	.542	518	604	Minnesota Vikings	14	20	.412	613	746
Miami Dolphins	17	15	.531	700	650	Tennessee Oilers▼	9	13	.409	371	533
Buffalo Bills	14	13	.519	648	612	St. Louis Rams†@	13	20	.394	501	697
Chicago Bears	14	14	.500	579	552	San Diego Chargers▲	7	11	.389	332	428
Indianapolis Colts■	10	10	.500	360	389	Cleveland Browns	11	19	.367	596	702
Jacksonville Jaguars	2	2	.500	83	116	Tampa Bay Buccaneers	2	4	.333	68	125
Carolina Panthers	1	1	.500	39	47	Atlanta Falcons	2	5	.286	139	181
New York Jets	5	6	.455	216	200	Arizona Cardinals∞	1	4	.200	81	134
Philadelphia Eagles	9	11	.450	356	369	New Orleans Saints	0	4	.000	56	123

*One game played when franchise was in Dallas (Texans); won 20-17.
†One game played when franchise was in Cleveland; won 15-14.
‡One game played when franchise was in Boston; lost 21-6.
§Two games played when franchise was in Boston; won 26-8, lost 51-10.
∞Two games played when franchise was in Chicago; won 28-21, lost 7-0. Three games played when franchise was in St. Louis; lost 35-23, lost 30-14, lost 41-16.
▲One game played when franchise was in Los Angeles; lost 24-16.
◆12 games played when franchise was in Los Angeles; record of 6-6.
■15 games played when franchise was in Baltimore; record of 8-7.
▼All 22 games played when franchise was in Houston; record of 9-13.
@32 games played when franchise was in Los Angeles; record of 12-20.

CHAMPIONS OF DEFUNCT PRO FOOTBALL LEAGUES

ALL-AMERICAN FOOTBALL CONFERENCE

Year	Winner	Coach	Loser	Coach	Score, Site
1946	Cleveland Browns	Paul Brown	N.Y. Yankees	Ray Flaherty	14-9, Cleveland
1947	Cleveland Browns	Paul Brown	N.Y. Yankees	Ray Flaherty	14-3, New York
1948	Cleveland Browns	Paul Brown	Buffalo Bills	Red Dawson	49-7, Cleveland
1949	Cleveland Browns	Paul Brown	S.F. 49ers	Buck Shaw	21-7, Cleveland

NOTE: Cleveland Browns and San Francisco 49ers joined the NFL after the AAFC folded in 1949.

WORLD FOOTBALL LEAGUE

Year	Winner	Coach	Loser	Coach	Score, Site
1974	Birmingham Americans	Jack Gotta	Florida Blazers	Jack Pardee	22-21, Birmingham
1975	League folded October 22				

UNITED STATES FOOTBALL LEAGUE

Year	Winner	Coach	Loser	Coach	Score, Site
1983	Michigan Panthers	Jim Stanley	Philadelphia Stars	Jim Mora	24-22, Denver
1984	Philadelphia Stars	Jim Mora	Arizona Wranglers	George Allen	23-3, Tampa
1985	Baltimore Stars	Jim Mora	Oakland Invaders	Charlie Sumner	28-24, E. Rutherford, N.J.

YEAR-BY-YEAR STANDINGS

1920

Team	W	L	T	Pct.
Akron Pros*	8	0	3	1.000
Decatur Staleys	10	1	2	.909
Buffalo All-Americans	9	1	1	.900
Chicago Cardinals	6	2	2	.750
Rock Island Independents	6	2	2	.750
Dayton Triangles	5	2	2	.714
Rochester Jeffersons	6	3	2	.667
Canton Bulldogs	7	4	2	.636
Detroit Heralds	2	3	3	.400
Cleveland Tigers	2	4	2	.333
Chicago Tigers	2	5	1	.286
Hammond Pros	2	5	0	.286
Columbus Panhandles	2	6	2	.250
Muncie Flyers	0	1	0	.000

*No official standings were maintained for the 1920 season, and the championship was awarded to the Akron Pros in a League meeting on April 30, 1921. Clubs played schedules which included games against non-league opponents. Records of clubs against all opponents are listed above.

1921

Team	W	L	T	Pct.
Chicago Staleys	9	1	1	.900
Buffalo All-Americans	9	1	2	.900
Akron Pros	8	3	1	.727
Canton Bulldogs	5	2	3	.714
Rock Island Independents	4	2	1	.667
Evansville Crimson Giants	3	2	0	.600
Green Bay Packers	3	2	1	.600
Dayton Triangles	4	4	1	.500
Chicago Cardinals	3	3	2	.500
Rochester Jeffersons	2	3	0	.400
Cleveland Indians	3	5	0	.375
Washington Senators	1	2	0	.333
Cincinnati Celts	1	3	0	.250
Hammond Pros	1	3	1	.250
Minneapolis Marines	1	3	1	.250
Detroit Heralds	1	5	1	.167
Columbus Panhandles	1	8	0	.111
Tonawanda Kardex	0	1	0	.000
Muncie Flyers	0	2	0	.000
Louisville Brecks	0	2	0	.000
New York Giants	0	2	0	.000

1922

Team	W	L	T	Pct.
Canton Bulldogs	10	0	2	1.000
Chicago Bears	9	3	0	.750
Chicago Cardinals	8	3	0	.727
Toledo Maroons	5	2	2	.714
Rock Island Independents	4	2	1	.667
Racine Legion	6	4	1	.600
Dayton Triangles	4	3	1	.571
Green Bay Packers	4	3	3	.571
Buffalo All-Americans	5	4	1	.556
Akron Pros	3	5	2	.375
Milwaukee Badgers	2	4	3	.333
Oorang Indians	2	6	0	.250
Minneapolis Marines	1	3	0	.250
Louisville Brecks	1	3	0	.250
Evansville Crimson Giants	0	3	0	.000
Rochester Jeffersons	0	4	1	.000
Hammond Pros	0	5	1	.000
Columbus Panhandles	0	7	0	.000

1923

Team	W	L	T	Pct.
Canton Bulldogs	11	0	1	1.000
Chicago Bears	9	2	1	.818
Green Bay Packers	7	2	1	.778
Milwaukee Badgers	7	2	3	.778
Cleveland Indians	3	1	3	.750
Chicago Cardinals	8	4	0	.667
Duluth Kelleys	4	3	0	.571
Columbus Tigers	5	4	1	.556
Buffalo All-Americans	4	4	3	.500
Racine Legion	4	4	2	.500
Toledo Maroons	2	3	2	.400
Rock Island Independents	2	3	3	.400
Minneapolis Marines	2	5	2	.286
St. Louis All-Stars	1	4	2	.200
Hammond Pros	1	5	1	.167
Dayton Triangles	1	6	1	.143
Akron Indians	1	6	0	.143
Oorang Indians	1	10	0	.091
Rochester Jeffersons	0	2	0	.000
Louisville Brecks	0	3	0	.000

1924

Team	W	L	T	Pct.
Cleveland Bulldogs	7	1	1	.875
Chicago Bears	6	1	4	.857
Frankford Yellow Jackets	11	2	1	.846
Duluth Kelleys	5	1	0	.833
Rock Island Independents	6	2	2	.750
Green Bay Packers	7	4	0	.636
Racine Legion	4	3	3	.571
Chicago Cardinals	5	4	1	.556
Buffalo Bisons	6	5	0	.545
Columbus Tigers	4	4	0	.500
Hammond Pros	2	2	1	.500
Milwaukee Badgers	5	8	0	.385
Akron Indians	2	6	0	.250
Dayton Triangles	2	6	0	.250
Kansas City Blues	2	7	0	.222
Kenosha Maroons	0	5	1	.000
Minneapolis Marines	0	6	0	.000
Rochester Jeffersons	0	7	0	.000

1925

Team	W	L	T	Pct.
Chicago Cardinals	11	2	1	.846
Pottsville Maroons	10	2	0	.833
Detroit Panthers	8	2	2	.800
New York Giants	8	4	0	.667
Akron Indians	4	2	2	.667
Frankford Yellow Jackets	13	7	0	.650
Chicago Bears	9	5	3	.643
Rock Island Independents	5	3	3	.625
Green Bay Packers	8	5	0	.615
Providence Steam Roller	6	5	1	.545
Canton Bulldogs	4	4	0	.500
Cleveland Bulldogs	5	8	1	.385
Kansas City Cowboys	2	5	1	.286
Hammond Pros	1	4	0	.200
Buffalo Bisons	1	6	2	.143
Duluth Kelleys	0	3	0	.000
Rochester Jeffersons	0	6	1	.000
Milwaukee Badgers	0	6	0	.000
Dayton Triangles	0	7	1	.000
Columbus Tigers	0	9	0	.000

1926

Team	W	L	T	Pct.
Frankford Yellow Jackets	14	1	1	.933
Chicago Bears	12	1	3	.923
Pottsville Maroons	10	2	1	.833
Kansas City Cowboys	8	3	0	.727
Green Bay Packers	7	3	3	.700
Los Angeles Buccaneers	6	3	1	.667
New York Giants	8	4	1	.667
Duluth Eskimos	6	5	3	.545
Buffalo Rangers	4	4	2	.500
Chicago Cardinals	5	6	1	.455
Providence Steam Roller	5	7	1	.417
Detroit Panthers	4	6	2	.400
Hartford Blues	3	7	0	.300
Brooklyn Lions	3	8	0	.273
Milwaukee Badgers	2	7	0	.222
Akron Pros	1	4	3	.200
Dayton Triangles	1	4	1	.200
Racine Tornadoes	1	4	0	.200
Columbus Tigers	1	6	0	.143
Canton Bulldogs	1	9	3	.100
Hammond Pros	0	4	0	.000
Louisville Colonels	0	4	0	.000

1927

Team	W	L	T	Pct.
New York Giants	11	1	1	.917
Green Bay Packers	7	2	1	.778
Chicago Bears	9	3	2	.750
Cleveland Bulldogs	8	4	1	.667
Providence Steam Roller	8	5	1	.615
New York Yankees	7	8	1	.467
Frankford Yellow Jackets	6	9	3	.400
Pottsville Maroons	5	8	0	.385
Chicago Cardinals	3	7	1	.300
Dayton Triangles	1	6	1	.143
Duluth Eskimos	1	8	0	.111
Buffalo Bisons	0	5	0	.000

1928

Team	W	L	T	Pct.
Providence Steam Roller	8	1	2	.889
Frankford Yellow Jackets	11	3	2	.786
Detroit Wolverines	7	2	1	.778
Green Bay Packers	6	4	3	.600
Chicago Bears	7	5	1	.583
New York Giants	4	7	2	.364
New York Yankees	4	8	1	.333
Pottsville Maroons	2	8	0	.200
Chicago Cardinals	1	5	0	.167
Dayton Triangles	0	7	0	.000

1929

Team	W	L	T	Pct.
Green Bay Packers	12	0	1	1.000
New York Giants	13	1	1	.929
Frankford Yellow Jackets	9	4	5	.692
Chicago Cardinals	6	6	1	.500
Boston Bulldogs	4	4	0	.500
Orange Tornadoes	3	4	4	.429
Staten Island Stapletons	3	4	3	.429
Providence Steam Roller	4	6	2	.400
Chicago Bears	4	9	2	.308
Buffalo Bisons	1	7	1	.125
Minneapolis Red Jackets	1	9	0	.100
Dayton Triangles	0	6	0	.000

1930

Team	W	L	T	Pct.
Green Bay Packers	10	3	1	.769
New York Giants	13	4	0	.765
Chicago Bears	9	4	1	.692
Brooklyn Dodgers	7	4	1	.636
Providence Steam Roller	6	4	1	.600
Staten Island Stapletons	5	5	2	.500
Chicago Cardinals	5	6	2	.455
Portsmouth Spartans	5	6	3	.455
Frankford Yellow Jackets	4	13	1	.222
Minneapolis Red Jackets	1	7	1	.125
Newark Tornadoes	1	10	1	.091

1931

Team	W	L	T	Pct.
Green Bay Packers	12	2	0	.857
Portsmouth Spartans	11	3	0	.786
Chicago Bears	8	5	0	.615
Chicago Cardinals	5	4	0	.556
New York Giants	7	6	1	.538
Providence Steam Roller	4	4	3	.500
Staten Island Stapletons	4	6	1	.400
Cleveland Indians	2	8	0	.200
Brooklyn Dodgers	2	12	0	.143
Frankford Yellow Jackets	1	6	1	.143

1932

Team	W	L	T	Pct.
Chicago Bears	7	1	6	.875
Green Bay Packers	10	3	1	.769
Portsmouth Spartans	6	2	4	.750
Boston Braves	4	4	2	.500
New York Giants	4	6	2	.400
Brooklyn Dodgers	3	9	0	.250
Chicago Cardinals	2	6	2	.250
Staten Island Stapletons	2	7	3	.222

NOTE: Chicago Bears and Portsmouth finished regularly scheduled games tied for first place. Bears won playoff game, which counted in standings, 9-0.

1933

EASTERN DIVISION

Team	W	L	T	Pct.	PF	PA
N.Y. Giants	11	3	0	.786	244	101
Brooklyn	5	4	1	.556	93	54
Boston	5	5	2	.500	103	97
Philadelphia	3	5	1	.375	77	158
Pittsburgh	3	6	2	.333	67	208

WESTERN DIVISION

Team	W	L	T	Pct.	PF	PA
Chicago Bears	10	2	1	.833	133	82
Portsmouth	6	5	0	.545	128	87
Green Bay	5	7	1	.417	170	107
Cincinnati	3	6	1	.333	38	110
Chi. Cardinals	1	9	1	.100	52	101

PLAYOFFS

NFL championship
Chicago Bears 23 vs. N.Y. Giants 21

1934

EASTERN DIVISION

Team	W	L	T	Pct.	PF	PA
N.Y. Giants	8	5	0	.615	147	107
Boston	6	6	0	.500	107	94
Brooklyn	4	7	0	.364	61	153
Philadelphia	4	7	0	.364	127	85
Pittsburgh	2	10	0	.167	51	206

WESTERN DIVISION

Team	W	L	T	Pct.	PF	PA
Chicago Bears	13	0	0	1.000	286	86
Detroit	10	3	0	.769	238	59
Green Bay	7	6	0	.538	156	112
Chi. Cardinals	5	6	0	.455	80	84
St. Louis	1	2	0	.333	27	61
Cincinnati	0	8	0	.000	10	243

PLAYOFFS

NFL championship

N.Y. Giants 30 vs. Chicago Bears 13

1935

EASTERN DIVISION

Team	W	L	T	Pct.	PF	PA
N.Y. Giants	9	3	0	.750	180	96
Brooklyn	5	6	1	.455	90	141
Pittsburgh	4	8	0	.333	100	209
Boston	2	8	1	.200	65	123
Philadelphia	2	9	0	.182	60	179

WESTERN DIVISION

Team	W	L	T	Pct.	PF	PA
Detroit	7	3	2	.700	191	111
Green Bay	8	4	0	.667	181	96
Chicago Bears	6	4	2	.600	192	106
Chi. Cardinals	6	4	2	.600	99	97

PLAYOFFS

NFL championship

Detroit 26 vs. N.Y. Giants 7

NOTE: One game between Boston and Philadelphia was cancelled.

1936

EASTERN DIVISION

Team	W	L	T	Pct.	PF	PA
Boston	7	5	0	.583	149	110
Pittsburgh	6	6	0	.500	98	187
N.Y. Giants	5	6	1	.455	115	163
Brooklyn	3	8	1	.273	92	161
Philadelphia	1	11	0	.083	51	206

WESTERN DIVISION

Team	W	L	T	Pct.	PF	PA
Green Bay	10	1	1	.909	248	118
Chicago Bears	9	3	0	.750	222	94
Detroit	8	4	0	.667	235	102
Chi. Cardinals	3	8	1	.273	74	143

PLAYOFFS

NFL championship

Green Bay 21, Boston 6, at New York.

1937

EASTERN DIVISION

Team	W	L	T	Pct.	PF	PA
Washington	8	3	0	.727	195	120
N.Y. Giants	6	3	2	.667	128	109
Pittsburgh	4	7	0	.364	122	145
Brooklyn	3	7	1	.300	82	174
Philadelphia	2	8	1	.200	86	177

WESTERN DIVISION

Team	W	L	T	Pct.	PF	PA
Chicago Bears	9	1	1	.900	201	100
Green Bay	7	4	0	.636	220	122
Detroit	7	4	0	.636	180	105
Chi. Cardinals	5	5	1	.500	135	165
Cleveland	1	10	0	.091	75	207

PLAYOFFS

NFL championship

Washington 28 at Chicago Bears 21

1938

EASTERN DIVISION

Team	W	L	T	Pct.	PF	PA
N.Y. Giants	8	2	1	.800	194	79
Washington	6	3	2	.667	148	154
Brooklyn	4	4	3	.500	131	161
Philadelphia	5	6	0	.455	154	164
Pittsburgh	2	9	0	.182	79	169

WESTERN DIVISION

Team	W	L	T	Pct.	PF	PA
Green Bay	8	3	0	.727	223	118
Detroit	7	4	0	.636	119	108
Chicago Bears	6	5	0	.545	194	148
Cleveland	4	7	0	.364	131	215
Chi. Cardinals	2	9	0	.182	111	168

PLAYOFFS

NFL championship

N.Y. Giants 23 vs. Green Bay 17

1939

EASTERN DIVISION

Team	W	L	T	Pct.	PF	PA
N.Y. Giants	9	1	1	.900	168	85
Washington	8	2	1	.800	242	94
Brooklyn	4	6	1	.400	108	219
Philadelphia	1	9	1	.100	105	200
Pittsburgh	1	9	1	.100	114	216

WESTERN DIVISION

Team	W	L	T	Pct.	PF	PA
Green Bay	9	2	0	.818	233	153
Chicago Bears	8	3	0	.727	298	157
Detroit	6	5	0	.545	145	150
Cleveland	5	5	1	.500	195	164
Chi. Cardinals	1	10	0	.091	84	254

PLAYOFFS

NFL championship

Green Bay 27 vs. N.Y. Giants 0

1940

EASTERN DIVISION

Team	W	L	T	Pct.	PF	PA
Washington	9	2	0	.818	245	142
Brooklyn	8	3	0	.727	186	120
N.Y. Giants	6	4	1	.600	131	133
Pittsburgh	2	7	2	.222	60	178
Philadelphia	1	10	0	.091	111	211

WESTERN DIVISION

Team	W	L	T	Pct.	PF	PA
Chicago Bears	8	3	0	.727	238	152
Green Bay	6	4	1	.600	238	155
Detroit	5	5	1	.500	138	153
Cleveland	4	6	1	.400	171	191
Chi. Cardinals	2	7	2	.222	139	222

PLAYOFFS

NFL championship

Chicago Bears 73 at Washington 0

1941

EASTERN DIVISION

Team	W	L	T	Pct.	PF	PA
N.Y. Giants	8	3	0	.727	238	114
Brooklyn	7	4	0	.636	158	127
Washington	6	5	0	.545	176	174
Philadelphia	2	8	1	.200	119	218
Pittsburgh	1	9	1	.100	103	276

WESTERN DIVISION

Team	W	L	T	Pct.	PF	PA
Chicago Bears	10	1	0	.909	396	147
Green Bay	10	1	0	.909	258	120
Detroit	4	6	1	.400	121	195
Chi. Cardinals	3	7	1	.300	127	197
Cleveland	2	9	0	.182	116	244

PLAYOFFS

Western Division playoff
Chicago Bears 33 vs. Green Bay 14

NFL championship
Chicago Bears 37 vs. N.Y. Giants 9

1942

EASTERN DIVISION

Team	W	L	T	Pct.	PF	PA
Washington	10	1	0	.909	227	102
Pittsburgh	7	4	0	.636	167	119
N.Y. Giants	5	5	1	.500	155	139
Brooklyn	3	8	0	.273	100	168
Philadelphia	2	9	0	.182	134	239

WESTERN DIVISION

Team	W	L	T	Pct.	PF	PA
Chicago Bears	11	0	0	1.000	376	84
Green Bay	8	2	1	.800	300	215
Cleveland	5	6	0	.455	150	207
Chi. Cardinals	3	8	0	.273	98	209
Detroit	0	11	0	.000	38	263

PLAYOFFS

NFL championship
Washington 14 vs. Chicago Bears 6

1943

EASTERN DIVISION

Team	W	L	T	Pct.	PF	PA
Washington	6	3	1	.667	229	137
N.Y. Giants	6	3	1	.667	197	170
Phil.-Pitt.	5	4	1	.556	225	230
Brooklyn	2	8	0	.200	65	234

NOTE: Cleveland Rams did not play in 1943.

WESTERN DIVISION

Team	W	L	T	Pct.	PF	PA
Chicago Bears	8	1	1	.889	303	157
Green Bay	7	2	1	.778	264	172
Detroit	3	6	1	.333	178	218
Chi. Cardinals	0	10	0	.000	95	238

PLAYOFFS

Eastern Division playoff
Washington 28 at N.Y. Giants 0

NFL championship
Chicago Bears 41 vs. Washington 21

1944

EASTERN DIVISION

Team	W	L	T	Pct.	PF	PA
N.Y. Giants	8	1	1	.889	206	75
Philadelphia	7	1	2	.875	267	131
Washington	6	3	1	.667	169	180
Boston	2	8	0	.200	82	233
Brooklyn	0	10	0	.000	69	166

WESTERN DIVISION

Team	W	L	T	Pct.	PF	PA
Green Bay	8	2	0	.800	238	141
Chicago Bears	6	3	1	.667	258	172
Detroit	6	3	1	.667	216	151
Cleveland	4	6	0	.400	188	224
Card-Pitt	0	10	0	.000	108	328

PLAYOFFS

NFL championship
Green Bay 14 at N.Y. Giants 7

1945

EASTERN DIVISION

Team	W	L	T	Pct.	PF	PA
Washington	8	2	0	.800	209	121
Philadelphia	7	3	0	.700	272	133
N.Y. Giants	3	6	1	.333	179	198
Boston	3	6	1	.333	123	211
Pittsburgh	2	8	0	.200	79	220

WESTERN DIVISION

Team	W	L	T	Pct.	PF	PA
Cleveland	9	1	0	.900	244	136
Detroit	7	3	0	.700	195	194
Green Bay	6	4	0	.600	258	173
Chicago Bears	3	7	0	.300	192	235
Chi. Cardinals	1	9	0	.100	98	228

PLAYOFFS

NFL championship
Cleveland 15 vs. Washington 14

1946

AAFC

EASTERN DIVISION

Team	W	L	T	Pct.	PF	PA
New York	10	3	1	.769	270	192
Brooklyn	3	10	1	.231	226	339
Buffalo	3	10	1	.231	249	370
Miami	3	11	0	.154	167	378

WESTERN DIVISION

Team	W	L	T	Pct.	PF	PA
Cleveland	12	2	0	.857	423	137
San Francisco	9	5	0	.643	307	189
Los Angeles	7	5	2	.583	305	290
Chicago	5	6	3	.455	263	315

PLAYOFFS

AAFC championship
Cleveland 14 vs. New York 9

NFL

EASTERN DIVISION

Team	W	L	T	Pct.	PF	PA
N.Y. Giants	7	3	1	.700	236	162
Philadelphia	6	5	0	.545	231	220
Washington	5	5	1	.500	171	191
Pittsburgh	5	5	1	.500	136	117
Boston	2	8	1	.200	189	273

WESTERN DIVISION

Team	W	L	T	Pct.	PF	PA
Chicago Bears	8	2	1	.800	289	193
Los Angeles	6	4	1	.600	277	257
Green Bay	6	5	0	.545	148	158
Chi. Cardinals	6	5	0	.545	260	198
Detroit	1	10	0	.091	142	310

PLAYOFFS

NFL championship
Chicago Bears 24 at N.Y. Giants 14

AAFC

EASTERN DIVISION						WESTERN DIVISION						PLAYOFFS
Team	W	L	T	Pct.	PF	PA						**AAFC championship**
New York	11	2	1	.846	378	239						Cleveland 14 at New York 3
Buffalo	8	4	2	.667	320	288						
Brooklyn	3	10	1	.231	181	340						
Baltimore	2	11	1	.154	167	377						

Team	W	L	T	Pct.	PF	PA
Cleveland	12	1	1	.923	410	185
San Francisco	8	4	2	.667	327	264
Los Angeles	7	7	0	.500	328	256
Chicago	1	13	0	.071	263	425

NFL

EASTERN DIVISION

Team	W	L	T	Pct.	PF	PA
Philadelphia	8	4	0	.667	308	242
Pittsburgh	8	4	0	.667	240	259
Boston	4	7	1	.364	168	256
Washington	4	8	0	.333	295	367
N.Y. Giants	2	8	2	.200	190	309

WESTERN DIVISION

Team	W	L	T	Pct.	PF	PA
Chi. Cardinals	9	3	0	.750	306	231
Chicago Bears	8	4	0	.667	363	241
Green Bay	6	5	1	.545	274	210
Los Angeles	6	6	0	.500	259	214
Detroit	3	9	0	.250	231	305

PLAYOFFS

Eastern Division playoff
Philadelphia 21 at Pittsburgh 0

NFL championship
Chicago Cardinals 28 vs. Philadelphia 21

AAFC

EASTERN DIVISION

Team	W	L	T	Pct.	PF	PA
Buffalo	7	7	0	.500	360	358
Baltimore	7	7	0	.500	333	327
New York	6	8	0	.429	265	301
Brooklyn	2	12	0	.143	253	387

WESTERN DIVISION

Team	W	L	T	Pct.	PF	PA
Cleveland	14	0	0	1.000	389	190
San Francisco	12	2	0	.857	495	248
Los Angeles	7	7	0	.500	258	305
Chicago	1	13	0	.071	202	439

PLAYOFFS

Eastern Division playoff
Buffalo 28 vs. Baltimore 17

AAFC championship
Cleveland 49 vs. Buffalo 7

NFL

EASTERN DIVISION

Team	W	L	T	Pct.	PF	PA
Philadelphia	9	2	1	.818	376	156
Washington	7	5	0	.583	291	287
N.Y. Giants	4	8	0	.333	297	388
Pittsburgh	4	8	0	.333	200	243
Boston	3	9	0	.250	174	372

WESTERN DIVISION

Team	W	L	T	Pct.	PF	PA
Chi. Cardinals	11	1	0	.917	395	226
Chicago Bears	10	2	0	.833	375	151
Los Angeles	6	5	1	.545	327	269
Green Bay	3	9	0	.250	154	290
Detroit	2	10	0	.167	200	407

PLAYOFFS

NFL championship
Philadelphia 7 vs. Chicago Cardinals 0

AAFC

Team	W	L	T	Pct.	PF	PA
Cleveland	9	1	2	.900	339	171
San Francisco	9	3	0	.750	416	227
Brooklyn-N.Y.	8	4	0	.667	196	206
Buffalo	5	5	2	.500	236	256
Chicago	4	8	0	.333	179	268
Los Angeles	4	8	0	.333	253	322
Baltimore	1	11	0	.083	172	341

PLAYOFFS

AAFC Semifinals
Cleveland 31 vs. Buffalo 21
San Francisco 17 vs. Brooklyn-N.Y. 7

AAFC championship
Cleveland 21 vs. San Francisco 7

NFL

EASTERN DIVISION

Team	W	L	T	Pct.	PF	PA
Philadelphia	11	1	0	.917	364	134
Pittsburgh	6	5	1	.545	224	214
N.Y. Giants	6	6	0	.500	287	298
Washington	4	7	1	.364	268	339
N.Y. Bulldogs	1	10	1	.091	153	365

WESTERN DIVISION

Team	W	L	T	Pct.	PF	PA
Los Angeles	8	2	2	.800	360	239
Chicago Bears	9	3	0	.750	332	218
Chi. Cardinals	6	5	1	.545	360	301
Detroit	4	8	0	.333	237	259
Green Bay	2	10	0	.167	114	329

PLAYOFFS

NFL championship
Philadelphia 14 at Los Angeles 0

AMERICAN CONFERENCE

Team	W	L	T	Pct.	PF	PA
Cleveland	10	2	0	.833	310	144
N.Y. Giants	10	2	0	.833	268	150
Philadelphia	6	6	0	.500	254	141
Pittsburgh	6	6	0	.500	180	195
Chi. Cardinals	5	7	0	.417	233	287
Washington	3	9	0	.250	232	326

NATIONAL CONFERENCE

Team	W	L	T	Pct.	PF	PA
Los Angeles	9	3	0	.750	466	309
Chicago Bears	9	3	0	.750	279	207
N.Y. Yanks	7	5	0	.583	366	367
Detroit	6	6	0	.500	321	285
Green Bay	3	9	0	.250	244	406
San Francisco	3	9	0	.250	213	300
Baltimore	1	11	0	.083	213	462

PLAYOFFS

American Conference playoff
Cleveland 8 vs. N.Y. Giants 3

National Conference playoff
Los Angeles 24 vs. Chicago Bears 14

NFL championship
Cleveland 30 vs. Los Angeles 28

1951

AMERICAN CONFERENCE

Team	W	L	T	Pct.	PF	PA
Cleveland	11	1	0	.917	331	152
N.Y. Giants	9	2	1	.818	254	161
Washington	5	7	0	.417	183	296
Pittsburgh	4	7	1	.364	183	235
Philadelphia	4	8	0	.333	234	264
Chi. Cardinals	3	9	0	.250	210	287

NATIONAL CONFERENCE

Team	W	L	T	Pct.	PF	PA
Los Angeles	8	4	0	.667	392	261
Detroit	7	4	1	.636	336	259
San Francisco	7	4	1	.636	255	205
Chicago Bears	7	5	0	.583	286	282
Green Bay	3	9	0	.250	254	375
N.Y. Yanks	1	9	2	.100	241	382

PLAYOFFS

NFL championship
Los Angeles 24 vs. Cleveland 17

1952

AMERICAN CONFERENCE

Team	W	L	T	Pct.	PF	PA
Cleveland	8	4	0	.667	310	213
N.Y. Giants	7	5	0	.583	234	231
Philadelphia	7	5	0	.583	252	271
Pittsburgh	5	7	0	.417	300	273
Chi. Cardinals	4	8	0	.333	172	221
Washington	4	8	0	.333	240	287

NATIONAL CONFERENCE

Team	W	L	T	Pct.	PF	PA
Detroit	9	3	0	.750	344	192
Los Angeles	9	3	0	.750	349	234
San Francisco	7	5	0	.583	285	221
Green Bay	6	6	0	.500	295	312
Chicago Bears	5	7	0	.417	245	326
Dallas Texans	1	11	0	.083	182	427

PLAYOFFS

National Conference playoff
Detroit 31 vs. Los Angeles 21

NFL championship
Detroit 17 at Cleveland 7

1953

EASTERN CONFERENCE

Team	W	L	T	Pct.	PF	PA
Cleveland	11	1	0	.917	348	162
Philadelphia	7	4	1	.636	352	215
Washington	6	5	1	.545	208	215
Pittsburgh	6	6	0	.500	211	263
N.Y. Giants	3	9	0	.250	179	277
Chi. Cardinals	1	10	1	.091	190	337

WESTERN CONFERENCE

Team	W	L	T	Pct.	PF	PA
Detroit	10	2	0	.833	271	205
San Francisco	9	3	0	.750	372	237
Los Angeles	8	3	1	.727	366	236
Chicago Bears	3	8	1	.273	218	262
Baltimore	3	9	0	.250	182	350
Green Bay	2	9	1	.182	200	338

PLAYOFFS

NFL championship
Detroit 17 vs. Cleveland 16

1954

EASTERN CONFERENCE

Team	W	L	T	Pct.	PF	PA
Cleveland	9	3	0	.750	336	162
Philadelphia	7	4	1	.636	284	230
N.Y. Giants	7	5	0	.583	293	184
Pittsburgh	5	7	0	.417	219	263
Washington	3	9	0	.250	207	432
Chi. Cardinals	2	10	0	.167	183	347

WESTERN CONFERENCE

Team	W	L	T	Pct.	PF	PA
Detroit	9	2	1	.818	337	189
Chicago Bears	8	4	0	.667	301	279
San Francisco	7	4	1	.636	313	251
Los Angeles	6	5	1	.545	314	285
Green Bay	4	8	0	.333	234	251
Baltimore	3	9	0	.250	131	279

PLAYOFFS

NFL championship
Cleveland 56 vs. Detroit 10

1955

EASTERN CONFERENCE

Team	W	L	T	Pct.	PF	PA
Cleveland	9	2	1	.818	349	218
Washington	8	4	0	.667	246	222
N.Y. Giants	6	5	1	.545	267	223
Chi. Cardinals	4	7	1	.364	224	252
Philadelphia	4	7	1	.364	248	231
Pittsburgh	4	8	0	.333	195	285

WESTERN CONFERENCE

Team	W	L	T	Pct.	PF	PA
Los Angeles	8	3	1	.727	260	231
Chicago Bears	8	4	0	.667	294	251
Green Bay	6	6	0	.500	258	276
Baltimore	5	6	1	.455	214	239
San Francisco	4	8	0	.333	216	298
Detroit	3	9	0	.250	230	275

PLAYOFFS

NFL championship
Cleveland 38 at Los Angeles 14

1956

EASTERN CONFERENCE

Team	W	L	T	Pct.	PF	PA
N.Y. Giants	8	3	1	.727	264	197
Chi. Cardinals	7	5	0	.583	240	182
Washington	6	6	0	.500	183	225
Cleveland	5	7	0	.417	167	177
Pittsburgh	5	7	0	.417	217	250
Philadelphia	3	8	1	.273	143	215

WESTERN CONFERENCE

Team	W	L	T	Pct.	PF	PA
Chicago Bears	9	2	1	.818	363	246
Detroit	9	3	0	.750	300	188
San Francisco	5	6	1	.455	233	284
Baltimore	5	7	0	.417	270	322
Green Bay	4	8	0	.333	264	342
Los Angeles	4	8	0	.333	291	307

PLAYOFFS

NFL championship
N.Y. Giants 47 vs. Chicago Bears 7

1957

EASTERN CONFERENCE

Team	W	L	T	Pct.	PF	PA
Cleveland	9	2	1	.818	269	172
N.Y. Giants	7	5	0	.583	254	211
Pittsburgh	6	6	0	.500	161	178
Washington	5	6	1	.455	251	230
Philadelphia	4	8	0	.333	173	230
Chi. Cardinals	3	9	0	.250	200	299

WESTERN CONFERENCE

Team	W	L	T	Pct.	PF	PA
Detroit	8	4	0	.667	251	231
San Francisco	8	4	0	.667	260	264
Baltimore	7	5	0	.583	303	235
Los Angeles	6	6	0	.500	307	278
Chicago Bears	5	7	0	.417	203	211
Green Bay	3	9	0	.250	218	311

PLAYOFFS

Western Conference playoff
Detroit 31 at San Francisco 27

NFL championship
Detroit 59 vs. Cleveland 14

1958

EASTERN CONFERENCE

Team	W	L	T	Pct.	PF	PA
N.Y. Giants	9	3	0	.750	246	183
Cleveland	9	3	0	.750	302	217
Pittsburgh	7	4	1	.636	261	230
Washington	4	7	1	.364	214	268
Chi. Cardinals	2	9	1	.182	261	356
Philadelphia	2	9	1	.182	235	306

WESTERN CONFERENCE

Team	W	L	T	Pct.	PF	PA
Baltimore	9	3	0	.750	381	203
Chicago Bears	8	4	0	.667	298	230
Los Angeles	8	4	0	.667	344	278
San Francisco	6	6	0	.500	257	324
Detroit	4	7	1	.364	261	276
Green Bay	1	10	1	.091	193	382

PLAYOFFS

Eastern Conference playoff
N.Y. Giants 10 vs. Cleveland 0

NFL championship
Baltimore 23 at N.Y. Giants 17 (OT)

1959

EASTERN CONFERENCE

Team	W	L	T	Pct.	PF	PA
N.Y. Giants	10	2	0	.833	284	170
Cleveland	7	5	0	.583	270	214
Philadelphia	7	5	0	.583	268	278
Pittsburgh	6	5	1	.545	257	216
Washington	3	9	0	.250	185	350
Chi. Cardinals	2	10	0	.167	234	324

WESTERN CONFERENCE

Team	W	L	T	Pct.	PF	PA
Baltimore	9	3	0	.750	374	251
Chicago Bears	8	4	0	.667	252	196
Green Bay	7	5	0	.583	248	246
San Francisco	7	5	0	.583	255	237
Detroit	3	8	1	.273	203	275
Los Angeles	2	10	0	.167	242	315

PLAYOFFS

NFL championship
Baltimore 31 vs. N.Y. Giants 16

1960

AFL

EASTERN DIVISION

Team	W	L	T	Pct.	PF	PA
Houston	10	4	0	.714	379	285
N.Y. Titans	7	7	0	.500	382	399
Buffalo	5	8	1	.385	296	303
Boston Patriots	5	9	0	.357	286	349

WESTERN DIVISION

Team	W	L	T	Pct.	PF	PA
L.A. Chargers	10	4	0	.714	373	336
Dallas Texans	8	6	0	.571	362	253
Oakland	6	8	0	.429	319	388
Denver	4	9	1	.308	309	393

PLAYOFFS

AFL championship
Houston 24 vs. L.A. Chargers 16

NFL

EASTERN CONFERENCE

Team	W	L	T	Pct.	PF	PA
Philadelphia	10	2	0	.833	321	246
Cleveland	8	3	1	.727	362	217
N.Y. Giants	6	4	2	.600	271	261
St. Louis	6	5	1	.545	288	230
Pittsburgh	5	6	1	.455	240	275
Washington	1	9	2	.100	178	309

WESTERN CONFERENCE

Team	W	L	T	Pct.	PF	PA
Green Bay	8	4	0	.667	332	209
Detroit	7	5	0	.583	239	212
San Francisco	7	5	0	.583	208	205
Baltimore	6	6	0	.500	288	234
Chicago	5	6	1	.455	194	299
L.A. Rams	4	7	1	.364	265	297
Dallas Cowboys	0	11	1	.000	177	369

PLAYOFFS

NFL championship
Philadelphia 17 vs. Green Bay 13

1961

AFL

EASTERN DIVISION

Team	W	L	T	Pct.	PF	PA
Houston	10	3	1	.769	513	242
Boston Patriots	9	4	1	.692	413	313
N.Y. Titans	7	7	0	.500	301	390
Buffalo	6	8	0	.429	294	342

WESTERN DIVISION

Team	W	L	T	Pct.	PF	PA
San Diego	12	2	0	.857	396	219
Dallas Texans	6	8	0	.429	334	343
Denver	3	11	0	.214	251	432
Oakland	2	12	0	.143	237	458

PLAYOFFS

AFL championship
Houston 10 at San Diego 3

NFL

EASTERN CONFERENCE

Team	W	L	T	Pct.	PF	PA
N.Y. Giants	10	3	1	.769	368	220
Philadelphia	10	4	0	.714	361	297
Cleveland	8	5	1	.615	319	270
St. Louis	7	7	0	.500	279	267
Pittsburgh	6	8	0	.429	295	287
Dallas Cowboys	4	9	1	.308	236	380
Washington	1	12	1	.077	174	392

WESTERN CONFERENCE

Team	W	L	T	Pct.	PF	PA
Green Bay	11	3	0	.786	391	223
Detroit	8	5	1	.615	270	258
Baltimore	8	6	0	.571	302	307
Chicago	8	6	0	.571	326	302
San Francisco	7	6	1	.538	346	272
Los Angeles	4	10	0	.286	263	333
Minnesota	3	11	0	.214	285	407

PLAYOFFS

NFL championship
Green Bay 37 vs. N.Y. Giants 0

1962

AFL

EASTERN DIVISION

Team	W	L	T	Pct.	PF	PA
Houston	11	3	0	.786	387	270
Boston Patriots	9	4	1	.692	346	295
Buffalo	7	6	1	.538	309	272
N.Y. Titans	5	9	0	.357	278	423

WESTERN DIVISION

Team	W	L	T	Pct.	PF	PA
Dallas Texans	11	3	0	.786	389	233
Denver	7	7	0	.500	353	334
San Diego	4	10	0	.286	314	392
Oakland	1	13	0	.071	213	370

PLAYOFFS

AFL championship
Dallas Texans 20 at Houston 17 (OT)

NFL

EASTERN CONFERENCE

Team	W	L	T	Pct.	PF	PA
N.Y. Giants	12	2	0	.857	398	283
Pittsburgh	9	5	0	.643	312	363
Cleveland	7	6	1	.538	291	257
Washington	5	7	2	.417	305	376
Dallas Cowboys	5	8	1	.385	398	402
St. Louis	4	9	1	.308	287	361
Philadelphia	3	10	1	.231	282	356

WESTERN CONFERENCE

Team	W	L	T	Pct.	PF	PA
Green Bay	13	1	0	.929	415	148
Detroit	11	3	0	.786	315	177
Chicago	9	5	0	.643	321	287
Baltimore	7	7	0	.500	293	288
San Francisco	6	8	0	.429	282	331
Minnesota	2	11	1	.154	254	410
Los Angeles	1	12	1	.077	220	334

PLAYOFFS

NFL championship
Green Bay 16 at N.Y. Giants 7

1963

AFL

EASTERN DIVISION

Team	W	L	T	Pct.	PF	PA
Boston Patriots	7	6	1	.538	327	257
Buffalo	7	6	1	.538	304	291
Houston	6	8	0	.429	302	372
N.Y. Jets	5	8	1	.385	249	399

WESTERN DIVISION

Team	W	L	T	Pct.	PF	PA
San Diego	11	3	0	.786	399	256
Oakland	10	4	0	.714	363	288
Kansas City	5	7	2	.417	347	263
Denver	2	11	1	.154	301	473

PLAYOFFS

Eastern Division playoff
Boston 26 at Buffalo 8
AFL championship
San Diego 51 vs. Boston 10

NFL

EASTERN CONFERENCE

Team	W	L	T	Pct.	PF	PA
N.Y. Giants	11	3	0	.786	448	280
Cleveland	10	4	0	.714	343	262
St. Louis	9	5	0	.643	341	283
Pittsburgh	7	4	3	.636	321	295
Dallas	4	10	0	.286	305	378
Washington	3	11	0	.214	279	398
Philadelphia	2	10	2	.167	242	381

WESTERN CONFERENCE

Team	W	L	T	Pct.	PF	PA
Chicago	11	1	2	.917	301	144
Green Bay	11	2	1	.846	369	206
Baltimore	8	6	0	.571	316	285
Detroit	5	8	1	.385	326	265
Minnesota	5	8	1	.385	309	390
Los Angeles	5	9	0	.357	210	350
San Francisco	2	12	0	.143	198	391

PLAYOFFS

NFL championship
Chicago 14 vs. N.Y. Giants 10

1964

AFL

EASTERN DIVISION

Team	W	L	T	Pct.	PF	PA
Buffalo	12	2	0	.857	400	242
Boston Patriots	10	3	1	.769	365	297
N.Y. Jets	5	8	1	.385	278	315
Houston	4	10	0	.286	310	355

WESTERN DIVISION

Team	W	L	T	Pct.	PF	PA
San Diego	8	5	1	.615	341	300
Kansas City	7	7	0	.500	366	306
Oakland	5	7	2	.417	303	350
Denver	2	11	1	.154	240	438

PLAYOFFS

AFL championship
Buffalo 20 vs. San Diego 7

NFL

EASTERN CONFERENCE

Team	W	L	T	Pct.	PF	PA
Cleveland	10	3	1	.769	415	293
St. Louis	9	3	2	.750	357	331
Philadelphia	6	8	0	.429	312	313
Washington	6	8	0	.429	307	305
Dallas	5	8	1	.385	250	289
Pittsburgh	5	9	0	.357	253	315
N.Y. Giants	2	10	2	.167	241	399

WESTERN CONFERENCE

Team	W	L	T	Pct.	PF	PA
Baltimore	12	2	0	.857	428	225
Green Bay	8	5	1	.615	342	245
Minnesota	8	5	1	.615	355	296
Detroit	7	5	2	.583	280	260
Los Angeles	5	7	2	.417	283	339
Chicago	5	9	0	.357	260	379
San Francisco	4	10	0	.286	236	330

PLAYOFFS

NFL championship
Cleveland 27 vs. Baltimore 0

1965

AFL

EASTERN DIVISION

Team	W	L	T	Pct.	PF	PA
Buffalo	10	3	1	.769	313	226
N.Y. Jets	5	8	1	.385	285	303
Boston Patriots	4	8	2	.333	244	302
Houston	4	10	0	.286	298	429

WESTERN DIVISION

Team	W	L	T	Pct.	PF	PA
San Diego	9	2	3	.818	340	227
Oakland	8	5	1	.615	298	239
Kansas City	7	5	2	.583	322	285
Denver	4	10	0	.286	303	392

PLAYOFFS

AFL championship
Buffalo 23 at San Diego 0

NFL

EASTERN CONFERENCE

Team	W	L	T	Pct.	PF	PA
Cleveland	11	3	0	.786	363	325
Dallas	7	7	0	.500	325	280
N.Y. Giants	7	7	0	.500	270	338
Washington	6	8	0	.429	257	301
Philadelphia	5	9	0	.357	363	359
St. Louis	5	9	0	.357	296	309
Pittsburgh	2	12	0	.143	202	397

WESTERN CONFERENCE

Team	W	L	T	Pct.	PF	PA
Green Bay	10	3	1	.769	316	224
Baltimore	10	3	1	.769	389	284
Chicago	9	5	0	.643	409	275
San Francisco	7	6	1	.538	421	402
Minnesota	7	7	0	.500	383	403
Detroit	6	7	1	.462	257	295
Los Angeles	4	10	0	.286	269	328

PLAYOFFS

Western Conference playoff
Green Bay 13 vs. Baltimore 10 (OT)

NFL championship
Green Bay 23 vs. Cleveland 12

1966

AFL

EASTERN DIVISION

Team	W	L	T	Pct.	PF	PA
Buffalo	9	4	1	.692	358	255
Boston Patriots	8	4	2	.667	315	283
N.Y. Jets	6	6	2	.500	322	312
Houston	3	11	0	.214	335	396
Miami	3	11	0	.214	213	362

WESTERN DIVISION

Team	W	L	T	Pct.	PF	PA
Kansas City	11	2	1	.846	448	276
Oakland	8	5	1	.615	315	288
San Diego	7	6	1	.538	335	284
Denver	4	10	0	.286	196	381

PLAYOFFS

AFL championship
Kansas City 31 at Buffalo 7

NFL

EASTERN CONFERENCE

Team	W	L	T	Pct.	PF	PA
Dallas	10	3	1	.769	445	239
Cleveland	9	5	0	.643	403	259
Philadelphia	9	5	0	.643	326	340
St. Louis	8	5	1	.615	264	265
Washington	7	7	0	.500	351	355
Pittsburgh	5	8	1	.385	316	347
Atlanta	3	11	0	.214	204	437
N.Y. Giants	1	12	1	.077	263	501

WESTERN CONFERENCE

Team	W	L	T	Pct.	PF	PA
Green Bay	12	2	0	.857	335	163
Baltimore	9	5	0	.643	314	226
Los Angeles	8	6	0	.571	289	212
San Francisco	6	6	2	.500	320	325
Chicago	5	7	2	.417	234	272
Detroit	4	9	1	.308	206	317
Minnesota	4	9	1	.308	292	304

PLAYOFFS

NFL championship
Green Bay 34 at Dallas 27

Super Bowl I
Green Bay 35, Kansas City 10, at Los Angeles.

1967

AFL

EASTERN DIVISION

Team	W	L	T	Pct.	PF	PA
Houston	9	4	1	.692	258	199
N.Y. Jets	8	5	1	.615	371	329
Buffalo	4	10	0	.286	237	285
Miami	4	10	0	.286	219	407
Boston Patriots	3	10	1	.231	280	389

WESTERN DIVISION

Team	W	L	T	Pct.	PF	PA
Oakland	13	1	0	.929	468	233
Kansas City	9	5	0	.643	408	254
San Diego	8	5	1	.615	360	352
Denver	3	11	0	.214	256	409

PLAYOFFS

AFL championship
Oakland 40 vs. Houston 7

NFL

EASTERN CONFERENCE

CAPITOL DIVISION

Team	W	L	T	Pct.	PF	PA
Dallas	9	5	0	.643	342	268
Philadelphia	6	7	1	.462	351	409
Washington	5	6	3	.455	347	353
New Orleans	3	11	0	.214	233	379

CENTURY DIVISION

Team	W	L	T	Pct.	PF	PA
Cleveland	9	5	0	.643	334	297
N.Y. Giants	7	7	0	.500	369	379
St. Louis	6	7	1	.462	333	356
Pittsburgh	4	9	1	.308	281	320

WESTERN CONFERENCE

COASTAL DIVISION

Team	W	L	T	Pct.	PF	PA
Los Angeles	11	1	2	.917	398	196
Baltimore	11	1	2	.917	394	198
San Francisco	7	7	0	.500	273	337
Atlanta	1	12	1	.077	175	422

CENTRAL DIVISION

Team	W	L	T	Pct.	PF	PA
Green Bay	9	4	1	.692	332	209
Chicago	7	6	1	.538	239	218
Detroit	5	7	2	.417	260	259
Minnesota	3	8	3	.273	233	294

PLAYOFFS

Conference championships
Dallas 52 vs. Cleveland 14
Green Bay 28 vs. Los Angeles 7

NFL championship
Green Bay 21 vs. Dallas 17

Super Bowl II
Green Bay 33, Oakland 14, at Miami.

1968

AFL

EASTERN DIVISION

Team	W	L	T	Pct.	PF	PA
N.Y. Jets	11	3	0	.786	419	280
Houston	7	7	0	.500	303	248
Miami	5	8	1	.385	276	355
Boston Patriots	4	10	0	.286	229	406
Buffalo	1	12	1	.077	199	367

WESTERN DIVISION

Team	W	L	T	Pct.	PF	PA
Oakland	12	2	0	.857	453	233
Kansas City	12	2	0	.857	371	170
San Diego	9	5	0	.643	382	310
Denver	5	9	0	.357	255	404
Cincinnati	3	11	0	.214	215	329

PLAYOFFS

Western Division playoff
Oakland 41 vs. Kansas City 6

AFL championship
N.Y. Jets 27 vs. Oakland 23

NFL

EASTERN CONFERENCE

CAPITOL DIVISION

Team	W	L	T	Pct.	PF	PA
Dallas	12	2	0	.857	431	186
N.Y. Giants	7	7	0	.500	294	325
Washington	5	9	0	.357	249	358
Philadelphia	2	12	0	.143	202	351

CENTURY DIVISION

Team	W	L	T	Pct.	PF	PA
Cleveland	10	4	0	.714	394	273
St. Louis	9	4	1	.692	325	289
New Orleans	4	9	1	.308	246	327
Pittsburgh	2	11	1	.154	244	397

WESTERN CONFERENCE

COASTAL DIVISION

Team	W	L	T	Pct.	PF	PA
Baltimore	13	1	0	.929	402	144
Los Angeles	10	3	1	.769	312	200
San Francisco	7	6	1	.538	303	310
Atlanta	2	12	0	.143	170	389

CENTRAL DIVISION

Team	W	L	T	Pct.	PF	PA
Minnesota	8	6	0	.571	282	242
Chicago	7	7	0	.500	250	333
Green Bay	6	7	1	.462	281	227
Detroit	4	8	2	.333	207	241

PLAYOFFS

Conference championships
Cleveland 31 vs. Dallas 20
Baltimore 24 vs. Minnesota 14

NFL championship
Baltimore 34 at Cleveland 0

Super Bowl III
N.Y. Jets 16, Baltimore 7, at Miami.

1969

AFL

EASTERN DIVISION

Team	W	L	T	Pct.	PF	PA
N.Y. Jets	10	4	0	.714	353	269
Houston	6	6	2	.500	278	279
Boston Patriots	4	10	0	.286	266	316
Buffalo	4	10	0	.286	230	359
Miami	3	10	1	.231	233	332

WESTERN DIVISION

Team	W	L	T	Pct.	PF	PA
Oakland	12	1	1	.923	377	242
Kansas City	11	3	0	.786	359	177
San Diego	8	6	0	.571	288	276
Denver	5	8	1	.385	297	344
Cincinnati	4	9	1	.308	280	367

PLAYOFFS

Divisional games
Kansas City 13 at N.Y. Jets 6
Oakland 56 vs. Houston 7

AFL championship
Kansas City 17 at Oakland 7

NFL

EASTERN CONFERENCE

CAPITOL DIVISION

Team	W	L	T	Pct.	PF	PA
Dallas	11	2	1	.846	369	223
Washington	7	5	2	.583	307	319
New Orleans	5	9	0	.357	311	393
Philadelphia	4	9	1	.308	279	377

CENTURY DIVISION

Team	W	L	T	Pct.	PF	PA
Cleveland	10	3	1	.769	351	300
N.Y. Giants	6	8	0	.429	264	298
St. Louis	4	9	1	.308	314	389
Pittsburgh	1	13	0	.071	218	404

WESTERN CONFERENCE

COASTAL DIVISION

Team	W	L	T	Pct.	PF	PA
Los Angeles	11	3	0	.786	320	243
Baltimore	8	5	1	.615	279	268
Atlanta	6	8	0	.429	276	268
San Francisco	4	8	2	.333	277	319

CENTRAL DIVISION

Team	W	L	T	Pct.	PF	PA
Minnesota	12	2	0	.857	379	133
Detroit	9	4	1	.692	259	188
Green Bay	8	6	0	.571	269	221
Chicago	1	13	0	.071	210	339

PLAYOFFS

Conference championships
Cleveland 38 at Dallas 14
Minnesota 23 vs. Los Angeles 20

NFL championship
Minnesota 27 vs. Cleveland 7

Super Bowl IV
Kansas City 23, Minnesota 7, at New Orleans.

1970

AMERICAN CONFERENCE

EASTERN DIVISION

Team	W	L	T	Pct.	PF	PA
Baltimore*	11	2	1	.846	321	234
Miami†	10	4	0	.714	297	228
N.Y. Jets	4	10	0	.286	255	286
Buffalo	3	10	1	.231	204	337
Boston Patriots	2	12	0	.143	149	361

CENTRAL DIVISION

Team	W	L	T	Pct.	PF	PA
Cincinnati*	8	6	0	.571	312	255
Cleveland	7	7	0	.500	286	265
Pittsburgh	5	9	0	.357	210	272
Houston	3	10	1	.231	217	352

WESTERN DIVISION

Team	W	L	T	Pct.	PF	PA
Oakland*	8	4	2	.667	300	293
Kansas City	7	5	2	.583	272	244
San Diego	5	6	3	.455	282	278
Denver	5	8	1	.385	253	264

*Division champion.
†Wild-card team.

NATIONAL CONFERENCE

EASTERN DIVISION

Team	W	L	T	Pct.	PF	PA
Dallas*	10	4	0	.714	299	221
N.Y. Giants	9	5	0	.643	301	270
St. Louis	8	5	1	.615	325	228
Washington	6	8	0	.429	297	314
Philadelphia	3	10	1	.231	241	332

CENTRAL DIVISION

Team	W	L	T	Pct.	PF	PA
Minnesota*	12	2	0	.857	335	143
Detroit†	10	4	0	.714	347	202
Chicago	6	8	0	.429	256	261
Green Bay	6	8	0	.429	196	293

WESTERN DIVISION

Team	W	L	T	Pct.	PF	PA
San Francisco*	10	3	1	.769	352	267
Los Angeles	9	4	1	.692	325	202
Atlanta	4	8	2	.333	206	261
New Orleans	2	11	1	.154	172	347

PLAYOFFS

AFC divisional games
Baltimore 17 vs. Cincinnati 0
Oakland 21 vs. Miami 14

AFC championship
Baltimore 27 vs. Oakland 17

NFC divisional games
Dallas 5 vs. Detroit 0
San Francisco 17 at Minnesota 14

NFC championship
Dallas 17 at San Francisco 10

Super Bowl V
Baltimore 16, Dallas 13, at Miami.

1971

AMERICAN CONFERENCE

EASTERN DIVISION

Team	W	L	T	Pct.	PF	PA
Miami*	10	3	1	.769	315	174
Baltimore†	10	4	0	.714	313	140
New England	6	8	0	.429	238	325
N.Y. Jets	6	8	0	.429	212	299
Buffalo	1	13	0	.071	184	394

CENTRAL DIVISION

Team	W	L	T	Pct.	PF	PA
Cleveland*	9	5	0	.643	285	273
Pittsburgh	6	8	0	.429	246	292
Houston	4	9	1	.308	251	330
Cincinnati	4	10	0	.286	284	265

WESTERN DIVISION

Team	W	L	T	Pct.	PF	PA
Kansas City*	10	3	1	.769	302	208
Oakland	8	4	2	.667	344	278
San Diego	6	8	0	.429	311	341
Denver	4	9	1	.308	203	275

*Division champion.
†Wild-card team.

NATIONAL CONFERENCE

EASTERN DIVISION

Team	W	L	T	Pct.	PF	PA
Dallas*	11	3	0	.786	406	222
Washington†	9	4	1	.692	276	190
Philadelphia	6	7	1	.462	221	302
St. Louis	4	9	1	.308	231	279
N.Y. Giants	4	10	0	.286	228	362

CENTRAL DIVISION

Team	W	L	T	Pct.	PF	PA
Minnesota*	11	3	0	.786	245	139
Detroit	7	6	1	.538	341	286
Chicago	6	8	0	.429	185	276
Green Bay	4	8	2	.333	274	298

WESTERN DIVISION

Team	W	L	T	Pct.	PF	PA
San Francisco*	9	5	0	.643	300	216
Los Angeles	8	5	1	.615	313	260
Atlanta	7	6	1	.538	274	277
New Orleans	4	8	2	.333	266	347

PLAYOFFS

AFC divisional games
Miami 27 at Kansas City 24 (OT)
Baltimore 20 at Cleveland 3

AFC championship
Miami 21 vs. Baltimore 0

NFC divisional games
Dallas 20 at Minnesota 12
San Francisco 24 vs. Washington 20

NFC championship
Dallas 14 vs. San Francisco 3

Super Bowl VI
Dallas 24, Miami 3, at New Orleans.

THE LONGEST DAY

In the longest game in NFL history, the Miami Dolphins defeated the Kansas City Chiefs, 27-24, on Christmas Day 1971 in the first round of the AFC playoffs. Garo Yepremian's 37-yard field goal won it for Miami in the second overtime—after 82 minutes and 40 seconds of play—after Chiefs counterpart Jan Stenerud missed a 31-yard attempt with 35 seconds left in regulation time. Kickers aside, the hero of the game was Chiefs running back Ed Podolak, who gained 350 yards on rushes, receptions and returns. It was the last game played at Kansas City's Municipal Stadium.

AMERICAN CONFERENCE

EASTERN DIVISION

Team	W	L	T	Pct.	PF	PA
Miami*	14	0	0	1.000[ce7]	385	171
N.Y. Jets	7	7	0	.500	367	324
Baltimore	5	9	0	.357	235	252
Buffalo	4	9	1	.321	257	377
New England	3	11	0	.214	192	446

CENTRAL DIVISION

Team	W	L	T	Pct.	PF	PA
Pittsburgh*	11	3	0	.786	343	175
Cleveland†	10	4	0	.714	268	249
Cincinnati	8	6	0	.571	299	229
Houston	1	13	0	.071	164	380

WESTERN DIVISION

Team	W	L	T	Pct.	PF	PA
Oakland*	10	3	1	.750	365	248
Kansas City	8	6	0	.571	287	254
Denver	5	9	0	.357	325	350
San Diego	4	9	1	.321	264	344

*Division champion.
†Wild-card team.

NATIONAL CONFERENCE

EASTERN DIVISION

Team	W	L	T	Pct.	PF	PA
Washington*	11	3	0	.786	336	218
Dallas†	10	4	0	.714	319	240
N.Y. Giants	8	6	0	.571	331	247
St. Louis	4	9	1	.321	193	303
Philadelphia	2	11	1	.179	145	352

CENTRAL DIVISION

Team	W	L	T	Pct.	PF	PA
Green Bay*	10	4	0	.714	304	226
Detroit	8	5	1	.607	339	290
Minnesota	7	7	0	.500	301	252
Chicago	4	9	1	.321	225	275

WESTERN DIVISION

Team	W	L	T	Pct.	PF	PA
San Francisco*	8	5	1	.607	353	249
Atlanta	7	7	0	.500	269	274
Los Angeles	6	7	1	.464	291	286
New Orleans	2	11	1	.179	215	361

PLAYOFFS

AFC divisional games
Pittsburgh 13 vs. Oakland 7
Miami 20 vs. Cleveland 14

AFC championship
Miami 21 at Pittsburgh 17

NFC divisional games
Dallas 30 at San Francisco 28
Washington 16 vs. Green Bay 3

NFC championship
Washington 26 vs. Dallas 3

Super Bowl VII
Miami 14, Washington 7, at Los Angeles.

AMERICAN CONFERENCE

EASTERN DIVISION

Team	W	L	T	Pct.	PF	PA
Miami*	12	2	0	.857	343	150
Buffalo	9	5	0	.643	259	230
New England	5	9	0	.357	258	300
Baltimore	4	10	0	.286	226	341
N.Y. Jets	4	10	0	.286	240	306

CENTRAL DIVISION

Team	W	L	T	Pct.	PF	PA
Cincinnati*	10	4	0	.714	286	231
Pittsburgh†	10	4	0	.714	347	210
Cleveland	7	5	2	.571	234	255
Houston	1	13	0	.071	199	447

WESTERN DIVISION

Team	W	L	T	Pct.	PF	PA
Oakland*	9	4	1	.679	292	175
Denver	7	5	2	.571	354	296
Kansas City	7	5	2	.571	231	192
San Diego	2	11	1	.179	188	386

*Division champion.
†Wild-card team.

NATIONAL CONFERENCE

EASTERN DIVISION

Team	W	L	T	Pct.	PF	PA
Dallas*	10	4	0	.714	382	203
Washington†	10	4	0	.714	325	198
Philadelphia	5	8	1	.393	310	393
St. Louis	4	9	1	.321	286	365
N.Y. Giants	2	11	1	.179	226	362

CENTRAL DIVISION

Team	W	L	T	Pct.	PF	PA
Minnesota*	12	2	0	.857	296	168
Detroit	6	7	1	.464	271	247
Green Bay	5	7	2	.429	202	259
Chicago	3	11	0	.214	195	334

WESTERN DIVISION

Team	W	L	T	Pct.	PF	PA
Los Angeles*	12	2	0	.857	388	178
Atlanta	9	5	0	.643	318	224
New Orleans	5	9	0	.357	163	312
San Francisco	5	9	0	.357	262	319

PLAYOFFS

AFC divisional games
Oakland 33 vs. Pittsburgh 14
Miami 34 vs. Cincinnati 16

AFC championship
Miami 27 vs. Oakland 10

NFC divisional games
Minnesota 27 vs. Washington 20
Dallas 27 vs. Los Angeles 16

NFC championship
Minnesota 27 at Dallas 10

Super Bowl VIII
Miami 24, Minnesota 7, at Houston.

AMERICAN CONFERENCE

EASTERN DIVISION

Team	W	L	T	Pct.	PF	PA
Miami*	11	3	0	.786	327	216
Buffalo†	9	5	0	.643	264	244
New England	7	7	0	.500	348	289
N.Y. Jets	7	7	0	.500	279	300
Baltimore	2	12	0	.143	190	329

CENTRAL DIVISION

Team	W	L	T	Pct.	PF	PA
Pittsburgh*	10	3	1	.750	305	189
Cincinnati	7	7	0	.500	283	259
Houston	7	7	0	.500	236	282
Cleveland	4	10	0	.286	251	344

WESTERN DIVISION

Team	W	L	T	Pct.	PF	PA
Oakland*	12	2	0	.857	355	228
Denver	7	6	1	.536	302	294
Kansas City	5	9	0	.357	233	293
San Diego	5	9	0	.357	212	285

*Division champion.
†Wild-card team.

NATIONAL CONFERENCE

EASTERN DIVISION

Team	W	L	T	Pct.	PF	PA
St. Louis*	10	4	0	.714	285	218
Washington†	10	4	0	.714	320	196
Dallas	8	6	0	.571	297	235
Philadelphia	7	7	0	.500	242	217
N.Y. Giants	2	12	0	.143	195	299

CENTRAL DIVISION

Team	W	L	T	Pct.	PF	PA
Minnesota*	10	4	0	.714	310	195
Detroit	7	7	0	.500	256	270
Green Bay	6	8	0	.429	210	206
Chicago	4	10	0	.286	152	279

WESTERN DIVISION

Team	W	L	T	Pct.	PF	PA
Los Angeles*	10	4	0	.714	263	181
San Francisco	6	8	0	.429	226	236
New Orleans	5	9	0	.357	166	263
Atlanta	3	11	0	.214	111	271

PLAYOFFS

AFC divisional games
Oakland 28 vs. Miami 26
Pittsburgh 32 vs. Buffalo 14

AFC championship
Pittsburgh 24 at Oakland 13

NFC divisional games
Minnesota 30 vs. St. Louis 14
Los Angeles 19 vs. Washington 10

NFC championship
Minnesota 14 vs. Los Angeles 10

Super Bowl IX
Pittsburgh 16, Minnesota 6, at New Orleans.

HISTORY *Year-by-year standings*

1975

AMERICAN CONFERENCE

EASTERN DIVISION

Team	W	L	T	Pct.	PF	PA
Baltimore*	10	4	0	.714	395	269
Miami	10	4	0	.714	357	222
Buffalo	8	6	0	.571	420	355
New England	3	11	0	.214	258	358
N.Y. Jets	3	11	0	.214	258	433

CENTRAL DIVISION

Team	W	L	T	Pct.	PF	PA
Pittsburgh*	12	2	0	.857	373	162
Cincinnati†	11	3	0	.786	340	246
Houston	10	4	0	.714	293	226
Cleveland	3	11	0	.214	218	372

WESTERN DIVISION

Team	W	L	T	Pct.	PF	PA
Oakland*	11	3	0	.786	375	255
Denver	6	8	0	.429	254	307
Kansas City	5	9	0	.357	282	341
San Diego	2	12	0	.143	189	345

*Division champion.
†Wild-card team.

NATIONAL CONFERENCE

EASTERN DIVISION

Team	W	L	T	Pct.	PF	PA
St. Louis*	11	3	0	.786	356	276
Dallas†	10	4	0	.714	350	268
Washington	8	6	0	.571	325	276
N.Y. Giants	5	9	0	.357	216	306
Philadelphia	4	10	0	.286	225	302

CENTRAL DIVISION

Team	W	L	T	Pct.	PF	PA
Minnesota*	12	2	0	.857	377	180
Detroit	7	7	0	.500	245	262
Chicago	4	10	0	.286	191	379
Green Bay	4	10	0	.286	226	285

WESTERN DIVISION

Team	W	L	T	Pct.	PF	PA
Los Angeles*	12	2	0	.857	312	135
San Francisco	5	9	0	.357	255	286
Atlanta	4	10	0	.286	240	289
New Orleans	2	12	0	.143	165	360

PLAYOFFS

AFC divisional games
Pittsburgh 28 vs. Baltimore 10
Oakland 31 vs. Cincinnati 28

AFC championship
Pittsburgh 16 vs. Oakland 10

NFC divisional games
Los Angeles 35 vs. St. Louis 23
Dallas 17 at Minnesota 14

NFC championship
Dallas 37 at Los Angeles 7

Super Bowl X
Pittsburgh 21, Dallas 17, at Miami.

1976

AMERICAN CONFERENCE

EASTERN DIVISION

Team	W	L	T	Pct.	PF	PA
Baltimore*	11	3	0	.786	417	246
New England†	11	3	0	.786	376	236
Miami	6	8	0	.429	263	264
N.Y. Jets	3	11	0	.214	169	383
Buffalo	2	12	0	.143	245	363

CENTRAL DIVISION

Team	W	L	T	Pct.	PF	PA
Pittsburgh*	10	4	0	.714	342	138
Cincinnati	10	4	0	.714	335	210
Cleveland	9	5	0	.643	267	287
Houston	5	9	0	.357	222	273

WESTERN DIVISION

Team	W	L	T	Pct.	PF	PA
Oakland*	13	1	0	.929	350	237
Denver	9	5	0	.643	315	206
San Diego	6	8	0	.429	248	285
Kansas City	5	9	0	.357	290	376
Tampa Bay	0	14	0	.000	125	412

*Division champion.
†Wild-card team.

NATIONAL CONFERENCE

EASTERN DIVISION

Team	W	L	T	Pct.	PF	PA
Dallas*	11	3	0	.786	296	194
Washington†	10	4	0	.714	291	217
St. Louis	10	4	0	.714	309	267
Philadelphia	4	10	0	.286	165	286
N.Y. Giants	3	11	0	.214	170	250

CENTRAL DIVISION

Team	W	L	T	Pct.	PF	PA
Minnesota*	11	2	1	.821	305	176
Chicago	7	7	0	.500	253	216
Detroit	6	8	0	.429	262	220
Green Bay	5	9	0	.357	218	299

WESTERN DIVISION

Team	W	L	T	Pct.	PF	PA
Los Angeles*	10	3	1	.750	351	190
San Francisco	8	6	0	.571	270	190
Atlanta	4	10	0	.286	172	312
New Orleans	4	10	0	.286	253	346
Seattle	2	12	0	.143	229	429

PLAYOFFS

AFC divisional games
Oakland 24 vs. New England 21
Pittsburgh 40 at Baltimore 14

AFC championship
Oakland 24 vs. Pittsburgh 7

NFC divisional games
Minnesota 35 vs. Washington 20
Los Angeles 14 at Dallas 12

NFC championship
Minnesota 24 vs. Los Angeles 13

Super Bowl XI
Oakland 32, Minnesota 14, at Pasadena, Calif.

JUICE WAS HOT

On December 16, 1973, O.J. Simpson of the Buffalo Bills rushed for 200 yards against the New York Jets, becoming the first player to rush for 2,000 in an NFL season. The feat has since been accomplished two more times—by Eric Dickerson in 1984 and Barry Sanders in 1997—but both of those players needed 16 games to reach the milestone. Simpson did it in 14. The 200-yard game was Simpson's third that season, and he still holds the league record with six career 200-yard games. The 1973 Bills became the first NFL team to rush for 3,000 yards in a season.

1977

AMERICAN CONFERENCE

EASTERN DIVISION

Team	W	L	T	Pct.	PF	PA
Baltimore*	10	4	0	.714	295	221
Miami	10	4	0	.714	313	197
New England	9	5	0	.643	278	217
N.Y. Jets	3	11	0	.214	191	300
Buffalo	3	11	0	.214	160	313

CENTRAL DIVISION

Team	W	L	T	Pct.	PF	PA
Pittsburgh*	9	5	0	.643	283	243
Houston	8	6	0	.571	299	230
Cincinnati	8	6	0	.571	238	235
Cleveland	6	8	0	.429	269	267

WESTERN DIVISION

Team	W	L	T	Pct.	PF	PA
Denver*	12	2	0	.857	274	148
Oakland†	11	3	0	.786	351	230
San Diego	7	7	0	.500	222	205
Seattle	5	9	0	.357	282	373
Kansas City	2	12	0	.143	225	349

*Division champion.
†Wild-card team.

NATIONAL CONFERENCE

EASTERN DIVISION

Team	W	L	T	Pct.	PF	PA
Dallas*	12	2	0	.857	345	212
Washington	9	5	0	.643	196	189
St. Louis	7	7	0	.500	272	287
Philadelphia	5	9	0	.357	220	207
N.Y. Giants	5	9	0	.357	181	265

CENTRAL DIVISION

Team	W	L	T	Pct.	PF	PA
Minnesota*	9	5	0	.643	231	227
Chicago†	9	5	0	.643	255	253
Detroit	6	8	0	.429	183	252
Green Bay	4	10	0	.286	134	219
Tampa Bay	2	12	0	.143	103	223

WESTERN DIVISION

Team	W	L	T	Pct.	PF	PA
Los Angeles*	10	4	0	.714	302	146
Atlanta	7	7	0	.500	179	129
San Francisco	5	9	0	.357	220	260
New Orleans	3	11	0	.214	232	336

PLAYOFFS

AFC divisional games
Denver 34 vs. Pittsburgh 21
Oakland 37 at Baltimore 31 (OT)

AFC championship
Denver 20 vs. Oakland 17

NFC divisional games
Dallas 37 vs. Chicago 7
Minnesota 14 at Los Angeles 7

NFC championship
Dallas 23 vs. Minnesota 6

Super Bowl XII
Dallas 27, Denver 10, at New Orleans.

1978

AMERICAN CONFERENCE

EASTERN DIVISION

Team	W	L	T	Pct.	PF	PA
New England*	11	5	0	.688	358	286
Miami†	11	5	0	.688	372	254
N.Y. Jets	8	8	0	.500	359	364
Buffalo	5	11	0	.313	302	354
Baltimore	5	11	0	.313	239	421

CENTRAL DIVISION

Team	W	L	T	Pct.	PF	PA
Pittsburgh*	14	2	0	.875	356	195
Houston†	10	6	0	.625	283	298
Cleveland	8	8	0	.500	334	356
Cincinnati	4	12	0	.250	252	284

WESTERN DIVISION

Team	W	L	T	Pct.	PF	PA
Denver*	10	6	0	.625	282	198
Oakland	9	7	0	.563	311	283
Seattle	9	7	0	.563	345	358
San Diego	9	7	0	.563	355	309
Kansas City	4	12	0	.250	243	327

*Division champion.
†Wild-card team.

NATIONAL CONFERENCE

EASTERN DIVISION

Team	W	L	T	Pct.	PF	PA
Dallas*	12	4	0	.750	384	208
Philadelphia†	9	7	0	.563	270	250
Washington	8	8	0	.500	273	283
St. Louis	6	10	0	.375	248	296
N.Y. Giants	6	10	0	.375	264	298

CENTRAL DIVISION

Team	W	L	T	Pct.	PF	PA
Minnesota*	8	7	1	.531	294	306
Green Bay	8	7	1	.531	249	269
Detroit	7	9	0	.438	290	300
Chicago	7	9	0	.438	253	274
Tampa Bay	5	11	0	.313	241	259

WESTERN DIVISION

Team	W	L	T	Pct.	PF	PA
Los Angeles*	12	4	0	.750	316	245
Atlanta†	9	7	0	.563	240	290
New Orleans	7	9	0	.438	281	298
San Francisco	2	14	0	.125	219	350

PLAYOFFS

AFC wild-card game
Houston 17 at Miami 9

AFC divisional games
Houston 31 at New England 14
Pittsburgh 33 vs. Denver 10

AFC championship
Pittsburgh 34 vs. Houston 5

NFC wild-card game
Atlanta 14 vs. Philadelphia 13

NFC divisional games
Dallas 27 vs. Atlanta 20
Los Angeles 34 vs. Minnesota 10

NFC championship
Dallas 28 at Los Angeles 0

Super Bowl XIII
Pittsburgh 35, Dallas 31, at Miami.

NO HEISMAN JINX FOR T.D.

In a case of the rich getting richer, the Dallas Cowboys—on the heels of a division-winning, 11-win season in 1976—used the second pick in the 1977 draft to select Heisman Trophy-winning running back Tony Dorsett of Pittsburgh. (The Cowboys had acquired the No. 2 pick in a trade with the Seattle Seahawks.) And Dorsett didn't disappoint, rushing for 1,007 yards and scoring 12 touchdown as a rookie and helping Dallas win its second Super Bowl. He was a consensus choice for NFL Rookie of the Year.

1979

AMERICAN CONFERENCE

EASTERN DIVISION

Team	W	L	T	Pct.	PF	PA
Miami*	10	6	0	.625	341	257
New England	9	7	0	.563	411	326
N.Y. Jets	8	8	0	.500	337	383
Buffalo	7	9	0	.438	268	279
Baltimore	5	11	0	.313	271	351

CENTRAL DIVISION

Team	W	L	T	Pct.	PF	PA
Pittsburgh*	12	4	0	.750	416	262
Houston†	11	5	0	.688	362	331
Cleveland	9	7	0	.563	359	352
Cincinnati	4	12	0	.250	337	421

WESTERN DIVISION

Team	W	L	T	Pct.	PF	PA
San Diego*	12	4	0	.750	411	246
Denver†	10	6	0	.625	289	262
Seattle	9	7	0	.563	378	372
Oakland	9	7	0	.563	365	337
Kansas City	7	9	0	.438	238	262

*Division champion.
†Wild-card team.

NATIONAL CONFERENCE

EASTERN DIVISION

Team	W	L	T	Pct.	PF	PA
Dallas*	11	5	0	.688	371	313
Philadelphia†	11	5	0	.688	339	282
Washington	10	6	0	.625	348	295
N.Y. Giants	6	10	0	.375	237	323
St. Louis	5	11	0	.313	307	358

CENTRAL DIVISION

Team	W	L	T	Pct.	PF	PA
Tampa Bay*	10	6	0	.625	273	237
Chicago†	10	6	0	.625	306	249
Minnesota	7	9	0	.438	259	337
Green Bay	5	11	0	.313	246	316
Detroit	2	14	0	.125	219	365

WESTERN DIVISION

Team	W	L	T	Pct.	PF	PA
Los Angeles*	9	7	0	.563	323	309
New Orleans	8	8	0	.500	370	360
Atlanta	6	10	0	.375	300	388
San Francisco	2	14	0	.125	308	416

PLAYOFFS

AFC wild-card game
Houston 13 vs. Denver 7

AFC divisional games
Houston 17 at San Diego 14
Pittsburgh 34 vs. Miami 14

AFC championship
Pittsburgh 27 vs. Houston 13

NFC wild-card game
Philadelphia 27 vs. Chicago 17

NFC divisional games
Tampa Bay 24 vs. Philadelphia 17
Los Angeles 21 at Dallas 19

NFC championship
Los Angeles 9 at Tampa Bay 0

Super Bowl XIV
Pittsburgh 31, Los Angeles 19, at Pasadena, Calif.

1980

AMERICAN CONFERENCE

EASTERN DIVISION

Team	W	L	T	Pct.	PF	PA
Buffalo*	11	5	0	.688	320	260
New England	10	6	0	.625	441	325
Miami	8	8	0	.500	266	305
Baltimore	7	9	0	.438	355	387
N.Y. Jets	4	12	0	.250	302	395

CENTRAL DIVISION

Team	W	L	T	Pct.	PF	PA
Cleveland*	11	5	0	.688	357	310
Houston†	11	5	0	.688	295	251
Pittsburgh	9	7	0	.563	352	313
Cincinnati	6	10	0	.375	244	312

WESTERN DIVISION

Team	W	L	T	Pct.	PF	PA
San Diego*	11	5	0	.688	418	327
Oakland†	11	5	0	.688	364	306
Kansas City	8	8	0	.500	319	336
Denver	8	8	0	.500	310	323
Seattle	4	12	0	.250	291	408

*Division champion.
†Wild-card team.

NATIONAL CONFERENCE

EASTERN DIVISION

Team	W	L	T	Pct.	PF	PA
Philadelphia*	12	4	0	.750	384	222
Dallas†	12	4	0	.750	454	311
Washington	6	10	0	.375	261	293
St. Louis	5	11	0	.313	299	350
N.Y. Giants	4	12	0	.250	249	425

CENTRAL DIVISION

Team	W	L	T	Pct.	PF	PA
Minnesota*	9	7	0	.563	317	308
Detroit	9	7	0	.563	334	272
Chicago	7	9	0	.438	304	264
Tampa Bay	5	10	1	.344	271	341
Green Bay	5	10	1	.344	231	371

WESTERN DIVISION

Team	W	L	T	Pct.	PF	PA
Atlanta*	12	4	0	.750	405	272
Los Angeles†	11	5	0	.688	424	289
San Francisco	6	10	0	.375	320	415
New Orleans	1	15	0	.063	291	487

PLAYOFFS

AFC wild-card game
Oakland 27 vs. Houston 7

AFC divisional games
San Diego 20 vs. Buffalo 14
Oakland 14 at Cleveland 12

AFC championship
Oakland 34 at San Diego 27

NFC wild-card game
Dallas 34 vs. Los Angeles 13

NFC divisional games
Philadelphia 31 vs. Minnesota 16
Dallas 30 at Atlanta 27

NFC championship
Philadelphia 20 vs. Dallas 7

Super Bowl XV
Oakland 27, Philadelphia 10, at New Orleans.

THE BIGGEST COMEBACK

In a harbinger of things to come, the San Francisco 49ers rallied from a 35-7 deficit to beat New Orleans, 38-35, on December 7, 1980. An otherwise meaningless late-season game became the biggest comeback in NFL history as the 49ers tied the game with a touchdown with 1:50 left and won it on Ray Wersching's 36-yard field goal at 7:40 of overtime. Second-year quarterback Joe Montana threw two touchdown passes for San Francisco to offset the three TD passes Archie Manning tossed for the Saints, who finished the season with the league's worst record (1-15).

1981

AMERICAN CONFERENCE

EASTERN DIVISION

Team	W	L	T	Pct.	PF	PA
Miami*	11	4	1	.719	345	275
N.Y. Jets†	10	5	1	.656	355	287
Buffalo†	10	6	0	.625	311	276
Baltimore	2	14	0	.125	259	533
New England	2	14	0	.125	322	370

CENTRAL DIVISION

Team	W	L	T	Pct.	PF	PA
Cincinnati*	12	4	0	.750	421	304
Pittsburgh	8	8	0	.500	356	297
Houston	7	9	0	.438	281	355
Cleveland	5	11	0	.313	276	375

WESTERN DIVISION

Team	W	L	T	Pct.	PF	PA
San Diego*	10	6	0	.625	478	390
Denver	10	6	0	.625	321	289
Kansas City	9	7	0	.563	343	290
Oakland	7	9	0	.438	273	343
Seattle	6	10	0	.375	322	388

*Division champion.
†Wild-card team.

NATIONAL CONFERENCE

EASTERN DIVISION

Team	W	L	T	Pct.	PF	PA
Dallas*	12	4	0	.750	367	277
Philadelphia†	10	6	0	.625	368	221
N.Y. Giants†	9	7	0	.563	295	257
Washington	8	8	0	.500	347	349
St. Louis	7	9	0	.438	315	408

CENTRAL DIVISION

Team	W	L	T	Pct.	PF	PA
Tampa Bay*	9	7	0	.563	315	268
Detroit	8	8	0	.500	397	322
Green Bay	8	8	0	.500	324	361
Minnesota	7	9	0	.438	325	369
Chicago	6	10	0	.375	253	324

WESTERN DIVISION

Team	W	L	T	Pct.	PF	PA
San Francisco*	13	3	0	.813	357	250
Atlanta	7	9	0	.438	426	355
Los Angeles	6	10	0	.375	303	351
New Orleans	4	12	0	.250	207	378

PLAYOFFS

AFC wild-card game
Buffalo 31 at New York Jets 27

AFC divisional games
San Diego 41 at Miami 38 (OT)
Cincinnati 28 vs. Buffalo 21

AFC championship
Cincinnati 27 vs. San Diego 7

NFC wild-card game
N.Y. Giants 27 at Philadelphia 21

NFC divisional games
Dallas 38 vs. Tampa Bay 0
San Francisco 38 vs. N.Y. Giants 24

NFC championship
San Francisco 28 vs. Dallas 27

Super Bowl XVI
San Francisco 26, Cincinnati 21, at Pontiac, Mich.

1982

AMERICAN CONFERENCE

Team	W	L	T	Pct.	PF	PA
L.A. Raiders	8	1	0	.889	260	200
Miami	7	2	0	.778	198	131
Cincinnati	7	2	0	.778	232	177
Pittsburgh	6	3	0	.667	204	146
San Diego	6	3	0	.667	288	221
N.Y. Jets	6	3	0	.667	245	166
New England	5	4	0	.556	143	157
Cleveland	4	5	0	.444	140	182
Buffalo	4	5	0	.444	150	154
Seattle	4	5	0	.444	127	147
Kansas City	3	6	0	.333	176	184
Denver	2	7	0	.222	148	226
Houston	1	8	0	.111	136	245
Baltimore	0	8	1	.056	113	236

NATIONAL CONFERENCE

Team	W	L	T	Pct.	PF	PA
Washington	8	1	0	.889	190	128
Dallas	6	3	0	.667	226	145
Green Bay	5	3	1	.611	226	169
Minnesota	5	4	0	.556	187	198
Atlanta	5	4	0	.556	183	199
St. Louis	5	4	0	.556	135	170
Tampa Bay	5	4	0	.556	158	178
Detroit	4	5	0	.444	181	176
New Orleans	4	5	0	.444	129	160
N.Y. Giants	4	5	0	.444	164	160
San Francisco	3	6	0	.333	209	206
Chicago	3	6	0	.333	141	174
Philadelphia	3	6	0	.333	191	195
L.A. Rams	2	7	0	.222	200	250

As a result of a 57-day players' strike, the 1982 NFL regular season schedule was reduced from 16 weeks to 9. At the conclusion of the regular season, a 16-team Super Bowl Tournament was held. Eight teams from each conference were seeded 1 through 8 based on their records during regular season play.

Miami finished ahead of Cincinnati based on a better conference record. Pittsburgh won common games tiebreaker with San Diego after New York Jets were eliminated from three-way tie based on conference record. Cleveland finished ahead of Buffalo and Seattle based on better conference record. Minnesota, Atlanta, St. Louis and Tampa Bay seeds were determined by best won-lost record in conference games. Detroit finished ahead of New Orleans and the New York Giants based on a better conference record.

PLAYOFFS

AFC first round
Miami 28 vs. New England 13
L.A. Raiders 27 vs. Cleveland 10
New York Jets 44 at Cincinnati 17
San Diego 31 at Pittsburgh 28

AFC second round
N.Y. Jets 17 at L.A. Raiders 14
Miami 34 vs. San Diego 13

AFC championship
Miami 14 vs. New York Jets 0

NFC first round
Washington 31 vs. Detroit 7
Green Bay 41 vs. St. Louis 16
Minnesota 30 vs. Atlanta 24
Dallas 30 vs. Tampa Bay 17

NFC second round
Washington 21 vs. Minnesota 7
Dallas 37 vs. Green Bay 26

NFC championship
Washington 31 vs. Dallas 17

Super Bowl XVII
Washington 27, Miami 17, at Pasadena, Calif.

A GAME FOR THE AGES

In a game voted the NFL's "Game of the '80s" by the Pro Football Hall of Fame, the San Diego Chargers beat the Miami Dolphins, 41-38, in an AFC divisional playoff game on January 2, 1982. The two teams combined to set 11 NFL playoff records, including most points (79) and most total yards (1,036). Five players caught passes for at least 100 yards, including Chargers tight end Kellen Winslow, who caught 13 passes for 166 yards. Winslow also blocked a 43-yard field goal attempt by the Dolphins' Uwe von Schamann on the final play of regulation time, enabling Rolf Benirschke to win it for San Diego with a 29-yard field goal at 13:52 of overtime.

1983

AMERICAN CONFERENCE

EASTERN DIVISION

Team	W	L	T	Pct.	PF	PA
Miami*	12	4	0	.750	389	250
New England	8	8	0	.500	274	289
Buffalo	8	8	0	.500	283	351
Baltimore	7	9	0	.438	264	354
N.Y. Jets	7	9	0	.438	313	331

CENTRAL DIVISION

Team	W	L	T	Pct.	PF	PA
Pittsburgh*	10	6	0	.625	355	303
Cleveland	9	7	0	.563	356	342
Cincinnati	7	9	0	.438	346	302
Houston	2	14	0	.125	288	460

WESTERN DIVISION

Team	W	L	T	Pct.	PF	PA
L.A. Raiders*	12	4	0	.750	442	338
Seattle†	9	7	0	.563	403	397
Denver†	9	7	0	.563	302	327
San Diego	6	10	0	.375	358	462
Kansas City	6	10	0	.375	386	367

*Division champion.
†Wild-card team.

NATIONAL CONFERENCE

EASTERN DIVISION

Team	W	L	T	Pct.	PF	PA
Washington*	14	2	0	.875	541	332
Dallas†	12	4	0	.750	479	360
St. Louis	8	7	1	.531	374	428
Philadelphia	5	11	0	.313	233	322
N.Y. Giants	3	12	1	.219	267	347

CENTRAL DIVISION

Team	W	L	T	Pct.	PF	PA
Detroit*	9	7	0	.563	347	286
Green Bay	8	8	0	.500	429	439
Chicago	8	8	0	.500	311	301
Minnesota	8	8	0	.500	316	348
Tampa Bay	2	14	0	.125	241	380

WESTERN DIVISION

Team	W	L	T	Pct.	PF	PA
San Francisco*	10	6	0	.625	432	293
L.A. Rams†	9	7	0	.563	361	344
New Orleans	8	8	0	.500	319	337
Atlanta	7	9	0	.438	370	389

PLAYOFFS

AFC wild-card game
Seattle 31 vs. Denver 7

AFC divisional games
Seattle 27 at Miami 20
L.A. Raiders 38 vs. Pittsburgh 10

AFC championship game
L.A. Raiders 30 vs. Seattle 14

NFC wild-card game
Los Angeles Rams 24 at Dallas 17

NFC divisional games
San Francisco 24 vs. Detroit 23
Washington 51 vs. L.A. Rams 7

NFC championship
Washington 24 vs. San Francisco 21

Super Bowl XVIII
L.A. Raiders 38, Washington 9, at Tampa, Fla.

1984

AMERICAN CONFERENCE

EASTERN DIVISION

Team	W	L	T	Pct.	PF	PA
Miami*	14	2	0	.875	513	298
New England	9	7	0	.563	362	352
N.Y. Jets	7	9	0	.438	332	364
Indianapolis	4	12	0	.250	239	414
Buffalo	2	14	0	.125	250	454

CENTRAL DIVISION

Team	W	L	T	Pct.	PF	PA
Pittsburgh*	9	7	0	.563	387	310
Cincinnati	8	8	0	.500	339	339
Cleveland	5	11	0	.313	250	297
Houston	3	13	0	.188	240	437

WESTERN DIVISION

Team	W	L	T	Pct.	PF	PA
Denver*	13	3	0	.813	353	241
Seattle†	12	4	0	.750	418	282
L.A. Raiders†	11	5	0	.688	368	278
Kansas City	8	8	0	.500	314	324
San Diego	7	9	0	.438	394	413

*Division champion.
†Wild-card team.

NATIONAL CONFERENCE

EASTERN DIVISION

Team	W	L	T	Pct.	PF	PA
Washington*	11	5	0	.688	426	310
N.Y. Giants†	9	7	0	.563	299	301
St. Louis	9	7	0	.563	423	345
Dallas	9	7	0	.563	308	308
Philadelphia	6	9	1	.406	278	320

CENTRAL DIVISION

Team	W	L	T	Pct.	PF	PA
Chicago*	10	6	0	.625	325	248
Green Bay	8	8	0	.500	390	309
Tampa Bay	6	10	0	.375	335	380
Detroit	4	11	1	.281	283	408
Minnesota	3	13	0	.188	276	484

WESTERN DIVISION

Team	W	L	T	Pct.	PF	PA
San Francisco*	15	1	0	.938	475	227
L.A. Rams†	10	6	0	.625	346	316
New Orleans	7	9	0	.438	298	361
Atlanta	4	12	0	.250	281	382

PLAYOFFS

AFC wild-card game
Seattle 13 vs. Los Angeles Raiders 7

AFC divisional games
Miami 31 vs. Seattle 10
Pittsburgh 24 at Denver 17

AFC championship
Miami 45 vs. Pittsburgh 28

NFC wild-card game
N.Y. Giants 16 at L.A. Rams 13

NFC divisional games
San Francisco 21 vs. N.Y. Giants 10
Chicago 23 at Washington 19

NFC championship
San Francisco 23 vs. Chicago 0

Super Bowl XIX
San Francisco 38, Miami 16, at Palo Alto, Calif.

DAN'S THE MAN

In 1984, Dan Marino of the Miami Dolphins had perhaps the greatest season of any quarterback in NFL history. In only his second year Marino led the league in attempts (564), completions (362), yards (5,084), average gain per pass attempt (9.0), percentage of TDs per attempt (8.5), touchdowns (48) and QB rating (108.9). His yards, TDs and completion totals set NFL records. It took Marino just eight games to break Bob Griese's team record for touchdown passes in a season and nine games to break Griese's yardage mark. At 23, Marino also became the youngest quarterback to take his team to the Super Bowl, where the Dolphins lost to the 49ers.

1985

AMERICAN CONFERENCE

EASTERN DIVISION

Team	W	L	T	Pct.	PF	PA
Miami*	12	4	0	.750	428	320
N.Y. Jets†	11	5	0	.688	393	264
New England†	11	5	0	.688	362	290
Indianapolis	5	11	0	.313	320	386
Buffalo	2	14	0	.125	200	381

CENTRAL DIVISION

Team	W	L	T	Pct.	PF	PA
Cleveland*	8	8	0	.500	287	294
Cincinnati	7	9	0	.438	441	437
Pittsburgh	7	9	0	.438	379	355
Houston	5	11	0	.313	284	412

WESTERN DIVISION

Team	W	L	T	Pct.	PF	PA
L.A. Raiders*	12	4	0	.750	354	308
Denver	11	5	0	.688	380	329
Seattle	8	8	0	.500	349	303
San Diego	8	8	0	.500	467	435
Kansas City	6	10	0	.375	317	360

*Division champion.
†Wild-card team.

NATIONAL CONFERENCE

EASTERN DIVISION

Team	W	L	T	Pct.	PF	PA
Dallas*	10	6	0	.625	357	333
N.Y. Giants†	10	6	0	.625	399	283
Washington	10	6	0	.625	297	312
Philadelphia	7	9	0	.438	286	310
St. Louis	5	11	0	.313	278	414

CENTRAL DIVISION

Team	W	L	T	Pct.	PF	PA
Chicago*	15	1	0	.938	456	198
Green Bay	8	8	0	.500	337	355
Minnesota	7	9	0	.438	346	359
Detroit	7	9	0	.438	307	366
Tampa Bay	2	14	0	.125	294	448

WESTERN DIVISION

Team	W	L	T	Pct.	PF	PA
L.A. Rams*	11	5	0	.688	340	277
San Francisco†	10	6	0	.625	411	263
New Orleans	5	11	0	.313	294	401
Atlanta	4	12	0	.250	282	452

PLAYOFFS

AFC wild-card game
New England 26 at N.Y. Jets 14

AFC divisional games
Miami 24 vs. Cleveland 21
New England 27 at L.A. Raiders 20

AFC championship
New England 31 at Miami 14

NFC wild-card game
N.Y. Giants 17 vs. San Francisco 3

NFC divisional games
Los Angeles Rams 20 vs. Dallas 0
Chicago 21 vs. New York Giants 0

NFC championship
Chicago 24 vs. Los Angeles Rams 0

Super Bowl XX
Chicago 46, New England 10, at New Orleans.

1986

AMERICAN CONFERENCE

EASTERN DIVISION

Team	W	L	T	Pct.	PF	PA
New England*	11	5	0	.688	412	307
N.Y. Jets†	10	6	0	.625	364	386
Miami	8	8	0	.500	430	405
Buffalo	4	12	0	.250	287	348
Indianapolis	3	13	0	.188	229	400

CENTRAL DIVISION

Team	W	L	T	Pct.	PF	PA
Cleveland*	12	4	0	.750	391	310
Cincinnati	10	6	0	.625	409	394
Pittsburgh	6	10	0	.375	307	336
Houston	5	11	0	.313	274	329

WESTERN DIVISION

Team	W	L	T	Pct.	PF	PA
Denver*	11	5	0	.688	378	327
Kansas City†	10	6	0	.625	358	326
Seattle	10	6	0	.625	366	293
L.A. Raiders	8	8	0	.500	323	346
San Diego	4	12	0	.250	335	396

*Division champion.
†Wild-card team.

NATIONAL CONFERENCE

EASTERN DIVISION

Team	W	L	T	Pct.	PF	PA
N.Y. Giants*	14	2	0	.875	371	236
Washington†	12	4	0	.750	368	296
Dallas	7	9	0	.438	346	337
Philadelphia	5	10	1	.344	256	312
St. Louis	4	11	1	.281	218	351

CENTRAL DIVISION

Team	W	L	T	Pct.	PF	PA
Chicago*	14	2	0	.875	352	187
Minnesota	9	7	0	.563	398	273
Detroit	5	11	0	.313	277	326
Green Bay	4	12	0	.250	254	418
Tampa Bay	2	14	0	.125	239	473

WESTERN DIVISION

Team	W	L	T	Pct.	PF	PA
San Francisco*	10	5	1	.656	374	247
L.A. Rams†	10	6	0	.625	309	267
Atlanta	7	8	1	.469	280	280
New Orleans	7	9	0	.438	288	287

PLAYOFFS

AFC wild-card game
N.Y. Jets 35 vs. Kansas City 15

AFC divisional games
Cleveland 23 vs. N.Y. Jets 20 (OT)
Denver 22 vs. New England 17

AFC championship
Denver 23 at Cleveland 20 (OT)

NFC wild-card game
Washington 19 vs. L.A. Rams 7

NFC divisional games
Washington 27 at Chicago 13
N.Y. Giants 49 vs. San Francisco 3

NFC championship
N.Y. Giants 17 vs. Washington 0

Super Bowl XXI
New York Giants 39, Denver 20, at Pasadena, Calif.

DOUBLE GRAND

In 1985, Roger Craig of the San Francisco 49ers did something no NFL player had done before or has done since—rush for more than 1,000 yards and catch passes for more than 1,000 in the same season. Craig's final numbers were 1,050 yards rushing on 214 attempts and 1,016 yards receiving on an NFL-high 92 receptions. Despite Craig's heroics, the 49ers had (for them) one of their most disappointing seasons of the 1980s. Although they won 10 games, the defending Super Bowl champions finished second to the Rams in the NFC West and lost in the first round of the playoffs.

1987

AMERICAN CONFERENCE

EASTERN DIVISION

Team	W	L	T	Pct.	PF	PA
Indianapolis*	9	6	0	.600	300	238
New England	8	7	0	.533	320	293
Miami	8	7	0	.533	362	335
Buffalo	7	8	0	.467	270	305
N.Y. Jets	6	9	0	.400	334	360

CENTRAL DIVISION

Team	W	L	T	Pct.	PF	PA
Cleveland*	10	5	0	.667	390	239
Houston†	9	6	0	.600	345	349
Pittsburgh	8	7	0	.533	285	299
Cincinnati	4	11	0	.267	285	370

WESTERN DIVISION

Team	W	L	T	Pct.	PF	PA
Denver*	10	4	1	.700	379	288
Seattle†	9	6	0	.600	371	314
San Diego	8	7	0	.533	253	317
L.A. Raiders	5	10	0	.333	301	289
Kansas City	4	11	0	.267	273	388

*Division champion.
†Wild-card team.

NOTE: The 1987 NFL regular season was reduced from 224 games to 210 (16 to 15 for each team) due to players' strike.

NATIONAL CONFERENCE

EASTERN DIVISION

Team	W	L	T	Pct.	PF	PA
Washington*	11	4	0	.733	379	285
Dallas	7	8	0	.467	340	348
St. Louis	7	8	0	.467	362	368
Philadelphia	7	8	0	.467	337	380
N.Y. Giants	6	9	0	.400	280	312

CENTRAL DIVISION

Team	W	L	T	Pct.	PF	PA
Chicago*	11	4	0	.733	356	282
Minnesota†	8	7	0	.533	336	335
Green Bay	5	9	1	.367	255	300
Tampa Bay	4	11	0	.267	286	360
Detroit	4	11	0	.267	269	384

WESTERN DIVISION

Team	W	L	T	Pct.	PF	PA
San Francisco*	13	2	0	.867	459	253
New Orleans†	12	3	0	.800	422	283
L.A. Rams	6	9	0	.400	317	361
Atlanta	3	12	0	.200	205	436

PLAYOFFS

AFC wild-card game
Houston 23 vs. Seattle 20 (OT)

AFC divisional games
Cleveland 38 vs. Indianapolis 21
Denver 34 vs. Houston 10

AFC championship
Denver 38 vs. Cleveland 33

NFC wild-card game
Minnesota 44 at New Orleans 10

NFC divisional games
Minnesota 36 at San Francisco 24
Washington 21 at Chicago 17

NFC championship
Washington 17 vs. Minnesota 10

Super Bowl XXII
Washington 42, Denver 10, at San Diego.

1988

AMERICAN CONFERENCE

EASTERN DIVISION

Team	W	L	T	Pct.	PF	PA
Buffalo*	12	4	0	.750	329	237
Indianapolis	9	7	0	.563	354	315
New England	9	7	0	.563	250	284
N.Y. Jets	8	7	1	.531	372	354
Miami	6	10	0	.375	319	380

CENTRAL DIVISION

Team	W	L	T	Pct.	PF	PA
Cincinnati*	12	4	0	.750	448	329
Cleveland†	10	6	0	.625	304	288
Houston†	10	6	0	.625	424	365
Pittsburgh	5	11	0	.313	336	421

WESTERN DIVISION

Team	W	L	T	Pct.	PF	PA
Seattle*	9	7	0	.563	339	329
Denver	8	8	0	.500	327	352
L.A. Raiders	7	9	0	.438	325	369
San Diego	6	10	0	.375	231	332
Kansas City	4	11	1	.281	254	320

*Division champion.
†Wild-card team.

NATIONAL CONFERENCE

EASTERN DIVISION

Team	W	L	T	Pct.	PF	PA
Philadelphia*	10	6	0	.625	379	319
N.Y. Giants	10	6	0	.625	359	304
Washington	7	9	0	.438	345	387
Phoenix	7	9	0	.438	344	398
Dallas	3	13	0	.188	265	381

CENTRAL DIVISION

Team	W	L	T	Pct.	PF	PA
Chicago*	12	4	0	.750	312	215
Minnesota†	11	5	0	.688	406	233
Tampa Bay	5	11	0	.313	261	350
Detroit	4	12	0	.250	220	313
Green Bay	4	12	0	.250	240	315

WESTERN DIVISION

Team	W	L	T	Pct.	PF	PA
San Francisco*	10	6	0	.625	369	294
L.A. Rams†	10	6	0	.625	407	293
New Orleans	10	6	0	.625	312	283
Atlanta	5	11	0	.313	244	315

PLAYOFFS

AFC wild-card game
Houston 24 at Cleveland 23

AFC divisional games
Cincinnati 21 vs. Seattle 13
Buffalo 17 vs. Houston 10

AFC championship
Cincinnati 21 vs. Buffalo 10

NFC wild-card game
Minnesota 28 vs. L.A. Rams 17

NFC divisional games
Chicago 20 vs. Philadelphia 12
San Francisco 34 vs. Minnesota 9

NFC championship
San Francisco 28 at Chicago 3

Super Bowl XXIII
San Francisco 20, Cincinnati 16, at Miami.

BENGALS HAD BITE

In one of the most improbable turnarounds in NFL history, the Cincinnati Bengals went from being a sack-sad, 4-11 team in 1987 to within 34 seconds of winning the Super Bowl a year later. Many players stepped up their level of play in 1988, as nine Cincinnati players were selected to the Pro Bowl. But it was someone who wasn't Pro Bowl-bound—rookie running back Ickey Woods—who sparked the turnaround. Woods, a second-round draft choice from UNLV, rushed for 1,066 yards that season and performed what came to be known as the "Ickey Shuffle" after every touchdown he scored. He performed it 15 times that year.

1989

AMERICAN CONFERENCE

EASTERN DIVISION

Team	W	L	T	Pct.	PF	PA
Buffalo*	9	7	0	.563	409	317
Indianapolis	8	8	0	.500	298	301
Miami	8	8	0	.500	331	379
New England	5	11	0	.313	297	391
N.Y. Jets	4	12	0	.250	253	411

CENTRAL DIVISION

Team	W	L	T	Pct.	PF	PA
Cleveland*	9	6	1	.594	334	254
Houston†	9	7	0	.563	365	412
Pittsburgh†	9	7	0	.563	265	326
Cincinnati	8	8	0	.500	404	285

WESTERN DIVISION

Team	W	L	T	Pct.	PF	PA
Denver*	11	5	0	.688	362	226
Kansas City	8	7	1	.531	318	286
L.A. Raiders	8	8	0	.500	315	297
Seattle	7	9	0	.438	241	327
San Diego	6	10	0	.375	266	290

*Division champion.
†Wild-card team.

NATIONAL CONFERENCE

EASTERN DIVISION

Team	W	L	T	Pct.	PF	PA
N.Y. Giants*	12	4	0	.750	348	252
Philadelphia†	11	5	0	.688	342	274
Washington	10	6	0	.625	386	308
Phoenix	5	11	0	.313	258	377
Dallas	1	15	0	.063	204	393

CENTRAL DIVISION

Team	W	L	T	Pct.	PF	PA
Minnesota*	10	6	0	.625	351	275
Green Bay	10	6	0	.625	362	356
Detroit	7	9	0	.438	312	364
Chicago	6	10	0	.375	358	377
Tampa Bay	5	11	0	.313	320	419

WESTERN DIVISION

Team	W	L	T	Pct.	PF	PA
San Francisco*	14	2	0	.875	442	253
L.A. Rams†	11	5	0	.688	426	344
New Orleans	9	7	0	.563	386	301
Atlanta	3	13	0	.188	279	437

PLAYOFFS

AFC wild-card game
Pittsburgh 26 at Houston 23 (OT)

AFC divisional games
Cleveland 34 vs. Buffalo 30
Denver 24 vs. Pittsburgh 23

AFC championship
Denver 37 vs. Cleveland 21

NFC wild-card game
L.A. Rams 21 at Philadelphia 7

NFC divisional games
L.A. Rams 19 at N.Y. Giants 13 (OT)
San Francisco 41 vs. Minnesota 13

NFC championship
San Francisco 30 vs. L.A. Rams 3

Super Bowl XXIV
San Francisco 55, Denver 10, at New Orleans.

1990

AMERICAN CONFERENCE

EASTERN DIVISION

Team	W	L	T	Pct.	PF	PA
Buffalo*	13	3	0	.813	428	263
Miami†	12	4	0	.750	336	242
Indianapolis	7	9	0	.438	281	353
N.Y. Jets	6	10	0	.375	295	345
New England	1	15	0	.063	181	446

CENTRAL DIVISION

Team	W	L	T	Pct.	PF	PA
Cincinnati*	9	7	0	.563	360	352
Houston†	9	7	0	.563	405	307
Pittsburgh	9	7	0	.563	292	240
Cleveland	3	13	0	.188	228	462

WESTERN DIVISION

Team	W	L	T	Pct.	PF	PA
L.A. Raiders*	12	4	0	.750	337	268
Kansas City†	11	5	0	.688	369	257
Seattle	9	7	0	.563	306	286
San Diego	6	10	0	.375	315	281
Denver	5	11	0	.313	331	374

*Division champion.
†Wild-card team.

NATIONAL CONFERENCE

EASTERN DIVISION

Team	W	L	T	Pct.	PF	PA
N.Y. Giants*	13	3	0	.813	335	211
Philadelphia†	10	6	0	.625	396	299
Washington†	10	6	0	.625	381	301
Dallas	7	9	0	.438	244	308
Phoenix	5	11	0	.313	268	396

CENTRAL DIVISION

Team	W	L	T	Pct.	PF	PA
Chicago*	11	5	0	.688	348	280
Tampa Bay	6	10	0	.375	264	367
Detroit	6	10	0	.375	373	413
Green Bay	6	10	0	.375	271	347
Minnesota	6	10	0	.375	351	326

WESTERN DIVISION

Team	W	L	T	Pct.	PF	PA
San Francisco*	14	2	0	.875	353	239
New Orleans†	8	8	0	.500	274	275
L.A. Rams	5	11	0	.313	345	412
Atlanta	5	11	0	.313	348	365

PLAYOFFS

AFC wild-card playoffs
Miami 17 vs. Kansas City 16
Cincinnati 41 vs. Houston 14

AFC divisional playoffs
Buffalo 44 vs. Miami 34
L.A. Raiders 20 vs. Cincinnati 10

AFC championship
Buffalo 51 vs. L.A. Raiders 3

NFC wild-card playoffs
Washington 20 at Philadelphia 6
Chicago 16 vs. New Orleans 6

NFC divisional playoffs
San Francisco 28 vs. Washington 10
N.Y. Giants 31 vs. Chicago 3

NFC championship
N.Y. Giants 15 at San Francisco 13

Super Bowl XXV
N.Y. Giants 20 vs. Buffalo 19, at Tampa, Fla.

A STACKED CUPBOARD

Some first-time NFL head coaches inherit terrible teams. In 1989, George Seifert inherited a great one. After succeeding Bill Walsh in San Francisco, Seifert did what his predecessor had done the year before: win a Super Bowl. The 49ers simply dominated the NFL in 1989, winning a league-high 14 games (10 of them by at least 10 points) and losing just twice (by a combined five points). They won their three playoff games by a combined score of 126-26, including 55-10 over Denver in the most lopsided Super Bowl ever.

AMERICAN CONFERENCE

EASTERN DIVISION

Team	W	L	T	Pct.	PF	PA
Buffalo*	13	3	0	.813	458	318
N.Y. Jets†	8	8	0	.500	314	293
Miami	8	8	0	.500	343	349
New England	6	10	0	.375	211	305
Indianapolis	1	15	0	.063	143	381

CENTRAL DIVISION

Team	W	L	T	Pct.	PF	PA
Houston*	11	5	0	.688	386	251
Pittsburgh	7	9	0	.438	292	344
Cleveland	6	10	0	.375	293	298
Cincinnati	3	13	0	.188	263	435

WESTERN DIVISION

Team	W	L	T	Pct.	PF	PA
Denver*	12	4	0	.750	304	235
Kansas City†	10	6	0	.625	322	252
L.A. Raiders†	9	7	0	.563	298	297
Seattle	7	9	0	.438	276	261
San Diego	4	12	0	.250	274	342

*Division champion.
†Wild-card team.

NATIONAL CONFERENCE

EASTERN DIVISION

Team	W	L	T	Pct.	PF	PA
Washington*	14	2	0	.875	485	224
Dallas†	11	5	0	.688	342	310
Philadelphia	10	6	0	.625	285	244
N.Y. Giants	8	8	0	.500	281	297
Phoenix	4	12	0	.250	196	344

CENTRAL DIVISION

Team	W	L	T	Pct.	PF	PA
Detroit*	12	4	0	.750	339	295
Chicago†	11	5	0	.688	299	269
Minnesota	8	8	0	.500	301	306
Green Bay	4	12	0	.250	273	313
Tampa Bay	3	13	0	.188	199	365

WESTERN DIVISION

Team	W	L	T	Pct.	PF	PA
New Orleans*	11	5	0	.688	341	211
Atlanta†	10	6	0	.625	361	338
San Francisco	10	6	0	.625	393	239
L.A. Rams	3	13	0	.188	234	390

PLAYOFFS

AFC wild-card playoffs
Kansas City 10 vs. L.A. Raiders 6
Houston 17 vs. N.Y. Jets 10

AFC divisional playoffs
Denver 26 vs. Houston 24
Buffalo 37 vs. Kansas City 14

AFC championship
Buffalo 10 vs. Denver 7

NFC wild-card playoffs
Atlanta 27 at New Orleans 20
Dallas 17 at Chicago 13

NFC divisional playoffs
Washington 24 vs. Atlanta 7
Detroit 38 vs. Dallas 6

NFC championship
Washington 41 vs. Detroit 10

Super Bowl XXVI
Washington 37 vs. Buffalo 24, at Minneapolis.

AMERICAN CONFERENCE

EASTERN DIVISION

Team	W	L	T	Pct.	PF	PA
Miami*	11	5	0	.688	340	281
Buffalo†	11	5	0	.688	381	283
Indianapolis	9	7	0	.563	216	302
N.Y. Jets	4	12	0	.250	220	315
New England	2	14	0	.125	205	363

CENTRAL DIVISION

Team	W	L	T	Pct.	PF	PA
Pittsburgh*	11	5	0	.688	299	225
Houston†	10	6	0	.625	352	258
Cleveland	7	9	0	.438	272	275
Cincinnati	5	11	0	.313	274	364

WESTERN DIVISION

Team	W	L	T	Pct.	PF	PA
San Diego*	11	5	0	.688	335	241
Kansas City†	10	6	0	.625	348	282
Denver	8	8	0	.500	262	329
L.A. Raiders	7	9	0	.438	249	281
Seattle	2	14	0	.125	140	312

*Division champion.
†Wild-card team.

NATIONAL CONFERENCE

EASTERN DIVISION

Team	W	L	T	Pct.	PF	PA
Dallas*	13	3	0	.813	409	243
Philadelphia†	11	5	0	.688	354	245
Washington†	9	7	0	.563	300	255
N.Y. Giants	6	10	0	.375	306	367
Phoenix	4	12	0	.250	243	332

CENTRAL DIVISION

Team	W	L	T	Pct.	PF	PA
Minnesota*	11	5	0	.688	374	249
Green Bay	9	7	0	.563	276	296
Tampa Bay	5	11	0	.313	267	365
Chicago	5	11	0	.313	295	361
Detroit	5	11	0	.313	273	332

WESTERN DIVISION

Team	W	L	T	Pct.	PF	PA
San Francisco*	14	2	0	.875	431	236
New Orleans†	12	4	0	.750	330	202
Atlanta	6	10	0	.375	327	414
L.A. Rams	6	10	0	.375	313	383

PLAYOFFS

AFC wild-card playoffs
San Diego 17 vs. Kansas City 0
Buffalo 41 vs. Houston 38 (OT)

AFC divisional playoffs
Buffalo 24 at Pittsburgh 3
Miami 31 vs. San Diego 0

AFC championship
Buffalo 29 at Miami 10

NFC wild-card playoffs
Washington 24 at Minnesota 7
Philadelphia 36 at New Orleans 20

NFC divisional playoffs
San Francisco 20 vs. Washington 13
Dallas 34 vs. Philadelphia 10

NFC championship
Dallas 30 at San Francisco 20

Super Bowl XXVII
Dallas 52 vs. Buffalo 17, at Pasadena, Calif.

QB III

In the final hurrah of his Hall of Fame coaching career, Joe Gibbs led the Washington Redskins to their third Super Bowl title in 10 years in January 1992. Chuck Noll and Bill Walsh also had coached as many Super Bowl winners, but Gibbs outdid both of them in one respect: he had different quarterbacks in every one. Whereas Noll won four Super Bowls with Terry Bradshaw calling the signals and Walsh won three with Joe Montana, Gibbs won his with Joe Theismann, Doug Williams and Mark Rypien.

HISTORY *Year-by-year standings*

1993

AMERICAN CONFERENCE

EASTERN DIVISION

Team	W	L	T	Pct.	PF	PA
Buffalo*	12	4	0	.750	329	242
Miami	9	7	0	.563	349	351
N.Y. Jets	8	8	0	.500	270	247
New England	5	11	0	.313	238	286
Indianapolis	4	12	0	.250	189	378

CENTRAL DIVISION

Team	W	L	T	Pct.	PF	PA
Houston*	12	4	0	.750	368	238
Pittsburgh†	9	7	0	.563	308	281
Cleveland	7	9	0	.438	304	307
Cincinnati	3	13	0	.188	187	319

WESTERN DIVISION

Team	W	L	T	Pct.	PF	PA
Kansas City*	11	5	0	.688	328	291
L.A. Raiders†	10	6	0	.625	306	326
Denver†	9	7	0	.563	373	284
San Diego	8	8	0	.500	322	290
Seattle	6	10	0	.375	280	314

*Division champion.
†Wild-card team.

NATIONAL CONFERENCE

EASTERN DIVISION

Team	W	L	T	Pct.	PF	PA
Dallas*	12	4	0	.750	376	229
N.Y. Giants†	11	5	0	.688	288	205
Philadelphia	8	8	0	.500	293	315
Phoenix	7	9	0	.438	326	269
Washington	4	12	0	.250	230	345

CENTRAL DIVISION

Team	W	L	T	Pct.	PF	PA
Detroit*	10	6	0	.625	298	292
Minnesota†	9	7	0	.563	277	290
Green Bay†	9	7	0	.563	340	282
Chicago	7	9	0	.438	234	230
Tampa Bay	5	11	0	.313	237	376

WESTERN DIVISION

Team	W	L	T	Pct.	PF	PA
San Francisco*	10	6	0	.625	473	295
New Orleans	8	8	0	.500	317	343
Atlanta	6	10	0	.375	316	385
L.A. Rams	5	11	0	.313	221	367

PLAYOFFS

AFC wild-card playoffs
Kansas City 27 vs. Pittsburgh 24 (OT)
L.A. Raiders 42 vs. Denver 24

AFC divisional playoffs
Buffalo 29 vs. L.A. Raiders 23
Kansas City 28 at Houston 20

AFC championship
Buffalo 30 vs. Kansas City 13

NFC wild-card playoffs
Green Bay 28 at Detroit 24
N.Y. Giants 17 vs. Minnesota 10

NFC divisional playoffs
San Francisco 44 vs. N.Y. Giants 3
Dallas 27 vs. Green Bay 17

NFC championship
Dallas 38 vs. San Francisco 21

Super Bowl XXVIII
Dallas 30 vs. Buffalo 13, at Atlanta.

1994

AMERICAN CONFERENCE

EASTERN DIVISION

Team	W	L	T	Pct.	PF	PA
Miami*	10	6	0	.625	389	327
New England†	10	6	0	.625	351	312
Indianapolis	8	8	0	.500	307	320
Buffalo	7	9	0	.438	340	356
N.Y. Jets	6	10	0	.375	264	320

CENTRAL DIVISION

Team	W	L	T	Pct.	PF	PA
Pittsburgh*	12	4	0	.750	316	234
Cleveland†	11	5	0	.688	340	204
Cincinnati	3	13	0	.188	276	406
Houston	2	14	0	.125	226	352

WESTERN DIVISION

Team	W	L	T	Pct.	PF	PA
San Diego*	11	5	0	.688	381	306
Kansas City†	9	7	0	.563	319	298
L.A. Raiders	9	7	0	.563	303	327
Denver	7	9	0	.438	347	396
Seattle	6	10	0	.375	287	323

*Division champion.
†Wild-card team.

NATIONAL CONFERENCE

EASTERN DIVISION

Team	W	L	T	Pct.	PF	PA
Dallas*	12	4	0	.750	414	248
N.Y. Giants	9	7	0	.563	279	305
Arizona	8	8	0	.500	235	267
Philadelphia	7	9	0	.438	308	308
Washington	3	13	0	.188	320	412

CENTRAL DIVISION

Team	W	L	T	Pct.	PF	PA
Minnesota*	10	6	0	.625	356	314
Detroit†	9	7	0	.563	357	342
Green Bay†	9	7	0	.563	382	287
Chicago†	9	7	0	.563	271	307
Tampa Bay	6	10	0	.375	251	351

WESTERN DIVISION

Team	W	L	T	Pct.	PF	PA
San Francisco*	13	3	0	.813	505	296
New Orleans	7	9	0	.438	348	407
Atlanta	7	9	0	.438	313	389
L.A. Rams	4	12	0	.250	286	365

PLAYOFFS

AFC wild-card playoffs
Miami 27 vs. Kansas City 17
Cleveland 20 vs. New England 13

AFC divisional playoffs
Pittsburgh 29 vs. Cleveland 9
San Diego 22 vs. Miami 21

AFC championship
San Diego 17 at Pittsburgh 13

NFC wild-card playoffs
Green Bay 16 vs. Detroit 12
Chicago 35 at Minnesota 18

NFC divisional playoffs
San Francisco 44 vs. Chicago 15
Dallas 35 vs. Green Bay 9

NFC championship
San Francisco 38 vs. Dallas 28

Super Bowl XXIX
San Francisco 49 vs. San Diego 26 at Miami.

FOUR IN A ROW

In 1993, the Buffalo Bills accomplished something unprecedented in NFL history: they played in the Super Bowl for a fourth successive year. Although they lost all four—joining the Minnesota Vikings and Denver Broncos as the only four-time Super Bowl losers—their achievement should not be minimized. Fifteen different Bills played in the Pro Bowl over the four-year span (1990 through '93), including perennials Cornelius Bennett, Jim Kelly, Andre Reed, Bruce Smith and Thurman Thomas.

1995

AMERICAN CONFERENCE

EASTERN DIVISION

	W	L	T	Pct.	Pts.	Opp.
Buffalo*	10	6	0	.625	350	335
Indianapolis†	9	7	0	.563	331	316
Miami†	9	7	0	.563	398	332
New England	6	10	0	.375	294	377
N.Y. Jets	3	13	0	.188	233	384

CENTRAL DIVISION

	W	L	T	Pct.	Pts.	Opp.
Pittsburgh*	11	5	0	.689	407	327
Cincinnati	7	9	0	.438	349	374
Houston	7	9	0	.438	348	324
Cleveland	5	11	0	.313	289	356
Jacksonville	4	12	0	.250	275	404

WESTERN DIVISION

	W	L	T	Pct.	Pts.	Opp.
Kansas City*	13	3	0	.813	358	241
San Diego†	9	7	0	.563	321	323
Seattle	8	8	0	.500	363	366
Denver	8	8	0	.500	388	345
Oakland	8	8	0	.500	348	332

*Division champion.
†Wild-card team.

NATIONAL CONFERENCE

EASTERN DIVISION

	W	L	T	Pct.	Pts.	Opp.
Dallas*	12	4	0	.750	435	291
Philadelphia†	10	6	0	.625	318	338
Washington	6	10	0	.375	326	359
N.Y. Giants	5	11	0	.313	290	340
Arizona	4	12	0	.250	275	422

CENTRAL DIVISION

	W	L	T	Pct.	Pts.	Opp.
Green Bay*	11	5	0	.689	404	314
Detroit†	10	6	0	.625	436	336
Chicago	9	7	0	.563	392	360
Minnesota	8	8	0	.500	412	385
Tampa Bay	7	9	0	.438	238	335

WESTERN DIVISION

	W	L	T	Pct.	Pts.	Opp.
San Francisco*	11	5	0	.688	457	258
Atlanta†	9	7	0	.563	362	349
St. Louis	7	9	0	.438	309	418
Carolina	7	9	0	.438	289	325
New Orleans	7	9	0	.438	319	348

PLAYOFFS

AFC wild-card playoffs
Buffalo 37 vs. Miami 22
Indianapolis 35 at San Diego 20

AFC divisional playoffs
Pittsburgh 40 vs. Buffalo 21
Indianapolis 10 at Kansas City 7

AFC championship
Pittsburgh 20 vs. Indianapolis 16

NFC wild-card playoffs
Philadelphia 58 vs. Detroit 37
Green Bay 37 vs. Atlanta 20

NFC divisional playoffs
Green Bay 27 at San Francisco 17
Dallas 30 vs. Philadelphia 11

NFC championship
Dallas 38 vs. Green Bay 27

Super Bowl XXX
Dallas 27 vs Pittsburgh 17, at Tempe, Ariz.

1996

AMERICAN CONFERENCE

EASTERN DIVISION

	W	L	T	Pct.	Pts.	Opp.
New England*	11	5	0	.687	418	313
Buffalo†	10	6	0	.625	319	266
Indianapolis†	9	7	0	.563	317	334
Miami	8	8	0	.500	339	325
N.Y. Jets	1	15	0	.063	279	454

CENTRAL DIVISION

	W	L	T	Pct.	Pts.	Opp.
Pittsburgh*	10	6	0	.625	344	257
Jacksonville†	9	7	0	.563	325	335
Cincinnati	8	8	0	.500	372	369
Houston	8	8	0	.500	345	319
Baltimore	4	12	0	.250	371	441

WESTERN DIVISION

	W	L	T	Pct.	Pts.	Opp.
Denver*	13	3	0	.813	391	275
Kansas City	9	7	0	.563	297	300
San Diego	8	8	0	.500	310	376
Oakland	7	9	0	.438	340	293
Seattle	7	9	0	.438	317	376

*Division champion.
†Wild-card team.

NATIONAL CONFERENCE

EASTERN DIVISION

	W	L	T	Pct.	Pts.	Opp.
Dallas*	10	6	0	.625	286	250
Philadelphia†	10	6	0	.625	363	341
Washington	9	7	0	.563	364	312
Arizona	7	9	0	.438	300	397
N.Y. Giants	6	10	0	.375	242	297

CENTRAL DIVISION

	W	L	T	Pct.	Pts.	Opp.
Green Bay*	13	3	0	.813	456	210
Minnesota†	9	7	0	.563	298	315
Chicago	7	9	0	.438	283	305
Tampa Bay	6	10	0	.375	221	293
Detroit	5	11	0	.313	302	368

WESTERN DIVISION

	W	L	T	Pct.	Pts.	Opp.
Carolina*	12	4	0	.750	367	218
San Francisco†	12	4	0	.750	398	257
St. Louis	6	10	0	.375	303	409
Atlanta	3	13	0	.188	309	465
New Orleans	3	13	0	.188	229	339

PLAYOFFS

AFC wild-card playoffs
Jacksonville 30, Buffalo 27
Pittsburgh 42, Indianapolis 14

AFC divisional playoffs
Jacksonville 30, Denver 27
New England 28, Pittsburgh 3

AFC championship
New England 20, Jacksonville 16

NFC wild-card playoffs
Dallas 40, Minnesota 15
San Francisco 14, Philadelphia 0

NFC divisional playoffs
Green Bay 35, San Francisco 14
Carolina 26, Dallas 17

NFC championship
Green Bay 30, Carolina 13

Super Bowl XXXI
Green Bay 35, New England 21, at New Orleans.

TWO FOR THE SHOW

The 1995 season marked the debut of two new teams for the first time in 19 seasons: the Carolina Panthers and the Jacksonville Jaguars. Although neither team was a serious contender (that would take a year), neither was an embarrassment, either. The Panthers went 7-9 in the NFC West and the Jaguars went 4-12 in the AFC Central. It was a far cry from 1976, when the expansion Seattle Seahawks and Tampa Bay Buccaneers—who were afforded few of the first-year perks given the Panthers and Jaguars—combined to go 2-26.

SUPER BOWLS

SUMMARIES

SUPER BOWL I
JANUARY 15, 1967, AT LOS ANGELES
```
Kansas City (AFL).................  0   10    0    0 — 10
Green Bay (NFL)...................  7    7   14    7 — 35
```
Winning coach—Vince Lombardi.
Most Valuable Player—Bart Starr.
Attendance—61,946.

SUPER BOWL II
JANUARY 14, 1968, AT MIAMI
```
Green Bay (NFL)...................  3   13   10    7 — 33
Oakland (AFL).....................  0    7    0    7 — 14
```
Winning coach—Vince Lombardi.
Most Valuable Player—Bart Starr.
Attendance—75,546.

SUPER BOWL III
JANUARY 12, 1969, AT MIAMI
```
New York (AFL)....................  0    7    6    3 — 16
Baltimore (NFL)...................  0    0    0    7 —  7
```
Winning coach—Weeb Ewbank.
Most Valuable Player—Joe Namath.
Attendance—75,389.

SUPER BOWL IV
JANUARY 11, 1970, AT NEW ORLEANS
```
Minnesota (NFL)...................  0    0    7    0 —  7
Kansas City (AFL).................  3   13    7    0 — 23
```
Winning coach—Hank Stram.
Most Valuable Player—Len Dawson.
Attendance—80,562.

SUPER BOWL V
JANUARY 17, 1971, AT MIAMI
```
Baltimore (AFC)...................  0    6    0   10 — 16
Dallas (NFC)......................  3   10    0    0 — 13
```
Winning coach—Don McCafferty.
Most Valuable Player—Chuck Howley.
Attendance—79,204.

SUPER BOWL VI
JANUARY 16, 1972, AT NEW ORLEANS
```
Dallas (NFC)......................  3    7    7    7 — 24
Miami (AFC).......................  0    3    0    0 —  3
```
Winning coach—Tom Landry.
Most Valuable Player—Roger Staubach.
Attendance—81,023.

SUPER BOWL VII
JANUARY 14, 1973, AT LOS ANGELES
```
Miami (AFC).......................  7    7    0    0 — 14
Washington (NFC)..................  0    0    0    7 —  7
```
Winning coach—Don Shula.
Most Valuable Player—Jake Scott.
Attendance—90,182.

SUPER BOWL VIII
JANUARY 13, 1974, AT HOUSTON
```
Minnesota (NFC)...................  0    0    0    7 —  7
Miami (AFC).......................  14   3    7    0 — 24
```
Winning coach—Don Shula.
Most Valuable Player—Larry Csonka.
Attendance—71,882.

SUPER BOWL IX
JANUARY 12, 1975, AT NEW ORLEANS
```
Pittsburgh (AFC)..................  0    2    7    7 — 16
Minnesota (NFC)...................  0    0    0    6 —  6
```
Winning coach—Chuck Noll.
Most Valuable Player—Franco Harris.
Attendance—80,997.

SUPER BOWL X
JANUARY 18, 1976, AT MIAMI
```
Dallas (NFC)......................  7    3    0    7 — 17
Pittsburgh (AFC)..................  7    0    0   14 — 21
```
Winning coach—Chuck Noll.
Most Valuable Player—Lynn Swann.
Attendance—80,187.

SUPER BOWL XI
JANUARY 9, 1977, AT PASADENA, CALIF.
```
Oakland (AFC).....................  0   16    3   13 — 32
Minnesota (NFC)...................  0    0    7    7 — 14
```
Winning coach—John Madden.
Most Valuable Player—Fred Biletnikoff.
Attendance—103,428.

SUPER BOWL XII
JANUARY 15, 1978, AT NEW ORLEANS
```
Dallas (NFC)......................  10   3    7    7 — 27
Denver (AFC)......................  0    0   10    0 — 10
```
Winning coach—Tom Landry.
Most Valuable Players—Harvey Martin and Randy White.
Attendance—75,804.

SUPER BOWL XIII
JANUARY 21, 1979, AT MIAMI
```
Pittsburgh (AFC)..................  7   14    0   14 — 35
Dallas (NFC)......................  7    7    3   14 — 31
```
Winning coach—Chuck Noll.
Most Valuable Player—Terry Bradshaw.
Attendance—78,656.

SUPER BOWL XIV
JANUARY 20, 1980, PASADENA, CALIF.
```
Los Angeles (NFC).................  7    6    6    0 — 19
Pittsburgh (AFC)..................  3    7    7   14 — 31
```
Winning coach—Chuck Noll.
Most Valuable Player—Terry Bradshaw.
Attendance—103,985.

SUPER BOWL XV
JANUARY 25, 1981, AT NEW ORLEANS
```
Oakland (AFC).....................  14   0   10    3 — 27
Philadelphia (NFC)................  0    3    0    7 — 10
```
Winning coach—Tom Flores.
Most Valuable Player—Jim Plunkett.
Attendance—75,500.

SUPER BOWL XVI
JANUARY 24, 1982, AT PONTIAC, MICH.
```
San Francisco (NFC)...............  7   13    0    6 — 26
Cincinnati (AFC)..................  0    0    7   14 — 21
```
Winning coach—Bill Walsh.
Most Valuable Player—Joe Montana.
Attendance—81,270.

SUPER BOWL XVII

JANUARY 30, 1983, AT PASADENA, CALIF.

Miami (AFC)	7	10	0	0 — 17
Washington (NFC)	0	10	3	14 — 27

Winning coach—Joe Gibbs.
Most Valuable Player—John Riggins.
Attendance—103,667.

SUPER BOWL XVIII

JANUARY 22, 1984, AT TAMPA

Washington (NFC)	0	3	6	0 — 9
Los Angeles (AFC)	7	14	14	3 — 38

Winning coach—Tom Flores.
Most Valuable Player—Marcus Allen.
Attendance—72,920.

SUPER BOWL XIX

JANUARY 20, 1985, AT PALO ALTO, CALIF.

Miami (AFC)	10	6	0	0 — 16
San Francisco (NFC)	7	21	10	0 — 38

Winning coach—Bill Walsh.
Most Valuable Player—Joe Montana.
Attendance—84,059.

SUPER BOWL XX

JANUARY 26, 1986, AT NEW ORLEANS

Chicago (NFC)	13	10	21	2 — 46
New England (AFC)	3	0	0	7 — 10

Winning coach—MIke Ditka.
Most Valuable Player—Richard Dent.
Attendance—73,818.

SUPER BOWL XXI

JANUARY 25, 1987, AT PASADENA, CALIF.

Denver (AFC)	10	0	0	10 — 20
N.Y. Giants (NFC)	7	2	17	13 — 39

Winning coach—Bill Parcells.
Most Valuable Player—Phil Simms.
Attendance—101,063.

SUPER BOWL XXII

JANUARY 31, 1988, AT SAN DIEGO

Washington (NFC)	0	35	0	7 — 42
Denver (AFC)	10	0	0	0 — 10

Winning coach—Joe Gibbs.
Most Valuable Player—Doug Williams.
Attendance—73,302.

SUPER BOWL XXIII

JANUARY 22, 1989, AT MIAMI

Cincinnati (AFC)	0	3	10	3 — 16
San Francisco (NFC)	3	0	3	14 — 20

Winning coach—Bill Walsh.
Most Valuable Player—Jerry Rice.
Attendance—75,179.

SUPER BOWL XXIV

JANUARY 28, 1990, AT NEW ORLEANS

San Francisco (NFC)	13	14	14	14 — 55
Denver (AFC)	3	0	7	0 — 10

Winning coach—George Seifert.
Most Valuable Player—Joe Montana.
Attendance—72,919.

SUPER BOWL XXV

JANUARY 27, 1991, AT TAMPA

Buffalo (AFC)	3	9	0	7 — 19
New York (NFC)	3	7	7	3 — 20

Winning coach—Bill Parcells.
Most Valuable Player—Ottis Anderson.
Attendance—73,813.

SUPER BOWL XXVI

JANUARY 26, 1992, AT MINNEAPOLIS

Washington (NFC)	0	17	14	6 — 37
Buffalo (AFC)	0	0	10	14 — 24

Winning coach—Joe Gibbs.
Most Valuable Player—Mark Rypien.
Attendance—63,130.

SUPER BOWL XXVII

JANUARY 31, 1993, AT PASADENA, CALIF.

Buffalo (AFC)	7	3	7	0 — 17
Dallas (NFC)	14	14	3	21 — 52

Winning coach—Jimmy Johnson.
Most Valuable Player—Troy Aikman.
Attendance—98,374.

SUPER BOWL XXVIII

JANUARY 30, 1994, AT ATLANTA, GA.

Dallas (NFC)	6	0	14	10 — 30
Buffalo (AFC)	3	10	0	0 — 13

Winning coach—Jimmy Johnson.
Most Valuable Player—Emmitt Smith.
Attendance—72,817.

SUPER BOWL XXIX

JANUARY 29, 1995, AT MIAMI, FLA.

San Diego (AFC)	7	3	8	8 — 26
San Francisco (NFC)	14	14	14	7 — 49

Winning coach—George Seifert.
Most Valuable Player—Steve Young.
Attendance—74,107.

SUPER BOWL XXX

JANUARY 28, 1996, AT TEMPE, ARIZ.

Dallas (NFC)	10	3	7	7 — 27
Pittsburgh (AFC)	0	7	0	10 — 17

Winning coach—Barry Switzer.
Most Valuable Player—Larry Brown.
Attendance—76,347.

SUPER BOWL XXXI

JANUARY 26, 1997, AT NEW ORLEANS

New England (AFC)	14	0	7	0 — 21
Green Bay (NFC)	10	17	8	0 — 35

Winning coach—Mike Holmgren.
Most Valuable Player—Desmond Howard.
Attendance—72,301.

SUPER BOWL XXXII

JANUARY 25, 1998, AT SAN DIEGO

Green Bay (NFC)	7	7	3	7 — 24
Denver (AFC)	7	10	7	7 — 31

Winning coach—Mike Shanahan.
Most Valuable Player—Terrell Davis.
Attendance—68,912.

HISTORY — Super Bowls

PRO BOWLS

RESULTS

Date	Site	Winning team, score	Losing team, score	Att.
1-15-39	Wrigley Field, Los Angeles	New York Giants, 13	Pro All-Stars, 10	†20,000
1-14-40	Gilmore Stadium, Los Angeles	Green Bay Packers, 16	NFL All-Stars, 7	†18,000
12-29-40	Gilmore Stadium, Los Angeles	Chicago Bears, 28	NFL All-Stars, 14	21,624
1-4-42	Polo Grounds, New York	Chicago Bears, 35	NFL All-Stars, 24	17,725
12-27-42	Shibe Park, Philadelphia	NFL All-Stars, 17	Washington Redskins, 14	18,671
1943-50	No game was played.			
1-14-51	Los Angeles Memorial Coliseum	American Conference, 28	National Conference, 27	53,676
1-12-52	Los Angeles Memorial Coliseum	National Conference, 30	American Conference, 13	19,400
1-10-53	Los Angeles Memorial Coliseum	National Conference, 27	American Conference, 7	34,208
1-17-54	Los Angeles Memorial Coliseum	East, 20	West, 9	44,214
1-16-55	Los Angeles Memorial Coliseum	West, 26	East, 19	43,972
1-15-56	Los Angeles Memorial Coliseum	East, 31	West, 30	37,867
1-13-57	Los Angeles Memorial Coliseum	West, 19	East, 10	44,177
1-12-58	Los Angeles Memorial Coliseum	West, 26	East, 7	66,634
1-11-59	Los Angeles Memorial Coliseum	East, 28	West, 21	72,250
1-17-60	Los Angeles Memorial Coliseum	West, 38	East, 21	56,876
1-15-61	Los Angeles Memorial Coliseum	West, 35	East, 31	62,971
1-7-62*	Balboa Stadium, San Diego	West, 47	East, 27	20,973
1-14-62	Los Angeles Memorial Coliseum	West, 31	East, 30	57,409
1-13-63*	Balboa Stadium, San Diego	West, 21	East, 14	27,641
1-13-63	Los Angeles Memorial Coliseum	East, 30	West, 20	61,374
1-12-64	Los Angeles Memorial Coliseum	West, 31	East, 17	67,242
1-19-64*	Balboa Stadium, San Diego	West, 27	East, 24	20,016
1-10-65	Los Angeles Memorial Coliseum	West, 34	East, 14	60,598
1-16-65*	Jeppesen Stadium, Houston	West, 38	East, 14	15,446
1-15-66*	Rice Stadium, Houston	AFL All-Stars, 30	Buffalo Bills, 19	35,572
1-15-66	Los Angeles Memorial Coliseum	East, 36	West, 7	60,124
1-21-67*	Oakland-Alameda County Coliseum	East, 30	West, 23	18,876
1-22-67	Los Angeles Memorial Coliseum	East, 20	West, 10	15,062
1-21-68*	Gator Bowl, Jacksonville, Fla.	East, 25	West, 24	40,103
1-21-68	Los Angeles Memorial Coliseum	West, 38	East, 20	53,289
1-19-69*	Gator Bowl, Jacksonville, Fla.	West, 38	East, 25	41,058
1-19-69	Los Angeles Memorial Coliseum	West, 10	East, 7	32,050
1-17-70*	Astrodome, Houston	West, 26	East, 3	30,170
1-18-70	Los Angeles Memorial Coliseum	West, 16	East, 13	57,786
1-24-71	Los Angeles Memorial Coliseum	NFC, 27	AFC, 6	48,222
1-23-72	Los Angeles Memorial Coliseum	AFC, 26	NFC, 13	53,647
1-21-73	Texas Stadium, Irving	AFC, 33	NFC, 28	37,091
1-20-74	Arrowhead Stadium, Kansas City	AFC, 15	NFC, 13	66,918
1-20-75	Orange Bowl, Miami	NFC, 17	AFC, 10	26,484
1-26-76	Louisiana Superdome, New Orleans	NFC, 23	AFC, 20	30,546
1-17-77	Kingdome, Seattle	AFC, 24	NFC, 14	64,752
1-23-78	Tampa Stadium	NFC, 14	AFC, 13	51,337
1-29-79	Los Angeles Memorial Coliseum	NFC, 13	AFC, 7	46,281
1-27-80	Aloha Stadium, Honolulu	NFC, 37	AFC, 27	49,800
2-1-81	Aloha Stadium, Honolulu	NFC, 21	AFC, 7	50,360
1-31-82	Aloha Stadium, Honolulu	AFC, 16	NFC, 13	50,402
2-6-83	Aloha Stadium, Honolulu	NFC, 20	AFC, 19	49,883
1-29-84	Aloha Stadium, Honolulu	NFC, 45	AFC, 3	50,445
1-27-85	Aloha Stadium, Honolulu	AFC, 22	NFC, 14	50,385
2-2-86	Aloha Stadium, Honolulu	NFC, 28	AFC, 24	50,101
2-1-87	Aloha Stadium, Honolulu	AFC, 10	NFC, 6	50,101
2-7-88	Aloha Stadium, Honolulu	AFC, 15	NFC, 6	50,113
1-29-89	Aloha Stadium, Honolulu	NFC, 34	AFC, 3	50,113
2-4-90	Aloha Stadium, Honolulu	NFC, 27	AFC, 21	50,445
2-3-91	Aloha Stadium, Honolulu	AFC, 23	NFC, 21	50,345
2-2-92	Aloha Stadium, Honolulu	NFC, 21	AFC, 15	50,209
2-7-93	Aloha Stadium, Honolulu	AFC, 23 (OT)	NFC, 20	50,007
2-6-94	Aloha Stadium, Honolulu	NFC, 17	AFC, 3	50,026
2-5-95	Aloha Stadium, Honolulu	AFC, 41	NFC, 13	49,121
2-4-96	Aloha Stadium, Honolulu	NFC, 20	AFC, 13	50,034
2-2-97	Aloha Stadium, Honolulu	AFC, 26 (OT)	NFC, 23	50,031
2-1-98	Aloha Stadium, Honolulu	AFC, 29	NFC, 24	49,995

*AFL game.
†Estimated figure.

HISTORY *Pro Bowls*

Year—Name, team

1951— Otto Graham, Cleveland Browns
1952— Dan Towler, Los Angeles Rams
1953— Dan Doll, Detroit Lions
1954— Chuck Bednarik, Philadelphia Eagles
1955— Billy Wilson, San Francisco 49ers
1956— Ollie Matson, Chicago Cardinals
1957— Bert Rechichar, Baltimore Colts (back)
     Ernie Stautner, Pittsburgh Steelers (lineman)
1958— Hugh McElhenny, San Francisco 49ers (back)
     Gene Brito, Washington Redskins (lineman)
1959— Frank Gifford, New York Giants (back)
     Doug Atkins, Chicago Bears (lineman)
1960— Johnny Unitas, Baltimore Colts (back)
     Gene Lipscomb, Baltimore Colts (lineman)
1961— Johnny Unitas, Baltimore Colts (back)
     Sam Huff, New York Giants (lineman)
1962— Cotton Davidson, Dallas Texans*
     Jim Brown, Cleveland Browns (back)
     Henry Jordan, Green Bay Packers (lineman)
1963— Curtis McClinton, Dallas Texans* (offense)
     Earl Faison, San Diego Chargers* (defense)
     Jim Brown, Cleveland Browns (back)
     Gene Lipscomb, Pittsburgh Steelers (lineman)
1964— Keith Lincoln, San Diego Chargers* (offense)
     Archie Matsos, Oakland Raiders* (defense)
     Johnny Unitas, Baltimore Colts (back)
     Gino Marchetti, Baltimore Colts (lineman)
1965— Keith Lincoln, San Diego Chargers* (offense)
     Willie Brown, Denver Broncos* (defense)
     Fran Tarkenton, Minnesota Vikings (back)
     Terry Barr, Detroit Lions (lineman)
1966— Joe Namath, New York Jets* (offense)
     Frank Buncom, San Diego Chargers* (defense)
     Jim Brown, Cleveland Browns (back)
     Dale Meinert, St. Louis Cardinals (lineman)
1967— Babe Parilli, Boston Patriots* (offense)
     Verlon Biggs, New York Jets* (defense)
     Gale Sayers, Chicago Bears (back)
     Floyd Peters, Philadelphia Eagles (lineman)
1968— Joe Namath, New York Jets* (offense)
     Don Maynard, New York Jets* (offense)
     Speedy Duncan, San Diego Chargers (defense)
     Gale Sayers, Chicago Bears (back)
     Dave Robinson, Green Bay Packers (lineman)

Year—Name, team

1969— Len Dawson, Kansas City Chiefs* (offense)
     George Webster, Houston* (defense)
     Roman Gabriel, Los Angeles Rams (back)
     Merlin Olsen, Los Angeles Rams (lineman)
1970— John Hadl, San Diego Chargers*
     Gale Sayers, Chicago Bears (back)
     George Andrie, Dallas Cowboys (lineman)
1971— Mel Renfro, Dallas Cowboys (back)
     Fred Carr, Green Bay Packers (lineman)
1972— Jan Stenerud, Kansas City Chiefs (offense)
     Willie Lanier, Kansas City Chiefs (defense)
1973— O.J. Simpson, Buffalo Bills
1974— Garo Yepremian, Miami Dolphins
1975— James Harris, Los Angeles Rams
1976— Billy Johnson, Houston Oilers
1977— Mel Blount, Pittsburgh Steelers
1978— Walter Payton, Chicago Bears
1979— Ahmad Rashad, Minnesota Vikings
1980— Chuck Muncie, New Orleans Saints
1981— Eddie Murray, Detroit Lions
1982— Kellen Winslow, San Diego Chargers
     Lee Roy Selmon, Tampa Bay Buccaneers
1983— Dan Fouts, San Diego Chargers
     John Jefferson, Green Bay Packers
1984— Joe Theismann, Washington Redskins
1985— Mark Gastineau, New York Jets
1986— Phil Simms, New York Giants
1987— Reggie White, Philadelphia Eagles
1988— Bruce Smith, Buffalo Bills
1989— Randall Cunningham, Philadelphia Eagles
1990— Jerry Gray, Los Angeles Rams
1991— Jim Kelly, Buffalo Bills
1992— Michael Irvin, Dallas Cowboys
1993— Steve Tasker, Buffalo Bills
1994— Andre Rison, Atlanta Falcons
1995— Marshall Faulk, Indianapolis Colts
1996— Jerry Rice, San Francisco 49ers
1997— Mark Brunell, Jacksonville Jaguars
1998— Warren Moon, Seattle Seahawks
     *AFL game.

RECORDS

INDIVIDUAL SERVICE
PLAYERS

Most years played
26—George Blanda, Chicago Bears, Baltimore, Houston, Oakland, 1949 through 1975, except 1959.
Most years with one club
20—Jackie Slater, L.A. Rams, St. Louis Rams, 1976 through 1995.
Most games played, career
340—George Blanda, Chicago Bears, Baltimore, Houston, Oakland, 1949 through 1975, except 1959.
Most consecutive games played, career
282—Jim Marshall, Cleveland, Minnesota, September 25, 1960 through December 16, 1979.

COACHES

Most years as head coach
40—George Halas, Chicago Bears, 1920 through 1929, 1933 through 1942, 1946 through 1955 and 1958 through 1967.
Most games won as head coach
328—Don Shula, Baltimore, 1963 through 1969; Miami, 1970 through 1995.
Most games lost as head coach
162—Tom Landry, Dallas, 1960 through 1988.

INDIVIDUAL OFFENSE
RUSHING
YARDS

Most yards, career
16,726—Walter Payton, Chicago, 1975 through 1987.
Most yards, season
2,105—Eric Dickerson, Los Angeles Rams, 1984.
Most years leading league in yards
8—Jim Brown, Cleveland, 1957 through 1965, except 1962.
Most consecutive years leading league in yards
5—Jim Brown, Cleveland, 1957 through 1961.
Most years with 1,000 or more yards
10—Walter Payton, Chicago, 1976 through 1986, except 1982.
Most consecutive years with 1,000 or more yards
9—Barry Sanders, Detroit, 1989 through 1997.
Most yards, game
275—Walter Payton, Chicago vs. Minnesota, November 20, 1977.
Most games with 200 or more yards, career
6—O.J. Simpson, Buffalo, San Francisco, 1969 through 1979.
Most games with 200 or more yards, season
4—Earl Campbell, Houston, 1980.
Most consecutive games with 200 or more yards, season
2—O.J. Simpson, Buffalo, December 9 through 16, 1973.
O.J. Simpson, Buffalo, November 25 through December 5, 1976.
Earl Campbell, Houston, October 19 through 26, 1980.
Most games with 100 or more yards, career
77—Walter Payton, Chicago, 1975 through 1987.
Most games with 100 or more yards, season
14—Barry Sanders, Detroit, 1997.
Most consecutive games with 100 or more yards, career
14—Barry Sanders, Detroit, September 14 through December 21, 1997.
Most consecutive games with 100 or more yards, season
14—Barry Sanders, Detroit, September 14 through December 21, 1997.
Longest run from scrimmage
99 yards—Tony Dorsett, Dallas at Minnesota, January 3, 1983 (touchdown).

ATTEMPTS

Most attempts, career
3,838—Walter Payton, Chicago, 1975 through 1987.

Most attempts, season
407—James Wilder, Tampa Bay, 1984.
Most attempts, game
45—Jamie Morris, Washington at Cincinnati, December 17, 1988, overtime.
43—Butch Woolfolk, New York Giants at Philadelphia, November 20, 1983.
James Wilder, Tampa Bay vs. Green Bay, September 30, 1984, overtime.
Most years leading league in attempts
6—Jim Brown, Cleveland, 1958 through 1965, except 1960 and 1962.
Most consecutive years leading league in attempts
4—Steve Van Buren, Philadelphia, 1947 through 1950.
Walter Payton, Chicago, 1976 through 1979.

TOUCHDOWNS

Most touchdowns, career
123—Marcus Allen, L.A. Raiders, Kansas City, 1982 through 1997.
Most touchdowns, season
25—Emmitt Smith, Dallas, 1995.
Most years leading league in touchdowns
5—Jim Brown, Cleveland, 1957 through 1959, 1963, 1965.
Most consecutive years leading league in touchdowns
3—Steve Van Buren, Philadelphia, 1947 through 1949.
Jim Brown, Cleveland, 1957 through 1959.
Abner Haynes, Dallas Texans, 1960 through 1962.
Cookie Gilchrist, Buffalo, 1962 through 1964.
Leroy Kelly, Cleveland, 1966 through 1968.
Most touchdowns, game
6—Ernie Nevers, Chicago Cardinals vs. Chicago Bears, November 28, 1929.
Most consecutive games with one or more touchdowns, career
13—John Riggins, Washington, December 26, 1982 through November 27, 1983.
George Rogers, Washington, November 24, 1985 through November 2, 1986.
Most consecutive games with one or more touchdowns, season
12—John Riggins, Washington, September 5 through November 27, 1983.

PASSING
PASSER RATING

Highest rating, career (1,500 or more attempts)
97.0—Steve Young, Tampa Bay, San Francisco, 1985 through 1997.
Highest rating, season (qualifiers)
112.8—Steve Young, San Francisco, 1994.

ATTEMPTS

Most attempts, career
7,452—Dan Marino, Miami, 1983 through 1997.
Most attempts, season
691—Drew Bledsoe, New England, 1994.
Most years leading league in attempts
5—Dan Marino, Miami, 1984, 1986, 1988, 1992, 1997.
Most consecutive years leading league in attempts
3—Johnny Unitas, Baltimore, 1959 through 1961.
George Blanda, Houston, 1963 through 1965.
Most attempts, game
70—Drew Bledsoe, New England vs. Minnesota, November 13, 1994 (overtime).
68—George Blanda, Houston vs. Buffalo, November 1, 1964.

COMPLETIONS

Most completions, career
4,453—Dan Marino, Miami, 1983 through 1997.
Most completions, season
404—Warren Moon, Houston, 1991.

Most years leading league in completions
6—Dan Marino, Miami, 1984, 1985, 1986, 1988, 1992, 1997.
Most consecutive years leading league in completions
3—George Blanda, Houston, 1963 through 1965.
Dan Marino, Miami, 1984 through 1986.
Most completions, game
45—Drew Bledsoe, New England vs. Minnesota, November 13, 1994 (overtime).
42—Richard Todd, New York Jets vs. San Francisco, September 21, 1980.

YARDS

Most yards, career
55,416—Dan Marino, Miami, 1983 through 1997.
Most yards, season
5,084—Dan Marino, Miami, 1984.
Most years leading league in yards
5—Sonny Jurgensen, Philadelphia, Washington, 1961, 1962, 1966, 1967, 1969.
Dan Marino, Miami, 1984 through 1986, 1988, 1992.
Most consecutive years leading league in yards
4—Dan Fouts, San Diego, 1979 through 1982.
Most years with 3,000 or more yards
12—Dan Marino, Miami, 1984 through 1997, except 1993 and 1996.
John Elway, Denver, 1985 through 1997, except 1992.
Most yards, game
554—Norm Van Brocklin, Los Angeles at New York Yanks, September 28, 1951.
Most games with 400 or more yards, career
13—Dan Marino, Miami, 1983 through 1996.
Most games with 400 or more yards, season
4—Dan Marino, Miami, 1984.
Most consecutive games with 400 or more yards, season
2—Dan Fouts, San Diego, December 11 through 20, 1982.
Dan Marino, Miami, December 2 through 9, 1984.
Phil Simms, New York Giants, October 6 through 13, 1985.
Most games with 300 or more yards, career
56—Dan Marino, Miami, 1983 through 1997.
Most games with 300 or more yards, season
9—Dan Marino, Miami, 1984.
Warren Moon, Houston, 1990.
Most consecutive games with 300 or more yards, season
5—Joe Montana, San Francisco, September 19 through December 11, 1982.
Longest pass completion
99 yards—Frank Filchock, Washington vs. Pittsburgh, October 15, 1939 (touchdown).
George Izo, Washington at Cleveland, September 15, 1963 (touchdown).
Karl Sweetan, Detroit at Baltimore, October 16, 1966 (touchdown).
Sonny Jurgensen, Washington at Chicago, September 15, 1968 (touchdown).
Jim Plunkett, Los Angeles Raiders vs. Washington, October 2, 1983 (touchdown).
Ron Jaworski, Philadelphia vs. Atlanta, November 10, 1985 (touchdown).
Stan Humphries, San Diego at Seattle, September 18, 1994 (touchdown).
Brett Favre, Green Bay at Chicago, September 11, 1995 (touchdown).

YARDS PER ATTEMPT

Most yards per attempt, career (1,500 or more attempts)
8.63—Otto Graham, Cleveland, 1950 through 1955 (13,499 yards, 1,565 attempts).
Most yards per attempt, season (qualifiers)
11.17—Tommy O'Connell, Cleveland, 1957 (1,229 yards, 110 attempts).
Most years leading league in yards per attempt
7—Sid Luckman, Chicago Bears, 1939 through 1943, 1946, 1947.
Most consecutive years leading league in yards per attempt
5—Sid Luckman, Chicago Bears, 1939 through 1943.

Most yards per attempt, game (20 or more attempts)
18.58—Sammy Baugh, Washington vs. Boston, October 31, 1948 (446 yards, 24 attempts).

TOUCHDOWNS

Most touchdowns, career
385—Dan Marino, Miami, 1983 through 1997.
Most touchdowns, season
48—Dan Marino, Miami, 1984.
Most years leading league in touchdowns
4—Johnny Unitas, Baltimore, 1957 through 1960.
Len Dawson, Dallas Texans, Kansas City, 1962 through 1966, except 1964.
Most consecutive years leading league in touchdowns
4—Johnny Unitas, Baltimore, 1957 through 1960.
Most touchdowns, game
7—Sid Luckman, Chicago Bears at New York Giants, November 14, 1943.
Adrian Burk, Philadelphia at Washington, October 17, 1954.
George Blanda, Houston vs. New York Titans, November 19, 1961.
Y.A. Tittle, New York Giants vs. Washington, October 28, 1962.
Joe Kapp, Minnesota vs. Baltimore, September 28, 1969.

INTERCEPTIONS

Most interceptions, career
277—George Blanda, Chicago Bears, Baltimore, Houston, Oakland, 1949 through 1975, except 1959.
Most interceptions, season
42—George Blanda, Houston, 1962.
Most interceptions, game
8—Jim Hardy, Chicago Cardinals vs. Philadelphia, September 24, 1950.
Most attempts with no interceptions, game
70—Drew Bledsoe, New England vs. Minnesota, November 13, 1994 (overtime).
63—Rich Gannon, Minnesota at New England, October 20, 1991 (overtime).
60—Davey O'Brien, Philadelphia at Washington, December 1, 1940.

INTERCEPTION PERCENTAGE

Lowest interception percentage, career (1,500 or more attempts)
2.10—Neil O'Donnell, Pittsburgh, N.Y. Jets, 1991 through 1997 (2,519 attempts, 53 interceptions).
Lowest interception percentage, season (qualifiers)
0.66—Joe Ferguson, Buffalo, 1976 (151 attempts, one interception).
Most years leading league in lowest interception percentage
5—Sammy Baugh, Washington, 1940, 1942, 1944, 1945, 1947.

SACKS (SINCE 1963)

Most times sacked, career
492—Dave Krieg, Seattle, Kansas City, Detroit, Arizona, Chicago, 1980 through 1996.
Most times sacked, season
72—Randall Cunningham, Philadelphia, 1986.
Most times sacked, game
12—Bert Jones, Baltimore vs. St. Louis, October 26, 1980.
Warren Moon, Houston vs. Dallas, September 29, 1985.

RECEIVING

RECEPTIONS

Most receptions, career
1,057—Jerry Rice, San Francisco, 1985 through 1997.
Most receptions, season
123—Herman Moore, Detroit, 1995.
Most years leading league in receptions
8—Don Hutson, Green Bay, 1936 through 1945, except 1938 and 1940.
Most consecutive years leading league in receptions
5—Don Hutson, Green Bay, 1941 through 1945.
Most receptions, game
18—Tom Fears, Los Angeles vs. Green Bay, December 3, 1950.

Most consecutive games with one or more receptions
183—Art Monk, Washington, N.Y. Jets, Philadelphia, January 2, 1983 through December 24, 1995.

YARDS

Most yards, career
16,455—Jerry Rice, San Francisco, 1985 through 1997.
Most yards, season
1,848—Jerry Rice, San Francisco, 1995.
Most years leading league in yards
7—Don Hutson, Green Bay, 1936 through 1944, except 1937 and 1940.
Most consecutive years leading league in yards
4—Don Hutson, Green Bay, 1941 through 1944.
Most years with 1,000 or more yards
11—Jerry Rice, San Francisco, 1986 through 1996.
Most yards, game
336—Willie Anderson, Los Angeles Rams at New Orleans, November 26, 1989 (overtime).
309—Stephone Paige, Kansas City vs. San Diego, December 22, 1985.
Most games with 200 or more yards, career
5—Lance Alworth, San Diego, Dallas, 1962 through 1972.
Most games with 200 or more yards, season
3—Charley Hennigan, Houston, 1961.
Most games with 100 or more yards, career
61—Jerry Rice, San Francisco, 1985 through 1996.
Most games with 100 or more yards, season
11—Michael Irvin, Dallas, 1995.
Most consecutive games with 100 or more yards, season
7—Charley Hennigan, Houston, 1961.
　　Bill Groman, Houston, 1961.
　　Michael Irvin, Dallas, 1995.
Longest reception
99 yards—Andy Farkas, Washington vs. Pittsburgh, October 15, 1939 (touchdown).
　　Bobby Mitchell, Washington at Cleveland, September 15, 1963 (touchdown).
　　Pat Studstill, Detroit at Baltimore, October 16, 1966 (touchdown).
　　Gerry Allen, Washington at Chicago, September 15, 1968 (touchdown).
　　Cliff Branch, Los Angeles Raiders vs. Washington, October 2, 1983 (touchdown).
　　Mike Quick, Philadelphia vs. Atlanta, November 10, 1985 (touchdown).
　　Tony Martin, San Diego at Seattle, September 18, 1994 (touchdown).
　　Robert Brooks, Green Bay at Chicago, September 11, 1995 (touchdown).

TOUCHDOWNS

Most touchdowns, career
155—Jerry Rice, San Francisco, 1985 through 1997.
Most touchdowns, season
22—Jerry Rice, San Francisco, 1987.
Most years leading league in touchdowns
9—Don Hutson, Green Bay, 1935 through 1944, except 1939.
Most consecutive years leading league in touchdowns
5—Don Hutson, Green Bay, 1940 through 1944.
Most touchdowns, game
5—Bob Shaw, Chicago Cardinals vs. Baltimore, October 2, 1950.
　　Kellen Winslow, San Diego at Oakland, November 22, 1981.
　　Jerry Rice, San Francisco at Atlanta, October 14, 1990.
Most consecutive games with one or more touchdowns
13—Jerry Rice, San Francisco, December 19, 1986 through December 27, 1987.

COMBINED NET YARDS

(Rushing, receiving, interception returns, punt returns, kickoff returns and fumble returns)

ATTEMPTS

Most attempts, career
4,368—Walter Payton, Chicago, 1975 through 1987.

Most attempts, season
496—James Wilder, Tampa Bay, 1984.
Most attempts, game
48—James Wilder, Tampa Bay at Pittsburgh, October 30, 1983.

YARDS

Most yards, career
21,803—Walter Payton, Chicago, 1975 through 1987.
Most yards, season
2,535—Lionel James, San Diego, 1985.
Most years leading league in yards
5—Jim Brown, Cleveland, 1958 through 1961, 1964.
Most consecutive years leading league in yards
4—Jim Brown, Cleveland, 1958 through 1961.
Most yards, game
404—Glyn Milburn, Denver vs. Seattle, December 10, 1995.

SCORING

POINTS

Most points, career
2,002—George Blanda, Chicago Bears, Baltimore, Houston, Oakland, 1949 through 1975, except 1959.
Most points, season
176—Paul Hornung, Green Bay, 1960.
Most years leading league in points
5—Don Hutson, Green Bay, 1940 through 1944.
　　Gino Cappelletti, Boston, 1961 through 1966, except 1962.
Most consecutive years leading league in points
5—Don Hutson, Green Bay, 1940 through 1944.
Most years with 100 or more points
11—Nick Lowery, Kansas City, 1981 through 1993, except 1982 and 1987.
　　Morten Andersen, New Orleans, Atlanta, 1985 through 1997, except 1990 and 1996.
Most points, game
40—Ernie Nevers, Chicago Cardinals vs. Chicago Bears, November 28, 1929.
Most consecutive games with one or more points
222—Morten Andersen, New Orleans, Atlanta, December 11, 1983 through December 21, 1997.

TOUCHDOWNS

Most touchdowns, career
166—Jerry Rice, San Francisco, 1985 through 1997.
Most touchdowns, season
25—Emmitt Smith, Dallas, 1995.
Most years leading league in touchdowns
8—Don Hutson, Green Bay, 1935 through 1938 and 1941 through 1944.
Most consecutive years leading league in touchdowns
4—Don Hutson, Green Bay, 1935 through 1938 and 1941 through 1944.
Most touchdowns, game
6—Ernie Nevers, Chicago Cardinals vs. Chicago Bears, November 28, 1929.
　　Dub Jones, Cleveland vs. Chicago Bears, November 25, 1951.
　　Gale Sayers, Chicago vs. San Francisco, December 12, 1965.
Most consecutive games with one or more touchdowns
18—Lenny Moore, Baltimore, October 27, 1963 through September 19, 1965.

EXTRA POINTS

Most extra points attempted, career
959—George Blanda, Chicago Bears, Baltimore, Houston, Oakland, 1949 through 1975, except 1959.
Most extra points made, career
943—George Blanda, Chicago Bears, Baltimore, Houston, Oakland, 1949 through 1975, except 1959.
Most extra points attempted, season
70—Uwe von Schamann, Miami, 1984.
Most extra points made, season
66—Uwe von Schamann, Miami, 1984.

Most extra points attempted, game
10—Charlie Gogolak, Washington vs. New York Giants, November 27, 1966.

Most extra points made, game
9—Pat Harder, Chicago Cardinals at New York Giants, October 17, 1948.
    Bob Waterfield, Los Angeles vs. Baltimore, October 22, 1950.
    Charlie Gogolak, Washington vs. New York Giants, November 27, 1966.

FIELD GOALS AND FIELD-GOAL PERCENTAGE

Most field goals attempted, career
637—George Blanda, Chicago Bears, Baltimore, Houston, Oakland, 1949 through 1975, except 1959.

Most field goals made, career
385—Gary Anderson, Pittsburgh, Philadelphia, San Francisco, 1982 through 1997.

Most field goals attempted, season
49—Bruce Gossett, Los Angeles, 1966.
    Curt Knight, Washington, 1971.

Most field goals made, season
37—John Kasay, Carolina, 1996.

Most field goals attempted, game
9—Jim Bakken, St. Louis at Pittsburgh, September 24, 1967.

Most field goals made, game
7—Jim Bakken, St. Louis at Pittsburgh, September 24, 1967.
    Rich Karlis, Minnesota vs. Los Angeles Rams, November 5, 1989 (overtime).
    Chris Boniol, Dallas vs. Green Bay, November 18, 1996.

Most field goals made, one quarter
4—Garo Yepremian, Detroit vs. Minnesota, November 13, 1966, second quarter.
    Curt Knight, Washington at New York Giants, November 15, 1970, second quarter.
    Roger Ruzek, Dallas vs. New York Giants, November 2, 1987, fourth quarter.

Most consecutive games with one or more field goals made, career
31—Fred Cox, Minnesota, November 17, 1968 through December 5, 1970.

Most consecutive field goals made, career
31—Fuad Reveiz, Minnesota, October 10, 1994 through September 17, 1995.

Most field goals of 50 or more yards, career
33—Morten Andersen, New Orleans, Atlanta, 1982 through 1997.

Most field goals of 50 or more yards, season
8—Morten Andersen, Atlanta, 1995.

Most field goals of 50 or more yards, game
3—Morten Andersen, Atlanta vs. New Orleans, December 10, 1995.

Longest field goal made
63 yards—Tom Dempsey, New Orleans vs. Detroit, November 8, 1970.

Highest field-goal percentage, career (100 or more made)
83.06—Chris Boniol, Dallas, Philadelphia, 1994 through 1997 (124 attempted, 103 made).

Highest field-goal percentage, season (qualifiers)
100.00—Tony Zendejas, Los Angeles Rams, 1991 (17 attempted, 17 made).

SAFETIES

Most safeties, career
4—Ted Hendricks, Baltimore, Green Bay, Oakland, Los Angeles Raiders, 1969 through 1983.
    Doug English, Detroit, 1975 through 1985, except 1980.

Most safeties, season
2—Held by many players.

Most safeties, game
2—Fred Dryer, Los Angeles vs. Green Bay, October 21, 1973.

PUNTING

Most punts, career
1,154—Dave Jennings, New York Giants, New York Jets, 1974 through 1987.

Most punts, season
114—Bob Parsons, Chicago, 1981.

Most seasons leading league in punting
4—Sammy Baugh, Washington, 1940 through 1943.
    Jerrel Wilson, Kansas City, 1965, 1968, 1972, 1973.

Most consecutive seasons leading league in punting
4—Sammy Baugh, Washington, 1940 through 1943.

Most punts, game
15— John Teltschik, Philadelphia at New York Giants, December 6, 1987 (overtime).
14—Dick Nesbitt, Chicago Cardinals at Chicago Bears, November 30, 1933.
    Keith Molesworth, Chicago Bears vs. Green Bay, December 10, 1933.
    Sammy Baugh, Washington vs. Philadelphia, November 5, 1939.
    Carl Kinscherf, New York Giants at Detroit, November 7, 1943.
    George Taliaferro, New York Yanks vs. Los Angeles, September 28, 1951.

Longest punt
98 yards—Steve O'Neal, New York Jets at Denver, September 21, 1969.

FUMBLES

Most fumbles, career
152—Warren Moon, Houston, Minnesota, Seattle, 1984 through 1997.

Most fumbles, season
21—Tony Banks, St. Louis, 1996.

Most fumbles, game
7—Len Dawson, Kansas City vs. San Diego, November 15, 1964.

PUNT RETURNS

Most punt returns, career
344—Dave Meggett, N.Y. Giants, New England, 1989 through 1997.

Most punt returns, season
70—Danny Reece, Tampa Bay, 1979.

Most years leading league in punt returns
3—Les "Speedy" Duncan, San Diego, Washington, 1965, 1966, 1971.
    Rick Upchurch, Denver, 1976, 1978, 1982.

Most punt returns, game
11—Eddie Brown, Washington at Tampa Bay, October 9, 1977.

YARDS

Most yards, career
3,668—Dave Meggett, N.Y. Giants, New England, 1989 through 1997.

Most yards, season
875—Desmond Howard, Green Bay, 1996.

Most yards, game
207—LeRoy Irvin, Los Angeles at Atlanta, October 11, 1981.

Longest punt return
103 yards—Robert Bailey, Los Angeles Rams at New Orleans, October 23, 1994 (touchdown).

FAIR CATCHES

Most fair catches, career
114—Dave Meggett, N.Y. Giants, New England, 1989 through 1997.

Most fair catches, season
27—Leo Lewis, Minnesota, 1989.

Most fair catches, game
7—Lem Barney, Detroit vs. Chicago, November 21, 1976.
    Bobby Morse, Philadelphia vs. Buffalo, December 27, 1987.

TOUCHDOWNS

Most touchdowns, career
9—Eric Metcalf, Cleveland, Atlanta, San Diego, 1989 through 1997.

Most touchdowns, season
4—Jack Christiansen, Detroit, 1951.
  Rick Upchurch, Denver, 1976.

Most touchdowns, game
2—Jack Christiansen, Detroit vs. Los Angeles, October 14, 1951.
  Jack Christiansen, Detroit vs. Green Bay, November 22, 1951.
  Dick Christy, New York Titans vs. Denver, September 24, 1961.
  Rick Upchurch, Denver vs. Cleveland, September 26, 1976.
  LeRoy Irvin, Los Angeles at Atlanta, October 11, 1981.
  Vai Sikahema, St. Louis vs. Tampa Bay, December 21, 1986.
  Todd Kinchen, Los Angeles Rams vs. Atlanta, December 27, 1992.
  Eric Metcalf, San Diego at Cincinnati, November 2, 1997.
  Darrien Gordon, Denver vs. Carolina, November 9, 1997.
  Jermaine Lewis, Baltimore vs. Seattle, December 7, 1997.

KICKOFF RETURNS

Most kickoff returns, career
421—Mel Gray, New Orleans, Detroit, Houston, Tennessee, Philadelphia, 1986 through 1997.

Most kickoff returns, season
70—Tyrone Hughes, New Orleans, 1996.

Most years leading league in kickoff returns
3—Abe Woodson, San Francisco, 1959, 1962, 1963.
  Tyrone Hughes, New Orleans, 1994 through 1996.

Most kickoff returns, game
10—Desmond Howard, Oakland at Seattle, October 26, 1997.

YARDS

Most yards, career
10,250—Mel Gray, New Orleans, Detroit, Houston, Tennessee, Philadelphia, 1986 through 1997.

Most yards, season
1,791—Tyrone Hughes, New Orleans, 1996.

Most years leading league in yards
3—Bruce Harper, New York Jets, 1977 through 1979.
  Tyrone Hughes, New Orleans, 1994 through 1996.

Most yards, game
304—Tyrone Hughes, New Orleans vs. Los Angeles Rams, October 23, 1994.

Longest kickoff return
106 yards—Al Carmichael, Green Bay vs. Chicago Bears, October 7, 1956 (touchdown).
  Noland Smith, Kansas City at Denver, December 17, 1967.
  Roy Green, St. Louis at Dallas, October 21, 1979.

TOUCHDOWNS

Most touchdowns, career
6—Ollie Matson, Chicago Cardinals, Los Angeles Rams, Detroit, Philadelphia, 1952 through 1964, except 1953.
  Gale Sayers, Chicago, 1965 through 1971.
  Travis Williams, Green Bay, Los Angeles, 1967 through 1971.
  Mel Gray, New Orleans, Detroit, Houston, Tennessee, Philadelphia, 1986 through 1997.

Most touchdowns, season
4—Travis Williams, Green Bay, 1967.
  Cecil Turner, Chicago, 1970.

Most touchdowns, game
2—Timmy Brown, Philadelphia vs. Dallas, November 6, 1966.
  Travis Williams, Green Bay vs. Cleveland, November 12, 1967.
  Ron Brown, Los Angeles Rams vs. Green Bay, November 24, 1985.
  Tyrone Hughes, New Orleans vs. Los Angeles Rams, October 23, 1994.

COMBINED KICK RETURNS

(KICKOFFS AND PUNTS)

Most kick returns, career
664—Mel Gray, New Orleans, Detroit, Houston, Tennessee, Philadelphia, 1986 through 1997.

Most kick returns, season
102—Glyn Milburn, Detroit, 1997.

Most kick returns, game
13—Stump Mitchell, St. Louis at Atlanta, October 18, 1981.
  Ron Harris, New England at Pittsburgh, December 5, 1993.

YARDS

Most yards, career
12,810—Mel Gray, New Orleans, Detroit, Houston, Tennessee, Philadelphia, 1986 through 1997.

Most yards, season
1,943—Tyrone Hughes, New Orleans, 1996.

Most yards, game
347—Tyrone Hughes, New Orleans vs. Los Angeles Rams, October 23, 1994.

TOUCHDOWNS

Most touchdowns, career
9—Ollie Matson, Chicago Cardinals, Los Angeles Rams, Detroit, Philadelphia, 1952 through 1966, except 1953.
  Mel Gray, New Orleans, Detroit, Houston, 1986 through 1997.

Most touchdowns, season
4—Jack Christiansen, Detroit, 1951.
  Emlen Tunnell, New York Giants, 1951.
  Gale Sayers, Chicago, 1967.
  Travis Williams, Green Bay, 1967.
  Cecil Turner, Chicago, 1970.
  Billy "White Shoes" Johnson, Houston, 1975.
  Rick Upchurch, Denver, 1976.

Most touchdowns, game
2—Held by many players.

INDIVIDUAL DEFENSE

INTERCEPTIONS

Most interceptions, career
81—Paul Krause, Washington, Minnesota, 1964 through 1979.

Most interceptions, season
14—Dick "Night Train" Lane, Los Angeles, 1952.

Most interceptions, game
4—Held by many players.

Most consecutive games with one or more interceptions
8—Tom Morrow, Oakland, 1962 through 1963.

Most yards on interceptions, career
1,282—Emlen Tunnell, New York Giants, Green Bay, 1948 through 1961.

Most yards on interceptions, season
349—Charlie McNeil, San Diego, 1961.

Most yards on interceptions, game
177—Charlie McNeil, San Diego vs. Houston, September 24, 1961.

Longest interception return
103—Vencie Glenn, San Diego vs. Denver, November 29, 1987.
  Louis Oliver, Miami vs. Buffalo, October 4, 1992.
  (Note: James Willis, 14 yards, and Troy Vincent, 90 yards, combined for a 104-yard interception return for Philadelphia vs. Dallas, November 3, 1996.)

TOUCHDOWNS

Most touchdowns, career
9—Ken Houston, Houston, Washington, 1967 through 1980.

Most touchdowns, season
4—Ken Houston, Houston, 1971.
  Jim Kearney, Kansas City, 1972.
  Eric Allen, Philadelphia, 1993.

Most touchdowns, game
2—Held by many players.

FUMBLES RECOVERED

Most fumbles recovered (own and opponents'), career
54—Warren Moon, Houston, Minnesota, Seattle, 1984 through 1997.

Most fumbles recovered (own), career
54—Warren Moon, Houston, Minnesota, Seattle, 1984 through 1997.

Most opponents' fumbles recovered, career
29—Jim Marshall, Cleveland, Minnesota, 1960 through 1979.
Most fumbles recovered (own and opponents'), season
9—Don Hultz, Minnesota, 1963.
  Dave Krieg, Seattle, 1989.
Most fumbles recovered (own), season
9—Dave Krieg, Seattle, 1989.
Most opponents' fumbles recovered, season
9—Don Hultz, Minnesota, 1963.
Most fumbles recovered (own and opponents'), game
4—Otto Graham, Cleveland at New York Giants, October 25, 1953.
  Sam Etcheverry, St. Louis at New York Giants, September 17, 1961.
  Roman Gabriel, Los Angeles at San Francisco, October 12, 1969.
  Joe Ferguson, Buffalo vs. Miami, September 18, 1977.
  Randall Cunningham, Philadelphia at Los Angeles Raiders, November 30, 1986 (overtime).
Most fumbles recovered (own), game
4—Otto Graham, Cleveland at New York Giants, October 25, 1953.
  Sam Etcheverry, St. Louis at New York Giants, September 17, 1961.
  Roman Gabriel, Los Angeles at San Francisco, October 12, 1969.
  Joe Ferguson, Buffalo vs. Miami, September 18, 1977.
  Randall Cunningham, Philadelphia at Los Angeles Raiders, November 30, 1986 (overtime).
Most opponents' fumbles recovered, game
3—Held by many players.
Longest fumble return
104 yards—Jack Tatum, Oakland at Green Bay, September 24, 1972 (touchdown).

TOUCHDOWNS

Most touchdowns (own and opponents' recovered), career
4—Bill Thompson, Denver, 1969 through 1981.
  Jessie Tuggle, Atlanta, 1987 through 1992.
Most touchdowns (own recovered), career
2—Held by many players.
Most touchdowns (opponents' recovered), career
4—Jessie Tuggle, Atlanta, 1987 through 1992.
Most touchdowns, season
2—Held by many players.
Most touchdowns, game
2—Fred "Dippy" Evans, Chicago Bears vs. Washington, November 28, 1948.

SACKS (SINCE 1982)

Most sacks, career
176.5—Reggie White, Philadelphia, Green Bay, 1985 through 1997.
Most sacks, season
22—Mark Gastineau, New York Jets, 1984.
Most sacks, game
7—Derrick Thomas, Kansas City vs. Seattle, November 11, 1990.

TEAM MISCELLANEOUS
CHAMPIONSHIPS

Most league championships won
12—Green Bay, 1929, 1930, 1931, 1936, 1939, 1944, 1961, 1962, 1965, 1966, 1967, 1996.
Most consecutive league championships won
3—Green Bay, 1929 through 1931.
  Green Bay, 1965 through 1967.
Most first-place finishes during regular season (since 1933)
18—Cleveland Browns, 1950 through 1955, 1957, 1964, 1965, 1967, 1968, 1969, 1971, 1980, 1985, 1986, 1987, 1989.
Most consecutive first-place finishes during regular season (since 1933)
7—Los Angeles, 1973 through 1979.

GAMES WON

Most games won, season
15—San Francisco, 1984.
  Chicago, 1985.
Most consecutive games won, season
14—Miami, September 17 through December 16, 1972.
Most consecutive games won from start of season
14—Miami, September 17 through December 16, 1972 (entire season).
Most consecutive games won at end of season
14—Miami, September 17 through December 16, 1972 (entire season).
Most consecutive undefeated games, season
14—Miami, September 17 through December 16, 1972 (entire season).
Most consecutive games won
17—Chicago Bears, November 26, 1933 through December 2, 1934.
Most consecutive undefeated games
25—Canton, 1921 through 1923 (won 22, tied three).
Most consecutive home games won
27—Miami, October 17, 1971 through December 15, 1974.
Most consecutive undefeated home games
30—Green Bay, 1928 through 1933 (won 27, tied three).
Most consecutive road games won
18—San Francisco, November 27, 1988 through December 30, 1990.
Most consecutive undefeated road games
18—San Francisco, November 27, 1988 through December 30, 1990 (won 18).

GAMES LOST

Most games lost, season
15—New Orleans, 1980.
  Dallas, 1989.
  New England, 1990.
  Indianapolis, 1991.
  New York Jets, 1996.
Most consecutive games lost
26—Tampa Bay, September 12, 1976 through December 4, 1977.
Most consecutive winless games
26—Tampa Bay, September 12, 1976 through December 4, 1977 (lost 26).
Most consecutive games lost, season
14—Tampa Bay, September 12 through December 12, 1976.
  New Orleans, September 7 through December 7, 1980.
  Baltimore, September 13 through December 13, 1981.
  New England, September 23 through December 30, 1990.
Most consecutive games lost from start of season
14—Tampa Bay, September 12 through December 12, 1976 (entire season).
  New Orleans, September 7 through December 7, 1980.
Most consecutive games lost at end of season
14—Tampa Bay, September 12 through December 12, 1976 (entire season).
  New England, September 23 through December 30, 1990.
Most consecutive winless games, season
14—Tampa Bay, September 12 through December 12, 1976 (lost 14; entire season).
  New Orleans, September 7 through December 7, 1980 (lost 14).
  Baltimore, September 13 through December 13, 1981 (lost 14).
  New England, September 23 through December 30, 1990 (lost 14).
Most consecutive home games lost
14—Dallas, October 9, 1988 through December 24, 1989.
Most consecutive winless home games
14—Dallas, October 9, 1988 through December 24, 1989 (lost 14).

Most consecutive road games lost
23—Houston, September 27, 1981 through November 4, 1984.
Most consecutive winless road games
23—Houston, September 27, 1981 through November 4, 1984 (lost 23).

TIE GAMES

Most tie games, season
6—Chicago Bears, 1932.
Most consecutive tie games
3—Chicago Bears, September 25 through October 9, 1932.

TEAM OFFENSE
RUSHING

Most years leading league in rushing
16—Chicago Bears, 1932, 1934, 1935, 1939, 1940, 1941, 1942, 1951, 1955, 1956, 1968, 1977, 1983, 1984, 1985, 1986.
Most consecutive years leading league in rushing
4—Chicago Bears, 1939 through 1942.
   Chicago Bears, 1983 through 1986.

ATTEMPTS

Most attempts, season
681—Oakland, 1977.
Most attempts, game
72—Chicago Bears vs. Brooklyn, October 20, 1935.
Most attempts by both teams, game
108—Chicago Cardinals 70, Green Bay 38, December 5, 1948.
Fewest attempts, game
6—Chicago Cardinals at Boston, October 29, 1933.
Fewest attempts by both teams, game
35—New Orleans 20, Seattle 15, September 1, 1991.

YARDS

Most yards, season
3,165—New England, 1978.
Fewest yards, season
298—Philadelphia, 1940.
Most yards, game
426—Detroit vs. Pittsburgh, November 4, 1934.
Most yards by both teams, game
595—Los Angeles 371, New York Yanks 224, November 18, 1951.
Fewest yards, game
-53—Detroit at Chicago Cardinals, October 17, 1943.
Fewest yards by both teams, game
-15—Detroit -53, Chicago Cardinals 38, October 17, 1943.

TOUCHDOWNS

Most touchdowns, season
36—Green Bay, 1962.
Fewest touchdowns, season
1—Brooklyn, 1934.
Most touchdowns, game
7—Los Angeles vs. Atlanta, December 4, 1976.
Most touchdowns by both teams, game
8—Los Angeles 6, New York Yanks 2, November 18, 1951.
   Chicago Bears 5, Green Bay 3, November 6, 1955.
   Cleveland 6, Los Angeles 2, November 24, 1957.

PASSING
ATTEMPTS

Most attempts, season
709—Minnesota, 1981.
Fewest attempts, season
102—Cincinnati, 1933.
Most attempts, game
70—New England vs. Minnesota, November 13, 1994 (overtime).
68—Houston at Buffalo, November 1, 1964.

Most attempts by both teams, game
112—New England 70, Minnesota 42, November 13, 1994 (overtime).
104—Miami 55, New York Jets 49, October 18, 1987 (overtime).
102—San Francisco 57, Atlanta 45, October 6, 1985.
Fewest attempts, game
0—Green Bay vs. Portsmouth, October 8, 1933.
   Detroit at Cleveland, September 10, 1937.
   Pittsburgh vs. Brooklyn, November 16, 1941.
   Pittsburgh vs. Los Angeles, November 13, 1949.
   Cleveland vs. Philadelphia, December 3, 1950.
Fewest attempts by both teams, game
4—Detroit 3, Chicago Cardinals 1, November 3, 1935.
   Cleveland 4, Detroit 0, September 10, 1937.

COMPLETIONS

Most completions, season
432—San Francisco, 1995.
Fewest completions, season
25—Cincinnati, 1933.
Most completions, game
45—New England vs. Minnesota, November 13, 1994 (overtime).
42—New York Jets vs. San Francisco, September 21, 1980.
Most completions by both teams, game
71—New England 45, Minnesota 26, November 13, 1994 (overtime).
68—San Francisco 37, Atlanta 31, October 6, 1985.
Fewest completions, game
0—Held by many teams. Last team: Buffalo vs. New York Jets, September 29, 1974.
Fewest completions by both teams, game
1—Philadelphia 1, Chicago Cardinals 0, November 8, 1936.
   Cleveland 1, Detroit 0, September 10, 1937.
   Detroit 1, Chicago Cardinals 0, September 15, 1940.
   Pittsburgh 1, Brooklyn 0, November 29, 1942.

YARDS

Most yards, season
5,018—Miami, 1984.
Most years leading league in yards
10—San Diego, 1965, 1968, 1971, 1978 through 1983, 1985.
Most consecutive years leading league in yards
6—San Diego, 1978 through 1983.
Fewest yards, season
302—Chicago Cardinals, 1934.
Most yards, game
554—Los Angeles at New York Yanks, September 28, 1951.
Most yards by both teams, game
884—New York Jets 449, Miami 435, September 21, 1986 (overtime).
883—San Diego 486, Cincinnati 397, December 20, 1982.
Fewest yards, game
-53—Denver at Oakland, September 10, 1967.
Fewest yards by both teams, game
-11—Green Bay -10, Dallas -1, October 24, 1965.

TOUCHDOWNS

Most touchdowns, season
49—Miami, 1984.
Fewest touchdowns, season
0—Cincinnati, 1933.
   Pittsburgh, 1945.
Most touchdowns, game
7—Chicago Bears at New York Giants, November 14, 1943.
   Philadelphia at Washington, October 17, 1954.
   Houston vs. New York Titans, November 19, 1961.
   Houston vs. New York Titans, October 14, 1962.
   New York Giants vs. Washington, October 28, 1962.
   Minnesota vs. Baltimore, September 28, 1969.
   San Diego at Oakland, November 22, 1981.
Most touchdowns by both teams, game
12—New Orleans 6, St. Louis 6, November 2, 1969.

INTERCEPTIONS

Most interceptions, season
48—Houston, 1962.
Fewest interceptions, season
5—Cleveland, 1960.
    Green Bay, 1966.
    Kansas City, 1990.
    New York Giants, 1990.
Most interceptions, game
9—Detroit vs. Green Bay, October 24, 1943.
    Pittsburgh vs. Philadelphia, December 12, 1965.
Most interceptions by both teams, game
13—Denver 8, Houston 5, December 2, 1962.

SACKS

Most sacks allowed, season
104—Philadelphia, 1986.
Most years leading league in fewest sacks allowed
10—Miami, 1973 and 1982 through 1990.
Most consecutive years leading league in fewest sacks allowed
9—Miami, 1982 through 1990.
Fewest sacks allowed, season
7—Miami, 1988.
Most sacks allowed, game
12—Pittsburgh at Dallas, November 20, 1966.
    Baltimore vs. St. Louis, October 26, 1980.
    Detroit vs. Chicago, December 16, 1984.
    Houston vs. Dallas, September 29, 1985.
Most sacks allowed by both teams, game
18—Green Bay 10, San Diego 8, September 24, 1978.

SCORING

POINTS

Most points, season
541—Washington, 1983.
Most points, game
72—Washington vs. New York Giants, November 27, 1966.
Most points by both teams, game
113—Washington 72, New York Giants 41, November 27, 1966.
Fewest points by both teams, game
0—Occurred many times. Last time: New York Giants 0, Detroit 0, November 7, 1943.
Most points in a shutout victory
64—Philadelphia vs. Cincinnati, November 6, 1934.
Fewest points in a shutout victory
2—Green Bay at Chicago Bears, October 16, 1932.
    Chicago Bears at Green Bay, September 18, 1938.
Most points in first half of game
49—Green Bay vs. Tampa Bay, October 2, 1983.
Most points in first half of game by both teams
70—Houston 35, Oakland 35, December 22, 1963.
Most points in second half of game
49—Chicago Bears at Philadelphia, November 30, 1941.
Most points in second half of game by both teams
65—Washington 38, New York Giants 27, November 27, 1966.
Most points in one quarter
41—Green Bay vs. Detroit, October 7, 1945, second quarter.
    Los Angeles vs. Detroit, October 29, 1950, third quarter.
Most points in one quarter by both teams
49—Oakland 28, Houston 21, December 22, 1963, second quarter.
Most points in first quarter
35—Green Bay vs. Cleveland, November 12, 1967.
Most points in first quarter by both teams
42—Green Bay 35, Cleveland 7, November 12, 1967.
Most points in second quarter
41—Green Bay vs. Detroit, October 7, 1945.
Most points in second quarter by both teams
49—Oakland 28, Houston 21, December 22, 1963.

Most points in third quarter
41—Los Angeles vs. Detroit, October 29, 1950.
Most points in third quarter by both teams
48—Los Angeles 41, Detroit 7, October 29, 1950.
Most points in fourth quarter
31—Oakland vs. Denver, December 17, 1960.
    Oakland vs. San Diego, December 8, 1963.
    Atlanta at Green Bay, September 13, 1981.
Most points in fourth quarter by both teams
42—Chicago Cardinals 28, Philadelphia 14, December 7, 1947.
    Green Bay 28, Chicago Bears 14, November 6, 1955.
    New York Jets 28, Boston 14, October 27, 1968.
    Pittsburgh 21, Cleveland 21, October 18, 1969.
Most consecutive games without being shut out
322—San Francisco, October 16, 1977 through December 21, 1997.

TIMES SHUT OUT

Most times shut out, season
8—Frankford, 1927 (lost six, tied two).
    Brooklyn, 1931 (lost eight).
Most consecutive times shut out
8—Rochester, 1922 through 1924 (lost eight).

TOUCHDOWNS

Most touchdowns, season
70—Miami, 1984.
Most years leading league in touchdowns
13—Chicago Bears, 1932, 1934, 1935, 1939, 1941, 1942, 1943, 1944, 1946, 1947, 1948, 1956, 1965.
Most consecutive years leading league in touchdowns
4—Chicago Bears, 1941 through 1944.
    Los Angeles, 1949 through 1952.
Most touchdowns, game
10—Philadelphia vs. Cincinnati, November 6, 1934.
    Los Angeles vs. Baltimore, October 22, 1950.
    Washington vs. New York Giants, November 27, 1966.
Most touchdowns by both teams, game
16—Washington 10, New York Giants 6, November 27, 1966.
Most consecutive games with one or more touchdowns
166—Cleveland, 1957 through 1969.

EXTRA POINTS

Most extra points, season
66—Miami, 1984.
Fewest extra points, season
2—Chicago Cardinals, 1933.
Most extra points, game
10—Los Angeles vs. Baltimore, October 22, 1950.
Most extra points by both teams, game
14—Chicago Cardinals 9, New York Giants 5, October 17, 1948.
    Houston 7, Oakland 7, December 22, 1963.
    Washington 9, New York Giants 5, November 27, 1966.

FIELD GOALS

Most field goals attempted, season
49—Los Angeles, 1966.
    Washington, 1971.
Most field goals made, season
37—Carolina, 1996.
Most field goals attempted, game
9—St. Louis at Pittsburgh, September 24, 1967.
Most field goals made, game
7—St. Louis at Pittsburgh, September 24, 1967.
    Minnesota vs. Los Angeles Rams, November 5, 1989 (overtime).
Most field goals attempted by both teams, game
11—St. Louis 6, Pittsburgh 5, November 13, 1966.
    Washington 6, Chicago 5, November 14, 1971.
    Green Bay 6, Detroit 5, September 29, 1974.
    Washington 6, New York Giants 5, November 14, 1976.

Most field goals made by both teams, game
8—Cleveland 4, St. Louis 4, September 20, 1964.
  Chicago 5, Philadelphia 3, October 20, 1968.
  Washington 5, Chicago 3, November 14, 1971.
  Kansas City 5, Buffalo 3, December 19, 1971.
  Detroit 4, Green Bay 4, September 29, 1974.
  Cleveland 5, Denver 3, October 19, 1975.
  New England 4, San Diego 4, November 9, 1975.
  San Francisco 6, New Orleans 2, October 16, 1983.
  Seattle 5, Los Angeles Raiders 3, December 18, 1988.

Most consecutive games with one or more field goals made
31—Minnesota, November 17, 1968 through December 5, 1970.

SAFETIES

Most safeties, season
4—Cleveland, 1927.
  Detroit, 1962.
  Seattle, 1993.

Most safeties, game
3—Los Angeles Rams vs. New York Giants, September 30, 1984.

Most safeties by both teams, game
3—Los Angeles Rams 3, New York Giants 0, September 30, 1984.

FIRST DOWNS

Most first downs, season
387—Miami, 1984.

Most first downs, game
39—New York Jets vs. Miami, November 27, 1988.
  Washington at Detroit, November 4, 1990 (overtime).

Most first downs by both teams, game
62—San Diego 32, Seattle 30, September 15, 1985.

PUNTING

Most punts, season
114—Chicago, 1981.

Fewest punts, season
23—San Diego, 1982.

Most punts, game
17—Chicago Bears vs. Green Bay, October 22, 1933.
  Cincinnati vs. Pittsburgh, October 22, 1933.

Most punts by both teams, game
31—Chicago Bears 17, Green Bay 14, October 22, 1933.
  Cincinnati 17, Pittsburgh 14, October 22, 1933.

Fewest punts, game
0—Held by many teams.

Fewest punts by both teams, game
0—Buffalo 0, San Francisco 0, September 13, 1992.

FUMBLES

Most fumbles, season
56—Chicago Bears, 1938.
  San Francisco, 1978.

Fewest fumbles, season
8—Cleveland, 1959.

Most fumbles, game
10—Philadelphia/Pittsburgh vs. New York, October 9, 1943.
  Detroit at Minnesota, November 12, 1967.
  Kansas City vs. Houston, October 12, 1969.
  San Francisco at Detroit, December 17, 1978.

Most fumbles by both teams, game
14—Washington 8, Pittsburgh 6, November 14, 1937.
  Chicago Bears 7, Cleveland 7, November 24, 1940.
  St. Louis 8, New York Giants 6, September 17, 1961.
  Kansas City 10, Houston 4, October 12, 1969.

LOST

Most fumbles lost, season
36—Chicago Cardinals, 1959.

Fewest fumbles lost, season
3—Philadelphia, 1938.
  Minnesota, 1980.

Most fumbles lost, game
8—St. Louis at Washington, October 25, 1976.
  Cleveland at Pittsburgh, December 23, 1990.

RECOVERED

Most fumbles recovered (own and opponents'), season
58—Minnesota, 1963.

Fewest fumbles recovered (own and opponents'), season
9—San Francisco, 1982.

Most fumbles recovered (own and opponents'), game
10—Denver vs. Buffalo, December 13, 1964.
  Pittsburgh vs. Houston, December 9, 1973.
  Washington vs. St. Louis, October 25, 1976.

Most fumbles recovered (own), season
37—Chicago Bears, 1938.

Fewest fumbles recovered (own), season
2—Washington, 1958.

TOUCHDOWNS

Most touchdowns on fumbles recovered (own and opponents'), season
5—Chicago Bears, 1942.
  Los Angeles, 1952.
  San Francisco, 1965.
  Oakland, 1978.

Most touchdowns on own fumbles recovered, season
2—Held by many teams. Last team: Miami, 1996.

Most touchdowns on fumbles recovered (own and opponents'), game
2—Held by many teams.

Most touchdowns on fumbles recovered (own and opponents'), game
3—Detroit 2, Minnesota 1, December 9, 1962.
  Green Bay 2, Dallas 1, November 29, 1964.
  Oakland 2, Buffalo 1, December 24, 1967.

Most touchdowns on own fumbles recovered, game
1—Held by many teams.

Most touchdowns on opponents' fumbles recovered by both teams, game
3—Green Bay 2, Dallas 1, November 29, 1964.
  Oakland 2, Buffalo 1, December 24, 1967.

TURNOVERS

Most turnovers, season
63—San Francisco, 1978.

Fewest turnovers, season
12—Kansas City, 1982.

Most turnovers, game
12—Detroit vs. Chicago Bears, November 22, 1942.
  Chicago Cardinals vs. Philadelphia, September 24, 1950.
  Pittsburgh vs. Philadelphia, December 12, 1965.

Most turnovers by both teams, game
17—Detroit 12, Chicago Bears 5, November 22, 1942.
  Boston 9, Philadelphia 8, December 8, 1946.

PUNT RETURNS

Most punt returns, season
71—Pittsburgh, 1976.
  Tampa Bay, 1979.
  Los Angeles Raiders, 1985.

Fewest punt returns, season
12—Baltimore, 1981.
  San Diego, 1982.

Most punt returns, game
12—Philadelphia at Cleveland, December 3, 1950.

Most punt returns by both teams, game
17—Philadelphia 12, Cleveland 5, December 3, 1950.

YARDS

Most yards, season
785—Los Angeles Raiders, 1985.
Fewest yards, season
27—St. Louis, 1965.
Most yards, game
231—Detroit vs. San Francisco, October 6, 1963.
Most yards by both teams, game
282—Los Angeles 219, Atlanta 63, October 11, 1981.

TOUCHDOWNS

Most touchdowns, season
5—Chicago Cardinals, 1959.
Most touchdowns, game
2—Held by many teams. Last team: Cleveland vs. Pittsburgh, October 24, 1993.
Most touchdowns by both teams, game
2—Occurred many times. Last time: Cleveland 2, Pittsburgh 0, October 24, 1993.

KICKOFF RETURNS

Most kickoff returns, season
88—New Orleans, 1980.
Fewest kickoff returns, season
17—New York Giants, 1944.
Most kickoff returns, game
12—New York Giants at Washington, November 27, 1966.
Most kickoff returns by both teams, game
19—New York Giants 12, Washington 7, November 27, 1966.

YARDS

Most yards, season
1,973—New Orleans, 1980.
Fewest yards, season
282—New York Giants, 1940.
Most yards, game
362—Detroit at Los Angeles, October 29, 1950.
Most yards by both teams, game
560—Detroit 362, Los Angeles 198, October 29, 1950.

TOUCHDOWNS

Most touchdowns, season
4—Green Bay, 1967.
  Chicago, 1970.
  Detroit, 1994.
Most touchdowns, game
2—Chicago Bears at Green Bay, September 22, 1940.
  Chicago Bears vs. Green Bay, November 9, 1952.
  Philadelphia vs. Dallas, November 6, 1966.
  Green Bay vs. Cleveland, November 12, 1967.
  Los Angeles Rams vs. Green Bay, November 24, 1985.
  New Orleans vs. Los Angeles Rams, October 23, 1994.
Most touchdowns by both teams, game (each team scoring)
2—Occurred many times. Last time: Houston 1, Pittsburgh 1, December 4, 1988.

PENALTIES

Most penalties, season
156—L.A. Raiders, 1994.
Fewest penalties, season
19—Detroit, 1937.
Most penalties, game
22—Brooklyn at Green Bay, September 17, 1944.
  Chicago Bears at Philadelphia, November 26, 1944.
Most penalties by both teams, game
37—Cleveland 21, Chicago Bears 16, November 25, 1951.
Fewest penalties, game
0—Held by many teams. Last team: San Francisco vs. Philadelphia, November 29, 1992.
Fewest penalties by both teams, game
0—Brooklyn 0, Pittsburgh 0, October 28, 1934.
  Brooklyn 0, Boston 0, September 28, 1936.
  Cleveland 0, Chicago Bears 0, October 9, 1938.
  Pittsburgh 0, Philadelphia 0, November 10, 1940.

YARDS PENALIZED

Most yards penalized, season
1,274—Oakland, 1969.
Fewest yards penalized, season
139—Detroit, 1937.
Most yards penalized, game
209—Cleveland vs. Chicago Bears, November 25, 1951.
Most yards penalized by both teams, game
374—Cleveland 209, Chicago Bears 165, November 25, 1951.
Fewest yards penalized, game
0—Held by many teams. Last team: San Francisco vs. Philadelphia, November 29, 1992.
Fewest yards penalized by both teams, game
0—Brooklyn 0, Pittsburgh 0, October 28, 1934.
  Brooklyn 0, Boston 0, September 28, 1936.
  Cleveland 0, Chicago Bears 0, October 9, 1938.
  Pittsburgh 0, Philadelphia 0, November 10, 1940.

TEAM DEFENSE

RUSHING

YARDS ALLOWED

Most yards allowed, season
3,228—Buffalo, 1978.
Fewest yards allowed, season
519—Chicago Bears, 1942.

TOUCHDOWNS ALLOWED

Most touchdowns allowed, season
36—Oakland, 1961.
Fewest touchdowns allowed, season
2—Detroit, 1934.
  Dallas, 1968.
  Minnesota, 1971.

PASSING

YARDS ALLOWED

Most yards allowed, season
4,751—Atlanta, 1995.
Fewest yards allowed, season
545—Philadelphia, 1934.

TOUCHDOWNS ALLOWED

Most touchdowns allowed, season
40—Denver, 1963.
Fewest touchdowns allowed, season
1—Portsmouth, 1932.
  Philadelphia, 1934.

YARDS ALLOWED

(RUSHING AND PASSING)

Most yards allowed rushing and passing, season
6,793—Baltimore, 1981.
Fewest yards allowed rushing and passing, season
1,539—Chicago Cardinals, 1934.

SCORING

POINTS ALLOWED

Most points allowed, season
533—Baltimore, 1981.
Fewest points allowed, season (since 1932)
44—Chicago Bears, 1932.

SHUTOUTS

Most shutouts, season
10—Pottsville, 1926 (won nine, tied one).
  New York Giants, 1927 (won nine, tied one).

Most consecutive shutouts
13—Akron, 1920 through 1921 (won 10, tied three).

TOUCHDOWNS ALLOWED

Most touchdowns allowed, season
68—Baltimore, 1981.
Fewest touchdowns allowed, season (since 1932)
6—Chicago Bears, 1932.
 Brooklyn, 1933.

FIRST DOWNS ALLOWED

Most first downs allowed, season
406—Baltimore, 1981.
Fewest first downs allowed, season
77—Detroit, 1935.
Most first downs allowed by rushing, season
179—Detroit, 1985.
Fewest first downs allowed by rushing, season
35—Chicago Bears, 1942.
Most first downs allowed by passing, season
230—Atlanta, 1995.
Fewest first downs allowed by passing, season
33—Chicago Bears, 1943.
Most first downs allowed by penalties, season
48—Houston, 1985.
Fewest first downs allowed by penalties, season
1—Boston, 1944.

INTERCEPTIONS

Most interceptions, season
49—San Diego, 1961.
Fewest interceptions, season
3—Houston, 1982.
Most interceptions, game
9—Green Bay at Detroit, October 24, 1943.
 Philadelphia at Pittsburgh, December 12, 1965.
Most yards returning interceptions, season
929—San Diego, 1961.
Fewest yards returning interceptions, season
5—Los Angeles, 1959.
Most yards returning interceptions, game
325—Seattle vs. Kansas City, November 4, 1984.
Most touchdowns returning interceptions, season
9—San Diego, 1961.
Most touchdowns returning interceptions, game
4—Seattle vs. Kansas City, November 4, 1984.
Most touchdowns returning interceptions by both teams, game
4—Philadelphia 3, Pittsburgh 1, December 12, 1965.
 Seattle 4, Kansas City 0, November 4, 1984.

FUMBLES

Most opponents' fumbles forced, season
50—Minnesota, 1963.
 San Francisco, 1978.
Fewest opponents' fumbles forced, season
11—Cleveland, 1956.
 Baltimore, 1982.

RECOVERED

Most opponents' fumbles recovered, season
31—Minnesota, 1963.
Fewest opponents' fumbles recovered, season
3—Los Angeles, 1974.
Most opponents' fumbles recovered, game
8—Washington vs. St. Louis, October 25, 1976.
 Pittsburgh vs. Cleveland, December 23, 1990.

TOUCHDOWNS

Most touchdowns on opponents' fumbles recovered, season
4—Held by many teams. Last team: Atlanta, 1991.
Most touchdowns on opponents' fumbles recovered, game
2—Held by many teams. Last team: Cincinnati at Seattle,
 September 6, 1992.

TURNOVERS

Most opponents' turnovers, season
66—San Diego, 1961.
Fewest opponents' turnovers, season
11—Baltimore, 1982.
Most opponents' turnovers, game
12—Chicago Bears at Detroit, November 22, 1942.
 Philadelphia at Chicago Cardinals, September 24, 1950.
 Philadelphia at Pittsburgh, December 12, 1965.

SACKS

Most sacks, season
72—Chicago, 1984.
Fewest sacks, season
11—Baltimore, 1982.
Most sacks, game
12—Dallas at Pittsburgh, November 20, 1966.
 St. Louis at Baltimore, October 26, 1980.
 Chicago at Detroit, December 16, 1984.
 Dallas at Houston, September 29, 1985.

PUNTS RETURNED

Most punts returned by opponents, season
71—Tampa Bay, 1976.
 Tampa Bay, 1977.
Fewest punts returned by opponents, season
7—Washington, 1962.
 San Diego, 1982.
Most yards allowed on punts returned by opponents, season
932—Green Bay, 1949.
Fewest yards allowed on punts returned by opponents, season
22—Green Bay, 1967.
Most touchdowns allowed on punts returned by opponents, season
4—New York, 1959.
 Atlanta, 1992.

KICKOFFS RETURNED

Most kickoffs returned by opponents, season
91—Washington, 1983.
Fewest kickoffs returned by opponents, season
10—Brooklyn, 1943.
Most yards allowed on kickoffs returned by opponents, season
2,045—Kansas City, 1966.
Fewest yards allowed on kickoffs returned by opponents, season
225—Brooklyn, 1943.
Most touchdowns allowed on kickoffs returned by opponents, season
3—Minnesota, 1963.
 Dallas, 1966.
 Minnesota, 1970.
 Detroit, 1980.
 Pittsburgh, 1986.
 Buffalo, 1997.

STATISTICAL LEADERS

CAREER MILESTONES

TOP 20 RUSHERS

Player	League	Years	Att.	Yds.	Avg.	Long	TD
Walter Payton	NFL	13	3838	16726	4.4	76	110
Barry Sanders*	NFL	9	2719	13778	5.1	85	95
Eric Dickerson	NFL	11	2996	13259	4.4	85	90
Tony Dorsett	NFL	12	2936	12739	4.3	99	77
Jim Brown	NFL	9	2359	12312	5.2	80	106
Marcus Allen*	NFL	16	3022	12243	4.1	61	123
Franco Harris	NFL	13	2949	12120	4.1	75	91
Thurman Thomas*	NFL	10	2720	11405	4.2	80	63
John Riggins	NFL	14	2916	11352	3.9	66	104
O.J. Simpson	AFL-NFL	11	2404	11236	4.7	94	61
Emmitt Smith*	NFL	8	2595	11234	4.3	75	112
Ottis Anderson	NFL	14	2562	10273	4.0	76	81
Joe Perry	AAFC-NFL	16	1929	9723	5.0	78	71
Earl Campbell	NFL	8	2187	9407	4.3	81	74
Jim Taylor	NFL	10	1941	8597	4.4	84	83
Earnest Byner*	NFL	14	2095	8261	3.9	54	56
Herschel Walker*	NFL	12	1954	8225	4.2	91	61
Roger Craig	NFL	11	1991	8189	4.1	71	56
Gerald Riggs	NFL	10	1989	8188	4.1	58	69
Larry Csonka	AFL-NFL	11	1891	8081	4.3	54	64

*Active through 1997 season.

TOP 20 PASSERS

Player	League	Years	Att.	Comp.	Yds.	TD	Int.	Rating Pts.
Steve Young*	NFL	13	3548	2300	28508	193	91	97.0
Joe Montana	NFL	15	5391	3409	40551	273	139	92.3
Brett Favre*	NFL	7	3206	1971	22591	182	95	89.3
Dan Marino*	NFL	15	7452	4453	55416	385	220	87.8
Otto Graham	AAFC-NFL	10	2626	1464	23584	174	135	86.6
Jim Kelly	NFL	11	4779	2874	35467	237	175	84.4
Roger Staubach	NFL	11	2958	1685	22700	153	109	83.4
Neil Lomax	NFL	8	3153	1817	22771	136	90	82.7
Sonny Jurgensen	NFL	18	4262	2433	32224	255	189	82.625
Len Dawson	NFL-AFL	19	3741	2136	28711	239	183	82.555
Troy Aikman*	NFL	9	3696	2292	26016	129	110	82.3
Ken Anderson	NFL	16	4475	2654	32838	197	160	81.9
Bernie Kosar	NFL	12	3365	1994	23301	124	87	81.8
Danny White	NFL	13	2950	1761	21959	155	132	81.7
Dave Krieg*	NFL	18	5290	3093	37948	261	199	81.5
Warren Moon*	NFL	14	6528	3827	47465	279	224	81.2
Boomer Esiason*	NFL	14	5205	2969	37920	247	184	81.1
Jeff Hostetler*	NFL	12	2338	1357	16430	94	71	80.480
Neil O'Donnell*	NFL	8	2519	1438	16810	89	53	80.471
Bart Starr	NFL	16	3149	1808	24718	152	138	80.465

*Active through 1997 season.

TOP 20 RECEIVERS

Player	League	Years	No.	Yds.	Avg.	Long	TD
Jerry Rice*	NFL	13	1057	16455	15.6	96	155
Art Monk	NFL	16	940	12721	13.5	79	68
Andre Reed*	NFL	13	826	11764	14.2	83	80
Steve Largent	NFL	14	819	13089	16.0	74	100
Henry Ellard*	NFL	15	807	13662	16.9	81	65
James Lofton	NFL	16	764	14004	18.3	80	75
Cris Carter*	NFL	11	756	9436	12.5	80	89
Charlie Joiner	AFL-NFL	18	750	12146	16.2	87	65
Gary Clark	NFL	11	699	10856	15.5	84	65
Irving Fryar*	NFL	14	736	11427	15.5	80	75
Ozzie Newsome	NFL	13	662	7980	12.1	74	47
Charley Taylor	NFL	13	649	9110	14.0	88	79
Andre Rison*	NFL	9	641	8839	13.8	75	73
Drew Hill	NFL	15	634	9831	15.5	81	60
Don Maynard	NFL-AFL	15	633	11834	18.7	87	88

Player	League	Years	No.	Yds.	Avg.	Long	TD
Raymond Berry	NFL	13	631	9275	14.7	70	68
Tim Brown*	NFL	10	599	8588	14.3	80	60
Sterling Sharpe	NFL	7	595	8134	13.7	79	65
Anthony Miller*	NFL	10	595	9148	15.4	76	63

*Active through 1997 season.

TOP 20 SCORERS

Player	League	Years	TD	XP Made	FG Made	Total
George Blanda	NFL-AFL	26	9	943	335	2002
Nick Lowery	NFL	18	0	562	383	1711
Jan Stenerud	AFL-NFL	19	0	580	373	1699
Gary Anderson*	NFL	16	0	526	385	1681
Morten Andersen*	NFL	16	0	507	378	1641
Lou Groza	AAFC-NFL	21	1	810	264	1608
Norm Johnson*	NFL	16	0	592	322	1558
Eddie Murray	NFL	17	0	521	337	1532
Pat Leahy	NFL	18	0	558	304	1470
Jim Turner	AFL-NFL	16	1	521	304	1439
Matt Bahr	NFL	17	0	522	300	1422
Mark Moseley	NFL	16	0	482	300	1382
Jim Bakken	NFL	17	0	534	282	1380
Fred Cox	NFL	15	0	519	282	1365
Jim Breech	NFL	14	0	517	243	1246
Al Del Greco*	NFL	14	0	435	263	1224
Chris Bahr	NFL	14	0	490	241	1213
Kevin Butler*	NFL	13	0	413	265	1208
Gino Cappelletti	AFL-NFL	11	42	350	†176	†1130
Ray Wersching	NFL	15	0	456	222	1122

*Active through 1997 season.
†Includes four two-point conversions.

YEAR BY YEAR

AFC

RUSHING
(Based on most net yards)

	Net Yds.	Att.	TD
1960—Abner Haynes, Dallas	875	156	9
1961—Billy Cannon, Houston	948	200	6
1962—Cookie Gilchrist, Buffalo	1096	214	13
1963—Clem Daniels, Oakland	1099	215	3
1964—Cookie Gilchrist, Buffalo	981	230	6
1965—Paul Lowe, San Diego	1121	222	7
1966—Jim Nance, Boston	1458	299	11
1967—Jim Nance, Boston	1216	269	7
1968—Paul Robinson, Cincinnati	1023	238	8
1969—Dick Post, San Diego	873	182	6
1970—Floyd Little, Denver	901	209	3
1971—Floyd Little, Denver	1133	284	6
1972—O.J. Simpson, Buffalo	1251	292	6
1973—O.J. Simpson, Buffalo	2003	332	12
1974—Otis Armstrong, Denver	1407	263	9
1975—O.J. Simpson, Buffalo	1817	329	16
1976—O.J. Simpson, Buffalo	1503	290	8
1977—Mark van Eeghen, Oakland	1273	324	7
1978—Earl Campbell, Houston	1450	302	13
1979—Earl Campbell, Houston	1697	368	19
1980—Earl Campbell, Houston	1934	373	13
1981—Earl Campbell, Houston	1376	361	10
1982—Freeman McNeil, N.Y. Jets	786	151	6
1983—Curt Warner, Seattle	1449	335	13
1984—Earnest Jackson, San Diego	1179	296	8
1985—Marcus Allen, L.A. Raiders	1759	380	11
1986—Curt Warner, Seattle	1481	319	13
1987—Eric Dickerson, Indianapolis	1288	283	6
1988—Eric Dickerson, Indianapolis	1659	388	14
1989—Christian Okoye, Kansas City	1480	370	12
1990—Thurman Thomas, Buffalo	1297	271	11

	Net Yds.	Att.	TD
1991—Thurman Thomas, Buffalo	1407	288	7
1992—Barry Foster, Pittsburgh	1690	390	11
1993—Thurman Thomas, Buffalo	1315	355	6
1994—Chris Warren, Seattle	1545	333	9
1995—Curtis Martin, New England	1487	368	14
1996—Terrell Davis, Denver	1538	345	13
1997—Terrell Davis, Denver	1750	369	15

PASSING
(Based on highest passer rating among qualifiers*)

	Att.	Com.	Yds.	TD	Int.	Rat.
1960— Jack Kemp, Chargers	406	211	3018	20	25	67.1
1961— George Blanda, Hou.	362	187	3330	36	22	91.3
1962— Len Dawson, Dal.	310	189	2759	29	17	98.3
1963— Tobin Rote, S.D.	286	170	2510	20	17	86.7
1964— Len Dawson, K.C.	354	199	2879	30	18	89.9
1965— John Hadl, S.D.	348	174	2798	20	21	71.3
1966— Len Dawson, K.C.	284	159	2527	26	10	101.7
1967— Daryle Lamonica, Oak.	425	220	3228	30	20	80.8
1968— Len Dawson, K.C.	224	131	2109	17	9	98.6
1969— Greg Cook, Cin.	197	106	1854	15	11	88.3
1970— Daryle Lamonica, Oak.	356	179	2516	22	15	76.5
1971— Bob Griese, Mia.	263	145	2089	19	9	90.9
1972— Earl Morrall, Mia.	150	83	1360	11	7	91.0
1973— Ken Stabler, Oak.	260	163	1997	14	10	88.5
1974— Ken Anderson, Cin.	328	213	2667	18	10	95.9
1975— Ken Anderson, Cin.	377	228	3169	21	11	94.1
1976— Ken Stabler, Oak.	291	194	2737	27	17	103.7
1977— Bob Griese, Mia.	307	180	2252	22	13	88.0
1978— Terry Bradshaw, Pit.	368	207	2915	28	20	84.8
1979— Dan Fouts, S.D.	530	332	4082	24	24	82.6
1980— Brian Sipe, Cle.	554	337	4132	30	14	91.4
1981— Ken Anderson, Cin.	479	300	3754	29	10	98.5
1982— Ken Anderson, Cin.	309	218	2495	12	9	95.5
1983— Dan Marino, Mia.	296	173	2210	20	6	96.0

Left margin: HISTORY Statistical leaders

	Att.	Com.	Yds.	TD	Int.	Rat.
1984— Dan Marino, Mia.	564	362	5084	48	17	108.9
1985— Ken O'Brien, NYJ	488	297	3888	25	8	96.2
1986— Dan Marino, Mia.	623	378	4746	44	23	92.5
1987— Bernie Kosar, Cle.	389	241	3033	22	9	95.4
1988— Boomer Esiason, Cin.	388	223	3572	28	14	97.4
1989— Boomer Esiason, Cin.	455	258	3525	28	11	92.1
1990— Jim Kelly, Buf.	346	219	2829	24	9	101.2
1991— Jim Kelly, Buf.	474	304	3844	33	17	97.6
1992— Warren Moon, Hou.	346	224	2521	18	12	89.3
1993— John Elway, Den.	551	348	4030	25	10	92.8
1994— Dan Marino, Mia.	615	385	4453	30	17	89.2
1995— Jim Harbaugh, Ind.	314	200	2575	17	5	100.7
1996— John Elway, Den.	466	287	3328	26	14	89.2
1997— Mark Brunell, Jac.	435	264	3281	18	7	†91.17

*This chart includes passer rating points for all leaders, although the same rating system was not used for determining leading quarterbacks prior to 1973. The old system was less equitable, yet similar to the new in that the rating was based on percentage of completions, touchdown passes, percentage of interceptions and average gain in yards.

†Brunell and Jeff George of Oakland (521, 290, 3917, 29, 9), tied with 91.2 rating points, but rounded to another decimal place, Brunell's rating is higher, 91.17 to 91.15.

RECEIVING

(Based on most receptions)

	No.	Yds.	TD
1960—Lionel Taylor, Denver	92	1235	12
1961—Lionel Taylor, Denver	100	1176	4
1962—Lionel Taylor, Denver	77	908	4
1963—Lionel Taylor, Denver	78	1101	10
1964—Charley Hennigan, Houston	101	1546	8
1965—Lionel Taylor, Denver	85	1131	6
1966—Lance Alworth, San Diego	73	1383	13
1967—George Sauer, N.Y. Jets	75	1189	6
1968—Lance Alworth, San Diego	68	1312	10
1969—Lance Alworth, San Diego	64	1003	4
1970—Marlin Briscoe, Buffalo	57	1036	8
1971—Fred Biletnikoff, Oakland	61	929	9
1972—Fred Biletnikoff, Oakland	58	802	7
1973—Fred Willis, Houston	57	371	1
1974—Lydell Mitchell, Baltimore	72	544	2
1975—Reggie Rucker, Cleveland	60	770	3
Lydell Mitchell, Baltimore	60	544	4
1976—MacArthur Lane, Kansas City	66	686	1
1977—Lydell Mitchell, Baltimore	71	620	4
1978—Steve Largent, Seattle	71	1168	8
1979—Joe Washington, Baltimore	82	750	3
1980—Kellen Winslow, San Diego	89	1290	9
1981—Kellen Winslow, San Diego	88	1075	10
1982—Kellen Winslow, San Diego	54	721	6
1983—Todd Christensen, L.A. Raiders	92	1247	12
1984—Ozzie Newsome, Cleveland	89	1001	5
1985—Lionel James, San Diego	86	1027	6
1986—Todd Christensen, L.A. Raiders	95	1153	8
1987—Al Toon, N.Y. Jets	68	976	5
1988—Al Toon, N.Y. Jets	93	1067	5
1989—Andre Reed, Buffalo	88	1312	9
1990—Haywood Jeffires, Houston	74	1048	8
Drew Hill, Houston	74	1019	5
1991—Haywood Jeffires, Houston	100	1181	7
1992—Haywood Jeffires, Houston	90	913	9
1993—Reggie Langhorne, Indianapolis	85	1038	3
1994—Ben Coates, New England	96	1174	7
1995—Carl Pickens, Cincinnati	99	1234	17
1996—Carl Pickens, Cincinnati	100	1180	12
1997—Tim Brown, Oakland	104	1408	5

SCORING

(Based on most total points)

	TD	PAT	FG	Tot.
1960— Gene Mingo, Denver	6	33	18	123
1961— Gino Cappelletti, Boston	8	48	17	147
1962— Gene Mingo, Denver	4	32	27	137
1963— Gino Cappelletti, Boston	2	35	22	113
1964— Gino Cappelletti, Boston	7	36	25	155
1965— Gino Cappelletti, Boston	9	27	17	132
1966— Gino Cappelletti, Boston	6	35	16	119
1967— George Blanda, Oakland	0	56	20	116
1968— Jim Turner, N.Y. Jets	0	43	34	145
1969— Jim Turner, N.Y. Jets	0	33	32	129
1970— Jan Stenerud, Kansas City	0	26	30	116
1971— Garo Yepremian, Miami	0	33	28	117
1972— Bobby Howfield, N.Y. Jets	0	40	27	121
1973— Roy Gerela, Pittsburgh	0	36	29	123
1974— Roy Gerela, Pittsburgh	0	33	20	93
1975— O.J. Simpson, Buffalo	23	0	0	138
1976— Toni Linhart, Baltimore	0	49	20	109
1977— Errol Mann, Oakland	0	39	20	99
1978— Pat Leahy, N.Y. Jets	0	41	22	107
1979— John Smith, New England	0	46	23	115
1980— John Smith, New England	0	51	26	129
1981— Jim Breech, Cincinnati	0	49	22	115
Nick Lowery, Kansas City	0	37	26	115
1982— Marcus Allen, L.A. Raiders	14	0	0	84
1983— Gary Anderson, Pittsburgh	0	38	27	119
1984— Gary Anderson, Pittsburgh	0	45	24	117
1985— Gary Anderson, Pittsburgh	0	40	33	139
1986— Tony Franklin, New England	0	44	32	140
1987— Jim Breech, Cincinnati	0	25	24	97
1988— Scott Norwood, Buffalo	0	33	32	129
1989— David Treadwell, Denver	0	39	27	120
1990— Nick Lowery, Kansas City	0	37	34	139
1991— Pete Stoyanovich, Miami	0	28	31	121
1992— Pete Stoyanovich, Miami	0	34	30	124
1993— Jeff Jaeger, L.A. Raiders	0	27	35	132
1994— John Carney, San Diego	0	33	34	135
1995— Norm Johnson, Pittsburgh	0	39	34	141
1996— Cary Blanchard, Indianapolis	0	27	36	135
1997— Mike Hollis, Jacksonville	0	41	31	134

FIELD GOALS

	No.
1960— Gene Mingo, Denver	18
1961— Gino Cappelletti, Boston	17
1962— Gene Mingo, Denver	27
1963— Gino Cappelletti, Boston	22
1964— Gino Cappelletti, Boston	25
1965— Pete Gogolak, Buffalo	28
1966— Mike Mercer, Oakland-Kansas City	21
1967— Jan Stenerud, Kansas City	21
1968— Jim Turner, N.Y. Jets	34
1969— Jim Turner, N.Y. Jets	32
1970— Jan Stenerud, Kansas City	30
1971— Garo Yepremian, Miami	28
1972— Roy Gerela, Pittsburgh	28
1973— Roy Gerela, Pittsburgh	29
1974— Roy Gerela, Pittsburgh	20
1975— Jan Stenerud, Kansas City	22
1976— Jan Stenerud, Kansas City	21
1977— Errol Mann, Oakland	20
1978— Pat Leahy, N.Y. Jets	22
1979— John Smith, New England	23
1980— John Smith, New England	26
Fred Steinfort, Denver	26
1981— Nick Lowery, Kansas City	26
1982— Nick Lowery, Kansas City	19
1983— Raul Allegre, Baltimore	30
1984— Gary Anderson, Pittsburgh	24
Matt Bahr, Cleveland	24
1985— Gary Anderson, Pittsburgh	33
1986— Tony Franklin, New England	32
1987— Dean Biasucci, Indianapolis	24
Jim Breech, Cincinnati	24
1988— Scott Norwood, Buffalo	32
1989— David Treadwell, Denver	27
1990— Nick Lowery, Kansas City	34
1991— Pete Stoyanovich, Miami	31
1992— Pete Stoyanovich, Miami	30
1993— Jeff Jaeger, L.A. Raiders	35
1994— John Carney, San Diego	34

	No.
1995— Norm Johnson, Pittsburgh	34
1996— Cary Blanchard, Indianapolis	36
1997— Cary Blanchard, Indianapolis	32

INTERCEPTIONS

	No.	Yds.
1960— Austin Gonsoulin, Denver	11	98
1961— Bill Atkins, Buffalo	10	158
1962— Lee Riley, N.Y. Jets	11	122
1963— Fred Glick, Houston	12	180
1964— Dainard Paulson, N.Y. Jets	12	157
1965— W.K. Hicks, Houston	9	156
1966— Johnny Robinson, Kansas City	10	136
Bobby Hunt, Kansas City	10	113
1967— Miller Farr, Houston	10	264
Tom Janik, Buffalo	10	222
Dick Westmoreland, Miami	10	127
1968— Dave Grayson, Oakland	10	195
1969— Emmitt Thomas, Kansas City	9	146
1970— Johnny Robinson, Kansas City	10	155
1971— Ken Houston, Houston	9	220
1972— Mike Sensibaugh, Kansas City	8	65
1973— Dick Anderson, Miami	8	136
Mike Wagner, Pittsburgh	8	134
1974— Emmitt Thomas, Kansas City	12	214
1975— Mel Blount, Pittsburgh	11	121
1976— Ken Riley, Cincinnati	9	141
1977— Lyle Blackwood, Baltimore	10	163
1978— Thom Darden, Cleveland	10	200
1979— Mike Reinfeldt, Houston	12	205
1980— Lester Hayes, Oakland	13	273
1981— John Harris, Seattle	10	155
1982— Ken Riley, Cincinnati	5	88
Bobby Jackson, N.Y. Jets	5	84
Dwayne Woodruff, Pittsburgh	5	53
Donnie Shell, Pittsburgh	5	27
1983— Ken Riley, Cincinnati	8	89
Vann McElroy, Los Angeles	8	68
1984— Kenny Easley, Seattle	10	126
1985— Eugene Daniel, Indianapolis	8	53
Albert Lewis, Kansas City	8	59
1986— Deron Cherry, Kansas City	9	150
1987— Mike Prior, Indianapolis	6	57
Mark Kelso, Buffalo	6	25
Keith Bostic, Houston	6	-14
1988— Erik McMillan, N.Y. Jets	8	168
1989— Felix Wright, Cleveland	9	91
1990— Richard Johnson, Houston	8	100
1991— Ronnie Lott, L.A. Raiders	8	52
1992— Henry Jones, Buffalo	8	263
1993— Nate Odomes, Buffalo	9	65
Eugene Robinson, Seattle	9	80
1994— Eric Turner, Cleveland	9	199
1995— Willie Williams, Pittsburgh	7	122
1996— Tyrone Braxton, Denver	9	128
1997— Mark McMillian, Kansas City	8	274
Darryl Williams, Seattle	8	172

PUNTING

(Based on highest average yardage per punt by qualifiers)

	No.	Avg.
1960— Paul Maguire, L.A. Chargers	43	40.5
1961— Bill Atkins, Buffalo	85	44.5
1962— Jim Fraser, Denver	55	43.6
1963— Jim Fraser, Denver	81	44.4
1964— Jim Fraser, Denver	73	44.2
1965— Jerrel Wilson, Kansas City	69	45.4
1966— Bob Scarpitto, Denver	76	45.8
1967— Bob Scarpitto, Denver	105	44.9
1968— Jerrel Wilson, Kansas City	63	45.1
1969— Dennis Partee, San Diego	71	44.6
1970— Dave Lewis, Cincinnati	79	46.2
1971— Dave Lewis, Cincinnati	72	44.8
1972— Jerrel Wilson, Kansas City	66	44.8

	No.	Avg.
1973— Jerrel Wilson, Kansas City	80	45.5
1974— Ray Guy, Oakland	74	42.2
1975— Ray Guy, Oakland	68	43.8
1976— Marv Bateman, Buffalo	86	42.8
1977— Ray Guy, Oakland	59	43.4
1978— Pat McInally, Cincinnati	91	43.1
1979— Bob Grupp, Kansas City	89	43.6
1980— Luke Prestridge, Denver	70	43.9
1981— Pat McInally, Cincinnati	72	45.4
1982— Luke Prestridge, Denver	45	45.0
1983— Rohn Stark, Baltimore	91	45.3
1984— Jim Arnold, Kansas City	98	44.9
1985— Rohn Stark, Indianapolis	78	45.9
1986— Rohn Stark, Indianapolis	76	45.2
1987— Ralf Mojsiejenko, San Diego	67	42.9
1988— Harry Newsome, Pittsburgh	65	45.4
1989— Greg Montgomery, Houston	56	43.3
1990— Mike Horan, Denver	58	44.4
1991— Reggie Roby, Miami	54	45.7
1992— Greg Montgomery, Houston	53	46.9
1993— Greg Montgomery, Houston	54	45.6
1994— Jeff Gossett, L.A. Raiders	77	43.9
1995— Rick Tuten, Seattle	83	45.0
1996— John Kidd, Miami	78	46.3
1997— Tom Tupa, New England	71	45.7

PUNT RETURNS

(Based on most total yards)

	No.	Yds.	Avg.
1960— Abner Haynes, Dallas	14	215	15.4
1961— Dick Christy, N.Y. Jets	18	383	21.3
1962— Dick Christy, N.Y. Jets	15	250	16.7
1963— Claude Gibson, Oakland	26	307	11.8
1964— Bobby Jancik, Houston	12	220	18.3
1965— Leslie Duncan, San Diego	30	464	15.5
1966— Leslie Duncan, San Diego	18	238	13.2
1967— Floyd Little, Denver	16	270	16.9
1968— Noland Smith, Kansas City	18	270	15.0
1969— Bill Thompson, Denver	25	288	11.5
1970— Ed Podolak, Kansas City	23	311	13.5
1971— Leroy Kelly, Cleveland	30	292	9.7
1972— Chris Farasopolous, N.Y. Jets	17	179	10.5
1973— Ron Smith, San Diego	27	352	15.0
1974— Lemar Parrish, Cincinnati	18	338	18.8
1975— Billy Johnson, Houston	40	612	18.8
1976— Rick Upchurch, Denver	39	536	13.7
1977— Billy Johnson, Houston	30	539	15.4
1978— Rick Upchurch, Denver	36	493	13.7
1979— Tony Nathan, Miami	28	306	10.9
1980— J.T. Smith, Kansas City	40	581	14.5
1981— James Brooks, San Diego	22	290	13.2
1982— Rick Upchurch, Denver	15	242	16.1
1983— Kirk Springs, N.Y. Jets	23	287	12.5
1984— Mike Martin, Cincinnati	24	376	15.7
1985— Irving Fryar, New England	37	520	14.1
1986— Bobby Joe Edmonds, Seattle	34	419	12.3
1987— Bobby Joe Edmonds, Seattle	20	251	12.6
1988— Jojo Townsell, N.Y. Jets	35	409	11.7
1989— Clarence Verdin, Indianapolis	23	296	12.9
1990— Clarence Verdin, Indianapolis	31	396	12.8
1991— Rod Woodson, Pittsburgh	28	320	11.4
1992— Rod Woodson, Pittsburgh	32	364	11.4
1993— Tim Brown, L.A. Raiders	40	465	11.6
1994— Tim Brown, L.A. Raiders	40	487	12.2
1995— Tamarick Vanover, Kansas City	51	540	10.6
1996— David Meggett, New England	52	588	11.3
1997— Leon Johnson, N.Y. Jets	51	619	12.1

KICKOFF RETURNS

(Based on most total yards)

	No.	Yds.	Avg.
1960— Ken Hall, Houston	19	594	31.3
1961— Dave Grayson, Dallas	16	453	28.3
1962— Bobby Jancik, Houston	24	726	30.3

	No.	Yds.	Avg.
1963—Bobby Jancik, Houston	45	1317	29.3
1964—Bo Roberson, Oakland	36	975	27.1
1965—Abner Haynes, Denver	34	901	26.5
1966—Goldie Sellers, Denver	19	541	28.5
1967—Zeke Moore, Houston	14	405	28.9
1968—George Atkinson, Oakland	32	802	25.1
1969—Bill Thompson, Denver	19	594	31.3
1970—Jim Duncan, Baltimore	20	707	35.4
1971—Mercury Morris, Miami	15	423	28.2
1972—Bruce Laird, Baltimore	29	843	29.1
1973—Wallace Francis, Buffalo	23	687	29.9
1974—Greg Pruitt, Cleveland	22	606	27.5
1975—Harold Hart, Oakland	17	518	30.5
1976—Duriel Harris, Miami	17	559	32.9
1977—Raymond Clayborn, New England	20	869	31.0
1978—Keith Wright, Cleveland	30	789	26.3
1979—Larry Brunson, Oakland	17	441	25.9
1980—Horace Ivory, New England	36	992	27.6
1981—Carl Roaches, Houston	28	769	27.5
1982—Mike Mosley, Buffalo	18	487	27.1
1983—Fulton Walker, Miami	36	962	26.7
1984—Bobby Humphrey, N.Y. Jets	22	675	30.7
1985—Glen Young, Cleveland	35	898	25.7
1986—Lupe Sanchez, Pittsburgh	25	591	23.6
1987—Paul Palmer, Kansas City	38	923	24.3
1988—Tim Brown, L.A. Raiders	41	1098	26.8
1989—Rod Woodson, Pittsburgh	36	982	27.3
1990—Kevin Clark, Denver	20	505	25.3

	No.	Yds.	Avg.
1991—Nate Lewis, San Diego	23	578	25.1
1992—Jon Vaughn, New England	20	564	28.2
1993—Clarence Verdin, Indianapolis	50	1050	21.0
1994—Andre Coleman, San Diego	49	1293	26.4
1995—Andre Coleman, San Diego	62	1411	22.8
1996—Mel Gray, Houston	50	1224	24.5
1997—Kevin Williams, Arizona	59	1459	24.7

SACKS

	No.
1982— Jesse Baker, Houston	7.5
1983— Mark Gastineau, N.Y. Jets	19.0
1984— Mark Gastineau, N.Y. Jets	22.0
1985— Andre Tippett, New England	16.5
1986— Sean Jones, L.A. Raiders	15.5
1987— Andre Tippett, New England	12.5
1988— Greg Townsend, L.A. Raiders	11.5
1989— Lee Williams, San Diego	14.0
1990— Derrick Thomas, Kansas City	20.0
1991— William Fuller, Houston	15.0
1992— Leslie O'Neal, San Diego	17.0
1993— Neil Smith, Kansas City	15.0
1994— Kevin Greene, Pittsburgh	14.0
1995— Bryce Paup, Buffalo	17.5
1996— Michael McCrary, Seattle	13.5
Bruce Smith, Buffalo	13.5
1997— Bruce Smith, Buffalo	15.0

NFC

RUSHING

(Based on most net yards)

	Net Yds.	Att.	TD
1960—Jim Brown, Cleveland	1257	215	9
1961—Jim Brown, Cleveland	1408	305	8
1962—Jim Taylor, Green Bay	1474	272	19
1963—Jim Brown, Cleveland	1863	291	12
1964—Jim Brown, Cleveland	1446	280	7
1965—Jim Brown, Cleveland	1544	289	17
1966—Gale Sayers, Chicago	1231	229	8
1967—Leroy Kelly, Cleveland	1205	235	11
1968—Leroy Kelly, Cleveland	1239	248	16
1969—Gale Sayers, Chicago	1032	236	8
1970—Larry Brown, Washington	1125	237	5
1971—John Brockington, Green Bay	1105	216	4
1972—Larry Brown, Washington	1216	285	8
1973—John Brockington, Green Bay	1144	265	3
1974—Lawrence McCutcheon, L.A. Rams	1109	236	3
1975—Jim Otis, St. Louis	1076	269	5
1976—Walter Payton, Chicago	1390	311	13
1977—Walter Payton, Chicago	1852	339	14
1978—Walter Payton, Chicago	1395	333	11
1979—Walter Payton, Chicago	1610	369	14
1980—Walter Payton, Chicago	1460	317	6
1981—George Rogers, New Orleans	1674	378	13
1982—Tony Dorsett, Dallas	745	177	5
1983—Eric Dickerson, L.A. Rams	1808	390	18
1984—Eric Dickerson, L.A. Rams	2105	379	14
1985—Gerald Riggs, Atlanta	1719	397	10
1986—Eric Dickerson, L.A. Rams	1821	404	11
1987—Charles White, L.A. Rams	1374	324	11
1988—Herschel Walker, Dallas	1514	361	5
1989—Barry Sanders, Detroit	1470	280	14
1990—Barry Sanders, Detroit	1304	255	13
1991—Emmitt Smith, Dallas	1563	365	12
1992—Emmitt Smith, Dallas	1713	373	18
1993—Emmitt Smith, Dallas	1486	283	9
1994—Barry Sanders, Detroit	1883	331	7
1995—Emmitt Smith, Dallas	1773	377	25
1996—Barry Sanders, Detroit	1553	307	11
1997—Barry Sanders, Detroit	2053	335	11

PASSING

(Based on highest passer rating among qualifiers*)

	Att.	Com.	Yds.	TD	Int.	Rat.
1960— Milt Plum, Cle.	250	151	2297	21	5	110.4
1961— Milt Plum, Cle.	302	177	2416	18	10	90.3
1962— Bart Starr, G.B.	285	178	2438	12	9	90.7
1963— Y.A. Tittle, NYG	367	221	3145	36	14	104.8
1964— Bart Starr, G.B.	272	163	2144	15	4	97.1
1965— Rudy Bukich, Chi.	312	176	2641	20	9	93.7
1966— Bart Starr, G.B.	251	156	2257	14	3	105.0
1967— Sonny Jurgensen, Was.	508	288	3747	31	16	87.3
1968— Earl Morrall, Bal.	317	182	2909	26	17	93.2
1969— Sonny Jurgensen, Was.	442	274	3102	22	15	85.4
1970— John Brodie, S.F.	378	223	2941	24	10	93.8
1971— Roger Staubach, Dal.	211	126	1882	15	4	104.8
1972— Norm Snead, NYG	325	196	2307	17	12	84.0
1973— Roger Staubach, Dal.	286	179	2428	23	15	94.6
1974— Sonny Jurgensen, Was.	167	107	1185	11	5	94.6
1975— Fran Tarkenton, Min.	425	273	2994	25	13	91.7
1976— James Harris, L.A.	158	91	1460	8	6	89.8
1977— Roger Staubach, Dal.	361	210	2620	18	9	87.1
1978— Roger Staubach, Dal.	413	231	3190	25	16	84.9
1979— Roger Staubach, Dal.	461	267	3586	27	11	92.4
1980— Ron Jaworski, Phi.	451	257	3529	27	12	90.0
1981— Joe Montana, S.F.	488	311	3565	19	12	88.4
1982— Joe Theismann, Was.	252	161	2033	13	9	91.3
1983— Steve Bartkowski, Atl.	432	274	3167	22	5	97.6
1984— Joe Montana, S.F.	432	279	3630	28	10	102.9
1985— Joe Montana, S.F.	494	303	3653	27	13	91.3
1986— Tommy Kramer, Min.	372	208	3000	24	10	92.6
1987— Joe Montana, S.F.	398	266	3054	31	13	102.1
1988— Wade Wilson, Min.	332	204	2746	15	9	91.5
1989— Joe Montana, S.F.	386	271	3521	26	8	112.4
1990— Phil Simms, NYG	311	184	2284	15	4	92.7
1991— Steve Young, S.F.	279	180	2517	17	8	101.8
1992— Steve Young, S.F.	402	268	3465	25	7	107.0
1993— Steve Young, S.F.	462	314	4023	29	16	101.5
1994— Steve Young, S.F.	461	324	3969	35	10	112.8
1995— Brett Favre, G.B.	570	359	4413	38	13	99.5
1996— Steve Young, S.F.	316	214	2410	14	6	97.2
1997— Steve Young, S.F.	356	241	3029	19	6	104.7

*This chart includes passer rating points for all leaders, although the same rating system was not used for determining leading quarterbacks prior to 1973. The old system was less equitable, yet similar to the new in that the rating was based on percentage of completions, touchdown passes, percentage of interceptions and average gain in yards.

RECEIVING
(Based on most receptions)

	No.	Yds.	TD
1960—Raymond Berry, Baltimore	74	1298	10
1961—Jim Phillips, L.A. Rams	78	1092	5
1962—Bobby Mitchell, Washington	72	1384	11
1963—Bobby Joe Conrad, St. Louis	73	967	10
1964—Johnny Morris, Chicago	93	1200	10
1965—Dave Parks, San Francisco	80	1344	12
1966—Charley Taylor, Washington	72	1119	12
1967—Charley Taylor, Washington	70	990	9
1968—Clifton McNeil, San Francisco	71	994	7
1969—Dan Abramowicz, New Orleans	73	1015	7
1970—Dick Gordon, Chicago	71	1026	13
1971—Bob Tucker, N.Y. Giants	59	791	4
1972—Harold Jackson, Philadelphia	62	1048	4
1973—Harold Carmichael, Philadelphia	67	1116	9
1974—Charles Young, Philadelphia	63	696	3
1975—Chuck Foreman, Minnesota	73	691	9
1976—Drew Pearson, Dallas	58	806	6
1977—Ahmad Rashad, Minnesota	51	681	2
1978—Rickey Young, Minnesota	88	704	5
1979—Ahmad Rashad, Minnesota	80	1156	9
1980—Earl Cooper, San Francisco	83	567	4
1981—Dwight Clark, San Francisco	85	1105	4
1982—Dwight Clark, San Francisco	60	913	5
1983—Roy Green, St. Louis	78	1227	14
Charlie Brown, Washington	78	1225	8
Earnest Gray, N.Y. Giants	78	1139	5
1984—Art Monk, Washington	106	1372	7
1985—Roger Craig, San Francisco	92	1016	6
1986—Jerry Rice, San Francisco	86	1570	15
1987—J.T. Smith, St. Louis	91	1117	8
1988—Henry Ellard, L.A. Rams	86	1414	10
1989—Sterling Sharpe, Green Bay	90	1423	12
1990—Jerry Rice, San Francisco	100	1502	13
1991—Michael Irvin, Dallas	93	1523	8
1992—Sterling Sharpe, Green Bay	108	1461	13
1993—Sterling Sharpe, Green Bay	112	1274	11
1994—Cris Carter, Minnesota	122	1256	7
1995—Herman Moore, Detroit	123	1686	14
1996—Jerry Rice, San Francisco	108	1254	8
1997—Herman Moore, Detroit	104	1293	8

SCORING
(Based on most total points)

	TD	PAT	FG	Tot.
1960— Paul Hornung, Green Bay	15	41	15	176
1961— Paul Hornung, Green Bay	10	41	15	146
1962— Jim Taylor, Green Bay	19	0	0	114
1963— Don Chandler, N.Y. Giants	0	52	18	106
1964— Lenny Moore, Baltimore	20	0	0	120
1965— Gale Sayers, Chicago	22	0	0	132
1966— Bruce Gossett, L.A. Rams	0	29	28	113
1967— Jim Bakken, St. Louis	0	36	27	117
1968— Leroy Kelly, Cleveland	20	0	0	120
1969— Fred Cox, Minnesota	0	43	26	121
1970— Fred Cox, Minnesota	0	35	30	125
1971— Curt Knight, Washington	0	27	29	114
1972— Chester Marcol, Green Bay	0	29	33	128
1973— David Ray, L.A. Rams	0	40	30	130
1974— Chester Marcol, Green Bay	0	19	25	94
1975— Chuck Foreman, Minnesota	22	0	0	132
1976— Mark Moseley, Washington	0	31	22	97
1977— Walter Payton, Chicago	16	0	0	96
1978— Frank Corral, L.A. Rams	0	31	29	118
1979— Mark Moseley, Washington	0	39	25	114
1980— Ed Murray, Detroit	0	35	27	116
1981— Ed Murray, Detroit	0	46	25	121
Rafael Septien, Dallas	0	40	27	121
1982— Wendell Tyler, L.A. Rams	13	0	0	78

	TD	PAT	FG	Tot.
1983— Mark Moseley, Washington	0	62	33	161
1984— Ray Wersching, S.F.	0	56	25	131
1985— Kevin Butler, Chicago	0	51	31	144
1986— Kevin Butler, Chicago	0	36	28	120
1987— Jerry Rice, San Francisco	23	0	0	138
1988— Mike Cofer, San Francisco	0	40	27	121
1989— Mike Cofer, San Francisco	0	49	29	136
1990— Chip Lohmiller, Washington	0	41	30	131
1991— Chip Lohmiller, Washington	0	56	31	149
1992— Morten Andersen, New Orleans	0	33	29	120
Chip Lohmiller, Washington	0	30	30	120
1993— Jason Hanson, Detroit	0	28	34	130
1994— Fuad Reveiz, Minnesota	0	30	34	132
1995— Emmitt Smith, Dallas	25	0	0	150
1996— John Kasay, Carolina	0	34	37	145
1997— Richie Cunningham, Dallas	0	24	34	126

FIELD GOALS

	No.
1960— Tommy Davis, San Francisco	19
1961— Steve Myhra, Baltimore	21
1962— Lou Michaels, Pittsburgh	26
1963— Jim Martin, Baltimore	24
1964— Jim Bakken, St. Louis	25
1965— Fred Cox, Minnesota	23
1966— Bruce Gossett, L.A. Rams	28
1967— Jim Bakken, St. Louis	27
1968— Mac Percival, Chicago	25
1969— Fred Cox, Minnesota	26
1970— Fred Cox, Minnesota	30
1971— Curt Knight, Washington	29
1972— Chester Marcol, Green Bay	33
1973— David Ray, L.A. Rams	30
1974— Chester Marcol, Green Bay	25
1975— Toni Fritsch, Dallas	22
1976— Mark Moseley, Washington	22
1977— Mark Moseley, Washington	21
1978— Frank Corral, L.A. Rams	29
1979— Mark Moseley, Washington	25
1980— Eddie Murray, Detroit	27
1981— Rafael Septien, Dallas	27
1982— Mark Moseley, Washington	20
1983— Ali Haji-Sheikh, N.Y. Giants	35
1984— Paul McFadden, Philadelphia	30
1985— Morten Andersen, New Orleans	31
Kevin Butler, Chicago	31
1986— Kevin Butler, Chicago	28
1987— Morten Andersen, New Orleans	28
1988— Mike Cofer, San Francisco	27
1989— Rich Karlis, Minnesota	31
1990— Chip Lohmiller, Washington	30
1991— Chip Lohmiller, Washington	31
1992— Chip Lohmiller, Washington	30
1993— Jason Hanson, Detroit	34
1994— Fuad Reveiz, Minnesota	34
1995— Morten Andersen, Atlanta	31
1996— John Kasay, Carolina	37
1997— Richie Cunningham, Dallas	34

INTERCEPTIONS

	No.	Yds.
1960— Dave Baker, San Francisco	10	96
Jerry Norton, St. Louis	10	96
1961— Dick Lynch, N.Y. Giants	9	60
1962— Willie Wood, Green Bay	9	132
1963— Dick Lynch, N.Y. Giants	9	251
Rosie Taylor, Chicago	9	172
1964— Paul Krause, Washington	12	140
1965— Bobby Boyd, Baltimore	9	78
1966— Larry Wilson, St. Louis	10	180
1967— Lem Barney, Detroit	10	232
Dave Whitsell, New Orleans	10	178
1968— Willie Williams, N.Y. Giants	10	103
1969— Mel Renfro, Dallas	10	118
1970— Dick Le Beau, Detroit	9	96
1971— Bill Bradley, Philadelphia	11	248

	No.	Yds.
1972— Bill Bradley, Philadelphia	9	73
1973— Bob Bryant, Minnesota	7	105
1974— Ray Brown, Atlanta	8	164
1975— Paul Krause, Minnesota	10	201
1976— Monte Jackson, L.A. Rams	10	173
1977— Rolland Lawrence, Atlanta	7	138
1978— Ken Stone, St. Louis	9	139
Willie Buchanon, Green Bay	9	93
1979— Lemar Parrish, Washington	9	65
1980— Nolan Cromwell, L.A. Rams	8	140
1981— Everson Walls, Dallas	11	133
1982— Everson Walls, Dallas	7	61
1983— Mark Murphy, Washington	9	127
1984— Tom Flynn, Green Bay	9	106
1985— Everson Walls, Dallas	9	31
1986— Ronnie Lott, San Francisco	10	134
1987— Barry Wilburn, Washington	9	135
1988— Scott Case, Atlanta	10	47
1989— Eric Allen, Philadelphia	8	38
1990— Mark Carrier, Chicago	10	39
1991— Ray Crockett, Detroit	6	141
Tim McKyer, Atlanta	6	24
Deion Sanders, Atlanta	6	119
Aeneas Williams, Phoenix	6	60
1992— Aubray McMillian, Minnesota	8	157
1993— Deion Sanders, Atlanta	7	91
1994— Aeneas Williams, Arizona	9	89
1995— Orlando Thomas, Minnesota	9	108
1996— Keith Lyle, St. Louis	9	152
1997— Ryan McNeil, St. Louis	9	127

PUNTING

(Based on highest average yardage per punt by qualifiers)

	No.	Avg.
1960— Jerry Norton, St. Louis	39	45.6
1961— Yale Lary, Detroit	52	48.4
1962— Tommy Davis, San Francisco	48	45.8
1963— Yale Lary, Detroit	35	48.9
1964— Bobby Walden, Minnesota	72	46.4
1965— Gary Collins, Cleveland	65	46.7
1966— David Lee, Baltimore	49	45.6
1967— Billy Lothridge, Atlanta	87	43.7
1968— Billy Lothridge, Atlanta	75	44.3
1969— David Lee, Baltimore	50	45.3
1970— Julian Fagan, New Orleans	77	42.5
1971— Tom McNeill, Philadelphia	73	42.0
1972— Dave Chapple, L.A. Rams	53	44.2
1973— Tom Wittum, San Francisco	79	43.7
1974— Tom Blanchard, New Orleans	88	42.1
1975— Herman Weaver, Detroit	80	42.0
1976— John James, Atlanta	101	42.1
1977— Tom Blanchard, New Orleans	82	42.4
1978— Tom Skladany, Detroit	86	42.5
1979— Dave Jennings, N.Y. Giants	104	42.7
1980— Dave Jennings, N.Y. Giants	94	44.8
1981— Tom Skladany, Detroit	64	43.5
1982— Carl Birdsong, St. Louis	54	43.8
1983— Frank Garcia, Tampa Bay	95	42.2
1984— Brian Hansen, New Orleans	69	43.8
1985— Rick Donnelly, Atlanta	59	43.6
1986— Sean Landeta, N.Y. Giants	79	44.8
1987— Rick Donnelly, Atlanta	61	44.0
1988— Jim Arnold, Detroit	97	42.4
1989— Rich Camarillo, Phoenix	76	43.4
1990— Sean Landeta, N.Y. Giants	75	44.1
1991— Harry Newsome, Minnesota	68	45.5
1992— Harry Newsome, Minnesota	72	45.0
1993— Jim Arnold, Detroit	72	44.5
1994— Sean Landeta, L.A. Rams	78	44.8
1995— Sean Landeta, St. Louis	83	44.3
1996— Matt Turk, Washington	75	45.1
1997— Mark Royals, New Orleans	88	45.9

PUNT RETURNS

(Based on most total yards)

	No.	Yds.	Avg.
1960— Abe Woodson, San Francisco	13	174	13.4
1961— Willie Wood, Green Bay	14	225	16.1
1962— Pat Studstill, Detroit	29	457	15.8
1963— Dick James, Washington	16	214	13.4
1964— Tommy Watkins, Detroit	16	238	14.9
1965— Leroy Kelly, Cleveland	17	265	15.6
1966— Johnny Roland, St. Louis	20	221	11.1
1967— Ben Davis, Cleveland	18	229	12.7
1968— Bob Hayes, Dallas	15	312	20.8
1969— Alvin Haymond, L.A. Rams	33	435	13.2
1970— Bruce Taylor, San Francisco	43	516	12.0
1971— Les Duncan, Washington	22	233	10.6
1972— Ken Ellis, Green Bay	14	215	15.4
1973— Bruce Taylor, San Francisco	15	207	13.8
1974— Dick Jauron, Detroit	17	286	16.8
1975— Terry Metcalf, St. Louis	23	285	12.4
1976— Eddie Brown, Washington	48	646	13.5
1977— Larry Marshall, Philadelphia	46	489	10.6
1978— Jackie Wallace, L.A. Rams	52	618	11.9
1979— John Sciarra, Philadelphia	16	182	11.4
1980— Kenny Johnson, Atlanta	23	281	12.2
1981— LeRoy Irvin, L.A. Rams	46	615	13.4
1982— Billy Johnson, Atlanta	24	273	11.4
1983— Henry Ellard, L.A. Rams	16	217	13.6
1984— Henry Ellard, L.A. Rams	30	403	13.4
1985— Henry Ellard, L.A. Rams	37	501	13.5
1986— Vai Sikahema, St. Louis	43	522	12.1
1987— Mel Gray, New Orleans	24	352	14.7
1988— John Taylor, San Francisco	44	556	12.6
1989— Walter Stanley, Detroit	36	496	13.8
1990— Johnny Bailey, Chicago	36	399	11.1
1991— Mel Gray, Detroit	25	385	15.4
1992— Johnny Bailey, Phoenix	20	263	13.2
1993— Tyrone Hughes, New Orleans	37	503	13.6
1994— Brian Mitchell, Washington	32	452	14.1
1995— Eric Guliford, Carolina	43	475	11.0
1996— Desmond Howard, Green Bay	58	875	15.1
1997— Karl Williams, Tampa Bay	46	597	13.0

KICKOFF RETURNS

(Based on most total yards)

	No.	Yds.	Avg.
1960— Tom Moore, Green Bay	12	397	33.1
1961— Dick Bass, L.A. Rams	23	698	30.3
1962— Abe Woodson, San Francisco	37	1157	31.3
1963— Abe Woodson, San Francisco	29	935	32.3
1964— Clarence Childs, N.Y. Giants	34	987	29.0
1965— Tommy Watkins, Detroit	17	584	34.4
1966— Gale Sayers, Chicago	23	718	31.2
1967— Travis Williams, Green Bay	18	739	41.1
1968— Preston Pearson, Baltimore	15	527	35.1
1969— Bobby Williams, Detroit	17	563	33.1
1970— Cecil Turner, Chicago	23	752	32.7
1971— Travis Williams, L.A. Rams	25	743	29.7
1972— Ron Smith, Chicago	30	924	30.8
1973— Carl Garrett, Chicago	16	486	30.4
1974— Terry Metcalf, St. Louis	20	623	31.2
1975— Walter Payton, Chicago	14	444	31.7
1976— Cullen Bryant, L.A. Rams	16	459	28.7
1977— Wilbert Montgomery, Phila.	23	619	26.9
1978— Steve Odom, Green Bay	25	677	27.1
1979— Jimmy Edwards, Minnesota	44	1103	25.1
1980— Rich Mauti, New Orleans	31	798	27.6
1981— Mike Nelms, Washington	37	1099	29.7
1982— Alvin Hall, Detroit	16	426	26.6
1983— Darrin Nelson, Minnesota	18	445	24.7
1984— Barry Redden, L.A. Rams	23	530	23.0
1985— Ron Brown, L.A. Rams	28	918	32.8
1986— Dennis Gentry, Chicago	20	576	28.8
1987— Sylvester Stamps, Atlanta	24	660	27.5

	No.	Yds.	Avg.
1988—Donnie Elder, Tampa Bay	34	772	22.7
1989—Mel Gray, Detroit	24	640	26.7
1990—Dave Meggett, N.Y. Giants	21	492	23.4
1991—Mel Gray, Detroit	36	929	25.8
1992—Deion Sanders, Atlanta	40	1067	26.7
1993—Tony Smith, Atlanta	38	948	24.9
1994—Tyrone Hughes, New Orleans	63	1556	24.7
1995—Tyrone Hughes, New Orleans	66	1617	24.5
1996—Tyrone Hughes, New Orleans	70	1791	25.6
1997—Glyn Milburn, Detroit	55	1315	23.9

SACKS

	No.
1982— Doug Martin, Minnesota	11.5
1983— Fred Dean, San Francisco	17.5
1984— Richard Dent, Chicago	17.5

	No.
1985— Richard Dent, Chicago	17.0
1986— Lawrence Taylor, N.Y. Giants	20.5
1987— Reggie White, Philadelphia	21.0
1988— Reggie White, Philadelphia	18.0
1989— Chris Doleman, Minnesota	21.0
1990— Charles Haley, San Francisco	16.0
1991— Pat Swilling, New Orleans	17.0
1992— Clyde Simmons, Philadelphia	19.0
1993— Renaldo Turnbull, New Orleans	13.0
Reggie White, Green Bay	13.0
1994— Ken Harvey, Washington	13.5
John Randle, Minnesota	13.5
1995— William Fuller, Philadelphia	13.0
Wayne Martin, New Orleans	13.0
1996— Kevin Greene, Carolina	14.5
1997— John Randle, Minnesota	15.5

COACHING RECORDS

COACHES WITH 100 CAREER VICTORIES

(Ranked according to career wins)

		REGULAR SEASON				POSTSEASON			CAREER			
	Yrs.	Won	Lost	Tied	Pct.	Won	Lost	Pct.	Won	Lost	Tied	Pct.
Don Shula	33	328	156	6	.676	19	17	.528	347	173	6	.665
George Halas	40	318	148	31	.671	6	3	.667	324	151	31	.671
Tom Landry	29	250	162	6	.605	20	16	.556	270	178	6	.601
Curly Lambeau	33	226	132	22	.624	3	2	.600	229	134	22	.623
Chuck Noll	23	193	148	1	.566	16	8	.667	209	156	1	.572
Chuck Knox	22	186	147	1	.558	7	11	.389	193	158	1	.550
Paul Brown	21	166	100	6	.621	4	9	.308	170	109	6	.607
Bud Grant	18	158	96	5	.620	10	12	.455	168	108	5	.607
*Dan Reeves	17	148	115	1	.563	8	7	.533	156	122	1	.561
Steve Owen	23	153	100	17	.598	2	8	.200	155	108	17	.584
*Marv Levy	17	143	112	0	.561	11	8	.579	154	120	0	.562
*Marty Schottenheimer	14	138	76	1	.644	5	11	.313	143	87	1	.621
Joe Gibbs	12	124	60	0	.674	16	5	.762	140	65	0	.683
Hank Stram	17	131	97	10	.571	5	3	.625	136	100	10	.573
Weeb Ewbank	20	130	129	7	.502	4	1	.800	134	130	7	.507
*Bill Parcells	13	118	88	1	.572	10	5	.667	128	93	0	.579
Sid Gillman	18	122	99	7	.550	1	5	.167	123	104	7	.541
George Allen	12	116	47	5	.705	4	7	.364	120	54	5	.684
*Mike Ditka	12	112	72	0	.609	6	6	.500	118	78	0	.602
Don Coryell	14	111	83	1	.572	3	6	.333	114	89	1	.561
John Madden	10	103	32	7	.750	9	7	.563	112	39	7	.731
George Seifert	8	98	30	0	.766	10	5	.667	108	35	0	.755
Buddy Parker	15	104	75	9	.577	3	2	.600	107	77	9	.578
Vince Lombardi	10	96	34	6	.728	9	1	.900	105	35	6	.740
Bill Walsh	10	92	59	1	.609	10	4	.714	102	63	1	.617

*Active NFL coaches in 1997.

ACTIVE COACHES CAREER RECORDS

(Ranked according to career NFL percentages)

		REGULAR SEASON				POSTSEASON			CAREER			
	Yrs.	Won	Lost	Tied	Pct.	Won	Lost	Pct.	Won	Lost	Tied	Pct.
Steve Mariucci	1	13	3	0	.813	1	1	.500	14	4	0	.778
Mike Holmgren	6	64	32	0	.667	9	4	.692	73	36	0	.670
Bill Cowher	6	64	32	0	.667	5	6	.455	69	38	0	.645
Marty Schottenheimer	14	138	76	1	.644	5	11	.313	143	87	1	.621
Jim Fassel	1	10	5	1	.667	0	1	.000	10	6	1	.618
Mike Shanahan	5	41	27	0	.603	4	1	.800	45	28	0	.616
Mike Ditka	12	112	72	0	.609	6	6	.500	118	78	0	.602
Bill Parcells	13	118	88	1	.572	10	5	.667	128	93	0	.579
Bobby Ross	6	56	40	0	.583	3	4	.429	59	44	0	.573
Jimmy Johnson	7	61	51	0	.545	7	2	.778	68	53	0	.562
Dan Reeves	17	148	115	1	.563	8	7	.533	156	122	1	.561
Dennis Green	6	56	40	0	.583	1	5	.167	57	45	0	.559
Jim Mora	11	93	74	0	.557	0	4	.000	93	78	0	.544
USFL Totals	3	41	12	1	.769	7	1	.875	48	13	1	.782
Dom Capers	3	26	22	0	.542	1	1	.500	27	23	0	.540
Ray Rhodes	3	26	21	1	.552	2	2	.333	27	23	1	.539
Pete Carroll	2	16	16	0	.500	1	1	.500	17	17	0	.500
Tom Coughlin	3	24	24	0	.500	2	2	.500	26	26	0	.500
Tony Dungy	2	16	16	0	.500	1	1	.500	17	17	0	.500
Dick Vermeil	8	59	58	0	.504	3	4	.429	62	62	0	.500
Dennis Erickson	3	23	25	0	.479	0	0	.000	23	25	0	.479
Ted Marchibroda	11	81	88	1	.479	2	4	.333	83	92	1	.474
Wade Phillips	3	17	19	0	.472	0	1	.000	17	20	0	.459
Dave Wannstedt	5	36	44	0	.450	1	1	.500	37	45	0	.451
Bruce Coslet	6	40	49	0	.449	0	1	.000	40	50	0	.444
Jeff Fisher	4	24	32	0	.429	0	0	.000	24	32	0	.429
Norv Turner	4	26	37	1	.414	0	0	.000	26	37	1	.414
Vince Tobin	2	11	21	0	.344	0	0	.000	11	21	0	.344
Kevin Gilbride	1	4	12	0	.250	0	0	.000	4	12	0	.333
Chan Gailey	0	0	0	0	.000	0	0	.000	0	0	0	.000
Jon Gruden	0	0	0	0	.000	0	0	.000	0	0	0	.000

HALL OF FAME

ROSTER OF MEMBERS
FIVE NEW INDUCTEES IN 1998

Paul Krause, Tommy McDonald, Anthony Munoz, Mike Singletary and Dwight Stephenson were inducted into Pro Football's Hall of Fame in 1998, expanding the list of former stars honored at Canton, Ohio, to 194.

Name	Elec. year	College	Pos.	NFL teams
Adderley, Herb	1980	Michigan State	CB	Green Bay Packers, 1961-69; Dallas Cowboys, 1970-72
Alworth, Lance†	1978	Arkansas	WR	San Diego Chargers, 1962-70; Dallas Cowboys, 1971-72.
Atkins, Doug	1982	Tennessee	DE	Cleveland Browns, 1953-54; Chicago Bears, 1955-66; New Orleans Saints, 1967-69
Badgro, Morris (Red)	1981	Southern California	E	New York Yankees, 1926; New York Giants, 1930-35
Barney, Lem	1992	Jackson State	CB	Detroit Lions, 1967-77
Battles, Cliff	1968	W. Virginia Wesleyan	HB/QB	Boston Braves, Boston Redskins, Washington Redskins, 1932-37; coach, Brooklyn Dodgers, 1946-47
Baugh, Sammy	1963	Texas Christian	QB	Washington Redskins, 1937-52; coach, New York Titans, 1960-61; Houston Oilers, 1964
Bednarik, Chuck	1967	Pennsylvania	C/LB	Philadelphia Eagles, 1949-62
Bell, Bert	1963	Pennsylvania	*	NFL Commissioner, 1946-59
Bell, Bobby	1983	Minnesota	LB	Kansas City Chiefs, 1963-74
Berry, Raymond†	1973	Southern Methodist	E	Baltimore Colts, 1955-67; coach, New England Patriots, 1984-89
Bidwill, Charles W.	1967	Loyola	*	Owner, Chicago Cardinals, 1933-47
Biletnikoff, Fred	1988	Florida State	WR	Oakland Raiders, 1965-78
Blanda, George†	1981	Kentucky	QB/PK	Chicago Bears, 1949-58; Baltimore Colts, 1950; Houston Oilers, 1960-66; Oakland Raiders, 1967-73
Blount, Mel†	1989	Southern	CB	Pittsburgh Steelers, 1970-83
Bradshaw, Terry†	1989	Louisiana Tech	QB	Pittsburgh Steelers, 1970-83
Brown, Jim†	1971	Syracuse	FB	Cleveland Browns, 1957-65
Brown, Paul	1967	Miami of Ohio	*	Coach, Cleveland Browns, 1946-62; Cincinnati Bengals, 1968-75
Brown, Roosevelt	1975	Morgan State	T	New York Giants, 1953-66
Brown, Willie†	1984	Grambling	DB	Denver Broncos, 1963-66; Oakland Raiders, 1967-78
Buchanan, Buck	1990	Grambling	DT	Kansas City Chiefs, 1963-75
Butkus, Dick†	1979	Illinois	LB	Chicago Bears, 1965-73
Campbell, Earl†	1991	Texas	RB	Houston Oilers, 1978-84; New Orleans Saints, 1984-85
Canadeo, Tony	1974	Gonzaga	HB	Green Bay Packers, 1941-44, 46-52
Carr, Joe	1963			NFL President, 1921-39
Chamberlin, Guy	1965	Nebraska	E/WB*	Player/coach, Canton Bulldogs, Cleveland, Frankford Yellowjackets, Chicago Bears, Chicago Cardinals, 1919-28
Christiansen, Jack	1970	Colorado A&M	DB	Detroit Lions, 1951-58; coach, San Francisco 49ers, 1963-67
Clark, Dutch	1963	Colorado College	QB	Portsmouth Spartans, Detroit Lions, 1931-38
Connor, George	1975	Notre Dame	T/LB	Chicago Bears, 1948-55
Conzelman, Jimmy	1964	Washington (Mo.)	HB*	Coach/executive, Decatur, Rock Island, Milwaukee, Detroit, Providence, Chicago Cardinals, 1920-48
Creekmur, Lou	1996	William & Mary	T/G	Detroit Lions, 1950-59
Csonka, Larry	1987	Syracuse	RB	Miami Dolphins, 1968-74, 79; New York Giants, 1976-78
Davis, Al	1992	Syracuse	*	Coach/general manager/president, Oakland-Los Angeles Raiders, 1963-present
Davis, Willie	1981	Grambling	DE	Cleveland Browns, 1958-59; Green Bay Packers, 1960-69
Dawson, Len	1987	Purdue	QB	Pittsburgh Steelers, 1957-58; Cleveland Browns, 1960-61; Dallas Texans, 1962; Kansas City Chiefs, 1963-75
Dierdorf, Dan	1996	Michigan	T/C	St. Louis Cardinals, 1971-83
Ditka, Mike	1988	Pittsburgh	TE	Chicago Bears, 1961-66; Philadelphia Eagles, 1967-68; Dallas Cowboys, 1969-72; coach, Chicago Bears, 1982-92; New Orleans Saints, 1997-present
Donovan, Art	1968	Boston College	DT	Baltimore Colts, New York Yanks, Dallas Texans, 1950-61
Dorsett, Tony	1994	Pittsburgh	RB	Dallas Cowboys, 1977-87; Denver Broncos, 1988
Driscoll, Paddy	1965	Northwestern	TB/HB/QB	Player/coach, Chicago Cardinals, Chicago Bears, 1919-31, 41-68
Dudley, Bill	1966	Virginia	HB	Pittsburgh Steelers, Detroit Lions, Washington Redskins, 1942-53
Edwards, Turk	1969	Washington State	T	Boston Braves, Boston Redskins, Washington Redskins, 1932-40
Ewbank, Weeb	1978	Miami of Ohio	*	Coach, Baltimore Colts, 1954-62; New York Jets, 1963-73
Fears, Tom	1970	Santa Clara	E	Los Angeles Rams, 1948-56; coach, New Orleans Saints, 1967-70
Finks, Jim	1995	Tulsa	QB*	Pittsburgh Steelers, 1949-55; administrator, Minnesota Vikings, 1964-73; Chicago Bears, 1974-86; New Orleans Saints, 1987-93
Flaherty, Ray	1976	Gonzaga	E*	Player/coach, Los Angeles Wildcats, New York Yankees, AFL; New York Giants, Boston Redskins, Washington Redskins, New York Yankees, AAFC; Chicago Hornets, 1926-49

Name	Elec. year	College	Pos.	NFL teams
Ford, Len	1976	Michigan	E	Los Angeles Dons, Cleveland Browns, 1948-58
Fortmann, Danny	1965	Colgate	G	Chicago Bears, 1936-43
Fouts, Dan†	1993	Oregon	QB	San Diego Chargers, 1973-87
Gatski, Frank	1985	Marshall	C	Cleveland Browns, 1946-56; Detroit Lions, 1957
George, Bill	1974	Wake Forest	LB	Chicago Bears, Los Angeles Rams, 1952-66
Gibbs, Joe	1996	San Diego State	*	Washington Redskins, 1981-92
Gifford, Frank	1977	Southern California	HB/E	New York Giants, 1952-60, 62-64
Gillman, Sid	1983	Ohio State	E*	Cleveland Rams, 1936; coach, Los Angeles Rams, 1955-59; Los Angeles Chargers, 1960; San Diego Chargers, 1961-69, 71; Houston Oilers, 1973-74
Graham, Otto	1965	Northwestern	QB	Cleveland Browns, 1946-55; coach, Washington Redskins, 1966-68
Grange, Red	1963	Illinois	HB	Chicago Bears, 1925, 29-34; New York Yankees, 1926-27
Grant, Bud	1994	Minnesota	WR*	Philadelphia Eagles, 1951-52; coach, Minnesota Vikings, 1967-83, 1985
Greene, Joe†	1987	North Texas State	DT	Pittsburgh Steelers, 1969-81
Gregg, Forrest†	1977	Southern Methodist	T	Green Bay Packers, Dallas Cowboys, 1956, 58-71; coach, Cleveland Browns, 1975-77; Cincinnati Bengals, 1980-83; Green Bay Packers, 1984-87
Griese, Bob	1990	Purdue	QB	Miami Dolphins, 1967-80
Groza, Lou	1974	Ohio State	T/PK	Cleveland Browns, 1946-59, 61-67
Guyon, Joe	1966	Carlisle, Georgia Tech	HB	Canton Bulldogs, Cleveland Indians, Oorang Indians, Rock Island Independents, Kansas City Cowboys, New York Giants, 1918-27
Halas, George	1963	Illinois	E*	Player/coach/ founder, Chicago Bears, 1920-83
Ham, Jack†	1988	Penn State	LB	Pittsburgh Steelers, 1971-82
Hannah, John†	1991	Alabama	G	New England Patriots, 1973-85
Harris, Franco†	1990	Penn State	RB	Pittsburgh Steelers, 1972-83; Seattle Seahawks, 1984
Haynes, Mike	1997	Arizona State	CB	New England Patriots, 1976-82; Los Angeles Raiders, 1983-89
Healey, Ed	1964	Dartmouth	T	Rock Island, Chicago Bears, 1920-27
Hein, Mel	1963	Washington State	C	New York Giants, 1931-45
Hendricks, Ted	1990	Miami, Fla.	LB	Baltimore Colts, 1969-73; Green Bay Packers, 1974; Oakland/Los Angeles Raiders, 1975-83
Henry, Wilbur	1963	Wash'ton & Jefferson	T	Canton Bulldogs, Akron Indians, New York Giants, Pottsville Maroons, Pittsburgh Steelers, 1920-30
Herber, Arnie	1966	Regis	HB	Green Bay Packers, New York Giants, 1930-45
Hewitt, Bill	1971	Michigan	E	Chicago Bears, 1932-36; Philadelphia Eagles, 1937-39; Philadelphia/Pittsburgh, 1943
Hinkle, Clarke	1964	Bucknell	FB	Green Bay Packers, 1932-41
Hirsch, Elroy (Crazylegs)	1968	Wisconsin	E/HB	Chicago Rockets, Los Angeles Rams, 1946-57
Hornung, Paul	1986	Notre Dame	RB	Green Bay Packers, 1957-62, 64-66
Houston, Ken†	1986	Prairie View	DB	Houston Oilers, 1967-72; Washington Redskins, 1973-80
Hubbard, Cal	1963	Centenary, Geneva	T/E	New York Giants, Green Bay Packers, Pittsburgh Steelers, 1927-36
Huff, Sam	1982	West Virginia	LB	New York Giants, 1956-63; Washington Redskins, 1964-67, 69
Hunt, Lamar	1972	Southern Methodist	*	Founder, American Football League, 1959; president, Dallas Texans, 1960-62; Kansas City Chiefs, 1963-present
Hutson, Don	1963	Alabama	E	Green Bay Packers, 1935-45
Johnson, Jimmy	1994	UCLA	DB	San Francisco 49ers, 1961-76
Johnson, John Henry	1987	Arizona State	FB	San Francisco 49ers, 1954-56; Detroit Lions, 1957-59; Pittsburgh Steelers, 1960-65; Houston Oilers, 1966
Joiner, Charlie	1966	Grambling	WR	Houston Oilers, 1969-72; Cincinnati Bengals, 1972-75; San Diego Chargers, 1976-86
Jones, Deacon†	1980	South Carolina State	DE	Los Angeles Rams, 1961-71; San Diego Chargers, 1972-73; Washington Redskins, 1974
Jones, Stan	1991	Maryland	G/DT	Chicago Bears, 1954-65; Washington Redskins, 1966
Jordan, Henry	1995	Virginia	DT	Cleveland Browns, 1957-58; Green Bay Packers, 1959-69
Jurgensen, Sonny	1983	Duke	QB	Philadelphia Eagles, 1957-63; Washington Redskins, 1964-74
Kelly, Leroy	1994	Morgan State	RB	Cleveland Browns, 1964-73
Kiesling, Walter	1966	St. Thomas	G/T*	Player/coach, Duluth Eskimos, Pottsville Maroons, Boston Braves, Chicago Cardinals, Chicago Bears, Green Bay Packers, Pittsburgh Steelers, 1926-56
Kinard, Frank (Bruiser)	1971	Mississippi	T	Brooklyn Dodgers, 1938-45; New York Yankees, 1946-47
Krause, Paul	1998	Iowa	S	Washington Redskins, 1964-67; Minnesota Vikings, 1968-79
Lambeau, Curly	1963	Notre Dame	TB/FB/E*	Founder/player/coach, Green Bay Packers, 1919-49
Lambert, Jack†	1990	Kent State	LB	Pittsburgh Steelers, 1974-84
Landry, Tom†	1990	Texas	*	Coach, Dallas Cowboys, 1960-88
Lane, Dick (Night Train)	1974	Scottsbluff J.C.	DB	Los Angeles Rams, Chicago Cardinals, Detroit Lions, 1952-65
Langer, Jim†	1987	South Dakota State	C	Miami Dolphins, 1970-79; Minnesota Vikings, 1980-81
Lanier, Willie †	1986	Morgan State	LB	Kansas City Chiefs, 1967-77
Largent, Steve†	1995	Tulsa	WR	Seattle Seahawks, 1976-89
Lary, Yale	1979	Texas A&M	DB	Detroit Lions, 1952-53, 56-64

Name	Elec. year	College	Pos.	NFL teams
Lavelli, Dante	1975	Ohio State	E	Cleveland Browns, 1946-56
Layne, Bobby	1967	Texas	QB	Chicago Bears, New York Bulldogs, Detroit Lions, Pittsburgh Steelers, 1948-62
Leemans, Tuffy	1978	George Washington	FB	New York Giants, 1936-43
Lilly, Bob†	1980	Texas Christian	DT	Dallas Cowboys, 1961-74
Little, Larry	1993	Bethune Cookman	G	San Diego Chargers, 1967-68; Miami Dolphins, 1969-80
Lombardi, Vince	1971	Fordham	*	Coach, Green Bay Packers, 1959-67; Washington Redskins, 1969
Luckman, Sid	1965	Columbia	QB	Chicago Bears, 1939-50
Lyman, Roy (Link)	1964		T	Canton Bulldogs, Cleveland, Chicago Bears, 1922-34
Mackey, John	1992	Syracuse	TE	Baltimore Colts, 1963-71; San Diego Chargers, 1972
Mara, Tim	1963		*	Founder, New York Giants, 1925-65
Mara, Wellington	1997	Fordham	*	President, New York Giants, 1965-present
Marchetti, Gino†	1972	San Francisco	DE	Dallas Texans, 1952; Baltimore Colts, 1953-66
Marshall, George Preston	1963		*	Founder, Washington Redskins, 1932-65
Matson, Ollie†	1972	San Francisco	HB	Chicago Cardinals, 1952, 54-58; Los Angeles Rams, 1959-62; Detroit Lions, 1963; Philadelphia Eagles, 1964-66
Maynard, Don	1987	Texas Western College	WR	New York Giants, 1958; New York Jets, 1960-72; St. Louis Cardinals, 1973
McAfee, George	1966	Duke	HB	Chicago Bears, 1940-41, 45-50
McCormack, Mike	1984	Kansas	T	New York Yanks, 1951; Cleveland Browns, 1954-62
McDonald, Tommy	1998	Oklahoma	WR	Philadelphia Eagles,1957-63; Dallas Cowboys, 1964; Los Angeles Rams, 1965-66; Atlanta Falcons, 1967; Cleveland Browns,1968
McElhenny, Hugh†	1970	Washington	HB	San Francisco 49ers, Minnesota Vikings, New York Giants, Detroit Lions, 1952-64
McNally, Johnny Blood	1963	St. John's	HB	Milwaukee Badgers, Duluth Eskimos, Pottsville Maroons, Green Bay Packers, Pittsburgh Steelers, 1925-39
Michalske, August (Mike)	1964	Penn State	G	New York Yankees, Green Bay Packers, 1927-37
Millner, Wayne	1968	Notre Dame	E	Boston Redskins, Washington Redskins, 1936-41, 45
Mitchell, Bobby	1983	Illinois	RB/FL/WR	Cleveland Browns, 1958-61; Washington Redskins, 1962-68
Mix, Ron	1979	Southern California	T	Los Angeles Chargers, 1960; San Diego Chargers, 1961-69; Oakland Raiders, 1971
Moore, Lenny	1975	Penn State	HB	Baltimore Colts, 1956-67
Motley, Marion	1968	Nevada	FB/LB	Cleveland Browns, Pittsburgh Steelers, 1946-55
Munoz, Anthony†	1998	Southern California	OT	Cincinnati Bengals, 1980-92
Musso, George	1982	Milliken	G/DT	Chicago Bears, 1933-44
Nagurski, Bronko	1963	Minnesota	FB/T	Chicago Bears, 1930-37, 43
Namath, Joe	1985	Alabama	QB	New York Jets, 1965-76; Los Angeles Rams, 1977
Neale, Earle (Greasy)	1969	W. Virginia Wesleyan	*	Coach, Philadelphia Eagles, 1941-50
Nevers, Ernie	1963	Stanford	FB	Duluth Eskimos, Chicago Cardinals, 1926-37
Nitschke, Ray†	1978	Illinois	LB	Green Bay Packers, 1958-72
Noll, Chuck†	1993	Dayton	*	Coach, Pittsburgh Steelers, 1969-91
Nomellini, Leo†	1969	Minnesota	DT	San Francisco 49ers, 1953-63
Olsen, Merlin†	1982	Utah State	DT	Los Angeles Rams, 1962-76
Otto, Jim†	1980	Miami, Fla.	C	Oaklland Raiders, 1960-74
Owen, Steve	1966	Phillips	T/G	Player/coach, Kansas City Cowboys, New York Giants, 1924-53
Page, Alan	1988	Notre Dame	DT	Minnesota Vikings, 1967-78; Chicago Bears, 1978-81
Parker, Clarence (Ace)	1972	Duke	HB	Brooklyn Dodgers, 1937-41; Boston Yanks; 1945; New York Yankees, 1946
Parker, Jim†	1973	Ohio State	G	Baltimore Colts, 1957-67
Payton, Walter†	1993	Jackson State	RB	Chicago Bears, 1975-87
Perry, Joe†	1969	Compton J.C.	FB	San Francisco 49ers, Baltimore Colts, 1948-63
Pihos, Pete	1970	Indiana	E	Philadelphia Eagles, 1947-55
Ray, Hugh (Shorty)	1966	Illinois	*	NFL technical adviser and supervisor of officials, 1938-56
Reeves, Daniel F.	1967	Georgetown	*	Founder, Los Angeles Rams, 1941-71
Renfro, Mel	1996	Oregon	DB	Dallas Cowboys, 1964-77
Riggins, John	1992	Kansas	FB	New York Jets, 1971-75; Washington Redskins, 1976-85
Ringo, Jim	1981	Syracuse	C	Green Bay Packers, 1953-63; Philadelphia Eagles, 1964-67
Robustelli, Andy	1971	Arnold	DE	Los Angeles Rams, 1951-55; New York Giants, 1956-64
Rooney, Arthur J.	1964	Georgetown	*	Founder, Pittsburgh Steelers, 1933-82
Rozelle, Pete	1985	San Francisco	*	NFL Commissioner, 1960-89
St. Clair, Bob	1990	Tulsa	T	San Francisco 49ers, 1953-63
Sayers, Gale†	1977	Kansas	RB	Chicago Bears, 1965-71
Schmidt, Joe	1973	Pittsburgh	LB	Detroit Lions, 1953-65; coach, Detroit Lions, 1967-72
Schramm, Tex	1991	Texas	*	President/general manager, Dallas Cowboys, 1960-88
Selmon, Lee Roy	1995	Oklahoma	DE	Tampa Bay Buccaneers, 1976-84
Shell, Art	1989	Md.-Eastern Shore	T	Oakland-Los Angeles Raiders, 1968-82; coach, Los Angeles Raiders, 1989-94
Shula, Don†	1997	John Carroll	DB	Cleveland Browns, 1951-52; Baltimore Colts, 1953-56; Washington Redskins, 1957; coach, Baltimore Colts, 1963-69, Miami Dolphins, 1970-95

Name	Elec. year	College	Pos.	NFL teams
Simpson, O.J.†	1985	Southern California	RB	Buffalo Bills, 1969-77; San Francisco 49ers, 1978
Singletary, Mike†	1998	Baylor	LB	Chicago Bears, 1981-92
Smith, Jackie	1994	N'western Louisiana	TE	St. Louis Cardinals, 1963-77; Dallas Cowboys, 1978
Starr, Bart†	1977	Alabama	QB	Green Bay Packers, 1956-71; coach, Green Bay Packers, 1975-83
Staubach, Roger†	1985	Navy	QB	Dallas Cowboys, 1969-79
Stautner, Ernie†	1969	West Virginia	DT	Pittsburgh Steelers, 1950-63
Stenerud, Jan†	1991	Montana State	PK	Kansas City Chiefs, 1967-79; Green Bay Packers, 1980-83; Minnesota Vikings, 1984-85
Stephenson, Dwight	1998	Alabama	C	Miami Dolphins, 1980-87
Strong, Ken	1967	New York U.	HB/PK	Staten Island Stapletons, New York Yankees, New York Giants, 1929-39, 44-47
Stydahar, Joe	1967	West Virginia	T	Chicago Bears, 1936-42, 45-46
Tarkenton, Fran	1986	Georgia	QB	Minnesota Vikings, 1961-66, 72-78; New York Giants, 1967-71
Taylor, Charley	1984	Arizona State	WR	Washington Redskins, 1964-75, 77
Taylor, Jim	1976	Louisiana State	FB	Green Bay Packers, 1958-66; New Orleans Saints, 1967
Thorpe, Jim	1963	Carlisle	HB	Canton Bulldogs, Oorang Indians, Cleveland Indians, Toledo Maroons, Rock Island Independents, New York Giants, 1915-26, 29
Tittle, Y.A.	1971	Louisiana State	QB	Baltimore Colts, 1948-50; San Francisco 49ers, 1951-60; New York Giants, 1961-64
Trafton, George	1964	Notre Dame	C	Chicago Bears, 1920-32
Trippi, Charlie	1968	Georgia	HB	Chicago Cardinals, 1947-55
Tunnell, Emlen	1967	Iowa	DB	New York Giants, Green Bay Packers, 1948-61
Turner, Clyde (Bulldog)	1966	Hardin-Simmons	C/LB	Chicago Bears, 1940-52; coach, New York Titans, 1962
Unitas, John†	1979	Louisville	QB	Baltimore Colts, 1956-72; San Diego Chargers, 1973
Upshaw, Gene†	1987	Texas A&I	G	Oakland Raiders, 1967-81
Van Brocklin, Norm	1971	Oregon	QB	Los Angeles Rams, 1949-57; Philadelphia Eagles, 1958-60; coach, Minnesota Vikings, 1961-66; Atlanta Falcons, 1968-74
Van Buren, Steve	1965	Louisiana State	HB	Philadelphia Eagles, 1944-51
Walker, Doak	1986	Southern Methodist	RB	Detroit Lions, 1950-55
Walsh, Bill	1993	San Jose State	*	Coach, San Francisco 49ers, 1979-88
Warfield, Paul†	1983	Ohio State	WR	Cleveland Browns, 1964-69, 76-77; Miami Dolphins, 1970-74
Waterfield, Bob	1965	UCLA	QB	Cleveland Rams, Los Angeles Rams, 1945-52; coach, Los Angeles Rams, 1960-62
Webster, Mike	1997	Wisconsin	C-G	Pittsburgh Steelers, 1974-88; Kansas City Chiefs, 1989-90
Weinmeister, Arnie	1984	Washington	T	New York Yankees, 1948-49; New York Giants, 1950-53
White, Randy	1994	Maryland	DT	Dallas Cowboys, 1975-88
Willis, Bill	1977	Ohio State	G	Cleveland Browns, 1946-53
Wilson, Larry†	1978	Utah	DB	St. Louis Cardinals, 1960-72
Winslow, Kellen	1995	Missouri	TE	San Diego Chargers, 1979-87
Wojciechowicz, Alex	1968	Fordham	C/LB	Detroit Lions, Philadelphia Eagles, 1938-50
Wood, Willie	1989	Southern California	S	Green Bay Packers, 1960-71

*Hall of Fame member was selected for contributions other than as a player.
†Elected his first year of eligibility.
Abbreviations of positions: C—Center, CB—Cornerback, DB—Defensive back, DE—Defensive end, DT—Defensive tackle, E—End, FB—Fullback, FL—Flanker, G—Guard, HB—Halfback, LB—Linebacker, PK—Placekicker, QB—Quarterback, RB—Running back, S—Safety, T—Tackle, TB—Tailback, TE—Tight end.

THE SPORTING NEWS AWARDS

PLAYER OF THE YEAR

1954—Lou Groza, OT/K, Cleveland
1955—Otto Graham, QB, Cleveland
1956—Frank Gifford, HB, N.Y. Giants
1957—Jim Brown, RB, Cleveland
1958—Jim Brown, RB, Cleveland
1959—Johnny Unitas, QB, Baltimore
1960—Norm Van Brocklin, QB, Philadelphia
1961—Paul Hornung, HB, Green Bay
1962—Y.A. Tittle, QB, N.Y. Giants
1963—Y.A. Tittle, QB, N.Y. Giants
1964—Johnny Unitas, QB, Baltimore
1965—Jim Brown, RB, Cleveland
1966—Bart Starr, QB, Green Bay
1967—Johnny Unitas, QB, Baltimore
1968—Earl Morrall, QB, Baltimore
1969—Roman Gabriel, QB, L.A. Rams
1970—NFC: John Brodie, QB, San Francisco
    AFC: George Blanda, QB/PK, Oakland
1971—NFC: Roger Staubach, QB, Dallas
    AFC: Bob Griese, QB, Miami
1972—NFC: Larry Brown, RB, Washington
    AFC: Earl Morrall, QB, Miami
1973—NFC: John Hadl, QB, L.A. Rams
    AFC: O.J. Simpson, RB, Buffalo
1974—NFC: Chuck Foreman, RB, Minnesota
    AFC: Ken Stabler, QB, Oakland
1975—NFC: Fran Tarkenton, QB, Minnesota
    AFC: O.J. Simpson, RB, Buffalo
1976—NFC: Walter Payton, RB, Chicago
    AFC: Ken Stabler, QB, Oakland

1977—NFC: Walter Payton, RB, Chicago
    AFC: Craig Morton, QB, Denver
1978—NFC: Archie Manning, QB, New Orleans
    AFC: Earl Campbell, RB, Houston
1979—NFC: Ottis Anderson, RB, St. Louis
    AFC: Dan Fouts, QB, San Diego
1980—Brian Sipe, QB, Cleveland
1981—Ken Anderson, QB, Cincinnati
1982—Mark Moseley, PK, Washington
1983—Eric Dickerson, RB, L.A. Rams
1984—Dan Marino, QB, Miami
1985—Marcus Allen, RB, L.A. Raiders
1986—Lawrence Taylor, LB, N.Y. Giants
1987—Jerry Rice, WR, San Francisco
1988—Boomer Esiason, QB, Cincinnati
1989—Joe Montana, QB, San Francisco
1990—Jerry Rice, WR, San Francisco
1991—Thurman Thomas, RB, Buffalo
1992—Steve Young, QB, San Francisco
1993—Emmitt Smith, RB, Dallas
1994—Steve Young, QB, San Francisco
1995—Brett Favre, QB, Green Bay
1996—Brett Favre, QB, Green Bay
1997—Barry Sanders, RB, Detroit
    NOTE: From 1970-79, a player was selected as Player of the Year for both the NFC and AFC. In 1980 The Sporting News reinstated the selection of one player as Player of the Year for the entire NFL.

ROOKIE OF THE YEAR

1955—Alan Ameche, FB, Baltimore
1956—J.C. Caroline, HB, Chicago
1957—Jim Brown, FB, Cleveland
1958—Bobby Mitchell, HB, Cleveland
1959—Nick Pietrosante, FB, Detroit
1960—Gail Cogdill, E, Detroit
1961—Mike Ditka, E, Chicago
1962—Ronnie Bull, HB, Chicago
1963—Paul Flatley, WR, Minnesota
1964—Charley Taylor, HB, Washington
1965—Gale Sayers, RB, Chicago
1966—Tommy Nobis, LB, Atlanta
1967—Mel Farr, RB, Detroit
1968—Earl McCullouch, WR, Detroit
1969—Calvin Hill, RB, Dallas
1970—NFC: Bruce Taylor, CB, San Francisco
    AFC: Dennis Shaw, QB, Buffalo
1971—NFC: John Brockington, RB, Green Bay
    AFC: Jim Plunkett, QB, New England
1972—NFC: Chester Marcol, PK, Green Bay
    AFC: Franco Harris, RB, Pittsburgh
1973—NFC: Chuck Foreman, RB, Minnesota
    AFC: Boobie Clark, RB, Cincinnati
1974—NFC: Wilbur Jackson, RB, San Francisco
    AFC: Don Woods, RB, San Diego
1975—NFC: Steve Bartkowski, QB, Atlanta
    AFC: Robert Brazile, LB, Houston
1976—NFC: Sammy White, WR, Minnesota
    AFC: Mike Haynes, CB, New England

1977—NFC: Tony Dorsett, RB, Dallas
    AFC: A.J. Duhe, DT, Miami
1978—NFC: Al Baker, DE, Detroit
    AFC: Earl Campbell, RB, Houston
1979—NFC: Ottis Anderson, RB, St. Louis
    AFC: Jerry Butler, WR, Buffalo
1980—Billy Sims, RB, Detroit
1981—George Rogers, RB, New Orleans
1982—Marcus Allen, RB, L.A. Raiders
1983—Dan Marino, QB, Miami
1984—Louis Lipps, WR, Pittsburgh
1985—Eddie Brown, WR, Cincinnati
1986—Rueben Mayes, RB, New Orleans
1987—Robert Awalt, TE, St. Louis
1988—Keith Jackson, TE, Philadelphia
1989—Barry Sanders, RB, Detroit
1990—Richmond Webb, T, Miami
1991—Mike Croel, LB, Denver
1992—Santana Dotson, DL, Tampa Bay
1993—Jerome Bettis, RB, L.A. Rams
1994—Marshall Faulk, RB, Indianapolis
1995—Curtis Martin, RB, New England
1996—Eddie George, RB, Houston
1997—Warrick Dunn, RB, Tampa Bay
    NOTE: In 1980, The Sporting News began selecting one rookie as Rookie of the Year for the entire NFL.

NFL COACH OF THE YEAR

1947—Jimmy Conzelman, Chi. Cardinals
1948—Earle (Greasy) Neale, Philadelphia
1949—Paul Brown, Cleveland (AAFC)
1950—Steve Owen, N.Y. Giants

1951—Paul Brown, Cleveland
1952—J. Hampton Pool, L.A. Rams
1953—Paul Brown, Cleveland
1954—None

1955—Joe Kuharich, Washington
1956—Jim Lee Howell, N.Y. Giants
1957—None
1958—None
1959—None
1960—None
1961—Vince Lombardi, Green Bay
1962—None
1963—George Halas, Chicago
1964—Don Shula, Baltimore
1965—George Halas, Chicago
1966—Tom Landry, Dallas
1967—George Allen, L.A. Rams
1968—Don Shula, Baltimore
1969—Bud Grant, Minnesota
1970—Don Shula, Miami
1971—George Allen, Washington
1972—Don Shula, Miami
1973—Chuck Knox, L.A. Rams
1974—Don Coryell, St. Louis
1975—Ted Marchibroda, Baltimore
1976—Chuck Fairbanks, New England

1977—Red Miller, Denver
1978—Jack Patera, Seattle
1979—Dick Vermeil, Philadelphia
1980—Chuck Knox, Buffalo
1981—Bill Walsh, San Francisco
1982—Joe Gibbs, Washington
1983—Joe Gibbs, Washington
1984—Chuck Knox, Seattle
1985—Mike Ditka, Chicago
1986—Bill Parcells, N.Y. Giants
1987—Jim Mora, New Orleans
1988—Marv Levy, Buffalo
1989—Lindy Infante, Green Bay
1990—George Seifert, San Francisco
1991—Joe Gibbs, Washington
1992—Bill Cowher, Pittsburgh
1993—Dan Reeves, N.Y. Giants
1994—George Seifert, San Francisco
1995—Ray Rhodes, Philadelphia
1996—Dom Capers, Carolina
1997—Jim Fassel, N.Y. Giants

NFL EXECUTIVE OF THE YEAR

1955—Dan Reeves, L.A. Rams
1956—George Halas, Chicago
1972—Dan Rooney, Pittsburgh
1973—Jim Finks, Minnesota
1974—Art Rooney, Pittsburgh
1975—Joe Thomas, Baltimore
1976—Al Davis, Oakland
1977—Tex Schramm, Dallas
1978—John Thompson, Seattle
1979—John Sanders, San Diego
1980—Eddie LeBaron, Atlanta
1981—Paul Brown, Cincinnati
1982—Bobby Beathard, Washington
1983—Bobby Beathard, Washington
1984—George Young, N.Y. Giants

1985—Mike McCaskey, Chicago
1986—George Young, N.Y. Giants
1987—Jim Finks, New Orleans
1988—Bill Polian, Buffalo
1989—John McVay, San Francisco
1990—George Young, N.Y. Giants
1991—Bill Polian, Buffalo
1992—Ron Wolf, Green Bay
1993—George Young, N.Y. Giants
1994—Carmen Policy, San Francisco
1995—Bill Polian, Carolina
1996—Bill Polian, Carolina
1997—George Young, N.Y. Giants
NOTE: The Executive of the Year Award was not given from 1957-71.

1997 NFL ALL-PRO TEAM

OFFENSE

WR—Herman Moore, Detroit
      Tim Brown, Oakland
TE— Shannon Sharpe, Denver
  T— Tony Boselli, Jacksonville
      Jonathan Ogden, Baltimore
  C— Dermontti Dawson, Pittsburgh
  G— Larry Allen, Dallas
      Randall McDaniel, Minnesota
QB— Brett Favre, Green Bay
RB— Terrell Davis, Denver
      Barry Sanders, Detroit

DEFENSE

DE— Michael Strahan, N.Y. Giants
      Bruce Smith, Buffalo
DT— Dana Stubblefield, San Francisco
      John Randle, Minnesota
LB— Jessie Armstead, N.Y. Giants
      Levon Kirkland, Pittsburgh
      John Mobley, Denver
CB— Aeneas Williams, Phoenix
      Deion Sanders, Dallas
  S— LeRoy Butler, Green Bay
      Carnell Lake, Pittsburgh

SPECIALISTS

PR— Darrien Gordon, Denver
KR— Michael Bates, Carolina
  K— Richie Cunningham, Dallas
  P— Matt Turk, Washington

TEAM BY TEAM

ARIZONA CARDINALS
YEAR-BY-YEAR RECORDS

	REGULAR SEASON							PLAYOFFS			
Year	W	L	T	Pct.	PF	PA	Finish	W	L	Highest round	Coach
1920*	6	2	2	.750	...	...	T4th				Paddy Driscoll
1921*	3	3	2	.500	...	...	T8th				Paddy Driscoll
1922*	8	3	0	.727	...	...	3rd				Paddy Driscoll
1923*	8	4	0	.667	...	...	6th				Arnold Horween
1924*	5	4	1	.556	...	...	8th				Arnold Horween
1925*	11	2	1	.846	...	...	1st				Norman Barry
1926*	5	6	1	.455	...	...	10th				Norman Barry
1927*	3	7	1	.300	...	...	9th				Guy Chamberlin
1928*	1	5	0	.167	...	...	9th				Fred Gillies
1929*	6	6	1	.500	...	...	T4th				Dewey Scanlon
1930*	5	6	2	.455	...	...	T7th				Ernie Nevers
1931*	5	4	0	.556	...	...	4th				LeRoy Andrews, E. Nevers
1932*	2	6	2	.250	...	...	7th				Jack Chevigny
1933*	1	9	1	.100	52	101	5th/Western Div.	—	—		Paul Schissler
1934*	5	6	0	.455	80	84	4th/Western Div.	—	—		Paul Schissler
1935*	6	4	2	.600	99	97	T3rd/Western Div.	—	—		Milan Creighton
1936*	3	8	1	.273	74	143	4th/Western Div.	—	—		Milan Creighton
1937*	5	5	1	.500	135	165	4th/Western Div.	—	—		Milan Creighton
1938*	2	9	0	.182	111	168	5th/Western Div.	—	—		Milan Creighton
1939*	1	10	0	.091	84	254	5th/Western Div.	—	—		Ernie Nevers
1940*	2	7	2	.222	139	222	5th/Western Div.	—	—		Jimmy Conzelman
1941*	3	7	1	.300	127	197	4th/Western Div.	—	—		Jimmy Conzelman
1942*	3	8	0	.273	98	209	4th/Western Div.	—	—		Jimmy Conzelman
1943*	0	10	0	.000	95	238	4th/Western Div.	—	—		Phil Handler
1944†	0	10	0	.000	108	328	5th/Western Div.	—	—		P. Handler-Walt Kiesling
1945*	1	9	0	.100	98	228	5th/Western Div.	—	—		Phil Handler
1946*	6	5	0	.545	260	198	T3rd/Western Div.	—	—		Jimmy Conzelman
1947*	9	3	0	.750	306	231	1st/Western Div.	1	0	NFL champ	Jimmy Conzelman
1948*	11	1	0	.917	395	226	1st/Western Div.	0	1	NFL championship game	Jimmy Conzelman
1949*	6	5	1	.545	360	301	3rd/Western Div.	—	—		P. Handler-Buddy Parker
1950*	5	7	0	.417	233	287	5th/American Conf.	—	—		Curly Lambeau
1951*	3	9	0	.250	210	287	6th/American Conf.	—	—		Curly Lambeau, P. Handler-Cecil Isbell
1952*	4	8	0	.333	172	221	T5th/American Conf.	—	—		Joe Kuharich
1953*	1	10	1	.091	190	337	6th/Eastern Conf.	—	—		Joe Stydahar
1954*	2	10	0	.167	183	347	6th/Eastern Conf.	—	—		Joe Stydahar
1955*	4	7	1	.364	224	252	T4th/Eastern Conf.	—	—		Ray Richards
1956*	7	5	0	.583	240	182	2nd/Eastern Conf.	—	—		Ray Richards
1957*	3	9	0	.250	200	299	6th/Eastern Conf.	—	—		Ray Richards
1958*	2	9	1	.182	261	356	T5th/Eastern Conf.	—	—		Pop Ivy
1959*	2	10	0	.167	234	324	6th/Eastern Conf.	—	—		Pop Ivy
1960‡	6	5	1	.545	288	230	4th/Eastern Conf.	—	—		Pop Ivy
1961‡	7	7	0	.500	279	267	4th/Eastern Conf.	—	—		Pop Ivy
1962‡	4	9	1	.308	287	361	6th/Eastern Conf.	—	—		Wally Lemm
1963‡	9	5	0	.643	341	283	3rd/Eastern Conf.	—	—		Wally Lemm
1964‡	9	3	2	.750	357	331	2nd/Eastern Conf.	—	—		Wally Lemm
1965‡	5	9	0	.357	296	309	T5th/Eastern Conf.	—	—		Wally Lemm
1966‡	8	5	1	.615	264	265	4th/Eastern Conf.	—	—		Charley Winner
1967‡	6	7	1	.462	333	356	3rd/Century Div.	—	—		Charley Winner
1968‡	9	4	1	.692	325	289	2nd/Century Div.	—	—		Charley Winner
1969‡	4	9	1	.308	314	389	3rd/Century Div.	—	—		Charley Winner
1970‡	8	5	1	.615	325	228	3rd/NFC Eastern Div.	—	—		Charley Winner
1971‡	4	9	1	.308	231	279	4th/NFC Eastern Div.	—	—		Bob Hollway
1972‡	4	9	1	.308	193	303	4th/NFC Eastern Div.	—	—		Bob Hollway
1973‡	4	9	1	.308	286	365	4th/NFC Eastern Div.	—	—		Don Coryell
1974‡	10	4	0	.714	285	218	1st/NFC Eastern Div.	0	1	NFC div. playoff game	Don Coryell
1975‡	11	3	0	.786	356	276	1st/NFC Eastern Div.	0	1	NFC div. playoff game	Don Coryell
1976‡	10	4	0	.714	309	267	3rd/NFC Eastern Div.	—	—		Don Coryell
1977‡	7	7	0	.500	272	287	3rd/NFC Eastern Div.	—	—		Don Coryell
1978‡	6	10	0	.375	248	296	T4th/NFC Eastern Div.	—	—		Bud Wilkinson
1979‡	5	11	0	.313	307	358	5th/NFC Eastern Div.	—	—		B. Wilkinson, Larry Wilson
1980‡	5	11	0	.313	299	350	4th/NFC Eastern Div.	—	—		Jim Hanifan
1981‡	7	9	0	.438	315	408	5th/NFC Eastern Div.	—	—		Jim Hanifan
1982‡	5	4	0	.556	135	170	T4th/NFC	0	1	NFC first-round pl. game	Jim Hanifan

	REGULAR SEASON							PLAYOFFS			
Year	W	L	T	Pct.	PF	PA	Finish	W	L	Highest round	Coach
1983‡	8	7	1	.531	374	428	3rd/NFC Eastern Div.	—	—		Jim Hanifan
1984‡	9	7	0	.563	423	345	T3rd/NFC Eastern Div.	—	—		Jim Hanifan
1985‡	5	11	0	.313	278	414	5th/NFC Eastern Div.	—	—		Jim Hanifan
1986‡	4	11	1	.281	218	351	5th/NFC Eastern Div.	—	—		Gene Stallings
1987‡	7	8	0	.467	362	368	T2nd/NFC Eastern Div.	—	—		Gene Stallings
1988§	7	9	0	.438	344	398	T3rd/NFC Eastern Div.	—	—		Gene Stallings
1989§	5	11	0	.313	258	377	4th/NFC Eastern Div.	—	—		G. Stallings, Hank Kuhlmann
1990§	5	11	0	.313	268	396	5th/NFC Eastern Div.	—	—		Joe Bugel
1991§	4	12	0	.250	196	344	5th/NFC Eastern Div.	—	—		Joe Bugel
1992§	4	12	0	.250	243	332	5th/NFC Eastern Div.	—	—		Joe Bugel
1993§	7	9	0	.438	326	269	4th/NFC Eastern Div.	—	—		Joe Bugel
1994	8	8	0	.500	235	267	3rd/NFC Eastern Div.	—	—		Buddy Ryan
1995	4	12	0	.250	275	422	5th/NFC Eastern Div.	—	—		Buddy Ryan
1996	7	9	0	.438	300	397	4th/NFC Eastern Div.	—	—		Vince Tobin
1997	4	12	0	.250	283	379	5th/NFC Eastern Div.	—	—		Vince Tobin

*Chicago Cardinals.
†Card-Pitt, a combined squad of Chicago Cardinals and Pittsburgh Steelers.
‡St. Louis Cardinals.
§Phoenix Cardinals.

FIRST-ROUND DRAFT PICKS

1936—Jim Lawrence, B, Texas Christian
1937—Ray Buivid, B, Marquette
1938—Jack Robbins, B, Arkansas
1939—Charles Aldrich, C, Texas Christian*
1940—George Cafego, B, Tennessee*
1941—John Kimbrough, B, Texas A&M
1942—Steve Lach, B, Duke
1943—Glenn Dobbs, B, Tulsa
1944—Pat Harder, B, Wisconsin*
1945—Charley Trippi, B, Georgia*
1946—Dub Jones, B, Louisiana State
1947—DeWitt (Tex) Coulter, T, Army
1948—Jim Spavital, B, Oklahoma A&M
1949—Bill Fischer, G, Notre Dame
1950—None
1951—Jerry Groom, C, Notre Dame
1952—Ollie Matson, B, San Francisco
1953—Johnny Olszewski, QB, California
1954—Lamar McHan, B, Arkansas
1955—Max Boydston, E, Oklahoma
1956—Joe Childress, B, Auburn
1957—Jerry Tubbs, C, Oklahoma
1958—King Hill, B, Rice*
1959—Billy Stacy, B, Mississippi State
1960—George Izo, QB, Notre Dame
1961—Ken Rice, T, Auburn
1962—Fate Echols, DT, Northwestern
    Irv Goode, C, Kentucky
1963—Jerry Stovall, DB, Louisiana State
    Don Brumm, E, Purdue
1964—Ken Kortas, DT, Louisville
1965—Joe Namath, QB, Alabama
1966—Carl McAdams, LB, Oklahoma
1967—Dave Williams, WR, Washington
1968—MacArthur Lane, RB, Utah State

1969—Roger Wehrli, DB, Missouri
1970—Larry Stegent, RB, Texas A&M
1971—Norm Thompson, DB, Utah
1972—Bobby Moore, RB, Oregon
1973—Dave Butz, DT, Purdue
1974—J.V. Cain, TE, Colorado
1975—Tim Gray, DB, Texas A&M
1976—Mike Dawson, DT, Arizona
1977—Steve Pisarkiewicz, QB, Missouri
1978—Steve Little, K, Arkansas
    Ken Greene, DB, Washington St.
1979—Ottis Anderson, RB, Miami (Fla.)
1980—Curtis Greer, DE, Michigan
1981—E.J. Junior, LB, Alabama
1982—Luis Sharpe, T, UCLA
1983—Leonard Smith, DB, McNeese State
1984—Clyde Duncan, WR, Tennessee
1985—Freddie Joe Nunn, LB, Mississippi
1986—Anthony Bell, LB, Michigan St.
1987—Kelly Stouffer, QB, Colorado St.
1988—Ken Harvey, LB, California
1989—Eric Hill, LB, Louisiana State
    Joe Wolf, G, Boston College
1990—None
1991—Eric Swann, DL, None
1992—None
1993—Garrison Hearst, RB, Georgia
    Ernest Dye, T, South Carolina
1994—Jamir Miller, LB, UCLA
1995—None
1996—Simeon Rice, DE, Illinois
1997—Tom Knight, DB, Iowa
1998—Andre Wadsworth, DE, Florida State
    *First player chosen in draft.

FRANCHISE RECORDS

Most rushing yards, career
7,999—Ottis Anderson

Most rushing yards, season
1,605—Ottis Anderson, 1979

Most rushing yards, game
214—LeShon Johnson at N.O., Sept. 22, 1996

Most rushing touchdowns, season
14—John David Crow, 1962

Most passing attempts, season
560—Neil Lomax, 1984

Most passing attempts, game
61—Neil Lomax at S.D., Sept. 20, 1987

Most passes completed, season
345—Neil Lomax, 1984

Most passes completed, game
37—Neil Lomax at Was., Dec. 16, 1984
    Kent Graham vs. St.L., Sept. 29, 1996 (OT)

Most passing yards, career
34,639—Jim Hart

Most passing yards, season
4,614—Neil Lomax, 1984

Most passing yards, game
522—Boomer Esiason at Was., Nov. 10, 1996 (OT)
468—Neil Lomax at Was., Dec. 16, 1984

Most touchdown passes, season
28—Charley Johnson, 1963
   Neil Lomax, 1984
Most pass receptions, career
522—Roy Green
Most pass receptions, season
101—Larry Centers, 1995
Most pass receptions, game
16—Sonny Randle at NYG, Nov. 4, 1962
Most receiving yards, career
8,497—Roy Green

Most receiving yards, season
1,555—Roy Green, 1984
Most receiving yards, game
256—Sonny Randle vs. NYG, Nov. 4, 1962
Most receiving touchdowns, season
16—Sonny Randle, 1960
Most touchdowns, career
66—Roy Green
Most field goals, season
30—Greg Davis, 1995

Longest field goal
55 yards—Greg Davis at Sea., Dec. 19,
   1993
   Greg Davis at Det., Sept. 17, 1995
Most interceptions, career
52—Larry Wilson
Most interceptions, season
12—Bob Nussbaumer, 1949

SERIES RECORDS

Arizona vs.: Atlanta 13-6; Baltimore, 1-0; Buffalo 3-3; Carolina 0-1; Chicago 25-54-6; Cincinnati 2-4; Dallas 23-47-1; Denver 0-4-1; Detroit 15-28-3; Green Bay 21-41-4; Indianapolis 6-6; Jacksonville 0-0; Kansas City 1-4-1; Miami 0-7; Minnesota 8-7; New England 6-3; New Orleans 11-10; N.Y. Giants 37-72-2; N.Y. Jets 2-2; Oakland 1-2; Philadelphia 47-49-5; Pittsburgh 21-30-3; St. Louis 13-16-2; San Diego 1-6; San Francisco 9-10; Seattle 5-0; Tampa Bay 7-7; Tennessee 4-3; Washington 39-61-1.
NOTE: Includes records for entire franchise, from 1920 to present.

COACHING RECORDS

LeRoy Andrews, 0-1-0; Norman Barry, 16-8-2; Joe Bugel, 20-44-0; Guy Chamberlain, 3-7-1; Jack Chevigny, 2-6-2; Jimmy Conzelman, 34-31-3 (1-1); Don Coryell, 42-27-1 (0-2); Paddy Driscoll, 16-26-4; Paddy Driscoll, 17-8-4; Chuck Drulis-Ray Prochaska-Ray Willsey*, 2-0-0; Fred Gillies, 1-5-0; Phil Handler, 1-29-0; Phil Handler-Cecil Isbell*, 1-1-0; Phil Handler-Buddy Parker*, 2-4-0; Jim Hanifan, 39-49-1 (0-1); Bob Hollway, 8-18-2; Arnold Horween, 13-8-1; Frank Ivy, 17-29-2; Joe Kuharich, 4-8-0; Hank Kuhlmann, 0-5-0; Curly Lambeau, 7-15-0; Wally Lemm, 27-26-3; Ernie Nevers, 11-19-2; Buddy Parker, 4-1-1; Ray Richards, 14-21-1; Buddy Ryan, 12-20-0; Dewey Scanlon, 6-6-1; Paul Schissler, 6-15-1; Gene Stallings, 23-34-1; Joe Stydahar, 3-20-1; Vince Tobin, 11-21-0; Bud Wilkinson, 9-20-0; Larry Wilson, 2-1-0; Charley Winner, 35-30-5.
NOTE: Playoff games in parentheses.
*Co-coaches.

RETIRED UNIFORM NUMBERS

No.	Player
8	Larry Wilson
77	Stan Mauldin
88	J.V. Cain
99	Marshall Goldberg

ATLANTA FALCONS
YEAR-BY-YEAR RECORDS

			REGULAR SEASON						PLAYOFFS		
Year	W	L	T	Pct.	PF	PA	Finish	W	L	Highest round	Coach
1966	3	11	0	.214	204	437	7th/Eastern Conf.	—	—		Norb Hecker
1967	1	12	1	.077	175	422	4th/Coastal Div.	—	—		Norb Hecker
1968	2	12	0	.143	170	389	4th/Coastal Div.	—	—		N. Hecker, N. Van Brocklin
1969	6	8	0	.429	276	268	3rd/Coastal Div.	—	—		Norm Van Brocklin
1970	4	8	2	.333	206	261	3rd/NFC Western Div.	—	—		Norm Van Brocklin
1971	7	6	1	.538	274	277	3rd/NFC Western Div.	—	—		Norm Van Brocklin
1972	7	7	0	.500	269	274	2nd/NFC Western Div.	—	—		Norm Van Brocklin
1973	9	5	0	.643	318	224	2nd/NFC Western Div.	—	—		Norm Van Brocklin
1974	3	11	0	.214	111	271	4th/NFC Western Div.	—	—		N. Van Brocklin, M. Campbell
1975	4	10	0	.286	240	289	3rd/NFC Western Div.	—	—		Marion Campbell
1976	4	10	0	.286	172	312	T3rd/NFC Western Div.	—	—		M. Campbell, Pat Peppler
1977	7	7	0	.500	179	129	2nd/NFC Western Div.	—	—		Leeman Bennett
1978	9	7	0	.563	240	290	2nd/NFC Western Div.	1	1	NFC div. playoff game	Leeman Bennett
1979	6	10	0	.375	300	388	3rd/NFC Western Div.	—	—		Leeman Bennett
1980	12	4	0	.750	405	272	1st/NFC Western Div.	0	1	NFC div. playoff game	Leeman Bennett
1981	7	9	0	.438	426	355	2nd/NFC Western Div.	—	—		Leeman Bennett
1982	5	4	0	.556	183	199	T4th/NFC	0	1	NFC first-round pl. game	Leeman Bennett
1983	7	9	0	.438	370	389	4th/NFC Western Div.	—	—		Dan Henning
1984	4	12	0	.250	281	382	4th/NFC Western Div.	—	—		Dan Henning
1985	4	12	0	.250	282	452	4th/NFC Western Div.	—	—		Dan Henning
1986	7	8	1	.469	280	280	3rd/NFC Western Div.	—	—		Dan Henning
1987	3	12	0	.200	205	436	4th/NFC Western Div.	—	—		Marion Campbell
1988	5	11	0	.313	244	315	4th/NFC Western Div.	—	—		Marion Campbell
1989	3	13	0	.188	279	437	4th/NFC Western Div.	—	—		M. Campbell, Jim Hanifan
1990	5	11	0	.313	348	365	T3rd/NFC Western Div.	—	—		Jerry Glanville
1991	10	6	0	.625	361	338	2nd/NFC Western Div.	1	1	NFC div. playoff game	Jerry Glanville
1992	6	10	0	.375	327	414	T3rd/NFC Western Div.	—	—		Jerry Glanville
1993	6	10	0	.375	316	385	3rd/NFC Western Div.	—	—		Jerry Glanville
1994	7	9	0	.438	313	389	T2nd/NFC Western Div.	—	—		June Jones
1995	9	7	0	.563	362	349	2nd/NFC Western Div.	0	1	NFC wild-card game	June Jones
1996	3	13	0	.188	309	465	T4th/NFC Western Div.	—	—		June Jones
1997	7	9	0	.438	320	361	T2nd/NFC Western Div.	—	—		Dan Reeves

FIRST-ROUND DRAFT PICKS

1966—Tommy Nobis, LB, Texas*
        Randy Johnson, QB, Texas A&I
1967—None
1968—Claude Humphrey, DE, Tennessee State
1969—George Kunz, T, Notre Dame
1970—John Small, LB, Citadel
1971—Joe Profit, RB, Northeast Louisiana State
1972—Clarence Ellis, DB, Notre Dame
1973—None
1974—None
1975—Steve Bartkowski, QB, California*
1976—Bubba Bean, RB, Texas A&M
1977—Warren Bryant, T, Kentucky
        Wilson Faumuina, DT, San Jose State
1978—Mike Kenn, T, Michigan
1979—Don Smith, DE, Miami (Fla.)
1980—Junior Miller, TE, Nebraska
1981—Bobby Butler, DB, Florida State
1982—Gerald Riggs, RB, Arizona State
1983—Mike Pitts, DE, Alabama

1984—Rick Bryan, DT, Oklahoma
1985—Bill Fralic, T, Pittsburgh
1986—Tony Casillas, DT, Oklahoma
        Tim Green, LB, Syracuse
1987—Chris Miller, QB, Oregon
1988—Aundray Bruce, LB, Auburn*
1989—Deion Sanders, DB, Florida State
        Shawn Collins, WR, Northern Arizona
1990—Steve Broussard, RB, Washington State
1991—Bruce Pickens, CB, Nebraska
        Mike Pritchard, WR, Colorado
1992—Bob Whitfield, T, Stanford
        Tony Smith, RB, Southern Mississippi
1993—Lincoln Kennedy, T, Washington
1994—None
1995—Devin Bush, DB, Florida State
1996—None
1997—Michael Booker, DB, Nebraska
1998—Keith Brooking, LB, Georgia Tech
        *First player chosen in draft.

FRANCHISE RECORDS

Most rushing yards, career
6,631—Gerald Riggs
Most rushing yards, season
1,719—Gerald Riggs, 1985
Most rushing yards, game
202—Gerald Riggs at N.O., Sept. 2, 1984
Most rushing touchdowns, season
13—Gerald Riggs, 1984
Most passing attempts, season
557—Jeff George, 1995
Most passing attempts, game
66—Chris Miller vs. Det., Dec. 24, 1989
Most passes completed, season
336—Jeff George, 1995
Most passes completed, game
37—Chris Miller vs. Det., Dec. 24, 1989
Most passing yards, career
23,468—Steve Bartkowski
Most passing yards, season
4,143—Jeff George, 1995

Most passing yards, game
416—Steve Bartkowski vs. Pit., Nov. 15,
        1981
Most touchdown passes, season
31—Steve Bartkowski, 1980
Most pass receptions, career
423—Andre Rison
Most pass receptions, season
111—Terance Mathis, 1994
Most pass receptions, game
15—William Andrews vs. Pit., Nov. 15,
        1981
Most receiving yards, career
6,257—Alfred Jenkins
Most receiving yards, season
1,358—Alfred Jenkins, 1981
Most receiving yards, game
193—Alfred Jackson vs. S.F., Dec. 2, 1984
        Andre Rison at Det., Sept. 4, 1994

Most receiving touchdowns, season
15—Andre Rison, 1993
Most touchdowns, career
56—Andre Rison
Most field goals, season
31—Morten Andersen, 1995
Longest field goal
59 yards—Morten Andersen vs. S.F.,
        Dec. 24, 1995
Most interceptions, career
39—Rolland Lawrence
Most interceptions, season
10—Scott Case, 1988
Most sacks, career
62.5—Claude Humphrey
Most sacks, season
16—Joel Williams, 1980

SERIES RECORDS

Atlanta vs.: Arizona 6-13; Buffalo 3-4; Carolina 2-4; Chicago 9-9; Cincinnati 2-7; Dallas 6-11; Denver 3-6; Detroit 6-20; Green Bay 9-10; Indianapolis 0-10; Jacksonville 0-1; Kansas City 0-4; Miami 1-6; Minnesota 6-13; New England 5-3; New Orleans 33-24; N.Y. Giants 6-6; N.Y. Jets 4-3; Oakland 3-6; Philadelphia 8-9-1; Pittsburgh 1-10; St. Louis 21-39-2; San Diego 5-1; San Francisco 22-39-1; Seattle 2-4; Tampa Bay 8-7; Tennessee 5-4; Washington 4-13-1.

COACHING RECORDS

Leeman Bennett, 46-41-0 (1-3); Marion Campbell, 17-51-0; Jerry Glanville, 27-37-0 (1-1); Jim Hanifan, 0-4-0; Norb Hecker, 4-26-1; Dan Henning, 22-41-1; June Jones, 19-29-0 (0-1); Pat Peppler, 3-6-0; Dan Reeves, 7-9-0; Norm Van Brocklin, 37-49-3. NOTE: Playoff games in parentheses.

RETIRED UNIFORM NUMBERS

No.	Player
10	Steve Bartkowski
31	William Andrews
57	Jeff Van Note
60	Tommy Nobis

BALTIMORE RAVENS
YEAR-BY-YEAR RECORDS

	REGULAR SEASON						PLAYOFFS			
Year	W	L	T	Pct.	PF	PA	Finish	W	L	Highest round	Coach
1996	4	12	0	.250	371	441	5th/AFC Central Div.	—	—		Ted Marchibroda
1997	6	9	1	.406	326	345	5th/AFC Central Div.	—	—		Ted Marchibroda

FIRST-ROUND DRAFT PICKS

1996—Jonathan Ogden, T, UCLA
    Ray Lewis, LB, Miami (Fla.)
1997—Peter Boulware, DE, Florida State

1998—Duane Starks, DB, Miami (Fla.)
*First player chosen in draft.

FRANCHISE RECORDS

Most rushing yards, career
1,511—Bam Morris
Most rushing yards, season
774—Bam Morris, 1997
Most rushing yards, game
176—Bam Morris at Was., Oct. 26, 1997
Most rushing touchdowns, season
4—Earnest Byner, 1996
    Bam Morris, 1996, 1997
Most passing attempts, season
549—Vinny Testaverde, 1996
Most passing attempts, game
51—Vinny Testaverde vs. St.L., Oct. 27, 1996 (OT)
50—Vinny Testaverde vs. Jac., Nov. 24, 1996 (OT)
47—Vinny Testaverde vs. Pit., Oct. 5, 1997
    Vinny Testaverde at Mia., Oct. 19, 1997
Most passes completed, season
325—Vinny Testaverde, 1996
Most passes completed, game
32—Vinny Testaverde vs. Mia., Oct. 19, 1997
Most passing yards, career
7,148—Vinny Testaverde

Most passing yards, season
4,177—Vinny Testaverde, 1996
Most passing yards, game
429—Vinny Testaverde vs. St.L., Oct. 27, 1996 (OT)
366—Vinny Testaverde vs. Jac., Nov. 24, 1996 (OT)
353—Vinny Testaverde vs. N.E., Oct. 6, 1996
Most touchdown passes, season
33—Vinny Testaverde, 1996
Most pass receptions, career
145—Michael Jackson
Most pass receptions, season
76—Michael Jackson, 1996
Most pass receptions, game
9—Michael Jackson vs. Jac., Nov. 24, 1996 (OT)
    Brian Kinchen vs. Jac., Nov. 24, 1996 (OT)
8—Michael Jackson vs. N.E., Oct. 6, 1996
    Michael Jackson vs. Jac., Aug. 31, 1997
Most receiving yards, career
2,119—Michael Jackson
Most receiving yards, season
1,201—Michael Jackson, 1996

Most receiving yards, game
198—Derrick Alexander vs. Pit., Dec. 1, 1996
Most receiving touchdowns, season
14—Michael Jackson, 1996
Most touchdowns, career
18—Derrick Alexander
    Michael Jackson
Most field goals, season
26—Matt Stover, 1997
Longest field goal
50 yards—Matt Stover vs. St.L., Oct. 27, 1996
Most interceptions, career
8—Antonio Langham
Most interceptions, season
5—Antonio Langham, 1996
    Eric Turner, 1996
Most sacks, career
11.5—Peter Boulware
Most sacks, season
11.5—Peter Boulware, 1997

SERIES RECORDS

Baltimore vs.: Arizona, 0-1; Carolina 0-1; Cincinnati 1-3; Denver 0-1; Indianapolis 0-1; Jacksonville 0-4; Miami, 0-1; New England 0-1; New Orleans 1-0; N.Y. Giants, 1-0; N.Y. Jets, 0-1; Oakland 1-0; Philadelphia, 0-0-1; Pittsburgh 1-3; St. Louis 1-0; San Diego, 0-1; San Francisco 0-1; Seattle, 1-0; Tennessee 2-2; Washington, 1-0.

COACHING RECORDS

Ted Marchibroda, 10-21-1.

RETIRED UNIFORM NUMBERS

No.	Player
	None

BUFFALO BILLS
YEAR-BY-YEAR RECORDS

	REGULAR SEASON							PLAYOFFS			
Year	W	L	T	Pct.	PF	PA	Finish	W	L	Highest round	Coach
1960*	5	8	1	.385	296	303	3rd/Eastern Div.	—	—		Buster Ramsey
1961*	6	8	0	.429	294	342	4th/Eastern Div.	—	—		Buster Ramsey
1962*	7	6	1	.538	309	272	3rd/Eastern Div.	—	—		Lou Saban
1963*	7	6	1	.538	304	291	2nd/Eastern Div.	0	1	E. Div. championship game	Lou Saban
1964*	12	2	0	.857	400	242	1st/Eastern Div.	1	0	AFL champ	Lou Saban
1965*	10	3	1	.769	313	226	1st/Eastern Div.	1	0	AFL champ	Lou Saban
1966*	9	4	1	.692	358	255	1st/Eastern Div.	0	1	AFL championship game	Joe Collier
1967*	4	10	0	.286	237	285	T3rd/Eastern Div.	—	—		Joe Collier
1968*	1	12	1	.077	199	367	5th/Eastern Div.	—	—		J. Collier, H. Johnson
1969*	4	10	0	.286	230	359	T3rd/Eastern Div.	—	—		John Rauch
1970	3	10	1	.231	204	337	4th/AFC Eastern Div.	—	—		John Rauch
1971	1	13	0	.071	184	394	5th/AFC Eastern Div.	—	—		Harvey Johnson
1972	4	9	1	.321	257	377	4th/AFC Eastern Div.	—	—		Lou Saban
1973	9	5	0	.643	259	230	2nd/AFC Eastern Div.	—	—		Lou Saban
1974	9	5	0	.643	264	244	2nd/AFC Eastern Div.	0	1	AFC div. playoff game	Lou Saban
1975	8	6	0	.571	420	355	3rd/AFC Eastern Div.	—	—		Lou Saban
1976	2	12	0	.143	245	363	5th/AFC Eastern Div.	—	—		Lou Saban, Jim Ringo
1977	3	11	0	.214	160	313	T4th/AFC Eastern Div.	—	—		Jim Ringo

REGULAR SEASON   PLAYOFFS

Year	W	L	T	Pct.	PF	PA	Finish	W	L	Highest round	Coach
1978	5	11	0	.313	302	354	T4th/AFC Eastern Div.	—	—		Chuck Knox
1979	7	9	0	.438	268	279	4th/AFC Eastern Div.	—	—		Chuck Knox
1980	11	5	0	.688	320	260	1st/AFC Eastern Div.	0	1	AFC div. playoff game	Chuck Knox
1981	10	6	0	.625	311	276	3rd/AFC Eastern Div.	1	1	AFC div. playoff game	Chuck Knox
1982	4	5	0	.444	150	154	T8th/AFC	—	—		Chuck Knox
1983	8	8	0	.500	283	351	T2nd/AFC Eastern Div.	—	—		Kay Stephenson
1984	2	14	0	.125	250	454	5th/AFC Eastern Div.	—	—		Kay Stephenson
1985	2	14	0	.125	200	381	5th/AFC Eastern Div.	—	—		Hank Bullough
1986	4	12	0	.250	287	348	4th/AFC Eastern Div.	—	—		H. Bullough, M. Levy
1987	7	8	0	.467	270	305	4th/AFC Eastern Div.	—	—		Marv Levy
1988	12	4	0	.750	329	237	1st/AFC Eastern Div.	1	1	AFC championship game	Marv Levy
1989	9	7	0	.563	409	317	1st/AFC Eastern Div.	0	1	AFC div. playoff game	Marv Levy
1990	13	3	0	.813	428	263	1st/AFC Eastern Div.	2	1	Super Bowl	Marv Levy
1991	13	3	0	.813	458	318	1st/AFC Eastern Div.	2	1	Super Bowl	Marv Levy
1992	11	5	0	.688	381	283	2nd/AFC Eastern Div.	3	1	Super Bowl	Marv Levy
1993	12	4	0	.750	329	242	1st/AFC Eastern Div.	2	1	Super Bowl	Marv Levy
1994	7	9	0	.438	340	356	4th/AFC Eastern Div.	—	—		Marv Levy
1995	10	6	0	.625	350	335	1st/AFC Eastern Div.	1	1	AFC div. playoff game	Marv Levy
1996	10	6	0	.625	319	266	2nd/AFC Eastern Div.	0	1	AFC wild-card night	Marv Levy
1997	6	10	0	.375	255	367	4th/AFC Eastern Div.	—	—		Marv Levy

*American Football League.

FIRST-ROUND DRAFT PICKS

1960—Richie Lucas, QB, Penn State
1961—Ken Rice, T, Auburn* (AFL)
1962—Ernie Davis, RB, Syracuse
1963—Dave Behrman, C, Michigan State
1964—Carl Eller, DE, Minnesota
1965—Jim Davidson, T, Ohio State
1966—Mike Dennis, RB, Mississippi
1967—John Pitts, DB, Arizona State
1968—Haven Moses, WR, San Diego St.
1969—O.J. Simpson, RB, Southern California*
1970—Al Cowlings, DE, Southern California
1971—J.D. Hill, WR, Arizona State
1972—Walt Patulski, DE, Notre Dame*
1973—Paul Seymour, T, Michigan
     Joe DeLamielleure, G, Michigan State
1974—Reuben Gant, TE, Oklahoma State
1975—Tom Ruud, LB, Nebraska
1976—Mario Clark, DB, Oregon
1977—Phil Dokes, DT, Oklahoma State
1978—Terry Miller, RB, Oklahoma State
1979—Tom Cousineau, LB, Ohio State*
     Jerry Butler, WR, Clemson
1980—Jim Ritcher, C, North Carolina State

1981—Booker Moore, RB, Penn State
1982—Perry Tuttle, WR, Clemson
1983—Tony Hunter, TE, Notre Dame
     Jim Kelly, QB, Miami (Fla.)
1984—Greg Bell, RB, Notre Dame
1985—Bruce Smith, DT, Virginia Tech*
     Derrick Burroughs, DB, Memphis State
1986—Ronnie Harmon, RB, Iowa
     Will Wolford, T, Vanderbilt
1987—Shane Conlan, LB, Penn State
1988—None
1989—None
1990—James Williams, DB, Fresno State
1991—Henry Jones, S, Illinois
1992—John Fina, T, Arizona
1993—Thomas Smith, DB, North Carolina
1994—Jeff Burris, DB, Notre Dame
1995—Ruben Brown, G, Pittsburgh
1996—Eric Moulds, WR, Mississippi State
1997—Antowain Smith, RB, Houston
1998—None
*First player chosen in draft.

FRANCHISE RECORDS

Most rushing yards, career
11,405—Thurman Thomas
Most rushing yards, season
2,003—O.J. Simpson, 1973
Most rushing yards, game
273—O.J. Simpson at Det., Nov. 25, 1976
Most rushing touchdowns, season
16—O.J. Simpson, 1975
Most passing attempts, season
508—Joe Ferguson, 1983
Most passing attempts, game
55—Joe Ferguson at Mia., Oct. 9, 1983
Most passes completed, season
304—Jim Kelly, 1991
Most passes completed, game
38—Joe Ferguson at Mia., Oct. 9, 1983
Most passing yards, career
35,467—Jim Kelly

Most passing yards, season
3,844—Jim Kelly, 1991
Most passing yards, game
419—Joe Ferguson at Mia., Oct. 9, 1983
Most touchdown passes, season
33—Jim Kelly, 1991
Most pass receptions, career
826—Andre Reed
Most pass receptions, season
90—Andre Reed, 1994
Most pass receptions, game
15—Andre Reed vs. G.B., Nov. 20, 1994
Most receiving yards, career
11,764—Andre Reed
Most receiving yards, season
1,312—Andre Reed, 1989
Most receiving yards, game
255—Jerry Butler vs. NYJ, Sept. 23, 1979

Most receiving touchdowns, season
11—Bill Brooks, 1995
Most touchdowns, career
83—Thurman Thomas
Most field goals, season
32—Scott Norwood, 1988
Longest field goal
59 yards—Steve Christie vs. Mia., Sept. 26, 1993
Most interceptions, career
40—George Byrd
Most interceptions, season
10—Billy Atkins, 1961
     Tom Janik, 1967
Most sacks, career
154—Bruce Smith
Most sacks, season
19—Bruce Smith, 1990

SERIES RECORDS

Buffalo vs.: Arizona 3-3; Atlanta 4-3; Carolina 1-0; Chicago 2-5; Cincinnati 8-10; Dallas 3-3; Denver 17-12-1; Detroit 2-3-1; Green Bay 5-2; Indianapolis 31-23-1; Jacksonville 0-1; Kansas City 17-14-1; Miami 22-41-1; Minnesota 2-6; New England 35-40-1; New Orleans 3-2; N.Y. Giants 5-2; N.Y. Jets 44-31; Oakland 14-15; Philadelphia 4-4; Pittsburgh 7-8; St. Louis 4-3; San Diego 7-16-2; San Francisco 3-3; Seattle 2-4; Tampa Bay 2-4; Tennessee 13-22; Washington 4-4.

COACHING RECORDS

Hank Bullough, 4-17-0; Joe Collier, 13-16-1 (0-1); Harvey Johnson, 2-23-1; Chuck Knox, 37-36-0 (1-2); Marv Levy, 112-70-0 (11-8); Buster Ramsey, 11-16-1; John Rauch, 7-20-1; Jim Ringo, 3-20-0; Lou Saban, 68-45-4 (2-2); Kay Stephenson, 10-26-0.
NOTE: Playoff games in parentheses.

RETIRED UNIFORM NUMBERS

No.	Player
	None

CAROLINA PANTHERS
YEAR-BY-YEAR RECORDS

		REGULAR SEASON							PLAYOFFS		
Year	W	L	T	Pct.	PF	PA	Finish	W	L	Highest round	Coach
1995	7	9	0	.438	289	325	T3rd/NFC Western Div.	—	—		Dom Capers
1996	12	4	0	.750	367	218	1st/NFC Western Div.	1	1	NFC championship game	Dom Capers
1997	7	9	0	.438	265	314	T2nd/NFC Western Div.	—	—		Dom Capers

FIRST-ROUND DRAFT PICKS

1995—Kerry Collins, QB, Penn State
Tyrone Poole, DB, Fort Valley (Ga.) St.
Blake Brockermeyer, T, Texas

1996—Tim Biakabutuka, RB, Michigan
1997—Rae Carruth, WR, Colorado
1998—Jason Peter, DT, Nebraska

FRANCHISE RECORDS

Most rushing yards, career
1,588—Anthony Johnson
Most rushing yards, season
1,120—Anthony Johnson, 1996
Most rushing yards, game
147—Fred Lane vs. Oak., Nov. 2, 1997
Most rushing touchdowns, season
7—Fred Lane, 1997
Most passing attempts, season
433—Kerry Collins, 1995
Most passing attempts, game
47—Kerry Collins vs. K.C., Sept. 21, 1997
Most passes completed, season
214—Kerry Collins, 1995
Most passes completed, game
26—Kerry Collins vs. Bal., Dec. 15, 1996
Most passing yards, career
7,295—Kerry Collins
Most passing yards, season
2,717—Kerry Collins, 1995

Most passing yards, game
335—Kerry Collins at N.O., Nov. 26, 1995
Most touchdown passes, season
14—Kerry Collins, 1995, 1996
Most pass receptions, career
157—Mark Carrier
Most pass receptions, season
66—Mark Carrier, 1995
Most pass receptions, game
9—Willie Green at Atl., Nov. 3, 1996
Most receiving yards, career
2,127—Mark Carrier
Most receiving yards, season
1,002—Mark Carrier, 1995
Most receiving yards, game
157—Willie Green at St.L., Nov. 12, 1995
Willie Green at S.F., Dec. 8, 1996
Most receiving touchdowns, season
10—Wesley Walls, 1996

Most touchdowns, career
16—Wesley Walls
Most field goals, season
37—John Kasay, 1996
Longest field goal
54 yards—John Kasay vs. Oak., Nov. 2, 1997
Most interceptions, career
10—Eric Davis
Most interceptions, season
6—Brett Maxie, 1995
Most sacks, career
21.5—Lamar Lathon
Most sacks, season
14.5—Kevin Greene, 1996

SERIES RECORDS

Carolina vs.: Arizona 1-0; Atlanta 4-2; Buffalo 0-1; Baltimore 1-0; Chicago 0-1; Cincinnati 0-0; Dallas 1-0; Denver 0-1; Detroit 0-0; Green Bay 0-1; Indianapolis 1-0; Jacksonville 0-1; Kansas City 0-1; Miami 0-0; Minnesota 0-2; New England 1-0; New Orleans 4-2; N.Y. Giants 1-0; N.Y. Jets 1-0; Oakland 1-0; Philadelphia 0-1; Pittsburgh 1-0; St. Louis 3-3; San Diego 1-0; San Francisco 3-3; Seattle 0-0; Tampa Bay 1-1; Tennessee 1-0; Washington 0-2.

COACHING RECORDS

Dom Capers, 26-22-0 (1-1).
NOTE: Playoff games in parentheses.

RETIRED UNIFORM NUMBERS

No.	Player
	None

CHICAGO BEARS
YEAR-BY-YEAR RECORDS

Year	W	L	T	Pct.	PF	PA	Finish	W	L	Highest round	Coach
		REGULAR SEASON							PLAYOFFS		
1920*	10	1	2	.909	...	...	2nd				George Halas
1921†	9	1	1	.900	...	...	1st				George Halas
1922	9	3	0	.750	...	...	2nd				George Halas
1923	9	2	1	.818	...	...	2nd				George Halas
1924	6	1	4	.857	...	...	2nd				George Halas
1925	9	5	3	.643	...	...	7th				George Halas
1926	12	1	3	.923	...	...	2nd				George Halas
1927	9	3	2	.750	...	...	3rd				George Halas
1928	7	5	1	.583	...	...	5th				George Halas
1929	4	9	2	.308	...	...	9th				George Halas
1930	9	4	1	.692	...	...	3rd				Ralph Jones
1931	8	5	0	.615	...	...	3rd				Ralph Jones
1932	7	1	6	.875	...	...	1st				Ralph Jones
1933	10	2	1	.833	133	82	1st/Western Div.	1	0	NFL champ	George Halas
1934	13	0	0	1.000	286	86	1st/Western Div.	0	1	NFL championship game	George Halas
1935	6	4	2	.600	192	106	T3rd/Western Div.	—	—		George Halas
1936	9	3	0	.750	222	94	2nd/Western Div.				George Halas
1937	9	1	1	.900	201	100	1st/Western Div.	0	1	NFL championship game	George Halas
1938	6	5	0	.545	194	148	3rd/Western Div.	—	—		George Halas
1939	8	3	0	.727	298	157	2nd/Western Div.	—	—		George Halas
1940	8	3	0	.727	238	152	1st/Western Div.	1	0	NFL champ	George Halas
1941	10	1	0	.909	396	147	1st/Western Div.	2	0	NFL champ	George Halas
1942	11	0	0	1.000	376	84	1st/Western Div.	0	1	NFL championship game	George Halas, Hunk Anderson-Luke Johnsos
1943	8	1	1	.889	303	157	1st/Western Div.	1	0	NFL champ	H. Anderson-L. Johnsos
1944	6	3	1	.667	258	172	T2nd/Western Div.	—	—		H. Anderson-L. Johnsos
1945	3	7	0	.300	192	235	4th/Western Div.	—	—		H. Anderson-L. Johnsos
1946	8	2	1	.800	289	193	1st/Western Div.	1	0	NFL champ	George Halas
1947	8	4	0	.667	363	241	2nd/Western Div.	—	—		George Halas
1948	10	2	0	.833	375	151	2nd/Western Div.	—	—		George Halas
1949	9	3	0	.750	332	218	2nd/Western Div.	—	—		George Halas
1950	9	3	0	.750	279	207	2nd/National Conf.	0	1	Nat. Conf. champ. game	George Halas
1951	7	5	0	.583	286	282	4th/National Conf.	—	—		George Halas
1952	5	7	0	.417	245	326	5th/National Conf.	—	—		George Halas
1953	3	8	1	.273	218	262	T4th/Western Conf.	—	—		George Halas
1954	8	4	0	.667	301	279	2nd/Western Conf.	—	—		George Halas
1955	8	4	0	.667	294	251	2nd/Western Conf.	—	—		George Halas
1956	9	2	1	.818	363	246	1st/Western Conf.	0	1	NFL championship game	Paddy Driscoll
1957	5	7	0	.417	203	211	5th/Western Conf.	—	—		Paddy Driscoll
1958	8	4	0	.667	298	230	T2nd/Western Conf.	—	—		George Halas
1959	8	4	0	.667	252	196	2nd/Western Conf.	—	—		George Halas
1960	5	6	1	.455	194	299	5th/Western Conf.	—	—		George Halas
1961	8	6	0	.571	326	302	T3rd/Western Conf.	—	—		George Halas
1962	9	5	0	.643	321	287	3rd/Western Conf.	—	—		George Halas
1963	11	1	2	.917	301	144	1st/Western Conf.	1	0	NFL champ	George Halas
1964	5	9	0	.357	260	379	6th/Western Conf.	—	—		George Halas
1965	9	5	0	.643	409	275	3rd/Western Conf.	—	—		George Halas
1966	5	7	2	.417	234	272	5th/Western Conf.	—	—		George Halas
1967	7	6	1	.538	239	218	2nd/Central Div.	—	—		George Halas
1968	7	7	0	.500	250	333	2nd/Central Div.	—	—		Jim Dooley
1969	1	13	0	.071	210	339	4th/Central Div.	—	—		Jim Dooley
1970	6	8	0	.429	256	261	T3rd/NFC Central Div.	—	—		Jim Dooley
1971	6	8	0	.429	185	276	3rd/NFC Central Div.	—	—		Jim Dooley
1972	4	9	1	.321	225	275	4th/NFC Central Div.	—	—		Abe Gibron
1973	3	11	0	.214	195	334	4th/NFC Central Div.	—	—		Abe Gibron
1974	4	10	0	.286	152	279	4th/NFC Central Div.	—	—		Abe Gibron
1975	4	10	0	.286	191	379	T3rd/NFC Central Div.	—	—		Jack Pardee
1976	7	7	0	.500	253	216	2nd/NFC Central Div.	—	—		Jack Pardee
1977	9	5	0	.643	255	253	2nd/NFC Central Div.	0	1	NFC div. playoff game	Jack Pardee
1978	7	9	0	.438	253	274	T3rd/NFC Central Div.	—	—		Neill Armstrong
1979	10	6	0	.625	306	249	2nd/NFC Central Div.	0	1	AFC wild-card game	Neill Armstrong
1980	7	9	0	.438	304	264	3rd/NFC Central Div.	—	—		Neill Armstrong
1981	6	10	0	.375	253	324	5th/NFC Central Div.	—	—		Neill Armstrong
1982	3	6	0	.333	141	174	T11th/NFC	—	—		Mike Ditka
1983	8	8	0	.500	311	301	T2nd/NFC Central Div.	—	—		Mike Ditka
1984	10	6	0	.625	325	248	1st/NFC Central Div.	1	1	NFC championship game	Mike Ditka

			REGULAR SEASON						PLAYOFFS	
Year	W	L	T	Pct.	PF	PA	Finish	W	L	Highest round	Coach
1985	15	1	0	.938	456	198	1st/NFC Central Div.	3	0	Super Bowl champ	Mike Ditka
1986	14	2	0	.875	352	187	1st/NFC Central Div.	0	1	NFC div. playoff game	Mike Ditka
1987	11	4	0	.733	356	282	1st/NFC Central Div.	0	1	NFC div. playoff game	Mike Ditka
1988	12	4	0	.750	312	215	1st/NFC Central Div.	1	1	NFC championship game	Mike Ditka
1989	6	10	0	.375	358	377	4th/NFC Central Div.	—	—		Mike Ditka
1990	11	5	0	.688	348	280	1st/NFC Central Div.	1	1	NFC div. playoff game	Mike Ditka
1991	11	5	0	.688	299	269	2nd/NFC Central Div.	0	1	NFC wild-card game	Mike Ditka
1992	5	11	0	.313	295	361	T3rd/NFC Central Div.	—	—		Mike Ditka
1993	7	9	0	.438	234	230	4th/NFC Central Div.	—	—		Dave Wannstedt
1994	9	7	0	.563	271	307	T2nd/NFC Central Div.	1	1	NFC div. playoff game	Dave Wannstedt
1995	9	7	0	.563	392	360	3rd/NFC Central Div.	—	—		Dave Wannstedt
1996	7	9	0	.438	283	305	3rd/NFC Central Div.	—	—		Dave Wannstedt
1997	4	12	0	.250	263	421	5th/NFC Central Div.	—	—		Dave Wannstedt

*Decatur Staleys.
†Chicago Staleys.

FIRST-ROUND DRAFT PICKS

1936—Joe Stydahar, T, West Virginia
1937—Les McDonald, E, Nebraska
1938—Joe Gray, B, Oregon State
1939—Sid Luckman, B, Columbia
　　　Bill Osmanski, B, Holy Cross
1940—C. Turner, C, Hardin-Simmons
1941—Tom Harmon, B, Michigan*
　　　Norm Standlee, B, Stanford
　　　Don Scott, B, Ohio State
1942—Frankie Albert, B, Stanford
1943—Bob Steuber, B, Missouri
1944—Ray Evans, B, Kansas
1945—Don Lund, B, Michigan
1946—Johnny Lujack, QB, Notre Dame
1947—Bob Fenimore, B, Oklahoma A&M*
1948—Bobby Layne, QB, Texas
　　　Max Baumgardner, E, Texas
1949—Dick Harris, C, Texas
1950—Chuck Hunsinger, B, Florida
1951—Bob Williams, B, Notre Dame
　　　Billy Stone, B, Bradley
　　　Gene Schroeder, E, Virginia
1952—Jim Dooley, B, Miami
1953—Billy Anderson, B, Compton (Ca.) J.C.
1954—Stan Wallace, B, Illinois
1955—Ron Drzewiecki, B, Marquette
1956—Menan (Tex) Schriewer, E, Texas
1957—Earl Leggett, DT, Louisiana State
1958—Chuck Howley, LB, West Virginia
1959—Don Clark, B, Ohio State
1960—Roger Davis, G, Syracuse
1961—Mike Ditka, E, Pittsburgh
1962—Ron Bull, RB, Baylor
1963—Dave Behrman, C, Michigan State
1964—Dick Evey, DT, Tennessee
1965—Dick Butkus, LB, Illinois
1965—Gale Sayers, RB, Kansas
　　　Steve DeLong, DE, Tennessee
1966—George Rice, DT, Louisiana State

1967—Loyd Phillips, DE, Arkansas
1968—Mike Hull, RB, Southern California
1969—Rufus Mayes, T, Ohio State
1970—None
1971—Joe Moore, RB, Missouri
1972—Lionel Antoine, T, Southern Illinois
　　　Craig Clemons, DB, Iowa
1973—Wally Chambers, DE, Eastern Kentucky
1974—Waymond Bryant, LB, Tennessee State
　　　Dave Gallagher, DE, Michigan
1975—Walter Payton, RB, Jackson State
1976—Dennis Lick, T, Wisconsin
1977—Ted Albrecht, T, California
1978—None
1979—Dan Hampton, DT, Arkansas
　　　Al Harris, DE, Arizona State
1980—Otis Wilson, LB, Louisville
1981—Keith Van Horne, T, Southern California
1982—Jim McMahon, QB, Brigham Young
1983—Jimbo Covert, T, Pittsburgh
　　　Willie Gault, WR, Tennessee
1984—Wilber Marshall, LB, Florida
1985—William Perry, DT, Clemson
1986—Neal Anderson, RB, Florida
1987—Jim Harbaugh, QB, Michigan
1988—Brad Muster, RB, Stanford
　　　Wendell Davis, WR, Louisiana State
1989—Donnell Woolford, DB, Clemson
　　　Trace Armstrong, DE, Florida
1990—Mark Carrier, DB, Southern California
1991—Stan Thomas, T, Texas
1992—Alonzo Spellman, DE, Ohio State
1993—Curtis Conway, WR, Southern California
1994—John Thierry, LB, Alcorn State
1995—Rashaan Salaam, RB, Colorado
1996—Walt Harris, DB, Mississippi State
1997—None
1998—Curtis Enis, RB, Penn State
*First player chosen in draft.

FRANCHISE RECORDS

Most rushing yards, career
16,726—Walter Payton
Most rushing yards, season
1,852—Walter Payton, 1977
Most rushing yards, game
275—Walter Payton vs. Min., Nov. 20, 1977

Most rushing touchdowns, season
14—Gale Sayers, 1965
　　　Walter Payton, 1977
　　　Walter Payton, 1979
Most passing attempts, season
522—Erik Kramer, 1995
Most passing attempts, game
60—Erik Kramer vs. NYJ, Nov. 16, 1997

Most passes completed, season
315—Erik Kramer, 1995
Most passes completed, game
33—Bill Wade at Was., Oct. 25, 1964
Most passing yards, career
14,686—Sid Luckman
Most passing yards, season
3,838—Erik Kramer, 1995

Most passing yards, game
468—Johnny Lujack vs. Chi. Cards, Dec. 11, 1949

Most touchdown passes, season
29—Erik Kramer, 1995

Most pass receptions, career
492—Walter Payton

Most pass receptions, season
93—Johnny Morris, 1964

Most pass receptions, game
14—Jim Keane at NYG, Oct. 23, 1949

Most receiving yards, career
5,059—Johnny Morris

Most receiving yards, season
1,301—Jeff Graham, 1995

Most receiving yards, game
214—Harlon Hill at S.F., Oct. 31, 1954

Most receiving touchdowns, season
13—Ken Kavanaugh, 1947
Dick Gordon, 1970

Most touchdowns, career
125—Walter Payton

Most field goals, season
31—Kevin Butler, 1985

Longest field goal
55 yards—Bob Thomas at L.A. Rams,

Nov. 23, 1975
Kevin Butler vs. Min., Oct. 25, 1993
Kevin Butler at T.B., Dec. 12, 1993

Most interceptions, career
38—Gary Fencik

Most interceptions, season
10—Mark Carrier, 1990

Most sacks, career
124.5—Richard Dent

Most sacks, season
17.5—Richard Dent, 1984

SERIES RECORDS

Chicago vs.: Arizona 54-25-6; Atlanta 9-9; Buffalo 5-2; Carolina 1-0; Cincinnati 2-4; Dallas 7-9; Denver 5-6; Detroit 71-53-3; Green Bay 82-67-6; Indianapolis 16-21; Jacksonville 1-0; Kansas City 4-3; Miami 3-5; Minnesota 32-39-2; New England 2-5; New Orleans 10-7; N.Y. Giants 25-16-2; N.Y. Jets 4-2; Oakland 4-5; Philadelphia 25-4-1; Pittsburgh 19-5-1; St. Louis 36-25-3; San Diego 3-4; San Francisco 25-25-1; Seattle 2-4; Tampa Bay 30-10; Tennessee 3-4; Washington 14-13.
NOTE: Includes records as Decatur Staleys in 1920 and Chicago Staleys in 1921.

COACHING RECORDS

Hunk Anderson-Luke Johnsos*, 23-11-2 (1-1); Neill Armstrong, 30-34-0 (0-1); Mike Ditka, 106-62-0 (6-6); Jim Dooley, 20-36-0; Paddy Driscoll, 14-9-1 (0-1); Abe Gibron, 11-30-1; George Halas, 318-148-31 (6-3); Ralph Jones, 24-10-7; Jack Pardee, 20-22-0 (0-1); Dave Wannstedt, 36-44-0 (1-1).
NOTE: Playoff games in parentheses.
*Co-coaches.

RETIRED UNIFORM NUMBERS

No.	Player
3	Bronko Nagurski
5	George McAfee
7	George Halas
28	Willie Galimore
34	Walter Payton
40	Gale Sayers
41	Brian Piccolo
42	Sid Luckman
51	Dick Butkus
56	Bill Hewitt
61	Bill George
66	Bulldog Turner
77	Red Grange

CINCINNATI BENGALS
YEAR-BY-YEAR RECORDS

| | | | REGULAR SEASON | | | | | | PLAYOFFS | |
Year	W	L	T	Pct.	PF	PA	Finish	W	L	Highest round	Coach
1968*	3	11	0	.214	215	329	5th/Western Div.	—	—		Paul Brown
1969*	4	9	1	.308	280	367	5th/Western Div.	—	—		Paul Brown
1970	8	6	0	.571	312	255	1st/AFC Central Div.	0	1	AFC div. playoff game	Paul Brown
1971	4	10	0	.286	284	265	4th/AFC Central Div.	—	—		Paul Brown
1972	8	6	0	.571	299	229	3rd/AFC Central Div.	—	—		Paul Brown
1973	10	4	0	.714	286	231	1st/AFC Central Div.	0	1	AFC div. playoff game	Paul Brown
1974	7	7	0	.500	283	259	T2nd/AFC Central Div.	—	—		Paul Brown
1975	11	3	0	.786	340	246	2nd/AFC Central Div.	0	1	AFC div. playoff game	Paul Brown
1976	10	4	0	.714	335	210	2nd/AFC Central Div.	—	—		Bill Johnson
1977	8	6	0	.571	238	235	T2nd/AFC Central Div.	—	—		Bill Johnson
1978	4	12	0	.250	252	284	4th/AFC Central Div.	—	—		B. Johnson, H. Rice
1979	4	12	0	.250	337	421	4th/AFC Central Div.	—	—		Homer Rice
1980	6	10	0	.375	244	312	4th/AFC Central Div.	—	—		Forrest Gregg
1981	12	4	0	.750	421	304	1st/AFC Central Div.	2	1	Super Bowl	Forrest Gregg
1982	7	2	0	.778	232	177	T2nd/AFC	0	1	AFC first-round pl. game	Forrest Gregg
1983	7	9	0	.438	346	302	3rd/AFC Central Div.	—	—		Forrest Gregg
1984	8	8	0	.500	339	339	2nd/AFC Central Div.	—	—		Sam Wyche
1985	7	9	0	.438	441	437	T2nd/AFC Central Div.	—	—		Sam Wyche
1986	10	6	0	.625	409	394	2nd/AFC Central Div.	—	—		Sam Wyche
1987	4	11	0	.267	285	370	4th/AFC Central Div.	—	—		Sam Wyche
1988	12	4	0	.750	448	329	1st/AFC Central Div.	2	1	Super Bowl	Sam Wyche
1989	8	8	0	.500	404	285	4th/AFC Central Div.	—	—		Sam Wyche
1990	9	7	0	.563	360	352	1st/AFC Central Div.	1	1	AFC div. playoff game	Sam Wyche
1991	3	13	0	.188	263	435	4th/AFC Central Div.	—	—		Sam Wyche
1992	5	11	0	.313	274	364	4th/AFC Central Div.	—	—		David Shula

			REGULAR SEASON						PLAYOFFS		
Year	W	L	T	Pct.	PF	PA	Finish	W	L	Highest round	Coach
1993	3	13	0	.188	187	319	4th/AFC Central Div.	—	—		David Shula
1994	3	13	0	.188	276	406	3rd/AFC Central Div.	—	—		David Shula
1995	7	9	0	.438	349	374	T2nd/AFC Central Div.	—	—		David Shula
1996	8	8	0	.500	372	369	T3rd/AFC Central Div.	—	—		D. Shula, B. Coslet
1997	7	9	0	.438	355	405	4th/AFC Central Div.	—	—		Bruce Coslet

*American Football League.

FIRST-ROUND DRAFT PICKS

1968—Bob Johnson, C, Tennessee
1969—Greg Cook, QB, Cincinnati
1970—Mike Reid, DT, Penn State
1971—Vernon Holland, T, Tennessee State
1972—Sherman White, DE, California
1973—Issac Curtis, WR, San Diego State
1974—Bill Kollar, DT, Montana State
1975—Glenn Cameron, LB, Florida
1976—Billy Brooks, WR, Oklahoma
    Archie Griffin, RB, Ohio State
1977—Eddie Edwards, DT, Miami (Fla.)
    Wilson Whitley, DT, Houston
    Mike Cobb, TE, Michigan State
1978—Ross Browner, DE, Notre Dame
    Blair Bush, C, Washington
1979—Jack Thompson, QB, Washington State
    Charles Alexander, RB, Louisiana State
1980—Anthony Munoz, T, Southern California
1981—David Verser, WR, Kansas
1982—Glen Collins, DE, Mississippi State
1983—Dave Rimington, C, Nebraska
1984—Ricky Hunley, LB, Arizona

    Pete Koch, DE, Maryland
    Brian Blados, T, North Carolina
1985—Eddie Brown, WR, Miami (Fla.)
    Emanuel King, LB, Alabama
1986—Joe Kelly, LB, Washington
    Tim McGee, WR, Tennessee
1987—Jason Buck, DT, Brigham Young
1988—Rickey Dixon, S, Oklahoma
1989—None
1990—James Francis, LB, Baylor
1991—Alfred Williams, LB, Colorado
1992—David Klingler, QB, Houston
    Darryl Williams, DB, Miami (Fla.)
1993—John Copeland, DE, Alabama
1994—Dan Wilkinson, DT, Ohio State*
1995—Ki-Jana Carter, RB, Penn State*
1996—Willie Anderson, T, Auburn
1997—Reinard Wilson, LB, Florida State
1998—Takeo Spikes, LB, Auburn
    Brian Simmons, LB, North Carolina
*First player chosen in draft.

FRANCHISE RECORDS

Most rushing yards, career
6,447—James Brooks
Most rushing yards, season
1,239—James Brooks, 1989
Most rushing yards, game
246—Corey Dillon vs. Ten., Dec. 4, 1997
Most rushing touchdowns, season
15—Ickey Woods, 1988
Most passing attempts, season
567—Jeff Blake, 1995
Most passing attempts, game
56—Ken Anderson at S.D., Dec. 20, 1982
Most passes completed, season
326—Jeff Blake, 1995
Most passes completed, game
40—Ken Anderson at S.D., Dec. 20, 1982
Most passing yards, career
32,838—Ken Anderson
Most passing yards, season
3,959—Boomer Esiason, 1986

Most passing yards, game
490—Boomer Esiason at L.A. Rams, Oct. 7, 1990
Most touchdown passes, season
29—Ken Anderson, 1981
Most pass receptions, career
417—Cris Collinsworth
Most pass receptions, season
100—Carl Pickens, 1996
Most pass receptions, game
12—James Brooks at Min., Dec. 25, 1989
    Carl Pickens vs. Pit., Nov. 10, 1996
Most receiving yards, career
7,101—Isaac Curtis
Most receiving yards, season
1,273—Eddie Brown, 1988
Most receiving yards, game
216—Eddie Brown vs. Pit., Nov. 16, 1988
Most receiving touchdowns, season
17—Carl Pickens, 1995

Most touchdowns, career
70—Pete Johnson
Most field goals, season
29—Doug Pelfrey, 1995
Longest field goal
55 yards—Chris Bahr vs. Hou., Sept. 23, 1979
Most interceptions, career
65—Ken Riley
Most interceptions, season
9—Ken Riley, 1976
Most sacks, career
84.5—Eddie Edwards
Most sacks, season
21.5—Coy Bacon, 1976

SERIES RECORDS

Cincinnati vs.: Arizona 4-2; Atlanta 7-2; Baltimore 3-1; Buffalo 10-8; Carolina 0-0; Chicago 4-2; Dallas 3-4; Denver 6-13; Detroit 3-3; Green Bay 4-4; Indianapolis 8-10; Jacksonville 4-2; Kansas City 9-11; Miami 3-12; Minnesota 4-4; New England 7-9; New Orleans 4-5; N.Y. Giants 4-2; N.Y. Jets 6-10; Oakland 7-15; Philadelphia 6-2; Pittsburgh 23-32; St. Louis 5-3; San Diego 9-14; San Francisco 1-7; Seattle 7-7; Tampa Bay 3-2; Tennessee 28-29-1; Washington 2-4.

COACHING RECORDS

Paul Brown, 55-56-1 (0-3); Bruce Coslet, 14-11; Forrest Gregg, 32-25-0 (2-2); Bill Johnson, 18-15-0; Homer Rice, 8-19-0; Dave Shula, 19-52-0; Sam Wyche, 61-66-0 (3-2). NOTE: Playoff games in parentheses.

RETIRED UNIFORM NUMBERS

No.	Player
54	Bob Johnson

DALLAS COWBOYS
YEAR-BY-YEAR RECORDS

	REGULAR SEASON						PLAYOFFS			
Year	W	L	T	Pct.	PF	PA	Finish	W	L	Highest round	Coach
1960	0	11	1	.000	177	369	7th/Western Conf.	—	—		Tom Landry
1961	4	9	1	.308	236	380	6th/Eastern Conf.	—	—		Tom Landry
1962	5	8	1	.385	398	402	5th/Eastern Conf.	—	—		Tom Landry
1963	4	10	0	.286	305	378	5th/Eastern Conf.	—	—		Tom Landry
1964	5	8	1	.385	250	289	5th/Eastern Conf.	—	—		Tom Landry
1965	7	7	0	.500	325	280	T2nd/Eastern Conf.	—	—		Tom Landry
1966	10	3	1	.769	445	239	1st/Eastern Conf.	0	1	NFL championship game	Tom Landry
1967	9	5	0	.643	342	268	1st/Capitol Div.	1	1	NFL championship game	Tom Landry
1968	12	2	0	.857	431	186	1st/Capitol Div.	0	1	E. Conf. championship game	Tom Landry
1969	11	2	1	.846	369	223	1st/Capitol Div.	0	1	E. Conf. championship game	Tom Landry
1970	10	4	0	.714	299	221	1st/NFC Eastern Div.	2	1	Super Bowl	Tom Landry
1971	11	3	0	.786	406	222	1st/NFC Eastern Div.	3	0	Super Bowl champ	Tom Landry
1972	10	4	0	.714	319	240	2nd/NFC Eastern Div.	1	1	NFC championship game	Tom Landry
1973	10	4	0	.714	382	203	1st/NFC Eastern Div.	1	1	NFC championship game	Tom Landry
1974	8	6	0	.571	297	235	3rd/NFC Eastern Div.	—	—		Tom Landry
1975	10	4	0	.714	350	268	2nd/NFC Eastern Div.	2	1	Super Bowl	Tom Landry
1976	11	3	0	.786	296	194	1st/NFC Eastern Div.	0	1	NFC div. playoff game	Tom Landry
1977	12	2	0	.857	345	212	1st/NFC Eastern Div.	3	0	Super Bowl champ	Tom Landry
1978	12	4	0	.750	384	208	1st/NFC Eastern Div.	2	1	Super Bowl	Tom Landry
1979	11	5	0	.688	371	313	1st/NFC Eastern Div.	0	1	NFC div. playoff game	Tom Landry
1980	12	4	0	.750	454	311	2nd/NFC Eastern Div.	2	1	NFC championship game	Tom Landry
1981	12	4	0	.750	367	277	1st/NFC Eastern Div.	1	1	NFC championship game	Tom Landry
1982	6	3	0	.667	226	145	2nd/NFC	2	1	NFC championship game	Tom Landry
1983	12	4	0	.750	479	360	2nd/NFC Eastern Div.	0	1	NFC wild-card game	Tom Landry
1984	9	7	0	.563	308	308	T3rd/NFC Eastern Div.	—	—		Tom Landry
1985	10	6	0	.625	357	333	1st/NFC Eastern Div.	0	1	NFC div. playoff game	Tom Landry
1986	7	9	0	.438	346	337	3rd/NFC Eastern Div.	—	—		Tom Landry
1987	7	8	0	.467	340	348	T2nd/NFC Eastern Div.	—	—		Tom Landry
1988	3	13	0	.188	265	381	5th/NFC Eastern Div.	—	—		Tom Landry
1989	1	15	0	.063	204	393	5th/NFC Eastern Div.	—	—		Jimmy Johnson
1990	7	9	0	.438	244	308	4th/NFC Eastern Div.	—	—		Jimmy Johnson
1991	11	5	0	.688	342	310	2nd/NFC Eastern Div.	1	1	NFC div. playoff game	Jimmy Johnson
1992	13	3	0	.813	409	243	1st/NFC Eastern Div.	3	0	Super Bowl champ	Jimmy Johnson
1993	12	4	0	.750	376	229	1st/NFC Eastern Div.	3	0	Super Bowl champ	Jimmy Johnson
1994	12	4	0	.750	414	248	1st/NFC Eastern Div.	1	1	NFC championship game	Barry Switzer
1995	12	4	0	.750	435	291	1st/NFC Eastern Div.	3	0	Super Bowl champ	Barry Switzer
1996	10	6	0	.625	286	250	1st/NFC Eastern Div.	1	1	NFC div. playoff game	Barry Switzer
1997	6	10	0	.375	304	314	4th/NFC Eastern Div.	—	—		Barry Switzer

FIRST-ROUND DRAFT PICKS

1961—Bob Lilly, DT, Texas Christian
1962—None
1963—Lee Roy Jordan, LB, Alabama
1964—Scott Appleton, DT, Texas
1965—Craig Morton, QB, California
1966—John Niland, G, Iowa
1967—None
1968—Dennis Homan, WR, Alabama
1969—Calvin Hill, RB, Yale
1970—Duane Thomas, RB, West Texas State
1971—Tody Smith, DE, Southern California
1972—Bill Thomas, RB, Boston College
1973—Billy Joe DuPree, TE, Michigan State
1974—Ed Jones, DE, Tennessee State*
    Charles Young, RB, North Carolina State
1975—Randy White, LB, Maryland
    Thomas Henderson, LB, Langston
1976—Aaron Kyle, DB, Wyoming
1977—Tony Dorsett, RB, Pittsburgh
1978—Larry Bethea, DE, Michigan State
1979—Robert Shaw, C, Tennessee
1980—None

1981—Howard Richards, T, Missouri
1982—Rod Hill, DB, Kentucky State
1983—Jim Jeffcoat, DE, Arizona State
1984—Billy Cannon Jr., LB, Texas A&M
1985—Kevin Brooks, DE, Michigan
1986—Mike Sherrard, WR, UCLA
1987—Danny Noonan, DT, Nebraska
1988—Michael Irvin, WR, Miami (Fla.)
1989—Troy Aikman, QB, UCLA*
1990—Emmitt Smith, RB, Florida
1991—Russell Maryland, DL, Miami (Fla.)*
    Alvin Harper, WR, Tennessee
    Kelvin Pritchett, DT, Mississippi
1992—Kevin Smith, DB, Texas A&M
    Robert Jones, LB, East Carolina
1993—None
1994—Shante Carver, DE, Arizona State
1995—None
1996—None
1997—David LaFleur, TE, Louisiana State
1998—Greg Ellis, DE, North Carolina
    *First player chosen in draft.

FRANCHISE RECORDS

Most rushing yards, career
12,036—Tony Dorsett
Most rushing yards, season
1,773—Emmitt Smith, 1995
Most rushing yards, game
237—Emmitt Smith at Phi., Oct. 31, 1993
Most rushing touchdowns, season
25—Emmitt Smith, 1995
Most passing attempts, season
533—Danny White, 1983
Most passing attempts, game
53—Troy Aikman at Cin., Dec. 14, 1997
Most passes completed, season
334—Danny White, 1983
Most passes completed, game
34—Troy Aikman at NYG, Oct. 5, 1997
Most passing yards, career
26,016—Troy Aikman

Most passing yards, season
3,980—Danny White, 1983
Most passing yards, game
460—Don Meredith at S.F., Nov. 10, 1963
Most touchdown passes, season
29—Danny White, 1983
Most pass receptions, career
666—Michael Irvin
Most pass receptions, season
111—Michael Irvin, 1995
Most pass receptions, game
13—Lance Rentzel vs. Was., Nov. 19, 1967
Most receiving yards, career
10,680—Michael Irvin
Most receiving yards, season
1,603—Michael Irvin, 1995
Most receiving yards, game
246—Bob Hayes at Was., Nov. 13, 1966

Most receiving touchdowns, season
14—Frank Clarke, 1962
Most touchdowns, career
119—Emmitt Smith
Most field goals, season
34—Richie Cunningham, 1997
Longest field goal
54 yards—Toni Fritsch at NYG,
Sept. 24, 1972
Ken Willis at Cle., Sept. 1, 1991
Most interceptions, career
52—Mel Renfro
Most interceptions, season
11—Everson Walls, 1981
Most sacks, career
113—Harvey Martin
Most sacks, season
20—Harvey Martin, 1977

SERIES RECORDS

Dallas vs.: Arizona 47-23-1; Atlanta 11-6; Buffalo 3-3; Carolina 0-1; Chicago 9-7; Cincinnati 4-3; Denver 4-2; Detroit 7-6; Green Bay 8-10; Indianapolis 7-3; Jacksonville 1-0; Kansas City 4-2; Miami 2-6; Minnesota 9-6; New England 7-0; New Orleans 14-3; N.Y. Giants 44-25-2; N.Y. Jets 5-1; Oakland 3-3; Philadelphia 45-29; Pittsburgh 14-11; St. Louis 8-9; San Diego 5-1; San Francisco 7-12-1; Seattle 4-1; Tampa Bay 6-0; Tennessee 5-4; Washington 41-31-2.

COACHING RECORDS

Jimmy Johnson, 44-36-0 (7-1); Tom Landry, 250-162-6 (20-16); Barry Switzer, 40-24-0 (5-2).
NOTE: Playoff games in parentheses.

RETIRED UNIFORM NUMBERS

No.	Player
None	

DENVER BRONCOS
YEAR-BY-YEAR RECORDS

	REGULAR SEASON							PLAYOFFS			
Year	W	L	T	Pct.	PF	PA	Finish	W	L	Highest round	Coach
1960*	4	9	1	.308	309	393	4th/Western Div.	—	—		Frank Filchock
1961*	3	11	0	.214	251	432	3rd/Western Div.	—	—		Frank Filchock
1962*	7	7	0	.500	353	334	2nd/Western Div.	—	—		Jack Faulkner
1963*	2	11	1	.154	301	473	4th/Western Div.	—	—		Jack Faulkner
1964*	2	11	1	.154	240	438	4th/Western Div.	—	—		J. Faulkner, M. Speedie
1965*	4	10	0	.286	303	392	4th/Western Div.	—	—		Mac Speedie
1966*	4	10	0	.286	196	381	4th/Western Div.	—	—		M. Speedie, Ray Malavasi
1967*	3	11	0	.214	256	409	4th/Western Div.	—	—		Lou Saban
1968*	5	9	0	.357	255	404	4th/Western Div.	—	—		Lou Saban
1969*	5	8	1	.385	297	344	4th/Western Div.	—	—		Lou Saban
1970	5	8	1	.385	253	264	4th/AFC Western Div.	—	—		Lou Saban
1971	4	9	1	.308	203	275	4th/AFC Western Div.	—	—		Lou Saban, Jerry Smith
1972	5	9	0	.357	325	350	3rd/AFC Western Div.	—	—		John Ralston
1973	7	5	2	.571	354	296	T2nd/AFC Western Div.	—	—		John Ralston
1974	7	6	1	.536	302	294	2nd/AFC Western Div.	—	—		John Ralston
1975	6	8	0	.429	254	307	2nd/AFC Western Div.	—	—		John Ralston
1976	9	5	0	.643	315	206	2nd/AFC Western Div.	—	—		John Ralston
1977	12	2	0	.857	274	148	1st/AFC Western Div.	2	1	Super Bowl	Red Miller
1978	10	6	0	.625	282	198	1st/AFC Western Div.	0	1	AFC div. playoff game	Red Miller
1979	10	6	0	.625	289	262	2nd/AFC Western Div.	0	1	AFC wild-card game	Red Miller
1980	8	8	0	.500	310	323	T3rd/AFC Western Div.	—	—		Red Miller
1981	10	6	0	.625	321	289	2nd/AFC Western Div.	—	—		Dan Reeves
1982	2	7	0	.222	148	226	12th/AFC	—	—		Dan Reeves
1983	9	7	0	.563	302	327	T2nd/AFC Western Div.	0	1	AFC wild-card game	Dan Reeves
1984	13	3	0	.813	353	241	1st/AFC Western Div.	0	1	AFC div. playoff game	Dan Reeves
1985	11	5	0	.688	380	329	2nd/AFC Western Div.	—	—		Dan Reeves
1986	11	5	0	.688	378	327	1st/AFC Western Div.	2	1	Super Bowl	Dan Reeves
1987	10	4	1	.700	379	288	1st/AFC Western Div.	2	1	Super Bowl	Dan Reeves
1988	8	8	0	.500	327	352	2nd/AFC Western Div.	—	—		Dan Reeves

		REGULAR SEASON						PLAYOFFS		
Year	W	L	T	Pct.	PF	PA	Finish	W	L	Highest round	Coach
1989	11	5	0	.688	362	226	1st/AFC Western Div.	2	1	Super Bowl	Dan Reeves
1990	5	11	0	.313	331	374	5th/AFC Western Div.	—	—		Dan Reeves
1991	12	4	0	.750	304	235	1st/AFC Western Div.	1	1	AFC championship game	Dan Reeves
1992	8	8	0	.500	262	329	3rd/AFC Western Div.	—	—		Dan Reeves
1993	9	7	0	.563	373	284	3rd/AFC Western Div.	0	1	AFC wild-card game	Wade Phillips
1994	7	9	0	.438	347	396	4th/AFC Western Div.	—	—		Wade Phillips
1995	8	8	0	.500	388	345	T3rd/AFC Western Div.	—	—		Mike Shanahan
1996	13	3	0	.813	391	275	1st/AFC Western Div.	0	1	AFC div. playoff game	Mike Shanahan
1997	12	4	0	.750	472	287	2nd/AFC Western Div.	4	0	Super Bowl champ	Mike Shanahan

*American Football League.

FIRST-ROUND DRAFT PICKS

1960—Roger Leclerc, C, Trinity (Conn.)
1961—Bob Gaiters, RB, New Mexico State
1962—Merlin Olsen, DT, Utah State
1963—Kermit Alexander, DB, UCLA
1964—Bob Brown, T, Nebraska
1965—None
1966—Jerry Shay, DT, Purdue
1967—Floyd Little, RB, Syracuse
1968—None
1969—None
1970—Bob Anderson, RB, Colorado
1971—Marv Montgomery, T, Southern California
1972—Riley Odoms, TE, Houston
1973—Otis Armstrong, RB, Purdue
1974—Randy Gradishar, LB, Ohio State
1975—Louis Wright, DB, San Jose State
1976—Tom Glassic, G, Virginia
1977—Steve Schindler, G, Boston College
1978—Don Latimer, DT, Miami (Fla.)
1979—Kevin Clark, T, Nebraska

1980—None
1981—Dennis Smith, DB, Southern California
1982—Gerald Willhite, RB, San Jose State
1983—Chris Hinton, G, Northwestern
1984—None
1985—Steve Sewell, RB, Oklahoma
1986—None
1987—Ricky Nattiel, WR, Florida
1988—Ted Gregory, DT, Syracuse
1989—Steve Atwater, DB, Arkansas
1990—None
1991—Mike Croel, LB, Nebraska
1992—Tommy Maddox, QB, UCLA
1993—Dan Williams, DE, Toledo
1994—None
1995—None
1996—John Mobley, LB, Kutztown (Pa.)
1997—Trevor Pryce, DT, Clemson
1998—Marcus Nash, WR, Tennessee

FRANCHISE RECORDS

Most rushing yards, career
6,323—Floyd Little
Most rushing yards, season
1,750—Terrell Davis, 1997
Most rushing yards, game
215—Terrell Davis vs. Cin., Sept. 21, 1997
Most rushing touchdowns, season
15—Terrell Davis, 1997
Most passing attempts, season
605—John Elway, 1985
Most passing attempts, game
59—John Elway at G.B., Oct. 10, 1993
Most passes completed, season
348—John Elway, 1993
Most passes completed, game
36—John Elway vs. S.D., Sept. 4, 1994
Most passing yards, career
48,669—John Elway
Most passing yards, season
4,030—John Elway, 1993

Most passing yards, game
447—Frank Tripucka at Buf., Sept. 15, 1962
Most touchdown passes, season
27—John Elway, 1997
Most pass receptions, career
543—Lionel Taylor
Most pass receptions, season
100—Lionel Taylor, 1961
Most pass receptions, game
13—Lionel Taylor vs. Oak., Nov. 29, 1964
   Robert Anderson vs. Chi., Sept. 30, 1973
   Shannon Sharpe vs. S.D., Oct. 6, 1996
Most receiving yards, career
6,872—Lionel Taylor
Most receiving yards, season
1,244—Steve Watson, 1981
Most receiving yards, game
199—Lionel Taylor vs. Buf., Nov. 27, 1960

Most receiving touchdowns, season
13—Steve Watson, 1981
Most touchdowns, career
54—Floyd Little
Most field goals, season
31—Jason Elam, 1995
Longest field goal
57 yards—Fred Steinfort vs. Was., Oct. 13, 1980
Most interceptions, career
44—Steve Foley
Most interceptions, season
11—Goose Gonsoulin, 1960
Most sacks, career
97.5—Simon Fletcher
Most sacks, season
16—Simon Fletcher, 1992

SERIES RECORDS

Denver vs.: Arizona 4-0-1; Atlanta 6-3; Baltimore 1-0; Buffalo 12-17-1; Carolina 1-0; Chicago 6-5; Cincinnati 13-6; Dallas 2-4; Detroit 4-3; Green Bay 4-3-1; Indianapolis 9-2; Jacksonville 1-0; Kansas City 32-43; Miami 2-5-1; Minnesota 4-5; New England 19-12; New Orleans 4-2; N.Y. Giants 3-3; N.Y. Jets 13-12-1; Oakland 24-49-2; Philadelphia 2-6; Pittsburgh 10-6-1; San Diego 40-35-1; St. Louis 4-4; San Francisco 4-4; Seattle 26-15; Tampa Bay 3-1; Tennessee 11-20-1; Washington 4-3.

COACHING RECORDS

Jack Faulkner, 9-22-1; Frank Filchock, 7-20-1; Ray Malavasi, 4-8-0; Red Miller, 40-22 (2-3); Wade Phillips, 16-16-0 (0-1); John Ralston, 34-33-3; Dan Reeves, 110-73-1 (7-6); Lou Saban, 20-42-3; Mike Shanahan, 33-15-0 (4-1); Jerry Smith, 2-3; Mac Speedie, 6-19-1.
NOTE: Playoff games in parentheses.

RETIRED UNIFORM NUMBERS

No.	Player
18	Frank Tripucka
44	Floyd Little

DETROIT LIONS
YEAR-BY-YEAR RECORDS

		REGULAR SEASON						PLAYOFFS			
Year	W	L	T	Pct.	PF	PA	Finish	W	L	Highest round	Coach
1930*	5	6	3	.455	...	...	T7th				Tubby Griffen
1931*	11	3	0	.786	...	...	2nd				Potsy Clark
1932*	6	2	4	.750	...	...	3rd				Potsy Clark
1933*	6	5	0	.545	128	87	2nd/Western Div.				Potsy Clark
1934	10	3	0	.769	238	59	2nd/Western Div.				Potsy Clark
1935	7	3	2	.700	191	111	1st/Western Div.	1	0	NFL champ	Potsy Clark
1936	8	4	0	.667	235	102	3rd/Western Div.	—	—		Potsy Clark
1937	7	4	0	.636	180	105	T2nd/Western Div.	—	—		Dutch Clark
1938	7	4	0	.636	119	108	2nd/Western Div.	—	—		Dutch Clark
1939	6	5	0	.545	145	150	3rd/Western Div.	—	—		Gus Henderson
1940	5	5	1	.500	138	153	3rd/Western Div.	—	—		Potsy Clark
1941	4	6	1	.400	121	195	3rd/Western Div.	—	—		Bill Edwards
1942	0	11	0	.000	38	263	5th/Western Div.	—	—		B. Edwards, John Karcis
1943	3	6	1	.333	178	218	3rd/Western Div.	—	—		Gus Dorais
1944	6	3	1	.667	216	151	T2nd/Western Div.	—	—		Gus Dorais
1945	7	3	0	.700	195	194	2nd/Western Div.	—	—		Gus Dorais
1946	1	10	0	.091	142	310	2nd/Western Div.	—	—		Gus Dorais
1947	3	9	0	.250	231	305	5th/Western Div.	—	—		Gus Dorais
1948	2	10	0	.167	200	407	5th/Western Div.	—	—		Bo McMillin
1949	4	8	0	.333	237	259	4th/Western Div.	—	—		Bo McMillin
1950	6	6	0	.500	321	285	4th/National Conf.	—	—		Bo McMillin
1951	7	4	1	.636	336	259	T2nd/National Conf.	—	—		Buddy Parker
1952	9	3	0	.750	344	192	1st/National Conf.	2	0	NFL champ	Buddy Parker
1953	10	2	0	.833	271	205	1st/Western Conf.	1	0	NFL champ	Buddy Parker
1954	9	2	1	.818	337	189	1st/Western Conf.	0	1	NFL championship game	Buddy Parker
1955	3	9	0	.250	230	275	6th/Western Conf.	—	—		Buddy Parker
1956	9	3	0	.750	300	188	2nd/Western Conf.	—	—		Buddy Parker
1957	8	4	0	.667	251	231	1st/Western Conf.	2	0	NFL champ	George Wilson
1958	4	7	1	.364	261	276	5th/Western Conf.	—	—		George Wilson
1959	3	8	1	.273	203	275	5th/Western Conf.	—	—		George Wilson
1960	7	5	0	.583	239	212	T2nd/Western Conf.	—	—		George Wilson
1961	8	5	1	.615	270	258	2nd/Western Conf.	—	—		George Wilson
1962	11	3	0	.786	315	177	2nd/Western Conf.	—	—		George Wilson
1963	5	8	1	.385	326	265	T4th/Western Conf.	—	—		George Wilson
1964	7	5	2	.583	280	260	4th/Western Conf.	—	—		George Wilson
1965	6	7	1	.462	257	295	6th/Western Conf.	—	—		Harry Gilmer
1966	4	9	1	.308	206	317	T6th/Western Conf.	—	—		Harry Gilmer
1967	5	7	2	.417	260	259	3rd/Central Div.	—	—		Joe Schmidt
1968	4	8	2	.333	207	241	4th/Central Div.	—	—		Joe Schmidt
1969	9	4	1	.692	259	188	2nd/Central Div.	—	—		Joe Schmidt
1970	10	4	0	.714	347	202	2nd/NFC Central Div.	0	1	NFC div. playoff game	Joe Schmidt
1971	7	6	1	.538	341	286	2nd/NFC Central Div.	—	—		Joe Schmidt
1972	8	5	1	.607	339	290	2nd/NFC Central Div.	—	—		Joe Schmidt
1973	6	7	1	.464	271	247	2nd/NFC Central Div.	—	—		Don McCafferty
1974	7	7	0	.500	256	270	2nd/NFC Central Div.	—	—		Rick Forzano
1975	7	7	0	.500	245	262	2nd/NFC Central Div.	—	—		Rick Forzano
1976	6	8	0	.429	262	220	3rd/NFC Central Div.	—	—		R. Forzano, T. Hudspeth
1977	6	8	0	.429	183	252	3rd/NFC Central Div.	—	—		Tommy Hudspeth
1978	7	9	0	.438	290	300	T3rd/NFC Central Div.	—	—		Monte Clark
1979	2	14	0	.125	219	365	5th/NFC Central Div.	—	—		Monte Clark
1980	9	7	0	.563	334	272	2nd/NFC Central Div.	—	—		Monte Clark
1981	8	8	0	.500	397	322	2nd/NFC Central Div.	—	—		Monte Clark
1982	4	5	0	.444	181	176	T8th/NFC	0	1	NFC first-round pl. game	Monte Clark
1983	9	7	0	.563	347	286	1st/NFC Central Div.	0	1	NFC div. playoff game	Monte Clark
1984	4	11	1	.281	283	408	4th/NFC Central Div.	—	—		Monte Clark
1985	7	9	0	.438	307	366	T3rd/NFC Central Div.	—	—		Darryl Rogers
1986	5	11	0	.313	277	326	3rd/NFC Central Div.	—	—		Darryl Rogers

	REGULAR SEASON							PLAYOFFS			
Year	W	L	T	Pct.	PF	PA	Finish	W	L	Highest round	Coach
1987	4	11	0	.267	269	384	T4th/NFC Central Div.	—	—		Darryl Rogers
1988	4	12	0	.250	220	313	T4th/NFC Central Div.	—	—		Darryl Rogers
1989	7	9	0	.438	312	364	3rd/NFC Central Div.	—	—		Wayne Fontes
1990	6	10	0	.375	373	413	T2nd/NFC Central Div.	—	—		Wayne Fontes
1991	12	4	0	.750	339	295	1st/NFC Central Div.	1	1	NFC championship game	Wayne Fontes
1992	5	11	0	.313	273	332	T3rd/NFC Central Div.	—	—		Wayne Fontes
1993	10	6	0	.625	298	292	1st/NFC Central Div.	0	1	NFC wild-card game	Wayne Fontes
1994	9	7	0	.563	357	342	T2nd/NFC Central Div.	0	1	NFC wild-card game	Wayne Fontes
1995	10	6	0	.625	436	336	2nd/NFC Central Div.	0	1	NFC wild-card game	Wayne Fontes
1996	5	11	0	.313	302	368	5th/NFC Central Div.	—	—		Wayne Fontes
1997	9	7	0	.563	379	306	T3rd/NFC Central Div.	0	1	NFC wild-card game	Bobby Ross

*Portsmouth Spartans.

FIRST-ROUND DRAFT PICKS

1936—Sid Wagner, G, Michigan State
1937—Lloyd Cardwell, B, Nebraska
1938—Alex Wojciechowicz, C, Fordham
1939—John Pingel, B, Michigan State
1940—Doyle Nave, B, Southern California
1941—Jim Thomason, B, Texas A&M
1942—Bob Westfall, B, Michigan
1943—Frank Sinkwich, B, Georgia*
1944—Otto Graham, B, Northwestern
1945—Frank Szymanski, B, Notre Dame
1946—Bill Dellastatious, B, Missouri
1947—Glenn Davis, B, Army
1948—Y.A. Tittle, B, Louisiana State
1949—John Rauch, B, Georgia
1950—Leon Hart, E, Notre Dame*
    Joe Watson, C, Rice
1951—None
1952—None
1953—Harley Sewell, G, Texas
1954—Dick Chapman, T, Rice
1955—Dave Middleton, B, Auburn
1956—Howard Cassidy, B, Ohio State
1957—Bill Glass, G, Baylor
1958—Alex Karras, DT, Iowa
1959—Nick Pietrosante, B, Notre Dame
1960—John Robinson, DB, Louisiana State
1961—None
1962—John Hadl, QB, Kansas
1963—Daryl Sanders, T, Ohio State
1964—Pete Beathard, QB, Southern California
1965—Tom Nowatzke, RB, Indiana
1966—None
1967—Mel Farr, RB, UCLA
1968—Greg Landry, QB, Massachusetts
    Earl McCullouch, E, Southern California

1969—None
1970—Steve Owens, RB, Oklahoma
1971—Bob Bell, DT, Cincinnati
1972—Herb Orvis, DE, Colorado
1973—Ernie Price, DE, Texas A&I
1974—Ed O'Neil, LB, Penn State
1975—Lynn Boden, G, South Dakota State
1976—James Hunter, DB, Grambling State
    Lawrence Gaines, FB, Wyoming
1977—None
1978—Luther Bradley, DB, Notre Dame
1979—Keith Dorney, T, Penn State
1980—Billy Sims, RB, Oklahoma*
1981—Mark Nichols, WR, San Jose State
1982—Jimmy Williams, LB, Nebraska
1983—James Jones, RB, Florida
1984—David Lewis, TE, California
1985—Lomas Brown, T, Florida
1986—Chuck Long, QB, Iowa
1987—Reggie Rogers, DE, Washington
1988—Bennie Blades, S, Miami (Fla.)
1989—Barry Sanders, RB, Oklahoma State
1990—Andre Ware, QB, Houston
1991—Herman Moore, WR, Virginia
1992—Robert Porcher, DE, South Carolina State
1993—None
1994—Johnnie Morton, WR, Southern California
1995—Luther Elliss, DT, Utah
1996—Reggie Brown, LB, Texas A&M
    Jeff Hartings, G, Penn State
1997—Bryant Westbrook, DB, Texas
1998—Terry Fair, DB, Tennessee
    *First player chosen in draft.

FRANCHISE RECORDS

Most rushing yards, career
13,778—Barry Sanders
Most rushing yards, season
2,053—Barry Sanders, 1997
Most rushing yards, game
237—Barry Sanders vs. T.B., Nov. 13, 1994
Most rushing touchdowns, season
16—Barry Sanders, 1991
Most passing attempts, season
583—Scott Mitchell, 1995
Most passing attempts, game
50—Eric Hipple at L.A. Rams, Oct. 19, 1986
    Scott Mitchell at Was., Oct. 22, 1995
    Scott Mitchell at Atl., Nov. 5, 1995

    Scott Mitchell at Oak., Oct. 13, 1996
    Scott Mitchell vs. T.B., Sept. 7, 1997
Most passes completed, season
346—Scott Mitchell, 1995
Most passes completed, game
33—Eric Hipple at Cle., Sept. 28, 1986
    Chuck Long vs. G.B., Oct. 25, 1987
Most passing yards, career
15,710—Bobby Layne
Most passing yards, season
4,338—Scott Mitchell, 1995
Most passing yards, game
410—Scott Mitchell vs. Min., Nov. 23, 1995

Most touchdown passes, season
32—Scott Mitchell, 1995
Most pass receptions, career
528—Herman Moore
Most pass receptions, season
123—Herman Moore, 1995
Most pass receptions, game
14—Herman Moore vs. Chi., Dec. 5, 1995
Most receiving yards, career
7,484—Herman Moore
Most receiving yards, season
1,686—Herman Moore, 1995
Most receiving yards, game
302—Cloyce Box vs. Bal., Dec. 3, 1950

Most receiving touchdowns, season
15—Cloyce Box, 1952
Most touchdowns, career
105—Barry Sanders
Most field goals, season
34—Jason Hanson, 1993

Longest field goal
56 yards—Jason Hanson vs. Cle., Oct. 8, 1995
Most interceptions, career
62—Dick LeBeau

Most interceptions, season
12—Don Doll, 1950
Jack Christiansen, 1953
Most sacks, season
23—Al Baker, 1978

SERIES RECORDS

Detroit vs.: Arizona 28-15-3; Atlanta 20-6; Buffalo 3-2-1; Carolina 0-0; Chicago 53-71-3; Cincinnati 3-3; Dallas 6-7; Denver 3-4; Green Bay 57-66-6; Indianapolis 19-17-2; Jacksonville 1-0; Kansas City 3-5; Miami 2-4; Minnesota 27-44-2; New England 3-3; New Orleans 6-8-1; N.Y. Giants 14-14-1; N.Y. Jets 5-3; Oakland 2-6; Philadelphia 11-10-2; Pittsburgh 13-12-1; St. Louis 27-32-1; San Diego 3-3; San Francisco 26-28-1; Seattle 3-4; Tampa Bay 22-18; Tennessee 3-4; Washington 3-24.
NOTE: Includes records only from 1934 to present.

COACHING RECORDS

Dutch Clark, 14-8-0; Monte Clark, 43-61-1 (0-2); Potsy Clark, 53-25-7 (1-0); Gus Dorais, 20-31-2; Bill Edwards, 4-9-1; Wayne Fontes, 66-67-0 (1-4); Rick Forzano, 15-17-0; Harry Gilmer, 10-16-2; Hal Griffen, 5-6-3; Elmer Henderson, 6-5-0; Tommy Hudspeth, 11-13-0; John Karcis, 0-8-0; Don McCafferty, 6-7-1; Alvin McMillin, 12-24-0; Buddy Parker, 47-23-2 (3-1); Darryl Rogers, 18-40-0; Bobby Ross, 9-7-0 (0-1); Joe Schmidt, 43-34-7 (0-1); George Wilson, 53-45-6 (2-0).
NOTE: Playoff games in parentheses.

RETIRED UNIFORM NUMBERS

No.	Player
7	Dutch Clark
22	Bobby Layne
37	Doak Walker
56	Joe Schmidt
85	Chuck Hughes
88	Charlie Sanders

GREEN BAY PACKERS
YEAR-BY-YEAR RECORDS

		REGULAR SEASON					PLAYOFFS			
Year	W	L	T	Pct.	PF	PA	Finish	W	L	Highest round	Coach
1921	3	2	1	.600	...	...	T6th				Curly Lambeau
1922	4	3	3	.571	...	...	T7th				Curly Lambeau
1923	7	2	1	.778	...	...	3rd				Curly Lambeau
1924	7	4	0	.636	...	...	6th				Curly Lambeau
1925	8	5	0	.615	...	...	9th				Curly Lambeau
1926	7	3	3	.700	...	...	5th				Curly Lambeau
1927	7	2	1	.778	...	...	2nd				Curly Lambeau
1928	6	4	3	.600	...	...	4th				Curly Lambeau
1929	12	0	1	1.000	...	...	1st				Curly Lambeau
1930	10	3	1	.769	...	...	1st				Curly Lambeau
1931	12	2	0	.857	...	...	1st				Curly Lambeau
1932	10	3	1	.769	...	...	2nd				Curly Lambeau
1933	5	7	1	.417	170	107	3rd/Western Div.				Curly Lambeau
1934	7	6	0	.538	156	112	3rd/Western Div.	—	—		Curly Lambeau
1935	8	4	0	.667	181	96	2nd/Western Div.	—	—		Curly Lambeau
1936	10	1	1	.909	248	118	1st/Western Div.	1	0	NFL champ	Curly Lambeau
1937	7	4	0	.636	220	122	T2nd/Western Div.				Curly Lambeau
1938	8	3	0	.727	223	118	1st/Western Div.	0	1	NFL championship game	Curly Lambeau
1939	9	2	0	.818	233	153	1st/Western Div.	1	0	NFL champ	Curly Lambeau
1940	6	4	1	.600	238	155	2nd/Western Div.	—	—		Curly Lambeau
1941	10	1	0	.909	258	120	2nd/Western Div.	0	1	W. Div. championship game	Curly Lambeau
1942	8	2	1	.800	300	215	2nd/Western Div.	—	—		Curly Lambeau
1943	7	2	1	.778	264	172	2nd/Western Div.	—	—		Curly Lambeau
1944	8	2	0	.800	238	141	1st/Western Div.	1	0	NFL champ	Curly Lambeau
1945	6	4	0	.600	258	173	3rd/Western Div.	—	—		Curly Lambeau
1946	6	5	0	.545	148	158	T3rd/Western Div.	—	—		Curly Lambeau
1947	6	5	1	.545	274	210	3rd/Western Div.	—	—		Curly Lambeau
1948	3	9	0	.250	154	290	4th/Western Div.	—	—		Curly Lambeau
1949	2	10	0	.167	114	329	5th/Western Div.	—	—		Curly Lambeau
1950	3	9	0	.250	244	406	T5th/National Conf.	—	—		Gene Ronzani
1951	3	9	0	.250	254	375	5th/National Conf.	—	—		Gene Ronzani
1952	6	6	0	.500	295	312	4th/National Conf.	—	—		Gene Ronzani
1953	2	9	1	.182	200	338	6th/Western Conf.	—	—		Gene Ronzani, Hugh Devore-S. McLean
1954	4	8	0	.333	234	251	5th/Western Conf.	—	—		Lisle Blackbourn
1955	6	6	0	.500	258	276	3rd/Western Conf.	—	—		Lisle Blackbourn
1956	4	8	0	.333	264	342	5th/Western Conf.	—	—		Lisle Blackbourn
1957	3	9	0	.250	218	311	6th/Western Conf.	—	—		Lisle Blackbourn
1958	1	10	1	.091	193	382	6th/Western Conf.	—	—		Scooter McLean
1959	7	5	0	.583	248	246	T3rd/Western Conf.	—	—		Vince Lombardi

	REGULAR SEASON							PLAYOFFS			
Year	W	L	T	Pct.	PF	PA	Finish	W	L	Highest round	Coach
1960	8	4	0	.667	332	209	1st/Western Conf.	0	1	NFL championship game	Vince Lombardi
1961	11	3	0	.786	391	223	1st/Western Conf.	1	0	NFL champ	Vince Lombardi
1962	13	1	0	.929	415	148	1st/Western Conf.	1	0	NFL champ	Vince Lombardi
1963	11	2	1	.846	369	206	2nd/Western Conf.	—	—		Vince Lombardi
1964	8	5	1	.615	342	245	T2nd/Western Conf.	—	—		Vince Lombardi
1965	10	3	1	.769	316	224	1st/Western Conf.	2	0	NFL champ	Vince Lombardi
1966	12	2	0	.857	335	163	1st/Western Conf.	2	0	Super Bowl champ	Vince Lombardi
1967	9	4	1	.692	332	209	1st/Central Div.	3	0	Super Bowl champ	Vince Lombardi
1968	6	7	1	.462	281	227	3rd/Central Div.	—	—		Phil Bengtson
1969	8	6	0	.571	269	221	3rd/Central Div.	—	—		Phil Bengtson
1970	6	8	0	.429	196	293	T3rd/NFC Central Div.	—	—		Phil Bengtson
1971	4	8	2	.333	274	298	4th/NFC Central Div.	—	—		Dan Devine
1972	10	4	0	.714	304	226	1st/NFC Central Div.	0	1	NFC div. playoff game	Dan Devine
1973	5	7	2	.429	202	259	3rd/NFC Central Div.	—	—		Dan Devine
1974	6	8	0	.429	210	206	3rd/NFC Central Div.	—	—		Dan Devine
1975	4	10	0	.286	226	285	T3rd/NFC Central Div.	—	—		Bart Starr
1976	5	9	0	.357	218	299	4th/NFC Central Div.	—	—		Bart Starr
1977	4	10	0	.286	134	219	4th/NFC Central Div.	—	—		Bart Starr
1978	8	7	1	.531	249	269	2nd/NFC Central Div.	—	—		Bart Starr
1979	5	11	0	.313	246	316	4th/NFC Central Div.	—	—		Bart Starr
1980	5	10	1	.344	231	371	T4th/NFC Central Div.	—	—		Bart Starr
1981	8	8	0	.500	324	361	3rd/NFC Central Div.	—	—		Bart Starr
1982	5	3	1	.611	226	169	3rd/NFC	1	1	NFC second-round pl. game	Bart Starr
1983	8	8	0	.500	429	439	T2nd/NFC Central Div.	—	—		Bart Starr
1984	8	8	0	.500	390	309	2nd/NFC Central Div.	—	—		Forrest Gregg
1985	8	8	0	.500	337	355	2nd/NFC Central Div.	—	—		Forrest Gregg
1986	4	12	0	.250	254	418	4th/NFC Central Div.	—	—		Forrest Gregg
1987	5	9	1	.367	255	300	3rd/NFC Central Div.	—	—		Forrest Gregg
1988	4	12	0	.250	240	315	T4th/NFC Central Div.	—	—		Lindy Infante
1989	10	6	0	.625	362	356	2nd/NFC Central Div.	—	—		Lindy Infante
1990	6	10	0	.375	271	347	T2nd/NFC Central Div.	—	—		Lindy Infante
1991	4	12	0	.250	273	313	4th/NFC Central Div.	—	—		Lindy Infante
1992	9	7	0	.563	276	296	2nd/NFC Central Div.	—	—		Mike Holmgren
1993	9	7	0	.563	340	282	T2nd/NFC Central Div.	1	1	NFC div. playoff game	Mike Holmgren
1994	9	7	0	.563	382	287	T2nd/NFC Central Div.	1	1	NFC div. playoff game	Mike Holmgren
1995	11	5	0	.689	404	314	1st/NFC Central Div.	2	1	NFC championship game	Mike Holmgren
1996	13	3	0	.813	456	210	1st/NFC Central Div.	3	0	Super Bowl champ	Mike Holmgren
1997	13	3	0	.813	422	282	1st/NFC Central Div.	2	1	Super Bowl	Mike Holmgren

FIRST-ROUND DRAFT PICKS

1936—Russ Letlow, G, San Francisco
1937—Ed Jankowski, B, Wisconsin
1938—Cecil Isbell, B, Purdue
1939—Larry Buhler, B, Minnesota
1940—Hal Van Every, B, Marquette
1941—George Paskvan, B, Wisconsin
1942—Urban Odson, T, Minnesota
1943—Dick Wildung, T, Minnesota
1944—Merv Pregulman, G, Michigan
1945—Walt Schlinkman, G, Texas Tech
1946—Johnny Strzykalski, B, Marquette
1947—Ernie Case, B, UCLA
1948—Earl Girard, B, Wisconsin
1949—Stan Heath, B, Nevada
1950—Clayton Tonnemaker, G, Minnesota
1951—Bob Gain, T, Kentucky
1952—Babe Parilli, QB, Kentucky
1953—Al Carmichael, B, Southern California
1954—Art Hunter, T, Notre Dame
    Veryl Switzer, B, Kansas State
1955—Tom Bettis, G, Purdue
1956—Jack Losch, B, Miami
1957—Paul Hornung, B, Notre Dame*
    Ron Kramer, E, Michigan
1958—Dan Currie, C, Michigan State
1959—Randy Duncan, B, Iowa*
1960—Tom Moore, RB, Vanderbilt
1961—Herb Adderley, DB, Michigan State

1962—Earl Gros, RB, Louisiana State
1963—Dave Robinson, LB, Penn State
1964—Lloyd Voss, DT, Nebraska
1965—Donny Anderson, RB, Texas Tech
    Larry Elkins, E, Baylor
1966—Jim Grabowski, RB, Illinois
    Gale Gillingham, G, Minnesota
1967—Bob Hyland, C, Boston College
    Don Horn, QB, San Diego State
1968—Fred Carr, LB, Texas-El Paso
    Bill Lueck, G, Arizona
1969—Rich Moore, DT, Villanova
1970—Mike McCoy, DT, Notre Dame
    Rich McGeorge, TE, Elon
1971—John Brockington, RB, Ohio State
1972—Willie Buchanon, DB, San Diego State
    Jerry Tagge, QB, Nebraska
1973—Barry Smith, WR, Florida State
1974—Barty Smith, RB, Richmond
1975—None
1976—Mark Koncar, T, Colorado
1977—Mike Butler, DE, Kansas
    Ezra Johnson, DE, Morris Brown
1978—James Lofton, WR, Stanford
    John Anderson, LB, Michigan
1979—Eddie Lee Ivery, RB, Georgia Tech
1980—Bruce Clark, DT, Penn State
    George Cumby, LB, Oklahoma

1981—Rich Campbell, QB, California
1982—Ron Hallstrom, G, Iowa
1983—Tim Lewis, DB, Pittsburgh
1984—Alphonso Carreker, DT, Florida State
1985—Ken Ruettgers, T, Southern California
1986—None
1987—Brent Fullwood, RB, Auburn
1988—Sterling Sharpe, WR, South Carolina
1989—Tony Mandarich, T, Michigan State
1990—Tony Bennett, LB, Mississippi
　　　Darrell Thompson, RB, Minnesota

1991—Vincent Clark, DB, Ohio State
1992—Terrell Buckley, DB, Florida State
1993—Wayne Simmons, LB, Clemson
　　　George Teague, DB, Alabama
1994—Aaron Taylor, T, Notre Dame
1995—Craig Newsome, DB, Arizona State
1996—John Michaels, T, Southern California
1997—Ross Verba, T, Iowa
1998—Vonnie Holliday, DT, North Carolina
*First player chosen in draft.

FRANCHISE RECORDS

Most rushing yards, career
8,207—Jim Taylor
Most rushing yards, season
1,474—Jim Taylor, 1962
Most rushing yards, game
190—Dorsey Levens vs. Dal., Nov. 23, 1997
Most rushing touchdowns, season
19—Jim Taylor, 1962
Most passing attempts, season
599—Don Majkowski, 1989
Most passing attempts, game
61—Brett Favre vs. S.F., Oct. 14, 1996 (OT)
59—Don Majkowski at Det., Nov. 12, 1989
Most passes completed, season
363—Brett Favre, 1994
Most passes completed, game
36—Brett Favre at Chi., Dec. 5, 1993
Most passing yards, career
24,718—Bart Starr

Most passing yards, season
4,458—Lynn Dickey, 1983
Most passing yards, game
418—Lynn Dickey at T.B., Oct. 12, 1980
Most touchdown passes, season
39—Brett Favre, 1996
Most pass receptions, career
595—Sterling Sharpe
Most pass receptions, season
112—Sterling Sharpe, 1993
Most pass receptions, game
14—Don Hutson at NYG, Nov. 22, 1942
Most receiving yards, career
9,656—James Lofton
Most receiving yards, season
1,497—Robert Brooks, 1995
Most receiving yards, game
257—Bill Howton vs. L.A. Rams, Oct. 21, 1956

Most receiving touchdowns, season
18—Sterling Sharpe, 1994
Most touchdowns, career
105—Don Hutson
Most field goals, season
33—Chester Marcol, 1972
Longest field goal
54 yards—Chris Jacke at Det., Jan. 2, 1994
Most interceptions, career
52—Bobby Dillon
Most interceptions, season
10—Irv Comp, 1943
Most sacks, career
84—Ezra Johnson
Most sacks, season
20.5—Ezra Johnson, 1978

SERIES RECORDS

Green Bay vs.: Arizona 41-21-4; Atlanta 10-9; Buffalo 2-5; Carolina 1-0; Chicago 67-82-6; Cincinnati 4-4; Dallas 10-8; Denver 3-4-1; Detroit 66-57-6; Indianapolis 18-19-1; Jacksonville 1-0; Kansas City 1-5-1; Miami 1-8; Minnesota 36-36-1; New England 3-3; New Orleans 13-4; N.Y. Giants 22-20-2; N.Y. Jets 2-5; Oakland 2-5; Philadelphia 20-9; Pittsburgh 21-11; St. Louis 27-40-1; San Diego 5-1; San Francisco 22-25-1; Seattle 4-3; Tampa Bay 24-13-1; Tennessee 3-3; Washington 9-11.

COACHING RECORDS

Phil Bengtson, 20-21-1; Lisle Blackbourn, 17-31-0; Dan Devine, 25-27-4 (0-1); Hugh Devore-Ray (Scooter) McLean, 0-2-0; Forrest Gregg, 25-37-1; Mike Holmgren, 64-32-0 (9-4); Lindy Infante, 24-40-0; Curly Lambeau, 209-104-21 (3-2); Vince Lombardi, 89-29-4 (9-1); Ray (Scooter) McLean, 1-10-1; Gene Ronzani, 14-31-1; Bart Starr, 52-76-3 (1-1).
NOTE: Playoff games in parentheses.

RETIRED UNIFORM NUMBERS

No.	Player
3	Tony Canadeo
14	Don Hutson
15	Bart Starr
66	Ray Nitschke

INDIANAPOLIS COLTS
YEAR-BY-YEAR RECORDS

			REGULAR SEASON					PLAYOFFS			
Year	W	L	T	Pct.	PF	PA	Finish	W	L	Highest round	Coach
1953*	3	9	0	.250	182	350	5th/Western Conf.	—	—		Keith Molesworth
1954*	3	9	0	.250	131	279	6th/Western Conf.	—	—		Weeb Ewbank
1955*	5	6	1	.455	214	239	4th/Western Conf.	—	—		Weeb Ewbank
1956*	5	7	0	.417	270	322	4th/Western Conf.	—	—		Weeb Ewbank
1957*	7	5	0	.583	303	235	3rd/Western Conf.	—	—		Weeb Ewbank
1958*	9	3	0	.750	381	203	1st/Western Conf.	1	0	NFL champ	Weeb Ewbank
1959*	9	3	0	.750	374	251	1st/Western Conf.	1	0	NFL champ	Weeb Ewbank
1960*	6	6	0	.500	288	234	4th/Western Conf.	—	—		Weeb Ewbank
1961*	8	6	0	.571	302	307	T3rd/Western Conf.	—	—		Weeb Ewbank
1962*	7	7	0	.500	293	288	4th/Western Conf.	—	—		Weeb Ewbank
1963*	8	6	0	.571	316	285	3rd/Western Conf.	—	—		Don Shula
1964*	12	2	0	.857	428	225	1st/Western Conf.	0	1	NFL championship game	Don Shula
1965*	10	3	1	.769	389	284	2nd/Western Conf.	0	1	W. Conf. champ. game	Don Shula

Year	W	L	T	Pct.	PF	PA	Finish	W	L	Highest round	Coach
							REGULAR SEASON			**PLAYOFFS**	
1966*	9	5	0	.643	314	226	2nd/Western Conf.	—	—		Don Shula
1967*	11	1	2	.917	394	198	2nd/Coastal Div.	—	—		Don Shula
1968*	13	1	0	.929	402	144	1st/Coastal Div.	2	1	Super Bowl	Don Shula
1969*	8	5	1	.615	279	268	2nd/Coastal Div.	—	—		Don Shula
1970*	11	2	1	.846	321	234	1st/AFC Eastern Div.	3	0	Super Bowl champ	Don McCafferty
1971*	10	4	0	.714	313	140	2nd/AFC Eastern Div.	1	1	AFC championship game	Don McCafferty
1972*	5	9	0	.357	235	252	3rd/AFC Eastern Div.	—	—		McCafferty, John Sandusky
1973*	4	10	0	.286	226	341	T4th/AFC Eastern Div.	—	—		Howard Schnellenberger
1974*	2	12	0	.143	190	329	5th/AFC Eastern Div.	—	—		H. Schnellenberger, Joe Thomas
1975*	10	4	0	.714	395	269	1st/AFC Eastern Div.	0	1	AFC div. playoff game	Ted Marchibroda
1976*	11	3	0	.786	417	246	1st/AFC Eastern Div.	0	1	AFC div. playoff game	Ted Marchibroda
1977*	10	4	0	.714	295	221	1st/AFC Eastern Div.	0	1	AFC div. playoff game	Ted Marchibroda
1978*	5	11	0	.313	239	421	T4th/AFC Eastern Div.	—	—		Ted Marchibroda
1979*	5	11	0	.313	271	351	5th/AFC Eastern Div.	—	—		Ted Marchibroda
1980*	7	9	0	.438	355	387	4th/AFC Eastern Div.	—	—		Mike McCormack
1981*	2	14	0	.125	259	533	T4th/AFC Eastern Div.	—	—		Mike McCormack
1982*	0	8	1	.056	113	236	14th/AFC	—	—		Frank Kush
1983*	7	9	0	.438	264	354	T4th/AFC Eastern Div.	—	—		Frank Kush
1984	4	12	0	.250	239	414	4th/AFC Eastern Div.	—	—		Frank Kush, Hal Hunter
1985	5	11	0	.313	320	386	4th/AFC Eastern Div.	—	—		Rod Dowhower
1986	3	13	0	.188	229	400	5th/AFC Eastern Div.	—	—		Rod Dowhower, Ron Meyer
1987	9	6	0	.600	300	238	1st/AFC Eastern Div.	0	1	AFC div. playoff game	Ron Meyer
1988	9	7	0	.563	354	315	T2nd/AFC Eastern Div.	—	—		Ron Meyer
1989	8	8	0	.500	298	301	T2nd/AFC Eastern Div.	—	—		Ron Meyer
1990	7	9	0	.438	281	353	3rd/AFC Eastern Div.	—	—		Ron Meyer
1991	1	15	0	.063	143	381	5th/AFC Eastern Div.	—	—		Ron Meyer, Rick Venturi
1992	9	7	0	.563	216	302	3rd/AFC Eastern Div.	—	—		Ted Marchibroda
1993	4	12	0	.250	189	378	5th/AFC Eastern Div.	—	—		Ted Marchibroda
1994	8	8	0	.500	307	320	3rd/AFC Eastern Div.	—	—		Ted Marchibroda
1995	9	7	0	.563	331	316	T2nd/AFC Eastern Div.	2	1	AFC championship game	Ted Marchibroda
1996	9	7	0	.563	317	334	3rd/AFC Eastern Div.	0	1	AFC wild-card game	Lindy Infante
1997	3	13	0	.188	313	401	5th/AFC Eastern Div.	—	—		Lindy Infante

*Baltimore Colts.

FIRST-ROUND DRAFT PICKS

1953—Billy Vessels, B, Oklahoma
1954—Cotton Davidson, B, Baylor
1955—George Shaw, B, Oregon*
　　　Alan Ameche, B, Wisconsin
1956—Lenny Moore, B, Penn State
1957—Jim Parker, T, Ohio State
1958—Lenny Lyles, B, Louisville
1959—Jackie Burkett, C, Auburn
1960—Ron Mix, T, Southern California
1961—Tom Matte, RB, Ohio State
1962—Wendell Harris, DB, Louisiana State
1963—Bob Vogel, T, Ohio State
1964—Marv Woodson, DB, Indiana
1965—Mike Curtis, LB, Duke
1966—Sam Ball, T, Kentucky
1967—Bubba Smith, DT, Michigan State*
　　　Jim Detwiler, RB, Michigan
1968—John Williams, G, Minnesota
1969—Eddie Hinton, WR, Oklahoma
1970—Norm Bulaich, RB, Texas Christian
1971—Don McCauley, RB, North Carolina
　　　Leonard Dunlap, DB, North Texas State
1972—Tom Drougas, T, Oregon
1973—Bert Jones, QB, Louisiana State
　　　Joe Ehrmann, DT, Syracuse
1974—John Dutton, DE, Nebraska
　　　Roger Carr, WR, Louisiana Tech
1975—Ken Huff, G, North Carolina
1976—Ken Novak, DT, Purdue

1977—Randy Burke, WR, Kentucky
1978—Reese McCall, TE, Auburn
1979—Barry Krauss, LB, Alabama
1980—Curtis Dickey, RB, Texas A&M
　　　Derrick Hatchett, DB, Texas
1981—Randy McMillan, RB, Pittsburgh
　　　Donnell Thompson, DT, North Carolina
1982—Johnie Cooks, LB, Mississippi State
　　　Art Schlichter, QB, Ohio State
1983—John Elway, QB, Stanford*
1984—L. Coleman, DB, Vanderbilt
　　　Ron Solt, G, Maryland
1985—Duane Bickett, LB, Southern California
1986—Jon Hand, DT, Alabama
1987—Cornelius Bennett, LB, Alabama
1988—None
1989—Andre Rison, WR, Michigan State
1990—Jeff George, QB, Illinois*
1991—None
1992—Steve Emtman, DE, Washington*
　　　Quentin Coryatt, LB, Texas A&M
1993—Sean Dawkins, WR, California
1994—Marshall Faulk, RB, San Diego State
　　　Trev Alberts, LB, Nebraska
1995—Ellis Johnson, DT, Florida
1996—Marvin Harrison, WR, Syracuse
1997—Tarik Glenn, T, California
1998—Peyton Manning, QB, Tennessee*
　　　*First player chosen in draft.

FRANCHISE RECORDS

Most rushing yards, career
5,487—Lydell Mitchell
Most rushing yards, season
1,659—Eric Dickerson, 1988
Most rushing yards, game
198—Norm Bulaich vs. NYJ, Sept. 19, 1971
Most rushing touchdowns, season
16—Lenny Moore, 1964
Most passing attempts, season
485—Jeff George, 1991
Most passing attempts, game
59—Jeff George at Was., Nov. 7, 1993
Most passes completed, season
292—Jeff George, 1991
Most passes completed, game
37—Jeff George at Was., Nov. 7, 1993
Most passing yards, career
39,768—Johnny Unitas
Most passing yards, season
3,481—Johnny Unitas, 1963

Most passing yards, game
401—Johnny Unitas vs. Atl., Sept. 17, 1967
Most touchdown passes, season
32—Johnny Unitas, 1959
Most pass receptions, career
631—Raymond Berry
Most pass receptions, season
85—Reggie Langhorne, 1993
Most pass receptions, game
13—Lydell Mitchell vs. NYJ, Dec. 15, 1974
    Joe Washington at K.C., Sept. 2, 1979
Most receiving yards, career
9,275—Raymond Berry
Most receiving yards, season
1,298—Raymond Berry, 1960
Most receiving yards, game
224—Raymond Berry at Was., Nov. 10, 1957
Most receiving touchdowns, season
14—Raymond Berry, 1959

Most touchdowns, career
113—Lenny Moore
Most field goals, season
36—Cary Blanchard, 1996
Longest field goal
58 yards—Dan Miller at S.D., Dec. 26, 1982
Most interceptions, career
57—Bob Boyd
Most interceptions, season
11—Tom Keane, 1953
Most sacks, career
56.5—Fred Cook
Most sacks, season
17—John Dutton, 1975

SERIES RECORDS

Indianapolis vs.: Arizona 6-6; Atlanta 10-0; Buffalo 23-31-1; Carolina 0-1; Chicago 21-16; Cincinnati 10-8; Dallas 3-7; Denver 2-9; Detroit 17-19-2; Green Bay 19-18-1; Jacksonville 1-0; Kansas City 5-6; Miami 19-37; Minnesota 11-7-1; New England 22-33; New Orleans 3-3; N.Y. Giants 5-5; N.Y. Jets 33-22; Oakland 2-5; Philadelphia 7-6; Pittsburgh 4-13; St. Louis 21-17-2; San Diego 6-11; San Francisco 22-16; Seattle 4-2; Tampa Bay 5-4; Tennessee 7-7; Washington 16-9.
NOTE: Includes records as Baltimore Colts from 1953 through 1983.

COACHING RECORDS

Rod Dowhower, 5-24-0; Weeb Ewbank, 59-52-1 (2-0); Hal Hunter, 0-1-0; Lindy Infante, 12-19-0 (0-1); Frank Kush, 11-28-1; Ted Marchibroda, 71-67-0 (2-4); Don McCafferty, 22-10-1 (4-1); Mike McCormack, 9-23-0; Ron Meyer, 36-35-0 (0-1); Keith Molesworth, 3-9-0; John Sandusky, 4-5-0; Howard Schnellenberger, 4-13-0; Don Shula, 71-23-4 (2-3); Joe Thomas, 2-9-0; Rick Venturi, 1-10.
NOTE: Playoff games in parentheses.

RETIRED UNIFORM NUMBERS

No.	Player
19	Johnny Unitas
22	Buddy Young
24	Lenny Moore
70	Art Donovan
77	Jim Parker
82	Raymond Berry
89	Gino Marchetti

JACKSONVILLE JAGUARS

YEAR-BY-YEAR RECORDS

			REGULAR SEASON						PLAYOFFS		
Year	W	L	T	Pct.	PF	PA	Finish	W	L	Highest round	Coach
1995	4	12	0	.250	275	404	5th/AFC Central Div.	—	—		Tom Coughlin
1996	9	7	0	.563	325	335	2nd/AFC Central Div.	2	1	AFC championship game	Tom Coughlin
1997	11	5	0	.688	394	318	2nd/AFC Central Div.	0	1	AFC wild-card game	Tom Coughlin

FIRST-ROUND DRAFT PICKS

1995—Tony Boselli, T, Southern California
    James Stewart, RB, Tennessee
1996—Kevin Hardy, LB, Illinois

1997—Renaldo Wynn, DT, Notre Dame
1998—Fred Taylor, RB, Florida
    Donovin Darius, DB, Syracuse

FRANCHISE RECORDS

Most rushing yards, career
1,803—James Stewart
Most rushing yards, season
823—Natrone Means, 1997
Most rushing yards, game
112—James Stewart at St.L., Oct. 20, 1996

Most rushing touchdowns, season
9—Natrone Means, 1997
Most passing attempts, season
557—Mark Brunell, 1996
Most passing attempts, game
52—Mark Brunell at St.L., Oct. 20, 1996

Most passes completed, season
353—Mark Brunell, 1996
Most passes completed, game
37—Mark Brunell at St.L., Oct. 20, 1996
Most passing yards, career
9,816—Mark Brunell

Most passing yards, season
4,367—Mark Brunell, 1996
Most passing yards, game
432—Mark Brunell at N.E., Sept. 22, 1996
Most touchdown passes, season
19—Mark Brunell, 1996
Most pass receptions, career
187—Jimmy Smith
Most pass receptions, season
85—Keenan McCardell, 1996, 1997
Most pass receptions, game
16—Keenan McCardell at St.L., Oct. 20, 1996

Most receiving yards, career
2,856—Jimmy Smith
Most receiving yards, season
1,244—Jimmy Smith, 1996
Most receiving yards, game
232—Keenan McCardell at St.L., Oct. 20, 1996
Most receiving touchdowns, season
7—Jimmy Smith, 1996
Most touchdowns, career
22—James Stewart
Most field goals, season
31—Mike Hollis, 1997

Longest field goal
53 yards—Mike Hollis vs. Pit., Oct. 8, 1995
Mike Hollis vs. Car., Sept. 29, 1996
Most interceptions, career
5—Deon Figures
Chris Hudson
Most interceptions, season
5—Deon Figures, 1997
Most sacks, career
16—Clyde Simmons
Most sacks, season
8.5—Clyde Simmons, 1997

SERIES RECORDS

Jacksonville vs.: Arizona 0-0; Atlanta 1-0; Baltimore 4-0; Buffalo 1-0; Carolina 1-0; Chicago 0-1; Cincinnati 2-4; Dallas 0-1; Denver 0-1; Detroit 0-1; Green Bay 0-1; Indianapolis 0-1; Kansas City 1-0; Miami 0-0; Minnesota 0-0; New England 0-2; New Orleans 0-1; N.Y. Giants 1-0; N.Y. Jets 1-1; Oakland 1-1; Philadelphia 1-0; Pittsburgh 3-3; St. Louis 0-1; San Diego 0-0; San Francisco 0-0; Seattle 1-1; Tampa Bay 0-1; Tennessee 3-3; Washington 0-1.

COACHING RECORDS

Tom Coughlin, 24-24-0 (2-2).
NOTE: Playoff games in parentheses.

RETIRED UNIFORM NUMBERS

No.   Player
None

KANSAS CITY CHIEFS
YEAR-BY-YEAR RECORDS

		REGULAR SEASON							PLAYOFFS		
Year	W	L	T	Pct.	PF	PA	Finish	W	L	Highest round	Coach
1960*†	8	6	0	.571	362	253	2nd/Western Div.	—	—		Hank Stram
1961*†	6	8	0	.429	334	343	2nd/Western Div.	—	—		Hank Stram
1962*†	11	3	0	.786	389	233	1st/Western Div.	1	0	AFL champ	Hank Stram
1963*	5	7	2	.417	347	263	3rd/Western Div.	—	—		Hank Stram
1964*	7	7	0	.500	366	306	2nd/Western Div.	—	—		Hank Stram
1965*	7	5	2	.583	322	285	3rd/Western Div.	—	—		Hank Stram
1966*	11	2	1	.846	448	276	1st/Western Div.	1	1	Super Bowl	Hank Stram
1967*	9	5	0	.643	408	254	2nd/Western Div.	—	—		Hank Stram
1968*	12	2	0	.857	371	170	2nd/Western Div.	0	1	W. Div. champ. game	Hank Stram
1969*	11	3	0	.786	359	177	2nd/Western Div.	3	0	Super Bowl champ	Hank Stram
1970	7	5	2	.583	272	244	2nd/AFC Western Div.	—	—		Hank Stram
1971	10	3	1	.769	302	208	1st/AFC Western Div.	0	1	AFC div. playoff game	Hank Stram
1972	8	6	0	.571	287	254	2nd/AFC Western Div.	—	—		Hank Stram
1973	7	5	2	.571	231	192	T2nd/AFC Western Div.	—	—		Hank Stram
1974	5	9	0	.357	233	293	T3rd/AFC Western Div.	—	—		Hank Stram
1975	5	9	0	.357	282	341	3rd/AFC Western Div.	—	—		Paul Wiggin
1976	5	9	0	.357	290	376	4th/AFC Western Div.	—	—		Paul Wiggin
1977	2	12	0	.143	225	349	5th/AFC Western Div.	—	—		Paul Wiggin, Tom Bettis
1978	4	12	0	.250	243	327	5th/AFC Western Div.	—	—		Marv Levy
1979	7	9	0	.438	238	262	5th/AFC Western Div.	—	—		Marv Levy
1980	8	8	0	.500	319	336	T3rd/AFC Western Div.	—	—		Marv Levy
1981	9	7	0	.563	343	290	3rd/AFC Western Div.	—	—		Marv Levy
1982	3	6	0	.333	176	184	11th/AFC	—	—		Marv Levy
1983	6	10	0	.375	386	367	T4th/AFC Western Div.	—	—		John Mackovic
1984	8	8	0	.500	314	324	4th/AFC Western Div.	—	—		John Mackovic
1985	6	10	0	.375	317	360	5th/AFC Western Div.	—	—		John Mackovic
1986	10	6	0	.625	358	326	2nd/AFC Western Div.	0	1	AFC wild-card game	John Mackovic
1987	4	11	0	.267	273	388	5th/AFC Western Div.	—	—		Frank Gansz
1988	4	11	1	.281	254	320	5th/AFC Western Div.	—	—		Frank Gansz
1989	8	7	1	.531	318	286	2nd/AFC Western Div.	—	—		Marty Schottenheimer
1990	11	5	0	.688	369	257	2nd/AFC Western Div.	0	1	AFC wild-card game	Marty Schottenheimer
1991	10	6	0	.625	322	252	2nd/AFC Western Div.	1	1	AFC div. playoff game	Marty Schottenheimer
1992	10	6	0	.625	348	282	2nd/AFC Western Div.	0	1	AFC wild-card game	Marty Schottenheimer
1993	11	5	0	.688	328	291	1st/AFC Western Div.	2	1	AFC championship game	Marty Schottenheimer
1994	9	7	0	.563	319	298	2nd/AFC Western Div.	0	1	AFC wild-card game	Marty Schottenheimer
1995	13	3	0	.813	358	241	1st/AFC Western Div.	0	1	AFC div. playoff game	Marty Schottenheimer
1996	9	7	0	.563	297	300	2nd/AFC Western Div.	—	—		Marty Schottenheimer
1997	13	3	0	.813	375	232	1st/AFC Western Div.	0	1	AFC div. playoff game	Marty Schottenheimer

*American Football League.
†Dallas Texans.

FIRST-ROUND DRAFT PICKS

1960—Don Meredith, QB, Southern Methodist
1961—E.J. Holub, C, Texas Tech
1962—Ronnie Bull, RB, Baylor
1963—Buck Buchanan, DT, Grambling* (AFL)
     Ed Budde, G, Michigan State
1964—Pete Beathard, QB, Southern California
1965—Gale Sayers, RB, Kansas
1966—Aaron Brown, DE, Minnesota
1967—Gene Trosch, DE, Miami
1968—Mo Moorman, G, Texas A&M
     George Daney, G, Texas-El Paso
1969—Jim Marsalis, DB, Tennessee State
1970—Sid Smith, T, Southern California
1971—Elmo Wright, WR, Houston
1972—Jeff Kinney, RB, Nebraska
1973—None
1974—Woody Green, RB, Arizona State
1975—None
1976—Rod Walters, G, Iowa
1977—Gary Green, DB, Baylor
1978—Art Still, DE, Kentucky
1979—Mike Bell, DE, Colorado State
     Steve Fuller, QB, Clemson

1980—Brad Budde, G, Southern California
1981—Willie Scott, TE, South Carolina
1982—Anthony Hancock, WR, Tennessee
1983—Todd Blackledge, QB, Penn State
1984—Bill Maas, DT, Pittsburgh
     John Alt, T, Iowa
1985—Ethan Horton, RB, North Carolina
1986—Brian Jozwiak, T, West Virginia
1987—Paul Palmer, RB, Temple
1988—Neil Smith, DE, Nebraska
1989—Derrick Thomas, LB, Alabama
1990—Percy Snow, LB, Michigan State
1991—Harvey Williams, RB, Louisiana State
1992—Dale Carter, DB, Tennessee
1993—None
1994—Greg Hill, RB, Texas A&M
1995—Trezelle Jenkins, T, Michigan
1996—Jerome Woods, DB, Memphis
1997—Tony Gonzalez, TE, California
1998—Victor Riley, T, Auburn
     *First player chosen in draft.

FRANCHISE RECORDS

Most rushing yards, career
4,897—Christian Okoye
Most rushing yards, season
1,480—Christian Okoye, 1989
Most rushing yards, game
200—Barry Word vs. Det., Oct. 14, 1990
Most rushing touchdowns, season
13—Abner Haynes, 1962
Most passing attempts, season
603—Bill Kenney, 1983
Most passing attempts, game
55—Joe Montana at S.D., Oct. 9, 1994
     Steve Bono at Mia., Dec. 12, 1994
Most passes completed, season
346—Bill Kenney, 1983
Most passes completed, game
37—Joe Montana at S.D., Oct. 9, 1994
Most passing yards, career
28,507—Len Dawson

Most passing yards, season
4,348—Bill Kenney, 1983
Most passing yards, game
435—Len Dawson vs. Den., Nov. 1, 1964
Most touchdown passes, season
30—Len Dawson, 1964
Most pass receptions, career
416—Henry Marshall
Most pass receptions, season
80—Carlos Carson, 1983
Most pass receptions, game
12—Ed Podolak vs. Den., Oct. 7, 1973
Most receiving yards, career
7,306—Otis Taylor
Most receiving yards, season
1,351—Carlos Carson, 1983
Most receiving yards, game
309—Stephone Paige vs. S.D., Dec. 22, 1985

Most receiving touchdowns, season
12—Chris Burford, 1962
Most touchdowns, career
57—Otis Taylor
Most field goals, season
34—Nick Lowery, 1990
Longest field goal
58 yards—Nick Lowery at Was., Sept. 18, 1983
     Nick Lowery vs. L.A. Raiders, Sept. 12, 1985
Most interceptions, career
58—Emmitt Thomas
Most interceptions, season
12—Emmitt Thomas, 1974
Most sacks, career
99.5—Derrick Thomas
Most sacks, season
20—Derrick Thomas, 1990

SERIES RECORDS

Kansas City vs.: Arizona 4-1-1; Atlanta 4-0; Buffalo 14-17-1; Carolina 1-0; Chicago 3-4; Cincinnati 11-9; Dallas 2-4; Denver 43-32; Detroit 5-3; Green Bay 5-1-1; Indianapolis 6-5; Jacksonville 0-1; Miami 10-10; Minnesota 3-3; New England 14-7-3; New Orleans 4-3; N.Y. Giants 3-6; N.Y. Jets 14-12-1; Oakland 37-36-2; Philadelphia 1-1; Pittsburgh 6-14; St. Louis 2-4; San Diego 39-35-1; San Francisco 3-4; Seattle 26-12; Tampa Bay 5-2; Tennessee 24-17; Washington 4-1.
NOTE: Includes records as Dallas Texans from 1960 through 1962.

COACHING RECORDS

Tom Bettis, 1-6-0; Frank Gansz, 8-22-1; Marv Levy, 31-42-0; John Mackovic, 30-34-0 (0-1); Marty Schottenheimer, 94-49-1 (3-7); Hank Stram, 124-76-10 (5-3); Paul Wiggin, 11-24-0.
NOTE: Playoff games in parentheses.

RETIRED UNIFORM NUMBERS

No.	Player
3	Jan Stenerud
16	Len Dawson
28	Abner Haynes
33	Stone Johnson
36	Mack Lee Hill
63	Willie Lanier
78	Bobby Bell
86	Buck Buchanan

MIAMI DOLPHINS
YEAR-BY-YEAR RECORDS

Year	W	L	T	Pct.	PF	PA	Finish	W	L	Highest round	Coach
					REGULAR SEASON					PLAYOFFS	
1966*	3	11	0	.214	213	362	T4th/Eastern Div.	—	—		George Wilson
1967*	4	10	0	.286	219	407	T3rd/Eastern Div.	—	—		George Wilson
1968*	5	8	1	.385	276	355	3rd/Eastern Div.	—	—		George Wilson
1969*	3	10	1	.231	233	332	5th/Eastern Div.	—	—		George Wilson
1970	10	4	0	.714	297	228	2nd/AFC Eastern Div.	0	1	AFC div. playoff game	Don Shula
1971	10	3	1	.769	315	174	1st/AFC Eastern Div.	2	1	Super Bowl	Don Shula
1972	14	0	0	1.000	385	171	1st/AFC Eastern Div.	3	0	Super Bowl champ	Don Shula
1973	12	2	0	.857	343	150	1st/AFC Eastern Div.	3	0	Super Bowl champ	Don Shula
1974	11	3	0	.786	327	216	1st/AFC Eastern Div.	0	1	AFC div. playoff game	Don Shula
1975	10	4	0	.714	357	222	2nd/AFC Eastern Div.	—	—		Don Shula
1976	6	8	0	.429	263	264	3rd/AFC Eastern Div.	—	—		Don Shula
1977	10	4	0	.714	313	197	2nd/AFC Eastern Div.	—	—		Don Shula
1978	11	5	0	.688	372	254	2nd/AFC Eastern Div.	0	1	AFC wild-card game	Don Shula
1979	10	6	0	.625	341	257	1st/AFC Eastern Div.	0	1	AFC div. playoff game	Don Shula
1980	8	8	0	.500	266	305	3rd/AFC Eastern Div.	—	—		Don Shula
1981	11	4	1	.719	345	275	1st/AFC Eastern Div.	0	1	AFC div. playoff game	Don Shula
1982	7	2	0	.778	198	131	T2nd/AFC	3	1	Super Bowl	Don Shula
1983	12	4	0	.750	389	250	1st/AFC Eastern Div.	0	1	AFC div. playoff game	Don Shula
1984	14	2	0	.875	513	298	1st/AFC Eastern Div.	2	1	Super Bowl	Don Shula
1985	12	4	0	.750	428	320	1st/AFC Eastern Div.	1	1	AFC championship game	Don Shula
1986	8	8	0	.500	430	405	3rd/AFC Eastern Div.	—	—		Don Shula
1987	8	7	0	.533	362	335	T2nd/AFC Eastern Div.	—	—		Don Shula
1988	6	10	0	.375	319	380	5th/AFC Eastern Div.	—	—		Don Shula
1989	8	8	0	.500	331	379	T2nd/AFC Eastern Div.	—	—		Don Shula
1990	12	4	0	.750	336	242	2nd/AFC Eastern Div.	1	1	AFC div. playoff game	Don Shula
1991	8	8	0	.500	343	349	3rd/AFC Eastern Div.	—	—		Don Shula
1992	11	5	0	.688	340	281	1st/AFC Eastern Div.	1	1	AFC championship game	Don Shula
1993	9	7	0	.563	349	351	2nd/AFC Eastern Div.	—	—		Don Shula
1994	10	6	0	.625	389	327	1st/AFC Eastern Div.	1	1	AFC div. playoff game	Don Shula
1995	9	7	0	.563	398	332	T2nd/AFC Eastern Div.	0	1	AFC wild-card game	Don Shula
1996	8	8	0	.500	279	454	4th/AFC Eastern Div.	—	—		Jimmy Johnson
1997	9	7	0	.563	339	327	T2nd/AFC Eastern Div.	0	1	AFC wild-card game	Jimmy Johnson

*American Football League.

FIRST-ROUND DRAFT PICKS

1966—Jim Grabowski, RB, Illinois*
    Rick Norton, QB, Kentucky
1967—Bob Griese, QB, Purdue
1968—Larry Csonka, RB, Syracuse
    Doug Crusan, T, Indiana
1969—Bill Stanfill, DE, Georgia
1970—None
1971—None
1972—Mike Kadish, DT, Notre Dame
1973—None
1974—Don Reese, DE, Jackson State
1975—Darryl Carlton, T, Tampa
1976—Larry Gordon, LB, Arizona State
    Kim Bokamper, LB, San Jose State
1977—A.J. Duhe, DE, Louisiana State
1978—None
1979—Jon Giesler, T, Michigan
1980—Don McNeal, DB, Alabama
1981—David Overstreet, RB, Oklahoma
1982—Roy Foster, G, Southern California

1983—Dan Marino, QB, Pittsburgh
1984—Jackie Shipp, LB, Oklahoma
1985—Lorenzo Hampton, RB, Florida
1986—None
1987—John Bosa, DE, Boston College
1988—Eric Kumerow, DE, Ohio State
1989—Sammie Smith, RB, Florida State
    Louis Oliver, DB, Florida
1990—Richmond Webb, T, Texas A&M
1991—Randal Hill, WR, Miami (Fla.)
1992—Troy Vincent, DB, Wisconsin
    Marco Coleman, LB, Georgia Tech
1993—O.J. McDuffie, WR, Penn State
1994—Tim Bowens, DT, Mississippi
1995—Billy Milner, T, Houston
1996—Daryl Gardener, DT, Baylor
1997—Yatil Green, WR, Miami (Fla.)
1998—John Avery, RB, Mississippi
    *First player chosen in draft.

FRANCHISE RECORDS

Most rushing yards, career
6,737—Larry Csonka
Most rushing yards, season
1,258—Delvin Williams, 1978
Most rushing yards, game
197—Mercury Morris vs. N.E., Sept. 30, 1973

Most rushing touchdowns, season
15—Karim Abdul-Jabbar, 1997
Most passing attempts, season
623—Dan Marino, 1986
Most passing attempts, game
60—Dan Marino vs. NYJ, Oct. 23, 1988
    Dan Marino at N.E., Nov. 23, 1997

Most passes completed, season
385—Dan Marino, 1994
Most passes completed, game
39—Dan Marino at Buf., Nov. 16, 1986
Most passing yards, career
55,416—Dan Marino

Most passing yards, season	Most receiving yards, career	Longest field goal
5,084—Dan Marino, 1984	8,869—Mark Duper	59 yards—Pete Stoyanovich at NYJ, Nov. 12, 1989

Most passing yards, game
521—Dan Marino vs. NYJ, Oct. 23, 1988

Most receiving yards, season
1,389—Mark Clayton, 1984

Most interceptions, career
35—Jake Scott

Most touchdown passes, season
48—Dan Marino, 1984

Most receiving yards, game
217—Mark Duper vs. NYJ, Nov. 10, 1985

Most interceptions, season
10—Dick Westmoreland, 1967

Most pass receptions, career
550—Mark Clayton

Most receiving touchdowns, season
18—Mark Clayton, 1984

Most sacks, career
67.5—Bill Stanfill

Most pass receptions, season
86—Mark Clayton, 1988

Most touchdowns, career
82—Mark Clayton

Most sacks, season
18.5—Bill Stanfill, 1973

Most pass receptions, game
12—Jim Jensen at N.E., Nov. 6, 1988

Most field goals, season
31—Pete Stoyanovich, 1991

SERIES RECORDS

Miami vs.: Arizona 7-0; Atlanta 6-1; Baltimore, 1-0; Buffalo 41-22-1; Carolina 0-0; Chicago 5-3; Cincinnati 12-3; Dallas 6-2; Denver 5-2-1; Detroit 4-2; Green Bay 8-1; Indianapolis 37-19; Jacksonville 0-0; Kansas City 10-10; Minnesota 4-2; New England 37-25; New Orleans 5-4; N.Y. Giants 1-3; N.Y. Jets 33-28-1; Oakland 6-15-1; Philadelphia 6-3; Pittsburgh 8-7; St. Louis 6-1; San Diego 6-10; San Francisco 4-3; Seattle 4-2; Tampa Bay 4-2; Tennessee 13-11; Washington 5-2.

COACHING RECORDS

Jimmy Johnson, 17-15-0 (0-1); Don Shula, 257-133-2 (17-14); George Wilson, 15-39-2.

RETIRED UNIFORM NUMBERS

No.	Player
12	Bob Griese

MINNESOTA VIKINGS
YEAR-BY-YEAR RECORDS

	REGULAR SEASON							PLAYOFFS		
Year	W	L	T	Pct.	PF	PA	Finish	W	L	Highest round	Coach
1961	3	11	0	.214	285	407	7th/Western Conf.	—	—		Norm Van Brocklin
1962	2	11	1	.154	254	410	6th/Western Conf.	—	—		Norm Van Brocklin
1963	5	8	1	.385	309	390	T4th/Western Conf.	—	—		Norm Van Brocklin
1964	8	5	1	.615	355	296	T2nd/Western Conf.	—	—		Norm Van Brocklin
1965	7	7	0	.500	383	403	5th/Western Conf.	—	—		Norm Van Brocklin
1966	4	9	1	.308	292	304	T6th/Western Conf.	—	—		Norm Van Brocklin
1967	3	8	3	.273	233	294	4th/Central Div.	—	—		Bud Grant
1968	8	6	0	.571	282	242	1st/Central Div.	0	1	W. Conf. champ. game	Bud Grant
1969	12	2	0	.857	379	133	1st/Central Div.	2	1	Super Bowl	Bud Grant
1970	12	2	0	.857	335	143	1st/NFC Central Div.	0	1	NFC div. playoff game	Bud Grant
1971	11	3	0	.786	245	139	1st/NFC Central Div.	0	1	NFC div. playoff game	Bud Grant
1972	7	7	0	.500	301	252	3rd/NFC Central Div.	—	—		Bud Grant
1973	12	2	0	.857	296	168	1st/NFC Central Div.	2	1	Super Bowl	Bud Grant
1974	10	4	0	.714	310	195	1st/NFC Central Div.	2	1	Super Bowl	Bud Grant
1975	12	2	0	.857	377	180	1st/NFC Central Div.	0	1	NFC div. playoff game	Bud Grant
1976	11	2	1	.821	305	176	1st/NFC Central Div.	2	1	Super Bowl	Bud Grant
1977	9	5	0	.643	231	227	1st/NFC Central Div.	1	1	NFC championship game	Bud Grant
1978	8	7	1	.531	294	306	1st/NFC Central Div.	0	1	NFC div. playoff game	Bud Grant
1979	7	9	0	.438	259	337	3rd/NFC Central Div.	—	—		Bud Grant
1980	9	7	0	.563	317	308	1st/NFC Central Div.	0	1	NFC div. playoff game	Bud Grant
1981	7	9	0	.438	325	369	4th/NFC Central Div.	—	—		Bud Grant
1982	5	4	0	.556	187	198	T4th/NFC	1	1	NFC second-round pl. game	Bud Grant
1983	8	8	0	.500	316	348	T2nd/NFC Central Div.	—	—		Bud Grant
1984	3	13	0	.188	276	484	5th/NFC Central Div.	—	—		Les Steckel
1985	7	9	0	.438	346	359	T3rd/NFC Central Div.	—	—		Bud Grant
1986	9	7	0	.563	398	273	2nd/NFC Central Div.	—	—		Jerry Burns
1987	8	7	0	.533	336	335	2nd/NFC Central Div.	2	1	NFC championship game	Jerry Burns
1988	11	5	0	.688	406	233	2nd/NFC Central Div.	1	1	NFC div. playoff game	Jerry Burns
1989	10	6	0	.625	351	275	1st/NFC Central Div.	0	1	NFC div. playoff game	Jerry Burns
1990	6	10	0	.375	351	326	T2nd/NFC Central Div.	—	—		Jerry Burns
1991	8	8	0	.500	301	306	3rd/NFC Central Div.	—	—		Jerry Burns
1992	11	5	0	.688	374	249	1st/NFC Central Div.	0	1	NFC wild-card game	Dennis Green
1993	9	7	0	.563	277	290	T2nd/NFC Central Div.	0	1	NFC wild-card game	Dennis Green
1994	10	6	0	.625	356	314	1st/NFC Central Div.	0	1	NFC wild-card game	Dennis Green
1995	8	8	0	.500	412	385	4th/NFC Central Div.	—	—		Dennis Green
1996	9	7	0	.563	298	315	2nd/NFC Central Div.	0	1	NFC wild-card game	Dennis Green
1997	9	7	0	.563	354	359	T3rd/NFC Central Div.	1	1	NFC div. playoff game	Dennis Green

FIRST-ROUND DRAFT PICKS

1961—Tommy Mason, RB, Tulane*
1962—None
1963—Jim Dunaway, T, Mississippi
1964—Carl Eller, DE, Minnesota
1965—Jack Snow, WR, Notre Dame
1966—Jerry Shay, DT, Purdue
1967—Clint Jones, RB, Michigan State
    Gene Washington, WR, Michigan State
    Alan Page, DT, Notre Dame
1968—Ron Yary, T, Southern California*
1969—None
1970—John Ward, DT, Oklahoma State
1971—Leo Hayden, RB, Ohio State
1972—Jeff Siemon, LB, Stanford
1973—Chuck Foreman, RB, Miami (Fla.)
1974—Fred McNeill, LB, UCLA
    Steve Riley, T, Southern California
1975—Mark Mullaney, DE, Colorado State
1976—James White, DT, Oklahoma State
1977—Tommy Kramer, QB, Rice
1978—Randy Holloway, DE, Pittsburgh
1979—Ted Brown, RB, North Carolina State

1980—Doug Martin, DT, Washington
1981—None
1982—Darrin Nelson, RB, Stanford
1983—Joey Browner, DB, Southern California
1984—Keith Millard, DE, Washington State
1985—Chris Doleman, LB, Pittsburgh
1986—Gerald Robinson, DE, Auburn
1987—D.J. Dozier, RB, Penn State
1988—Randall McDaniel, G, Arizona State
1989—None
1990—None
1991—None
1992—None
1993—Robert Smith, RB, Ohio State
1994—DeWayne Washington, CB, North Carolina State
    Todd Steussie, T, California
1995—Derrick Alexander, DE, Florida State
    Korey Stringer, T, Ohio State
1996—Duane Clemons, DE, California
1997—Dwayne Rudd, LB, Alabama
1998—Randy Moss, WR, Marshall
    *First player chosen in draft.

FRANCHISE RECORDS

Most rushing yards, career
5,879—Chuck Foreman
Most rushing yards, season
1,266—Terry Allen, 1997
Most rushing yards, game
200—Chuck Foreman at Phi., Oct. 24, 1976
Most rushing touchdowns, season
13—Chuck Foreman, 1975
    Chuck Foreman, 1976
    Terry Allen, 1992
Most passing attempts, season
606—Warren Moon, 1995
Most passing attempts, game
63—Rich Gannon at N.E., Oct. 20, 1991
Most passes completed, season
377—Warren Moon, 1995
Most passes completed, game
38—Tommy Kramer vs. Cle., Dec. 14, 1980
    Tommy Kramer vs. G.B., Nov. 29, 1981

Most passing yards, career
33,098—Fran Tarkenton
Most passing yards, season
4,264—Warren Moon, 1994
Most passing yards, game
490—Tommy Kramer at Was., Nov. 2, 1986
Most touchdown passes, season
33—Warren Moon, 1995
Most pass receptions, career
667—Cris Carter
Most pass receptions, season
122—Cris Carter, 1994, 1995
Most pass receptions, game
15—Rickey Young at N.E., Dec. 16, 1979
Most receiving yards, career
7,986—Anthony Carter
Most receiving yards, season
1,371—Cris Carter, 1995

Most receiving yards, game
210—Sammy White vs. Det., Nov. 7, 1976
Most receiving touchdowns, season
17—Cris Carter, 1995
Most touchdowns, career
76—Bill Brown
Most field goals, season
46—Fred Cox, 1970
Longest field goal
54 yards—Jan Stenerud vs. Atl., Sept. 16, 1984
Most interceptions, career
53—Paul Krause
Most interceptions, season
10—Paul Krause, 1975
Most sacks, career
130—Carl Eller
Most sacks, season
21—Chris Doleman, 1989

SERIES RECORDS

Minnesota vs.: Arizona 7-8; Atlanta 13-6; Buffalo 6-2; Carolina 2-0; Chicago 39-32-2; Cincinnati 4-4; Dallas 6-9; Denver 5-4; Detroit 44-27-2; Green Bay 36-36-1; Indianapolis 7-11-1; Jacksonville 0-0; Kansas City 3-3; Miami 2-4; New England 3-4; New Orleans 13-6; N.Y. Giants 7-5; N.Y. Jets 1-5; Oakland 3-6; Philadelphia 11-6; Pittsburgh 8-4; St. Louis 15-11-2; San Diego 3-4; San Francisco 16-17-1; Seattle 2-4; Tampa Bay 27-13; Tennessee 4-3; Washington 4-6.

COACHING RECORDS

Jerry Burns, 52-43-0 (3-3); Bud Grant, 158-96-5 (10-12); Dennis Green, 56-40-0 (1-5); Les Steckel, 3-13-0; Norm Van Brocklin, 29-51-4.
NOTE: Playoff games in parentheses.

RETIRED UNIFORM NUMBERS

No.	Player
10	Fran Tarkenton
88	Alan Page

NEW ENGLAND PATRIOTS
YEAR-BY-YEAR RECORDS

			REGULAR SEASON						PLAYOFFS		
Year	W	L	T	Pct.	PF	PA	Finish	W	L	Highest round	Coach
1960*†	5	9	0	.357	286	349	4th/Eastern Div.	—	—		Lou Saban
1961*†	9	4	1	.692	413	313	2nd/Eastern Div.	—	—		Lou Saban, Mike Holovak
1962*†	9	4	1	.692	346	295	2nd/Eastern Div.	—	—		Mike Holovak

Year		REGULAR SEASON								PLAYOFFS		
	W	L	T	Pct.	PF	PA	Finish	W	L	Highest round	Coach
1963*†	7	6	1	.538	327	257	1st/Eastern Div.	1	1	AFL championship game	Mike Holovak
1964*†	10	3	1	.769	365	297	2nd/Eastern Div.	—	—		Mike Holovak
1965*†	4	8	2	.333	244	302	3rd/Eastern Div.	—	—		Mike Holovak
1966*†	8	4	2	.667	315	283	2nd/Eastern Div.	—	—		Mike Holovak
1967*†	3	10	1	.231	280	389	5th/Eastern Div.	—	—		Mike Holovak
1968*†	4	10	0	.286	229	406	4th/Eastern Div.	—	—		Mike Holovak
1969*†	4	10	0	.286	266	316	T3rd/Eastern Div.	—	—		Clive Rush
1970†	2	12	0	.143	149	361	5th/AFC Eastern Div.	—	—		Clive Rush, John Mazur
1971	6	8	0	.429	238	325	T3rd/AFC Eastern Div.	—	—		John Mazur
1972	3	11	0	.214	192	446	5th/AFC Eastern Div.	—	—		J. Mazur, Phil Bengtson
1973	5	9	0	.357	258	300	3rd/AFC Eastern Div.	—	—		Chuck Fairbanks
1974	7	7	0	.500	348	289	T3rd/AFC Eastern Div.	—	—		Chuck Fairbanks
1975	3	11	0	.214	258	358	T4th/AFC Eastern Div.	—	—		Chuck Fairbanks
1976	11	3	0	.786	376	236	2nd/Eastern Div.	0	1	AFC div. playoff game	Chuck Fairbanks
1977	9	5	0	.643	278	217	3rd/AFC Eastern Div.	—	—		Chuck Fairbanks
1978	11	5	0	.688	358	286	1st/AFC Eastern Div.	0	1	AFC div. playoff game	Chuck Fairbanks, Hank Bullough-R. Erhardt
1979	9	7	0	.563	411	326	2nd/AFC Eastern Div.	—	—		Ron Erhardt
1980	10	6	0	.625	441	325	2nd/AFC Eastern Div.	—	—		Ron Erhardt
1981	2	14	0	.125	322	370	T4th/AFC Eastern Div.	—	—		Ron Erhardt
1982	5	4	0	.556	143	157	7th/AFC	0	1	AFC first-round pl. game	Ron Meyer
1983	8	8	0	.500	274	289	T2nd/AFC Eastern Div.	—	—		Ron Meyer
1984	9	7	0	.563	362	352	2nd/AFC Eastern Div.	—	—		R. Meyer, R. Berry
1985	11	5	0	.688	362	290	T2nd/AFC Eastern Div.	3	1	Super Bowl	Raymond Berry
1986	11	5	0	.688	412	307	1st/AFC Eastern Div.	0	1	AFC div. playoff game	Raymond Berry
1987	8	7	0	.533	320	293	T2nd/AFC Eastern Div.	—	—		Raymond Berry
1988	9	7	0	.563	250	284	T2nd/AFC Eastern Div.	—	—		Raymond Berry
1989	5	11	0	.313	297	391	4th/AFC Eastern Div.	—	—		Raymond Berry
1990	1	15	0	.063	181	446	5th/AFC Eastern Div.	—	—		Rod Rust
1991	6	10	0	.375	211	305	4th/AFC Eastern Div.	—	—		Dick MacPherson
1992	2	14	0	.125	205	363	5th/AFC Eastern Div.	—	—		Dick MacPherson
1993	5	11	0	.313	238	286	4th/AFC Eastern Div.	—	—		Bill Parcells
1994	10	6	0	.625	351	312	2nd/AFC Eastern Div.	0	1	AFC wild-card game	Bill Parcells
1995	6	10	0	.375	294	377	4th/AFC Eastern Div.	—	—		Bill Parcells
1996	11	5	0	.687	418	313	1st/AFC Eastern Div.	2	1	Super Bowl	Bill Parcells
1997	10	6	0	.625	369	289	1st/AFC Eastern Div.	1	1	AFC div. playoff game	Pete Carroll

*American Football League.
†Boston Patriots.

FIRST-ROUND DRAFT PICKS

1960—Ron Burton, RB, Northwestern
1961—Tommy Mason, RB, Tulane
1962—Gary Collins, WR, Maryland
1963—Art Graham, E, Boston College
1964—Jack Concannon, QB, Boston College* (AFL)
1965—Jerry Rush, DE, Michigan State
    Dave McCormick, T, Louisiana State
1966—Karl Singer, T, Purdue
    Willie Townes, T, Tulsa
1967—John Charles, DB, Purdue
1968—Dennis Byrd, DE, North Carolina State
1969—Ron Sellers, WR, Florida State
1970—Phil Olsen, DT, Utah State
1971—Jim Plunkett, QB, Stanford*
1972—None
1973—John Hannah, G, Alabama
    Sam Cunningham, RB, Southern California
    Darryl Stingley, WR, Purdue
1974—None
1975—Russ Francis, TE, Oregon
1976—Mike Haynes, DB, Arizona State
    Pete Brock, C, Colorado
    Tim Fox, DB, Ohio State
1977—Raymond Clayborn, DB, Texas
    Stanley Morgan, WR, Tennessee
1978—Bob Cryder, G, Alabama

1979—Rick Sanford, DB, South Carolina
1980—Roland James, DB, Tennessee
    Vagas Ferguson, RB, Notre Dame
1981—Brian Holloway, T, Stanford
1982—Kenneth Sims, DT, Texas*
    Lester Williams, DT, Nebraska
1983—Tony Eason, QB, Illinois
1984—Irving Fryar, WR, Nebraska*
1985—Trevor Matich, C, Brigham Young
1986—Reggie Dupard, RB, Southern Methodist
1987—Bruce Armstrong, G, Louisville
1988—J. Stephens, RB, Northwestern Louisiana State
1989—Hart Lee Dykes, WR, Oklahoma State
1990—Chris Singleton, LB, Arizona
    Ray Agnew, DL, North Carolina State
1991—Pat Harlow, T, Southern California
    Leonard Russell, RB, Arizona State
1992—Eugene Chung, T, Virginia Tech
1993—Drew Bledsoe, QB, Washington State*
1994—Willie McGinest, DE, Southern California
1995—Ty Law, DB, Michigan
1996—Terry Glenn, WR, Ohio State
1997—Chris Canty, DB, Kansas State
1998—Robert Edwards, RB, Georgia
    Tebucky Jones, DB, Syracuse
    *First player chosen in draft.

FRANCHISE RECORDS

Most rushing yards, career
5,453—Sam Cunningham

Most rushing yards, season
1,487—Curtis Martin, 1995

Most rushing yards, game
212—Tony Collins vs. NYJ, Sept. 18, 1983

Most rushing touchdowns, season
14—Curtis Martin, 1995, 1996

Most passing attempts, season
691—Drew Bledsoe, 1994

Most passing attempts, game
70—Drew Bledsoe vs. Min., Nov. 13, 1994 (OT)
60—Drew Bledsoe at Pit., Dec. 16, 1995

Most passes completed, season
400—Drew Bledsoe, 1994

Most passes completed, game
45—Drew Bledsoe vs. Min., Nov. 13, 1994 (OT)
39—Drew Bledsoe at Pit., Dec. 16, 1995

Most passing yards, career
26,886—Steve Grogan

Most passing yards, season
4,555—Drew Bledsoe, 1994

Most passing yards, game
426—Drew Bledsoe vs. Min., Nov. 13, 1994 (OT)
421—Drew Bledsoe at Mia., Sept. 5, 1994

Most touchdown passes, season
31—Babe Parilli, 1964

Most pass receptions, career
534—Stanley Morgan

Most pass receptions, season
96—Ben Coates, 1994

Most pass receptions, game
12—Ben Coates at Ind., Nov. 27, 1994

Most receiving yards, career
10,352—Stanley Morgan

Most receiving yards, season
1,491—Stanley Morgan, 1986

Most receiving yards, game
182—Stanley Morgan vs. Mia., Nov. 8, 1981

Most receiving touchdowns, season
12—Stanley Morgan, 1979

Most touchdowns, career
68—Stanley Morgan

Most field goals, season
32—Tony Franklin, 1986

Longest field goal
55 yards—Matt Bahr at Mia., Nov. 12, 1995

Most interceptions, career
36—Raymond Clayborn

Most interceptions, season
11—Ron Hall, 1964

Most sacks, career
100—Andre Tippett

Most sacks, season
18.5—Andre Tippett, 1984

SERIES RECORDS

New England vs.: Arizona 3-6; Atlanta 3-5; Baltimore 1-0; Buffalo 40-35-1; Carolina 0-1; Chicago 5-2; Cincinnati 9-7; Dallas 0-7; Denver 12-19; Detroit 3-3; Green Bay 3-3; Indianapolis 33-22; Jacksonville 2-0; Kansas City 7-14-3; Miami 25-37; Minnesota 4-3; New Orleans 5-3; N.Y. Giants 2-3; N.Y. Jets 34-40-1; Oakland 12-13-1; Philadelphia 2-5; Pittsburgh 3-11; St. Louis 3-3; San Diego 16-11-2; San Francisco 1-7; Seattle 6-7; Tampa Bay 3-1; Tennessee 17-14-1; Washington 1-5.
NOTE: Includes records as Boston Patriots from 1960 through 1970.

COACHING RECORDS

Phil Bengtson, 1-4-0; Raymond Berry, 48-39-0 (3-2); Hank Bullough, 0-1-0; Pete Carroll, 10-6-0 (1-1); Ron Erhardt, 21-27-0; Chuck Fairbanks, 46-39-0 (0-2); Mike Holovak, 52-46-9 (1-1); Dick MacPherson, 8-24-0; John Mazur, 9-21-0; Ron Meyer, 18-15-0 (0-1); Bill Parcells, 32-32-0 (2-2); Clive Rush, 5-16-0; Rod Rust, 1-15-0; Lou Saban, 7-12-0. NOTE: Playoff games in parentheses.

RETIRED UNIFORM NUMBERS

No.	Player
14	Steve Grogan
20	Gino Cappelletti
57	Steve Nelson
73	John Hannah
79	Jim Hunt
89	Bob Dee

NEW ORLEANS SAINTS
YEAR-BY-YEAR RECORDS

	REGULAR SEASON						PLAYOFFS			
Year	W	L	T	Pct.	PF	PA	Finish	W	L	Highest round	Coach
1967	3	11	0	.214	233	379	4th/Capitol Div.	—	—		Tom Fears
1968	4	9	1	.308	246	327	3rd/Century Div.	—	—		Tom Fears
1969	5	9	0	.357	311	393	3rd/Capitol Div.	—	—		Tom Fears
1970	2	11	1	.154	172	347	4th/NFC Western Div.	—	—		Tom Fears, J.D. Roberts
1971	4	8	2	.333	266	347	4th/NFC Western Div.	—	—		J.D. Roberts
1972	2	11	1	.179	215	361	4th/NFC Western Div.	—	—		J.D. Roberts
1973	5	9	0	.357	163	312	T3rd/NFC Western Div.	—	—		John North
1974	5	9	0	.357	166	263	3rd/NFC Western Div.	—	—		John North
1975	2	12	0	.143	165	360	4th/NFC Western Div.	—	—		J. North, Ernie Hefferle
1976	4	10	0	.286	253	346	T3rd/NFC Western Div.	—	—		Hank Stram
1977	3	11	0	.214	232	336	4th/NFC Western Div.	—	—		Hank Stram
1978	7	9	0	.438	281	298	3rd/NFC Western Div.	—	—		Dick Nolan
1979	8	8	0	.500	370	360	2nd/NFC Western Div.	—	—		Dick Nolan
1980	1	15	0	.063	291	487	4th/NFC Western Div.	—	—		Dick Nolan, Dick Stanfel
1981	4	12	0	.250	207	378	4th/NFC Western Div.	—	—		Bum Phillips
1982	4	5	0	.444	129	160	T8th/NFC	—	—		Bum Phillips
1983	8	8	0	.500	319	337	3rd/NFC Western Div.	—	—		Bum Phillips
1984	7	9	0	.438	298	361	3rd/NFC Western Div.	—	—		Bum Phillips
1985	5	11	0	.313	294	401	3rd/NFC Western Div.	—	—		B. Phillips, Wade Phillips
1986	7	9	0	.438	288	287	3rd/NFC Western Div.	—	—		Jim Mora
1987	12	3	0	.800	422	283	2nd/NFC Western Div.	0	1	NFC wild-card game	Jim Mora
1988	10	6	0	.625	312	283	3rd/NFC Western Div.	—	—		Jim Mora
1989	9	7	0	.563	386	301	3rd/NFC Western Div.	—	—		Jim Mora

			REGULAR SEASON					PLAYOFFS		
Year	W	L	T	Pct.	PF	PA	Finish	W	L	Highest round	Coach
1990	8	8	0	.500	274	275	2nd/NFC Western Div.	0	1	NFC wild-card game	Jim Mora
1991	11	5	0	.688	341	211	1st/NFC Western Div.	0	1	NFC wild-card game	Jim Mora
1992	12	4	0	.750	330	202	2nd/NFC Western Div.	0	1	NFC wild-card game	Jim Mora
1993	8	8	0	.500	317	343	2nd/NFC Western Div.	—	—		Jim Mora
1994	7	9	0	.438	348	407	T2nd/NFC Western Div.	—	—		Jim Mora
1995	7	9	0	.438	319	348	T3rd/NFC Western Div.	—	—		Jim Mora
1996	3	13	0	.188	229	339	T4th/NFC Western Div.	—	—		Jim Mora, Rick Venturi
1997	6	10	0	.375	237	327	4th/NFC Western Div.	—	—		Mike Ditka

FIRST-ROUND DRAFT PICKS

1967—Les Kelley, RB, Alabama
1968—Kevin Hardy, DE, Notre Dame
1969—John Shinners, G, Xavier (Ohio)
1970—Ken Burrough, WR, Texas Southern
1971—Archie Manning, QB, Mississippi
1972—Royce Smith, G, Georgia
1973—None
1974—Rick Middleton, LB, Ohio State
1975—Larry Burton, WR, Purdue
    Kurt Schumacher, G, Ohio State
1976—Chuck Muncie, RB, California
1977—Joe Campbell, DE, Maryland
1978—Wes Chandler, WR, Florida
1979—Russell Erxleben, P, Texas
1980—Stan Brock, T, Colorado
1981—George Rogers, RB, South Carolina*
1982—Lindsay Scott, WR, Georgia
1983—None

1984—None
1985—Alvin Toles, LB, Tennessee
1986—Jim Dombrowski, T, Virginia
1987—Shawn Knight, DE, Brigham Young
1988—Craig Heyward, RB, Pittsburgh
1989—Wayne Martin, DE, Arkansas
1990—Renaldo Turnbull, DE, West Virginia
1991—None
1992—Vaughn Dunbar, RB, Indiana
1993—Willie Roaf, T, Louisiana Tech
    Irv Smith, TE, Notre Dame
1994—Joe Johnson, DE, Louisville
1995—Mark Fields, LB, Washington State
1996—Alex Molden, DB, Oregon
1997—Chris Naeole, G, Colorado
1998—Kyle Turley, T, San Diego State
   *First player chosen in draft.

FRANCHISE RECORDS

Most rushing yards, career
4,267—George Rogers
Most rushing yards, season
1,674—George Rogers, 1981
Most rushing yards, game
206—George Rogers vs. St.L., Sept. 4, 1983
Most rushing touchdowns, season
13—George Rogers, 1981
    Dalton Hilliard, 1989
Most passing attempts, season
567—Jim Everett, 1995
Most passing attempts, game
55—Jim Everett at S.F., Sept. 25, 1994
Most passes completed, season
346—Jim Everett, 1994
Most passes completed, game
33—Archie Manning at G.B., Sept. 10, 1978
Most passing yards, career
21,734—Archie Manning

Most passing yards, season
3,970—Jim Everett, 1995
Most passing yards, game
377—Archie Manning at S.F., Dec. 7, 1980
Most touchdown passes, season
26—Jim Everett, 1995
Most pass receptions, career
532—Eric Martin
Most pass receptions, season
85—Eric Martin, 1988
Most pass receptions, game
14—Tony Galbreath at G.B., Sept. 10, 1978
Most receiving yards, career
7,854—Eric Martin
Most receiving yards, season
1,090—Eric Martin, 1989
Most receiving yards, game
205—Wes Chandler vs. Atl., Sept. 2, 1979
Most receiving touchdowns, season
9—Henry Childs, 1977

Most touchdowns, career
53—Dalton Hilliard
Most field goals, season
31—Morten Andersen, 1985
Longest field goal
63 yards—Tom Dempsey vs. Det., Nov. 8, 1970
Most interceptions, career
37—Dave Waymer
Most interceptions, season
10—Dave Whitsell, 1967
Most sacks, career
115—Rickey Jackson
Most sacks, season
17—Pat Swilling, 1991

SERIES RECORDS

New Orleans vs.: Arizona 10-11; Atlanta 24-33; Baltimore 0-1; Buffalo 2-3; Carolina 2-4; Chicago 7-10; Cincinnati 5-4; Dallas 3-14; Denver 2-4; Detroit 8-6-1; Green Bay 4-13; Indianapolis 3-3; Jacksonville 1-0; Kansas City 3-4; Miami 4-5; Minnesota 6-13; New England 3-5; N.Y. Giants 8-11; N.Y. Jets 4-4; Philadelphia 8-12; Oakland 3-4-1; Pittsburgh 5-6; St. Louis 23-31; San Diego 1-6; San Francisco 15-40-2; Seattle 4-2; Tampa Bay 12-5; Tennessee 4-4-1; Washington 5-12.

COACHING RECORDS

Mike Ditka, 6-10-0; Tom Fears, 13-34-2; Ernie Hefferle, 1-7-0; Jim Mora, 93-74-0 (0-4); Dick Nolan, 15-29-0; John North, 11-23-0; Bum Phillips, 27-42-0; Wade Phillips, 1-3-0; J.D. Roberts, 7-25-3; Dick Stanfel, 1-3-0; Hank Stram, 7-21-0; Rick Venturi, 1-7-0.
NOTE: Playoff games in parentheses.

RETIRED UNIFORM NUMBERS

No.	Player
31	Jim Taylor
81	Doug Atkins

NEW YORK GIANTS
YEAR-BY-YEAR RECORDS

	REGULAR SEASON						PLAYOFFS			
Year	W	L	T	Pct.	PF	PA	Finish	W	L	Highest round	Coach
1925	8	4	0	.667	122	67	T4th				Bob Folwell
1926	8	4	1	.667	147	51	T6th				Joe Alexander
1927	11	1	1	.917	197	20	1st				Earl Potteiger
1928	4	7	2	.364	79	136	6th				Earl Potteiger
1929	13	1	1	.929	312	86	2nd				LeRoy Andrews
1930	13	4	0	.765	308	98	2nd				L. Andrews, Benny Friedman-Steve Owen
1931	7	6	1	.538	154	100	5th				Steve Owen
1932	4	6	2	.400	93	113	5th				Steve Owen
1933	11	3	0	.786	244	101	1st/Eastern Div.	0	1	NFL championship game	Steve Owen
1934	8	5	0	.615	147	107	1st/Eastern Div.	1	0	NFL champ	Steve Owen
1935	9	3	0	.750	180	96	1st/Eastern Div.	0	1	NFL championship game	Steve Owen
1936	5	6	1	.455	115	163	3rd/Eastern Div.	—	—		Steve Owen
1937	6	3	2	.667	128	109	2nd/Eastern Div.	—	—		Steve Owen
1938	8	2	1	.800	194	79	1st/Eastern Div.	1	0	NFL champ	Steve Owen
1939	9	1	1	.900	168	85	1st/Eastern Div.	0	1	NFL championship game	Steve Owen
1940	6	4	1	.600	131	133	3rd/Eastern Div.	—	—		Steve Owen
1941	8	3	0	.727	238	114	1st/Eastern Div.	0	1	NFL championship game	Steve Owen
1942	5	5	1	.500	155	139	3rd/Eastern Div.				Steve Owen
1943	6	3	1	.667	197	170	2nd/Eastern Div.	0	1	E. Div. champ. game	Steve Owen
1944	8	1	1	.889	206	75	1st/Eastern Div.	0	1	NFL championship game	Steve Owen
1945	3	6	1	.333	179	198	T3rd/Eastern Div.	—	—		Steve Owen
1946	7	3	1	.700	236	162	1st/Eastern Div.	0	1	NFL championship game	Steve Owen
1947	2	8	2	.200	190	309	5th/Eastern Div.	—	—		Steve Owen
1948	4	8	0	.333	297	388	T3rd/Eastern Div.	—	—		Steve Owen
1949	6	6	0	.500	287	298	3rd/Eastern Div.	—	—		Steve Owen
1950	10	2	0	.833	268	150	2nd/American Conf.	0	1	Am. Conf. champ. game	Steve Owen
1951	9	2	1	.818	254	161	2nd/American Conf.	—	—		Steve Owen
1952	7	5	0	.583	234	231	T2nd/American Conf.	—	—		Steve Owen
1953	3	9	0	.250	179	277	5th/Eastern Conf.	—	—		Steve Owen
1954	7	5	0	.583	293	184	3rd/Eastern Conf.	—	—		Jim Lee Howell
1955	6	5	1	.545	267	223	3rd/Eastern Conf.	—	—		Jim Lee Howell
1956	8	3	1	.727	264	197	1st/Eastern Conf.	1	0	NFL champ	Jim Lee Howell
1957	7	5	0	.583	254	211	2nd/Eastern Conf.	—	—		Jim Lee Howell
1958	9	3	0	.750	246	183	1st/Eastern Conf.	1	1	NFL championship game	Jim Lee Howell
1959	10	2	0	.833	284	170	1st/Eastern Conf.	0	1	NFL championship game	Jim Lee Howell
1960	6	4	2	.600	271	261	3rd/Eastern Conf.	—	—		Jim Lee Howell
1961	10	3	1	.769	368	220	1st/Eastern Conf.	0	1	NFL championship game	Allie Sherman
1962	12	2	0	.857	398	283	1st/Eastern Conf.	0	1	NFL championship game	Allie Sherman
1963	11	3	0	.786	448	280	1st/Eastern Conf.	0	1	NFL championship game	Allie Sherman
1964	2	10	2	.167	241	399	7th/Eastern Conf.	—	—		Allie Sherman
1965	7	7	0	.500	270	338	T2nd/Eastern Conf.	—	—		Allie Sherman
1966	1	12	1	.077	263	501	8th/Eastern Conf.	—	—		Allie Sherman
1967	7	7	0	.500	369	379	2nd/Century Div.	—	—		Allie Sherman
1968	7	7	0	.500	294	325	2nd/Capitol Div.	—	—		Allie Sherman
1969	6	8	0	.429	264	298	2nd/Century Div.	—	—		Alex Webster
1970	9	5	0	.643	301	270	2nd/NFC Eastern Div.	—	—		Alex Webster
1971	4	10	0	.286	228	362	5th/NFC Eastern Div.	—	—		Alex Webster
1972	8	6	0	.571	331	247	3rd/NFC Eastern Div.	—	—		Alex Webster
1973	2	11	1	.179	226	362	5th/NFC Eastern Div.	—	—		Alex Webster
1974	2	12	0	.143	195	299	5th/NFC Eastern Div.	—	—		Bill Arnsparger
1975	5	9	0	.357	216	306	4th/NFC Eastern Div.	—	—		Bill Arnsparger
1976	3	11	0	.214	170	250	5th/NFC Eastern Div.	—	—		B. Arnsparger, J. McVay
1977	5	9	0	.357	181	265	T4th/NFC Eastern Div.	—	—		John McVay
1978	6	10	0	.375	264	298	T4th/NFC Eastern Div.	—	—		John McVay
1979	6	10	0	.375	237	323	4th/NFC Eastern Div.	—	—		Ray Perkins
1980	4	12	0	.250	249	425	5th/NFC Eastern Div.	—	—		Ray Perkins
1981	9	7	0	.563	295	257	3rd/NFC Eastern Div.	1	1	NFC div. playoff game	Ray Perkins
1982	4	5	0	.444	164	160	T8th/NFC	—	—		Ray Perkins
1983	3	12	1	.219	267	347	5th/NFC Eastern Div.	—	—		Bill Parcells
1984	9	7	0	.563	299	301	2nd/NFC Eastern Div.	1	1	NFC div. playoff game	Bill Parcells
1985	10	6	0	.625	399	283	2nd/NFC Eastern Div.	1	1	NFC div. playoff game	Bill Parcells
1986	14	2	0	.875	371	236	1st/NFC Eastern Div.	3	0	Super Bowl champ	Bill Parcells
1987	6	9	0	.400	280	312	5th/NFC Eastern Div.	—	—		Bill Parcells
1988	10	6	0	.625	359	304	2nd/NFC Eastern Div.	—	—		Bill Parcells
1989	12	4	0	.750	348	252	1st/NFC Eastern Div.	0	1	NFC div. playoff game	Bill Parcells
1990	13	3	0	.813	335	211	1st/NFC Eastern Div.	3	0	Super Bowl champ	Bill Parcells

			REGULAR SEASON						PLAYOFFS		
Year	W	L	T	Pct.	PF	PA	Finish	W	L	Highest round	Coach
1991	8	8	0	.500	281	297	4th/NFC Eastern Div.	—	—		Ray Handley
1992	6	10	0	.375	306	367	4th/NFC Eastern Div.	—	—		Ray Handley
1993	11	5	0	.688	288	205	2nd/NFC Eastern Div.	1	1	NFC div. playoff game	Dan Reeves
1994	9	7	0	.563	279	305	2nd/NFC Eastern Div.	—	—		Dan Reeves
1995	5	11	0	.313	290	340	4th/NFC Eastern Div.	—	—		Dan Reeves
1996	6	10	0	.375	242	297	5th/NFC Eastern Div.	—	—		Dan Reeves
1997	10	5	1	.656	307	265	1st/NFC Eastern Div.	0	1	NFC wild-card game	Jim Fassel

HISTORY Team by team

FIRST-ROUND DRAFT PICKS

1936—Art Lewis, T, Ohio
1937—Ed Widseth, T, Minnesota
1938—George Karamatic, B, Gonzaga
1939—Walt Nielson, B, Arizona
1940—Grenville Lansdell, B, Southern California
1941—George Franck, B, Minnesota
1942—Merle Hapes, B, Mississippi
1943—Steve Filipowicz, B, Fordham
1944—Billy Hillenbrand, B, Indiana
1945—Elmer Barbour, B, Wake Forest
1946—George Connor, T, Notre Dame
1947—Vic Schwall, B, Northwestern
1948—Tony Minisi, B, Pennsylvania
1949—Paul Page, B, Southern Methodist
1950—Travis Tidwell, B, Auburn
1951—Kyle Rote, B, Southern Methodist*
　　　Kim Spavital, B, Oklahoma A&M
1952—Frank Gifford, B, Southern California
1953—Bobby Marlow, B, Alabama
1954—None
1955—Joe Heap, B, Notre Dame
1956—Henry Moore, B, Arkansas
1957—None
1958—Phil King, B, Vanderbilt
1959—Lee Grosscup, B, Utah
1960—Lou Cordileone, G, Clemson
1961—None
1962—Jerry Hillebrand, LB, Colorado
1963—None
1964—Joe Don Looney, RB, Oklahoma
1965—T. Frederickson, RB, Auburn*
1966—Francis Peay, T, Missouri
1967—None
1968—None

1969—Fred Dryer, DE, San Diego State
1970—Jim Files, LB, Oklahoma
1971—Rocky Thompson, RB, West Texas State
1972—Eldridge Small, DB, Texas A&I
　　　Larry Jacobson, DT, Nebraska
1973—None
1974—John Hicks, G, Ohio State
1975—None
1976—Troy Archer, DE, Colorado
1977—Gary Jeter, DT, Southern Cal
1978—Gordon King, T, Stanford
1979—Phil Simms, QB, Morehead State
1980—Mark Haynes, DB, Colorado
1981—Lawrence Taylor, LB, North Carolina
1982—Butch Woolfolk, RB, Michigan
1983—Terry Kinard, DB, Clemson
1984—Carl Banks, LB, Michigan State
　　　Bill Roberts, T, Ohio State
1985—George Adams, RB, Kentucky
1986—Eric Dorsey, DT, Notre Dame
1987—Mark Ingram, WR, Michigan State
1988—Eric Moore, T, Indiana
1989—Brian Williams, G, Minnesota
1990—Rodney Hampton, RB, Georgia
1991—Jarrod Bunch, FB, Michigan
1992—Derek Brown, TE, Notre Dame
1993—None
1994—Thomas Lewis, WR, Indiana
1995—Tyrone Wheatley, RB, Michigan
1996—Cedric Jones, DE, Oklahoma
1997—Ike Hilliard, WR, Florida
1998—Shaun Williams, DB, UCLA
　　　*First player chosen in draft.

FRANCHISE RECORDS

Most rushing yards, career
6,897—Rodney Hampton
Most rushing yards, season
1,516—Joe Morris, 1986
Most rushing yards, game
218—Gene Roberts vs. Chi. Cardinals,
　　　Nov. 12, 1950
Most rushing touchdowns, season
21—Joe Morris, 1985
Most passing attempts, season
533—Phil Simms, 1984
Most passing attempts, game
62—Phil Simms at Cin., Oct. 13, 1985
Most passes completed, season
286—Phil Simms, 1984
Most passes completed, game
40—Phil Simms at Cin., Oct. 13, 1985
Most passing yards, career
33,462—Phil Simms

Most passing yards, season
4,044—Phil Simms, 1984
Most passing yards, game
513—Phil Simms at Cin., Oct. 13, 1985
Most touchdown passes, season
36—Y.A. Tittle, 1963
Most pass receptions, career
395—Joe Morrison
Most pass receptions, season
78—Earnest Gray, 1983
Most pass receptions, game
12—Mark Bavaro at Cin., Oct. 13, 1985
Most receiving yards, career
5,434—Frank Gifford
Most receiving yards, season
1,209—Homer Jones
Most receiving yards, game
269—Del Shofner vs. Was., Oct. 28, 1962

Most receiving touchdowns, season
13—Homer Jones, 1967
Most touchdowns, career
50—Rodney Hampton
Most field goals, season
35—Ali Haji-Sheikh, 1983
Longest field goal
56 yards—Ali Haji-Sheikh at Det.,
　　　Nov. 7, 1983
Most interceptions, career
74—Emlen Tunnell
Most interceptions, season
11—Otto Schellbacher, 1951
　　　Jimmy Patton, 1958
Most sacks, career
132.5—Lawrence Taylor
Most sacks, season
20.5—Lawrence Taylor, 1986

SERIES RECORDS

N.Y. Giants vs.: Arizona 72-37-2; Atlanta 6-6; Baltimore, 0-1; Buffalo 2-5; Carolina 0-1; Chicago 16-25-2; Cincinnati 2-4; Dallas 25-44-2; Denver 3-3; Detroit 14-14-1; Green Bay 20-22-2; Indianapolis 5-5; Jacksonville 0-1; Kansas City 6-3; Miami 3-1; Minnesota 5-7; New England 3-2; New Orleans 11-8; N.Y. Jets 4-4; Oakland 2-5; Philadelphia 65-59-2; Pittsburgh 44-28-3; St. Louis 7-20; San Diego 4-3; San Francisco 11-11; Seattle 5-3; Tampa Bay 8-4; Tennessee 5-1; Washington 67-50-3.

COACHING RECORDS

Joe Alexander, 8-4-1; LeRoy Andrews, 24-5-1; Bill Arnsparger, 7-28-0; Jim Fassel, 10-5-1 (0-1); Bob Folwell, 8-4-0; Benny Friedman, 2-0-0; Ray Handley, 14-18-0; Jim Lee Howell, 53-27-4 (2-2); John McVay, 14-23-0; Steve Owen, 153-100-17 (2-8); Bill Parcells, 77-49-1 (8-3); Ray Perkins, 23-34-0 (1-1); Earl Potteiger, 15-8-3; Dan Reeves, 31-33-0 (1-1); Allie Sherman, 57-51-4 (0-3); Alex Webster, 29-40-1.
NOTE: Playoff games in parentheses.

RETIRED UNIFORM NUMBERS

No.	Player
1	Ray Flaherty
7	Mel Hein
11	Phil Simms
14	Y.A. Tittle
32	Al Blozis
40	Joe Morrison
42	Charlie Conerly
50	Ken Strong
56	Lawrence Taylor

NEW YORK JETS
YEAR-BY-YEAR RECORDS

			REGULAR SEASON					PLAYOFFS		
Year	W	L	T	Pct.	PF	PA	Finish	W	L	Highest round	Coach
1960*†	7	7	0	.500	382	399	2nd/Eastern Div.	—	—		Sammy Baugh
1961*†	7	7	0	.500	301	390	3rd/Eastern Div.	—	—		Sammy Baugh
1962*†	5	9	0	.357	278	423	4th/Eastern Div.	—	—		Bulldog Turner
1963*	5	8	1	.385	249	399	4th/Eastern Div.	—	—		Weeb Ewbank
1964*	5	8	1	.385	278	315	3rd/Eastern Div.	—	—		Weeb Ewbank
1965*	5	8	1	.385	285	303	2nd/Eastern Div.	—	—		Weeb Ewbank
1966*	6	6	2	.500	322	312	3rd/Eastern Div.	—	—		Weeb Ewbank
1967*	8	5	1	.615	371	329	2nd/Eastern Div.	—	—		Weeb Ewbank
1968*	11	3	0	.786	419	280	1st/Eastern Div.	2	0	Super Bowl champ	Weeb Ewbank
1969*	10	4	0	.714	353	269	1st/Eastern Div.	0	1	Div. playoff game	Weeb Ewbank
1970	4	10	0	.286	255	286	3rd/AFC Eastern Div.	—	—		Weeb Ewbank
1971	6	8	0	.429	212	299	T3rd/AFC Eastern Div.	—	—		Weeb Ewbank
1972	7	7	0	.500	367	324	2nd/AFC Eastern Div.	—	—		Weeb Ewbank
1973	4	10	0	.286	240	306	T4th/AFC Eastern Div.	—	—		Weeb Ewbank
1974	7	7	0	.500	279	300	T3rd/AFC Eastern Div.	—	—		Charley Winner
1975	3	11	0	.214	258	433	T4th/AFC Eastern Div.	—	—		C. Winner, Ken Shipp
1976	3	11	0	.214	169	383	4th/AFC Eastern Div.	—	—		Lou Holtz, Mike Holovak
1977	3	11	0	.214	191	300	T4th/AFC Eastern Div.	—	—		Walt Michaels
1978	8	8	0	.500	359	364	3rd/AFC Eastern Div.	—	—		Walt Michaels
1979	8	8	0	.500	337	383	3rd/AFC Eastern Div.	—	—		Walt Michaels
1980	4	12	0	.250	302	395	5th/AFC Eastern Div.	—	—		Walt Michaels
1981	10	5	1	.656	355	287	2nd/AFC Eastern Div.	0	1	AFC wild-card game	Walt Michaels
1982	6	3	0	.667	245	166	T4th/AFC	2	1	AFC championship game	Walt Michaels
1983	7	9	0	.438	313	331	T4th/AFC Eastern Div.	—	—		Joe Walton
1984	7	9	0	.438	332	364	3rd/AFC Eastern Div.	—	—		Joe Walton
1985	11	5	0	.688	393	264	T2nd/AFC Eastern Div.	0	1	AFC wild-card game	Joe Walton
1986	10	6	0	.625	364	386	2nd/AFC Eastern Div.	1	1	AFC div. playoff game	Joe Walton
1987	6	9	0	.400	334	360	5th/AFC Eastern Div.	—	—		Joe Walton
1988	8	7	1	.531	372	354	4th/AFC Eastern Div.	—	—		Joe Walton
1989	4	12	0	.250	253	411	5th/AFC Eastern Div.	—	—		Joe Walton
1990	6	10	0	.375	295	345	4th/AFC Eastern Div.	—	—		Bruce Coslet
1991	8	8	0	.500	314	293	2nd/AFC Eastern Div.	0	1	AFC wild-card game	Bruce Coslet
1992	4	12	0	.250	220	315	4th/AFC Eastern Div.	—	—		Bruce Coslet
1993	8	8	0	.500	270	247	3rd/AFC Eastern Div.	—	—		Bruce Coslet
1994	6	10	0	.375	264	320	5th/AFC Eastern Div.	—	—		Pete Carroll
1995	3	13	0	.188	233	384	5th/AFC Eastern Div.	—	—		Rich Kotite
1996	1	15	0	.063	279	454	5th/AFC Eastern Div.	—	—		Rich Kotite
1997	9	7	0	.563	348	287	T2nd/AFC Eastern Div.	—	—		Bill Parcells

*American Football League.
†New York Titans.

FIRST-ROUND DRAFT PICKS

1960—George Izo, QB, Notre Dame
1961—Tom Brown, G, Minnesota
1962—Sandy Stephens, QB, Minnesota
1963—Jerry Stovall, RB, Louisiana State

1964—Matt Snell, RB, Ohio State
1965—Joe Namath, QB, Alabama
        Tom Nowatzke, RB, Indiana
1966—Bill Yearby, DT, Michigan

1967—Paul Seiler, G, Notre Dame
1968—Lee White, RB, Weber State
1969—Dave Foley, T, Ohio State
1970—Steve Tannen, DB, Florida
1971—John Riggins, RB, Kansas
1972—Jerome Barkum, WR, Jackson State
1972—Mike Taylor, LB, Michigan
1973—Burgess Owens, DB, Miami
1974—Carl Barzilauskas, DT, Indiana
1975—None
1976—Richard Todd, QB, Alabama
1977—Marvin Powell, T, Southern California
1978—Chris Ward, T, Ohio State
1979—Marty Lyons, DT, Alabama
1980—Lam Jones, WR, Texas
1981—Freeman McNeil, RB, UCLA
1982—Bob Crable, LB, Notre Dame
1983—Ken O'Brien, QB, California-Davis

1984—Russell Carter, DB, Southern Methodist
   Ron Faurot, DE, Arkansas
1985—Al Toon, WR, Wisconsin
1986—Mike Haight, T, Iowa
1987—Roger Vick, FB, Texas A&M
1988—Dave Cadigan, T, Southern California
1989—Jeff Lageman, LB, Virginia
1990—Blair Thomas, RB, Penn State
1991—None
1992—Johnny Mitchell, TE, Nebraska
1993—Marvin Jones, LB, Florida State
1994—Aaron Glenn, DB, Texas A&M
1995—Kyle Brady, TE, Penn State
   Hugh Douglas, DE, Central State (O.)
1996—Keyshawn Johnson, WR, Southern California*
1997—James Farrior, LB, Virginia
1998—None
   *First player chosen in draft.

FRANCHISE RECORDS

Most rushing yards, career
8,074—Freeman McNeil
Most rushing yards, season
1,331—Freeman McNeil, 1985
Most rushing yards, game
199—Adrian Murrell at Ariz., Oct. 27, 1996
Most rushing touchdowns, season
11—Emerson Boozer, 1972
   Johnny Hector, 1987
   Brad Baxter, 1991
Most passing attempts, season
518—Richard Todd, 1983
Most passing attempts, game
62—Joe Namath vs. Bal., Oct. 18, 1970
Most passes completed, season
308—Richard Todd, 1983
Most passes completed, game
42—Richard Todd vs. S.F., Sept. 21, 1980
Most passing yards, career
27,057—Joe Namath

Most passing yards, season
4,007—Joe Namath, 1967
Most passing yards, game
496—Joe Namath at Bal., Sept. 24, 1972
Most touchdown passes, season
26—Al Dorow, 1960
   Joe Namath, 1967
Most pass receptions, career
627—Don Maynard
Most pass receptions, season
93—Al Toon, 1988
Most pass receptions, game
17—Clark Gaines vs. S.F., Sept. 21, 1980
Most receiving yards, career
11,732—Don Maynard
Most receiving yards, season
1,434—Don Maynard, 1967
Most receiving yards, game
228—Don Maynard at Oak., Nov. 17, 1968

Most receiving touchdowns, season
14—Art Powell, 1960
   Don Maynard, 1965
Most touchdowns, career
88—Don Maynard
Most field goals, season
34—Jim Turner, 1968
Longest field goal
55 yards—Pat Leahy vs. Chi., Dec. 14,
   1985
   John Hall at Sea., Aug. 31,
   1997
Most interceptions, career
34—Bill Baird
Most interceptions, season
12—Dainard Paulson, 1964
Most sacks, career
107.5—Mark Gastineau
Most sacks, season
22—Mark Gastineau, 1984

SERIES RECORDS

N.Y. Jets vs.: Arizona 2-2; Atlanta 3-4; Baltimore, 1-0; Buffalo 31-44; Carolina 0-1; Chicago 2-4; Cincinnati 10-6; Dallas 1-5; Denver 12-13-1; Detroit 3-5; Green Bay 5-2; Indianapolis 22-33; Jacksonville 1-1; Kansas City 12-14-1; Miami 28-33-1; Minnesota 5-1; New England 40-34-1; New Orleans 4-4; N.Y. Giants 4-4; Oakland 10-16-2; Philadelphia 0-6; Pittsburgh 1-12; St. Louis 2-6; San Diego 9-17-1; San Francisco 1-6; Seattle 5-8; Tampa Bay 6-1; Tennessee 12-20-1; Washington 1-5.
NOTE: Includes records as New York Titans from 1960 through 1962.

COACHING RECORDS

Sammy Baugh, 14-14-0; Pete Carroll, 6-10-0; Bruce Coslet, 26-38-0 (0-1); Weeb Ewbank, 71-77-6 (2-1); Mike Holovak, 0-1-0; Lou Holtz, 3-10-0; Rich Kotite, 4-28-0; Walt Michaels, 39-47-1 (2-2); Bill Parcells, 9-7-0; Ken Shipp, 1-4-0; Clyde Turner, 5-9-0; Joe Walton, 53-57-1 (1-2); Charley Winner, 9-14-0.
NOTE: Playoff games in parentheses.

RETIRED UNIFORM NUMBERS

No.	Player
12	Joe Namath
13	Don Maynard

OAKLAND RAIDERS
YEAR-BY-YEAR RECORDS

	REGULAR SEASON							PLAYOFFS			
Year	W	L	T	Pct.	PF	PA	Finish	W	L	Highest round	Coach
1960*	6	8	0	.429	319	388	3rd/Western Div.	—	—		Eddie Erdelatz
1961*	2	12	0	.143	237	458	4th/Western Div.	—	—		E. Erdelatz, Marty Feldman
1962*	1	13	0	.071	213	370	4th/Western Div.	—	—		M. Feldman, Red Conkright
1963*	10	4	0	.714	363	288	2nd/Western Div.	—	—		Al Davis
1964*	5	7	2	.417	303	350	3rd/Western Div.	—	—		Al Davis

			REGULAR SEASON						PLAYOFFS		
Year	W	L	T	Pct.	PF	PA	Finish	W	L	Highest round	Coach
1965*	8	5	1	.615	298	239	2nd/Western Div.	—	—		Al Davis
1966*	8	5	1	.615	315	288	2nd/Western Div.	—	—		John Rauch
1967*	13	1	0	.929	468	233	1st/Western Div.	1	1	Super Bowl	John Rauch
1968*	12	2	0	.857	453	233	1st/Western Div.	1	1	AFL championship game	John Rauch
1969*	12	1	1	.923	377	242	1st/Western Div.	1	1	AFL championship game	John Madden
1970	8	4	2	.667	300	293	1st/AFC Western Div.	1	1	AFC championship game	John Madden
1971	8	4	2	.667	344	278	2nd/AFC Western Div.	—	—		John Madden
1972	10	3	1	.750	365	248	1st/AFC Western Div.	0	1	AFC div. playoff game	John Madden
1973	9	4	1	.679	292	175	1st/AFC Western Div.	1	1	AFC championship game	John Madden
1974	12	2	0	.857	355	228	1st/AFC Western Div.	1	1	AFC championship game	John Madden
1975	11	3	0	.786	375	255	1st/AFC Western Div.	1	1	AFC championship game	John Madden
1976	13	1	0	.929	350	237	1st/AFC Western Div.	3	0	Super Bowl champ	John Madden
1977	11	3	0	.786	351	230	2nd/AFC Western Div.	1	1	AFC championship game	John Madden
1978	9	7	0	.563	311	283	T2nd/AFC Western Div.	—	—		John Madden
1979	9	7	0	.563	365	337	T3rd/AFC Western Div.	—	—		Tom Flores
1980	11	5	0	.688	364	306	2nd/AFC Western Div.	4	0	Super Bowl champ	Tom Flores
1981	7	9	0	.438	273	343	4th/AFC Western Div.	—	—		Tom Flores
1982†	8	1	0	.889	260	200	1st/AFC	1	1	AFC second-round pl. game	Tom Flores
1983†	12	4	0	.750	442	338	1st/AFC Western Div.	3	0	Super Bowl champ	Tom Flores
1984†	11	5	0	.688	368	278	3rd/AFC Western Div.	0	1	AFC wild-card game	Tom Flores
1985†	12	4	0	.750	354	308	1st/AFC Western Div.	0	1	AFC div. playoff game	Tom Flores
1986†	8	8	0	.500	323	346	4th/AFC Western Div.	—	—		Tom Flores
1987†	5	10	0	.333	301	289	4th/AFC Western Div.	—	—		Tom Flores
1988†	7	9	0	.438	325	369	3rd/AFC Western Div.	—	—		Mike Shanahan
1989†	8	8	0	.500	315	297	3rd/AFC Western Div.	—	—		Mike Shanahan, Art Shell
1990†	12	4	0	.750	337	268	1st/AFC Western Div.	1	1	AFC championship game	Art Shell
1991†	9	7	0	.563	298	297	3rd/AFC Western Div.	0	1	AFC wild-card game	Art Shell
1992†	7	9	0	.438	249	281	4th/AFC Western Div.	—	—		Art Shell
1993†	10	6	0	.625	306	326	2nd/AFC Western Div.	1	1	AFC div. playoff game	Art Shell
1994†	9	7	0	.563	303	327	3rd/AFC Western Div.	—	—		Art Shell
1995	8	8	0	.500	348	332	T3rd/AFC Western Div.	—	—		Mike White
1996	7	9	0	.438	340	293	T4th/AFC Western Div.	—	—		Mike White
1997	4	12	0	.250	324	419	T4th/AFC Western Div.	—	—		Joe Bugel

*American Football League.
†Los Angeles Raiders.

FIRST-ROUND DRAFT PICKS

1960—Dale Hackbart, DB, Wisconsin
1961—Joe Rutgens, DT, Illinois
1962—Roman Gabriel, QB, North Carolina State* (AFL)
1963—None
1964—Tony Lorick, RB, Arizona State
1965—Harry Schuh, T, Memphis State
1966—Rodger Bird, DB, Kentucky
1967—Gene Upshaw, G, Texas A&I
1968—Eldridge Dickey, QB, Tenn. State
1969—Art Thoms, DT, Syracuse
1970—Raymond Chester, TE, Morgan State
1971—Jack Tatum, DB, Ohio State
1972—Mike Siani, WR, Villanova
1973—Ray Guy, P, So. Mississippi
1974—Henry Lawrence, T, Florida A&M
1975—Neal Colzie, DB, Ohio State
1976—None
1977—None
1978—None
1979—None
1980—Marc Wilson, QB, Brigham Young
1981—Ted Watts, DB, Texas Tech
      Curt Marsh, G, Washington

1982—Marcus Allen, RB, Southern California
1983—Don Mosebar, T, Southern California
1984—None
1985—Jessie Hester, WR, Florida State
1986—Bob Buczkowski, DT, Pittsburgh
1987—John Clay, T, Missouri
1988—Tim Brown, WR, Notre Dame
      Terry McDaniel, CB, Tennessee
      Scott Davis, DE, Illinois
1989—None
1990—Anthony Smith, DE, Arizona
1991—Todd Marinovich, QB, Southern California
1992—Chester McGlockton, DT, Clemson
1993—Patrick Bates, DB, Texas A&M
1994—Rob Fredrickson, LB, Michigan State
1995—Napoleon Kaufman, RB, Washington
1996—Rickey Dudley, TE, Ohio State
1997—Darrell Russell, DT, Southern California
1998—Charles Woodson, DB, Michigan
      Mo Collins, T, Florida
*First player chosen in draft.

FRANCHISE RECORDS

Most rushing yards, career
8,545—Marcus Allen

Most rushing yards, season
1,759—Marcus Allen, 1985

Most rushing yards, game
221—Bo Jackson at Sea., Nov. 30, 1987

Most rushing touchdowns, season
16—Pete Banaszak, 1975

Most passing attempts, season
521—Jeff George, 1997

Most passing attempts, game
59—Todd Marinovich vs. Cle., Sept. 20, 1992

Most passes completed, season
304—Ken Stabler, 1979

Most passes completed, game
34—Jim Plunkett at K.C., Sept. 12, 1985

Most passing yards, career
19,078—Ken Stabler

Most passing yards, season
3,917—Jeff George, 1997

Most passing yards, game
424—Jeff Hostetler vs. S.D., Oct. 18, 1993

Most touchdown passes, season
34—Daryle Lamonica, 1969

Most pass receptions, career
599—Tim Brown

Most pass receptions, season
104—Tim Brown, 1997

Most pass receptions, game
14—Tim Brown vs. Jac., Dec. 21, 1997

Most receiving yards, career
8,974—Fred Biletnikoff

Most receiving yards, season
1,408—Tim Brown, 1997

Most receiving yards, game
247—Art Powell vs. Hou., Dec. 22, 1963

Most receiving touchdowns, season
16—Art Powell, 1964

Most touchdowns, career
95—Marcus Allen

Most field goals, season
35—Jeff Jaeger, 1993

Longest field goal
54 yards—George Fleming vs. Den., Oct. 2, 1961

Most interceptions, career
39—Willie Brown
Lester Hayes

Most interceptions, season
13—Lester Hayes, 1980

Most sacks, career
107.5—Greg Townsend

Most sacks, season
17.5—Tony Cline, 1970

SERIES RECORDS

Oakland vs.: Arizona 2-1; Atlanta 6-3; Baltimore 0-1; Buffalo 15-14; Carolina 0-1; Chicago 5-4; Cincinnati 15-7; Dallas 3-3; Denver 49-24-2; Detroit 6-2; Green Bay 5-2; Indianapolis 5-2; Jacksonville 1-1; Kansas City 36-37-2; Miami 15-6-1; Minnesota 6-3; New England 13-12-1; New Orleans 4-3-1; N.Y. Giants 5-2; N.Y. Jets 16-10-2; Philadelphia 3-4; Pittsburgh 7-5; St. Louis 7-2; San Diego 45-29-2; San Francisco 5-3; Seattle 21-19; Tampa Bay 3-1; Tennessee 20-14; Washington 6-2.
NOTE: Includes records as Los Angeles Raiders from 1982 through 1994.

COACHING RECORDS

Joe Bugel, 4-12-0; Red Conkright, 1-8-0; Al Davis, 23-16-3; Eddie Erdelatz, 6-10-0; Marty Feldman, 2-15-0; Tom Flores, 83-53-0 (8-3); John Madden, 103-32-7 (9-7); John Rauch, 33-8-1 (2-2); Mike Shanahan, 8-12-0; Art Shell, 54-38-0 (2-3); Mike White, 15-17-0.
NOTE: Playoff games in parentheses.

RETIRED UNIFORM NUMBERS

No.	Player
	None

PHILADELPHIA EAGLES
YEAR-BY-YEAR RECORDS

	REGULAR SEASON							PLAYOFFS			
Year	W	L	T	Pct.	PF	PA	Finish	W	L	Highest round	Coach
1933	3	5	1	.375	77	158	4th/Eastern Div.	—	—		Lud Wray
1934	4	7	0	.364	127	85	T3rd/Eastern Div.	—	—		Lud Wray
1935	2	9	0	.182	60	179	5th/Eastern Div.	—	—		Lud Wray
1936	1	11	0	.083	51	206	5th/Eastern Div.	—	—		Bert Bell
1937	2	8	1	.200	86	177	5th/Eastern Div.	—	—		Bert Bell
1938	5	6	0	.455	154	164	4th/Eastern Div.	—	—		Bert Bell
1939	1	9	1	.100	105	200	T4th/Eastern Div.	—	—		Bert Bell
1940	1	10	0	.091	111	211	5th/Eastern Div.	—	—		Bert Bell
1941	2	8	1	.200	119	218	4th/Eastern Div.	—	—		Greasy Neale
1942	2	9	0	.182	134	239	5th/Eastern Div.	—	—		Greasy Neale
1943*	5	4	1	.556	225	230	3rd/Eastern Div.	—	—		G. Neale-Walt Kiesling
1944	7	1	2	.875	267	131	2nd/Eastern Div.	—	—		Greasy Neale
1945	7	3	0	.700	272	133	2nd/Eastern Div.	—	—		Greasy Neale
1946	6	5	0	.545	231	220	2nd/Eastern Div.	—	—		Greasy Neale
1947	8	4	0	.667	308	242	1st/Eastern Div.	1	1	NFL championship game	Greasy Neale
1948	9	2	1	.818	376	156	1st/Eastern Div.	1	0	NFL champ	Greasy Neale
1949	11	1	0	.917	364	134	1st/Eastern Div.	1	0	NFL champ	Greasy Neale
1950	6	6	0	.500	254	141	T3rd/American Conf.	—	—		Greasy Neale
1951	4	8	0	.333	234	264	5th/American Conf.	—	—		Bo McMillin, Wayne Millner
1952	7	5	0	.583	252	271	T2nd/American Conf.	—	—		Jim Trimble
1953	7	4	1	.636	352	215	2nd/Eastern Conf.	—	—		Jim Trimble
1954	7	4	1	.636	284	230	2nd/Eastern Conf.	—	—		Jim Trimble
1955	4	7	1	.364	248	231	T4th/Eastern Conf.	—	—		Jim Trimble
1956	3	8	1	.273	143	215	6th/Eastern Conf.	—	—		Hugh Devore
1957	4	8	0	.333	173	230	5th/Eastern Conf.	—	—		Hugh Devore
1958	2	9	1	.182	235	306	T5th/Eastern Conf.	—	—		Buck Shaw
1959	7	5	0	.583	268	278	T2nd/Eastern Conf.	—	—		Buck Shaw
1960	10	2	0	.833	321	246	1st/Eastern Conf.	1	0	NFL champ	Buck Shaw
1961	10	4	0	.714	361	297	2nd/Eastern Conf.	—	—		Nick Skorich
1962	3	10	1	.231	282	356	7th/Eastern Conf.	—	—		Nick Skorich
1963	2	10	2	.167	242	381	7th/Western Conf.	—	—		Nick Skorich
1964	6	8	0	.429	312	313	T3rd/Eastern Conf.	—	—		Joe Kuharich
1965	5	9	0	.357	363	359	T5th/Eastern Conf.	—	—		Joe Kuharich

			REGULAR SEASON						PLAYOFFS		
Year	W	L	T	Pct.	PF	PA	Finish	W	L	Highest round	Coach
1966	9	5	0	.643	326	340	T2nd/Eastern Conf.	—	—		Joe Kuharich
1967	6	7	1	.462	351	409	2nd/Capitol Div.	—	—		Joe Kuharich
1968	2	12	0	.143	202	351	4th/Capitol Div.	—	—		Joe Kuharich
1969	4	9	1	.308	279	377	4th/Capitol Div.	—	—		Jerry Williams
1970	3	10	1	.231	241	332	5th/NFC Eastern Div.	—	—		Jerry Williams
1971	6	7	1	.462	221	302	3rd/NFC Eastern Div.	—	—		J. Williams, Ed Khayat
1972	2	11	1	.179	145	352	5th/NFC Eastern Div.	—	—		Ed Khayat
1973	5	8	1	.393	310	393	3rd/NFC Eastern Div.	—	—		Mike McCormack
1974	7	7	0	.500	242	217	4th/NFC Eastern Div.	—	—		Mike McCormack
1975	4	10	0	.286	225	302	5th/NFC Eastern Div.	—	—		Mike McCormack
1976	4	10	0	.286	165	286	4th/NFC Eastern Div.	—	—		Dick Vermeil
1977	5	9	0	.357	220	207	T4th/NFC Eastern Div.	—	—		Dick Vermeil
1978	9	7	0	.563	270	250	2nd/NFC Eastern Div.	0	1	NFC wild-card game	Dick Vermeil
1979	11	5	0	.688	339	282	2nd/NFC Eastern Div.	1	1	NFC div. playoff game	Dick Vermeil
1980	12	4	0	.750	384	222	1st/NFC Eastern Div.	2	1	Super Bowl	Dick Vermeil
1981	10	6	0	.625	368	221	2nd/NFC Eastern Div.	0	1	NFC wild-card game	Dick Vermeil
1982	3	6	0	.333	191	195	T11th/NFC	—	—		Dick Vermeil
1983	5	11	0	.313	233	322	4th/NFC Eastern Div.	—	—		Marion Campbell
1984	6	9	1	.406	278	320	5th/NFC Eastern Div.	—	—		Marion Campbell
1985	7	9	0	.438	286	310	4th/NFC Eastern Div.	—	—		M. Campbell, Fred Bruney
1986	5	10	1	.344	256	312	4th/NFC Eastern Div.	—	—		Buddy Ryan
1987	7	8	0	.467	337	380	T2nd/NFC Eastern Div.	—	—		Buddy Ryan
1988	10	6	0	.625	379	319	1st/NFC Eastern Div.	0	1	NFC div. playoff game	Buddy Ryan
1989	11	5	0	.688	342	274	2nd/NFC Eastern Div.	0	1	NFC wild-card game	Buddy Ryan
1990	10	6	0	.625	396	299	T2nd/NFC Eastern Div.	0	1	NFC wild-card game	Buddy Ryan
1991	10	6	0	.625	285	244	3rd/NFC Eastern Div.	—	—		Rich Kotite
1992	11	5	0	.688	354	245	2nd/NFC Eastern Div.	1	1	NFC div. playoff game	Rich Kotite
1993	8	8	0	.500	293	315	4th/NFC Eastern Div.	—	—		Rich Kotite
1994	7	9	0	.438	308	308	4th/NFC Eastern Div.	—	—		Rich Kotite
1995	10	6	0	.625	318	338	2nd/NFC Eastern Div.	1	1	NFC div. playoff game	Ray Rhodes
1996	10	6	0	.625	363	341	2nd/NFC Eastern Div.	0	1	NFC wild-card game	Ray Rhodes
1997	6	9	1	.406	317	372	3rd/NFC Eastern Div.	—	—		Ray Rhodes

*Phil-Pitt "Steagles," a combined squad of Philadelphia Eagles and Pittsburgh Steelers.

FIRST-ROUND DRAFT PICKS

1936—Jay Berwanger, B, Chicago*
1937—Sam Francis, B, Nebraska*
1938—John McDonald, B, Nebraska
1939—Davey O'Brien, QB, Texas Christian
1940—Wes McAfee, B, Duke
1941—None
1942—Pete Kmetovic, B, Stanford
1943—Joe Muha, B, Virginia Military
1944—Steve Van Buren, B, Louisiana State
1945—John Yonaker, E, Notre Dame
1946—Leo Riggs, B, Southern California
1947—Neil Armstrong, E, Oklahoma A&M
1948—Clyde Scott, B, Arkansas
1949—Chuck Bednarik, C, Pennsylvania*
      Frank Tripucka, QB, Notre Dame
1950—Bud Grant, E, Minnesota
1951—Ebert Van Buren, B, Louisiana State
      Chet Mutryn, B, Xavier
1952—John Bright, B, Drake
1953—None
1954—Neil Worden, B, Notre Dame
1955—Dick Bielski, B, Maryland
1956—Bob Pellegrini, C, Maryland
1957—Clarence Peaks, B, Michigan State
1958—Walter Kowalczyk, B, Michigan State
1959—None
1960—Ron Burton, B, Northwestern
1961—Art Baker, B, Syracuse
1962—None
1963—Ed Budde, T, Michigan State
1964—Bob Brown, T, Nebraska
1965—None
1966—Randy Beisler, T, Indiana
1967—Harry Jones, RB, Arkansas

1968—Tim Rossovich, DE, Southern California
1969—Leroy Keyes, RB, Purdue
1970—Steve Zabel, E, Oklahoma
1971—Richard Harris, DE, Grambling State
1972—John Reaves, QB, Florida
1973—Jerry Sisemore, T, Texas
      Charle Young, TE, Southern California
1974—None
1975—None
1976—None
1977—None
1978—None
1979—Jerry Robinson, LB, UCLA
1980—Roynell Young, DB, Alcorn State
1981—Leonard Mitchell, DE, Houston
1982—Mike Quick, WR, North Carolina State
1983—Michael Haddix, RB, Mississippi State
1984—Kenny Jackson, WR, Penn State
1985—Kevin Allen, T, Indiana
1986—Keith Byars, RB, Ohio State
1987—Jerome Brown, DT, Miami (Fla.)
1988—Keith Jackson, TE, Oklahoma
1989—None
1990—Ben Smith, DB, Georgia
1991—Antone Davis, T, Tennessee
1992—None
1993—Lester Holmes, T, Jackson State
      Leonard Renfro, DT, Colorado
1994—Bernard Williams, T, Georgia
1995—Mike Mamula, DE, Boston College
1996—Jermane Mayberry, T, Texas A&M-Kingsville
1997—Jon Harris, DE, Virginia
1998—Tra Thomas, T, Florida State
  *First player chosen in draft.

FRANCHISE RECORDS

Most rushing yards, career
6,538—Wilbert Montgomery
Most rushing yards, season
1,512—Wilbert Montgomery, 1979
Most rushing yards, game
205—Steve Van Buren vs. Pit., Nov. 27, 1949
Most rushing touchdowns, season
15—Steve Van Buren, 1945
Most passing attempts, season
560—Randall Cunningham, 1988
Most passing attempts, game
62—Randall Cunningham at Chi., Oct. 2, 1989
Most passes completed, season
301—Randall Cunningham, 1988
Most passes completed, game
34—Randall Cunningham at Was., Sept. 17, 1989
Most passing yards, career
26,963—Ron Jaworski

Most passing yards, season
3,808—Randall Cunningham, 1988
Most passing yards, game
447—Randall Cunningham at Was., Sept. 17, 1989
Most touchdown passes, season
32—Sonny Jurgensen, 1961
Most pass receptions, career
589—Harold Carmichael
Most pass receptions, season
88—Irving Fryar, 1996
Most pass receptions, game
14—Don Looney at Was., Dec. 1, 1940
Most receiving yards, career
8,978—Harold Carmichael
Most receiving yards, season
1,409—Mike Quick, 1983
Most receiving yards, game
237—Tommy McDonald vs. NYG, Dec. 10, 1961

Most receiving touchdowns, season
13—Tommy McDonald, 1960
Tommy McDonald, 1961
Mike Quick, 1983
Most touchdowns, career
79—Harold Carmichael
Most field goals, season
30—Paul McFadden, 1984
Longest field goal
59 yards—Tony Franklin at Dal., Nov. 12, 1979
Most interceptions, career
34—Bill Bradley
Most interceptions, season
11—Bill Bradley, 1971
Most sacks, career
124—Reggie White
Most sacks, season
21—Reggie White, 1987

SERIES RECORDS

Philadelphia vs.: Arizona 49-47-5; Atlanta 9-8-1; Baltimore, 0-0-1; Buffalo 4-4; Carolina 1-0; Chicago 4-25-1; Cincinnati 2-6; Dallas 29-45; Denver 6-2; Detroit 10-11-2; Green Bay 9-20; Indianapolis 6-7; Jacksonville 0-1; Kansas City 1-1; Miami 3-6; Minnesota 6-11; New England 5-2; New Orleans 12-8; N.Y. Giants 59-65-2; N.Y. Jets 6-0; Oakland 4-3; Pittsburgh 44-26-3; St. Louis 12-14-1; San Diego 2-4; San Francisco 6-14-1; Seattle 4-2; Tampa Bay 3-2; Tennessee 6-0; Washington 54-64-6.
NOTE: Includes records when team combined with Pittsburgh squad and was known as Phil-Pitt in 1943.

COACHING RECORDS

Bert Bell, 10-44-2; Fred Bruney, 1-0-0; Marion Campbell, 17-29-1; Hugh Devore, 7-16-1; Ed Khayat, 8-15-2; Rich Kotite, 36-28-0 (1-1); Joe Kuharich, 28-41-1; Mike McCormack, 16-25-1; Alvin McMillin, 2-0-0; Wayne Millner, 2-8-0; Earle (Greasy) Neale, 63-43-5 (3-1); Ray Rhodes, 26-21-1 (1-2); Buddy Ryan, 43-35-1 (0-3); Buck Shaw, 19-16-1 (1-0); Nick Skorich, 15-24-3; Jim Trimble, 25-20-3; Dick Vermeil, 54-47-0 (3-4); Jerry Williams, 7-22-2; Lud Wray, 9-21-1.

RETIRED UNIFORM NUMBERS

No.	Player
15	Steve Van Buren
40	Tom Brookshier
44	Pete Retzlaff
60	Chuck Bednarik
70	Al Wistert
99	Jerome Brown

PITTSBURGH STEELERS
YEAR-BY-YEAR RECORDS

Year	W	L	T	Pct.	PF	PA	Finish	W	L	Highest round	Coach
1933*	3	6	2	.333	67	208	5th/Eastern Div.	—	—		Jap Douds
1934*	2	10	0	.167	51	206	5th/Eastern Div.	—	—		Luby DiMello
1935*	4	8	0	.333	100	209	3rd/Eastern Div.	—	—		Joe Bach
1936*	6	6	0	.500	98	187	2nd/Eastern Div.	—	—		Joe Bach
1937*	4	7	0	.364	122	145	3rd/Eastern Div.	—	—		Johnny Blood
1938*	2	9	0	.182	79	169	5th/Eastern Div.	—	—		Johnny Blood
1939*	1	9	1	.100	114	216	T4th/Eastern Div.	—	—		J. Blood-W. Kiesling
1940*	2	7	2	.222	60	178	4th/Eastern Div.	—	—		Walt Kiesling
1941	1	9	1	.100	103	276	5th/Eastern Div.	—	—		Bert Bell-Buff Donelli-Walt Kiesling
1942	7	4	0	.636	167	119	2nd/Eastern Div.	—	—		Walt Kiesling
1943†	5	4	1	.556	225	230	3rd/Eastern Div.	—	—		W. Kiesling-Greasy Neale
1944‡	0	10	0	.000	108	328	5th/Western Div.	—	—		W. Kiesling-Phil Handler
1945	2	8	0	.200	79	220	5th/Eastern Div.	—	—		Jim Leonard
1946	5	5	1	.500	136	117	T3rd/Eastern Div.	—	—		Jock Sutherland
1947	8	4	0	.667	240	259	2nd/Eastern Div.	0	1	E. Div. champ. game	Jock Sutherland
1948	4	8	0	.333	200	243	T3rd/Eastern Div.	—	—		John Michelosen
1949	6	5	1	.545	224	214	2nd/Eastern Div.	—	—		John Michelosen
1950	6	6	0	.500	180	195	T3rd/American Conf.	—	—		John Michelosen
1951	4	7	1	.364	183	235	4th/American Conf.	—	—		John Michelosen
1952	5	7	0	.417	300	273	3rd/American Conf.	—	—		Joe Bach
1953	6	6	0	.500	211	263	4th/Eastern Conf.	—	—		Joe Bach

Year	W	L	T	Pct.	PF	PA	Finish	W	L	Highest round	Coach
							REGULAR SEASON			**PLAYOFFS**	
1954	5	7	0	.417	219	263	4th/Eastern Conf.	—	—		Walt Kiesling
1955	4	8	0	.333	195	285	6th/Eastern Conf.	—	—		Walt Kiesling
1956	5	7	0	.417	217	250	5th/Eastern Conf.	—	—		Walt Kiesling
1957	6	6	0	.500	161	178	3rd/Eastern Conf.	—	—		Buddy Parker
1958	7	4	1	.636	261	230	3rd/Eastern Conf.	—	—		Buddy Parker
1959	6	5	1	.545	257	216	4th/Eastern Conf.	—	—		Buddy Parker
1960	5	6	1	.455	240	275	5th/Eastern Conf.	—	—		Buddy Parker
1961	6	8	0	.429	295	287	5th/Eastern Conf.	—	—		Buddy Parker
1962	9	5	0	.643	312	363	2nd/Eastern Conf.	—	—		Buddy Parker
1963	7	4	3	.636	321	295	4th/Eastern Conf.	—	—		Buddy Parker
1964	5	9	0	.357	253	315	6th/Eastern Conf.	—	—		Buddy Parker
1965	2	12	0	.143	202	397	7th/Eastern Conf.	—	—		Mike Nixon
1966	5	8	1	.385	316	347	6th/Eastern Conf.	—	—		Bill Austin
1967	4	9	1	.308	281	320	4th/Century Div.	—	—		Bill Austin
1968	2	11	1	.154	244	397	4th/Century Div.	—	—		Bill Austin
1969	1	13	0	.071	218	404	4th/Century Div.	—	—		Chuck Noll
1970	5	9	0	.357	210	272	3rd/AFC Central Div.	—	—		Chuck Noll
1971	6	8	0	.429	246	292	2nd/AFC Central Div.	—	—		Chuck Noll
1972	11	3	0	.786	343	175	1st/AFC Central Div.	1	1	AFC championship game	Chuck Noll
1973	10	4	0	.714	347	210	2nd/AFC Central Div.	0	1	AFC div. playoff game	Chuck Noll
1974	10	3	1	.750	305	189	1st/AFC Central Div.	3	0	Super Bowl champ	Chuck Noll
1975	12	2	0	.857	373	162	1st/AFC Central Div.	3	0	Super Bowl champ	Chuck Noll
1976	10	4	0	.714	342	138	1st/AFC Central Div.	1	1	AFC championship game	Chuck Noll
1977	9	5	0	.643	283	243	1st/AFC Central Div.	0	1	AFC div. playoff game	Chuck Noll
1978	14	2	0	.875	356	195	1st/AFC Central Div.	3	0	Super Bowl champ	Chuck Noll
1979	12	4	0	.750	416	262	1st/AFC Central Div.	3	0	Super Bowl champ	Chuck Noll
1980	9	7	0	.563	352	313	3rd/AFC Central Div.	—	—		Chuck Noll
1981	8	8	0	.500	356	297	2nd/AFC Central Div.	—	—		Chuck Noll
1982	6	3	0	.667	204	146	T4th/AFC	0	1	AFC first-round pl. game	Chuck Noll
1983	10	6	0	.625	355	303	1st/AFC Central Div.	0	1	AFC div. playoff game	Chuck Noll
1984	9	7	0	.563	387	310	1st/AFC Central Div.	1	1	AFC championship game	Chuck Noll
1985	7	9	0	.438	379	355	T2nd/AFC Central Div.	—	—		Chuck Noll
1986	6	10	0	.375	307	336	3rd/AFC Central Div.	—	—		Chuck Noll
1987	8	7	0	.533	285	299	3rd/AFC Central Div.	—	—		Chuck Noll
1988	5	11	0	.313	336	421	4th/AFC Central Div.	—	—		Chuck Noll
1989	9	7	0	.563	265	326	T2nd/AFC Central Div.	1	1	AFC div. playoff game	Chuck Noll
1990	9	7	0	.563	292	240	3rd/AFC Central Div.	—	—		Chuck Noll
1991	7	9	0	.438	292	344	2nd/AFC Central Div.	—	—		Chuck Noll
1992	11	5	0	.688	299	225	1st/AFC Central Div.	0	1	AFC div. playoff game	Bill Cowher
1993	9	7	0	.563	308	281	2nd/AFC Central Div.	0	1	AFC wild-card game	Bill Cowher
1994	12	4	0	.750	316	234	1st/AFC Central Div.	1	1	AFC championship game	Bill Cowher
1995	11	5	0	.689	407	327	1st/AFC Central Div.	2	1	Super Bowl	Bill Cowher
1996	10	6	0	.625	344	257	1st/AFC Central Div.	1	1	AFC div. playoff game	Bill Cowher
1997	11	5	0	.688	372	307	1st/AFC Central Div.	1	1	AFC championship game	Bill Cowher

*Pittsburgh Pirates.

†Phil-Pitt "Steagles," a combined squad of Philadelphia Eagles and Pittsburgh Steelers.

‡Card-Pitt, a combined squad of Chicago Cardinals and Pittsburgh Steelers.

FIRST-ROUND DRAFT PICKS

1936—Bill Shakespeare, B, Notre Dame
1937—Mike Basrak, C, Duquesne
1938—Byron White, B, Colorado
    Frank Filchock, B, Indiana
1939—None
1940—Kay Eakin, B, Arkansas
1941—Chet Gladchuk, C, Boston College
1942—Bill Dudley, B, Virginia*
1943—Bill Daley, B, Minnesota
1944—Johnny Podesto, B, St. Mary's (Calif.)
1945—Paul Duhart, B, Florida
1946—Doc Blanchard, B, Army
1947—Hub Bechtol, E, Texas
1948—Dan Edwards, E, Georgia
1949—Bobby Gage, B, Clemson
1950—Lynn Chandnois, B, Michigan State
1951—Clarence Avinger, B, Alabama
1952—Ed Modzelewski, B, Maryland
1953—Ted Marchibroda, QB, St. Bonaventure

1954—John Lattner, B, Notre Dame
1955—Frank Varrichione, T, Notre Dame
1956—Gary Glick, B, Colorado State*
    Art Davis, B, Mississippi State
1957—Len Dawson, QB, Purdue
1958—None
1959—None
1960—Jack Spikes, B, Texas Christian
1961—None
1962—Bob Ferguson, RB, Ohio State
1963—None
1964—Paul Martha, RB, Pittsburgh
1965—None
1966—Dick Leftridge, RB, West Virginia
1967—None
1968—Mike Taylor, T, Southern California
1969—Joe Greene, DT, North Texas State
1970—Terry Bradshaw, QB, Louisiana Tech*
1971—Frank Lewis, WR, Grambling State

1972—Franco Harris, RB, Penn State
1973—James Thomas, DB, Florida State
1974—Lynn Swann, WR, Southern California
1975—Dave Brown, DB, Michigan
1976—Bennie Cunningham, TE, Clemson
1977—Robin Cole, LB, New Mexico
1978—Ron Johnson, DB, Eastern Michigan
1979—Greg Hawthorne, RB, Baylor
1980—Mark Malone, QB, Arizona State
1981—Keith Gary, DE, Oklahoma
1982—Walter Abercrombie, RB, Baylor
1983—Gabriel Rivera, DT, Texas Tech
1984—Louis Lipps, WR, Southern Mississippi
1985—Darryl Sims, DT, Wisconsin
1986—John Rienstra, G, Temple

1987—Rod Woodson, DB, Purdue
1988—Aaron Jones, DE, Eastern Kentucky
1989—Tim Worley, RB, Georgia
    Tom Ricketts, T, Pittsburgh
1990—Eric Green, TE, Liberty (Va.)
1991—Huey Richardson, LB, Florida
1992—Leon Searcy, T, Miami (Fla.)
1993—Deon Figures, DB, Colorado
1994—Charles Johnson, WR, Colorado
1995—Mark Bruener, TE, Washington
1996—Jermain Stephens, T, North Carolina A&T
1997—Chad Scott, DB, Maryland
1998—Alan Faneca, G, Louisiana State
    *First player chosen in draft.

FRANCHISE RECORDS

Most rushing yards, career
11,950—Franco Harris
Most rushing yards, season
1,690—Barry Foster, 1992
Most rushing yards, game
218—John Fuqua at Phi., Dec. 20, 1970
Most rushing touchdowns, season
14—Franco Harris, 1976
Most passing attempts, season
486—Neil O'Donnell, 1993
Most passing attempts, game
55—Neil O'Donnell vs. G.B., Dec. 24, 1995
Most passes completed, season
270—Neil O'Donnell, 1993
Most passes completed, game
34—Neil O'Donnell at Chi., Nov. 5, 1995 (OT)
31—Joe Gilliam at Den., Sept. 22, 1974 (OT)
30—Terry Bradshaw vs. Cle., Nov. 25, 1979 (OT)
29—Terry Bradshaw vs. Cin., Sept. 19, 1982 (OT)
28—Kent Nix vs. Dal., Oct. 22, 1967

Most passing yards, career
27,989—Terry Bradshaw
Most passing yards, season
3,724—Terry Bradshaw, 1979
Most passing yards, game
409—Bobby Layne vs. Chi. Cardinals, Dec. 13, 1958
Most touchdown passes, season
28—Terry Bradshaw, 1978
Most pass receptions, career
537—John Stallworth
Most pass receptions, season
85—Yancey Thigpen, 1995
Most pass receptions, game
12—J.R. Wilburn vs. Dal., Oct. 22, 1967
Most receiving yards, career
8,723—John Stallworth
Most receiving yards, season
1,398—Yancey Thigpen, 1997
Most receiving yards, game
235—Buddy Dial vs. Cle., Oct. 22, 1961

Most receiving touchdowns, season
12—Buddy Dial, 1961
    Louis Lipps, 1985
Most touchdowns, career
100—Franco Harris
Most field goals, season
34—Norm Johnson, 1995
Longest field goal
55 yards—Gary Anderson vs. S.D., Nov. 25, 1984
Most interceptions, career
57—Mel Blount
Most interceptions, season
11—Mel Blount, 1975
Most sacks, career
73.5—L.C. Greenwood
Most sacks, season
15—Mike Merriweather, 1984

SERIES RECORDS

Pittsburgh vs.: Arizona 30-21-3; Atlanta 10-1; Baltimore 3-1; Buffalo 8-7; Carolina 0-1; Chicago 5-19-1; Cincinnati 32-23; Dallas 11-14; Denver 6-10-1; Detroit 12-13-1; Green Bay 11-21; Indianapolis 13-4; Jacksonville 3-3; Kansas City 14-6; Miami 6-8; Minnesota 4-8; New England 11-3; New Orleans 6-5; N.Y. Giants 28-44-3; N.Y. Jets 13-1; Oakland 5-7; Philadelphia 26-44-3; St. Louis 6-17-2; San Diego 16-5; San Francisco 7-9; Seattle 5-6; Tampa Bay 4-0; Tennessee 35-20; Washington 25-39-4.
NOTE: Includes records as Pittsburgh Pirates from 1933 through 1940; also includes records when team combined with Philadelphia squad and was known as Phil-Pitt in 1943 and when team combined with Chicago Cardinals squad and was known as Card-Pitt in 1944.

COACHING RECORDS

Bill Austin, 11-28-3; Joe Bach, 21-27-0; Bert Bell, 0-2-0; Bill Cowher, 64-32-0 (5-6); Luby DiMelio, 2-10-0; Aldo Donelli, 0-5-0; Forrest Douds, 3-6-2; Walt Kiesling, 30-55-5; Jim Leonard, 2-8-0; Johnny (Blood) McNally, 6-19-0; Johnny Michelosen, 20-26-2; Mike Nixon, 2-12-0; Chuck Noll, 193-148-1 (16-8); Buddy Parker, 51-47-6 (0-1); Jock Sutherland, 13-9-1 (0-1).

RETIRED UNIFORM NUMBERS

No.	Player
	None

ST. LOUIS RAMS
YEAR-BY-YEAR RECORDS

| | | | REGULAR SEASON | | | | | | PLAYOFFS | | |
Year	W	L	T	Pct.	PF	PA	Finish	W	L	Highest round	Coach
1937*	1	10	0	.091	75	207	5th/Western Div.	—	—		Hugo Bezdek
1938*	4	7	0	.364	131	215	4th/Western Div.	—	—		Hugo Bezdek, Art Lewis
1939*	5	5	1	.500	195	164	4th/Western Div.	—	—		Dutch Clark
1940*	4	6	1	.400	171	191	4th/Western Div.	—	—		Dutch Clark

			REGULAR SEASON					PLAYOFFS		
Year	W	L	T	Pct.	PF	PA	Finish	W	L	Highest round	Coach
1941*	2	9	0	.182	116	244	5th/Western Div.	—	—		Dutch Clark
1942*	5	6	0	.455	150	207	3rd/Western Div.	—	—		Dutch Clark
1943*	Rams did not play in 1943.										
1944*	4	6	0	.400	188	224	4th/Western Div.	—	—		Buff Donelli
1945*	9	1	0	.900	244	136	1st/Western Div.	1	0	NFL champ	Adam Walsh
1946†	6	4	1	.600	277	257	2nd/Western Div.	—	—		Adam Walsh
1947†	6	6	0	.500	259	214	4th/Western Div.	—	—		Bob Snyder
1948†	6	5	1	.545	327	269	3rd/Western Div.	—	—		Clark Shaughnessy
1949†	8	2	2	.800	360	239	1st/Western Div.	0	1	NFL championship game	Clark Shaughnessy
1950†	9	3	0	.750	466	309	1st/National Conf.	1	1	NFL championship game	Joe Stydahar
1951†	8	4	0	.667	392	261	1st/National Conf.	1	0	NFL champ	Joe Stydahar
1952†	9	3	0	.750	349	234	2nd/National Conf.	0	1	Nat. Conf. champ. game	J. Stydahar, Hamp Pool
1953†	8	3	1	.727	366	236	3rd/Western Conf.	—	—		Hamp Pool
1954†	6	5	1	.545	314	285	4th/Western Conf.	—	—		Hamp Pool
1955†	8	3	1	.727	260	231	1st/Western Conf.	0	1	NFL championship game	Sid Gillman
1956†	4	8	0	.333	291	307	6th/Western Conf.	—	—		Sid Gillman
1957†	6	6	0	.500	307	278	4th/Western Conf.	—	—		Sid Gillman
1958†	8	4	0	.667	344	278	T2nd/Western Conf.	—	—		Sid Gillman
1959†	2	10	0	.167	242	315	6th/Western Conf.	—	—		Sid Gillman
1960†	4	7	1	.364	265	297	6th/Western Conf.	—	—		Bob Waterfield
1961†	4	10	0	.286	263	333	6th/Western Conf.	—	—		Bob Waterfield
1962†	1	12	1	.077	220	334	7th/Western Conf.	—	—		B. Waterfield, H. Svare
1963†	5	9	0	.357	210	350	6th/Western Conf.	—	—		Harland Svare
1964†	5	7	2	.417	283	339	5th/Western Conf.	—	—		Harland Svare
1965†	4	10	0	.286	269	328	7th/Western Conf.	—	—		Harland Svare
1966†	8	6	0	.571	289	212	3rd/Western Conf.	—	—		George Allen
1967†	11	1	2	.917	398	196	1st/Coastal Div.	0	1	W. Conf. champ. game	George Allen
1968†	10	3	1	.769	312	200	2nd/Coastal Div.	—	—		George Allen
1969†	11	3	0	.786	320	243	1st/Coastal Div.	0	1	W. Conf. champ. game	George Allen
1970†	9	4	1	.692	325	202	2nd/NFC Western Div.	—	—		George Allen
1971†	8	5	1	.615	313	260	2nd/NFC Western Div.	—	—		Tommy Prothro
1972†	6	7	1	.464	291	286	3rd/NFC Western Div.	—	—		Tommy Prothro
1973†	12	2	0	.857	388	178	1st/NFC Western Div.	0	1	NFC div. playoff game	Chuck Knox
1974†	10	4	0	.714	263	181	1st/NFC Western Div.	1	1	NFC championship game	Chuck Knox
1975†	12	2	0	.857	312	135	1st/NFC Western Div.	1	1	NFC championship game	Chuck Knox
1976†	10	3	1	.750	351	190	1st/NFC Western Div.	1	1	NFC championship game	Chuck Knox
1977†	10	4	0	.714	302	146	1st/NFC Western Div.	0	1	NFC div. playoff game	Chuck Knox
1978†	12	4	0	.750	316	245	1st/NFC Western Div.	1	1	NFC championship game	Ray Malavasi
1979†	9	7	0	.563	323	309	1st/NFC Western Div.	2	1	Super Bowl	Ray Malavasi
1980†	11	5	0	.688	424	289	2nd/NFC Western Div.	0	1	NFC wild-card game	Ray Malavasi
1981†	6	10	0	.375	303	351	3rd/NFC Western Div.	—	—		Ray Malavasi
1982†	2	7	0	.222	200	250	14th/NFC	—	—		Ray Malavasi
1983†	9	7	0	.563	361	344	2nd/NFC Western Div.	1	1	NFC div. playoff game	John Robinson
1984†	10	6	0	.625	346	316	2nd/NFC Western Div.	0	1	NFC wild-card game	John Robinson
1985†	11	5	0	.688	340	277	1st/NFC Western Div.	1	1	NFC championship game	John Robinson
1986†	10	6	0	.625	309	267	2nd/NFC Western Div.	0	1	NFC wild-card game	John Robinson
1987†	6	9	0	.400	317	361	3rd/NFC Western Div.	—	—		John Robinson
1988†	10	6	0	.625	407	293	2nd/NFC Western Div.	0	1	NFC wild-card game	John Robinson
1989†	11	5	0	.688	426	344	2nd/NFC Western Div.	2	1	NFC championship game	John Robinson
1990†	5	11	0	.313	345	412	T3rd/NFC Western Div.	—	—		John Robinson
1991†	3	13	0	.188	234	390	4th/NFC Western Div.	—	—		John Robinson
1992†	6	10	0	.375	313	383	T3rd/NFC Western Div.	—	—		Chuck Knox
1993†	5	11	0	.313	221	367	4th/NFC Western Div.	—	—		Chuck Knox
1994†	4	12	0	.250	286	365	4th/NFC Western Div.	—	—		Chuck Knox
1995	7	9	0	.438	309	418	T3rd/NFC Western Div.	—	—		Rich Brooks
1996	6	10	0	.375	303	409	3rd/NFC Western Div.	—	—		Rich Brooks
1997	5	11	0	.313	299	359	5th/NFC Western Div.	—	—		Dick Vermeil

*Cleveland Rams.
†Los Angeles Rams.

FIRST-ROUND DRAFT PICKS

1937—Johnny Drake, B, Purdue
1938—Corbett Davis, B, Indiana*
1939—Parker Hall, B, Mississippi
1940—Ollie Cordill, B, Rice
1941—Rudy Mucha, C, Washington
1942—Jack Wilson, B, Baylor

1943—Mike Holovak, B, Boston College
1944—Tony Butkovich, B, Illinois
1945—Elroy Hirsch, B, Wisconsin
1946—Emil Sitko, B, Notre Dame
1947—Herman Wedemeyer, B, St. Mary's (Cal.)
1948—None

1949—Bobby Thomason, B, Virginia Military
1950—Ralph Pasquariello, B, Villanova
       Stan West, G, Oklahoma
1951—Bud McFadin, G, Texas
1952—Bill Wade, B, Vanderbilt*
       Bob Carey, E, Michigan State
1953—Donn Moomaw, C, UCLA
       Ed Barker, E, Washington State
1954—Ed Beatty, C, Cincinnati
1955—Larry Morris, C, Georgia Tech
1956—Joe Marconi, B, West Virginia
       Charlie Horton, B, Vanderbilt
1957—Jon Arnett, B, Southern California
       Del Shofner, B, Baylor
1958—Lou Michaels, T, Kentucky
       Jim Phillips, E, Auburn
1959—Dick Bass, B, Pacific
       Paul Dickson, G, Baylor
1960—Billy Cannon, RB, Louisiana State*
1961—Marlin McKeever, LB, Southern California
1962—Roman Gabriel, QB, North Carolina State
       Merlin Olsen, DT, Utah State
1963—Terry Baker, QB, Oregon State*
       Rufus Guthrie, G, Georgia Tech
1964—Bill Munson, QB, Utah State
1965—Clancy Williams, DB, Washington State
1966—Tom Mack, G, Michigan
1967—None
1968—None
1969—Larry Smith, RB, Florida
       Jim Seymour, E, Notre Dame
       Bob Klein, TE, Southern California
1970—Jack Reynolds, LB, Tennessee
1971—Isiah Robertson, LB, Southern
       Jack Youngblood, DE, Florida

1972—None
1973—None
1974—John Cappelletti, RB, Penn State
1975—Mike Fanning, DT, Notre Dame
       Dennis Harrah, G, Miami (Fla.)
       Doug France, T, Ohio State
1976—Kevin McLain, LB, Colorado State
1977—Bob Brudzinski, LB, Ohio State
1978—Elvis Peacock, RB, Oklahoma
1979—George Andrews, LB, Nebraska
       Kent Hill, G, Georgia Tech
1980—Johnnie Johnson, DB, Texas
1981—Mel Owens, LB, Michigan
1982—Barry Redden, RB, Richmond
1983—Eric Dickerson, RB, Southern Methodist
1984—None
1985—Jerry Gray, DB, Texas
1986—Mike Schad, T, Queens College (Ont.)
1987—None
1988—Gaston Green, RB, UCLA
       Aaron Cox, WR, Arizona State
1989—Bill Hawkins, DE, Miami (Fla.)
       Cleveland Gary, RB, Miami (Fla.)
1990—Bern Brostek, C, Washington
1991—Todd Lyght, CB, Notre Dame
1992—Sean Gilbert, DE, Pittsburgh
1993—Jerome Bettis, RB, Notre Dame
1994—Wayne Gandy, T, Auburn
1995—Kevin Carter, DE, Florida
1996—Lawrence Phillips, RB, Nebraska
       Eddie Kennison, WR, Louisiana State
1997—Orlando Pace, T, Ohio State*
1998—Grant Wistrom, DE, Nebraska
    *First player chosen in draft.

FRANCHISE RECORDS

Most rushing yards, career
7,245—Eric Dickerson
Most rushing yards, season
2,105—Eric Dickerson, 1984
Most rushing yards, game
247—Willie Ellison vs. N.O., Dec. 5, 1971
Most rushing touchdowns, season
18—Eric Dickerson, 1983
Most passing attempts, season
554—Jim Everett, 1990
Most passing attempts, game
55—Mark Rypien vs. Buf., Dec. 10, 1995
Most passes completed, season
308—Jim Everett, 1988
Most passes completed, game
35—Dieter Brock vs. S.F., Oct. 27, 1985
Most passing yards, career
23,758—Jim Everett
Most passing yards, season
4,310—Jim Everett, 1989

Most passing yards, game
554—Norm Van Brocklin at N.Y. Yanks,
     Sept. 28, 1951
Most touchdown passes, season
31—Jim Everett, 1988
Most pass receptions, career
593—Henry Ellard
Most pass receptions, season
119—Isaac Bruce, 1995
Most pass receptions, game
18—Tom Fears vs. G.B., Dec. 3, 1950
Most receiving yards, career
9,761—Henry Ellard
Most receiving yards, season
1,781—Isaac Bruce, 1995
Most receiving yards, game
336—Willie Anderson at N.O., Nov. 26,
    1989
Most receiving touchdowns, season
17—Elroy Hirsch, 1951

Most touchdowns, career
58—Eric Dickerson
Most field goals, season
30—David Ray, 1973
Longest field goal
54 yards—Tony Zendejas vs. Pit., Sept. 12,
    1993
Most interceptions, career
46—Ed Meador
Most interceptions, season
14—Night Train Lane, 1952
Most sacks, career
151.5—Deacon Jones
Most sacks, season
22—Deacon Jones, 1964
    Deacon Jones, 1968

SERIES RECORDS

St. Louis vs.: Arizona 16-13-2; Atlanta 39-21-2; Baltimore 0-1; Buffalo 3-4; Carolina 3-3; Chicago 25-36-3; Cincinnati 3-5; Dallas 9-8; Denver 4-4; Detroit 32-27-1; Green Bay 40-27-1; Indianapolis 17-21-2; Jacksonville 1-0; Kansas City 4-2; Miami 1-6; Minnesota 11-15-2; New England 3-3; New Orleans 31-23; N.Y. Giants 20-7; N.Y. Jets 6-2; Oakland 2-7; Philadelphia 14-12-1; Pittsburgh 17-6-2; San Diego 3-3; San Francisco 47-45-2; Seattle 4-2; Tampa Bay 8-3; Tennessee 5-2; Washington 7-16-1.
NOTE: Includes records as Los Angeles Rams from 1946 through 1994.

COACHING RECORDS

George Allen, 47-17-4 (2-2); Hugo Bezdek, 1-13-0; Rich Brooks, 13-19-0; Dutch Clark, 16-26-2; Aldo Donelli, 4-6-0; Sid Gillman, 28-31-1 (0-1); Chuck Knox, 69-48-1 (3-5); Art Lewis, 4-4-0; Ray Malavasi, 40-33-0 (3-3); Hamp Pool, 23-10-2 (0-1); Tommy Prothro, 14-12-2; John Robinson, 75-68-0 (4-6); Clark Shaughnessy, 14-7-3 (0-1); Bob Snyder, 6-6-0; Joe Stydahar, 17-8-0 (2-1); Harland Svare, 14-31-3; Dick Vermeil, 5-11-0; Adam Walsh, 15-5-1 (1-0); Bob Waterfield, 9-24-1.

SAN DIEGO CHARGERS
YEAR-BY-YEAR RECORDS

	REGULAR SEASON								PLAYOFFS			
Year	W	L	T	Pct.	PF	PA	Finish	W	L	Highest round	Coach
1960*†	10	4	0	.714	373	336	1st/Western Div.	0	1	AFL championship game	Sid Gillman
1961*	12	2	0	.857	396	219	1st/Western Div.	0	1	AFL championship game	Sid Gillman
1962*	4	10	0	.286	314	392	3rd/Western Div.	—	—		Sid Gillman
1963*	11	3	0	.786	399	256	1st/Western Div.	1	0	AFL champ	Sid Gillman
1964*	8	5	1	.615	341	300	1st/Western Div.	0	1	AFL championship game	Sid Gillman
1965*	9	2	3	.818	340	227	1st/Western Div.	0	1	AFL championship game	Sid Gillman
1966*	7	6	1	.538	335	284	3rd/Western Div.	—	—		Sid Gillman
1967*	8	5	1	.615	360	352	3rd/Western Div.	—	—		Sid Gillman
1968*	9	5	0	.643	382	310	3rd/Western Div.	—	—		Sid Gillman
1969*	8	6	0	.571	288	276	3rd/Western Div.	—	—		S. Gillman, C. Waller
1970	5	6	3	.455	282	278	3rd/AFC Western Div.	—	—		Charlie Waller
1971	6	8	0	.429	311	341	3rd/AFC Western Div.	—	—		Harland Svare
1972	4	9	1	.308	264	344	4th/AFC Western Div.	—	—		Harland Svare
1973	2	11	1	.179	188	386	4th/AFC Western Div.	—	—		H. Svare, Ron Waller
1974	5	9	0	.357	212	285	T3rd/AFC Western Div.	—	—		Tommy Prothro
1975	2	12	0	.143	189	345	4th/AFC Western Div.	—	—		Tommy Prothro
1976	6	8	0	.429	248	285	3rd/AFC Western Div.	—	—		Tommy Prothro
1977	7	7	0	.500	222	205	3rd/AFC Western Div.	—	—		Tommy Prothro
1978	9	7	0	.563	355	309	T2nd/AFC Western Div.	—	—		T. Prothro, Don Coryell
1979	12	4	0	.750	411	246	1st/AFC Western Div.	0	1	AFC div. playoff game	Don Coryell
1980	11	5	0	.688	418	327	1st/AFC Western Div.	1	1	AFC championship game	Don Coryell
1981	10	6	0	.625	478	390	1st/AFC Western Div.	1	1	AFC championship game	Don Coryell
1982	6	3	0	.667	288	221	T4th/AFC	1	1	AFC second-round pl. game	Don Coryell
1983	6	10	0	.375	358	462	T4th/AFC Western Div.	—	—		Don Coryell
1984	7	9	0	.438	394	413	5th/AFC Western Div.	—	—		Don Coryell
1985	8	8	0	.500	467	435	T3rd/AFC Western Div.	—	—		Don Coryell
1986	4	12	0	.250	335	396	5th/AFC Western Div.	—	—		D. Coryell, Al Saunders
1987	8	7	0	.533	253	317	3rd/AFC Western Div.	—	—		Al Saunders
1988	6	10	0	.375	231	332	4th/AFC Western Div.	—	—		Al Saunders
1989	6	10	0	.375	266	290	5th/AFC Western Div.	—	—		Dan Henning
1990	6	10	0	.375	315	281	4th/AFC Western Div.	—	—		Dan Henning
1991	4	12	0	.250	274	342	5th/AFC Western Div.	—	—		Dan Henning
1992	11	5	0	.688	335	241	1st/AFC Western Div.	1	1	AFC div. playoff game	Bobby Ross
1993	8	8	0	.500	322	290	4th/AFC Western Div.	—	—		Bobby Ross
1994	11	5	0	.688	381	306	1st/AFC Western Div.	2	1	Super Bowl	Bobby Ross
1995	9	7	0	.563	321	323	2nd/AFC Western Div.	0	1	AFC wild-card game	Bobby Ross
1996	8	8	0	.500	310	376	3rd/AFC Western Div.	—	—		Bobby Ross
1997	4	12	0	.250	266	425	T4th/AFC Western Div.	—	—		Kevin Gilbride

*American Football League.
†Los Angeles Chargers.

FIRST-ROUND DRAFT PICKS

1960—Monty Stickles, E, Notre Dame
1961—Earl Faison, E, Indiana
1962—Bob Ferguson, RB, Ohio State
1963—Walt Sweeney, E, Syracuse
1964—Ted Davis, E, Georgia Tech
1965—Steve DeLong, DE, Tennessee
1966—Don Davis, T, Los Angeles State
1967—Ron Billingsley, DT, Wyoming
1968—Russ Washington, T, Missouri
       Jim Hill, DB, Texas A&I
1969—Marty Domres, QB, Columbia
       Bob Babich, LB, Miami of Ohio
1970—Walker Gillette, WR, Richmond

1971—Leon Burns, RB, Long Beach State
1972—None
1973—Johnny Rodgers, WR, Nebraska
1974—Bo Matthews, RB, Colorado
       Don Goode, LB, Kansas
1975—Gary Johnson, DT, Grambling State
       Mike Williams, DB, Louisiana State
1976—Joe Washington, RB, Oklahoma
1977—Bob Rush, C, Memphis State
1978—John Jefferson, WR, Arizona State
1979—Kellen Winslow, TE, Missouri
1980—None
1981—James Brooks, RB, Auburn

1982—None
1983—Billy Ray Smith, LB, Arkansas
    Gary Anderson, WR, Arkansas
    Gill Byrd, DB, San Jose State
1984—Mossy Cade, DB, Texas
1985—Jim Lachey, G, Ohio State
1986—Leslie O'Neal, DE, Oklahoma State
    Jim FitzPatrick, T, Southern California
1987—Rod Bernstine, TE, Texas A&M
1988—Anthony Miller, WR, Tennessee
1989—Burt Grossman, DE, Pittsburgh

1990—Junior Seau, LB, Southern California
1991—Stanley Richard, CB, Texas
1992—Chris Mims, DT, Tennessee
1993—Darrien Gordon, DB, Stanford
1994—None
1995—None
1996—None
1997—None
1998—Ryan Leaf, QB, Washington State

FRANCHISE RECORDS

Most rushing yards, career
4,963—Paul Lowe

Most rushing yards, season
1,350—Natrone Means, 1994

Most rushing yards, game
217—Gary Anderson vs. K.C., Dec. 18, 1988

Most rushing touchdowns, season
19—Chuck Muncie, 1981

Most passing attempts, season
609—Dan Fouts, 1981

Most passing attempts, game
58—Mark Herrmann at K.C., Dec. 22, 1985

Most passes completed, season
360—Dan Fouts, 1981

Most passes completed, game
37—Dan Fouts vs. Mia., Nov. 18, 1984 (OT)
    Mark Herrmann at K.C., Dec. 22, 1985

Most passing yards, career
43,040—Dan Fouts

Most passing yards, season
4,802—Dan Fouts, 1981

Most passing yards, game
444—Dan Fouts vs. NYG, Oct. 19, 1980
    Dan Fouts at S.F., Dec. 11, 1982

Most touchdown passes, season
33—Dan Fouts, 1981

Most pass receptions, career
586—Charlie Joiner

Most pass receptions, season
90—Tony Martin, 1995

Most pass receptions, game
15—Kellen Winslow at G.B., Oct. 7, 1984

Most receiving yards, career
9,585—Lance Alworth

Most receiving yards, season
1,602—Lance Alworth, 1965

Most receiving yards, game
260—Wes Chandler vs. Cin., Dec. 20, 1982

Most receiving touchdowns, season
14—Lance Alworth, 1965
    Tony Martin, 1996

Most touchdowns, career
83—Lance Alworth

Most field goals, season
34—John Carney, 1994

Longest field goal
54 yards—John Carney vs. Sea., Nov. 10, 1991

Most interceptions, career
42—Gill Byrd

Most interceptions, season
9—Charlie McNeil, 1961

Most sacks, career
105.5—Leslie O'Neal

Most sacks, season
17.5—Gary Johnson, 1980

SERIES RECORDS

San Diego vs.: Arizona 6-1; Atlanta 1-5; Baltimore, 1-0; Buffalo 16-7-2; Carolina 0-1; Chicago 4-3; Cincinnati 14-9; Dallas 1-5; Denver 35-40-1; Detroit 3-3; Green Bay 1-5; Indianapolis 11-6; Jacksonville 0-0; Kansas City 35-39-1; Miami 10-6; Minnesota 4-3; New England 11-16-2; New Orleans 6-1; N.Y. Giants 3-4; N.Y. Jets 17-9-1; Oakland 29-45-2; Philadelphia 4-2; Pittsburgh 5-16; St. Louis 3-3; San Francisco 3-5; Seattle 20-18; Tampa Bay 6-1; Tennessee 18-13-1; Washington 0-5.
NOTE: Includes records as Los Angeles Chargers in 1960.

COACHING RECORDS

Don Coryell, 69-56-0 (3-4); Kevin Gilbride, 4-12-0; Sid Gillman, 86-53-6 (1-4); Dan Henning, 16-32-0; Tommy Prothro, 21-39-0; Bobby Ross, 47-33-0 (3-3); Al Saunders, 17-22-0; Harland Svare, 7-17-2; Charlie Waller, 9-7-3; Ron Waller, 1-5-0.

RETIRED UNIFORM NUMBERS

No.	Player
14	Dan Fouts

SAN FRANCISCO 49ERS
YEAR-BY-YEAR RECORDS

		REGULAR SEASON							PLAYOFFS		
Year	W	L	T	Pct.	PF	PA	Finish	W	L	Highest round	Coach
1946*	9	5	0	.643	307	189	2nd/Western Div.	—	—		Buck Shaw
1947*	8	4	2	.667	327	264	2nd/Western Div.	—	—		Buck Shaw
1948*	12	2	0	.857	495	248	2nd/Western Div.	—	—		Buck Shaw
1949*	9	3	0	.750	416	227	2nd	—	—		Buck Shaw
1950	3	9	0	.250	213	300	T5th/National Conf.	—	—		Buck Shaw
1951	7	4	1	.636	255	205	T2nd/National Conf.	—	—		Buck Shaw
1952	7	5	0	.583	285	221	3rd/National Conf.	—	—		Buck Shaw
1953	9	3	0	.750	372	237	3rd/Western Conf.	—	—		Buck Shaw
1954	7	4	1	.636	313	251	3rd/Western Conf.	—	—		Buck Shaw
1955	4	8	0	.333	216	298	5th/Western Conf.	—	—		Red Strader
1956	5	6	1	.455	233	284	3rd/Western Conf.	—	—		Frankie Albert
1957	8	4	0	.667	260	264	2nd/Western Conf.	0	1	W. Conf. champ. game	Frankie Albert
1958	6	6	0	.500	257	324	4th/Western Conf.	—	—		Frankie Albert
1959	7	5	0	.583	255	237	T3rd/Western Conf.	—	—		Red Hickey
1960	7	5	0	.583	208	205	T2nd/Western Conf.	—	—		Red Hickey

	REGULAR SEASON						PLAYOFFS			
Year	W	L	T	Pct.	PF	PA	Finish	W	L	Highest round	Coach

Year	W	L	T	Pct.	PF	PA	Finish	W	L	Highest round	Coach
1961	7	6	1	.538	346	272	5th/Western Conf.	—	—		Red Hickey
1962	6	8	0	.429	282	331	5th/Western Conf.	—	—		Red Hickey
1963	2	12	0	.143	198	391	7th/Western Conf.	—	—		R. Hickey, J. Christiansen
1964	4	10	0	.286	236	330	7th/Western Conf.	—	—		Jack Christiansen
1965	7	6	1	.538	421	402	4th/Western Conf.	—	—		Jack Christiansen
1966	6	6	2	.500	320	325	4th/Western Conf.	—	—		Jack Christiansen
1967	7	7	0	.500	273	337	3rd/Coastal Div.	—	—		Jack Christiansen
1968	7	6	1	.538	303	310	3rd/Coastal Div.	—	—		Dick Nolan
1969	4	8	2	.333	277	319	4th/Coastal Div.	—	—		Dick Nolan
1970	10	3	1	.769	352	267	1st/NFC Western Div.	1	1	NFC championship game	Dick Nolan
1971	9	5	0	.643	300	216	1st/NFC Western Div.	1	1	NFC championship game	Dick Nolan
1972	8	5	1	.607	353	249	1st/NFC Western Div.	0	1	NFC div. playoff game	Dick Nolan
1973	5	9	0	.357	262	319	T3rd/NFC Western Div.	—	—		Dick Nolan
1974	6	8	0	.429	226	236	2nd/NFC Western Div.	—	—		Dick Nolan
1975	5	9	0	.357	255	286	2nd/NFC Western Div.	—	—		Dick Nolan
1976	8	6	0	.571	270	190	2nd/NFC Western Div.	—	—		Monte Clark
1977	5	9	0	.357	220	260	3rd/NFC Western Div.	—	—		Ken Meyer
1978	2	14	0	.125	219	350	4th/NFC Western Div.	—	—		Pete McCulley, Fred O'Connor
1979	2	14	0	.125	308	416	4th/NFC Western Div.	—	—		Bill Walsh
1980	6	10	0	.375	320	415	3rd/NFC Western Div.	—	—		Bill Walsh
1981	13	3	0	.813	357	250	1st/NFC Western Div.	3	0	Super Bowl champ	Bill Walsh
1982	3	6	0	.333	209	206	T11th/NFC	—	—		Bill Walsh
1983	10	6	0	.625	432	293	1st/NFC Western Div.	1	1	NFC championship game	Bill Walsh
1984	15	1	0	.938	475	227	1st/NFC Western Div.	3	0	Super Bowl champ	Bill Walsh
1985	10	6	0	.625	411	263	2nd/NFC Western Div.	0	1	NFC wild-card game	Bill Walsh
1986	10	5	1	.656	374	247	1st/NFC Western Div.	0	1	NFC div. playoff game	Bill Walsh
1987	13	2	0	.867	459	253	1st/NFC Western Div.	0	1	NFC div. playoff game	Bill Walsh
1988	10	6	0	.625	369	294	1st/NFC Western Div.	3	0	Super Bowl champ	Bill Walsh
1989	14	2	0	.875	442	253	1st/NFC Western Div.	3	0	Super Bowl champ	George Seifert
1990	14	2	0	.875	353	239	1st/NFC Western Div.	1	1	NFC championship game	George Seifert
1991	10	6	0	.625	393	239	3rd/NFC Western Div.	—	—		George Seifert
1992	14	2	0	.875	431	236	1st/NFC Western Div.	1	1	NFC championship game	George Seifert
1993	10	6	0	.625	473	295	1st/NFC Western Div.	1	1	NFC championship game	George Seifert
1994	13	3	0	.813	505	296	1st/NFC Western Div.	3	0	Super Bowl champ	George Seifert
1995	11	5	0	.688	457	258	1st/NFC Western Div.	0	1	NFC div. playoff game	George Seifert
1996	12	4	0	.750	398	257	2nd/NFC Western Div.	1	1	NFC div. playoff game	George Seifert
1997	13	3	0	.813	375	265	1st/NFC Western Div.	1	1	NFC championship game	Steve Mariucci

*All-America Football Conference.

FIRST-ROUND DRAFT PICKS

1950—Leo Nomellini, T, Minnesota
1951—Y.A. Tittle, QB, Louisiana State
1952—Hugh McElhenny, RB, Washington
1953—Harry Babcock, E, Georgia*
    Tom Stolhandske, E, Texas
1954—Bernie Faloney, QB, Maryland
1955—Dick Moegel, HB, Rice
1956—Earl Morrall QB, Michigan State
1957—John Brodie, QB, Stanford
1958—Jim Pace, RB, Michigan
    Charles Krueger, T, Texas A&M
1959—Dave Baker, RB, Oklahoma
    Dan James, C, Ohio State
1960—Monty Stickles, E, Notre Dame
1961—Jim Johnson, RB, UCLA
    Bernie Casey, RB, Bowling Green State
    Billy Kilmer, QB, UCLA
1962—Lance Alworth, RB, Arkansas
1963—Kermit Alexander, RB, UCLA
1964—Dave Parks, E, Texas Tech*
1965—Ken Willard, RB, North Carolina
    George Donnelly, DB, Illinois
1966—Stan Hindman, DE, Mississippi
1967—Steve Spurrier, QB, Florida
    Cas Banaszek, LB, Northwestern
1968—Forrest Blue, C, Auburn
1969—Ted Kwalick, TE, Penn State
    Gene Washington, WR, Stanford

1970—Cedrick Hardman, DE, North Texas State
    Bruce Taylor, DB, Boston University
1971—Tim Anderson, DB, Ohio State
1972—Terry Beasley, WR, Auburn
1973—Mike Holmes, DB, Tex. Southern
1974—Wilbur Jackson, RB, Alabama
    Bill Sandifer, DT, UCLA
1975—Jimmy Webb, DT, Mississippi State
1976—None
1977—None
1978—Ken McAfee, TE, Notre Dame
    Dan Bunz, LB, Long Beach State
1979—None
1980—Earl Cooper, RB, Rice
    Jim Stuckey, DE, Clemson
1981—Ronnie Lott, DB, Southern California
1982—None
1983—None
1984—Todd Shell, LB, Brigham Young
1985—Jerry Rice, WR, Mississippi Valley State
1986—None
1987—Harris Barton, T, North Carolina
    Terrence Flager, RB, Clemson
1988—None
1989—Keith DeLong, LB, Tennessee
1990—Dexter Carter, RB, Florida State
1991—Ted Washington, DL, Louisville
1992—Dana Hall, DB, Washington

1993—Dana Stubblefield, DT, Kansas
    Todd Kelly, DE, Tennessee
1994—Bryant Young, DT, Notre Dame
    William Floyd, RB, Florida State
1995—J.J. Stokes, WR, UCLA

1996—None
1997—Jim Druckenmiller, QB, Virginia Tech
1998—R.W. McQuarters, DB, Oklahoma State
*First player chosen in draft.

FRANCHISE RECORDS

Most rushing yards, career
7,344—Joe Perry
Most rushing yards, season
1,502—Roger Craig, 1988
Most rushing yards, game
194—Delvin Williams at St.L., Dec. 31, 1976
Most rushing touchdowns, season
10—Joe Perry, 1953
    J.D. Smith, 1959
    Billy Kilmer, 1961
    Ricky Watters, 1993
    Derek Loville, 1995
Most passing attempts, season
578—Steve DeBerg, 1979
Most passing attempts, game
60—Joe Montana at Was., Nov. 17, 1986
Most passes completed, season
347—Steve DeBerg, 1979
Most passes completed, game
37—Joe Montana at Atl., Nov. 6, 1985

Most passing yards, career
35,142—Joe Montana
Most passing yards, season
4,023—Steve Young, 1993
Most passing yards, game
476—Joe Montana at Atl., Oct. 14, 1990
Most touchdown passes, season
35—Steve Young, 1994
Most pass receptions, career
1,057—Jerry Rice
Most pass receptions, season
122—Jerry Rice, 1995
Most pass receptions, game
16—Jerry Rice at L.A. Rams, Nov. 20, 1994
Most receiving yards, career
16,455—Jerry Rice
Most receiving yards, season
1,848—Jerry Rice, 1995
Most receiving yards, game
289—Jerry Rice vs. Min., Dec. 18, 1995

Most receiving touchdowns, season
22—Jerry Rice, 1987
Most touchdowns, career
166—Jerry Rice
Most field goals, season
30—Jeff Wilkins, 1996
Longest field goal
56 yards—Mike Cofer at Atl., Oct. 14, 1990
Most interceptions, career
51—Ronnie Lott
Most interceptions, season
10—Dave Baker, 1960
    Ronnie Lott, 1986
Most sacks, career
111.5—Cedrick Hardman
Most sacks, season
18—Cedrick Hardman

SERIES RECORDS

San Francisco vs.: Arizona 10-9; Atlanta 39-22-1; Baltimore 1-0; Buffalo 3-3; Carolina 3-3; Chicago 25-25-1; Cincinnati 7-1; Dallas 12-7-1; Denver 4-4; Detroit 28-26-1; Green Bay 25-22-1; Indianapolis 16-22; Jacksonville 0-0; Kansas City 4-3; Miami 3-4; Minnesota 17-16-1; New England 7-1; New Orleans 40-15-2; N.Y. Giants 11-11; N.Y. Jets 6-1; Oakland 3-5; Philadelphia 14-6-1; Pittsburgh 9-7; St. Louis 45-47-2; San Diego 5-3; Seattle 4-2; Tampa Bay 12-2; Tennessee 6-3; Washington 11-6-1.
NOTE: Includes records only from 1950 to present.

COACHING RECORDS

Frankie Albert, 19-16-1 (0-1); Jack Christiansen, 26-38-3; Monte Clark, 8-6-0; Red Hickey, 27-27-1; Steve Mariucci, 13-3-0 (1-1); Pete McCulley, 1-8-0; Ken Meyer, 5-9-0; Dick Nolan, 54-53-5 (2-3); Fred O'Connor, 1-6-0; George Seifert, 98-30-0 (10-5); Buck Shaw, 33-25-2; Red Strader, 4-8-0; Bill Walsh, 92-59-1 (10-4).

RETIRED UNIFORM NUMBERS

No.	Player
12	John Brodie
16	Joe Montana
34	Joe Perry
37	Jimmy Johnson
39	Hugh McElhenny
70	Charlie Krueger
73	Leo Nomellini
87	Dwight Clark

SEATTLE SEAHAWKS
YEAR-BY-YEAR RECORDS

		REGULAR SEASON						PLAYOFFS			
Year	W	L	T	Pct.	PF	PA	Finish	W	L	Highest round	Coach
1976	2	12	0	.143	229	429	5th/NFC Western Div.	—	—		Jack Patera
1977	5	9	0	.357	282	373	4th/AFC Western Div.	—	—		Jack Patera
1978	9	7	0	.563	345	358	T2nd/AFC Western Div.	—	—		Jack Patera
1979	9	7	0	.563	378	372	T3rd	—	—		Jack Patera
1980	4	12	0	.250	291	408	5th/AFC Western Div.	—	—		Jack Patera
1981	6	10	0	.375	322	388	5th/AFC Western Div.	—	—		Jack Patera
1982	4	5	0	.444	127	147	T8th/AFC	—	—		J. Patera, Mike McCormack
1983	9	7	0	.562	403	397	T2nd/AFC Western Div.	2	1	AFC championship game	Chuck Knox
1984	12	4	0	.750	418	282	2nd/AFC Western Div.	1	1	AFC div. playoff game	Chuck Knox
1985	8	8	0	.500	349	303	T3rd/AFC Western Div.	—	—		Chuck Knox
1986	10	6	0	.625	366	293	T2nd/AFC Western Div.	—	—		Chuck Knox
1987	9	6	0	.600	371	314	2nd/AFC Western Div.	0	1	AFC wild-card game	Chuck Knox
1988	9	7	0	.563	339	329	1st/AFC Western Div.	0	1	AFC div. playoff game	Chuck Knox
1989	7	9	0	.438	241	327	4th/AFC Western Div.	—	—		Chuck Knox
1990	9	7	0	.563	306	286	3rd/AFC Western Div.	—	—		Chuck Knox

			REGULAR SEASON						PLAYOFFS		
Year	W	L	T	Pct.	PF	PA	Finish	W	L	Highest round	Coach
1991	7	9	0	.438	276	261	4th/AFC Western Div.	—	—		Chuck Knox
1992	2	14	0	.125	140	312	5th/AFC Western Div.	—	—		Tom Flores
1993	6	10	0	.375	280	314	5th/AFC Western Div.	—	—		Tom Flores
1994	6	10	0	.375	287	323	5th/AFC Western Div.	—	—		Tom Flores
1995	8	8	0	.500	363	366	T3rd/AFC Western Div.	—	—		Dennis Erickson
1996	7	9	0	.438	317	376	T4th/AFC Western Div.	—	—		Dennis Erickson
1997	8	8	0	.500	365	362	3rd/AFC Western Div.	—	—		Dennis Erickson

FIRST-ROUND DRAFT PICKS

1976—Steve Niehaus, DT, Notre Dame
1977—Steve August, G, Tulsa
1978—Keith Simpson, DB, Memphis State
1979—Manu Tuiasosopo, DT, UCLA
1980—Jacob Green, DE, Texas A&M
1981—Kenny Easley, DB, UCLA
1982—Jeff Bryant, DE, Clemson
1983—Curt Warner, RB, Penn State
1984—Terry Taylor, DB, Southern Illinois
1985—None
1986—John L. Williams, RB, Florida
1987—Tony Woods, LB, Pittsburgh

1988—None
1989—Andy Heck, T, Notre Dame
1990—Cortez Kennedy, DT, Miami (Fla.)
1991—Dan McGwire, QB, San Diego State
1992—Ray Roberts, T, Virginia
1993—Rick Mirer, QB, Notre Dame
1994—Sam Adams, DE, Texas A&M
1995—Joey Galloway, WR, Ohio State
1996—Pete Kendall, T, Boston College
1997—Shawn Springs, CB, Ohio State
     Walter Jones, T, Florida State
1998—Anthony Simmons, LB, Clemson

FRANCHISE RECORDS

Most rushing yards, career
6,706—Chris Warren

Most rushing yards, season
1,545—Chris Warren, 1994

Most rushing yards, game
207—Curt Warner vs. K.C., Nov. 27, 1983 (OT)
192—Curt Warner vs. Den., Dec. 20, 1986

Most rushing touchdowns, season
15—Chris Warren, 1995

Most passing attempts, season
532—Dave Krieg, 1985

Most passing attempts, game
51—Dave Krieg vs. Atl., Oct. 13, 1985

Most passes completed, season
313—Warren Moon, 1997

Most passes completed, game
33—Dave Krieg vs. Atl., Oct. 13, 1985

Most passing yards, career
26,132—Dave Krieg

Most passing yards, season
3,678—Warren Moon, 1997

Most passing yards, game
418—Dave Krieg vs. Den., Nov. 20, 1983

Most touchdown passes, season
32—Dave Krieg, 1984

Most pass receptions, career
819—Steve Largent

Most pass receptions, season
81—Brian Blades, 1994

Most pass receptions, game
15—Steve Largent vs. Det., Oct. 18, 1987

Most receiving yards, career
13,089—Steve Largent

Most receiving yards, season
1,287—Steve Largent, 1985

Most receiving yards, game
261—Steve Largent vs. Det., Oct. 18, 1987

Most receiving touchdowns, season
13—Daryl Turner, 1985

Most touchdowns, career
101—Steve Largent

Most field goals, season
28—Todd Peterson, 1996

Longest field goal
55 yards—John Kasay vs. K.C., Jan. 2, 1994

Most interceptions, career
50—Dave Brown

Most interceptions, season
10—John Harris, 1981
     Kenny Easley, 1984

Most sacks, career
116.0—Jacob Green

Most sacks, season
16.0—Jacob Green, 1983

SERIES RECORDS

Seattle vs.: Arizona 0-5; Atlanta 4-2; Baltimore, 0-1; Buffalo 4-2; Carolina 0-0; Chicago 4-2; Cincinnati 7-7; Dallas 1-4; Denver 15-26; Detroit 4-3; Green Bay 3-4; Indianapolis 2-4; Jacksonville 1-1; Kansas City 12-26; Miami 2-4; Minnesota 4-2; New England 7-6; New Orleans 2-4; N.Y. Giants 3-5; N.Y. Jets 8-5; Oakland 19-21; Philadelphia 2-4; Pittsburgh 6-5; St. Louis 2-4; San Diego 18-20; San Francisco 2-4; Tampa Bay 4-0; Tennessee 6-4; Washington 3-5.

COACHING RECORDS

Dennis Erickson, 23-25-0; Tom Flores, 14-34-0; Chuck Knox, 80-63-0 (3-4); Mike McCormack, 4-3-0; Jack Patera, 35-59-0.

RETIRED UNIFORM NUMBERS

No.	Player
80	Steve Largent

TAMPA BAY BUCCANEERS
YEAR-BY-YEAR RECORDS

			REGULAR SEASON						PLAYOFFS		
Year	W	L	T	Pct.	PF	PA	Finish	W	L	Highest round	Coach
1976	0	14	0	.000	125	412	5th/AFC Western Div.	—	—		John McKay
1977	2	12	0	.143	103	223	5th/NFC Central Div.	—	—		John McKay
1978	5	11	0	.313	241	259	5th/NFC Central Div.	—	—		John McKay
1979	10	6	0	.625	273	237	1st/NFC Central Div.	1	1	NFC championship game	John McKay

			REGULAR SEASON					PLAYOFFS		
Year	W	L	T	Pct.	PF	PA	Finish	W	L	Highest round	Coach
1980	5	10	1	.344	271	341	T4th/NFC Central Div.	—	—		John McKay
1981	9	7	0	.563	315	268	1st/NFC Central Div.	0	1	NFC div. playoff game	John McKay
1982	5	4	0	.556	158	178	T4th/NFC	0	1	NFC first-round pl. game	John McKay
1983	2	14	0	.125	241	380	5th/NFC Central Div.	—	—		John McKay
1984	6	10	0	.375	335	380	3rd/NFC Central Div.	—	—		John McKay
1985	2	14	0	.125	294	448	5th/NFC Central Div.	—	—		Leeman Bennett
1986	2	14	0	.125	239	473	5th/NFC Central Div.	—	—		Leeman Bennett
1987	4	11	0	.267	286	360	T4th/NFC Central Div.	—	—		Ray Perkins
1988	5	11	0	.313	261	350	3rd/NFC Central Div.	—	—		Ray Perkins
1989	5	11	0	.313	320	419	5th/NFC Central Div.	—	—		Ray Perkins
1990	6	10	0	.375	264	367	T2nd/NFC Central Div.	—	—		R. Perkins, R. Williamson
1991	3	13	0	.188	199	365	5th/NFC Central Div.	—	—		Richard Williamson
1992	5	11	0	.313	267	365	T3rd/NFC Central Div.	—	—		Sam Wyche
1993	5	11	0	.313	237	376	5th/NFC Central Div.	—	—		Sam Wyche
1994	6	10	0	.375	251	351	5th/NFC Central Div.	—	—		Sam Wyche
1995	7	9	0	.438	238	335	5th/NFC Central Div.	—	—		Sam Wyche
1996	6	10	0	.375	221	293	4th/NFC Central Div.	—	—		Tony Dungy
1997	10	6	0	.625	299	263	3rd/AFC Western Div.	1	1	NFC div. playoff game	Tony Dungy

FIRST-ROUND DRAFT PICKS

1976—Lee Roy Selmon, DE, Oklahoma*
1977—Ricky Bell, RB, Southern California*
1978—Doug Williams, QB, Grambling State
1979—None
1980—Ray Snell, T, Wisconsin
1981—Hugh Green, LB, Pittsburgh
1982—Sean Farrell, G, Penn State
1983—None
1984—None
1985—Ron Holmes, DE, Washington
1986—Bo Jackson, RB, Auburn*
     Rod Jones, DB, Southern Methodist
1987—Vinny Testaverde, QB, Miami (Fla.)*
1988—Paul Gruber, T, Wisconsin

1989—Broderick Thomas, LB, Nebraska
1990—Keith McCants, LB, Alabama
1991—Charles McRae, T, Tennessee
1992—None
1993—Eric Curry, DE, Alabama
1994—Trent Dilfer, QB, Fresno State
1995—Warren Sapp, DT, Miami (Fla.)
     Derrick Brooks, LB, Florida State
1996—Regan Upshaw, DE, California
     Marcus Jones, DT, North Carolina
1997—Warrick Dunn, RB, Florida State
     Reidel Anthony, WR, Florida
1998—None
    *First player chosen in draft.

FRANCHISE RECORDS

Most rushing yards, career
5,957—James Wilder
Most rushing yards, season
1,544—James Wilder, 1984
Most rushing yards, game
219—James Wilder at Min., Nov. 6, 1983
Most rushing touchdowns, season
13—James Wilder, 1984
Most passing attempts, season
521—Doug Williams, 1980
Most passing attempts, game
56—Doug Williams vs. Cle., Sept. 28, 1980
Most passes completed, season
308—Steve DeBerg, 1984
Most passes completed, game
31—Vinny Testaverde at Hou., Dec. 10, 1989
Most passing yards, career
14,820—Vinny Testaverde

Most passing yards, season
3,563—Doug Williams, 1981
Most passing yards, game
486—Doug Williams at Min., Nov. 16, 1980
Most touchdown passes, season
21—Trent Dilfer, 1997
Most pass receptions, career
430—James Wilder
Most pass receptions, season
86—Mark Carrier, 1989
Most pass receptions, game
13—James Wilder vs. Min., Sept. 15, 1985
Most receiving yards, career
5,018—Mark Carrier
Most receiving yards, season
1,422—Mark Carrier, 1989
Most receiving yards, game
212—Mark Carrier at N.O., Dec. 6, 1987

Most receiving touchdowns, season
9—Kevin House, 1981
    Bruce Hill, 1988
    Mark Carrier, 1989
Most touchdowns, career
46—James Wilder
Most field goals, season
25—Michael Husted, 1996
Longest field goal
57 yards—Michael Husted at L.A. Raiders, Dec. 19, 1993
Most interceptions, career
29—Cedric Brown
Most interceptions, season
9—Cedric Brown, 1981
Most sacks, career
78.5—Lee Roy Selmon
Most sacks, season
13—Lee Roy Selmon, 1977

SERIES RECORDS

Tampa Bay vs.: Arizona 7-7; Atlanta 7-8; Buffalo 4-2; Carolina 1-1; Chicago 10-30; Cincinnati 2-3; Dallas 0-6; Denver 1-3; Detroit 18-22; Green Bay 13-24-1; Indianapolis 4-5; Jacksonville 1-0; Kansas City 2-5; Miami 2-4; Minnesota 13-27; New England 1-3; New Orleans 5-12; N.Y. Giants 4-8; N.Y. Jets 1-6; Oakland 1-3; Philadelphia 2-3; Pittsburgh 0-4; St. Louis 3-8; San Diego 1-6; San Francisco 2-12; Seattle 0-4; Tennessee 1-4; Washington 4-4.

COACHING RECORDS

Leeman Bennett, 4-28-0; Tony Dungy, 16-16-0 (1-1); John McKay, 44-88-1 (1-3); Ray Perkins, 19-41-0; Richard Williamson, 4-15-0; Sam Wyche, 23-41-0.

RETIRED UNIFORM NUMBERS

No.	Player
63	Lee Roy Selmon

TENNESSEE OILERS
YEAR-BY-YEAR RECORDS

	REGULAR SEASON							PLAYOFFS			
Year	W	L	T	Pct.	PF	PA	Finish	W	L	Highest round	Coach
1960*†	10	4	0	.714	379	285	1st/Eastern Div.	1	0	AFL champ	Lou Rymkus
1961*†	10	3	1	.769	513	242	1st/Eastern Div.	1	0	AFL champ	L. Rymkus, Wally Lemm
1962*†	11	3	0	.786	387	270	1st/Eastern Div.	0	1	AFL championship game	Pop Ivy
1963*†	6	8	0	.429	302	372	3rd/Eastern Div.	—	—		Pop Ivy
1964*†	4	10	0	.286	310	355	4th/Eastern Div.	—	—		Sammy Baugh
1965*†	4	10	0	.286	298	429	4th/Eastern Div.	—	—		Hugh Taylor
1966*†	3	11	0	.214	335	396	T4th/Eastern Div.	—	—		Wally Lemm
1967*†	9	4	1	.692	258	199	1st/Eastern Div.	0	1	AFL championship game	Wally Lemm
1968*†	7	7	0	.500	303	248	2nd/Eastern Div.	—	—		Wally Lemm
1969*†	6	6	2	.500	278	279	2nd/Eastern Div.	0	1	Div. playoff game	Wally Lemm
1970†	3	10	1	.231	217	352	4th/AFC Central Div.	—	—		Wally Lemm
1971†	4	9	1	.308	251	330	3rd/AFC Central Div.	—	—		Ed Hughes
1972†	1	13	0	.071	164	380	4th/AFC Central Div.	—	—		Bill Peterson
1973†	1	13	0	.071	199	447	4th/AFC Central Div.	—	—		B. Peterson, S. Gillman
1974†	7	7	0	.500	236	282	T2nd/AFC Central Div.	—	—		Sid Gillman
1975†	10	4	0	.714	293	226	3rd/AFC Central Div.	—	—		Bum Phillips
1976†	5	9	0	.357	222	273	4th/AFC Central Div.	—	—		Bum Phillips
1977†	8	6	0	.571	299	230	T2nd/AFC Central Div.	—	—		Bum Phillips
1978†	10	6	0	.625	283	298	2nd/AFC Central Div.	2	1	AFC championship game	Bum Phillips
1979†	11	5	0	.688	362	331	2nd/AFC Central Div.	2	1	AFC championship game	Bum Phillips
1980†	11	5	0	.688	295	251	2nd/AFC Central Div.	0	1	AFC wild-card game	Bum Phillips
1981†	7	9	0	.438	281	355	3rd/AFC Central Div.	—	—		Ed Biles
1982†	1	8	0	.111	136	245	13th/AFC	—	—		Ed Biles
1983†	2	14	0	.125	288	460	4th/AFC Central Div.	—	—		Ed Biles, Chuck Studley
1984†	3	13	0	.188	240	437	4th/AFC Central Div.	—	—		Hugh Campbell
1985†	5	11	0	.313	284	412	4th/AFC Central Div.	—	—		H. Campbell, J. Glanville
1986†	5	11	0	.313	274	329	4th/AFC Central Div.	—	—		Jerry Glanville
1987†	9	6	0	.600	345	349	2nd/AFC Central Div.	1	1	AFC div. playoff game	Jerry Glanville
1988†	10	6	0	.625	424	365	T2nd/AFC Central Div.	1	1	AFC div. playoff game	Jerry Glanville
1989†	9	7	0	.563	365	412	T2nd/AFC Central Div.	0	1	AFC wild-card game	Jerry Glanville
1990†	9	7	0	.563	405	307	2nd/AFC Central Div.	0	1	AFC wild-card game	Jack Pardee
1991†	11	5	0	.688	386	251	1st/AFC Central Div.	1	1	AFC div. playoff game	Jack Pardee
1992†	10	6	0	.625	352	258	2nd/AFC Central Div.	0	1	AFC wild-card game	Jack Pardee
1993†	12	4	0	.750	368	238	1st/AFC Central Div.	0	1	AFC div. playoff game	Jack Pardee
1994†	2	14	0	.125	226	352	4th/AFC Central Div.	—	—		Jack Pardee, Jeff Fisher
1995†	7	9	0	.438	348	324	T2nd/AFC Central Div.	—	—		Jeff Fisher
1996†	8	8	0	.500	345	319	T3rd/AFC Central Div.	—	—		Jeff Fisher
1997†	8	8	0	.500	333	310	3rd/AFC Central Div.	—	—		Jeff Fisher

*American Football League.
†Houston Oilers.

FIRST-ROUND DRAFT PICKS

1960—Billy Cannon, RB, Louisiana State
1961—Mike Ditka, E, Pittsburgh
1962—Ray Jacobs, DT, Howard Payne
1963—Danny Brabham, LB, Arkansas
1964—Scott Appleton, DT, Texas
1965—Lawrence Elkins, WR, Baylor* (AFL)
1966—Tommy Nobis, LB, Texas
1967—George Webster, LB, Michigan State
    Tom Regner, G, Notre Dame
1968—None
1969—Ron Pritchard, LB, Arizona State
1970—Doug Wilkerson, G, North Carolina Central
1971—Dan Pastorini, QB, Santa Clara
1972—Greg Sampson, DE, Stanford
1973—John Matuszak, DE, Tampa*
    George Amundson, RB, Iowa State
1974—None
1975—Robert Brazile, LB, Jackson State
    Don Hardeman, RB, Texas A&I

1976—None
1977—Morris Towns, T, Missouri
1978—Earl Campbell, RB, Texas*
1979—None
1980—None
1981—None
1982—Mike Munchak, G, Penn State
1983—Bruce Matthews, G, Southern California
1984—Dean Steinkuhler, G, Nebraska
1985—Ray Childress, DE, Texas A&M
    Richard Johnson, DB, Wisconsin
1986—Jim Everett, QB, Purdue
1987—Alonzo Highsmith, FB, Miami (Fla.)
    Haywood Jeffires, WR, North Carolina State
1988—Lorenzo White, RB, Michigan State
1989—David Williams, T, Florida
1990—Lamar Lathon, LB, Houston
1991—None
1992—None

1993—Brad Hopkins, G, Illinois
1994—Henry Ford, DE, Arkansas
1995—Steve McNair, QB, Alcorn State
1996—Eddie George, RB, Ohio State

1997—Kenny Holmes, DE, Miami (Fla.)
1998—Kevin Dyson, WR, Utah
*First player chosen in draft.

FRANCHISE RECORDS

Most rushing yards, career
8,574—Earl Campbell
Most rushing yards, season
1,934—Earl Campbell, 1980
Most rushing yards, game
216—Billy Cannon at N.Y. Titans, Dec. 10, 1961
Eddie George vs. Oak., Aug. 31, 1997 (OT)
Most rushing touchdowns, season
19—Earl Campbell, 1979
Most passing attempts, season
655—Warren Moon, 1991
Most passing attempts, game
68—George Blanda at Buf., Nov. 1, 1964
Most passes completed, season
404—Warren Moon, 1991
Most passes completed, game
41—Warren Moon vs. Dal., Nov. 10, 1991
Most passing yards, career
33,685—Warren Moon

Most passing yards, season
4,690—Warren Moon, 1991
Most passing yards, game
527—Warren Moon at K.C., Dec. 16, 1990
Most touchdown passes, season
36—George Blanda, 1961
Most pass receptions, career
542—Ernest Givins
Most pass receptions, season
101—Charlie Hennigan, 1964
Most pass receptions, game
13—Charlie Hennigan at Boston, Oct. 13, 1961
Haywood Jeffires at NYJ, Oct. 13, 1991
Most receiving yards, career
7,935—Ernest Givins
Most receiving yards, season
1,746—Charlie Hennigan, 1961

Most receiving yards, game
272—Charlie Hennigan at Boston, Oct. 13, 1961
Most receiving touchdowns, season
17—Bill Groman, 1961
Most touchdowns, career
73—Earl Campbell
Most field goals, season
32—Al Del Greco, 1996
Longest field goal
56 yards—Al Del Greco vs. S.F., Oct. 27, 1996
Most interceptions, career
45—Jim Norton
Most interceptions, season
12—Freddy Glick, 1963
Mike Reinfeldt, 1979
Most sacks, season
15.5—Jesse Baker, 1979

SERIES RECORDS

Tennessee vs.: Arizona 3-4; Atlanta 4-5; Baltimore 2-2; Buffalo 22-13; Carolina 0-1; Chicago 4-3; Cincinnati 29-28-1; Dallas 4-5; Denver 20-11-1; Detroit 4-3; Green Bay 3-3; Indianapolis 7-7; Jacksonville 3-3; Kansas City 17-24; Miami 11-13; Minnesota 3-4; New England 14-17-1; New Orleans 4-4-1; N.Y. Giants 1-5; N.Y. Jets 20-12-1; Oakland 14-20; Philadelphia 0-6; Pittsburgh 20-35; St. Louis 2-5; San Diego 13-18-1; San Francisco 3-6; Seattle 4-6; Tampa Bay 4-1; Washington 4-3.
NOTE: Includes records as Houston Oilers from 1960 through 1996.

COACHING RECORDS

Sammy Baugh, 4-10-0; Ed Biles, 8-23-0; Hugh Campbell, 8-22-0; Jeff Fisher, 24-30-0; Sid Gillman, 8-15-0; Jerry Glanville, 33-32-0 (2-3); Ed Hughes, 4-9-1; Frank Ivy, 17-11-0 (0-1); Wally Lemm, 37-38-4 (1-2); Jack Pardee, 43-31-0 (1-4); Bill Peterson, 1-18-0; Bum Phillips, 55-35-0 (4-3); Lou Rymkus, 11-7-1 (1-0); Chuck Studley, 2-8-0; Hugh Taylor, 4-10-0.

RETIRED UNIFORM NUMBERS

No.	Player
34	Earl Campbell
43	Jim Norton
63	Mike Munchak
65	Elvin Bethea

WASHINGTON REDSKINS
YEAR-BY-YEAR RECORDS

		REGULAR SEASON							PLAYOFFS		
Year	W	L	T	Pct.	PF	PA	Finish	W	L	Highest round	Coach
1932*	4	4	2	.500	55	79	4th				Lud Wray
1933†	5	5	2	.500	103	97	3rd/Eastern Div.	—	—		Lone Star Dietz
1934†	6	6	0	.500	107	94	2nd/Eastern Div.	—	—		Lone Star Dietz
1935†	2	8	1	.200	65	123	4th/Eastern Div.	—	—		Eddie Casey
1936†	7	5	0	.583	149	110	1st/Eastern Div.	0	1	NFL championship game	Ray Flaherty
1937	8	3	0	.727	195	120	1st/Eastern Div.	1	0	NFL champ	Ray Flaherty
1938	6	3	2	.667	148	154	2nd/Eastern Div.	—	—		Ray Flaherty
1939	8	2	1	.800	242	94	2nd/Eastern Div.	—	—		Ray Flaherty
1940	9	2	0	.818	245	142	1st/Eastern Div.	0	1	NFL championship game	Ray Flaherty
1941	6	5	0	.545	176	174	3rd/Eastern Div.	—	—		Ray Flaherty
1942	10	1	0	.909	227	102	1st/Eastern Div.	1	0	NFL champ	Ray Flaherty
1943	6	3	1	.667	229	137	1st/Eastern Div.	1	1	NFL championship game	Dutch Bergman
1944	6	3	1	.667	169	180	3rd/Eastern Div.	—	—		Dudley DeGroot
1945	8	2	0	.800	209	121	1st/Eastern Div.	0	1	NFL championship game	Dudley DeGroot
1946	5	5	1	.500	171	191	T3rd/Eastern Div.	—	—		Turk Edwards
1947	4	8	0	.333	295	367	4th/Eastern Div.	—	—		Turk Edwards
1948	7	5	0	.583	291	287	2nd/Eastern Div.	—	—		Turk Edwards
1949	4	7	1	.364	268	339	4th/Eastern Div.	—	—		John Whelchel, H. Ball
1950	3	9	0	.250	232	326	6th/American Conf.	—	—		Herman Ball

	REGULAR SEASON						PLAYOFFS			
Year	W	L	T	Pct.	PF	PA	Finish	W	L	Highest round	Coach
1951	5	7	0	.417	183	296	3rd/American Conf.	—	—		Herman Ball, Dick Todd
1952	4	8	0	.333	240	287	T5th/American Conf.	—	—		Curly Lambeau
1953	6	5	1	.545	208	215	3rd/Eastern Conf.	—	—		Curly Lambeau
1954	3	9	0	.250	207	432	5th/Eastern Conf.	—	—		Joe Kuharich
1955	8	4	0	.667	246	222	2nd/Eastern Conf.	—	—		Joe Kuharich
1956	6	6	0	.500	183	225	3rd/Eastern Conf.	—	—		Joe Kuharich
1957	5	6	1	.455	251	230	4th/Eastern Conf.	—	—		Joe Kuharich
1958	4	7	1	.364	214	268	4th/Eastern Conf.	—	—		Joe Kuharich
1959	3	9	0	.250	185	350	5th/Eastern Conf.	—	—		Mike Nixon
1960	1	9	2	.100	178	309	6th/Eastern Conf.	—	—		Mike Nixon
1961	1	12	1	.077	174	392	7th/Eastern Conf.	—	—		Bill McPeak
1962	5	7	2	.417	305	376	4th/Eastern Conf.	—	—		Bill McPeak
1963	3	11	0	.214	279	398	6th/Eastern Conf.	—	—		Bill McPeak
1964	6	8	0	.429	307	305	T3rd/Eastern Conf.	—	—		Bill McPeak
1965	6	8	0	.429	257	301	4th/Eastern Conf.	—	—		Bill McPeak
1966	7	7	0	.500	351	355	5th/Eastern Conf.	—	—		Otto Graham
1967	5	6	3	.455	347	353	3rd/Capitol Div.	—	—		Otto Graham
1968	5	9	0	.357	249	358	3rd/Capitol Div.	—	—		Otto Graham
1969	7	5	2	.583	307	319	2nd/Capitol Div.	—	—		Vince Lombardi
1970	6	8	0	.429	297	314	4th/NFC Eastern Div.	—	—		Bill Austin
1971	9	4	1	.692	276	190	2nd/NFC Eastern Div.	0	1	NFC div. playoff game	George Allen
1972	11	3	0	.786	336	218	1st/NFC Eastern Div.	2	1	Super Bowl	George Allen
1973	10	4	0	.714	325	198	2nd/NFC Eastern Div.	0	1	NFC div. playoff game	George Allen
1974	10	4	0	.714	320	196	2nd/NFC Eastern Div.	0	1	NFC div. playoff game	George Allen
1975	8	6	0	.571	325	276	3rd/NFC Eastern Div.	—	—		George Allen
1976	10	4	0	.714	291	217	2nd/NFC Eastern Div.	0	1	NFC div. playoff game	George Allen
1977	9	5	0	.643	196	189	2nd/NFC Eastern Div.	—	—		George Allen
1978	8	8	0	.500	273	283	3rd/NFC Eastern Div.	—	—		Jack Pardee
1979	10	6	0	.625	348	295	3rd/NFC Eastern Div.	—	—		Jack Pardee
1980	6	10	0	.375	261	293	3rd/NFC Eastern Div.	—	—		Jack Pardee
1981	8	8	0	.500	347	349	4th/NFC Eastern Div.	—	—		Joe Gibbs
1982	8	1	0	.889	190	128	1st/NFC	4	0	Super Bowl champ	Joe Gibbs
1983	14	2	0	.875	541	332	1st/NFC Eastern Div.	2	1	Super Bowl	Joe Gibbs
1984	11	5	0	.688	426	310	1st/NFC Eastern Div.	0	1	NFC div. playoff game	Joe Gibbs
1985	10	6	0	.625	297	312	3rd/NFC Eastern Div.	—	—		Joe Gibbs
1986	12	4	0	.750	368	296	2nd/NFC Eastern Div.	2	1	NFC championship game	Joe Gibbs
1987	11	4	0	.733	379	285	1st/NFC Eastern Div.	3	0	Super Bowl champ	Joe Gibbs
1988	7	9	0	.438	345	387	T3rd/NFC Eastern Div.	—	—		Joe Gibbs
1989	10	6	0	.625	386	308	3rd/NFC Eastern Div.	—	—		Joe Gibbs
1990	10	6	0	.625	381	301	T2nd/NFC Eastern Div.	1	1	NFC div. playoff game	Joe Gibbs
1991	14	2	0	.875	485	224	1st/NFC Eastern Div.	3	0	Super Bowl champ	Joe Gibbs
1992	9	7	0	.563	300	255	3rd/NFC Eastern Div.	1	1	NFC div. playoff game	Joe Gibbs
1993	4	12	0	.250	230	345	5th/NFC Eastern Div.	—	—		Richie Petitbon
1994	3	13	0	.188	320	412	5th/NFC Eastern Div.	—	—		Norv Turner
1995	6	10	0	.375	326	359	3rd/NFC Eastern Div.	—	—		Norv Turner
1996	9	7	0	.563	364	312	3rd/NFC Eastern Div.	—	—		Norv Turner
1997	8	7	1	.533	327	289	2nd/NFC Eastern Div.	—	—		Norv Turner

*Boston Braves.
†Boston Redskins.

FIRST-ROUND DRAFT PICKS

1936—Riley Smith, QB, Alabama
1937—Sammy Baugh, QB, Texas Christian
1938—Andy Farkas, B, Detroit
1939—I.B. Hale, T, Texas Christian
1940—Ed Boell, B, New York University
1941—Forrest Evashevski, B, Michigan
1942—Orban Sanders, B, Texas
1943—Jack Jenkins, B, Missouri
1944—Mike Micka, B, Colgate
1945—Jim Hardy, B, Southern California
1946—Cal Rossi, B, UCLA
1947—Cal Rossi, B, UCLA
1948—Harry Gilmer, QB, Alabama*
1949—Rob Goode, RB, Texas A&M
1950—George Thomas, RB, Oklahoma
1951—Leon Heath, RB, Oklahoma
1952—Larry Isbell, QB, Baylor

1953—Jack Scarbath, QB, Maryland
1954—Steve Meilinger, TE, Kentucky
1955—Ralph Guglielmi, QB, Notre Dame
1956—Ed Vereb, RB, Maryland
1957—Don Bosseler, RB, Miami (Fla.)
1958—None
1959—Don Allard, QB, Boston College
1960—Richie Lucas, QB, Penn State
1961—Joe Rutgens, T, Illinois
　　　Norm Snead, QB, Wake Forest
1962—Ernie Davis, RB, Syracuse*
　　　Leroy Jackson, RB, Illinois Central
1963—Pat Richter, TE, Wisconsin
1964—Charley Taylor, RB, Arizona State
1965—None
1966—Charlie Gogolak, K, Princeton
1967—Ray McDonald, RB, Idaho

1968—Jim Smith, DB, Oregon
1969—None
1970—None
1971—None
1972—None
1973—None
1974—None
1975—None
1976—None
1977—None
1978—None
1979—None
1980—Art Monk, WR, Syracuse
1981—Mark May, T, Pittsburgh
1982—None
1983—Darrell Green, DB, Texas A&I

1984—None
1985—None
1986—None
1987—None
1988—None
1989—None
1990—None
1991—Bobby Wilson, DT, Michigan State
1992—Desmond Howard, WR, Michigan
1993—Tom Carter, DB, Notre Dame
1994—Heath Shuler, QB, Tennessee
1995—Michael Westbrook, WR, Colorado
1996—Andre Johnson, T, Penn State
1997—Kenard Lang, DE, Miami (Fla.)
1998—None
*First player chosen in draft.

FRANCHISE RECORDS

Most rushing yards, career
7,472—John Riggins

Most rushing yards, season
1,353—Terry Allen, 1996

Most rushing yards, game
221—Gerald Riggs vs. Phi., Sept. 17, 1989

Most rushing touchdowns, season
24—John Riggins, 1983

Most passing attempts, season
541—Jay Schroeder, 1986

Most passing attempts, game
58—Jay Schroeder vs. S.F., Dec. 1, 1985

Most passes completed, season
293—Joe Theismann, 1981

Most passes completed, game
32—Sonny Jurgensen at Cle., Nov. 26, 1967
John Friesz at NYG, Sept. 18, 1994

Most passing yards, career
25,206—Joe Theismann

Most passing yards, season
4,109—Jay Schroeder, 1986

Most passing yards, game
446—Sammy Baugh vs. N.Y. Yanks, Oct. 31, 1948

Most touchdown passes, season
31—Sonny Jurgensen, 1967

Most pass receptions, career
888—Art Monk

Most pass receptions, season
106—Art Monk, 1984

Most pass receptions, game
13—Art Monk vs. Cin., Dec. 15, 1985
Kelvin Bryant vs. NYG, Dec. 7, 1986
Art Monk at Det., Nov. 4, 1990

Most receiving yards, career
13,026—Art Monk

Most receiving yards, season
1,436—Bobby Mitchell, 1963

Most receiving yards, game
255—Anthony Allen vs. St.L., Oct. 4, 1987

Most receiving touchdowns, season
12—Hugh Taylor, 1952
Charley Taylor, 1966
Jerry Smith, 1967
Ricky Sanders, 1988

Most touchdowns, career
90—Charley Taylor

Most field goals, season
33—Mark Moseley, 1983

Longest field goal
57 yards—Steve Cox vs. Sea., Sept. 28, 1986

Most interceptions, career
44—Darrell Green

Most interceptions, season
13—Dan Sandifer, 1948

Most sacks, career
97.5—Dexter Manley

Most sacks, season
18.0—Dexter Manley, 1986

SERIES RECORDS

Washington vs.: Arizona 61-39-1; Atlanta 13-4-1; Baltimore, 0-1; Buffalo 4-4; Carolina 2-0; Chicago 13-14; Cincinnati 4-2; Dallas 31-41-2; Denver 3-4; Detroit 24-3; Green Bay 11-9; Indianapolis 9-16; Jacksonville 1-0; Kansas City 1-4; Miami 2-5; Minnesota 6-4; New England 5-1; New Orleans 12-5; N.Y. Giants 50-67-3; N.Y. Jets 5-1; Oakland 2-6; Philadelphia 64-54-6; Pittsburgh 39-25-4; St. Louis 16-7-1; San Diego 5-0; San Francisco 6-11-1; Seattle 5-3; Tampa Bay 4-4; Tennessee 3-4.
NOTE: Includes records only from 1937 to present.

COACHING RECORDS

George Allen, 67-30-1 (2-5); Bill Austin, 6-8-0; Herman Bell, 4-16-0; Dutch Bergman, 6-3-1 (1-1); Eddie Casey, 2-8-1; Dudley DeGroot, 14-5-1 (0-1); William Dietz, 11-11-2; Turk Edwards, 16-18-1; Ray Flaherty, 54-21-3 (2-2); Joe Gibbs, 124-60-0 (16-5); Otto Graham, 17-22-3; Joe Kuharich, 26-32-2; Curly Lambeau, 10-13-1; Vince Lombardi, 7-5-2; Bill McPeak, 21-46-3; Mike Nixon, 4-18-2; Jack Pardee, 24-24-0; Richie Petitbon, 4-12-0; Dick Todd, 5-4-0; Norv Turner, 26-37-1; John Whelchel, 3-3-1; Lud Wray, 4-4-2.

RETIRED UNIFORM NUMBERS

No.	Player
33	Sammy Baugh

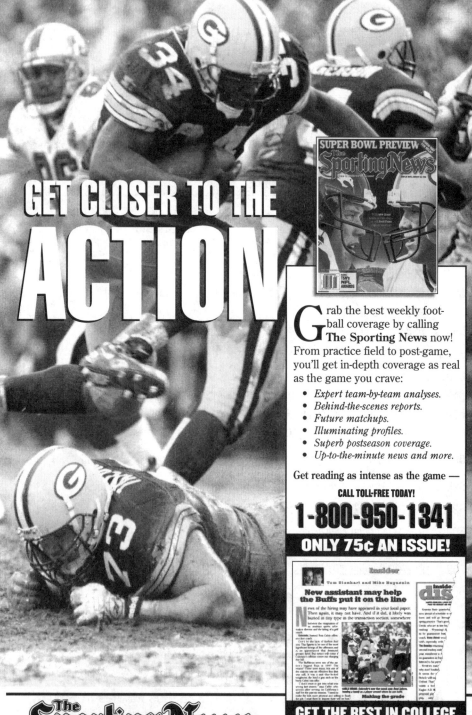